W9-AWC-620

Government Has Changed Over the Last 75 Years.

We've Changed With It.

PRENTICE HALL

75th Anniversary Edition

Magruder's AMERICAN GOVERNMENT

William A. McClenaghan

It's Still Changing, and So Are We . . .

. . . *Resolved,* that you deserve the NEW

NEW!

ABC News InterActive™: The "Powers" Series

➢ **Three interactive videodiscs** that explore the powers of the Presidency, Congress, and the Supreme Court—fully correlated to *Magruder's*

NEW!

Government in Action Transparencies

➢ A brand new package of **100 color transparencies,** including political cartoons, up-to-date maps, graphs, and charts with overlays, and more

NEW!

Teacher's Edition

➢ A new **wraparound format** with le son plans, high-interest backgroun notes, and student-oriented activiti located where they're most useful - around easy-to-read student pages

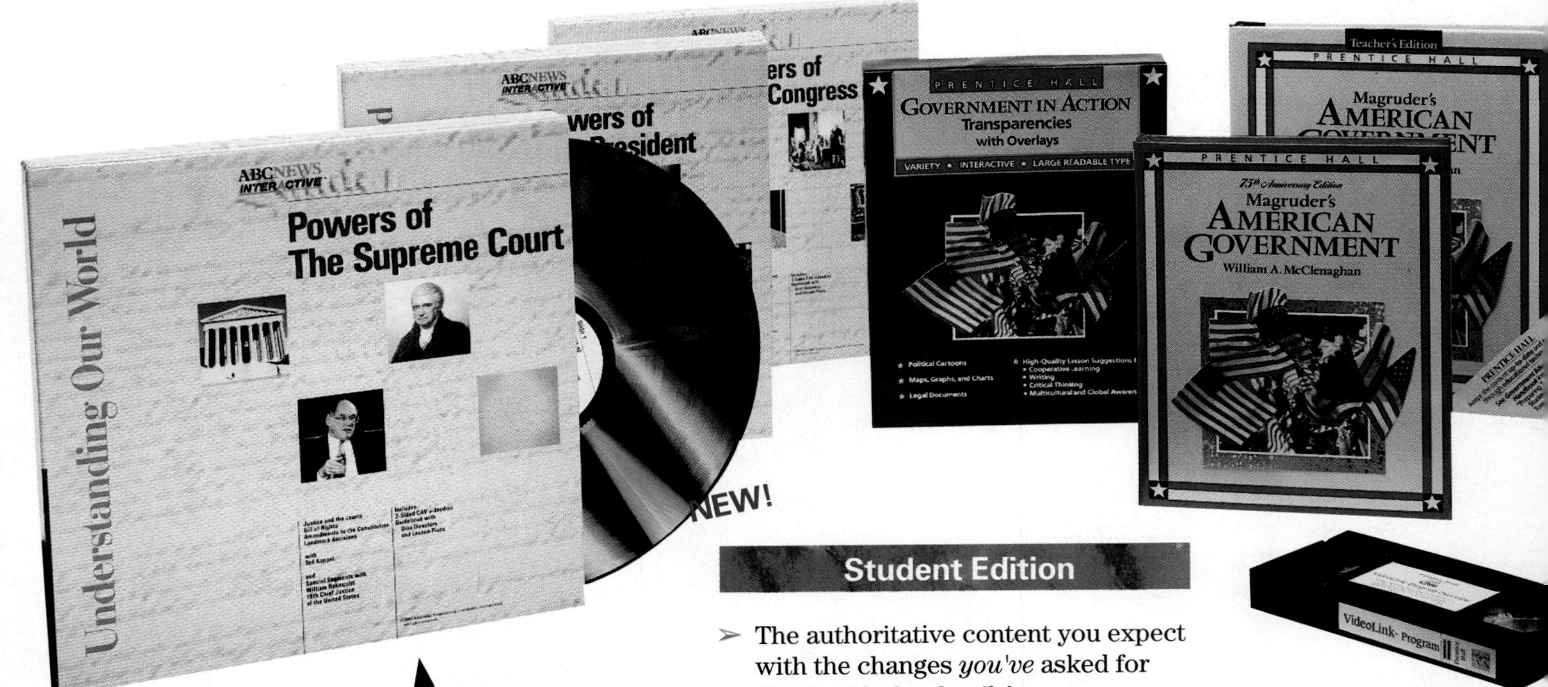

NEW!

Student Edition

➢ The authoritative content you expect with the changes *you've* asked for (See inside for details)

CNN VideoLink™

➢ **Video broadcasts** of CNN's "The Week in Review," accompanied by weekly Teaching Guides correlate to *Magruder's*, bring today's news into your classroom

The Trusted Authority

Magruder's AMERICAN GOVERNMENT

NEW! **Teacher's Resource File**

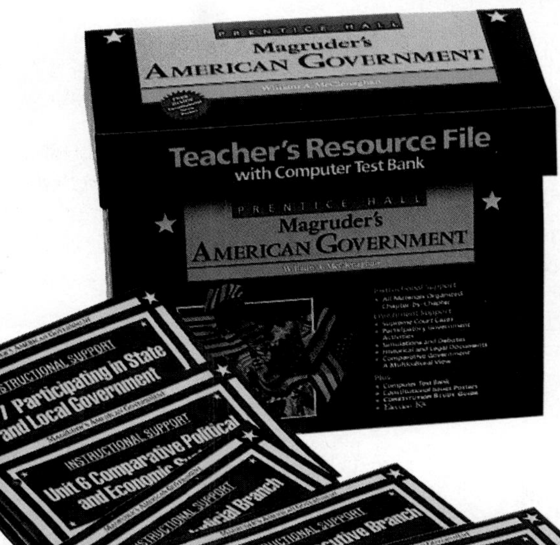

➢ **Instructional Support Files (7)**
All the instructional support you need, organized chapter by chapter. Includes case studies on *contemporary issues* for each chapter!

➢ **Enrichment Support Files (5)**
- Participatory Government
- Simulations and Debates
- Supreme Court Cases
- Historical and Legal Documents
- Comparative Government: A Multicultural Perspective

➢ **Constitution Study Guide**
An easy-to-understand overview

➢ **Computer Test Bank/Assessment**
Offers all you need to create high-quality, multiple versions of tests in minutes, *correlated to your state and local objectives.* Includes Alternative Assessment Guidelines and Forms.

➢ **Prentice Hall Election Kit**
For analyzing and participating in elections

➢ **Constitutional Issues Posters**
With political cartoons and quotes

Since 1917 . . .

PRENTICE HALL

75th Anniversary Edition

The Government Educator's Handbook

TABLE OF CONTENTS

The Need for Civic Understanding

by Ernest L. Boyer

Today, the world's 165 independent nations and sixty-odd political units are interlocked. High interest rates in the United States hurt Common Market countries; bad harvests in the Soviet Union help Canadian farmers; a Middle East oil glut means less pressure in Brazil to aid capital-starved Africa; unemployment in Germany sends ripples through Spain and Yugoslavia; a robotics breakthrough in Tokyo makes a difference in Detroit. Pretoria and Peoria are connected.

As conditions have changed both at home and abroad, our political agenda has come to include increasingly complicated questions. For example, how can we reduce our reliance on fossil fuels? Should we limit imports from other countries to protect our own industries? To what extent should human rights violations in other countries influence our foreign policy? How can we come to an agreement on international standards for atmospheric pollution? Even the metaphysical question of when a human life begins and ends has become a topic of political debate.

These fundamental issues, and many others, will continue to press in, shaping the public agenda and even the private lives of most Americans. And yet the information needed to think constructively about these issues seems increasingly beyond our grasp. To put it plainly, we are becoming civically illiterate as a nation. Unable to make informed judgments on complicated issues and debates, many Americans are tempted to turn to simple answers, to slogans, or to nostalgia for a world that never was. They succumb to the blandishments of glib electronic soothsayers, or simply withdraw, convinced that nothing can be done.

If public opinion surveys are to be believed, half of all Americans do not believe that important national problems such as energy shortages, inflation, and crime can be solved through traditional American political institutions. Many argue that it is no longer possible to resolve complex public issues through the democratic process because citizens are not sufficiently informed to debate policy choices of consequence. Further, the proportion of citizens professing "great confidence" in the leaders of major social institutions has declined dramatically. A recent survey of college freshmen revealed that a significant percentage of these students distrust many of the nation's most basic social institutions. Confidence in the executive branch of government continues to go down, and roughly half of our citizens do not believe that the electoral process is the principal determinant of how the country is actually run.

For those . . . who care about government "by the people," this increase in apathy and decline in public confidence cannot go unchallenged. In a world where human survival is at stake, cynicism and ignorance are not acceptable alternatives. The replacement of democratic government by a technocracy and the control of policy by special-interest groups cannot be tolerated. Thus the need to help all students become intelligent and informed citizens is self-evident. . . . If education cannot help students see beyond themselves and better understand issues of national and international significance, then each new generation will remain ignorant, and its capacity to live intelligently and responsibly will be diminished . . .

Civic Understanding Requires Communication

[First] I am convinced that the destiny of this country may indeed be threatened not so much by weapons systems, but by the inclination of public officials to obscure the truth. And, further, I am convinced that if our students are to become responsible citizens for a new century, civic education must be concerned, above all, with the quality of communication. The work of democracy is carried on through thoughtful discourse through town meetings, city councils, study groups, informal conversations, and television screens. And citizenship training, if it means anything at all, means teaching students to think critically, listen with discernment, and communicate with power and precision. If students learn to listen, speak, read, and write more carefully, they will not only be civically empowered, but also they will know how to distinguish between the authentic and the fraudulent in human discourse. A better grounding in rhetoric and logic and in the techniques of discussion and debate would also help prepare them for responsible citizenship.

Dr. Boyer is the President of the Carnegie Foundation for the Advancement of Teaching. This essay is adapted by permission from CIVITAS, published by the Center for Civic Education, 1991, pp. xv–xvii.

Civic Understanding Requires Knowledge

Second, civic education for a new century also must provide students with a core of basic knowledge about social issues and institutions, to allow them to put their understanding of democracy in perspective. Civic understanding means a study of history and literature. It means that students would encounter the classic political thinkers, from Plato, Hobbes, Locke, and Montesquieu to John Adams, James Madison, and John C. Calhoun. Equally important, it means they should study government today, not just by examining its theory and machinery, but also by exploring current public issues.

Civic Understanding Is Active, Not Passive

Third, I'm convinced that civic education means classrooms that are active, not passive, places. We must begin to recognize that students are already members of an institution, the school; and that they need to understand how this place works, and to participate in school decisions that affect their lives, just as they will be asked to do so later on, in other institutions and in society at large. If we fail to give students these experiences while they are young, there is a high probability that they will be deferred for a lifetime.

Civic Understanding Is for Living

Finally, education for citizenship means helping students make connections between what they learn and how they live. In the American high school, too many young people feel unwanted, unneeded, and unconnected to the larger world. Further, there is a serious gap between the young and the old in our society, an intergenerational separation in which youth and their elders are not seriously engaged in common discourse.

As an essential part of civic education, students need to understand that learning is for living, and that education means developing the capacity to make judgments, form convictions, and act boldly on values held.

We must help them understand that all choices, in thought or in action, are equally valid. Such an education does not dictate solutions or suggest that there are simple answers for every complicated question. Rather, it means helping students develop responsible ways of thinking, believing, and acting.

On a related matter, it is becoming increasingly important in our diversified culture that students be encouraged to deal thoughtfully with our deepest differences. The harsh truth is that society today is characterized by such divisiveness that consensus often seems almost impossible, and this puts the nation's schools squarely in the middle. Indeed, teachers are often criticized if they try to examine sensitive issues in the classroom. Yet to ignore controversial issues is to offer students an incomplete education, an incapacity to think carefully about life's most important concerns. I remain convinced that even in matters where society is sharply divided, schools have an especially important role to play, one that goes beyond silence or the extension of the status quo. If we hope to make progress toward resolving deep conflicts in the culture, we must encourage open and sensitive classroom discussion about choices, even in such controversial areas as sex, drugs, cultural differences, and religious beliefs. Finding a way to deal thoughtfully with our deepest differences is perhaps the greatest challenge citizenship education now confronts. And in the guidance of such inquiry, teachers must be trusted.

The focus of civic education must be extended beyond the American agenda to the world beyond our shores. That world may not yet be a global village, but surely our sense of neighborhood includes more people and cultures than ever before. Refugees flow from one country to another, but too many students can neither point to the locations of these great migrations on a map nor talk about the famines or wars or poverty that caused them. Philosophers, statesmen, inventors, and artists from around the world enrich our lives, and the contributions should be taught and celebrated.

Obviously, formal eduction cannot single-handedly deal with the massive challenge of civic education. Beyond the classroom, churches, libraries, youth groups, labor unions, senior citizen's organizations, and many other groups must become greater sources of civic education, though not to the exclusion of more direct political participation. The media—newspapers, journals, radio, and television—also have a powerful role to play. Still, the nation's schools have a special obligation to combat growing illiteracy about public issues. . . . Schools and colleges simply must help students understand the process by which public policy is shaped and prepare them to make informed, discriminating judgments on questions that will affect their futures, as well as those of the nation and the world.

Multicultural EDUCATION

Valuing Differences

WHAT IS MULTICULTURAL EDUCATION? It is a curriculum and a way of teaching that acknowledges the cultural diversity of the United States and the world and sees this diversity as a positive fact of life. Multicultural education strives for more complex understandings and more sensitivity to issues of diversity than has ever been evidenced in the past. At its foundation is the recognition of the intrinsic worth of each individual, regardless of race, ethnic background, gender, religion, socioeconomic status, or physical or mental condition.

Multicultural education is being incorporated in all content areas. This movement for educational reform is not without controversy, however. Many proponents of multicultural education differ greatly in their proposals for teaching and content reform.

The Melting Pot and the Salad Bowl

At the heart of the multicultural movement is the recognition that the United States is a multiracial, multiethnic, and multicultural society. This view contrasts sharply with the view prevalent in American education for many decades—the vision of the United States as a melting pot. This assimilationist view held that, over time, all nationalities and ethnicities would give up their original culture and mix in the American melting pot, producing a uniquely American culture. In the interest of serving this point of view, American educators intentionally ignored or devalued differences and sought to minimize their expression.

In the past few decades, however, social scientists have determined that the melting pot idea does not adequately describe American society. All ethnic and cultural groups have retained some aspects of their culture, even after moving into the American mainstream.

Thus, a new model was proposed to describe American society—that of "the salad bowl," or cultural pluralism. In this view, the different ethnic groups in the United States retain many of their traditions, such as language and social customs. At the same time, however, ethnic groups adopt many characteristics of the predominant Anglo-American culture, such as obedience to laws and participation in the mainstream government and economic systems. In this view of cultural pluralism, ethnic identification continues to be important to all Americans and is central to both self-identification and to group identification.

The Debate Leads to Action

The debate between the melting-pot theorists and the cultural pluralists would have been largely academic, except for evidence that educational practices based on the melting pot theory were negatively affecting the performance of students in our schools. Educators noted that the failure to include diverse cultural perspectives—and to treat these perspectives with respect—was undermining the self-confidence and motivation of minority students. The result was a high rate of failure and alienation from the school environment in minority populations. Also, the narrow cultural focus in the curriculum meant that students from majority groups lacked the knowledge they needed to overcome prejudice and to participate successfully in our multicultural society.

Proponents of multicultural education argued that educators must teach about the diverse nature of our society and our world to fulfill their mission. For without sensitivity to and appreciation for ethnic, racial, and cultural differences, educational excellence and equality of opportunity could not be achieved.

The multiculturalists' arguments have had a great effect on the educational community. Iowa and Minnesota have mandated that multicultural approaches be part of all content instruction. In California and New York, cultural pluralism and multicultural education have been placed at the core of the states' social studies instruction. In large urban areas, which have the greatest cultural diversity, the need for multicultural education is being addressed through changes in the curriculum, teacher awareness, and a search for new multicultural materials.

The Goals of Multicultural Education

MULTICULTURAL EDUCATION is a broad educational reform movement and therefore seeks to achieve many goals. The list below draws upon many of the published goals of state and local educational agencies as well as the writings of multicultural educators such as James A. Banks and Christine I. Bennett. *Magruder's American Government* shares these goals and used them as an overall guide in incorporating multicultural education into this program.

- To develop positive self-images by helping students understand their own cultures.
- To help students gain greater self-understanding by viewing their cultures from the perspectives of other groups.
- To help students develop an appreciation of individual and cultural differences.
- To enrich students' experience with the diverse historical, artistic, and literary contributions of other groups.
- To provide students with the ability to function within other cultures.
- To combat racism, prejudice, and discrimination.
- To build social-action skills and inspire students to participate in a culturally diverse nation and world.
- To help students master essential content and skills.

The Government and Multicultural Education

The study of American government provides an ideal opportunity to inject the perspectives of multiculturalism into the curriculum. Our American government is a government of many peoples from a variety of culturally diverse backgrounds. Our American government is a problem-solving government. Its laws and the interpretation of its Constitution seek to guarantee rights and ensure liberties that might otherwise be denied—or have historically been denied—on the basis of ethnocentric, biased, and prejudiced views of groups.

By focusing on diversity, the *Student Edition* of *Magruder's American Government* broadens students' horizons. Besides a narrative that explores American government from the point of view of all its people, two *Student Edition* features, "Voices on Government" and "Global Awareness" help students to better understand the multiracial, multiethnic, and multicultural nation in which they live. The *Teacher's Edition* offers special help to teachers for heightening student awareness of cultural diversity. Of special interest are the notes called "Spotlights On: Multiculturalism." These notes offer teachers high-interest background information on multicultural aspects of the government content. Finally, the *Teacher's Resource File* includes "Case Studies on Contemporary Issues," "Debates," and "Comparative Government: A Multicultural View" activities.

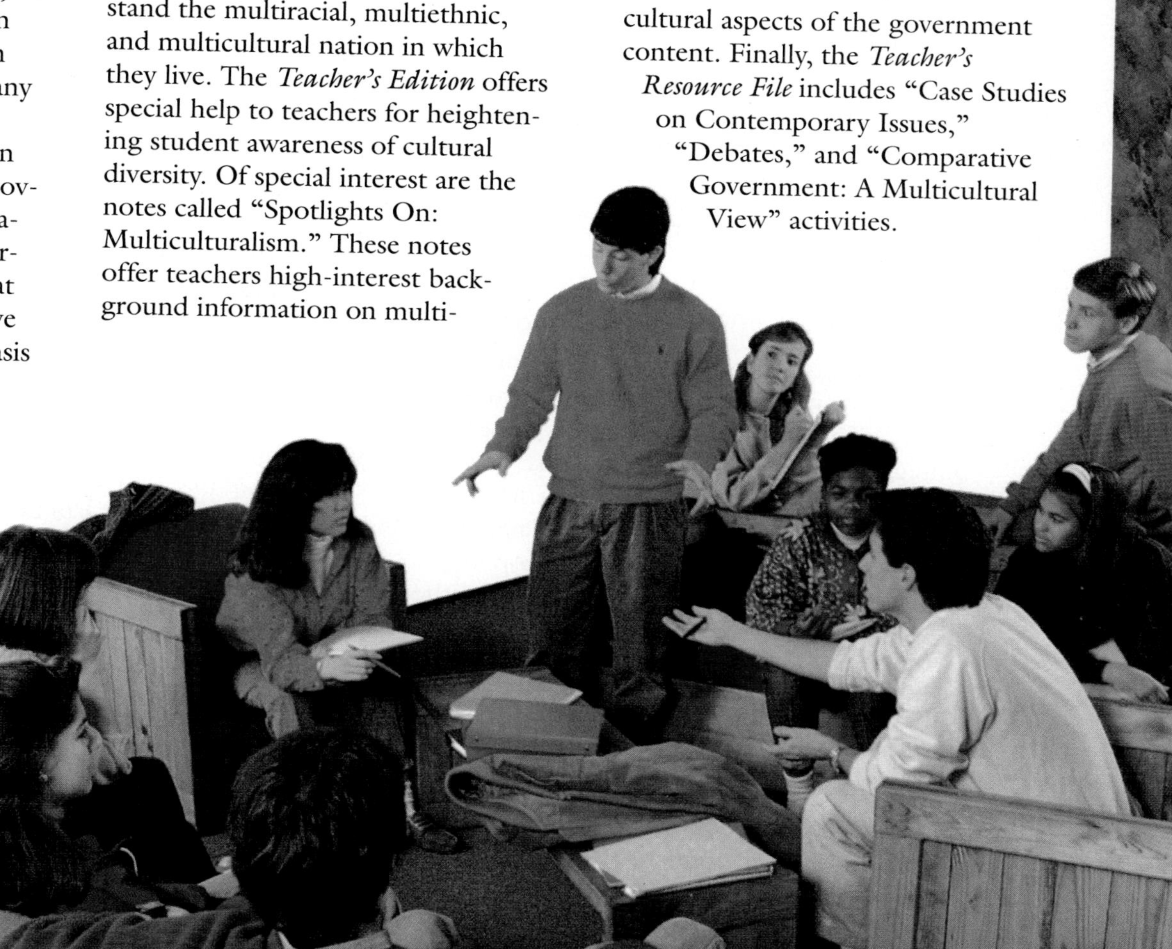

COOPERATIVE LEARNING

Prentice Hall interviews Robert Slavin

Cooperative learning is being used now more than ever before. But what is cooperative learning, and why should you incorporate it into your classroom activities?

For a clearer picture, we talked with Robert Slavin, Director of the Johns Hopkins University Center for Social Organization of Schools and one of the nation's leading researchers on the use of cooperative learning in the classroom.

Q. What are we talking about when we say "cooperative learning"?

A. Cooperative learning actually refers to a wide range of different methods. What is common to all of them is the idea that kids of the same age are working together to help each other learn.

Q. How does that happen? How does cooperative learning reinforce or expand learning?

A. One of the things that cooperative learning does is motivate students to be concerned about each other's learning, so that students feel that their peers are supporting their learning efforts.

Another thing is that students, in the process of discussing the material that the teacher has presented, get to voice their own current understanding, which helps them in the sense that people learn by teaching. Cooperative learning also helps other kids by filling in gaps. Explaining ideas to each other may help kids to grasp ideas that they may have only dimly understood at the end of the teacher's lesson.

Q. Why should cooperative learning be used in the classroom? For example, what are its benefits?

A. The main benefit of cooperative learning is that it improves student achievement. Many studies that have compared it to traditional learning have found that cooperative learning improves the achievement of high achievers, of average achievers, and of low achievers in many different circumstances.

Cooperative learning also fosters improved intergroup relations, acceptance of mainstreamed, academically handicapped kids, and self-esteem. Since kids enjoy working cooperatively, I think they would feel good about a class in which they are able to work together in this way.

Q. Are there any drawbacks to using cooperative learning?

A. Well, I suppose some people would say that it's noisy. You've got to be prepared for some noise. Also, in many forms of cooperative learning there is scoring to be done, so there's some paperwork that may be involved, but not a great deal. Other than that, I'm not sure that there are any serious drawbacks.

Q. How can cooperative learning be structured so that one student doesn't do all the work?

A. There are many ways to do it. In our methods, the groups are working to earn certificates or other kinds of recognition based on the learning of all members of the group. . . . What this means is that the only way for the group to succeed is if everybody learns, so there's no way for one student to do all the work. You rarely want to give the group a single task, or a single activity that they all have to do, because then it is possible for one kid to do all the work.

Q. You've said that group success should depend on individual learning. How does that work?

A. If there's something that can be traced back to each individual student, then the sum of those individual assessments is used to determine teams that get certificates or special recognition, or bonus points on their grades—something to indicate that the teacher values group performance. But the success of the group is dependent on things that show the individual learning or the individual participation of the student.

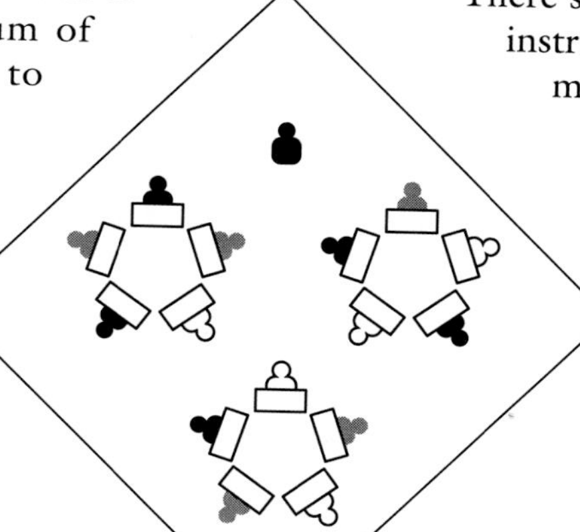

In cooperative learning activities, students work together to help each other learn.

Q. Some people are opposed to the idea of using rewards and certificates. How do you feel about that?

A. I think there are some kinds of objectives for which they may not be necessary, such as composition, because kids enjoy that anyway, but for most school subjects, some kind of a group reward is necessary. It doesn't have to be big, just something to communicate to the kids that the activity is important and valuable. Because without that, the students don't see as clearly the need to help each other. There has to be something that they're trying to work toward as a group. Most often, simple recognition is sufficient to tell the group that its success matters.

Q. How often should cooperative learning be used?

A. It should be used pretty extensively. Even when you're using cooperative learning, the kids are not working in groups all day or all the time. There's a cycle of activities that includes instruction, individual assessment, and may include some individual work. I think that we certainly have many, many classrooms where cooperative learning is used essentially all year. But it also makes sense to use it for shorter periods, as long as you're not using it on, say, every other Thursday when it's raining. If you are going to use it, it's important to use it consistently for some period of time, maybe six weeks, rather than to do it just from time to time.

Q. Should the groups be constant over that period?

A. We recommend changing them after every six weeks. . . . We definitely recommend against the use of ad hoc groups, of just saying, "Everybody find a partner." There's a major benefit to having a group that kids really identify with and think is important. If you're changing groups every day, then that's not going to happen.

How It Works

To give you a wide range of options, there is at least one cooperative learning activity for every chapter of *Magruder's American Government*. You are the best judge of how often to use them. These guidelines will help you get started:

Group Size: 4–6 students.

Group Make-Up: Combination of high, average, and low achievers, with a balance of sex, ethnicity, and personalities.

Duration of Groups: Change after about six weeks

Frequency of Use: As often as practical; consistency is important.

Accountability: Group success should depend on individual learning—measured by one evaluation, or by improvement over time.

Recognition: Just something small to show you value group success—praise and public recognition are often enough; bonus points are good, too.

Writing as a Process

Today we think of writing as a complex process that involves the application of a wide range of thinking skills and language abilities. Thinking of the process as a series of steps, we can focus on the techniques and tools writers need, the knowledge they must develop, and the choices they must learn to make at each of these steps. From this understanding of what writers must be able to do, we can begin to devise some instructional strategies, some direct activities to teach appropriate skills and knowledge.

The process theory proposes that writers practice very different skills and undertake very different activities at each of the following five productive stages:

Prewriting

Writers get warmed up, choose a focus, gather ideas and details, record, and begin to sort out their data, seeing how the data fit together in useful ways. This stage is a time of discovery and of invention. It is rich, productive, and extravagant.

Writing

Writers need to get their ideas recorded in some sort of tentative, first-draft shape as easily and as quickly as possible. Fluency with written English is critical to this stage, as is the knowledge of what choices are available to writers and what factors influence their judgment about these options. Therefore, writers must learn how to turn streams of thoughts and ideas into coherent, organized written streams, and they need to have much experience in making the choices and in having their judgments work effectively in the written piece.

Revising

From revision that is supported by the positive, informed response of outside readers and by the rethinking and revising by the writers themselves, writers learn that writing benefits from being scrutinized again (and again) after that first draft. This stage involves revising for sense and editing for word choice and sentence style. Writers need to learn how to review a draft with an eye to revision; they need to learn to be editors. In addition, they need to learn to proofread—to spot errors and make corrections in spelling, capitalization, punctuation, and grammar. These are complicated skills that require much learning and much teaching.

Evaluating

After a student's final draft is turned in, there is still opportunity for teaching and learning to occur. Students may be involved in evaluating their writing and the writing of others by using scoring sheets or rubrics and by emphasizing one of several different methods of scoring.

Publishing

Writers benefit when the classroom is a place where writing is valued as more than a pointless exercise, where it is honored, put on display, kept in a student file or portfolio, or presented in a classroom book. Yet, although honoring student writing can be done quite simply, it seems to be overlooked in many classrooms. Publishing seeks to give credibility and value to the act of writing and to its product. As the final step in the writing process, it demonstrates to the student that the written piece (and indirectly its author) is valued by other people.

Benefits

Following these steps can involve students deeply in a process in which they have a reasonably good chance of success. The steps teach them how to make the process useful and operational in their own writing experience.

The Writing Process

Prewriting

Developing Ideas

- Observing
- Mapping
- Listening
- Cueing
- Imagining
- Clustering
- Outlining
- Reading
- Log-keeping
- Researching
- Brainstorming
- Remembering
- Journal Writing
- Dramatizing
- Questioning
- Free Writing

Organizing

- Developing with details, reasons, examples, incidents, or arguments
- Ordering by chronology, importance, or other logic
- Classifying
- Deductive-Inductive order

Writing

Setting Rhetorical Stance

- Voice
- Audience
- Purpose
- Form

Making Linguistic Choices

- Diction/Choice of words
- Phrase/Clause structure
- Sentence structure
- Modification and subordination
- Connections/ Transitions
- Figurative language

Revising

Proofreading

- Catching copy errors
- Checking mechanics
- Proofing spelling
- Revising sentence structure

Editing

- Peer editing
- Response groups
- Self-Revision
- Yes-No
- Questionnaire
- Written responses

Evaluating

- Grading
- Correcting
- Holistic scoring
- Primary-trait scoring

Publishing

- Sharing
- Posting
- Filing
- Dispatching

Critical Thinking

A Key to Good Citizenship

By Susan Feibelman
Program Specialist, Dallas Independent School District

Like clockwork at the start of each school year, students in classrooms across the country raise their hands and ask about the number of dates that they will be required to memorize over the term. Unfortunately, for them civic education has become synonymous with memorization—the study of government seems composed of an endless number of names, dates, legislation, and processes that must be committed to memory.

But as we know, government education involves much more than that. In addition to knowing how a bill becomes a law, students need to possess the skills to evaluate and analyze the positions of their government and its leaders. They need to be able to recognize bias, to determine relevance, test conclusions, and demonstrate reasoned judgment to participate effectively in our democratic society. In other words, students need to think critically.

Critical Thinking and Government

Over the past fifteen years educators in all disciplines have been constantly reminded that they should be teaching students to develop both *convergent* and *divergent* thinking. The 1989 report of the National Council for the Social Studies Task Force on Scope and Sequence identified numerous critical thinking strategies that should be a part of any social studies curriculum. Recent regional and national conferences for the social studies have offered countless numbers of "how-to" workshops for integrating critical thinking into the social studies classroom. Staff development sessions in local school districts have placed special emphasis on preparing students of all abilities to think critically in all content areas. And social studies textbooks have highlighted critical thinking as a part of their instructional package.

All this attention and discussion has been invaluable, but we must be careful not to lose sight of the original intent—to teach students to think. Sometimes we have regarded critical thinking as something outside the regular curriculum that must be added to our already overflowing instructional "plate." Yet, critical thinking is not a separate instructional agenda that must be added on; instead, it can be smoothly integrated into almost any lesson. And, luckily, the study of government has always been an exercise in critical thinking—teaching the process of critical thinking is the natural outgrowth of this study.

A Multi-Purpose Approach

Magruder's American Government provides teachers with a variety of critical thinking activities and questions. Throughout the text, students will be presented with many opportunities to consider critically various aspects of the content. Each one of the 17 critical thinking skills listed in the chart at right is taught in detail in skill lessons, then reinforced throughout the text in section and chapter reviews. Each question in the reviews has a critical thinking label, and students are referred to the Critical Thinking/How to Solve Problems chart on page 19 of the their text to learn the definition of the skill that is being reinforced.

In each instance the critical thinking approach is driven by the content. The critical thinking questions have been developed to offer an instructional focus for the unit of study, as an extension to daily instruction, and as a process for achieving instructional closure.

By using these instructional materials teachers will be able to provide students with ample practice in the art and science of critical thinking. Only through practice do we actually build communication, organization, and leadership skills in our students. These skills are invaluable, and will help prepare students for their roles as active citizens into the twenty-first century, rather than becoming mere "storehouses" of reluctantly learned, and quickly forgotten, isolated bits of information.

Critical Thinking Skills: Program Correlation

Skill	Definition	Page on which skill is taught	Pages on which skill is reinforced
IDENTIFY AND CLARIFY THE PROBLEM			
Expressing problems clearly	To succinctly describe a complex situation or body of information	Page 20	Pages 49, 117, 209, 244, 257, 526, 571, 627, 671, 685
Identifying central issues	To identify the main ideas in a piece of information	Page 124	Pages 95, 103, 220, 253, 294, 375, 379, 403, 497, 505, 559, 599
Making comparisons	To identify how different ideas, objects, historical figures, or situations are alike and/or different	Page 376	Pages 30, 209, 231, 290, 379, 393, 453, 571, 581, 603, 617, 637, 661, 685
Determining relevance	To decide if and how events, situations, or items are related to one another	Page 152	Pages 95, 114, 151, 155, 196, 365, 411
Formulating questions	To create questions that seek answers to specific objectives and lead to a deeper understanding of an issue	Page 540	Pages 18, 227, 281, 311, 326, 603, 627, 685
JUDGE INFORMATION RELATED TO THE PROBLEM			
Distinguishing fact from opinion	To separate those statements that can be proven to be true from those that reflect a personal viewpoint	Page 228	Pages 179, 183, 231, 321, 427
Checking consistency	To compare two or more items and determine whether they agree or disagree with each other	Page 92	Pages 23, 53, 71, 351, 422, 438, 479, 483, 508, 515, 520, 543, 549, 642
Distinguishing false from accurate images	To examine a widely held belief about a person, place, or thing and determine whether or not the belief is based in fact	Page 206	Pages 53, 209, 214, 257
Identifying assumptions	To recognize unstated beliefs that may underlie a statement, action, or event	Page 480	Pages 46, 127, 247, 355, 403, 434, 483, 489, 515, 535, 543, 627, 648
Recognizing bias	To identify a stated or unstated viewpoint or slant that is designed to promote one set of beliefs over another	Page 180	Pages 127, 155, 339
Recognizing ideologies	To identify underlying beliefs from actions or statements	Page 600	Pages 8, 23, 35, 86, 131, 189, 257, 329, 403, 457, 543, 603, 661
DRAW CONCLUSIONS AND SOLVE THE PROBLEM			
Drawing conclusions	To find an answer or to form an opinion based on available information	Page 50	Pages 14, 38, 53, 59, 71, 95, 123, 140, 183, 231, 307, 379, 419, 466, 470, 555, 567, 590, 623, 661, 674
Recognizing cause and effect	To examine one event or idea causes other events or ideas to occur	Page 278	Pages 155, 183, 205, 261, 281, 351, 399, 585, 611, 667
Predicting consequences	To determine the likely effect of an event or action on the outcome of future events or actions	Page 512	Pages 80, 91, 127, 144, 171, 209, 273, 302, 311, 351, 368, 414, 422, 457, 515
Identifying alternatives	To identify one or more methods to achieve a goal and to solve a problem; to recognize the possibility of other goals	Page 454	Pages 23, 107, 127, 136, 165, 257, 347, 457, 483, 511, 571, 681
Testing conclusions	To examine a conclusion and determine whether or not it is supported by known facts	Page 348	Pages 67, 71, 277, 351, 422, 447, 483, 603, 657
Demonstrating reasoned judgment	To present evidence or reasoning that supports a given opinion or statement	Page 568	Pages 63, 231, 238, 271, 281, 335, 360, 379, 385, 476, 539

Teaching Heterogeneous Groups

Meeting the Challenge:

Take a look around your classroom. If it's anything like the vast majority of other American classrooms, it probably includes students from several different ethnic backgrounds and cultural groups. In all likelihood it also includes gifted students as well as students with learning disabilities, native speakers as well as students for whom English is a second language, and visual learners as well as verbal learners.

The range of abilities, languages, cultural perspectives, and learning styles found in the typical American classroom is enough to challenge the most accomplished teacher. Yet it is imperative that today's teachers meet this challenge. They must provide meaningful instruction to all students and they must do so within the confines of an existing social studies curriculum.

How can teachers accomplish this task? First, they must look to their diverse student populations as a source of tremendous opportunity. They also must take their students' differences into account and plan their curriculum accordingly. To help teachers with this task *Magruder's American Government* presents several special features.

THE CHALLENGE

To provide students with meaningful and significant instruction that recognizes different learning abilities.

THE SOLUTION

Students successfully meet the challenge of intellectual development and subject mastery when instruction makes sense to them. However, what makes sense to one student does not always make sense to another. One student may grasp difficult and complicated concepts very quickly, while another may learn more slowly and thus require guided instruction and frequent opportunities for remediation. Still another student may have difficulty reading.

Using a variety of activities geared to different ability levels helps teachers achieve a balance between the need for enrichment and the need for remediation. For example, presenting students who need more intellectual stimulation with more than one perspective on an issue or problem increases their opportunities for discovering, analyzing, and evaluating relationships between ideas. Similarly, using special reading strategies with slower readers enhances—before, during, and after reading—their comprehension of key issues.

"If possible, give students choices on some projects so they can work in ways that are most meaningful to them."

Magruder's American Government Teacher's Edition provides an abundance of teaching notes and activities for students of all abilities. "Teaching Heterogeneous Groups" suggests ways to tailor content to meet the instructional needs of students of varying abilities, while the activities "For Gifted Students" present strategies for challenging students who need more intellectual stimulation. "Enrichment" activities provide opportunities for learning at three different levels of difficulty: easy, average, and challenging. "Reteaching" strategies in every lesson provide activities for students needing remediation.

THE CHALLENGE

To communicate content to students who have limited English proficiency or use English as a second language.

THE SOLUTION

The greatest challenge in teaching students for whom English is a second language lies in the creation of materials and experiences that do not rely heavily on the printed word. Often, students with limited English proficiency have average or above-average ability, but lack the cultural background or language skills necessary to build a framework for learning and for clearly expressing themselves. These students need assistance in building prior knowledge and overcoming language barriers. By providing background knowledge missing from a student's personal experience, by using visual cues to illustrate key points, and by reviewing the meaning of unfamiliar idiomatic phrases and words, teachers can help non-native speakers overcome these barriers to learning.

Magruder's American Government can help you tailor instruction to the needs of students with limited English proficiency. The wide array of charts, photos, and other graphic organizers in the *Student Edition* provides visual learning cues. "LEP" activities in the *Teacher's Edition* utilize visual, non-verbal means to teach content, while "Vocabulary" activities suggest strategies for developing students' understanding of key terms.

THE CHALLENGE

To focus discussions in a manner that capitalizes on different cultural perspectives.

THE SOLUTION

Since we live in a pluralistic society, the study of American government is in itself a study of different cultural perspectives. As students learn about the structure and function of government, they learn how early Iroquois nations influenced the development of American government, why the struggle for civil rights continues to this day, and what the multicultural goals of the 1990s are. Students are led to understand and recognize that our government is built upon, and continually strengthened by, the contributions of all Americans, including those of varying ethnic and cultural backgrounds.

The *Student Edition* includes two culturally informed narrative features — "Voices on Government" and "Global Awareness" — that highlight the contributions to government by Americans from different backgrounds. *Magruder's American Government* also includes "Spotlight On: Global Awareness" and "Spotlight On: Multiculturalism" —multicultural teaching notes in the *Teacher's Edition*.

THE CHALLENGE

To accommodate students with different learning styles.

THE SOLUTION

One of the most recent developments in education addresses the reality that, just as teachers have different teaching styles, students have different learning styles. Students in the same class often have different methods of assimilating the same information. The explanation of a concept may be clear to one student, while it escapes another, equally intelligent learner. What may seem like a "left-field" question from a student may be an attempt to fit content into a unique learning perspective.

What this phenomenon means for educators is that learning styles must be considered when planning and implementing lessons. The simplest strategy for meeting this objective is to create a class atmosphere that fosters tolerance for individual differences and focuses on strengths rather than weaknesses. But that strategy is not enough. Providing a variety of materials and activities so that all students have a chance to learn in a manner suited to their preferred way of learning is also critical.

Magruder's American Government provides a plentiful source of materials to meet the needs of students with different learning styles. The *Student Edition* includes numerous graphs, charts, and political cartoons that will appeal to visual learners. The *Teacher's Edition* suggests activities for "Cooperative Learning," while the *Teacher's Resource File* provides "Simulations and Debates," and "Participatory Government" files to challenge students who are active learners. In addition, Government in Action Transparencies provide class activities for visual learners, and new video and video disk components are available to challenge all students in ways never before possible.

Different Learning Styles

General—Student needs to focus on the big picture before addressing specific information.

Specific—Student needs to understand details before grasping the whole concept.

Active—Hands-on, exploratory interaction with the subject is preferred by the student.

Social—Student needs to focus on personal relationships and may prefer to learn in a group.

Verbal—Student needs to verbalize current understanding and to think through ideas aloud.

Structured—Learner uses a systematic approach to solving any problem and works in an orderly fashion from start to finish.

Strategies for Reading in the Content Area

You Don't Have to Be a Reading Teacher to Encourage Good Reading Habits

To participate fully in the study of American government, all students, not just good readers, need to be *active readers.* Active readers interact with the text before, during, and after reading. They use proven reading strategies, such as "Question Writing" and "Relating to the Topic," to integrate what they already know with what they are about to learn, and build a framework for the various facts and ideas they are studying. As a result, active or strategic readers achieve a far greater and more personal understanding of what they read.

Magruder's American Government has been designed to help your students become active and strategic readers. The following reading strategies, identified as appropriate in each section of the *Teacher's Edition*, will help students focus before they actually begin to read, and monitor their comprehension *as* they read. Using these strategies will enable all your students—not just your good readers—to take responsibility for their reading and become active, strategic readers.

Question Writing

This activity introduces students to the main ideas of a section before they begin to read. It is a good strategy to use with students who need help focusing their attention on reading.

To use this strategy, follow these steps:

1. Have students read the section's main headings and/or each of the subheadings.
2. Invite students to turn each heading into a question. Write all questions on the chalkboard, or have students write them at their desks.
3. Have students skim the text to find the answers to their questions, or answer questions as they read the section.

Structured Overview and Graphic Organizer

The structured overview and graphic organizer use an outline and a diagram, respectively, to introduce students to the major concepts and important terms in a section. This reading strategy is especially effective for sections with a heavy concept or vocabulary load and for visual learners.

To set up the structured overview or graphic organizer, follow these steps:

1. Ask students to skim the section for key words and concepts. You may wish to list these items on the chalkboard.
2. Ask students to skim the section headings and create an outline of the section using both main headings and subheadings, and including important words or "Key Terms." Students can then revise their outlines as they read the section.
3. Or, create a chart on the chalkboard and ask students to suggest concepts and important

Example

If the section deals with:
"Formally Amending the Constitution,"
you might put the following words on the chalkboard:

Process	The 26 Amendments
amendment	Bill of Rights
formal amendment	13th Amendment
four methods	19th Amendment

words or "Key Terms" from the section to be placed under appropriate headings on the chart. Students can add to the chart or revise it as they read the section.

Problem-Solving

Creating a problem provides an imaginative entry into a text selection and a reason to become familiar with text content. It can stimulate curiosity and motivate students to seek a solution.

Follow these steps to implement this strategy:

1. Identify a single concept or topic from the text.
2. Present a hypothetical problem that can be solved by using that concept or information related to the concept or topic. The problem could be drawn from current events, past issues in government, or your own fertile imagination!
3. Invite students to generate solutions to the problem. Encourage them to think creatively, since there are no correct answers. You may want to write students' solutions on the chalkboard.
4. Ask students to keep the problem and their solutions in mind as they read the section. If the problem is solved in the text, you might invite students to compare that solution to their own.

Example

If the topic is:
"State and Local Revenues,"

the problem might be:
"You are a city official. You need more funds for the schools, but you do not wish to raise property taxes. How can you raise or find the money you need?"

Relating to the Topic

This strategy enables students to prepare for their reading assignment by relating the topic they will read about to a similar topic or a situation they have encountered in their own lives.

This strategy may he used in the following way:

1. Choose a topic or concept in the section on which students might focus.
2. Without telling students what the topic or concept is, pose a question that illustrates the topic and draws upon students' personal experiences or knowledge.
3. Encourage students to consider the question in pairs or as a class, and have students elaborate on the topic or concept being discussed.
4. Introduce the section topic or concept. Encourage students to compare the concept they just discussed with what they read in the text. Point out to students that this activity helps them to understand how government affects their daily lives.

Reinforcing Key Terms

As students read, have them find facts in the text that reinforce or prove each Key Term.

Predicting Content

This activity may combine pre-reading and during-reading activities. Before reading, have students read the boldfaced headings found throughout the section. Point out that these headings form an outline of the content. Then have students predict the content of the section in one sentence. Direct students to read the section to test their predictions.

Who? What? When? Where? How? Why?

While reading each section, have students write short answers to focus questions beginning *Who, What, When, Where, How*, and *Why*. With practice, students can learn to pose their own questions.

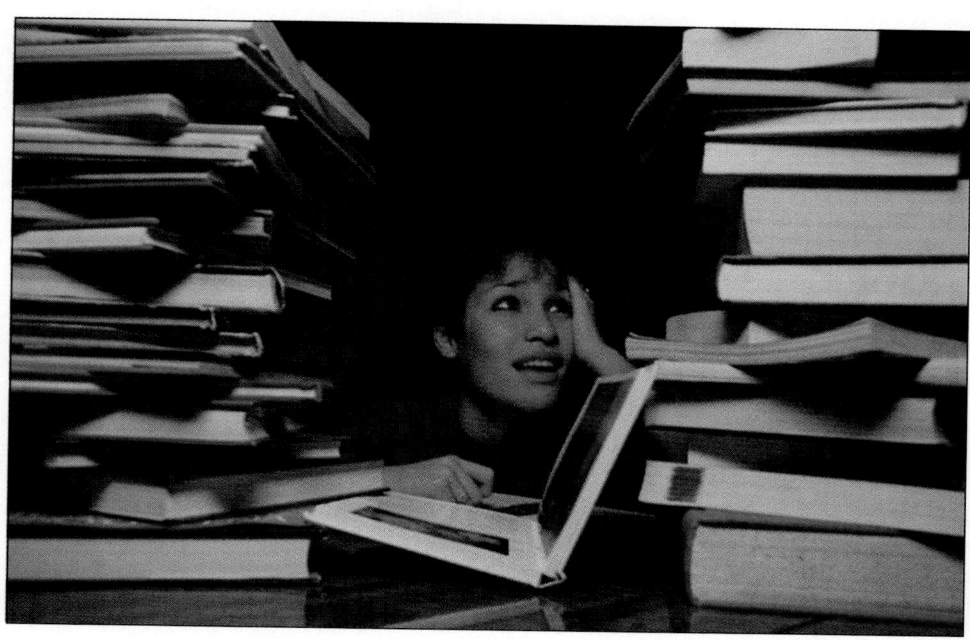

Assessing Student Knowledge

"WILL THIS BE ON THE TEST?" If you've heard that question once, you probably have heard it a thousand times. For, in the eyes of many students, test scores and grades are the ultimate measure of academic success.

Recent research into the process by which students learn is leading to changes in the science of classroom assessment.

Assessment and alternative assessment tools have come of age, and teachers like yourself are being encouraged to include new methods of analyzing and interpreting student performance in their assessment program. Many schools even are requesting alternative assessment programs that are structured to assess students' strengths and accomplishments, as well as their weaknesses or failures.

What Is Informal Assessment?

What is alternative assessment and how do you communicate informal learning to students—and their parents? Alternative assessment methods are designed to enable teachers like yourselves to make informed decisions regarding instruction, to provide direction, and to help bring students' performance in line with their potential. Thus, unlike formal assessment, informal assessment is individualized. It is ongoing, and perhaps even done daily. It relies upon, among other things, your observations and the student's own reports and self-evaluation of progress. It includes many "new" methods of student assessment that are not really new at all. In fact, it's likely that you have used many of the tools of informal assessment—talking with students, observing and listening to students, reading and evaluating student writing. Nevertheless, it is worth examining some of the informal assessment tools we have included in Magruder's American Government, especially since these methods have been designed to help you discover how students think, not just what they know.

Observation and Interview

Informal observation can be a valuable assessment tool revealing a student's success or frustration in approaching a learning task. You might wish to try the following observation activities:

- When students provide verbal explanations, evaluate them for reasonableness.
- Probe to discover student strategies and methods for coming up with answers.
- Listen for thoughts expressed in the student's own words.
- Watch for comments and actions—including those that you haven't formally tried to elicit—that indicate insight into the concepts.

Interviews also can produce a body of assessment information. When you ask planned questions about a student's approach to an assignment, you can evaluate the student's skills. For example, the assignment might be to research a particular aspect of the local government.

Here are some tips for conducting interviews:

- Begin with broad questions about the processes the student used and then focus on specifics.
- Keep it short, and be sure to probe for successful strategies as well as areas for improvement.
- Conduct interviews with individuals while the rest of the class is focused on a task.

If you wish to be systematic, you can develop an observation/interview checklist for some or all students. Include such behaviors as time on task, attention to task, ability to work cooperatively, and ability to ask questions. (See the "Computer Test Bank and Assessment" file in the Teacher's Resource File for an example of such a form.)

Student Writing

Student writing can provide many clues to student needs. Writing enables students to put into words their frustrations as well as their successes, as they approach an assignment or reflect upon an activity, an assignment, or a test. You can then use this information to learn about the student's needs.

When reading student writing, you may wish to do the following:

- Provide positive feedback and reassurance to the student.
- Write suggestions for overcoming barriers to learning, for reducing frustration, or for pursuing activities and assignments in greater depth.
- Use questions to stimulate thought about a topic.

Here again, if you wish to be systematic, you can develop a checklist to evaluate the journal writing of some or all students. The Teacher's Resource File includes a sample form you can use to evaluate students' writing in terms of content, organization, usage, mechanics, and style.

Portfolios

Composition teachers have been using portfolios—individualized collections of significant student work—for some time. Portfolios help to instill pride of ownership and a sense of accomplishment in writing, to chart individual progress, and to provide diagnosis for improving instruction.

Portfolios can be used in government classes for similar purposes.

Consider the following tips for using portfolios

- Encourage students to assist you in selecting material for their portfolios.
- Provide opportunities for students to review, discuss, and informally evaluate their own portfolios.
- Emphasize pride in the accomplishments demonstrated by the contents of the portfolio.

Student Self-Assessment

One important contributor to your store of assessment information is the students themselves. Students can verbally express and comment on their own learning and progress; they can also write about it. To assess their own progress in working through individual activities, students can use the Student Self-Assessment Form found in the Teacher's Resource File entitled "Computer Test Bank and Assessment."

Don't Throw Out Formal Testing

Of course, traditional methods of formal assessment still have their place in the classroom. *Magruder's American Government* provides you with a variety of formal testing options outlined below.

Chapter Tests

Each chapter has a three-page ready-made test that reviews Key Terms, tests students' understanding of Main Ideas, assesses students' ability to interpret graphic information, and evaluates students' ability to use critical thinking skills. Chapter Tests are found in the Unit booklets contained in the Teacher's Resource File.

Additional Test Questions

For every chapter, three pages of Additional Test Questions for each of the categories tested by the Chapter Tests (Key Terms, Main Ideas, interpreting graphic information, and using critical thinking skills) are also available in the Instructional Support File found in the Teacher's Resource File. Because the additional test questions are coded to ability levels, you can tailor your tests to fit individual and specific classroom needs.

Computer Test Bank

The Computer Test Bank contains all the Chapter Tests and all the Additional Test Questions. It provides the ultimate flexibility to create a variety of tests geared to your students' ability levels, or your state and local curriculum requirements.

Putting It All Together

No one method of assessment can adequately identify the successes and failures of all students. The suggestions and materials for formal and informal assessment available to users of *Magruder's American Government* offer teachers a wide range of activities and assessment tools. You'll want to use these ideas as a springboard for developing your own assessment materials and taking a fresh look at your students.

Putting Technology to Work in the Classroom

The most rewarding moments for any teacher are those in which that flicker of understanding and recognition registers on the student's face—those moments when the previously struggling student "gets it" for the first time. And as any teacher can confirm, there are few things more frustrating than the repeated failure to engage that student who just does not seem to be thriving on traditional pedagogical fare.

The challenge of achieving the rewards and overcoming the frustrations of teaching has never been greater. Yet at the same time, the tools with which teachers can approach this challenge have never been more potent. For with the help of the latest educational technologies, teachers can overcome the obstacles that stand in the way of learning and understanding. They can address the specific needs of students with different learning styles. And, rather than being overwhelmed by the rapidity of change in knowledge and information, they can use that change as a device for inspiring and motivating their students.

Technological Solutions for the Teacher—and Student

Research tells us that different students have different learning styles. Some learners need to get a general overview of a topic before they can grasp its details; others need to build from a group of details to develop their own generalizations or to understand those that others make. Some learners need a structured approach to learning; other learners are restricted by such structure. Still others prefer group work, and some must verbalize their ideas to understand them or use hands-on learning in order to achieve a concrete understanding of an abstract idea.

Technology offers many ways to make issues in American government come alive and to engage students of different learning styles. Computers, CD-ROM, and other technologies place vast sources of information and information-processing capabilities at students' fingertips. Audiovisual tools such as television documentaries, cable news broadcasts, and videodiscs help make events come to life by presenting images and sounds that command attention.

For example, interactive video products, such as ABCNews InterActive™, to which the Teacher's Edition is correlated, give students a chance to view video presentations of factual information about the Supreme Court, Congress, the presidency, and other topics. This technology also gives students a chance to construct their own presentations, using the product's visual, audio, and printed information. Thus, students gain exposure to different methods of receiving knowledge; and they also learn new ways of producing, expressing, building, reshaping, and sharing that knowledge. Students can be freed to use talents besides writing—and responses can take such forms as concept maps, charts, graphs, edited newscasts, slides, digitized sounds and pictures, and recorded interviews or debates.

Such technologies offer students of varying learning styles an opportunity to interact with information on their own terms, in ways that enable them to utilize their particular intellectual strengths.

Keeping Pace in a Changing World

Another challenge of teaching today is the rapid pace of change in knowledge and information. This challenge is partially the result of technology that enables huge amounts of information to be transferred over vast distances in tiny fragments of time. Yet it is that same technology that will allow teachers to use that information to their advantage—and to the advantage of their students.

Access to cable news programs, such as the CNN VideoLink™, available with *Magruder's American Government,* can help teachers manage in this age of information and keep their classrooms well informed about the latest developments in this country and around the world. Students can benefit from the latest global newsgathering technology and stay on top of the changes that continually sweep the globe. And they can do so through a medium that stimulates their interest and their willingness to learn.

Real-Life Learning

The lessons learned with the help of current and future technology promise to serve the student for a lifetime. Students who learn by using technology to present their own ideas will be those best prepared for their lives in the twenty-first century. Students who have experience working with networked computers and databases, as well as those who have learned how to work cooperatively, will enter the workplace of tomorrow with some of the requisite skills for success.

Perhaps there is also an even greater potential in technology—to equalize opportunity. For once information is freed from the control of a single individual, it becomes less authoritarian and prescriptive in its essence. Also, the technology itself becomes an aid to cooperation and collaboration as students learn to work interactively with information and with other people.

The Promise of Technology

When students use technology to learn, to share, and to express themselves, they become more actively involved in their own learning. Instead of merely receiving instruction, they can follow their own paths to discovery. Instead of relying on a single source or perhaps just a few sources for information, they can tap into huge reservoirs of information, playing ideas off other net worked users, interacting with and communicating by new means, and sharing approaches to problem solving.

Teachers, too, are empowered. The teacher is no longer the sole presenter of the information, but the manager of a special learning environment. Instead of needing to direct the experience, he or she need only help to keep it smoothly on track. Many teachers report great personal satisfaction and a heightening of their own self-concept when they use various options in technology to solve problems and facilitate student learning. These reports are helping to overcome some of the barriers that have heretofore limited the availability and use of technological resources in many schools and classrooms.

Technology promises great rewards to both teacher and student. So invite technology into your classroom, and watch this new world unfold.

Managing CONTENT and INSTRUCTION

Course Plans and Pacing Guide

We know from talking with teachers like yourself that the time constraints, course focus, and ability level of students in government classrooms varies widely. So, we designed *Magruder's American Government* to give you practical tools—tools you can use to manage content and time, and adapt instruction to suit your specific needs.

Student Edition

Clear, Flexible Organization

A logically organized, newly designed text helps you manage the demands of a content-heavy, time-constrained course.

- Each chapter contains three to six **manageable sections,** making it easy for you to cover a chapter a week. (See the Table of Contents on pp. *vii-xiv*.)
- Each section follows a **three-step lesson format** (Preview, Read, Review) and lists "Key Terms" at the beginning of each section, ensuring mastery of key terms and concepts. (See page 25.)
- Each chapter includes a **Chapter-in-Brief** , allowing you to:
  - **Preview** the chapter or individual sections
  - **Review** the chapter or individual sections
  - **Survey** omitted chapters or sections (For example, you may wish to skip Chapter 5 and assign the Chapter-in-Brief on page 125 as a quick survey of that chapter before moving on to other chapters.)
- Each chapter concludes with a **Chapter Review** that contains four carefully sequenced parts. For your convenience and easy assignment, the "Main Idea" questions are divided by section, and the "Getting Involved" activities can be completed in one class period or less. (See page 155.)

Engaging Narrative, Active Learning

Magruder's helps you manage instruction by directing your television-age students to do more than just read the text. It invites them to get involved in the classroom and the world beyond the classroom.

- Each unit opens with a **Unit Introduction** that includes three to four "Did you Know. . ." facts to stimulate student interest. (See page 233.)
- Each chapter begins with a **Chapter Preview** that links chapter content to prior knowledge and the contemporary world. (See page 184.) "Describe" and "Predict" questions provoke lively discussion and thought. Chapter objectives are clearly stated, and are related to each section in the chapter.
- Every chapter includes **Debating Key Issues,** a feature based on key Supreme Court decisions, or **What You Can Do,** a case study of students' participation in government—features that invite students to "get involved."
- **Government Resources Handbook** orients your young citizens to valuable information that can help them make good decisions. Chapter Review activities provide practice in using the handbook.

Consistent Skill Development

- Every chapter includes a skill lesson that helps you refine students' **Critical Thinking Skills** (See page152.) and **Citizenship Skills.** (See page 308.)
- Every visual in the *Student Edition* includes a skill caption. (See page 398.)
- Every unit contains two "How to" **citizenship charts.** (See page 658.)
- **How to Solve Problems** chart in Chapter 1 defines 17 common critical thinking skills used to solve problems. (See page 19.) All 17 skills are taught step by step in the text. Students are referred back to the chart whenever a critical thinking question appears in a section or chapter review so that they can see the context in which critical thinking is used to solve problems.

Teacher's Edition

The new wraparound format includes lesson plans, high-interest background notes, and student-oriented activities located where they're most useful —around easy-to-read student pages — so you can plan, instruct, and assess more effectively than ever.

> ***"Students can be directed to do so much by the text. They don't just have to read."***

Plan More Easily

- **Course plans and pacing charts** on pages T27-T31 help you select the units, chapters, and sections you need to cover or omit.
- **Managing the Unit** suggestions, with references to the course plans and pacing charts noted above, give you a bird's-eye view of the content in each unit, and help you budget your time. (See page 232.) To survey a unit, simply assign the "Chapter-in-Brief" pages from that unit and distribute the lesson outlines for each chapter in the unit from the Teacher's Resource File.
- **Chapter Resources** guide acts as the nerve center for *Magruder's*. (See page 210.) Whenever possible, cross references to other components are provided to help facilitate planning. Look for these symbols:

Teaching Resources File

Computer Test Bank

Government in Action Transparencies

- **Lesson Plans** include clearly labeled activities designed to help schools adapt the same text for basic, heterogeneous, and gifted or AP classes.
- **Bibliography/Multimedia Resources,** located on the Chapter-in- Brief page of each chapter, "Additional Resources," includes literature and new educational software to enrich instruction. (See page 255.)

Instruct More Effectively

With everything you need to plan at your fingertips, you are ready to begin instruction.

- **Unit Focus** prompts you to activate prior knowledge, discuss the unit opener, assign a journal writing activity, and discuss bulletin board ideas or assignments.
- **Chapter Focus** helps you introduce the chapter and motivate learning.
- **Section Focus** lists the section's purpose and objectives and includes a creative **Bellringer Activity** to get students on task the moment class begins.
- **Vocabulary** and **Reading Strategies** help you work with basic, LD, or LEP students.
- **Teaching the visuals and features** tips help you extend content.
- **Guided practice** and **independent practice** suggestions help you ensure mastery of Key Terms and concepts.
- Lesson plans prompt you to **monitor comprehension** by reviewing answers.
- A **Closure** statement helps you review the section and, when appropriate, segue into the next section.

Remediate and Enrich More Sensitively

- A **Reteaching activity** for every section helps you remediate students who need it while others complete the **Enrichment activity.**
- Activities for additional enrichment appear below the student pages:
  - **Cooperative Learning**
  - **Teaching Heterogeneous Groups**
  - **For Gifted Students**
  - **Multicultural Awareness**
- **Spotlight On** background notes also appear below the student pages to help you shine in the classroom:
  - **Roots of Democracy**
  - **Political Talk**
  - **Constitutional Issues**
  - **Economics**
  - **Global Awareness**
  - **Multiculturalism**
  - **Behind the Scenes**

- ***Magruder's:* A Witness to Change** provides William McClenaghan's special historical perspective of each chapter, helping you and your students see how government works. (See page 314.)

Teacher's Resource File

Instructional Support Files

All basic instructional materials you need to teach a chapter are organized chapter by chapter—the way you teach.

- **Lesson Outlines** (one per section) can be used to survey complete sections, chapters, or units.
- **Guided Reading and Review Worksheets** (one per section) check mastery of key terms and concepts.
- **Quizzes** (one per section) provide opportunties for informal assessment—and can be graded quickly.
- **Critical Thinking** or **Citizenship Skill Application** (one per chapter) reinforce skills taught in the text.

- **Case Study on Contemporary Issues** (one per chapter) enriches learning and includes:
  - Primary source reading
  - Political cartoon, and
  - Graph/chart study for each case study.
- **Chapter Tests** include visual interpretation skill section and questions coded by ability level and objective.
- **Additional Test Questions** help you design tests suited to your needs.

Enrichment Support Files

Magruder's offers valuable backup on your favorite topics to suit your course focus and teaching style.

- **Participatory Government Activities File** includes public-policy handbook, a guide to student and summer government programs, and more.
- **Simulations and Debates File** includes a guide to debating and to short role-plays, debates, and simulations.
- **Supreme Court Cases File** includes over 50 landmark cases, plus extension activities for each "Debating Key Issues" feature in the text.
- **Historical and Legal Documents File** includes over 60 teacher-requested favorites.
- **Comparative Government: A Multicultural View File** includes ten comparative government case studies to improve students' global awareness.

Computer Test Bank

Magruder's lets you create a variety of high-quality tests—all suited to the ability level of your students—in minutes. Just request our free software or call our free Dial-A-Test service.

- **Ability level codes** help you select questions appropriate for your students.
- **Objective codes** before each test item allows you to match test items with the section objective code listed in the *Teacher's Edition* lesson plan. Testing to your state or local objectives is as simple as matching the section objective to your state or local objective.
- **Alternative Assessment Guidelines** and Forms offer suggestions for assessing student knowledge and writing.

Election Kit

Helps students analyze and participate in elections.

Constitutional Issues Posters

Uses political cartoons and quotes to highlight an enduring Constitutional issue linked to the Bulletin Board suggestions for each unit in the *Teacher's Edition.*

Constitution Study Guide

Offers in-depth study of the Constitution plus a 96-page teacher's manual.

GOVERNMENT IN ACTION TRANSPARENCIES

A set of 100 transparencies helps students become active participants in government and learning. The set includes:

- **Political cartoons** on your favorite topics (one per chapter).
- **Up-to-date maps, graphs, and charts** with overlays for dynamic instruction (one per chapter).
- **Legal documents** that help prepare students for the future.
- **High-quality lesson suggestions** for cooperative learning, writing, critical thinking, multicultural and global awareness, and participation in government.

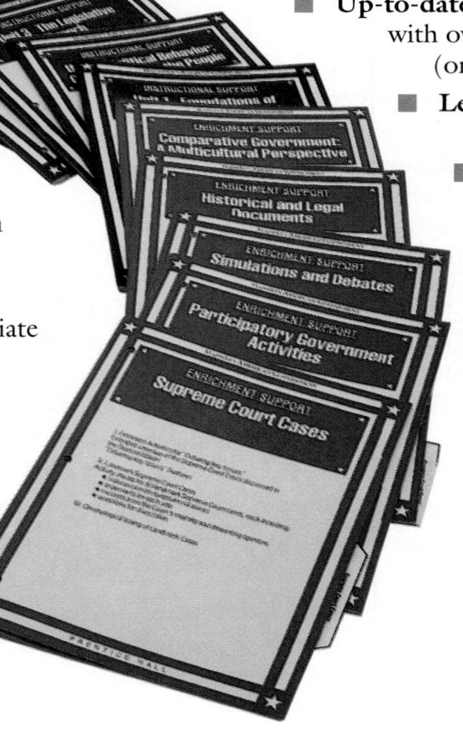

COURSE PLANS AND PACING GUIDE

The following pages show how the units and chapters of *Magruder's American Government* and accompanying components can be adapted to fit your specific course focus, time constraints and state or district curriculum requirements for government. One-semester course plans (Courses B - G) are based on a total of 18 weeks and 90 class days while the full-year course plan (Course A) is based on 36 weeks and 180 days.

COURSE A

U.S. Government Survey Course (1 year)

COURSE B:

U.S. Government Survey course (1 semester)

Course B pacing chart suggests sections that can be omitted in order to survey all units in one semester. Use the Chapter-in-Brief pages and Teacher's Resource File outlines for each section to help you survey omitted sections.

COURSE C

Participation in Government/Political Behavior (1 semester)

Focus on Unit 2, "Political Behavior" and Unit 7, "Participating in State and Local Government." Use the Chapter-in-Brief pages to help you quickly survey the other units. Omit Unit 6, "Comparative Political and Economic Systems" if constrained by time. Use the Participatory Government, Case Studies on Contemporary Issues, Simulations and Debates, and Election Kit in the Teacher's Resource File to supplement your instruction.

COURSE D

Principles of Democracy (1 semester)

Cover the first three chapters of Unit 1, "Foundations of American Government." Follow with Unit 5, "The Judicial Branch." Use the Chapter-in-Brief pages to help you survey Units 2 through 4. Now cover Chapter 4, "Federalism" and Unit 7, "Participating in State and Local Government." Conclude with Unit 6, "Comparative Political and Economic Systems." Use the Supreme Court Cases, Historical and Legal Documents, Case Studies on Contemporary Issues, and Comparative Government: A Multicultural View files in the Teacher's Resource File to supplement your instruction.

COURSE E

Structure of National and State Governments (1 semester)

Omit Unit 2, "Political Behavior" and Unit 6, "Comparative Political and Economic Systems."

COURSE F:

Comparative Government/ World Affairs (1 semester)

Focus on Unit 1, "Foundations of American Government," Unit 6, "Comparative Political and Economic Systems," and Unit 4, "The Executive Branch." Omit all other units. Use the Comparative Government: A Multicultural View file in the Teacher's Resource File and Global Awareness background notes in the *Teacher's Edition* to supplement your instruction.

COURSE G:

Constitutional Law/ Law Education (1 semester)

Cover the first three chapters of Unit 1, "Foundations in American Government." Follow with Unit 5, "The Judicial Branch," Chapter 25, "State and Local Government in Action," and possibly Unit 3, "The Legislative Branch." Omit Unit 2 , "Political Behavior," Unit 4 , "The Executive Branch," and Unit 6, "Comparative Political and Economic Systems." Cover all Debating Key Issues features. Use the Supreme Court Cases, Historical and Legal Documents, and Case Studies on Contemporary Issues files in the Teacher's Resource File to supplement your instruction.

Daily Pacing Guide

Chapter/Section	Course A	Course B	Course C	Course D	Course E	Course F	Course G
CHAPTER 1 Principles of Government							
1 Government and the State	2 days	2	.5	1	1.5	3	1
2 Forms of Government	2	1	1	1	1	3.5	1
3 Basic Concepts of Democracy	2	1	.5	1	1.5	2.5	1
Chapter-in-Brief	1		.5	1			1
CHAPTER 2 Origins of American Government							
1 Our Political Beginnings	1	1	1	1	1	2.5	1.5
2 The Coming of Independence	2		.5	1	1	2.5	1
3 The Critical Period	1		.5	1	1	1.5	1
4 Creating the Constitution	2		.5	1	1.5	2.5	1
5 Ratifying the Constitution	1		.5	.5	.5	1	.5
Chapter-in-Brief	1	1		.5			1
CHAPTER 3 The Constitution							
1 The Six Basic Principles	2	1	1	1.5	1.5	3.5	1.5
2 Formally Amending the Constitution	1	1	.5	.5	.5	1.5	.5
3 Informal Amendment	1	1	.5	.5	.5	1	.5
Chapter-in-Brief	1			.5			.5
CHAPTER 4 Federalism							
1 Federalism and the Division of Power	2	1	1	1			
2 The National Government and the 50 States	1		1	.5	1		
3 Interstate Relations	1		.5	.5	.5		
Chapter-in-Brief	1	1		1			
CHAPTER 5 Political Parties							
1 Parties and What They Do	2	1	2				
2 The Two-Party System	1	1	2				
3 The Two-Party System in American History	1		1				
4 The Minor Parties	1	.5	1				
5 The Organization of Political Parties	1	.5	.5				
Chapter-in-Brief	1			1.5			
CHAPTER 6 Voters and Voter Behavior							
1 The Constitution and the Right to Vote	2		1				
2 Voter Qualifications Among the States	1		.5				
3 Suffrage and Civil Rights	2		1				
4 Nonvoting	1	1	.5				
5 Voter Behavior	1	1	.5				
Chapter-in-Brief	1	1		1.5			

A = Survey/Full Year
B = Survey/1 Semester
C = Participation in Government
D = Principles of Democracy
E = Structure of National and State Governments
F = Comparative Government
G = Constitutional Law

Chapter/Section	Course A	Course B	Course C	Course D	Course E	Course F	Course G
CHAPTER 7 The Electoral Process							
1 The Nominating Process	1 day	1	1				
2 Elections	2	.5	1.5				
3 Money and the Election Process	1	.5	1				
Chapter-in-Brief	1			1.5			
CHAPTER 8 Mass Media and Public Opinion							
1 The Formation of Public Opinion	2	.5	1				
2 The Measurement of Public Opinion	1	.5	.5				
3 The Mass Media and Politics	1	.5	1.5				
Chapter-in-Brief	1			1.5			
CHAPTER 9 Interest Groups							
1 The Nature of Interest Groups	2	.5	1				
2 Types of Interest Groups	1	.5	1				
3 Interest Groups at Work	1	.5	1.5				
Chapter-in-Brief	1			1.5			
CHAPTER 10 Congress							
1 The National Legislature	2	1			2		1
2 The House of Representatives	2	1	1		1		1
3 The Senate	1	1	1		1		1
4 The Members of Congress	2	1	1		2		1
Chapter-in-Brief	1	.5		1.5			1
CHAPTER 11 Powers of Congress							
1 The Scope of Congressional Powers	2	1	.5		2		1
2 The Expressed Powers	2	1	1		2		1
3 The Implied Powers	2	1	1		2		1
4 The Nonlegislative Powers	2	1	1		1		1
Chapter-in-Brief	1	.5		1.5			1
CHAPTER 12 Congress in Action							
1 Congress Organizes	2	1	.5		2		1
2 Committees in Congress	2	1	1		2		1
3 How a Bill Becomes a Law: The House	2	1	1		2		1
4 The Bill in the Senate and the Final Stages	2	1	1		1		1
Chapter-in-Brief	1	.5		1.5			1
CHAPTER 13 The Presidency							
1 The President's Job Description	2	1	.5		1.5	1.5	
2 Presidential Succession and the Vice Presidency	2	1	.5		.5	.5	
3 Presidential Selection: The Framers' Plan	1	1	.5		1	1	
4 Nominating Presidential Candidates Today	1	1	.5		1	1	

A = Survey/Full Year
B = Survey/1 Semester
C = Participation in Government
D = Principles of Democracy
E = Structure of National and State Governments
F = Comparative Government
G = Constitutional Law

Daily Pacing Guide (continued)

Chapter/Section	Course A	Course B	Course C	Course D	Course E	Course F	Course G
5 At the National Convention	2 days	.5	.5		1	1	
6 The Election	2	.5	.5		.5	.5	
Chapter-in-Brief	1	.5	1	1.5			
CHAPTER 14 The Presidency in Action							
1 The Changing View of Presidential Power	2	.5	.5		1.5	2.5	
2 The President's Executive Powers	2	.5	1		1	1	
3 The Diplomatic and Military Powers	1	.5	.5		1	1.5	
4 The Legislative and Judicial Powers	1	.5	.5		1	1.5	
5 The Executive Office of the President and the Cabinet	2	1	.5		1	1	
Chapter-in-Brief	1	.5		1.5			
CHAPTER 15 Government at Work: The Bureaucracy							
1 The Federal Bureaucracy	2	1	.5		1	1	
2 The Executive Departments and the Independent Agencies	1	1	1		1	1	
3 The Civil Service	1	1	.5		.5	.5	
Chapter-in-Brief	1	.5		1.5			
CHAPTER 16 Financing Government							
1 Where the Money Comes From: Taxes	1	1	.5		1	2	
2 Nontax Revenues and Borrowing	1	.5	.5		.5	.5	
3 Spending and the Budget	1	1.5	1		1	2	
Chapter-in-Brief	1	.5		1.5			
CHAPTER 17 Foreign Policy and National Defense							
1 Foreign and Defense Policy: An Overview	1	1	1		1	2	
2 The Departments of State and Defense	1	.5	.5		1	1	
3 Other Foreign/Defense Policy Agencies	1	.5	.5		.5	.5	
4 American Foreign Policy: Past and Present	1		1		1.5	1.5	
5 Foreign Aid, Defense Alliances, and the United Nations	1	.5	1		1	1	
Chapter-in-Brief	1	1		1.5			
CHAPTER 18 The Federal Court System							
1 The National Judiciary	2	1	1	2.5	1		2
2 The Inferior Courts	1	1	.5	2.5	.5		2
3 The Supreme Court	1	1	2	2	2		3
4 The Special Courts	1	1	.5	1.5	.5		2
Chapter-in-Brief	1	.5		2			2
CHAPTER 19 Civil Liberties: First Amendment Freedoms							
1 The Unalienable Rights	2	1	1	2	1		3.5
2 Freedom of Religion	2	1	.5	2	1.5		3
3 Freedom of Speech and Press	2	1	1	3	1.5		3
4 Freedom of Expression and National Security	1	1	.5	2	1.5		2.5

A = Survey/Full Year
B = Survey/1 Semester
C = Participation in Government
D = Principles of Democracy
E = Structure of National and State Governments
F = Comparative Government
G = Constitutional Law

Daily Pacing Guide (continued)

Chapter/Section	Course A	Course B	Course C	Course D	Course E	Course F	Course G
5 Freedom of Assembly and Petition	1 day	1	.5	2	1		2
Chapter-in-Brief	1	.5		2			3
CHAPTER 20 Civil Liberties: Protecting Individual Freedoms							
1 Due Process	2	1	1	1.5	2		3
2 Freedom and Security of the Person	2	1	.5	1	1		2.5
3 Rights of the Accused	2	1	.5	1	1		3
4 Rights of the Accused: Punishment	1	1	.5	1	1		3
Chapter-in-Brief	1	.5	.5				1.5
CHAPTER 21 Civil Rights: Equal Justice Under Law							
1 Diversity and Discrimination in American Society	1	1	1	1	1.5		2
2 Equality Before the Law	2	1	1	1	1.5		2
3 Federal Civil Rights Laws	1	.5	1.5	2	1		3
4 American Citizenship	2	1	1	1	.5		1
Chapter-in-Brief	1	1		2			3
CHAPTER 22 Comparative Political Systems							
1 Great Britain	2			2		5	
2 Japan	2			2		5	
3 Mexico	2			2		5	
4 The Former Soviet Union	2	2		2		10	
Chapter-in-Brief	1	1		3			
CHAPTER 23 Comparative Economic Systems							
1 Capitalism	2			2		5	
2 Socialism	2			2		5	
3 Communism	2			2		5	
Chapter-in-Brief	1	2		2			
CHAPTER 24 Organization of State and Local Government							
1 The State Legislatures	2	1.5	2.5	1	2		
2 The Governor and State Administration	2	1.5	2.5	.5	2		
3 Counties, Towns, Townships, and Special Districts	2	1	2	.5	2		
4 Cities and Metropolitan Areas	2	.5	2	.5	2		
Chapter-in-Brief	1		1	1			
CHAPTER 25 State and Local Government in Action							
1 Providing Important Services	3	1.5	2.5		2		1
2 Financing State Government	2	1	2		1		1
3 In the Courtroom	2	1	2		2		2
4 The Courts and Their Judges	3	1.5	2.5		2		2
Chapter-in-Brief	1		1				2

A = Survey/Full Year
B = Survey/1 Semester
C = Participation in Government
D = Principles of Democracy
E = Structure of National and State Governments
F = Comparative Government
G = Constitutional Law

Credits

Teacher Writers/Reviewers

Robert J. Cormier, Teacher
Shrewsbury High School, Shrewsbury, Massachusetts

Susan Feibelman, Program Specialist
Dallas Independent School District, Dallas, Texas

Cathy L.Nelson, Teacher
Fridley High School, Fridley, Minnesota

Multicultural Reviewer

Dr. Charles Hancock
Department of Educational Studies
The Ohio State University, Columbus, Ohio

Staff

Editorial: David Lippman
Marie E. Norris
Marisa Sibio Shuff

Art and Design: L. Christopher Valente
Samuel S. Wallace
Jonathan Pollard

Cover Design: L. Christopher Valente
Martucci Studio

Electronic Page Makeup: Will Hirschowitz
Pearl B. Weinstein

Production: Pauline Wright
Shyamol Bhattacherya

Photo Research: Russell Lappa

Marketing: Jeffrey M. Ikler
Laura Asermily

Pre-press Production: Roger Powers
Leanne Cordischi

Manufacturing: Valerie Rhoades

PHOTO CREDITS **Page T7**, Robert Kelly/Life Picture Service; **T10**, File photo; **T17**, © Bob Daemmrich; **T19**, © Tony Freeman/PhotoEdit; **T21**, © Larry Lawfer; **T23**, © Bob Daemmirch

Prentice Hall A Division of Simon & Schuster
Englewood Cliffs, New Jersey 07632

ISBN 0-13-544545-0

Printed in the United States of America

3 4 5 6 7 8 9 99 98 97 96 95 94 93 92

Teacher's Edition

1992

75th Anniversary Edition

Magruder's AMERICAN GOVERNMENT

With this edition, *Magruder's American Government* marks its 75th year of publication. First published in 1917, the earliest edition of *Magruder's* numbered 562 pages and contained 101 black-and-white photographs. The pages themselves were no larger than a page from a paperback. Government in the United States has changed dramatically since 1917, and, as you can tell from this edition, *Magruder's* has changed with it. The original goal of the text, however, remains the same: to describe, analyze, and explain the American system of government and how it relates to you, the reader.

Shown above: A reproduction of the engraving that appeared on the cover of the first edition of *Magruder's*.

1992

75th Anniversary Edition

Magruder's AMERICAN GOVERNMENT

REVISED BY

William A. McClenaghan

DEPARTMENT OF POLITICAL SCIENCE
OREGON STATE UNIVERSITY

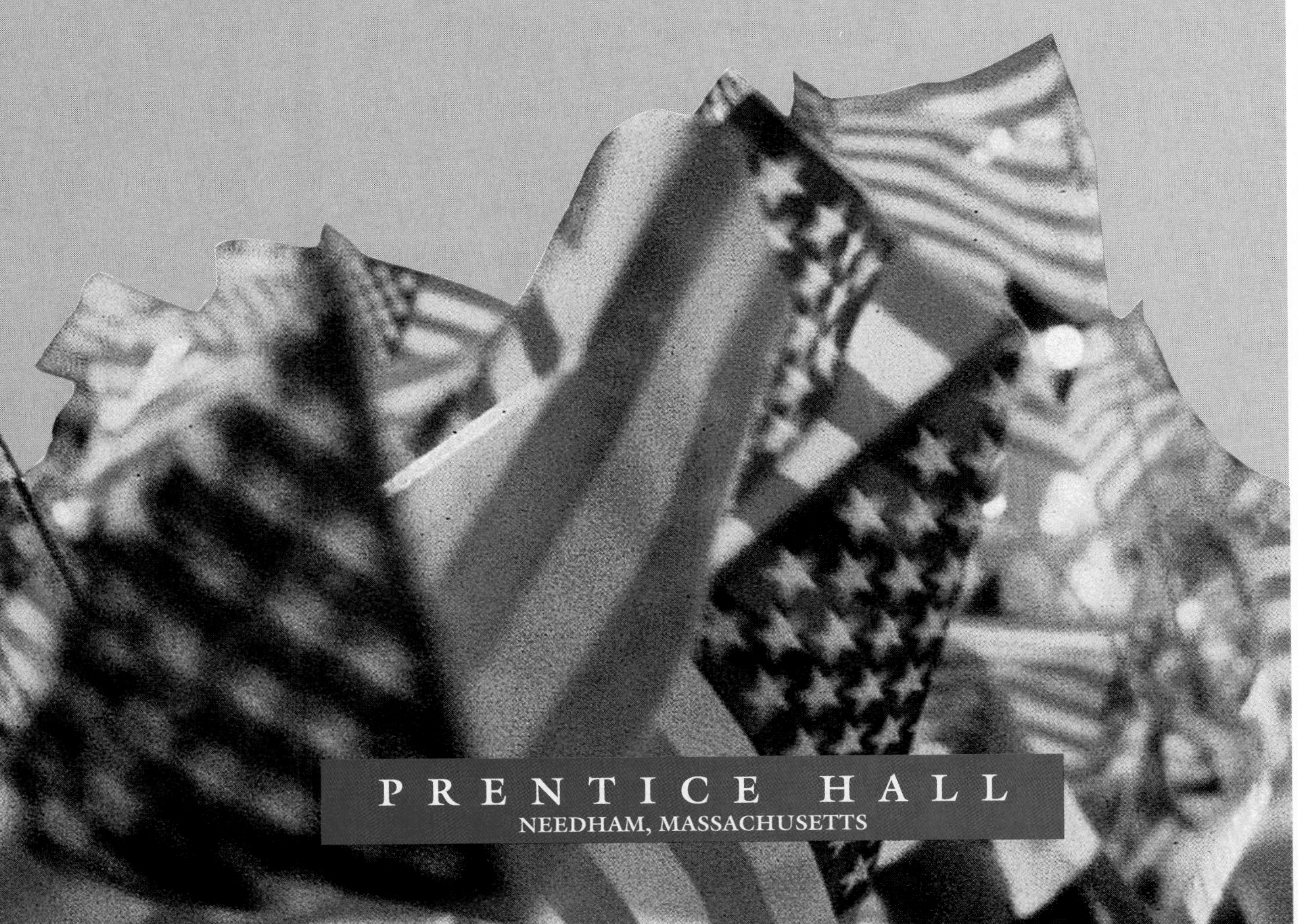

PRENTICE HALL
NEEDHAM, MASSACHUSETTS

American Government,

first published in 1917 and revised annually, is an enduring symbol of the author's faith in American ideals and American institutions. The life of Frank Abbott Magruder (1882–1949) was an outstanding example of Americanism at its very best. His career as a teacher, author, and tireless worker in civic and religious undertakings remains an inspiring memory to all who knew him.

STAFF CREDIT

Editorial:	David Lippman Nancy Rogier Marisa Sibio Shuff
Art and Design:	L. Christopher Valente Samuel S. Wallace Linda Johnson
Cover Design:	L. Christopher Valente Martucci Studio
Electronic Page Makeup:	Edwin Zeitz Linda Johnson
Production:	Pauline Wright
Photo Research:	Russell Lappa
Marketing:	Jeffrey M. Ikler Laura Asermily
Pre-press Production:	Roger Powers Leanne Cordischi
Manufacturing:	Valerie Rhoades

Library of Congress Catalog Card Number: 17-13472

PRENTICE HALL
A Division of Simon & Schuster
Englewood Cliffs, New Jersey 07632

ISBN 0-13-544529-9

Printed in the United States of America

3 4 5 6 7 8 9 99 98 97 96 95 94 93 92

PROGRAM REVIEWERS AND ADVISORS

Barbara C. Adams	Government Teacher Coronado High School Lubbock, Texas
Thomas Bass	Chairman, Political Science Department University of St. Thomas Houston, Texas
William J. Bialobrzeski	Political Science Instructor Southgate Anderson High School Southgate, Michigan
Connie Hankins	Government Teacher Miami Carol City High School Miami, Florida
Melva Ruth Jones	Teacher/Social Studies Department Chair Lincoln High School Dallas, Texas
William E. Law	AP Government Teacher Morse High School San Diego, California
James I. Malone	Government Teacher Rancho Buena Vista High School Vista, California
Dick Parsons	Government Teacher El Dorado High School Placerville, California
Ninfa Anita Sepulveda	Social Studies Department Chairperson S. F. Austin Senior High School Houston, Texas
Dr. Shelly K. Singer	Divisional Chair, Social Studies/Foreign Language Larkin High School Elgin, Illinois
Ellen Stone	Government Teacher McAllen High School McAllen, Texas

PREFACE

If a nation expects to be ignorant and free, . . .
it expects what never was and never will be.

THOMAS JEFFERSON

THIS IS A BOOK ABOUT GOVERNMENT—and, more particularly, about government in the United States. Over the course of its 25 chapters and more than 800 pages, you will consider the ways in which government in this country is organized, the ways in which it is controlled by the people, the many things that it does, and the various ways in which it does them.

Magruder's American Government, 1992, is the latest in a long line of editions of this book. The first one appeared in 1917, making this one the 75th anniversary edition. Every edition of this book has had one basic purpose: to describe, analyze, and explain the American system of government.

All of the many changes made in each edition of this book illustrate a very important point:

The American system of government is extraordinarily dynamic. Change—growth, adaptation, innovation—is a basic element of its character. While it is true that our government's fundamental principles and its basic structure have remained constant over time, many of its other characteristics have changed. They continue to do so—from year to year and, frequently, from one day to the next, and sometimes remarkably.

To underscore the critical importance of this fact of continuing change, dwell for a moment on the phrase "the American system of government." You will come across it again and again, for it is an apt description of government in the United States. As you will soon discover, that system is a very complex one.

It is complex because it is made up of many different parts, performing many different functions. It is a system because all of its many different parts are interrelated. The whole cannot be understood without a knowledge of its several interacting parts; and those parts cannot be understood without a knowledge of the whole. Given all of this, the vital effects of ongoing change in the system are obvious.

Every effort has been made to see that this book is as accurate, as up-to-date, as readable, and as interesting and usable as possible. The wealth of factual information it contains has been drawn from the most current and reliable of sources. This is not a book on current events, however. It does contain much data and draws many examples from the contemporary scene. But they are purposefully woven into the context of its primary objective: the description, analysis, and explanation of the American system of government. Another major objective is to provide a basis for understanding how other nations are governed through a careful examination of other political and economic systems.

Textbooks are sometimes criticized as being "too large," "too factual," or "not interpretive enough." *This* textbook includes that material which we believe to be absolutely necessary to a basic knowledge and understanding of the American governmental system. If the book is a "large" one, it is because its subject is a very large *and* a very *important* one.

Every book, regardless of its subject, reflects, to at least some degree, the biases of its author. This book is no exception. We have made a very conscious effort to minimize their appearance and to present a fair and balanced view of government in the United States. But, inevitably, those biases are present. Whenever they appear, they should be examined critically by the reader, of course. One of them is outstandingly obvious: the conviction that the American system of government, despite its imperfections, is in fact and should be government of the people, by the people, and for the people.

One final comment here—from both the original author, the late Frank Abbott Magruder, and the present one: Over the years we have received much valuable help from the many teachers and students who have used this book in classrooms across the nation. Their comments, suggestions, criticisms, and questions have played a large part in the making of each new edition—and they continue to be more than welcome, of course.

WILLIAM A. McCLENAGHAN

Department of Political Science
Oregon State University
Corvallis, Oregon

TABLE OF CONTENTS

UNIT 1

UNIT 2

Political Behavior: Government by the People

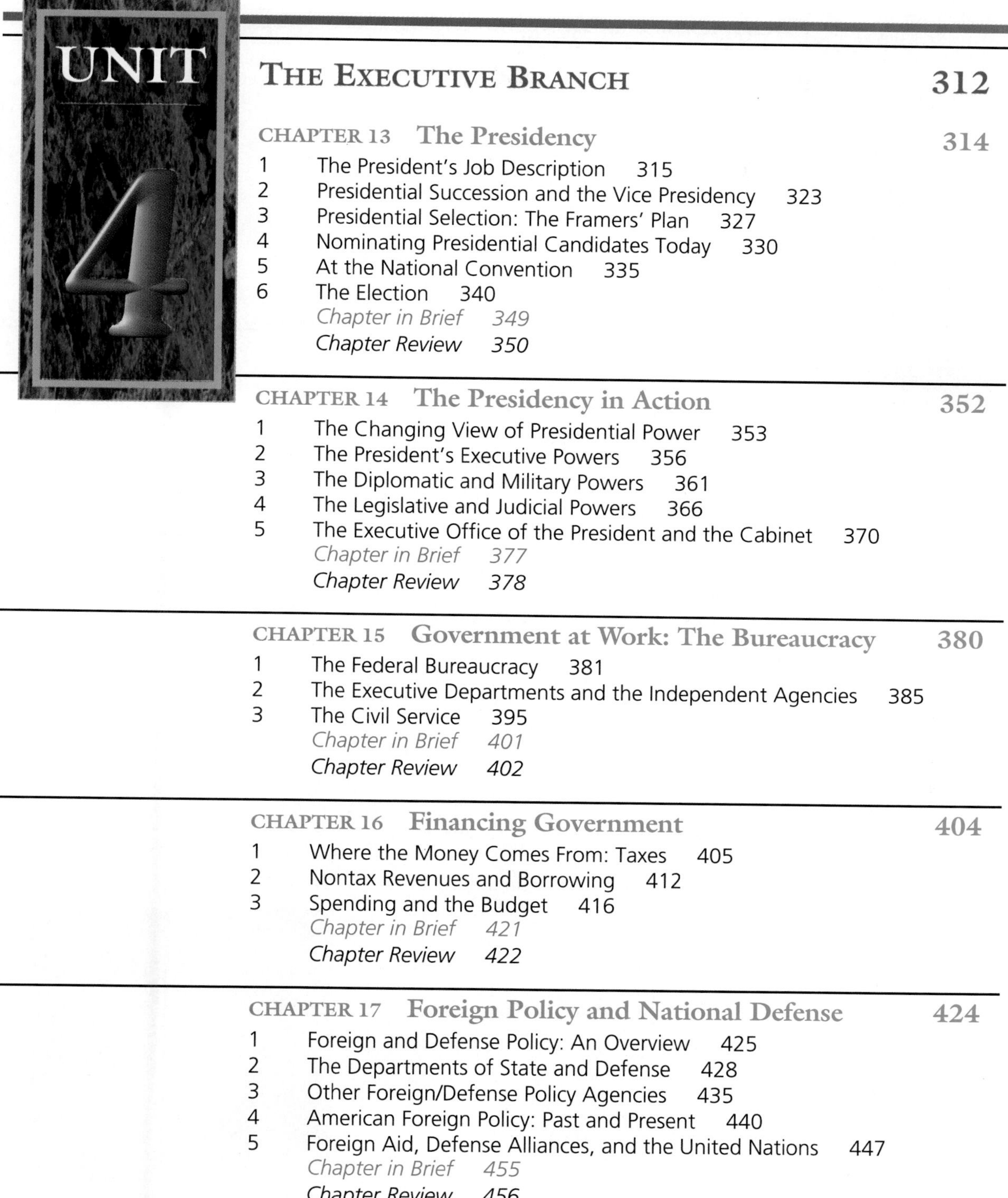

The Executive Branch 312

The Judicial Branch 458

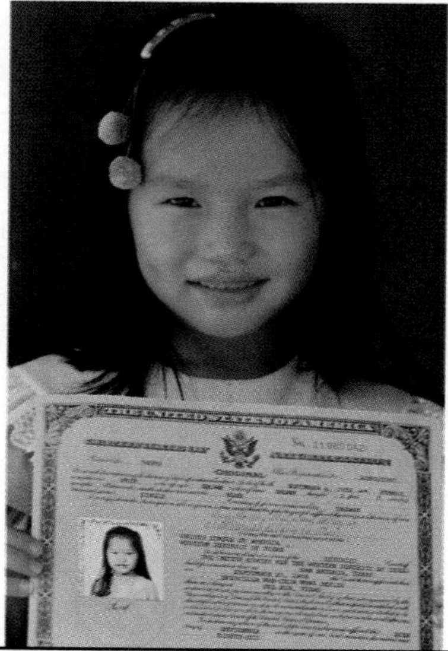

UNIT 6

Comparative Political and Economic Systems 572

UNIT 7

Participating in State and Local Government 628

Reference Section

Special Features

Debating Key Issues

Background information and key arguments on landmark Supreme Court cases

What You Can Do

Examples of student participation in government

Voices on Government

Opinions, views, and comments on the American political system

Global Awareness

Charts and graphs that compare governments around the world

Political Art

Artists' views on the American political scene, past and present

Skill Lessons

Critical Thinking

Citizenship

Maps, Charts, Graphs, Diagrams, Tables

Maps

Graphs, Charts, Diagrams

Tables

Citizenship Charts

Managing the Unit

You may wish to review the following materials before beginning the unit to help plan your instruction.

Each chapter ends with a Chapter-in-Brief with suggestions for previewing, reviewing, or omitting the chapter.

Unit 1 Outline

Pacing Charts,
pp. T28–T31

Unit 1

An American Tradition An explosion of fireworks illuminates the Statue of Liberty during an Independence Day celebration.

Skills and Features

The following skill lessons and features are included in this unit.

Skill Lessons

Critical Thinking: Expressing Problems Clearly (p. 20)
Critical Thinking: Drawing Conclusions (p. 50)
Citizenship: How to Use Different Sources of Government Information (p. 68)
Critical Thinking: Checking Consistency (p. 92)

Debates/Case Studies

What *You* Can Do: Campaigning for the Environment (p. 9)
Debating Key Issues: Should School Officials Have the Right to Censor Student Newspapers? (*Hazelwood* v. *Kuhlmeier*) (p. 39)
Debating Key Issues: Should the Death Penalty Be Declared Unconstitutional? (*Gregg* v. *Georgia*) (p. 64)
Debating Key Issues: Should Congress Set a National Drinking Age? (*South Dakota* v. *Elizabeth H. Dole*) (p. 87)

Foundations of American Government

On July 3, 1776, John Adams wrote to his wife, Abigail, his thoughts on how America's Declaration of Independence ought to be observed in the years to come. Adams wrote, "[the day] ought to be solemnized with Pomp and Parade, with Shews, Games, Sports, Guns, Bells, Bonfires and Illuminations from one End of this Continent to the other . . ." A year and a day later, Americans did indeed celebrate the first anniversary of Independence Day in some of the major cities of the 13 States, Philadelphia among them. Beginning at one o'clock in the afternoon, the discharge of cannons boomed from every ship in the river. Parades and banquets were held, accompanied by music and the thunder of guns. Bells rang and fireworks rocketed into the sky. Today, Independence Day remains a day of celebration—a day when Americans look back to mark one of the initial steps in the building of American government.

Did You Know That . . .

- As the Constitutional Convention sat in 1787, a woman was being tried for witchcraft on the north side of Philadelphia.
- The majority of the members of the Constitutional Convention were lawyers, while none of them were farmers.
- Fifty-one percent of the American people today believe that the American form of government is admired by people throughout the world.

Unit Focus

Activate Prior Knowledge Ask students to define the word *tradition*; then ask them to describe traditions in their families or in some other group to which they belong. Then ask: Why might tradition be important to the existence of many institutions?

Interpreting the Visual Point out the photo of the Statue of Liberty during a July 4th celebration. Tell students that the formal name of the statue is *Liberty Enlightening the World*. Ask: What sort of symbol has the Statue of Liberty become?

Did You Know That . . . Direct students to the items under "Did You Know That . . . ." How much do students think the members of the Constitutional Convention were influenced by their fellow Americans?

Journal Writing A journal may serve as a record of students' personal impressions, thoughts, and ideas about their course work and related current events in the world and in their lives. It is an opportunity for students to be creative; to create political cartoons, songs, poems, and stories as well as editorials and essays. Suggest to students that they keep a notebook exclusively as a journal. Students should make entries at least once a week, and be sure to date each entry. (You may want them to write more frequently, but they should not write less than once a week to ensure some continuity.) Although journal writing generally is not graded, you should collect and review the journals at regular intervals. A suggested journal topic will be provided for each unit. Suggested topics for the first entry include students' thoughts on the necessity of government or ideas for needed amendments to the Constitution.

You may also want to utilize **CNN Video-link** to generate ideas for journal writing.

Bulletin Board Idea

Using the Poster Ask students to consider this statement: "That government is best which governs least." What does it mean? Do students agree or disagree with the statement? Direct students to the wall poster titled "American Ideals: Liberty and Order." Ask them to consider whether the two ideals—liberty and order—are complimentary or contradictory. Ask: Is it possible to have liberty without order? What limits does the need for order place on individual liberty? Then have students examine the poster to see if any of its quotes or cartoons express the same idea as the above statement. Discuss the cartoon showing two shipwreck survivors: Is order necessary for survival, as the cartoon implies? Ask students to find two quotes that have similar messages. Tell the class that Confucius' statement dates to about 500 B.C. while that of Ronald Reagan is contemporary, illustrating that the debate of the proper role of government began in ancient times and continues to the present. Ask students to locate news articles, editorials, cartoons, or photographs that further illustrate the question of the proper role of government in people's lives. Display these on the bulletin board with the poster.

Chapter 1 Resources

In the Teacher's Resource File
The following materials are found in the Teacher's Resource File box.

Instructional Support: Unit 1 File

For the Section
Outlines, pp. 2, 5, 8
Guided Reading and Reviews, pp. 3, 6, 9
Quizzes, pp. 4, 7, 10

For the Chapter
Skill Application, p. 11
Case Study on Contemporary Issues, pp. 12–14
Chapter Test, pp. 15–17
Additional Test Questions, pp. 18–20

Enrichment Support Files

Participatory Government Activities, pp. 28–39, 40–43
Simulations and Debates: Majority Rule; The Rule of Law
Historical and Legal Documents, pp. 7, 10

Computer Test Bank and Assessment

Transparency Package, pp. 1, 26

Chapter 1 Focus

Introduce the Chapter Tell students that in this chapter they will learn about the purposes of government, its major forms, and the basic concepts of democracy. Read with students the Chapter Preview and Objectives.

Writing Activity Direct students' attention to "Describe." Have students describe five ways that government is involved in their lives. Then have them write a description of how their lives would be different if government were not involved in those ways.

Motivate for Learning Direct students' attention to "Predict." Lead students in a discussion of their definitions of *democracy*. You may wish to write some student definitions on the board for students to keep in mind as they read. Then, when the class is completed, ask students to re-evaluate their definition.

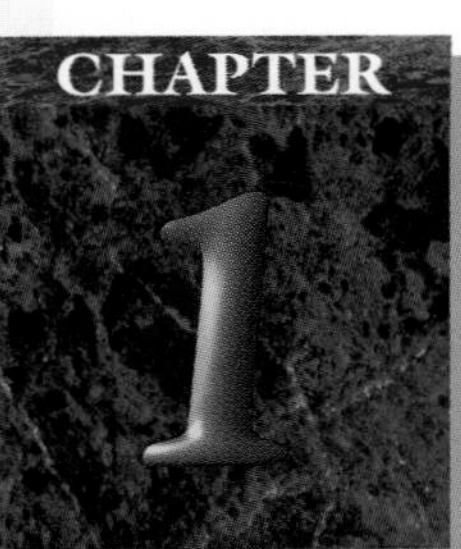

Principles of Government

Chapter Preview

Hair streaming behind her and the wind in her face, a woman is cruising along on her motorcycle, well within the posted speed limit of 45 miles per hour. She is stopped by a police officer and issued a citation because she is in violation of a State law that requires the wearing of protective helmets. A young father is on the way to the park, his two small children bouncing on the back seat. A police officer pulls him over and gives him a ticket for breaking the law that requires the use of seat belts or car-seats for all occupants of a vehicle.

In recent years, many Americans have questioned the right and responsibility of government to be involved in matters of personal safety. Some fear that the freedom to make many personal choices, even ones that are unhealthy or unsafe, will be eroded. Others disagree. The larger issue is this: What are the roles and the limits of government in a democracy? This chapter is about the purposes of government, its major forms, and the basic concepts of democracy.

Before you read this chapter:

- **Describe** five ways that government is involved in your life.
- **Predict** what you think is the exact meaning of "democracy."

As you read, focus on the main objective for each section. Understand:

1. The purposes for which government exists.
2. The major forms of government in the world today.
3. The major concepts of American democracy.

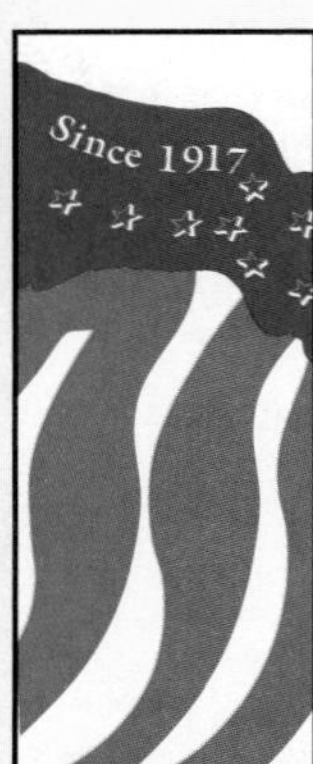

Magruder's American Government: *A Witness to Change* by William A. McClenaghan

For 75 years now, this book has been a witness to change—in fact, to a great many changes.

None of those changes has been more extraordinary or of more far-reaching consequence than the recent disintegration of the Soviet Union. Through more than 40 editions, this book reflected the fact of the cold war. Editions in the 1950s and 1960s carried these blunt words from President Eisenhower: "The threat to our safety, and the hopes of a peaceful world, can be simply stated. It is communist imperialism." And, in the 1980s, these from President Reagan—aimed specifically at the Soviets: "We are not a warlike people. Quite the opposite... But neither are we naive or foolish. We know only too well that war comes not when the forces of freedom are strong, but when they are weak. It is then that tyrants are tempted."

Suddenly, the cold war was over. Communism had collapsed. The Soviet Union had disappeared. And, once again, we were able to see the wisdom in Diogenes' plaintive plea: "Bury me on my face; for in a little while everything will be turned upside down."

Popular Patriotism Father and child express support for the United States and its government. Such support was overwhelming during the Persian Gulf War of 1991, during which this picture was taken.

1 Government and the State

Find Out:

- What are the four basic characteristics of a state?
- What are the four most influential theories about the origin of the state?
- For what purposes does government exist?

Key Terms:

government, public policies, state, sovereign

What is government, and why does it exist? One good way to answer those questions is to ask these: What would life be like if there were no government—no police, no public schools, no President, no Congress, no courts? Who would pave the streets? Who would punish those who rob or kill? Who would protect the nation against foreign dangers? Government does those things and much more.

What Is Government?

1.a **Government** is the institution through which a society makes and enforces its public policies. Government is made up of those people who exercise government's powers, those who have authority and control over other people.

1.b The **public policies** of a government are, in short, all of those things a government decides to do. Here are but a few examples of public policies: imposing an income tax, setting a minimum wage, maintaining large, combat-ready armed forces, protecting the environment.

In the United States and many other countries, the people who exercise the powers of government are legislators, who make public policy in the form of law; executives and administrators, who enforce and administer those laws; and judges, who apply those laws to court cases. In some countries, government is in the hands of religious leaders, or royal families, or tribal chiefs, or soldiers with guns.

Government is among the oldest of all human inventions. Early records of government

SECTION 1
Government and the State

FOCUS

Teacher's Resource File See the Unit 1 File, p. 2, for the Section 1 Outline.

Objectives

1.1 Describe the four basic characteristics of a state.
1.2 Outline the four most influential theories of the origins of the state.
1.3 Explain the purposes for which government exists.

Bellringer Activity Before you begin the section, ask students: Do we need a government? Explore with students the notion of society without government, or *anarchy*. Lead them in a discussion of why governments are established.

State the Purpose In Section 1, students will learn the characteristics of a state and the reasons why states establish governments. Special attention is given to the purposes underlying the U.S. system of government.

ABCNEWS INTERACTIVE

The following video segments may be used to highlight aspects of elements of government.

POWERS OF THE CONGRESS GUIDEBOOK
Chapter 3: Elements of Government, p. 78
Chapter 7: Democracy, p. 82

Vocabulary

Point out "Key Terms" on page 3. Have volunteers look them up in the Glossary (page 772) and then read the definition of each term to the class. Have other students suggest an example of each term. LEP

Reading Strategy: Question Writing

As a preparation for reading, have students read the section's main headings. Then ask students to write a question about each heading and look for the answers to their questions as they read.

INSTRUCT

Explain Have a volunteer read aloud the Preamble to the Constitution on page 7. On the board, draw a circle graph with the label *state* above it. Divide it into four sections, representing the four basic characteristics of a state, and, with students, label the sections *population, territory, sovereignty,* and *government.* Draw a line out from the *government* section, and at the end of the line draw another circle graph labeled *Government.* Divide it into three sections, and, with students, label the sections *legislators, executives and administrators,* and *judges.* Beneath the *Government* circle graph, write the word *Purposes.* Have students suggest various purposes of the U.S. Government, drawing from pp. 7–8. List them on the board. (*Possible answers: to create a strong union, to provide justice, to maintain order, to defend the nation, to promote the general welfare, to safeguard individual rights.*)

date back to ancient Egypt and the 6th century, B.C. More than 2,300 years ago, Aristotle observed that "man is by nature a political animal."[1] When he wrote those words, Aristotle was recording what had been obvious for thousands of years.

The State

Over the course of human history, the state has emerged as the dominant political unit in the
1.c world. The **state** can be defined as a body of people, living in a defined territory, organized politically—that is, under a government—and having the power to make and enforce law without the consent of any higher authority.

There are more than 160 states in the world today. They vary greatly in size, military power, natural resources, economic importance, and in many other ways. Each of them, however, has all four of the characteristics of a state: population, territory, sovereignty, and government.[2]

Population Clearly, a state must have people. The size of the population has nothing to do with the existence of a state, however. The smallest state in terms of population is San Marino. Nestled high in the Apennines and bounded on all sides by Italy, it has some 22,000 people. The People's Republic of China is the most populous state. Its population is now well over one billion—one in five of all the world's people are Chinese.

The population of a state may be quite homogeneous—that is, composed of people who are much alike. Or that population may be heterogeneous—that is, made up of people of different races, languages, religions, and customs.

[1]In most of the world's written political record, the words *man* and *men* have been widely used to refer to all of humankind. This text follows that form when presenting excerpts from historical writings or documents and in references to them.

[2]Note that what has been defined here—the state—is a legal entity. In popular usage, a state is often called a "nation" or a "country." In a strict sense, however, the word *nation* is an ethnic term, referring to races or other large groups of people. The word *country* is a geographic term, referring to a particular place, region, or area of land.

Territory Just as a state must have people, so must it have land—territory with known and recognized boundaries. Here, too, Vatican City ranks as the smallest state in the world. It covers only .17 square mile. The largest state in the world has been the Soviet Union—that is, the Soviet Union as it existed through the early 1990s. It spread across more than 8,000,000 square miles—nearly one-sixth of all the land surface of the earth. The total area of the United States is 3,618,770 square miles.

1.d **Sovereignty** Every state is **sovereign**. That is, it has supreme and absolute power within its own territory. Each state can decide its own foreign and domestic policies. It is neither subordinate nor responsible to any other authority.

Thus, as a sovereign state, the United States can determine its form of government. It can frame its economic system and shape its own foreign policies.[3] Sovereignty is the one characteristic that distinguishes the state from all other, lesser political units. For example, the Virgin Islands and Guam are not states. They are not sovereign; each of them is, instead, a territorial possession of the United States.

The States within the United States are not sovereign and so are not states in the international, legal sense. Each State is subordinate to the Constitution of the United States.

The location of sovereignty within a state is of supreme importance. If the people are sovereign, then the government is democratic. If, on the other hand, a single person or a small group holds the power, a dictatorship exists.

Government Every state, by definition, is politically organized. That is, every state has a government. Recall, a government is the institution through which society makes and enforces its public policies. It is the agency through which the state exerts its will and works to accomplish its goals. Government consists of the machinery and the personnel by which the state is ruled.

[3]In this book, *state* printed with a small "s" denotes a state in the family of nations, such as the United States. *State* printed with a capital "S" refers to a State in the American union.

As you will see shortly, governments in the world today take a number of different forms. But whatever form a government takes, it has the authority to make and enforce public policies. That is, it has the power to rule—including the power to use force if necessary to compel people to accept its rule.

Origins of the State

For centuries, historians, political scientists, philosophers, and others have pondered the question of the origin of the state. What factor or set of circumstances first brought it into being?

Over time, many different answers have been offered, but history provides no conclusive evidence to support any of them. However, four theories have emerged as the most widely accepted explanations for the origin of the state.

The Force Theory Many scholars have long believed that the state was born of force. They hold that one person or group claimed control over an area and forced all within it to submit to that person's or group's rule. When that rule was established, all the basic elements of the state—population, territory, sovereignty, and government—were present.

The Evolutionary Theory Others claim that the state developed naturally out of the early family. They hold that the primitive family, of which one person was the head and thus the "government," was the first stage in political development. Over countless years the original family became a network of related families—a clan. In time the clan became a tribe. When the tribe first turned to agriculture and gave up its nomadic ways, the state was born.

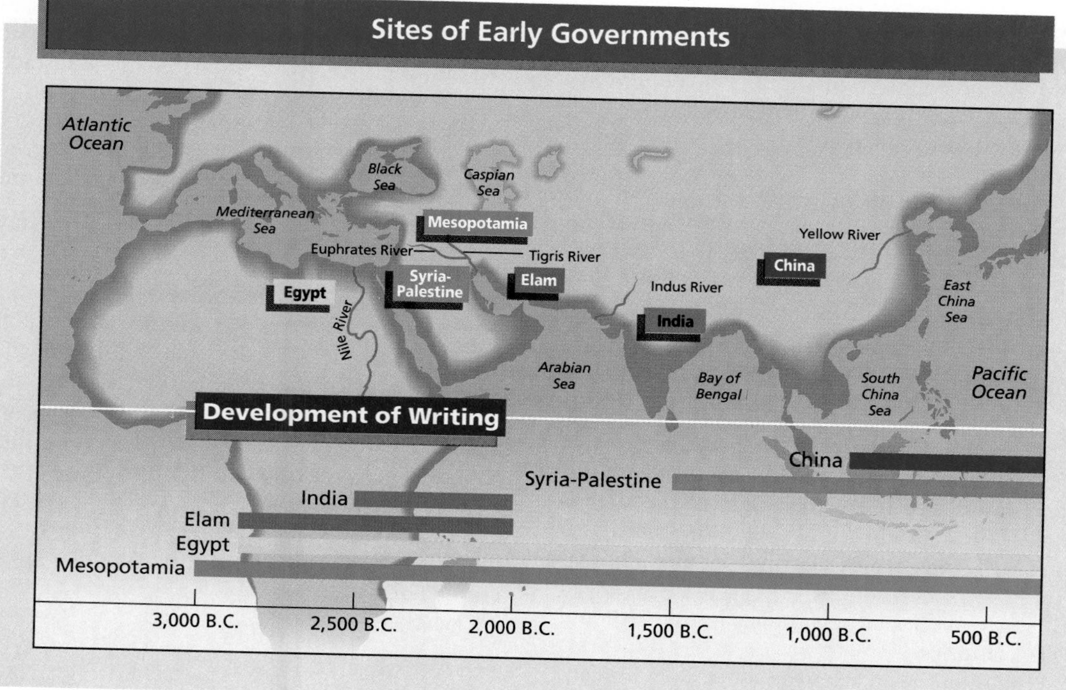

Interpreting Maps: Multicultural Awareness The map shows the areas where the earliest governments are believed to have formed. How would early writing (inset) have played a key part in the development of government?

Interpreting Maps Ask students to list ways in which government depends on writing (and reading) today. (*Possible answers: record keeping, legislation, communication, media.*) Have them use these ideas to answer the question in the map caption.

Caption Answer The development of writing allowed civilizations to store records, build on earlier knowledge, spread ideas, and facilitate government.

Provide Guided Practice Have students differentiate between *state* and *government*. (*A state is a body of people living in a defined territory under government. Government is an institution through which a society makes and enforces public policy.*) Ask what is the difference between a state and a State. (*A state has sovereignty.*) Have students explain briefly the four main theories of the origin of the state. (*These theories are: the Force Theory, the Evolutionary Theory, the Divine Right Theory, and the Social Contract Theory.*)

Provide Independent Practice

TRF **Teacher's Resource File** You may wish to assign the Section 1 Guided Reading and Review, Unit 1 File, p. 3, to help students master section objective content.

Enrichment

In small groups, or individually, have students do research on one ancient government, such as the Greek, Roman, Persian, Chinese, or Egyptian, and report their findings to the class. A good place to start would be an encyclopedia. In their reports, students should identify the country, the time period of the government, major political figures, and one or two aspects unique to that government. Students might also describe the form of government. (Average)

Interpreting Political Cartoons After students have read the cartoon ask: What is the probable attitude of the artist toward government? (*Most likely, the artist feels that government complicates the lives of citizens.*) Discuss with students this view of government.

Caption Answer By implying that government does not improve conditions, but makes them worse.

Interpreting Political Cartoons American government was strongly influenced by the social contract theory. How does this cartoon poke fun at that theory?

The Divine Right Theory The theory of divine right was widely accepted in much of the Western world from the 15th through the 18th centuries. It held that the state was created by God and that God had given those of royal birth a "divine right" to rule. The people were bound to obey their ruler as they would God; opposition to "the divine right of kings" was both treason and mortal sin.

Much of the thought upon which present-day democratic government rests was first developed as a challenge to the theory of divine right.

The notion of divine right was not unique to European history. The rulers of many ancient civilizations—including the Chinese, Egyptian, Aztec, and Mayan civilizations—were held to be gods or at least to have been chosen by the gods. The Japanese emperor, the *mikado*, governed by divine right for centuries until 1945.

The Social Contract Theory In terms of the American political system, the most significant of the theories of the origin of the state is that of the "social contract." Philosophers such as John Locke, James Harrington, and Thomas Hobbes in England and Jean Jacques Rousseau in France developed this theory in the 17th and 18th centuries.

Hobbes wrote that in earliest history humans lived in a "state of nature." No government existed; no person was subject to any superior power. That which people could take by force belonged to them. However, all people were similarly free in this state of nature. No authority existed to protect one person from the aggressive or violent actions of another. Thus, individuals were only as safe as their own physical prowess could make them. Human life in the state of nature, wrote Hobbes, was "nasty, brutish, and short."

Human beings overcame their unpleasant condition, says the theory, by agreeing with one another to create a state. By contract, people within a given area agreed to give up to the state as much power as was needed to promote the well-being of all. In the contract—that is, through a constitution—the members of the state created a government to exercise the powers they had granted to the state.

In short, the social contract theory argues that the state arose out of a voluntary act of free people. It holds that the state exists only to serve the will of the people, that they are the sole source of political power, and that they are free to give or to withhold that power as they choose. The great concepts that this theory promoted—popular sovereignty, limited government, and individual rights—were immensely important to the shaping of the American governmental system.[4]

[4]The Declaration of Independence (see page 720) laid its justification for revolution on the social contract theory, arguing that the king and his ministers had violated the contract. Thomas Jefferson called the document "pure Locke."

Spotlight on: Global Awareness

The ancient Chinese felt that a single ruler should govern all of humanity with a universal code of principles. The Chinese emperor, called the "Son of Heaven," was believed by the Chinese people to be able to communicate with both Heaven and Earth. The emperor ruled through a complex bureaucracy of educated professionals. But although the government was based on a "mandate of heaven," if the emperor's rule was found to be unjust, the people were justified in rebelling against him. It was believed, too, that Heaven could show its displeasure by sending famine and other natural disasters.

The Purpose of Government

What does government do? You can find the best answer to that question in the Preamble to the Constitution of the United States. The American governmental system was created to serve the purposes set out there.

> "We the People of the United States, in Order to form a more perfect Union, establish Justice, insure domestic Tranquility, provide for the common defence, promote the general Welfare, and secure the Blessings of Liberty to ourselves and our Posterity, do ordain and establish this Constitution for the United States of America."

To Form a More Perfect Union The United States, which had just won its independence from Great Britain, faced an altogether uncertain future in the postwar 1780s. In 1781 the Articles of Confederation, the nation's first constitution, had created "a firm league of friendship" among the 13 States. But that league soon proved to be neither very firm nor even very friendly. The 1780s were marked by intense rivalries and jealousies among the States; and the government that the Articles had established was powerless to confront the chaos and confusion of the time.

The Constitution of today was written in 1787, and it was adopted by the original States in order to link them, and the American people, more closely together. That Constitution was built in the belief that in union there is strength.

To Establish Justice To provide justice is, said Thomas Jefferson, "the most sacred of the duties of government." No purpose, no goal of public policy, can be of greater importance in a democracy.

But what, precisely, is justice? The term is difficult to define, for justice is a concept. Like truth, liberty, good, and other concepts, justice means what people make it mean.

As the concept of justice has developed over time in American thought and practice, it has come to mean this: The law, in both its content and its administration, must be reasonable, fair, and impartial. Those standards of justice have not always been met in this country. We have not attained our professed goal of "equal justice for all." But this, too, must be said: The history of this country can be told largely in terms of our continuing attempts to reach that goal.

"Injustice anywhere," said Martin Luther King, Jr., "is a threat to justice everywhere." You will encounter this idea again and again in this book.

To Insure Domestic Tranquility Order is essential to the well-being of any society, and keeping the peace at home has always been a prime function of government.

Most people can only imagine what it would be like to live in a state of anarchy—that is, without government, without law and order. But people do live that way in some parts of the world today. For years now, the government of Lebanon has been too weak to control the actions of several warring religious factions. The street fighting in strife-torn Beirut suggests what life without government is like.

In *The Federalist* No. 51, James Madison observed: "If men were angels no government would be necessary." But Madison, who was perhaps the most thoughtful of the Framers of the Constitution, knew that most human beings fall far short of this standard.

To Provide for the Common Defense Defending the nation against foreign enemies has always been one of government's major responsibilities. You can see its importance in this striking fact: Defense is mentioned far more often in the Constitution than any of the other functions of the government it created. The nation's defense and foreign policies are but two sides of the same coin—the security of the United States.

The cold war is now history. It came to an end with the collapse of communism in Eastern Europe and the Soviet Union. That conflict, which lasted for more than 40 years, pitted the United States and its allies in the free world against the Soviet Union and its satellites in the Communist world. For all of those years the world lived with the threat of World War III and nuclear holocaust.

Even with the end of the cold war, the world remains a dangerous place, and the United States must maintain its vigilance and its armed strength. Iraq's invasion of Kuwait in the summer of 1990

Caption Answer It may suggest the multicultural nature of American society.

MONITOR COMPREHENSION

Answers to Section 1 Review
1. "Key Terms" are defined on the following pages:
 a. government, p. 3
 b. public policies, p. 3
 c. state, p. 4
 d. sovereign, p. 4
2. population, territory, sovereignty, and government **3.** It determines who controls the state. **4.** force theory, evolutionary theory, divine right theory, social contract theory. **5.** To form a more perfect Union; establish justice; maintain order; provide national defense; promote the general welfare; secure individual rights.
6. Answers will vary. Students should observe that "We, the People," suggests the idea behind the social contract.

Teacher's Resource File See the Unit 1 File, p. 4, for the Section 1 Quiz.

CLOSURE

Remind students that government is one aspect of a state, and that governments may serve a variety of purposes. The purposes described in Section 1 are those of the U.S. and other democratic governments and reflect certain ideas about human nature and human rights. In Section 2 students will learn how various types of government are structured to fulfill particular purposes.

Assignment Assign Section 2, pp. 10–14, for the next class period.

National Museumof American Art - Smithsonian

Interpreting Political Art This handmade quilt hangs in the Smithsonian Institution. What might have been the artist's intent in using multicolored pieces of fabric surrounding the Statue of Liberty?

and the ensuing war in the Persian Gulf in early 1991 furnish abundant proof of that fact.

To Promote the General Welfare Few people realize the extent to which government acts as the servant of its citizens, yet you can see examples everywhere.

Public schools are a leading illustration of our government's work to promote the general welfare. So, too, are the government's efforts to protect the quality of the air you breathe, the water you drink, and the food you eat. The list of tasks the government performs for your benefit goes on and on.

Some governmental functions that are common in other countries—operating railroads, airlines, and coal mines, for example—are not carried out by the government in this country. In general, the services that government provides in the United States are those that benefit all or most people and are not likely to be provided by the voluntary acts of private individuals or groups.

To Secure the Blessings of Liberty This nation was founded by those who loved liberty and prized it above all earthly possessions. They believed with Thomas Jefferson that "the God who gave us life gave us liberty at the same time." They subscribed to Benjamin Franklin's maxim: "They that can give up essential liberty to obtain a little temporary safety deserve neither liberty nor safety."

As you will see shortly, the American dedication to freedom for the individual recognizes that liberty cannot be absolute. It is, instead, a relative matter. No person can be free to do whatever he or she pleases—for that behavior would interfere with the freedoms of others. As Clarence Darrow, the great defense lawyer, once said: "You can only be free if I am free."

Both the Federal Constitution and the State constitutions set out many guarantees of rights and liberties for the individual in this country. But that does not mean that those guarantees are so firmly established that they exist forever. To preserve and protect them, each generation must learn and understand them anew, and be willing to stand up for them when necessary. You, too, must agree with Jefferson: "Eternal vigilance is the price of liberty."

Section 1 Review

1. Define: government, public policies, state, sovereign
2. What are the four main characteristics of a state?
3. For what reason is the location of sovereignty within a state so important?
4. What are the four most widely held theories about the origin of the state?
5. What are the six purposes of government outlined in the Preamble to the Constitution?

Critical Thinking

6. Recognizing Ideologies (p. 19) Explain how the language of the Preamble reflects the concept of the social contract.

SPOTLIGHT ON: Economics

If the Federal Government handed every U.S. citizen a check for $100, the total would equal a little more than the amount the U.S. Government earmarked in 1991 for the Department of Education alone! A large portion of each year's federal budget is allocated to this and other federal departments that seek in some way to promote the general welfare. The Environmental Protection Agency, for example, was allocated $5.8 billion in 1991 to restore and preserve the quality of the environment, while the Food and Drug Administration received $663 million to test various foods and medicines to insure their safety for public use.

Reteach

Have students write their own version of the Preamble to the Constitution, listing why they think the U.S. Government should exist and what its purposes should be.

What You Can Do

Campaigning for the Environment

In 1987, a civics class at the Tenakill School in Closter, New Jersey, formed a campaign to urge their school to stop using polystyrene in the cafeteria. Polystyrene is the soft, lightweight, plastic foam that is used to make many disposable food containers and trays. The school's group, Kids Against Pollution, attacked the material for two reasons. Polystyrene is nonbiodegradable—that is, it does not readily decay over a few years when disposed of in landfills. In addition, polystyrene gives off toxic fumes when it is burned. The food industry, including many school cafeterias, uses more than one billion pounds of polystyrene each year, mostly for packaging.

With persistence and hard work, the students at the Tenakill School succeeded in their efforts to end polystyrene use in the cafeteria. Their success inspired similar groups in the United States and Europe. In 1988, the students at West Milford High School in New Jersey were also able to ban polystyrene in their school by winning over a reluctant school board and most of their fellow students. Buoyed by their victory, the West Milford group set their sights even higher. They joined a national movement to stop the use of polystyrene containers by the world's largest consumer of the material—McDonald's. The 8,400 McDonald's restaurants across the United States were estimated to use a total of 3.5 billion foam boxes each year, or between 7 to 8 percent of all polystyrene foam products sold in the United States.

Kurtiz Schneid, the leader of the movement in West Milford, and other citizens got involved in this national movement to reduce the use of polystyrene. They demonstrated in front of the United Nations to urge a worldwide boycott of McDonald's restaurants. Schneid dressed as "Ronald McToxic," and his followers spread a message based on the restaurant's advertising slogan: "The planet deserves a break today." Other West Milford residents organized letter-writing campaigns to urge McDonald's to stop using polystyrene.

In November 1990, McDonald's Corp. decided to stop using polystyrene containers for its hamburgers and other sandwiches. This translated into a savings of more than 45 million pounds of the plastic waste a year. Six months later, working with the Environmental Defense Fund, the company launched a major waste-reduction effort, including composting and recycling. The company aimed to reduce the daily generation of garbage by 80 percent.

Groups of citizens spoke out strongly on this issue. The success they achieved in achieving their goals indicates that they were heard.

Getting Involved

1. Identify a need in your school or community similar to the one addressed by the students in this case.

2. Formulate a plan for how you might organize volunteer efforts to help remedy this problem and identify resources that could be used in your plan.

3. Predict any problems or objections you might encounter in implementing your plan.

TEACHING
What You Can Do

Campaigning for the Environment

Objective

Understand the importance of participation in civic affairs.

INSTRUCT

After students have read the feature, have them point out the various methods by which the students in the reading pursued their goals. Below are some possible questions for discussion:

- What can be accomplished through each method?
- What are the risks, if any, of each method?
- If you wanted to support reform in your community, which method would you personally feel most comfortable using? Why?

Then divide the class into small groups to work through the "Getting Involved" section. Have each group present its plan to the class.

TRF **Teacher's Resource File**
See the Participatory Government Activities file, pp. 28–39, for "A Citizen's Guide to Public and Private Resources."

SECTION 2
Forms of
Government

FOCUS

Teacher's Resource File
See the Unit 1 File, p. 5, for the Section 2 Outline.

Objectives

1.4 Outline the characteristics of unitary, federal, and confederate systems of government.

1.5 Describe differences between presidential and parliamentary systems of government.

1.6 Compare dictatorship and democracy.

Bellringer Activity Before you begin the section, write the words 1. *Presidential,* 2. *Parliamentary,* 3. *Dictatorship* on the board. Then ask students to provide examples for each category. (*Examples may include: 1. U.S., France, Egypt, Switzerland, Mexico. 2. U.K., Canada, Israel, Zimbabwe. 3. Cuba, Libya, China.*)

State the Purpose Governments are organized in a variety of forms. In Section 2, students will learn three different ways of classifying these forms: according to the geographic distribution of power, the relationship between legislative and executive branches, and the number of persons who can participate in the governing process.

2 Forms of Government

Find Out:

- What are the characteristics of unitary, federal, and confederate governments?
- How do presidential and parliamentary governments differ?
- How do a dictatorship and a democracy differ?

Key Terms:

unitary government, federal government, confederation, presidential government, parliamentary government, dictatorship, democracy, direct democracy, representative democracy

Does the form a government takes, the way in which it is structured, have any importance? Political scientists, historians, and other social commentators have long argued that question. The English poet Alexander Pope weighed in with this couplet in 1733:

> “For forms of government let fools contest: Whate'er is best adminster'd is best.”

Was Pope right? Does it matter what form a government takes? In this section, which focuses on forms of government, you will find some help in framing your own response to those questions.

Classifying Governments

No two governments are, or ever have been, exactly alike, for governments are the products of human needs and experiences. But all governments can be classified according to one or more of their basic features. Over time, political scientists have developed many bases upon which to classify—and so to describe, compare, and analyze—governments. Three of those classifications are especially important and useful. These are classifications according to: (1) the geographic distribution of governmental power within the state, (2) the relationship between the legislative (lawmaking) and the executive (law-executing) branches of the government, and (3) the number of persons who can take part in the governing process.[5]

Geographic Distribution of Power

In every system of government the power to govern is located in one or more places, geographically. From this standpoint, three basic forms of government exist: unitary, federal, and confederate governments.

Unitary Government A **unitary government** is often described as a centralized government. It is a government in which all powers held by the government belong to a single, central agency. The central government creates local units of government for its own convenience. Whatever powers those local governments have come only from that central source.

Most governments in the world are unitary in form, including the governments of the individual 50 States. Great Britain is another illustration of the type. A single central organ—the Parliament—holds all of the power of the British government. Local governments do exist but solely to relieve Parliament of burdens it could perform only with difficulty and inconvenience. Though hardly likely, Parliament could do away with all agencies of local government at any time.

Be careful not to confuse the unitary form of government with one in which the government holds absolute power, such as a dictatorship. In the unitary form all of the powers rightfully held by the government are concentrated in the central government. But that government might not have *all* power. In Great Britain, for example, the powers held by the government are limited. British government is unitary and, at the same time, democratic.

Federal Government A **federal government** is one in which the powers of government are divided between a central government and several local governments. An authority superior to both the central and local governments makes this division of powers on a geographic basis; and that division cannot be changed by either the local or national level acting alone.

[5]Note that these classifications are not mutually exclusive. Thus, as you will see, the government of the United States is federal, presidential, and democratic; British government is unitary, parliamentary, and democratic; and so on.

Reading Strategy: Graphic Organizer

As a preparation for reading, point out that this section is about three ways of classifying governments. Have students read the headings to find the three ways, along with examples or concepts under each one. Have students use these headings, subheadings, and concepts to create graphic organizers for this section.

Vocabulary

Point out "Key Terms" on page 10. Below are some additional words whose meanings may help students understand the section content.

—**monolithic:** huge, massive
—**militaristic:** having a policy of aggressive military preparedness LEP

Both levels of government act directly on the people through their own sets of laws, officials, and agencies.

In the United States, for example, the National Government has certain powers and the 50 States have others. This division of powers is set out in the Constitution of the United States. The Constitution stands above both levels of government; and it cannot be changed unless the people, acting through both the National Government and the States, agree to that change.

Australia, Canada, Mexico, Switzerland, Germany, India, and some 20 other states also have federal forms of government today.

Confederate Government A **confederation** is an alliance of independent states. A central organ—the confederate government—has the power to handle only those matters that the member states have assigned to it. Typically, confederate governments have had limited powers and only in such fields as defense and foreign commerce. Most often, they have not had the power to make laws that apply directly to individuals, at least not without some further action by the member states. A confederate structure makes it possible for the several states to cooperate in matters of common concern and also retain their separate identities.

The United States under the Articles of Confederation (1781–1789) and the Confederate States (1861–1865) are examples of confederations. The Commonwealth of Independent States, which emerged in 1991 after the breakup of the Soviet Union, is a modern-day example of a confederation.

Relationship Between Legislative and Executive Branches

Viewing governments from the standpoint of the relationship between their legislative and executive agencies yields two basic forms of government: presidential and parliamentary.

Presidential Government A **presidential government** features a separation of powers between the executive and legislative branches of the government. The two branches are independent of one another and coequal. The chief executive—president—is chosen independently of the legislature, holds office for a fixed term,

Tribal Council: Multicultural Awareness Native Americans such as these Apache leaders have governed the internal affairs of their group for centuries. The Iroquois of the 1500s were known for their confederate form of government.

and has broad powers not subject to the direct control of the legislative branch. The two branches regularly have several powers with which each can check—block or restrain—actions by the other branch.

Usually, as in the United States and each of the 50 States, a written constitution provides for the separation of powers between the branches of government.

Parliamentary Government In **parliamentary government**, the executive is made up of the prime minister or premier and that official's cabinet. The members of the executive are members of the legislative branch, the parliament. The prime minister is the leader of the majority party or of a coalition of parties in parliament and is chosen to be the executive by that body. With parliament's approval, the prime minister selects the members of the cabinet from among the members of parliament. The executive is thus chosen by the legislature, is a part of it, and is subject to its direct control.

The prime minister and the cabinet—often called "the government"—remain in office only as long as their policies and administration have the confidence of a majority in parliament. If parliament defeats the prime minister and cabinet on an important matter—if the government receives a "vote of no confidence"—the government must resign from office. Then a

INSTRUCT

Analyze/Discuss Begin by asking students how governments can be classified (*By geographic distribution of power, by the relationship between the legislative and executive branches of government, and by the number of people who participate in governing.*) To help students understand the significance of these criteria discuss with them the following scenarios:

1. There are no State governments; all governmental authority rests with the National Government in Washington, D.C.
2. The President is elected by the Senate, not by the people.
3. The country is ruled by one self-appointed legislative body.

Explore with students the ramifications, personal and public, of each of these scenarios. (*Students will probably acknowledge the loss of fair representation and attention to local issues that would be the result of the first item and also the danger to personal freedoms of the second and third items.*)

ABCNEWS INTERACTIVE

The following video segment may be used to highlight aspects of forms of government.

POWERS OF THE CONGRESS GUIDEBOOK
Chapter 8: Comparing Governments, p. 83

ACTIVITY: For Gifted Students

Theme: Systems Political scientists use a system for defining the state and classifying forms of government. These systems rely on specific sets of variables to provide their definition. Have students compare and contrast the systems used by a fiction writer to describe states and forms of government, for example, in George Orwell's *Animal Farm* or *1984*, Aldous Huxley's *Brave New World*, or Charlotte Perkins Gillman's *Herland*, etc., with the systems described in this section. Students should be encouraged to present their findings to the class.

SPOTLIGHT ON: Multiculturalism

Over two centuries before the Articles of Confederation, the Native American Iroquois nation forged the first viable confederate government in North America. The Iroquois Confederacy (or League) united five tribes—Mohawk, Oneida, Onondaga, Cayuga, and Seneca—in a defensive alliance, much like the Articles, in the area of today's New York State. A sixth tribe, the Tuscarora, joined the league in 1722. A council of representatives—chosen by leading women from each of the tribes—made key decisions on war and peace. Each tribe retained control over its own affairs and none could be compelled to obey council directives against its will.

Interpreting Graphs Point out that the arrows extending from the voters box indicate which offices are chosen directly by voters. In the presidential model, voters choose directly both the legislature and the chief executive. In the parliamentary model, voters choose directly only the legislature; the legislature then chooses the chief executive. Ask: What do the two systems have in common? (*The judiciary is appointed indirectly and the legislatures are chosen by the people.*)

Caption Answer
Parliamentary.

Provide Guided Practice In three columns on the board, list the three ways of classifying governments: *Geographic Distribution, Relationship of Legislative to Executive Branches, Number Who Can Participate.* Under each one, write the relevant subheadings from the text. Then have students volunteer the names of countries given in the text as examples for each subheading. Write the names in the appropriate places. If you wish, have students volunteer names of other countries to add to the various categories, drawing on their prior knowledge.

Provide Independent Practice
TRF Teacher's Resource File You may wish to assign the Section 2 Guided Reading and Review, Unit 1 File, p. 6, to help students master the section objective content.

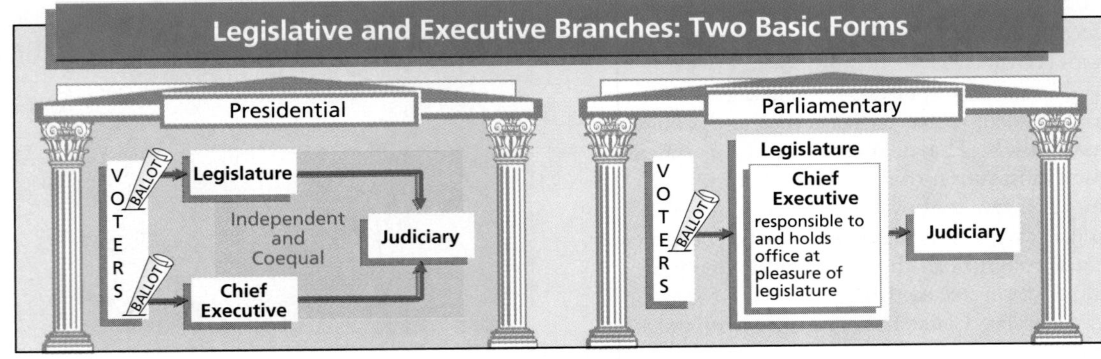

Interpreting Graphs Compare parliamentary and presidential forms of government. In which form of government is the chief executive both elected from and part of the legislature?

new government must be formed. Either parliament chooses a new prime minister or, as often happens, all the seats of parliament go before the voters in a general election.

A parliamentary government does not experience one of the major problems of the presidential form—prolonged conflict and sometimes deadlock between the executive and legislative branches. But, notice, that is another way of saying that the checks and balances of presidential government are not a part of the parliamentary system. Most governments in the world today are parliamentary in form.

The Number Who Can Participate

To most people, the most meaningful of these classifications of governments is the one that depends on the number of persons who can take part in the governing process. Here there are two basic forms to consider: dictatorships and democracies.

Dictatorship A **dictatorship** exists where those who rule cannot be held responsible to the will of the people. The government is not accountable for its policies, nor for the ways in which they are carried out. Dictatorship is probably the oldest, and it is certainly the most common, form of government known.[6]

All dictatorships are authoritarian. That is, they are governmental systems in which those in power hold absolute and unchallengeable authority over the people. Modern dictatorships have tended to be totalitarian, as well. That is, they exercise dictatorial (authoritarian) power over just about every aspect of human affairs.

The leading examples of dictatorship in the 20th century have been those in Fascist Italy (from 1922 to 1943), in Nazi Germany (from 1933 to 1945), and in the Soviet Union (from 1917 until the late 1980s), and one that still exists in the People's Republic of China (where the present regime came to power in 1949).

The Soviet political system has experienced extraordinary change since Mikhail Gorbachev gained power in 1985—and, clearly, the Soviet government of today is not the repressive dictatorship that existed for some 70 years.

Although they do exist, one-person dictatorships are not at all common today. A close approach to such a regime now exists in Libya, which has been dominated by Muammar al-Qaddafi since 1969.

---

[6]The word *dictatorship* comes from the Latin *dictare*, meaning to dictate, issue orders, authoritative commands. *Dictator* was the ancient Roman republic's title for the leader who was given extraordinary powers in times of crisis. Julius Caesar (100–44 B.C.) became the first of the Roman dictators, in 49 B.C.

Dictatorships are sometimes identified as either autocracies or oligarchies. An autocracy is a government in which a single person holds unlimited political power. An oligarchy is a government in which the power to rule is held by a small, usually self-appointed elite.

Enrichment

Have students work in small groups to discuss the following question: On the basis of the description on pp. 11–12, who do you think has more power, a president or a prime minister? When they have finished, you may wish to have groups present their conclusions. Then lead a class discussion comparing each group's ideas. (Average)

Spotlight on: Behind the Scenes

Economic depression and social dislocation were the major causes of fascism in Germany in the 1930s. As the country blamed for World War I, Germany was forced to pay reparations (or damages), crippling the nation's economy, causing food shortages and spiraling inflation in the 1920s, and desperate unemployment after the Great Depression struck. These conditions, combined with national grief over the thousands killed in battle and a national pride stung by defeat, created a sense of frustration that made the nation receptive to Hitler's spellbinding oratory and reactionary tactics, and to Nazism's promise of a glorious future.

Most present-day dictatorships are not nearly so monolithic, not nearly so absolutely controlled by a single person or by a very small group as may appear to be the case. Regularly, outward appearances hide the fact that several groups—the army, religious leaders, industrialists, and others—compete for power in the political system.

Dictatorships often present the outward appearance of control by the people. The people often vote in popular elections; but the vote is closely controlled, and ballots usually contain the candidates of but one political party. An elected legislative body often exists, but only to rubber-stamp the policies of the dictatorship.

Typically, dictatorial regimes are militaristic in character. They usually gain power by force. The military holds many of the major posts in the government. After crushing all effective opposition at home, these regimes may turn to foreign aggression to enhance the country's military power and prestige.

Absolute Dictator Nazi leader Adolf Hitler was the ruthless dictator of Germany from 1933 to 1945.

Democracy In a **democracy**, supreme political authority rests with the people. The people hold the sovereign power, and government is conducted only by and with the consent of the people.[7]

Abraham Lincoln gave immortality to this definition of democracy in his Gettysburg Address in 1863: "government of the people, by the people, for the people." Nowhere is there a better, more concise statement of the American understanding of democracy.

A democracy can be either direct or indirect in form. A **direct democracy**—also called a 1.a pure democracy—exists where the will of the people is translated into public policy (law) directly by the people themselves, in mass meetings. Clearly, such a direct democracy system can work only in very small communities where the problems of government are relatively few and simple.

Direct democracy does not exist at the national level anywhere in the world today. But the New England town meeting which you will read about in Chapter 24, and the *Landsgemeinde* in a few of the smaller Swiss cantons are excellent examples of direct democracy in action.[8]

The United States is more familiar with the indirect form of democracy—that is, with representative democracy. In a **representative** 1.b **democracy**, a small group of persons chosen by the people to act as their representatives expresses the popular will. These agents of the people are responsible for the day-to-day conduct of government—the making and executing of laws and so on. They are accountable to the people for that conduct, especially at periodic elections. At these elections the people have an opportunity to express their approval or disapproval of their representatives by casting ballots

[7]The word *democracy* is derived from the Greek words *demos* meaning "the people" and *kratia* meaning "rule" or "authority." The Greek word *demokratia* means "rule by the people."

[8]The *Landsgemeinde*, like the original New England town meeting, is an assembly open to all local citizens qualified to vote. In a more limited sense, lawmaking by initiative petition is also an example of direct democracy; see Chapter 24.

Interpreting Graphs Point out that each country on the graph on page 14 has been given one check for each question, except for one country. Which country is neither presidential nor parliamentary? (*Cuba*).

Caption Answer Thailand, Egypt, and Botswana.

ACTIVITY: Teaching Heterogeneous Groups

Review with students that government is the institution through which society makes and enforces its public policies. Then have students list the following words or phrases on a sheet of paper: *social contract theory, federal government, democracy,* and *compromise.* Have students define the terms and add any important examples to help them understand basic principles of American government. LEP

Reteach

Have students choose the three terms in the following list that accurately describe the U.S. government: unitary, **federal,** confederate, **presidential,** parliamentary, dictatorship, **democracy.** As they choose each term, have them explain briefly in their own words what it means. (Federal *describes a government in which power is shared;* presidential *describes a government wherein there is a separation of powers between the executive and legislative branches;* democracy *decribes a government whose authority rests with the people.*)

Monitor Comprehension

Answers to Section 2 Review
1. "Key Terms" are defined on the following pages:
a. direct democracy, p. 13
b. representative democracy, p. 13
2. (a) All powers held belong to a single, central agency. (b) The power of the central government is limited to only those matters which the member states have assigned it. (c) Power is divided between a central government and local governments on a geographic basis according to a constitution. **3.** (a) Separation of powers between executive and legislative branches. (b) The authority of the executive is conditional upon the approval of the legislature. (c) Parliamentary. **4.** (a) Those who rule are not accountable to the popular will. (b) Supreme political authority resides in the people and government is conducted only by and with their consent. (c) Democracy. **5.** Students' answers should demonstrate an understanding of the operations of those forms of government discussed.

Closure

In this section students have learned that governments differ in where governing power is located, in the relationship between legislative and executive agencies, and in the number of people who take part in governing. Using these distinctions, governments can be analyzed in a variety of ways.

Assignment Assign Section 3, pp. 15–18, for the next class period.

Global Awareness

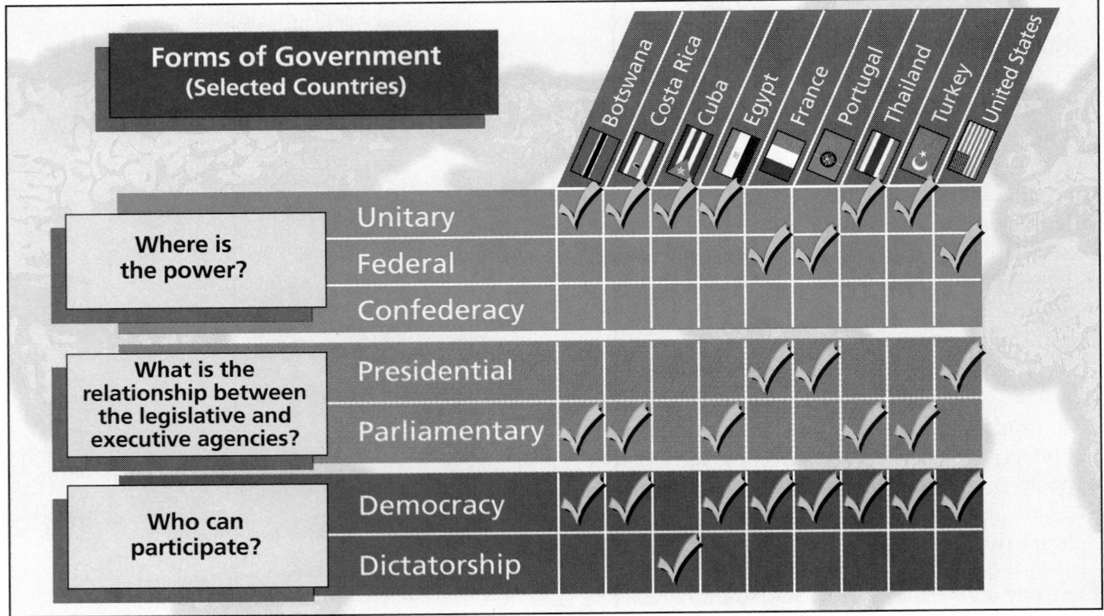

Interpreting Graphs: Multicultural Awareness Different forms of government in several countries are described above. Which Southeast Asian country and two African countries are parliamentary democracies?

for or against them. To put it another way, representative democracy is government with the consent of the governed.

Some people insist that the United States is more properly called a republic rather than a democracy. They hold that in a republic the sovereign power is held by the electorate—those eligible to vote—and that the political power is exercised by representatives chosen by and held responsible to the electorate. For them, democracy can be defined only in terms of direct democracy. To most Americans, however, the terms *democracy*, *republic*, *representative democracy*, and *republican form of government* generally mean the same thing.

Whatever the terms used, remember that in a democracy the people are sovereign. They are the only source for any and all of the government's power. In other words, the people rule. That is one idea upon which all Americans agree.

Section 2 Review

1. Define: direct democracy, representative democracy
2. (a) What is the basic characteristic of a unitary government? (b) A confederate government? (c) A federal government?
3. (a) What is the basic characteristic of a presidential government? (b) A parliamentary government? (c) Which is the most common today?
4. (a) What is the basic characteristic of a dictatorial government? (b) A democratic government? (c) Which is the most common today?

Critical Thinking

5. Drawing Conclusions (p. 19) Which combination of governmental forms would best fulfill the purposes of government?

★

Spotlight on: Political Talk

The word *republic* is derived from the Latin words *res,* meaning "thing" and *publica,* meaning " the people." Therefore, the Latin word *respublica* means literally "thing of the people." The derivation of the word *republic* demonstrates the importance of the idea to the pre-Empire Romans that government belonged to the governed.

Teacher's Resource File
See the Unit 1 File, p. 7, for the Section 2 Quiz.

3 Basic Concepts of Democracy

Find Out:

- What are the basic concepts on which American democracy is built?
- How does the operation of American government illustrate these basic concepts?

Key Terms:

compromise, anarchy

What do you make of the following assessment of democracy? "No government demands so much from the citizen as Democracy and none gives back so much."[9] What does democratic government demand from you? What does it give you in return? Can you cite any concrete examples in answer to either of these questions? You may find some of those examples as you read this section.

The Foundations of Democracy

Democracy is not inevitable. It does not exist in the United States simply because Americans regard it as the best of all possible political systems. Nor will it continue to exist for that reason.[10] Rather, democracy exists in this country because the American people believe in its basic concepts. It will continue to exist only for as long as we, the people, continue to subscribe to—and practice—those concepts.

The basic concepts of democracy, as they are understood and applied in the United States, can be described this way:

1. A recognition of the fundamental worth and dignity of every person.
2. A respect for the equality of all persons.
3. A faith in majority rule and an insistence upon minority rights.
4. An acceptance of the necessity of compromise.
5. An insistence upon the widest possible degree of individual freedom.

Of course, these ideas can be worded in other ways. No matter what the wording, however, they form the very minimum that anyone who professes to believe in democracy must agree to. Some people will argue that other concepts belong in such a list—for example, the right of each person to a certain minimum level of economic security. But the point here is that, no matter what else might be included, at least these must be.

These concepts present the American people with a number of problems and challenges. In order to preserve democracy, each generation must develop the skills with which to solve these problems. (You will find a discussion of problem-solving skills on page 19.)

Fundamental Worth of the Individual

Democracy is firmly based upon a belief in the fundamental importance of the individual. Each individual, no matter what his or her station in life, is a separate and distinct being. Democracy insists that each person's worth and dignity must be recognized and respected by all other individuals, and by society, at all times.

This concept of the dignity and worth of the individual is of overriding importance in democratic thought. Everything a democratic society does must and should be done within the limits of this great concept. American society is constantly striving to fulfill it.

At various times, of course, the welfare of one or a few individuals is subordinated to the interests of the many in a democracy. People can be forced to do certain things whether they want to or not. The examples are many, and they range from paying taxes or registering for the draft to stopping at a stop sign.

When a democratic society forces people to pay a tax or obey traffic signals, it is serving the interests of the many. But the democracy is *not* serving the many simply as the interests of a

[9]James Bryce, *Modern Democracies* (Macmillan, 1921), Vol. II, p. 608.

[10]The late Sir Winston Churchill (1874–1965) once argued for democracy in these terms: "No one pretends that democracy is perfect or all-wise. Indeed, it has been said that democracy is the worst form of government except all of those other forms which have been tried from time to time."

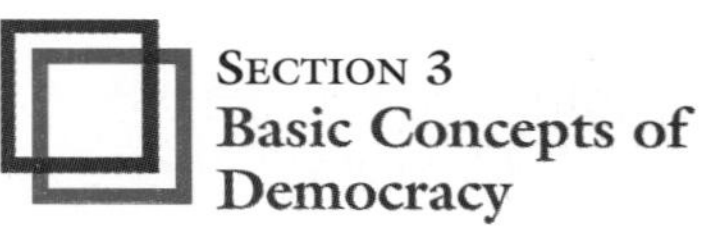

SECTION 3
Basic Concepts of Democracy

Objectives

1.7 Understand the basic concepts on which American democracy is built.

1.8 Analyze how the operation of American government illustrates these basic concepts.

Bellringer Activity Write the word *democracy* on the board. Ask students to brainstorm, as in word-associations games, terms they would relate to the word democracy. (*Possible responses: America, freedom, liberty, Greece, people, government.*)

State the Purpose The U.S. Government is a democracy. In Section 3, students will learn the beliefs about the individual and about society that underlie this political philosophy. They will explore the implications and limitations of those beliefs.

ABCNEWS INTERACTIVE

The following video segment may be used to highlight aspects of civic values.

POWERS OF THE CONGRESS GUIDEBOOK
Chapter 57: Development of Democracy, p. 134

Vocabulary

Point out to students "Key Terms" on page 15. Ask volunteers to look up the definitions of these words in a dictionary. Then ask students: How might these two terms be related? Discuss with students the necessity of compromise in government and the necessity for government. LEP

Reading Strategy: Role-Playing in Writing

After students have read the section, ask them to imagine they are the writers of the U.S. Constitution. Have them make a short statement to the class explaining why they are in favor of a democratic system of government.

Instruct

Analyze For each of the five basic concepts of democracy (p. 15), have students write one sentence that best expresses the idea behind it, using the text and their own words. (*Example: In a democracy, the dignity and work of each individual must be respected.*) Write volunteer's sentences in five columns across the board. Below each sentence, write the word *But* and have students suggest important qualifications or limitations upon the idea—things that the original sentence does not imply. (*Example: But sometimes the welfare of an individual must take second place to that of the majority.*) As you write each qualification on the board, have students explain why that particular qualification is necessary.

Provide Guided Practice On the board, write the five headings from the book representing the five basic concepts of democracy (pp. 15–17). Then have students skim the material under each heading to find key terms and ideas. As students call out terms and ideas, write them under the appropriate heading. Have students explain the significance of each suggestion.

Provide Independent Practice

TRF **Teacher's Resource File** You may wish to assign the Section 3 Guided Reading and Review, Unit 1 File, p. 9, to help students master section objective content.

mass of people who happen to outnumber the few. Rather, it is serving the many who, as individuals, together make up that society.

The distinction here between a single individual and all individuals may be a very fine one. It is, however, critically important to a true understanding of the meaning of democracy.

Equality of All Persons

Hand-in-hand with the belief in the worth of the individual, democracy stresses the equality of all individuals. It holds, with Jefferson, that "all men are created equal."

Certainly, democracy does *not* insist on an equality of condition for all persons. Thus, it does not claim that all are born with the same mental or physical abilities. Nor does it argue that all persons have a right to an equal share of worldly goods.

Rather, the democratic concept of equality insists that all are entitled to (1) equality of opportunity and (2) equality before the law. That is, the democratic concept of equality holds that no person should be held back for any such arbitrary reasons as those based on race, color, religion, or sex. The concept holds that each person must be free to develop himself or herself as fully as he or she can (or cares to) and that each person should be treated as the equal of all other persons by the law.

We have come a great distance toward reaching the goal of equality for all in this country. But, clearly, we are still a considerable distance from a genuine, universally recognized and respected equality for all.

Political Equality Every person in a democratic society, regardless of race, color, religion, or gender, is entitled to live freely and equally and to fulfill his or her potential.

Spotlight on: Constitutional Issues

The concept of equality we now uphold is quite different from the one the Framers had in mind when the Bill of Rights was ratified in 1791. At that time, neither African Americans, who were enslaved in the South and in much of the North, nor women were "equal" under the law. Almost 80 years passed before the Constitution was amended to uphold the legal equality of males of all races—although it was still seldom upheld in fact—and nearly 50 more before women received the right to vote. Only in the last 40 years has our present concept of equality for all people taken shape, two centuries after the Bill of Rights was passed.

Enrichment

Have students read the Bill of Rights, and identify passages that express any of the five basic concepts of democracy. (Average)

OR

Teacher's Resource File
See the Unit 1 File for the Case Study on Contemporary Issues.

Majority Rule and Minority Rights

In a democracy, it is the will of the people and not the dictate of the ruling few that determines public policy. But what is the popular will, and how is it determined? How is the democratic society to decide and make public policies? Some standard, some device must exist, by which these crucial questions can be answered. The only satisfactory device democracy knows is that of majority rule. Democracy argues that a majority of the people will be right more often than they will be wrong, and that the majority will also be right more often than will any one person or small group.

Democracy can be described as an experiment—a trial-and-error process—designed to find satisfactory ways to order human relations. Notice that it does *not* say that the majority will always be "right," that it will always arrive at the best of all possible decisions on public matters. In fact, the democratic process—the process of majority rule—does not intend to come up with "right" or "best" answers. Rather, the democratic process searches for satisfactory solutions to public problems.

Of course, democracy insists that the majority's decisions will more often be more, rather than less, satisfactory. Democracy does admit the possibility of mistakes, however—the possibility that "wrong" or less satisfactory answers will sometimes be found. Democracy also recognizes that seldom is any solution to a public problem so satisfactory that it cannot be improved upon. It knows, too, that circumstances can change over time. So, the process of experimentation, of seeking answers to public questions, is really a never-ending one.

Certainly, a democracy cannot work without the principle of majority rule. Unchecked, however, a majority could destroy its opposition and, in the process, destroy democracy as well. Thus, democracy insists upon majority rule restrained by minority rights. The majority must always recognize the right of any minority to become, by fair and lawful means, the majority. The majority must always be willing to listen to a minority's argument, to hear its objections, to bear its criticisms, and to welcome its suggestions. Anything less contradicts the very meaning of democracy.

Necessity of Compromise

In a democracy, public decision-making must be largely a matter of give-and-take among the various competing interests. It is a matter of **com-**
1.a **promise**—the process of blending and adjusting, of reconciling competing views and interests—in order to find the position most acceptable to the largest number.

Compromise is an essential part of the democratic concept for two major reasons. First, remember that democracy puts the individual first and, at the same time, insists that each individual is the equal of all others. In a democratic society made up of many individuals and groups with many different opinions and interests, how can the people make public decisions except by compromise?

Second, few public questions have only two sides. Most can be answered in several ways. As a case in point, take the apparently simple question of how a city should pay for the paving of a public street. Should it charge the costs to those who own property along the street? Or should all of the city's residents pay the costs from the city's general treasury? Or should the city and the adjacent property owners share the costs? What about those who will use the street but do not live in the city? Should they have to pay a toll or buy a license for that use?

Again, the point is that most public policy questions have several possible answers. The fact remains, however, that the democratic society must find some answer.

Remember, compromise is a process, a way of achieving majority agreement. It is never an end in itself. Not all compromises are good, and not all are necessary. Some things—such as the equality of all persons—should never be the subject of any kind of compromise if democracy is to survive.

Individual Freedom

It should be clear by this point that democracy can thrive only in an atmosphere of individual freedom. But democracy does not and cannot insist on complete freedom for the individual. Absolute freedom can exist only in a state of
1.b **anarchy**—in the total absence of government.

Teacher's Resource File
See the Simulations and Debates file for "Majority Rule" and "The Rule of Law" to support this section.

Monitor Comprehension

Answers to Section 3 Review
1. "Key Terms" are defined on the following pages:
a. compromise, p. 17
b. anarchy, p. 17
2. A recognition of each person's fundamental worth; respect for the equality of all; faith in majority rule with minority rights; acceptance of the need to compromise; insistence on the widest possible degree of individual freedom. **3.** Because democracy puts individuals first while at the same time insisting on the equality of all. Also, since few questions have only "two sides," compromise is often needed to find majority agreement.
4. Society places the highest value on the guarantees necessary to the free exchange of ideas—expression and thought.
5. Answers will vary. Students might question what steps the nation is taking to achieve equality for all; how the nation is working to listen to the voice of the minority. Students might also ask about specific issues, such as poverty, hunger, and unemployment, and how those factors relate to the fundamental worth of each individual.

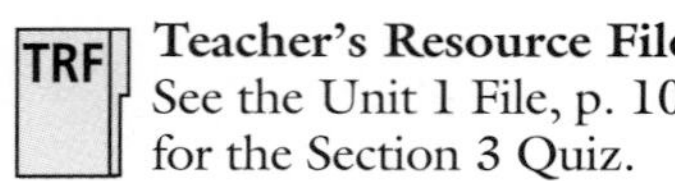

Teacher's Resource File
See the Unit 1 File, p. 10, for the Section 3 Quiz.

VOICES *on Government*

Antonia Hernandez, president and general counsel of the Mexican American Legal Defense and Educational Fund

On Multicultural Goals for the 1990s

"The '90s is a threshold decade. . . . We need to grab control of our destiny. . . . I see a lot of young people in their 30s and 40s who've taken advantage of the educational opportunities. We have lots of leaders. Now it is incumbent upon us to demand our share of power. . . . We need to register and vote, participate from the lowest level to the highest level. Our success will be determined by our willingness to be a part of the solution."

Anarchy can only lead, inevitably and quickly, to rule by the strong and ruthless.

Democracy does insist, however, that each individual must be as free to do as he or she pleases as far as the freedom of all will allow. Justice Oliver Wendell Holmes once had this to say about the relative nature of each individual's rights: "The right to swing my fist ends where the other man's nose begins."

Drawing the line between the rights of one individual and those of another is far from easy. But the drawing of that line is a continuous and vitally important function of democratic government. As John F. Kennedy put it: "The rights of every man are diminished when the rights of one man are threatened."

Striking the proper balance between freedom for the individual and the rights of society as a whole is similarly difficult—and vital. Abraham Lincoln once stated democracy's problem in these words:

> "Must a government of necessity be too *strong* for the liberties of its own people, or too *weak* to maintain its own existence?"

The problem goes to the very heart of democracy. Human beings desire both liberty and authority. Democratic government must work constantly to strike the proper balance between the two. The authority of government must be adequate to the needs of society. But that authority must never be allowed to become so great that it restricts the individual beyond necessity.

Democracy views all rights as vital, but it places its highest value on those necessary to the free exchange of ideas. Several years ago, the President's Committee on Civil Rights made the point:

> "In a free society there is faith in the ability of the people to make sound, rational judgments. But such judgments are possible only when the people have access to all relevant facts and to all prevailing interpretations of the facts. How can such judgments be formed on a sound basis if arguments, viewpoints, or opinions are arbitrarily suppressed? How can the concept of the marketplace of thought in which truth ultimately prevails retain its validity if the thought of certain individuals is denied the right of circulation?"

You will return to the subject of individual rights later, especially in chapters 19 and 20. You will also return to the other basic democratic concepts throughout this book.

Section 3 Review

1. **Define:** compromise, anarchy
2. What does the text suggest are the basic concepts of democracy?
3. For what reasons is compromise an essential part of the democratic process?
4. Upon which individual freedoms does democracy place its highest values?

Critical Thinking

5. **Formulating Questions** (p. 19) Based on the five concepts of democratic government, write a list of questions you would like to ask the President about democracy in America.

★

Activity: Cooperative Learning
Time: one class period **Activity:** Respond to a quotation from the chapter. **Grouping:** pairs **Purpose:** Have partners select one of the many quotations from Chapter 1 and work together to write a reaction to it. Reactions should explain what students think the quotation means and why they agree or disagree with it. **Roles:** Have partners determine the roles of recorder and spokesperson. **Outcome:** Have the spokesperson for each pair read the quotation and the reaction statement to the class. Invite the rest of the class to comment.

How to Solve Problems

Identify and Clarify the Problem

SKILL	DEFINITION	Page on which skill is taught
Expressing problems clearly	To succinctly describe a complex situation or body of information	Page 20
Identifying central issues	To identify the main ideas in a piece of information	Page 124
Making comparisons	To identify how different ideas, objects, historical figures, or situations are alike and/or different	Page 376
Determining relevance	To decide if and how events, situations, or items relate to one another	Page 152
Formulating questions	To create questions that seek answers to specific objectives and lead to a deeper understanding of an issue	Page 540

Judge Information Related to the Problem

SKILL	DEFINITION	Page on which skill is taught
Distinguishing fact from opinion	To separate those statements that can be proven to be true from those that reflect a personal viewpoint	Page 228
Checking consistency	To compare two or more items or ideas and determine whether they agree or disagree with each other	Page 92
Distinguishing false from accurate images	To examine a widely held belief about a person, place, or thing and determine whether or not the belief is based in fact	Page 206
Identifying assumptions	To recognize unstated beliefs that may underlie a statement, action, or event	Page 480
Recognizing bias	To identify a stated or unstated viewpoint or slant that is designed to promote one set of beliefs over another	Page 180
Recognizing ideologies	To identify underlying beliefs from actions or statements	Page 600

Draw Conclusions and Solve the Problem

SKILL	DEFINITION	Page on which skill is taught
Drawing conclusions	To find an answer or to form an opinion based on available information	Page 50
Recognizing cause and effect	To examine how one event or idea causes other events or ideas to occur	Page 278
Predicting consequences	To determine the likely effect of an event or action on the outcome of future events or actions	Page 510
Identifying alternatives	To identify one or more methods to achieve a goal or solve a problem; to recognize the possibility of other goals	Page 452
Testing conclusions	To examine a conclusion and determine whether or not it is supported by known facts	Page 346
Demonstrating reasoned judgment	To present evidence or reasoning that supports a given opinion or statement	Page 564

CLOSURE

Point out that although the five basic concepts of democracy may not be expressed in the everyday operations of government, they underlie our entire governmental system. Some may argue that our government does not express these principles perfectly. Nevertheless, they are the principles to which our country generally subscribes and that we strive to follow.

Assignment Assign Chapter 2, Section 1, pp. 24–30, for the next class period.

How to Solve Problems Tell students that this chart provides them with a description of all critical thinking skills taught in this book. In every section review, students will be asked a question with a critical thinking label. Students will be referred to this page (p. 19) to learn the definition of the particular critical thinking skill.

Reteach

Have students draw a single-frame cartoon that visually expresses one of the basic concepts of democracy outlined in the section. You may wish to display finished work on a bulletin board organized around the five basic concepts.

TEACHING
Critical Thinking

Expressing Problems Clearly

Objective
Organize information to express ideas clearly.

INSTRUCT

After students have worked through the four steps of the exercise, have them write a short, one-paragraph answer to the question in 4. You may want to extend discussion of the problem between Citizens A and B by exploring the concept of compromise raised in Chapter 1, Section 3.

Answers 1. (a) Disturbing the peace. (b) Citizen A has been abusive and aggressive. **2.** (a) A quiet dinner period. (b) To be able to practice. **3.** (a) That she plays the oboe only. (b) Citizen B also practices on weekend mornings; destroyed plants. **4.** Citizen A accuses Citizen B of disturbing his dinner period by practicing the oboe.

TRF **Teacher's Resource File** See the Unit 1 File, p. 11, for the Skill Application to reinforce the lesson.

Critical Thinking

Expressing Problems Clearly

Expressing problems clearly means succinctly describing a complex situation or body of information. When you express a problem clearly, you have taken the first step toward solving that problem. The table on the previous page includes some of the other critical thinking skills you can use to solve problems.

You have read that "no government demands so much of citizens as democracy." Indeed, your role as a citizen in a democracy will require you to participate in solving many problems. Use the following steps to practice expressing problems clearly.

1. Analyze the information. When you are confronted with a problem, you must make yourself familiar with the information involved. Read the sample police report on the right. (a) What is the nature of the complaint made by Citizen A? (b) What is the information given by Citizen B?

2. Identify the basic concepts involved. All problems arise out of a specific set of circumstances. However, they often revolve around a general principle, such as fairness. To identify this concept, try to express the problem in terms of what each side wants for itself. (a) What benefit does Citizen A want to achieve for himself by making the complaint? (b) What does Citizen B want ?

3. Identify the function of the supporting details. In any problem, there are details that are part of the story, but not really part of the overall problem. (a) In the police report below, is it an important part of the problem that Citizen B plays the oboe or that she plays poorly? (b) What other details in this report do not relate to the basic issue of disagreement between Citizen A and Citizen B?

4. Express the problem clearly. Now that you have identified the main area of dispute and stripped away the details, you are ready to express the problem clearly. What is a succinct description of the dispute between Citizen A and Citizen B?

Police Report

Citizen A has lodged a formal complaint about his neighbor, Citizen B. According to Citizen A, Citizen B has been playing her oboe in such a way as to deny Citizen A his peace and quiet. For example, Citizen B regularly practices her oboe near an open window at 6 P.M., when Citizen A and his family are eating dinner. Citizen B also practices on weekend mornings. Citizen A further complains that Citizen B is not a very accomplished oboe player, which makes the annoyance even worse.

Citizen B claims that Citizen A has never tried to work out an agreement by which she could continue practicing at a time more convenient for Citizen A. Instead, Citizen A has made threatening and abusive phone calls. She even suspects that Citizen A is responsible for the destruction of some garden plants, which she found destroyed after a particularly angry phone call from Citizen A. She has no solid evidence to support this accusation, however.

Chapter-in-Brief

Scan all headings, photographs, charts, and other visuals in the chapter before reading the section summaries below.

Section 1 Government and the State (pp. 3–8) Government is the institution through which a society makes and enforces public policies. It is one of humankind's oldest inventions.

The state has emerged as the dominant political unit in the world. A state is a body of people living in a defined area, having a government, and having the power to govern themselves without the consent of any higher authority.

Major theories that seek to explain the origin of the state include (1) the force theory, which holds that the state grew out of the forceful takeover of authority by a person or group; (2) the evolutionary theory, which sees the state as the natural extension of the family system over increasingly large and complex communities; (3) the divine right theory, which says that a god or gods created the state; and (4) the social contract theory, which holds that humans agreed to form states to ensure their own survival.

The social contract theory had the greatest influence on the founders of the United States. The Framers expressed their beliefs in the purposes of government in the Preamble to the Constitution.

Section 2 Forms of Government (pp. 10–14) Governments can be classified by one or more of their basic features. These include (1) the geographic distribution of power, (2) the relationship between the legislative and executive branches, and (3) the number of persons who take part in governmental processes.

The geographic distribution of power in a government gives it one of three basic forms: (1) a unitary government, in which all governmental power is held by a central government; (2) a federal government, in which governmental powers are divided between a central and local governments; and (3) a confederation, which is an alliance of independent states.

Depending on the relationship between the legislative and executive branch, government may take a presidential or parliamentary form. In the presidential form, each branch is independent and coequal. In a parliamentary form, the executive consists of members of the legislative branch.

The number of people who can take part in the governmental process is also a basis by which to classify governments. In a dictatorship, government is not accountable to the people. In a democracy, the people hold supreme political authority, either directly or, more commonly, through elected representatives.

Section 3 Basic Concepts of Democracy (pp. 15–18) The basic concepts of democracy in the United States are: (1) a recognition of the worth and dignity of each person; (2) respect for the equality of each person; (3) faith in majority rule and insistence on minority rights; (4) an acceptance of the need to compromise; and (5) an insistence upon the widest possible degree of individual freedom.

To ensure its survival as a democracy, this country must respect and apply these principles. This task requires the society to respect the worth of each person without allowing individual needs to injure the interests of the many. The democracy must ensure equal opportunity and equality for all; it must respect majority rule without allowing the majority to crush the minority; and it must use compromise to reach the most satisfactory decisions without compromising basic principles.

Teaching Suggestions for CHAPTER-IN-BRIEF

Below are some of the possible uses for the Chapter-in-Brief:

To Preview the Chapter You may want to assign the Chapter-in-Brief page and the Section Outlines from the Teacher's Resource File before beginning Chapter 1 to introduce students to "Key Terms" and concepts in each section.

To Review the Chapter When students have completed Chapter 1, you might want to assign the Chapter-in-Brief as a tool for review, along with the Guided Reading and Reviews from the Teacher's Resource File.

To Omit the Chapter If you wish to skip Chapter 1, it may be helpful to assign the Chapter-in-Brief to students as a review before beginning another chapter. You may also want to assign the Chapter 1 Test to assess student knowledge of the material. Then specific portions of Chapter 1 may be assigned to students needing reinforcement of "Key Terms" and concepts.

Teacher's Resource File See the Unit 1 File for the following materials:

- Section Outlines, pp. 2, 5, 8
- Guided Reading and Reviews, pp. 3, 6, 9
- Chapter 1 Test, pp. 15–17.

ADDITIONAL RESOURCES

Barone, Michael. *Our Country: The Shaping of America from Roosevelt to Reagan.* Free Press, 1990.

Brown, Lester R. and Alan B Durning. *State of the World.* Worldwatch Institute, annual.

Communism: Its Rise and Fall in the 20th Century. Christian Science Monitor, 1990.

Dahl, Robert A. *Democracy and Its Critics.* Yale University Press, 1989.

Moyers, Bill. *A World of Ideas.* Doubleday, 1989.

Paxton, John E. (ed.) *The Statesman's Yearbook.* St. Martin's Press, annual.

Roskin, Michael G. *Countries and Concept: An Introduction to Comparative Politics.* Prentice Hall, 3rd ed., 1989.

Roskin, Michael G., et al. *Political Science: An Introduction.* Prentice Hall, 4th ed., 1991.

Shafritz, Jay M. *Dictionary of American Government and Politics.* Dorsey, 1988.

Soe, Christian (ed.). *Comparative Politics.* Dushkin, annual.

Tinder, Glenn. *Political Thinking: The Perennial Questions.* HarperCollins, 5th ed., 1991.

Animal Farm. 16mm film. Phoenix Films, 1974. Color. 75 min. An animation in two parts based on the novel.

Answers to

Chapter 1 Review

Vocabulary and Key Terms

Matching

1. sovereign
2. government
3. public policies
4. confederation
5. dictatorship

True or False

1. False—the correct term is *public policies.*
2. False—correct term is *parliamentary government.*
3. False—correct term is *state.*
4. True.

Word Relationships

1. *Unitary government* refers to a system in which all existing governmental powers are held by the central government; a *federal government* is one in which powers are distributed among a central and several regional governments.
2. A *direct democracy* is one in which each individual has a direct voice in votes. *Representative democracy* involves the popular election of representatives to function on behalf of all the people.
3. A *dictatorship* is a form of government in which the government is not responsible to the will of the people. *Anarchy* is the absence of governmental authority.
4. *Presidential government* is a system characterized by separation of powers between coequal legislative and executive branches. In a *parliamentary government,* the executive is chosen by and responsible to the legislative branch.

Main Ideas

Section 1

1. Population, territory, sovereignty, and government. **2.** Force theory holds that an individual or group created a state by forcing others to submit to the aggressor's authority; evolutionary theory says that the state emerged as a natural extension of the family structure; divine right theory says that the state was created by a god; and social contract theory says that people agreed to form a state for their mutual benefit. **3.** Social contract theory. **4.** People form governments to create a more perfect union, to establish justice, to insure domestic tranquility, provide for a common defense, promote the general welfare, and to secure the blessings of liberty.

Section 2

5. Geographic distribution of power; the relationship between the legislative and executive; and the number of persons who can take part in the governing process. **6.** Unitary government, in which all existing governmental power is held by one central government; federal government, in which governmental powers are divided among a central government and several regional governments; or a confederation, in which several independent states join together and delegate limited powers to a

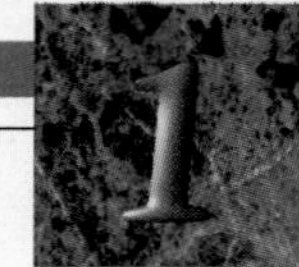

Chapter Review

Vocabulary and Key Terms

government (p. 3)	confederation (p. 11)	democracy (p. 13)
public policies (p. 3)	presidential government (p. 11)	direct democracy (p. 13)
state (p. 4)	parliamentary government (p.11)	representative democracy (p. 13)
sovereign (p. 4)	dictatorship (p. 12)	compromise (p. 17)
unitary government (p. 10)		anarchy (p. 17)
federal government (p. 10)		

Matching: *Review the key terms in the list above. If you are not sure of a term's meaning, look up the term and review its definition. Choose a term from the list above that best matches each description.*

1. a state that has supreme power within its own territory
2. the institution through which society makes and enforces its policies
3. that which a government decides to do
4. an alliance of independent states that expressly delegates limited powers to a central government
5. a form of government that is often totalitarian and authoritarian

True or False: *Determine whether each statement is true or false. If it is true, write "true." If it is false, change the underlined word or words to make the statement true.*

1. Compromise can be described as all those things that a government does.
2. Presidential governments do not have to contend with issues of prolonged deadlock and conflict between the executive and legislative branches.
3. A government is a sovereign member of the world community.
4. Democracy comes from Greek words meaning "rule by the people."

Word Relationships: *Distinguish between words in each pair.*

1. unitary government/federal government
2. direct democracy/representative democracy
3. dictatorship/anarchy
4. presidential government/parliamentary government

Main Ideas

Section 1 (pp. 3–8)

1. What characteristics define a state?
2. Briefly describe the four most widely held theories that attempt to explain the origin of the state.
3. Which theory on the origin of the state was most influential in the founding of the United States?
4. For what reasons do people form governments?

Section 2 (pp. 10–14)

5. On what three general bases can governments be classified?
6. Name and briefly describe the three forms of government that can result depending on how governmental power is distributed.
7. Name and briefly describe the two forms of government that can result depending on the relationship between the legislative and executive branches.

8. Name and briefly describe what forms of government can result depending on the number of people who can participate in the governmental process.

Section 3 (pp. 15–18)

9. Briefly describe the five basic concepts of democracy.
10. For what reasons is compromise such an essential part of democracy?
11. Describe the relationship between the rights of the individual and the rights of the overall society.
12. (a) In what sense must a democratic society provide for the rights of the minority? (b) What obligation does this place upon the majority?

Critical Thinking

1. **Recognizing Ideologies** (p. 19) Consider Martin Luther King, Jr.'s statement that "injustice anywhere is a threat to justice everywhere." (a) What is your understanding of that statement? (b) Why is such a belief necessary in order to maintain a democratic society?
2. **Checking Consistency** (p. 19) Review the ideas of Thomas Hobbes regarding the social contract theory and the origin of the state. (a) What is Hobbes's view about the nature of human beings? Explain why you agree or disagree with this view. (b) Given Hobbes's view, do you think it makes sense for people to enter into a contract with other human beings for their mutual protection?
3. **Identifying Alternatives** (p. 19) One of the five basic concepts of democracy is majority rule with minority rights. (a) What is the record of the United States in ensuring minority rights? (b) What do you think the United States might do to improve its protection of the rights of the minority?

Getting Involved

1. **Writing Your Opinion** Write your own "social contract" in which you express your feelings about what should be required of members of a political society, and what the government should provide the people. Start by creating a chart with two columns. In one column, list the responsibilities of the citizens in your proposed social contract. In the other column, list what you feel the government should provide its citizens. Begin your contract with a statement about the need for people to join together for their mutual benefit. Then detail your ideas for the contract. Proofread and revise for corrections. Then, prepare a final copy.
2. **Cooperative Activity** Conduct a classroom convention in which you discuss the different classifications of government as described in Section 2. The goal of the convention will be to decide as a class what you consider to be the best possible form of government. Start by creating a chart for each of the three bases of classification: (1) geographic distribution of power; (2) relationship between the legislative and executive; and (3) the number of persons who can take part in the governing process. For each category, discuss the pros and cons of each variation. After you have finished debating, write a profile of your ideal government that explains that government's characteristics.
3. **Creating a Poster** Create a poster that illustrates one of the five basic concepts of democracy discussed in Section 3. The poster should contain both words and images to communicate your ideas about how American society can best fulfill the concept you have chosen.

central government. **7.** Parliamentary, in which the executive is part of and responsible to the legislative; and presidential, in which the executive and legislative are separate and coequal. **8.** Dictatorship, in which the government has no responsibility to the people and is controlled completely by a small number of people; or a democracy, in which the people hold ultimate political power.

Section 3

9. Equality of all persons; fundamental worth of the individual; majority rule with minority rights; necessity of compromise; and individual freedom.
10. Democracy insists that individuals be respected and also insists that all people are equal. Therefore, compromise must exist so that both of these concepts are preserved.
11. Individual freedom exists only in so far as they do not infringe on the rights of others.
12. (a) A democratic society must enable the minority to be heard and to become the majority if it is able. (b) The majority must not use its power to crush the minority.

Critical Thinking

1. (a) Answers will vary. Students might note that justice itself does not exist if it is not available to everyone.
(b) Answers will vary. Students might note that democracy requires all individuals to be equal. When inequality exists, democracy itself is threatened.
2. (a) Answers will vary. Students might observe that Hobbes views people in a state of nature as self-interested.
(b) Answers will vary. Based on Hobbes's view, students might question the trustworthiness of other people; or students might suggest that most people would see little choice but to give up their self-interests in order to achieve more security against those who are stronger.
3. (a) Answers will vary. Students might suggest that minorities have fared poorly in the United States. Others would suggest that the United States has done well at providing minority groups the opportunity to become a part of a political majority. (b) Answers will vary. Students might observe the difficulty of providing for minority rights without unjustly limiting the rule of the majority.

Getting Involved

1–3. Answers and results will vary, but students should demonstrate an understanding of the concepts in this chapter.

23

Chapter 2 Resources

IN THE TEACHER'S RESOURCE FILE
The following materials are found in the Teacher's Resource File box.

Instructional Support: Unit 1 File

For the Section
Outlines, pp. 21, 24, 27, 30, 33
Guided Reading and Reviews, pp. 22, 25, 28, 31, 34
Quizzes, pp. 23, 26, 29, 32, 35

For the Chapter
Skill Application, p. 36
Case Study on Contemporary Issues pp. 37–39
Chapter Test, pp. 40–42
Additional Test Questions, pp. 43–45

Enrichment Support Files

Supreme Court Cases, p.2
Historical and Legal Documents, pp. 3, 6–7, 9–10, 13

Computer Test Bank and Assessment

Transparency Package, pp. 2, 27

Chapter 2 Focus

Introduce the Chapter Tell students that in this chapter they will learn about the origins and development of the American system of government from the time of the Roman Empire through the Continental Congresses held before and during the Revolutionary War. Read with students the Chapter Preview and Objectives.

Writing Activity Direct students' attention to "Describe" under "Before you read this chapter." Have students brainstorm to create a list of important governmental principles. Have students choose one about which to write descriptions.

Motivate for Learning Direct students' attention to "Predict." Lead students in a discussion of events that exemplify the strength of the U.S. government, then discuss what might have happened had the government not shown strength.

Origins of American Government

Chapter Preview

A Russian artist, having been allowed to travel abroad for the first time in 1991, commented about his country, "It's amazing to me that so much freedom could lead to so much *poshlost.*" *Poshlost* is a Russian word that is said to be untranslatable, but in the artist's sentence it means "chaos."

In 1991 revolutionary changes took place in what the world once knew as the Soviet Union. From the chaos emerged a new nation—the Commonwealth of Independent States. Similarly, the men and women who created the American system of government in 1787 needed to create order out of post-revolutionary chaos. They built a system that served the distinct needs of a new country. This chapter is about the origins of American government, from its historical development through the creation of the Constitution.

Before you read this chapter:

- **Describe** what you think is the most important principle of a new government.
- **Predict** some problems the United States would face if it lacked a strong central government.

As you read, focus on the main objective for each section. Understand:

1. The origins of the American governmental system.
2. The development of that system through the colonial period to the coming of Independence.
3. The Critical Period and the governmental arrangements set up by the Articles of Confederation.
4. The events and the processes involved in the creation and adoption of the Constitution of the United States.

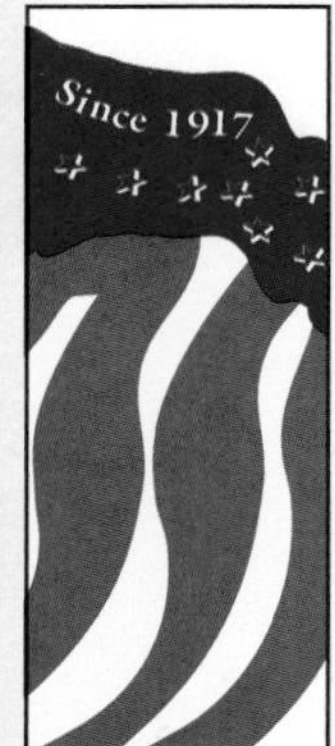

Magruder's American Government: *A Witness to Change* by William A. McClenaghan

In 1917 this book carried a Constitution with only 17 amendments. The 18th Amendment, establishing prohibition, was added two years later, and was repealed by the 21st Amendment in 1933.

Seven other amendments have been added to the Constitution over the lifespan of this book. Can you imagine a Constitution

—that did not provide for women's suffrage (19th Amendment, 1920)?
—under which the President was inaugurated in March, not January (20th Amendment, 1933)?
—that contained no limit on the number of terms a President could serve (22nd Amendment, 1951)?
—that excluded the District of Columbia from the electoral college system (23rd Amendment, 1961)?
—that allowed poll taxes (24th Amendment, 1964)?
—under which a vacancy in the Vice Presidency went unfilled through the term (25th Amendment, 1967)?
—that did not provide for voting by 18-year-olds (26th Amendment, 1971)?

Note that four of these amendments deal with expanding suffrage, demonstrating the importance of this issue to twentieth century Americans.

Our Strength: Diversity Those who formed the American government crafted a system flexible enough to respond to the needs of the ever-growing and diversifying American population of today.

1 Our Political Beginnings

Find Out:

- What were the basic ideas about government that English colonists brought to America?
- How did governments first develop in the 13 colonies?

Key Terms:

limited government, representative government, Magna Carta, Petition of Right, English Bill of Rights, charter, bicameral, unicameral

For most Americans, the Fourth of July is the time to celebrate this nation's birthday. Every year, people recall 1776 and the coming of Independence with fireworks and picnics and other festivities.

Of course, the story of the United States begins long before 1776. It starts no later than the mid-1500s when explorers, traders, and settlers first made their way to North America. The French, Dutch, Spanish, Swedes, and others contributed to European domination of the continent—and to the domination of the Native Americans who were here for untold centuries before the Europeans came.

It was the English, however, who came in the largest numbers. And they soon controlled the 13 colonies that stretched some 1,300 miles along the Atlantic seaboard.

Basic Concepts of Government

The earliest English settlers brought with them the knowledge of a political system—established laws, customs, and practices—that had been developing for centuries. The political system the settlers knew was from 17th-century England, but many ideas that contributed

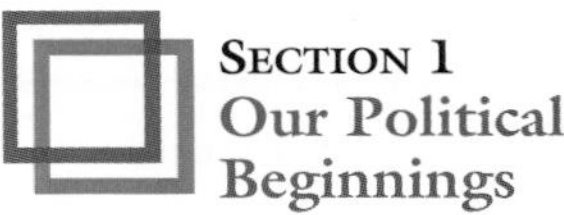

Section 1
Our Political Beginnings

Focus

Objectives

2.1 Understand the basic ideas about government that English colonists brought to America.

2.2 Examine how governments first developed in the 13 colonies.

Bellringer Activity Before you begin the section, ask students: If you were one of the early colonists, name three important laws on which you would want to base your government.

State the Purpose The government of the United States was built upon three basic ideas acquired by the English from ancient civilizations. In Section 1, students will learn what those ideas are, the names of important documents in which those ideas were expressed, and how the three ideas contributed to the character of the American colonial governments.

ABCNEWS INTERACTIVE

The following video segments can be used to highlight Powers of Congress

POWERS OF THE CONGRESS GUIDEBOOK
Chapter 51: Historical Figures, p.57
Chapter 52: Documents, p.58

See also Enrichment Questions and Activities starting on p. 161.

Vocabulary

Point out the "Key Terms" on page 25 to the students. Below are additional words whose meanings may help students better understand the section content.

—**diversity:** variety
—**landmark:** describes an important turning point or stage LEP

Reading Strategy: Problem-Solving

As a preparation for reading, ask students where they would get ideas if they were to create a new government. Discuss with students government concepts and terms they may know from television, periodicals, or books. How might this information help them form a new government? During this discussion, you might refer to students to events after the break up of the Soviet Union.

INSTRUCT

Explain/Analyze Explain to students that the way the United States government is organized, its powers, and its limitations, are based on ideas about government that were brought to these shores by the English colonists. The three ideas of ordered, limited, and representative government are found in several important documents of English history: the Magna Carta (1215), the Petition of Right (1628), and the English Bill of Rights (1689). Many of the provisions in these documents were included in the charters of the 13 colonies. Further, explain that three different types of government developed in the 13 colonies. Royal, or Crown, colonies were subject to the direct control of the King; proprietary colonies were set up as business ventures, and were ruled in the manner chosen by the owner; and charter colonies were governed by the colonists themselves. At the time of the revolution, New Hampshire, Massachusetts, New York, New Jersey, Virginia, North Carolina, South Carolina, and Georgia were royal colonies. Maryland, Pennsylvania, and Delaware were proprietary colonies, and Connecticut and Rhode Island were charter colonies.
Have students analyze the author's statement at the end of the section about how the Revolution might never have occured if all the colonies had had charter governments. Do students agree or disagree with the statement? Why or why not?

Foundations of American Rights

Rights	Sources of Rights			
	Magna Carta (1215)	English Bill of Rights (1689)	Virginia Declaration of Rights (1776)	Bill of Rights (1791)
Trial by jury		✔		✔
Due process	✔	✔		✔
Private property	✔			✔
No unreasonable searches or seizures			✔	✔
No cruel punishment		✔	✔	✔
No excessive bail or fines		✔		✔
Right to bear arms		✔		✔
Right to petition		✔		✔
Freedom of speech			✔	✔
Freedom of the press			✔	✔
Freedom of religion			✔	✔

▲ **Interpreting Tables: Multicultural Awareness** Although revolutionary in their day, these rights did not extend to all people. Which group gained the most through these rights?

to it came from other times and places. For example, the concept of the rule of law that influenced English political ideas had its roots in the early river civilizations of Africa and Asia.[1] And the ancient Romans actually occupied much of England, leaving their direct legacy of law, religion, and custom on the people. Most importantly, the English colonists brought three ideas that were to loom large in the shaping of government in the United States.

[1]For example, King Hammurabi of Babylonia developed a codified system of laws known as Hammurabi's Code around 1750 B.C. Its 285 laws covered real estate, trade, and business transactions, as well as criminal law. The code distinguished between major and minor offenses, established the state as the authority that would enforce the law, and tried to guarantee social justice. Because of the Babylonians' close contact with the Hebrews, many of their laws became part of the Hebrew law and thus later a part of the Old Testament of the Bible—for example, "An eye for an eye." The English and the English colonists were, of course, familiar with and devoutly attracted to this Biblical concept of the rule of law.

Ordered Government The first English colonists saw the need for an orderly regulation of their relationships with one another—that is, for government. They created local governments, based on those they had known in England. Many of the offices and units of government the early settlers established are still found at the local level today: the offices of sheriff, coroner, assessor, and justice of the peace, the grand jury, counties, townships, and several others.

Limited Government Those first English colonists also brought with them the idea that government is not all-powerful. That is, government is limited in what it may do, and each individual has certain rights that government cannot take away.

1.a The concept of **limited government** described above was deeply rooted in English belief and practice by the time the first English ships reached the Americas. It had been introduced in England with the signing of the Magna Carta in 1215, and it had been developing there for nearly 400 years before Jamestown was settled in 1607.

ACTIVITY: Cooperative Learning

Time: two class periods **Activity:** List and describe local government offices **Grouping:** groups of four to six students **Purpose:** Using outside resources, have students work together to prepare a list of five offices found in their own city or town today and write a brief description of the function of each office. **Roles:** Have students assign the following roles: manager, researcher(s), recorder, and spokesperson. **Outcome:** When researchers have presented their information to the group, have the spokesperson read the group's list of offices. As different groups report, compile a class list of local government offices on the chalkboard.

Representative Government The early English settlers also carried another important concept to America: **representative govern-** 1.a **ment**. This idea that government should serve the will of the people had also been developing in England for centuries. With it had come a growing insistence that the people should have a voice in deciding what government should and should not do. As with the concept of limited government, this notion of "government of, by, and for the people" found fertile soil in America, and it flourished here.

Landmark English Documents

These basic notions of ordered government, of limited government, and of representative government can be traced to several landmark documents in English history.

The Magna Carta A group of determined barons forced King John to sign the **Magna** 1.b **Carta**—the Great Charter—at Runnymede in 1215. Weary of John's military campaigns and heavy taxes, the barons were seeking protection against arbitrary acts by the king.

The Magna Carta included such fundamental rights as trial by jury and due process of law—protection against the arbitrary taking of life, liberty, or property.

These protections against the absolute power of the king were originally intended only for the privileged classes. Over time, they became the rights of all English people and were incorporated into other documents. The Magna Carta established the principle that the power of the monarchy was not absolute.

The Petition of Right The Magna Carta 1.d was respected by some monarchs and ignored by others for 400 years. During this time, England's Parliament, a representative body with the power to make laws, slowly grew in influence. In 1628, when Charles I asked Parliament for more money in taxes, Parliament refused until he signed the Petition of Right.

The **Petition of Right** limited the king's power by demanding that the king not imprison political critics without trial by jury; not declare martial law, or rule by the military, during peacetime; nor require people to shelter troops without the homeowner's consent. In addition, the document stated that no man should be:

> "compelled to make or yield any gift, loan, benevolence, tax, or such like charge, without common consent by act of parliament."

The Petition challenged the idea of the divine right of kings, declaring that even a monarch must obey the law of the land.

The Bill of Rights In 1688, after years of revolt and turmoil, Parliament offered the crown to William and Mary of Orange. The events surrounding their ascent to the throne are known in English history as the Glorious Revolution. To prevent abuse of power by William and Mary and all future monarchs, Parliament, in 1689, drew up the Bill of Rights to which William and Mary had to agree.

The **English Bill of Rights** prohibited a 1.e standing army in peacetime, except with the consent of Parliament, and required that all parliamentary elections be free. The document also declared

> "that the pretended power of suspending of laws, or the execution of laws, by regal authority, without consent of Parliament is illegal . . .
>
> that levying money for or to the use of the crown . . . without grant of Parliament . . . is illegal . . .

Life, Liberty, Property English philosopher John Locke's argument that these were natural rights rather than privileges heavily influenced 18th-century America.

Interpreting Tables Direct students' attention to the table "Foundations of American Rights" on p. 26. Have them analyze the chart to find out which rights were extended in what order and in what documents. Ask: What document introduced the right to freedom of speech? (*Virginia Declaration of Rights*)

Caption Answer White males.

Provide Guided Practice
Write on the board the three basic concepts of government—*limited government*, *ordered government*, and *representative government*. Have students volunteer examples from real life that illustrate each concept. List students' examples on the board under the concepts.

Provide Independent Practice
TRF **Teacher's Resource File**
Assign the Section 1 Guided Reading and Review in the Unit 1 File, p. 22, to help students master section objective content.

SPOTLIGHT ON: Roots of Democracy

A medieval lord might be an unlikely contributor to the development of constitutional government, but Simon de Monfort (c. 1208-1265), a powerful Anglo-Norman baron, did just that! In 1264, de Monfort led a group of barons against Henry III of England to force the king's adherence to the Provisions of Oxford. The Provisions, written to limit the monarchy, included the establishment of a baronial council that could veto the king's decisions and tri-annual meetings with representatives from the lesser nobility. De Monfort briefly held power during the ensuing civil war and, true to his beliefs in the Provisions, he summoned what became known as the Model Parliament. This parliament included not only the great barons and two knights from each shire, but, remarkably, two representatives from each town. This was the first time in parliamentary history that members of the commons had been included in the government. Though de Monfort and his supporters were killed by royal forces at Evesham in 1265, his belief that the commons should be involved in government set an important precedent for the development of modern representative institutions.

that it is the right of the subjects to petition the king . . . and that prosecutions for such petitioning are illegal . . . ”

In addition, the English Bill of Rights included such guarantees as the right to a fair and speedy trial, and freedom from excessive bail and from cruel and unusual punishment.

Our nation has built on, changed, and added to those ideas and institutions that settlers brought here from England. Still, much in American government and politics today is based on these early English ideas.

Government in the Colonies

England's colonies in North America have been described as "13 schools of government." The colonies were the settings in which Americans first began to learn the difficult art of government.[2]

The 13 colonies were established separately, over a span of 125 years. Over that long period, outlying trading posts and isolated farm settlements developed into organized communities. The first colony, Virginia, was founded with the first permanent English settlement in North America at Jamestown in 1607.[3] Georgia was the last to be formed, with the settlement of Savannah in 1733.

Each of the colonies was born out of a particular set of circumstances, and so each had its own character. Virginia was originally organized as a commercial venture. Its first colonists were employees of the Virginia Company, a private trading corporation. Massachusetts was first settled by people who came to North America in search of greater personal and religious freedom. Georgia was founded largely as a haven for debtors—a refuge for the victims of England's harsh poor laws.

But the differences between and among the colonies are really of little importance. Of much greater significance is the fact that all of them were shaped by their English origins. The many similarities among all 13 colonies far outweighed the differences.

Each colony was established on the basis of
1.f a **charter**, a written grant of authority from the king.[4] Over time, these instruments of government led to the establishment of three different kinds of colonies: royal, proprietary, and charter.

Royal Colonies The royal colonies were subject to the direct control of the Crown. On the eve of the Revolution in 1775, there were eight: New Hampshire, Massachusetts, New York, New Jersey, Virginia, North Carolina, South Carolina, and Georgia.

The Virginia colony was not the quick success its sponsors had promised. So, in 1624, the king revoked the London Company's charter, and Virginia became the first royal colony. Later, as the original charters of other colonies were canceled or withdrawn, they became royal colonies. Georgia was the last to join the list, in 1754.

Over time, a pattern of government emerged for each of the royal colonies. The king named a governor to serve as the colony's chief executive. A council, also named by the king, served as an advisory body to the royal governor. In time, the governor's council became the upper
1.g house of the colonial legislature. It also became the highest court in the colony. The lower house of a **bicameral** (two-house) legislature was elected by those property owners qualified

[2]The Europeans who came to the Americas brought with them their own views of government, but this does not mean that they brought the idea of government to the Americas. Native Americans had governments. They had political institutions that worked to accomplish the goals of the state; they had political leaders; and they had policies toward other states.

Some Native-American political organizations were very complex. For example, five Native-American groups in present-day New York State—the Seneca, Cayuga, Oneida, Onondaga, and Mohawk—formed a confederation known as the Iroquois League. The League was set up to end conflicts among the groups, but it was so successful as a form of government that it lasted for over 200 years.

[3]St. Augustine, Florida, is the oldest continuously populated European settlement in what is now the United States. St. Augustine was founded by Pedro Menendez in 1565 to establish Spanish authority in the region.

[4]Except for Georgia. Its charter was granted by Parliament in 1732.

Spotlight on: Multiculturalism

In 1619, a year before the *Mayflower* reached Plymouth, the first African settlers in English North America arrived at Jamestown. These settlers, numbering about twenty, were indentured servants, not slaves. At the time, African slavery was common in the American colonies of Portugal and Spain, but the practice did not become widespread in the English colonies until after the establishment, in 1672, of the Royal African Company. Thereafter, the number of Africans, who were now being brought to the colonies as slaves, rose sharply.

Enrichment

Have students write an explanation of what they think the true nature and purpose of government are. Students should begin their writing with a summary of what government is and why it exists. Students should illustrate points they make by referring to problems faced by emerging nations today. (Challenging)

Early Colonial Government Fiery orator Patrick Henry addresses the Virginia House of Burgesses—the first representative body, or elected legislature, to meet in America.

to vote.[5] It owed much of its influence to the fact that it shared with the governor and his council the power of the purse—that is, the power to tax and the power to spend. The governor, advised by the council, appointed the judges for the colony's courts.

The laws passed by the legislature had to be approved by the governor and the Crown. Royal governors often ruled with a stern hand, following instructions from London. Much of the resentment that finally flared into revolution was fanned by their actions.

The Proprietary Colonies At the time of the Revolution, there were three proprietary colonies: Maryland, Pennsylvania, and Delaware. A proprietor was a person to whom the king had made a grant of land. By charter, that land could be settled and governed much as the proprietor (owner) chose.

In 1632 the king had granted Maryland to Lord Baltimore and in 1681, Pennsylvania to William Penn. In 1682 Penn also acquired Delaware.[6]

The governments of these three colonies were much like those in the royal colonies. The governor, however, was appointed by the proprietor. In Maryland and Delaware, the legislatures were bicameral. In Pennsylvania, the legislature
1.h was a **unicameral** (one-house) body. There, the governor's council did not act as one house of the legislature. As in the royal colonies, appeals from the decisions of the proprietary colonies could be carried to the king in London.

[5]The Virginia legislature held its first meeting in the church at Jamestown on July 30, 1619, and was the first representative body to meet in the English colonies. It was made up of burgesses—that is, representatives—elected from each settlement in the colony. Virginia called the lower house of its colonial legislature the House of Burgesses; South Carolina, the House of Commons; Massachusetts, the House of Representatives.

[6]New York, New Jersey, North Carolina, South Carolina, and Georgia also began as proprietary colonies. Each of them later became a royal colony.

Reteach

Have students review the section by creating an outline representing the important ideas in the section. You may want to provide them with the beginning of the outline:

Our Political Beginnings

I. Basic concepts of government
   A. Ordered government
   B. Limited government
   C. Representative government

Monitor Comprehension

Answers to Section 1 Review

1. "Key Terms" are defined on the following pages:
- **a.** limited government, p. 26
- **b.** representative government, p. 27
- **c.** Magna Carta, p. 27
- **d.** Petition of Right, p. 27
- **e.** English Bill of Rights, p. 27
- **f.** charter, p. 28
- **g.** bicameral, p. 28
- **h.** unicameral, p. 29

2. ordered, limited; representative government; guarantees and freedoms promised in the Magna Carta, Petition of Right, English Bill of Rights; writings of John Locke **3.** Royal colonies under more direct control of the Crown; Proprietary colonies governed by the owner; Charter colonies enjoyed a large degree of self-government.
4. (a) All started with charters; based on English government. (b) They all had varying degrees of self-government.

Closure

The American system of government is based on ideas that originated in Africa and Asia and traveled to England with the Roman conquest, and from England to the colonies. The English colonists lived under three types of government: royal, proprietary, and charter. In the next section, students will learn about the changes in the relationship between the colonies and England in the 1700s.

Assignment Assign Section 2, pp. 30–35 for the next class period.

The Charter Colonies Connecticut and Rhode Island were charter colonies. They were based on charters granted in 1662 and 1663, respectively, to the colonists themselves.[7] Thus, they were largely self-governing.

The governors of Connecticut and Rhode Island were elected each year by the white, male property owners in each colony. Although the king's approval was required before the governor could take office, it was not often asked. Laws made by their bicameral legislatures were not subject to the governor's veto nor was the Crown's approval needed. Colonial judges were appointed by the legislature, but appeals could be taken from the colonial courts to the king.

The Connecticut and the Rhode Island charters were so liberal for their time that, with independence, they served for many years as State constitutions, with only minor changes. In fact, many historians say that had Britain allowed the other colonies the same freedom and self-government, the Revolution might never have occurred.

Section 1 Review

1. Define: limited government, representative government, Magna Carta, Petition of Right, English Bill of Rights, charter, bicameral, unicameral
2. What major political ideas did the early English settlers bring to America?
3. Identify and describe the three types of colonial government in pre-Revolutionary America.

Critical Thinking

4. Making Comparisons (p. 19) (a) In what ways were the colonial governments similar? (b) How were they different?

[7]The Massachusetts Bay Colony was established as the first charter colony in 1629. Its charter was later revoked and Massachusetts became a royal colony in 1691. Religious dissidents from Massachusetts founded Connecticut in 1633 and Rhode Island in 1636.

2 The Coming of Independence

Find Out:
- How did the relationship between the colonies and Great Britain change in the pre-Revolutionary period?
- For what reasons is the Declaration of Independence considered a revolutionary document?
- What was government like in the newly independent United States?

Key Terms:

Albany Plan of Union, boycott, constitution, popular sovereignty

"We must hang together, or assuredly we shall all hang separately." Benjamin Franklin spoke these words on July 4, 1776, as he and the other members of the Second Continental Congress adopted the Declaration of Independence. Those who heard him may well have chuckled. But they also may have felt a shiver, for the good doctor's humor carried a deadly serious message.

In this section, you will follow the events that led to the momentous decision to break with Great Britain,[8] and you will also read about the new State governments that were established with the coming of Independence.

Royal Control

The 13 colonies, which had been separately established, were separately controlled under the king, largely through the Privy Council and the Board of Trade in London. Parliament took little part in the management of the colonies. Although it did become more and more interested in matters of

[8]England became Great Britain by the Act of Union with Scotland in 1707.

Teacher's Resource File
See the Unit 1 File, p. 23, for the Section 1 Quiz.

trade, it left matters of colonial administration almost entirely to the Crown.[9]

Over the century and a half that followed the first settlement at Jamestown, the colonies developed within that framework of royal control. In theory, they were governed in all important matters from London. But London was 3,000 miles away, and it took nearly two months to sail that distance across a peril-filled Atlantic. So, in practice, the colonists became used to a large measure of self-government.

In time, each colonial legislature assumed broad lawmaking powers. Many found the power of the purse to be very effective. They often bent a governor to their will by not voting the money for his salary until he came to terms with them. As one member of New Jersey's Assembly put it: "Let us keep the dogges poore, and we'll make them do as we please."

By the mid-1700s, the relationship between Britain and the colonies had become, in fact if not in form, federal. This means that the central government in London was responsible for colonial defense and for foreign affairs. It also provided a uniform system of money and credit and a common market for colonial trade. Beyond that, the colonies were allowed a fairly wide amount of self-rule. Little was taken from them in direct taxes to pay for the central government. And, the few regulations set by Parliament, mostly about trade, were largely ignored.

This was soon to change. Shortly after George III came to the throne in 1760, Britain began to deal more firmly with the colonies. Restrictive trading acts were expanded and enforced. New taxes were imposed, mostly to support British troops in North America.

Many colonists took strong exception to these moves. They objected to taxes they had had no part in levying. This arrangement, they claimed, was "taxation without representation."

They saw little need for the costly presence of British troops since the French had been defeated and their power broken in the French and Indian War (1754–1763). The colonists considered themselves British subjects loyal to the Crown. They refused, however, to accept Parliament's claim that it had a right to control their own local affairs.

The king's ministers were poorly informed and stubborn. They pushed ahead with their policies, despite the resentments they stirred in America. Within a few years, the colonists were to be forced to a fateful choice: to submit or to revolt.

Growing Colonial Unity

Long before the 1770s, several attempts had been made to promote cooperation among the colonies.

The Road to Revolution, 1765–1766
British enforcement of the Stamp Act led to angry protests against "taxation without representation" in colonial America.

[9]Much of English political history can be told in terms of the centuries-long struggle for supremacy between king and Parliament. But despite its growing power in British government, Parliament paid little attention to the colonies until late in the colonial period.

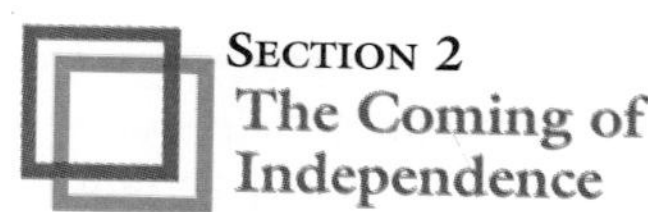

Section 2
The Coming of Independence

Focus

Objectives

2.3 Explain how the relationship between the colonies and Great Britain changed in the pre-Revolutionary period.

2.4 Understand why the Declaration of Independence is considered a revolutionary document.

2.5 Describe what government was like in the newly independent United States.

Bellringer Activity Before you begin the section, ask: Suppose you have worked on writing the Declaration of Independence. When it is published, you might be arrested and executed. Other people will die in defending these ideas. What are you thinking as you sign this document? Discuss students' responses.

State the Purpose For a period of more than 100 years, from the formation of colonial governments in the 1600s until 1760, the colonies were very much like sovereign states, although they were united under the central government in England. In Section 2, students will learn how the colonies' relationships with each other and with England changed in the mid-1700s and what caused these changes.

Vocabulary

Point out the "Key Terms" on page 30 to the students. Below are some additional words whose meanings may help students better understand the section content.

—**continental:** of or relating to the colonies that later formed the U.S.

—**momentous:** very important; of great consequence

—**minister:** a high officer of state

LEP

Reading Strategy: Predicting Content

Before reading, have students read the boldfaced headings found throughout the section. Point out to students that these headings form an outline of the content. Then have students predict the content of the section in one sentence. Direct students to read the section to test their predictions.

Early Attempts In 1643 the Massachusetts Bay, Plymouth, New Haven, and Connecticut settlements formed the New England Confederation, a "league of friendship" for defense against the Native Americans. However, as the danger from Native Americans passed and friction among the settlements grew, the confederation lost importance and finally died in 1684. In 1696 William Penn offered an elaborate plan for intercolonial cooperation, largely in trade, defense, and criminal matters. It received little attention and was soon forgotten.

The Albany Plan In 1754 the British Board of Trade called a meeting of seven of the northern colonies at Albany[10] The main purpose of the meeting was to discuss the problems of colonial trade and the danger of attacks by the French and their Native-American allies. Here, Benjamin Franklin offered what came to be
1.a known as the **Albany Plan of Union**.

Franklin proposed the formation of an annual congress of delegates from each of the 13 colonies. That body would have the power to raise military and naval forces, make war and peace with the Native Americans, regulate trade with them, levy taxes, and collect customs duties.

Franklin's plan was ahead of its time. It was agreed to by the Albany meeting, but it was turned down by the colonies and by the Crown. Franklin's plan was to be remembered later, however.

The Stamp Act Congress Britain's harsh tax and trade policies of the 1760s fanned resentment in the colonies. Parliament had passed a number of new laws, among them the Stamp Act of 1765. That law required the use of tax stamps on all legal documents, on certain business agreements, and on newspapers.

The new taxes were widely denounced, in part because the rates were perceived as severe, but largely because they amounted to "taxation without representation." In October of 1765 nine colonies[11] sent delegates to the Stamp Act Congress in New York. They prepared a strong protest, called the Declaration of Rights and Grievances, against the new British policies and sent it to the king. Their actions marked the first time a significant number of the colonies had joined to oppose the British government.

Parliament repealed the Stamp Act, but frictions mounted. New laws were passed and new policies were made to tie the colonies more closely to London. Colonists showed their resentment and anger in wholesale evasion of the laws. Mob violence erupted at several ports,
1.b and many colonists supported a **boycott**—a refusal to buy or sell—English goods. On March 3, 1770, British troops in Boston fired on a jeering crowd, killing five, in what came to be known as the Boston Massacre.

Organized resistance was carried on through Committees of Correspondence, which had grown out of a group formed by Samuel Adams in Boston in 1772. Within a year these committees existed throughout the colonies, providing a network for cooperation and the exchange of information among the patriots.

Protests multiplied. The famous Boston Tea Party came on December 16, 1773. A group of men, disguised as Native Americans, boarded three ships in Boston harbor and dumped their cargo into the sea in protest of a new tea monopoly.

The First Continental Congress

In the spring of 1774, Parliament passed yet another set of laws, this time to punish the colonists for the troubles in Boston and elsewhere. These new laws, denounced in America as the Intolerable Acts, caused the Massachusetts and Virginia assemblies to call a meeting of all the colonies.

Fifty-five delegates, from every colony except Georgia, met in Philadelphia on September 5, 1774. For nearly two months, the members of this First Continental Congress discussed the worsening situation and debated plans for action.

[10]Connecticut, Maryland, Massachusetts, New Hampshire, New York, Pennsylvania, and Rhode Island.

[11]All except Georgia, New Hampshire, North Carolina, and Virginia.

INSTRUCT

Explain/Discuss Help students recognize the importance of the positive aspects of cooperation that already had been established when it came time to form a new nation. Explain that the New England Confederation and the Albany Plan represented positive attempts by the colonists to improve their lives by combining resources and working toward common purposes. Also, the Stamp Act Congress, the Declaration of Rights and Grievances that resulted from it, and the boycott of English goods all unified the colonies against England.

Then discuss with students whether it might have been possible for the colonies to have had a more succesful relationship with the British government, and how this could have been accomplished. (*Students should understand that the relationship between the British Crown and the colonies might have been more successful had the British not suspended colonist's rights—rights they expected as British citizens.*)

ABCNEWS INTERACTIVE

The following video segments can be used to highlight aspects of colonial government.

POWERS OF THE CONGRESS GUIDEBOOK
Chapter 51: Historical Figures, p. 57
Chapter 53: Development of Democracy, p. 58

See also Enrichment Questions and Activities beginning on page 161.

Enrichment

Have students draw cartoons representing ideas in the excerpt from the Declaration of Independence on page 34. Ask students to consider the fact that many of the ideas in the document come from the English tradition of government. (Average)

SPOTLIGHT ON: Political Talk

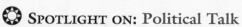

While angry colonists did indeed boycott British goods in the 1760s and '70s, that is not what they would have called it—the word "boycott" had not been invented yet. The term comes from the name of Captain C. C. Boycott, an unfortunate English landlord. Boycott was the first among a number of absentee landlords against whom the Irish Land League protested in the 1870s. The word *boycott*, originally written with a capital "B," gained wide popularity in the United Kingdom in the 1880s, and was subsequently adopted into American usage.

They sent a Declaration of Rights, protesting Britain's colonial policies, to George III. The delegates urged each of the colonies to refuse all trade with England until the hated taxes and trade regulations were repealed. The delegates also called for the creation of local committees to enforce that boycott.

The meeting adjourned on October 26, with a call for a second congress the following May. Over the next several months, all the colonial legislatures, including Georgia's, gave their support to the actions of the First Continental Congress.

The Second Continental Congress

During the fall and winter of 1774–75, the British government continued to refuse to compromise, let alone reverse, its colonial policies. It reacted to the Declaration of Rights as it had to other expressions of colonial discontent—with even stricter and more repressive measures.

The Second Continental Congress met in Philadelphia on May 10, 1775. By then, the Revolution had begun. The "shot heard 'round the world" had been fired. The battles of Lexington and Concord had been fought three weeks earlier, on April 19.

Each of the 13 colonies sent representatives to the Congress. Most of those who had attended the First Continental Congress were again present. Most notable among the newcomers were Benjamin Franklin of Pennsylvania and John Hancock of Massachusetts.

Hancock was chosen president of the Congress.[12] Almost at once, a continental army was organized, and George Washington was appointed its commander in chief. Thomas Jefferson then took Washington's place in the Virginia delegation.

The Second Continental Congress became, by force of circumstance, the nation's first national government. However, it rested on no constitutional base. It was condemned by the British as an unlawful assembly and a den of traitors. But it was supported by the force of public opinion and practical necessity.

Preparing for Victory George Washington, appointed commander in chief by the Second Continental Congress, plans the next move against British forces.

The Second Continental Congress served as the first government of the United States for five fateful years, from the signing of the Declaration of Independence in July 1776 until the Articles of Confederation went into effect on March 1, 1781. During that time it fought a war, raised armies and a navy, borrowed money, bought supplies, created a monetary system, made treaties with foreign powers, and did those other things that any government would have had to do in the circumstances.

The unicameral Congress exercised both legislative and executive powers. In legislative matters, each colony—later, State—had one vote. Executive functions were handled by committees of delegates.

[12]Peyton Randolph, who had also served as president of the First Continental Congress, was originally chosen for the office. He resigned on May 24, however, because the Virginia House of Delegates, of which he was the speaker, had been called into session. Hancock was then elected to succeed him.

Provide Guided Practice
Write the headings "First Continental Congress," "Second Continental Congress,"and "First State Constitutions." Have students volunteer facts from the section for each heading. (*Answers will vary, but students should be able to suggest material found on pp. 32–35.*)

Provide Independent Practice

TRF **Teacher's Resource File** You may wish to assign the Section 2 Guided Reading and Review from the Unit 1 File, p. 25, to help students master section objective content.

SPOTLIGHT ON: Economics

The Second Continental Congress had not only to invent a new system of government during a war, but it also had to cope with the worst period of inflation in U.S. history. Between 1775 and 1779, the value of the $191 million in Continental bills the Congress printed to finance the war sank dramatically. In 1777, it took $3 in bills to purchase goods worth $1 in gold or silver. By 1779, the ratio had shot up 42 to 1, skyrocketed to 100 to 1 in 1780, and 146 to 1 in 1781. In that year, the Congress offered to buy back the bills at a rate of 40 to 1—an inglorious end for the first national currency.

Monitor Comprehension

Answers to Section 2 Review
1) "Key Terms" are defined on the following pages:

a. Albany Plan of Union, p. 32
b. boycott, p. 32
c. constitution, p. 35
d. popular sovereignty, p. 35

2. Britain exercised little direct control before 1760. After 1760, Britain began to take a more active role in the affairs of the colonies, and colonists began to resent it. **3.** The Second Continental Congress directed the war effort, borrowed money to finance the war, coined money, bought supplies, and made treaties with other governments. **4.** (a) Benjamin Franklin, John Adams, Roger Sherman, Robert Livingston, and Thomas Jefferson; Jefferson did most of the work. (b) It explains the reasons behind the break with Britain, and uses language and ideas from English political thought. **5.** All followed the principles of popular sovereignty and limited government, supported the concept of civil liberties, and had a system of separation of powers and checks and balances. **6.** (a) Students should note that the colonists evidently believed that laws that were not just need not be respected or obeyed. (b) Answers will vary, but students would probably respond positively.

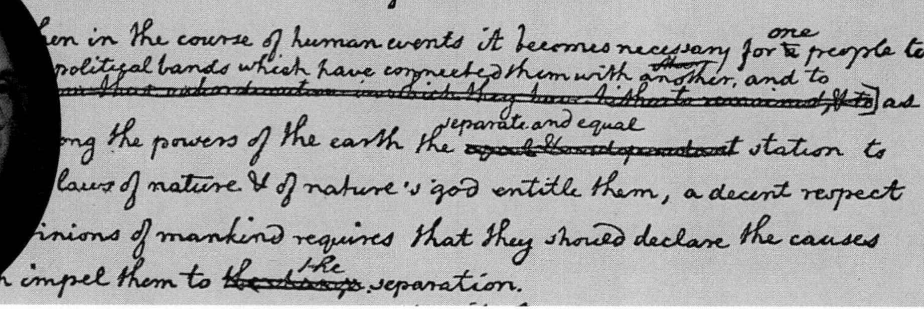

Declaration of Independence.
A Declaration by the Representatives of the UNITED STATES
AMERICA, in General Congress assembled.

"An expression of the American mind" So Thomas Jefferson (left) described his Declaration of Independence, shown in the author's own hand.

The Declaration of Independence

On June 7, 1776, Richard Henry Lee of Virginia proposed to the Congress:

> "*Resolved*, That these United Colonies are, and of right ought to be, free and independent States, that they are absolved from all allegiance to the British Crown, and that all political connection between them and the State of Great Britain is, and ought to be, totally dissolved."

Congress named a committee of five—Benjamin Franklin, John Adams, Roger Sherman, Robert Livingston, and Thomas Jefferson—to prepare a proclamation of independence. Their momentous product, the Declaration of Independence, was almost wholly the work of Jefferson.

On July 2, the final break came. The delegates unanimously agreed to Lee's resolution. Two days later, on July 4, 1776, they adopted the Declaration of Independence and announced it to the world.

The Declaration announces the independence of the United States in its first paragraph. Much of the balance of the document—nearly two-thirds of it—speaks of "the repeated injuries and usurpations" that led the colonists to revolt. At its heart, the Declaration proclaims:

> "We hold these truths to be self-evident, that all men are created equal, that they are endowed by their Creator with certain unalienable Rights, that among these are Life, Liberty and the pursuit of Happiness. That to secure these rights, Governments are instituted among Men, deriving their just powers from the consent of the governed; That whenever any Form of Government becomes destructive of these ends it is the Right of the People to alter or to abolish it, and to institute new Government, laying its foundations on such principles and organizing its power in such form, as to them shall seem most likely to effect their Safety and Happiness."

With these brave words, the United States of America was born. The 13 colonies became free and independent States. The 56 men who signed the Declaration sealed it with this final sentence:

> "And for the support of this Declaration, with a firm reliance on the protection of Divine Providence, we mutually pledge to each other, our lives, our Fortunes, and our sacred Hono·."

Activity: Cooperative Learning

Time: one class period **Activity:** Paraphrase the first paragraph of the Declaration of Independence **Grouping:** groups of three to four students **Purpose:** Have group members discuss the meaning of the opening paragraph of the Declaration . Then have students work together to rewrite the paragraph to express what they understand it to mean. **Roles:** Assign the following roles: discussion leader, recorder, and spokesperson. **Outcome:** When the recorder has prepared the final draft, have the spokesperson read the group's paragraph to the class. Invite the class to discuss the group's interpretation.

Reteach

Have students suppose that the Declaration of Independence was published today and that they are television or newspaper commentators. Have students write a short commentary explaining the importance of the event, where the ideas in the Declaration came from, and what is likely to happen next.

The First State Governments

In January 1776, New Hampshire adopted a constitution to replace its royal charter. Less than three months later, South Carolina followed suit. Then, on May 10, the Congress urged each of the colonies to adopt:

> "such governments as shall, in the opinion of the representatives of the people, best conduce to the happiness and safety of their constituents."

In 1776 and 1777, most of the States adopted written **constitutions**—bodies of fundamental laws setting out the principles, structures, and processes of the governments. 1.c Assemblies or conventions were commonly used to draft and then adopt these new documents. Massachusetts set a lasting precedent in the constitution-making process. There, a convention submitted its work to the voters for ratification. The Massachusetts constitution of 1780 is the oldest of the present-day State constitutions. In fact, it is the oldest written constitution in force anywhere in the world today.

Common Features of New States

The first State constitutions differed, sometimes widely, in detail. Yet they shared many common features.

Popular Sovereignty Each of the new constitutions was based on the principle of **popular sovereignty**. 1.d This principle insists that government can exist and function *only* with the consent of the governed. It is the people who hold power; it is the people who are sovereign.

Limited Government The concept of limited government was a major feature of each document. The powers delegated to government were at best reluctantly granted and hedged with many restrictions.

Civil Rights and Liberties Seven of the new documents[13] contained a bill of rights, setting out the "unalienable rights" held by the people. In every State it was made clear that the sovereign people held certain rights that government must at all times respect.

Separation of Powers and Checks and Balances The powers granted to the new State governments were purposely divided among three branches: executive, legislative, and judicial. Each branch was given powers with which to check the other branches of the government.

The new State constitutions were rather brief documents. For the most part, they were declarations of principle and statements of limitation on governmental power. Memories of the royal governors were fresh and the new State governors were given little real power. Most of the authority that was granted to State government was placed in the legislature. Elective terms of office were made purposely short, seldom more than one or two years. The right to vote was limited to those adult males who could meet property ownership and other rigid qualifications.

Yet with all their limits, these documents would have a large influence on those who would shape a government for the new United States.

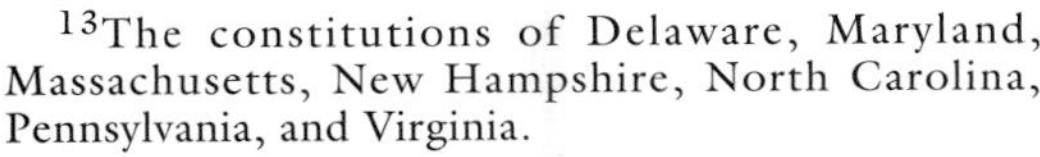

[13]The constitutions of Delaware, Maryland, Massachusetts, New Hampshire, North Carolina, Pennsylvania, and Virginia.

Section 2 Review

1. **Define:** Albany Plan of Union, boycott, constitution, popular sovereignty
2. What was the relationship between Britain and the colonies like in the mid-1700s, and how did it change in the 1760s?
3. In what ways did the Second Continental Congress serve as the first national government?
4. (a) Who wrote the Declaration of Independence? (b) For what reasons are the opening lines of its second paragraph so important?
5. List the common features of the first State constitutions.

Critical Thinking

6. **Recognizing Ideologies** (p. 19) The Second Continental Congress met in violation of the law. (a) What does this say about the colonists' view of governmental authority? (b) How would you respond to such a gathering today?

Teacher's Resource File See the Unit 1 File, p. 26, for the Section 2 Quiz

CLOSURE

Remind students that the Declaration of Independence both announces a break with England and states a theory about what a government should be. The fact that the colonies already had been governing themselves for all practical purposes may have made the colonists particularly intolerant of English repression. In the next section, students will see how difficult it was for the colonies to form a strong nation without surrendering their own hard-won sovereignty.

Assignment Assign Section 3, pp. 36–38 for the next class period.

SPOTLIGHT ON: Constitutional Issues

The colonial governors made a lasting impression on the colonists—strong enough to ensure weak executives in both State and national constitutions. In every colony, save Connecticut and Rhode Island, the governor had become the symbol of royal tyranny to the Americans. Colonial governors wielded extraordinary powers. With full authority over the State militias, a seat on the colonies' highest court, and the power to dismiss State legislatures at their discretion, governors could pardon the convicted, appoint and dismiss judges and other officials, regulate trade, conduct diplomacy, grant lands, and even supervise religious activities! Limitations on the powers of the executive thus became an article of faith for State and national constitution-makers. In fact, as you will see in the next section, the Framers of the first national constitution, the Articles of Confederation, were so suspicious of executive authority that the first National Government had no executive at all.

SECTION 3
The Critical Period

FOCUS

Teacher's Resource File
See the Unit 1 File, p. 27, for the Section 3 Outline.

Objectives

2.6 Demonstrate an understanding of the basic provisions and major weaknesses of the Articles of Confederation

2.7 Explain reasons why the 1780s are known as the Critical Period in American history.

2.8 Examine the steps that led to the Constitutional Convention in 1787.

Bellringer Activity Write the statement "It is important for a country to have a strong central government." Ask students to express their opinions about this statement, and to explain why they think as they do.

State the Purpose The first years of the United States were very difficult ones. Although the colonies had agreed that they wanted independence from England, no real and permanent National Government existed. In Section 3, students will learn about early steps taken to form a National Government, what problems arose during the Critical Period, and what events led to the Constitutional Convention.

3 The Critical Period

Find Out:

- What were the basic provisions and major weaknesses of the Articles of Confederation?
- For what reasons are the 1780s known as the Critical Period in American history?
- What steps led to the Constitutional Convention in 1787?

Key Terms:
ratification, Articles of Confederation

The First and Second Continental Congresses rested on no legal base. They were called in haste to meet an emergency, and they were intended to be temporary. Something more regular and permanent was clearly needed. In this section, you will read about the first attempt to establish a lasting government for the new nation.

The First National Constitution

Richard Henry Lee's resolution that had led to the Declaration of Independence also called on the Second Continental Congress to propose "a plan of confederation." Off and on, for 17 months, that body considered the problem of uniting the former colonies. Finally, on November 15, 1777, they approved the Articles of Confederation.

The Articles did not go into effect immediately, however. The **ratification**—formal approv- 1a.
al—of each of the 13 States was needed first. Eleven States agreed to the document within a year. Delaware added its approval in mid-1779. But Maryland did not ratify until February 27, 1781. The Second Continental Congress then set March 1, 1781, as the date when the Articles were finally to become effective.

The **Articles of Confederation** established 1.b
"a firm league of friendship" among the States. Each State kept "its sovereignty, freedom, and independence, and every power, jurisdiction, and right . . . not . . . expressly delegated to the United States, in Congress assembled." The States came together "for their common defense, the security of their liberties, and their mutual and general welfare."

Governmental Structure The government set up by the Articles was simple indeed. A Congress was the sole body created. It was unicameral, made up of delegates chosen yearly by the States in whatever way their legislatures might direct. Each State had one vote in the Congress, whatever its population or wealth.

There was no executive or judicial branch. These functions were to be handled by committees of the Congress. Each year the Congress would choose one of its members as its president. That person would be its presiding officer, but not the president of the United States. Civil officers such as postmasters were to be appointed by the Congress.

Powers of Congress Several important powers were given to the Congress. It could make war and peace; send and receive ambassadors; make treaties; borrow money; set up a monetary system; build a navy; raise an army by asking the States for troops; fix uniform standards of weights and measures; and settle disputes among the States.

State Obligations By agreeing to the Articles, the States had pledged to obey the Articles and acts of the Congress; provide the funds and troops requested by the Congress; treat citizens of other States fairly and equally with their own; give full faith and credit to the public acts, records, and judicial proceedings of every other State; surrender fugitives from justice to each other; submit their disputes to Congress for settlement; and allow open travel and trade between and among the States.

Beyond these few obligations, the States retained those powers not explicitly given to the Congress. They, not the Congress, were primarily responsible for protecting life and property and for promoting the general welfare—"the safety and happiness"—of the people.

Reading Strategy: Relating to Topic

As a preparation for reading, point out that in 1990 East and West Germany, by mutual agreement, merged to form one country. Although the two countries had been one before 1945, over the next 45 years they developed significant economic and social differences. Ask students to identify some of the problems faced in reuniting the two countries.

Vocabulary

Point out the "Key Terms" on page 36 to the students. Ask students to explain the difference between the use of the word *articles* in Articles of Confederation and the use of that word in the sense of "newspaper articles." Ask students to explain what a confederation is. Does it imply a strong federal government? (*No*) Is it the same thing as a union? (*No; it is much more loosely organized.*) LEP

Weaknesses The powers of the Congress appear, at first glance, to have been considerable. Several important powers were missing, however. Their lack, together with other weaknesses, soon proved the Articles inadequate to the needs of the time.

The Congress did not have the power to tax. It could raise money only by borrowing and by asking the States for funds. Borrowing was, at best, a poor source. The Second Continental Congress had borrowed heavily to support the Revolution, and many of those debts had not been paid. And, while the Articles were in force, not one State came close to meeting the financial requests made by the Congress.

Nor did the Congress have the power to regulate trade between the States. This lack of a central mechanism to regulate the young nation's commerce was one of the major factors that led to the adoption of the Constitution, as you will see.

The Congress had no power to make the States obey the Articles of Confederation or the laws it made. Congress could exercise the powers it did have only with the consent of 9 of the 13 State delegations. Finally, the Articles themselves could be changed only with the consent of all 13 of the State legislatures. This procedure proved an impossible task; not one amendment was ever added to the Articles of Confederation.

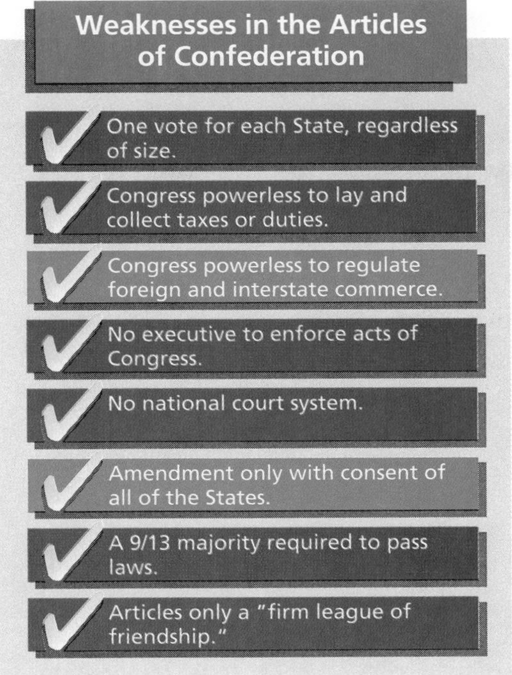

Weaknesses in the Articles of Confederation
One vote for each State, regardless of size.
Congress powerless to lay and collect taxes or duties.
Congress powerless to regulate foreign and interstate commerce.
No executive to enforce acts of Congress.
No national court system.
Amendment only with consent of all of the States.
A 9/13 majority required to pass laws.
Articles only a "firm league of friendship."

Interpreting Charts The thirst for independence made Americans wary of strong central government. How is this caution reflected in the chart?

The Critical Period, the 1780s

The long Revolutionary War finally ended on October 19, 1781. America's victory was confirmed by the Treaty of Paris in 1783. With peace, however, the new nation's economic and political problems came into sharp focus. The weaknesses of the Articles of Confederation soon surfaced.

With a central government unable to act, the States bickered among themselves and grew increasingly jealous and suspicious of one another. They refused to support the new central government, financially and in almost every other way. Several of them made agreements with foreign governments, even though that was forbidden by the Articles. Most even organized their own military forces. George Washington complained, "We are one nation today and 13 tomorrow. Who will treat with us on such terms?"

The States taxed each other's goods and even banned some trade. They printed their own money, often with little backing. Economic chaos spread throughout the colonies as prices soared and sound credit vanished. Debts, public and private, went unpaid. Violence broke out in a number of places as a result of the economic chaos. Shays's Rebellion in western Massachusetts in 1786 was only the most spectacular of several incidents.

The Articles had not created a government able to deal with the nation's troubles. Inevitably, demand grew for a stronger, more effective national government. Those who were most threatened by economic and political instability—large property owners, merchants, traders,

INSTRUCT

Discuss Discuss with students the ways in which weaknesses in the Articles of Confederation led to problems during the Critical Period and, then, to the need for a constitutional convention. For example, Congress did not have the power to tax or to regulate interstate trade. These two weaknesses created economic chaos. This economic instability led to pressure for reform from merchants, bankers, etc., which led to meetings of state delegates in Mt. Vernon and Annapolis, culminating in the Convention at Philadelphia in 1787.

Interpreting Charts Explain to students that every item in the chart is a "no" to central government.

Caption Answer The chart shows that there was no strength in the National Government.

ABCNEWS INTERACTIVE

The following video segment may be used to highlight aspects of the Articles of Confederation.

POWERS OF THE CONGRESS GUIDEBOOK
Chapter 52: Documents, p. 58

Provide Guided Practice On the board write *Articles of Confederation*, *Critical Period*, and *Constitutional Convention*. Have students list provisions in the Articles of Confederation, problems they caused during the Critical Period, and associated reasons why States attended the Constitutional Convention. (*See pp. 37–38.*)

Provide Independent Practice

TRF **Teacher's Resource File** You may wish to assign Section 3 Guided Reading and Review, Unit 1 File, p. 28.

Enrichment

Have students imagine they are merchants living under the Articles of Confederation, during the Critical Period. Have them create a letter to their congressman explaining how they feel about the effectiveness of the new government, and why. Tell students to be sure to include information from the section, and to conclude their letters with a recommendation for improving the government. (Average)

Monitor Comprehension

Answers to Section 3 Review
1. "Key terms" are defined on the following page:
  a. ratification, p. 36
  b. Articles of Confederation, p. 36
2. Second Continental Congress, November 15, 1777.
3. (a) It consisted solely of Congress. (b) To make treaties, exchange ambassadors, make war and peace, borrow money, set up a monetary system, build a navy and army, fix standards of weights and measures, settle disputes among States.
4. Congress could not tax or regulate trade, could not make States cooperate, required near-unanimous consent to pass laws, unanimous consent to amend Articles. **5.**After the Revolution the new nation had to focus on its problems,but the existing government was not up to the task. The nation seemed on the verge of breaking apart.

Closure

Point out to students that the Critical Period helped to clarify the need for a central government and may have helped to define many of the issues discussed at the Constitutional Convention. As students read the next section they will see how representatives to the Convention went about trying to create a document that would help resolve those issues

Assignment Assign Section 4, pp. 40–46 for the next class period.

Shays's Rebellion To protest the loss of their properties to tax collectors, angry farmers seized courthouses in Massachusetts in 1786.

and other creditors—soon took the lead in efforts to that end. The movement for change began to take concrete form in 1785.

The Meetings at Mount Vernon and Annapolis

Maryland and Virginia, plagued by bitter trade disputes, took the first step in the movement for change. Ignoring the Congress, the two States agreed to a conference on their trade problems. Representatives from the two States met at Alexandria, Virginia, in March 1785. At George Washington's invitation, they moved their sessions to his home at nearby Mount Vernon. Their negotiations proved so successful that on January 21, 1786, the Virginia Assembly called for "a joint meeting of [all of] the States to recommend a federal plan for regulating commerce."

That joint meeting opened at Annapolis, Maryland, on September 11, 1786. Representatives from only 5 of the 13 States attended[14] Disappointed, but still hopeful, the Annapolis Convention called for yet another meeting of the States

> "at Philadelphia on the second Monday in May next, to take into consideration the situation of the United States, to devise such further provisions as shall appear to them necessary to render the constitution of the Federal Government adequate to the exigencies of the Union."

By mid-February of 1787, seven of the States had named delegates to the Philadelphia meeting. These were Delaware, Georgia, New Hampshire, New Jersey, North Carolina, Pennsylvania, and Virginia. Then, on February 21 the Congress, which had been hesitating, also called upon the States to send delegates to Philadelphia

> "for the sole and express purpose of revising the Articles of Confederation and reporting to Congress and the several legislatures such alterations and provisions therein as shall when agreed to in Congress and confirmed by the States render the [Articles] adequate to the exigencies of Government and the preservation of the Union."

That Philadelphia meeting became the Constitutional Convention.

Section 3 Review

1. Define: ratification, Articles of Confederation
2. When and by whom were the Articles of Confederation prepared?
3. (a) Describe the government set up by the Articles. (b) What powers were given to Congress?
4. What were the major weaknesses of the government under the Articles?

Critical Thinking

5. Drawing Conclusions (p. 19) For what reasons is the period during which the Articles were in force called the Critical Period in American history?

[14]New York, New Jersey, Pennsylvania, Delaware, and Virginia. Although New Hampshire, Massachusetts, Rhode Island, and North Carolina had appointed delegates, none attended the Annapolis meeting.

Reteach

Have students create a timeline of the events discussed in Section 3 that led to the Constitutional Convention in 1787.

Teacher's Resource File
See the Unit 1 File, p. 29, for the Section 3 Quiz.

Debating Key Issues

Should Schools Have the Right to Censor Student Newspapers?

Hazelwood v. *Kuhlmeier*

In 1983, the principal at Hazelwood Central High School in Missouri removed two pages from the student newspaper that carried stories about divorce and teen pregnancy. He did not notify the student editors or reporters. Although the students and their faculty-adviser strongly objected to the school's censorship, the principal maintained that the stories were "inappropriate, personal, sensitive, and unsuitable for student readers."

After consulting with her faculty-adviser and the American Civil Liberties Union, Cathy Kuhlmeier and a group of fellow students sued the school district in the United States district court. Their lawyer cited the 1st Amendment, which provides for freedom of speech and freedom of the press. The court ruled that the school newspaper was not a public forum. Censorship, therefore, was permissible because the articles would have made it appear that the entire school endorsed the values they projected.

On appeal to the district court of appeals, the ruling was reversed and decided in favor of the students. At this point, the Hazelwood School District appealed to the United States Supreme Court.

Review the following evidence and arguments presented to the U.S. Supreme Court:

Arguments for Hazelwood School District

1. Students' 1st Amendment rights are not violated if educators exercise editorial control over school-sponsored publications, especially when they do so because of educational concerns.
2. The school newspaper is not a public forum. Therefore, so long as the school remained neutral on socially and politically controversial matters, the censorship was warranted.
3. Educators are responsible for guiding and controlling school-sponsored publications and other creative endeavors when such activities are sanctioned by, and reflect on, the school itself.

Arguments for Cathy Kuhlmeier

1. The students' 1st Amendment rights were violated. The right of free student speech is protected by the Constitution when such speech does not disrupt class work or infringe on the rights of others.
2. The school newspaper is a public forum, and does not reflect the school's viewpoint. Therefore, the students had the right to express their own opinions to the community.
3. The educator's responsibility to instill moral and political values is not meant to stifle free student thought and expression. Students should not be forced to limit themselves to state-approved subjects or opinions.

Getting Involved

1. Identify the constitutional grounds on which each side based its arguments in the case.
2. Debate the opposing viewpoints presented in the case.
3. Predict how you think the Supreme Court ruled in this case and why. Now refer to the Supreme Court Glossary on page 764 to read about the decision. Discuss the impact of the Court's ruling on free student speech and expression in general.

TEACHING
Debating Key Issues

***Hazelwood v. Kuhlmeier:* Should Schools Have the Right to Censor Student Newspapers?**

Objective
Demonstrate reasoned judgement

Instruct

Before reading the feature, you might want to elicit student answers to the question in the title. When students have finished reading the feature, ask if their answers have changed and if so, why. Then work through the "Getting Involved" section, starting with identifying the constitutional grounds for each side in the case.

During the class discussion, encourage students to explain which arguments they found most compelling and why.

Supreme Court Decision

The Court upheld the principal's action, since the school official occupied the place of "publisher" of the newspaper. "First Amendment rights of students...are not automatically coextensive with the rights of adults in other settings...and... must be applied in light of the special characteristics of the school environment..." School officials had full control over school-sponsored activities "so long as their actions are reasonably related to legitimate pedagogical concerns..." and "had valid educational purpose."

Teacher's Resource File
See the Supreme Court Case file for an activity that extends coverage of this case.

SECTION 4
Creating the Constitution

FOCUS

Teacher's Resource File See the Unit 1 File, p. 30, for the Section 4 Outline.

Objectives

2.9 Describe how the Constitution was written.
2.10 Explain why compromises were necessary.
2.11 List three major compromises incorporated into the Constitution.

Bellringer Activity Before you begin the section, ask students to think of conflicts they have witnessed in local, State, or National Government. Examples may include funding, nuclear power safety, or environmental issues. On the board, list the conflicts and briefly summarize the opposing sides of each conflict. Have students suggest a compromise that might resolve each of these situations.

State the Purpose Although the Framers came from different parts of the country and had different specific interests, they shared the same basic beliefs about government. In Section 4, students will learn what an arduous process creating the Constitution was, and how problems were resolved through compromise.

4 Creating the Constitution

Find Out:

- How was the Constitution written?
- For what reasons were compromises necessary?
- What major compromises were involved?

Key Terms:

Framers, Virginia Plan, New Jersey Plan, Connecticut Compromise, Three-Fifths Compromise, Commerce and Slave Trade Compromise

Picture this scene. It's hot—sweltering, in fact. Yet the windows are closed to discourage eavesdroppers. The atmosphere is tense as the men exchange their views. Indeed, some become so angry that they threaten to leave the hall. A few carry out their threats.

This was the scene throughout much of the Philadelphia meeting that began on Friday, May 25, 1887. In this section, you will read about that meeting and its work.

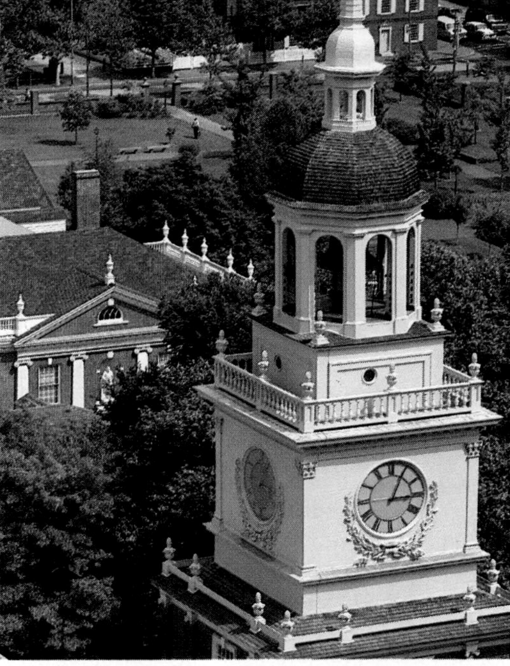

Seat of Liberty The Philadelphia Convention met in Independence Hall during the hot summer of 1787. The document crafted by the convention is still regarded as the supreme law of the land today.

The Framers

Twelve of the 13 States, all but Rhode Island, sent delegates to Philadelphia.[15] In total, 74 delegates were chosen by the legislatures in those 12 states. For a number of reasons, however, only 55 of them actually attended the convention.

Of that 55, this much can be said: Never, before or since, has so remarkable a group been brought together in this country. Thomas Jefferson, who was not among them, later called the delegates "an assembly of demigods."

1.a The group—the **Framers** of the Constitution—included these outstanding personalities: George Washington, James Madison, Edmund Randolph, and George Mason from Virginia; Benjamin Franklin, Gouverneur Morris, Robert Morris, and James Wilson from Pennsylvania; Alexander Hamilton from New York; William Paterson from New Jersey; Elbridge Gerry and Rufus King from Massachusetts; Luther Martin from Maryland; Oliver Ellsworth and Roger Sherman from Connecticut; John Dickinson from Delaware; and John Rutledge and Charles Pinckney from South Carolina.

These were men of wide knowledge and public experience, of wealth and prestige. Many of them had fought in the Revolution; 39 had been members of the Continental Congress or the Congress of the Confederation, or both. Eight had served in constitutional conventions

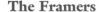

[15]The Rhode Island legislature was controlled by the soft-money forces—mostly debtors and small farmers who were helped by inflation and so were against a stronger central government. The New Hampshire delegation, delayed mostly by lack of funds, did not reach Philadelphia until late July.

Reading Strategy: Focus Questions

Before reading the section, have students write six focus questions beginning with Who, What, When, Where, How, and Why. While reading, have students answer their questions.

Vocabulary

Point out the "Key Terms" on page 40 to the students. Ask students to elaborate on the meaning of the word *compromise*. Does one side always lose something in a compromise? Is there such a thing as a win-win compromise?

in their own States, and seven had been State governors. Eight had signed the Declaration of Independence. Thirty-one of the delegates had attended college in a day when there were but a few colleges in the land, and their number also included two college presidents and three professors. Two were to become Presidents of the United States, and one a Vice President. Seventeen later served in the Senate and 11 in the House of Representatives.

Is it any wonder that the product of such a gathering was described by English statesman William E. Gladstone, nearly a century later, as "the most wonderful work ever struck off at a given time by the brain and purpose of man"?

Remarkably, the average age of the delegates was only 44, and nearly half were only in their 30s. Indeed, most of the real leaders were in that age group—Madison was 36, Gouverneur Morris 35, Randolph 34, and Hamilton 32. At 81, Franklin was the oldest. He was failing, however, and not able to attend many of the meetings. George Washington, at 55, was one of the few older members who played a key role at the meetings.

By and large, the Framers of the Constitution were of a new generation in American politics. Several of the better-known leaders of the Revolutionary period were not in Philadelphia. Patrick Henry said he "smelt a rat" and refused to attend. Samuel Adams, John Hancock, and Richard Henry Lee were not selected as delegates by their States. Thomas Paine was in Paris. So, too, was Thomas Jefferson—as American minister to France. John Adams was our envoy to England and Holland at the time.

Given the fact that white males then held complete control of the political process, it is not surprising that no women, no African Americans, and no Native Americans are found among the Framers of the Constitution.

VOICES *on Government*

On the Task of Writing a Constitution

James Madison, architect of the Constitution and fourth President of the United States

"The [writing of the Constitution] formed a task more difficult than can be well conceived by those who were not concerned in the execution of it. Adding to [the difficulty] the natural diversity of human opinions on all new and complicated subjects, it is impossible to consider the degree of concord which ultimately prevailed as less than a miracle."

Organization and Procedure

The Framers met in Independence Hall, probably in the same room in which the Declaration of Independence had been signed 11 years earlier.

They organized immediately on May 25, unanimously electing George Washington president of the convention [16] Then, and at the second session on Monday, May 28, they adopted several rules of procedure. A majority of the States would be needed to conduct business. Each State delegation was to have one vote and a majority would carry any proposal.

The convention had drawn much public attention. So, to protect themselves from outside pressures, the delegates adopted a rule of secrecy. On the whole, the rule was well kept.

A secretary, William Jackson, kept the convention's *Journal.* That official record, however, was quite sketchy and often inaccurate. Most of what is known of the work of the convention

[16]Twenty-eight delegates from seven States were present on that first day. The full number of 55 was not reached until August 6, when John Francis Mercer of Maryland arrived. In the meantime, some delegates had departed, and others were absent from time to time. Some 40 members attended most of the daily sessions of the convention.

INSTRUCT

Discuss Point out where, on page 40, the author writes of the Constitutional Convention, "Never, before or since, has so remarkable a group been brought together in this country." Explain that this brilliant assembly of political and military leaders was able to temper their differences and work out compromises that resulted in a workable Constitution for the new nation.

Several different blueprints for government were proposed and vigorously debated, the most notable being the Virginia and New Jersey plans. The Connecticut Compromise brought together these two different proposals. Other important areas of compromise were in commerce and the slave trade as well as representation based on slaves, the Three-Fifths clause.

The completed Constitution reflected the best ideas of many philosophies on government. It also reflected the experiences of the assembled leaders, both in colonial governments and under Articles of Confederation.

ABCNEWS INTERACTIVE

The following video segments may be used to highlight aspects of the Constitutional Convention.

POWERS OF THE CONGRESS GUIDEBOOK
Chapter 53: Constitutional Convention of 1787, p. 130
Chapter 55: Historical Figures, p. 132
Chapter 56: Documents, p. 133

SPOTLIGHT ON: Behind the Scenes

Is it possible that the Framers created the Constitution to enhance their own financial positions? This controversial question was asked in 1913 by historian Charles A. Beard in his *An Economic Interpretation of the Constitution of the United States.* In that work, Beard argued that the Framers acted as "a consolidated economic group" to protect their financial security. Beard pointed out that of the 55 delegates, 34 were lawyers; 40 owned public securities, 14 held land for speculation, 24 had money loaned at interest, 11 were investors in mercantile, manufacturing, or shipping businesses, while 15 owned slaves. At least five-sixths of the delegates, Beard contended, stood to benefit financially from the new Constitution. Although later historians have refuted the idea that the Framers put self-interest entirely over principle, Beard's ideas stimulated discussion about the Constitution and the motivations of the men who created it.

Analyze Ask students to evaluate the Connecticut Compromise. Do they think smaller States are hurt because larger States have greater representation in the House of Representatives, or are larger States hurt in any way because smaller States have equal representation in the Senate? (*Answers will vary, but students should demonstrate an understanding of the importance of the Compromise, and a knowledge of its provisions.*)

comes from James Madison's voluminous *Notes.* His brilliance and depth of knowledge led his colleagues to hold him in great respect. Quickly, he became the convention's floor leader. Madison contributed more to the Constitution than did any of the others, and still he was able to keep a close record of its work. Certainly, he deserves the title "Father of the Constitution."

The Framers met on 89 of the 116 days from May 25 through their final meeting on September 17. They did most of their work on the floor of the convention. They handled some matters in committees, but all questions were ultimately settled by the full body.

The Decision to Write a New Constitution

The Philadelphia Convention was called to recommend revisions in the Articles of Confederation. However, almost at once the delegates agreed that they were, in fact, meeting to create a new government for the United States. On May 30 they adopted this proposal, put by Edmund Randolph of Virginia:

> "*Resolved*, . . . that a *national* Government ought to be established consisting of a *supreme* Legislative, Executive and Judiciary."

With this momentous decision, the Framers redefined the purpose of the convention. From that point on, they set about the writing of a new constitution. This new constitution was intended to replace the Articles of Confederation. Their debates were spirited, even bitter. At times the convention seemed near collapse. Once they had passed Governor Randolph's resolution, however, the goal of a majority of the convention never changed.

The Virginia Plan

No State had more to do with the calling of the convention than Virginia. It was not surprising, then, that its delegates should offer the first plan for a new constitution. On May 29 the Virginia Plan, largely the work of Madison, was presented by Randolph.

1.b The **Virginia Plan** called for a new government with three separate branches: legislative, executive, and judicial. The legislature—Congress—would be bicameral. Representation in each house was to be based either upon each State's population or upon the amount of money it gave for the support of the central government. The members of the lower house, the House of Representatives, were to be popularly elected in each State. Those of the upper house, the Senate, were to be chosen by the House from lists of persons nominated by the State legislatures.

Congress was to be given all of the powers it held under the Articles. In addition, it was to have the power to legislate "in all cases in which the separate States are incompetent" to act, to veto any State law in conflict with national law, and to use force if necessary to make a State obey national law.

Under the Virginia Plan, Congress would choose a national executive and a national judiciary. Together, these two branches would form a "council of revision." They could veto acts of Congress, but a veto could be overridden by the two houses. The executive would have "a general authority to execute the national laws." The judiciary would "consist of one or more supreme tribunals [courts], and of inferior tribunals."

The Virginia Plan also provided that all State officers should take an oath to support the Union, that each State be guaranteed a republican form of government, and that Congress have the power to admit new States to the Union.

The Virginia Plan, then, called for the creation of a truly national government with greatly expanded powers and, importantly, the power to enforce its decisions.

The Virginia Plan set the agenda for much of the convention's work. But some delegates—especially those from the smaller States of Delaware, Maryland, and New Jersey, and from New York[17]—found it too radical. Soon they

[17]The Virginia Plan's major support came from the three largest States: Virginia, Pennsylvania, and Massachusetts. New York was then only the fifth largest. Alexander Hamilton, the convention's most outspoken champion of a stronger central government, was regularly outvoted by his fellow delegates from New York.

developed their counterproposals. On June 15 William Paterson of New Jersey presented the position of the small States.

The New Jersey Plan

Paterson and his colleagues offered several amendments to the Articles, but not nearly so thorough a revision as that proposed by the Virginia Plan. The **New Jersey Plan** would 1.c
have kept the unicameral Congress of the Confederation, with each of the States equally represented. To those powers Congress already had would be added closely limited powers to tax and to regulate trade between the States.

The New Jersey Plan also called for a federal executive of more than one person. This plural executive would be chosen by Congress and could be removed by it at the request of a majority of the States' governors. The federal judiciary would be composed of a single supreme tribunal, appointed by the executive.

Among their several differences, the major point of disagreement between the two plans centered on this question: How should the States be represented in Congress? Would it be on the basis of their populations or financial contributions, as in the Virginia Plan? Or would it be on the basis of State equality, as in the Articles and the New Jersey Plan?

For weeks the delegates returned to this conflict. The lines were sharply drawn. Several delegates, on both sides of the issue, threatened to withdraw. Finally, the dispute was settled by one of the key compromises the Framers were to make as they built the Constitution.

The Connecticut Compromise

The disagreement over representation in Congress was critical. The large States expected to dominate the new government. The small States feared that they would not be able to protect their interests. Tempers flared on both sides. The debate became so intense that Benjamin Franklin was moved to suggest that

> "henceforth prayers imploring the assistance of Heaven . . . be offered in this Assembly every morning before we proceed to business."

"It is unthinkable that the citizens of Rhode Island should ever surrender their sovereignty to some central authority way off in Philadelphia."—

Interpreting Political Cartoons By 1787, Rhode Island had been self-governing for 124 years. In light of this, what sense can you make of this cartoon?

The conflict was finally settled by a compromise suggested by the Connecticut delegation. Under the **Connecticut Compromise**, it was 1.d
agreed that Congress should be composed of two houses. In the smaller Senate, the States would be represented equally. In the House, the representation of each State would be based upon its population.

Thus, by combining basic features of the rival Virginia and New Jersey Plans, the convention's most serious dispute was resolved. The agreement satisfied the smaller States in particular, and it made it possible for them to support the creation of a strong central government.

The Connecticut Compromise was so pivotal to the writing of the Constitution that it has often been called the Great Compromise.

The Three-Fifths Compromise

Once it had been agreed to base the seats in the House on each State's population, this question arose: Should slaves be counted in the populations of the southern States?

Again debate was fierce. Most delegates from the slave-holding States argued that slaves should be counted. Most of the Northerners took the opposing view. The table on the next page shows the significant percentage of enslaved people among the populations of the southern States.

Interpreting Political Cartoons
Ask: What is ironic about what the man in the cartoon is saying? Lead students to understand the idea that in the over two hundred years since the Constitution was ratified the *relative* distance from Rhode Island to Pennsylvania has shrunk considerably. In the 1780s it could take up to six or seven days to travel between Providence and Philadelphia. Today it is only minutes by airplane. What was once "way off" in Philadelphia or Washington, D.C., no longer is.

Caption Answer Rhode Island was accustomed to State sovereignty and hostile to the idea of a National Government.

SPOTLIGHT ON: Global Awareness
Over half of the nations of the world have bicameral legislatures, but only a handful base membership in the upper house on the principle of equal representation for each state, as described in the Connecticut Compromise. Switzerland's Council of States—like the U.S. Senate—provides for two seats from each of the country's 22 cantons (or states). The Argentine Senate, the French Senate, and the German Bundesrat, also follow this approach. In other nations with bicameral legislatures, including Italy, India, Canada, and Japan, the number of seats in both houses is based upon population, as described by the Virginia Plan.

Interpreting Tables Have students examine the table. Then explain that in the case of Virginia, adding three-fifths of its slave population would give Virginia the greatest representation in the union. In this way, owning slaves increased an individual's and the State's political power. Have students analyze the table to determine which five States benefitted most from the Three-Fifths Compromise. (*Virginia, South Carolina, Maryland, North Carolina, Georgia*)

Caption Answer To give their States greater representation in the House.

Slavery in the United States, 1790

State	Total Population	Slaves in Population	% Slaves
Connecticut	237,946	2,648	1.11
Delaware	59,096	8,837	14.95
Georgia	82,548	29,624	35.89
Maryland	319,728	103,036	32.23
Massachusetts	475,307	0	0.00
New Hampshire	141,885	157	0.11
New Jersey	184,139	11,423	6.20
New York	340,120	21,193	6.23
North Carolina	393,751	100,783	25.60
Pennsylvania	434,373	3,707	0.85
Rhode Island	68,825	958	1.39
South Carolina	249,073	107,094	43.00
Virginia	747,600	292,627	39.14

Source: Census Bureau, *Historical Statistics of the United States, Colonial Times to 1970*, Part I, pages 24-36

Interpreting Tables This table shows the slave populations of each State in 1790. Why did the southern States want enslaved people counted in their States' total population?

Finally, the Framers agreed to the **Three-**
1.e **Fifths Compromise**. It provided that all "free persons" should be counted, and so should "three-fifths of all other persons."[18] For the three-fifths won by the Southerners, the Northerners exacted a price. That formula was also to be used in fixing the amount of money to be raised in each State by any direct tax levied by Congress. This unusual compromise disappeared from the Constitution along with slavery itself with the 13th Amendment of 1865. For more than 120 years now, there have been no "all other persons" in this country.

The Commerce and Slave Trade Compromise

The convention agreed that Congress had to have the power to regulate foreign and interstate trade. To many Southerners, that power carried a real danger, however. They worried that Congress, likely to be controlled by northern commercial interests, would act against the interests of the white agricultural South.

They were particularly fearful that Congress would try to pay for the new government out of export duties—and southern tobacco was the major American export of the time. They also feared that Congress would interfere with the slave trade.

Before they would agree to the commerce power, the white Southerners insisted on certain protections. So, according to the **Commerce and**
1.f **Slave Trade Compromise**, Congress was forbidden the power to tax the export of goods from any State. It was also forbidden the power to act on the slave trade for a period of at least 20 years.[19]

A "Bundle of Compromises"

The convention spent much of its time, said Franklin, "sawing boards to make them fit."

[18]Article I, Section 2, Clause 3. For "all other persons" read "slaves."

[19]Article I, Section 9, Clause 1. Congress promptly banned the importation of people to be enslaved in 1808, and in 1820 it declared the slave trade to be piracy. The smuggling of the enslaved into this country continued until the outbreak of the Civil War, however.

The Constitution drafted at Philadelphia has often been called a "bundle of compromises." These descriptions are apt, if they are properly understood.

There were differences of opinion among the delegates, certainly. After all, the delegates came from 12 different States which were widely separated in geographic and economic terms. The delegates often reflected the interests of their States. Bringing these interests together did require compromise. Indeed, final decisions on issues such as selection of the President, the treaty-making process, the structure of the national court system, and the amendment process were reached as a result of compromise.

But by no means did all, or even most, of what shaped the document come from compromises. The Framers agreed on many of the basic issues they faced. Thus, nearly all the delegates were convinced that they wanted a new central government. The Framers were also dedicated to the concepts of popular sovereignty and of limited government. None questioned for a moment the wisdom of representative government. The principles of separation of powers and of checks and balances were accepted almost as a matter of course.

Sources of the Constitution

The Framers were well educated and widely read. They were familiar with the governments of ancient Greece and Rome and those of contemporary Great Britain and Europe. They knew the political writings of their time, of such works as William Blackstone's *Commentaries on the Laws of England*, the Baron de Montesquieu's *The Spirit of the Laws*, Jean Jacques Rousseau's *Social Contract*, John Locke's *Two Treatises of Government*, and many others.

More immediately, the Framers drew on their own experiences. Remember, they were familiar with the Second Continental Congress, the Articles of Confederation, and their own State governments. Much that went into the Constitution came directly, sometimes word for word, from the Articles. A number of provisions were drawn from the several State constitutions, as well.

The Convention Completes Its Work

For several weeks, through the hot Philadelphia summer, the delegates took up resolution after resolution. Finally, on September 8, a committee was named "to revise the stile of and arrange the articles which had been agreed to" by the convention. That group, the Committee of Stile headed by Gouverneur Morris, put the Constitution in its final form.

Then, on September 17, the convention approved its work and 39 names were placed on the finished document.[20]

Perhaps none of the Framers were completely satisfied with their work. Nevertheless, wise old Benjamin Franklin put into words what many of the Framers must have thought on that final day:

> "Sir, I agree with this Constitution with all its faults, if they are such; because I think a general Government necessary for us . . . I doubt . . . whether any Convention we can obtain, may be able to make a better Constitution. For when you assemble a number of men to have the advantage of their joint wisdom, you inevitably assemble with those men, all their prejudices, their passions, their errors of opinion, their local interests, and their selfish views. From such an assembly can a perfect production be expected? It therefore astonishes me, Sir, to find this system approaching so near to perfection as it does . . . "

On Franklin's motion, the 39 consenting Framers put their names to the Constitution. Madison tells us that

> " . . . Doctor Franklin, looking toward the President's chair, at the back of which a rising sun happened to be painted, observed to a few members near him, that Painters had found it difficult to distinguish in their art a rising from a setting sun. I have, said he, often and often in the course of the Session . . . looked at that behind the President without being able to tell whether it was rising or setting. But now at length I have the happiness to know that it is a rising and not a setting sun."

[20]Three of the delegates present on that last day refused to sign the proposed Constitution: Edmund Randolph of Virginia, who later did support ratification; Elbridge Gerry of Massachusetts, who later became Vice President under Madison; and George Mason of Virginia, who continued to oppose the Constitution until his death in 1792.

Provide Guided Practice On the board write the names of the three major compromises: Connecticut Compromise, Three-fifths Compromise, and Commerce and Slave Trade Compromise. Have students state the opposing sides of each compromise and how the issue was resolved. *(Connecticut: Virginia Plan and New Jersey Plans benefitted large States and small States, respectively. The Compromise offered a two-house legislature; the Senate in which States would be equally represented and the House in which States were represented by population. Three-fifths: slave-holding States wanted slaves counted for representation purposes, non-slave holding States did not want slaves counted. The Compromise provided for the counting of any slave as three-fifths of a person. Commerce and Slave Trade: Southerners worried that a northern-controlled Congress would put high duties on tobacco. The Compromise forbid Congress the power to put an export tax on goods from any State.)*

Provide Independent Practice

TRF **Teacher's Resource File** You may wish to assign Section 4 Guided Reading and Review, Unit 1 File, p. 31, to help students master section content.

Enrichment

Have students choose one of the Framers about whom they will do research to write a three-page biography. The biographies should focus especially on the subjects' contributions to the Constitution. (Average)

OR

TRF **Teacher's Resource File**
See the Unit 1 File for the Case Study on Contemporary Issues for this chapter.

Monitor Comprehension

Answers to Section 4 Review
1. "Key Terms" are defined on the following pages:
a. Framers, p. 40
b. Virginia Plan, p. 42
c. New Jersey Plan, p. 43
d. Connecticut Compromise, p. 43
e. Three-Fifths Compromise, p. 44
f. Commerce and Slave Compromises, p. 44
2. Philadelphia between May and September, 1787 **3.** (a) James Madison. (b) Kept careful notes of the proceedings; acted as floor leader of the convention; contributed more to the Constitution than any other Framer.
4. To create an entirely new constitution. **5.** The Constitution represents a consensus of opinion, which was achieved through numerous compromises.
6. European thinkers, their own experiences, ideas from the Articles, and State constitutions.
7. Some students might say that the compromise represents the pragmatism of the Framers.

Teacher's Resource File See the Unit 1 File, p. 32, for the Section 4 Quiz.

Closure

Point out to students that writing the Constitution was the next step in creating the American nation. However, as students read the next section they will see that not everyone immediately favored the Constitution when it was first published.

Assignment Assign Section 5, pp. 46–49, for the next class period.

Philadelphia Convention An artist portrays the gathering that produced our Constitution. The painting highlights Washington's presence, which, though he rarely took part in the debates, was a strong influence on the proceedings.

Section 4 Review

1. Define: Framers, Virginia Plan, New Jersey Plan, Connecticut Compromise, Three-Fifths Compromise, Commerce and Slave Trade Compromise
2. When and where was the Constitution written?
3. (a) Who is known as the "Father of the Constitution"? (b) Why does he have this title?
4. What momentous decision did the Framers make at the beginning of the Convention?
5. In what sense was the Constitution a "bundle of compromises"?
6. From what sources did the Framers draw in writing the Constitution?

Critical Thinking

7. Identifying Assumptions (p. 19) Populations of African Americans serving as slaves were counted at three-fifths of their total to determine congressional representation. What does this fact suggest about the Framers' views on slavery?

★

5 Ratifying the Constitution

Find Out:

- What were the Anti-Federalists' objections to the ratification of the Constitution?
- How was the Constitution ratified?

Key Terms:

Federalists, Anti-Federalists

Today, the Constitution of the United States is the object of extraordinary respect and admiration, both here and abroad. But in 1787 and 1788, it was widely criticized, and in every State there were many who opposed its adoption.

As you will see in this section, the battle over the ratification of the Constitution was not easily decided.

Ratification

Remember, the Articles of Confederation provided that changes could be made in them only if all

Reteach

Have students imagine they are one of the convention delegates. Have them write a brief letter describing the three major compromises in the Constitution and the importance of compromise to the process of creating the document.

Activity: For Gifted Students

Theme: Rights After having studied the ratification process for the United States Constitution, have students evaluate the power of compromise by analyzing primary source material, literary selection, and interpreting demographic data to describe the impact of the Constitution's ratification on the new nation's diverse citizenry: a middle-class Boston merchant, the wife of a Maryland tobacco planter and a Virginia house slave. Students may present their findings in a role-play format.

of the State legislatures agreed. But the new Constitution was intended to replace, not amend, the Articles. The Framers had seen how crippling the unanimity requirement could be. So, the new Constitution (in Article VII) provided that

> "The ratification of the conventions of nine States shall be sufficient for the establishment of this Constitution between the States so ratifying the same."

The Congress of the Confederation agreed to this irregular procedure. After a short debate, it sent the new document to the States on September 28, 1787.

Federalists and Anti-Federalists The proposed Constitution was printed, circulated, and debated vigorously. Two groups quickly emerged
in each of the States: the **Federalists**, who 1.a
favored ratification, and the **Anti-Federalists**, 1.b
who opposed it.

The Federalists were led by many of those who had attended the Philadelphia Convention. Among them, the most active and the most effective were James Madison and Alexander Hamilton. Their opposition was headed by such well-known Revolutionary War figures as Patrick Henry, Richard Henry Lee, John Hancock, and Samuel Adams.

The Federalists stressed the weaknesses of the Articles. They argued that the many difficulties facing the Republic could be overcome only by a new government based on the proposed Constitution.

The Anti-Federalists attacked nearly every part of the new document. Many objected to the ratification process, to the absence of any mention of God, to the denial to the States of a power to print money, and to other features of the Framers' proposals.

Two of the major features of the proposed Constitution drew the heaviest fire, however: (1) the greatly increased powers of the central government and (2) the lack of a bill of rights. The proposed document did not provide for such basic liberties as freedom of speech, press, and religion, nor for the rights of fair trial. Patrick Henry said of the proposed Constitution:

> "I look upon that paper as the most fatal plan that could possibly be conceived to enslave a free people."

Global Awareness

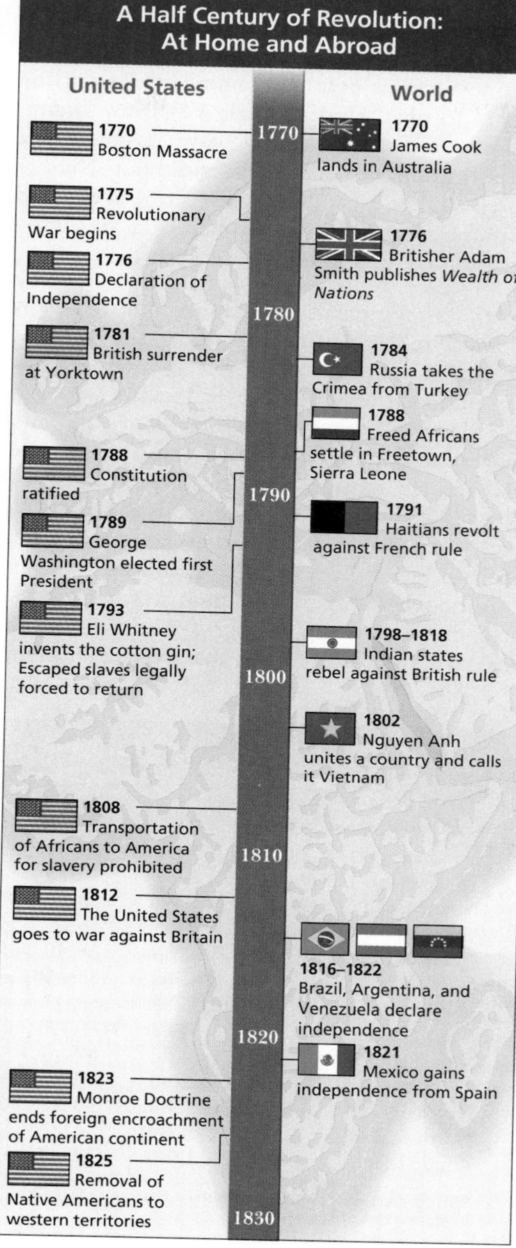
A Half Century of Revolution: At Home and Abroad
United States
World
1770
1780
1790
1800
1810
1820
1830
1770 Boston Massacre
1775 Revolutionary War begins
1776 Declaration of Independence
1781 British surrender at Yorktown
1788 Constitution ratified
1789 George Washington elected first President
1793 Eli Whitney invents the cotton gin; Escaped slaves legally forced to return
1808 Transportation of Africans to America for slavery prohibited
1812 The United States goes to war against Britain
1823 Monroe Doctrine ends foreign encroachment of American continent
1825 Removal of Native Americans to western territories
1770 James Cook lands in Australia
1776 Britisher Adam Smith publishes *Wealth of Nations*
1784 Russia takes the Crimea from Turkey
1788 Freed Africans settle in Freetown, Sierra Leone
1791 Haitians revolt against French rule
1798–1818 Indian states rebel against British rule
1802 Nguyen Anh unites a country and calls it Vietnam
1816–1822 Brazil, Argentina, and Venezuela declare independence
1821 Mexico gains independence from Spain

Interpreting Charts Do you think this global turmoil was coincidence, or were the events in various countries connected?

Section 5 Ratifying the Constitution

Focus

Teacher's Resource File See the Unit 1 File, p. 33, for the Section 5 outline.

Objectives

2.12 State Anti-Federalists objections to ratification.
2.13 Describe how the Constitution was ratified.

Bellringer Activity Before you begin the section, ask: Does a strong central government automatically take away individual freedom? Why or why not? Have students defend their positions.

State the Purpose Although the Constitution is today regarded as one of the greatest achievements of political philosophy ever, when it was first published and put to the States for approval, it met with a huge opposition from Anti-Federalists. In Section 5, students will learn who the Federalists and Anti-Federalists were, why the Anti-Federalists at first rejected the Constitution, and the drama of the debate and ratification of the Constitution.

Interpreting Charts Have students analyze the chart and ask volunteers to explain any relationships among events they might notice.

Caption Answer Ideas of independence from colonial powers might have spread so that one independence movement led to another.

Vocabulary

Point out the "Key Terms" on page 46 to the students. Ask students to analyze the words *Federalists* and *Anti-Federalists* based on what they know about the prefix *anti-*, the suffix *-ist,* and the word *Federal.* Have students predict to which group George Washington and Patrick Henry each belonged. **LEP**

Reading Strategy: Question Writing

As a preparation for reading, ask students to read the section's main headings and subheadings and write a question about each one.

INSTRUCT

Analyze With students, analyze the Federalist and the Anti-Federalist positions throughout the process of ratification. It is clear that the Federalists wanted the Constitution ratified and that the Anti-Federalists did not. However, it is less clear what the Anti-Federalists wanted in its place. You might analyze with students the provisions of the Articles and the Constitution, and see if there is something in between that students feel might have satisfied the Anti-Federalists.

Interpreting Tables Caption Answer New Hampshire, New York, and Rhode Island

Interpreting Graphs Caption Answer Article VII provided for ratification by nine, rather than thirteen, States

ABCNEWS INTERACTIVE

The following video segment may be used to highlight aspects of the ratification of the Constitution.

POWERS OF THE CONGRESS GUIDEBOOK
Chapter 54: Ratification of the Constitution, p. 131

Provide Guided Practice On the board write the words *Federalists* and *Anti-Federalists.* Have volunteers name the Federalists and Anti-Federalists identified in the section. Write their names in lists in each column. Then discuss the people on the lists in terms of their ideas and accomplishments, and the effects they had on the ratification process.

Success The contest for ratification was close in several States, but the Federalists finally won in all of them.

The table below shows that Delaware was the first State to ratify. On June 21, 1788, New Hampshire brought the number of ratifying States to nine. Under Article VII, New Hampshire's ratification should have brought the Constitution into effect, but it did not. Neither Virginia nor New York had yet ratified, and without either of these key states the new government could not hope to succeed.

VIRGINIA Virginia's ratification followed New Hampshire's by just four days. The brilliant debates in its convention were followed closely throughout the State. The Federalists were led by Madison, the young John Marshall, and Governor Edmund Randolph (even though he had refused to sign the Constitution). Patrick Henry, leading the opposition, was joined by such outstanding Virginians as James Monroe, Richard Henry Lee, and George Mason.

Although George Washington was not a delegate, his strong support for ratification proved vital. With Madison, he was able to get a reluctant Jefferson to support the document. Had Jefferson fought on the side of the Anti-Federalists, Virginia might never have ratified the Constitution.

NEW YORK A narrow vote in the New York convention brought the number of States to 11. New York ratified only after a long battle. The Anti-Federalists were led by Governor George Clinton and by two of the State's three delegates to the Philadelphia Convention [21]

Ratification of the Constitution

State	Date	Vote
Delaware	Dec. 7, 1787	30-0
Pennsylvania	Dec. 12, 1787	46-23
New Jersey	Dec. 18, 1787	38-0
Georgia	Jan. 2, 1788	26-0
Connecticut	Jan. 9, 1788	128-40
Massachusetts	Feb. 6, 1788	187-168
Maryland	Apr. 28, 1788	63-11
South Carolina	May 23, 1788	149-73
New Hampshire	June 21, 1788	57-46
Virginia	June 25, 1788	89-79
New York	July 26, 1788	30-27
North Carolina	Nov. 21, 1789*	184-77
Rhode Island	May 29, 1790	34-32

*Second vote; ratification was originally defeated on August 4, 1788, by a vote of 184-84.

Interpreting Tables Virginia's ratification came only after a long struggle. In what other States was ratification won by only a narrow margin?

Steps to a More Perfect Union

1765	Stamp Act Congress
1770s	Committees of Correspondence
1774	First Continental Congress
1775–81	Second Continental Congress
1776	Declaration of Independence
1781	Articles of Confederation Adopted
1783	Treaty of Paris
1785	Mount Vernon Convention
1786	Annapolis Convention
1787	Constitutional Convention
1788	Ninth State (New Hampshire) ratifies Constitution
1789	Constitution becomes effective
1790	Thirteenth State (Rhode Island) ratifies Constitution

1775–1783 War for Independence

Interpreting Graphs The steps to ratification are illustrated above. Why was the Constitution not effective after ratification by New Hampshire, rather than Rhode Island?

[21] Robert Yates and John Lansing had quit Philadelphia in July, arguing that the convention had gone beyond its authority. Like many other Anti-Federalist leaders, Governor Clinton later supported the Constitution.

Enrichment

Have students think about the role of the Constitution in deciding a matter like *Hazelwood* v. *Kuhlmeier*. See "Debating Key Issues" on page 39. Have students write summaries of the position of a Federalist and an Anti-Federalist with respect to that case. (Average)

Reteach

Have students summarize the positions of the Federalists and the Anti-Federalists and the milestones in ratification.

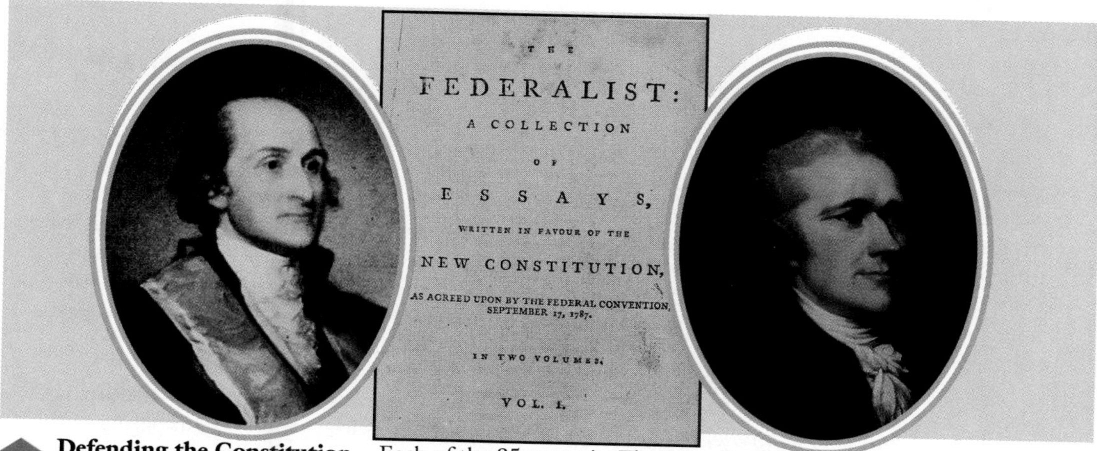
THE

FEDERALIST:

A COLLECTION

OF

ESSAYS,

WRITTEN IN FAVOUR OF THE

NEW CONSTITUTION,

AS AGREED UPON BY THE FEDERAL CONVENTION, SEPTEMBER 17, 1787.

IN TWO VOLUMES.

VOL. I.

Defending the Constitution Each of the 85 essays in *The Federalist* were signed with the pen name *Publius.* Fifty-one are attributed to Alexander Hamilton (right), eight to John Jay (left) and the rest to James Madison.

The contest in New York gave rise to a remarkable campaign document: *The Federalist.* It was a collection of 85 essays written in support of the Constitution by Alexander Hamilton, James Madison, and John Jay. Those essays were first published as letters to the people in various newspapers of the State and soon were collected in book form. Though written in haste, they remain an excellent commentary on the Constitution, and are among the best political writings in the English language.

Inauguration of the New Government

On September 13, 1788, with 11 of the 13 States "under the federal roof," the Congress of the Confederation paved the way for its successor. It chose New York as the temporary capital [22] It set the first Wednesday in January as the date on which the States would choose presidential electors. The first Wednesday in February was set as the date on which those electors would vote, and the first Wednesday in March as the date for the inauguration of the new government.

The new Congress convened on March 4, 1789. It met in Federal Hall, on Wall Street in New York City. Because it lacked a quorum, however, it could not count the electoral votes until April 6. Finally, on that day, it found that George Washington had been elected President by a unanimous vote, and John Adams Vice President, with a substantial majority. On April 30, after an historic trip from Mount Vernon to New York, Washington took the oath of office as the first President of the United States.

Section 5 Review

1. **Define:** Federalist, Anti-Federalist
2. (a) How was the Constitution ratified? (b) What was "irregular" about that process?
3. The Anti-Federalists centered their opposition to the Constitution on what two main points?

Critical Thinking

4. **Expressing Problems Clearly** (p. 19) (a) Why might the failure of New York and Virginia to ratify have doomed the Constitution? (b) What did the nation stand to lose by losing those key States?

★

[22]The District of Columbia did not become the nation's capital until 1800. Congress moved its sessions to Philadelphia in December, 1790. It held its first meeting in the new "federal city," Washington, D.C., on November 17, 1800.

Provide Independent Practice

TRF Teacher's Resource File You may wish to assign the Section 5 Guided Reading and Review, Unit 1 File, p. 34, to help students master section content.

Monitor Comprehension

Answers to Section 5 Review
1. "Key Terms" are defined on the following pages:
a. Federalist, p. 47
b. Anti-Federalist, p. 47
2. (a) Ratification required the approval of nine of the States. (b) Unanimity.was not required. **3.** Increased power of the central government and lack of a bill of rights. **4.** (a) They were among the leading States in terms of economics and political leadership. (b) Without them in the Union, the young nation would have suffered economically and politically.

Teacher's Resource File See the Unit 1 File, p. 35, for the Section 5 Quiz.

Closure

Remind students that the Anti-Federalists and reluctant supporters of the Constitution included two future Presidents, Thomas Jefferson and James Monroe. The Federalist versus Anti-Federalist debate remains in American politics to this day.

Assignment Assign Section 1 of Chapter 3, pp. 55–59, for the next class period.

Activity: Teaching Heterogeneous Groups

Have students write each of the following on one side of an index card: Magna Carta, Petition of Right, Bill of Rights, Albany Plan of Union, Stamp Act Congress, First Continental Congress, Second Continental Congress, Declaration of Independence, Article of Confederation, the Virginia Plan, the New Jersey Plan, the Connecticut Compromise, and the Constitution. Then have students write dates and important facts about each document on the reverse side of its card. Encourage students to organize the cards chronologically, thus creating a timeline of key events in the creation of American government. Suggest that students use the cards to review the key points of the chapter.

TEACHING
Critical Thinking

Drawing Conclusions
Compare information to draw a conclusion.

INSTRUCT

As an aid to drawing conclusions, you might have students copy the chart on a sheet of paper and then use colors to highlight the provisions of each plan in the Constitution.

Answers 1. (a) two houses; representation by population or financial support; representatives of lower house chosen by popular vote; in upper house nominated by State legislators and chosen by lower house. (b) one house; equal representation; representatives elected by State legislators. (c) two houses; equal representation in upper house, by population in lower house; lower house chosen by popular vote; upper house chosen by State legislators. **2.** (a) In number of houses, types of representation, process of choosing representatives. (b) The Constitution is the same as, or close to, the Virginia Plan regarding number of houses and methods of choosing representatives; close to New Jersey Plan in basis for determining representation. **3.** (a) Yes. (b) Virginia Plan. (c) Number of houses, basis of representation in lower house, election of representatives in both houses. (d) basis of representation in the upper house, election of representatives in the lower house.

Drawing Conclusions

A conclusion is a judgment based on reason. Drawing a conclusion, therefore, means finding an answer or forming an opinion based on available information. Being able to draw conclusions is an important skill that all citizens need in order to evaluate information and solve problems.

The table below outlines the two major plans put forward at the Constitutional Convention for the legislative branch, as well as the provisions that the Framers finally agreed upon at the Convention. Follow the steps and the information on the table to practice drawing conclusions.

1. Read and summarize the information on the table. Before you can draw a conclusion, you must have a firm grasp of the information you are considering. Read down each column of the table and answer the following questions (a) What were the basic features of the Virginia Plan? (b) What were the basic features of the New Jersey Plan? (c) What was the plan finally adopted by the Convention?

2. Compare the information in each of the rows of the table. Read across the rows of the table and ask: (a) In what ways do the three plans differ? (b) In what ways are they similar?

3. Draw conclusions based on the information in the table. Comparing the information on the table should raise some questions in your mind. As you answer these questions based on the information in the table, you are drawing conclusions. Answer the following questions: (a) Did both the Virginia and New Jersey plans contribute to the features actually adopted in the Constitution? (b) Which plan, if any, contributed more to the Constitution? (c) What would you expect the proponents of the Virginia Plan to have liked about the Constitution? (d) What about the proponents of the New Jersey Plan?

	Virginia Plan	New Jersey Plan	Constitution's Provisions
Number of houses in legislature	2	1	2
Basis for determining representation in legislature	each State's population OR amount of each State's financial support for the central government	equal representation for each State	equal representation for each State in upper house; representation by each State's population in lower house
Basis for choosing representatives for legislature	representatives in lower house chosen by popular vote; representatives in upper house nominated by State legislators and chosen by lower house	elected by State legislatures	representatives in lower house chosen by popular vote in each State; representatives in upper house chosen by State legislatures*

*17th Amendment provided for popular election of senators.

Teacher's Resource file
See the Unit 1 File, p. 36, for the Skill Application to reinforce this lesson.

Chapter-in-Brief

Scan all headings, photographs, charts, and other visuals in the chapter before reading the section summaries below.

Section 1 Our Political Beginnings (pp. 25–30) Europeans began coming to North America in the mid-1500s. While many nations sought to colonize America, the English emerged as the dominant force.

American colonists benefitted from a developing English tradition of ordered, limited, and representative government. This heritage served as the basis of the colonial governments. In turn, these governments helped provide training for the colonists in the art of government.

Section 2 The Coming of Independence (pp. 30–35) After 150 years of colonial rule in America, Great Britain began taking a more active role in the colonies in the 1760s. For example, the British increased taxes in the colonies. The colonists resented this "taxation without representation." Twelve of the 13 colonies joined in the First Continental Congress to plan opposition to British policies.

A follow-up to the First Continental Congress met in May of 1775. By that time, the Revolution had begun. The Second Continental Congress became the government of the new United States, and it produced the Declaration of Independence.

The newly formed States now began to write their own constitutions. Portions of these documents would later influence the Constitution of the United States.

Section 3 The Critical Period (pp. 36–38) In order to provide a more lasting plan of government, the Second Continental Congress created the Articles of Confederation. The Articles established "a firm league of friendship" among the States. This friendship was not very strong, and bickering among the States soon threatened the new nation. People began to explore new ways to meet the needs of the nation. Ultimately, this movement led to a convention in May 1787, in Philadelphia. This meeting became the Constitutional Convention.

Section 4 Creating the Constitution (pp. 40–46) The Philadelphia meeting involved delegates from every State but Rhode Island. The delegates quickly agreed that the nation needed a new government. However, there were many disagreements, as each State sought to protect its own interests.

Among the compromises that made the Constitution possible was the Connecticut Compromise. It led to the creation of the current configuration of Congress. Compromise also helped settle troublesome questions about slavery, the selection of the President, and other issues.

Section 5 Ratifying the Constitution (pp. 46–49) The convention created the Constitution; now it was up to the States to accept or reject it. The Constitution was promoted by the Federalists. The Anti-Federalists attacked the document out of fear of the plan's strong central government and because it lacked a bill of rights. One key feature of the debate was the publication of the pro-Constitution *The Federalist*.

The Constitution finally gained the needed support of the States. The new Congress convened in what was then the capital, New York, in March 1789. On April 30, George Washington became the nation's first President.

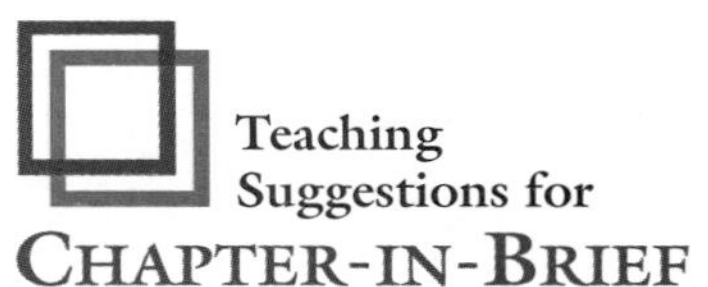

Teaching Suggestions for CHAPTER-IN-BRIEF

Below are some of the possible uses for the Chapter-in-Brief:

To Preview the Chapter You may want to assign the Chapter-in-Brief page and the Section Outlines from the Teacher's Resource File before beginning Chapter 2 to introduce students to the "Key Terms" and concepts in each section.

To Review the Chapter When students have completed Chapter 2, you might want to assign the Chapter-in-Brief as a tool for review, along with the Guided Reading and Review from the Teacher's Resource File.

To Omit the Chapter If you want to skip Chapter 2, it may be helpful to assign the Chapter-in-Brief to students as a review before continuing to another chapter. You may also want to assign the Chapter 2 Test to assess student knowledge of the material. Then specific portions of Chapter 2 may be assigned to students needing reinforcement of "Key Terms" and concepts.

TRF **Teacher's Resource File** See the Unit 1 File for the following materials:

- Section Outlines, pp. 21, 24, 27, 30, 33.
- Guided Reading and Reviews, pp. 22, 25, 28, 31, 34.
- Chapter 3 Test, pp. 40–42.

ADDITIONAL RESOURCES

Allen, W.B., et al. (eds.). *The Essential AntiFederalist.* University Press of America, 1987.

America: A Personal History of the United States, No. 4 - Inventing a Nation. 16mm film. Time-Life Films, 1972. Color. 52 min.

The Background of the Constitution: Where Historians Disagree. Sound filmstrip. Random House Media, 1986.

Bernstein, Richard B. *Are We to Be a Nation? The Making of the Con stitution.* Harvard University Press, 1987.

Bowen, Catherine Drinker. *Miracle at Philadelphia: The Story of the Constitution.* Little, Brown, 1966, 1986.

The Constitution in Action. Sound filmstrip. Random House Media, 1986.

Huston, J.A. *Logistics of Liberty.* University of Delaware Press, 1991.

Independence. Video. National Archives. Color. 30 minutes.

Levy, Michael (ed.). *Political Thought in America: An Anthology.* Dorsey, 2nd ed., 1988.

Mansfield, H.C. *America's Constitutional Soul.* Johns Hopkins Uni versity Press, 1991.

Rossiter, Clinton. 1787: *The Grand Convention.* Norton, 1987.

U.S. Constitution. Tutor. Computer software. Micro Lab, 1981. Apple II/II+/IIe, 48k.

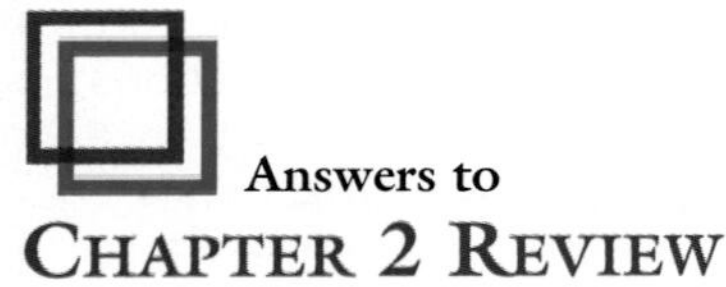

Answers to
Chapter 2 Review

Vocabulary and Key Terms

Matching
1. charter
2. constitution
3. bicameral
4. Articles of Confederation
5. Three-Fifths Compromise
6. Commerce and Slave Trade Compromise

True or False
1. true
2. false—the correct term is Connecticut Compromise
3. false—the correct term is Magna Carta
4. true
5. false—the correct term is boycott

Word Relationships
1. b does not belong; a, c, and d all refer to components of the English political tradition that influenced the colonists in America. **2.** a does not belong; b, c, and d all relate to plans put forth at the Constitutional Convention for the legislature. **3.** c does not belong; a, b, and d each refer to principles of government with which the colonists were familiar. **4.** d does not belong; a, b, and c refer to people or groups that played a part in the Constitution.

Main Ideas

1. Ordered government, limited government, representative government. **2.** Basic beliefs that a monarch must obey the laws and that the people have a right to expect government to protect their property and rights. **3.** (a) Some started as commercial ventures; others as havens for those seeking religious freedom. (b) Eventually, each took one of three forms: Royal charters, proprietary colonies, and charter colonies. **4.** (a) Prior to the 1760s, the British did not bother to exert too much direct control over the colonies. (b) After the 1760s, Britain began to take a more active role in the colonies. **5.** The colonists were angered. The different colonies began to come together to plan a response. **6.** Each was based on the principles of popular sovereignty, limited government, civil liberties, and separation of powers and checks and balances **7.** (a) Sought to form a "firm league of friendship" among the States. (b) Articles did not grant enough power to the national government. Consequently, that government was powerless, and the 13 States were for all practical purposes without the benefit of a central government. **8.** Consisted of a unicameral Congress. Congress chose a president, but only over the Congress itself. The powers of Congress included the power to make war, borrow money, build a navy and raise an army. Congress could not tax or regulate trade. it also had no real power to force the States to obey its laws or the Articles. **9.** Several leaders recognized the need for a change in the

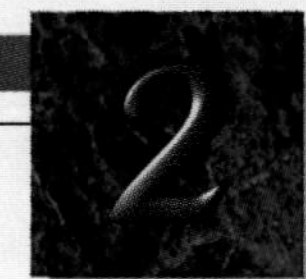

Chapter-in-Brief

Vocabulary and Key Terms

limited government (p. 26)
representative government (p. 27)
Magna Carta (p. 27)
Petition of Right (p. 27)
English Bill of Rights (p. 27)
charter (p. 28)
bicameral (p. 28)
unicameral (p. 29)
Albany Plan of Union (p. 32)
boycott (p. 32)
constitution (p. 35)
popular sovereignty (p. 35)
ratification (p. 36)
Articles of Confederation (p. 36)
Framers (p. 40)
Virginia Plan (p. 42)
New Jersey Plan (p. 43)
Connecticut Compromise (p. 43)
Three-Fifths Compromise (p. 44)
Commerce and Slave Trade Compromise (p. 44)
Federalists (p. 47)
Anti-Federalists (p. 47)

Matching: *Review the key terms in the list above. If you are not sure of a term's meaning, look up the term and review its definition. Choose a term from the list above that best matches each description.*

1. the written grants that authorized the formation of the colonies
2. the body of fundamental laws that sets out the principles, structures, and processes of government
3. legislative body that has two houses
4. attempted to establish a "firm league of friendship" among the original States
5. enabled the Framers to resolve the dispute over whether or not slaves would be counted among each State's population
6. an agreement that forbade Congress to act against the slave trade for 20 years

True or False: *Determine whether each statement is true or false. If it is true, write "true." If it is false, change the underlined word or words to make the statement true.*

1. Pennsylvania's colonial legislature had only one chamber, and so was unicameral.
2. The Virginia Plan outlined the structure of Congress that was ultimately accepted by the Framers.
3. The Petition of Right represented the earliest expression of the rights of the people of England against abuse from the Crown.
4. The Federalists supported the ratification of the Constitution.
5. The policies of the British in the 1760s led to a ratification of English goods in the the colonies.

Word Relationships: *Three of the terms in each of the following sets of terms are related. Choose the term that does not belong and explain why it does not belong.*

1. (a) Magna Carta (b) Albany Plan of Union (c) English Bill of Rights (d) Petition of Right
2. (a) Articles of Confederation (b) Virginia Plan (c) New Jersey Plan (d) Connecticut Compromise
3. (a) limited government (b) popular sovereignty (c) ratification (d) representative government
4. (a) Framers (b) Federalists (c) Anti-Federalists (d) boycott

Main Ideas

Section 1 (pp. 25–30)

1. What three ideas about government did the colonists take with them from England?
2. What concepts did the colonists derive from the Magna Carta, the Petition of Right, and the English Bill of Rights?
3. (a) How did the colonial governments develop? (b) What shape did they take?

Section 2 (pp. 30–35)

4. (a) Describe how the British governed the colonies before the 1760s. (b) After the 1760s?
5. What was the colonists' response to the change in British policies in the 1760s?
6. What were the common features of the first State constitutions?

Section 3 (pp. 36–38)

7. (a) What was the goal of the Articles of Confederation? (b) How well did it succeed?
8. What were the major characteristics of the Articles?
9. How did the nation respond to the shortcomings of the Articles?

Section 4 (pp. 40–46)

10. (a) Who were the Framers of the Constitution? (b) In what sense did they represent a new generation in American politics?
11. What was the role of compromise in the framing of the Constitution?
12. What were the major areas of agreement at the Constitutional Convention?

Section 5 (pp. 46–49)

13. (a) Who were the Federalists? (b) What was their argument in favor of the Constitution?
14. What were the main arguments used by the Anti-Federalists?
15. What were their main battlegrounds in the debate over ratification?

Critical Thinking

1. **Distinguishing False from Accurate Images** (p. 19) What does the fact that the nation needed a stronger central government during the Critical Period suggest about the sense of unity among the States?
2. **Drawing Conclusions** (p. 19) Patrick Henry, a leading patriot during the Revolution, refused to attend the Constitutional Convention, saying ". . . I smell a rat in Philadelphia tending toward monarchy." Why might Henry have felt this way?
3. **Checking Consistency** (p. 19) How does the history of America between the 1600s and 1789 demonstrate that "questions of politics and economics are, in fact, inseparable"?

Getting Involved

1. **Writing Your Opinion** It is 1789. Write a letter to one of the Framers in which you express your opinion on the Constitution. First, create a list of what you see as the positive aspects of the document. Then, list the negative features. Note any suggestions you have for improvements. Next, write a draft of the letter in which you politely offer your ideas. Revise your letter, making certain that each idea is clearly explained. Proofread your letter and draft a final copy.
2. **Class Debate** Conduct a class debate on the following: *Resolved,* that whenever any form of government becomes destructive of the people's life, liberty, and pursuit of happiness, the people have a right and a duty to abolish it. Select one team to debate in favor of this statement and one team to debate against it. The rest of the class can evaluate each side's presentation.
3. **Creating a Political Cartoon** Draw a political cartoon that illustrates the concept of a constitution. Be sure to consider the ideals and beliefs that helped inspire the Framers. In other words, consider what the Framers hoped to accomplish and the means by which they achieved their goal.

government as the one set up in the proposed Constitution. They also did not like the absence of a bill of rights. **15.** New York and Virginia. Their support was vital to the success of the new Constitution.

Critical Thinking

1. Answers will vary, but students might observe that the States were driven by conflict and competition, and unable to formulate effective policy for the nation. **2.** Answers will vary. Students might observe that the concept of a central, powerful government might have seemed too much like monarchy for many former colonists. **3.** Answers will vary. Students might observe that the growing colonial dissatisfaction that ultimately led to revolution grew out of increased involvement by the British in the colonial economies. Much of the conflict during the Critical Period that led to the Constitutional Convention grew out of the economic competition between the States.

Getting Involved

1–3. Answers and results will vary, but students should demonstrate an understanding of the concepts in this chapter.

Articles. They called several meetings for the purpose of discussing plans to revise and improve the Articles. **10.** With the notable exceptions of George Washington and Ben Franklin, the Framers were not of the men who guided America up to and through the Revolutionary War, but a younger breed—averaging only 44 years of age at the time of the Convention. **11.** Many of the major decisions agreed upon at the convention came as a result of compromise. **12.** The participants agreed on the need for a new government. There was also no disagreement about the importance of popular sovereignty and limited government. **13.** (a) The Federalists were led by many of those who attended the Constitutional Convention, notably Alexander Hamilton and James Madison. (b) Their main argument was against the Articles of Confederation. **14.** Anti-Federalists did not want such a strong central

Chapter 3 Resources

In the Teacher's Resource File
The following materials are found in the Teacher's Resource File box.

Instructional Support: Unit 1 File

For the Section	For the Chapter
Outlines, pp. 46, 49, 52	Skill Application, p. 55
Guided Reading and Reviews, pp. 47, 50, 53	Case Study on Contemporary Issues, pp. 56–58
Quizzes, pp. 48, 51, 54	Chapter Test, pp. 59–61
	Additional Test Questions, pp. 62–64

Enrichment Support Files

Participatory Government Activities, pp. 28–39
Supreme Court Cases, pp. 3, 17–18
Simulations and Debates: The War Powers Act
Historical and Legal Documents, p. 39

Computer Test Bank and Assessment

Transparency Package, pp. 3, 28, 59

Chapter 3 Focus

Introduce the Chapter Tell students that in this chapter they will learn about the six basic principles embodied in the United States Constitution and the process by which the Constitution is formally and informally amended. Read with students the Chapter Preview and Objectives.

Writing Activity Direct students' attention to "Describe" under "Before you read this chapter." Ask them to think about their reactions to the statement, then write a paragraph that reflects their opinions about whether or not the statement is true.

Motivate for Learning Direct students to "Predict." Ask them to predict which of the following courses Americans would be likely to take if the Constitution no longer met our needs: armed rebellion, specific amendments, a complete rewrite of the document. Have students defend their choices.

The Constitution

Chapter Preview

Should TV cameras be excluded from courtrooms during trials? Is evidence obtained by illegal wiretaps admissible in court? How legal is professional baseball's reserve clause? Believe it or not, the answers to these twentieth century questions can be found in the Constitution.

You are probably asking yourself, "What did the founding fathers know about wiretaps, or TV cameras, or professional baseball?" The answer, realistically, is "nothing." It is more correct to say, then, that the answers to those questions are found in the interpretation of the Constitution. The basic principles of the United States Constitution have served as the framework of United States law and government for more than 200 years. In this chapter you will read about the American constitutional system and examine the issue of constitutional growth.

Before you read this chapter:

- **Describe** your reaction to this statement: "In the United States, all citizens can do whatever they wish to do."
- **Predict** what might occur if the Constitution no longer met the needs of the people of the United States.

As you read, focus on the main objective for each section. Understand:

1. The meaning of the basic principles of the American constitutional system in both their historical and current settings.
2. The processes of constitutional change and development by formal amendment.
3. The processes of constitutional change and development by informal amendment.

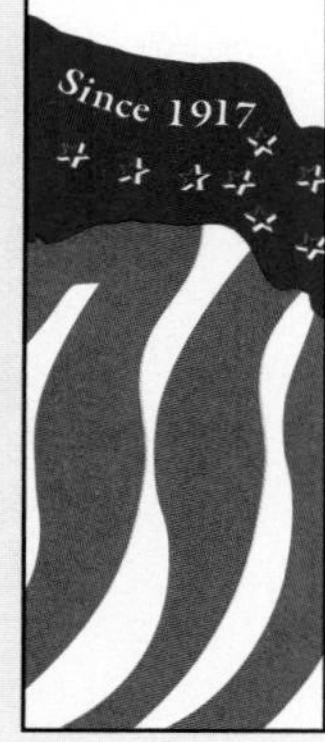

Magruder's American Government: *A Witness to Change* by William A. McClenaghan

Today we think of the system of checks and balances as an integral part of constitutional government. Yet in 1917, some commentators worried more about obstacles to effective government than about the unchecked power of government officials. As the 1917 edition of *Magruder's* observed:

The principle of checks and balances in government is not held in such high esteem today as it was a century ago. The people no longer fear the officers whom they elect every year. They admit that mistakes or evil designs of one department might be checked by another, but they have also come to realize that well-planned honest policies of one department can be checked by ...another if the latter are unfavorable to them. (p. 47)

It is obvious that we live in a much different political world today—a world colored by such experiences as the war in Vietnam, the Watergate scandal, and the Iran-Contra affair. We know, once again, that effective checks against the aggregation of power are absolutely essential to the maintenance of constitutional government in the United States.

"The wise CONSTITUTION let's truly revere,/It points out the course of our Empire to steer" went the words of a 1787 song about the new Constitution, written in Philadelphia's Independence Hall, shown above.

SECTION 1
The Six Basic Principles

FOCUS

Teacher's Resource File
See the Unit 1 File, p. 46, for the Section 1 Outline

Objectives
3.1 Examine the six basic principles upon which the U.S. Constitution is built.
3.2 Analyze the operation of the system of checks and balances.
3.3 Explain how the principle of federalism came to be embodied in the Constitution.

Bellringer Activity Have students turn to page 726 and read the Preamble to the Constitution. After they have finished ask: What was the purpose of the Preamble? What, in your opinion, is the most important part?

State the Purpose The Constitution was founded on six basic principles. In this section, students will examine these six principles, and how they are embodied in the Constitution, and understand their bearing on the workings of the United States government.

ABCNEWS INTERACTIVE
The following video segment may be used to highlight aspects of the Constitution and individual amendments.

POWERS OF THE CONGRESS GUIDEBOOK
Chapter 3: Constitutional Government, p. 4

1 The Six Basic Principles

Find Out:

- What are the six basic principles on which the Constitution of the United States is built?
- How does the American system of separation of powers and checks and balances operate?
- How did the principle of federalism come to be embodied in the Constitution?

Key Terms:
popular sovereignty, limited government, constitutionalism, rule of law, separation of powers, checks and balances, judicial review, unconstitutional, federalism

Perhaps you have heard the phrase "less is more." Although the Framers of the Constitution probably did not have this exact phrase in mind, the amazing document they created reflects its meaning.

The Constitution of the United States is this nation's fundamental law—in its own terms it is "the supreme law of the land." As such, you might expect the document to fill volumes. The Framers, however, wrote a document of only about 7,000 words that you can read in about half an hour. You will find the text of the Constitution beginning on page 724. As you read it, think about the surprising fact that this brief document has successfully guided this nation through two centuries of tremendous growth and change.

One of the Constitution's strengths is that it does not go into great detail about how the government should be run. Instead, the Constitution is built on six basic principles which are explored in detail in this section. These basic principles are: popular sovereignty, limited government, separation of powers, checks and balances, judicial review, and federalism.

Popular Sovereignty

In the United States, all political power belongs to the people. The people are sovereign. **Popular sovereignty** means that people are the 1.a
only source of governmental power. Government can govern only with the consent of the governed.

Vocabulary

Point out the "Key Terms" above. Below are some additional words whose meanings may help students understand the section content.
— **principle:** a general and basic rule
— **compromise:** a settlement of differences through mutual concessions
— **majority:** a number greater than half the total LEP

Reading Strategy: Question Writing

Have students read the section's main headings. Then ask students to write a question about each heading, and look for the answers to their questions as they read.

INSTRUCT

Explain/Discuss Explain to students that the U.S. Constitution, though brief, has proven powerful because its built-in flexibility has allowed it to grow and change with time. Instead of including very detailed descriptions of what the government should be, the Framers based the Constitution on six broad and basic governmental principles: popular sovereignty, limited government, separation of powers, checks and balances, judicial review, and federalism.

Discuss with students the importance and benefits of each of the principles, and how these principles are still in evidence today. For example, you might cite the struggle between the President and Congress over the declaration of war in the Persian gulf and the controversy over Supreme Court nominees.

Also discuss with students the idea that federalism, the system of government under which we operate, is essentially a compromise between the chaos of a loose federation like the Articles of Confederation and an all-powerful central government under which the colonies had labored. The Framers had lived under both systems and wanted in the Constitution the benefits of both without the inefficiency or loss of freedoms of either. The six principles allowed the Framers to create a government under which central control was diffuse and the concentration of power difficult.

This principle of popular sovereignty, so boldly stated in the Declaration of Independence, is woven throughout the Constitution. In the Preamble, its opening words, the Constitution declares: "We the People of the United States...do ordain and establish this Constitution for the United States of America."

By creating the Constitution, the sovereign people created the Government of the United States and gave to it certain powers. Through the Constitution and its own fundamental law, each State government received its powers from the people.

Limited Government

1.b The principle of **limited government** holds that government is *not* all-powerful, that it may do *only* those things that the people have given it the power to do.

In effect, the principle of limited government is the other side of the coin of popular sovereignty. It is that principle stated the other way around: The people are the only source of any and all of government's authority; and government has only that authority the people have given to it.

The concept of limited government can be expressed another way: Government must obey the law. Stated this way, the principle is often called **constitutionalism**—that is, that government must be conducted according to constitutional principles. The concept of limited government is also described as the **rule of**
1.c **law**—that is, government and its officers are always subject to—never above—the law.

In large part, the Constitution is a statement of limited government. Much of it reads as explicit prohibitions of power to government.[1] For example, notice the Constitution's guarantees of freedom of expression. Those great guarantees—of freedom of religion, of speech, of press, of assembly, and of petition—are vital to democratic government. They are set out in the 1st Amendment, which begins with the words: "Congress shall make no law...."

[1]See, especially, Article I, Sections 9 and 10; the 1st through the 10th Amendments; and the 13th, 14th, 15th, 19th, 24th, and 26th Amendments.

Separation of Powers

Recall the brief discussion of the parliamentary and the presidential forms of government in Section 2 of Chapter 1. In a parliamentary system the basic powers of a government—its legislative, executive, and judicial powers—are all gathered in the hands of a single agency. British government is a leading example. In a presidential system, these basic powers are distributed—separated—among three distinct and independent branches of the government as in the United States.

The Constitution distributes the powers of the National Government among the Congress (the legislative branch), the President (the executive branch), and the courts (the judicial
1.d branch). This **separation of powers** is clearly set forth in specific places in the Constitution.

Article I, Section 1 declares:

> "All legislative powers herein granted shall be vested in a Congress of the United States..."

Thus, Congress is the lawmaking branch of the National Government.

Article II, Section 1 declares:

> "The Executive power shall be vested in a President of the United States..."

Thus, the President is given the law-executing, law-enforcing, law-administering powers of the National Government.

Article III, Section 1 declares:

> "The judicial power of the United States shall be vested in one Supreme Court, and in such inferior courts as the Congress may from time to time establish."

Thus, the federal courts, and most importantly the Supreme Court, interpret and apply the laws of the United States in cases brought before them.

Remember, the Framers of the Constitution intended to create a stronger government for the United States. But they also intended to limit the powers of that government. The doctrine of separation of powers was designed to achieve that end result.

Defending this arrangement, James Madison wrote in *The Federalist* No. 47:

SPOTLIGHT ON: Roots of Democracy

As Americans we take great pride in the ringing phrases of the Declaration of Independence, but few realize how heavily Thomas Jefferson relied on the works of John Locke (1632-1704)—the great philosopher who hailed from, of all places, England. The Framers' ideas on limited government and popular sovereignty were influenced by Locke's most important work, *Two Treatises on Government* (1690), in which Locke rejected the "divine right" of kings—the belief that monarchy derived its legitimacy from God. Instead, Locke argued that the legitimacy of government sprang from the individual or, as Jefferson would later write, from "the consent of the governed." Locke argued that the individual was born free and was entitled to the Natural Rights of "life, liberty, and estate"—a phrase Jefferson refashioned as the "certain inalienable rights" among which were "life, liberty, and the pursuit of happiness." If governments failed to protect these rights, subjects were entitled to withdraw their support, according to Locke. The American Declaration of Independence that Locke's ideas inspired did exactly that.

"The accumulation of all powers, legislative, executive, and judiciary, in the same hands, whether one, a few, or many...may justly be pronounced the very definition of tyranny."

Checks and Balances

The National Government is organized around three separate branches. As you have read, the Constitution gives to each branch its own field of governmental authority: legislative, executive, and judicial.

These three branches are not entirely separated nor completely independent of one another, however. Rather, they are tied together by a complex system of **checks and balances**. This 1.a
means that each branch is subject to a number of constitutional checks, or restraints, by the other branches. In other words, each branch has certain powers with which it can check the operations and balance the power of the other two.

The chart on the next page describes the major features of the check-and-balance arrangement. As you can see, the Congress has the power to make law, but the President may veto, or reject, any act of Congress. In its turn, Congress can override a veto by a two-thirds vote in each house. Congress can refuse to provide funds requested by the President, or the Senate may refuse to approve a treaty or an appointment made by the President.

Unemployment Line During the recession of the early 1990s, President Bush used his veto power to overrule a bill passed by Congress to extend unemployment benefits.

The chart also shows how the system of checks and balances links the judicial branch to Congress and the executive branch. The President has the power to name all federal judges. Each appointment, however, must be approved by a majority vote in the Senate. At the same time, the courts have the power to determine the constitutionality of acts of Congress and of presidential actions, and to strike down those they find unconstitutional.

Head-on clashes between the branches do occur periodically. The check-and-balance system operates all the time, however. And the very fact that it does exist—that each branch has its several checks—affects much of what happens in Washington.

For example, when the President picks someone to serve in some important office in the executive branch—as, say, Secretary of State or Director of the Federal Bureau of Investigation (FBI) or the Central Intelligence Agency (CIA)—the President is quite aware that the Senate must confirm that appointment. So, quite purposely, the President picks someone who will very likely be approved by the Senate. In a similar sense, when Congress makes law, it does so with a careful eye on both the President's veto power and the power of the courts to review its actions.

Spectacular clashes—direct applications of the check-and-balance system—do sometimes occur, of course. The President does veto some acts of Congress. On rare occasions, Congress does override one of those vetoes. Even more rarely, the Senate does reject one of the President's appointees.

But, again, these and other direct confrontations are not common. Congress, the President, and even the courts try to avoid them. The check-and-balance system makes compromise necessary—and as you may expect, compromise is a vital part of democratic government.

Over time, the check-and-balance system has worked quite well. It has done what the Framers intended it to do. It has prevented "an

Provide Guided Practice List the six basic principles on one side of the chalkboard. Then write the following terms, out of order, in a list beside the six principles: "*We the people,*" *rule of law, three branches of government, veto override,* Marbury *v.* Madison, *American governmental system.* Have students match the terms to the related principles. (*"We the people"/popular sovereignty; rule of law/limited government; three branches of government/separation of powers; veto override/checks and balances;* Marbury *v.* Madison*/judicial review; American government system/federalism.*)

Provide Independent Practice

TRF **Teacher's Resource File** You may wish to assign Section 1 Guided Reading and Review, Unit File 1, p.47, to help students master section objective content.

Enrichment

Ask volunteers to provide real-life examples to support the presense of each principle in today's government. (Average)

OR

Teacher's Resource File
See the Unit 1 File for the Case Study on Contemporary Issues for Chapter 3.

Interpreting Charts Have students study the chart on page 58. Then ask what might happen if certain checks and balances were removed. (*Answers will vary, but students should see how power is controlled and protected through the system of checks and balances.*)

Caption Answer Checks upon the judicial branch are the power of Congress to impeach and remove judges and to approve judicial appointments.

MONITOR COMPREHENSION

Answers to Section 1 Review
1. "Key Terms" are defined on the following pages:
- **a.** popular sovereignty, p.55
- **b.** limited government, p.56
- **c.** rule of law, p.56
- **d.** separation of powers, p.56
- **e.** checks and balances, p.57
- **f.** judicial review, p.58
- **g.** unconstitutional, p.59
- **h.** federalism, p.59

2. The need for a stronger, central government and the need to respect self-government at the State level. **3.** Popular sovereignty, limited government, separation of powers, checks and balances, judicial review, federalism **4.** Those in government are bound by the Constitution. **5.** Congress can override a veto, remove a President, refuse funds; Senate can refuse to approve treaties or presidential appointments. **6.** It can declare acts of Congress unconstitutional. **7.** Emphasis on the capacity of people to govern themselves shows respect for human potential; a system in which branches of government check each other shows suspicion of government.

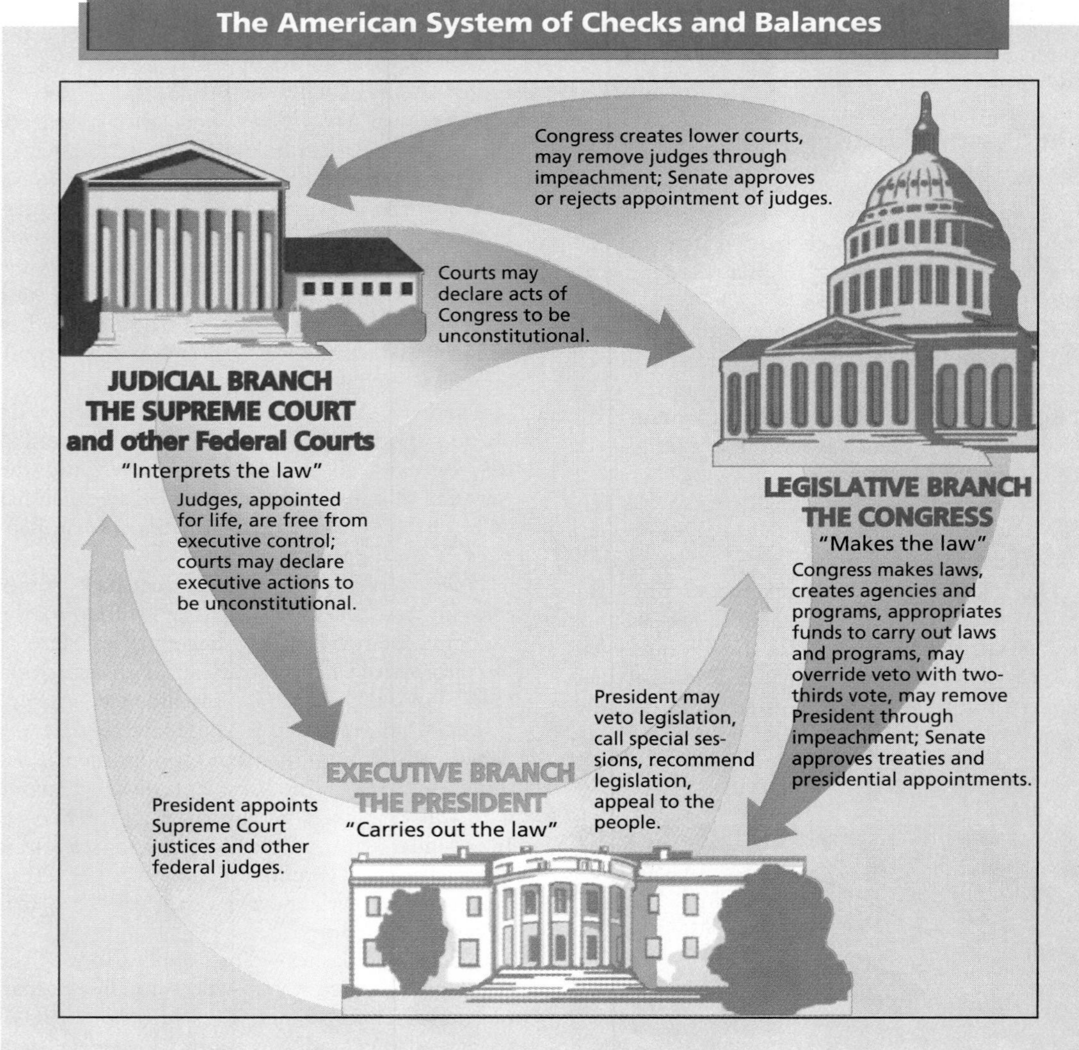
The American System of Checks and Balances
Congress creates lower courts, may remove judges through impeachment; Senate approves or rejects appointment of judges.
Courts may declare acts of Congress to be unconstitutional.
JUDICIAL BRANCH
THE SUPREME COURT
and other Federal Courts
"Interprets the law"
Judges, appointed for life, are free from executive control; courts may declare executive actions to be unconstitutional.
LEGISLATIVE BRANCH
THE CONGRESS
"Makes the law"
Congress makes laws, creates agencies and programs, appropriates funds to carry out laws and programs, may override veto with two-thirds vote, may remove President through impeachment; Senate approves treaties and presidential appointments.
President may veto legislation, call special sessions, recommend legislation, appeal to the people.
EXECUTIVE BRANCH
THE PRESIDENT
"Carries out the law"
President appoints Supreme Court justices and other federal judges.

Interpreting Charts Under the system of checks and balances, each branch of government can check the actions of the others. In what way can the power of the judiciary be checked by the other branches?

unjust combination of the majority." At the same time, it has not very often stalled a close working relationship between the executive, legislative, and judicial branches.

The good working relationship has been especially true when the President and a majority in both houses of Congress have been of the same political party. When the other party controls one or both houses, conflicts play a larger than usual part in that relationship—as they have in recent years.

Judicial Review

As part of the system of checks and balances,
1.f courts have the power of **judicial review**—the

ACTIVITY: Teaching Heterogeneous Groups

Have students write each power of the branches of government (See the chart above.) on one 3x5 index card. Then distribute the cards among three students so that each student has all the cards for one branch. Then one student begins the activity by reading one of the cards for his or her branch of government. Each of the other students must find the card in his or her hand that checks or balances the power chosen by the first student. Students should confirm each other's choices. The game continues, with students taking turns, until all powers in each hand have been read. LEP power to decide whether what government does is in accord with what the Constitution provides.

More precisely, judicial review may be defined this way: It is the power of a court to determine the constitutionality of a governmental action. In part, then, judicial review is the power to declare **unconstitutional**—to declare illegal, null and 1.g
void, of no force and effect—a governmental action found to violate some provision in the Constitution. The power of judicial review is held by all federal courts and by most state courts, as well.[2]

The Constitution does not provide for judicial review in so many words. Yet the Framers clearly meant that the federal courts, especially the Supreme Court, should have that power.

In practice, the Supreme Court established the power of judicial review in the landmark case of *Marbury* v. *Madison* in 1803. (See Chapter 18 for a close look at that case.) Since then, the Supreme Court and other federal and State courts have used the power in thousands of cases. Mostly, the courts have upheld challenged governmental actions. That is, in most cases in which the power of judicial review is exercised, the actions of government are found to be constitutional.

That is not always the case, however. To date, the Supreme Court has decided more than 130 cases in which it has found an act or some part of an act of Congress to be unconstitutional. It has struck down several presidential and other executive branch actions as well. The Court has also voided hundreds of actions of the States and their local governments, including more than 1,000 State laws.

Federalism

As you have read, the American governmental system is federal in form. The powers held by government are distributed on a territorial basis. The National Government holds some of those powers, and others belong to the 50 States.

The principle of **federalism**—the division of 1.h
power among a central government and several regional governments—came to the Constitution out of both experience and necessity. In Philadelphia, the Framers faced a number of difficult problems, including a major one: How to build a new, stronger, more effective National Government while preserving the existing States and the concept of local self-government.

The colonists had rebelled against the harsh rule of a powerful and distant central government. They had fought for the right to manage their local affairs without the meddling and dictation of the king and his ministers in far-off London. Surely, they would not now agree to another such government.

The Framers found their solution in federalism. In short, they constructed the federal arrangement, with its division of powers, as a compromise. It was an alternative to the system of nearly independent States, loosely tied to one another in the weak Articles of Confederation, and a much feared, too powerful central government. The next chapter explores the federal system at length.

[2]Generally, the power is held by all courts of record. These are courts that keep a record of their proceedings and have the power to punish for contempt of court. Usually, only the lowest state courts—justice of the peace courts, for example—are not courts of record.

Section 1 Review

1. **Define:** popular sovereignty, limited government, rule of law, separation of powers, checks and balances, judicial review, unconstitutional, federalism
2. What two factors led the Framers to create a federal system of government?
3. Upon what six basic principles is the Constitution built?
4. What is the principle of constitutionalism?
5. How does the legislative branch check and balance the executive?
6. How does the judicial branch check and balance the Congress?

Critical Thinking

7. **Drawing Conclusions** (p. 19) The Constitution reflects the Framers' beliefs about people and their need for government. Based on the six basic principles of the Constitution, what can you conclude about the Framers' view of human nature?

Teacher's Resource File
See the Unit 1 File, p. 48, for the Section 1 Quiz.

CLOSURE

Remind students that the Constitution is a broad explanation of the limits of government, based on six principles. The fact that the Constitution is not a rigid, detailed document has allowed our government to change and grow over more than two hundred years. As students read the next section, they will learn how the Framers made provisions for change in the Constitution and how those changes are brought about.

Assignment Assign Section 2, pages 60–63 for the next class period.

Reteach

List the six principles on the chalkboard. Next to the principles, but out of order, list their definitions. Have students match the examples to the correct principle.

SPOTLIGHT ON: Constitutional Issues

Although the Civil War was certainly the best-known dispute over the concept of federalism, it was not the first threat to the Union. In 1815, New England State delegates met at the Hartford Convention to protest the War of 1812 and recommend secession for the region unless Federal power was curtailed. In 1830 South Carolina threatened secession after the Federal Government blocked its attempt to invoke a doctrine of "nullification," which would have exempted the State from paying a tariff Southerners believed to favor the North.

SECTION 2
Formally Amending the Constitution

FOCUS

Teacher's Resource File
See the Unit 1 File, p.49, for the Section 1 Outline

Objectives

3.4 Determine how the Constitution has been able to endure more than 200 years of extraordinary change and growth in this country.

3.5 Examine the Bill of Rights and the reasons it was added to the Constitution.

3.6 Explain the processes by which formal changes can be made in the Constitution.

Bellringer Activity Ask students: What, in your opinion, is your most important right? Use students' responses to list a "Student Bill of Rights" on the chalkboard. Conclude the activity by pointing out that when the original Constitution was written, it did not contain rights we commonly associate with it. Explain that this section will describe how we secured those rights and other changes to the constitution.

State the Purpose When the Constitution was written, provisions were made to allow for amendments that would reflect the changing needs of the people. In Section 2, students will learn about the four methods of formal amendment, and will examine the Bill of Rights.

2 Formally Amending the Constitution

Find Out:

- How has the Constitution been able to endure more than 200 years of extraordinary change and growth in this country?
- What is the Bill of Rights and why was it added to the Constitution?
- What are the processes by which formal changes can be made in the Constitution?

Key Terms:
amendment, formal amendment, Bill of Rights

Think about living in a country where there are few good roads, no cars, telephones or televisions, and few cities. There are no factories, few stores, and almost everyone lives and works on a farm. Chances are, living in such a place would represent a big change from the life you live today.

The country described above is the United States—as it was in 1787 when the Constitution was written. Obviously, the needs and concerns of the people at that time were quite different from ours today. Yet the Constitution that those first Americans wrote continues to guide the actions of our government in the 1990s. In fact, it has been in force for more than 200 years—longer than the written constitution of any other nation of the world [3] It has survived and thrived as the nation changed from a scattered collection of about 4 million people into the far-flung home of over 250 million. The same Constitution has guided the United States through its transformation from a struggling nation on the fringe of survival into the most powerful country on earth.

[3]The British constitution dates from well before the Norman Conquest of 1066, but it is not a single, written document. Rather, it is an "unwritten constitution," a collection of principles, customs, traditions, and significant parliamentary acts that guide British government and practice. Israel, which has existed only since 1948, is the only other state in the world without a written constitution.

How has the Constitution endured and kept up with that astounding change? The answer lies in this highly important fact: The Constitution of today *is*, and at the same time *is not*, the document of 1787. Many of its words are the same, and much of their meaning remains the same. But some of its words have been changed, some have been eliminated, and some have been added. And the meanings of many of its provisions have been modified as well.

This process of constitutional change has come about in two basic ways: (1) by formal amendment and (2) by informal amendment. In this section, you will read about the formal process of amending the Constitution.

Formal Amendment Process

The Framers knew that even the wisest of constitution-makers cannot build for all time. Thus, the Constitution provides for its own **amend-
1.a ment**—that is, for changes in its written words.

Article V sets out two methods for the proposal and two methods for the ratification of constitutional amendments. So, there are four
1.b methods of **formal amendment**—changes or additions that become part of the written language of the Constitution itself. The diagram on the next page sets out these four methods.

First Method An amendment may be proposed by a two-thirds vote in each house of Congress and be ratified by three-fourths of the State legislatures. Today, 38 State legislatures must approve an amendment in order to make it a part of the Constitution. Twenty-five of the Constitution's now 26 amendments were adopted in this manner.

Second Method An amendment may be proposed by Congress and then ratified by conventions, called for that purpose, in three-fourths of the States. Only the 21st Amendment, added in 1933, was adopted in this way [4]

[4]The 21st Amendment repealed the 18th, which had established national prohibition. Conventions were used to ratify the amendment largely because Congress felt that the convention's popularly elected delegates would be more likely to reflect public opinion on the question of repeal than would State legislators.

Reading Strategy: Problem Solving

Ask: How would students feel or react if they were found in violation of a law they believed was unjust, but could not be changed. Lead students into a discussion of the importance of being able to amend the law.

Vocabulary

Have students look at the three "Key Terms" on page 60. Write the word *amendment* on the board; then ask students to find the small word in the larger word. (*mend*) Ask what this word means and how it might apply to the Constitution. **LEP**

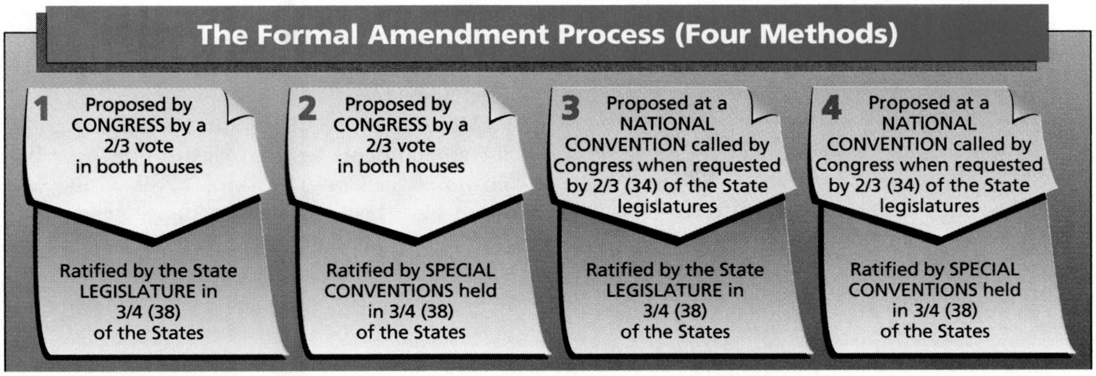

The Formal Amendment Process (Four Methods)

1 Proposed by CONGRESS by a 2/3 vote in both houses
Ratified by the State LEGISLATURE in 3/4 (38) of the States
2 Proposed by CONGRESS by a 2/3 vote in both houses
Ratified by SPECIAL CONVENTIONS held in 3/4 (38) of the States
3 Proposed at a NATIONAL CONVENTION called by Congress when requested by 2/3 (34) of the State legislatures
Ratified by the State LEGISLATURE in 3/4 (38) of the States
4 Proposed at a NATIONAL CONVENTION called by Congress when requested by 2/3 (34) of the State legislatures
Ratified by SPECIAL CONVENTIONS held in 3/4 (38) of the States

Interpreting Charts The four different ways in which amendments may be added to the Constitution are shown here. How does the formal amendment process illustrate federalism?

Third Method An amendment may be proposed by a national convention, called by Congress at the request of two-thirds of the State legislatures—today, 34. And, as you can see in the diagram, it must then be ratified by three-fourths of the State legislatures. To date, Congress has not called such a convention [5]

Fourth Method An amendment may be proposed by a national convention and ratified by conventions in three-fourths of the States. Remember that the Constitution itself was adopted in much this same way.

The Constitution places only one restriction on the subjects with which a proposed amendment may deal. Article V declares that "no State, without its consent, shall be deprived of its equal suffrage in the Senate."

Note that the formal amendment process emphasizes the federal character of the governmental system. Proposal takes place at the national level and ratification is a State-by-State matter. Also note that when the Constitution is amended, that action represents the expression of the people's sovereign will—the people have spoken.

When both houses of Congress pass a resolution proposing an amendment, Congress does not send it to the President to be signed or vetoed, though the Constitution would seem to require it [6] When Congress proposes an amendment, it is not making law (not legislating).

Some criticize the practice of sending proposed amendments to the State legislatures rather than to ratifying conventions, especially because it permits a constitutional change without a clear-cut expression by the people. The critics point out that State legislators, who do the ratifying, are elected to office for a mix of reasons—party membership; name familiarity; incumbency; their stands on such matters as taxes, schools, welfare programs; and a host of other things. They are almost never chosen because of their stand on a proposed amendment to the Federal Constitution. On the other hand, critics claim, the delegates to a ratifying convention would be chosen by the people on the basis of one particular factor: a yes-or-no stand on the proposed amendment.

The Supreme Court has held that a State cannot require an amendment proposed by Congress to be approved by a vote of the people of the State

[5]The calling of a convention has been a near thing twice in recent years. Between 1963 and 1969, 33 State legislatures, one short of the necessary two-thirds, sought an amendment to erase the Supreme Court's "one-person, one-vote" decisions; see Chapter 10. Also, between 1975 and 1991, 32 States asked for a convention to propose an amendment that would require that the federal budget be balanced each year, except in time of war or other national emergency.

[6]See Article I, Section 7, Clause 3. This practice of not submitting proposed amendments to the President is an example of the many "informal amendments" to the Constitution, a matter we shall turn to shortly.

INSTRUCT

Discuss The United States has changed dramatically over the more than 200 years since the Constitution was ratified. Despite these many changes, the nation has survived, in part, because of the adaptability of the document that established it. The Constitution's amendment provisions—notwithstanding the bicentury argument over the practice—interpreted to fit the times. Since 1789, 26 formal amendments have been made to it. The first ten are known as the Bill of Rights, and protect individual rights. Point out that there are four different processes for formally amending the United States Constitution. Ask students to discuss the reasons why there might be four methods—Why has one method been used more often than the other three?

ABCNEWS INTERACTIVE

The following video segments may be used to highlight aspects of the formal amendment processes.

POWERS OF THE CONGRESS GUIDEBOOK
Chapter 10: Amending the Constitution, p. 13
Chapter 48: Methods of Amendment, p. 54

Interpreting Charts Have students study the chart. Discuss student opinions about why the process was made so difficult.

Caption Answer The amendment process involves both the Federal Government and the States.

SPOTLIGHT ON: Global Awareness

Most of the world's 160 constitutions can also be amended, but the procedures differ from country to country. In Australia, Ireland, and Japan, for example, amendments are submitted to popular referendum after passage in the legislature. In Denmark after an amendment passes, parliament is dissolved, an election is held, and the new parliament must approve the amendment. In Belgium, no sitting legislature may amend the constitution. Both houses must be dissolved, new elections held, and the new legislature must approve the amendment with a two-thirds majority in both houses.

Enrichment

Have students analyze the years in which constitutional amendments were passed. Then have students use these dates to create a timeline. What events in history may have spurred the amendment process in each case? Have students add related events to their timelines to show cause and effect. (Challenging)

Provide Guided Practice Ask volunteers to describe and then list on the board the four methods of proposing and ratifying an amendment to the Constitution.

Provide Independent Practice

TRF **Teacher's Resource File** You may wish to assign the Section 2 Guided Reading and Review from the Unit 1 File, p.50, to help students master section content.

Interpreting Tables Have students study the table on p. 63, and ask them to indicate amendments ratified to expand voting rights. Then have them discuss reasons why these amendments were necessary.

Caption Answer The 10th Amendment, "Powers Reserved to the States," which clarified States' rights in the Union.

Monitor Comprehension

Answers to Section 2 Review
1. "Key Terms" are defined on the following pages:
a. amendment, p. 60
b. formal amendment, p. 60
c. Bill of Rights, p. 62
2. The Framers knew that they could not build a document that would last for all time.
3. (a) two-thirds vote in each house and national convention called by Congress when requested by two-thirds of the States. (b) by legislatures of three-fourths of the States and conventions in three-fourths of the States. **4.** Answers will vary. Students might note that the difficult process has ensured that only amendments with nearly universal support are ratified. If it were easier, the Constitution

VOICES on Government

Susan B. Anthony, advocate of women's rights, declares her belief in women's equality.

On the Importance of the 19th Amendment

"It may be delayed longer than we think; it may be here sooner than we expect; but the day will come when man will recognize woman as his peer, not only at the fireside but in the councils of the nation. Then, and not until then, will there be the perfect comradeship, the ideal union between the sexes that shall result in the highest development of the race. What this shall be we may not attempt to define, but this we know, that only good can come to the individual or to the nation through the rendering of exact justice."

before it can be ratified by the State legislature. It made that ruling in *Hawke* v. *Smith* in 1920. But a State legislature can call for an advisory vote by the people before it acts, as the Court most recently held in *Kimble* v. *Swackhamer* in 1978.

If a State rejects a proposed amendment, it is not forever bound by that action. It may later reconsider and ratify the proposal. But most constitutional scholars agree that the reverse is not true. Once a State has approved an amendment, that action is final and unchangeable.

More than 10,000 joint resolutions calling for amendments to the Constitution have been proposed in Congress since 1789. Only 33 of them have been sent on to the States. And, of those, only 26 have been finally ratified.[7]

The 26 Amendments

Congress proposed all of the first 10 amendments in 1789. Each of them arose from the controversy surrounding the ratification of the Constitution itself. Many people, including Thomas Jefferson, had agreed to support the Constitution only on condition that a listing of the basic rights of the people be added to the document immediately. As you can see in the table on the following page, all 10 of these amendments were ratified by the States in 1791.

Collectively, the first 10 amendments are
1.c known as the **Bill of Rights**. They set out the great constitutional guarantees of freedom of expression and belief, of freedom and security of the person, and of fair and equal treatment before the law. You will read about the Bill of Rights in detail in Chapters 19 and 20. The 10th Amendment does not deal with civil rights as such. Rather, it spells out the concept of reserved powers in the federal system.

Another cluster of amendments came out of the aftermath of the Civil War. The 13th, 14th, and 15th Amendments are often called the Civil War Amendments. The 13th (1865) ended slavery and prohibits most other forms of "involuntary servitude." The 14th (1868)

[7]Two of the seven unratified amendments were offered in 1789, along with the 10 that became the Bill of Rights. One dealt with the distribution of seats in the House of Representatives, the other with congressional pay. A third, proposed in 1810, would have voided the citizenship of anyone accepting a foreign title or other honor. Another, in 1861, would have prohibited any amendment relating to slavery. A fifth, in 1924, would have given Congress the power to regulate child labor. A sixth one, proclaiming the equal rights of women (ERA), was proposed in 1972, but it fell three States short of ratification and died in 1982. A seventh, to give the District of Columbia seats in Congress, was proposed in 1978; only 16 States ratified it; it died in 1985.

One of the unratified amendments from 1789, the congressional pay measure, has gained new life in recent years. Thirty-four States have now ratified it, 26 of them since the late 1970s. The text of the long-pending proposal: "No law varying the compensation for the services of the Senators and Representatives shall take effect, until an election of Representatives shall have intervened."

Spotlight on: Multiculturalism

While most Northern States abolished slavery 60 years before passage of the 13th amendment—beginning within the Vermont constitution in 1777—African Americans in the North seldom enjoyed the rights accorded to whites. Discriminatory hiring and segregation of public facilities kept African Americans seperate and unequal, as many northern States required cash bonds to gaurantee good behavior, thus barring African Americans entry. Also, in most northern States, African Americans could neither vote nor serve on a jury. Five States refused African Americans the right to testify against whites and one refused their right to own property or sue.

Activity: For Gifted Students

Theme: Change After students have studied the processes for amending the Constitution, have them select an amendment from the last half of the twentieth century (amendments 22–26) to research to learn why and how the amendment was passed. Students should use resources such as newspaper accounts, debates from the Congressional Record, interviews, and documentaries. Students should then present their findings in the form of a short narrative that focuses on the importance of being able to change the Constitution.

Amendments to the Constitution

Amendment	Subject Adopted	Year	Purpose
1	Freedom of Religion, Speech, Press, Assembly, and Petition	1791	Established civil rights guarantees
2	Right to Bear Arms	1791	
3	Lodging Troops in Private Homes	1791	
4	Search and Seizure	1791	
5	Rights of the Accused	1791	
6	Right to Speedy Trial by Jury	1791	
7	Jury Trial in Civil Cases	1791	
8	Bail and Punishment	1791	
9	Powers Reserved to the People	1791	
10	Powers Reserved to the State	1791	
11	Immunity of States from certain suits	1795	Overturned Court decision
12	Changes in Electoral College procedure	1804	Altered election rules
13	Prohibition of slavery	1865	Reflected social values
14	Citizenship, due process, equal protection	1868	Overturned Court decision
15	No denial of vote due to race, color, or previous condition of servitude	1870	Expanded voting rights
16	Power of Congress to tax incomes	1913	Overturned Court decision
17	Popular election of U.S. Senators	1913	Altered election rules
18	Prohibition of alcoholic beverages	1919	Reflected social values
19	Women's suffrage	1920	Expanded voting rights
20	Presidential terms; sessions of Congress	1933	Altered election rules
21	Repeal of Prohibition (18th Amendment)	1933	Reflected social values
22	Limit on number of President's terms	1951	Altered election rules
23	District of Columbia electoral vote	1961	Expanded voting rights
24	Prohibition of poll tax as voter qualification	1964	Expanded voting rights
25	Presidential succession and disability	1967	Altered election rules
26	Minimum voting age no higher than age 18	1971	Expanded voting rights

Interpreting Tables Of the 33 constitutional amendments proposed, only these 26 were ratified. Which amendment specifically addresses federalism?

defined American citizenship and granted it to former slaves. It also contains the Due Process and Equal Protection clauses, which protect basic civil rights from infringement by the States. The 15th Amendment (1870) forbids any restrictions on the right to vote based upon "race, color, or previous condition of servitude."

The table above shows the number, subject, year of adoption, and purpose of all of the 26 formal amendments. You can also read the full text of each amendment, along with an explanation of their meanings, on pages 736–742. In addition, you will return to the amendments many times in later chapters.

Section 2 Review

1. Define: amendment, formal amendment, Bill of Rights

2. Why did the Framers provide for amendment of the Constitution?

3. (a) By what two methods can amendments to the Constitution be proposed? (b) Ratified?

Critical Thinking

5. Demonstrating Reasoned Judgment (p. 19) Did the Framers make it too hard to amend the Constitution?

★

might not represent the views of a large percentage of Americans.

Teacher's Resource File See the Unit 1 File, p. 51, for the Section 2 Quiz.

Closure

Remind students that the Constitution is the longest-living framework for national government in the world. The Framers understood that society would change over time, and so made provisions for amendments to be formally proposed and ratified by both the State and Federal goverments. In the last 200 years, there have been 26 amendments to the Constitution, including the Bill of Rights. In the next section, students will learn about the informal processes of making amendments to the Constitution.

Assignment Assign Section 3, pages 65–67 for the next class period.

Activity: Cooperative Learning

Time: one class period **Activity:** Propose an amendment to the Constitution **Grouping:** groups of four to six students **Purpose:** Have students reach consensus on an amendment they would like to see made to the Constitution, and choose the process they think could most likely result in ratification. **Roles:** Assign the following roles: discussion leader, recorder, and spokesperson. **Outcome:** Have the spokesperson read the group's proposed amendment to the class and explain the group's choice of amendment method.

Reteach

Have students create four flow charts showing the four amendment processes.

TEACHING

Debating Key Issues

Gregg v. Georgia:
Should the Death Penalty Be Declared Unconstitutional?

Objective

Analyze and evaluate evidence

INSTRUCT

Before reading the feature, you may want to ask students to give their opinions about the death penalty. After they have read the selection, ask them to analyze both sides of the argument and write a paragraph in support of Troy Leon Gregg and a paragraph in support of the State of Georgia. Then have them evaluate both sides of the issue to see if they can predict how the Court decided.

SUPREME COURT DECISION

The Supreme Court upheld the sentence imposed on Gregg. In a 7–2 decision, with Justices Marshall and Brennan dissenting, the majority argued that "punishment of death does not invariably violate the Constitution." The risk that the death penalty "will be inflicted in an arbitrary manner" is greatly reduced if a State follows a strict, two-step process, and this process had been fairly applied to Gregg's sentencing, according to the Court.

TRF **Teacher's Resource File** See the Supreme Court Case File for an activity that extends coverage of this case.

Debating Key Issues

Should the Death Penalty Be Declared Unconstitutional?

Gregg v. *Georgia*

In November 1976, the bullet-ridden bodies of two men were found lying in a ditch near a highway rest stop in Georgia. Two days later Troy Leon Gregg and Floyd Allen were located by police driving a stolen car in North Carolina. In Gregg's pocket was a 0.25-caliber pistol, later identified as the murder weapon.

Allen stated that Gregg had killed the men in order to rob them and steal their car. Gregg denied this, claiming that he fired the gun in self-defense. Gregg was charged with murder and armed robbery.

In accordance with Georgia procedure in capital cases—crimes punishable by death—the trial was in two stages. In the first, the jury found Gregg guilty. At the second stage, the judge instructed the jury that it could recommend a death sentence under certain specific circumstances. The alternative was life in prison. The jury found that these circumstances were present and sentenced Gregg to death.

Gregg appealed to the Georgia Supreme Court. His lawyers cited the 8th Amendment, which forbids "cruel and unusual punishment" as well as a 1972 case, *Furman* v. *Georgia*, in which the U.S. Supreme Court ruled that the death penalty, as it was carried out, was unfair and arbitrary. Nonetheless, the Georgia Supreme Court upheld Gregg's death sentence. Gregg then appealed to the Supreme Court.

Review the following evidence and arguments presented to the United States Supreme Court:

Arguments for Troy Leon Gregg

1. The death penalty is cruel and unusual punishment, and therefore violates the 8th Amendment.

2. The death penalty discriminated against racial minorities and the poor, violating the 14th Amendment.

3. Because the jury had the discretion to choose the death penalty or life imprisonment, the capital-sentencing decision may have been made in an arbitrary manner.

Arguments for Georgia

1. The cruel and unusual punishment clause of the 8th Amendment was aimed at preventing punishments that were disproportionate to the crimes. Capital punishment for the crime of murder cannot always be viewed as disproportionate.

2. In *Furman* v. *Georgia* the Supreme Court left open the possibility that States could again enact death penalty laws, provided those laws followed objective, nondiscriminatory guidelines.

3. The Georgia death-penalty statute was based on carefully described standards, including a two-stage trial, thus passing the constitutional test.

Getting Involved

1. Identify the constitutional grounds upon which each side based its arguments.

2. Debate the opposing viewpoints presented in *Gregg* v. *Georgia.*

3. Predict how you think the Supreme Court ruled in this case and why. Then refer to the Supreme Court Glossary on page 764 to read about the decision in this case. Discuss the impact that you think the Court's ruling has on the incidence of violent crime in the United States.

3 Informal Amendment

Find Out:

- For what reasons is the informal amendment process the real key to two centuries of constitutional change and development in this country?
- What are the several means of informal change?

Key Terms:

informal amendment, executive agreement

As you read through the Constitution, you will notice that it deals in large part with matters of principle and of basic organization and structure. Most of its sections are brief, even skeletal in nature. Because this is true, it becomes clear that to understand the Constitution and the process of constitutional change, you must understand a key point: There is much in the Constitution that cannot be seen with the naked eye. Much has been put there, not by formal amendment, but by **informal amendment**—the process by which 1.a
many changes have been made in the Constitution that have not led to changes in the document's written words. These informal amendments are the result of the day-to-day, year-to-year experiences of government under the Constitution.

This highly important process of informal amendment has taken place—and continues to take place—in five basic ways: through (1) the passage of basic legislation by Congress; (2) actions taken by the President; (3) decisions of the Supreme Court; (4) the activities of political parties; and (5) custom. In this section, you will read about these five basic means of informal amendment, and how they have enabled the Constitution to grow and change with the country.

Basic Legislation

Congress has been a major agent of informal amendment in two ways. First, it has passed many laws to spell out several of the Constitution's brief provisions. That is, Congress has added flesh to the bones of those sections of the Constitution the Framers left purposely skeletal for Congress to add details and meaning as circumstances have required.

Take the structure of the federal court system as an example. In Article III, Section 1, the Constitution provides for "one Supreme Court, and...such inferior courts as the Congress may from time to time ordain and establish." Beginning with the Judiciary Act of 1789, all of the federal courts, except the Supreme Court, have been set up by acts of Congress. Or, similarly, Article II creates only the offices of President and Vice President. The many departments, agencies, and offices in the huge executive branch have been created by acts of Congress.

Second, Congress has added to the Constitution by the way in which it has used many of its powers. For example, the Constitution gives to Congress the expressed power to regulate foreign and interstate commerce.[8] But what is "foreign commerce"? What is "interstate commerce"? What, exactly, does Congress have the power to regulate? The Constitution does not directly answer these questions. In passing thousands of statutes under the Commerce Clause, however, Congress has done much to define the meaning of these words. And, in doing so, it has informally amended—in fact, added a great deal to—the Constitution.

Executive Action

The manner in which different Presidents have used their powers has also produced a number of important informal amendments. For example, the Constitution states that only Congress can declare war.[9] But the Constitution also makes the President the Commander in Chief of the nation's armed forces.[10] Acting under that authority, several Presidents have made war

---

[8]Article I, Section 8, Clause 3.
[9]Article I, Section 8, Clause 11.
[10]Article II, Section 2, Clause 1.

SECTION 3
Informal Amendment

FOCUS

TRF **Teacher's Resource File**
See the Unit 1 File, p.52, for the Section 3 Outline.

Objectives

3.7 Examine the reasons why the informal amendment process is the real key to two centuries of constitutional development.

3.8 Determine the several means of informal change to the Constitution.

Bellringer Activity Hold up a photo of a house and ask students: Could you build this house from this photo? Ask students why they could not. Lead them to understand the need for detailed plans. Then explain that the Constitution is a "picture" of government, but details have had to be worked out to complete day-to-day work.

State the Purpose The Constitution is only a brief outline of the basic tenets of government. Day-to-day implementation is possible through a broad process of informal amendment. In Section 3, students will examine why the informal amendment process is important to government, and they will learn five ways in which informal amendments affect the Constitution.

ABCNEWS INTERACTIVE

The following video segment may be used to highlight aspects of informal amendment.

POWERS OF THE SUPREME COURT GUIDEBOOK
Chapter 33: Landmark Decisions of the Supreme Court, p. 50

Vocabulary

Direct students to the "Key Terms" on page 65. As they read Section 3, have them keep a list of similarities and differences between the processes of formal and informal amendment. LEP

Reading Strategy: Who? What? When? Where? How? Why?

As students read Section 3, have them write and answer six focus questions using who, what, when, where, how, and why to determine facts about the informal amendment process.

INSTRUCT

Explain Explain to students that informal amendment differs considerably from formal amendment. To understand how, ask students to envision constitutional government as a process, evolving and growing to meet changing public needs. Informal amendment facilitates this process, keeping government up-to-date without formal modification of the blueprint—the Constitution—upon which the system is based.

Provide Guided Practice List the following examples of informal amendment on the board: commerce laws, executive agreements, Democrats and Republicans, Marbury *v.* Madison, the Cabinet. then have students match them to one of the ways of informally amending the Constititution. (*commerce laws/legislation; executive agreements/executive actions; Democrats and Republicans/party policies;* Marbury *v.* Madison/*court decisions; the Cabinet/custom*)

Provide Independent Practice

TRF **Teacher's Resource File** You may wish to assign the Section 3 Guided Reading and Review, Unit 1 File, p. 53, to help students master section objective content.

Interpreting Political Cartoons Ask students to interpret the cartoon on p. 67. Why have so few changes been made to the Constitution?

Caption Answer Only a small percentage of formally proposed amendments to the Constitution are ratified.

Truman Takes Executive Action As Commander in Chief of the armed forces, President Truman sent troops to Korea without a formal declaration of war by Congress.

National Conventions Since the mid-1800s, the informal method of nominating presidential candidates has been through the national convention.

without the benefit of a congressional declaration of war. In fact, Presidents have used the armed forces abroad in combat without such a declaration on no fewer than 200 separate occasions in American history.

Among many other examples is the use of an
1.b **executive agreement**—a pact made by the President directly with the head of a foreign state. The principal difference between these executive agreements and treaties is that they need not be approved by the Senate. Executive agreements are as legally binding as treaties, however. Recent Presidents have often used them in the conduct of foreign affairs instead of the more cumbersome treaty-making process outlined in Article II, Section 2 of the Constitution.

Court Decisions

The nation's courts, most tellingly the United States Supreme Court, interpret and apply the Constitution in many cases they hear. You have already read about several of these instances of constitutional interpretation—that is, informal amendment—by the Court, such as in *Marbury* v. *Madison*, 1803. You will encounter many more examples in this text, for the Supreme Court is, as Woodrow Wilson once put it, "a constitutional convention in continuous session."

Party Practices

The nation's political parties have also been a major source of informal amendment over the course of American political history.

The Constitution makes no mention of political parties. In fact, most of the Framers were opposed to their growth. In his Farewell Address in 1796, George Washington warned the people against what he called "the baneful effect of the spirit of party." Washington feared the divisive effect of party politics. Yet, even as he spoke, parties were developing in this country. They have played a major role in the shaping of government and its processes ever since. There are numerous examples of that point.

Neither the Constitution nor any law provides for the nomination of candidates for the presidency. From the 1830s on, however, the

Enrichment

Have students explain in a brief paragraph how a law, if passed, might add "flesh and bones" to the Constitution. (Average)

SPOTLIGHT ON: Behind the Scenes

When Washington warned of the "baneful effects of parties" he knew what he was talking about! While history correctly records his unanimous election to the presidency in 1789, the victory came without electoral votes from New York. Federalists controlling the State Senate and Anti-Federalists controlling the Assembly (House) could not reach an agreement on whom to elect to the State's electoral college delegation, so New York didn't send one and, therefore, didn't participate in Washington's election.

major parties have held national conventions to do just that. The parties have converted the Electoral College, the body that makes the formal selection of the nation's President, from what the Framers intended into a "rubber stamp" for the popular vote in presidential elections. (You will read more about the role of the Electoral College in Chapter 13.) Both houses of Congress are organized and conduct much of their business on the basis of party. The President makes appointments to office with an eye to party politics. In short, government in the United States is in many ways government through party.

Custom

Unwritten customs may be as strong as written laws, and many customs have developed in our governmental system.

Again, there are many examples. By custom, not because the Constitution says so, the heads of the 14 executive departments make up the Cabinet, an advisory body to the President.

On each of the eight occasions when a President died in office, the Vice President succeeded to that office—most recently in 1963. Yet, the written words of the Constitution did not provide for this practice until the adoption of the 25th Amendment in 1967. Until then, the Constitution said only that the powers and duties of the Presidency—but *not* the office itself—should be transferred to the Vice President.[11]

Both the strength and the importance of unwritten customs can be seen in the reaction to the rare circumstances in which one of them has not been observed. For nearly 150 years, the "no-third-term tradition" was a closely followed rule in presidential politics. The tradition began in 1796, when George Washington refused to seek another term as President. In 1940, and again in 1944, however, Franklin Roosevelt broke the no-third-term custom. He sought and won a third and then a fourth term in the White House. As a direct result, the 22nd Amendment was added to the Constitution in 1951. So, what had been an unwritten custom, an informal amendment, became a written part of the Constitution itself.

IF I HAVE THE CONSTITUTION WHAT'S ALL THIS OTHER STUFF?
PROPOSED CONSTITUTIONAL AMENDMENTS.
CIVICS

Interpreting Political Cartoons The Constitution is constantly changed through informal amendments. How does this cartoon view changes made by formal amendments?

Section 3 Review

1. **Define:** informal amendment, executive agreement
2. Describe the informal amendment process.
3. Why is this process of informal amendment important to understanding constitutional change?
4. What are the five ways (agents) by which the Constitution has been informally amended?

Critical Thinking

5. **Testing Conclusions** (p. 19) When Franklin Roosevelt ran for a third term, he violated the "no-third-term tradition." (a) Do you think that Roosevelt was wrong to violate this informal amendment? (b) What would happen if other informal amendments were also ignored by people in government?

[11]Read, carefully, Article II, Section 1, Clause 5, and hen Section 1 of the 25th Amendment.

Monitor Comprehension

Answers for Section 3 Review
1. "Key Terms" are defined on the following pages
a. informal amendment, p 65
b. executive agreement, p. 66
2. The way in which the Constitution has changed as a result of the day-to-day and year-to-year function of government. **3.** Formal changes to the Constitution are rare; informal amendment accounts for the means by which government keeps up with change in society. **4.** (a) passage of laws by Congress, (b) actions taken by the President, (c) decisions of the Supreme Court, (d) the activities of political parties, (e) custom. **5.** (a) and (b) Answers will vary, especially with respect to whether or not Roosevelt was right or wrong.

TRF **Teacher's Resource File** See the Unit 1 File, p.54, for the Section 3 Quiz.

Closure

In this section, students have examined the five ways by which the Constitution can be interpreted and amended through the informal processes: basic legislation, executive action, court decisions, party practices, and custom.

Assignment Assign Chapter 4, Section 1, pages 73–80 for the next class period.

Spotlight On: Economics

Among the departments created outside of what is provided in the Constitution is an entire office dedicated to handling the Federal budget. After the White House, the Office of Management and Budget is the largest office in the executive branch, with more than 500 employees and its own annual budget of more than $50 million. OMB also exercises an oversight function, tracking how and how effectively various Federal agencies spend their share of the Federal Government's $1.45-trillion annual budget.

Reteach

Have students review the questions they wrote for the Reading Strategy on p. 65. Have students ask their questions and discuss their answers with them.

TEACHING
Citizenship

Objective
Investigate types of government sources

INSTRUCT

Before students read the Citizenship feature, ask them to think of various ways they can keep informed about issues taking place in government. Discuss how an in-depth look at the issues prepares them to be better citizens. Have students write a brief essay that outlines the key reasons why it is important to be informed. Have them include the best ways to find information about the government.

Answers **1.** Answers will vary; students may or may not be familiar with the resources. **2.** (a) Examples: public/*The Congressional Record*; private/*The New York Times.* (b) Examples: public/ *The Congressional Record Index*; private/*The Almanac of American Politics.* **3.** (a) Primary. (b) Answers may vary; a senator's speech will tell students that senator's views, and may also express the views of many Americans at the time of the speech. (c) Secondary. (d) Examples: *The Congressional Record*, various periodicals, such as the *Wall Street Journal* or *Newsweek.* **4.** Answers will vary, but students should demonstrate, with examples, how they would use the four types of information.

Citizenship

How to Use Different Sources of Government Information

Information about Federal and State governments is available from many sources. Knowing how to use these sources is important to good citizenship. It is a key skill that enables you to be better informed and better equipped to participate in the democratic process.

For example, suppose you wanted to research how your representatives in Congress stood on the 1990–1991 conflict in the Persian Gulf. You might research speeches they made and votes they cast in the House or Senate. Such information is available from many sources. Follow these steps to practice using different sources of information.

1. Know what information is available. Each branch of the Federal Government collects and publishes great quantities of information. State and local governments also gather and distribute much material. In addition, private publishers produce material about government and its activities. Locate the Government Resources Handbook on page 690. This handbook lists just a few of the more popular and widely available sources of information on government and its activities. Have you used any of these resources before?

2. Know the differences between public and private sources. Public sources are those published by the Federal Government, a State government, or some other public agency. A private source is one published by a publisher that is not connected to any government agency.

Look in the Government Resources Handbook. (a) Can you find one public and one private source that might include the results of the vote in Congress authorizing the use of force in the Persian Gulf conflict? (b) Can you find one private and one public source that might include a representative's thoughts about the conflict?

3. Know the differences between primary and secondary sources. Primary sources are direct, firsthand accounts of an event, such as a court decision, the transcript of a committee debate, or an eyewitness account of an event. Primary sources provide insight into a person's views or attitudes. Secondary sources are secondhand summaries and interpretations of primary sources. Often, secondary sources include the author's opinion and bias. (a) Is the text of a senator's speech a primary or a secondary source? (b) For what kind of information is such a source useful? (c) If you wanted to read an analysis of the actions of Congress during the crisis in the Persian Gulf, would you look for a primary or a secondary source? (d) Can you identify possible sources for these pieces of information in the Government Resources Handbook?

4. Determine the reliability of your sources. Each source offers benefits and drawbacks. For example, a primary source gives firsthand information, but might reflect the strong bias of its author. A secondary source might distort the information it summarizes. Public sources might not offer as critical a view of the government as a private source might. A private source might reflect its author's bias. Because each source has benefits and drawbacks, it is always best to check several sources. How might you use all four types of information to complete your research on your representatives in Congress?

TRF **Teacher's Resource File**
See the Unit 1 File, p. 55, for the Skill Application for this lesson.

Chapter-in-Brief

Scan all headings, photographs, charts, and other visuals in the chapter before reading the section summaries below.

Section 1 The Six Basic Principles (pp. 55–59) The Constitution of the United States is the "supreme law of the land," the nation's fundamental law. It is the framework on which the government is built. The Constitution does not describe in great detail how the government is to work. Rather, the Constitution sets out six basic principles that shape and guide its operations.

1. Popular sovereignty: The people are sovereign; they are the only source for the authority of government.
2. Limited government: Government is not all-powerful; it may do only those things the people have given it the power to do.
3. Separation of powers: Government's legislative, executive, and judicial powers are divided among three independent, coequal branches.
4. Checks and balances: The three branches are tied together through a complex system of checks, restraints, each can use against the other.
5. Judicial review: The courts (most importantly, the Supreme Court) have the power to determine the constitutionality of governmental actions.
6. Federalism: The powers of government are distributed on a territorial basis, between the National Government and the several States.

Section 2 Formally Amending the Constitution (pp. 60–63) Since 1787, when the Constitution was written, this nation's population has grown from about 4 million people to over 250 million. The nation was then 13 States stretched along the Atlantic seaboard; it now extends across the continent and beyond. How has the Constitution survived such change?

One reason the Constitution has endured is that it contains a built-in mechanism by which it can be adjusted to meet the changing needs of the nation. This is the constitutional amendment process, which includes four formal methods of amending the Constitution. Each of these methods reflects the principle of federalism—proposals for amendments must be made at the national level, and amendments must be ratified at the State level.

The process of amending the Constitution is not easy. More than 10,000 resolutions calling for amendments have been introduced over the years. Only 26 amendments have thus far been added to the Constitution. The first 10 amendments—the Bill of Rights—were all ratified at the same time, in 1791.

Section 3 Informal Amendment (pp. 65–67) The Framers wrote much of the Constitution in brief, even outline-like terms. So, the real key to 200 years of constitutional change and development in the United States lies in the informal amendment process, the many changes that have been made in the Constitution but that have not involved changes in its written words.

An almost countless number of informal amendments have been added to the Constitution in five ways: (1) the passage of basic legislation by Congress, (2) actions taken by Presidents, (3) decisions of the Supreme Court, (4) the activities of political parties, and (5) custom.

These informal amendments are the product of the day-to-day, year-to-year experiences of government under the Constitution.

Teaching Suggestions for CHAPTER-IN-BRIEF

Below are some of the possible uses for the Chapter-in-Brief:

To Preview the Chapter You may want to assign the Chapter-in-Brief page and the Section Outlines from the Teacher's Resource File before beginning Chapter 3 to introduce students to the "Key Terms" and concepts in each section.

To Review the Chapter When students have completed Chapter 3, you might want to assign the Chapter-in-Brief as a tool for review, along with the Guided Reading and Reviews from the Teacher's Resource File.

To Omit the Chapter If you want to skip Chapter 3, it may be helpful to assign the Chapter-in-Brief to students as a review before continuing to another chapter. You may also want to assign the Chapter 3 Test to assess student knowledge of the material. Then specific portions of Chapter 3 may be assigned to students needing reinforcement of "Key Terms" and concepts.

Teacher's Resource File See the Unit 1 File for the following materials:

- Section Outlines, pp. 46, 49, 52.
- Guided Reading and Reviews, pp. 47, 50, 53.
- Chapter 3 Test, pp. 59–61.

ADDITIONAL RESOURCES

Cox, Archibald. *The Court and the Constitution.* Houghton Mifflin, 1987.

Keenan, Joseph. *The Constitution of the United States: Origins, Documents, and Interpretation.* Dorsey Press, 2nd ed., 1988.

Rossum, Ralph A. and G. Alan Tarr. *American Constitutional Law: Cases and Interpretation.* St. Martin's Press, 2nd ed., 1987.

America: A Personal History of the United States, No. 4—Inventing a Nation. 16 mm film. Time-Life Films, 1972. Color. 52 min.

The Background of the Constitution: Where Historians Disagree. Sound filmstrip. Random House Media, 1986.

The Constitution in Action. Sound filmstrip. Random House Media, 1986. Color. 8 parts.

Answers to CHAPTER 3 REVIEW

Vocabulary and Key Terms

Matching
1. judicial review
2. formal amendment
3. unconstitutional
4. federalism
5. separation of powers

True or False
1. false—the correct term is separation of powers.
2. false—the correct term is amendment.
3. true
4. false—the correct term is informal amendment.
5. true

Word Relationships
1. Limited government refers to basic principle of American government that says that government is not all powerful. Popular sovereignty is the related idea that the people hold the ultimate power in government.
2. Checks and balances helps ensure that each of the branches of government does not gain too much power or control over the government. Checks and balances helps fulfill the principle of separation of powers, which states that the three branches of government (executive, legislative, and judicial) must be independent and equal.
3. Judicial review refers to the judicial branch's power to judge the constitutionality of acts of Congress or the executive branch. As a result of judicial review, a court might find an act of Congress or the executive unconstitutional—that is, invalid.
4. Rule of law refers to the principle that states that no person is above the law. The Bill of Rights consists of the first 10 amendments to the Constitution, and it deals mostly with guarantees of individual rights

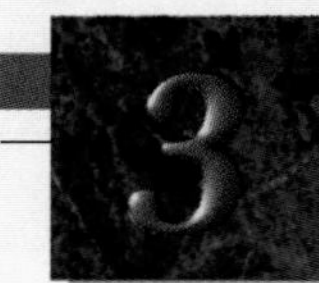

Chapter Review

Vocabulary and Key Terms

popular sovereignty (p. 55)	checks and balances (p. 57)	formal amendment (p. 60)
limited government (p.56)	judicial review (p. 58)	Bill of Rights (p. 62)
constitutionalism (p. 56)	unconstitutional (p. 59)	informal amendment (p. 65)
rule of law (p.56)	federalism (p.59)	executive agreement (p. 66)
separation of powers (p. 56)	amendment (p. 60)	

Matching: *Review the key terms in the list above. If you are not sure of a term's meaning, look up the term and review its definition. Choose a term from the list above that best matches each description.*

1. an example of the judicial branch's check on the legislative branch
2. an official change in the language of the Constitution
3. what a law that violates the Constitution is declared
4. the principle that explains why States hold many powers in the American system of government
5. the principle that divides the executive, legislative, and judicial powers of the government into separate but equal branches

True or False: *Determine whether each statement is true or false. If it is true, write "true." If it is false, change the underlined word or words to make the statement true.*

1. Under the principle of popular sovereignty the National Government has three equal branches.
2. Executive agreement is the process by which the Constitution has been changed and added to during the course of United States history.
3. The first 10 amendments to the United States Constitution are known as the Bill of Rights.
4. Formal amendments have resulted from laws passed by Congress, decisions of the Supreme Court, and the activities of political parties.
5. The principle of constitutionalism states that government must be bound by a fundamental law.

Word Relationships: *Distinguish between the words in each pair.*

1. limited government/popular sovereignty
2. checks and balances/separation of powers
3. judicial review/unconstitutional
4. rule of law/Bill of Rights

Main Ideas

Section 1 (pp. 55–59)

1. How does the Constitution's length and its absence of detail help explain its strength?
2. (a) Who holds the ultimate power in the United States system of government? (b) What two guiding principles of the Constitution serve as the basis for that fact?
3. (a) What are the remaining basic principles upon which the Constitution is built? (b) How do those principles operate in American government?

70

Main Ideas

Section 1
1. The Constitution is relatively short. It is short because it provides general principles about the shape and form of government rather than many specific details. The focus on principles rather than details has helped the Constitution survive the growth and change of the nation. **2.** (a) People hold the ultimate political power in the United States government. (b) popular sovereignty and limited government **3.** (a) rule of law, separation of powers, judicial review, and federalism. (b) Rule of law requires that all people be subject to the law. The separation of powers divides the judicial, legislative, and executive powers of government among three coequal branches. Judicial review enables the judicial branch to declare unconstitutional the actions of any other branch of decisions of government. And federalism divides governmental power between a

Section 2 (pp. 60–63)

4. (a) In what ways has the United States changed in its more than 200-year history? (b) how has this change affected the Constitution?
5. (a) For what reasons is there a need for the formal amendment of the Constitution? (b) How many times has that process taken place?
6. For what reason was the Bill of Rights added to the Constitution?

Section 3 (pp. 65–67)

7. (a) How does an informal amendment differ from a formal amendment? (b) Which is more common?
8. For what reason is the process of informal amendment necessary?
9. What are the major means for informally amending the Constitution?

Critical Thinking

1. **Drawing Conclusions** (p. 19) The Preamble to the Constitution begins with the words "We the people." This collective "we," however, did not extend far enough to include suffrage and equal rights for women, African Americans, and Native Americans. (a) How has this omission affected constitutional history in the United States? (b) Which, if any, of the 26 amendments to the Constitution remedied this situation?
2. **Checking Consistency** (p. 19) The concept of majority rule with minority rights, argued in *The Federalist* No. 10 on page 758, protects the few from the actions of the many. Find examples of the success and failure of the United States to live up to that concept over the course of its history.
3. **Testing Conclusions** (p. 19) The text says that the United States Constitution is a flexible document. Find evidence from the text that you believe supports the validity of that conclusion.

Getting Involved

1. **Writing Your Opinion** You are a newspaper editor in the late 1700s. Alexander Hamilton has just made a statement in which he referred to democracy as "mobocracy." Write an editorial in response to Hamilton's statement. Define the opinion that you want to take in the editorial. Next, list the arguments you will use. As you revise your editorial, make certain that your arguments are as persuasive as possible. Finally, proofread and make a final copy.
2. **Cooperative Activity** Conduct a mini-Constitutional Convention to update the Bill of Rights. Working in small groups, create a chart to organize your revisions and ideas. List the contents of the current Bill of Rights in one column. In the second column, identify which amendments you want to revise. Explain the reasons behind each suggested revision in the third column. As you make your decisions, think about current issues of debate such as gun control and the death penalty, and how they are addressed in the original Bill of Rights.
3. **Class Debate** Hold a debate on the following: *Resolved,* That the Constitution be amended to fix the terms for Supreme Court Justices. Select one team to debate in favor of the proposed amendment and one to debate against it. The rest of the class can evaluate each side's presentation.
4. **Gathering Information** (a) Using the Government Resources Handbook beginning on page 690, identify what sources you could use to find the names and addresses of your representatives and senators in Congress. (b) What sources might you be able to use to check their past voting records on civil rights, gun control, or other issues?

central government and several State governments.

Section 2

4. (a) The nation has grown from a rural, coastal nation of 4 million to a population of 250 million spread across a continent and beyond. (b) The Constitution has had to change to meet the changing needs of the nation. This change has come about via amendment. **5.** (a) The Framers understood that their document could not stand as it was written for all time. They anticipated changes in the nation and devised a method for changing the document. (b) Twenty-six times. **6.** It arose out of the controversy surrounding the ratification of the Constitution. Many people had agreed to support the Constitution only if the Bill of Rights was added.

Section 3

7. (a) Informal amendment refers to the process by which the meaning of the Constitution has changed without a corresponding change in the written language of the document itself. (b) Informal amendment **8.** The Constitution and its amendments deal with issues of principle and basic organization. Informal amendment allows the government to address the many day-to-day concerns of a functioning government. The Constitution is not easily amended formally. **9.** Informal amendment has taken place through the passage of laws by Congress, the actions taken by the President, the the Supreme Court, by the activities of political parties, and by the evolution of customs widely observed in each branch of government.

Critical Thinking

1. (a) The failure to grant equal justice under the law to women and minorities ensured agitation for equal rights and a sometimes turbulent constitutional history. (b) The 13th, 14th, 15th, 19th, and 24th amendments applied expressly to either women or minorities. **2.** Examples of tyranny of the majority include the U.S. Government's internment of those of Japanese descent during World War II, Alien and Sedition Acts passed by Presidents Adams and Wilson, and various Jim Crow laws.

3. Answers will vary, but students should be able to find material in the text, especially in Sections 2 and 3 about the formal and informal amendment processes.

Getting Involved

1–4. Answers and results will vary, but students should demonstrate an understanding of the concepts in this chapter.

Chapter 4 Resources

In the Teacher's Resource File
The following materials are found in the Teacher's Resource File box.

Instructional Support: Unit 1 File

For the Section
Outlines, pp. 65, 68, 71
Guided Reading and Reviews, pp. 66, 69, 72
Quizzes, pp. 67, 70, 73

For the Chapter
Skill Application, p. 74
Case Study on Contemporary Issues, pp. 76–77
Chapter Test, pp. 78–80
Additional Test Questions, pp. 81–83

Enrichment Support Files

Supreme Court Cases, pp. 4, 19–20, 21–22
Historical and Legal Documents, p. 22
Simulations and Debates: National Health Insurance

Computer Test Bank and Assessment

Transparency Package, pp. 4, 29

Chapter 4 Focus

Introduce the Chapter Tell students that in this chapter they will learn about the division of powers between the National Government and the States. Read with students the Chapter Preview and Objectives.

Writing Activity Direct students' attention to "Describe." Have students list three functions that the Federal Government performs that the States do not. Then have students write why they think the Federal Government was given powers different from the States.

Motivate for Learning Direct students' attention to "Predict." Elicit students' ideas about possible reasons why the Framers felt it was necessary to divide power between the National and State governments. Write them on the board to return to when students have completed the section so that students may check their predictions.

Federalism

Chapter Preview

Alaska and Hawaii attained Statehood more than 30 years ago, increasing the number of stars on the American flag from 48 to 50. The American flag might display one more star some day, if Puerto Rico is admitted by Congress as the 51st State.

The people of Puerto Rico voted to retain the island's status as a U.S. commonwealth in 1967. In late 1991, however, a significant number wished to become what one journalist called "a full-fledged part of a wealthy country," but Congress refused to grant them the opportunity to vote again. What are the National Government's obligations to "full-fledged" States and what is the process of admitting new States to the Union? Those issues were defined by the Framers of the Constitution when they created a Federal system of government and are discussed in this chapter.

Before you read this chapter:

- **Describe** three functions that the Federal Government performs that the States may not.
- **Predict** why the Framers felt it was necessary to divide power between the National and State governments.

As you read, focus on the main objective for each section. Understand:

1. The division of powers between the National Government and the States.
2. The National Government's obligations to the States.
3. The constitutional provisions that promote cooperation between and among the States.

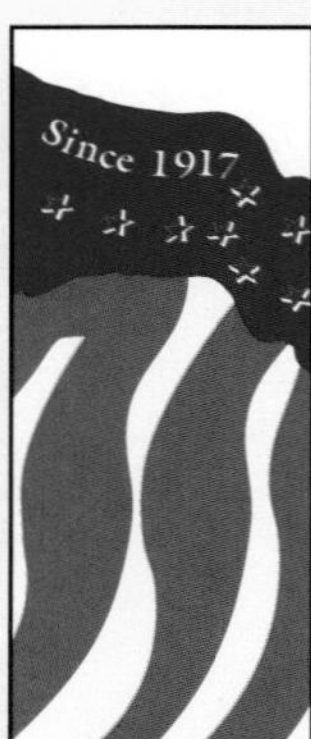

Magruder's American Government: *A Witness to Change* by William A. McClenaghan

In every edition of this book, several examples have been used to illustrate the reserved powers of the States in the federal system. On page 77 of this edition, these examples are used: "Any State can forbid persons under 18 to marry without parental consent or those under 21 to buy liquor. A State may require that doctors, lawyers, hairdressers, or plumbers be licensed..." (p. 77)

As incredible as it may now seem, the 1931 edition said that any State "could make laws requiring the consent of police officers to hold a church service; could pay the salaries of Catholic priests; could require all news items to be approved by a State censor before being published..." (p. 64)

The reserved powers of the States have been reshaped in hugely important ways since those words were written. In particular, the Supreme Court has many times applied the 14th Amendment's Due Process Clause to the ability of the States to interfere with individual rights—and, clearly, none of those examples from 1931 would be valid today.

Fifty Plus One? The Puerto Rican flag floats above this rally held in support of Puerto Rico's present commonwealth status. Other Puerto Ricans support being admitted to the United States as the 51st state.

1 Federalism and the Division of Power

Find Out:

- What is federalism and why does this country have a federal form of government?
- What are the delegated powers of the National Government? What powers are denied to it?
- What powers belong to the States? To the National Government? What powers are held concurrently by the National Government and the States?
- What role does the Supreme Court play in the federal system?

Key Terms:

federalism, division of powers, delegated powers, expressed powers, implied powers, inherent powers, reserved powers, exclusive powers, concurrent powers

When the Framers met at the Philadelphia Convention, they had a complex problem to solve: How could they design a strong, national government with the power to meet the nation's needs and, at the same time, preserve the existing States? The authors of the Constitution were dedicated to the concept of limited government. They believed that to divide governmental power is to restrict it and thus prevent its abuse.

You probably know that according to federal law young men must register for the draft at age 18; most employers must pay their workers at least $4.25 an hour; no one can be denied a job because he or she is African American, Hispanic, or Asian American.

You almost certainly know, too, that according to State law you must have a driver's license in order to drive a car; it is illegal for anyone under 21 to buy beer, wine, or liquor.

These few examples illustrate a complex arrangement: the division of governmental

Section 1
Federalism and the Division of Power

Focus

Teacher's Resource File See the Unit 1 File, p. 65, for the Section 1 Outline.

Objectives

4.1 Define the concept of federalism and why this country has a federal form of government.
4.2 Identify the powers delegated and denied to the National Government.
4.3 Analyze the division of powers and concurrent powers between National and State governments.
4.4 Demonstrate understanding of the role of the Supreme Court in the federal system.

Bellringer Activity Before you begin the section, ask students: Name three State or federal laws that affect you in your day-to-day activities. Use student suggestions to create a class list on the chalkboard. You may want to have students indicate which are federal and which are State laws.

State the Purpose Federalism is a system of government in which a written constitution divides the powers of government on a territorial basis. In Section 1, students will learn about the division of powers between the National Government and the States, how those powers are embodied in the Constitution, and the role of the Supreme Court in the federal system.

Vocabulary

Point out to students "Key Terms" on page 73. Discuss with students the concept of power in relation to their own experiences as students. Who has the power over aspects of their daily lives, and where is the power derived from? Work toward a definition of power as the ability to influence or control something or someone. You may wish to discuss why the Framers of the Constitution were so concerned about issues of power. LEP

Reading Strategy: Structured Overview/Graphic Organizer

Put "Key Terms" on one side of the chalkboard. Have students preview the section headings and identify the main concept as federalism. Write *Federalism: Division of Powers* on the other side of the chalkboard as the main heading in a chart. You might include National Government and State Government as subheadings. Work with students to choose the words and concepts most closely related to the headings.

INSTRUCT

Discuss/Analyze Briefly outline the division of powers between the Federal Government and the State government as provided by the Constitution. To clarify the various divisions of power, have students turn to the graph "The Division of Powers Between the National Government and the States" on p. 76. Divide students into groups representing each of the six categories in the graph. Have each group study the text to create a definition and give examples of its category. The group should choose a recorder to write down the definition and examples and a speaker to read this information to the other groups. As groups share their work, encourage students to challenge any questionable definitions or examples.

Interpreting Political Cartoons Ask students what other item, besides welfare, the cartoonist might have had the man carry. *(Education, health care, etc.)*

Caption Answer The cartoon shows that some powers overlap and that conflicts often arise concerning which level of government has responsibility.

powers in the American federal system. This section will help you to understand that complicated matter.

Federalism Defined

1.a **Federalism** is a system of government in which a written constitution divides the powers of government on a territorial basis. The division is made between a central, or national, government and several regional or local governments. Each level of government has its own area of powers. Neither level, acting alone, can change the basic division of powers the constitution makes between them. Each level operates through its own agencies and acts directly on the people through its own officials and laws.

The Constitution sets out the basic design of the American federal system. The document provides for a division of powers between the National Government and the States. That
1.b **division of powers** was implied in the original Constitution and then spelled out in the 10th Amendment:

"The powers not delegated to the United States by the Constitution, nor prohibited by it to the States, are reserved to the States respectively, or to the people."

In effect, federalism produces a dual system of government. It provides for two basic levels of government, each with its own sphere of authority. Each operates over the same people and territory at the same time.

Federalism's major strength is that it allows local actions in matters of local concern and national action in matters of wider concern. Local traditions, needs, and desires vary from one State to another, and federalism allows for this very significant fact.

Illustrations of the point are nearly endless. For example, most forms of gambling are legal in Nevada but are against the law in most other States. New Jersey buses private as well as public school students free of charge, but most States do not. Nebraska is the only State with a one-house, or unicameral, legislature. Only in North Carolina does the governor not have the power to veto acts of the legislature; only North Dakota does not require voter registration.

Federalism allows and encourages local choice in many matters. It also provides for the strength that comes from union. National defense and foreign affairs offer useful illustrations of the point. So, too, do domestic affairs. Take, for example, a natural disaster.

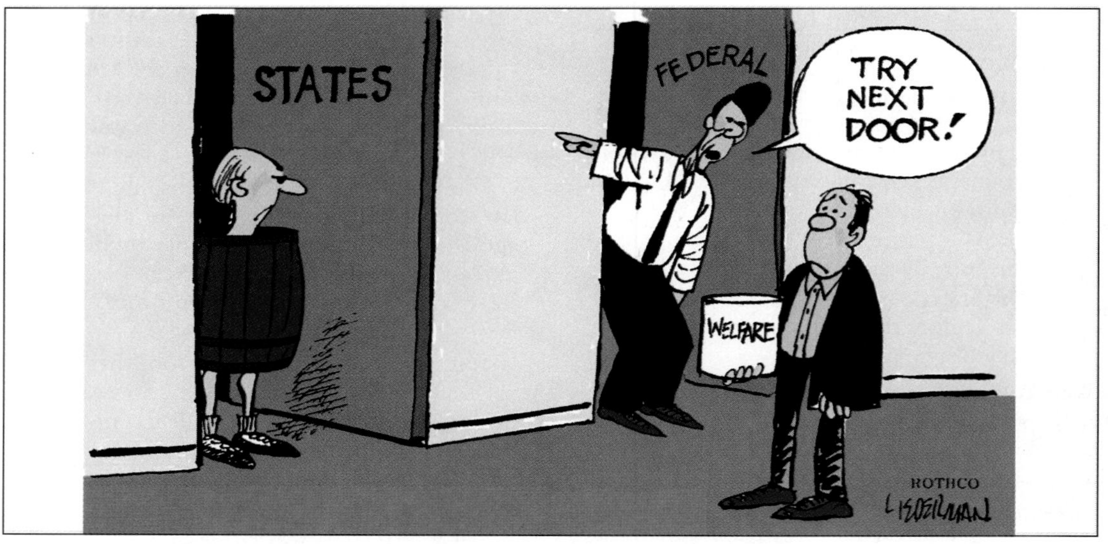

Interpreting Political Cartoons Federalism, like any governmental system, is not without its problems. What particular problem does this cartoon illustrate?

SPOTLIGHT ON: Roots of Democracy

The roots of the federal system can be traced back over 3000 years to the ancient Israelites, who combined their tribes to maintain national unity in the 13th century B.C. Ten centuries later, the Greeks applied federal principles in forming leagues of city-states, primarily for defensive purposes. The Achaen League (280-146 B.C.) was foremost among these. Taxes were collected, an army was raised from Achae's eleven member states, and the federal government—headed by a general who was elected president and served also as commander-in-chief—established uniform weights and measures and a federal judiciary.

When a flood, drought, winter storm, or other catastrophe hits some State, the resources of the National Government and all of the other States may be mobilized to aid the stricken area.

The National Government Is One of Delegated Powers

The National Government is a government of **delegated powers**. That is, it has only those 1.c
powers granted to it in the Constitution. Three distinct types of delegated powers exist: the expressed, the implied, and the inherent powers.

The Expressed Powers The **expressed** 1.d
powers are those delegated to the National Government in so many words—spelled out expressly in the Constitution.

You can find most of the expressed powers in Article I, Section 8. There, in 18 clauses, the Constitution expressly gives 27 powers to Congress. They include the power to lay and collect taxes, to coin money, to regulate foreign and interstate commerce, to raise and maintain armed forces, to declare war, to fix standards of weights and measures, to grant patents and copyrights, and to do many other things.

Note that the Constitution sets out several powers in other places, too. Thus, Article II, Section 2 gives several powers to the President. They include the power to act as commander in chief of the armed forces, to grant reprieves and pardons, to make treaties, and to name major federal officials. Article III grants "the judicial power of the United States" to the Supreme Court and other courts in the federal judiciary. Various amendments to the Constitution also contain several of the expressed powers; for example, the 16th Amendment gives Congress the power to levy an income tax.

The Implied Powers The **implied powers** 1.e
are those that are not expressly stated in the Constitution but are reasonably implied by those powers that are.

The constitutional basis for the implied powers is found in one of the expressed powers. Article I, Section 8, Clause 18 gives to Congress the "necessary and proper" power. The Necessary and Proper Clause says that Congress shall have the power:

> "to make all laws which shall be necessary and proper for carrying into execution the foregoing powers, and all other powers vested by this Constitution in the Government of the United States, or in any department or officer thereof."

Through congressional and court interpretation, the words "necessary and proper" have come to mean, in effect, "convenient and expedient." Indeed, the Necessary and Proper Clause is sometimes called the Elastic Clause because, over time, it has been stretched to cover so much.

Here are but a few of the thousands of examples of the exercise of implied powers: Congress has provided for the regulation of labor-management relations, the building of hydroelectric power dams, and the building of a 42,000-mile interstate highway system. It has made federal crimes of such acts as moving stolen goods, gambling devices, and kidnapped persons across State lines. It has prohibited racial discrimination in access to such places as restaurants, theaters, hotels, and motels. Congress has taken these actions, and many more, because the power to do so is reasonably implied by just *one* of the expressed powers: the power to regulate foreign and interstate commerce.[1]

The Inherent Powers The **inherent pow-** 1.f
ers are those that belong to the National Government because it is the national government of a sovereign state in the world community. Although the Constitution does not expressly provide for them, they are powers that national governments have historically possessed. It stands to reason that the Framers intended that the National Government they created would hold these powers.

The inherent powers are few in number. The chief ones include the power to regulate immigration, to deport aliens, to acquire territory, to give diplomatic recognition to other states, and to protect the nation against rebellion or internal subversion.

---

[1]Article I, Section 8, Clause 3. The doctrine of implied powers is treated in greater detail in Chapter 11.

ABC NEWS INTERACTIVE

The following video segments may be used to highlight aspects of federalism.

POWERS OF THE CONGRESS GUIDEBOOK
Chapter 11: The Federal System, p. 87
Chapter 12: Division of Powers, p. 88
Chapter 13: Powers of the Federal Government, p. 89
Chapter 14: Powers of State Government, p. 89
Chapter 15: Shared Powers, p. 91
Chapter 16: Powers of Local Government, p. 92

See also Enrichment Questions and Activities Guidebook beginning on page 161.

SPOTLIGHT ON: Economics

Presidents have declared an average of 24 disaster areas annually, with funding to each site averaging $12 million since 1979, when the Federal Emergency Management Office (FEMA) was formed to oversee federal disaster relief. According to FEMA, the number of disasters can vary dramatically from year to year. In 1991, for example, 36 sites were declared disaster areas, but in 1988 there were only 11. The largest single federal relief package ever created totaled $2.6 billion and followed Hurricane Hugo, which devastated the Carolinas, Puerto Rico, and the Virgin Islands in September of 1989.

Interpreting Graphs Ask students to name one concurrent power, as directed in the caption. You may want to ask the students to identify one power in each area of the graph.

Caption Answer Concurrent powers include: laying and collecting taxes, defining crimes and setting punishments, and taking private property for public use.

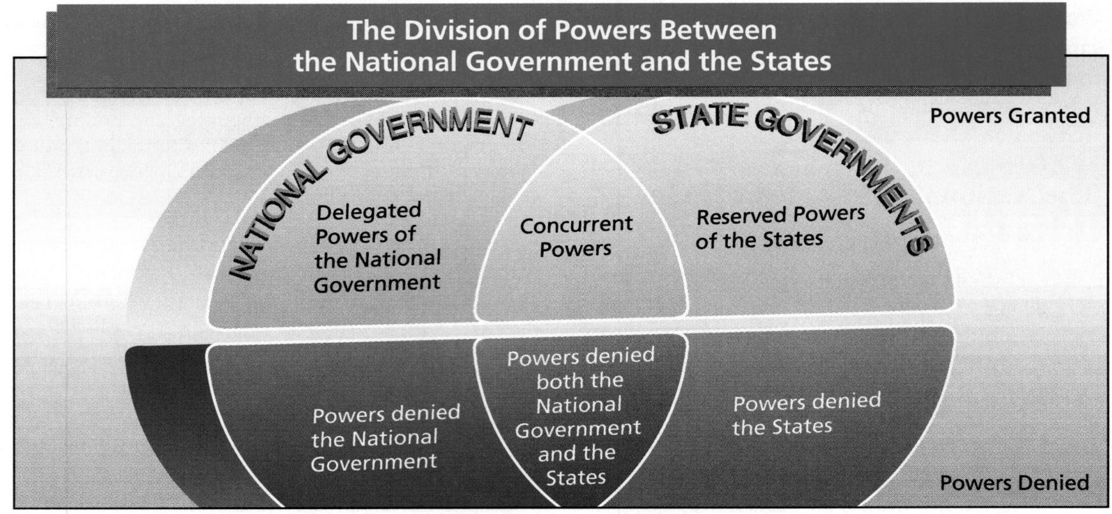

Interpreting Graphs Federalism determines the way that powers are divided between and shared among the National and State governments. Name one concurrent power.

One can argue that most of the inherent powers are implied by one or more of the expressed powers. For example, the power to regulate immigration is suggested by the expressed power to regulate foreign trade. The power to acquire territory can be drawn from the treaty-making power and the several war powers. But the doctrine of inherent powers holds that it is not necessary to go to those lengths to find these powers in the Constitution. In short, these powers exist because the United States exists.

Powers Denied to the National Government

Although the Constitution delegates certain powers to the National Government, it also denies certain powers to it. The Constitution does so in three distinct ways.

First, the Constitution denies some powers to the National Government in so many words—expressly.[2] Among them are the power to levy duties on exports; to deny freedom of religion, speech, press, or assembly; to conduct illegal searches or seizures; and to deny to any person a speedy and public trial, or a trial by jury.

Second, several powers are denied to the National Government because of the silence of the Constitution. Recall, the National Government is a government of delegated powers; it has only those powers the Constitution gives to it. Among the many powers not granted to the National Government are these: to create a public school system for the nation, to enact uniform marriage and divorce laws, and to set up units of local government. The Constitution says nothing that would give the National Government the power to do any of these things—expressly, implicitly, or inherently.

Third, some powers are denied to the National Government because the Constitution established a federal system for the United States. Clearly the Constitution does not intend that the National Government should have any power to do those things that would threaten the existence of that system. For example, in the exercise of its power to tax, Congress cannot tax any of the States or their local units in the carrying out of their governmental

[2]Most of the expressed denials of power are found in Article I, Section 9 and in the 1st through the 8th amendments.

Spotlight on: Muticulturalism

The Federal Government set its first broad immigration restrictions in 1924, with the passage of the National Origins Act. Before that, ethnic groups were selectively excluded from immigration to America, beginning with the Chinese Exclusion Act of 1882. The National Origins Act established a uniform quota system to stem the tide that brought some 28 million immigrants to the U.S. between 1860 and World War I. The quota system allowed entry to only 165,000 immigrants per year, heavily favoring English-speaking and German immigrants over all other immigrants. The 1976 Immigration and Naturalization Act replaced the quota system, making skill-level and the reuniting of families the primary criteria for immigration to the United States.

functions. If it could, it would have the power to destroy the States by taxing them out of existence.[3]

The States Are Governments of Reserved Powers

The Constitution reserves power to each of the States. The **reserved powers** are the powers held by the States in the federal system. They are those powers not given to the National Government and yet, at the same time, are not denied to the States. Read again the words of the 10th Amendment in the Constitution on page 738.

Thus, any State can forbid persons under 18 to marry without parental consent or those under 21 to buy liquor. A State can require that doctors, lawyers, hairdressers, or plumbers be licensed in order to practice in the State. The State can set up public school systems and units of local government, set the conditions under which it grants divorces, and permit certain forms of gambling and outlaw others.

The sphere of powers held by each State is huge. They can do all of those things just mentioned and much more because the Constitution does not forbid them to do so. At the same time, the National Government can do none of those things because the Constitution does not give it the power to do so. The power to do those things is reserved to the States.

Powers Denied to the States

As you know, the Constitution denies many powers to the National Government. Similarly, it forbids the States the power to do a great number of things.

The Constitution denies some powers to the States in so many words.[4] For example, no State can enter into any treaty, alliance, or confederation. Nor can a State print or coin money or deprive any person of life, liberty, or property without due process of law.

Some powers are also denied to the States by the existence of the federal system. Thus, no State or local government can tax any of the agencies or functions of the National Government. 1.g Remember, too, that each State has its own constitution—and that document also denies many powers to the State.[5]

The Federal System and Local Governments

Government in the United States is often discussed in terms of three layers: national, State, and local. However convenient this view may be, it is at best misleading. Recall, there are *two* basic levels in the federal system: the National Government and the 50 States.

Governments do exist at the local level all across the country, of course. In fact, there are more than 80,000 units of local government in the United States today. You will take a look at them later in this book; but for now, keep this important point in mind: All of these thousands of local governments are parts—subunits—of the various States.

Each of these local units is located within one of the 50 States. None has an existence apart from its parent State. In its constitution and in its laws, each of the States has created these units. To whatever extent any of these local governments can provide services, regulate activities, collect taxes, or do anything else, they can do so only because the State has established them and given them the power to do so. In short, as local governments exercise the powers they possess, they are actually exercising State powers. Another way of putting all of this is to remind you of a point that was first made in Chapter 1. Each of the 50 States has a unitary form of government.

---

[3]But note that when a State, or one of its local units, performs a so-called nongovernmental function—for example, operating liquor stores, a bus system, a farmer's market, and so forth—it is liable to federal taxes.

[4]Most of the expressed prohibitions of power to the States and, so, to their local governments are found in Article I, Section 10 and in the 13th, 14th, 15th, 19th, 24th, and 26th amendments.

[5]Study your own State's constitution on this point, and note the significance of the words "or to the people" in the 10th Amendment of the United States Constitution.

Provide Guided Practice On the chalkboard write the headings "Expressed Powers," "Implied Powers," and "Inherent Powers." List the following examples of each power and ask students to indicate in what category each example fits:

regulate immigration *(inherent)*
collect taxes *(expressed)*
coin money *(expressed)*
regulation of labor relations *(implied)*
building of dams *(implied)*
building highways *(implied)*
give diplomatic recognition *(inherent)*
prohibit discrimination *(implied)*
declare war *(expressed)*

You may also ask volunteers to provide additional examples for each category.

Provide Independent Practice

TRF **Teacher's Resource File** You may wish to assign the Section 1 Guided Reading and Review, Unit 1 File, p. 66, to help students master section objective content.

Enrichment

Have students create a simulation of the case *McCulloch* v. *Maryland.* Have nine students act as Supreme Court justices while others prepare verbal arguments outlining the dispute between the state of Maryland and the Federal Government. Students should draw upon the Constitution and the actual court decision in preparing their written and verbal arguments. (Challenging)

Interpreting Tables Ask students to identify the types of governments included in the table, and to name the basic structures of their own local government.

Caption Answer No. Local governments exercise only those powers granted to them by the State.

Governments in the United States

Type of Government	Number of Governments
Federal	1
State	50
Local	
County	3,042
Municipality	19,200
Township	16,691
School district	14,721
Other special district	29,532
Total	**83,237**

Source: Bureau of the Census, Census of Governments, 1987. The Census Bureau surveys all units of government in the United States every five years. The next census of governments will be conducted in 1992.

Interpreting Tables The table shows how federalism divides the powers of government. Do the thousands of local governments have powers other than those granted to them by the States?

The Exclusive Powers

1.h The **exclusive powers** are those that can be exercised only by the National Government. They include most of the delegated powers.

Some of the delegated powers are also expressly denied to the States—for example, the powers to coin money, make treaties with foreign states, and lay import duties. Thus, these powers belong solely to the National Government.

Some of the powers given to the National Government but not expressly denied to the States are also among the exclusive powers because of the nature of the particular powers involved. For example, the States are not expressly denied the power to regulate interstate commerce. However, if they could do so, trade would be at best chaotic, and at worst impossible. Therefore, States cannot exercise this power.[6]

[6]The States cannot regulate interstate commerce as such, but they do affect it. For example, in regulating highway speeds, the States regulate vehicles not only operating wholly within the State, but also those operating from State to State. Generally, the States can affect interstate commerce, but they may not impose an unreasonable burden on it.

The Concurrent Powers

1.i The **concurrent powers** are those that both the National Government and the States possess and exercise. They include, for example, the power to lay and collect taxes, to define crimes and set punishments for them, and to take private property for public use.

The concurrent powers are not held and exercised jointly by the two basic levels of the Federal Government. Rather, they are held and exercised separately and simultaneously. To rephrase the definition: The concurrent powers are those powers that the Constitution does not grant exclusively to the National Government and that, at the same time, it does not deny to the States.

The Supreme Law of the Land

The division of powers in the American federal system is a very complicated matter, as the diagram on page 76 shows. Again, it produces a dual system of government, one in which two basic levels of government operate over the same territory and the same people at the same time.

Clearly, such an arrangement is bound to result in conflicts between national law and State law. The Framers anticipated those conflicts—and so, they wrote the Supremacy Clause into the Constitution.

In Article VI, Section 2 the Constitution declares:

"This Constitution, and the laws of the United States which shall be made in pursuance thereof, and all treaties made, or which shall be made, under the authority of the United States, shall be the supreme law of the land . . . ."

Significantly, Article VI goes on to add:

". . . and the judges in every State shall be bound thereby, anything in the constitution or laws of any State to the contrary notwithstanding."

The Constitution and the laws and treaties of the United States are "the supreme law of the land." This means that the Constitution stands above all other forms of law in the United

TRF **Teacher's Resource File**
See the Supreme Court Cases File, pp. 19–22, for cases to support this section.

ACTIVITY: For Gifted Students
Theme: Systems After students have studied the concept of concurrent powers, remind them that both State governments and the Federal Government have shared power for defining educational standards and obligations for all public school systems. Have students survey teachers, school administrators, parents, and students to determine their school or community's attitude toward the development of a national curriculum to be used in all public schools. Have students present their findings through the publication of an informative newsletter.

States. Acts of Congress and treaties stand immediately beneath it.[7]

In other words, the Supremacy Clause creates a "ladder of laws" in the United States. The Constitution stands on the topmost rung. Then come the acts of Congress and treaties. Each State's constitution, supreme over all other forms of that State's law, stands beneath all forms of federal law. State statutes are on the next rung. At the base of the ladder are the different forms of local law: city and county charters and ordinances, and so forth.

The Supremacy Clause has been called the "linchpin of the Constitution," for it joins the National Government and the States into a single governmental unit, a federal state.

The Supreme Court and the Federal System The Supreme Court is the umpire in the federal system—for one of its chief duties is to apply the Supremacy Clause to the conflicts which that dual system of government inevitably produces.

The Court was first called on to play this role—to settle a clash between a national and a State law—in 1819. The case, *McCulloch* v. *Maryland*, involved the controversial Second Bank of the United States. The Bank had been chartered by Congress in 1816. In 1818 the Maryland legislature, hoping to cripple the bank, placed a tax on all notes issued by its Baltimore branch. James McCulloch, the branch cashier, refused to pay the tax, and the Maryland courts convicted him for that refusal.

The Supreme Court unanimously reversed the Maryland courts, however. Speaking for the Court, Chief Justice John Marshall based the decision squarely on the Constitution's Supremacy Clause:

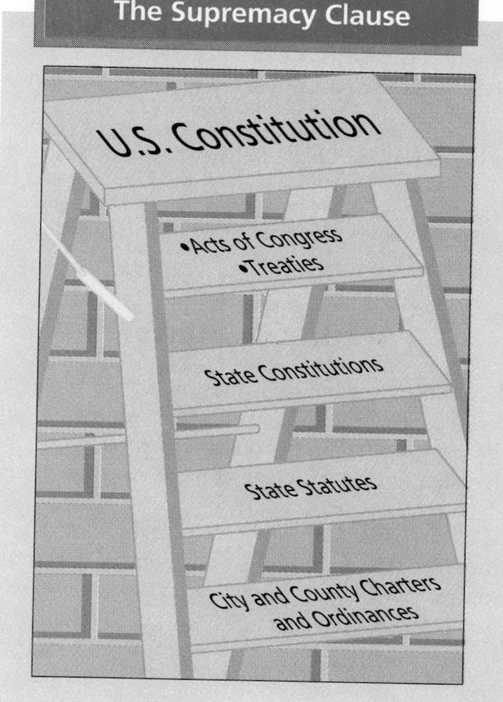

Interpreting Graphs This "ladder of laws" was created by the Supremacy Clause of the Constitution. Which branch of government decides conflicts between National and State governments?

"If any one proposition could command the universal assent of mankind we might expect it to be this—that the government of the Union, though limited in its powers, is supreme within its sphere of action . . . . [T]he States have no power to retard, impede, burden, or in any manner control, the operation of the constitutional laws enacted by Congress."[8]

It is impossible to overstate the significance of the Court's function—past and present—as the umpire of the federal system. Had the Court not

[7]Acts of Congress and treaties stand on equal planes with one another. Neither can conflict with any provision in the Constitution. In the rare case of conflict between the provisions of an act and those of a treaty, the one more recently adopted takes precedence—as the latest expression of the sovereign people's will. The Supreme Court has regularly held to that position from the first case it decided on the point, *The Head Money Cases,* 1884.

[8]The case is also critically important in the development of the constitutional system because, in deciding it, the Court for the first time upheld the doctrine of implied powers. It also held the National Government to be immune from any form of State taxation.

Interpreting Graphs Discuss with students the importance of the Supreme Court. Ask: Why might it be so important to have a supremely authoritative body of law? *(Possible answer: To avoid endless legal conflict within a federal system.)*

Caption Answer Conflicts between National and State governments are decided by the Supreme Court.

SPOTLIGHT ON: Constitutional Issues

When the Supreme Court, as "umpire" of the federal system, renders judgments unpopular with the States, the rules can be changed. The 11th Amendment, which prevents citizens of a State, or from a foreign country, from suing another State, was born in this fashion in 1795. When two South Carolinians sued the State of Georgia over confiscated property in 1793, in the case of *Chisolm* v. *Georgia*, the Court held that the Constitution gives federal courts explicit jurisdiction in "controversies between a state and citizens of another state," and ruled in favor of the plaintiff (Chisolm, *et. al.*). Disgruntled representatives in Congress quickly proposed the first post-Bill of Rights amendment to the Constitution to protect the long-established right of any sovereignty not to be sued without its own consent.

MONITOR COMPREHENSION

Answers to Section 1 Review

1. "Key Terms" are defined on the following pages:

a. federalism, page 74
b. division of powers, page 74
c. delegated powers, page 75
d. expressed powers, page 75
e. implied powers, page 75
f. inherent powers, page 75
g. reserved powers, page 77
h. exclusive powers, page 78
i. concurrent powers, page 78

2. Allows local action in matters of local concern, national action in matters of wider concern.
3. National Government has only those powers delegated to it. All other powers are reserved for States, except those specifically denied. **4.** (a) Powers are denied expressly, by the silence of the Constitution, and the federal system. (b) The federal system. **5.** The Constitution.
6. First time the Court settled a clash between State and federal law. **7.** (a) To ensure National Government's authority. (b) States might compete economically or militarily.

CLOSURE

Remind students that federalism is a system of government in which a written constitution divides power between the National Government and the States. In the next section students will learn how the Constitution defines the relationship between the National Government and the States.

Assignment Assign Section 2, pages 80–86, for the next class period.

taken this role, the federal system and probably the United States itself could not have survived its early years. Justice Oliver Wendell Holmes once made the point in these words:

> "I do not think that the United States would come to an end if we [the Court] lost our power to declare an act of Congress void. I do think the Union would be imperiled if we could not make that declaration as to the laws of the several States."[9]

Section 1 Review

1. Define: federalism, division of powers, expressed powers, implied powers, inherent powers, exclusive powers, concurrent powers
2. What is the chief advantage of the federal system?
3. For what reason is the National Government properly described as a government of delegated powers and the States as governments of reserved powers?
4. (a) On what three bases are powers denied to the National Government? (b) To the States?
5. What is the "supreme law of the land"?
6. What is the significance of *McCulloch* v. *Maryland* in the development of the federal system?

Critical Thinking

7. Predicting Consequences (p. 19) The States are denied the power to make treaties. (a) In your opinion, what is the reason for this denial of power? (b) What might happen if States had this power?

★

[9] *Collected Legal Papers* (New York: Harcourt, 1920), pp. 295–296. The Supreme Court first held a State law unconstitutional in a case from Georgia, *Fletcher v. Peck,* 1810. The Court found that a Georgia law of 1795, making a grant of land to John Peck, amounted to a contract between the State and Peck. It ruled that the legislature's later repeal of that law violated the Constitution's Contract Clause (Article I, Section 10, Clause 1): "No State shall . . . pass any . . . law impairing the obligations of contracts." Since then, the Court has found more than 1,000 State laws unconstitutional (and has upheld the constitutionality of thousands of others).

2 The National Government and the 50 States

Find Out:

- What are the obligations of the National Government to the States under the Constitution?
- What kinds of aid does the National Government grant to the States?
- What kinds of aid do the States provide the National Government?

Key Terms:

enabling act, act of admission, grants-in-aid program, block grant

Have you ever thought about, analyzed, or really focused on the words "the United States"? The United States is a union of States, the several States joined together, the States united.

The Constitution created and intends to preserve that Union. To that end, as you will see in this section, the Constitution (1) requires the National Government to guarantee certain things to the several States and (2) makes it possible for the National Government to do several things for the States.

The Nation's Obligations to the States

The Constitution places several obligations on the National Government for the benefit of the States. Most of them are to be found in Article IV.

Guarantee of a Republican Form of Government The Constitution requires the National Government to "guarantee to every State in this Union a republican form of government."[10] The Constitution does not define "republican form of government," and the Supreme Court has regularly refused to do so. The term is generally understood to mean a representative government, however.

[10] Article IV, Section 4.

Reteach

Refer students back to the graph on page 76 and have them reproduce it in larger format. Then have students add at least two examples of each type of power in the appropriate section of the graph. Students may retain these graphs as tools for review.

Teacher's Resource File
See the Unit 1 File, page 67, for the Section 1 Quiz.

SPOTLIGHT ON: Political Talk

The way that ordinary citizens have used the noun *United States* shows how popular attitudes on the concept of federalism have changed over time. From the birth of the nation until the Civil War, for example, people generally used the name as a plural noun—saying "The United States are..." This usage emphasized the individuality of the States at a time when people thought of themselves as citizens of their State. Since then, people have referred to the nation in the singular—i.e. "The United States is..."—a usage stressing the singularity of the Union rather than the separateness of the States.

The Supreme Court has held that the question of whether or not a State has a republican form of government is a political question. That is, it is one to be decided by the political branches of the government—the President and Congress—and not by the courts.

The leading case here is *Luther* v. *Borden*, 1849. It grew out of Dorr's Rebellion, a revolt led by Thomas W. Dorr against the State of Rhode Island in 1841–1842. Dorr and his followers had written and proclaimed a new constitution for the State.[11] When they tried to put the new document into operation, however, the governor in office under the original constitution declared martial law—temporary rule by military authorities. The governor also called on the Federal Government for help. President John Tyler then took steps to put down the revolt, and it quickly collapsed.

The question of which of the competing governments was the legitimate one was a major issue in *Luther* v. *Borden*. But, again, the Supreme Court refused to decide the matter.

The only extensive use ever made of the republican-form guarantee came in the years following the Civil War. Congress declared that several southern States did not have governments of a republican form. It refused to admit Senators and Representatives from those States until the States had ratified the 13th, 14th, and 15th amendments and broadened their laws to recognize the voting and other rights of African Americans.

Protection Against Invasion and Domestic Violence The National Government must also "protect each of them [States] against invasion; and on application of the legislature, or of the executive (when the legislature cannot be convened), against domestic violence."[12]

Today it is clear that an invasion of any one of the 50 States would be met as an attack on the United States itself. Hence, this constitutional guarantee is now of little, if any, significance.

However, that was not the case in the late 1780s. Then, it was not at all certain that all 13 States would stand together if a foreign power attacked one of them. So, before the 13 States agreed to give up their war-making powers, each demanded an ironclad pledge that an attack on any of them would be met as an attack on all.

The federal system assumes that each of the 50 States will keep the peace within its own borders. Thus, the primary responsibility for curbing insurrection, riot, or other internal disorder rests with the individual States. However, the Constitution does accept the fact that a State might not be able to control some situations. So, it guarantees protection against domestic violence in each of them.

Historically, the use of federal force to restore order within a State has been a rare event. Several instances did occur in the 1960s, however. When racial unrest exploded into violence

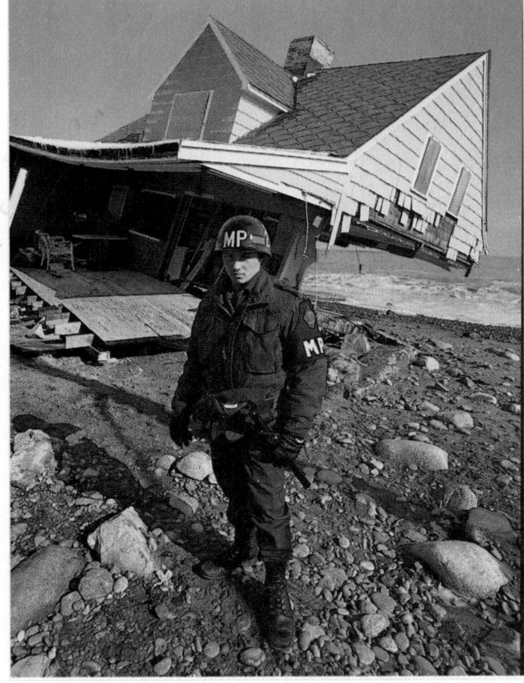

Nature's "Domestic Violence" When natural disasters strike, the federal government is obligated to send troops in to help devastated States recover.

[11]Rhode Island had not written a new constitution at the time of independence in 1775. Rhode Island's present constitution, which became effective in 1843, came as a direct result of Dorr's rebellion.

[12]Article IV, Section 4.

SECTION 2
The National Government and the 50 States

FOCUS

Teacher's Resource File See the Unit 1 File, p. 68, for the Section 2 Outline.

Objectives

4.5 Understand the obligations of the National Government to the States under the Constitution.

4.6 Identify the kinds of aid the National Government grants to the States.

4.7 Identify the kinds of aid the States provide the National Government.

Bellringer Activity Read the following quotation from Ronald Reagan's 1982 State of the Union Address: "The growth in Federal programs has...made the Federal Government 'more pervasive, more intrusive, more unmanageable, more ineffective and costly, and above all, more [un]accountable.'" Elicit student opinions about the quotation, and guide them into a discussion about the level of obligation the Federal Government has to the States.

State the Purpose The Constitution defines the relationship between the National Government and the States. In Section 2, students will learn about the obligations of the National Government to the States and ways they aid one another.

Vocabulary

Point out "Key Terms" on page 80 to students. Below are some additional words whose meanings may help students understand section content

—**obligation:** a duty or responsibility
—**ironclad:** so strong as to be unbreakable
—**plea:** a desperate appeal
—**revenue:** income for public use

LEP

Reading Strategy: Question Writing

As a preparation for reading, have students read the section's main headings. Then ask them to write down a question about each heading, and look for the answers to their questions as they read.

INSTRUCT

Explain Explain to students that the U.S. Constitution places several obligations on the National Government to the States and that there are also large areas of cooperation between the Federal Government and State governments. Then have students skim the section to find what the National Government's obligations are. *(Guarantee of a republican form of government, protection against invasion and domestic violence, and respect for the territorial integrity of each State.)* Write each on the board as students give the answers. Then ask students for examples of how the National Government has met each example. Then write the term *cooperative federalism* on the board, and ask students to name examples of this term. *(Grants-in-aid; block grants; State aid to National Government in the form of elections, naturalization and assistance in catching and holding criminals.)*

Other examples of cooperative federalism include the FBI, "lulu payments" (payments to local governments where there are large federal landholdings paid in lieu of taxes), Census Bureau data, administration of elections and naturalization procedures, and local police support for seeking fugitives from federal justice.

in Detroit during the "long, hot summer" of 1967, President Lyndon Johnson ordered units of the regular army into the city. He acted at the request of Michigan's Governor George Romney, and only after Detroit's police and firefighters, supported by State Police and National Guard units, could not control riots, arson, and looting in the city. In 1968, again at the request of the governors involved, federal troops were sent into Chicago and Baltimore to help put down the violence that erupted following the assassination of Martin Luther King, Jr.

Normally, a President has sent troops into a State only in answer to a request from its governor or legislature. But when national laws are being broken, national functions interfered with, or national property endangered, a President does not need to wait for such a plea.[13]

The ravages of nature—storms, floods, drought, forest fires, and such—can be more destructive than human violence. Here, too, acting to protect the States against "domestic violence," the Federal Government stands ready to aid stricken areas.

Respect for Territorial Integrity

The National Government is constitutionally bound to respect the territorial integrity of each of the States. That is, the National Government must recognize the legal existence and the physical boundaries of each State.

The whole scheme of the Constitution imposes this obligation. Several of its provisions do so, as well. For example, Congress must include, in both of its houses, members chosen in each one of the States.[14] Acting alone, Congress cannot create a new State from territory belonging to any one of the existing States. To do so, Congress first must have the consent of the legislature of the State involved.[15] Recall, also, Article V of the Constitution declares that no State can be deprived of its equal representation in the United States Senate without its own consent.

Admitting New States

Only Congress has the power to admit new States to the Union. The Constitution places only one restriction on that power. A new State cannot be created by taking territory from one or more of the existing States without the consent of the legislature(s) of the State(s) involved.[16]

Congress has admitted 37 States since the original 13 formed the Union. Five States—Vermont, Kentucky, Tennessee, Maine, and West Virginia—were created from parts of already existing States. Texas was an independent republic before admission. California was admitted shortly after being ceded to the United States by Mexico. Each of the other 30 States entered the Union only after a longer period of time, frequently more than 15 years, as an organized territory.

Admission Procedure The process of admission is usually simple. The area desiring Statehood first petitions Congress for admission.

[13]President Grover Cleveland ordered federal troops to put an end to rioting in the Chicago railyard during the Pullman Strike in 1894 despite the objections of Governor William Altgeld of Illinois. The Supreme Court upheld his actions in *In re Debs,* 1896. The Court found that rioters had threatened federal property and impeded the flow of the mails and interstate commerce. Thus, more than domestic violence was involved. Since then, several Presidents have acted without a request from the State involved. Most recently, President Dwight Eisenhower did so at Little Rock, Arkansas, in 1957, and President John Kennedy at the University of Mississippi in 1962 and at the University of Alabama in 1963. In each of those instances, the President acted to halt the unlawful obstruction of school integration orders issued by federal courts.

[14]In the House, Article I, Section 2, Clause 1; in the Senate, Article I, Section 3, Clause 1 and the 17th Amendment.

[15]Article IV, Section 3, Clause 1.

[16]Article IV, Section 3, Clause 1. Some argue that this provision was violated with West Virginia's admission in 1863. That State was formed from the 40 western counties that had broken away from Virginia over the issue of secession from the Union. The consent required by the Constitution was given by a minority of the members of the Virginia legislature—those who represented the 40 western counties. Congress accepted their action, holding that they were the only group legally capable of acting as the Virginia legislature at the time.

SPOTLIGHT ON: Behind the Scenes

George Washington set the precedent for federal intervention in unruly States in 1794. Frontier farmers in western Pennsylvania who distilled whiskey from surplus grain often flagrantly evaded an excise tax the Federal Government had imposed on the spirits, and in July mobs of farmers prevented a federal marshal from summoning violators to court. Without a request from the governor of the State, Washington sent 15,000 troops to the region to put down the rebellion—even leading them part of the way! Although the troops met no resistance and Washington pardoned the two ringleaders convicted of treason, this show of force during the Whiskey Rebellion conveyed the clear message that violence would not be permitted as a means of protest against national law.

Teacher's Resource File
See the Simulations and Debates file for an activity to support this section.

If and when Congress chooses, it passes an **enabling act**, which directs the framing of 1.a
a proposed State constitution. A convention prepares the constitution, which is then put to a popular vote in the proposed State. If the voters approve the constitution, it is then submitted to Congress for its consideration. If Congress still agrees to Statehood after reviewing the document, it passes an **act of admission**. If the Pres- 1.b
ident signs the act, the new State enters the Union.

The two newest States, Alaska and Hawaii, abbreviated the usual process of gaining admission to the Union. Each adopted a proposed constitution without waiting for an enabling act—Alaska in 1956 and Hawaii in 1950. Both became States in 1959.

Conditions for Admission Before finally admitting a new State, Congress has often established certain conditions. For example, in 1896 Utah was admitted as a State on the condition that its constitution outlaw polygamy—the practice of having more than one spouse at the same time. In the act admitting Alaska to the Union as the 49th State, Congress forever prohibited that State from claiming title to any lands legally held by any Native American.

Each State enters the Union on an equal footing with each of the other States. Thus, although Congress can set certain conditions like those just described, it cannot impose conditions of a political nature on the States. For example, when Oklahoma was admitted to the Union in 1907, Congress said the State could not remove its capital from Guthrie to any other place before 1913. In 1910, however, the Oklahoma legislature moved the State's capital to Oklahoma City. When this step was challenged, the United States Supreme Court held, in *Coyle* v. *Smith*, 1911, that Congress can set conditions for a prospective State's

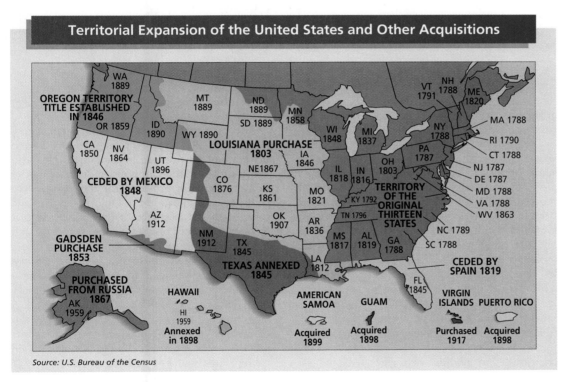

Territorial Expansion of the United States and Other Acquisitions

Interpreting Maps Thirty-seven States have joined the original 13 that formed the United States. Who must sign the act of admission of a new State?

ABCNEWS INTERACTIVE

The following video segments may be used to highlight aspects of the relationship between the National Government and State governments.

POWERS OF THE CONGRESS GUIDEBOOK
Chapter 61: Directory of States, page 67
Chapter 62: The Federal System, page 68

See also Enrichment Questions and Activities beginning on page 161.

Interpreting Maps As students analyze the map, you may wish to ask the following questions: In what year did our State became part of the United States? (*Answers will vary.*) What appears to be the relationship between geographical location and admission to the United States? (*States tended to be admitted from east to west.*) What States appear to be exceptions to that pattern?(*Exceptions are Florida, Arizona, New Mexico, and California.*)

Caption Answer The President must sign this act.

Teacher's Resource File
See the Historical and Legal Documents File, p. 22, for material to support this section.

VOICES *on Government*

L. Douglas Wilder, governor of Virginia and the first elected African-American governor in the United States

On the Federal Government and Education

"...there's an important federal role in education. I'm not talking about a federal curriculum, or federal regulations dictating what schools should teach. But the federal government has the responsibility to make sure that people are not denied educational opportunities because of their geographic location or their economic status."

admission. But, held the Court, the conditions cannot be enforced when they compromise the independence of a State to manage its own internal affairs.

Consider one more example here: President William Howard Taft vetoed a resolution to admit Arizona to the Union in 1911 because its proposed constitution provided that members of the State's judiciary could be recalled—removed from office—by popular vote. This provision meant, said Taft, that a judge would have to keep one eye on public opinion rather than leaving both eyes firmly focused onto matters of the law. In response to Taft's concern, Arizona then removed the recall section from the document. In 1912 Congress passed, and the President signed, another act of admission for Arizona. Almost immediately upon admission to the Union, however, the new State amended its new constitution to provide for the recall of judges. That provision remains a valid part of Arizona's constitution today.

Cooperative Federalism

As you know, federalism produces a dual system of government in the United States. Given this complex arrangement, it should come as no surprise that competition, tensions, and conflicts are a regular part of American federalism. In short, the American governmental system is like a tug-of-war—a continuing power struggle between the National Government and the States.

Keep in mind the central importance of the concept of divided powers in the American governmental system. Add to it this vital point: The American federal arrangement also involves a broad area of shared powers. That is, in addition to the two separate spheres of power held and exercised by the two basic levels of government, there are large and growing areas of cooperation between them.

Federal Grants-in-Aid Perhaps the best-known examples of this intergovernmental cooperation are the many federal **grants-in-aid**
1.c **programs**—grants of federal money or other resources to the States and/or their cities, counties, and other local units. These grants provide those levels of government with the funds often needed to carry out many of their functions.

The history of grants-in-aid programs goes back some 200 years—in fact, to the period before the Constitution. In the Northwest Ordinance of 1787, the Congress under the Articles of Confederation provided for the government of the territory beyond the Ohio River. Looking forward to the existence of new States on that frontier, the Congress set aside sections of land for the support of public education in those future States. On through the 19th century, States received grants of federal lands for a number of purposes—schools and colleges, roads and canals, flood control work, and several others. A large number of the major State universities, for example, were founded as land-grant colleges—schools built out of the sale of public lands given to the States by the Morrill Act of 1862.

Congress began to make grants of federal money quite early, too. In 1808 it gave the

Cooperation At Work This raffle provided much needed fix-up homes for just one dollar. The program was a cooperative venture between Federal and State agencies.

States $200,000 to support their militia. Cash grants did not come to play a large role until the Depression years of the 1930s, however. Much of the New Deal program aimed at bringing the nation out of its economic crisis was built around cash grants.

Since then, Congress has set up hundreds of grants-in-aid programs. In fact, more than 500 are now in operation. Dozens of programs function in many different areas: in education, mass transit, highway construction, health care, on-the-job training, and many others.

Grants-in-aid are based on the National Government's taxing power. Article I, Section 8, Clause 1 in the Constitution gives Congress that power in order

"... to pay the debts, and provide for the common defense and general welfare ...."

Over time, most grants have been both categorical and conditional. That is, Congress has made them for certain closely defined purposes, 1.d and it has set certain conditions that the States must meet in order to receive them. Most often, the major "strings" attached to a grant have required a State to (1) use the federal funds only for the purpose specified, (2) make its own contribution, often of an equal amount, sometimes much less, (3) set up an agency and procedures to manage the grant, and (4) obey the federal guidelines for which the aid is given.

In effect, the grants-in-aid process blurs the division-of-powers line in the federal system. It permits the Federal Government to operate in many areas in which it would otherwise have no constitutional authority—for example, public education and mental health programs.

Critics have long made that point in opposition to grant programs. Many also object to the narrowly defined, or categorical, nature of most grants. They insist that those factors give Washington too much control over policy matters that, they claim, should be set at the State and local levels.

Block Grants To meet this latter objection, some categorical grants have been combined into larger programs. Congress has converted them into **block grants**. These are grants to State and local governments with more broadly defined purposes and fewer strings attached.

By the early 1980s, federal grants accounted for approximately 25 percent of all State and local governmental expenditures. But, beginning

Provide Guided Practice
Write on the chalkboard: obligation of the National Government to the States(*republican government, protection against invasion and domestic violence, respect for territorial integrity, admittance of new States*), National Government aid to the States (*grants-in-aid, block grants, revenue sharing, "lulu payments," census information, National Guard equipment and training*), and States' aid to the National Government (*conduct elections, law enforcement aid, naturalization*). Have students provide specific examples for each category.

Provide Independent Practice
TRF **Teacher's Resource File**
You may wish to assign the Section 2 Guided Reading and Review, Unit 1 File, p. 69, to help students master section objective content.

Enrichment

Have students imagine they are current members of Congress. The people of Puerto Rico are requesting that Congress reconsider their refusal to grant them the opportunity to vote on whether or not they would like to become the 51st State. Have students write a speech to deliver to their colleagues that conveys their views on the subject. (Average)

OR

Teacher's Resource File
See the Unit 1 File, pp. 75–77, for the Case Study on Contemporary Issues for this chapter.

Activity: Cooperative Learning

Time: Two class periods **Activity:** Debate the issue of federal grants-in-aid. **Grouping:** Teams of four students **Purpose:** Have half the teams list arguments supporting federal grants-in-aid and the other teams list arguments opposing them. Suggest that groups use information obtained from local education, health, transportation, law enforcement, and other agencies receiving these grants to support their arguments. **Roles:** Have students assign the following roles: team leader, recorder. **Outcome:** Invite two teams to debate the issue in front of the class, then have the class evaluate the arguments of each team and vote on the winning team.

MONITOR COMPREHENSION

Answers to Section 2 Review
1. "Key Terms" are defined on the following pages:
a. enabling act, p. 83.
b. act of admission, p. 83
c. grants-in-aid program, p.84
d. block grant, page 85
2. (a) It was not clear that an attack on one State would be regarded as an attack on all. (b) States might need assistance. **3.** Congress may not create new States from existing ones without consent; include representatives from each State; each State has equal representation in Senate. **4.** (a) Congress. (b) Area desiring Statehood petitions Congress; which passes an enabling act; constitution approved, Congress passes act of admission. **5.** (a) Gives the National Government authority where Constitution did not intend. (b) Taxing power of Congress. **6.** Federal Government gave States a share of tax revenue. Reagan ended it to reduce the deficit. **7.** Regulate national elections; naturalization; help capture federal criminal suspects. **8.** Students may believe the Framers would disapprove because the grant gives the Federal Government power within States.

CLOSURE

Remind students that the Constitution defines the relationship between the National Government and the States. In the next section students will learn how several of the Constitution's provisions promote cooperation among the States.

Assignment Assign Section 3, pages 88–91, for the next class period.

in 1981, the Reagan Administration pushed hard for two major changes here: (1) a sharp cutback in overall grant spending, and (2) the conversion of most grant programs from a categorical to a block-grant format. As a result, federal grant monies now account for less than 20 percent of total State and local spending.

Revenue Sharing A different form of federal money aid, the revenue sharing program, was in place from 1972 to 1987. Under that arrangement, Congress gave an annual share of the huge federal tax collection to the States and their cities, counties, and townships. Altogether, those "shared revenues" amounted to more than $83 billion over the years the program was in force.

The revenue sharing program differed from the traditional grants-in-aid approach in a number of ways. Virtually no strings were attached to the money. The "shared revenues" could be spent very largely as the States and their local units chose to spend them.

Needless to say, revenue sharing was quite popular with and strongly supported by many governors, mayors, and other State and local officials. It was opposed by the Reagan Administration, however, and it fell victim to the financial needs of the deficit-ridden Federal Government.

Other Forms of Federal Aid The Federal Government aids the States in several other important ways. Some of the many illustrations are well known—for example, the FBI's extensive help to State and local police. But many forms of aid are not nearly so visible—for example, "lulu payments." These are federal monies that go to local governments in those areas in which there are large federal landholdings. These direct payments are made in lieu of—to take the place of—the property taxes that those local governments cannot collect from the Federal Government.

Other examples include: The army and the air force equip and train each State's National Guard units. The Census Bureaus are essential to State and local school, housing, and transportation officials as they plan for the future.

State Aid to the National Government Intergovernmental cooperation is a two-way street. That is, the States and their local units of government also aid the National Government in many ways. Thus, State and local election officials conduct national elections in each State. These elections are financed with State and local funds and are largely regulated by State laws.

The legal process by which aliens can become citizens, called naturalization, takes place most often in State, not federal, courts. Those who commit federal crimes and are sought by the FBI are often picked up by State and local police officers and then held in local jails. And the examples go on and on.

Section 2 Review

1. Define: enabling act, act of admission, grants-in-aid program, block grant
2. (a) For what reason does the Constitution obligate the National Government to protect each State against foreign invasion? (b) Domestic violence?
3. In what sense does the Constitution require the National Government to respect the territorial integrity of each State?
4. (a) Who has the exclusive power to admit new States? (b) How does that process generally work?
5. (a) On what grounds do some people oppose federal grants-in-aid? (b) Support them?
6. What was the revenue sharing program? What became of it?
7. In what ways do the States aid the National Government?

Critical Thinking

8. Recognizing Ideologies (p. 19) If the Framers were alive today, how do you think they would feel about a federal law that required States to raise the legal drinking age in order to receive federal grants for highway construction?

★

SPOTLIGHT ON: Political Talk

Changes in the allocation of federal monies to the States reflect a program known as "the New Federalism." New Federalism, a concept introduced by President Richard Nixon in 1969, is a response to the steady growth in the size and scope of federal programs since the Great Depression. In essence, New Federalism maintains that the States know best how to provide relief and other services to their own citizens; therefore, Federal Government programs should be reduced in these areas and authority transferred to the States.

Reteach

Write the following terms on the chalkboard in a random order: republican form of government, conduct national elections, block grants, protection/relief, naturalization. Ask volunteers to categorize individual items as either national obligations to the States or State obligations to the Union.

Teacher's Resource File
See the Unit 1 File, p. 70, for the Section 2 Quiz.

Debating Key Issues

Should Congress Set a National Drinking Age?

South Dakota v. *Elizabeth H. Dole*

Every year in the United States, 20,000 drunk drivers are involved in fatal accidents. Of that number, more than 3,000 are under the legal drinking age. In the early 1980s, many people attributed the high death rate to the variance in the legal drinking age from State to State. Young people often drove across a State border to legally buy and drink alcohol. While traveling back home, these intoxicated drivers frequently caused fatal accidents.

In an attempt to reduce the death toll, Congress passed the National Minimum Drinking Age Act in 1984. This statute mandated that any State that did not raise its legal drinking age to 21 would be denied a portion of its annual federal highway funds, a sum which could translate to tens of millions of dollars. Nine States, led by South Dakota, disputed the law. They said that it violated both the repeal of Prohibition and the sovereignty of the States.

In the United States district court, the lawyer for South Dakota argued that the measure exceeded the boundaries of congressional power and violated the 21st Amendment, which disposed of Prohibition. However, the State's claims were denied in both the district court and, later, on appeal. At this point, South Dakota appealed to the U.S. Supreme Court, naming Elizabeth H. Dole, United States Secretary of Transportation, as the defendant.

Review the following evidence and arguments presented to the United States Supreme Court:

Arguments for Elizabeth H. Dole

1. Congress did not overstep its bounds. It wrote the measure to provide for and advance the general welfare of United States citizens.
2. The statute was closely linked to the national concern for safe interstate travel, which falls under the jurisdiction of the Department of Transportation. The provisions concerning liquor were merely incidental to creating safe highways.
3. The percentage of highway funds withheld from the States was small. Any State could forgo the funds and set whatever drinking age it wished.

Arguments for South Dakota

1. Congress infringed on the sovereign rights of the States when it passed the National Minimum Drinking Age Act.
2. The act violates the 21st Amendment, which gave the States control over drinking ages. The concern for safe travel does not give the Federal Government the power to dictate drinking age.
3. The withholding of highway funds to influence the States is federal blackmail and abridges the States' constitutional rights.

Getting Involved

1. Identify the constitutional grounds on which each side based its arguments in this case.
2. Debate the opposing viewpoints presented in this case.
3. Predict how the Supreme Court ruled in this case and why. Now turn to the Supreme Court Glossary that begins on page 764 to read the decision. Discuss the effect of the Court's ruling on future struggles between Federal and State Governments.

TEACHING

Debating Key Issues

***South Dakota* v. *Elizabeth H. Dole*: Should Congress Set a National Drinking Age?**

Objective

Analyze and evaluate evidence.

INSTRUCT

Before students read the feature, you might want to elicit their answers to the question in the title. Ask students what might have caused Congress to consider a national drinking age. Students might also be asked what they think have been the effects of drinking and driving on young people. When students have finished reading the feature, work through the "Getting Involved" section.

SUPREME COURT DECISION

The Court upheld the right of the National Government to limit highway funds to States that did not qualify under the rules of "entitlement," thus requiring all States that wished to continue to receive full federal highway aid to raise to 21 years the legal age to purchase and consume alcohol. In recent years the Federal Government has attached similar "strings" to federal aid in a number of instances, including speed limits on interstate highways.

Teacher's Resource File
See the Supreme Court Cases file for an activity that extends coverage of this case.

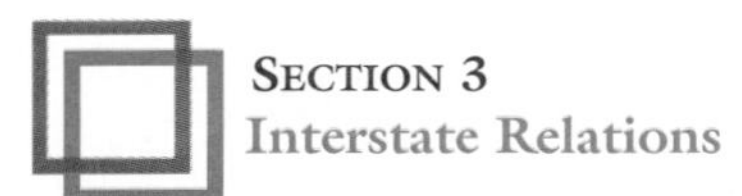

SECTION 3
Interstate Relations

FOCUS

Teacher's Resource File
See the Unit 1 File, page 71, for the Section 3 Outline.

Objective
4.8 Analyze how provisions of the Constitution promote cooperation between and among the States.

Bellringer Activity Before reading this section, write the word *cooperation* on the board and ask students to suggest definitions or synonyms, which may also be written on the board. Ask a volunteer to find the word in the dictionary and compare that definition with the class's.

State the Purpose The U.S. Constitution increased the power of the National Government and reduced conflict among the States. In Section 3, students will learn how provisions of the Constitution promote cooperation among the States.

ABCNEWS INTERACTIVE

The following video segment may be used to highlight aspects of interstate relations.

POWERS OF THE CONGRESS GUIDEBOOK
Chapter 62: The Federal System, page 68

See also Enrichment Questions and Activities beginning on page 161.

3 Interstate Relations

Find Out:

- How do several of the Constitution's provisions promote cooperation between and among the States?

Key Terms:

interstate compact, full faith and credit, extradition

You know that conflict among the States was a major reason for the adoption of the Constitution in 1789. The fact that the new document strengthened the hand of the National Government, especially in the field of commerce, lessened many of those interstate frictions. So, too, did several of the Constitution's provisions that deal directly with the States' relationships with one another. This section is concerned with those provisions.

Interstate Compacts

1.a No State can enter into any treaty, alliance, or confederation. The States may, however, with the consent of Congress, enter into **interstate compacts**—agreements among themselves and with foreign states.[17]

The States made only 26 compacts until 1920. Since then, however, and especially since the mid-1930s, they have been growing in number. New York and New Jersey led the way in 1921 with a compact creating the New York Port Authority to manage and develop the harbor facilities of that great metropolis.

[17]Article I, Section 10, Clause 3. The Supreme Court has held that congressional consent is not needed for compacts that do not "tend to increase the political power of the States," *Virginia* v. *Tennessee,* 1893. But it is often difficult to decide whether an agreement is political or nonpolitical. So, most interstate agreements are submitted to Congress as a matter of course.

Taming the Raging Colorado River The Glen Canyon Dam in Arizona is part of an extensive interstate compact that diverts the water of the river to 20 million people. Dams like this provide hydroelectricity for large areas.

Reading Strategy: Problem-Solving

Tell students: You are governor, and the governor of another State has requested that a parent and child in your State be extradited. That parent was not awarded custody in a recent divorce case, and moved to your State in an attempt to retain custody of the child. You have reason to believe that the court case was unfair. What should you do? Ask students to keep the problem in mind as they read, and make a decision when they have completed reading the section.

Vocabulary

Point out to students "Key Terms" on page 88. Discuss with students the concept of extradition as it relates to interstate relations. What do students think might be the importance of the process to the justice system? *(Possible answer: It would be too easy for criminals to escape punishment if extradition did not exist.)*

Some 200 compacts are now in force, and many involve several States. In fact, all 50 States have joined in two of them: the Compact for the Supervision of Parolees and Probationers and the Compact on Juveniles. These compacts enable States to share important law-enforcement data. Other agreements, many with multi-State membership, cover a widening range of subjects. They include, for example, compacts designed to coordinate the development and conservation of such resources as water, oil, wildlife, and fish; forest fire protection; stream and harbor pollution; tax collections; motor vehicle safety; the licensing of drivers; and the cooperative use of public universities.

Full Faith and Credit

The Constitution commands

> "Full faith and credit shall be given in each State to the public acts, records, and judicial proceedings of every other State."[18]

The words *public acts* refer to the laws of a State. *Records* refers to such documents as birth certificates, marriage licenses, deeds to property, car registrations, and the like. The words *judicial proceedings* relate to the outcome of court actions: judgments for debt, criminal convictions, divorce decrees, and so forth.

Suppose that a person dies in Baltimore and leaves a will disposing of some property in Chicago. The State of Illinois must give **full faith and credit** to—that is, respect the validity of—the proving of that will as a judicial proceeding of the State of Maryland. A person can prove age, place of birth, marital status, title to property, and similar facts by securing the necessary documents from the State where the record was made. 1.b

Exceptions The Full Faith and Credit Clause is regularly observed and usually operates in a routine way between and among the States. This rule has two exceptions, however. First, it applies only to civil, not criminal, matters. One State cannot enforce another State's criminal law. Second, full faith and credit need not be given to certain divorces granted by one State to residents of another State.

On the second exception, the key question is always this: Was the person who obtained the divorce in fact a resident of the State that granted it? If so, the divorce will be accorded full faith and credit in other States. If not, then the State granting the divorce did not have the authority to do so and another State can refuse to recognize it.

The matter of interstate "quickie" divorces has been a troublesome one for years. It has been so especially since the Supreme Court's decision in a 1945 case, *Williams* v. *North Carolina.* In that case, a man and a woman had traveled to Nevada, where each wanted to obtain a divorce so they could marry each other. They lived in Las Vegas for six weeks, the minimum period of State residence required by Nevada's divorce law. The couple received their divorces, were married, and then immediately returned to North Carolina. But that State's authorities refused to recognize their Nevada divorces. North Carolina brought the couple to trial and a jury convicted each of them of the crime of bigamous cohabitation—marrying and living together while a previous marriage is still legally in effect.

On appeal, the Supreme Court upheld North Carolina's denial of full faith and credit to the Nevada divorces. It ruled that the couple had not in fact established *bona fide*—good faith, or valid—residence in Nevada. Rather, the Court held that through all of this the couple had remained legal residents of North Carolina. In short, the Court found that Nevada did not have the authority to grant them divorces.

A divorce granted by a State court to a *bona fide* resident of that State must be given full faith and credit in all other States. To become a legal resident of a State, a person must intend to reside there permanently, or at least indefinitely. Clearly, the Williamses had not intended to do so.

The *Williams* case, and later ones, cast dark clouds of doubt over the validity of thousands of other interstate divorces. The later marriages of persons involved in them, and the frequently

---

[18]Article IV, Section 1.

INSTRUCT

Discuss Discuss with students the importance and benefits of each of the provisions in the U.S. Constitution regarding the States' relationships with one another. These provisions include: interstate compacts, the Full Faith and Credit Clause, extradition, and the Privileges and Immunities Clause.

Also, discuss the relative benefits to the States and to the National Government of their constitutional relationship to each other. Why has this system endured? *(The strong National Government and various constitutional provisions have made it possible for interstate conflicts to be settled peaceably.)* How have conflicts been handled? *(Through the courts and interstate compacts.)*

Provide Guided Practice Give students a list of situations and ask them to indicate whether or not each situation falls within the guidelines of the Constitution. Situations could include: marriage of two teenagers in the state of Michigan is ruled null and void when they return to their home in Pennsylvania, or Minnesota signs a treaty with Canada over fishing rights. You may want to have students identify the provision in the Constitution that relates to each example or generate additional situations to pose to classmates.

Provide Independent Practice

TRF **Teacher's Resource File** You may wish to assign Section 3 Guided Reading and Review, Unit 1 File, p. 72, to help students master section objective content.

Interpreting Graphs Have students analyze the graph describing the extradition process. Have volunteers describe each step in the process for the class.

Caption Answer The "executive authority of the State" referred to in the United States Constitution is the governor.

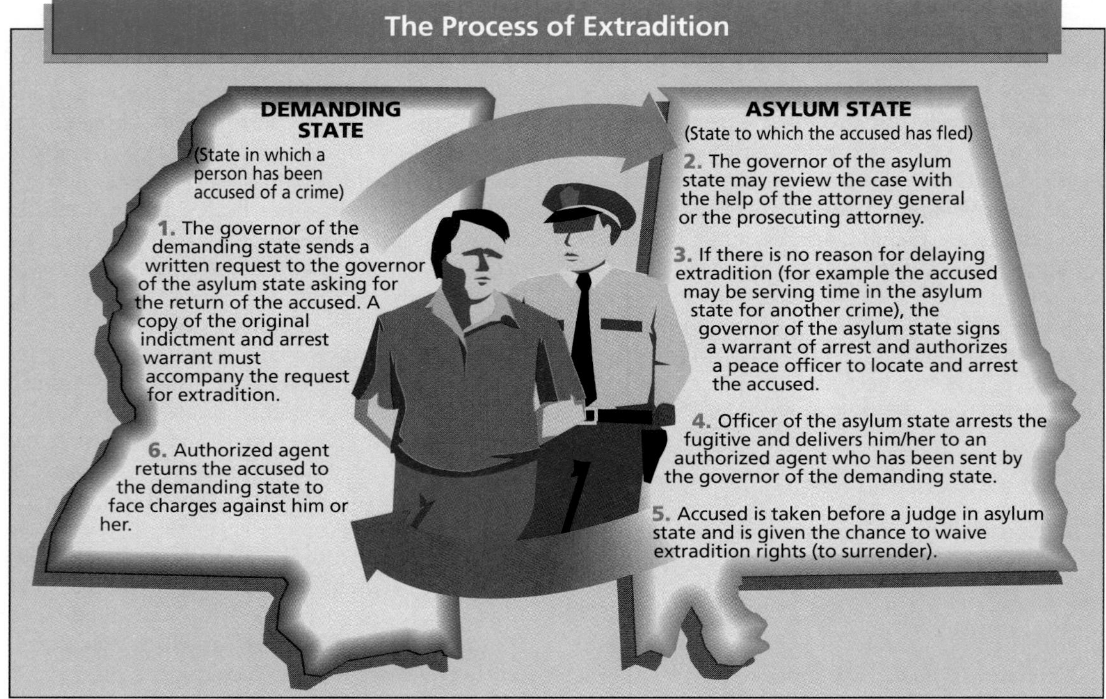

The Process of Extradition
DEMANDING STATE
(State in which a person has been accused of a crime)
1. The governor of the demanding state sends a written request to the governor of the asylum state asking for the return of the accused. A copy of the original indictment and arrest warrant must accompany the request for extradition.
6. Authorized agent returns the accused to the demanding state to face charges against him or her.
ASYLUM STATE
(State to which the accused has fled)
2. The governor of the asylum state may review the case with the help of the attorney general or the prosecuting attorney.
3. If there is no reason for delaying extradition (for example the accused may be serving time in the asylum state for another crime), the governor of the asylum state signs a warrant of arrest and authorizes a peace officer to locate and arrest the accused.
4. Officer of the asylum state arrests the fugitive and delivers him/her to an authorized agent who has been sent by the governor of the demanding state.
5. Accused is taken before a judge in asylum state and is given the chance to waive extradition rights (to surrender).

Interpreting Graphs When a person charged with a crime flees from one State to another, these steps are taken to bring the accused to face charges. Who is the "executive authority of the State" referred to in the Constitution?

tangled estate problems produced by their deaths, suggest the confused and serious nature of the matter.

Extradition

According to the Constitution

"A person charged in any State with treason, felony, or other crime, who shall flee from justice, and be found in another State, shall, on demand of the executive authority of the State from which he fled, be delivered up, to be removed to the State having jurisdiction of the crime."[19]

1.c **Extradition** is a legal process in which a fugitive from justice in a State is returned to that State from another. Extradition is designed to prevent a person from being able to escape justice by fleeing a State. The return of a fugitive from justice in a State is usually a routine matter; governors regularly approve the extradition requests they receive from other States' chief executives. Some of those requests are contested, however—especially in those cases with strong racial or political overtones, and in those increasingly frequent instances of parental kidnapping of children involved in custody disputes as a result of a divorce.

Until recently, governors could, and on occasion did, refuse to return fugitives. In *Kentucky* v. *Dennison*, 1861, for example, the Supreme Court held that the Constitution did not give the Federal Government any power with which to compel a governor to act in an extradition

[19]Article IV, Section 2, Clause 2. Extradition has been carried on between sovereign states for centuries. The word *extradition* is the term popularly used in the United States for what is technically known in the law as interstate rendition.

Enrichment

Have students write an editorial calling for more interstate cooperation to solve a current issue, such as gun or drug trafficking or nonpayment of child support. Students should refer to constitutional provisions and use historical examples of interstate cooperation when and if appropriate to support their positions. (Average) case. So, for more than a century, the Constitution's word "shall" in the Extradition Clause had to be read as "may."

The Supreme Court overturned that ruling in 1987, however. In *Puerto Rico* v. *Branstad,* a unanimous Court held that the federal courts can indeed order an unwilling governor to extradite a fugitive.

Privileges and Immunities

The Constitution provides:

> "The citizens of each State shall be entitled to all privileges and immunities of citizens of the several States."[20]

In short, this means that a resident of one State will not be discriminated against unreasonably by another State.

The courts have never handed down a full list of the privileges and immunities of "interstate citizenship." However, here is a partial list: the right to pass through or reside in any other State for the purpose of trade, agriculture, professional pursuits, or otherwise; the right to use the courts; the right to make contracts; the right to buy, own, rent, and sell property; and the right to marry.

Of course, the provision does not mean that a resident of one State need not obey the laws of another State while in that State. Nor does it mean that a State cannot reasonably discriminate against residents of other States. Thus, any State can require that a person live in that State for a certain period of time before he or she can vote or hold any public office. A State can also require a period of residence before it grants a person a license to practice law, medicine, dentistry, and so on.

In another example, the wild fish and game in a State are considered to be the common property of the people of that State. So, a State can require nonresidents to pay higher fees for fishing or hunting licenses than those paid by residents—who pay taxes to provide fish hatcheries, enforce game laws, and so on. By the same token, a State university often charges higher tuition to students from other States than it does to residents.

Interstate Rights The right to marry is one of the privileges each State is required to extend to citizens of any other State.

Section 3 Review

1. Define: interstate compacts, full faith and credit, extradition

2. What agreements does the Constitution prohibit the States from making?

3. (a) For what does the Full Faith and Credit Clause provide? (b) The Extradition Clause? (c) The Privileges and Immunities Clauses?

Critical Thinking

4. Predicting Consequences (p. 19) What might result if each State was not required to give full faith and credit to the public acts, records, and judicial proceedings of the other States?

★

[20]Article IV, Section 2, Clause 1. The provision is reinforced in the 14th Amendment.

Monitor Comprehension

Answers to Section 3 Review
1. "Key Terms" are defined on the following pages:
a. interstate compact, p. 88
b. full faith and credit, p. 89
c. extradition, p. 90
2. Treaties, alliances, and confederations. **3.** (a) It requires that each State accept the public acts, records, and judicial proceedings of every other State. (b) The return of fugitives from justice from one State to the State from which they fled. (c) It means that the resident of one State will not be discriminated against unreasonably by another State. **4.** Answers may vary. Students might say that each State would strive to respect each other's public acts; others might predict that a State would begin to disregard certain public acts in order to provide economic advantage to itself or its residents. The result would be that each State would become more isolated from the other States.

Closure

Remind students that the U.S. Constitution increased the power of the National Government and reduced conflict among the States. Provisions of the Constitution promote cooperation between and among the States. These include interstate compacts, the Full Faith and Credit Clause, the Privileges and Immunities Clause, and extradition.

Assignment Assign section 1 of Chapter 5 for the next class period.

Reteach

Have volunteers name each of the four provisions in the Constitution for interstate cooperation, and provide an example of each from the text. *(Examples: interstate compacts/Compact on Juveniles; full faith and credit/marital status; extradition/a person accused of robbery in Connecticut flees to New York and is arrested and returned; privileges and immunities/the right to buy property.)*

TRF **Teacher's Resource File**
See the Unit 1 File, p. 73, for the Section 3 Quiz.

Activity: Teaching Heterogeneous Groups

Review that federalism provides for a dual system of government—that is, two levels that govern the same people and territory at the same time. Provide students with several laws or areas of power, and have them divide the laws or areas into three groups—those under the jurisdiction of the Federal Government, those under the jurisdiction of the individual States, and those that may be governed by both. Examples of areas include: national defense, gambling, public education, voter registration, foreign affairs, natural disasters, imposing and collecting taxes, coining money, declaring war, divorce, making treaties, interstate commerce, hunting and fishing laws, buying or renting property, and environmental protection.

TEACHING
Critical Thinking

Checking Consistency

Objective
Analyze data to determine consistency.

INSTRUCT
Ask students to work independently or in groups to add one or two examples to columns A and B. You may want students to share examples with other students in order to check items for consistency.

Answers 1. (a) Freedom of religion; respect for legal and public acts between States; makes the constitution the supreme law of the land. (b) Answers will vary, but students will most likely expect government actions to comply with the requirements. **2.** (a) The first two actions are unconstitutional. (b) Answers will vary, but students might predict civil unrest as a result of the first two actions. (c) Constitutional rights are being abridged by the first two actions. **3.** (a) Most students will feel the first two actions did not live up to their expectations. (b) The first two actions are exactly contrary to constitutional requirements; the third is in compliance with the Constitution.

Critical Thinking

Checking Consistency

Checking consistency means comparing two or more items or ideas and determining whether or not they agree with one another. Being able to check consistency can help you determine if your government is operating the way it was intended to, and if your leaders are living up to the promises they have made. Use the following steps to practice checking the consistency of the actions of your government.

1. Identify the belief, principle, or rule that applies. American government is ordered government; it has a clear set of rules that govern its behavior. The overriding statement of beliefs, goals, and principles for American government is the Constitution. Read the excerpts from the Constitution in Column A below. (a) What is the requirement that the Constitution makes in each excerpt? (b) How might you expect a person or organization to act in response to this constitutional requirement?

2. Note the action taken by the official or governmental body. Read the statements in Column B, which represent imaginary actions taken by government officials or organizations. For each action taken, answer the following questions. (a) What actions are being taken? (b) What are the likely consequences of this action? (c) What impact will this action have on citizens?

3. Check for consistency between the action taken and the applicable belief, principle, and rule. Each statement in Column A relates to the corresponding action in Column B. For each of the three examples, compare the expected or required behavior from Column A with the corresponding action taken in Column B. Ask yourself: (a) Did the action taken live up to your expectations from Column A? (b) If not, in what way is the action inconsistent with the requirement listed in Column A?

Column A Constitutional Requirement	Column B Government Action
"Congress shall make no law respecting an establishment of religion, or prohibiting free exercise thereof." —1st Amendment	Congress requires by law any territory wishing to become a State to adopt an official religion.
"Full faith and credit shall be given in each State to the public acts, records, and judicial proceedings of every other State." —Article IV, Section 1	A State requires all residents not married within State borders to obtain a State marriage license in order to be considered legally married.
"The Judges in every State shall be bound [by the Constitution], anything in the constitution or laws of any State to the contrary notwithstanding." —Article VI, Section 2	A judge in a State court rules a State law denying residents the right to free speech to be unconstitutional.

TRF **Teacher's Resource File**
See the Unit 1 File, page 74, for the Skill Application for this lesson.

Chapter-in-Brief

Scan all headings, photographs, charts, and other visuals in the chapter before reading the section summaries below.

Section 1 Federalism and the Division of Powers (pp. 73–80) There are two basic levels of government in the American federal system—national and State.

The National Government is one of delegated powers—powers specifically granted by the Constitution itself. The delegated powers are of three types: expressed, implied, and inherent.

The States are governments of reserved powers. That is, the Constitution reserves to the States those powers that the Constitution does not grant to the National Government and does not deny to the States.

The Framers expected conflict between the two basic levels of government, and so made the Constitution the nation's supreme law. The Supreme Court is the umpire in the federal system.

Section 2 The National Government and the 50 States (pp. 80–86) The Constitution obligates the National Government to ensure that each State has a republican form of government. Also, the National Government must protect the States against foreign invasion and against domestic violence. Thus, if a State cannot protect itself from internal disorder, the National Government may step in.

The Constitution also requires the National Government to respect the territorial integrity of the States. For example, Congress may not create a new State out of an existing one without the existing State's consent.

Congress has the power to admit new States. Usually, the prospective State petitions Congress, which then passes an enabling act. This act directs the prospective State to draft a constitution. If voters approve of the constitution, and Congress still agrees to Statehood, Congress must then pass an act of admission. With the President's signature, the act creates a new State.

Congress can place conditions on the admission of a prospective State. For example, Congress required Utah to outlaw polygamy before admission. However, Congress cannot make requirements that compromise a State's right to manage its own internal affairs.

The National Government provides financial assistance to the States. Grants-in-aid programs are a major example of this help. Grants take two forms: categorical or block. Block grants generally involve fewer requirements States must satisfy to receive the monies.

States provide numerous services to the National Government, as well. For example, States administer national elections and assist federal law-enforcement efforts.

Section 3 Interstate Relations (pp. 88–91) The States cannot enter into treaties, alliances, or confederations. However, they can form interstate compacts—agreements among themselves and with foreign states. These compacts enable States to cooperate on matters of mutual concern.

The Constitution requires each State to give full faith and credit to—respect the validity of—the laws, official records, and court actions of other States. The obligation applies only to civil matters.

The Constitution also requires each State to return fugitives from justice to the State from which they fled.

Teaching Suggestions for CHAPTER-IN-BRIEF

Below are some of the possible uses for the Chapter-in-Brief:

To Preview the Chapter You may want to assign the Chapter-in-Brief page and the Section Outlines from the Teacher's Resource File before beginning Chapter 4 to introduce students to "Key Terms" and concepts in each section.

To Review the Chapter When students have completed Chapter 4, you might want to assign the Chapter-in-Brief as a tool for review, along with the Guided Reading and Reviews from the Teacher's Resource File.

To Omit the Chapter If you wish to skip Chapter 4, it may be helpful to assign the Chapter-in-Brief to students as a review before continuing to another chapter. You may also want to assign the Chapter 4 Test to assess student knowledge of the material. Then specific portions of Chapter 4 may be assigned to students needing reinforcement of "Key Terms" and concepts.

Teacher's Resource File See the Unit 1 File for the following materials:

- Section Outlines, pp. 65, 68, 71.
- Guided Reading and Reviews, pp. 66, 69, 72.
- Chapter 4 Test, pp. 78–80.

ADDITIONAL RESOURCES

Barone, Michael and Grant Ujifusa. *The Almanac of American Politics*, 1990. National Journal, 1989.

Conway, Jill K., et al. *Learning About Women: Gender, Politics, and Power*. University of Michigan Press, 1989.

Conway, M. Margaret. *Political Participation in the United States.* Prentice Hall, 1991.

Dunham, Pat. *Electoral Behavior in the United States.* Prentice Hall, 1991.

Flanigan, William H. and Nancy H. Zingale. *Political Behavior of the American Electorate.* Allyn and Bacon, 6th ed., 1987.

Jelen, Ted G. (ed.). *Religion and Political Behavior in the United States.* Greenwood Press, 1989.

Piven, Francis F. and Richard A. Cloward. *Why Americans Don't Vote.* Pantheon, 1989.

Pohlmann, Marcus D. *Black Politics in Conservative America.* Longman, 1990.

Salmore, Stephen A. and Barbara G. Salmore. *Candidates, Parties, and Campaigns: Electoral Politics in America.* CQ Press, 2nd ed., 1989.

The Women Get the Vote. Film/McGraw-Hill, 1989. Black and white. 27 min.

Answers to

CHAPTER 4 REVIEW

Vocabulary and Key Terms

Matching

1. expressed powers
2. act of admission
3. block grant
4. federalism
5. inherent powers
6. implied powers
7. interstate compact

True or False

1. True.
2. True.
3. False—the correct term is grant-in-aid program.
4. False—the correct term is enabling act.
5. True.

Word Relationships

1. Item B refers to a Constitutional principle. The other three items identify types of delegated powers.
2. Item A refers to the process by which a territory becomes a State. The other three items refer to types of interstate relations among the 50 States.
3. Item D refers to interstate relations. The other three items refer to the relationship between the Federal Government and the governments of the 50 States.

Main Ideas

Section 1

1. It enabled the Framers to create a strong central government while respecting the concerns of each of the existing States. **2.** The National Government's powers are delegated powers. Some are expressed powers, some are implied, others are inherent. The National Government is also denied certain powers—either expressly, because the Constitution does not grant the power to the National Government, or implicitly because of the nature of the federal system itself.
3. The powers of the States are the reserved powers. These are any and all powers that the Constitution does not give to the National Government or explicitly deny the States. The Constitution denies States the power to enter into any treaty, alliance or confederation. They cannot print or coin money or deny citizens due process. States may not tax agencies or functions of the National Government, or do anything else that works against the existence of the federal system. **4.** The Constitution is the supreme law of the land, the "linchpin" that holds the National Government and the States together. The Supreme Court is the umpire that interprets the Constitution in cases of conflict between the States and the National Government.

Section 2

5. The National Government must guarantee to each State a republican form of government; protect each State from foreign invasion and domestic violence; and respect territorial integrity.
6. An area desiring Statehood petitions Congress to pass an enabling act to direct the fram-

Chapter Review

Vocabulary and Key Terms

federalism (p. 74)
division of powers (p. 74)
delegated powers (p. 75)
expressed powers (p. 75)
implied powers (p. 75)
inherent powers (p. 75)
reserved powers (p. 77)
exclusive powers (p. 78)
concurrent powers (p. 78)
enabling act (p. 83)
act of admission (p. 83)
grants-in-aid program (p. 84)
block grant (p. 85)
interstate compact (p. 88)
full faith and credit (p. 89)
extradition (p. 90)

Matching: *Review the key terms in the list above. If you are not sure of a term's meaning, look up the term and review its definition. Choose a term from the list above that best matches each description.*

1. those powers granted by the Constitution to the National Government in so many words
2. congressional measure admitting a United States territory into the Union as a State
3. a type of federal grants-in-aid; monies from which are to be used in a particular but broadly defined area
4. a system of government in which a constitution divides the powers of government on a territorial basis
5. those powers that belong to the National Government because it is the national government of a sovereign state
6. those powers of the National Government that are necessary and proper to the exercise of the expressed powers
7. agreements made by States among themselves and with foreign states

True or False: *Determine whether each statement is true or false. If it is true, write "true." If it is false, change the underlined word or words to make the statement true.*

1. Reserved powers are those powers held by the States in the federal system.
2. Delegated powers are those powers granted to the National Government in the Constitution.
3. Some people have questioned whether or not block grants give the federal government too much say in matters of State and local concern.
4. Congress directs an area desiring Statehood to frame a proposed State constitution in an act of admission.
5. Those powers that can only be exercised by the National Government are called exclusive powers.

Word Relationships: *Three of the terms in each of the following sets of terms are related. Choose the term that does not belong and explain why it does not belong.*

1. (a) expressed powers (b) division of powers (c) implied powers (d) inherent powers
2. (a) act of admission (b) extradition (c) interstate compact (d) full faith and credit
3. (a) federalism (b) division of powers (c) grants-in-aid program (d) full faith and credit

Main Ideas

Section 1 (pp. 73–80)

1. How did the principle of federalism enable the Framers to solve the problems they faced at the Constitutional Convention?
2. Briefly describe the powers of the National Government under the Constitution.
3. Briefly describe the powers of the States under the Constitution.

4. What is the role of the Constitution and the Supreme Court in the federal system?

Section 2 **(pp. 80–86)**

5. According to the Constitution, what must the National Government provide to the States?
6. Outline the role of Congress in admitting new States to the Union.
7. What is cooperative federalism?
8. Give some examples of cooperative federalism at work in the United States.

Section 3 **(pp. 88–91)**

9. In what two general ways did the Constitution resolve some of the interstate conflicts experienced under the Articles of Confederation?
10. What specific provisions does the Constitution include to encourage cooperation among the States?
11. Under what circumstances can a State deny another State full faith and credit?

Critical Thinking

1. **Drawing Conclusions** (p. 19) For what reason might a governor of a State be reluctant to call for federal troops in the event that violence breaks out in a city in his or her State?

2. **Identifying Central Issues** (p. 19) (a) Would the United States be better off if there were not as much variety in the laws and customs of different States? (b) Does the fact that different States have different laws lead to unfairness and inequality in the overall legal system?

3. **Determining Relevance** (p. 19) As you read in this chapter, before a new State can be admitted into the Union, Congress must approve its constitution. Do you think Congress should have this power over the internal affairs and government of a State? Give reasons for your answer.

Getting Involved

1. **Writing Your Opinion** Write a letter to a friend, relative, or acquaintance who lives in another State, explaining some of the features that you feel make your State unique among the 50 States. Start by making a list of some of the features of your State that you like and dislike. Consider such factors as the weather, location, the businesses and industries commonly found there, unusual holidays, and the type of people who live there. Also consider the history of the State and any noteworthy current events that have taken place in your State. Next try to identify those features of your State that are not commonly associated with any of the other States. As you write the first draft of your letter, strive to make a convincing argument that your State has a distinct character. Finally, proofread the letter, correct any errors, and make a final copy.
2. **Class Debate** Hold a debate on one of the following topics: (a) *Resolved,* That the Supreme Court of the United States be denied the power to declare any form of State law unconstitutional; (b) *Resolved,* That grants-in-aid programs undermine the federal system and reduce the power and importance of the States. Choose one team to debate each side of the topic you select. The rest of the class can evaluate each team's presentation.
3. **Gathering Information** (a) Using the Government Resources Handbook on page 690 of your textbook, identify what sources you could use to find out about a grants-in-aid program recently passed by the National Government. (b) What sources might you consult to find the address of a government agency that could provide information about the grants?

ing of a proposed State constitution. After the voters of the proposed State have approved the new constitution, Congress can pass an act of admission. **7.** The term refers to the area of of shared powers and cooperation between the Federal and State governments. **8.** Federal grants-in-aid programs and other block grants. Also, the States aid the Federal Government by helping to conduct, finance, and regulate elections, and by helping to handle Federal criminals.

Section 1

9. The Constitution helped resolve the conflict by creating a stronger National Government and by specifically addressing many aspects of interstate relations. **10.** It enables the States to enter into interstate compacts; it requires each State to grant full faith and credit to the public acts, records, and judicial proceedings of other States; it requires States to extradite fugitives from justice in other States; it entitles citizens of each State to all the privileges and immunities of citizens of all the States. **11.** One State cannot enforce another State's criminal law, and in certain cases of divorce.

Critical Thinking

1. Answers will vary. Students might suggest that a governor would want voters to think he or she was capable of handling the problems of the State.
2. (a) Answers will vary. Students might note that a lack of variety of laws would create less confusion, but that diversity in customs helps make the nation stronger and richer. (b) Answers will vary. Students should note that no law may violate any provision of the Constitution.
3. Answers will vary. Students might note that Congress has the responsibility to ensure a republican form of government, but that the arrangement does call into question the legitimate extent of the power of Congress over the States.

Getting Involved

1–3. Answers and results will vary, but students should demonstrate an understanding of the concepts in this chapter.

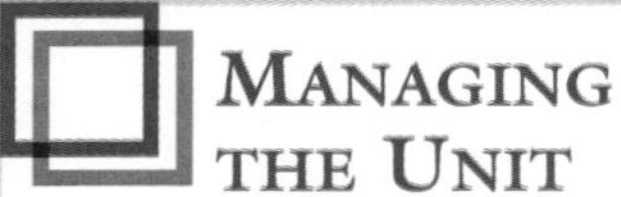

Managing the Unit

You may wish to review the following materials before beginning the unit to help plan your instruction.

Each chapter ends with a Chapter-in-Brief with suggestions for previewing, reviewing, or omitting the chapter.

Unit 2 Outline

Pacing Charts,
pp. T28–T31

Unit 2

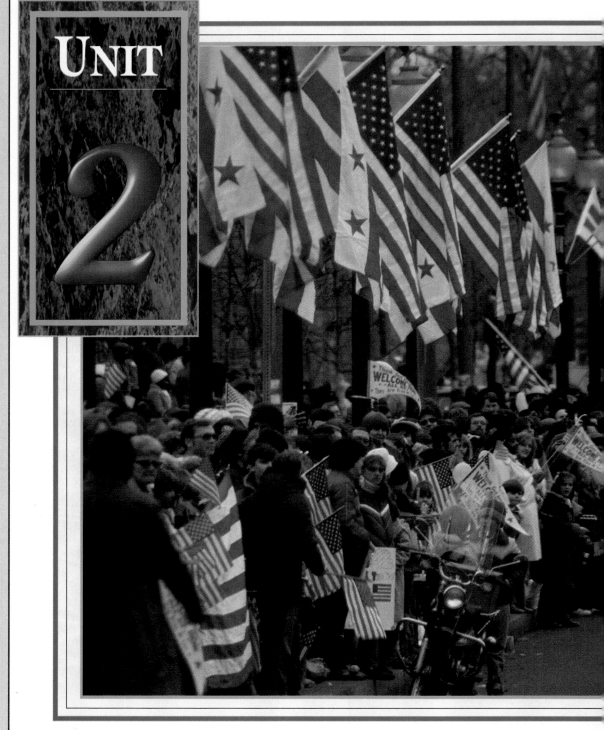

Welcome Home Parade Government by the people includes participating in such events as this parade in Washington, D.C., which celebrated the release of hostages from Iran in 1981.

Skills and Features The following skill lessons and features are included in this unit.

Skill Lessons

Critical Thinking: Identifying Central Issues (p. 124)
Critical Thinking: Determining Relevance (p. 152)
Critical Thinking: Recognizing Bias (p. 180)
Critical Thinking: Distinguishing False from Accurate Images (p. 206)
Critical Thinking: Distinguishing Fact from Opinion (p. 228)

Debates/Case Studies

What *You* Can Do: Tackling Politics (p. 108)
Debating Key Issues: Should Free Speech Ever Be Suppressed? (*Feiner* v. *New York*) (p. 137)
What *You* Can Do: Working to Change State Law (p. 172)
Debating Key Issues: Should the Government Have the Power to Restrict the Press? (*New York Times* v. *U.S.*) (p. 197)
Debating Key Issues: Should Federal Projects Be Allowed to Violate the Law? (*Tennessee Valley Authority* v. *Hill*) (p. 221)

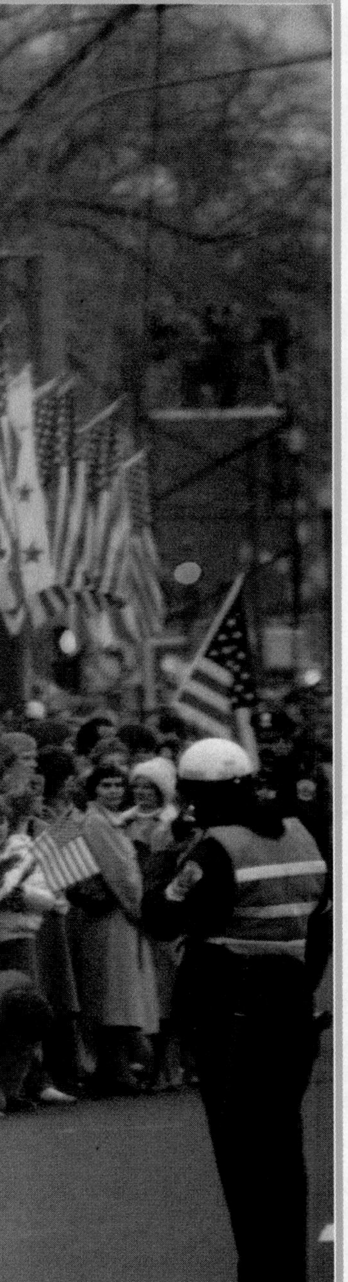

Political Behavior: Government by the People

The morning after the 1876 presidential election, newspapers in New York confidently announced, "Tilden Elected." In the 1916 presidential election, the *New York Sun* ("It Shines for All") went to press with this headline: "Hughes Elected by Narrow Margin; Sweeps West." And then there was Mr. Dewey, whom the *Chicago Daily Tribune* announced to be the new President in 1948. For the record, voters in those elections actually picked Rutherford B. Hayes, Woodrow Wilson, and Harry S Truman, respectively. In today's electronic age, television and radio are the first to break the news of presidential election results. Television election analysts have often been guilty of offering confident predictions long before they should. But they have never broadcast the wrong winners. Political candidates, the parties that run them, the voters who turn out on election day, and the mass media that track, analyze, and report on politics—all this falls under the broad topic of American political behavior.

Did You Know That . . .

- By October 1991, more than 115 contenders had declared their candidacies for the 1992 presidential election.
- Television broadcast its first coverage of a presidential election in 1932.
- Young people between the ages of 18 and 21 are statistically the least likely to vote.
- Spending by House and Senate campaigns dropped to $445 million in the 1990 congressional elections.

Unit Focus

Activate Prior Knowledge Ask students: How many people do you think would buy lottery tickets if a winner had already been selected? Tell students that in most of the presidential elections since 1964, while polling places were still open in California, television stations had already announced the winner of the election. Ask: Do you think that early projections of election results and pre-election polling discourage voter participation?

Interpreting the Visual Point out the photo of the parade in the unit opener. Tell students that when children attend events such as this, they are becoming "socialized" to politics and are laying the foundation for their later political opinions and ideas.

Did You Know That . . . Direct students to the items under "Did You Know That . . . ." Do students think that, if some of these statistics were general knowledge, elections in the United States would substantially differ from what they now are? In what ways?

Journal Writing Suggested topics for the second unit include creating a political cartoon about voting and elections, expressing opinions about the quality of the mass media, or writing a short story about a candidate running for political office.

You may also want to utilize **CNN Video-link** to generate ideas for journal writing.

Bulletin Board Idea

Using the Poster Direct students' attention to the wall poster titled "Politics: A Vehicle for Choice and Change." Tell them to take a minute to read the quotes and examine the cartoons. Then, write the word *politics* on the board. Ask students to supply a list of words that they associate with politics as you write their ideas on the board. You may wish to start them off by writing *choice, change, election, democracy,* and so on. Have them notice that some of the impressions on the poster are somewhat humorous or cynical. Ask students if they think that such a cynical view of the American political system is widespread. Discuss what might be meant by Abraham Lincoln's statement, "The ballot is stronger than the bullet"—especially in light of recent political changes in other parts of the world. Students can write their words on strips of construction paper for display on the bulletin board, striving to keep a balance of positive and humorous descriptions.

Chapter 5 Resources

In the Teacher's Resource File
The following materials are found in the Teacher's Resource File box.

Instructional Support: Unit 2 File

For the Section	For the Chapter
Outlines, pp. 2, 5, 8, 11, 14	Skill Application, p. 17
Guided Reading and Reviews, pp. 3, 6, 9, 12, 15	Case Study on Contemporary Issues, pp. 18–20
Quizzes, pp. 4, 7, 10, 13, 16	Chapter Test, pp. 21–23
	Additional Test Questions, pp. 24–26

Enrichment Support Files

Participatory Government Activities, pp. 28–39
Historical and Legal Documents, pp. 19, 27

Computer Test Bank and Assessment

Transparency Package, pp. 5, 30

Election Kit, pp. 8, 30–31

Chapter 5 Focus

Introduce the Chapter Tell students that in this chapter they will learn about the nature, functions, reasons for existence, and evolution of American political parties. Read with students the Chapter Preview and Objectives.

Writing Activity Direct students' attention to "Describe." Have students generate a list of party headquarters, posters, billboards, and pamphlets they may have seen, and candidate appearances of which they may have been aware.

Motivate for Learning Direct students' attention to "Predict." Lead students in a discussion of issues on which the two parties might differ: for example, day care, gun control, and the defense budget. For each category, ask students how they predict the two parties will differ. Have students check them again after they have finished reading the chapter.

Chapter 5 Political Parties

Chapter Preview

What political party nominated Ron Paul as its 1988 presidential candidate? Count yourself wrong if you answered either the Democratic or Republican party. The correct answer is the Libertarian party—the third largest political party in the United States, founded only 20 years ago.

Political parties are one of the major vehicles of popular participation in the American political system. With some exceptions at the local level, every candidate who runs for public office is nominated by a political party. As you will read in this chapter, their nature and function and the role they play in American politics provide living proof that government in the United States is, in fact, "government by the people."

Before you read this chapter:

- **Describe** any evidence of political parties that you have seen in your community.
- **Predict** what you think are the differences between the Democratic and Republican parties.

As you read, focus on the main objective for each section. Understand:

1. The nature and functions of parties in American politics.
2. The reasons for the existence of the American two-party system.
3. The evolution of American political parties.
4. The nature and role of minor parties in American politics.
5. The organizational structure and composition of the two major parties.

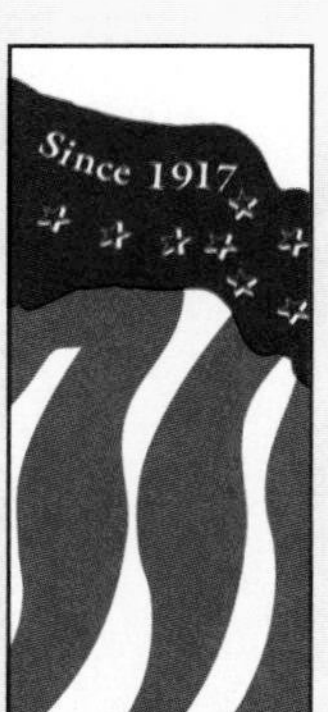

Magruder's American Government: *A Witness to Change* by William A. McClenaghan

In the 1920s through the 1940s this book's definition of *political parties* emphasized party principles and a party's stand on public policy questions. Thus, the 1936 edition declared: "A political party is an organization of many people, united by common principles or a common policy, and having for its immediate end the control of the government through the carrying of elections and the possession of office (p. 401).

That definition was presented as universal and all-inclusive. It was meant to apply to all political parties—here and abroad, without regard to major or minor party status.

Clearly, that definition could not be applied to either of the two major parties in American politics today. To all the minor parties—to the Libertarians, the Socialists, the Prohibitionists, and so on—yes. But, as we point out on page 99 (and elsewhere), the Republicans and the Democrats today are not primarily principle- or issue-oriented. They are, instead, election-oriented: that is, they are concerned with winning elections.

Campaign Fever Political campaigns provide an opportunity for people of all ages to rally to the support of the party that best expresses their beliefs and hopes for the future.

1 Parties and What They Do

Find Out:

- What is a political party?
- What do political parties do?

Key Terms:

political party, major parties, coalition

"Winning isn't everything, it's the only thing." So said legendary football coach Vince Lombardi. Lombardi was talking about his NFL teams. But those words could also be used to describe the Republican and Democratic parties. They, too, are in the business of winning.

In this section, you will look at political parties—what they are and what they do in the American political system.

What Is a Party?

1.a A **political party** can be defined as a group of persons who seek to control government through winning elections and holding public office. This definition of a political party is a broad one, and it will fit any political party—including the two major parties in American politics.

Another, more specific definition can be used to describe most political parties, both here and abroad: a group of persons, joined together on the basis of certain common principles, who seek to control government in order to bring about the adoption of certain public policies and programs.

But this definition, with its emphasis on principles and public policy positions, will not fit the
1.b two **major parties**, the dominant political parties in the United States. The Republican and Democratic parties are not primarily principle- or issue-oriented. They are, instead, *election*-oriented.

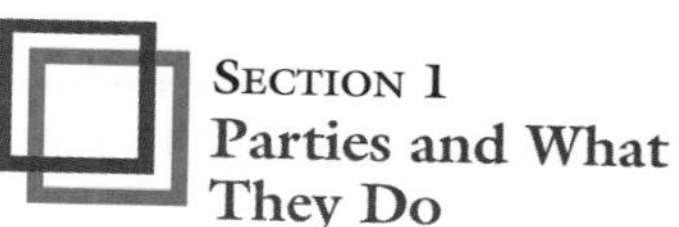

SECTION 1
Parties and What They Do

FOCUS

Teacher's Resource File See the Unit 2 File, p. 2, for the Section 1 Outline.

Objectives

5.1 Define political party.
5.2 Identify the functions of political parties.

Bellringer Activity Raise an issue that is close to student experience, such as a longer school year or abolishing of sports teams. Ask students to write down on a piece of paper a statement indicating their position on the issue. Next, have students relate their position to the class. Have students who took similar positions form groups on opposite sides of the room. Point out to them that they have polarized into two (or three) "parties."

State the Purpose Political parties are not collections of people who always agree, but are rather facilitators of the political process. In Section 1, students will learn the functions performed by political parties. They will also learn how political parties serve to clarify and moderate positions and to make government more responsive to people.

ABCNEWS INTERACTIVE

The following video segment may be used to highlight aspects of the functions of political parties.

POWERS OF THE CONGRESS GUIDEBOOK
Chapter 17: Political Party System, p. 93

Vocabulary

Point out "Key Terms" on page 99. Explain to students that the word *coalition* derives from the same word as *coalesce,* which means "to grow together" or "unite into a single body." For example, the two halves of a broken bone coalesce as they mend. Thus, a coalition is a group of diverse individuals who coalesce, or come together, to try to get a candidate elected to office. LEP

Reading Strategy: Reinforcing Key Ideas

Point out to students the following statement made by the author on page 100: "It is clear . . . that the political parties are essential to democratic government." As students read Section 1, have them write down every statement they can find that supports this general idea.

INSTRUCT

Analyze/Discuss To demonstrate the role of a political party, discuss students' reactions to the issue posed in the "Bellringer Activity." Then ask students to write down one reason why they feel the way they do. Have each of the two groups formed during the "Bellringer Activity" discuss these reasons. Students should not be surprised if differences of opinion exist within their group.

Use this discussion as a means of explaining to students that, in a similar way, political parties in the United States do not always agree or represent consensus, but instead provide a forum or "platform" for ideas.

Have each group develop its own platform of ideas on which their party is based. Then each group should write and act out a brief skit in which they illustrate each of the five functions—nominating, informer-stimulator, "seal of approval," governmental, and watchdog functions—of political parties.

In other words, neither the Republicans nor the Democrats can be properly described as a group of like-minded persons who regularly agree with one another on public questions. To illustrate the point, compare the public policy positions taken by various leading Republicans or Democrats. Senators Phil Gramm of Texas and Mark Hatfield of Oregon are both Republicans. Yet they often disagree on important issues and take opposing sides in the Senate. So, too, do such other Republicans as Jesse Helms of North Carolina and William Cohen of Maine, and Orrin Hatch of Utah and John Danforth of Missouri. Much the same can be said of many Democrats—for example, Senators Edward Kennedy of Massachusetts and Wendell Ford of Kentucky, or Daniel Moynihan of New York and Sam Nunn of Georgia.

Again, neither of the two major parties is made up of persons who are all of one mind in politics. Instead, each party is a **coalition**—a union of many persons of diverse interests—who have joined together to try to get candidates elected to public office. Each of them includes within its ranks a substantial share of nearly every economic, racial, religious, regional, and ideological grouping in this country. 1.c

What Do Parties Do?

It is clear from American history, and that of other people, as well, that political parties are essential to democratic government. Parties are the only mechanisms that develop broad policy and leadership choices and that then present those options to the people. By offering their alternatives, parties make it possible for the people to determine the course that government should take in this country.

Political parties are a vital link between the people and their government, between the governed and those who govern. Many argue that they are the principal means by which the will of the people is made known to government and by which government is held accountable to the people.

Parties serve the democratic ideal in another important way. They work to blunt conflict; they are "power brokers." They bring conflicting groups together. They modify and compromise the contending views of different interests and groups, and so help to unify the people. They soften the impact of extremists at both ends of the political spectrum.

Again, political parties are indispensable to American government. This fact can be underscored by a look at the major functions they perform.

The Nominating Function The major function of a political party is to nominate, or name, candidates for public office. That is, the parties recruit and choose candidates and then present them to the voters. Parties also provide those candidates with a solid base of votes and other forms of support.

The nominating function is almost exclusively a party function in this country.[1] It is the one particular activity that most clearly sets political parties apart from all of the other groups operating in politics.[2]

The Informer-Stimulator Function Parties inform the people and stimulate their interest and participation in public affairs. Other groups also perform this function—in particular, the news media and interest groups.

Parties try to inform and stimulate votes in several ways. Most of all, they campaign for their candidates, take stands on issues, and criticize the candidates and stands of their opponents.

Of course, each party tries to inform the people as it thinks they should be informed—to the party's advantage. It conducts its "educational" process through pamphlets, signs, buttons, and stickers; with advertisements in newspapers and magazines and on radio and television; in speeches, rallies, and conventions; and in many other ways.

Remember, both parties want to win elections, and that consideration has much to do with the positions they take on most issues.

[1]The exceptions are in nonpartisan elections and in those rare instances in which an independent candidate enters a partisan contest. Nominations are covered at length in Chapter 7.

[2]Including, most especially, the many kinds of interest groups (special interest organizations) described in Chapter 9.

SPOTLIGHT ON: Roots of Democracy

U.S. development of the modern Democratic party set an example for the entire world. The Democratic-Republicans formed the first truly popular party, organized at the grass-roots level by local party "regulars," who entered politics as a profession rather than as a function of their class. The party of Jefferson and Madison, unlike Hamilton's Federalists, was thus made responsive and responsible to public opinion. With the extension of the vote, the growth of the Democratic-Republican party was ensured, while Federalist fortunes declined.

Winning Republican Votes This 1900 campaign poster uses powerful imagery to win Republican votes. What does it say about what the Republican party stood for and what it opposed in that election year?

Both parties try to shape stands that will attract as many voters as possible—and that will, at the same time, offend as few as possible.

The "Seal of Approval" Function A party grants seals of approval, so to speak, to its candidates. It serves, in a sense, as a "bonding agent" to ensure the good performance of its candidates and officeholders. In choosing its candidates, the party tries to see that they are men and women who are both qualified and of good character—or, at least, that they are not unqualified and that they have no serious blemishes on their records. The party also prompts its successful candidates to perform well in office. The democratic process imposes this bonding agent function on a party, whether it really wants to perform it or not. If it fails to do so, both the party and its candidates may suffer the consequences in future elections.

The Governmental Function In several respects, government in the United States can be correctly described as government by party. For example, public officeholders—those who govern—are regularly chosen on the basis of party. Congress and the State legislatures conduct much of their business on a partisan basis. Most appointments to executive offices, both federal and State, are also made on the basis of party—so much so that the party in control of the legislature has some influence on the work it performs.

In yet another sense, parties provide a basis for the conduct of government. Under the system of separation of powers, the party is usually the major agent through which the executive and legislative branches cooperate with one another. For example, a President of one party knows he can usually count on the support of his party members in Congress and so acts accordingly.

Provide Guided Practice In order to reinforce the complicated and vital functions of parties, list the five functions of political parties on the chalkboard—*nominating, informer-stimulator, "seal of approval," governmental, and watchdog.* Have students explain the importance of each of the five functions.

Provide Independent Practice

TRF **Teacher's Resource File** You may wish to assign Section 1 Guided Reading and Review, Unit 2 File, p. 3, to help students master section objective content.

Caption Answer For: business and industry, a strong economy, protecting American interests in the Americas. Against: slower growth in business and industry, a poor economy, and an isolationist foreign policy.

Enrichment

Provide a newspaper and have students look for references in it. Then have students identify one or more of the functions of political parties implied in these references. Students should summarize each reference—for example, whether the party was choosing a candidate, confronting the opposition-party President in Congress, uniting to pass a bill—and then explain to the class the contribution to our political system of the event reported in the articles. (Average)

Monitor Comprehension

Answers to Section 1 Review
1. "Key Terms" are defined on the following pages:
a. political party, p. 99
b. major parties, p. 99
c. coalition, p. 100
2. That of power brokers bringing conflicting groups together. **3.** Nominating function, informer-stimulator function, "seal of approval" function, governmental function, and watchdog function. **4.** Students may suggest that in this list, one element cannot exist without the other, that they are all linked. America and democracy would not exist without compromise.

Teacher's Resource File See the Unit 2 File, p. 4, for the Section 1 Quiz .

Closure

Remind students that political parties are not necessarily made up of people who share the same philosophy or support the same causes, but rather are made up of people who want to see certain candidates elected. By carrying out five basic functions, political parties help to ensure that the government represents the people and that the people who elect the government are themselves making informed choices. As students read the next section, they will learn why the United States has a two-party system and how that system compares with one-party and multiparty systems.

Assignment Assign Section 2, pages 102–107, for the next class period.

Also, remember the discussion of constitutional change by informal amendment in Chapter 3. Political parties have played a large part in that process. As a leading illustration of that fact, the Constitution's cumbersome system of electing the President works principally because political parties reshaped it in its early years and have made it work ever since.

The Watchdog Function Parties act as watchdogs over the conduct of the public's business. This is particularly the function of the party out of power. It plays this role as it criticizes the policies and behavior of the party in power.[3] In effect, the party out of power attempts to convince the voters that they should "throw the rascals out," that the "outs" should become the "ins" and the "ins" the "outs." Its attacks tend to make the rascals more careful of their public charge and more responsive to the wishes and concerns of the people. In short, the party out of power plays the important role of "the loyal opposition."

Section 1 Review

1. Define: political party, major parties, coalition
2. What pivotal role do parties play in democratic government?
3. What are the most important functions performed by parties in American politics?

Critical Thinking

4. Identifying Central Issues (p. 19) Clinton Rossiter once noted, "No America without democracy, no democracy without politics, no politics without parties, no parties without compromise and moderation. . ." Explain your understanding of this statement using information from the section.

[3]In American politics the "party in power" is the party that controls the executive branch—i.e., the presidency at the national level, or the governorship at the State level.

2 The Two-Party System

Find Out:

- For what reasons does the United States have a two-party system?
- What are multiparty and one-party systems?
- What is the nature of party membership?

Key Terms:

minor party, two-party system, single-member district, plurality, pluralistic society, consensus, multiparty, one-party system

Does the name Earl Dodge mean anything to you? Probably not. Yet, Earl Dodge has been the Prohibition party's candidate for President of the United States three times—in 1984, 1988, and 1992.

One of the reasons why Mr. Dodge is not
1.a very well known is that he belongs to a **minor party**, one of the less widely supported parties in the political system. The two major parties dominate American politics. That is to say, this
1.b country has a **two-party system**. In a typical election, only the Republican or the Democratic party's candidates have a reasonable chance of winning public office.

In this section, you will examine the factors that have produced the American two-party system.

Reasons for the Two-Party System

In some States, and in many local communities, one of the two major parties may be overwhelmingly dominant, and for a long period of time—as, for example, the Democrats were throughout the South for decades. But, on the whole, and through most of history, the United States has been a two-party nation.

A number of factors help to explain why America has and continues to have a two-party system. No one reason, taken alone, offers a wholly satisfactory explanation for the phenomenon. But, taken together, several do stand as a quite persuasive answer.

Activity: Cooperative Learning

Time: Two class periods **Activity:** Locate examples of the "informer-stimulator" and "watchdog" functions of political parties. **Grouping:** Groups of three to four students **Purpose:** Have students work together to accumulate newspapers or news magazines and then locate at least one example of a political party acting as a watchdog over the opposition party. **Roles:** Have students assign the following roles: manager, researcher(s), spokesperson. **Outcome:** Have the spokesperson read the group's examples and invite class discussion.

Reteach

Have students form five groups and assign one of the five functions of political parties to each group. Then have the group nominate one person to be "newscaster." This person should assume the personality of one of the well-known news personalities. Using a statement prepared by the entire group, the newscaster should make a "newsflash" statement about some activity of a political party that epitomizes the function that was assigned to the group. For example, the nominating function group may simply show that the party has nominated someone for office; the watchdog group may announce changes the candidate has promised to make.

The Historical Basis The two-party system is rooted in the beginnings of the nation itself. The Framers of the Constitution were opposed to political parties. As you read in Chapter 2, however, the ratification of the Constitution saw the birth of America's first two parties: the Federalists, led by Alexander Hamilton, and the Anti-Federalists, who followed Thomas Jefferson.[4] In short, the American party system began as a two-party system.

The Force of Tradition Once established, human institutions are likely to become self-perpetuating—and so it has been with the two-party system. The very fact that the nation began with a two-party system has been a leading reason for its retention, and it has become over time an increasingly important, self-reinforcing reason.

The point can be made this way: Most Americans accept the idea of a two-party system simply because there has always been one. This inbred support for the arrangement is a principal reason why challenges to it have made so little headway in the nation's politics. In other words, America has a two-party system because America has a two-party system.

The Electoral System Several features of the American electoral system tend to promote the existence of but two major parties. That is to say, the basic shape, and many of the details, of the election process work in that direction.

[4]The Framers hoped to create a unified country; they sought to bring order out of the chaos of the Critical Period of the 1780s. To most of them, parties were "factions," agents of divisiveness and disunity. George Washington reflected this view when, in his Farewell Address in 1796, he warned the new nation against "the baneful effect of the spirit of party." In this light, it is hardly surprising that the Constitution made no provision for political parties. The Framers could not foresee the ways in which the governmental system they set up would develop. Thus, they could not possibly know that two major parties would emerge as prime instruments of government in the United States. Nor could they know that those two major parties would tend to be moderate, to choose middle-of-the-road positions, and so help to unify rather than divide the nation.

VOICES *on Government*

On Political Parties in the 1990s

Jack F. Kemp, Secretary of Housing and Urban Development under the Bush administration

"Democrats today are beginning to think more in terms of utilizing the private sector and Republicans are now talking about seeking solutions to some of the social and economic problems of poverty. All too long in the past the Democratic Party has simply thought of redistributing wealth, and the Republican Party has had a kind of *laissez-faire* attitude. . . . But I think there are leaders and thinkers in both parties who want to come and find *el otro sendero,* another path."

The single-member district arrangement is among the most prominent of these features. Nearly all of the elections held in this country—from the presidential contest on down to those at the most local of levels—are **single-member**
1.c **district** elections. That is, they are contests in which only one candidate from the district is elected to each office on the ballot. They are winner-take-all elections; the winning candidate
1.d is the one who receives a **plurality**—the largest number of votes cast for the office. Note that a plurality need not be a majority, which is more than half of all votes cast.

The single-member district pattern works to discourage minor parties. Because only one winner can come out of each contest, voters usually face only two viable choices: They can vote for the candidate of the party holding the office, or they can vote for the candidate of the party with

SECTION 2
The Two-Party System

FOCUS

Teacher's Resource File See the Unit 2 File, p. 5, for the Section 2 Outline.

Objectives

5.3 Explain why the U.S. has a two-party system.
5.4 Compare the characteristics of one-party and multiparty systems.
5.5 Describe the nature of party membership.

Bellringer Activity Ask students to consider what a presidential election would be like if only one candidate ran. How do students think a single-candidate race would affect issues and public policy, as well as voter participation?

State the Purpose Although the two-party system is partly the result of tradition, it also has notable advantages over multiparty and one-party systems in combining democracy and flexibility with political stability. In Section 2, students will explore why the United States has a two-party system, some problems with other systems, and the make-up of the two major American political parties.

ABCNEWS INTERACTIVE

The following video segment may be used to highlight aspects of the two-party system.

POWERS OF THE CONGRESS GUIDEBOOK
Chapter 17: Political Party System, p. 93

Vocabulary

Point out "Key Terms" on page 102 to students. Below is an additional word whose meaning may help students understand the section content.

— **ideology:** the way of thinking or ideas on which a particular political, economic, or social system is based. LEP

Reading Strategy: Question Writing

As a preparation for reading, ask students to list the main headings and each of the subheadings in the section and then turn each subheading into a question. Write all questions on the board. Have students skim the section to find answers to their questions. Invite students to tell you the answers they have found as you list them on the board.

INSTRUCT

Analyze/Explain Guide students through the historical basis for the two-party system, and the forces that have supported its continuation.

Explain that the strength of the two major parties keeps those parties strong and works to the exclusion of other parties. With their large memberships and their resulting financial resources, the Democratic and Republican parties are able to maintain their visibility, to perform their inform-and-stimulate functions, and to thereby maintain their membership.

Draw a chart on the board that lists *two-party system* and *multiparty system* down the left side and + and - along the top. Then have the class fill in the chart, by listing the positives and negatives associated with both the two-party and the multiparty systems.

Interpreting Political Cartoons Ask students what is the main objective of the characters in this cartoon. Point out that winning votes is the fuel that runs political parties, not issues.

Caption Answer By transposing the mascots of the candidates, the artist says there seems to be no perceptible difference between the parties.

the best chance of replacing the incumbent. In short, most voters think of a vote for a minor party candidate as a "wasted" one.

Another important aspect of the electoral system works to the same end. Much of American election law is purposely written to discourage minor parties and minor-party candidates.[5] Or, to put the point the other way around, much of American election law is intentionally framed to preserve, protect, and defend the two major parties and the two-party system. Thus, for example, in most States it is far more difficult for minor parties to get their candidates listed on the ballot than it is for the major parties to do so.

The 1988 presidential election offered a striking illustration of this intentional discrimination against minor parties. Both George Bush and Michael Dukakis were on the ballot in all 50 States and in the District of Columbia. But only one of the dozen or more other, and serious, presidential hopefuls was also listed everywhere. Only Leonora B. Fulani, the presidential nominee of the New Alliance party, also appeared on ballots cast in each of the 50 States and the District of Columbia.

To this point, minor party candidates have been able to make it to the ballot everywhere only four times. Eugene V. Debs of the Socialist party was the first to do so, in 1912. The Socialist party's candidate in 1916, Allan L. Benson, also appeared on the ballots of all of the then 48 States. And in 1980 two non-major party candidates were listed everywhere: Ed Clark, the Libertarian party's nominee, and John Anderson, who ran as an independent that year.

In 1988 the Libertarians' Ron Paul also did far better than minor party nominees usually do. He made it to the ballots of 47 States and the District of Columbia. But the other minor party candidates suffered their usual fate in 1988; none of the rest of them was able to gain the ballot in even half of the States.

[5]Nearly all election law in this country is State, not federal, law—a point discussed at length in the next two chapters. But, here, note this very important point: Nearly all of the close to 7,500 State legislators—nearly all of those persons who make State law—are either Democrats or Republicans. Only a handful of minor party members or independents now sit, or have ever sat, in State legislatures.

Interpreting Political Cartoons This cartoon depicts the presidential campaign of 1988. What opinion is the artist expressing about the American ideological consensus?

The American Ideological Consensus

Americans are, on the whole, an ideologically homogeneous people. That is, over time, Americans have shared much the same ideals, the same basic principles, and the same patterns of belief. This is not to say that we are all alike. Clearly, this is not the case. The United States is
1.e a **pluralistic society**—one consisting of several distinct cultures and groups. Increasingly, the members of various ethnic, racial, religious, and other social groups compete for and share in the exercise of political power in this country. Still,
1.f there is a broad **consensus**—a general agreement among various groups—on fundamental matters.

Nor is this to say that Americans have always agreed with one another in all matters. Far from it. The nation has been deeply divided at times: during the Civil War and in the years of the Great Depression, for example; and over such critical issues as racial discrimination and the war in Vietnam.

However, the nation has not been regularly plagued by sharp cleavages in politics. America has been free of long-standing, bitter disputes based on such factors as economic class, social status, religious beliefs, or national origins.

Those conditions that could produce several strong rival parties simply do not exist in this

ACTIVITY: Cooperative Learning

Time: Two class periods **Activity:** Research and report on State requirements for listing a candidate on the ballot in a presidential election. **Grouping:** Groups of three to four students **Purpose:** Have students use outside resources to prepare a brief report on regulations in their State governing the listing of presidential candidates on the ballot. **Roles:** Assign the following roles: manager, researcher(s), recorder, spokesperson. **Outcome:** Have the group spokesperson summarize each group's findings. Then lead a class discussion on whether or not the State regulations discriminate against minor party candidates and, if so, the pros and cons of such discrimination.

country, unlike the situation in most other democracies. In short, the realities of American society and politics simply will not permit more than two major parties.

This ideological consensus has had another very important impact on American parties. It has given the nation two major parties that look very much alike. Both tend to be moderate. Both are built on compromise and regularly try to occupy "the middle of the road."

Both parties seek the same prize: the votes of a majority of the voters. To do so, they must woo essentially the same people. Inevitably, each party takes policy stands much like those taken by the other. Often, and for very good reason, the competition between them becomes a struggle between competing political personalities rather than ideas.

Multiparty Systems

Some critics argue that the American two-party system should be scrapped. They would replace it with a **multiparty** arrangement, a system in which several major and many lesser parties exist. That arrangement exists in most European democracies today.

In the typical multiparty system, the various parties are each based on some particular interest, such as economic class, religious belief, sectional attachment, or political ideology. Those who favor such an arrangement here say that it would be more representative and more responsive to the will of the people. They insist that a multiparty system would give voters a real choice among candidates and policy alternatives.

The practical effect of two of the factors just noted—single-member districts and the American ideological consensus—seems to make such an arrangement impossible, however. Beyond that, a multiparty system tends to produce instability in government. One party is often unable to win the support of a majority of the voters. As a result, the power to govern must be shared by a number of parties, in a coalition. Several of the multiparty nations of Western Europe have long been plagued by governmental crises. They have experienced frequent shifts in party control as coalitions shift and dissolve. Italy furnishes an almost nightmarish example: It has had a new government on the average of once every nine months since the end of World War II.

One-Party Systems

In nearly all dictatorships today, only one political party—the party of the ruling clique—is allowed. For all practical purposes, it is quite accurate to say that in those circumstances the resulting **one-party system** is really a "no-party" system.

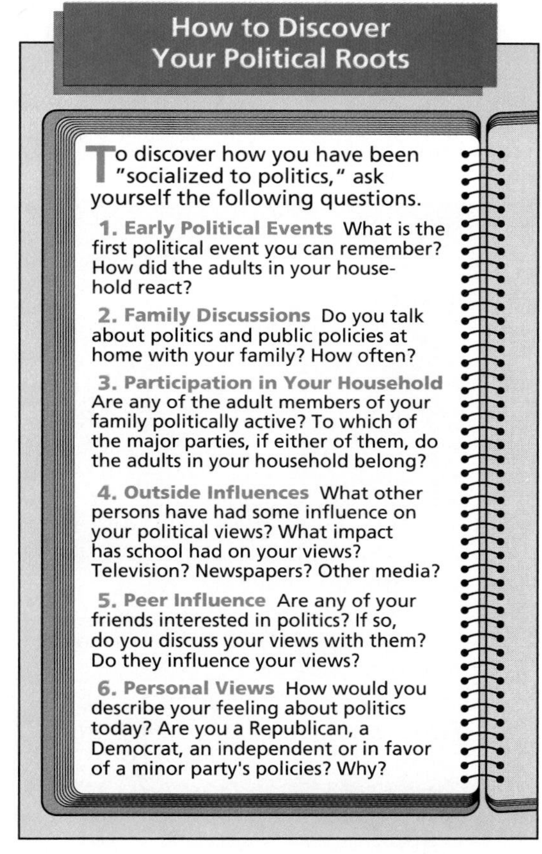

How to Discover Your Political Roots
To discover how you have been "socialized to politics," ask yourself the following questions.
1. Early Political Events What is the first political event you can remember? How did the adults in your household react?
2. Family Discussions Do you talk about politics and public policies at home with your family? How often?
3. Participation in Your Household Are any of the adult members of your family politically active? To which of the major parties, if either of them, do the adults in your household belong?
4. Outside Influences What other persons have had some influence on your political views? What impact has school had on your views? Television? Newspapers? Other media?
5. Peer Influence Are any of your friends interested in politics? If so, do you discuss your views with them? Do they influence your views?
6. Personal Views How would you describe your feeling about politics today? Are you a Republican, a Democrat, an independent or in favor of a minor party's policies? Why?

Interpreting Charts After studying the various ways to discover your political roots, name one or two other possibilities that are not on the chart.

Interpreting Charts Ask students to interview an older person and ask that person to choose what they think has had the most significant influences on their political views and to explain why those influences have been so strong. Have them report the responses to the class.

Caption Answer Students may suggest comparing the American system to that of another country or comparing this system to that of the country their ancestors are from or they have visited. Or, students may add, "Have you ever been involved in a political campaign yourself, whether at school or through membership in an organization?"

SPOTLIGHT ON: Global Awareness

Minor parties sometimes exercise astonishing influence in a multiparty system—far beyond the seeming strength of their small numbers. Israel's two major parties, Likud and Labor, dominate the 120 seat Knesset (the Israeli parliament), yet in June 1990 neither had sufficient votes to form a ruling coalition government. After 42 days of interparty haggling and deal-making, a government was assembled only after the tiny Moledet party, one of the smallest of the 16 parties represented in the Knesset with just two seats, threw its support to the Likud-led coalition.

Interpreting Photos and Political Cartoons

Caption Answer The cartoon shows a political candidate announcing that he will change parties in order to be loyal, or "get votes." Thus, he is attempting to attract votes from the opposition party as candidates from one party may support items in the other party's platform to attract more voters.

Provide Guided Practice On the board, write the four factors that explain the two-party system in America. (*historical basis, tradition, electoral system, ideological consensus*) Have students explain how each one of these factors helped develop or reinforce the two-party system in this country.

Provide Independent Practice

TRF **Teacher's Resource File** You may wish to assign the Section 2 Guided Reading and Review from the Unit 2 File, p. 6, to help students master section content.

In quite another sense, several States and many local areas in this country were, and many can still be, described in one-party terms. Until the late 1950s, the Democrats dominated the politics of the South. The Republican party was almost always the winner in New England and in the upper Middle West.

But effective two-party competition has spread fairly rapidly in the past 25 years or so. Democrats have won many offices in every northern State. Republican candidates have become more and more successful throughout the once "Solid South."[6]

Membership of the Parties

Membership in a party is purely voluntary. A person is a Republican or a Democrat, or belongs to a minor party or is an independent, because that is what he or she chooses to be.[7]

Remember, the two major parties are broadly based. In order to gain more votes than their opponents, they must attract as much support as they possibly can. Each party has always been composed, in greater or lesser degree, of a cross section of the nation's population. Each is made up of Protestants, Catholics, and Jews; whites,

[6]Nevertheless, about a third of the States can still be said to have a modified one-party system. That is, one of the major parties regularly wins most elections in those States. Also, while most States have vigorous two-party competition at the Statewide level, within them are many locales dominated by one party.

[7]In most States a person must declare a preference for a particular party in order to vote in that party's primary election. That declaration is usually made as a part of the voter registration process, and it is often said to make one "a registered Republican (or Democrat)." The requirement is only a procedural one, however, and wholly a matter of individual choice.

"And I promise to always be loyal to my party, even if I have to change parties to do it!"

Dunagin's People by Ralph Dunagin. Reprinted with special permission of NAS, Inc.

Interpreting Photos and Political Cartoons Political candidates try to attract as much support from as many groups as they can—thus this photo showing Republican George Bush with traditionally Democratic law enforcement officers. How does the cartoon reinforce this concept?

Enrichment

Have students research, through local newspapers and town reports, a list of at least ten electoral offices for which people in their community can vote, including local, state, and national offices. Next, have students list offices for which party affiliation is given on the ballot and note when affiliation is not given. Then have students record whether they agree or disagree with the following statement and why: All elected officials should be declared members of a party. (Challenging)

Political Party Identification, 1940–1991

Year	Independent	Republican	Democrat
1940	20%	38%	42%
1950	22%	33%	45%
1960	23%	30%	47%
1964	22%	25%	53%
1968	27%	27%	46%
1970	26%	29%	45%
1972	29%	28%	43%
1974	33%	24%	44%
1976	30%	23%	47%
1978	29%	23%	48%
1980	30%	24%	46%
1982	29%	26%	45%
1984	29%	31%	40%
1986	30%	30%	40%
1988	28%	30%	42%
1990	30%	31%	39%
1991	35%	33%	32%

Registered Voters (10–100%)

Source: Gallup Poll, May 26, 1991

Interpreting Graphs This graph shows the percentage of voters who identify with the two major parties, and the percentage of Independents. Which group shows the biggest gain in support between 1940 and 1990?

African Americans, Hispanics, and other minorities; professionals, farmers, and union members. Each numbers the young, the middle-aged, and the elderly; city-dwellers, suburbanites, and rural residents among its members.

It is true that the members of certain segments of the electorate tend to align themselves more solidly with one or the other of the major parties, at least for a time. Thus, in recent decades, African Americans, Catholics and Jews, and union members have voted more often for Democrats. In the same way, white males, Protestants, and the business community have been inclined to back the GOP.[8] Yet, never have all members of any group tied themselves permanently to either party.

Individuals identify themselves with a party for many reasons. Family is almost certainly the most important among them. Studies show that nearly two out of every three Americans follow the party allegiance of their parents.

Major events can also have a decided influence on party choice. Of these, the Civil War and the Depression of the 1930s have been the most significant in American political history.

Economic status also influences party choice, although generalizations are quite risky. Clearly, though, those in higher income groups are more likely to be Republicans, while those with lower incomes tend to be Democrats.

Several other factors also feed into the mix of both party choice and voting behavior—including age, place of residence, level of education, and the work environment. Some of those factors may conflict with one another in the case of any individual—and they often do.

You will read more about the matter of partisan preference and voting behavior in later chapters.

[8]GOP is common shorthand for the Republican party. The initials stand for Grand Old Party, a nickname acquired in the latter part of the last century.

Section 2 Review

1. **Define:** minor party, two-party system, single-member district, plurality, pluralistic society, consensus
2. What four factors help to explain the existence of America's two-party system?
3. (a) What is a multiparty system? (b) A one-party system?
4. For what reasons does each party represent a cross section of the American population?

Critical Thinking

5. **Identifying Alternatives** (p. 19) Imagine that you are a campaign official for one of the two major parties. Think of a slogan that your party's candidate can use to appeal to large numbers of voters.

★

Interpreting Graphs Caption Answer Independents show the biggest gain between 1940 and 1991.

Monitor Comprehension

Answers to Section 2 Review
1. "Key Terms" are defined on the following pages:
- **a.** minor party, p. 102
- **b.** two-party system, p. 102
- **c.** single-member district, p. 103
- **d.** plurality, p. 103
- **e.** pluralistic society, p. 104
- **f.** consensus, p. 104

2. History, tradition, the electoral system, ideological consensus. **3.** (a) One in which there are many parties, each usually based on some distinctive interest. (b) One in which only one party exists. **4.** In order to gain power, a party must appeal to as many different types of people as possible. **5.** Answers will vary, but slogans should make an appeal to several groups.

Closure

The two-party system in the U.S. has resulted from a combination of history, tradition, electoral laws, and the ideological consensus of Americans. Also, each of the major parties consists of a cross-section of people, and cannot claim the unfailing allegiance of any one group. As students read the next section, they will learn more about the changes that have taken place within the two-party system.

Assignment Assign Section 3, pp. 109–114, for the next class period.

Teacher's Resource File
See the Unit 2 File for the Section 2 Quiz on page 7.

Reteach

Have students make a campaign poster or political cartoon that emphasizes both the strength of the two-party system and the kinds of changes taking place in the two major parties, represented in "Voices on Government" and in the political cartoons and photograph on pages 103–106.

TEACHING

What You Can Do

Get Involved in Politics

Objective

Understand how young people, even those who are not old enough to vote, can become politically active.

INSTRUCT

Ask if any students in the class have been involved in politics in school or in their community. Invite students to share their experiences. Ask students to name some political activities other than voting and ask why they think they could or could not become involved in such activities.

Below is a possible question for post-reading discussion.

- How might experiences in other countries and cultures inspire one to become involved in politics?

What You Can Do

Tackling Politics

Only 37 percent of Americans who were between 18 and 24 years old voted in the November 1988 elections. Yet many teens are discovering that they can play some important roles in politics, and others are following their examples. Read about how some students are claiming a place for themselves in the political arena.

Students Take Action

Richard Taylor of Louisiana first became involved in politics when he was 14 years old. At that time, he ran a campaign that resulted in establishing a student position on the Louisiana State Board of Education. Richard has been elected governor of the Louisiana Youth Legislature and a youth leadership group called Louisiana Boy's State. The current high point of Richard's political career occurred when he was 17 years old and was elected as a delegate to the 1988 Democratic National Convention. Richard even defeated some elected officials for this honor and was privileged to cast his vote for the party's presidential nominee.

Subsequently, Richard worked for the 1988 Dukakis presidential campaign. He encourages other teens to become involved in politics, saying "It's your future. So why let someone else determine your destiny? You can play a significant role in determining it yourself."

Doris Wart, also from Louisiana, first became interested in politics when she visited the Soviet Union at age 13. At that time, she thought that the Soviet government and lifestyle were oppressive, and she began to truly appreciate her own government. When she returned home, Doris began working for the local Republican party. At 19, she founded a Republican Club at Louisiana State University and was elected as an alternate delegate to the 1988 Republican National Convention. Doris is active in registering high school and college students to vote and often participates.

Although Doris sometimes fantasizes about what it would be like to become the first woman President, her current goal is to become a member of the House of Representatives.

Not Just for Future Presidents

Like Richard and Doris, thousands of teens across America are becoming involved in politics at many levels. They volunteer to do everything from stuffing envelopes for their favorite candidates to starting political clubs in their schools.

As politically active 18-year-old Steve Densely of Utah remarks, "I could have listened to all the people who told me I was too young to make a difference in . . . politics. But I knew better. Don't let anyone tell you you can't do it, because I've learned from my experiences that you can." Perhaps the most important advice of all comes from 17-year-old Georgia resident Johnny Martinez: "Don't worry if you're too young to vote. It's incredible how much one volunteer can do."

Getting Involved

1. Identify an organization involved in national, State, or local politics in which you would like to be involved.
2. Formulate a plan for how you might become involved and identify resources that will help you implement your plan.
3. Predict what you think you can accomplish by becoming involved with this organization.

Teacher's Resource File
See the Participatory Government Activities file, pp. 28–39, for material to extend or support this feature.

3 The Two-Party System in American History

Find Out:

- How have political parties developed during the history of this country?
- Which two American political parties have dominated the nation's politics for more than 125 years?

Key Term:

electorate

Henry Ford, the great automaker, once said that all history is "bunk." Ford knew a great deal about automobiles and mass production, and much else. But he did not know much about history or its importance.

Listen, instead, to Shakespeare: "The past is prologue." Today is the product of yesterday. You are what you are today because of your history. The more you know about your past, the better prepared you are for today, and for tomorrow.

Much the same can be said about the two-party system in American politics. The more you know about its past, the better you understand its workings today.

In this section, you will take a look at the development of political parties in American history.

The Nation's First Parties

The beginnings of the American two-party system can be traced to the battle over the ratification of the Constitution. The conflicts of the time, centering on the proper form and role of government in the United States, were not stilled by the adoption of the work of the Framers at the Philadelphia Convention. Rather, those conflicts were carried over into the early years of the Republic, and they led directly to the formation of the nation's first full-blown political parties.

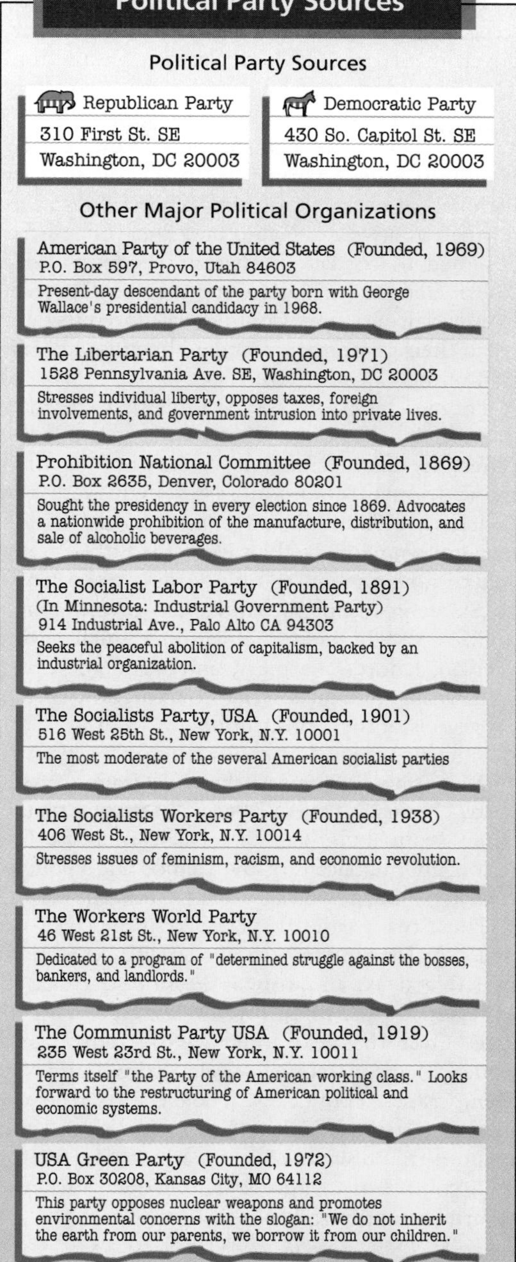

Political Party Sources
Political Party Sources
Republican Party
310 First St. SE
Washington, DC 20003
Democratic Party
430 So. Capitol St. SE
Washington, DC 20003
Other Major Political Organizations
American Party of the United States (Founded, 1969)
P.O. Box 597, Provo, Utah 84603
Present-day descendant of the party born with George Wallace's presidential candidacy in 1968.
The Libertarian Party (Founded, 1971)
1528 Pennsylvania Ave. SE, Washington, DC 20003
Stresses individual liberty, opposes taxes, foreign involvements, and government intrusion into private lives.
Prohibition National Committee (Founded, 1869)
P.O. Box 2635, Denver, Colorado 80201
Sought the presidency in every election since 1869. Advocates a nationwide prohibition of the manufacture, distribution, and sale of alcoholic beverages.
The Socialist Labor Party (Founded, 1891)
(In Minnesota: Industrial Government Party)
914 Industrial Ave., Palo Alto CA 94303
Seeks the peaceful abolition of capitalism, backed by an industrial organization.
The Socialists Party, USA (Founded, 1901)
516 West 25th St., New York, N.Y. 10001
The most moderate of the several American socialist parties
The Socialists Workers Party (Founded, 1938)
406 West St., New York, N.Y. 10014
Stresses issues of feminism, racism, and economic revolution.
The Workers World Party
46 West 21st St., New York, N.Y. 10010
Dedicated to a program of "determined struggle against the bosses, bankers, and landlords."
The Communist Party USA (Founded, 1919)
235 West 23rd St., New York, N.Y. 10011
Terms itself "the Party of the American working class." Looks forward to the restructuring of American political and economic systems.
USA Green Party (Founded, 1972)
P.O. Box 30208, Kansas City, MO 64112
This party opposes nuclear weapons and promotes environmental concerns with the slogan: "We do not inherit the earth from our parents, we borrow it from our children."

Interpreting Charts Only the largest minor parties are shown here. Which party shown has the narrowest political platform?

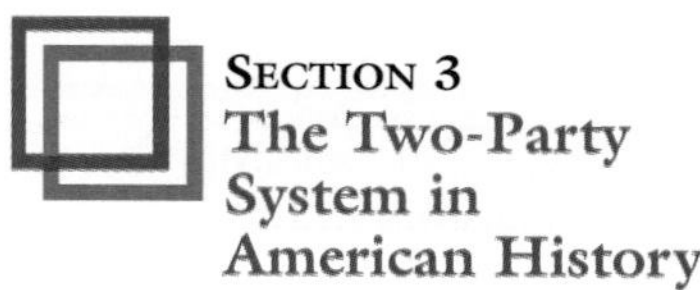

Section 3 The Two-Party System in American History

Focus

Teacher's Resource File See the Unit 2 File, p. 8, for the Section 3 Outline.

Objectives

5.6 Describe how political parties have developed in this country.

5.7 Name the two political parties that have dominated the nation's politics for more than 125 years.

Bellringer Activity Ask students to describe any kind of an era; e.g., an era centered around world events, popular music, or fashion. Invite students to speculate about what factors contribute to the domination of a musical star, an ideology, or, especially, a political party over a certain period.

State the Purpose The roots of today's Democratic and Republican parties began during the ratification of the U.S. Constitution. Each party has had two eras of domination in American history. In Section 3, students will read about the major political parties in the four eras of American political history.

Interpreting Charts Study the platforms of each of the minor parties. Ask: Why have these parties not become as large as the Republican and Democratic parties? (*Most represent the interests of a relatively small number of voters.*)

Caption Answer The Prohibition party.

Vocabulary

Point out the "Key Term" above. Explain to students that one of the meanings of the suffix *-ate* is "group." The word *senate*, for example, originally meant "group of elders." Ask students to consider this information as they give a possible definition for *electorate*. LEP

Reading Strategy: Relating to Topic

Refer students to the opening paragraphs of Section 3. Have them read the quotations from both Henry Ford and William Shakespeare and agree or disagree with each, explaining their opinions on the importance of history and its relevance to understanding the present.

INSTRUCT

Explain Clarify for students that the history of the two-party system in the United States began with the history of the government. The origins of the earliest parties, the Federalists and the Anti-Federalists, can be traced directly to the battle over the ratification of the Constitution. Since 1800, the history of the American party system can be divided into four periods dominated by two parties, the Democrats and the Republicans: the era of the Democrats, 1800–1860; the era of the Republicans, 1860–1932; the return of the Democrats, 1932–1968; and a "new era," 1968–?, during which presidential politics have been largely dominated by the Republican party, while Congress has been controlled by the Democrats.

ABCNEWS INTERACTIVE

The following video segments may be used to highlight aspects of the history of U.S. political parties.

POWERS OF THE PRESIDENT GUIDEBOOK
Chapter 7: Political Party System, p. 8
Chapter 40: Historical Figures, p. 48
Chapter 42: Presidents of the United States, p. 50

The Federalist party was the first to appear. It formed around Alexander Hamilton, who served as secretary of the treasury in the new government organized by George Washington. The Federalists were, by and large, the party of "the rich and the well-born." Most of them had supported the Constitution. Now, led by Hamilton, they worked to make a stronger national government a reality. They favored vigorous executive leadership and a set of policies designed to correct the nation's economic ills. The Federalists' program appealed to financial, manufacturing, and commercial interests. To reach their goals, they urged a liberal interpretation of the Constitution.

Thomas Jefferson, the nation's first secretary of state, led the opposition to the Federalists.[9] Jefferson and his followers were more sympathetic to the "common man" than were the Federalists. They favored a limited role for the new government. In their view, the States, not a central government, should dominate the United States government. And, that government's policies should help the nation's small shopkeepers, laborers, farmers, and planters. Jeffersonians insisted on a strict construction of the provisions of the Constitution.

Jefferson resigned from Washington's cabinet in 1793 to give his time to the organization of his party. Originally, the Anti-Federalist party took the name Republicans. Then it was known as the Jeffersonian Republicans or the Democratic-Republicans. By 1828, it was called the Democratic party.

These two parties first clashed in the elections of 1796. John Adams, the Federalists' candidate to succeed Washington as President, defeated Jefferson by just three votes in the electoral college. Over the next four years, Jefferson and James Madison worked tirelessly to build the Democratic-Republicans. Their efforts paid off in the elections of 1800. Jefferson defeated the incumbent President Adams, and his party also won control of Congress. The Federalists never returned to power.

[9] Given his opposition to the rise of parties, President Washington named arch foes Hamilton and Jefferson to his new cabinet to get them to work together—in an unsuccessful attempt to avoid the creation of formally organized and opposing groups.

The Eras of One-Party Domination

The history of the American party system since 1800 can be divided into four major periods. Through the first three of them, one or the other of the two major parties regularly held the presidency and, usually, both houses of Congress. The nation is now in a fourth period, which has been marked by divided government, as you will see.

In the first of these periods, from 1800 to 1860, the Democrats won 13 of 15 presidential elections. They lost the office only in the elections of 1840 and 1848. In the second era, from 1860 to 1932, the Republicans won 14 of 18 elections, losing only in 1884, 1892, 1912, and 1916. The third period, from 1932 to 1968, began with the Democrats' return to power and Franklin Roosevelt's first election to the presidency. The Democrats won five of the seven presidential elections held over those years, losing only in 1952 and 1956. Through the fourth period, which began in 1968, the Republicans have won five of six presidential elections, and they hold the White House today. But the Democrats have controlled both houses of Congress over most of the period, and they do so today.

The Era of the Democrats, 1800–1860

As you have read, Jefferson's election in 1800 marked the beginning of a period of Democratic domination that was to last until the Civil War. As the chart on the following page shows, the Federalists, shattered in 1800, had disappeared altogether by 1816.

For a time, through the Era of Good Feeling, the Democratic-Republicans were unopposed in national politics. They had split into factions by the mid-1820s, however. By the time of Andrew Jackson's administration (1829–1837), a potent National Republican (Whig) party had arisen to form a significant challenge to the Democrats. The major issues of the day—conflicts over public lands, the Second Bank of the United States, high tariffs, and slavery—all had made new party alignments inevitable.

The Democrats, led by Jackson, were a coalition of small farmers, debtors, frontier pioneers, and slaveholders. Their main area of political strength lay in the South and West. The years of

ACTIVITY: For Gifted Students

Theme: Leadership Partisan leadership and the legacy of the two-party system have become American political traditions. Have students evaluate the impact of partisan leadership on social and economic reforms over the past 15 years. For example, students might examine President Reagan's leadership on income tax reform in the 1980s. Students may present their conclusions by writing letters to the editor of the local paper.

Teacher's Resource File
See the Historical and Legal Documents file, p. 19, for material to support the section.

Jacksonian democracy saw the coming of universal white male suffrage, a large increase in the number of elective offices around the country, and the spread of the spoils system. (You will read more about the influence of Jacksonian Democracy in Chapter 15.)

The Whig party was led by the widely popular Henry Clay and the great orator, Daniel Webster. A loose coalition of eastern bankers, merchants and industrialists, and southern planters, the Whigs were opposed to the tenets of Jacksonian democracy and dedicated to the high tariff. However, the Whigs' victories were few. As the other major party from the mid-1830s to the 1850s, they were able to elect only two Presidents, both of them war heroes: William Henry Harrison in 1840 and Zachary Taylor in 1848.

By the 1850s the growing crisis over slavery split both major parties. Left leaderless by the deaths of Clay and Webster, the Whigs fell apart. Meanwhile, the Democrats split into two sharply divided camps, North and South. Through the decade the nation drifted toward civil war.

Of the several groupings that arose to compete for supporters during this time, the Republican party was the most successful. Born in 1854, it drew many Whigs and antislavery Democrats. The Republicans nominated their first presidential candidate, John C. Frémont, in 1856 and elected their first President, Abraham Lincoln, in 1860. With those accomplishments, the Republican party became the only party in the history of American politics to make the jump from third-party to major-party status. As you will shortly see, even greater things were in store for the Republican party.

The Era of the Republicans, 1860–1932

The Civil War signaled the beginning of the second era of one-party domination. For nearly 75 years, the Republicans—supported by business and financial interests, and by farmers, laborers, and newly freed African Americans—dominated the national scene.

The Democrats, crippled by the war, were able to survive mainly through their hold on the "Solid South." For the balance of the century, they slowly rebuilt their electoral base. In all that

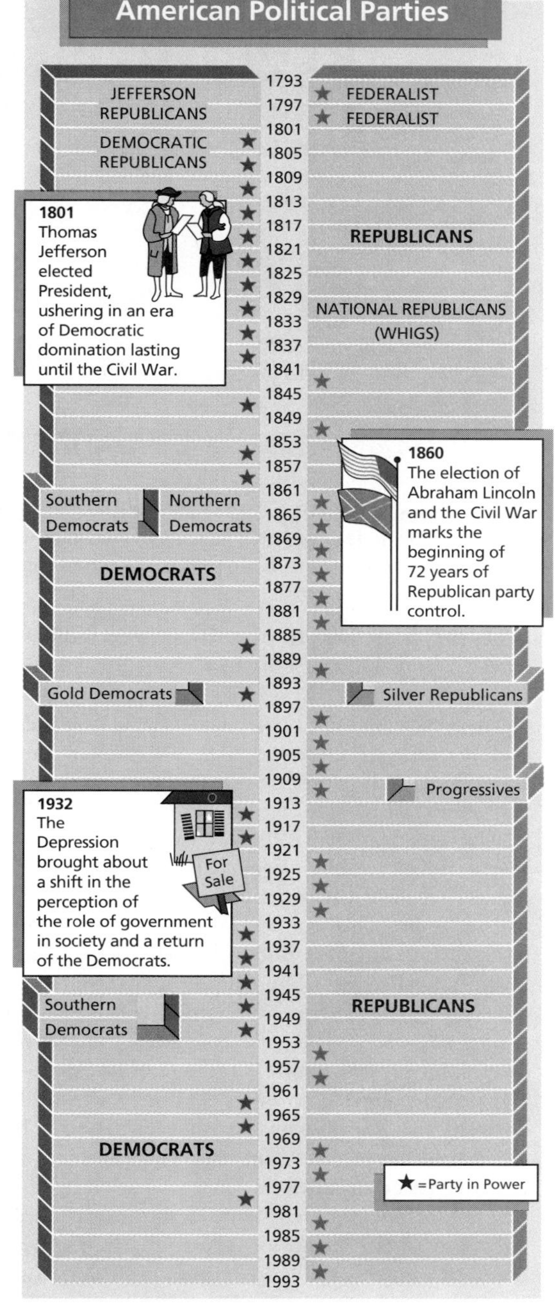

Interpreting Charts Three of the four eras of party domination are highlighted here. Which party had the longest period of control?

Interpreting Charts Ask: Which one of the four eras is not highlighted on this chart. (*The "new era."*) What events may be associated with the beginning of the new era? (*Students may suggest that the Vietnam War, civil rights, or a weak economy may be associated with the beginning of the new era.*)

Caption Answer The Republicans had the longest period of control from 1860 to 1932.

Spotlight on: Behind the Scenes

As unbelievable as it may seem today, Abraham Lincoln barely made it to the presidency. Although his election in 1860 marked the start of 72 years of Republican-dominated government, the Great Emancipator himself was elected President of the United States with the second smallest plurality ever recorded. In a four-way race, with the electorate badly divided over slavery, states rights, and possible secession by the Southern States, Lincoln took only 39.8 % of the popular vote versus Northern Democrat Stephen A. Douglas's 29.5%. Only John Quincy Adams, whose 1824 election was decided in the House of Representatives, became President with a smaller share of the popular vote, 31.9%.

Provide Guided Practice As a way to organize and distinguish events of the four eras, draw a time line on the board and have students supply the dates of each era. (*1800–1860; 1860–1932; 1932–1968; 1968 to the present*) Then have students supply the name of the dominant party during each era and any prominent figures and related events, while you write the information on the board. (*For example: 1800–1860: Democrats, Jackson, Second Bank, public lands, Whig party, etc.*)

A Voter for FDR The holder of this ticket to the Franklin Field ceremonies, part of the Democratic National Convention at Philadelphia in 1936, helped nominate President Roosevelt for a second time.

time, they were able to place only one candidate in the White House: Grover Cleveland in 1884 and again in 1892. Those elections marked only short breaks in Republican supremacy, however. Riding the crest of popular acceptance and unprecedented prosperity, the GOP remained the dominant party well into this century.

The election of 1896 was especially critical in the development of the party system. It climaxed years of protest by small business owners, farmers, and the emerging labor unions against big business and financial monopolies and the railroads. The Republicans regained the presidency with William McKinley. In doing so, they were able to gather new support from several segments of the **electorate**— 1.a the people eligible to vote. This new strength allowed the Republicans to maintain their role as the dominant party in national politics for another three decades.

The Democrats also made a significant contribution in this election. Although the Democratic nominee, William Jennings Bryan, lost the election, he presented himself as a powerful champion of the "little man"—and so helped to push the nation's party politics back toward the economic arena, and away from the divisions of sectionalism that had plagued the nation for so many years.

The Republicans suffered their worst setback of the era in 1912, when they renominated incumbent President William Howard Taft. Former President Theodore Roosevelt, denied the nomination of his party, left the Republicans to become the candidate of his "Bull Moose" Progressive party. With Republican support divided between Taft and Roosevelt, the Democratic nominee, Woodrow Wilson, was able to capture the presidency. And Wilson managed to keep the office, by a narrow margin, four years later.

But, again, the Democratic successes of 1912 and 1916 proved only a brief interlude. The GOP reasserted its control of the nation's politics by winning each of the next three presidential elections—with Warren Harding in 1920, Calvin Coolidge in 1924, and Herbert Hoover in 1928.

The Return of the Democrats, 1932 to 1968 The Great Depression, which began in 1929, had a massive impact on nearly all aspects of American life. Its effect on the American political landscape was considerable indeed. The

Enrichment

Have students pair off and research important problems and issues of any election year in American history. Have one student in each pair research the positions of one of the major party's candidates on those issues. The other student in the pair should research the positions of the opposing candidate. Have each student prepare and give a campaign speech that includes information about how this candidate sets him- or herself apart from opponents with respect to the issues. Following each pair of speeches, hold a vote for each pair of candidates, using a show of hands. Compare the results of the class straw poll with the actual election results. (Average)

OR

TRF **Teacher's Resource File**
See the Unit 2 file, pp. 18–20, for the Case Study on Contemporary Issues for Chapter 5.

landmark election of 1932 brought Franklin Roosevelt to the presidency and the Democrats back to power at the national level. Also, and of fundamental importance, that election marked a basic shift in the public's attitude toward the proper place of government in the nation's social and economic life.

Franklin Roosevelt and the Democrats engineered their victory in 1932 with a new electoral base. It was built largely of Southerners, small farmers, organized labor, and big-city political organizations. Roosevelt's revolutionary economic and social welfare programs, which formed the heart of the New Deal of the 1930s, further strengthened that coalition; and it soon brought increasing support from African Americans and other minorities to the Democrats.

President Roosevelt won reelection in 1936. He secured an unprecedented third term in 1940 and yet another term in 1944, each time by heavy majorities. Roosevelt's Vice President, Harry S Truman, completed the fourth term following FDR's death in 1945. Truman was elected to a full term of his own in 1948, when he turned back the GOP challenge led by Governor Thomas E. Dewey.

The Republicans did manage to regain the White House in 1952, and they kept it in 1956. The Republicans were led to victory in both elections by World War II hero Dwight Eisenhower, who both times defeated Democrat Adlai Stevenson.

Like other interludes in the eras of one-party domination, the Republican return to power was short-lived. In 1960 John F. Kennedy recaptured the presidency for the Democrats with a razor-thin plurality over the Republicans' nominee, then Vice President Richard M. Nixon. Lyndon Johnson became President following President Kennedy's assassination in 1963. In 1964, Johnson won by an overwhelming margin over his Republican opponent, Senator Barry Goldwater of Arizona.

The Start of a New Era Richard Nixon made a successful return to presidential politics in 1968. In that year's election he defeated Hubert Humphrey, the candidate of a Democratic party torn apart by conflicts over the war in Vietnam, civil rights, and a variety of social welfare issues. The Republican victory came with only a bare plurality over Humphrey and the strong third-party effort of the American Independent party nominee, Governor George Wallace of Alabama.

President Nixon remained in power when he routed the choice of the still-divided Democrats, Senator George McGovern, in 1972. Nixon's role in the Watergate scandal forced him from office in 1974, however. Vice President Gerald Ford then became President, and he filled out the balance of that presidential term. Beset by problems in the economy, by the continuing effects of Watergate, and by his pardon of former President Nixon, Ford lost the presidency to Jimmy Carter and the resurgent Democrats in 1976.

A steadily worsening economy, political fallout from the Iranian hostage crisis, and his own inability to establish himself as an effective President spelled defeat for Mr. Carter in 1980, however. Led by Ronald Reagan, the former governor of California, the Republicans scored an impressive victory that year; and Mr. Reagan won a second term by a landslide in 1984, overwhelming a Democratic ticket headed by former Vice President Walter Mondale.

The GOP kept control of the White House with a third straight win in 1988. Their candidate, George Bush, had served in the vice-presidency through the Reagan years, and he was able to turn back the Democrats and their nominee, Governor Michael Dukakis of Massachusetts.

Ronald Reagan's first election, in 1980, triggered wide-ranging efforts to alter the shape of many of the nation's foreign and domestic policies. His reelection in 1984, and then the election of President Bush in 1988, lend strong support to the claim that a majority of the nation's voters now favor more conservative rather than liberal stands on most public policy questions.

Nixon's victory in 1968 marked the beginning not only to a new era of one-party control, but also a period of divided government. During this time, Republicans regularly held the

Provide Independent Practice

TRF **Teacher's Resource File**
You may wish to assign the Section 3 Guided Reading and Review from the Unit 2 File, p. 9, to help students master section content.

TRF **Teacher's Resource File**
See the Historical and Legal Documents file, p. 27 , for material to support the section.

SPOTLIGHT ON: Political Talk

Neoconservatism—a rising new ideology—was partially responsible for the Republican resurrection of the 1980s. A hybrid ideology, neoconservatism was articulated first in the 1970s by disenchanted liberal thinkers in the quarterly journal, *Public Interest.* While accepting many features of the New Deal, neoconservatives were dismayed by what they saw as too much reliance on government. The many Democrats who voted for Ronald Reagan and the emergence of a more conservative Democratic party in the 1990s may attest to the pervasive impact of neoconservative ideas in the U.S.

MONITOR COMPREHENSION

Answers for Section 3 Review
1. The "Key Term" is defined on the following page:
a. electorate, p. 112
2. (a) The two major parties arose out of the battle for ratification of the Constitution. (b) Federalists and Anti-Federalists **3.** Democrats/1800–1860, Republicans/1860–1932, Return of the Democrats/ 1932–1968, and Return of the Republicans/1968–present. **4.** The present era is one of divided government; Republicans control the executive office, Democrats control Congress. **5.** Students may suggest that voters have preferred the national platform of the Republicans, but the views on local issues of the Democrats.

Teacher's Resource File See the Unit 2 File, p. 10, for the Section 3 Quiz.

CLOSURE

Remind students that the philosophies of the two major parties, the Republicans and the Democrats, have dominated politics in the United States for two hundred years. Each party has dominated national government for periods of time called Eras of One-Party Domination. As students read the next section, they will learn about the minor parties and their importance in American politics.

Assignment Assign Section 4, pp. 114–117, for the next class period.

White House while the Democrats have controlled Congress.[10] The present era of divided government is without precedent in American history. In earlier periods, a newly elected President almost always carried large numbers of his party's candidates into office with him. Thus, for example, the Democrats picked up 63 seats in the House when Woodrow Wilson won the presidency in 1912, and they gained 90 House seats when Franklin Roosevelt was elected for the first time in 1932.

Neither Nixon nor Reagan nor Bush brought many Republicans into office with him, however. In fact, the GOP lost seats in both the House and Senate when Bush won the presidency in 1988. Thus, President Bush, like Nixon and Reagan before him, has had to govern with a Congress solidly controlled by the opposition party.

Section 3 Review

1. Define: electorate
2. (a) Out of what circumstances did the nation's first two parties arise? (b) What were those parties?
3. Since 1800 the history of the American party system can be divided into what four eras?
4. What unique feature exists in the present era of one-party control?

Critical Thinking

5. Determining Relevance (p. 19) In recent years, the GOP has controlled the White House while the Democrats have controlled Congress. What does this fact suggest about voter opinions of each party?

★

[10]The Democrats have had almost uninterrupted control of Congress ever since their landslide victories of 1932. Over the years since then, the Republicans have controlled both houses for only two two-year periods—first following the congressional elections of 1946 and then 1952. The GOP did win control of the Senate (but not the House) in 1980; the Democrats recaptured the upper chamber in 1986, however, and have held it since.

4 The Minor Parties

Find Out:
- What are the different types of minor parties?
- What is the importance of minor parties?

Key Terms:
ideological parties, single-issue parties, economic protest parties, splinter parties

Peace and Freedom, Workers World, New Alliance, American Independent, Citizens, Workers League, Socialist Labor—these are only some of the parties whose candidates seek the presidency in 1992.

You know that none of these parties or their candidates have any real chance of winning. This is not to say that minor parties are unimportant, however. The bright light created by the two major parties too often blinds us to the vital role several minor parties have played in American politics.

In this section, you will read about the place of minor parties in the American political system.

Minor Parties in the United States

Their number and variety make minor parties difficult to describe and classify. Some have limited their efforts to a particular locale, others to a single State, and some to one region of the country. Still others have tried to woo the entire nation. Most have been short-lived, but a few have existed for decades. And, while most have lived mothlike around the flame of a single idea, some have had a broader, more practical base.

Still, four distinct types of minor parties can be identified:

1.a (1) The **ideological parties**—those based on a particular set of beliefs, a comprehensive view of social, economic, and political matters. Most of these minor parties have been built on some shade of Marxist thought—for example, the Socialist, Socialist Labor, Socialist Worker, and Communist parties. Some

ACTIVITY: Teaching Heterogeneous Groups

To clarify the information from Section 3, have students create two graphic organizers featuring the two major parties. Each organizer should have "Democrats" and "Republicans" as its main heading, and should include the original party name, any related parties (Whigs, Silver Democrats), major party figures, and periods of political domination. Students may also wish to include important events in each party's history mentioned in this section. LEP

Reteach

Share with students the following lyrics from a song popular during the election of 1800. The song is pro-Adams: "Then rally strong and you'll defeat, / Their schemes of wicked action; / And trample down beneath your feet, / The Jeffersonian faction. / Be staunch and true on freedom's side, / And keep a firm connection; / Let not the Democrats divide / Your votes at next election." Ask students to change the words of a song they know to support either the Democrats or the Republicans. Students may use traditional, jazz, rap, or any other musical genre, but their song must characterize the party they choose to write about.

have had a quite different color, however—especially the Libertarian party of today, which emphasizes individualism and calls for doing away with most of government's present functions and programs.

The ideological parties have not often been able to win many votes. But, as a rule, they have been long-lived.

(2) The **single-issue parties**—those concen- 1.b
trating on a single public policy matter. Their names have usually indicated their primary concern—for example, the Free Soil party opposed the spread of slavery in the 1840s and 1850s; the American party, the "Know Nothings"—opposed Irish-Catholic immigration in the 1850s; and the Right to Life party, opposed to abortion today.

Most of the single-issue parties have faded into history as events have passed them by, as their themes have failed to attract voters, or as one or both of the major parties have taken their key issues as their own.

(3) The **economic protest parties**—those 1.c
rooted in periods of economic discontent. Unlike the socialist parties, these groups have not had any clear-cut ideological base. Rather, they have proclaimed their disgust with the major parties, demanded better times, and focused their anger on such real or imagined enemies as the monetary system, "Wall Street bankers," the railroads, or foreign imports. Most often, they have been sectional parties, drawing their strength from the agricultural South and West. Thus, the Greenback party tried to take advantage of agrarian discontent from 1876 through 1884. It appealed to struggling farmers by calling for the free coinage of silver, federal regulation of the railroads, an income tax, and labor legislation. Its descendant, the Populist party of the 1890s, also demanded public ownership of railroads, telephone and telegraph companies, lower tariffs, and the adoption of the initiative and referendum.

Each of these economic protest parties has disappeared as the nation has climbed out of the difficult economic period in which that party was born.

(4) The **splinter parties**—those which have 1.d
split away from one of the major parties. Most

American Political Parties Since 1789

Party	From	To
Federalist	**1790**	**1816**
Anti-Federalist	**1790**	*
Democratic-Republican	**1796**	**1828**
Democrat	**1828**	**Present**
National Republican	**1828**	**1832**
Whig	**1836**	**1852**
Republican	**1856**	**Present**
Anti-Masonic	1832	1836
Liberty	1840	1848
Free Soil	1848	1852
American (Know Nothing)	1856	*
Constitutional Union	1860	*
Southern Democrat	1860	*
Prohibition	1869	1988
Liberal Republican	1872	*
Greenback	1876	1884
Socialist Labor	1892	1972
Populist	1892	1908
National Democrat	1896	*
Socialist	1904	1956
Progressive (Bull Moose)	1912	*
Progressive (La Follette)	1924	*
Communist	1928	1940
Union	1936	*
Progressive (H. Wallace)	1948	1952
Socialist Workers	1948	1988
States' Rights Democrats	1948	*
Workers World	1960	1988
American Independent (G. Wallace)	1968	1988
Communist	1968	1988
Libertarian	1972	1988
Peoples	1976	1980
U.S. Labor	1976	1984
Socialist	1980	1984
National Unity	1984	1988
Citizens'	1984	1988
Populist	1984	*

Boldface entries are major parties; all others are third parties; * Represents parties that were only in existence for one presidential election.
Note: The lifespan for many political parties can only be approximated since many existed at the State and local levels before they ran candidates in presidential elections and continued to exist at the State and local levels long after they dropped out of presidential races.

▲ **Interpreting Tables** This table shows how many parties have tried to challenge the supremacy of the two-party system since 1789. Which of the minor parties has survived the longest?

SECTION 4
The Minor Parties

FOCUS

Teacher's Resource File
See the Unit 2 File, p. 11, for the Section 4 Outline.

Objectives

5.8 Describe the different types of minor parties.

5.9 Explain the importance of minor parties.

Bellringer Activity Before you begin, ask students to list the possible effects of a third-party candidate in a presidential election. (*Possible responses: Force discussion of certain issues; draw votes from major-party candidates.*)

State the Purpose Many minor parties exist in the U.S. in addition to the two major political parties. While no candidate from a minor party has ever won a major election, minor parties serve important functions in American politics. In Section 4, students will read about types of minor parties and their place in the political process.

ABCNEWS INTERACTIVE

The following video segment may be used to highlight aspects of minor parties.

POWERS OF THE PRESIDENT GUIDEBOOK
Chapter 40: Historical Figures, p. 48

Interpreting Tables Caption Answer The Prohibition Party.

Vocabulary

Point out "Key Terms" on page 114. Using the descriptive word(s) in each term, ask students to predict the definition of each type of party.
LEP

Reading Strategy: Who? What? When? Where? How? Why?

While reading the section, have students write short answers to six focus questions they have written beginning *Who, What, When, Where, How* and *Why.* If necessary, write the answer to one of the questions on the board to help students get started.

INSTRUCT

Discuss Discuss with students the existence of minor parties in U.S. politics. As an aid to discussion, you may wish to ask the following questions: What contributions can minor parties make? (*Raise controversial issues, present voters with clear choices, offer new approaches.*) Do students think a strong showing major elections is possible for minor parties today? (*Students may feel that due to the innovation function of minor parties, strong ideas that might give them enormous support are usually incorporated into the platforms of the major parties, leading to an inability of minor parties to sustain enough support for a strong showing in elections.*)

Interpreting Tables Caption Answer The success of Roosevelt's Progressives split the Republican vote, taking votes from Taft that he would otherwise have won.

Provide Guided Practice On the board, list the four types (ideological, single issue, economic protest, and splinter) of minor parties. Invite students to describe and give an example of each. Then have students list the key roles of minor parties. (*Spoiler, critic, innovator.*)

Provide Independent Practice

TRF **Teacher's Resource File** You may wish to assign the Section 4 Guided Reading and Review from the Unit 2 File, p. 12, to help students master section content.

The 1912 Presidential Election

Party and Candidate	Popular Vote	%	Electoral Vote
Democrat—Woodrow Wilson	6,293,152	41.8	435
Progressive—Theodore Roosevelt	4,119,207	27.4	88
Republican—William H. Taft	3,486,333	23.2	8
Socialist—Eugene V. Debs	900,369	6.0	—
Prohibition—Eugene Chafin	207,972	1.4	—

Interpreting Tables These figures show that Theodore Roosevelt's Progressives did better than the Republicans in 1912. Why did this pave the way to the election of Woodrow Wilson?

of the more important minor parties in our politics have been of this kind. Among the leading groups that have split away from the Republicans are Theodore Roosevelt's "Bull Moose" Progressive party of 1912, and Robert La Follette's Progressive party of 1924. From the Democrats have come Henry Wallace's Progressive party and the States' Rights (Dixiecrat) party, both of 1948, and George Wallace's American Independent party of 1968.

Most splinter parties have formed around some strong personality—most often one who has failed to win his major party's presidential nomination. They have faded or collapsed when that leader has stepped aside. Thus, the Bull Moose Progressive party passed away when Theodore Roosevelt returned to the Republican fold after the election of 1912. And the American Independent party lost nearly all of its brief strength when Governor George Wallace rejoined the Democrats following his strong showing in the 1968 election.

A few of the minor parties have been successful at the State or local level. Some have elected a few members of Congress and occasionally won some electoral votes in the presidential contest; but, needless to say, none has ever won the presidency.

The Key Role of Minor Parties

Though most Americans do not support them, minor parties have nonetheless had an impact on American politics and on the major parties. For example, it was a minor party, the Anti-Masons in 1831, that first used a national convention to nominate a presidential candidate. The Whigs and then the Democrats followed suit in 1832. Ever since, the national convention has been the means by which the Democrats and Republicans have picked their presidential tickets.

A strong third-party candidacy can play a decisive role—often a "spoiler role"—in an election. This can be true in national, State, or local politics, and especially where the two major parties compete on roughly equal terms. In such situations, a third party can effectively deny one of the major parties a majority—and an election. The point was dramatically illustrated in the presidential election of 1912. A split in the Republican party and the resulting third-party candidacy of Theodore Roosevelt produced the results shown in the table above. Almost certainly had Theodore Roosevelt not quit the Republican party, Taft would have enjoyed a better showing, and Woodrow Wilson would not have become President.

Historically, however, the most important roles of the minor parties have been those of critic and innovator. Unlike the major parties, the minor parties have been ready, willing, and able to take quite clear-cut stands on the controversial issues of their day. Though such stands rarely lead to any sustained political success for any minor party, these actions have often drawn attention to some issue that the major parties have preferred to ignore or straddle. Over the years, many of the more important issues of American politics were first

Enrichment

Have students choose one of the following minor parties (from the table on page 115): Anti-Masonic, Free Soil, American (Know Nothing), Prohibition, Greenback, Socialist Labor, Populist, Progressive (Bull Moose), Progressive (La Follette), Communist, Socialist Workers, States' Rights Democrats, Libertarian. Ask students to prepare a three-minute campaign speech for the party they have been assigned, in which the purpose and goals of the party are described. (Challenging)

SPOTLIGHT ON: Constitutional Issues

To "civilize, Christianize, and Americanize" new immigrants through the passage of temperance laws: such was the original goal of the Prohibition party. Founded in 1869, the party helped whip up prohibition fever in the U.S. after World War I, leading to passage of the 18th Amendment. This amendment prohibited the manufacture, sale, and distribution of liquor. However, as the 1920s wore on, "wets"—those who favored repeal of Prohibition—began to outnumber the "dries," and the hardship of the Great Depression sped the repeal of Prohibition with the 21st Amendment in 1933.

Significant Minor Parties in Presidential Elections, 1880-1988*

Year	Party and Candidate	Percent of Popular Vote	Electoral Votes
1880	Greenback James B. Weaver	3.72	—
1888	Prohibition Clinton B. Fisk	2.19	—
1892	Populist James B. Weaver	8.50	22
	Prohibition John Bidwell	2.25	—
1904	Socialist Eugene V. Debs	2.98	—
1908	Socialist Eugene V. Debs	2.82	—
1912	Progressive (Bull Moose) Theodore Roosevelt	27.39	88
	Socialist Eugene V. Debs	5.99	—
1916	Socialist Allan L. Benson	3.18	—
1920	Socialist Eugene V. Debs	3.42	—
1924	Progressive Robert M. La Follette	16.56	13
1932	Socialist Norman M. Thomas	2.22	—
1948	States' Rights (Dixiecrat) Strom Thurmond	2.40	39
	Progressive Henry A. Wallace	2.38	—
1968	American Independent George C. Wallace	13.53	46

* Includes all minor parties that polled at least 2% of the popular vote. No minor party did so in the years not shown, including 1972, 1976, 1980, 1984, and 1988.

Interpreting Tables The Progressive party is followed closely by the American Independents in terms of high voter appeal. What might have accounted for the success of these parties?

brought to the public's attention by a minor party—for example, the progressive income tax, women's suffrage, railroad and banking regulation, and old-age pensions.

But this very important innovator function of the minor parties has also been a major source of their frustration. When their proposals have gained any real degree of popular support, one and then both of the major parties have taken them over and presented them as their own. After all, when there is a significant pool of votes to be had by supporting some idea, both major parties cannot resist the temptation. The late Norman Thomas, six times the Socialist party's candidate for President, complained that "the major parties are stealing from my platform."

The presidential nominees of more than a dozen minor parties made it to the ballots of various States in 1988—and at least that many will likely do so in the 1992 election. In 1988 the more (or at least somewhat) visible minor party presidential campaigns were those of the American Independent, Communist, Consumer, Libertarian, New Alliance, Prohibition, and Socialist Workers parties. More than 1,000 minor party candidates from a wide variety of minor parties also sought seats in Congress or ran for various State and local offices, as well.

Section 4 Review

1. **Define:** ideological parties, single-issue parties, economic protest parties, splinter parties
2. What are the major characteristics of the typical minor party in American politics?
3. In what ways have minor parties been important in politics in the United States?
4. Why is the innovator function a source of frustration to minor parties?

Critical Thinking

5. **Expressing Problems Clearly** (p. 19) Imagine you are a voter considering casting your ballot for a presidential candidate from a minor party. Explain the benefits and drawbacks of casting your vote that way.

★

Interpreting Tables
Caption Answer The leaders of the minor parties with high voter appeal addressed issues that the major parties were ignoring.

MONITOR COMPREHENSION

Answers for Section 4 Review
1. "Key Terms" are defined on the following pages:
a. ideological parties, p. 114
b. single-issue parties, p. 115
c. economic protest parties, p. 115
d. splinter parties, p. 115
2. Short-lived, based on a single issue, and formed around a strong personality. **3.** In their roles as critic and innovator. **4.** When their proposals have gained significant popular support, the major parties have taken them over. **5.** Benefit: one can make a statement on an issue. Drawback: the candidate has virtually no chance of being elected.

CLOSURE

Remind students that minor parties have contributed both ideas and motivation to the two major parties. Minor parties can be classified into four basic types—ideological, single-issue, economic protest, and splinter. As students read the next section they will learn how political parties are organized, the elements of a major party, and factors that explain the state of political parties today.

Assignment Assign Section 5, pages 118–123 for the next class period.

TRF **Teacher's Resource File**
See the Unit 2 File for the Section 4 Quiz on page 13.

Reteach

Have students write the four types of minor parties evenly across a piece of paper. Under each type of party have students write a description in their own words and two examples from the section.

SECTION 5
The Organization of Political Parties

FOCUS

Teacher's Resource File See the Unit 2 File, p. 14, for the Section 5 Outline.

Objectives

5.10 Describe the factors that make the major parties highly decentralized.
5.11 Explain how the major parties are organized.
5.12 Analyze the three elements of a major party.
5.13 Understand the factors that explain the current state of parties and the party system.

Bellringer Activity Ask students to identify three major national issues, such as health care financing, and ask students to associate a major party with each issue. Then, ask students to vote *pro* or *con* on each issue. Point out that although they may consider themselves Republicans or Democrats, they probably considered issues, not party, when they voted. This tendency has helped lead to decentralized party structure.

State the Purpose The Republican and Democratic parties are powerful organizations, yet they are highly decentralized. They do, however, have specific forms of organization, directed toward nominating candidates and getting candidates elected. In Section 5, students will learn how the major political parties are organized and the challenges they face.

5 The Organization of Political Parties

Find Out:

- What factors make both major parties such highly decentralized organizations?
- How are the major parties organized?
- What are the three basic elements of a major party?
- What factors explain the current state of parties and the party system?

Key Terms:
ward, precinct, split-ticket voting

How strong, how active, how well organized are the Republican and Democratic parties in your community? Contact the county chairperson or another official in one or both of the major parties. They are usually not very difficult to find. For starters, try the telephone directory. You might be surprised by what you discover.

In this section, you will take a look at the overall shape of party organization in the United States; and you will also consider the future of parties and the party system.

The Reality of Political Parties

You often read of the two major parties in terms that suggest that they are highly organized, close-knit, well-disciplined groups. Even though they may look that way on paper—as in the chart on page 119—neither party is anything of the kind. Rather, both are highly decentralized. They are fragmented, disjointed; and they are often beset by factions and internal squabbling.

In neither party is there a chain of command running from the national through the State to the local level. Each of the State party organizations is only loosely tied to the party's national structure. And local party organizations are often quite independent of their parent State organizations. These various party units usually cooperate with one another, of course—but that is not always the case.

The Role of the Presidency The President's party is usually more solidly united and more cohesively organized than is the opposition. The President is automatically the party leader. He asserts that leadership with a number of weapons, among them the President's access to the media, his popularity, and his power to make appointments to federal office and to dispense other favors.

The other party has no one in an even faintly comparable position. Indeed, in the American party system, there is almost never any one personality in the opposition party who can be called, in fact, its leader. Rather, a number of personalities, frequently in competition with one another, form a more or less loosely identifiable leadership group in the party out of power.[11]

The Impact of Federalism Federalism is a major reason for the decentralized nature of the two major political parties. Remember, the basic goal of the major parties is to gain control of government, and they try to do this by winning elective offices. There are today more than half a million elective offices in the United States—and, in the American federal system, those offices are widely distributed at the national, the State, and the local levels. In short, because the governmental system is decentralized, so, too, are the major parties that serve it.

The Role of the Nominating Process The nominating process is also a major cause of party decentralization. As you recall from Section 1, the nominating process has a central role in the life of political parties. You will read about the selection of candidates at some length in Chapter 7, but, for now, look at two related aspects of that process.

First, candidate selection is an intraparty process. That is, nominations are made within the party. Second, that process can be, and often is, a divisive one. Where there is a fight

[11]The party does have a temporary leader for a brief time every fourth year: its presidential candidate, from nomination to election day. A defeated presidential candidate is often called the party's "titular leader"—a leader in title, by custom, but not in fact.

Reading Strategy: Problem Solving

As a preparation for reading, ask students to imagine they are part of a team of advisers to the head of any huge organization. Have students visualize how they might seek out suggestions for improvements in the organization from all levels of workers. Ask students to write down how they would go about gaining support for a proposal or a change that they wanted to see implemented throughout the organization.

Vocabulary

Direct students to "Key Terms" on page 118. Ask students to predict which of these terms might be one contributing factor in the weakening of the two major parties (*split-ticket voting*).

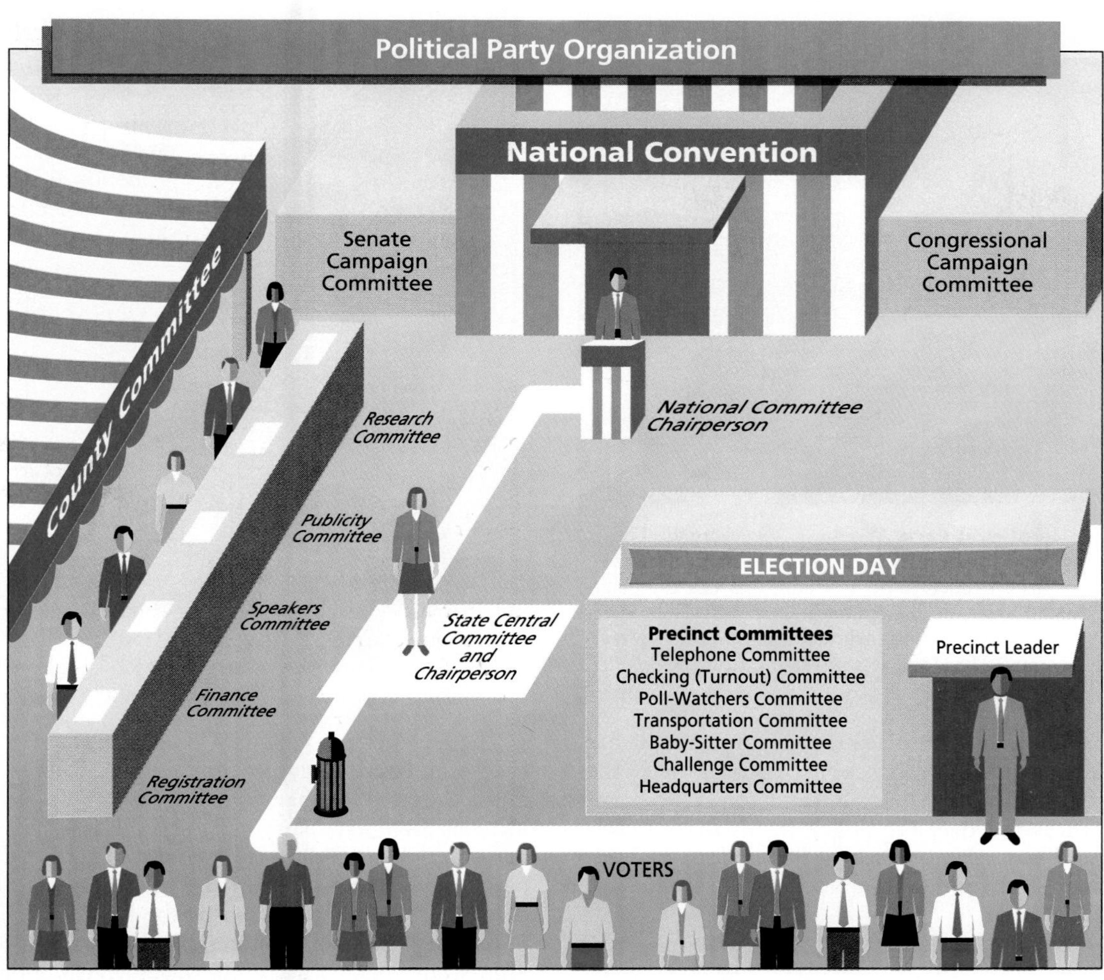

Interpreting Charts This chart shows the complexity of party organization at the national, State, and local levels. What accounts for the highly decentralized structures of the political party system?

over a nomination, that contest pits members of the same party against one another; Republicans fight Republicans, Democrats battle Democrats. In short, the prime function of the major parties—the making of nominations—is also a prime cause of their highly fragmented character.

National Party Machinery

As the chart above shows, there are four elements in the structure of both major parties at the national level. They are the national convention, the national committee, the national chairperson, and the congressional campaign committees.

The National Convention The national convention is often described as the party's national voice. It meets in the summer of every presidential election year to nominate the party's presidential and vice-presidential candidates. It also performs some other functions, including the adoption of the party's rules and

Interpreting Charts Ask students what is the primary purpose of the Election Day Precinct Committees? How do those functions contribute to the party's goal of electing candidates? *(Their primary purpose to ensure that as many voters as possible turnout to cast their vote. This contributes to the party's goal of electing candidates by increasing voter turnout and thus increasing their candidate's chances of winning.)*

Caption Answer The autonomy of the States and the nominating process account for the highly decentralized structure of the political party system.

ABCNEWS INTERACTIVE

The following video segments may be used to highlight aspects of party organization.

PARTIES OF THE PRESIDENT GUIDEBOOK
Chapter 7: Political Party System, p. 8
Chapter 10: Nominating a Candidate, p. 13

POWERS OF THE CONGRESS GUIDEBOOK
Chapter 22: Electing a Representative, p. 98
Chapter 23: Electing a Senator, p. 99
Chapter 66: The Federal System, p. 143

See also Enrichment Questions and Activities beginning on page 161.

Enrichment

Have students develop a comprehensive campaign strategy for the candidate of their choice. Assign different groups to study and make recommendations in such areas as media relations, direct mail, volunteer recruitment, candidate scheduling, issue briefs, fund-raising, etc. Have students form a central policy-making committee composed of one representative from each group to consolidate the recommendations into a campaign plan. You might wish to adapt this activity to a school election or, with another class, carry it through to a mock election. (Challenging)

Teacher's Resource File
See the Election Kit, pp. 30–31, for material to support the section.

INSTRUCT

Explain Explain to students that both the Republican and Democratic parties are highly decentralized and fragmented, largely as a result of the role of the presidency, federalism, and the potentially divisive nature of the nominating process.

There are four major elements in the structure of both parties at the national level: the national convention, the national committee, the national chairperson, and the congressional campaign committees.

State and local party organization is generally built along geographic and electoral lines.

The major parties may also be viewed as a three-part structure consisting of the party as an organization, the party in the electorate, and the party in the government.

Analyze Have students turn to the party organization chart on p. 119 and study the elements of party organization at different levels. Discuss how the chart reflects the federalist system and emphasize the fact that the lines between national, State, and local party organizations are not well-defined, representing areas of cooperation and communication rather than lines of authority.

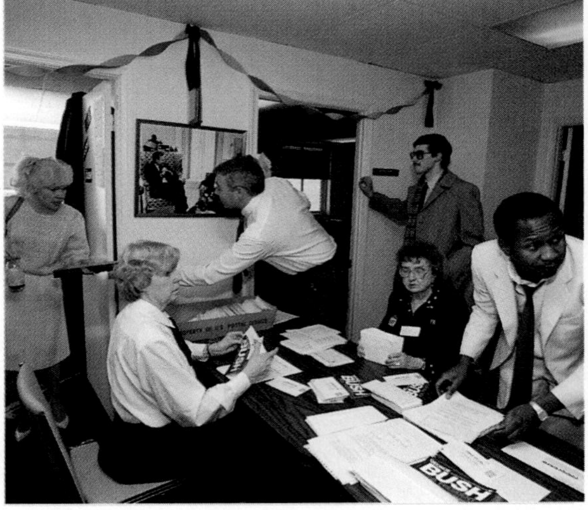

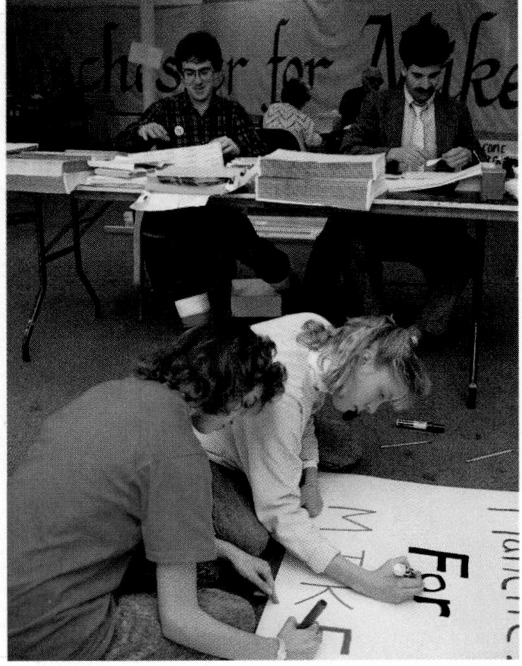

Political Party Workers At every level of party organization, the work of many individuals is needed to prepare and carry out campaign strategy. Both Republican (left) and Democratic (right) parties maintain their national committee headquarters in Washington, D.C.

the writing of its platform. Beyond that, it has little authority. It has no control over the selection of the party's candidates for other offices nor over the policy stands those nominees take. You will take a longer look at both parties' national nominating conventions in Chapter 13.

The National Committee Between conventions, the party's affairs are handled, at least in theory, by the national committee and by the national chairperson.

For years, each party's national committee was composed of a committeeman and a committeewoman chosen by the party organization in each State and several of the territories. Both parties have expanded the committee's membership in recent years, however.

Today, the Republican National Committee (RNC) also seats several of the party's State chairpersons—party leaders from those States that voted for the party's presidential candidate or that elected a Republican to the Senate, a majority of Republicans to the House, or a GOP governor in the preceding election.

The Democratic National Committee (DNC) is an even larger body. In addition to the committeeman and -woman from each State, it now includes each State party's chair- and vice-chairperson, several additional members from the party organizations of the larger States, and 33 at-large members chosen by the DNC itself. Several members of Congress, as well as governors, mayors, and Young Democrats, also have seats.

On paper, the national committee appears to be a powerful organ loaded with many of the party's leading figures. In fact, it does not have a great deal of clout. Most of its work centers on staging the party's national convention every four years.

The National Chairperson In each party, the national chairperson heads up the national committee. In form, he or she is chosen to a four-year term by the national committee, at a meeting held right after the national convention. In fact, the choice is made by the just-nominated presidential candidate and is then ratified by the national committee.

SPOTLIGHT ON: Economics

The national party committees also raise funds to support candidates for office and to make sure that the party's message gets out to the voters. For the election cycle 1989–1990, the RNC raised $207.2 million (86% of which came from individuals, 2% from PACs, and 12% from other sources), while the DNC raised $86.7 million (64% from individuals, 13% from PACs, and 22% from other sources) over the same period. The RNC spent $7.7 million on Senate races and about $3 million on races for the House, while the DNC spent about $5 million on behalf of Senate candidates, and some $3.3 million on races for the House.

To date, the Democrats and Republicans have each picked only one woman for its top post. Jean Westwood of Utah chaired the DNC from the 1972 convention until early 1973, and Mary Louise Smith of Iowa headed the RNC from 1974 to early 1977. Each was replaced soon after her party lost a presidential election, however. That is the usual fate of the national chairperson in the losing party every fourth year.

The chairperson directs the work of the party's headquarters and its small staff in Washington. In presidential election years, the committee's attention is focused on the national convention and then the campaign. In between, the chairperson and the committee work to strengthen the party and its fortunes—promoting party unity, raising money, recruiting new voters, and otherwise preparing for the next presidential season.

The Congressional Campaign Committees As the chart on page 119 shows, each party also has a campaign committee in each house of Congress.[12] These committees work to reelect incumbents and to save the seats given up by retiring party members. The committees also take a hand in some campaigns to unseat incumbents in the other party, at least in those House or Senate races where the chances for success seem to justify such efforts.

In both parties and in both houses, the members of these campaign committees are chosen by their colleagues. They serve for two years—that is, for a term of Congress.

[12]In the House, the National Republican Campaign Committee and the Democratic Congressional Campaign Committee; in the Senate, the National Republican Senatorial Campaign Committee and the Democratic Senatorial Campaign Committee.

Party Leaders Democratic National Committee Chairman Ron Brown (right) works to prevent a fourth straight presidential defeat for his party in 1992, while his Republican counterpart, Clayton Yeutter (left), strives to maintain Republican supremacy at the polls.

Provide Guided Practice On the board, list the components of the national party machinery. *(The national convention, the national committee, the national chairperson, and the congressional campaign committees.)* Invite students to provide one fact about the role of each as you write their comments on the board.

In light of the functions of the different parts of the party machinery, guide students to understand that the party is more a coordinating body than an executive body.

Provide Independent Practice

TRF **Teacher's Resource File** You may wish to assign the Section 5 Guided Reading and Review from the Unit 2 File, p. 15, to help students master section content.

SPOTLIGHT ON: Multiculturalism

Ronald H. Brown became the first African American appointed to serve as chairman of either of the national parties when he assumed the chair of the Democratic National Committee (DNC) in 1989. A Washington lawyer, former Senate staffer, and long-time Democratic party activist, Brown has served as a member of the DNC executive committee, as deputy chair, and as chief counsel, among other assignments, since 1982. Brown was a captain in the U.S. Army and, after his discharge, began his political career as an official of the National Urban League.

Interpreting Graphics Have students look at the graphic on page 123. Ask them to explain why none of the three elements can exist without the other two.

Caption Answer The party in government is the most visible.

MONITOR COMPREHENSION

Answers for Section 5 Review
1. "Key Terms" are defined on the following pages:
a. ward, p. 122
b. precinct, p. 122
c. split-ticket voting, p. 122
2. The national convention, the national committee, the national chairperson, and the congressional campaign committees.
3. (a) State central committee headed by a State chairperson. (b) County committees, precinct leaders and workers, and a variety of election-day precinct committees. **4.** Party organization, party in the electorate, and party in government. **5.** A sharp drop in the number of voters willing to identify with one of the major parties, an increase in split-ticket voting, structural changes and reforms, technological changes in campaigning, and the growth of single-issue organizations.
6. Students may suggest that local party organizations differ because each community has different needs and if the party does not look out for the community, it will not be able to get votes for its candidates.

TRF Teacher's Resource File See the Unit 2, p. 16, for the Section 5 Quiz.

State and Local Party Machinery

National party organization is largely the product of custom and the rules adopted by national conventions. At the State and local levels, however, party structure is largely set by State law.

The State Organization Look again at the chart on page 119. At the State level, party machinery is built around a State central committee, headed by a State chairperson.

The chairperson may be an important political figure in his or her own right. More often than not, however, the chairperson fronts for the governor, a U.S. senator, or some other powerful leader or group in the politics of the State.

Together, the chairperson and the central committee work to further the party's interests in the State. Most of the time they attempt to do so by building an effective organization and party unity, finding candidates and campaign funds, and so on. Remember, however, both major parties are highly decentralized, fragmented, and sometimes torn by struggles for power. This can complicate the chairperson's and the committee's job.

Local Organization Local party structures vary so widely that they nearly defy even a brief description. Generally, they follow the electoral map of the State, with a party unit for each district in which elective offices are to be filled: congressional and legislative districts, counties,
1.a cities and towns, wards, and precincts. A **ward** is a unit into which cities are often divided for the
1.b election of city council members. A **precinct** is the smallest unit of election administration—the voters in each precinct report to one polling place. In most larger cities a party's organization is further broken down by residential blocks and sometimes even apartment buildings.

In some places, local party organizations are active year-round, but most often they are inactive except for those few hectic months before an election.

The Three Elements of the Party

Look at the structure of the two major parties from another angle: the roles of their members, rather than their organizational charts. From this perspective, they are made up of three basic and closely interrelated elements:

1. The party organization: the leaders, the activists, and the hangers-on who control and run the party machinery.
2. The party in the electorate: the party's loyalists who vote the straight party ticket or usually vote for its candidates.
3. The party in government: the party's officeholders at all levels of government.

The Future of the Major Parties

Political parties have never been very popular in this country. Rather, over time, most Americans have had very mixed feelings about political parties. Most of us have accepted parties as necessary institutions, but, at the same time, people feel that they should be closely watched and controlled. To many, they have seemed little better than necessary evils.

Political parties have been in a period of decline since at least the late 1960s. Their decline has led some analysts to conclude that not only are the parties in serious trouble, the party system itself may be on the point of collapse.

The present, weakened state of the parties can be traced to several factors. They include:

1. A sharp drop in the number of voters willing to identify themselves as Republicans or Democrats, and a growing number who regard themselves as independents.
2. 1.c A big increase in **split-ticket voting**—voting for candidates of both parties for different offices at the same election.
3. Various structural changes and reforms—from the introduction of the direct primary in the early 1900s to recent and far-reaching changes in campaign finance laws—that have made the parties more "open" but have also led to greater internal conflict and disorganization.
4. Changes in the technology of campaigning for office—especially the heavy use of television and of such other devices as professional campaign managers and direct-mail advertising. These changes have made candidates much less dependent on party organizations.
5. The growth of single-issue organizations. These groups take sides for or against

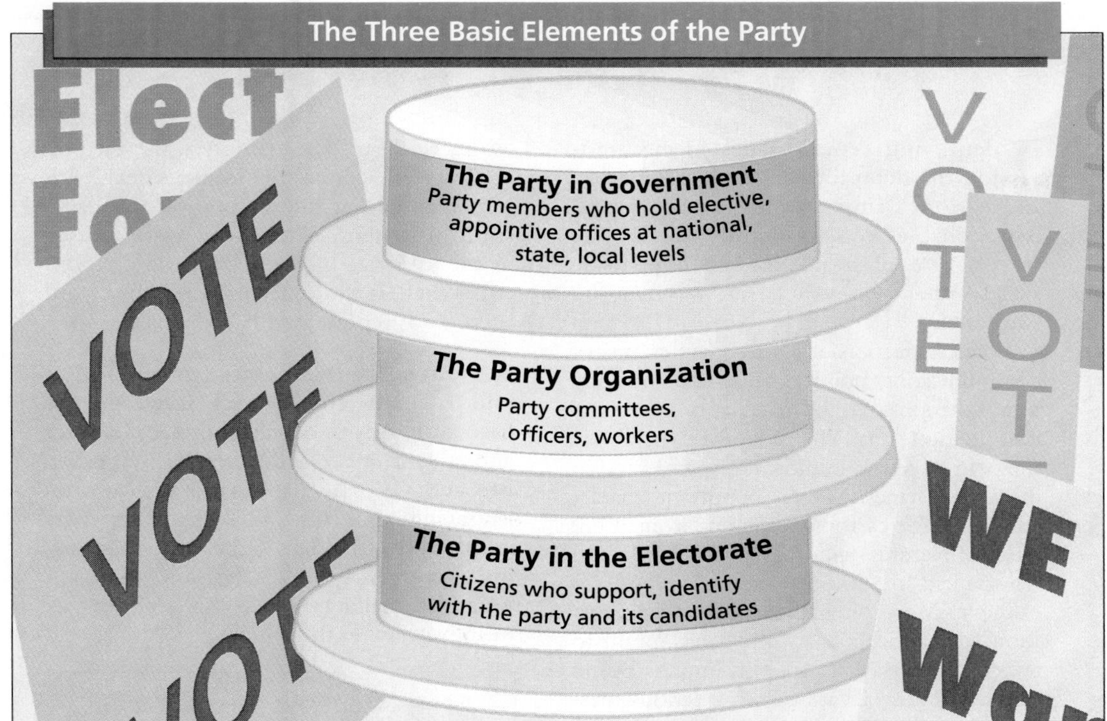

Interpreting Graphics This graphic shows how members fit into the political party structure. Which group receives the most attention from the public and the media?

candidates based on their own views in some specific area of public policy. One way such groups are making their presence felt is through political action committees (PACs). PACs raise and distribute money to candidates who will further their goals. Again, PACs have lessened candidates' reliance on party organizations for financial support.

You will look at the matters affecting the condition of the parties in the later chapters. As you do so, remember that political parties are indispensable to democratic government. The major parties have existed longer than have any other party anywhere in the world. And, as you have seen, they perform a number of necessary functions. In short, reports of their passing may be premature—and even farfetched.

Section 5 Review

1. Define: ward, precinct, split-ticket voting
2. What are the main elements of major party organization at the national level?
3. (a) What is the basic shape of party organization at the State level? (b) At the local level?
4. What are the three elements of the parties in terms of the roles of their members?
5. What features have led some observers to predict the collapse of the party system?

Critical Thinking

6. Drawing Conclusions (p. 19) Based on what you know about parties, their goals, and the American people, why do you think local party organizations vary so widely?

★

CLOSURE

Remind students that the major parties are decentralized organizations due to the role of the presidency, the system of federalism, and the nature of the nominating process. The nomination process involves finding candidates who are interested in running and who have support. A centralized organization might prevent many viable candidates from emerging. In the next chapter, students will examine "the party in the electorate"—voters and their behavior.

Assignment Assign Chapter 6, Section 1, beginning on page 129, for the next class period.

Reteach

Have students write imaginary journal entries as the National Committee Chairman for one or the other of the two major parties planning the national convention. Students' entries should address the problems and changes the political parties face today.

TEACHING
Critical Thinking

Identifying Central Issues

Objective
Interpret a political cartoon to identify central issues.

INSTRUCT

Before you introduce this lesson, you might review with students the political cartoons in this chapter on pages 104 and 106. Review the messages of these cartoons and discuss their elements.

When students have completed each step on the page, invite them to share their responses, which you might list on the board, before going on to the next step. Discuss different interpretations that may be offered as to the meanings of the symbols, and help students to clarify their statements of the message or main idea.

Answers 1. (a) The literal meaning is that in the past, which was a bad time, there existed machines of some sort that had to do with politics. (b) The items represent the media, funding, public opinion polls, and mailings. **2.** (a) In the sentence the word means "mechanisms," or "means to an end." (b) In the picture, the word is used literally. **3.** (a) The cartoon is saying that politics have not changed much over the years. (b) The cartoon is saying that these items are the mechanisms that parties use to achieve their desired results. (c) This is a negative view of these items.

Identifying Central Issues

Identifying central issues means finding the main ideas in a piece of information. Being able to identify central issues enables you to identify quickly the true nature of problems and controversies so that you can begin working on solutions.

Political cartoons are a frequent means of communicating political ideas and information. Cartoons have been a part of the American political scene since colonial days. Today they can be found in most newspapers and in many magazines. Several important characteristics make cartoons different from other kinds of pictures—photographs in books and newspapers or images on television, for example. More often than not, political cartoons are satirical. That is, they are meant to criticize, and they do so with humor. But, a cartoon almost always carries a serious message. In addition, cartoons frequently use caricature. That is, they use purposeful distortions or exaggerations to make a point or to attract attention.

Follow the steps below to practice identifying central issues in a political cartoon.

1. Examine the cartoon to identify and determine the meaning of the symbols. Cartoons use pictures and words to symbolize ideas or things. For example, an eagle in a cartoon usually symbolizes the United States. Examine the cartoon on this page. Read any captions or labels. (a) What is the literal meaning of the sentence at the top of the cartoon? (b) What do each of the items in the cartoon represent?

2. Identify the message or main idea. Each component of a cartoon generally relates to one basic message or main idea. By pointing out how different objects or events relate to that main idea, the cartoon achieves its comic or ironic effect. For example, look at the cartoon on this page. (a) In what sense is the word *machine* used in the sentence at the top of the cartoon? (b) What is the meaning of the word *machine* as represented by the objects?

3. Summarize the message or main idea, and identify the central issue of the cartoon. Any good cartoon makes a point and tries to make the viewer feel a certain way about a topic. (a) What is the cartoonist saying about the politics of yesterday and today? (b) What is the cartoonist saying about PACs, polls, television, and computerized mailings? (c) Is this a positive or negative view of these items?

Teacher's Resource File
See the Unit 2 File, p. 17, for the Skill Application to reinforce this skill lesson.

Chapter-in-Brief

Scan all headings, photographs, charts, and other visuals in the chapter before reading the section summaries below.

Section 1 Parties and What They Do (pp. 99–102) Political parties are groups of people who join together to elect candidates to public office. Unlike many other parties, the two major parties in the United States do not rest on any common ideological foundation.

Parties serve key functions in the political system: They select and support most candidates, and they help to keep the public informed on important issues, including the actions of the rival party. Parties grant a sort of seal of approval to candidates, thus assuring the public of the candidate's fitness. Indeed, parties are so important that they have even become instrumental in the administration of government.

Section 2 The Two-Party System (pp. 102–107) America's two-party system is the result of history and tradition; from its beginning, this nation has had two strong parties.

The American electoral system has several features that enable only two parties to compete. Election laws are written by officials who are usually members of the major parties. These laws tend to make it difficult for minor parties to flourish.

Another cause of the two-party system is that the United States is ideologically homogeneous. Most people have similar feelings about the broad issues of the day. Thus, there is little room or need for more than two parties.

Section 3 The Two-Party System in American History (pp. 109–114) The first parties in the United States formed during George Washington's administration. They became a force in the election of 1796. The nation has had strong political parties ever since.

Between 1800 and today, there have been four eras in which one party or the other has dominated national politics. The most recent era has been marked by Republican control of the White House and Democratic control of Congress.

Section 4 The Minor Parties (pp. 114–117) Minor parties have enjoyed little success in national politics. However, they have had an impact on the American political system.

Minor parties tend to fall into one of four categories: ideological parties, which are devoted to an overriding set of beliefs; single-issue parties; economic protest parties, which develop during times of economic hardship; and splinter parties—factions of one of the major parties.

The fate of most minor parties is failure. When they are successful, their ideas are often adopted by the major parties.

Section 5 The Organization of Political Parties (pp. 118–123) Political parties are not unified groups. National, State, and local branches of each party are only thinly connected. One reason for this is that the goal of electing officials requires different actions at different levels. Also, the act of choosing candidates often results in division within the party.

The national party machinery is generally devoted to trying to fill national offices. Their tasks include organizing the national convention.

State organizations are devoted to looking after the parties' interests in the States. Local organizations vary widely in structure. They tend to be most active at election time.

Teaching Suggestions for

Chapter-in-Brief

Below are some of the possible uses for the Chapter-in-Brief:

To Preview the Chapter You may want to assign the Chapter-in-Brief page and the Section Outlines from the Teacher's Resource File before beginning Chapter 5 to introduce students to the "Key Terms" and concepts in each section.

To Review the Chapter When students have completed Chapter 5, you might want to assign the Chapter-in-Brief as a tool for review, along with the Guided Reading and Reviews from the Teacher's Resource File.

To Omit the Chapter If you wish to skip Chapter 5, it may be helpful to assign the Chapter-in-Brief to students as a review before continuing to another chapter. You may also want to assign the Chapter 5 Test to assess student knowledge of the material. Then specific portions of Chapter 5 may be assigned to students needing reinforcement of "Key Terms" and concepts.

Teacher's Resource File See the Unit 2 File for the following materials:

- Section Outlines, pp. 2, 5, 8, 11, 14.
- Guided Reading and Reviews, pp. 3, 6, 9, 12, 15.
- Chapter 5 Test, pp. 21–23.

Additional Resources

Abramson, Paul R., *et al. Change and Continuity in the 1988 Elections.* CQ Press, 1990.

Anatomy of U.S. Political Parties. Filmstrips. Guidance Associates, 1989.

Barone, Michael and Grant Ujifusa. *The Almanac of American Politics, 1991.* National Journal, 1990.

Ginsberg, Benjamin and Martin Shafter. *Politics By Other Means: The Declining Importance of Elections in America.* Basic Books, 1990.

Maisel, L. Sandy (ed.). *The Parties Respond: Developments in the American Party System.* Westview Press, 1990.

Martis, Kenneth C. *The Historical Atlas of Political Parties in the United States Congress 1789–1989.* Macmillan, 1989.

Political Parties in America. 16mm film. Encyclopaedia Britannica Educational Corporation, 1973. Color. 20 min.

Sabato, Larry J. *The Party's Just Begun: Shaping Political Parties for America's Future.* Little, Brown, 1988.

Answers to CHAPTER 5 REVIEW

Vocabulary and Key Terms

Matching
1. political party
2. ideological party
3. consensus
4. minor party
5. precinct

True or False
1. True.
2. True.
3. False—the correct term is *coalition*.
4. False—the correct term is *single-member district*.
5. True.

Word Relationships
1. Item *d* does not belong. Items *a, b,* and *c* all refer to electoral units. Item *d* refers to the block of votes that a political party can consistently count on.
2. Item *b* does not belong. Items *a, c,* and *d* all refer to minor parties. Item *b* refers to the major parties in the American system of government.
3. Item *b* does not belong. Items *a, c,* and *d* all refer to either the two-party system itself or reasons for its existence. Item *d* refers to a system in which only one party holds significant political power.

Main Ideas

Section 1
1. Parties form to control government by holding political offices. **2.** The two major parties are primarily interested in electing officials. There is little in the way of ideology or concern for issues that binds all of the members together. **3.** Parties nominate candidates, stimulate the voters, certify the quality of candidates, provide a framework for much governmental conduct, and keep an eye on the rival parties.

Section 2
4. Two parties emerged out of the beginnings of American political history. The electoral system, with its single-member districts and requirement that a mere plurality be necessary for election, also contribute to the two-party system. The fact that the two parties control the process by which election laws are made also contributes, as does an ideological consensus in American society. **5.** The two parties each include a cross-section of racial, social, and political groups. **6.** Each party is election-oriented and tailors its message to as broad a base as possible. **7.** A multiparty system, common in Europe, involves parties based on a particular interest. Typically, several parties join together in a coalition to form a government. One-party systems are really no-party systems.

Section 3
8. The debate over the Constitution in the late 1780s set the stage for the first parties. **9.** Each party has taken turns enjoying extended periods of widespread control of the White House. There have been four such eras of one-party domination. **10.** The current era is unusual in that the party that is in control of the White House does

Chapter Review

Vocabulary and Key Terms

political party (p. 99)
major parties (p. 99)
coalition (p. 100)
minor party (p. 102)
two-party system (p. 102)
single-member district (p. 103)
plurality (p. 103)
pluralistic society (p. 104)
consensus (p. 104)
multiparty (p. 105)
one-party system (p. 105)
electorate (p. 112)
ideological parties (p. 114)
single-issue parties (p. 115)
economic protest parties (p. 115)
splinter parties (p. 115)
ward (p. 122)
precinct (p. 122)
split-ticket voting (p. 122)

Matching: *Review the key terms in the list above. If you are not sure of a term's meaning, look up the term and review its definition. Choose a term from the list above that best matches each description.*

1. a group of people who seek to control government by winning elections
2. a minor party that is based primarily on one set of beliefs
3. a general agreement among people
4. an American political party other than the Democrats or Republicans
5. the smallest electoral unit

True or False: *Determine whether each statement is true or false. If it is true, write "true." If it is false, change the underlined word or words to make the statement true.*

1. Split-ticket voting involves casting ballots for candidates of different parties in the same election.
2. Economic protest parties generally have no clear-cut ideological base, but are motivated by a demand for "better times."
3. A group of people with different interests who unite together is a consensus.
4. In a single-issue party, only one candidate is elected to each office on the ballot.
5. Candidates in many elections need not get more than half of all votes cast in order to win; a plurality is all that is necessary.

Word Relationships: *Three of the terms in each of the following sets of terms are related. Choose the term that does not belong and explain why it does not belong.*

1. (a) ward (b) precinct (c) single-member district (d) electorate
2. (a) single-issue parties (b) major party (c) ideological parties (d) splinter parties
3. (a) two-party system (b) one-party system (c) pluralistic society (d) single-member district

Main Ideas

Section 1 (pp. 99–102)

1. What is the purpose of a political party?
2. What does it mean to say that the two major parties are more election-oriented than issue-oriented?
3. What roles do the major parties play in the American political system?

Section 2 (pp. 102–107)

4. Explain why only two parties successfully compete in the American political system.

5. In general, what kind of voters do each of the major parties attract?
6. Give reasons for your answer to question number 5.
7. Describe the alternatives to the two-party system.

Section 3 **(pp. 109–114)**

8. When and under what circumstances did political parties first become a part of the American political process?
9. Describe the pattern that has characterized the two-party system over the course of American political history.
10. What feature makes the current era of one-party domination unusual?
11. Describe the differing views about the future of the two major parties.

Section 4 **(pp. 114–117)**

12. Into what basic categories do most minor parties fall?
13. In general, how have the minor parties been able to influence American politics?
14. Describe the fate of most minor parties.

Section 5 **(pp. 118–123)**

15. What factors contribute to the lack of organization of the major political parties?
16. Describe the organization of the parties at the national level.
17. Describe the organization of the parties at the State and local levels.

Critical Thinking

1. **Identifying Assumptions** (p. 19) The text refers to the party out of power as the "loyal opposition." (a) What is your understanding of this concept? (b) What does it suggest about the relationship of political parties with each other and the government?
2. **Recognizing Bias** (p. 19) For what reasons do you think that most election laws are written in a way that discourages the success of minor parties?
3. **Identifying Alternatives** (p. 19) What further steps do you think might be taken to limit the role that money plays in American politics?
4. **Predicting Consequences** (p. 19) What do you think would be the consequences if laws were changed to make it easier for candidates from minor parties to get on ballots and receive government funding for their campaigns?

Getting Involved

1. **Writing Your Opinion** Write a speech to introduce a new political party to the American voting public. Before you begin writing, make a list of the ideals your party will represent. Then make another list of the specific policies and programs you will promote. Use your lists to write a three-part speech. Open your speech with a statement that presents the name of your party and ideals that your new party will pursue. Then present each of your proposed policies and programs. Conclude by encouraging voters to support the new minor party, and explain why you believe their votes will not be "wasted." Proofread and revise the speech to correct errors. Draft a final copy.
2. **Class Debate** Hold a debate on the following topic: *Resolved*, That all political parties have equal opportunity to get on the ballot in all elections. Select teams to debate each side of the topic. The rest of the class can evaluate each of the teams' presentation.
3. **Gathering Information** Suppose you want to find out which of the two major political parties had controlled government in your State during a particular era in history. Use the Government Resources Handbook that begins on page 690 to find some sources you could use to find this information.

not control the Congress or the States. **11.** Some have predicted the collapse of the two parties based on such factors as a decline in party identification, an increase in split-ticket voting, the growing intra-party conflict stemming from primaries, changes in campaign technology that make candidates less dependent on parties, and the growth of special interest groups. Others point out the key role of parties in American government and predict that parties will remain.

Section 4

12. Ideological parties, single-issue parties, economic protest parties, and splinter parties. **13.** Generally, they have only been able to influence the outcome of elections in favor of one of the major parties. They have played the roles of "spoiler" and critic and innovator. **14.** Most parties disappear as their issue or the conditions or person that gave birth to them fade away. Any ideas they have that gather significant support are soon adopted by one or both of the major parties.

Section 5

15. Federalism, with the separate political units of the country and the States, fragments the party. The nominating process, which pits members of a party against each other, also fragments the parties. **16.** The party in power has the President to serve as party head. There is also the convention, the national committee, and the national chairperson, which direct and shape the national efforts of the party. **17.** The parties in each State have a State central committee and a State chairperson. These help further the party goals at the State level. Local organization varies widely. Often, local units exist for each electoral unit. Their efforts are primarily devoted to a particular election.

Critical Thinking

1. (a) Students should note the seeming contradiction between the terms *loyal* and *opposition*. (b) Students might suggest that the phrase indicates the adversarial nature of parties within a system to which they are both loyal. **2.** Students should recall that parties are election oriented, and are likely to pass laws that will limit the threat to their election. **3.** Students might suggest ideas such as making more radio and television time available for free to qualified candidates; etc. **4.** Students might suggest a further decline in the power of the two major parties. Others might point out that the factors that contribute to the domination of two parties would continue to make third-party success difficult.

Getting Involved

1–3. Answers and results will vary, but students should demonstrate an understanding of the concepts in this chapter.

Chapter 6 Resources

In the Teacher's Resource File
The following materials are found in the Teacher's Resource File box.

Instructional Support: Unit 2 File

For the Section
Outlines, pp. 27, 30, 33, 36, 39
Guided Reading and Reviews, pp. 28, 31, 34, 37, 40
Quizzes, pp. 29, 32, 35, 38, 41

For the Chapter
Skill Application, p. 42
Case Study on Contemporary Issues, pp. 43–45
Chapter Test, pp. 46–48
Additional Test Questions, pp. 49–51

Enrichment Support

Supreme Court Cases, p. 5
Historical and Legal Documents, pp. 8, 14, 23, 30, 32, 48–49

Computer Test Bank and Assessment
Transparency Package, pp. 6, 31, 53

Chapter 6 Focus

Introduce the Chapter Tell students that in this chapter they will learn about the evolution and execution of voting rights in the United States. Read with students the Chapter Preview and Objectives.

Writing Activity Direct students' attention to "Describe." Discuss with students what might motivate people to vote, then ask them to think about why it is that only slightly more than one half of eligible Americans vote in presidential elections. Then have them write their opinions about the importance of voting.

Motivate for Learning Direct students' attention to "Predict." Discuss with students why they might vote, as a way to develop ideas for their predictions. Then have the students predict three factors that they think might affect voting behavior among Americans.

Voters and Voter Behavior

Chapter Preview

In the face of tanks and guns, people in every corner of the globe—the countries of Eastern Europe, China, and Haiti, to name just a few places—have risked their lives for the right to vote in free elections. Those who have failed will undoubtedly try to win a voice in government at some point in the future.

Citizens of the United States won the right to vote in several suffrage movements over the course of this country's history. But, do all qualified Americans exercise their hard-won right to vote every time they have the opportunity? Regrettably, the answer is "No." This chapter is about *who* has the right to vote in elections in the United States, and about *how* and *why* the American public votes as it does.

Before you read this chapter:

- **Describe** why you do or do not think it is important for every eligible American to exercise his or her right to vote.
- **Predict** three factors that affect voting behavior among Americans.

As you read, focus on the main objective for each section. Understand:

1. The historical development of the right to vote in the United States.
2. The diversity of voter qualifications among the States.
3. The necessity for and effects of civil rights laws on suffrage.
4. Voter turnout and nonvoting in American elections.
5. The factors that affect the behavior of the American voter.

Magruder's American Government: *A Witness to Change* by William A. McClenaghan

In the 1917 edition, Frank Magruder offered these seven arguments in favor of women's suffrage:

1. Women need the ballot because of new industrial conditions. The discovery of steam power and electricity and the invention of machinery have shifted the production of most articles... from the home to the factory ... 2. The minds of men and women differ only slightly by nature... 3. When women are given the ballot they take more interest in civic duties than in idle pastimes. 4. More girls than boys are [now] being educated... 5. Persons who [as teachers] train citizens should understand the political duties of citizens... 6. Both by nature and by necessity women have better moral habits than men... 7. The most dignified way for women to influence legislation is by the secret ballot. (pp. 358 and 359)

Since the passage of the 19th Amendment in 1920, the "women's vote" has represented an important political force; it is difficult to believe that only decades ago women were denied this fundamental right.

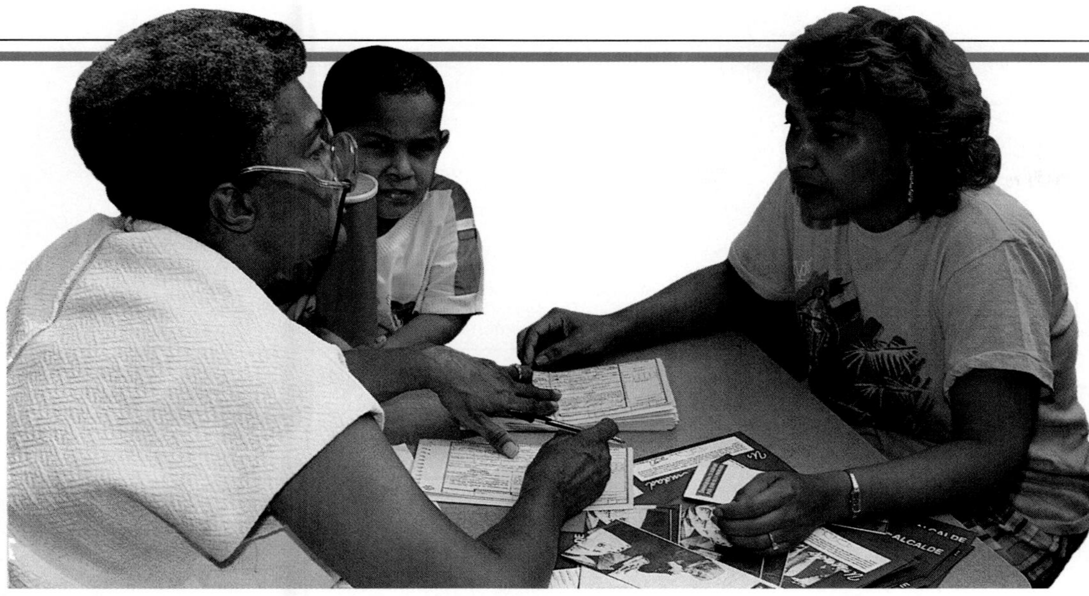

Becoming an Involved Citizen Registering to vote is an important step along the way to becoming a responsible and active participant in the democratic process of government.

1 The Constitution and the Right to Vote

Find Out:

- How did the right to vote evolve in the United States?
- What does the Constitution currently say about the right to vote?

Key Terms:

suffrage, franchise, electorate

Try this simple exercise in free association: What is the first word that comes to mind when you read the word *democracy*? Obviously, several thoughts might have occurred to you. Quite possibly, one that did had something to do with voting or elections—for the right to vote is at the very heart of the democratic process.

In this section, you will see how the right to vote has developed over the course of the nation's history.

The History of Voting Rights

Because the Framers disagreed on specific requirements, the Constitution left the power to set suffrage qualifications to each State.
1.a **Suffrage** means the right to vote. **Franchise** is
1.b another term with the same meaning.[1]

When the Constitution went into effect in 1789, the right to vote was everywhere restricted to white male property owners. In fact, probably not one in fifteen adult white males could vote in elections in the different States. Thomas Paine had ridiculed this situation in 1776. In *Common Sense*, he observed that a man whose only property was a jackass would lose his right to vote if the jackass died.

[1]Originally, the Constitution had only two suffrage provisions. Article I, Section 2, Clause 1 requires each State to allow anyone qualified to vote for members of "the most numerous branch" of its own legislature to vote as well for members of the national House of Representatives. Article II, Section I, Clause 2 provides that presidential electors be chosen in each State "in such manner as the legislature thereof may direct."

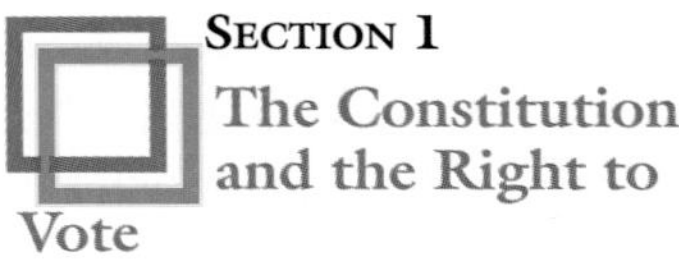

SECTION 1 The Constitution and the Right to Vote

FOCUS

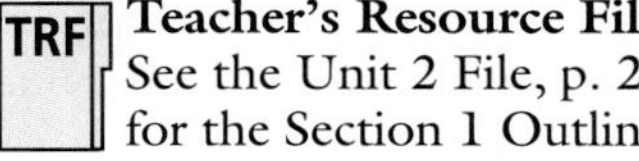

Teacher's Resource File See the Unit 2 File, p. 27, for the Section 1 Outline.

Objectives

6.1 Examine the ways in which the right to vote evolved in the United States.

6.2 Determine what the Constitution currently says about the right to vote.

Bellringer Activity Have the name *Susan B. Anthony* on the board as students come into class. Write the words *Who?* and *Why?* below her name. Have students use the index of this book to find answers to the questions. Use the fact that the Constitution did not grant suffrage to women until 1920 as a way to begin the lesson.

State the Purpose The right to vote—a fundamental activity in a democracy—has evolved since the Constitution was written over 200 years ago. In Section 1, students will examine two trends that have affected voting rights in the United States. They will also trace the evolution of voting rights through five stages, and understand how the Constitution protects those rights today.

ABCNEWS INTERACTIVE
The following video segment may be used to highlight aspects of voting rights.

POWERS OF THE CONGRESS GUIDEBOOK
Chapter 47: Amendments, p. 53

Vocabulary

Point out "Key Terms" on page 129. Below are some additional terms whose meanings might help students understand section content.

— **potential:** possible
— **servitude:** a condition under which a person is not free
— **deprive:** to take something from someone

LEP

Reading Strategy: Predicting Content

Before students read Section 1, have them look at the boldfaced headings. Remind them that these headings form an outline for each important idea. Have students write one sentence that predicts the content under each heading. As they read, have them refer to their sentences to check their predictions.

INSTRUCT

Discuss/Analyze In discussion, emphasize the expansion of suffrage from the early restrictions to the nearly universal suffrage for all people over 18 today. Remind students that many of the Framers were uneasy about granting very much power to ordinary people. (See Chapter 2)

Ask students to consider why the Framers might have felt this way. (*Most were wealthy land owners; they were concerned about incidents like Shays' Rebellion; there was no precedent for universal suffrage.*) Be sure students also understand that the Constitution leaves the setting of voter qualification to the States, but that the Federal Government has increasingly limited the States' options.

Interpreting Graphs Caption Answer Because the United States is a democracy, and voting denotes commitment to majority rule.

Provide Guided Practice With students, list the five stages of voting rights extension. (*1800s, religion; 1870, race or color; 1920, sex; 1960s, further security to voting rights based on race and extension of voting rights to the District of Columbia; 1971, persons over 18.*)

Provide Independent Practice

TRF Teacher's Resource File You may wish to assign the Section 1 Guided Reading and Review, Unit 2 File, p. 28, to help students master section objective content.

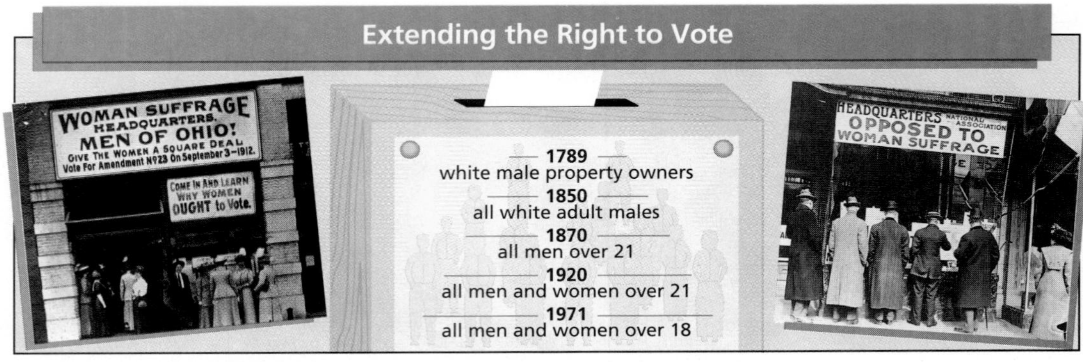

Interpreting Graphs As shown, universal suffrage took almost 200 years and faced strong opposition (right). Why are voting rights an essential component of the American system?

Asked Paine, "Now tell me, which was the voter, the man or the jackass?"

Today, the size of the American **electorate**—the potential voting population—is truly impressive. Nearly 190 million people, nearly all citizens who are at least 18 years of age, can qualify to vote. That huge number is a direct result of the legal definition of suffrage. That is, it is the result of those laws that determine who can and cannot vote. The large electorate is also the result of some 200 years of continuing, often bitter, and sometimes violent struggle over the issue of voting rights. 1.c

The long history of the development of suffrage since 1789 has been marked by two long-term trends: First, the nation has experienced the gradual elimination of a number of restrictions on the right to vote based on such factors as religious belief, property ownership, tax payment, race, and sex. Second, a significant share of what was originally the States' power over the right to vote has been assumed by the Federal Government.

The growth of the American electorate to its present size and shape has come in five fairly distinct stages—and these two trends have woven through them.

The Five Stages The first stage of the struggle to extend voting rights came in the early part of the 1800s. Religious qualifications, born in colonial days, quickly disappeared. No State has had a religious test since 1810. Property ownership and tax payment qualifications then began to fall, one by one, among the States. By mid-century, almost all white adult males could vote.

The second major effort to broaden the electorate followed the Civil War. The 15th Amendment, ratified in 1870, was intended to protect any citizen from being denied the right to vote because of race or color. Despite that amendment, African Americans were until recently the largest group of disfranchised citizens in the nation's population.

The ratification of the 19th Amendment in 1920—prohibiting the denial of the right to vote because of sex—completed the third expansion of suffrage. Wyoming, while still a territory, had been the first to give women the vote in 1869. By 1920 more than half of the States had followed that lead.

A fourth major extension took place during the 1960s, as federal legislation and court decisions centered on securing to African Americans a full role in the electoral process in all States. With the passing and vigorous enforcement of several civil rights acts, especially the Voting Rights Act of 1965 and its several later extensions, racial equality finally became possible in polling booths throughout the country.[2] The 23rd Amendment, added in 1961, included the voters of the District

[2]See Section 3.

Enrichment

Have students choose one of the five stages of the extension of voting rights and research it to discover ten facts about each extension. Facts may include names of important participants, events, legislation, etc. Students should write down their ten facts to share with the class. (Average)

SPOTLIGHT ON: Global Awareness

The extension of women's suffrage in the U.S. was part of a worldwide movement for women's equality brought about in part by World War I. Having proved themselves capable of doing "men's work" while the men were away at the front, women in Belgium, the Netherlands, Britain, France, Germany, Italy, Poland, Japan, and Canada, as well as in the U.S., demanded, and some achieved, the right to vote between 1918-1920. In Britain, only women over 30 were allowed to vote until 1928, after which age 18 became the standard for all voters. In Italy, France, and Japan, however, higher minimum voting ages for women were the rule as late as the 1940s.

of Columbia in the presidential electorate. The 24th Amendment, ratified in 1964, eliminated the poll tax (and any other tax) as a condition for voting in any federal election.

The fifth and latest expansion of the electorate came with the adoption of the 26th Amendment in 1971. It provides that no State can set any age above 18 as the minimum age at  which a person can qualify to vote.

The Power to Set Voting Qualifications

The Constitution does not give to the Federal Government the power to set suffrage qualifications. Rather, that matter is reserved to the States. The Constitution does, however, place five restrictions on the States in the use of that power.

1. Any person whom a State allows to vote for members of the "most numerous branch" of its own legislature must also be allowed to vote for representatives and senators in Congress.[3] This restriction is of little real meaning today. With only minor exceptions, each of the States allows the same voters to vote in all elections within the State.
2. No State can deprive any person of the right to vote "on account of race, color, or previous condition of servitude."[4]
3. No State can deprive any person of the right to vote on account of sex.[5]
4. No State can require the payment of any tax as condition for taking part in the nomination or election of any federal officeholder. That is, no State can levy any tax in connection with any process involved in the selection of the President, the Vice President, or members of Congress.[6]
5. No State can deprive any person who is at least 18 years of age of the right to vote because of age.[7]

Beyond these five restrictions, remember that no State can violate any other provision in the Constitution in the setting of suffrage qualifications—or in anything else that it does. A case decided by the Supreme Court in 1975, *Hill* v. *Stone*, illustrates the point. The Court struck down a section of the Texas constitution that declared that only those persons who owned taxable property could vote in city bond elections. The Court found the drawing of such a distinction for voting purposes—between those who do and those who do not own taxable property—to be an unreasonable classification, prohibited by the 14th Amendment's Equal Protection Clause.

[3]Article I, Section 2, Clause 1; the 17th Amendment extended the "most numerous branch" provision to the election of Senators.

[4]15th Amendment. The phrase "previous condition of servitude" refers to slavery. Note that this amendment does not guarantee the right to vote to African Americans, or to anyone else. Instead, it forbids the States to discriminate against any person on these grounds in the setting of suffrage qualifications.

[5]19th Amendment. Note that this amendment does not guarantee the right to vote to women as such. Technically, it forbids States the power to discriminate against males or females in establishing suffrage qualifications.

Section 1 Review

1. **Define:** suffrage, franchise, electorate
2. How large is the American electorate?
3. What two long-term trends have marked the development of the right to vote in the United States?
4. What specific restrictions does the Constitution place upon the States in the setting of suffrage qualifications?

Critical Thinking

5. **Recognizing Ideologies** (p. 19) Consider the extent of voting rights in 1789. (a) What do the voting restrictions of that time suggest about the first Americans' views of citizenship? (b) How have those views changed?

★

[6]24th Amendment.

[7]26th Amendment. Note that this amendment does not prevent any State from allowing persons younger than age 18 to vote. But it does prohibit a State from setting a maximum age for voting.

Monitor Comprehension

Answers to Section 1 Review
1. "Key Terms" are defined on the following pages:
a. suffrage, p. 129
b. franchise, p. 129
c. electorate, p. 130
2. Nearly 190 million
3. Gradual elimination of restrictions and assumption by the Federal Government of the States' power **4.** States must not (1) deny anyone who votes for members of the State legislature's most numerous branch the right to vote for members of Congress; (2) deny suffrage on the basis of race, color, or previous condition of servitude; (3) deny the vote based on sex; (4) levy a tax in connection with the election of President, Vice President, or Congresspersons; (5) deny anyone over 18 the vote **5.** (a) The old rules suggest that citizenship was viewed as belonging to white males with economic power. (b) Today, suffrage is considered the right of nearly all people over 18.

Closure

Remind students that voting rights have changed since 1789 to reflect evolving standards of justice. These changes appear as two trends: the end of restrictions based on ownership, tax payment, religion, race, and sex, and the exercise of power by the Federal Government to protect voting rights. In the next section, students will learn about voter qualifications and past restrictions in the States.

Assignment Assign Section 2, pages 132–136 for the next class period.

Activity: Teaching Heterogeneous Groups

Have students create a timeline, including the following dates: 1810, 1870, 1920, 1965, and 1971. Next to each date on the timeline have students write a statement to show how, in that year, the right to vote was extended in the United States. Statements should include information about which group of people secured its right to vote at that time. LEP

Reteach

Have students create a sketch for a poster representing each of the groups struggling for suffrage during the five stages of voting rights expansion. Students should include the dates and major arguments and any pertinent legislation in their sketches.

Teacher's Resource File
See the Unit 2 File, p. 29, for the Section 1 Quiz.

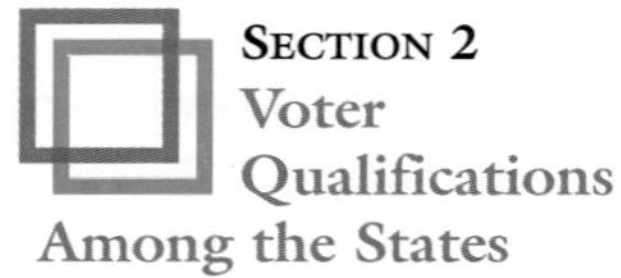

SECTION 2 Voter Qualifications Among the States

FOCUS

Teacher's Resource File See the Unit 2 File, p. 30, for the Section 2 Outline.

Objectives

6.3 Determine who may vote in the United States.
6.4 Examine the ways in which States have restricted voting rights in the past.

Bellringer Activity Write the names of your U.S. senators and your Congressperson on the board. Ask students to identify these names. Tally the responses to get the percentage of students who recognize these officials. Then have students turn to the table on page 133 to compare class percentages with national statistics.

State the Purpose The Constitution provides many voter rights guidelines. Individual States, however, have certain guidelines that apply to the voters in their States. In Section 2, students will learn more about the voter guidelines imposed by individual States, and will examine past restrictions imposed by the States.

ABCNEWS INTERACTIVE
The following video segments may be used to highlight aspects of voter qualification.

POWERS OF CONGRESS GUIDEBOOK
Chapter 50: Right to Vote, p. 127

Chapter 51: Amendments to the Constitution, p. 128

2 Voter Qualifications Among the States

Find Out:

- Who may vote in the United States?
- How have states restricted voting rights in the past?

Key Terms:
registration, literacy, poll tax

Are you eligible to vote? Probably not—at least not yet. But you will be, and fairly soon. In this section, you will see how the States, including yours, determine who is qualified to vote. You will also see how those qualifications have changed over the years.

Citizenship, Residence, and Age

Today, each State requires all voters to meet qualifications based on two factors: citizenship and residence.

Citizenship Aliens are generally denied the right to vote in the United States. Still, nothing in the Constitution says that aliens cannot vote, and any State could allow them to do so if it chose.[8]

Only one State now draws any distinction between native-born and naturalized citizens with regard to suffrage. The Minnesota constitution requires a person to have been an American citizen for at least three months before he or she can vote.

In practice, a few aliens do vote—though in what number no one knows. They either wrongly believe that they are citizens or unlawfully pass themselves off as citizens when they report to their polling place.

Residence Each State requires that a person live within the State for at least some period of time in order to qualify to vote. The States adopted residence requirements for two reasons: (1) The residence requirement was in part meant to keep a political machine from importing—bribing—enough outsiders to affect the outcome of local elections. The enforcement of residence rules ended that once common practice. (2) Every State has accepted the view that every voter should have at least some time in which to become familiar with the candidates and issues in an election before making a final choice at the polls.

Residence requirements are now quite brief. The details vary, but only slightly, among the 50 States. Today, in 23 States voters must live within the State for at least 30 days before an election.[9] In Colorado, however, the minimum period is slightly longer—32 days. Nine States require a somewhat shorter period: 29 days in California; 20 days in Minnesota, Oregon, and Tennessee; 15 days in South Dakota; 10 days in New Hampshire and Wisconsin; one day in Alabama and Kansas. The other 17 States set no fixed period, but a voter must be a legal resident of the State.

The fact that the residence requirement is a fairly uniform one today is a direct result of a 1972 decision by the Supreme Court. Until then, every State had required a much longer period—typically, a year in the State, 60 or 90 days in the county, and 30 days in the local ward or precinct.[10] But in the Voting Rights Act Amendments of 1970, Congress prohibited any requirement of longer than 30 days for voting in presidential elections.[11] In *Dunn* v. *Blumstein*, 1972, the

[8]At one time about a fourth of the States permitted those aliens who had applied for naturalization to vote. Typically, the western States did so to help attract settlers. Arkansas, the last State in which aliens could vote, adopted a citizenship requirement in 1926. In a few States, local governments can permit noncitizens to vote in local contests—e.g., city council elections—and a handful do.

[9]Alaska, Arizona, Georgia, Idaho, Illinois, Indiana, Kentucky, Maryland, Michigan, Mississippi, Montana, Nevada, New Jersey, New York, North Carolina, North Dakota, Ohio, Pennsylvania, Rhode Island, Texas, Utah, West Virginia, Washington. The Arizona requirement is 50 days for voting in State and local elections and 30 days for presidential elections.

[10]Recall from Chapter 5, Section 5: The precinct is the basic, smallest unit of election administration. The ward is a unit into which cities are often divided for the election of members of the city council.

[11]The Supreme Court upheld the provision in *Oregon* v. *Mitchell* in 1970, which you will read about shortly.

Reading Strategy: Structured Overview

As a preparation for reading, have students preview the headings in Section 2. They can then create an outline based on these headings. As students read the text, have them make notes under each heading, in an outline form, to help them remember the details of each section.

Vocabulary

Point out "Key Terms" on page 132. Ask students to explain what they think each one of the terms might have to do with voter rights or restrictions. **LEP**

Political Participation and Awareness in America

Percentage of Americans who. . .	
Vote in presidential elections	50%
Vote in congressional elections	35-40
Know name of congressional representative	36
Know names of both U.S. senators	29
Occasionally contact local officials	28
Vote in local elections	10-30
Occasionally attend public meetings	19
Occasionally contact federal or state officials	16
Know name of state senator	13
Give money to candidate or party	13
Know name of state representative	12

Source: Selected polls, including Gallup, *Denver Post* Poll, University of Michigan, and *The New York Times, 1989.*

Interpreting Tables Do the percentages shown here seem compatible with the number of citizens eligible to vote based on citizenship, residence, and age qualifications?

1972, the Supreme Court found Tennessee's requirement—at the time, a year in the State and 90 days in the county—unconstitutional. It held such a lengthy requirement to be an unsupportable discrimination against new residents and so in conflict with the 14th Amendment's Equal Protection Clause. The Supreme Court said that "30 days appears to be an ample period of time." Election law and practice among the States quickly accepted that standard.

Nearly every State does prohibit transients—persons living in the State for only a short time—from gaining a legal residence there. Thus, a traveling salesperson, a member of the armed services, or a college student usually cannot vote in a State where he or she has only a temporary physical residence. In several States, however, the courts have held that college students who claim the campus community as their legal residence can vote there.

Age The 26th Amendment sets 18 as the cap on the minimum age for voting in any election. Prior to its adoption in 1971, the generally accepted standard was 21 years of age.

In fact, up to 1970 only four States had put the voting age at under 21. Georgia first allowed 18-year-olds to vote in 1943, and then Kentucky did so in 1955. Alaska entered the Union in 1959 with the voting age set at 19, and Hawaii did so later that same year with the age set at 20. Both Alaska and Hawaii set the age above 18 but below 21 to avoid any problems that might be caused by high school students voting in local school-district elections. But, whatever the fears on that score, they have not been borne out by experience under the 26th Amendment.

In a growing number of States, some 17-year-olds can now cast ballots in primary elections. Those States allow anyone whose 18th birthday falls after the primary but before the general election to vote in the primary election—provided that person meets all other qualifications, of course.

One State, Nebraska, has come very close to effectively lowering the voting age to 17 for all elections. There, any person who will be 18 by the Tuesday following the first Monday in November can qualify to vote in any election held during that calendar year.

Other Qualifications

A few other qualifications, notably registration, are found in several States.

Interpreting Tables As students look at the table, ask them what it demonstrates about voter awareness and participation in the United States. (*They are low.*) Have students suggest ways that might encourage more people to participate in politics.

Caption Answer No, there are many more people who are eligible to vote than do.

INSTRUCT

Discuss/Examine Discuss with students that within the limits set by the Constitution, States may determine who may and may not vote. All States require citizenship and some length of residency as qualifications for voting. All States, except North Dakota, require registration before voting. Other restrictions vary, but may include mental incompetence, dishonorable military discharge, transient student status, or conviction for a serious crime.

Have students skim the section to identify past and present voter qualifications required by the States. List them on the board. (*Citizenship, residence, age, registration, literacy, tax payment; also people who are otherwise qualified may be disqualified due to mental incompetence, dishonorable military discharge, conviction of a serious crime.*)

When complete, examine the list, and at students' direction, circle all requirements still held by at least one State. (*Citizenship, residence, age, registration.*)

Now examine the requirements that have not been circled. How has the elimination of these requirements expanded suffrage? *(The elimination of literacy tests and poll taxes has expanded voting rights to African Americans and other minorities as well as immigrant citizens, against whom these requirements were used to keep them from voting.)* If time permits, discuss whether or not the Federal Government should establish uniform voting requirements for all 50 States. (*States' rights versus equal protection.*)

Interpreting Political Cartoons In many parts of the world, the right to vote is still a privilege rather than a right. How is the American attitude toward the right to vote viewed by this artist?

Registration Forty-nine States—all except North Dakota—require that most or all voters
1.a be registered to vote. **Registration** is a procedure of voter identification, intended to prevent fraudulent voting.[12] It gives election officials a list of those persons who are qualified to vote in an election. In a few States, the voter registration process is known as enrollment. Most of the States require all voters to register. But in a few—Wisconsin, for example—only those in urban areas must register to vote. Typically, a prospective voter must register his or her name, age, place of birth, present address, length of residence, and similar facts with some local official—usually a registrar of elections or the county clerk.

Every State except North Dakota now has some form of permanent registration. Typically, a voter remains registered unless or until he or she moves, dies, is convicted of a serious crime, is committed to a mental institution, or fails to vote for a certain number of years or elections.

The registration requirement has become somewhat controversial in recent years. In fact, some people argue that it should be done away with. They view registration as a bar to voter turnout, especially among the poor and the less-educated.

Most people who have studied the problem favor keeping the requirement as a necessary defense against fraud. But they also favor making the process a more convenient one. In short, they see the problem in these terms: Where

[12]Several States also use their voter registration to identify voters in terms of their party preference and, hence, their eligibility to take part in closed primaries. In most States voters must be registered in order to vote in any election held within the State, but a few do not impose the requirement for all elections—for example, registration is not required for voting in some school district elections in Minnesota.

Enrichment

Have all students find out where and how they can register to vote. They may want to obtain a voter registration card at the city or town hall or, in many States, at the Department of Motor Vehicles. Have those who are 18 actually register if they have not, and have students who are not yet 18 obtain cards to fill out as practice. (Easy) should the line be drawn between making it so easy to vote that fraud is encouraged and making it so difficult that legitimate voting is discouraged?

In fact, most States have eased the registration process over the last several years. More than half of the States now permit voters to register through the mail. And a growing number of States provide for voter registration at the many local offices of the State's department of motor vehicles and at local employment and social services agencies, too.

Maine and Wisconsin allow voters to register at any time, up to and including election day. Elsewhere, there is a deadline; a voter must be registered by some date before an election, often 20 or 30 days beforehand.[13] That cutoff gives election officials time to prepare the poll books—the lists of all registered voters in each precinct—for an upcoming election. States have now computerized their registration lists, and so the cutoff period has been shortened nearly everywhere.

Literacy Today, no State has a suffrage qualification based on voter **literacy**—a person's ability to read or write. 1.b

The literacy requirement could be, and in many places was, used to make sure that a qualified voter had at least some capacity to cast an informed ballot. But it also was used unfairly in many places to prevent or discourage certain groups from voting. The device was used in just that way to keep African Americans from voting for many years in many parts of the South.

Its unfair use finally led Congress to eliminate literacy as a suffrage qualification in the Voting Rights Act Amendments of 1970. The Supreme Court upheld that ban in *Oregon* v. *Mitchell*, 1970:

"In enacting the literacy ban . . . Congress had before it a long history of discriminatory use of literacy tests to disfranchise voters on account of their race."

[13]In Minnesota the deadline is 20 days before an election; however, any qualified person who misses that deadline can register, and then vote, on election day. Wyoming has a 30-day cutoff; but voters also may register on primary—but not on general—election day.

VOICES on Government

Demanding an End to Voting Restrictions

Martin Luther King, Jr., civil rights leader and winner of the Nobel Peace Prize in 1964

"We can never be satisfied as long as a Negro in Mississippi cannot vote and a Negro in New York believes he has nothing for which to vote. No, we are not satisfied, and we will not be satisfied until justice rolls down like waters and righteousness like a mighty stream. . . . I say to you, my friends, that even though we must face the difficulties of today and tomorrow, I still have a dream. It is a dream deeply rooted in the American dream that one day this nation will rise up and live out the true meaning of its creed—we hold these truths to be self-evident, that all men are created equal."

At the time Congress banned literacy tests, 18 States had some form of a literacy requirement. Some required potential voters to prove they had the ability to read; other States the ability to read and write. Still others required the ability to read, write, and "understand" some printed material—usually a passage taken from the State or Federal Constitution. Often, whites were asked simple questions; African Americans were asked questions so complex they would stump even a judge who was familiar with the passage.

Connecticut adopted the first literacy qualifications in 1855. Massachusetts followed in 1857. The actions of these States were aimed at limiting voting by Irish Catholic immigrants. Mississippi adopted a literacy requirement in

Provide Guided Practice On the chalkboard, write the two questions from the "Find Out" at the beginning of this section. (*1. Who may vote in the United States? 2. How have States restricted voting rights in the past?*) Then have volunteers answer them by listing information from the section. Write their answers under the appropriate question.(*1. Generally, citizens who are over 18 and have established residency in a State may vote. 2. States have restricted voting rights in the past with literacy tests and tax payments.*)

Provide Independent Practice

TRF Teacher's Resource File You may wish to assign the Section 2 Guided Reading and Review, Unit 2 File, p. 31, to students master section objective content.

SPOTLIGHT ON: Political Talk

Poll taxes, literacy tests, and other practices designed to disenfranchise, segregate, or degrade African Americans, are commonly referred to as "Jim Crow" laws. An eighteenth-century Kentucky plantation song was the source of the term, popularized by Thomas Dartmouth, a Louisville vaudevillian who wore blackface in a performance of the song in 1829. In 1840, a Boston railroad designated its "blacks only" car the Jim Crow, demonstrating the prevalence of the term. The term remained common in the post-Civil War South until segregation was challenged during the 1950s and 60s civil rights movement.

Monitor Comprehension

Answers to Section 2 Review
1. "Key Terms" are defined on the following pages:
a. registration, p. 134
b. literacy, p. 135
c. poll tax, p. 136.
2. Citizenship and residency.
3. 30 days. **4.** (a) It is supposed to prevent fraud in elections. (b) Some people believe it prevents the poor and members of minority groups from voting.
5. Literacy tests had been used often to deny qualified voters suffrage. **6.** (a) Was used to disfranchise African Americans. (b) It was outlawed in federal elections by the 24th Amendment; the Supreme Court later ruled the use of a poll tax unconstitutional. **7.** Answers will vary. Students should be able to predict the effects of their proposed rules and be able to defend them.

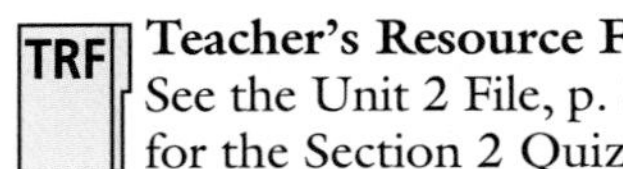
Teacher's Resource File See the Unit 2 File, p. 32, for the Section 2 Quiz.

Closure

Remind students that while the Constitution provides suffrage guidelines for the whole country, each State has its own guidelines. State guidelines are primarily related to citizenship, residence, age, and registration.

In Section 3, students will examine how various civil rights laws have extended suffrage in the United States.

Assignment Assign Section 3, pages 138–140 for the next class period.

1890, and shortly, most of the other southern States followed suit, usually with an "understanding clause."[14]

A number of States outside the South also adopted literacy qualifications of various sorts. Wyoming did so in 1889, California in 1894, Washington in 1896, New Hampshire in 1902, Arizona in 1913, New York in 1921, Oregon in 1924, and Alaska in 1949.

Tax Payment The **poll tax** was a tax payment required by some States before a person was allowed to vote. Property ownership, as proved by the payment of property taxes, was once a common suffrage requirement. That requirement and others that also called for the payment of a tax have now disappeared.

The poll tax was once found throughout the South. Beginning with Florida in 1889, each of the 11 southern States adopted the poll tax as part of an effort to discourage voting by African Americans. The device proved to be of only limited effectiveness, however. That fact, and opposition to the use of the poll tax from within the South as well as elsewhere, led most of those States to abandon it.[15]

The 24th Amendment, ratified in 1964, outlawed the poll tax, or any other tax, as a condition for voting in any federal election. The Supreme Court finally eliminated the poll tax as a qualification for voting in all elections in 1966. In *Harper* v. *Virginia State Board of Elections*, the Court held the Virginia poll tax to be in conflict with the 14th Amendment's Equal Protection Clause. The Court could find no reasonable relationship between the act of voting on the one hand, and the payment of a tax on the other.

Who May Not Vote Clearly, democratic
1.c government can exist only where the right to vote is very widely held. Still, every State does purposely deny the vote to certain persons. Thus, none of the 50 States allow people in mental institutions, or any other persons who have been legally found to be mentally incompetent, to vote. Nearly all States also disqualify those who have been convicted of serious crimes. A few States also do not allow anyone dishonorably discharged from the armed forces to vote. In some States, a few groups like duelists, the homeless, or polygamists are also disqualified.

Section 2 Review

1. Define: registration, literacy, poll tax
2. On what two bases does each State now set voter qualifications?
3. In general, how long must a person be a resident of a place before becoming a qualified voter?
4. (a) What is the essential purpose of voter registration? (b) For what reasons do some people urge its elimination?
5. For what reasons did Congress decide that literacy cannot be used as a voting qualification anywhere in the United States?
6. (a) How was the poll tax used as a voting qualification? (b) What finally became of this device?

Critical Thinking

7. Identifying Alternatives (p. 19) Imagine that you are a State lawmaker. On what grounds do you feel it is fair to deny someone the right to vote? Make a list of voter qualifications for your State that would meet constitutional standards.

★

[14]A "grandfather clause" was added to the Louisiana constitution in 1895, and Alabama, Georgia, Maryland, North Carolina, Oklahoma, and Virginia soon added them, as well. These clauses stated that any man, or his male descendants, who had voted in the State before the adoption of the 15th Amendment (1870) could become a legal voter without regard to any literacy or taxpaying qualifications. Those qualifications had been aimed at disfranchising African Americans, and the grandfather clauses were designed to enfranchise those white males who were unintentionally disqualified by their failure to meet the literacy or taxpaying requirements. The Supreme Court found the Oklahoma provision, the last to be adopted (in 1910), in conflict with the 15th Amendment in *Guinn* v. *United States* in 1915.

[15]By 1966, the poll tax was still in use only in Alabama, Mississippi, Texas, and Virginia. It had been abolished in North Carolina (1924), Louisiana (1934), Florida (1937), Georgia (1945), South Carolina (1950), Tennessee (1951), and Arkansas (1964).

Reteach

Have students write the subheadings in Section 2—citizenship, residence, age, registration, literacy, and poll tax—on a sheet of paper. Then have them review the section and summarize the key points for each heading.

Spotlight on: Roots of Democracy

While the right to vote is nearly universal and those not permitted to vote are the exception in democracy as we know it today, in Athens, Greece, the birthplace of democracy, voting was restricted to the privileged few. Only citizens could vote, and only men could be citizens. Although there were occasional exceptions, one generally had to be born into the citizen class, and while not all citizens were rich, none were paupers. Even at the height of Athenian democracy in the fourth century B.C., when citizenship extended more broadly than ever before, only 40,000 of an estimated population of 275,000 were citizens, about 1 out of 7.

Debating Key Issues

Should Free Speech Ever Be Suppressed?

Feiner v. *New York*

The primary purpose of the free speech clause of the 1st Amendment was to ensure the right of all people to express their views without the fear of persecution. Does this right extend to people who are expressing radical and unpopular ideas? Furthermore, does this right prevent police from intervening when they believe that those radical ideas threaten to incite listeners to violence?

In 1949, Irving Feiner, a student at Syracuse University in New York State, was speaking to a crowd on a Syracuse street corner. Feiner was inviting the crowd of about 75 listeners to attend a meeting of the Progressive party that evening.

The Progressives were a group that split off from the Democratic party during the 1948 presidential election. Their platform called for repeal of the military draft, strong civil rights laws, cooperation with the Soviet Union banning atomic bombs, and freedom of speech and of political action for communists. The Progressive candidate in that election was endorsed by the Communist party. The winner in 1948, however, was Harry S Truman.

In the course of his speech that night, Irving Feiner made insulting remarks about President Truman and the mayor of Syracuse. He also urged the African Americans in the crowd to fight for equal rights. Someone complained to the police, who sent two officers to investigate. The crowd was restless and some passersby were jostled and forced into the street. The police asked Feiner to stop speaking. When Feiner refused they arrested him for breach of the peace and he was later convicted. When the lower courts upheld that verdict, Feiner appealed to the United States Supreme Court.

Review the following arguments and evidence presented to the Supreme Court.

Arguments for Feiner

1. The 1st Amendment guarantees the right to free speech and applies it to the States through the 14th Amendment.
2. Police cannot be used as an instrument to suppress unpopular views.
3. The ordinary murmurings and objections of an unsympathetic audience cannot be allowed to silence a speaker.

Arguments for New York

1. Neither the 1st Amendment nor 14th Amendment has been violated.
2. The police acted not to suppress speech but to preserve public order, which is a legitimate reason for limiting speech.
3. The crowd was not merely unsympathetic, but clearly threatened to become riotous.

Getting Involved

1. Identify the constitutional grounds on which each side based its arguments.
2. Debate the opposing viewpoints presented in this case.
3. Predict how you think the Supreme Court ruled in this case and why. Then refer to the Supreme Court Glossary that begins on page 764 to read about the decision. Discuss the impact of the Court's decision on free speech.

TEACHING

Debating Key Issues

***Feiner* v. *New York*:**
Should Free Speech Ever Be Suppressed?

Objective
Apply problem-solving and decision-making skills.

Instruct

Before beginning the feature, you may want to ask students what their interpretation is of free speech. Have students volunteer any situations in which they think free speech could be suppressed justifiably. As they read the feature, have students decide which argument they feel is most compelling and why.

Work through "Getting Involved" with the class, and have students write down their predictions. After the decision is known, discuss with students how they would have decided the case had they been on the Court in 1951.

Supreme Court Decision

The Court upheld the disorderly conduct conviction of Feiner, observing that "it is one thing to say that the police cannot be used as an instrument of suppression of unpopular views, and another to say that they are powerless to prevent a breach of the peace."

TRF **Teacher's Resource File**
See the Supreme Court Case file, p. 5, for an activity that extends coverage of this case.

SECTION 3
Suffrage and Civil Rights

FOCUS

Teacher's Resource File See the Unit 2 File, p. 33, for the Section 3 Outline.

Objectives

6.5 Examine reasons why civil rights laws were necessary to secure the right to vote for African Americans.

6.6 Determine what have been the effects of civil rights laws on qualifications for voters.

Bellringer Activity Hold up a picture of Martin Luther King Jr., or have students turn to pages 135 or 553. Have students identify him, and ask them: Why would Dr. King have been concerned about voting rights?

State the Purpose Until recently, many African Americans of both sexes were barred from participating in the election process. In Section 3, students will learn about the reasons African Americans were denied the right to vote, and they will learn about the civil rights laws that have been passed to assure African Americans equal access to the polls.

ABCNEWS INTERACTIVE

The following video segments may be used to highlight aspects of civil rights and voting.

POWERS OF THE SUPREME COURT GUIDEBOOK
Chapter 22: Amendment 15, p. 35

POWERS OF THE CONGRESS GUIDEBOOK
Chapter 21: Apportionment, p. 97

3 Suffrage and Civil Rights

Find Out:

- For what reasons were civil rights laws necessary to secure the right to vote for African Americans?
- What have been the effects of civil rights laws on voting qualifications?

Key Terms:

gerrymandering, injunction

How important is the right to vote? For those who do not have it, that right can seem as important as life itself. Indeed, in the Deep South of the 1960s, civil rights workers suffered arrest, beatings, shocks with electric cattle prods, even death—all in the name of the right to vote. Their efforts inspired the nation and led to large-scale federal efforts to secure suffrage for African Americans and other minority groups in the United States.

In this section, you will read about that historic struggle and the landmark federal laws it produced.

The 15th Amendment

The 15th Amendment was ratified in 1870. It declares that the right to vote cannot be denied to any citizen of the United States because of race, color, or previous condition of servitude. The amendment was plainly intended to ensure that African-American men, nearly all of them former slaves and nearly all of them living in the South, could vote.

The 15th Amendment is not self-executing, however. To make it effective, Congress had to act. Yet for almost 90 years the Federal Government paid little attention to voting rights for African Americans.

Over that period, African Americans were generally and systematically kept from the polls in much of the South. White supremacists employed a number of tactics to that end. Their major weapon was violence; others included more subtle threats and social pressures—for example, firing an African-American man who did try to register or vote, or denying his family credit at local stores.

More formal—"legal"—devices were used, as well. The most effective were the literacy tests. White officials regularly manipulated these tests to disfranchise African-American citizens.

Registration laws served the same end. As written, they applied to all potential voters. In practice, however, they were often administered to keep African Americans from qualifying to vote. Poll taxes, "white primaries," gerrymandering, and several other devices were also used to that
1.a end. **Gerrymandering** is the practice of drawing the lines of electoral districts in order to limit the voting strength of a particular group or party.[16]

Led by decisions of the Supreme Court, the lower federal courts began to strike down many of these practices in the 1940s and 1950s. But those courts could act only in suits filed by those who claimed to be victims of discrimination. That case-by-case method was, at best, agonizingly slow.

Finally, Congress was moved to act—very largely in response to the civil rights movement led by Dr. Martin Luther King, Jr. It has passed several civil rights laws since the late 1950s. Those statutes are treated in some detail in Chapter 21. They do contain a number of sections specifically intended to implement the 15th Amendment, however, and those provisions are dealt with here.

[16]The Supreme Court outlawed gerrymandering when used for purposes of racial discrimination in a case from Alabama, *Gomillion* v. *Lightfoot,* in 1960. The white primary arose out of the decades-long Democratic domination of the politics of the South. Almost always, only the Democrats nominated candidates for office, and generally in primaries. In several southern States, political parties were defined by law as "private associations." As such, they could exclude members as they chose, and the Democrats regularly refused to admit African Americans. Because only party members could vote in the party's primary, African Americans were then excluded from the critical step in the public election process. The Supreme Court finally outlawed the white primary in a case from Texas, *Smith* v. *Allwright,* 1944.

Reading Strategy: Who? What? When? Where? How? Why?

Before they begin reading, have students make a list of questions beginning with who, what, when, where, how, and why on a piece of paper. As they read Section 3, have them answer these questions to help organize the information.

Vocabulary

Point out "Key Terms" on page 138. Explain to students that the word *gerrymandering* dates back to 1812, and is a combination of two words—Gerry, after Elbridge Gerry, the governor of Massachusetts, and salamander, a lizard-like reptile. The map of an election district redrawn during Gerry's governorship to benefit his party was said by one observer to resemble a salamander. Locate a picture of this cartoon on page 242. LEP LEP

The Civil Rights Acts of 1957 and 1960

The first such law passed by Congress, the Civil Rights Act of 1957, set up the United States Civil Rights Commission. One of the Commission's major duties is to inquire into claims of voter discrimination. It reports its findings to Congress and the President and, through the media, to the public. The Act also gave to the attorney general the power to seek **injunctions**—federal court orders—to prevent interference with any person's right to vote in federal elections. 1.b

The Civil Rights Act of 1960 added another safeguard. It provided for the appointment of federal voting referees. These officers were to serve anywhere a federal court found voter discrimination. They were given the power to help qualified persons to register and to vote in federal elections.

The Civil Rights Act of 1964

The Civil Rights Act of 1964 is a much broader measure than either of the two earlier ones. It outlaws discrimination in several areas, and especially in job-related matters. With regard to voting rights, its most important section forbids the use of any registration requirement in an unfair or discriminatory manner.

The 1964 law continued a pattern set in the earlier laws. For example, it relied on judicial action to overcome racial barriers and emphasized the use of federal court orders. These injunctions are backed by the power of the courts to punish for contempt any person who refuses to obey those orders.

Dramatic events in Selma, Alabama, soon pointed up the shortcomings of this approach, however. Dr. King mounted a voter registration drive in that city in early 1965. He and his supporters hoped that they could focus national attention on the issue of African-American voting rights—and they most certainly did. Their registration efforts were met with insults and violence—by local whites, city and county police, and then by State troopers. The nation saw much of the drama on television and was shocked. An outraged President Lyndon Johnson urged Congress to pass new and stronger legislation to ensure the voting rights of African Americans, and Congress acted quickly.

March on Montgomery, Alabama Martin Luther King, Jr. led this peaceful protest against voter discrimination in 1965.

The Voting Rights Act of 1965 and Its Amendments

The Voting Rights Act of 1965 made the 15th Amendment, at long last, a truly effective part of the Constitution. Unlike its predecessors, this act applies to all elections held anywhere in this country—State and local, as well as federal. The law has now been extended three times, in the Voting Rights Act Amendments of 1970, 1975, and 1982.

The 1965 law directed the attorney general to attack the constitutionality of the remaining State poll tax laws. That provision led directly to *Harper* v. *Virginia State Board of Elections*, in 1966 (see page 136).

The law also suspended the use of any literacy test or similar device in any State or county where less than half of the electorate had been registered or had voted in the 1964 elections. The law authorized the attorney general to appoint voting examiners to serve in any of those States or counties. It also gave these federal officers the power to register voters and otherwise oversee the conduct of elections in those areas. The

INSTRUCT

Explain/Discuss Explain to students that even though the 15th Amendment was passed in 1870, it was still possible for individual States to impose restrictions that could bar African Americans from voting. A series of civil rights laws enacted since 1957 have assured African Americans their present-day status as active participants in the American electorate.

Discuss with students the various civil rights laws and amendments, and point out to them the effects of each new piece of legislation. (*15th Amendment; Civil Rights Act of 1957 and 1960; Civil Rights Act of 1964; and Voting Rights Act of 1965 and its amendments of 1970, 1975, and 1982.*)

You may also want students to turn to the Constitution on page 726 and read the 15th Amendment to examine why the amendment could not hold up without the support of the civil rights laws enacted during the 1950s, 1960s, and 1970s.

Provide Guided Practice On the board, write as headings 1957, 1960, 1964, and 1965 Have students explain what civil rights legislation was passed in each year. List their responses under the appropriate heading.(*1957, 1960, 1964: Civil Rights Acts; 1965: Voting Rights Act*)

Provide Independent Practice

TRF **Teacher's Resource File** You may wish to assign Section 3 Guided Reading and Review, Unit 2 File, p. 34, to help students master section objective content.

SPOTLIGHT ON: Constitutional Issues

The crisis in Selma forced President Johnson to choose between protecting the rights of African Americans in the short run or extending them in the long run. While Alabama State police clearly violated the free assembly rights of civil rights workers, Johnson feared that sending Federal troops to Alabama would make "a State's rights martyr" of Governor George Wallace, and destroy vital Southern support for the Voting Rights Act in Congress. Despite criticism, Johnson waited before he sent the troops, a delay which avoided generating Southern resentment of a federal invasion and kept Southern support for the Voting Rights Act intact.

TRF **Teacher's Resource File**
See Historical and Legal Documents, pp. 30, 32, for material to support this section.

Monitor Comprehension

Answers to Section 3 Review
1. "Key Terms" are defined on the following pages:
a. gerrymandering, p. 138
b. injunction, p. 139
2. (a) and (b) Civil Rights Act of 1957 established Civil Rights Commission; Civil Rights Act of 1960 provided for the appointment of federal voting referees; Civil Rights Act of 1964 outlawed discrimination and forbade the use of registration requirements in a discriminatory manner; Voting Rights Act of 1965 applied antidiscrimination measures to all elections. **3.** (a) The civil rights movement helped inspire Congress to act. (b) He played a large leadership role in the civil rights movement. **4.** 1975 amendments to the Voting Rights Act of 1965. **5.** Students might note that repeated attempts to disfranchise African Americans suggests that racists recognized the power of the right to vote.

Closure

Remind students that although the Constitution provided suffrage for African-American men under the 15th Amendment, suffrage was often denied them in many places until the passage of civil rights laws during the 1950s and 1960s. In Section 4, students will examine the reasons why many Americans choose not to vote.

Assignment Assign Section 4, pages 141–144 for the next class period.

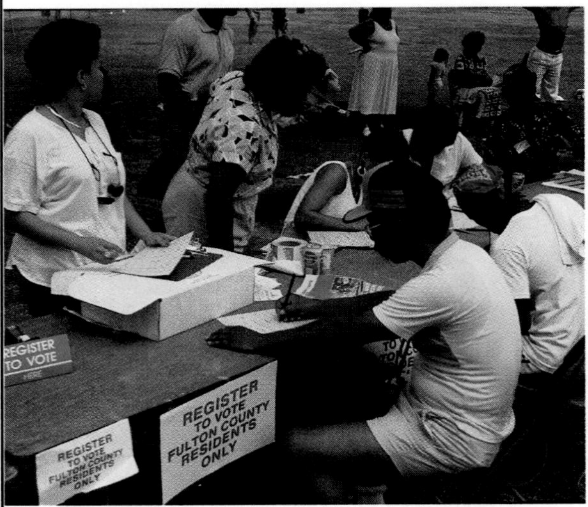

Civil Rights in Action Since the passage of the Voting Rights Act, the number of African-American voters has risen dramatically. Here, residents of Atlanta, Georgia, fill out voter registration forms.

1965 law also declared that no new election laws can go into effect in any of those States unless first approved—given "preclearance"—by the Department of Justice.

Any State or county subject to the voter-examiner and preclearance provisions can be removed from the law's coverage through a "bail-out" process. That relief can come if the State can show the United States District Court in the District of Columbia that it has not applied any of its voting procedures in a discriminatory way for at least the past 10 years.

The voter-examiner and preclearance provisions of the 1965 act applied to six entire States—Alabama, Georgia, Louisiana, Mississippi, South Carolina, and Virginia, and also to 40 North Carolina counties.

The Voting Rights Act was upheld by the Supreme Court in 1966. In *South Carolina* v. *Katzenbach*, the Court ruled that Congress had chosen both "rational and appropriate" means to implement the 15th Amendment.

The 1970 amendments extended the law for another five years. Based on the results of the 1968 elections, several counties in six more States—Alaska, Arizona, California, Idaho, New Mexico, and Oregon—were added to the law's coverage.

The 1970 law also provided that, for five years, no State could use literacy as the basis for any voting requirement. That temporary ban and the law's residence provisions were upheld by the Court in *Oregon* v. *Mitchell* in 1970.

The law was extended again in 1975, this time for seven years. The five-year ban on literacy tests became a permanent one, and the law's voter-examiner and preclearance provisions were broadened. Since 1975 they have also covered any State or county where more than 5 percent of the voting-age population belongs to certain "language minorities." These groups are defined to include all persons of Spanish heritage, Native Americans, Asian Americans, and Alaskan Natives. This addition spread the law's coverage to all of Alaska and Texas and to several counties in 24 other States, as well. In each of these areas, all ballots and official election materials must be printed both in English and in the language of the minority, or minorities, involved.

The 1982 amendments extended the basic features of the Voting Rights Act for another 25 years, with this major exception: Its language-minority provisions are to remain in effect only until mid-1992.

Section 3 Review

1. Define: gerrymandering, injunction
2. (a) Identify the major civil rights laws enacted by Congress over the past 30 years. (b) Describe their voting rights provisions.
3. (a) For what reasons did Congress pass the civil rights laws? (b) What role did Dr. Martin Luther King, Jr. play?
4. What voting rights provision pertains to "language minorities"?

Critical Thinking

5. Drawing Conclusions (p. 19) Racial prejudice in the United States often took the form of attempts to disfranchise African Americans. For what reasons do you think this was so?

★

Enrichment

Have students interview one person concerning his or her memories of the civil rights movement of the 1950s and 1960s. Questions should include: How did you first become aware of the movement? Were you personally involved? What do you remember about media coverage of the events? Students may compile their interviews into a class book. If video equipment is available, students may wish to tape their interviews. (Average)

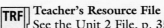

Teacher's Resource File
See the Unit 2 File, p. 35, for the Section 3 Quiz.

Reteach

Have students review the section and write 10 true or false questions about the section content. Students should then exchange their questions with a partner and answer the questions.

4 Nonvoting

Find Out:

- What is the scope of the nonvoter problem?
- For what reasons do people not vote?

Key Term:

political efficacy

The word *idiot* came to our language from the Greek. In ancient Athens, an idiot (*idiotes*) was a citizen who did not vote or take part in public life and was, therefore, ignorant of current affairs. Of course, the word *idiot* has other negative meanings in American culture, and it would be foolish to label all nonvoters so harshly. There are many special circumstances and reasons why some people do not vote. The troubling fact remains, however: Many of the millions of nonvoters in this country do not vote because they *choose* not to do so. How can this situation be improved? What steps should be taken to encourage full voter participation in this country? As you read, think about possible answers to these questions.

The Size of the Problem

The table and the graph on page 143 display the major facts of the nonvoter problem in American elections. On election day in 1988 there were an estimated 182.6 million persons of voting age in the United States. But only some 91.6 million persons—only 50.2 percent—actually voted in the presidential election. More than 91 million persons who *might* have voted did not vote.

In 1988 voters cast an estimated 81.6 million votes in the elections held across the country to fill the 435 seats in the House of Representatives. That is, over 55 percent of the electorate did not vote in the congressional elections of 1988. Note the even lower rate of voter turnout in the "off-year" House races in 1990 when a full two-thirds of eligible voters did not vote.

Little-Recognized Aspects of the Problem The fact that the United States has a nonvoter problem is widely recognized. But it is important to note that several aspects of the problem are not so widely known. For example, millions of nonvoters actually do vote. Ten million persons who did vote in the 1988 presidential election did not vote, in that same election, for a candidate for a seat in the House of Representatives.

"Nonvoting voters" are not limited to federal elections. In fact, they are much more common in State and local elections. As a general rule, the further down the ballot an office is, the fewer the number of votes that will be cast for it. This phenomenon is sometimes called "ballot fatigue." The expression suggests that many voters exhaust their patience or their knowledge as they work their way down the list of offices and measures on the ballot.

Some quick illustrations of the point: More votes are regularly cast in the presidential election than in the gubernatorial election in every State. More votes are generally cast for the governorship than for such other Statewide offices as lieutenant governor or secretary of state. More voters in a county usually vote in the races for Statewide offices than vote in the contests for such county offices as sheriff, county clerk, or district attorney, and so on.

There are other little-recognized facets of the problem, too. Thus, the table on page 143 shows that turnout in congressional elections is consistently higher in presidential years than it is in "off-year elections."

That same pattern holds among the States in terms of the types of elections held; more people vote in general elections than in either primary or special elections.

Why People Do Not Vote

Why do we have so many nonvoters? Why, even in a presidential election, do nearly half of all those who could vote stay away from the polls?

"Cannot-Voters" To begin with, look at another of those little-recognized aspects of the nonvoter problem: Several million persons who

SECTION 4
Nonvoting

FOCUS

Teacher's Resource File See the Unit 2 File, p. 36, for the Section 4 Outline.

Objectives

6.7 Determine the scope of the nonvoter problem in the United States.
6.8 Examine reasons why people do not vote.

Bellringer Activity Write the following question on the board: Is it a right, a duty, or a privilege to vote? Give students a few moments to think of reasons, then elicit responses, to foster a discussion of voter participation.

State the Purpose Out of 182.6 million people of voting age in the United States, only 91.6 million, or about 50 percent, participate in presidential elections. In Section 4, students will learn about the extent of the nonvoter problem in the U.S., and the reasons behind it.

ABCNEWS INTERACTIVE

The following video segment may be used to highlight aspects of voter participation.

POWERS OF CONGRESS GUIDEBOOK
Chapter 20: Rules for Elections, p. 96

Vocabulary

Point out "Key Term" on page 141, *political efficacy.* Have a volunteer look the term up in the Glossary and read the definition aloud. Then discuss with students their opinions about their own political efficacy.

Reading Strategy: Question Writing

Before students begin Section 4, have them skim the headings and subheadings throughout. Ask students to turn each heading into a question. You may want to write some of the questions on the board. Then have students skim Section 4 for answers to the questions.

INSTRUCT

Explain Explain to students that nonvoting in the United States has reached epidemic proportions. Only about half the people of voting age actually cast ballots in presidential elections, and only a third voted in the 1990 mid-term election. In some cases people do not vote because they cannot. They are restricted by residence status, sickness, incarceration, religious beliefs, or sudden emergencies. Others choose not to vote because of apathy, indecision, and a lack of feeling of political efficacy.

As students discuss nonvoting in the United States, have them consider the reasons why some people choose not to vote. Ask them to analyze what nonvoting reflects about the present mood and morale among the American people.

To aid discussion, you may want to have students also think about what factors might encourage voter participation. What discourages them from or encourages them to vote?

Interpreting Political Cartoons Ask students to identify the reasons why this cartoon is amusing. Ask them what it says about the election process and voter attitudes (*The cartoon shows that the candidates are both unsatisfactory, or are too similar to choose between.*)

Caption Answer By depicting voters as flipping coins to decide which way to vote.

Interpreting Political Cartoons Nonvoting has many issues at its roots. How is one issue—a lack of confidence in the candidates—conveyed in this cartoon?

are regularly identified as "nonvoters" can be more accurately described as "cannot-voters." That is, although it is true that they do not vote, the fact is that they cannot do so. The 1988 data support the point. In that figure of some 91 million who did not vote in the last presidential election, nearly 6 million are resident aliens—and, remember, they are barred from the polls in every State. Another 5 to 6 million citizens were so ill or otherwise physically disabled that they simply could not vote in an election. And an additional 2 or 3 million persons were traveling suddenly and unexpectedly, and so could not vote.

Other groups of cannot-voters include, for example: some 500,000 persons in mental health care facilities or under some other form of legal restraint because of their mental condition; more than 800,000 adults in jails and prisons; and perhaps as many as 100,000 who cannot vote because of their religious beliefs, such as beliefs that do not permit participation in the affairs of government.

Racial, religious, and other discrimination still plays a part in voter turnout, too—despite the many recent federal statutes, court decisions, and enforcement actions aimed at eliminating discrimination. An unknown number—but, certainly, more than a million persons—could not vote in 1988 because of (1) the purposeful administration of election laws to keep them from doing so, and/or (2) "informal" local pressures applied to that same end.

In short, that figure of about 91 million nonvoters in 1988 counts at least 17 million persons who, in fact, really should not be included in that number.

Actual Nonvoters Even so, there are millions of actual nonvoters in the United States. Thus, in 1988 more than 70 million Americans who could have voted in the presidential election did not.

There are any number of reasons for that behavior. As a leading example: Many deliberately choose not go to the polls. They do not vote because they are convinced that it makes no real difference who wins a certain election. Some are satisfied with the political world as they see it. They believe that, no matter who wins elections, things will continue to go well for themselves and for the country.

But a large number of those who deliberately stay away from the polls do so because they distrust politics and politicians. They have no sense
1.a of **political efficacy**. That is, they lack any sense of their own influence or effectiveness in politics. Many of them believe that they have been squeezed out of the political process, that the system that the people should control has been taken over by entrenched politicians, powerful special interests, and the media.

Cumbersome election procedures are another factor here—for example, inconvenient registration requirements, long ballots, and long lines at polling places. Bad weather also tends to discourage turnout. Another possible, though hotly debated, factor is the so-called "time-zone fallout" problem. This refers to the fact that in presidential elections, polls in the East close before polls in the West. Based on the early returns from the East, the news media often predict the outcome of a race before all the voters in the West have gone to the polls. Some people fear that such reports have discouraged western voters from casting their ballots.

Factors Affecting Turnout On the surface, the chief causes of nonvoting appear to be a lack of interest, indifference, and apathy.

ACTIVITY: Cooperative Learning

Time: One class period **Activity:** Create a public service television advertisement. **Grouping:** Groups of four to six students **Purpose:** Have students work together to write a one-minute television advertisement encouraging people to vote. Explain that group members should discuss what people will see and hear in the advertisement and how it will be presented to the class. **Roles:** Have students assign the following roles: manager, recorder, visual display preparer(s), spokesperson(s). **Outcome:** Have the spokesperson(s) present the group's ad to the class. The class may vote on the most effective advertisement.

A solution to the problem of nonvoting, though, requires a deeper look at its roots and causes.

The people most likely to vote display such characteristics as higher levels of income, education, and occupational status. They are usually well integrated into community life. They tend to be long-time residents who are active in or at least comfortable with their surroundings. They are likely to have a strong sense of party identification, believe that voting is an important act, and are subject to few cross-pressures—contra-

Voter Turnout, 1932-1960

Year	Population of Voting Age[a] (in millions)	Votes Cast for President (in millions)	(percent)	Votes Cast for U.S. Representatives (in millions)	(percent)
1932	75.768	39.732	52.4	37.657	49.7
1934	77.997	—	—	32.256	41.4
1936	80.174	45.643	56.9	42.886	53.5
1938	82.354	—	—	36.236	44.0
1940	84.728	49.900	58.9	46.951	55.4
1942	86.465	—	—	28.074	32.5
1944	85.654	47.977	56.0	45.103	52.7
1946	92.659	—	—	34.398	37.1
1948	95.573	48.794	51.1	45.933	48.1
1950	98.134	—	—	40.342	41.1
1952	99.929	61.551	61.6	57.571	57.6
1954	102.075	—	—	42.580	41.7
1956	104.515	62.067	59.3	58.428	55.9
1958	106.447	—	—	45.818	43.0
1960	109.672	68.838	62.8	64.133	58.5

[a]As estimated by Census Bureau. Population 18 years of age and over since ratification of 26th Amendment in 1971; prior to 1971, 21 years and over in all States, except: 18 years and over in Georgia since 1943 and Kentucky since 1955, 19 years and over in Alaska and 20 and over in Hawaii since 1959.

Sources: Statistical Abstract; Congressional Quarterly; Clerk of the House of Representatives.

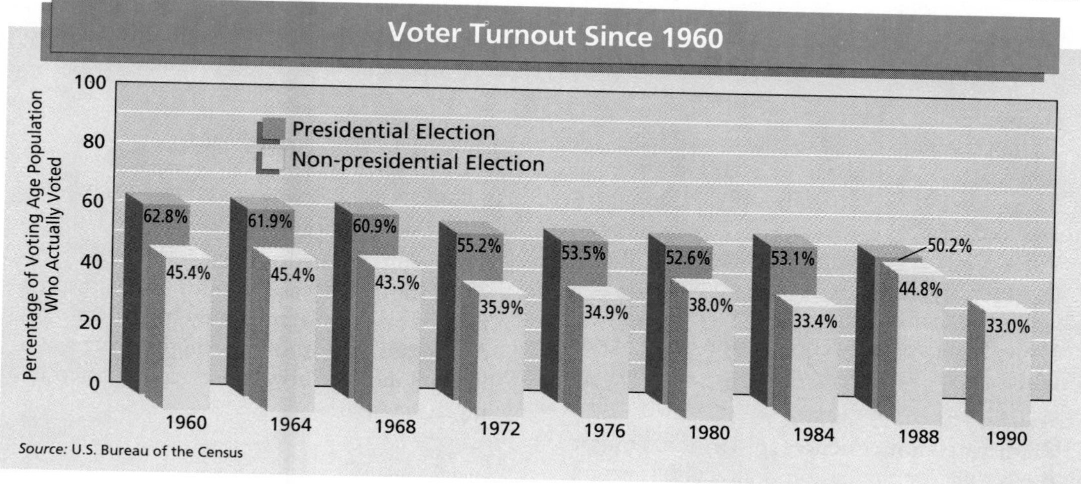

Interpreting Tables and Graphs Voter turnout peaked in 1960 then steadily decreased to the present. What are some of the factors that might account for this decline?

Interpreting Tables and Graphs Ask students to analyze the reasons why more people vote presidential candidates than Statewide candidates, even in the same election.(*Possible answers include: choosing the President seems more important than choosing State or Congressional officials.*)

Caption Answer Possible answers include disillusionment with politics, lack of interest, poor access to polls, participation taken for granted.

Provide Guided Practice Write the headings "Cannot Vote," "Actual Nonvoters" and "Factors Affecting Turnout" on the chalkboard. For each heading, have students suggest sentences or phrases that detail the key points of each head. (Cannot Vote: *ill, disabled, aliens;* Actual Nonvoters: *political efficacy;* Factors Affecting Turnout: *party competition; apathy.*)

Provide Independent Practice

TRF **Teacher's Resource File** You may wish to assign Section 4 Guided Reading and Review, Unit 2 File, p. 37, to help students master section objective content.

Enrichment

Have students interview three voting-age people to determine their voting habits and attitudes, and then present the findings to the class as an oral or written report. Students should attempt to understand the roots of interviewees' motivation or apathy. (Average)

MONITOR COMPREHENSION

Answers to Section 4 Review
1.) "Key Term" is defined on the following page:
a. political efficacy, p. 142
2. (a) 57% (b) 40% **3.** To the many voters who do not vote in the same elections for all the offices or measures on a ballot. **4.** (a) Illness, and unexpected events, apathy, and low income and education level, youth, and lack of party identification. (b) Apathy, apparent lack of political efficacy. **5.** It increases it. **6.** Answers will vary. Students might expect to see a dramatic change in the composition of government; students might also predict civil unrest.

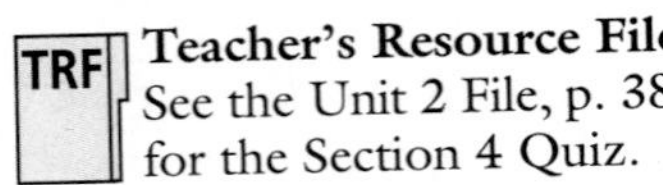

Teacher's Resource File See the Unit 2 File, p. 38, for the Section 4 Quiz.

CLOSURE

Remind students that while there are over 182 million people of voting age in the United States, at most only about half of them participate in the election process. Although there are "cannot voters," there are also many "actual nonvoters," people who choose not to vote because they lack a sense of political efficacy, among other factors.

In Section 5, students will examine the specific sociological and psychological factors that effect voter behavior.

Assignment Assign Section 5, pages 144–151 for the next class period.

dictory, competing influences—that would discourage their participation. They also are likely to live in those States and locales where laws, customs, and competition between the parties all work to promote turnout. The opposite characteristics produce a profile of those who are less likely to vote. Nonvoters are likely to be younger than age 35, unmarried, and unskilled. More nonvoters live in the South and in rural, rather than urban or suburban, locales.

A few of the factors are so important that they influence turnout even when they are not supported by, or are in conflict with, other factors. Thus, those persons with a high sense of political efficacy are likely to vote—no matter what their income, education, age, race, and so on. The degree of two-party competition has much the same kind of general, across-the-board effect. It, too, has an extraordinary impact on participation. Thus, the greater the degree of competition between candidates, the higher the rate of voter turnout will be, regardless of other factors.

Despite the greater weight of some factors, however, notice this important point: It is the combined presence of several of them, rather than of one of them alone, that tends to characterize a voter or nonvoter.

Section 4 Review

1. Define: political efficacy
2. (a) On average, about what percentage of eligible voters have taken part in presidential elections since 1932? (b) In off-year congressional elections?
3. What does "nonvoting by voters" refer to?
4. (a) Identify the causes for nonvoting. (b) Which is the major one?
5. How does two-party competition affect voter turnout?

Critical Thinking

6. Predicting Consequences (p. 19) What might be the results for the nation if all eligible voters were required to cast ballots?

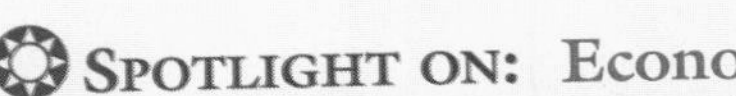

★

5 Voter Behavior

Find Out:
- How do sociological and psychological factors work to determine how a person will vote?
- How much does party identification affect voter behavior?

Key Terms:
political socialization, party identification, straight-ticket voting, split-ticket voting, independents

Today, many election campaigns begin months, even years before the election itself. Voters are bombarded with information about the candidates—what they have done or not done in their careers, what they are for and what they are against, and countless other pieces of information. Much of it is presented by the candidates themselves with the hope that it makes them look good; some of it comes from their opponents and is aimed at making them look bad.

Out of this mass of information, potential voters are supposed to make decisions. As you have seen, many of them choose not to choose. Millions of voters, however, do go to the polls. In this section, you will encounter the major factors that influence their decisions.

The Study of Voting Behavior

Most of what observers know about voter behavior comes from three sources:[17]

1. The results of particular elections. As a quick illustration: The careful study of the returns from areas populated largely by African Americans or Catholics or high-income families will indicate how those groups voted in a given election.

[17]Much of the most useful research on voter behavior is done by the Center for Political Studies at the University of Michigan.

Reteach
Ask students to imagine that they are chairpersons of a major political party. What steps would they take in a campaign to motivate people to vote? Based on the reasons cited in the section, have students write a plan that they think would encourage people to vote. The plan can take the form of a list or outline.

SPOTLIGHT ON: Economics
Who pays for the bombardment of commercials during the late summer and early fall of a presidential election year? Curiously enough, American taxpayers do. Since 1976, general elections for President have been publicly financed by the Federal Elections Commission. The FEC also matches contributions up to $250 for candidates in the party primaries, and finances the Republican and Democratic national conventions as well. In 1988, the Bush and Dukakis campaigns each received $46.1 million for the general election. The total FEC outlay for the 1988 campaign, including the primaries and the conventions, was $177.5 million.

2. The field of survey research—the polling (questioning, interviewing) of scientifically determined cross sections of the population. It is the method by which public opinion is most often identified and measured. The Gallup Poll is perhaps the best known survey research organization today.
3. Studies of **political socialization**—the process by which people gain their political attitudes and opinions. That very complex process begins in early childhood and continues on through each person's life. Political socialization involves all of the experiences and relationships that lead people to see the political world, and to act in it, as they do. 1a.

Here you will read about voter behavior—based on what those studies tell us about how and why people vote as they do. In Chapter 8, you will turn to the broader subject of public opinion and take a closer look at the techniques of survey research and the process of political socialization.

Factors That Influence Voters Observers still have much to learn about voter behavior, but many sociological and psychological factors quite clearly influence the way people vote.

Sociology is the study of groups and how people behave within groups. The sociological factors affecting voter behavior are really the many pieces of a voter's social and economic life. Those pieces are of two broad kinds: (1) a voter's personal characteristics—age, race, income, occupation, education, religion, and so on, and (2) a voter's group affiliations—family, co-workers, friends, and the like.

Psychology is the study of the mind and of individual behavior. The psychological factors that influence voter behavior are a voter's perceptions of politics. That is, how the voter sees the parties, the candidates, and the issues in an election.

The differences between these two kinds of influences are not so great as they might seem. In fact, they are closely related and constantly interact with one another. How voters look at parties, candidates, or issues is often shaped by their social and economic backgrounds. Or, to put it another way, each person tends to look at politics through the glasses of his or her own life.

Global Awareness

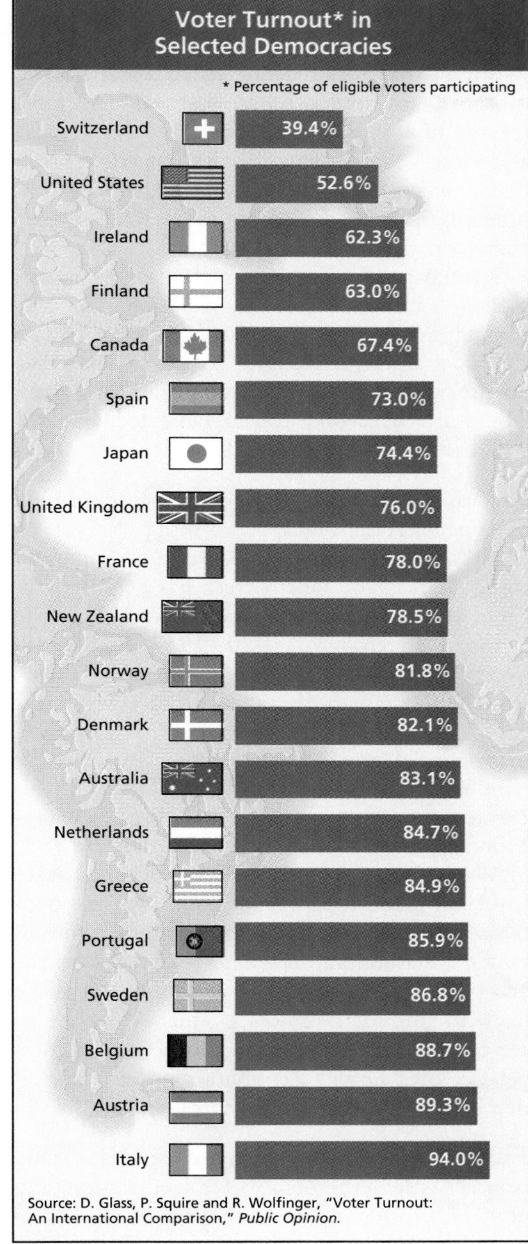

Interpreting Graphs Democracy does not ensure high voter turnout. Why might turnout be low in the United States?

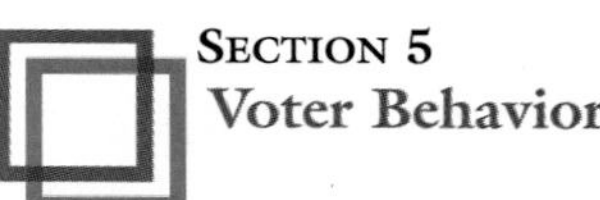

SECTION 5 Voter Behavior

FOCUS

TRF **Teacher's Resource File** See the Unit 2 File, p. 39, for the Section 5 Outline.

Objectives

6.9 Examine how sociological and psychological factors work to determine how a person will vote.

6.10 Determine how much party identification effects voter behavior.

Bellringer Activity Ask students: Why would the size of the town you live in effect how you vote? Use responses to this question to begin discussion of the sociological and psychological factors in voter behavior.

State the Purpose Why voters choose to vote the way they do is determined by several factors, some sociological and some psychological. These factors include a person's background, geographic location, party identification, income, and occupation.

In Section 5, students will learn about these sociological and psychological factors and how they, with party affiliation, influence how people vote.

Interpreting Graphs As students look at the graph on page 145, they will see that no country has 100% voter participation. Ask students to speculate about why this is so.

Caption Answer Possible answers include voter apathy, cumbersome registration requirements, noncompulsory voting, etc.

Vocabulary

Direct students' attention to "Key Terms" on page 144. As they read, have students make a list of these words and then make notes as they read about how each of these terms relates to the section title. LEP

Reading Strategy: Graphic Organizer

Create a chart that contains the two headings: *Sociological Factors* and *Psychological Factors.* Ask students to skim the headings and "Key Terms" in Section 5 for concepts that might be included under each heading.

INSTRUCT

Analyze/Explain/Discuss To help students understand group membership, have them write ten things about themselves on a piece of paper. While they do this, write ten things about yourself on the board. (*Examples might include your age group, sex, part of the country in which you live, occupation, race, religion, etc.*) Then go through your list, demonstrating how these facts about yourself make you a member of specific groups by writing the name of the group (i.e., female—women) next to each item on your list. Have students do this with their own lists, and have volunteers share some of their group affiliations with the class.

To further clarify the concept, explain that extensive studies of voter behavior indicate that how people vote is heavily influenced by a number of sociological factors—voters' income level, occupation, education, age, race, etc., and their primary group affiliations, especially family, coworkers, and friends—and by a number of psychological factors—how the voter views the parties, candidates, and issues in an election. Of these factors, the single most important and lasting predictor of a person's voting behavior is still party identification. This is true despite indications that some of this impact may have been lost in recent years.

Discuss with students how membership in various groups might or might not influence their own voting behavior.

The Sociological Factors

From the table on page 147, you can draw a composite picture of the American voter in terms of a number of sociological factors.

But a word of caution here: Do not make too much of any one of these factors. The table reports how voters, identified by a single characteristic, voted in each of the last eight presidential elections, from 1960 through 1988. But, remember, each voter possesses several of the characteristics shown in the table.

To make the point, consider these examples: College graduates are more likely to vote Republican. So are persons over 50 years of age. Catholics are more likely to vote for Democrats. So are members of labor unions. How, then, would a 55-year-old college-educated Catholic who belongs to the AFL-CIO vote?

Income, Occupation Voters in the middle- to upper-income brackets are more likely to be Republicans. Voters with lower incomes tend to be Democrats. This pattern has held up over time; as you can see, it even showed up in the lopsided elections of 1980, 1984, and 1988: Voters with incomes above $35,000 backed Ronald Reagan, both times, by better than 2 to 1, and they voted for George Bush by a margin of nearly 3 to 2. A majority of those with incomes of less than $15,000 voted for Democrats Jimmy Carter in 1980, Walter Mondale in 1984, and Michael Dukakis in 1988.

Most often, income and occupation are closely related matters. Professional and business people, and others with higher incomes, tend to vote for Republican candidates. Manual workers, and others from lower income groups, are more likely to vote for Democrats. Thus, with the single exception of 1964, professional and business people voted heavily Republican in the ten presidential elections from 1952 through 1988.

Education There is also a close relationship between the level of a voter's education and how he or she votes. A number of studies of voter behavior show that college graduates vote for Republicans in higher percentages than do high-school graduates. Those studies also show that high-school graduates vote more often Republican than do those who have only gone through grade school.

Sex, Age On the whole, sex does not appear to be a major factor in partisan voting behavior. That is, men are no more or less likely to favor one party and its candidates than are women. A number of studies, however, do suggest this: Men and women do vote in measurably different ways when issues related to war and national defense or human rights are prominent in an election.

Several analysts argue that there is now a "gender gap" in national politics. Since 1980, they say, women have become noticeably less likely than men to vote Republican, at least in presidential elections. Support for their view can be found in the table on page 147, where you can see a lessening of the gender gap in 1988 but still a difference of 4 percentage points.

Age is another matter, however. Younger voters usually have been more likely to be Democrats than Republicans. Older voters are likely to find the GOP and its candidates more attractive. Thus, in every presidential election from 1952 through 1980, the Democratic candidate received a larger percentage of the votes cast by the under-30 age group than of those cast by voters age 50 and over. But, notice, that long-standing pattern was broken by President Reagan's appeal to younger voters in 1984. George Bush kept their support in 1988.

Religious, Ethnic Background A majority of northern Protestants prefer the GOP. Catholics and Jews are much more likely to be Democrats.

Historical factors account for much of this pattern. Most of those who first came from Europe to settle this country were of English stock, and Protestant. The later tides of immigration, from southern and eastern Europe, brought many Catholics and Jews to the United States. Those later immigrants were often treated as minority groups by the largely Protestant establishment. And they most often settled in the larger cities, where local Democratic party organizations helped them to become citizens and voters. From the New Deal period of the

ACTIVITY: For Gifted Students

Theme: Rights Although the right to use the secret ballot is guaranteed to all citizens eligible to vote in the U.S., voters are still bombarded by aggressive political campaigning. Students may extend their study of voter behavior through research of voting trends as related to ethnicity, class, gender, religious affiliation, level of education, and family or other group affiliation(s). Students may wish to consult statistical abstracts, public opinion polls, social science journals, the Bill of Rights, etc., in order to plan and participate in a debate over the question: Does membership in a group really influence an individual's voting behavior?

Voting by Groups in Presidential Elections, 1960–1988 (By Percentage of Votes Reported Cast)

	1960		1964		1968			1972		1976		1980			1984		1988	
	D	R	D	R	D	R	AIP	D	R	D	R	D	R	I	D	R	D	R
National	50.1	49.9	61.3	38.7	43.0	43.4	13.6	37.5	60.7	50	48	41	50.7	6.6	41	59	46	54
Sex																		
Men	52	48	60	40	41	43	16	37	63	53	45	38	53	7	36	64	44	56
Women	49	51	62	38	45	43	12	38	62	48	51	44	49	6	45	55	48	52
Race																		
White	49	51	59	41	38	47	15	32	68	46	52	36	56	7	34	66	41	59
Nonwhite	68	32	94	6	85	12	3	87	13	85	15	86	10	2	84	13	82	18
Education																		
College	39	61	52	48	37	54	9	37	63	42	55	35	53	10	39	61	42	58
High school	52	48	62	38	42	43	15	34	66	54	46	43	51	5	43	57	46	54
Grade school	55	45	66	34	52	33	15	49	51	58	41	54	42	3	51	49	55	45
Occupation																		
Professional/ business	42	58	54	46	34	56	10	31	69	42	56	33	55	10	34	66		
White-collar	48	52	57	43	41	47	12	36	64	50	48	40	51	9	47	53	NA	NA
Manual	60	40	71	29	50	35	15	43	57	58	41	48	46	5	46	54		
Union family members	65	35	73	27	56	29	15	46	54	63	36	50	43	5	52	48		
Age																		
Under 30	54	46	64	36	47	38	15	48	52	53	45	47	41	11	40	60	37	63
30–49	54	46	63	37	44	41	15	33	67	48	49	38	52	8	40	60	45	55
50 and older	46	54	59	41	41	47	12	36	64	52	48	41	54	4	41	59	49	51
Religion																		
Protestants	38	62	55	45	35	49	16	30	70	46	53	39	54	6	39	61	42	58
Catholics	78	22	76	24	59	33	8	48	52	57	42	46	47	6	39	61	51	49
Politics																		
Republicans	5	95	20	80	9	86	5	5	95	9	91	8	86	5	4	96	7	93
Democrats	84	16	87	13	74	12	14	67	33	82	18	69	26	4	79	21	85	15
Independents	43	57	56	44	31	44	25	31	69	38	57	29	55	14	33	67	43	57
Region																		
East	53	47	68	32	50	43	7	42	58	51	47	43	47	9	46	54	51	49
Midwest	48	52	61	39	44	47	9	40	60	48	50	41	51	7	42	58	47	53
South	51	49	52	48	31	36	33	29	71	54	45	44	52	3	37	63	40	60
West	49	51	60	40	44	49	7	41	59	46	51	35	54	9	40	60	46	54

D = Democratic candidate; R = Republican candidate; AIP = American Independent Party candidate (George Wallace, 1968); I = Independent candidate (John B. Anderson, 1980). Figures do not add to 100% in some groups because of rounding and/or minor party votes. *Less than 1%.

Source: The Gallup Report, No. 278, November, 1988.

Interpreting Tables: Multicultural Awareness Groups have historic loyalties to particular parties. Which racial group has voted largely Democratic since 1960?

1930s on, social welfare programs have strengthened the ties of most minority groups to the Democratic party.

In 1960 John Kennedy became the first Roman Catholic President. His election marked a sharper split between Catholic and Protestant voters than that found in any of the other elections covered by the table.

Nonwhites support the Democratic party—consistently and massively. They form the only

ABCNEWS INTERACTIVE

The following video segments may be used to highlight aspects of voter behavior.

POWERS OF THE PRESIDENT GUIDEBOOK
Chapter 13: Electing a President, p.17

POWERS OF CONGRESS GUIDEBOOK
Chapter 17: Political Party System, p. 93

Interpreting Tables Direct students to the age category in the table. What does the table say about the party affiliation among younger voters? Among older voters? *(For a long time, older voters were more likely to vote Republican, and younger voters Democrat. Recently, more younger voters have voted Republican and some older voters have begun to vote Democratic.)*

Caption Answer Nonwhite.

TRF **Teacher's Resource File**
See page 19 of the Election Kit for an activity to support this section.

Interpreting Tables As students look at the table on page 148, ask them to note any consistencies in geographic distribution among Democrats and Republicans. (*Students may suggest that people seem more likely to vote Democrat in the East and South, while people in the Midwest and Southwest might be more likely to vote Republican.*)

Outcome of Selected Presidential Elections

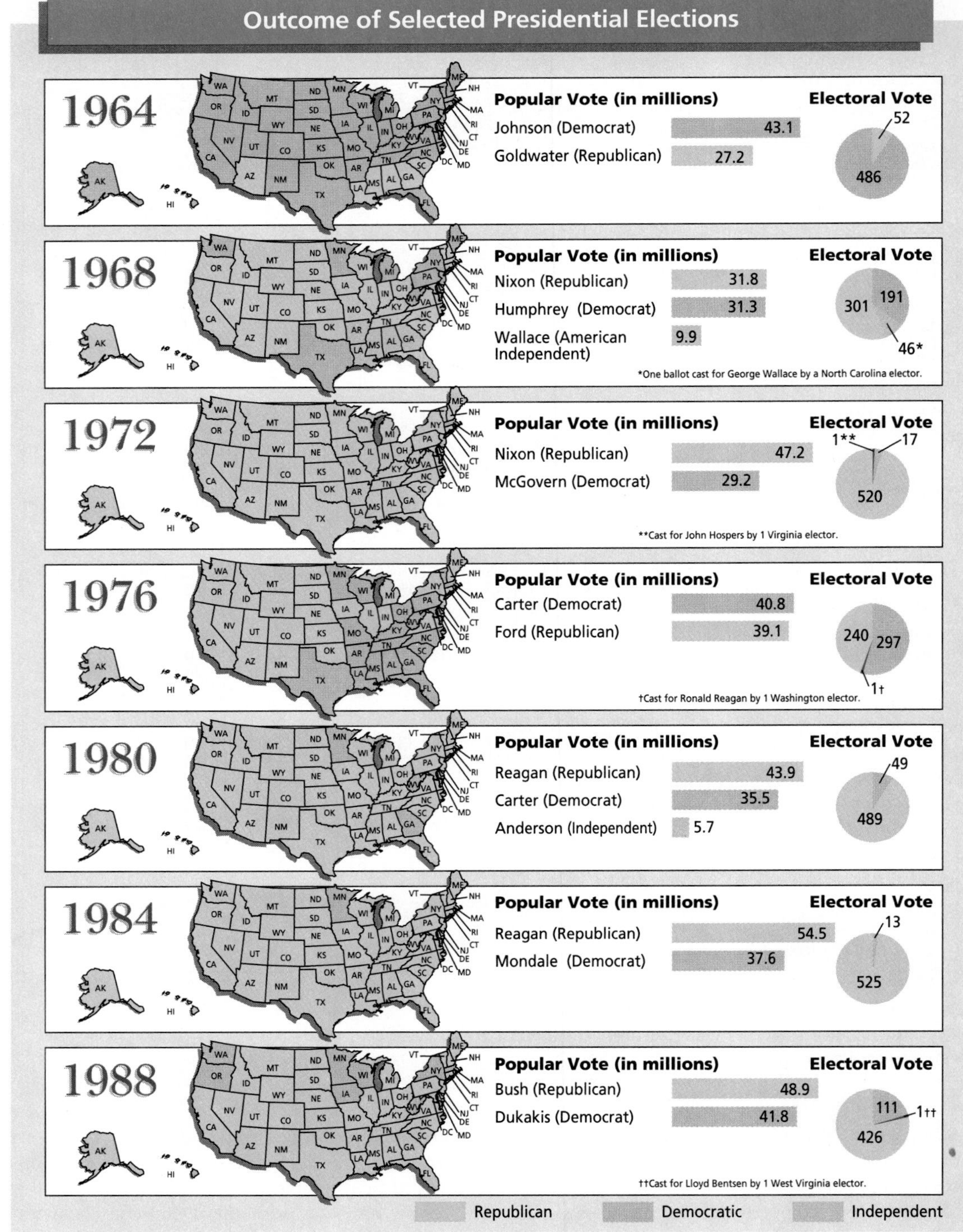

group that has given the Democratic candidate a clear majority in every presidential election since 1952. There are now more than 30 million African Americans, and they make up the single most important racial minority in the country. In the North, African Americans generally voted Republican until the 1930s. They moved away from the party of Abraham Lincoln with the coming of the New Deal, however. The civil rights movement of the 1960s led to greater African-American participation in the South—and there, too, African Americans now vote overwhelmingly Democratic.

There are now more than 23 million Hispanic Americans, people with Spanish-speaking backgrounds. To this point, Hispanics have tended to favor Democratic candidates. But, note, the label "Hispanic" conceals differences among Cuban Americans, who most often vote Republican, and Mexican Americans and Puerto Ricans, who are strongly Democratic. The rate of turnout among Hispanics is comparatively low—less than 30 percent in 1988.

Geography Geography—the part of the country, the State, and/or the locale in which a person lives—has an impact on voter behavior.

After the Civil War, the States of the old Confederacy voted so consistently Democratic that the Southeast quarter of the nation became known as the Solid South. For more than a hundred years now, most Southerners, regardless of any other factor, have been Democrats. The Solid South has disappeared in terms of presidential elections, but the Democrats still dominate most of the southern political scene.

Over time, the strongest and most consistent support for the Republicans by States can be found in Maine and Vermont in the Northeast and in Kansas, Nebraska, and the Dakotas in the Midwest. Lately, there has been much speculation about voting patterns in the "Sunbelt"—that area stretching from the southeastern States westward to California. Some analysts see the region as a base for increased conservatism and new strength for the Republican party in national politics.

Voters' attitudes also vary in terms of the size of the communities in which they live. In general, the Democrats draw strength from the big cities of the North and East. Many white Democrats have moved from the central cities and taken their political preferences with them, but Republican voters still dominate much of suburban America. Outside the South, voters in the smaller cities and rural areas are likely to be Republicans.

Family, Other Group Affiliations To this point, you have seen the American voter in terms of several broad social and economic characteristics. You can also consider voters on the basis of much smaller and more personal groupings, especially such primary groups as family, co-workers, and friends.

Typically, the members of a family vote in strikingly similar ways. Nine out of ten married couples share the same partisan leanings. As many as two out of every three voters follow the political attachments of their parents. Those who work together and circles of friends vote very much alike.

The Psychological Factors

In order to understand the voting process, you must look beyond such factors as occupation, level of education, ethnic background, and place of residence. You must also take into account a number of psychological factors. That is, you must look at the voters' perceptions of politics: how they see and how they react to the parties, the candidates, and the issues in an election.

Party Identification Most Americans identify themselves with one or the other of the two major parties early in life. Many never change. They support that party with little or no regard for either the candidates or the issues.

1b. The hefty impact of **party identification**—the loyalty of people to a political party—is the single most significant and lasting predictor of how a person will vote. A person who is a Democrat or a Republican will, for that reason, very likely vote for all or most of that party's candidates in an election. The practice of voting for candidates of but one party in an election is
1c. called **straight-ticket voting**.

Provide Guided Practice With students, review the section to find sociological and psychological factors in voter behavior, and write those factors in a list on the board. Then have students identify which factors would make someone more likely to vote Democratic and which Republican. (*Sociological factors: income, occupation, education, sex, age, religion, ethnicity, geography, family and other group affiliations. Psychological factors: party identification, candidates, issues. Democrat: Catholic, union member. Republican: White collar, Protestant, midwestern.*)

Provide Independent Practice

TRF **Teacher's Resource File** You may wish to assign the Section 5 Guided Reading and Review, in the Unit 2 File, p. 40, to help students master section objective content.

SPOTLIGHT ON: Multiculturalism

Although African Americans have strongly identified with the Democratic party since the New Deal and gave vital support to the last two Democrats elected to the presidency (94% for Lyndon B. Johnson in 1964 and 90% for Jimmy Carter in 1976), a recent survey by the Joint Center for Political Studies indicates that these days younger African Americans are less inclined than their parents to favor the Democratic party. According to the study, only 37% of African Americans under 30 identified themselves as "strong Democrats," while 59% of those over 50 identified themselves as such.

Enrichment

Have students research to create a voter behavior profile for their State, county, and/or city. Students might begin by analyzing the results of the last few elections and comparing the election results and party affiliations of the winners to various demographic studies of the area. Students should present their findings in the form of an oral report. (Challenging)

MONITOR COMPREHENSION

Answers to Section 5 Review
1. "Key Terms" are defined on the following pages:
a. political socialization,.p.145
b. party identification, p.149
c. straight-ticket voting, p.149
d. split-ticket voting, p. 150
e. independents, p.150
2. Answers include: income, occupation, education, sex, age, religious or ethnic background, geography, family and other group affiliations. **3.** Individual voters belong to different groups which may have different characteristic voting behaviors. Therefore, the characteristic voting behavior of any one group cannot be expected to hold for every single member of that group. **4.** Party identification, candidate appeal, and issues. **5.** Party identification. **6.** Answers will vary. (a) The most likely answer would be a change in the voters perception of the candidates or issues. (b) Psychological.

Teacher's Resource File See the Unit 2 File, p. 41, for the Section 5 Quiz.

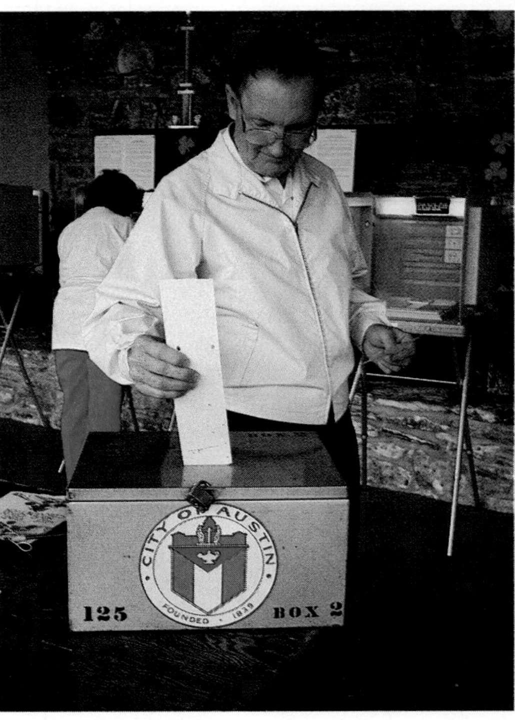

A Lifelong Responsibility An eighteen-year old exercises her right to vote (left) as does a veteran of the electoral system (right).

Party identification is, then, a key factor in American politics. Among many other things, it means that each of the major parties can regularly count on the votes of millions of faithful supporters in every election. The Democrats have enjoyed a substantial advantage over the Republicans in this matter for more than 50 years now.

Several signs suggest that, while it remains a major factor, party identification has lost some of its impact in recent years. One of those signs is the weakened condition of the parties themselves. Another is the marked increase in **split-**
1.d **ticket voting**—voting for candidates of both parties at the same election. That practice has increased remarkably since the 1960s.

Another telling sign is the large number of
1.e voters who now call themselves **independents**. This term identifies people with no party affiliation. But "independent" is a tricky term.[18] Many who claim to be independents actually support one or the other of the major parties quite regularly.

The loose nature of party membership makes it difficult to determine just what proportion of the electorate is independent. The best guesses put the number of independents at some-

[18]Voting behavior has been studied more extensively than any other form of political participation in the United States. It has (1) because of the obvious importance of the topic and (2) because of the almost unlimited amount of data available (innumerable elections in which millions of voters have cast billions of votes). Notice that the term *independent* is sometimes mistakenly used in ways that suggest that independents form a more or less cohesive group in politics that can be readily compared with Republicans and/or Democrats. However, independents are not only independent of Republicans and Democrats; independents are also independent of all other independents.

Reteach

Have students write several fill-in-the-blank paragraphs as a summary of Section 5. Blanks may be used for important ideas, facts, or key terms. When summaries are complete, have students exchange papers and fill in the missing words.

where between a fourth and a third of the all voters today.

Until recently, the typical independent was less concerned, less well informed, and less active in politics than those voters who identified themselves as Republicans or Democrats. That description still fits many independents. A new breed appeared in the 1960s and 1970s, however. Largely because of the political events and personalities of that period, these "new" independents preferred not to join either major party. Still, they are much like the party identifiers—except that they are often young and above average in education, income, and job status.

Candidates and Issues From much of what you have read about party identification, you might very well ask this question: How does the Republican party ever win a presidential election? A very large part of the answer can be put in these terms: candidates and issues.

Party identification is a long-term factor. Most voters identify with one or the other of the major parties, and over time, they most often support its candidates. But they do not always vote that way. One or more short-term factors can cause them to switch sides in a particular election—or, at the least to vote a split ticket. Look again at the table on page 147—15 percent of those voters who normally vote Democratic voted for George Bush in 1988.

The most important of these short-term factors are the candidates and the issues in an election. Clearly, the impressions a candidate makes on the voters can have an impact on how they vote. What image does a candidate project? How is he or she seen in terms of personality, character, style, appearance, past record, abilities, and so on?

Just as clearly, issues can also have a large impact on voter behavior. Their role varies from election to election, however, depending on such things as the emotional content of the issues themselves, the voters' awareness of them, and the ways in which they are presented to the electorate.

Issues have become an increasingly important part of the voter-decision mix in recent years.

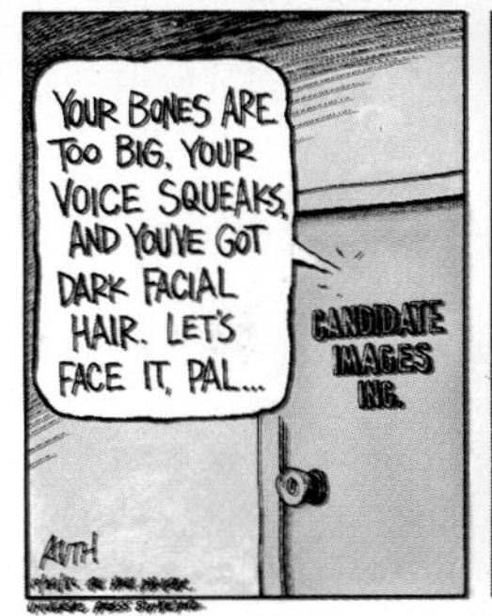

Interpreting Political Cartoons Many factors affect voting behavior. At which factor is the cartoonist poking fun?

The tumultuous nature of politics over the past 25 years or so—highlighted by the civil rights movement, the Vietnam War, the Watergate scandal, and ongoing economic problems—is likely responsible for this heightened concern with issues.

Section 5 Review

1. **Define:** political socialization, party identification, straight-ticket voting, split-ticket voting, independents
2. List three of the sociological factors that affect voting behavior.
3. Why is it important not to give too much weight to any one of these factors?
4. List three of the psychological factors that affect voting behavior.
5. What is the most significant, lasting indicator of an individual's voting behavior?

Critical Thinking

6. **Determining Relevance** (p. 19) Imagine that in a particular presidential election, the gender gap grew to 20 percent. (a) What would be the most likely explanation for this dramatic change? (b) Would sociological factors or psychological factors more likely be involved?

★

Interpreting Political Cartoons Ask students to speculate about why there is such an emphasis today on personal appearance compared to Lincoln's day.

Caption Answer The cartoon makes fun of the emphasis placed on physical appearance.

Closure

Remind students that many factors contribute to the behavior of voters in the United States. These factors, both sociological and psychological, include family background, income, occupation, geography, and party affiliation, to name a few. These factors, and the voting blocks formed by them, create a pluralistic society of often competing interests, but because the United States is a democracy the political process provides a venue for those interests.

Assignment Assign Chapter 7, Section 1, pp. 157–165, for the next class period.

Spotlight on: Behind the Scenes

The American electorate votes in a relatively predictable, 30-year cycle, says historian Arthur M. Schlesinger, Jr. According to his theory, Americans elect activist, reform governments for a period of about 15 years, followed by 15 years of the election of more conservative governments. While the cycles do not fall exactly on every fifteenth year, election patterns of the twentieth century tend to support Schlesinger's theory. Progressive era reformers dominated the government from the turn-of-the-century until the U.S. entered World War I, but fell out of favor with the voters during the Roaring 20s that followed. During the Great Depression, reform government returned in the form of the New Deal, but with the end of the Depression and of World War II issues of peace and prosperity dominated voter concerns. Reformers were returned again in 1960, but the crisis atmosphere of the years that followed with war in Vietnam, scandal over Watergate, and stagnation in the economy primed voters for the appeals of Ronald Reagan and the new conservatism.

TEACHING
Critical Thinking

Determining Relevance

Objective

Determining relevance through interpreting visual materials

INSTRUCT

Have students study the graphs. Ask them to examine the trends that appear in each of the categories under "Elected Officials," and have them summarize the information provided. For example, have them tell which category includes the greatest number of African Americans. After they have summarized the information, have students discuss why they think that there are more African American office holders in city and county offices than in federal offices.

Answers 1. (a) Registration of African Americans has increased since 1960. (b) There has been an increase in the participation of African Americans in several areas. **2.** (a) Political participation of African Americans. (b) That political participation among African Americans has increased since 1960. **3.**(a) Information in Graph A may explain information in some categories in Graph B, such as "U.S. Congress," "State Legislatures," and "City County & Offices." (b) Large increases in African American participation in education and local politics might have caused an increase in registration.

Critical Thinking

Determining Relevance

Determining relevance means deciding if and how events, situations, or items relate to or have an effect on one another. Determining relevance between pieces of information is an important skill in understanding relationships in the study of American Government and the political process. By determining whether information is relevant, it is possible to decide which information is important to consider and which information is not essential in the process of solving a problem. Follow the steps below and use the graph and the table to practice determining relevance between different pieces of information. The graph is on the left and gives information about voter registration. The table on the right is titled Elected Officials.

1. Identify the main idea represented by each piece of information. Look at the graph and the table shown on this page. Then, answer the following questions: (a) What is the basic idea communicated by the graph? (b) What is the main idea communicated by the table?

2. Look for connections between the main ideas. Compare your answers to the questions above about the graph and the table. Answer the following questions: (a) What ideas, concepts, or subjects do the graph and the table share in common with each other? (b) What conclusions can you draw from each one?

3. Determine the relevance of the two pieces of information. Once you have identified the similarities and differences between the graph and the table and the information they contain, you are ready to determine if and in what way the information relates. Ask yourself: (a) Does the information in the graph offer any possible explanation for the information in table? (b) Does the information in the table help explain the graph?

Political Participation of African-Americans in the South

VOTER REGISTRATION IN ELEVEN SOUTHERN STATES

(in millions)

Year	Registration
1960	1.5
1964	2.2
1968	3.1
1972	3.65
1976	4.15
1980	4.25
1984	5.6
1988	5.8

ELECTED OFFICIALS

STATE	U.S. Congress		State Legislature		City & County Offices		Law Enforcement		Education		TOTALS	
	1970	1990	1970	1990	1970	1990	1970	1990	1970	1990	1970	1990
Alabama	0	0	0	23	52	526	27	67	7	89	86	705
Arkansas	0	0	0	6	14	190	4	43	37	105	55	344
Florida	0	0	1	11	31	124	2	23	2	19	36	177
Georgia	0	1	14	30	18	352	1	23	7	89	40	495
Louisiana	0	0	1	20	34	313	20	65	9	129	64	527
Mississippi	0	1	1	23	57	450	18	81	5	114	81	669
North Carolina	0	0	1	17	50	324	1	28	10	84	62	453
South Carolina	0	0	0	21	32	237	4	6	2	132	38	396
Tennessee	0	1	8	13	9	97	17	16	4	22	38	149
Texas	0	1	3	14	16	155	0	40	10	95	29	305
Virginia	0	0	3	11	27	127	6	11	0	0	36	149
TOTALS	0	4	32	189	340	2,895	100	403	93	878	565	4,369

Latest figures available as of November, 1990. Sources: U.S. Bureau of the Census, Current Population Survey; Joint Center for Political Studies

TRF **Teacher's Resource File**
See page 42 of the Unit 2 File for the Skill Application for this lesson.

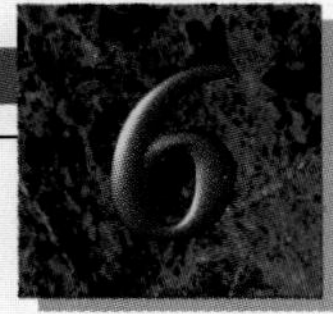

Chapter-in-Brief

Scan all headings, photographs, charts, and other visuals in the chapter before reading the section summaries below.

Section 1 The Constitution and the Right to Vote (pp. 129–131) The Constitution says very little about the rights of citizens to vote. For the most part, suffrage qualifications are left to the States.

Early in United States history, suffrage was enjoyed by a very few white, male property owners. Over time, the franchise has been extended. This has happened in two major ways: (1) through the gradual elimination of restrictive requirements to voting rights, and (2) by the ever-increasing authority of the Federal Government in the area of suffrage. Examples of federal control include Constitutional amendments that outlaw restricting voting rights based on race (15th), sex (19th), age (26th), and ability to pay a tax (24th).

Section 2 Voter Qualifications Among the States (pp. 132–136) Historically, States have set most suffrage restrictions. Today, every state requires voters to meet citizenship and residence requirements. Residence requirements have been reduced in recent years to about 30 days or less in most States.

Most States also require voters to register to vote. Again, the trend in this area has been toward easier, less restrictive registration.

In the past, States frequently required voters to meet literacy standards and to pay a tax in order to vote. However, the use of these devices to deny minorities suffrage led Congress and the courts to act against them.

Section 3 Suffrage and Civil Rights (pp. 138–140) The 15th Amendment of 1870 was intended to outlaw voting restrictions based on race. However, the amendment was never backed sufficiently by Congress.

Congress first put its muscle behind civil rights with the Civil Rights Acts of 1957 and 1960. These acts aimed at ending discrimination in federal elections. The Civil Rights Act of 1964 expanded on these provisions.

Still, neither act fully solved the discrimination problem, so Congress passed the Voting Rights Act of 1965. This act applied to all elections in the nation. Congress has extended and broadened this act several times.

Section 4 Nonvoting (pp. 141–144) In many elections, at least half of all eligible voters do not cast ballots. The problem is worse for offices low down on the ballot and for elections held in years of no presidential election.

A number of the nonvoters have legitimate reasons for not taking part. The large percentage, however, simply lack the interest or motivation to vote. A number of factors are associated with nonvoters, including low income level, relative youth, and many others.

Section 5 Voter Behavior (pp. 144–151) Millions of Americans do cast ballots. Their behavior is closely studied.

A number of sociological and political factors that influence a voter's decision exist. Sociological factors include a voter's income and occupation, education, age, and sex. The nature of these characteristics appears to have some effect on a voter's choice.

Psychological factors include the voter's perception of the candidates and the issues. Another key factor is party identification, for voters often cast their ballots for the same party in election after election.

Teaching Suggestions for Chapter-in-Brief

Below are some of the possible uses for the Chapter-in-Brief:

To Preview the Chapter You may want to assign the Chapter-in-Brief page and the Section Outlines from the Teacher's Resource File before beginning Chapter 6 to introduce students to "Key Terms" and concepts in each section.

To Review the Chapter When students have completed Chapter 6, you might want to assign the Chapter-in-Brief as a tool for review, along with the Guided Reading and Review from the Teacher's Resource File.

To Omit the Chapter If you wish to skip Chapter 6, it may be helpful to assign the Chapter-in-Brief to students as a review before continuing to another chapter. You may also want to assign the Chapter 6 Test to assess student knowledge of the material. Then specific portions of Chapter 6 may be assigned to students needing reinforcement of "Key Terms" and concepts.

Teacher's Resource File See the Unit 2 File for the following materials:

- Section Outlines, pp. 27, 30, 33, 36, 39
- Guided Reading and Reviews, pp. 28, 31, 34, 37, 40
- Chapter 6 Test, pp. 46–48.

Additional Resources

Conway, M. Margaret. *Political Participation in the United States.* Prentice Hall, 1991.

Darcy, R. *et al. Women, Elections, and Representation.* Longman, 1987.

Dunham, Pat. *Electoral Behavior in the United States.* Prentice Hall, 1991.

Elect I, II, and III. Computer software. MECC, 1982. Apple II+/IIe/IIc, 48k.

Flanigan, William H. and Nancy H. Zingale. *Political Behavior of the American Electorate.* Allyn and Bacon, 6th ed., 1987.

Nogel, Jack H. *Participation.* Prentice Hall, 1987.

Piven, Francis F. and Richard A. Cloward. *Why Americans Don't Vote.* Pantheon, 1989.

Pohlmann, Marcus D. *Black Politics in Conservative America.* Longman, 1990.

Salmore, Stephen A. and Barbara G. Salmore. *Candidates, Parties, and Campaigns: Electoral Politics in America.* CQ Press, 2nd ed., 1989.

The Women Get the Vote. McGraw-Hill, 1989. Black and white. 27 min.

Walton, Hanes. *Invisible Politics: Black Political Behavior.* State University of New York Press, 1987.

Answers to

CHAPTER 6 REVIEW

Vocabulary and Key Terms

Matching
1. gerrymandering
2. suffrage or franchise
3. literacy
4. injunction
5. electorate

True or False
1. True.
2. False—the correct term is poll tax.
3. False—the correct term is political efficacy.
4. True
5. False—the correct term is independents.

Word Relationships
1. Registration is a process by which voters establish their eligibility to vote. A poll tax is a now-unconstitutional tax required of anyone who wanted to vote. It was a device widely used to disfranchise African Americans.
2. Political efficacy is a person's impact on the political process. Political socialization is the process by which people acquire their political beliefs.
3. Party identification is loyalty to a certain party. Independents have no party loyalty.
4. Straight-ticket voting is the practice of voting for only the candidates of a single party. Split-ticket voting is the practice of casting votes for candidates in two or more parties.

Main Ideas

Section 1
1. The elimination of many voting restrictions and the assumption by the Federal Government of many of the State's powers over suffrage qualifications.
2. (1) In the early 1800s, many restrictive suffrage qualifications from the colonial era disappeared; (2) following the Civil War, the passage of the 15th Amendment attempted to protect the voting rights of African Americans; (3) the 19th Amendment of 1920 ensured that no one could be denied the vote based on sex; (4) the civil rights movement of the 1950s and 1960s; (5) the 26th Amendment, which provides that no one 18 or older can be denied the vote because of age.
3. (a) State (b) The U. S. Constitution sets five restrictions on the States: States must not (1) deny anyone who votes for members of the State legislature's most numerous branch the right to vote for members of Congress; (2) deny anyone the right to vote on account of race, color, or previous condition of servitude; (3) deny anyone the vote based on sex; (4) levy a tax in connection with the selection of President, Vice President, or member of Congress; (5) deny anyone who is at least 18 the right to vote.

Section 2
4. (a) Citizenship and residence. (b) Most States also require registration. And, different States prohibit people from voting for a variety or reasons such as con-

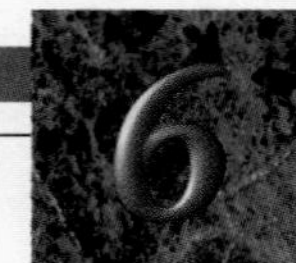

Chapter Review

Vocabulary and Key Terms

suffrage (p. 129)
franchise (p. 129)
electorate (p. 130)
registration (p. 134)
literacy (p. 135)
poll tax (p. 136)
gerrymandering (p. 138)
injunction (p. 139)
political efficacy (p. 142)
political socialization (p. 145)
party identification (p. 149)
straight-ticket voting (p.149)
split-ticket voting (p. 150)
independents (p. 150)

Matching: *Review the key terms in the list above. If you are not sure of a term's meaning, look up the term and review its definition. Choose a term from the list above that best matches each description.*

1. the drawing of electoral district lines to the advantage of a party or other group
2. the right to vote
3. the ability to read or write
4. a court order requiring or forbidding some action
5. all the people entitled to vote in a given election

True or False: *Determine whether each statement is true or false. If it is true, write "true." If it is false, change the underlined word or words to make the statement true.*

1. Voters who support only those candidates of one party are likely to practice <u>straight-ticket voting</u>.
2. <u>Registration</u> is a now-unconstitutional method of keeping certain people from voting.
3. People who doubt their own ability to influence the political process have little sense of <u>party identification</u>.
4. <u>Political socialization</u> is a complex process by which a person acquires his or her political attitudes.
5. The <u>electorate</u> does not identify with or support one of the two major parties.

Word Relationships: *Distinguish between the words in each pair.*

1. registration/poll tax
2. political efficacy/political socialization
3. party identification/independents
4. straight-ticket voting/split-ticket voting

Main Ideas

Section 1 (pp. 129–131)

1. What two trends explain the growth in the size of the American electorate?
2. What major events or eras contributed to those trends?
3. (a) At what level of government are voter qualifications set? (b) What restrictions does the Constitution place on the power to set voter qualifications?

Section 2 (pp. 132–136)

4. (a) On what two factors do each of the States set qualifications to vote? (b) What additional restrictions presently exist in the States?
5. What are some of the suffrage qualifications States used in the past, but no longer use today?

154

6. What was the purpose of literacy tests and poll taxes?

Section 3 **(pp. 138–140)**

7. What was the purpose of the 15th Amendment?
8. For what reasons did the 15th Amendment prove inadequate at protecting the suffrage of many African Americans?
9. (a) How did the civil rights movement of the 1950s and 1960s seek to solve the problem of disfranchisement among African Americans? (b) Were these efforts effective?

Section 4 **(pp. 141–144)**

10. What does it mean to say that the United States has a nonvoter problem?
11. (a) Who are the "cannot voters"? (b) What is the significance of their impact on the nonvoter problem?
12. What are the major reasons that people do not vote?

Section 5 **(pp. 144–151)**

13. What are the sociological factors that influence a person's voting decisions?
14. What are the psychological factors that influence a person's voting decisions?
15. For what reason is it difficult to predict how any one voter will vote based on an analysis of his or her psychological and sociological profile?

Critical Thinking

1. **Determining Relevance** (p. 19) What relationship, if any, can you see between these two facts: Changes in law and custom in recent years have made it possible for a wider range of citizens to vote. Yet at the same time, smaller percentages of voters take part in elections.
2. **Recognizing Bias** (p. 19) For what reasons do you think that all women were not granted the right to vote by the United States until 1920?
3. **Recognizing Cause and Effect** (p. 19) How would you expect the historical denial of voting rights to African Americans and other minority groups to have influenced the make-up of the Congress and the State legislatures?

Getting Involved

1. **Writing Your Opinion** Write a letter to a member of Congress about ways to increase voter turnout. Start by setting up a chart with two columns. In one column, brainstorm a list of reasons why you think people do not vote. In the second column, try to come up with solutions to each reason for not voting. Select your three best solutions for increasing voter turnout.

   Start your letter by introducing yourself as a concerned citizen and stating the purpose of your letter. Then describe your three ideas to improve voter turnout. For each idea, explain how it addresses a specific cause of low voter turnout. Revise your letter to make sure it is clear and to the point. Then, proofread and make a final copy.
2. **Class Debate** Hold a class debate on the following topic: *Resolved*, That your state should pass a compulsory voting law. Select one team to debate each side of the topic. The rest of the class can evaluate each team's presentation.
3. **Gathering Information** Using the Government Resources Handbook in the Reference Section beginning on page 690, identify what sources you could use to find detailed information about voter turnout in a recent national election.

155

viction of crimes, dishonorable discharge from the armed forces, mental incompetence, and so on. **5.** Many States used poll taxes and literacy requirements. **6.** These devices were aimed primarily at preventing African Americans from voting.

Section 3

7. The 15th Amendment says that no person can be denied the vote on the basis of race, color, or previous condition of servitude. **8.** Congress did not support the 15th Amendment with necessary laws. **9.** (a) In general, the civil rights movement led Congress to pass laws that empowered the Federal Government to take action against discriminatory practices. (b) The various acts got the government directly involved in securing suffrage for all people. The movement succeeded in providing African Americans who had been denied voting rights the franchise.

Section 4

10. In a typical election, 50 percent or more of the eligible voters do not vote. In addition, many of those who do vote do not vote for many of the offices on the ballot. **11.** (a) Cannot voters are those who have legitimate or legal reasons for not voting. (b) They constitute a significant block of nonvoters, although they are not the largest block. **12.** Many feel that they have no impact on the process. Others do not care who wins; others distrust the political process and feel it is hopelessly corrupted and compromised.

Section 5

13. Sociological factors include: income and occupation, education, sex and age, religious and ethnic background, geography, family and other group affiliations. **14.** Psychological factors include party identification, particular candidates, and issues involved. **15.** Many of the factors that seem to be associated with certain voting behavior overlap. Individuals may possess several characteristics that conflict in terms of their influence on voting behavior.

Critical Thinking

1. Answers will vary. Students might suggest that people who have long been denied access to the political process may have a low sense of political efficacy. **2.** Answers will vary. Students might suggest that the the denial of voting rights to women reveals a widespread lack of regard for women's ability to take part in politics. **3.** Answers will vary. Students might observe that the lack of voting rights for minority groups could be expected to result in low representation by minorities in Congress and State legislatures.

Getting Involved

1–3) Answer and results will vary, but students should demonstrate an understanding of the concepts in this chapter.

Chapter 7 Resources

In the Teacher's Resource File The following materials are found in the Teacher's Resource File box.

Instructional Support: Unit 2 File

For the Section
Outlines, pp. 52, 55, 58
Guided Reading and Reviews, pp. 53, 56, 59
Quizzes, pp. 54, 57, 60

For the Chapter
Skill Application, p. 61
Case Study on Contemporary Issues, pp. 62–64
Chapter Test, p. 65–67
Additional Test Questions, pp. 68–70

Enrichment Support Files

Participatory Government Activities, pp. 28–39, 44–69
Historical and Legal Documents, pp. 48, 49

Computer Test Bank and Assessment

Transparency Package, pp. 7, 32, 53, 54

Election Kit, pp. 7, 8, 28–29, 30–31, 40

Chapter 7 Focus

Introduce the Chapter Tell students that in Chapter 7, they will learn about the process by which candidates for public office are nominated and elected in the United States. They will also examine the influence of money in the electoral process. Read with students the Chapter Preview and Objectives.

Writing Activity Direct students' attention to "Describe." Ask them to describe in writing two facts or details that they can recall from a recent national or local election. Then have students explain in writing what it was about their two facts or details that were memorable.

Motivate for Learning Direct students' attention to "Predict." Discuss with students reasons why money might be so important in the electoral process, then have students make the predictions.

The Electoral Process

Chapter Preview

Twice the Democratic nominee for President in the 1950s, Adlai Stevenson once said this about the process of selecting candidates for an upcoming election: "It's exhausting physically; you burn up yourself, you burn up your ammunition, you burn up your [money]." Stevenson's description makes running for office sound more like war than politics.

The idea that the electoral process is a form of combat is evident in many words that describe it. *Contenders* who are ready to *fight* in the political *arena* are those who throw their hats in the *ring*. Even the word *campaign* has a military origin. This chapter is about running for office—the two basic stages of the electoral process and the very complex role that money plays in the electoral process.

Before you read this chapter:

- **Describe** two activities that take place during a presidential campaign.
- **Predict** what might occur if running for public office cost less money.

As you read, focus on the main objective for each section. Understand:

1. The methods by which candidates are nominated to run for public office.
2. The conduct of elections in the United States.
3. The place of money and the regulation of its use in the electoral process.

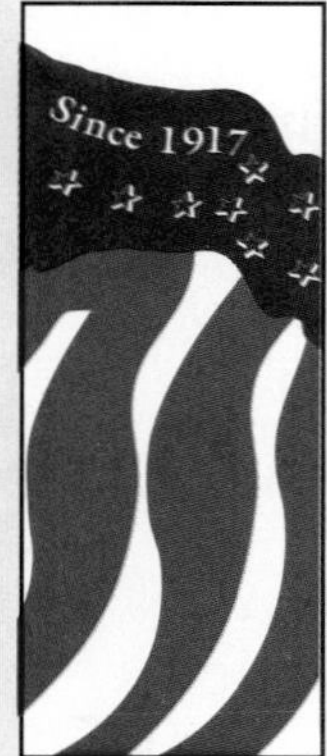

Magruder's American Government: *A Witness to Change* by William A. McClenaghan

The extremely lengthy, or "bed-sheet ballot," has been a problem for a long time in American politics. In fact, it has been a problem since the 1830s, and it has been discussed in every edition of this book.

This comment, on page 375 in the 1917 edition, is not remarkably different from what you will find on page 169 in this edition: "The present method of electing officers is a puzzle, the intricacies of which are understood only by politicians. Those who favor a shorter ballot would make the election process so simple that even the voter might understand it and be able to know something about those for whom he is to vote."

But this discussion question from several editions in the 1930s and 1940s might give you some pause: "Have your father, or your brother who votes, make a list of the National, State, county, township, city or village, and school officers elected by the people in your State. If they cannot do this, is that not a strong indication that more officers are being elected than the voters are capable of electing wisely?"

Can you imagine a question of that sort in terms of "your father, or your brother" today?

Electricity and Excitement — Perhaps no other political event in America can match the glamour of the national convention. The picture above shows a scene from the 1988 Democratic National Convention.

1 The Nominating Process

Find Out:

- What is the importance of the nominating stage in the electoral process?
- For what reasons did the caucus give way to the convention as the dominant nominating method?
- What are the different forms of the direct primary?
- How are petitions used in the nominating process?

Key Terms:

nomination, general election, caucus, direct primary, closed primary, open primary, blanket primary, runoff primary

Suppose your teacher stood in front of the class and said: "Here's a $1,000 bill. Who'd like to have it?" You, and everyone else in the room, would promptly say, or at least think: "Me!" Suppose the teacher then said: "Okay, we'll hold an election. The person who wins the most votes gets the money."

What would happen? If the election were held immediately, it is likely that each member of the class would vote for him- or herself. A few might vote for a friend. But, almost certainly, the election would still end in a tie. No one would win the money.

But suppose the teacher said: "We'll hold the election tomorrow." What do you think would happen then? As you think about the answer to that question, you begin to get a sense of the practical importance of the topic of this section: the nominating process—the first step in the process of electing candidates to office.

Section 1
The Nominating Process

Focus

Teacher's Resource File See the Unit 2 File, p. 52, for the Section 1 Outline.

Objectives

7.1 Determine the importance of the nominating stage in the electoral process.
7.2 Examine the reasons why the caucus gave way to the convention as the dominant nominating method.
7.3 Determine the different forms of direct primary.
7.4 Examine the ways in which petitions are used in the nominating process.

Bellringer Activity Have students respond to the following: What would you think if the principal announced that he or she alone would decide who could run for schoolwide offices? Would that be fair or unfair? Have students explain their responses. Tell students that the process of naming of candidates for office is called the *nominating process.*

State the Purpose The nomination of candidates is a vital step in the democratic process. In Section 1, students will examine five methods for making nominations as they have evolved over the course of United States history, and they will analyze the direct primary method—the method most widely used today.

Vocabulary

Direct students' attention to "Key Terms" on page 157. Explain to students that all these words have to do with the nominating process. Ask students to keep a list of words, and as they read, to jot down their definitions. Remind them to look for the similarities and differences among the definitions.

Reading Strategy: Question Writing

To better understand the key concepts of the lesson, have students read the main headings in Section 1. Then have them convert each of these headings into a question and write them down on a sheet of paper. As they read, ask students to answer the questions.

INSTRUCT

Explain/Discuss/Analyze
Refer back to the "Bellringer Activity," and explain that the principal in the hypothetical situation was in fact making nominations. By controlling the nominations, the principal controlled the electoral process. Ask students to recall their reactions to the question and consider fairer ways to make nominations.

Explain that nominations for public office are extremely important in a democratic system, and that there are five main methods of nomination. Ask students to analyze and then discuss the advantages and disadvantages of each method. They may want to begin by tracing the evolution of each method and answering such questions as: Why did the convention replace the caucus? (*Caucuses were seen as unrepresentative.*) What criticism of the convention did the direct primary attempt to address? (*Domination by party bosses.*) What might happen if self-announcement or petition were used for State- or nationwide campaigns? (*An unmanageable number of candidates might emerge.*)

ABCNEWS INTERACTIVE

The following video segment may be used to highlight aspects of the nominating process.

POWERS OF THE PRESIDENT GUIDEBOOK
Chapter 10: Nominating a Candidate, p. 13

The Importance of Nominations

The nominating process is the process of candi-
1.a date selection. **Nomination**—the naming of those who will seek office—is made in a number of different ways in American politics. Before turning to those several methods, however, consider this significant point: The making of nominations is a critically important matter in the American democratic system.

You have already seen two major illustrations of that point. In Chapter 5, you read about the making of nominations (1) as a prime function of political parties in the United States; and (2) as a leading reason for the decentralized character of the major parties.

The nominating process also has a very real impact on the exercise of the right to vote. In the typical election in this country, voters can make one of only two choices for each office. They can vote for the Republican candidate or they can vote for the Democratic candidate.[1] This is another way of saying that the United States has a two-party system. It is also another way to say that the nominating process is critically important. Those who make nominations place real, very practical limits on the choices that voters can make in an election. In one-party constituencies—those areas where one party regularly wins elections—the nominating process is the only point at which there is usually any real contest for a public office. Once the dominant party has made its nomination, the general election is little more than a formality.

Dictatorial regimes underscore the importance of the nominating process. Many hold
1.b **general elections**—regularly scheduled elections at which voters make the final selection of officeholders—much as the United States does. However, the ballots used in those elections usually list only one candidate for each office, and those candidates regularly win with majorities approaching 100 percent.

[1]The exception is nonpartisan elections. Other choices are sometimes listed, of course—minor party or independent nominees. But these are not often meaningful alternatives, and most voters choose not to "waste" their votes on candidates who cannot win.

For purposes of description and analysis, the various ways in which nominations are made in this country can be grouped in five broad categories: (1) self-announcement, (2) caucus, (3) convention, (4) direct primary, and (5) petition.

Self-announcement

Self-announcement is the oldest form of the nominating process in American politics. First used in colonial times, it is still often found at the small-town and rural levels in many parts of the country.

The method is actually quite simple. A person who wants to run for an office simply announces that fact. Modesty or local custom may dictate that someone else make the candidate's announcement, but the process amounts to the same thing.

Self-announcement is sometimes used by someone who failed to win a regular party nomination or by someone unhappy with the party's choice. Note that whenever a write-in candidate appears in an election, the self-announcement process has been used.

Three prominent presidential contenders have made use of the process in recent history: George Wallace, the American Independent party's nominee in 1968, and independent candidates Eugene McCarthy in 1976 and John Anderson in 1980.

The Caucus

1.c As a nominating device, a **caucus** is a group of like-minded persons who meet to select the candidates they will support in an upcoming election.

The first caucus nominations were made toward the end of the colonial period, probably in Boston in the mid-1720s. One of the earliest descriptions of the device can be found in John Adams's diary, in an entry he made in February 1763:

"This day learned that the Caucus club meets at certain times in the garret of Tom Dawes, the Adjutant of the Boston regiment. He has a large house, and he has a movable partition which he takes down, and the whole club meets in one room. There they smoke tobacco

SPOTLIGHT ON: Behind the Scenes
Five times in the last ten presidential elections (1952–1988) incumbents have been challenged for their party's nomination. Four of those times, the incumbent's reelection bid failed. Both Harry Truman (1952) and Lyndon Johnson (1968) withdrew from contention after challengers made strong showings in the New Hampshire primary. Gerald Ford (1976) and Jimmy Carter (1980) defeated opponents in their party primaries but lost the general election. Richard Nixon, who defeated two challengers for the Republican nomination before defeating George McGovern in 1972, is the exception.

ACTIVITY: Teaching Heterogeneous Groups
In order that students understand the nominating process and its importance, ask students to create a comparison chart to list the five ways in which nominations have been and are made in the United States. Have them complete the chart by indicating similarities and differences. You might want to conclude the activity with a discussion in which students state their opinions on the fairness of the nomination process.

Tammany Hall Named for a Delaware Native American known for his wisdom, this painting depicts the headquarters of Tammany, a Democratic political organization. The Democratic National Convention was held in the hall in 1868.

until you cannot see from one end of the garret to the other. There they drink flip, I suppose, and they choose a moderator who puts questions to the vote regularly; and selectmen, assessors, collectors, fire-wards, and representatives are regularly chosen before they are chosen in the town.”[2]

Originally the caucus was a private meeting consisting of a few influential figures. As political parties appeared, they soon took over the device and began to broaden the membership of the caucus.

[2]Charles Francis Adams (ed.), *The Works of John Adams* (Boston: Little, Brown, 1856), vol. II, p. 144. The origin of the term *caucus* is not clear. Most authorities suggest that it comes from the word *caulkers*, because the Boston Caucus Club met at times in a room formerly used as a meeting place by caulkers in Boston's shipyards. (Caulkers made ships watertight by filling seams or cracks in the hulls of sailing vessels with tar or oakum.)

The coming of independence brought the need to nominate candidates for State offices—for governor, lieutenant governor, and others above the local level. The legislative caucus—a meeting of a party's members in the State legislature—took on the job. At the national level, both the Federalists and the Democratic-Republicans in Congress were, by 1800, choosing their presidential and vice-presidential candidates through the congressional caucus.

The legislative and congressional caucuses were quite practical in their day. Transportation and communication were difficult at best, and legislators regularly came together in a central place. The spread of democracy, especially in the newer States on the frontier, spurred opposition to caucuses, however. More and more, people condemned them for their closed and unrepresentative character.

SPOTLIGHT ON: Roots of Democracy

While historians are unable to trace the evolution of electoral processes to their points of origin, the practice of acclamation of a victorious leader in tribal wars is believed to have been a major step in their development. The works of ancient writers suggest that, after battles between Indo-European tribes, vanquished warriors were expected to acclaim—that is, to praise or show approval of—the leader of the victorious tribe by loud cheering or the clashing together of shields and swords. Very little choice was involved, but the practice served to reduce tensions and integrate the formerly warring communities.

Criticism of the caucus reached its peak in the early 1820s. The supporters of three of the leading contenders for the presidency in 1824—Andrew Jackson, Henry Clay, and John Quincy Adams—boycotted the Democratic-Republicans' congressional caucus that year. In fact, Jackson and his supporters made "King Caucus" a leading campaign issue. The other major aspirant, William H. Crawford of Georgia, became the caucus nominee at a meeting attended by fewer than one-third of the Democratic-Republican party's members in Congress.

Crawford ran a poor third in the electoral college balloting in 1824, and the reign of King Caucus at the national level was ended. With its death in presidential politics, the caucus system soon withered at the State and local levels, as well.

The caucus is still used to make local nominations in some places, especially in New England. There, a caucus is open to all members of a party, and it looks only faintly like the original device.

Campaigning With Ribbons These precursors to political lapel buttons promoted Whig Party candidates nominated by convention in the 1840s.

The Convention

As the caucus method collapsed, the convention system took its place. The first national convention to nominate a presidential candidate was held by a minor party, the Anti-Masons, in Baltimore in 1831. The newly formed Whig party also held a convention later that same year, and the Democrats picked up the practice in 1832. All major party presidential nominees have been chosen by conventions ever since. By the 1840s conventions had become the major means for making nominations at every level in American politics.

On paper, the convention process seems ideally suited to representative government. A party's members meet in a local caucus to pick candidates for local offices and, at the same time, to select delegates to represent them at a county convention.[3] At the county convention, the delegates nominate candidates for county offices and also select delegates to the next rung on the convention ladder, usually the State convention. There, the delegates from the county conventions pick the party's nominees for governor and other State-wide offices. State conventions also send delegates to the party's national convention, where those delegates select its presidential and vice-presidential candidates.

In the theory of the convention system, the will of the party's rank and file membership is passed up through each of its representative levels. Practice soon pointed up the weaknesses of the theory, however, as party bosses found ways to manipulate the process. By playing with the selection of delegates at the local levels, they soon dominated the entire system.

[3]The meetings at which delegates to local conventions are chosen are still often called caucuses. Earlier, they were also known as primaries—that is, first meetings. The use of that name gave rise to the term ***direct primary***, to distinguish that newer nominating method from the convention process.

Enrichment

The nominating process is a critical part of the democratic system of government. All States use one or several of the five nominating methods discussed in the section. Ask students to find out what method of nominations are used for Statewide and national offices in their State. They may begin by calling the voter registration office or the Democratic or Republican committees. (Easy)

Teacher's Resource File
See the Election Kit, pp. 30–31, for materials to support this section.

The caliber of most conventions, at all levels, declined, especially in the late 1800s. How low some of them fell can be seen in this description of a Cook County (Chicago) convention in 1896:

“Of [723] delegates, those who had been on trial for murder numbered 17; sentenced to the penitentiary for murder or manslaughter and served sentence, 7; served terms in the penitentiary for burglary, 36; served terms in the penitentiary for picking pockets, 2; served terms in the penitentiary for arson, 1; . . . jailbirds identified by detectives, 84; keepers of gambling houses, 7; keepers of houses of ill-fame, 2; convicted by mayhem, 3; ex-prize fighters, 11; poolroom operators, 2; saloon keepers, 265; . . . political employees, 148; no occupation, 71; . . . ”[4]

By the 1870s, the convention system was under attack as a major source of evil in American politics. And by the 1910s, the direct primary had replaced the convention as the principal nominating method.

Most States now use the direct primary for all or at least most nominations in the State. A few States still use the convention, however—Connecticut, Michigan, Utah, and Virginia, for example, where it is closely regulated by State law. In addition, no adequate substitute for the convention has yet been found for making nominations at the presidential level, as you will read in Chapter 13.

The Direct Primary

A **direct primary** is an election held within the party to pick the party's candidates for the general election. 1.d

Wisconsin adopted the first Statewide direct primary law in 1903, and several other States soon followed its lead. Every State now makes at least some provision for its use.

In most States, State law requires that the major parties use the primary to choose their candidates for the United States Senate and House, for the governorship and all other State offices, and for most local offices, as well. In a few States, however, different combinations of convention and primary are used to pick candidates for the top offices. In Michigan, for example, the major parties choose their candidates for the U.S. Senate and House, the governorship, and the State legislature in primaries; their nominees for lieutenant governor, secretary of state, and attorney general are picked by conventions.[5]

Although the primaries are party nominating elections, they are now closely regulated in most States. The State usually sets the dates on which they are held, and it regularly conducts them, too. The State, not the parties, provides polling places and election officials, registration lists and ballots, and otherwise polices the process.

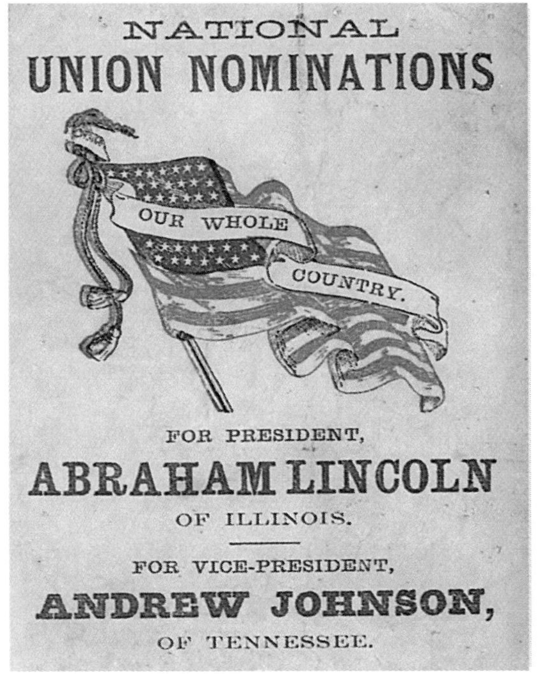

Campaign Ticket: 1864 This election took place before primary laws went into effect. Sometimes tickets such as this one actually were cast as ballots.

[4]R. M. Easley, "The Sine qua Non of Caucus Reform," *Review of Reviews*, September, 1897, p. 322.

[5]In most States, minor parties are required to make their nominations by other, more difficult processes—usually in conventions or by petition. For the significance of this point, see Chapter 5, Section 4.

Provide Guided Practice Ask students to name the five nominating methods discussed in the section. Write each method on the board, and ask volunteers to explain how each method is used today. (Suggested answers include: *Self Announcement: Candidates declare their intention to run; Caucus: Party members meet to select candidates; Convention: Voters elect delegates to nominating conventions; Direct Primary: Voters directly select candidates, may be "closed" to all but party members or "open" to all voters; Petition: Candidates are nominated by petitions signed by a certain number of qualified voters.*) Record student responses under each heading.

Provide Independent Practice

TRF **Teacher's Resource File** You may wish to assign Section 1 Guided Reading and Review, Unit 2 File, p. 53, to help students master section objective content.

ACTIVITY: Cooperative Learning

Time: Two class periods **Activity:** Report on an example of a nomination battle within a party during a recent presidential campaign. **Grouping:** Groups of four to six students **Purpose:** Have students use outside resources, such as periodical articles and books on presidential elections or candidates, to research and report on one example of an intraparty nomination fight. **Roles:** Assign the following roles: manager, researchers, recorder, spokesperson. **Outcome:** When the work is completed, have the spokesperson summarize the group's findings for the class.

There are two basic forms of the direct primary in use today: (1) the closed primary and (2) the open primary. The major difference between the two lies in the answer to this question: Who can vote in a party's primary—only qualified voters who are also party members, or any qualified voter?

The Closed Primary Thirty-eight States and the District of Columbia now use the
1.e **closed primary**—a party nominating election in which only declared party members can vote.[6] The primary is closed to all others.

In most of the closed primary States, party membership is established by registration (see Chapter 6, Section 2). When voters appear at the polling places on primary election day, their names are checked against the poll books—the lists of registered voters for each precinct. Each voter is then handed the ballot of the party in which he or she is registered.

In the other closed primary States, voters simply declare their party preference at the polling place. In some of them, that settles the matter; the person may vote in that party's primary. In others, however, that person can be challenged by a party's poll watcher—the person who has been designated by each party to ensure the fairness of the election process at the polls. If that happens, the voter is most often required to take an oath of party loyalty, swearing that he or she has supported that party and its candidates in the past and/or now does so.

The Open Primary Although it is the form in which the direct primary first appeared, the open primary is now found in only twelve States
1.f (see footnote 6). The **open primary** is a party nominating election in which any qualified voter can take part. It is open to anyone qualified to vote. No one has to declare a party choice at registration or at any other time.

When voters appear at the polling place, they are handed either the ballots of all the parties holding primaries or one large ballot containing the separate ballots of the various parties. Voters then pick the party primary in which they wish to vote.

A different version of the open primary is used in Alaska and Washington, where it is known as the wide-open primary or **blanket**
1.g **primary**. In each of those States, the voter receives a single large ballot listing each party's contenders for each nomination. The voter can vote in a single party's primary, as in the typical open primary. Or the voter can vote to nominate a Democrat for one office, a Republican for another, and so on.

Louisiana has yet another form of the open primary. Its unique "open-election law" provides for what amounts to a combination primary and election. The names of all persons who seek nominations are listed by office on a single primary ballot. A contender who wins more than 50 percent of the primary votes wins the office. In short, the primary in some cases becomes the election. In those contests where there is no majority winner, the two top vote-getters, regardless of party, face off in the general election.

The Closed vs. the Open Primary The two basic forms of the primary have excited arguments for decades. Those who favor the closed primary regularly make three arguments for it: (1) that it keeps the members of one party from raiding the other's primary in the hope of nominating weak candidates in the other party; (2) that the closed primary helps to make candidates more responsive and responsible to the party, its platform, and its members; and (3) that it helps to make voters more thoughtful because they must choose between the parties in order to vote in the primaries.

The critics of the closed primary contend that it (1) compromises the secrecy of the ballot, because it forces voters to make their party preferences known in public, and (2) tends to

[6]Every State but Alaska, Hawaii, Idaho, Louisiana, Michigan, Minnesota, Montana, North Dakota, Utah, Vermont, Washington, and Wisconsin. The Supreme Court has held that a State's closed primary law cannot forbid a party to allow independent voters to participate in its primary if the party chooses to do so. In *Tashjian* v. *Republican Party of Connecticut*, 1986, the Court struck down such a State law. Note that the Court did not outlaw the closed primary in this case, nor did it hold that a political party must allow independents to vote in its primary.

SPOTLIGHT ON: Global Awareness

In contrast to the closed primary, in which votes are cast for candidates on the basis of party, votes in some other democracies are actually counted on the basis of party. In other words, the results are expressed in terms of how each party fared, not each candidate. Nations employ this method of vote counting to insure what is called *proportional representation*—that is, the distribution of seats or offices in approximate proportion to the number of votes cast for a particular party. Denmark, Norway, Sweden, Austria, Belgium, Italy, and Finland are among those countries that use the proportional method to decide elections.

exclude independent voters from the partisan nomination process.[7] Advocates of the open primary believe that their system of nominating addresses both of these criticisms.

The opponents of the open primary insist that it (1) permits primary "raiding" and (2) undercuts the concepts of party loyalty and party responsibility.

The Runoff Primary In most States, candidates need to win only a plurality of the votes cast in the primary to win their party's nomination.[8]

In ten States,[9] however, an absolute majority is needed to carry a primary. If no one wins a majority in a race, a **runoff primary** takes place 1.h
a few weeks later. In the runoff primary, the two top vote-getters in the first direct primary face one another, and the winner of that vote becomes the nominee.

The Nonpartisan Primary In most States all or nearly all of the elective school and municipal offices are filled in nonpartisan elections in which candidates are not identified by party labels. About half of all State judges are chosen on nonpartisan ballots, as well.

The nomination of candidates for these offices takes place on a nonpartisan basis, too—often in nonpartisan primaries.

Typically, a contender who wins a clear majority in a nonpartisan primary then runs unopposed in the general election—subject only to write-in opposition. In many States, however, a candidate who wins a majority in the primary is declared elected at that point. If there is no majority winner, the names of the two top contenders are placed on the general election ballot.

The direct primary first appeared as a partisan nominating device, as you have seen. Many have long argued that it is really not well suited for use in nonpartisan election situations. They favor, instead, the petition method, of which you will read in a moment.

Evaluation of the Primary The direct primary, whether it is open or closed, is an intraparty nominating election. It came to American politics early in this century as a progressive reform in direct reaction to the boss-dominated and often corrupt convention system of nominating candidates. The direct primary method was intended to take the nominating function away from the party organization and put it in the hands of the party's membership.

Dunagin's People by Ralph Dunagin. Reprinted with special permission of NAS, Inc.

"My former opponent is supporting me in the general election. Please disregard all the things I said about him in the primary."

Interpreting Political Cartoons What aspect of political primary campaigning is hinted at in this cartoon?

[7]But see the discussion of *Tashjian* v. *Republican Party of Connecticut*, 1986 in footnote 6. Most closed-primary States have now amended their primary laws to comply with that decision.

[8]Recall, a plurality is a greater number of votes than those won by any other candidate, whether a majority or not. In Iowa, if no candidate wins at least 35 percent of the votes in a primary, the party must then nominate its candidate for that office by convention. In South Dakota, if no one who seeks a party's nomination for governor, or U.S. senator, or U.S. representative wins at least 35 percent, the party's candidate for that office must be picked in a runoff primary two weeks later. In North Carolina a runoff is held when no candidate wins 40 percent of the primary vote.

[9]Alabama, Arizona, Arkansas, Florida, Georgia, Mississippi, Oklahoma, South Carolina, Texas—and Louisiana under its unique "open election" law.

Interpreting Political Cartoons Ask students to discuss what the cartoon tells about possible conflict within a party during a primary election. (*Attacking the opposing candidate to win the primary—even though he or she is a member of the same party—is common practice during a primary.*)

Caption Answer The cartoon refers to the intraparty conflict that can take place during a primary.

Teacher's Resource File
See the Historical and Legal Documents file, p. 48, for materials to support this section.

Monitor Comprehension

Answers to Section 1 Review
1. "Key Terms" are defined on the following pages:
- **a.** nomination, p. 158
- **b.** general election, p. 158
- **c.** caucus, p. 158
- **d.** direct primary, p. 161
- **e.** closed primary, p. 162
- **f.** open primary, p. 162
- **g.** blanket primary, p. 162
- **h.** runoff primary, p. 163

2. It places practical limits on the choices voters have in a general election. **3.** Self-announcement. **4.** The wishes of the party's membership are passed up through each of several representative levels. **5.** Only declared party members can vote in a closed primary, whereas any eligible voter can vote in an open primary. **6.** A primary in which the voter may vote for a Republican for one office, a Democrat for another, etc. **7.** A primary in which candidates are not identified by party labels. **8.** Answers will vary. Students may suggest that its key purpose is to present the most qualified candidates; thus a convention might offer the best opportunity to deliberate over candidates and select the most qualified. Others might say that the process should select candidates with the widest appeal, in which case direct primaries would be the best method.

Teacher's Resource File
See the Unit 2 File, p. 54, for the Section 1 Quiz.

However, these basic facts about the primary have never been well understood by most of the electorate. Thus, for example, many voters resent having to declare their party preferences in those States that have a closed primary. Where the typical open primary is used, many are upset because they cannot express their choices for nominations in more than one party. Many voters are also annoyed by the "bed-sheet" ballot—the long list of candidates that typically appear on the primary ballot—not understanding that the use of the primary almost automatically means a long ballot.

Whatever the cause of voter dissatisfaction, it seems rather obvious that a large part of the electorate does not see the critical importance of the nominating stage. Thus, the turnout in the primaries in most States is usually less than half of that in general elections.

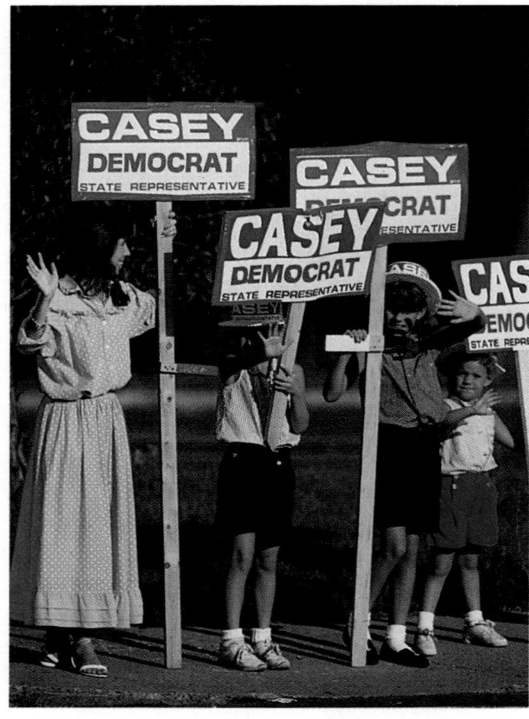

Day of Reckoning Campaigners appeal to voters up to the very last minute. Each State has its own rules on campaign tactics at polling places.

That fact leads into this little recognized point: There are actually two quite different electorates involved in the electoral process. One of them, the smaller of the two, is that group of voters who vote in the various open and closed primaries. It is very largely made up of those persons who are most likely to vote. The other electorate, the larger one, is that group of voters who take part only in the general election. To really grasp the significance of this point, review the discussion of those factors that affect voter turnout on page 142.

Another commonly cited drawback of primaries is their cost. When two or more candidates seek the same nomination, primary campaigns can be quite expensive. The fact that successful contenders for the nomination must mount—and find the money for—yet another campaign for the general election adds to the money problems that so many candidates face. It is unfortunately true that the financial facts of political life in the United States mean that some well-qualified people do not seek public office simply because they cannot muster the necessary funds. You will read more about the matter of money and politics shortly.

As you have read, the nominating process takes place within the party. So, when there are conflicts, they occur among the members of the same party. The direct primary magnifies this divisive aspect of the nominating process, because primaries are so public in nature. A bitter contest in the primaries can so wound and divide a party that it cannot recover in time to present a united front for the general election. Many a primary fight has cost a party an election.

A final criticism of the primary is that, because many voters are not very well informed, the primary places a premium on name familiarity. That is, it often gives an edge to a contender who has a well-known name or a name that sounds like that of some well-known person. A well-known name can help a candidate in any electoral situation, but name familiarity in and of itself has little or nothing to do with a candidate's qualifications.

The primary is not without its problems—nor is any other nominating device. Still, it does

Reteach

Have students reread the questions under "Find Out" in the beginning of Section 1. Ask them to write answers to each of the questions.

 **Presidential Primary** Jesse Jackson crisscrossed the country in 1988, speaking to voters about his platform as a Democratic presidential candidate.

give a party's members the opportunity to participate at the very core of the political process.

The Presidential Primary The presidential primary developed as an offshoot of the direct primary. It is not a nominating device, however. Rather, the presidential primary is an election that is held as a part of the process by which presidential candidates are chosen.

The presidential primary is a very complex device. It is one or both of two things, depending on the State involved. It is a process in which a party's voters elect some or all of a State party organization's delegates to that party's national convention; and/or it is a preference election in which voters can choose—vote their preference—among various contenders for a party's presidential nomination.

Much of what happens in presidential politics in the early months of every fourth year centers on this complicated process. You will read more about it in Chapter 13.

Nomination by Petition

One other nominating method is fairly widely used in American politics today—nomination by petition. With this method, candidates for public office are nominated by petitions signed by a certain number of qualified voters in the election district.[10]

Nomination by petition is found most widely at the local level, chiefly for nonpartisan school posts and municipal offices in middle-sized and smaller communities. It is also the process usually required by State law for the nomination of minor party and independent candidates. As noted in Chapter 5, the States frequently make the process of getting on the ballot purposely difficult for those candidates.

The details of the petition process vary widely from State to State, and even from one city to the next. Usually, however, the higher the office and/or the larger the constituency represented by the office, the greater the number of signatures needed for nomination.

Section 1 Review

1. Define: nomination, general election, caucus, direct primary, closed primary, open primary, blanket primary, runoff primary
2. In what ways is the nominating process key to the electoral process?
3. Which nominating method is the oldest?
4. In what ways do conventions seem well suited to democracy?
5. What is the difference between an open primary and a closed primary?
6. What is a wide-open primary?
7. What is a nonpartisan primary?

Critical Thinking

8. **Identifying Alternatives** (p. 19) In your opinion, what should be the key purpose of the nominating process? Which of the methods discussed in this section come closest to fulfilling this purpose?

★

[10]The petition device is also used in several other aspects of the electoral process. Thus, it and/or a filing fee is generally the method by which an aspirant's name is placed on the direct primary ballot.

Closure

The process of nominating candidates can take five forms: self-announcement, caucus, convention, direct primary, and petition. However, these methods have evolved over time, and today, most States use the direct primary method.

In Section 2, students will learn more about the importance of the nominating process in the context of elections.

Assignment Assign Section 2, pp. 166–171, for the next class period.

Section 2
Elections

Focus

Teacher's Resource File See the Unit 2 File, p. 55, for the Section 2 Outline.

Objectives

7.5 Examine the reasons why the details of the election process are so important.

7.6 Determine where and when elections take place.

7.7 Understand what a ballot is and determine the many forms it takes.

Bellringer Activity Have students respond to the following situation: You and a group of friends are trying to decide what to do together on Saturday night. Some of you want to go to a party, others want to go to a movie. How do you decide what to do? Why did you choose this method?

State the Purpose A democratic system of government cannot survive without free, honest, and accurate elections. In Section 2, students will examine how federal and State laws seek to insure the integrity of the vital process of elections. They will also examine the mechanics of an election to see how fairness and honesty are maintained.

2 Elections

Find Out:

- For what reasons are the details of the election process so important?
- Where and when do elections take place?
- What is the ballot and what are the many forms it takes?

Key Terms:

coattail effect, precinct, polling place, ballot

Most high school students are not old enough to vote. But high school students can serve on local election boards in some parts of the country. First in Hawaii and Oregon and now in several States, 16- and 17-year-olds can become full-fledged members of these official bodies—the panels that administer the elections at which public officeholders are chosen.

Americans hold more elections and vote more often than most people realize. Indeed, Sundays and holidays are about the only days in any year on which people do not go to the polls somewhere in the United States. Americans also elect far more officeholders than most people realize—in fact, more than 500,000 of them.

Obviously, the election of public officials is very serious business. In this section, you will read about the federal and state laws that seek to insure the integrity of this vital process.

The Administration of Elections

Once candidates have been nominated, they must face their opponents and the voters in the general election—in what H. G. Wells once called democracy's "feast, its great function."

Democratic government cannot succeed unless elections are free, honest, and accurate. Too many people look at the details of the election process as too complicated, too legalistic, too dry and boring, to worry about. But those people miss the vital part those details play in making democracy work. The often lengthy and closely detailed provisions of election law are designed to protect the integrity of that process. And they often have a very telling effect on the outcome of elections, as well.

You have read several illustrations showing that the details of election law can have real impacts—for example, when you read about voter qualifications and registration in the last chapter. You saw another only a few pages back, when you considered the details of the direct primary.

The Extent of Federal Control Nearly all elections in this country are held to choose the more than 500,000 persons who hold elective offices in the more than 83,000 units of government at the State and local levels. It is quite understandable, then, that most election law in the United States is State law.

There is a body of federal election law, however. The Constitution gives Congress the power to fix "the times, places, and manner of holding elections" of members of Congress.[11] Congress also has the power to set the time for choosing presidential electors, to set the date for casting electoral votes, and to regulate other aspects of the presidential election process.[12]

Congress has set the date for holding congressional elections as the first Tuesday following the first Monday in November of every even-numbered year. It has set the same date every fourth year for the presidential elections.[13]

Congress has required the use of secret ballots and allowed the use of voting machines in federal elections. It has also passed several laws to protect the right to vote in all elections, as you saw in Chapter 6, Section 3. And it has also prohibited various corrupt practices and regulated the financing of campaigns for federal office, as you will see in the pages ahead.

All other matters relating to national elections, and all of the details involved in choosing the thousands of State and local officials, are dealt with in the laws of the States.

[11]Article I, Section 4, Clause 1; 17th Amendment; see Chapter 10, Section 2.

[12]Article II, Section 1, Clause 3; 12th Amendment; see Chapter 13, Section 6.

[13]Congress has made an exception for Alaska, which may, if it chooses, elect its congressional delegation and cast its presidential vote in October. So far, however, Alaska has used the November date.

Reading Strategy: Who? What? When? Where? How? Why?

Have students skim the headings in Section 2. Then have them make a list of the questions: Who? What? When? Where? How? and Why? As they read, have them fill in information about the election process under each question heading. Make sure students make at least one entry under each heading, and ensure that they understand that the "who" can be both the voters and the candidates running for office.

Vocabulary

Point out "Key Terms" on page 166. Ask students to create a heading titled "Elections." Under the heading, have them list the "Key Terms". Tell students to write brief explanations of how each term relates to elections as they encounter each term in the text. LEP

When Elections Are Held Most States hold their elections to fill State offices on the same date Congress has set for national elections—in November of every even-numbered year.[14] Some States do fix other dates for at least some offices. Thus, Louisiana, Mississippi, New Jersey, and Virginia elect the governor, other executive officers, and State legislators in November of the odd-numbered year. Other local election dates vary from State to State. Where those elections are not held in November, they generally take place in the spring.

The Coattail Effect The **coattail effect** occurs when a strong candidate running for an office at the top of the ballot helps attract voters to other candidates on the party's ticket. In effect, the lesser known office seekers "ride the coattails" of the more prestigious personalities. In 1980 and 1984, for example, Ronald Reagan's coattails helped many Republican candidates win office. The coattail effect is usually most apparent in presidential elections. But a popular candidate for senator or governor can have the same kind of pulling power. 1.a

There can be a reverse coattail effect, too. It comes when a candidate for high office is less than popular with many voters—for example, Barry Goldwater as the Republican presidential nominee in 1964, and George McGovern for the Democrats in 1972. President Carter's coattails were also of the reverse variety in 1980.

Some have long held that all State and local elections should be held on dates other than those set for federal elections. This, they say, would help make voters pay more attention to State and local candidates and issues and lessen the coattail effects of presidential contests.

Precincts and Polling Places

A **precinct** is a voting district. Precincts are the 1.b
basic and smallest geographic units for the conduct of elections. State law regularly restricts their size, generally to an area with no more than 500 to 1,000 or so qualified voters. A **polling place**—where the voters who live in a 1.c
precinct actually vote—is located somewhere in or near each precinct.

A precinct election board supervises the polling place and the voting process in each precinct. Typically, the county clerk or county board of elections draws precinct lines, fixes the location of each polling place, and picks the members of the precinct boards.

The precinct board opens and closes the polls at the times set by State law. In most States, the polls are open from 7:00 or 8:00 A.M. to 7:00 or 8:00 P.M. The precinct election board must also see that the ballots and the ballot boxes or voting machines are available. It must make certain that only qualified voters cast ballots in the precinct. Often the board also counts the votes cast in the precinct and then sends the results to the proper place—usually to the county clerk or county board of elections.

VOICES *on Government*

On Taking Part in the Electoral Process

David N. Dinkins, elected mayor of New York City in January 1990

"Our society is a gorgeous mosaic of race and religious faith, of national origin. . . . No one person and no one group possibly can understand the ways and the worries of all. A government that includes all in the process will exclude fewer in the result. Representation . . . will reduce the alienation and frustration that too often characterize our society. Broad-based government is better government."

---

[14]The "Tuesday-after-the-first-Monday" formula prevents election day from falling on Sundays—to maintain the principle of separation of church and state—and on the first day of the month, which is often payday and therefore peculiarly subject to campaign pressures.

INSTRUCT

Discuss/Explain Ask students to recall the "Bellringer Activity" and how they proposed making a group decision. Explain to students that each community, each State, and the United States itself also faces group decisions. Many of these decisions are made at elections.

The goal of each election is to select the people's choice for public office and to do so in a free, honest, and accurate way. Have students explain how governments ensure the integrity of the election process.

They might begin their discussion by examining the role of the federal and the State government in elections. Then they may consider the key elements of an election—the ballot and the process and equipment by which a vote is cast. Ask: How do each of these elements ensure the integrity of the election process? *(They ensure uniformity and security.)* What are some ways that the election process could be corrupted without strict controls on the voting procedure? *(The integrity of an election could be compromised at all stages of the process, including scheduling, balloting, and counting.)*

ABCNEWS INTERACTIVE

The following video segment may be used to highlight aspects of the election process.

POWERS OF THE CONGRESS GUIDEBOOK
Chapter 20: Rules for Elections, p. 96

Poll watchers, one from each party, are allowed at each polling place. They may challenge any person they believe is not qualified to vote, check to be sure that as many as possible of their own party's supporters do vote, and monitor the whole process, including the counting of the ballots.

The Ballot

1.d The **ballot** is the device by which a voter registers a choice in an election [15] It can take a number of different forms.

Each of the States now provides for a secret ballot. That is, each requires that ballots be cast in such manner that others cannot know how a voter has voted.

Voting was a public process through much of the nation's earlier history. Paper ballots were used in some colonial elections, but voting was commonly *viva voce*—by voice. With suffrage limited to the privileged few, many defended oral voting as the only "manly" way in which to participate. Whatever the merits of that view, the expansion of the electorate brought with it a marked increase in intimidation, vote buying, and other corruptions of the voting process.

Paper ballots came into general use by the mid-1800s. The first ones were slips of paper that voters prepared themselves and dropped in the ballot box. Soon candidates and parties began to prepare ballots and hand them to voters to cast—sometimes paying them to do so. Those ballots were often printed on colored paper, and anyone watching could tell for whom voters were voting.

Political machines fought all attempts to make voting a more dependably fair and honest process. The political corruption of the post-Civil War years brought widespread demand for ballot reforms, however.

The Australian Ballot A new voting arrangement was devised in Australia, where it was first used in an election in Victoria in 1856. Its successes there led to its use in other countries. By 1900 nearly all of the States were using it, and it remains the basic form of the ballot today.

The Australian Ballot has four essential features: (1) it is printed at public expense; (2) it lists the names of all candidates in an election; (3) it is given out only at the polls, one to each qualified voter; and (4) it is voted in secret.

Two basic varieties of the Australian ballot have developed over the years. Nearly half the States now use the office-group version; the rest of the States use the party-column ballot.

The Office-Group Ballot The office-group ballot is the original form of the Australian ballot. It is also sometimes called the Massachusetts ballot because of its early (1888) use there. On the office-group ballot, the candidates for each office are grouped together. At first, the names of the candidates were listed in alphabetical order. Most States using the form now rotate the names—so that each candidate will have whatever psychological advantage there may be in having his or her name at the top of the list.

The Party-Column Ballot The party-column ballot is also known as the Indiana ballot, from its early (1889) use in that State. It lists

[15]The word comes from the Italian *ballotta*—"little ball," and reflects the practice of dropping black or white balls into a box to indicate a choice. The term *blackball* comes from the same practice.

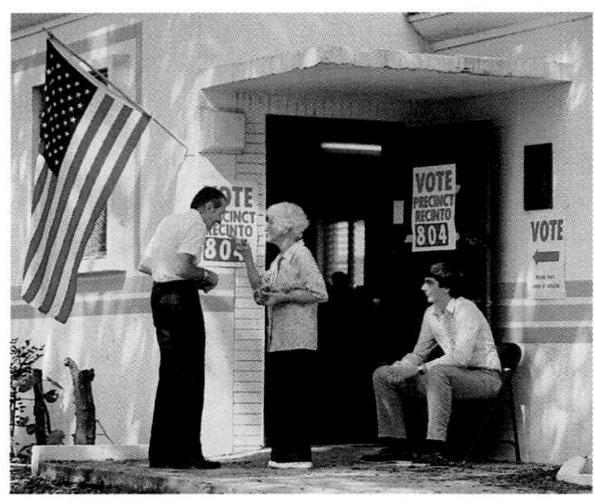

Election Day Citizens wait to cast votes in Coral Gables, Florida. What does the picture indicate about the people living in this particular community?

Caption Answer The presence of Spanish on the posters indicate that some portion of the community speaks Spanish.

Spotlight on: Political Talk

The reform effort that brought the Australian ballot to the U.S. was led by a group of elitist Republicans known as the Mugwumps. The term has become a common description for party members who object to the party line. The first Mugwumps were a group that split from the Republican party in 1884 to protest their party's nomination of the notorious James G. Blaine for President. Legend has it that the term derives from a little bird that sits on a fence "with his mug on one side and his wump on the other," but in fact the term comes from the Algonquin language, in which it means "chief or person of honor."

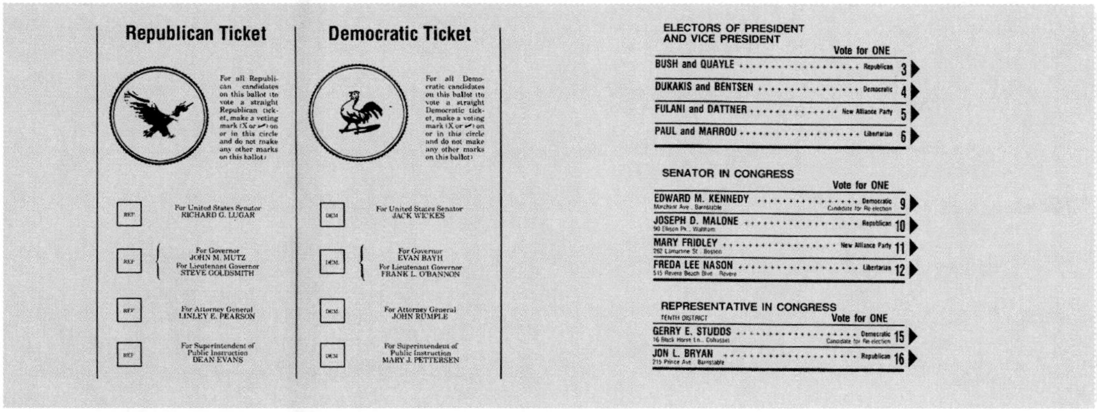

Presidential Election Ballots How did Indiana (left) and Massachusetts (right) ballots differ in the 1988 elections?

each party's candidates in a column under the party's name. Often there is a place at the top of each column where, with a single X, the voter can vote for all of that party's candidates.

Professional politicians tend to favor the party-column ballot. It encourages straight-ticket voting, especially if the party has a strong candidate at the head of the ticket. Most students of the political process favor the office-group form because it encourages voter judgment and split-ticket voting.

Sample Ballots Sample ballots, clearly marked as such, are available in most States prior to an election. In some they are mailed to all voters, and they appear in most newspapers. They cannot be cast, but they can help voters prepare for an election.[16]

The Long and the Short of It The ballot in a typical American election is a lengthy one, often and aptly called a "bed-sheet" ballot. It frequently lists so many offices, candidates, and measures that even the most well-informed voters have a difficult time marking it intelligently.

The long ballot came to American politics in the era of Jacksonian Democracy in the 1830s. Many held the view at the time that the greater the number of elective offices, the more democratic the governmental system. The idea remains widely accepted today.

Generally, the longest ballots are found at the local level, especially among the nation's 3,000-odd counties. In most counties, it is not unusual to find a large number of elected offices listed on ballots—including several commissioners, a clerk, a sheriff, one or more judges, a prosecutor, coroner, treasurer, assessor, surveyor, school superintendent, engineer, sanitarian, and even the proverbial dogcatcher.

Critics of the long ballot do not accept the argument that the more you elect the more democratic you are. They believe that quite the reverse is true; with a smaller number of elected offices to fill, the voter can better know the candidates and their qualifications. Critics also point to "ballot fatigue"—the drop-off in voting that can run as high as 20 to 30 percent at or near the bottom of the typical lengthy ballot.

There seems little, if any, good reason to elect such local officials as clerks, coroners, surveyors, and engineers. Their jobs do not carry basic policy-making responsibilities. Rather, they carry out policies made by others. For good

[16]First in Oregon (1907), and now in several States, an official voter's pamphlet is mailed to voters before an election. It lists all candidates and measures that will appear on the ballot. In Oregon each candidate is allowed space to present his or her qualifications and position on the issues, and supporters and opponents of ballot measures are allowed space to present their arguments, as well.

Provide Guided Practice Write the words "Honest, accurate, and free" on the board. Ask volunteers to answer the following: How does governmental administration of elections help fulfill this ideal? (*By providing uniform standards.*) What about polling places and precincts? (*Precinct boards and poll watchers ensure integrity within each locality.*) Australian ballots? (*Given in secret; identical for each voter.*) Voting machines and other innovations? (*Increase accuracy, speed, turnout.*)

Provide Independent Practice

TRF **Teacher's Resource File** You may wish to assign the Section 2 Guided Reading and Review from the Unit 2 File, p. 56, to help the students master section content.

Caption Answer Massachusetts listed candidates by office; Indiana listed the candidates by party affiliation.

Enrichment

Have students hold an election for celebrity of the month. Ask volunteers to act as election officials, to schedule the votes, and to draw up ballots. Generate a list of candidates by using the self-announcement form of nomination. Then hold a primary to narrow the list of candidates to two. Next, have the class hold a general election. Encourage students to "campaign" for their choices. After the election, have students evaluate the process and discuss how honest, free, and accurate the election was. (Easy)

Interpreting Charts The chart on this page outlines general voting procedures. Ask students to find out the specific voting procedures in their area, for example, when and where to register, and where the nearest polling place is located. Make sure students understand that these procedures will generally be the same for most local, State, and federal elections.

MONITOR COMPREHENSION

Answers to Section 2 Review
1. "Key Terms" are defined on the following pages:
- **a.** coattail effect, p. 167
- **b.** precinct, p. 167
- **c.** polling place, p. 167
- **d.** ballot, p. 168

2. The details help to keep elections free, honest, and accurate at every step. **3.** The majority of elective offices are at the State and local levels. **4.** (a) National elections are held on the Tuesday after the first Monday in November of even-numbered years. (b) State general elections are usually held the same day as the national election. A few States elect in odd-numbered years and/or in the spring. **5.** So that voters will pay more attention to State and local elections and to lessen the coattail effect. **6.** (a) The Australian ballot is printed at public expense, lists the names of all candidates, is given out only at the polls, and is voted in secret. (b) The office-group ballot groups the candidates for each office and the party-column ballot lists each party's candidates in a column under the party's name.

How to Vote

Before Election Day

1. Determine whether you are qualified to vote. To qualify to vote in the United States, you must be
- ☐ an American citizen and
- ☐ at least 18 years of age.

2. Register to vote. In every state except North Dakota, you must register to vote.
- ☐ **When?** In most states, registration must take place several weeks before election day. To find out the requirements in your state, telephone your local election board or officials.
- ☐ **Where?** In most states, you can register at the town or municipal hall. In some instances, registration tables or booths are set up at public places that are convenient for most voters to find and reach, such as shopping centers, supermarkets, or public libraries. Some states allow registration by mail.
- ☐ **How?** To register you will need proof of your age (such as a birth certificate). Registration forms are simple to fill out, requiring basic information such as your name, address, date and place of birth, and social security number. Some states ask registering voters to declare a party preference.

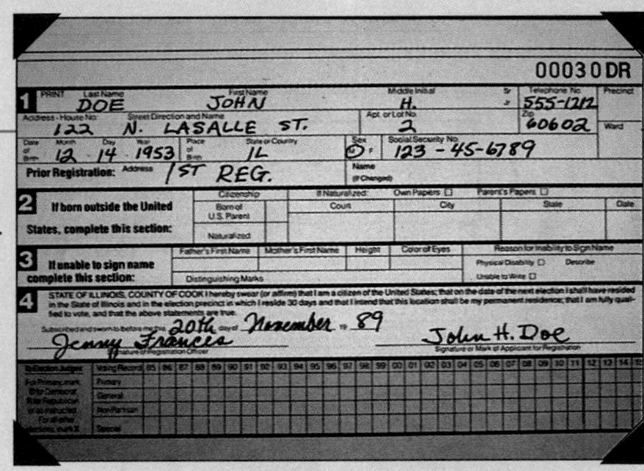

00030 DR

1 PRINT Last Name DOE First Name JOHN Middle Initial H. Telephone No. 555-1212 Precinct
Address - House No. 122 Street Direction and Name N. LASALLE ST. Apt. or Lot No. 2 Zip 60602 Ward
Date of Birth Month 12 Day 14 Year 1953 Place of Birth State or Country IL Sex M F Social Security No. 123-45-6789
Prior Registration: Address 1ST REG. Name (If Changed)

2 If born outside the United States, complete this section: Citizenship Born of U.S. Parent Naturalized If Naturalized: Own Papers ☐ Parent's Papers ☐ Court City State Date

3 If unable to sign name complete this section: Father's First Name Mother's First Name Height Color of Eyes Distinguishing Marks Reason for Inability to Sign Name Physical Disability ☐ Describe Unable to Write ☐

4 STATE OF ILLINOIS, COUNTY OF COOK I hereby swear (or affirm) that I am a citizen of the United States; that on the date of the next election I shall have resided in the State of Illinois and in the election precinct in which I reside 30 days and that I intend that this location shall be my permanent residence; that I am fully qualified to vote, and that the above statements are true.
Subscribed and sworn to before me this 20th day of November 19 89
Jenny Frances Signature of Registration Officer
John H. Doe Signature or Mark of Applicant for Registration

Voting Record: Primary, General, NonPartisan, Special

On Election Day

3. Go to your polling place to cast your vote. In most states you will be told at registration to which polling place you should go to cast your vote. If you need to find this information, however, you can call your town or municipal hall. Officials there can also tell you what the voting hours are at your polling place (typical voting hours are 7 A.M. to 7 P.M.).

"THERE GO THE KRAVITZES TO VOTE... WE BETTER GO CANCEL THEM OUT."

4. Check in with election officials at your polling place. When you arrive, there will usually be a line of people waiting to check in. When your turn comes, tell the election officials your address and name. They will then check your name off their list and hand you a ballot or punch card and direct you to a voting booth. If your state uses a lever machine, officials will simply direct you to a booth. If you have questions, feel free to ask these officials.

5. Cast your vote. To cast your vote, you will use a paper ballot, a lever machine, or a punch card, depending on your state's method. Read your ballot carefully, making your choices based on the research you have done into the candidates and issues involved in this election. When you are sure you have finished voting, place your completed card in the envelope you were given and hand it to the election judge.

Congratulations! You have just exercised one of your most important rights as a citizen in a democratic nation!

Reteach

Ask students to discuss the importance of honest, free, accurate elections in a democracy and the steps taken to ensure the integrity of elections. Have them look over Section 2 for key points that support this discussion.

government, the rule should be: Elect those who make public policies; appoint those who administer them.

Voting Machines and Innovations

Thomas Edison took out the first American patent for a voting machine. The community of Lockport, New York, first used his invention in 1892. The use of similar devices has long since spread to the polling places of every State.

Only a handful of States make the use of voting machines mandatory. Most often the machines are used only in some—usually the more populous—areas of a State. All told, however, more than half of all the votes in national elections today are cast on some form of voting machine.

The typical voting machine serves as its own booth. By pulling a lever, the voter encloses himself or herself within a curtain and unlocks the machine. The ballot appears on the face of the machine, and the voter makes his or her choices by pulling down the small levers over the names of the candidates he or she favors. In most States using the party-column ballot, the voter can pull a master lever to vote a straight ticket.

The machine is programmed so that a voter can cast only one vote per contest. Once all levers are in the desired positions, the voter opens the curtain. That action records the votes and, at the same time, clears the machine for the next voter.

The use of voting machines does away with the need for manual vote counting, reduces the number of persons needed to administer elections, and speeds the voting process. It also increases the number of voters who can be handled per precinct, makes ballot mutilation impossible, and minimizes fraud and counting errors.

Electronic Vote Counting Electronic data processing (EDP) techniques have been applied to the voting process in recent years—first in California and Oregon and now, to some degree, in more than two-thirds of the States.

The most widely used adaptation of EDP in elections involves punch-card ballots, which are counted by computers. Another involves paper ballots marked with sensitized ink and counted by optical scanners.

Vote-by-Mail Elections Some local elections are now conducted with mail-in ballots in a handful of States around the country.

Monterey County, California held the first vote-by-mail election in 1977. San Diego was the first locality to make large-scale use of the process in 1981. Since then, mail-in ballots have been used in local elections in several other places.

Vote-by-mail elections have stirred a growing controversy. Critics fear that the process threatens the principle of the secret ballot and invites fraud. Its supporters say that it can be as fraud-proof as any other method of voting. They also cite this fact: The process increases voter turnout in local elections and, at the same time, reduces the costs of conducting them.

The use of mail-in ballots has been confined to local-issue elections—except in Oregon and Montana, where State law now allows their use in some local candidate elections.

Section 2 Review

1. **Define:** coattail effect, precinct, polling place, ballot
2. In what ways are the details of the electoral process vital to the success of democratic government?
3. For what reason is most election law in this country State rather than federal?
4. (a) When are national elections held? (b) When are most State general elections held?
5. For what reasons do some people favor separate dates for national and for State and local elections?
6. (a) What is the Australian ballot? (b) How do office-group and party-column ballots differ?

Critical Thinking

7. **Predicting Consequences** (p. 19) Think about elections in your school for class president and student council. How might these elections be affected if there were no secret ballot?

★

7. Students may suggest that people could be pressured more easily into voting a certain way or harassed for voting a certain way.

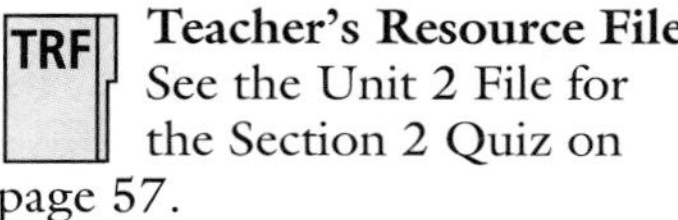
Teacher's Resource File See the Unit 2 File for the Section 2 Quiz on page 57.

Closure

In order for a democratic system to succeed, elections must be honest, free, and accurate. The administration of elections, the federal and State laws, and the mechanics of voting all serve to maintain the integrity of the election process.

In Section 3, students will look at the problematic role of money in the election process and how government regulates its use.

Assignment Assign Section 3, pp. 173–179 for the next class period.

Spotlight on: Multiculturalism

Another recent innovation at many polls is the use of the bilingual ballot. The Voting Rights Act, as amended in 1975, requires States to make bilingual ballots available in areas where 5 percent of the citizens of voting age are of a single-language minority and either do not speak English proficiently enough to participate in the electoral process or suffer low literacy rates. The law requires alternative ballots in Spanish, and several Asian languages, for example. In election year 1988, the law was put into effect in almost 400 jurisdictions in 19 different States.

TEACHING

What You Can Do

Working to Change State Law

Objective

Understand that individuals can work within the political system to change the law.

INSTRUCT

Before students begin reading the feature, ask them to discuss how citizens should respond if they feel a law is unfair. Ask students if they can think of an individual or group that has committed time and effort to changing existing law. They may cite the example of Martin Luther King, Jr., and the thousands of people who committed themselves to challenging legal discrimination in the 1950s and 1960s.

Below are some possible questions for postreading discussion:

- What are the resources necessary to "make a difference"?
- Why is it important that individuals participate in civic affairs?
- What issues or laws can students think of that they might like to change?

What You Can Do

Working to Change State Law

Citizens working actively together *can* make a difference. Their participation informs government of their priorities and concerns. Read about how a group of high-school students brought about a change in State law.

Students Take Action

Dean Neff teaches an American government course at Central High School in Omaha, Nebraska. He and some of his students are largely responsible for allowing most 17-year-olds in Nebraska to vote.

Over the past several years, Neff became more and more convinced that 17-year-olds who would be 18 by the following November—the time when general elections take place—ought to be able to vote in the primary elections in May. It seemed only fair, he felt, to give anyone who could vote in a general election the chance to help choose the candidates for that election.

Neff believed this so firmly that he decided to get involved. That decision turned into a student project in the fall of 1987. A number of high school seniors got deeply involved in research. They discovered that several States recently have allowed 17-year-olds to vote in the primary—including Indiana, Kentucky, Maryland, North and South Carolina, Ohio, Virginia, and West Virginia. Armed with good information and strong commitment, Neff and his students approached their State legislators.

LR 253 Becomes Law

Senator Carol Prisch of Omaha was so impressed by their presentation that she agreed to support their cause in the 1988 session of Nebraska's legislature. On January 6, 1988, Senator Prisch and three other legislators introduced Legislative Resolution 253, to amend Article VI, Section 1 of Nebraska's constitution. LR 253 was referred to the legislature's Committee on Government, Military, and Veterans Affairs and the students now became lobbyists. They wrote letters to or called on most of the other members of the legislature, urging them to support the bill. They contacted lawmakers, wrote letters to newspapers, and sought the backing of students and teachers in other schools around the State. Through their efforts they won endorsements from both major political parties and many civic organizations in Nebraska. When the bill finally reached the floor of the legislature on March 25, it was approved by an overwhelming vote, 43 to 3.

Little opposition, none of it organized, emerged after the legislature adjourned. Nebraska voters approved the proposed amendment by a comfortable margin at the general election on November 8, 1988. Students like yourselves made a difference. They changed State law.

Getting Involved

1. Identify a current issue on the State or local level of government similar to the one addressed in this case.

2. Formulate a plan for ways that you can get involved and identify resources that could be used in your plan.

3. Predict any problems or objections you might encounter in carrying out your plan.

172

Teacher's Resource File

See the Participatory Government Activities file, pp. 28–39, 44–69, for materials to support or extend this feature.

3 Money and the Election Process

Find Out:

- Why is money an indispensable campaign resource?
- What problems does money pose in the election process?
- How is the use of money regulated in elections today?

Key Term:

political action committee

Some believe that this is the golden rule of politics: The person who has the gold rules. That is not true. But this is: Running for public office costs money, and often a lot of it. And that fact creates some of the most difficult problems in American politics. It leaves open the possibility that candidates will try to buy their way into public office. And special interest groups may try to buy favors from those who are in office.

Clearly, government by the people must be protected from these dangers. But how? Parties and candidates must have money. Without it, they cannot campaign or do any of the many things they must do to win elections.

In short, money is an absolutely necessary campaign resource. Yet, the getting and the spending of campaign funds can corrupt the entire political process.

In this section, you will read about the role of money in elections and about the ongoing efforts to regulate campaign finance.

Campaign Spending Amounts

No one really knows how much money is spent on elections in the United States. Reliable estimates of total spending in recent presidential election years—including nominations and general elections for offices at all levels—are shown in the table on page 174.

The presidential election eats up by far the largest share of campaign dollars: For 1988, total spending for all of the major and minor party efforts—for the primaries, conventions, presidential campaign, everything—came to just about $500 million.

Some $445 million was spent in all of the U.S. House and Senate races in 1990—including the more than $21 million spent in a single Senate contest—in North Carolina.[17]

Radio and television time, professional campaign managers and consultants, newspaper advertisements, pamphlets, buttons, posters and

VOTE FOR
"IF WE RAISE ENOUGH CAMPAIGN FUNDS—
WE MIGHT BE ELECTED TO CONGRESS—
GIVE
WHERE WE CAN SPEND MOST OF OUR TIME RAISING MORE CAMPAIGN FUNDS"
©1987 HERBLOCK

Drawing by Schoenbaum; ©1984, The New Yorker Magazine, Inc.

Interpreting Political Cartoons The high cost of running for office is often criticized by the media. What message does the cartoon convey about this issue?

[17]Principal sources for the data in this section are Herbert E. Alexander, Citizens' Research Foundation; *Congressional Quarterly*; and the Federal Election Commission.

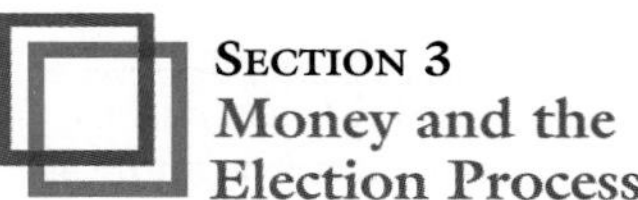

SECTION 3
Money and the Election Process

FOCUS

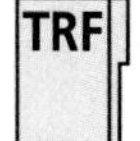

Teacher's Resource File See the Unit 2 File, p. 58, for the Section 3 Outline.

Objectives

7.8 Examine the reasons why money is an indispensable campaign resource.
7.9 Determine the problems that money poses in the election process.
7.10 Examine the ways in which the use of money is regulated in elections today.

Bellringer Activity Ask students to respond to this statement: "People who have lots of money are probably smarter and better qualified to hold political office." Discuss with students the problem of the enormous cost of running for office.

State the Purpose In Section 3, students will examine the role of money in electoral politics and the restrictions on the raising and spending of money in campaigns. These restrictions seek to ensure that money does not have a negative influence on the electoral process.

Interpreting Political Cartoons As students look at the cartoon, ask them to discuss whether or not it is fair to criticize members of Congress for raising the campaign money they need.

Caption Answer That representatives spend too much of their time trying to raise campaign funds.

Vocabulary

Direct students' attention to "Key Term" on page 173. Ask them to define separately each word of the term *political action committee.* Based on these definitions, have students predict what the term means in the context of money and elections. Have students check their prediction when they encounter the term in the text. LEP

Reading Strategy: Predicting Content

Have students read the boldfaced headings throughout Section 3. Point out that these headings present an outline of information on the use of money in the election process. Have students predict the content of each heading in one sentence. Then have them read the section to test their predictions.

INSTRUCT

Discuss/Explain Explain to students that money is an indispensable campaign resource. Ask students to discuss why this is so, and what issues and concerns are raised by that fact. (*The need for money introduces the possibility that those who have it will be able to "buy" elective office and that those who do not have it will be corrupted in the pursuit of it.*)

To aid in this discussion, students might answer the following: What is the danger of making fund-raising such an important part of getting elected? (*The risk of candidates being "bought" increases; officials spend less time running government and more time raising money.*) What might happen if only wealthy people could run for office? (*The pool of quality candidates would shrink*)

Ask students to explain why they think it might be necessary to have regulations about the use of money in an election. As part of the discussion, have them explain the role of the Federal Election Commission in the regulation process. (*The FEC regulates federal elections by enforcing disclosure requirements, setting spending and contribution guidelines; and by providing funding for presidential elections.*)

Interpreting Tables As students look at the table, ask them to review where the money for election campaigns comes from. Have them speculate how the sources for funding have changed from 1952 to 1988.

Caption Answer Possible answer: the high cost of media coverage, especially television time.

bumper strips, office rent, polls, data processing, mass mailings, travel—these and a host of other items make up the huge sums spent in campaigns. Television is by far the largest item in a typical campaign budget today. A single half hour of network TV time can run as much as $500,000, and a 30-second spot in prime time now runs to at least $150,000. As Will Rogers put it years ago, "You have to be loaded just to get beat."

The total amount spent in particular races varies, of course, and widely. How much depends on many factors: the office involved, the candidate and whether he or she is the incumbent, the opposition, and, not least, the availability of campaign funds.

Sources of Campaign Funding

In the broadest sense, parties and their candidates draw their money from two sources—private contributors and from the public treasury. Recent campaign finance laws have had a large impact on both of these sources, as you will see.

Private Givers Private givers have always been the major source of campaign funds in American politics. Those givers come in several different shapes and sizes:

Total Campaign Spending, 1952–1988

	Estimated Spending	Vote Cast for President	Cost per Voter
1952	$140 million	61.6 million	$2.28
1956	155 million	62.0 million	2.50
1960	175 million	68.8 million	2.54
1964	200 million	70.6 million	2.83
1968	300 million	73.2 million	4.10
1972	425 million	77.7 million	5.47
1976	540 million	81.6 million	6.62
1980	1.2 billion	86.5 million	13.87
1984	1.8 billion	92.6 million	19.38
1988	3.0 billion	91.6 million	32.75

Interpreting Tables What factors might account for the astronomical rise in the cost of campaign spending in the last three elections?

1. Small contributors—those who give $5 or $10 or so, and only occasionally. Clearly, the democratic ideal would be best served if all campaigns were entirely supported by the small contributions of millions of American voters. But only about 10 percent of all persons of voting age ever make such contributions; so, parties and candidates must look to other places for much of their funding.
2. Wealthier persons and families—the so-called "angels" or "fat cats," who can afford large donations and find it in their best interest to make them.
3. Candidates themselves—both incumbents and challengers, and their families, and, importantly, people who hold and want to keep appointive public offices.
4. Various nonparty groups—especially **political action committees (PACs)**—the political arms of special interest groups that have a major stake in public policy.
5. Temporary organizations—groups formed for the immediate purposes of a campaign, including fund-raising. Hundreds of these short-lived units spring up every two years, and at every level in American politics. Victory '88 (a pro-Bush/Quayle organization) and Hispanic Women for Dukakis-Bentsen were but two of these groups that operated in the 1988 presidential contest.

1.a

Then, too, parties and their candidates often hold fund-raising events of various sorts. The most common of these social-electioneering affairs are $25-, $100-, or $1,000-a-plate luncheons, dinners, picnics, concerts, receptions, cocktail parties, and rallies. Other commonly used fund-raising events include telethons and direct-mail campaigns.

To these traditional sources, a newer one—public subsidies from federal and/or State treasuries—has lately been added. To this point in time, subsidies have been most important at the presidential level.[18]

[18]Public funds for presidential campaigns come from the federal treasury. Several States now also have some form of public financing for parties and/or candidates at the State and even the local level.

ACTIVITY: Cooperative Learning

Time: One class period **Activity:** Write questions relating to a graph or table from the chapter. **Grouping:** 4 to 6 students **Purpose:** Assign one of the graphs or tables in Chapter 7 to each group. Have students work together to write three to five questions that can be answered using the information in the assigned graph or table. Then have groups exchange questions and write answers to them. **Roles:** Have students assign the following roles: discussion leader, recorder, spokesperson. **Outcome:** Have group spokespersons take turns reading a question and the group's answer. The class may use the appropriate graph or table in their texts to verify the answer.

SPOTLIGHT ON: Constitutional Issues

Since the Supreme Court struck down many FEC spending limits on congressional races (*Buckley* v. *Valeo,* 1976), some observers note an increase in the amounts that wealthy candidates are spending in their own bids for office, particularly for the Senate. Among large contributors to their successful campaigns for the Senate are the late John Heinz III(R-PA), who gave $2.5 million to his own campaign in 1976; Frank Lautenberg(D-NJ), $5 million in 1982; Jay Rockefeller (D-WV), $9 million in 1984; and Herbert Kohl(D-WI), $6.1 million in 1988. Senate leaders estimate that between one-half and two - thirds of the Senate membership are millionaires.

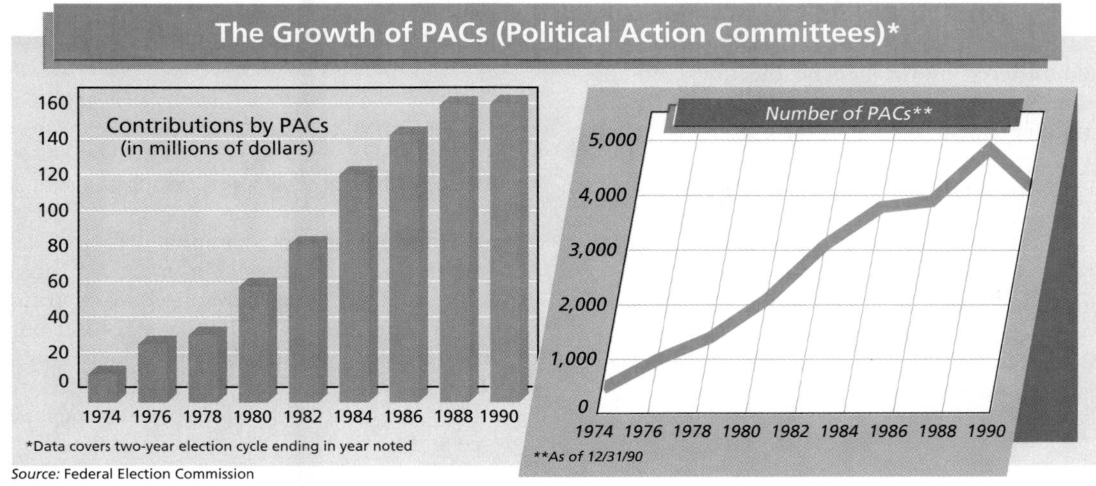

Interpreting Graphs Political action committees, only one source of funds for potential candidates, contribute millions of dollars to elections. Why do you think incumbents—those who seek reelection—receive a large share of PAC money?

Why People Give Campaign donations are a form of political participation. Those who make them do so for a number of reasons. Many small contributors give simply because they believe in a party or a candidate. But most of those who give want something in return. They want access to government, and they hope to get it by helping their "friends" win elections. Among the better demonstrations of the point: Some contributors give to both sides in a contest: heads they win and tails they still win.

Some big donors want appointments to public office, and others want to keep the ones they have. Some long for social recognition. For them, dinner at the White House, meeting with a cabinet official, or knowing the governor on a first-name basis may be enough. Organized labor, business, professional, and various other groups have particular policy aims. They want certain laws passed, changed, or repealed, or certain administrative actions taken.[19]

[19]Among those "various other groups" is organized crime, which, although not a PAC, has an obvious stake in public policy and in those who make it. Large-scale operations in narcotics, prostitution, gambling, loan-sharking, and other illegal activities cannot survive without close ties to at least some public officials.

Regulating Campaign Finance

Congress first began to regulate the use of money in the federal election process in 1907. In that year it became unlawful for any corporation or national bank to make "a money contribution in any election" of candidates for federal office. Since then, Congress has passed several laws to regulate the use of money in presidential and congressional campaigns.

Today, these regulations are found in three detailed laws: the Federal Election Campaign Act (FECA) of 1971, the FECA Amendments of 1974, and the FECA Amendments of 1976.[20]

[20]The earlier federal laws were loosely drawn, not often obeyed, and almost never enforced. The 1971 law replaced them. The 1974 law marked the major legislative response to the Watergate scandal. The 1976 law was passed in direct response to the Supreme Court's decision in *Buckley* v. *Valeo*, 1976. A number of minor changes were made in these laws in 1980.

Congress does not have the power to regulate the use of money in State and local elections. Every State now regulates at least some aspects of campaign finance. A useful summary of current State campaign finance laws can be found in *The Book of the States*, a biennial publication of the Council of State Governments.

Interpreting Graphs The number of political action committees has risen dramatically since 1974. Ask students if they think there is any correlation between the rise in PACs and the imposition of regulations by the Federal Election Commission. (*Possible answer: The limits placed on individual contributions in the 1970s helped create the demand for more funding, which PACs help fill.*)

Caption Answer Incumbents have a better chance for re-election.

ACTIVITY: For Gifted Students

Theme: Systems After students have completed their examination of the system used by the Federal Government to regulate the use of money by candidates for federal office, have them compare this regulating system with the system of other federal regulatory agencies. Using card catalogs, interviews, periodicals, etc., collect notes on federal regulation of the country's communications system, its aviation system, its securities industry, or some other target of federal regulation. Students will note both similarities and differences in the goals and practices of each regulatory system, presenting their findings in the form of a brief oral or written report.

ABCNEWS INTERACTIVE

The following video segments may be used to highlight aspects of money in political campaigns.

Powers of the Congress Guidebook
Chapter 18: Interest Groups, p.94
Chapter 20: Rules for Elections, p.96

See also Enrichment Questions and Activities beginning on page 161.

The Federal Election Commission All federal law dealing with campaign finance is administered by the Federal Election Commission. Set up by Congress in 1974, the FEC is an independent agency in the executive branch. Its six members are appointed by the President, with Senate confirmation.[21]

The laws that the commission enforces cover four broad areas. They (1) require the timely disclosure of campaign finance data, (2) place limits on campaign contributions, (3) place limits on campaign expenditures, and (4) provide public funding for several parts of the presidential election process.

Disclosure Requirements Congress first required the reporting of certain campaign finance information in 1910. Today, the disclosure requirements are very detailed. They are intended to spotlight the place of money in federal campaigns. In fact, the reports that candidates must file with the FEC are so comprehensive that nearly all candidates for federal office find that their campaign organizations must include at least one certified public accountant.

[21]The clerk of the House of Representatives and the secretary of the Senate also serve on the FEC; they are *ex officio*, nonvoting members of the commission.

Union Endorsement The AFL-CIO, represented here by president Lane Kirkland, backed Michael Dukakis in the 1988 presidential election.

No person or group can make a contribution in the name of another. Cash gifts of more than $100 are prohibited. So, too, are contributions from any foreign source. All newspaper, radio, and television ads, circulars, and all other materials promoting a candidate for a federal office must carry the name of the persons or groups that sponsor them.

All contributions to a candidate for federal office must be made through a single campaign committee. Only that committee can spend that candidate's campaign money. All contributions and spending must be closely accounted for by that one committee. Any contribution or loan of more than $200 must be identified by source and by date. So, too, must any spending over $200—by the name of the person or firm to whom payment was made, by date, and by purpose.

Any contribution of more than $5,000 must be reported to the FEC no later than 48 hours after it is received. So, too, must any sum of $1,000 or more received in the last 20 days of a campaign. A cash contribution of more than $100 cannot be accepted under any circumstances.

Any independent committee or person spending more than $250 for a candidate on its own—outside of that candidate's organization—must also file with the FEC. It must report the financial details of its operations and must swear, subject to perjury, that none of its activities was carried on in collusion with that candidate or his or her organization.

Neither corporations nor labor unions can themselves make contributions to federal candidates. But their political action committees can, and do.

The Role of PACs There were only some 600 PACs in 1974. Today, as the graph on page 175 shows, there are more than 4,000—including, for example, COPE (the AFL-CIO's Committee on Political Education), BANKPAC (the American Bankers Association's Political Action Committee), and NEAPAC (the National Education Association's Political Action Committee).

PACs fill their war chests with the voluntary contributions of their members—the executives, stockholders, and employees of a corporation; union members; doctors or dentists or teachers;

Top PAC Contributors to Candidates for Federal Office, 1988

National Association of Realtors	$3,000,000
International Brotherhood of Teamsters	$2,900,000
American Medical Association	$2,300,000
National Education Association	$2,100,000
National Association of Retired Federal Employees	$2,000,000
United Auto Workers	$1,900,000
Association of Trial Lawyers of America	$1,900,000
National Association of Letter Carriers	$1,700,000
American Federation of State, County, and Municipal Employees	$1,600,000
International Association of Machinists and Aerospace Workers	$1,500,000

Source: New York Times, June 5, 1989

Interpreting Tables The top ten highest financial contributors to 1988 candidates are shown in this table. Why is public access to this information important?

those who favor or oppose gun control or abortion; and so on. The PACs pool all these small sums into a single, larger fund. Then they distribute their monies to favored candidates. PACs put more than $170 million into the presidential and congressional campaigns of 1988—and millions more into State and local races.

No PAC may give more than $5,000 to any one federal candidate. But there is no overall limit on PAC giving. Each may contribute up to the $5,000 ceiling to as many different candidates as it chooses.[22]

Limits on Contributions Congress first began to regulate campaign contributions in 1907, when it outlawed donations by corporations and national banks. A similar ban was first applied to unions in 1943. Individual contributions first became subject to regulation in 1939.

Today, no person can give more than $1,000 to any federal candidate in a primary election, and no more than $1,000 to any federal candidate's general election campaign. Also, no person can give more than $5,000 in any year to a political action committee, or $20,000 to a national party committee. The total of any person's contributions to federal candidates and committees must be limited to no more than $25,000 in any one year.

These limits have been in place since 1974. They have finally curbed the long-standing and substantial impact of the "fat-cats" in federal elections.[23] But remember, the limits do not apply to campaigns of candidates for State and local offices.

Limits on Expenditures Congress first began to limit campaign spending in 1925. Most of the spending limitations that are now law apply only to the presidential election process.[24]

[22]An independent PAC, one operating on its own, without the approval of or any connection to a candidate, may spend—not contribute to, but spend on its own for a candidate—an unlimited amount. This point is particularly important in terms of presidential campaign financing.

[23]The limits may seem generous; in fact, they are very tight. Before the limits, many wealthy persons made contributions far larger than those amounts. For example, in 1972, W. Clement Stone, a Chicago insurance executive, gave more than $2 million. Furthermore, inflation has had a dramatic impact on these limits. Today, $1,000 will buy less than half of what it did in 1974.

[24]In *Buckley* v. *Valeo*, 1976, the Supreme Court struck down several restrictions that the 1974 FECA Amendments had placed on spending. The Court held each of them to be contrary to the 1st Amendment's guarantees of freedom of expression. In effect, said the Court, in politics "money is speech." The voided provisions (1) limited House and Senate campaign expenditures, (2) limited how much of their own money candidates could put into their own campaigns, and (3) said no person or group (independent committee) could spend more than $1,000 on behalf of a candidate without that candidate's authorization. The Court also struck down limits on presidential campaign spending, except for candidates who accept FEC subsidies for their campaigns.

Interpreting Tables Have students examine the various kinds of special interests that these contributors represent. Ask students to predict what a group such as the United Auto Workers might hope to achieve by contributing to election campaigns. (*Possible answers: The UAW might hope to promote policies that would favor the success of the auto industry.*) What kind of influence might a group such as the American Medical Association seek? (*Possible answer: The AMA would represent the concerns of physicians.*)

Caption Answer Because contributions can have a direct influence on public policy, citizens must be aware of the amount of influence wielded by these groups.

SPOTLIGHT ON: Economics

Political action committees (PACs) have come to play an increasingly central role in congressional fund-raising over the past decade as the costs of campaigning have soared. In 1986, 82% of the members of the House of Representatives depended on PACs for at least one-third of their campaign money, up from only 28% in 1974. PACs also play an important fund-raising role in the Senate, where the average senator must raise over $10,000 every week of his or her six-year term in order to accumulate the average "war chest" for the next campaign. A successful Senate race cost about $4 million in 1988 and is expected to cost between $6 and $10 million by the mid-90s.

Interpreting Tables Ask students what relationship they see between spending and electoral success. (*In four of six elections in which there was a significant difference, the candidate who spent more won.*)

Caption Answer Public funding of campaigns requires those who accept the funds to obey spending limits.

Provide Guided Practice Have students reread the predictions they made in creating a reading strategy. Ask them how their predictions were different from what they learned under each of the headings.

Provide Independent Practice

TRF **Teacher's Resource File** You may wish to assign the Section 3 Guided Reading and Review from the Unit 2 File, p. 59, to help students master section objective content.

Campaign Spending, Major Party Presidential Candidates, 1952–1988

(in millions of dollars)

Year				
1952	$ 6.61	Eisenhower*	$5.03	Stevenson
1956	7.78	Eisenhower*	5.11	Stevenson
1960	10.13	Nixon	9.80	Kennedy*
1964	16.03	Goldwater	8.76	Johnson*
1968	25.40	Nixon*	11.60	Humphrey
1972	61.40	Nixon*	30.00	McGovern
1976	21.79	Ford	21.80	Carter*
1980	29.19	Reagan*	29.35	Carter
1984	40.40	Reagan*	40.40	Mondale
1988	46.10	Bush*	46.10	Dukakis

*Indicates winner of presidential election.

Source: Adapted from Herbert E. Alexander, ***Financing Politics: Money, Elections and Reform*** (Washington, D.C.: Congressional Quarterly Press, 3rd ed., 1984), p. 7; 1984 and 1988 data from Federal Election Commission.

Interpreting Tables Since 1972, both parties have spent about the same amount of money in their campaigns. Why do you think this has been the case?

Those presidential contenders who accept federal campaign subsidies are subject to limits on their campaign spending. These limits apply in both the preconvention primaries and in the general election campaign.[25]

For 1988, no contender could spend more than $23.05 million in the preconvention period. After the conventions, the Dukakis and Bush campaigns could spend $46.1 million. And each of the major party's national committees could spend no more than $9.22 million in the presidential campaign.

Public Funding of Presidential Campaigns Congress first began to provide for the public funding of presidential campaigns in the Revenue Act of 1971. It broadened sections of that law in 1974 and again in 1976.

The 1971 law set up the Presidential Election Campaign Fund. It also provided that each person who files a federal income tax return can give one dollar of his or her tax payment (two dollars on a joint return) to the fund.

As the law now stands, the monies in the fund are to be used to pay for public subsidies for (1) the preconvention campaigns, (2) national conventions, and (3) presidential election campaigns.[26] The FEC administers the public subsidy process.

Preconvention Period The presidential primary and caucus campaigns are now supported by the private contributions a candidate raises plus the public money he or she receives from the FEC.

To be eligible for the public funds, a presidential hopeful must first get past a rather complicated barrier. He or she must raise at least $100,000 in contributions from individuals (not organizations). That amount must be gathered in $5,000 lots in each of at least 20 States, with each of those lots built from individual donations of not more than $250. This requirement is meant to discourage hopeless and frivolous candidates.

For each contender who passes that test, the FEC will match the first $250 of each individual's donation to that candidate—up to a total of half of the overall limit on primary spending. Thus, in 1988 the FEC gave some contenders as much as $11.5 million because the ceiling was $23.05 million for each candidate. The FEC does not match contributions from PACs or other political organizations.

These subsidies have had several impacts on the nominating process, in both major parties. Among other things, the availability of public money usually prompts more presidential hopefuls to enter the preconvention struggle now than was the case before the subsidies were put in place.

In 1988, all presidential hopefuls, combined, spent more than $210 million in the preconvention period—including more than $65 million in matching funds the FEC gave to six

[25] Through 1988, only one major party aspirant has not accepted federal funds, former Governor John B. Connally of Texas.

[26] The Revenue Act of 1971 also tried to stimulate campaign giving. It allowed a federal income-tax payer to take a credit—a subtraction from the total tax due—of up to $50, or $100 on a joint return, for political contributions. However, at President Reagan's urging, Congress eliminated this tax credit when it passed the Tax Reform Act of 1986. Several States allow State income tax credits or deductions for political contributions.

Enrichment

Have students write a newspaper editorial criticizing or supporting the role of money in the electoral process. The editorial should include discussion of FEC regulations. Ask students to make recommendations for additional governmental regulation (or deregulation) of campaign financing. (Average)

OR

TRF **Teacher's Resource File**
See the Unit 2 File for the Case Study or Contemporary Issues for Chapter 7.

contenders for the Republican nod, and eight for the Democrats' prize.

National Conventions If a major party applies for the money—and both did in 1976, 1980, 1984, and 1988—it automatically receives a grant to pay for its national convention. The two parties each got $9.22 million from the FEC for that purpose in 1988.

Presidential Campaigns Every major party presidential nominee automatically qualifies for a public subsidy to cover the costs of the general election campaign. For 1988, the Bush and the Dukakis campaigns each received $46.1 million from the FEC. A candidate can refuse that money, of course. Should that ever happen, the candidate would be free to raise however much he or she could from private sources.

So far, the nominees of both major parties have taken the public money each time. Because they did so, each automatically (1) could spend no more than the amount of the subsidy and (2) could not accept campaign funds from any other source.[27]

A minor party candidate can also qualify for public funding, but not automatically. To be eligible, the minor party must either (1) have won at least five percent of the popular vote in the last presidential election or (2) win at least that much of the vote in the election.[28]

[27]Independent PACs can spend unlimited sums in any federal campaign; see footnote 22.

Also, federal law neither limits nor requires the reporting of so-called soft money—money raised by State and local party organizations for such party-building activities as voter registration and get-out-the-vote drives. (Political money raised and/or spent subject to FEC regulation is known as hard money.)

[28]In the latter case, the public money would be received after the election and could not possibly help the candidate in that election. Again, many provisions of election law are purposely drawn to discourage minor-party efforts. To this point, two minor-party nominees have received FEC money: Sonia Johnson, the Citizens Party's presidential candidate in 1984, and Lenora Fulani, the New Alliance Party's candidate in 1988. Neither Johnson's subsidy of nearly $200,000, nor Fulani's of nearly $1 million, was for the general election campaign, however. Rather, each of them qualified for the money by meeting the preconvention triggering formula.

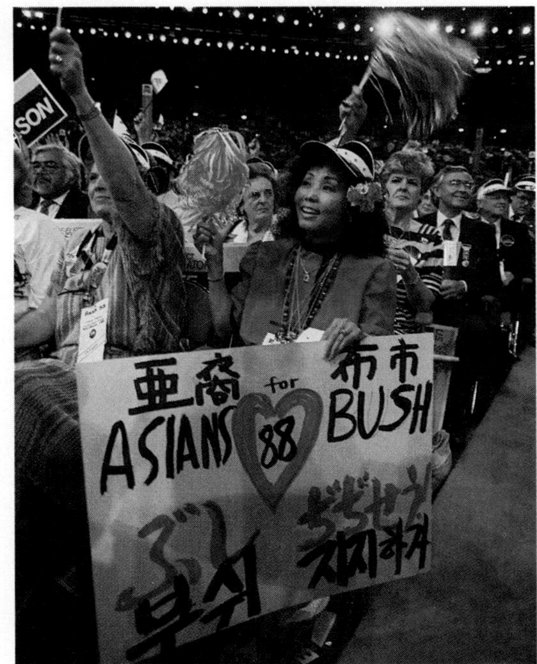

Multicultural Awareness Many delegates to the 1988 national conventions linked political support and ethnic heritage.

Section 3 Review

1. **Define:** political action committee (PAC)
2. What makes money so important to the election process?
3. Why are campaign finances regulated by law?
4. What are the major sources of campaign contributions in American politics?
5. What is the Federal Election Commission?
6. What four major areas of campaign finance are now covered by federal election laws?

Critical Thinking

7. **Distinguishing Fact From Opinion** (p. 19) The text says that "the democratic ideal would be best served if all campaigns were supported by the small contributions of millions of American voters." Explain why you agree or disagree with this statement.

★

Monitor Comprehension

Answers to Section 3 Review
1. "Key Term" is defined on the following page:
a. political action committee (PAC), p. 174
2. Campaigning, especially buying media time, is costly.
3. To ensure that campaigns for certain public offices are not corrupted. **4.** Private contributors and public treasuries. **5.** It is a federal agency that administers federal campaign finance laws. **6.** Federal election laws cover (a) disclosure, (b) limits on contributions, (c) limits on expenditures, and (d) public funding of presidential campaigns. **7.** Answers will vary. Some might say that "democracy" means that the greater the number of supporters of the political process, the closer it is to the democratic ideal.

Closure

Money plays a necessary but problematic role in elections. Candidates obtain money through contributions, their parties, from personal income, political action committees, and in some cases public sources. Today the Federal Election Commission helps ensure that candidates for federal office use money honestly.

In the next chapter, students will read about the role of the media and public opinion in electoral politics.

Assignment Assign Chapter 8, Section 1, pages 185–189, for the next class period.

Reteach

Ask students to discuss ways in which money can be a positive tool in people's lives and ways in which it can be a negative influence. Then have them answer the questions under "Find Out" in the beginning of the section.

Teacher's Resource File
See the Unit 2 File for the Section 3 Quiz on page 60.

TEACHING
Critical Thinking

Recognizing Bias

Objective:

Recognizing bias by distinguishing false from accurate images.

INSTRUCT

As students read the feature, have them list factors that can help them recognize bias. Then, as they read the ads, have them pick out words or phrases that aim to influence the reader's opinion, such as statements that trumpet a candidate's qualifications or an opponent's failures.

Ask students to discuss what effects biased advertising has on the voting public. Which of the ads on page 180 is the most persuasive? Why? (*Opinions will vary. Make sure students explain their answers.*)

Answers 1. (a) Ad A: opponent is unworthy; B: boasts of the candidate's record; C: notes candidate's qualifications. (b) Ad A is most negative. (c) Ad B is most straightforward. **2.** (a) Examples: A: opponent's attendance record; B: candidate's years in office; C: candidate's background. (b) Examples: A: opponent does not care; C: candidate is "successful." (c) All. **3.** (a) No. (b) A and B could be easily checked. (c) In A: opponent is unworthy. In B: voters like the candidate. In C: candidate is qualified. (d) Answers will vary. **4.** Ad A. **5.** (a) All three. (b) A criticizes opponent; B praises the candidate; C praises the candidate and criticizes the opponent.

Recognizing Bias

Recognizing bias means identifying a stated or unstated viewpoint or slant that is designed to promote one set of beliefs over another. As you read and watch political advertising, be on guard for signs of bias. Political advertising might be biased because it does not include all the information the viewer needs to make a good decision. Or, an ad might be biased as a result of a misleading use of statistics or "facts." Follow the steps below to help you identify bias in political advertising.

1. Watch for overly negative or overly positive ads. Every ad tries to persuade. But if an ad makes a candidate sound too good or too bad to be true, the ad is probably unbalanced—and biased. (a) What is the overall message of each ad below? (b) Is the message in any of the ads overwhelmingly positive or negative? (c) Do any of the ads present information in a straightforward manner?

2. Carefully separate fact from opinion. It might be a fact that candidate X is a scientist. But when an ad calls candidate X a "brilliant scientist," the fact becomes an opinion in disguise. When opinions are presented as facts in this way, it may be a sign of bias. Ask yourself (a) What are the facts presented in the ads below? (b) What are the opinions? (c) Are any opinions reported as facts?

3. Evaluate the use and accuracy of facts. Facts and statistics are useful. However, they can also be used unfairly to draw false conclusions. Look at the facts in the ads below. (a) Is there a source given? (b) Can the facts be supported or checked in any way? (c) Are the facts used to support some conclusion? (d) Do the facts actually do so?

4. Consider what information does not appear. Recall that bias is designed to promote one view over another. An ad can achieve this effect by leaving out key information. Do any of the ads include information on any rival candidates?

5. Identify the bias in the advertisements. Now you are ready to evaluate the ads below. (a) Which of these ads are biased? (b) In what ways do they promote one viewpoint over another?

A Do You Know Where Your Senator Is?	B David Lee Offers Solid Leadership	C Maria Hernandez For Governor
During the last session, Senator Jones was absent from the Senate floor 30 percent of the time! Don't you think you deserve a full-time Senator, a Senator who cares about the people of the State? Voters, it's time for a change!	As sheriff, Lee has served the people of Green County for 10 years. Five times, voters have elected Lee as their county's chief law enforcement officer. Why not make it six? Reelect Lee for sheriff.	Leading citizen, successful businesswoman, devoted mother—Hernandez offers the qualities and skills we need to recover from the disastrous reign of the Tax and Spend party. A record of accomplishment, a reputation for integrity, a promise of performance—that's Hernandez for governor!

TRF **Teacher's Resource File**
See the Unit 2 File, p. 61, for the Skill Application to reinforce the skill lesson.

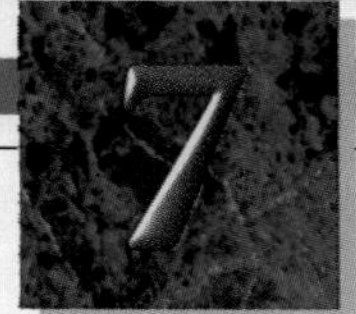

Chapter-in-Brief

Scan all headings, photographs, charts, and other visuals in the chapter before reading the section summaries below.

Section 1 The Nominating Process (pp. 157–165) The nominating process is critically important to democratic government. This is especially true in a two-party system, where voters usually find only two candidates for each office on the general-election ballot. In one-party areas, the nominating contests are regularly more important than the general election.

Five major nominating methods are used in American politics. They are: (1) self-announcement, (2) the caucus, (3) the delegate convention, (4) the direct primary, and (5) petition.

The direct primary, which developed at the turn of the century in reaction to the boss-dominated convention system, is the most widely used nominating method today. It is an intraparty nominating election. It takes two major forms among the States: (1) the open primary, in which any qualified voter may vote, and (2) the closed primary, where only declared party members may vote. Runoff primaries are widely used in the South. Nonpartisan primaries are often used to pick candidates for nonpartisan offices. Presidential primaries are not nominating devices; they are elections held to allow voters to express candidate preferences and/or to select delegates to the national conventions.

Section 2 Elections (pp. 166–171) In the United States, there are more than 500,000 elected offices, most of them at the local level across the country. There is only a limited amount of federal control of the election process. It is highly regulated by State law.

Presidential and congressional elections are held on the Tuesday following the first Monday in November in even-numbered years. Most States hold their general elections at the same time; local elections are generally held then, too, or in the spring. Voting takes place in local precincts and polling places.

Every State now uses the Australian ballot, which is either of the party-column or the office-group type. Long ballots are common in American elections.

Voting machines and electronic vote-counting systems are in wide use among the States. Vote-by-mail elections are being held with increasing frequency at the local level in a number of States.

Section 3 Money and the Election Process (pp. 173–179) Money plays a key role in politics and presents serious problems to democratic government.

Most campaign money comes from private sources. Today, the main sources are: (1) small individual contributors, (2) wealthier persons and families, (3) the candidates themselves, (4) nonparty private organizations—special interest groups and their political action committees (PACs), (5) temporary party organizations, and (6) party fund-raising events. The presidential election process is partially subsidized with public funds; so, too, are some State and local campaigns. Most of those persons and groups who make political contributions want something in return.

Federal campaign finance laws are administered by the Federal Election Commission. Those laws apply only to the federal—that is, to presidential and congressional—elections, not to State and local contests. They (1) require timely disclosure of campaign finance data, (2) limit campaign contributions, (3) limit campaign expenditures, and (4) provide public funding for several aspects of the presidential election process.

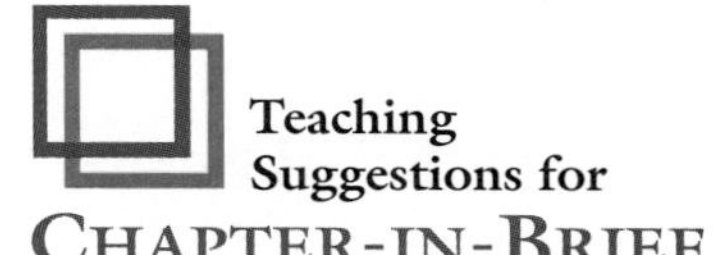

Teaching Suggestions for Chapter-in-Brief

Below are some of the possible uses for the Chapter-in-Brief:

To Preview the Chapter You may want to assign the Chapter-in-Brief page and the Section Outlines from the Teacher Resource File before beginning Chapter 7 to introduce students to the key terms and concepts in each section.

To Review the Chapter When students have completed Chapter 7, you might want to assign the Chapter-in-Brief as a tool for review, along with the Guided Reading and Reviews from the Teacher's Resource File.

To Omit the Chapter If you wish to skip Chapter 7, it may be helpful to assign the Chapter-in-Brief as a review before continuing to another chapter. You may also want to assign the Chapter 7 Test to assess student knowledge of the material. Then specific portions of Chapter 7 may be assigned to students needing reinforcement of "Key Terms" and concepts.

Teacher's Resource File See the Unit 2 File for the following materials:

- Section Outlines, pp. 52, 55, 58.
- Guided Reading and Reviews, pp. 53, 56, 59.
- Chapter 7 Test, pp. 65–67.

Additional Resources

Decisions, Decisions: On the Campaign Trail. Computer software. Tom Snyder Productions, 1991. Apple II/Macintosh/IBM.

Dinkin, Robert J. *Campaigning in America: A History of Election Practice.* Praeger, 1989.

Dunham, P. *Electoral Behavior in the United States.* Prentice Hall, 1991.

Edge of the Arena: Portrait of a Black Candidate. 16mm film. Rediscovery Productions, 1972. Color. 28 min.

Elect I, II, and III. Computer Software. MECC, 1982. Apple II+/IIe/IIc, 48k.

Electing the President. EBDC, 1983. Color. 29 min.

Magleby, David and Candice J. Nelson. *The Money Chase: Congressional Campaign Finance Reform.* Brookings, 1990.

Sherrill, Robert. *Why They Call It Politics.* Harcourt Brace Jovanovich, 5th ed., 1990.

Sorauf, Frank J., *Money in American Elections.* Little, Brown, 1988.

Chapter Review

Vocabulary and Key Terms

nomination (p. 158)
general election (p. 158)
caucus (p. 158)
direct primary (p. 161)
closed primary (p. 162)
open primary (p. 162)
blanket primary (p. 162)
runoff primary (p. 163)
coattail effect (p. 167)
precinct (p. 167)
polling place (p. 167)
ballot (p. 168)
political action committee (PAC) (p. 174)

Matching: *Review the key terms in the list above. If you are not sure of a term's meaning, look up the term and review its definition. Choose a term from the list above that best matches each description.*

1. a group of like-minded persons who meet to choose candidates for office
2. the political arm of a special interest group that seeks to influence the outcome of elections
3. an election held within a political party at which the voters choose candidates who will appear on the ballot in an upcoming general election
4. the phenomenon in which one candidate favorably influences the quantity of the vote cast for other candidates on the ballot from the same party
5. the place where the voters cast their ballots
6. the device by which voters register their choices in an election

True or False: *Determine whether each statement is true or false. If it is true, write "true." If it is false, change the underlined word or words to make the statement true.*

1. In a <u>runoff primary</u>, voters must choose between the two top finishers in an earlier primary election.
2. Because of <u>political action committees</u>, candidates of one party can benefit from the popularity of another candidate from their party on the ballot.
3. In a <u>general election</u>, voters must select the persons they want to hold certain public offices.
4. Each <u>precinct</u> has one polling place.
5. One commonly heard criticism of the blanket primary is that it encourages "raiding."

Word Relationships: *Distinguish between the words in each pair.*

1. caucus/direct primary
2. nomination/general election
3. precinct/polling place
4. blanket primary/closed primary

Main Ideas

Section 1 (pp. 157–165)

1. In what sense does the nominating process have an impact on the voters' right to vote in the American political system?
2. What are the five broad categories that describe the way that most nominations are made?
3. How has the nominating process in American politics changed over the course of American history?
4. Describe the different types of direct primaries that have been used in American politics.

Answers to CHAPTER 7 REVIEW

Vocabulary and Key Terms

Matching
1. caucus
2. political action committee (PAC)
3. direct primary
4. coattail effect
5. polling place
6. ballot

True or False
1. True.
2. False—the correct term is *coattail effect.*
3. True.
4. True.
5. False—the correct term is *open primary.*

Word Relationships
1. A caucus is a meeting of like-minded people who meet to select candidates they will support in an election. A direct primary is an election held within a political party in which voters select candidates for an election.
2. Nomination is the process of naming a candidate in a general election. A general election is the regularly scheduled election at which voters choose among the nominated candidates.
3. A precinct is the smallest unit of election administration. A polling place is where voters cast their ballots; there is one polling place per precinct.
4. A blanket primary is a nominating election in which voters can switch from one party's primary to another on an office-by-office basis. A closed primary is one in which only party members can participate.

Main Ideas

Section 1
1. In most elections, voters have at best two choices: Democrat or Republican. In areas of one-party control, nomination is tantamount to election. **2.** Self-announcement, caucus, convention, direct primary, and petition. **3.** At first, self-announcement and then the caucus were the major means of nomination. In an effort to make the process more democratic, conventions and then primaries emerged as dominant nominating devices. The petition is also used widely today—for example, in local elections. **4.** Closed primaries are those in which only party members may vote. Open primaries are those in which any qualified voter may take part. The blanket primary is a version of the open primary in which voters may switch between the two parties for each office on the ballot.

Section 2
5. Election laws are necessary to ensure fair elections. Fair elections are the foundation of democracy. **6.** Most elections take place at the State level, therefore most election law is State law. **7.** Congress fixes the "time, place, and manner" for the election of members of Congress. Congress also sets the time for the choosing of presidential electors as well as the date electors cast their ballots.

Section 2 (pp. 166–171)

5. What is the overall purpose and importance of election law in the American political process?
6. To what extent are States involved in governing elections?
7. To what extent is the Federal Government involved in governing elections?
8. Describe the basic differences between paper ballots and the other means of casting votes in this country.

Section 3 (pp. 173–179)

9. Briefly describe the role and importance of money in the election process.
10. What are the major sources of campaign funding in American politics?
11. For what basic reasons do individuals contribute money to political candidates?
12. How has the federal government become involved in the regulation of the financing of campaigns?

Critical Thinking

1. **Drawing Conclusions** (p. 19) Use what you have read in the chapter to make an argument for or against the following statement: The nomination of candidates is more important in the American political system than the election of candidates for office.
2. **Distinguishing Fact from Opinion** (p. 19) (a) Do you agree with the text statement that the election of officials such as clerks and coroners is not necessary in a democratic society? (b) Can you make any argument for the election of such public officials?
3. **Recognizing Cause and Effect** (p. 19) (a) How might the changes in laws regarding contributions to candidates have influenced the growth of PACs? (b) Explain why you would favor or oppose legislation that limited the amount candidates could spend on campaigns.

Getting Involved

1. **Writing Your Opinion** Write a letter to the governor of your State in which you express your opinion about public financing for election of State and local officials. Before you start your letter, list the reasons why you think your opinion is correct.

   Begin your letter by stating your purpose in writing. Then, write one paragraph for each of the reasons for your opinion. Review your first draft, checking to see that each paragraph is as persuasive as possible. Try to address any possible criticisms or questions the reader might have about your argument. Conclude the letter by thanking the governor for considering your ideas. Proofread and correct errors. Then prepare a final copy.
2. **Cooperative Activity** As a class, create an overall plan for elections in your State. Divide the class into three committees: One committee can debate the different methods of nominating candidates and determine the means by which minor parties can get candidates on the ballot. Another committee can decide how elections should be administered, including such questions as what public officials should be elected, what kind of ballot to use, and whether or not to allow voting by mail. The third committee should consider issues of campaign finance, such as limits on contributions, spending, public financing, and the role of PACs. When all three committees are finished, work as a class to organize the results into a single plan.
3. **Create a Political Cartoon** Draw a political cartoon that illustrates the role of money in the election process. Try to focus on some humorous or ironic aspect of the issue. Remember that the cartoon can use a combination of words and pictures to make its point.

Congress requires the secret ballot, and it has passed several laws to ensure voting rights. Finally, it has outlawed certain corrupt practices and become involved in the regulation of federal campaign finances.
8. The Australian ballot is the basic form of ballot used today. It is printed at public expense, lists the names of all candidates, is given out only at the polls (one to each voter), and is voted in secret. The original Australian ballot was the office group ballot, in which all candidates for each office are listed together. In the party-column ballot, all the candidates of each party are listed in a single column. Today, many States use voting machines. A very few States are experimenting with vote-by-mail elections.

Section 3

9. Money is vital to the election process. It is used to buy advertising, which is vital to any candidate hoping to win election.
10. Small contributors, wealthier persons, candidates themselves, various groups such as PACs, and temporary organizations set up to support candidates. Money is also raised via party fund-raising events. Also, the Federal Government has become a major source of funds at the federal level. **11.** Many give money because they believe in a candidate. Others hope to win friends in government so they can retain their office, influence policy, or achieve other personal rewards. **12.** The Federal Government limits how candidates for federal office can raise and spend money. The Federal Government also requires candidates to publicly disclose campaign finance information. Finally, the government provides funding for presidential elections.

Critical Thinking

1. For: Students may suggest that the nominating process is often the only time during which there is a real contest involving multiple choices. Against: Students may say that it is during the general election that the officeholder is chosen.
2. Answers will vary. Make sure students explain their answers.
3. Groups not allowed to give money formed PACs as a way of being able to contribute campaign funds. For example, the AFL-CIO, a labor union, is not allowed to give money, but COPE, the AFL-CIO's Committee on Political Education, is allowed to give money.

Getting Involved

1–3. Answers and results will vary, but students should demonstrate an understanding of the concepts in this chapter.

Chapter 8 Resources

In the Teacher's Resource File
The following materials are found in the Teacher's Resource File box.

Instructional Support: Unit 2 File

For the Section
Outlines, pp. 71, 74, 77
Guided Reading and Review, pp. 72, 75, 78
Quizzes, pp. 73, 76, 79

For the Chapter
Skill Application, p. 80
Case Study on Contemporary Issues, pp. 81–83
Chapter Test, p. 84–86
Additional Test Questions, pp. 87–89

Enrichment Support Files

Supreme Court Case, p. 6
Participatory Government Activities, pp. 20–27, 42–43, 44–67

Computer Test Bank and Assessment

Transparency Package, pp. 8, 33

Election Kit, pp. 15–17

Chapter 8 Focus

Introduce the Chapter Tell students that in this chapter they will learn how public opinion is formed, how it is measured, and the role that the mass media play in shaping it. Read with students the Chapter Preview and Objectives.

Writing Activity Direct students' attention to "Describe." Have students identify an opinion they share with those in their households and an opinion they share with a friend. Ask students to write a brief explanation of how family and friends may have influenced their opinions.

Motivate for Learning Direct students' attention to "Predict." Discuss specific examples of television being used in political campaigns or other current events. Ask what unique effect television might have. Ask whether television has ever helped them form opinions.

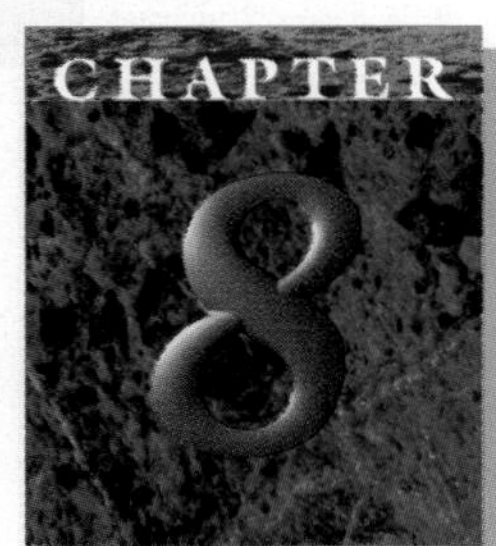

Mass Media and Public Opinion

Chapter Preview

For many bleak and frightening months of 1991, Americans were mesmerized by the sights and sounds of a war taking place thousands of miles away in the Persian Gulf. Who among us did not witness the sight of military men and women leaving family behind? Who did not hear the wail of warning sirens as another SCUD missile approached? Who did not see the sickening smoke blackening the skies of Kuwait or the surrender of Iraq's armies? Who did not share in the welcome accorded the returning troops? The power of the media—television in particular—to inform has never been more apparent.

But, the media does more than inform the public of unfolding events at home and abroad. It plays a very large role in forming the thoughts and opinions of the American public. This chapter is about the place of public opinion in American politics and the immense power of the mass media.

Before you read this chapter:

- **Describe** how family and friends have an effect on forming your opinions.
- **Predict** how political campaigning has changed since the development of television.

As you read, focus on the main objective for each section. Understand:

1. Public opinion and its role in American politics.
2. The means by which opinions are expressed and measured.
3. The impact of the mass media on politics.

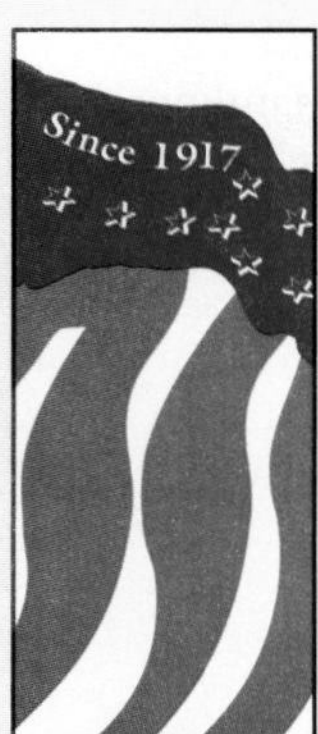

Magruder's American Government: *A Witness to Change* by William A. McClenaghan

It does not seem likely that textbooks have had much of an effect on television. But television has certainly had an extraordinary impact on textbooks—including this one. Some of that impact can be seen in terms of the content of this book. Television became a major force in American politics in the 1960s—and every edition of *American Government* since then has paid increasing attention to that medium, and to other mass media, as well.

But television's largest, most visible impact on textbooks has been on their format—on their overall shape and appearance. Television, and especially color television, has forced textbooks to become much more physically attractive, much more appealing than they were before the advent of the "tube." Comparing earlier editions of this book, and especially those before the 1960s, with this edition and other recent ones, is much like comparing early black-and-white television with what you regularly see on television screens today.

Media Blitz The enormity of the media presence in today's society brings to bear the question: To what extent is American public opinion shaped by the media?

1 The Formation of Public Opinion

Find Out:

- What is public opinion?
- What factors influence the making of public opinion?

Key Terms

public opinion, opinion leader

Do you like broccoli? Blue jeans? Spring vacation? Sports? What about cold weather? Old cars?

You have an opinion on each of those things, of course. In some cases, those opinions may be very strong and very important to you. But each of those opinions is your own view, your private opinion. As you will see, none of them is the kind of opinion discussed in this section—that is, public opinion.

What Is Public Opinion?

Few terms in American politics are more widely used, and less well understood, than the term *public opinion*. It appears regularly in newspapers and magazines and you hear it frequently on radio and television.

Quite often, the phrase is used in a way that suggests that all or most of the American people hold the same view on some public matter. Thus, time and again, politicians say that "the people" want such and such, television commentators tell us that "the public" favors this or opposes that, and so on.

In fact, there are very few matters in which all or nearly all of "the people" think alike. "The public" holds many different and often conflicting views on nearly every public question.

To understand what public opinion is, you must recognize this important point: Public opinion is a complex collection of the opinions of many different persons. It is the sum total of all of their views. It is *not* the single and undivided view of some mass mind.

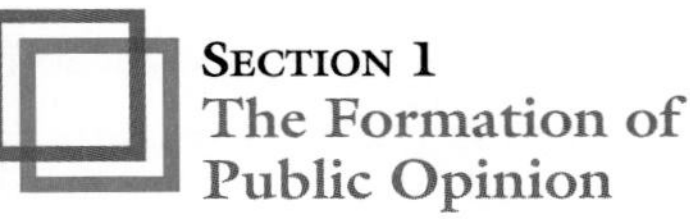

SECTION 1
The Formation of Public Opinion

FOCUS

Teacher's Resource File See the Unit 2 File, p. 71, for the Section 1 Outline.

Objectives

8.1 Define public opinion.
8.2 Outline the major factors that shape public opinion.

Bellringer Activity Before you begin the section, hold up newspaper headlines dealing with controversial issues that you have cut from the front page. Ask students to write down their opinion on each issue. Explore the reasons for their responses. Where do students think their opinions originated? Do they reach them regardless of outside influences, or do outside influences such as the family and the school help students form opinions?

State the Purpose In Section 1, students will learn what public opinion is and which factors influence it the most, including the family, schools, opinion leaders, and the mass media.

ABCNEWS INTERACTIVE

The following video segments may be used to highlight aspects of public opinion.

POWERS OF THE CONGRESS GUIDEBOOK
Chapter 18: Interest Groups, p. 94

POWERS OF THE PRESIDENT GUIDEBOOK
Chapter 8: Interest Groups, p. 10
Chapter 11: The Election Campaign, p. 15

Vocabulary

Point out "Key Terms" on page 185. Review with students the definition of the term *opinion leader*. (*Any person who, for any reason, has a more than usual influence on the views of others.*) Then ask them to name some people they believe are opinion leaders in their community or school. LEP

Reading Strategy: Graphic Organizer

Have students place the phrase *Public Opinion* on the center of a sheet of paper. Ask students to skim the subheadings of this section to identify the factors that shape public opinion—family, schools, opinion leaders, and mass media—and to place those factors around the phrase *Public Opinion* on their papers. Also ask students to think of any other factors that influence public opinion.

INSTRUCT

Analyze To explore the concepts raised in Section 1, have students generate a list of current public issues such as raising the legal driving age or lowering the legal age for consuming alcoholic beverages. Have students indicate which of the "shapers" of public opinion have influenced them the most on each of the issues: household members, friends, school, opinion leaders, or the mass media. Select one issue from the list and ask students to consider as a class or in small groups: Which group(s) of the population would probably support this issue and why? Which groups would probably oppose it? Why? What other factors, such as race, class, geographic location, and sex, often influence people's opinions on public issues?

Interpreting Graphs and Cartoons Point out to students the similarities between the positions of the radical left and the reactionary right. Ask: What characteristics do they share? (*They both favor extreme change.*)

Caption Answer The cartoonist is pointing out that, as the text states, "there are many publics in the United States."

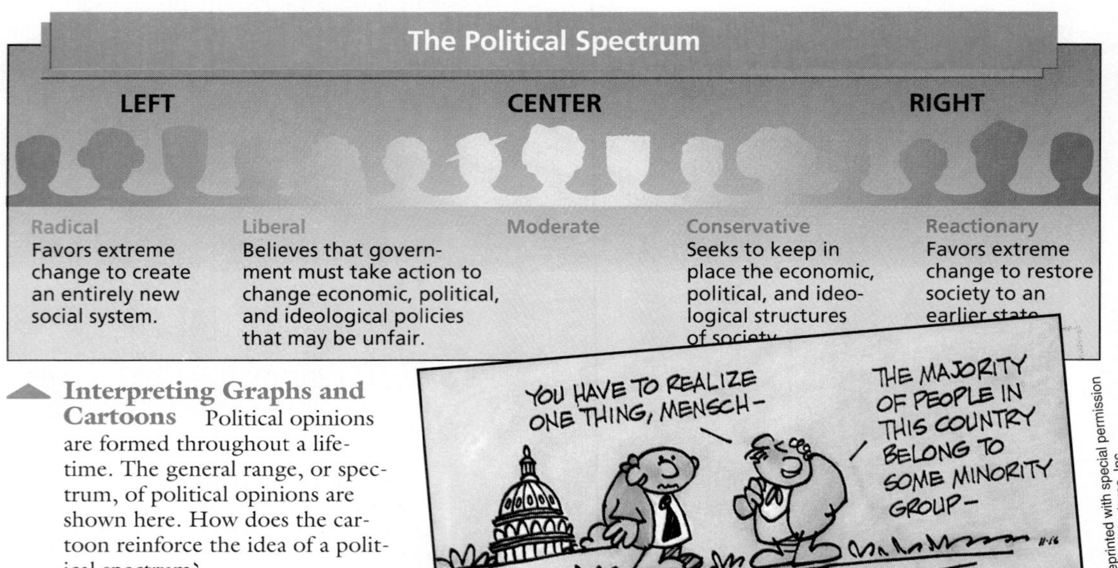
The Political Spectrum
LEFT
CENTER
RIGHT
Radical
Favors extreme change to create an entirely new social system.
Liberal
Believes that government must take action to change economic, political, and ideological policies that may be unfair.
Moderate
Conservative
Seeks to keep in place the economic, political, and ideological structures
Reactionary
Favors extreme change to restore society to an
YOU HAVE TO REALIZE ONE THING, MENSCH—
THE MAJORITY OF PEOPLE IN THIS COUNTRY BELONG TO SOME MINORITY GROUP—
small society
By Brickman
Reprinted with special permission of King Features, Inc.

Interpreting Graphs and Cartoons Political opinions are formed throughout a lifetime. The general range, or spectrum, of political opinions are shown here. How does the cartoon reinforce the idea of a political spectrum?

There are many publics in the United States—in fact, an uncountable number of them. Each public is made up of all those persons who hold the same view on some particular public question. Each group of people with a differing point of view is a separate public with regard to that matter.

To illustrate: All persons who think that Congress should establish a national health-insurance program belong to the public that holds that view. All who believe that the President is doing an excellent job as chief executive, or that capital punishment should be abolished, or that prayers should be permitted in the public schools are members of the separate publics with those particular opinions. Clearly, many persons belong to more than one of those 1.a
publics; but almost certainly only a very few belong to all four of them.

This point is crucial, too: In its proper sense, public opinion includes only those views that relate to matters of public affairs—to politics, to public issues, and to the making of public policies. To be an opinion in the public sense, a view must involve something of general concern, something of interest to a significant portion of the people as a whole.

Of course, the people as a whole are interested in many things—in rock groups and symphony orchestras, the New York Yankees and the Dallas Cowboys, candy bars and green vegetables, and a great deal more. People have opinions on each of these things, views that are sometimes loosely called "public opinion." But, again, in its proper sense, public opinion involves only those views that people hold on such things as parties and candidates, taxes, unemployment, welfare programs, national defense, foreign policy, and so on.

Definition Clearly, public opinion is so complex that it cannot be readily defined. But, for purposes of this book, **public opinion** can be described this way: Those attitudes held by a significant number of persons on matters of government and politics.

As suggested, you can better understand the term in the plural—that is, as public opinions, the opinions of publics. Or, to put it another way, public opinion is made up of expressed group attitudes.

SPOTLIGHT ON: Roots of Democracy

Public opinion—and how to shape it—has been an issue for hundreds of years. Jean-Jacques Rousseau (1712–1778), a towering figure of the French Enlightenment, was among the first political philosophers to devote serious attention to problems of "public opinion." In his major work, *The Social Contract*, Rousseau introduced the concept of the "general will," to which government was obliged to respond—while safeguarding the rights of the majority. "Whoever makes it his business to give laws to a people," he wrote, "must know how to sway opinions, and through them govern the passions of men."

A view must be expressed in order to be an opinion in the public sense. Unless an opinion is expressed in some way, it cannot be known by others. If others cannot know the opinion, it cannot be identified with any public.

Factors That Shape Public Opinion

No one is born with a set of attitudes about government and politics. Instead, each person learns his or her political opinions, and does so in a lifelong "classroom" and from many different "teachers." In other words, public opinion is formed out of a very complex process, and the factors involved in it are almost without number.

You have already considered much of this—in Chapter 6 with regard to voting behavior. In effect, that extensive look at why people vote as they do amounted to an extensive look at how public opinions form.

There, remember, you read about the process by which each person acquires political opinions as the process of political socialization. That complex process begins in early childhood and continues on through a person's lifetime. It involves all of the experiences and relationships that lead people to see the political world and to act in it as they do.[1]

There are many different agents of political socialization at work in the opinion-shaping process. Again, you looked at these agents at some length in Chapter 6: age, race, income, occupation, residence, group affiliations, and many others. But two of them—the family and education—have such a vital impact that they deserve another look here.

The Family Most parents do not think of themselves as agents of political socialization, nor do the other members of most families. They are, nonetheless, and very importantly so.

Children first see the political world from within the family and through the family's eyes. They begin to learn about politics much as they begin to learn about most other things—from what their parents have to say, from the stories that their older brothers and sisters bring home from school, from watching television with the family, and so on.

Most of what smaller children learn in the family setting are not really political opinions. Clearly, toddlers are not concerned with the wisdom of spending billions of dollars on Star Wars antimissile defense system or the pros and cons of the monetary policies of the Federal Reserve Board. Children do pick up some basic attitudes, however, and with those attitudes, a basic slant toward such things as authority and rules of behavior, property, neighbors, people of other racial or religious groups, and the like. In short, children lay some important foundations on which they will later build their political opinions.

A large number of scholarly studies report what common sense also suggests. The strong

"From the Mouths of Babes" Participating in public demonstrations—such as this anti-fur protest—helps socialize people to politics at a very early age.

[1]The concept of socialization comes from the fields of sociology and psychology. It is used to describe all of the ways in which a society transforms individuals into members of that society.

Provide Guided Practice Select one or two well-known political figures (Cuomo, Bush, Quayle, Clinton, etc.) and poll class members on their opinions of these figures. On the board, use the following scale to quantify each person's opinion: highly favorable, favorable, no opinion, unfavorable, highly unfavorable. After the political figures are rated, ask interviewees to account for their opinions. How much of this response can be attributed to the family, the school, the media? Other influences?

Provide Independent Practice

TRF **Teacher's Resource File** You may wish to assign Section 1 Guided Reading and Review, Unit 2 File, p. 72, to help students master section objective content.

Activity: Teaching Heterogeneous Groups

To guide students to a better understanding of the factors that shape public opinion, ask them to make a list of ten things that they learned to do from birth to age ten. The list should include such things as "learned to talk," "learned to tie my shoes," "learned to read," etc. Ask students where they learned to do these things in order to bring students to the realization that they learned most of these skills at home or in school. Then point out that, in the same way, we begin to form our first political opinions through the family and school.

Enrichment

Have students analyze the opinion page(s) of newspapers and identify the public issues the articles, cartoons, and letters raise. Students may use any recent edition of a local newspaper or a nationally distributed paper such as the *Washington Post* or the *New York Times.* Then have students write one or two paragraphs in which they choose the piece that they think would be most effective in shaping the opinions of others and explain why. (Easy)

Interpreting Graphs Ask students if they can think of any drawbacks to TV as a means of conveying factual information.

Caption Answer TV reaches people in their homes and is a more passive activity than reading.

Monitor Comprehension

Answers to Section 1 Review
1. "Key Terms" are defined on the following pages:
a. public opinion, p. 186
b. opinion leader, p. 188
2. Government and politics. **3.** Family, schools, opinion leaders, the mass media, age, race, income, occupation, and residence. **4.** The process by which each person acquires political opinions. **5.** Children spend most of their formative years close to families and schools. **6.** Television, radio, film, books, magazines, and newspapers. **7.** Some students may say that the family should share this responsibility.

TRF **Teacher's Resource File** See the Unit 2 File, p. 73, for the Section 1 quiz.

Closure

Remind students that public opinion refers to opinions on matters of public affairs. Individuals develop public opinions through contact with the family, schools, opinion leaders, and the mass media. In the next section, students will learn how public opinion is measured.

Assignment Assign Section 2, pp. 189–196, for the next class period.

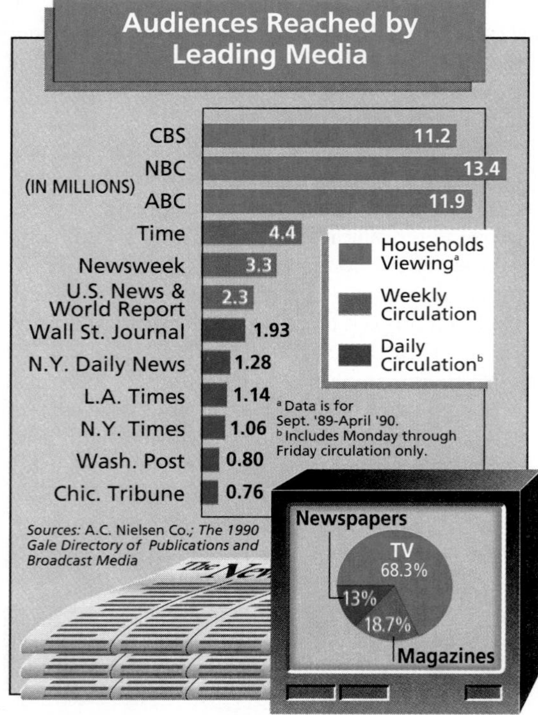

Interpreting Graphs This graph shows the influence of the mass media on the lives of Americans. Why does television reach a larger audience than print media?

influence the family has on the development of political opinions is largely a result of the near monopoly the family has on the child in his or her earliest, most impressionable years. Those studies also show that:

> "The orientations acquired in early childhood tend to be the most intensely and permanently held of all political views. They serve as the base on which all later political learning is built. . . . Adult political behavior is the logical extension of values, knowledge, and identification formed during childhood and youth."[2]

The Schools The start of formal schooling marks the first break in the force of family influence. For the first time children become regularly involved in activities outside the home.

From the first day, schools teach children the values of the American political system. They purposely work to indoctrinate the young and train them to become "good citizens." Schoolchildren salute the flag, recite the Pledge of Allegiance, and sing patriotic songs. They learn about George Washington, Susan B. Anthony, Martin Luther King, Jr., and other great Americans. From the early grades on, they pick up growing amounts of specific political knowledge, and they begin to form political opinions. In high school, they are often required to take a course in American government and to read books such as this one.

School involves much more than books and classes, of course. It is a complex bundle of experiences and a place where a good deal of informal learning occurs. School is a place where students encounter other students—and find that some of those other persons are like themselves, and some of them are different.

1.b **Opinion Leaders** The views expressed by certain people—opinion leaders—also bear heavily on public opinion. An **opinion leader** is any person who, for any reason, has a more than usual influence on the views of others.

Many opinion leaders hold public office. Some write for newspapers or magazines or broadcast their opinions on radio or television. Others are prominent in business, labor, agriculture, civic organizations, and so on. Many are in professional occupations—doctors, lawyers, teachers, ministers, and the like—and have contact with fairly large numbers of people on a regular basis. Many others are active members of their neighborhood or church, or have leadership roles in their local community.

Whoever they may be, opinion leaders are persons to whom others listen and from whom others draw ideas and convictions. Whatever their political, economic, or social standing or outlook may be, opinion leaders play a significant role in the formation of public opinion.

The Mass Media Obviously the mass media—which includes television, radio, film,

[2]Richard Dawson, Kenneth Previtt, and Karen Dawson, *Political Socialization,* 2nd ed. (Boston: Little, Brown, 1977), page 48.

Reteach

Have students keep a log of all the public or political issues that are referred to as they are watching one evening of television, excluding news broadcasts. Point out that political issues may be referred to in comedy or drama shows, talk shows, public interest messages, paid political announcements, and even commercials. Have students compare their findings in class.

Activity: Cooperative Learning

Time: Two class periods **Activity:** Respond to views of an opinion leader. **Grouping:** Groups of three to four students. **Purpose:** Have group members identify opinion leaders, for example, a local radio broadcaster, a national political figure, or a newspaper columnist. Have the group discuss their reactions to that person's views on a particular topic. Have the group recorder keep track of the discussion by listing supporting and opposing arguments from the group members. **Roles:** Assign the following roles: discussion leader, recorder, spokesperson. **Outcome:** Have the spokesperson summarize for the class the views expressed by the opinion leader and the responses of group members to those views. Invite comments and discussion.

books, magazines, and newspapers—have a large influence on the formation of public opinion. Take this as but one indication of that fact: The Census Bureau reports that there is at least one television set in 98 percent of the nation's 95 million households. There are two or more sets in 60 million homes and millions more in many other places. Most of those sets are turned on for at least seven hours a day—for a mind-boggling total of a billion hours a day.

A Mix of Factors No one factor, by itself, shapes any person's opinion on any matter. Some play a larger role than others, however. Thus, in addition to family and education, occupation and race are usually much more significant than, say, gender or place of residence.

But this is not always the case. On the question of national health insurance, for example, the job a person has—how well-paying it is, whether it includes coverage by a private health-insurance plan, and so on—will almost certainly have a greater impact on that person's view than his or her sex or where he or she happens to live. On the other hand, if the question involves equal pay for women, then sex will almost certainly loom much larger in the opinion-making mix. In short, the relative weight of each of the many factors that influence public opinion depends a great deal on the nature of the particular issue involved.

Section 1 Review

1. **Define:** public opinion, opinion leader
2. Public opinion includes views on what kinds of matters?
3. What factors shape public opinion?
4. What is political socialization?
5. What makes the family and schools such important agents in the opinion-shaping process?
6. What constitutes the mass media?

Critical Thinking

7. **Recognizing Ideologies** (p. 19) The text states that schools aim to socialize students so that they become "good citizens." Should this be a function of the educational system?

2 The Measurement of Public Opinion

Find Out:

- How is public opinion measured?
- For what reason is public opinion measured?

Key Terms:

mandate, interest group, public opinion poll, straw vote, sample, random sample, quota sample

How many times have you heard this phrase: "According to a recent poll. . ."? Probably more than you can count. It becomes especially common in the months leading up to an important election. If public policy is to be based on public opinion, it has to be possible to find the answers to these questions: What is the content of public opinion on a particular issue? How many people share a given view on that matter? How firmly do they hold that view? That is to say, it must be possible to "measure" public opinion—and, as you will see in this section, it is.

The Challenge of Measuring Public Opinion

The general content of public opinion on some matter—what different groups of people say they think about it—can be found by consulting the means by which people usually express opinions in American society. Those means are both many and varied. They include voting, lobbying, books, pamphlets, magazine and newspaper articles, editorial comments in the press and on radio and television, paid advertisements, letters to editors and public officials, and so on.

These and other means of expression are the devices through which the general shape of public opinion becomes known. But, usually, the means by which a view is expressed tells little—and often nothing reliable—about the size of the group that holds that opinion or how strongly it is held. In the American political system, these questions are vital ones. To find

Section 2
The Measurement of Public Opinion

Focus

Teacher's Resource File
See the Unit 2 File, p. 74, for the Section 2 Outline.

Objectives

8.3 Explain how public opinion is measured.
8.4 Analyze the reasons for measuring public opinion.

Bellringer Activity Choose a current public issue in your school or community and ask four students in the class to state their opinions on the issue. Then draw an illogical conclusion from their responses, such as the following: "So X percent of the students are opposed." When students disagree with your conclusion, have them discuss their reasoning.

State the Purpose Public opinion can be measured through several different means, including elections, interest groups, the media, personal contacts, and polls. Section 2 examines the value of each of these indicators and outlines the steps involved in scientific polling. The section also analyzes the ways in which public opinion does not determine public policy in the United States.

ABCNEWS INTERACTIVE

The following video segment may be used to highlight aspects of public opinion.

POWERS OF THE CONGRESS GUIDEBOOK
Chapter 18: Interest Groups, p. 94

Vocabulary

Point out "Key Terms" on page 189. Ask students which terms they think relate to scientific polling techniques? (*Sample, random sample, quota sample.*)

Reading Strategy: Problem-Solving

Ask students to consider individually or in small groups the following problem: You are considering running for public office. One of your biggest concerns is how the public would react to your candidacy. How might you go about gathering information to make a decision as to whether or not to run?

INSTRUCT

Explain/Analyze On the board, write in a column the first letters of the five methods of measuring public opinion discussed in this section: *E*lections, *I*nterest Groups, *M*edia, *P*ersonal Contacts, and *P*olls. Call on volunteers to supply the five methods as you write them on the board.

Ask students to identify a public issue. Which of the ways to measure public opinion would be most useful in gathering information on the issue which they have identified?

Refer students back to the "Bellringer Activity." Ask students to consider the five steps of polling and to specify in what ways your "poll" in that activity fell short of being a high-quality scientific poll.

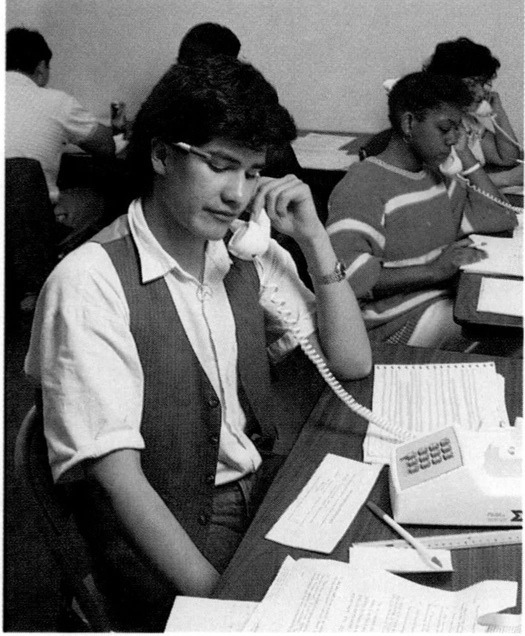

Measuring Public Opinion by Phone A telephone poll, conducted at the Texas Democratic headquarters, helps predict support for gubernatorial candidate Ann Richards.

answers to these questions you must make some effort to measure public opinion.

Measurement Through Elections In a democracy the voice of the people is supposed to express itself through the ballot box. Election results are very often said to be indicators of public opinion. The votes cast for rival candidates are regularly taken as evidences of the people's approval or rejection of the stands taken by those candidates and their parties. A party and its victorious candidates regularly claim to have received a mandate to carry out their campaign promises. In American politics a
1.a **mandate** refers to the instructions or commands a constituency gives to its elected officials.[3]

In fact, however, election results are seldom an accurate measure of public opinion. Voters make the choices they do in elections for any of several reasons, as you have seen. Very often, those choices have little or nothing to do with the candidates' stands on public questions. Then, too, candidates often disagree with some of the planks of their party's platform. And, as you have also seen, candidates and parties often express their positions in broad, vague terms.

In short, much of what you have read about voting behavior, and about the nature of parties, adds up to this: Elections are, at best, only useful indicators of public opinion. To call the typical election a mandate for much of anything other than a general direction in public policy is to be on very shaky ground.[4]

Measurement Through Interest Groups Interest groups are treated at length in the next
1.b chapter. For now, remember that **interest groups** are private organizations whose members share certain views and work to shape the making and content of public policy. These organizations are also very aptly known as pressure groups and special interest groups.

Interest groups are a chief means by which public opinion is made known. They present their views—exert their pressures—through their lobbyists, by letters, telephone calls, in political campaigns, and by a number of other methods. In dealing with them, however, public officials often find it difficult to determine two things: How many people does an interest group really represent? And just how strongly do those people hold the views that an organization says they do?

Measurement Through the Media Earlier you read some very impressive numbers about television. Those huge numbers help describe the place of the media in the opinion process; and you will read more of those numbers later. But, here, recognize the point that the media are a gauge for assessing public opinion.

[3]The term *mandate* comes from the Latin *mandare*—literally, "to place in one's hand or to commit to one's charge."

[4]Initiative and referendum elections, at which voters approve or reject specific measures, are elections in which public opinion is registered much more directly on specific public policy questions. See Chapter 24, Section 1.

Enrichment

Have students locate a public opinion poll, including the questions that were asked and the responses given. Then have students critique the questions as to their validity, based on the information given in step 3 of scientific polling on page 193. Finally, have students look at the results of the poll in light of their critique of the questions. Do they think the wording of the questions may have influenced the poll? Each individual should write one page in which they present their group's critique. (Challenging)

The media are frequently described as "mirrors" as well as "molders" of opinion. It is often said that the views expressed in newspaper editorials, syndicated columns, news magazines, television commentaries, and so on, are fairly good indicators of public opinion. The media are *not* very accurate mirrors, as you will soon see.

Measurement Through Personal Contacts

Most public officials have frequent and wide-ranging contacts in many different forms with large numbers of people. In each of these contacts, they try to read the public's mind. In fact, their jobs demand that they do so.

Members of Congress receive bags of mail, stacks of telegrams, and hundreds of phone calls. Many of them make frequent trips "to keep in touch with the folks back home." Top administration figures are often on the road, selling the President's programs and sensing the people's reactions. Even the President does some of this, with speaking trips to different parts of the country.

Governors, State legislators, mayors, and other officials also have any number of contacts with the public. These officials encounter the public in their offices, in public meetings, at social gatherings, at ball games, and so on.

Can public officials find "the voice of the people" in all of those contacts? Many can and do, and often with surprising accuracy. But some public officials cannot. They fall into an ever-present trap: They find only what they want to find—only those views that support and agree with their own.

Polls—the Best Measure of Public Opinion

The public's opinions are best measured by public opinion polls. A **public opinion poll** is a 1.c device that attempts to collect information about public opinion by asking people questions.[5] The more accurate polls are based on scientific polling techniques.

[5]The word *poll* comes from the old Teutonic word *polle*, meaning the top or crown of the head, the part that shows when heads are counted.

Public opinion polls have existed in this country for more than a century. Until the 1930s, however, they were far from scientific. Most earlier polling efforts were of the **straw** 1.d **vote** variety. That is, they were polls that sought to read the public's mind simply by asking the same question of a large number of people. Straw votes are still fairly common. Newspapers often run "clip-out and mail-in" ballots; radio talk shows ask listeners to respond to questions with phone calls; and so on.

The straw-vote technique is highly unreliable, however. It rests on the false assumption that a relatively large number of responses will give a fairly accurate picture of the public's views on a given question. But nothing in the process ensures that those who do respond will in fact represent a reasonably accurate cross section of the total population. The straw vote emphasizes the quantity rather than the quality of the sample to which its question is posed.

The most famous of all straw-polling mishaps took place in 1936. A periodical called the *Literary Digest* mailed postcard ballots to more than 10 million people and received answers from more than 2,376,000 of them. Based on that huge return, the magazine confidently predicted the outcome of the presidential election that year. It said that Governor Alfred Landon, the Republican nominee, would easily defeat incumbent Franklin Roosevelt. Instead, Roosevelt won

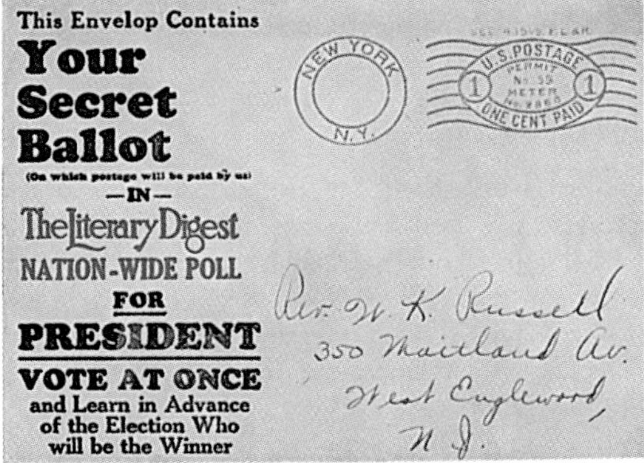

Choose Your Sample Carefully! More than two million people responded to this 1936 *Literary Digest* survey. Why do you think the poll was proven to be misleading?

Provide Guided Practice
Have students identify several school or public issues about which students can be polled. Then have students discuss how each step in the polling process could be implemented to measure opinion on those issues.

Provide Independent Practice
TRF **Teacher's Resource File** You may wish to assign the Section 2 Guided Reading and Review, Unit 2 File, p. 75, to help students master section objective content.

Caption Answer Because the sample was not randomly selected, it did not truly represent all eligible voters.

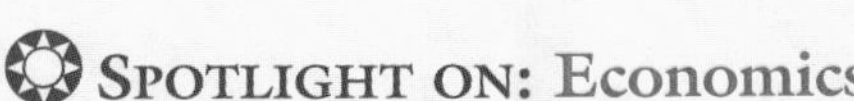

SPOTLIGHT ON: Economics
To help elected representatives in Washington "keep in touch with the folks back home," the federal budget for fiscal year 1992 has set aside almost 129 million taxpayer dollars for "expenses necessary for official mail costs" for members of Congress. The House budgeted $93,361,000 of that total—an average of $214,622.98 for every member. On the Senate side, the 1992 budget appropriates $35.5 million for official mail costs, an average of $355,000 per member.

Interpreting Political Cartoons Have students compare this cartoon to the quote from George Gallup in "Voices on Government" on page 193. Ask students if the cartoon and quote relay the same or differing messages. (*The cartoon and quote seem to be relaying conflicting information, with the cartoon downplaying the importance of answering polls and the quote emphasizing the importance of polls to the democratic process.*)

Caption Answer By implying that many eligible voters confuse voting and participating in government with merely participating in polls.

By Luckovich for the Times-Picayune, New Orleans

Interpreting Political Cartoons Public opinion polls are now followed closely by millions of Americans. How does the cartoon convey this as a *negative* phenomenon?

in a landslide. He captured more than 60 percent of the popular vote and carried every State but Maine and Vermont.

The *Digest* had drawn its sample on an altogether faulty basis: from automobile registration lists and from telephone directories. The *Digest* had failed to consider that in the mid-Depression year of 1936, millions of people could not afford to own cars or have private telephones. In short, its poll failed to reach most of the vast pool of the poor and unemployed, millions of blue-collar workers, and most of the ethnic minorities in the country. Those were the very segments of the population from which FDR and the Democrats drew their greatest support.[6]

Scientific Polling Serious efforts to take the public's pulse on a scientific basis date from the mid-1930s. They began with the work of such early pollsters as George Gallup and Elmo Roper. The techniques that they and others have developed since then have reached a highly sophisticated level.

There are now more than 1,000 national and regional polling organizations in this country. Many of them do mostly commercial work. That is, they tap the public's preferences on everything from toothpastes and headache remedies to television shows and thousands of other things. However, at least 200 of these polling outfits poll the political preferences of the American people. Among the best known of the national pollsters today are the Gallup Organization (the Gallup Poll) and Louis Harris and Associates (the Harris Survey).

The Polling Process Scientific poll-taking is an extremely complex process that can best be described in five basic steps. In their efforts to discover and report public opinion, pollsters must (1) define the universe to be surveyed; (2) construct a sample; (3) prepare valid questions; (4) select and control the means by which the poll will be taken; and (5) report their findings to the public.

Step 1: DEFINE THE UNIVERSE TO BE SURVEYED. The ***universe*** is a term that means the whole population that the poll aims to measure, the group whose opinions the poll will seek to discover. That universe can be all voters in Chicago, or every high school student in North Carolina, or all Republicans in New England, or all Democrats in Georgia, or all Catholic women over age 35 in the United States, and so on.

Step 2: CONSTRUCT A REPRESENTATIVE SAMPLE. If a poll's universe is very small—say, the 25 members of a high school class—the best way to find out what that universe thinks about some issue would be to poll every one of them. In most cases, however, it is not possible to interview a complete universe. This is certainly the case in matters of public policy that affect all the people in the nation. There are simply too many people in that universe to talk to. So, the
1.e poll-taker must select a **sample**—a representative slice of the total universe.

Most professional pollsters now draw a random sample, also called a probability sample. In a random sample, the poll-taker interviews a certain number of randomly selected people who live in a certain number of randomly
1.f selected places. In short, **random sample** is a

[6]The magazine had predicted the winner of each of the three previous presidential elections, but its failure to do so in 1936 was so colossal that it ceased publication not long thereafter.

sample in which each member of the universe and each geographic area within it have a mathematically equal chance of being included within the sample.

Most major national polls interview just over 1,500 people to represent the universe of the nation's entire adult population—some 185 million people.

How can the views of so few people represent the opinions of so many? The answer to that question lies in the mathematical law of probability. Flip a coin 1,000 times. The law of probability says that, given an honest coin and an honest flip, heads will come up 500 times. Furthermore, the law states that the results of this test will be the same—no matter how often you perform it, and no matter what kind of coin you use. The law of probability is regularly applied in a great many situations: by insurance companies to compute life expectancies, by a food inspector to check the quality of a farmer's truckload of beans, and by others who "play the odds"—including pollsters who draw random samples.

In short, if the sample is of sufficient size and is properly selected at random from the entire universe, the law of probability says that the result will be accurate to within a small and predictable margin of error. Mathematicians tell us that a properly drawn random sample of some 1,500 people will reflect the opinions of all the nation's adult population and will be accurate to within a margin of plus or minus (±) 3 percent.[7]

Some pollsters do use a less complicated, but less reliable, sampling method. They draw a **quota sample**, a sample deliberately constructed to reflect several of the major characteristics of the universe. For example, if 51.3 percent of that overall group is female, 17.5 percent of it is African American, and so on, then the sample will be made up of 51.3 percent females, 17.5 percent African Americans, and so on. Of course, most of the people in the sample will belong to more than one of the categories on which it is built. This fact
1.g explains why such a sample is less reliable than random samples.

Step 3: PREPARE VALID QUESTIONS. The way in which questions are worded is a very important matter. Wording can affect the reliability of any poll. For example, most people will probably say "yes" to a question put this way: "Should local taxes be reduced?" But many of those same persons will also give the same answer to this question: "Should the city's police force be increased to fight the rising tide of crime in our community?" Yet, expanding the police force almost certainly would require more local tax dollars. Responsible pollsters

[7]Pollsters acknowledge that it is impossible to construct a sample that would be an absolutely accurate reflection of a large universe—hence, the allowance for error. A margin of ±3 percent means a spread of 6 percentage points, of course. To bring the sampling error down from ± 3 percent to ± 1 percent, the size of the sample would have to be 9,500 people. The time and money needed to interview that big a sample make that a practical impossibility.

VOICES *on Government*

On the Value of Public Opinion Polls

"As students, scholars, and the general public gain a better understanding of polls, they will have a greater appreciation of the service polls can perform in a democracy. . . . [M]odern polls are the chief hope of lifting government to a higher level, by showing that the public supports the reforms that will make this possible, by providing a *modus operandi* for testing new ideas. . . . Polls can help make government more efficient and responsive; . . . they can make this a truer democracy."

George Gallup,
founder of the Gallup Poll

SPOTLIGHT ON: Multiculturalism

Since 1958, in an annual survey of voter attitudes on race, the Gallup organization has asked white Americans whether they would elect an African-American President. In 1958, only 35% responded that they would. By the late 1980s, the number rose to over 80%. In the 1988 Democratic primaries, Jesse Jackson, the party's first African-American presidential candidate, received a plurality of the vote in seven States and the District of Columbia, won 29% of the popular vote (6.7 million votes) and 27% (1,123 of 3,300) of the delegates. In total among a field of seven candidates, Jackson received 15% of the white vote.

Interpreting Charts Point out that this is a succinct summary of the five points outlined in the section, and that it would be helpful when studying for a quiz or exam.

Caption Answer Because public opinion—what the people think—is one of the most important factors in determining government policy.

acknowledge these issues and phrase their questions very carefully. They purposely try not to use "loaded" words, terms that are difficult to understand, and questions that are worded in a way that will tend to shape the answers that are given to them.

Step 4: SELECT AND CONTROL THE POLLING PROCESS. In part, this point relates to how the pollsters communicate with the sample. Most polls are taken face-to-face. That is, the interviewers question the respondents in person. However, pollsters conduct an increasing number of surveys by telephone, and others by mail. Professional pollsters see both advantages and drawbacks in each of these approaches. They all agree, however, that whichever technique they use to gather information, they must employ the same technique in the questioning of all of the respondents in a sample.

The interview itself is a very sensitive point in the process. The poll-taker's appearance, dress, apparent attitude, or tone of voice in asking questions can influence the replies he or she receives—and thus alter the validity of the poll's results. If the questions are not carefully worded, some of the respondent's replies may be snap judgments or emotional reactions. Others may be of the sort that the person being interviewed thinks "ought" to be given; or they may be answers that the respondent thinks will please—or offend—the interviewer. Thus, polling organizations try to hire and train their interviewing staffs very carefully.

Step 5: REPORT THEIR FINDINGS. Polls, whether scientific or not, try to measure the attitudes of people. To be of any real value, however, someone must analyze and report the results. Scientific polling organizations collect huge amounts of raw data today. In order to handle these data, computers and other electronic hardware have become routine parts of the processes by which pollsters tabulate and then interpret their data, draw their conclusions, and then publish their findings.

How to Take a Poll

1. Define the population to be polled. Decide what group you need to poll in order to find the answer to your question. For example, if you are seeking to learn what percentage of registered voters in Lexington, North Carolina actually voted, then it would not be sensible to poll anyone who did not register to vote.

2. Construct a sample. You may choose to construct either a *random sample*, in which you randomly choose the members of the group to be polled, or a *quota sample*, in which you poll a representative number of people from each subgroup in your survey.

3. Prepare valid questions. Try to ask objective questions, questions that can be answered in one word, and questions that do not include terms that are difficult to understand.

4. Select and control the means by which the poll will be taken. Decide whether you will conduct an in-person interview, a telephone interview, or a mail interview. Be sure to interview all members of the group in the same manner. Choose interviewers who are careful not to influence the responses by their dress, attitude, or tone of voice.

5. Report your findings. Make a table of the results of your poll and then analyze this data to determine the answer to your original question.

Interpreting Charts The most important steps to taking a poll are outlined here. Why do you think measuring public opinion is an acceptable part of the democratic process?

Evaluation of Polls

How good are the polls? On balance, the major national polls are fairly reliable. So, too, are most of the regional surveys around the country. Still, they are far from perfect. Fortunately, most responsible pollsters themselves are quite aware of that fact. Many of them are involved in continuing efforts to refine every aspect of the polling process to acknowledge the limits of their polls.

For example, pollsters know that they have difficulty measuring these qualities of the opinions they report: intensity, stability, and relevance. Intensity is the strength of feeling with which an opinion is held. Stability (or fluidity) is the relative permanence or changeableness of an opinion. Relevance (or salience) is how

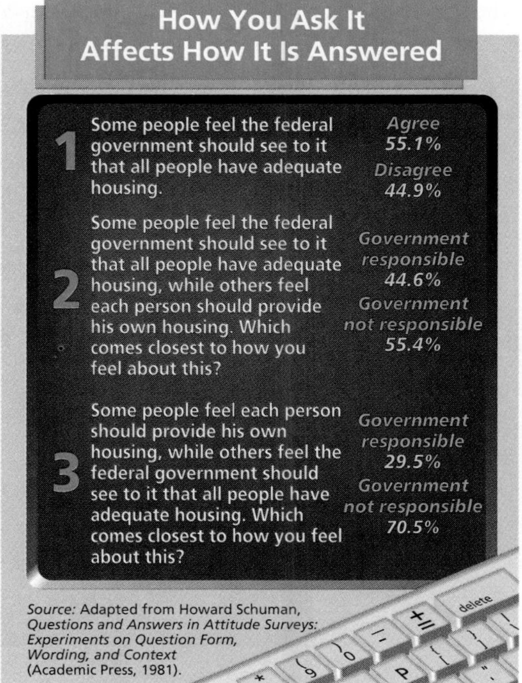

How You Ask It Affects How It Is Answered

1	Some people feel the federal government should see to it that all people have adequate housing.	Agree 55.1% Disagree 44.9%
2	Some people feel the federal government should see to it that all people have adequate housing, while others feel each person should provide his own housing. Which comes closest to how you feel about this?	Government responsible 44.6% Government not responsible 55.4%
3	Some people feel each person should provide his own housing, while others feel the federal government should see to it that all people have adequate housing. Which comes closest to how you feel about this?	Government responsible 29.5% Government not responsible 70.5%

Source: Adapted from Howard Schuman, *Questions and Answers in Attitude Surveys: Experiments on Question Form, Wording, and Context* (Academic Press, 1981).

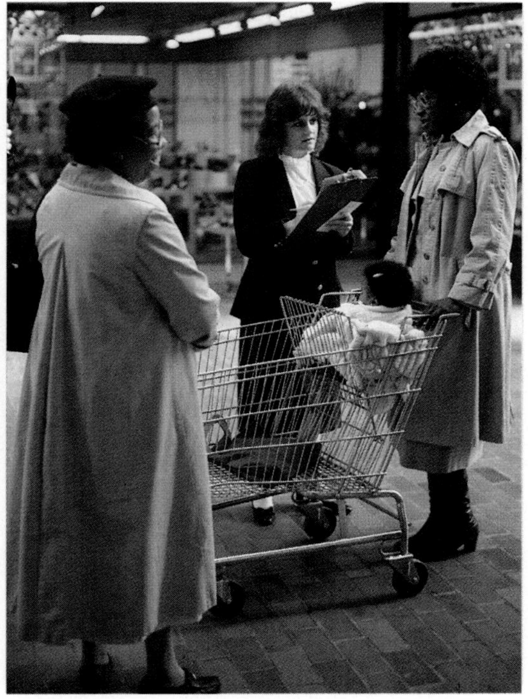

Interpreting Tables This table demonstrates the importance of how each question on a poll is worded. Which question above is worded in the least biased manner?

important a particular opinion is to the person who holds it.

Polls and pollsters are sometimes said to shape the opinions they are supposed to measure. Some critics of the polls say that in an election, for example, pollsters often create a "bandwagon effect." That is, some voters, wanting to be with the winner, jump on the bandwagon of the candidate who is ahead in the polls. The charge is most often leveled against those polls that appear as syndicated columns in many newspapers.

In spite of these criticisms, it is clear that scientific polls are the most useful tools there are for the difficult task of measuring public opinion. Though they may not be always or precisely accurate, they do offer reasonably reliable guides to public thought. Moreover, they help to focus attention on public questions and to stimulate discussion of them.

Limits on the Force of Public Opinion

More than a century ago, Lord Bryce, a very wise Englishman, described government in the United States as "government by public opinion."[8] Clearly, the energy devoted to the measuring of public opinion suggests something of its powerful role in American politics. However, Lord Bryce's opinion is true only if that description is understood to mean that public opinion is the major, but by no means the only, influence on public policy in this country. Its force is tempered by a number of other factors—for example, by interest groups, which you will read about in the next chapter.

Most importantly, however, remember this vital point: Our system of constitutional govern-

[8]James Bryce, *The American Commonwealth* (New York: Macmillan, 1888), vol. 2, page 251.

Interpreting Tables Help students understand that example 1 simply makes one statement and asks respondents if they agree or disagree. In examples 2 and 3, two options are offered, and respondents are asked which option they agree with more.

Caption Answer The first example is least biased. Examples 2 and 3 suggest that the two options they offer are mutually exclusive, which they need not be, and that there is no third (or fourth) option that someone might find preferable. Note, too, that the option offered first in each of these cases receives the most favorable response.

MONITOR COMPREHENSION

Answers to Section 2 Review
1. "Key Terms" are defined on the following pages:
- **a.** mandate, p. 190
- **b.** interest group, p. 190
- **c.** public opinion poll, p. 191
- **d.** straw vote, p. 191
- **e.** sample, p. 192
- **f.** random sample, p. 192
- **g.** quota sample, p. 193

2. To see how people feel about a particular subject and to enable leaders to base public policy on public opinion.
3. Scientific polls. **4.** Elections, interest groups, the media, and personal contacts. **5.** Wording can affect the answer and thus the reliability of a poll.
6. Pollsters (a) have difficulty measuring intensity, stability, and relevance of the opinions they report; and (b) are said to shape the opinions they are supposed to measure. **7.** An opposition candidate may be inspired to work harder; people who do not like the leader in the polls might be encouraged to go vote against him.

Teacher's Resource File See the Unit 2 File, p. 76, for the Section 2 Quiz.

CLOSURE

Remind students that measuring public opinion can help educate the public about important issues. In the next section, students will learn about the forms of mass media and analyze their impact on politics.

Assignment Assign Section 3, pp. 198–205, for the next class period.

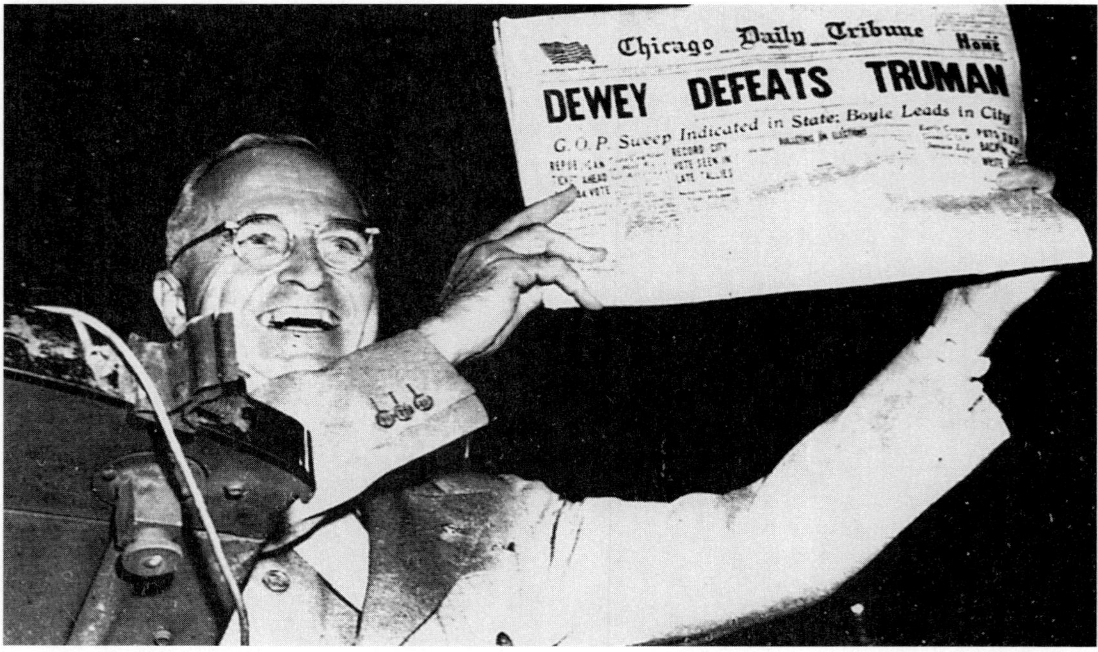

Poorly Predicted An elated Harry Truman holds up a newspaper headline wrongly announcing his defeat in 1948. Pollsters and others had predicted a landslide victory for Thomas E. Dewey in that election.

ment is not designed to give free and unrestricted play to public opinion—and especially not to majority opinion. In particular, the doctrines of separation of powers and of checks and balances and the constitutional guarantees of civil rights and liberties are intended to protect minority interests against the excesses of majority views and actions.

Finally, note that polls are not elections, or substitutes for elections. It is when faced with a ballot that voters must decide what is important and what is not. Voters must be able to tell the difference between opinions and concrete information, and should know the difference between personalities and platforms. Democracy is more than a simple measurement of opinion. Democracy is also about making careful choices among leaders and their positions on certain issues, and among the governmental actions that may follow. Ideally, democracy is the thoughtful participation of citizens in the political process.

Section 2 Review

1. **Define:** mandate, interest group, public opinion poll, straw vote, sample, random sample, quota sample
2. For what reasons is public opinion measured?
3. What device best measures public opinion?
4. What are the other major means of measuring public opinion?
5. Why is the wording of questions a critically important fact in the scientific polling process?
6. Name two shortcomings of scientific polling.

Critical Thinking

7. **Determining Relevance** (p. 19) What are some good reasons for knowing which candidate in an upcoming election is ahead in the polls?

★

SPOTLIGHT ON: Political Talk

"The people," said Thomas Jefferson, "may be safely trusted to hear everything true and false, and to form a correct judgment between them." Jefferson's legendary faith in a well-informed public was lost on most of his contemporaries. But Alexander Hamilton, Jefferson's bitter rival, objected most adamantly to the Republican tendency to bend to public opinion. "The voice of the people has been said to be the voice of God," Hamilton once wrote, adding "this maxim, however . . . is not true in fact. The people are turbulent and changing; they seldom judge or determine right." On another occasion, he stated his concern more succinctly, declaring: "The people, sir, is a great beast."

Reteach

Ask students to assume the role of an aide to a United States senator. The senator has asked them to prepare a memo recommending how to vote on a recent bill. Have each student write a memo explaining how they depended on the five measurements of public opinion to reach their recommendation. Be sure students refer to each of the five measures: elections, interest groups, media, personal contacts, and polls.

Debating Key Issues

Should the Government Have the Power to Restrict the Press?

New York Times v. *United States*

The United States experienced varying degrees of public unrest over this country's involvement in Vietnam from the early 1960s to 1973. Political scientist Daniel Ellsberg was vehemently against U.S. involvement. In 1971, Ellsberg stole and copied a Pentagon study known as the Pentagon Papers in which he had participated four years earlier. Ellsberg delivered the document to the *New York Times.* The newspaper began to publish excerpts from the study on June 13, 1971, causing outrage among many American citizens.

The document revealed that the American people and Congress had been deliberately deceived about United States presence and purposes in Vietnam. The administration of President Lyndon Johnson had made all major decisions to escalate the war months before they were put into action, and these decisions were independent of actual circumstances in Southeast Asia.

President Johnson was succeeded by Richard Nixon in 1968. When the *Times* began to publish excerpts from the Pentagon Papers, Nixon's administration quickly sought to stop it. On June 15, the U.S. district court issued a temporary restraining order against the *Times* after the Federal Government claimed that the publication of the document threatened national security. The *Times* petitioned the Supreme Court on June 24, and only six days later, the Court delivered its ruling.

Review the following evidence and arguments presented to the United States Supreme Court:

Arguments for *New York Times*

1. The 1st Amendment states that "Congress shall make no law . . . abridging the freedom of speech or of the press."
2. One of the few restraints on executive power in matters of national defense is a knowledgeable population. The press must be free to inform the American people.
3. The government has in no way shown that the publication of the Pentagon Papers would have dangerous consequences.

Arguments for United States

1. The 1st Amendment's guarantee of freedom of the press is not absolute when cases of national security are involved.
2. There must be a balance between the rights of the free press and the powers of the President to restrict this right when national security is involved.
3. If the press is allowed total freedom to print such documents, there is a danger that tragic consequences could result.

Getting Involved

1. Identify the constitutional grounds on which each side based its arguments.
2. Debate the opposing viewpoints in this case.
3. Predict how you think the Supreme Court ruled in this case and why. Then refer to the Supreme Court Glossary that begins on page 764 to read about the decision. Discuss the impact of the Court's decision on executive power and executive abuses.

TEACHING
Debating Key Issues

New York Times v. *United States:*
Should the Government Have the Power to Restrict the Press?

Objective
Use problem-solving and decision-making skills to predict the effects of a Supreme Court ruling.

INSTRUCT

Before students read the feature, elicit answers to the question posed in the title. Have students explain their responses.

After students read the Supreme Court's decision, have them write one or two paragraphs about the consequences of this Supreme Court decision.

SUPREME COURT DECISION

The Supreme Court refused to uphold the injunction against the publication, observing that ". . . it is the obligation of the government to prove that actual harm to the nation's security would be caused by the publication. . . ." The decision limited "prior restraint" of the press by government agencies claiming that secrecy was essential to "national security."

Teacher's Resource File
See the Supreme Court Cases file, p. 6, for an activity that extends coverage of this case.

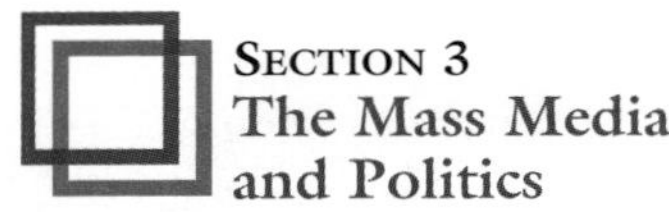

SECTION 3
The Mass Media and Politics

FOCUS

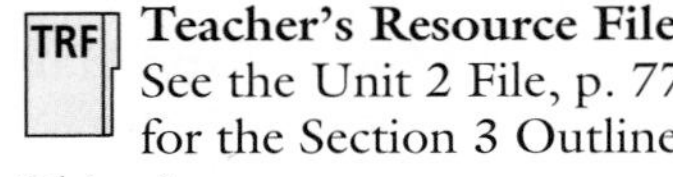

Teacher's Resource File See the Unit 2 File, p. 77, for the Section 3 Outline.

Objectives

8.5 Outline the major forms of mass media.

8.6 Analyze the impact of mass media on politics.

Bellringer Activity Ask students to indicate with thumbs up or thumbs down whether or not they do the following: Read the newspaper, listen to news on the radio, watch TV news, read news magazines, know who the opinion leaders in the mass media are. You may wish to have students verbally identify opinion leaders in the media such as Tom Brokaw, Peter Jennings, Leslie Stahl, etc.

State the Purpose The mass media play a major role in the political life of the United States. In Section 3, students will learn how the mass media provide information and opinion, shape the public agenda, and provide candidates with essential tools for political campaigns. Students will also explore the limits of media influence.

3 The Mass Media and Politics

Find Out:

- What are the major forms of mass media?
- What is mass media's impact on politics?

Key Terms:

medium, mass media, sound bite

How much television do you watch each day? Little or none? Two hours a day? Three hours? More? However much you watch, you no doubt know that your peers spend a great deal of time in front of the tube. Studies show that by the time the average person graduates from high school today, he or she has spent 11,000 hours in classrooms and 15,000 hours watching television.

Television has an extraordinary impact on the lives of everyone in this country. And, as you will see in this section, so do the other elements of the mass media.

An Overview of the Mass Media

A **medium** is a means of communication; it 1.a transmits some kind of information. And media is the plural of medium. The **mass media** 1.b include those means of communication that can reach large, widely dispersed audiences—masses of people—simultaneously.

Four major mass media are particularly important in American politics. Ranked in terms of impact, they are television, newspapers, radio, and magazines. Other media—books, films, and audiocassettes, for example—play a lesser role. So, too, do computers—though their communicating capabilities are becoming increasingly important.

The mass media are not a part of government; and, unlike political parties and interest groups, they do not exist primarily to influence government. They are, nonetheless, an important force in politics. Along with entertainment, the media provide people with political information. They do so directly when they report the news—in a newscast or in the news columns of a paper, for example. They also provide a large amount of political information less directly—for example, in radio and television programs, newspaper stories, and magazine articles that deal with such public topics as crime, nuclear power, or the federal deficit. Either way, people acquire most of the information they know about government and politics from the various forms of media.

Television

Politics and television have gone hand in hand since the new technology first appeared. The first public demonstration of television occurred at the New York World's Fair in 1939. President Franklin Roosevelt opened the fair on camera, and viewers watched him on tiny five- and seven-inch screens. World War II interrupted the development of the new medium, but it began to become generally available in the late 1940s. Television boomed in the 1950s. The first transcontinental broadcast came in 1951, when President Harry Truman, speaking in Washington, addressed the delegates attending the Japanese Peace Treaty Conference in San Francisco.

Today, television is all-pervasive. As you read earlier, there is at least one television set in 98 percent of the nation's 95 million households. In fact, there are more homes in this country with a television set than with indoor plumbing facilities.

The more than 1,400 television stations include more than 1,000 commercial outlets and over 300 public broadcasters. Three major national networks have dominated television from its infancy: the Columbia Broadcasting System (CBS), the American Broadcasting Company (ABC), and the National Broadcasting Company (NBC). Those three giants furnish about 90 percent of the programming of some 700 local stations. That programming accounts for about 65 percent of all television viewing time today.

The major networks' audience share has been declining in recent years, however. The main challenges to their domination have come from three sources: (1) several independent broadcast-

Reading Strategy: Relating to Topic

Choose a public issue that has been in the news for at least several days recently. Have students briefly write what they know about the issue. Then have them specify which elements they learned from one or more of the mass media. Discuss with students the various kinds of mass media.

Vocabulary

Point out "Key Terms" on page 198. Direct students' attention to the term *sound bite.* What do students think it means out of context? What do they think it means in the context of radio and television? LEP

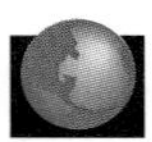

Global Awareness

Access to Media in Selected Countries

	U.S.A.	Japan	Indonesia	Bangladesh	Nigeria	Mexico	Italy	Czechoslovakia	Chile	Nicaragua
Population in millions	245.4	122.4	175.0	109.6	105.5	84.9	57.3	15.6	12.7	3.6
Number of daily newspapers	1,687	125	55	47	22	312	70	27	38	4
Circulation per 1000	268	562	18	6	18	120	96	298	96	82
Radios per 1000	2,126	824	118	40	162	197	697	577	335	257
TV sets per 1000	813	585	39	3.1	5.6	117	385	281	164	59

Source: United Nations' World Media Handbook, 1990

Interpreting Tables: Multicultural Awareness Access to media varies considerably from country to country. From the data on the graph, which country appears to be least influenced by television? Which country sells the most newspapers per thousand people?

ing groups—for example, the Fox Network; (2) cable broadcasters[9]—for example, Turner Broadcasting, and especially its Cable News Network (CNN); and (3) the Public Broadcasting System (PBS) and its more than 300 local stations.

Some of the most highly touted presentations on television—a Super Bowl game, for example, or a debate between the major parties' presidential candidates—are seen by as many as 100 million people. From 15 to 40 million watch the more popular sitcoms. Each of the three major network's nightly news programs draw 12 to 14 million viewers. Some 6 million places, including nearly two-thirds of the nation's households, are now hooked up to cable systems.

Television replaced newspapers as the principal source of political information for a majority of the American people in the early 1960s. In fact, television is now the principal source for an estimated 80 percent of the population.

Newspapers

The first regularly published newspaper in America, the *Boston News-Letter*, appeared in 1704.[10] Other papers soon followed, in Boston

[9]C-SPAN, the Cable-Satellite Public Affairs Network, has begun to attract a significant audience. C-SPAN presents both live and taped coverage of a broad and growing range of public events—including major floor debates and committee hearings in Congress, presidential and other press conferences, and speeches by notable public figures.

[10]The world's first newspaper was almost certainly *Tsing Pao*, a court journal in Beijing. Press historians believe that its first issues, printed from stone blocks, were published some time in the 6th century; its last issue appeared in 1935.

INSTRUCT

Analyze/Discuss Bring to class the front pages from two or more newspapers from the same day. Have students identify the issues addressed on each front page. Compare how many issues are treated by both newspapers. You also may wish to compare the depth of the information relayed and the tone of the articles on the same issue.

Ask students to identify the other forms of mass media besides newspapers. Identify examples of how television, magazines, and the radio have recently influenced the public agenda and how they are involved in electoral politics.

Have students individually or in groups create a public service announcement focusing on an issue they feel should concern the public. You may wish to bring in samples for students to examine. Explain to students that they should pay attention to the setting (if TV) and the wording of their pieces.

Interpreting Tables Lead a discussion on the following topic: Since the United States leads the countries listed in access to both radio and TV, does it follow that the American people are the most well informed? Have students consider how media is used in this country.

Caption Answer Bangladesh; Japan.

Teacher's Resource File
See the Participatory Government Activities file, pp. 20–27, for an activity that supports this section.

SPOTLIGHT ON: Global Awareness
Unlike the largely privately owned and commercially operated broadcast media in the United States, the major medium in Britain, the British Broadcasting Corporation, is state-owned and operated. The BBC operates two television stations and four radio channels, and, until the 1950s, held a monopoly on all broadcasting in Britain. BBC's news division broadcasts around the world in 40 languages, 24 hours a day. Publicly owned, BBC news is known for its editorial impartiality, integrity, and independence. Parliament has the authority to veto a BBC broadcast, but it has never exercised that prerogative.

ABCNEWS INTERACTIVE

The following video segments may be used to highlight aspects of public opinion.

POWERS OF THE CONGRESS GUIDEBOOK
Chapter 19: Congress and the Media, p. 95

POWERS OF THE SUPREME COURT GUIDEBOOK
Chapter 9: Freedom of the Press, p. 13

POWERS OF THE PRESIDENT GUIDEBOOK
Chapter 11: The Election, p. 15

and then in Philadelphia, New York, Annapolis, and elsewhere. By 1775, 35 newspapers were being published in the colonies. All of them were weekly papers, and they were printed on one sheet that was folded to make four pages. The nation's first daily newspaper, the *Philadelphia Evening Post and Daily Advertiser*, began publication in 1783.

Those first papers carried mostly political news and several spurred the colonists to revolution. They carried the news of independence and the text of the Declaration to people throughout the colonies. Thomas Jefferson marked the vital role of the press in the earliest years of the nation when, in 1787, he wrote to a friend:

> "Were it left to me to decide whether you should have a government without newspapers, or newspapers without a government, I should not hesitate a moment to prefer the latter."

The 1st Amendment, added to the Constitution in 1791, made the same point with its guarantee of the freedom of the press.

Today, more than 10,000 newspapers are published in the United States—including nearly 1,800 dailies, some 570 semiweeklies, more than 7,600 weeklies, and several hundred foreign-language papers. Those publications have a combined circulation of more than 150 million copies per issue. Surveys indicate that some 95 million people, just about half of the nation's adult population, read a newspaper every day; and they spend, on the average, a half-hour doing so.

Contrary to a widespread belief, the number of daily papers in the United States has not declined in recent years. In fact, just about as many dailies are published today as were published 40 years ago. The total circulation of

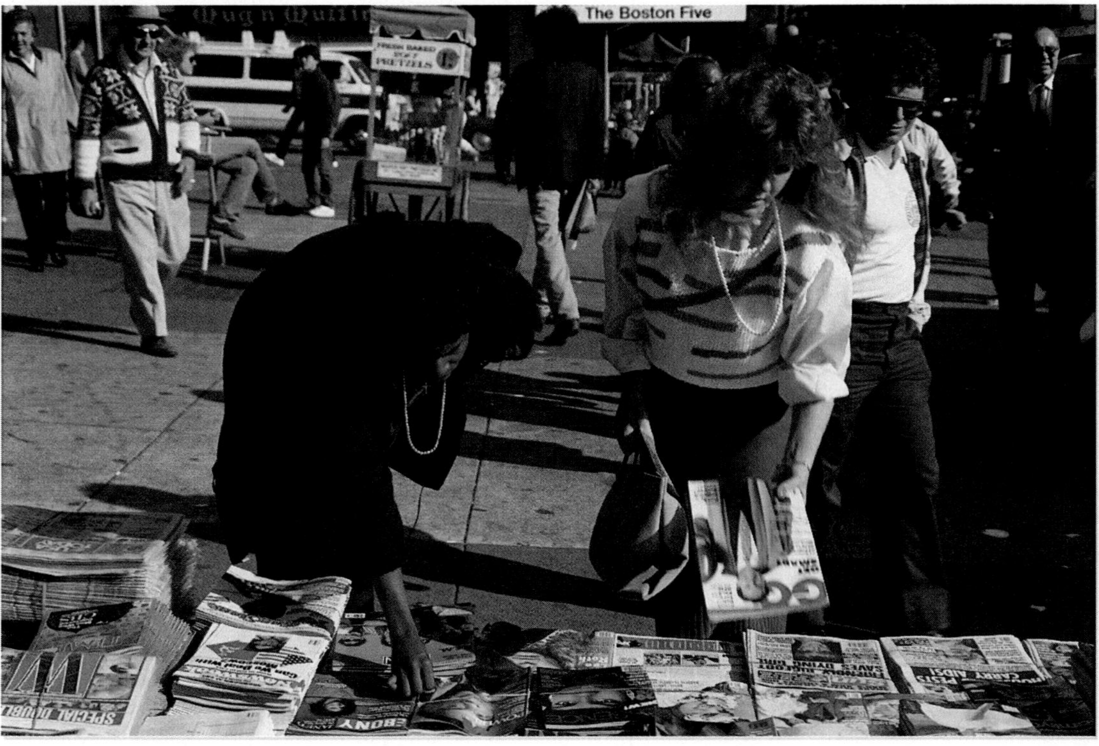

Newsstand Variety This newsstand in Boston displays the wide selection of print materials readily available in most American cities. Many of these publications provide the public with political information.

those papers has gone up about 20 percent in that period—to over 63 million copies today. There has been a marked decline, however, in the number of cities with competing newspapers. Most of the largest cities do have at least two major papers today, but a growing number of other cities do not.

Newspapers rank second only to television as the people's primary source of information about government and politics. Most papers cover stories in much greater depth than television does, and many try to present various points of view in their editorial sections. Those newspapers that have the most substantial reputations and national influence today include the *New York Times*, the *Washington Post*, the *Chicago Tribune*, the *Los Angeles Times*, the *Wall Street Journal*, and the *Christian Science Monitor*.

Most newspapers are local papers. That is, most of their readers live in or near the communities in which they are published. While most papers do carry a substantial amount of national and international news, most focus on their own locales. Advances in telecommunications and computerized operations are working a change in that basic fact, however. Today, each day's editions of the *New York Times*, the *Wall Street Journal*, and the *Christian Science Monitor* are generally available on the day of publication around the country; and *USA Today*, which began publication in the early 1980s, has become a popular national newspaper.

Radio

Radio as it exists today began in 1920. On November 2nd of that year, station KDKA in Pittsburgh went on the air with presidential election returns. Radio soon became immensely popular. By 1927, 733 commercial stations were on the air, Americans owned more than seven million radio sets, and two national networks were in operation. NBC was established in 1926 and CBS in 1927. The Mutual Broadcasting System was formed in 1934 and ABC in 1943. The advent of networks made it possible for broadcasters to present their programs and advertising messages to millions of people all over the country.

National Public Radio Because they are largely supported by listener contributions, NPR newscasters are respected for less biased reporting than that of commercial stations. Shown above is Nina Totenberg, NPR's legal affairs correspondent.

By the 1930s, radio had assumed much of the role in American society that television has today. It was a major entertainment medium, and millions planned their daily schedules around their favorite network programs. The networks also provided the nation with dramatic coverage of important events, and radio exposed the American people to national and international politics as never before. President Franklin Roosevelt was the first major public figure to use radio effectively. Author David Halberstam has described the impact of FDR's famous fireside chats:

> "He was the first great American radio voice. For most Americans of [that] generation, their first memory of politics would be of sitting by a radio and hearing *that* voice, strong, confident, totally at ease. . . . Most Americans in the previous 160 years had never seen a

Provide Guided Practice
Write *radio, television, magazines,* and *newspapers* on the board. Ask students to rank these items from most widely used to least widely used as a source of information. Then ask students to rank the items in terms of value: Which provides the most comprehensive coverage to which provides the least comprehensive coverage?

Provide Independent Practice
Teacher's Resource File
You may wish to assign the Section 3 Guided Reading and Review, Unit 2 File, p. 78, to help students master section objective content.

Enrichment

Divide the class into groups of three. Each person in the group should watch a different TV evening news broadcast for two days. On the basis of their observations, have each person list the top news stories reported by their program. As a group, have students compare their three programs. Lead a class discussion regarding whether the programs cover the same agendas. Have students write one page comparing newspaper coverage to the television news show. Which medium provides the most comprehensive information?(Average)

OR

Teacher's Resource File
See the Unit 2 File, pp. 81–83, for the Case Study on Contemporary Issues for Chapter 8.

President; now almost all of them were hearing him, *in their own homes.* It was literally and figuratively electrifying.”[11]

Many thought that the arrival of television would bring the end of radio as a major medium. But radio has survived, in large part because it is so conveniently available. People can hear music, news, sports, and other radio programs in many places where they cannot watch television—in their cars, at work, in the country, and so on.

Radio remains a major source of news and other political information. The average person hears 20 hours of radio each week. No one knows how many hundreds of millions of radios there are in this country—in homes, offices, cars, backpacks, and a great many other places. Those radios can pick up more than 10,000 stations on the AM and FM dials.

Many AM stations are affiliated with one or another of the national networks. Unlike television, however, most radio programming is local. There are now more than 300 public radio stations, most of them on the FM dial. These noncommercial outlets are part of National Public Radio (NPR), which is radio's counterpart of television's PBS.

In most large cities there is at least one station that broadcasts nothing but news and public affairs programs. In addition, many stations serve the preferences of African-American, Hispanic-American, or other minority audiences.

Magazines

Several magazines were published in colonial America. Benjamin Franklin began one of the very first, his *General Magazine*, in Philadelphia in 1741. On into the early 1900s, most magazines published in the United States were generally devoted to literature and the social graces. The first political magazines—among them, *Harper's Weekly* and the *Atlantic Monthly*—appeared in the mid-1800s. The progressive reform period in the early years of this century spawned several journals of opinion, including a number that featured articles by the leading muckrakers of the day.[12] For decades before radio and then television, magazines constituted the only national medium.

Some 10,000 magazines are published in the United States today. Most are trade publications—for example, *Veterinary Forum* and the *Automotive Executive*—or periodicals that target some special personal interest, such as *Golf Digest*, *Teen* and the *American Rifleman*. The top sellers today are *Modern Maturity*, *TV Guide*, and *Reader's Digest*; they each sell from 15 to 20 million or more copies per issue. Three news magazines, *Time*, *Newsweek*, and *U.S. News & World Report*, rank in the top 25 periodicals in terms of circulation. They have a combined circulation of nearly 10 million copies a week, and they are important sources of political news and comment. There are several other magazines devoted to public affairs, most of them vehicles of opinion—including the *Nation*, the *New Republic*, and *National Review*.

The Media's Impact on Politics

Clearly, the media play a significant role in American politics. But just how significant that role is, just how much influence the media have is the subject of long, still unsettled debate.

Whatever its weight, the media's influence can be seen in any number of situations. It is most visible, most often has its greatest weight in two areas: (1) the public agenda and (2) electoral politics.

The Public Agenda The media play a very large role in shaping the public agenda. As they report and comment on events, issues, problems, and personalities, the media determine to a very large extent what public matters the people will think and talk about—and, so, those matters that public policymakers will be concerned

[11]David Halberstam, *The Powers That Be* (New York: Knopf, 1979), page 15.

[12]The muckrakers were journalists who exposed wrongdoing in politics, business, and industry. The term was coined by Theodore Roosevelt in 1906 and is derived from the raking of muck—that is, manure and other barnyard debris. The muckrakers set the pattern for what is now called investigative reporting.

Activity: For Gifted Students

Theme: Power After students have completed their study of the power of media's impact on politics, students may choose to investigate the newspaper editorialist's perception of power to influence national politics. Students may identify two nationally or locally recognized editorial writers (e.g., William F. Buckley, George Will, Molly Ivins, etc.) for this investigation. Students should complete a style analysis for each editorialist, focusing on their use of powerful language, color, personalization of content, audience, etc. In a one- or two-page paper, students should compare the techniques of the two personalities whom they studied.

about. To put the point another way, the media have the power to focus the public's attention on a particular issue. And they do so by emphasizing some things and ignoring or downplaying others, by featuring certain items on the front page or at the top of the newscast and burying others.

It is not correct to say that the media tell the people *what* to think; but it is clear that they do tell the people what to think *about*. A look at any issue of a daily paper or a quick review of the content of any television news program will demonstrate that point. Remember, people rely on the media for most of the information they receive on public issues.

The mass media also has a direct impact on the nation's leaders. A widely respected authority has identified 11 news organizations that form the "inner ring" of influence in Washington, D.C. They are the three major television networks, CBS, ABC, and NBC; three newspapers, the *New York Times*, the *Washington Post*, and the *Wall Street Journal*; the two leading news wire services, the Associated Press (AP) and United Press International (UPI); and the three major news weeklies, *Time*, *Newsweek*, and *U.S. News & World Report*.[13] CNN has recently joined that select group. Top political figures in and out of government pay close attention to those sources and the President receives a daily digest of the news reports, analyses, and editorial comments broadcast and published by them and by other media.

Electoral Politics You have seen a number of illustrations of the media's importance in electoral politics as you have read this book. Thus, on page 122, you encountered the point that the media, and in particular television, have contributed to a decline in the place of parties in American politics.

[13] Stephen Hess, *The Washington Reporters* (Washington, D.C.: The Brookings Institution, 1981).

Image-Makers Political candidates and their staffs do their best to manipulate media coverage in order to project an image as appealing and attractive as possible to their constituents.

TRF **Teacher's Resource File**
See pages 15–17 of the Election Kit for material that supports this section.

SPOTLIGHT ON: Constitutional Issues
Since the late 1960s, the aggressiveness with which the media goes behind the scenes to "get a story" has increased significantly—e.g., as seen in the Iran-Contra affair and the Hart campaign of 1988. The Supreme Court's landmark decision in the case of *New York Times* v. *Sullivan* in 1964 cleared the way for this trend by making the charge of libel increasingly difficult to prove. In its ruling, the court established a stringent precedent requiring plaintiffs not only to prove the media wrong, but to show a deliberate intent of malice. The ruling, in effect, ensured the news media's right to be wrong, as long as it was not wrong on purpose.

Interpreting Political Cartoons This cartoon pokes fun at the influence of the media on public opinion. How?

Take as an example of that point the fact that television has made candidates far less dependent on party organizations than they once were. Before television, the major parties generally dominated the election process. They recruited most candidates who ran for office, and they ran those candidates' campaigns. The candidates depended on party organizations in order to reach the voters. Now, television allows candidates to appeal directly to the people, without the help of a party organization. Candidates for major office need not be experienced politicians who have worked their way up a party's political ladder over several elections. Today it is not at all unusual for candidates to assemble their own campaign organizations and operate with only loose connections with their political parties.

Recall, too, that in Chapter 6, Section 5 you read that how voters see a candidate—the impressions they have of that candidate's personality, character, abilities, and so on—is one of the major factors that influence voting behavior. Candidates and professional campaign managers are quite aware of this. They know that the kind of "image" a candidate projects in all of the media can have a telling effect on the outcome of an election.

Candidates regularly try to manipulate media coverage to their advantage. Campaign strategists know that almost everything most people know about candidates they learn from television; so they plan campaigns that emphasize television exposure. Such technical considerations as timing, location, lighting, and camera angles loom large, often at the expense of such substantive matters as the issues involved in an election or a candidate's qualifications for public office.

Good campaign managers also know that most television news programs are built out of stories that (1) take no more than a minute or two of air time and (2) show people doing something interesting or exciting. Newscasts seldom feature "talking heads"—speakers who drone on and on about some complex issue. Instead, their stories are usually short, sharply
1.c focused **sound bites**—snappy reports that can be aired in 30 or 45 seconds or so. Staged and carefully orchestrated visits to historic sites, factory gates, toxic-waste dumps, football games, and the like have become a standard part of the electoral scene.

Limits on Media Influence

It is all too easy to overstate the media's role in American politics. A number of built-in factors work to limit the media's impact on the behavior of the American voting public.

For one thing, not very many people follow international, national, or even local political events very closely. Many studies of voting behavior show that in the typical election, only about 10 percent of those who can vote and

Interpreting Political Cartoons As students study the cartoon, remind them of the author's comment: "[Most people] watch, listen to, and read those sources that generally agree with their own viewpoints." Have students compare this comment with the message in the cartoon. Which view do students support? (*These two messages conflict to some degree. The cartoon implies that most people form an opinion based on the media, while the text says that most people's opinions are already formed and they choose media that support those opinions.)*

Caption Answer By implying that the average person needs the input of the media in order to form an opinion.

Monitor Comprehension

Answers for Section 3 Review
1. "Key Terms" are defined on the following pages:
- **a.** medium, p. 198
- **b.** mass media, p. 198
- **c.** sound bite, p. 204

2. Television, newspapers, radio, and magazines. **3.** Television. **4.** The media has its greatest impact on the public agenda and electoral politics. **5.** Most people ignore sources that disagree with their opinions, most television programs have little or nothing to do with public affairs, and radio and TV news only highlight events. **6.** Answers will vary, but students should demonstrate an understanding of both the impact and the limits of media influence on public opinion.

Spotlight on: Behind the Scenes

The importance of a candidate's appearance was demonstrated during the Kennedy-Nixon debates of 1960—a formative political event in the age of television. The weekend before the first debate, John F. Kennedy took time out to relax at the beach. Richard Nixon, however, kept a hectic travel schedule until the day of the debate, despite fatigue from the flu and a minor leg injury. Nixon consequently looked drawn and pale, while the tanned Kennedy appeared at ease and healthy. Interestingly, while radio listeners tended to judge Nixon the winner, most TV viewers thought that Kennedy won.

only about 15 percent of those who do vote are well informed on the many candidates and issues under consideration in that election. In short, only a small part of the public actually takes in and understands much of what the media have to say about public affairs.

Moreover, most of those who do pay some attention to politics are likely to be selective about it. That is, they most often watch, listen to, and read those sources that generally agree with their own viewpoints. They regularly ignore those sources that disagree. Thus, for example, many Democrats do not watch the televised campaign appearances of Republican candidates. Nor do many Republicans read newspaper stories about the campaign efforts of Democratic candidates.

Another important limit on the media's impact on the public can be seen in the content of much of what they carry. This is especially true of radio and television. Most television programs, for example, have little or nothing to do with public affairs.[14] Advertisers who pay the high costs of television air time want to reach the largest possible audiences. So, because most people are far more interested in being entertained than they are in being informed about public issues, few public-affairs programs air in prime time. There are a few exceptions: "60 Minutes" on CBS, "20/20" on ABC, and "Exposé" on NBC, for example. But they are just that—exceptions.

Radio and television mostly "skim" the news. They report only what their news editors judge to be the most important and/or the most interesting stories of the day. Even on the widely watched evening news programs most reports are presented in 60-to 90-second time slots. In short, the broadcast media, or at least most of them, seldom give the kind of in-depth coverage that a good newspaper can supply to the interested reader.

[14]At least not directly. A number of popular programs do relate to public affairs in an indirect way, however. Thus, many are "crime shows," and crime is certainly a matter of public concern. Many also carry a political message—for example, that police are hardworking public servants who need the public's support and deserve the public's respect.

Newspapers are not as hampered as many other media in their ability to cover public affairs. Still, much of the content of most papers is nonpolitical. Newspaper readers are often more interested in the comics, the sports pages, and the social, travel, advertising, and entertainment sections of a paper than they are in its news and editorial pages. Like nearly all of television and radio, newspapers are business ventures dedicated to making a profit. They depend on their advertising revenues, which in turn depend on producing a product with the widest possible appeal.

All of this is not meant to say that in-depth coverage of public affairs is not available in the media. It is, to those who want it and will seek it out. There are a number of good newspapers around the country. In-depth coverage can also be found in several magazines and on a number of radio and television stations, including public broadcast outlets.

Remember, however, there is nothing about democracy that guarantees an alert and informed public. Like voting and other forms of political participation, being an informed citizen does require some effort.

Section 3 Review

1. Define: medium, mass media, sound bite

2. What are the four major media in terms of importance to American politics?

3. What is the most powerful form of mass media?

4. In what two areas does the media have its greatest impact?

5. What limits exist on the impact of mass media?

Critical Thinking

6. Recognizing Cause and Effect (p. 19) Which do you think happened first: The public was not interested in public affairs, so television and radio did not air such programming? Or, did television choose not to air public affairs programs, so the public did not develop much interest in such information?

Teacher's Resource File See the Unit 2 File, p. 79, for the Section 3 Quiz.

Closure

Remind students that because the mass media are pervasive in the United States, they have the ability to shape the public agenda and can be used (or manipulated) very effectively by public officials and candidates. Point out, however, that people may overestimate the power of the media. Passive observance of the media is often not enough to provide broad insight into a given issue. In the next chapter, students will learn about interest groups and how they influence public opinion and public policy.

Assignment Assign Chapter 9, Section 1, pp. 211–214, for the next class period.

Reteach

Have students prepare a two-page "Guide for Using the Mass Media to Find Out About Public Issues" that would be useful for a newcomer to the United States. Have them include specific information such as names of newspapers and magazines and TV and radio networks with local channel and radio frequencies. The guide should provide brief descriptions of what each source offers relating to public issues.

TEACHING
Critical Thinking

Distinguishing False from Accurate Images

Objective
Determine whether a widely held belief is based in fact.

INSTRUCT

Before introducing this lesson, have students offer a definition of the term *overstatement* and suggest words that often signal an overstatement. (*All, every, none, always, never.*) Ask for an example of an overstatement on the weather or the school lunchroom.

When students have completed the lesson, have them work in small groups to rewrite the boxed passage, eliminating or revising unjustified generalizations and overstatements.

Answers 1. The main message is the poor quality of television news programs. **2.** (a) Indicators of generalizations include: "A large percentage"; "many observers"; "the public has stopped reading newspapers"; "ignorant of politics." (b) Yes. The use of the following indicates overstatement: "always," "never," devastating effects," "catastrophic decline." **3.** (a) No specific facts are given in the passage. (b) One can conclude that the passage may present a false or inaccurate image.

Distinguishing False from Accurate Images

Distinguishing false from accurate images means examining a widely held belief about a person, place, thing, or situation and determining whether or not the belief is based in fact. This skill enables you to identify stereotypes or other misleading ideas so you can make your own decisions. As a participant in government, you will encounter both false and accurate images in a number of situations and settings—such as when you read a newspaper or magazine or tune in to the news on television or radio, or when you decide which issue or candidate to support in an election. To practice distinguishing between false and accurate images in the passage below, use the following steps.

1. Summarize the main message of the presentation. The first step in evaluating a piece of information is to understand exactly what its main point is. Read the boxed paragraph on this page and answer the following question: What is the main message of the piece?

2. Look for generalizations and overstatements in the presentation. Generalizations are statements that are presented as being accurate in all cases. Overstatements exaggerate, or enlarge on the truth. Words such as *all, every, none, always,* and *never* often indicate the presence of generalizations or overstatements. People frequently use these techniques to communicate ideas for which they have no hard evidence. In other words, people often use generalizations and overstatements to communicate false images. (a) What indicators of generalizations can you find in the boxed paragraph? (b) In your opinion, does the paragraph include any overstatements? Give support for your answer.

3. Look for supporting facts or evidence. People presenting accurate information can back up their statements with evidence—facts such as statistics and direct quotations. Of course, facts can be used in a misleading way, and you must always check facts for accuracy. In general, however, arguments or statements supported by facts are more likely to be accurate than those without facts. (a) What, if any, specific facts are given in the passage below? (b) Based on the use of facts in the passage below, what can you conclude about the accuracy of the passage?

A large percentage of the American people rely on nightly television news programs as their main source of information. Yet many observers have grave concerns about the accuracy and depth of political reporting on television newscasts. These observers say that television news always emphasizes style over substance. Newscasts typically seem to be devoid of any real content, and the opinions expressed never have any real value. News reporters frequently use propaganda techniques to appeal to viewers' emotions rather than to their intellect. As a result of the devastating effects of television news, the public has stopped reading newspapers. They have become ignorant of politics and have completely lost interest in political contests. Television news, these observers say, is to blame for a catastrophic decline in voter participation.

TRF **Teacher's Resource File**
See the Unit 2 File, p. 80, for the Skill Application to reinforce the skill lesson.

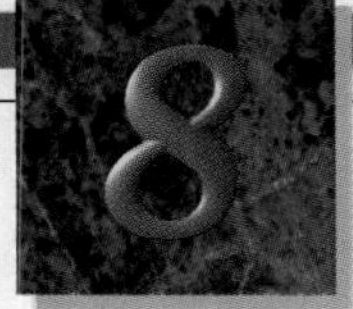

Chapter-in-Brief

Scan all headings, photographs, charts, and other visuals in the chapter before reading the section summaries below.

Section 1 The Formation of Public Opinion (pp. 185–189) Public opinion is a concept that is both widely used and widely misunderstood. The term does not refer to any opinion shared by all the American people. Nor does public opinion properly include people's views on nonpublic issues. It includes those attitudes held by a significant number of persons on matters of government and politics. In reality, "the public" holds many different and often conflicting views on nearly every public question.

Individuals come by their public opinions through the combined influence of several factors. Children undergo the first, crucial steps of political socialization in the family. Later, in school, students are trained to be "good citizens," a further step in political socialization.

Another factor that influences the acquisition of opinions on public issues is the influence of opinion leaders. The mass media is another force in the formation of public opinions.

Section 2 The Measurement of Public Opinion (pp. 189–196) The content of public opinion can be determined to some degree by checking the various means by which the public expresses its opinions.

One vehicle for the expression of public opinions is election returns. However, so many factors influence the behavior of voters that it is impossible to claim that election results are accurate indicators of public opinion.

The activities of interest groups are another public opinion indicator. Yet it is not always possible to determine for whom an interest group is acting, or how strongly the group's members support the group's action. Likewise, the mass media is often regarded as a mirror for public opinion, though in fact it is not very accurate.

Many officials rely on contact with the public to get a feel for public opinion. This method is limited by the extent to which officials are willing to hear views that disagree with their own.

The best way to measure public opinion is by opinion polls. Scientifically designed polls are effective instruments for measuring public opinion.

It is important to measure public opinion, but it is also important to know that public opinion is but one factor shaping public policy.

Section 3 The Mass Media and Politics (pp. 198–205) The American public gets information on public issues through the several forms of mass media. Television is the most significant supplier of public information.

Newspapers are another mass medium; before the age of television, they served as the public's primary source of information. Radio and magazines are also major mass media.

The media influences American politics mostly in two areas: (1) The media helps set the public agenda, and (2) mass media plays a central role in the field of electoral politics. Television especially has influenced the electoral process. It has changed the role of political parties; it has also altered the way candidates present themselves to the public, shifting the emphasis toward style over substance.

The power of the mass media is not all-encompassing. For one thing, people actually absorb little of what the mass media communicates. Many people use the mass media as sources of entertainment rather than information.

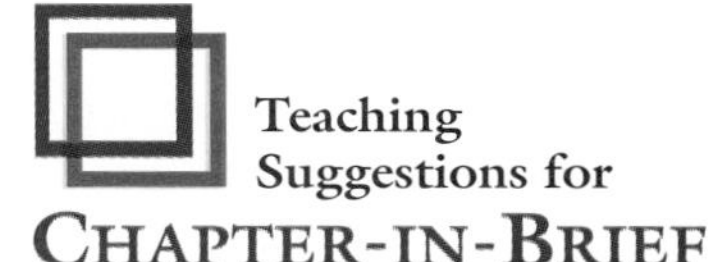

Teaching Suggestions for Chapter-in-Brief

Below are some of the possible uses for the Chapter-in-Brief:

To Preview the Chapter You may want to assign the Chapter-in-Brief page and the Section Outlines from the Teacher's Resource File before beginning Chapter 8 to introduce students to the key terms and concepts in each section.

To Review the Chapter When students have completed Chapter 8, you might want to assign the Chapter-in-Brief as a tool for review, along with the Guided Reading and Reviews from the Teacher's Resource File.

To Omit the Chapter If you wish to skip Chapter 8, it may be helpful to assign the Chapter-in-Brief to students as a review before continuing to another chapter. You may also want to assign the Chapter 8 Test to assess students' knowledge of the material. Then specific portions of Chapter 8 may be assigned to students needing reinforcement of key terms and concepts.

Teacher's Resource File
See the Unit 2 File for the following materials:

- Section Outlines, pp. 71, 74, 77.
- Guided Reading and Reviews, pp. 72, 75, 78.
- Chapter 8 Test, pp. 84–86.

Additional Resources

Abramson, Jeffrey and Gary R. Orren. *The Electronic Commonwealth: The Impact of News Media Technologies on Democratic Politics.* Basic Books, 1990.

Asher, Herbert B. *Polling and the Public: What Every Citizen Should Know.* CQ Press, 1987.

Crespi, Irving. *Public Opinion, Polls, and Democracy.* Westview Press, 1989.

Graber, Doris (ed.). *Media Power in Politics.* CQ Press, 2nd ed., 1989.

Iyengar, Shanto and Donald S. Kinder. *News That Matters: Television and American Opinion.* University of Chicago Press, 1989.

Kern, Montague. *30-Second Politics: Political Advertising in the Eighties.* Praeger, 1989.

Media in Politics. Videotape. Films for the Humanities, 1989. Color. 90 min.

Media Politics: The Big Hype. Sound filmstrip. Current Affairs, 1980. Color. 18 min.

Mickelson, Sig. *From Whistle Stop to Sound Bite: Four Decades of Politics and Television.* Praeger, 1989.

The Media in the 1984 and 1988 Presidential Campaigns. Greenwood Press, 1991.

Answers to
CHAPTER 8 REVIEW

Vocabulary and Key Terms

Matching
1. interest groups
2. medium
3. sample
4. opinion leader
5. sound bite
6. public opinion

True or False
1. True.
2. False—the correct term is *quota sample.*
3. True.
4. False—the correct term is *interest group.*
5. True.

Word Relationships
1. A medium is any means of communication; mass media are any kind of medium that are capable of reaching a widely dispersed audience.
2. A public opinion poll is a device for measuring the opinions of people by asking them questions; a straw vote is a type of poll in which a large, unrepresentative group of people is asked to respond to a particular question.
3. Public opinion is those attitudes held by a significant number of people on matters of public concern; a mandate is the instructions a constituency gives to its elected officials.

Main Ideas

Section 1
1. There are few matters on which all the American people agree. Rather, the public holds many different and conflicting views on most questions.
2. The family and the school.
3. The family is the place where most people begin to acquire their views on the political world; these views tend to be long-lasting. School is a place where most people acquire their training in being "good citizens." **4.** People also acquire political views from opinion leaders and the mass media; views also are shaped by occupation, sex, and other factors.

Section 2
5. Possible answers: elections, activities of interest groups, the media, personal contacts with the public, and polls.**6.** Elections are influenced by many factors, so that they can rarely be interpreted as an expression of public opinion on any one issue. It is often difficult to determine how well interest groups represent the views of their membership. Personal contacts are unlikely to comprise a representative sample of U.S. public opinion. Polls may not be scientific, and even scientific polls often do not accurately measure intensity, stability, and relevance of an opinion. **7.** Scientifically conducted public opinion polls.
8. Because the United States Constitution guarantees civil rights and liberties to those holding minority opinions. This curbs the views and actions of the majority when they interfere unjustly with minority interests.

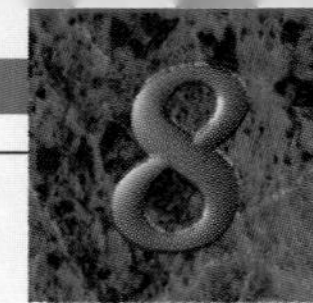

Chapter Review

Vocabulary and Key Terms

public opinion (p. 186)	public opinion poll (p. 191)	quota sample (p. 193)
opinion leader (p. 188)	straw vote (p. 191)	medium (p. 198)
mandate (p. 190)	sample (p. 192)	mass media (p. 198)
interest group (p. 190)	random sample (p. 192)	sound bite (p. 204)

Matching: *Review the key terms in the list above. If you are not sure of a term's meaning, look up the term and review its definition. Choose a term from the list above that best matches each description.*

1. an organization that tries to influence public policy
2. a means of communication
3. a representative slice of the population that a poll aims to evaluate
4. a person who possesses an unusual amount of influence on the views held by other people
5. news reports that are brief and sharply focused
6. those attitudes held by significant numbers of persons on public issues

True or False: *Determine whether each statement is true or false. If it is true, write "true." If it is false, change the underlined word or words to make the statement true.*

1. A public opinion poll aims at measuring the opinions of a group of people by asking them questions.
2. A type of sample that is carefully constructed to reflect the major characteristics of a particular universe is called a random sample.
3. Winners of elections often claim that their victories at the polls represent a mandate to carry out their proposed programs.
4. Any group that tries to influence public policy is an opinion leader.
5. Mass media are those means of communication that can reach large numbers of people.

Word Relationships: *Distinguish between words in each pair.*

1. medium/mass media
2. public opinion poll/straw vote
3. public opinion/mandate

Main Ideas

Section 1 (pp. 185–189)

1. Why is it incorrect to say that public opinion represents the single, undivided view of the American people?
2. What are the two most important agents of political socialization?
3. What makes the influence of the school and family so powerful in the development of political attitudes?
4. Besides the school and family, what other forces help influence public opinion in American society?

Section 2 (pp. 189–196)

5. Name four means of measuring public opinion.
6. List the limitations of each of these different means.
7. What is the most reliable means of measuring public opinion?

8. Why is it only partly true to say that government in the United States is "government by public opinion"?

Section 3 **(pp. 198–205)**

9. In what two ways do the mass media provide the American people with political information?
10. What is the impact of the mass media on the public agenda?
11. What is the impact of the mass media in electoral politics?
12. What factors limit the impact of the mass media on American politics?

Critical Thinking

1. **Expressing Problems Clearly** (p. 19) Recall that the text states that schools are key agents of political socialization. What are the key elements of citizenship in American society that you think students ought to learn in school?
2. **Predicting Consequences** (p. 19) Suppose that television stations were required to devote a large percentage of their air time to discussion of public policy issues. What effects would you expect this change to have on the viewing habits of Americans?
3. **Making Comparisons** (p. 19) Compare the advantages and disadvantages of newspapers and television as a means of providing the public with information on important public issues.
4. **Distinguishing False from Accurate Images** (p. 19) In spite of its powerful and important role in American society, television is often criticized for its lack of content on important issues. (a) Considering what you have read in this chapter, do you feel that it is accurate to characterize television as lacking in real content? (b) If so, what do you think is to blame for the quality of television programming?

Getting Involved

1. **Writing Your Opinion** Write the text to a public service announcement urging people to spend more time educating themselves on public issues. To prepare, write down three reasons why you think people should become more informed on matters of public concern. Also, create a list of ways that people can efficiently educate themselves. As you write your announcement, remember that your purpose is to encourage citizens. State the reasons why you think people should become more involved, and then present your suggestions. Revise your announcement to make sure your ideas are persuasive and encouraging. Correct any errors, then draft a final copy.
2. **Cooperative Activity** Work as a class to publish a school newspaper. First, decide together upon the name for your paper. Then divide the class into four groups. One group will identify, write, and illustrate a story about an issue of national concern to students. A second group will identify, write, and illustrate a story of local concern to all students. A third group will work on a story about a schoolwide issue that is of concern to all students. The fourth group will write an editorial explaining the purpose of the newspaper. Then, the fourth group will collect all the articles, combine them into a single issue, and copy and distribute the paper.
3. **Gathering Information** Use the Government Resources Handbook on page 690 to answer the following questions. (a) What sources might you use if you wanted to find out what public opinion polls predicted for a particular presidential race? (b) What sources might you consult to discover the actual results in that election?

Section 3

9. The mass media provides information directly, in the form of news, and indirectly, in the form of programming that deals with public issues, such as crime. **10.** The mass media helps shape the public agenda—what people talk about. However, it does not tell them what to think about these issues. **11.** The mass media has made candidates less dependent on parties. It has also changed the way people campaign, placing the emphasis more on matters of style than on substance. **12.** Few people follow politics directly. Also, many people only selectively seek information from the media. Finally, many media contain little substantive material on public issues.

Critical Thinking

1. Answers will vary. Students might suggest that schools should teach people to become informed citizens, to vote, to be patriotic, etc. **2.** Answers will vary. Students might predict that the public would become more informed on public questions. Others might suggest that the public would pay little attention to the new programming and seek other forms of entertainment. **3.** Answers will vary. Students might say that newspapers provide much information but take more time to digest. Television exposes viewers to a wide range of information but provides little depth. **4.** (a) Some may say that in spite of providing limited coverage, television does provide some degree of valuable information. Others will say that the television-influenced shift from substance to style has left television useless as a means of communicating real information. (b) Students might suggest that viewers' tolerance and appetite for content-light television is to blame.

Getting Involved

1–3. Answers and results will vary, but students should demonstrate an understanding of the concepts in this chapter.

Chapter 9 Resources

In the Teacher's Resource File
The following materials are found in the Teacher's Resource File box.

Instructional Support: Unit 2 File

For the Section
Outlines, pp. 90, 93, 96
Guided Reading and Reviews, pp. 91, 94, 97
Quizzes, pp. 92, 95, 98

For the Chapter
Skill Application, p. 99
Case Study on Contemporary Issues, pp. 100–102
Chapter Test, pp. 103–105
Additional Test Questions, pp. 106–108

Enrichment Support Files

Participatory Government Activities, pp. 42–43, 44–49
Supreme Court Cases, p. 7

Computer Test Bank and Assessment

Transparency Package, pp. 9, 34

Chapter 9 Focus

Introduce the Chapter Tell students that in this chapter they will learn about the nature and role of interest groups in the American political system, types of interest groups, and the methods used by interest groups to achieve their goals. Read with students the Chapter Preview and Objectives.

Writing Activity Direct students' attention to "Describe." Have students write down what they think public opinion is. Then ask students to write how they think groups might be more effective than individuals at influencing public opinion.

Motivate for Learning Direct students' attention to "Predict." Discuss ways in which people try to influence others. Discuss what methods are most effective at influencing others to change their minds.

Interest Groups

Chapter Preview

SURGEON GENERAL'S WARNING: Smoking Causes Lung Cancer, Heart Disease, Emphysema, And May Complicate Pregnancy. Versions of this message have appeared on cigarette packages since 1964. Evidence pointing to the health and environmental risks associated with smoking seems powerful.

Since the 1970s, many interest groups have worked persistently to demand laws that discourage smoking. Yet, on the opposite side of the smoking issue stand equally large and persistent forces: the farmers who grow and sell $3.5 billion worth of tobacco to the industry that produces $17 billion worth of tobacco products each year. These opposing efforts represent interest groups—any groups that try to promote their own interests by exerting pressure on legislators. This chapter is about interest groups and the way they work.

Before you read this chapter:

- **Describe** methods an interest group might use to influence public opinion.
- **Predict** some factors that might determine an interest group's success.

As you read, focus on the main objective for each section. Understand:

1. The nature of interest groups and their role in politics.
2. The several types of interest groups.
3. The means used by interest groups to influence public opinion and public policy.

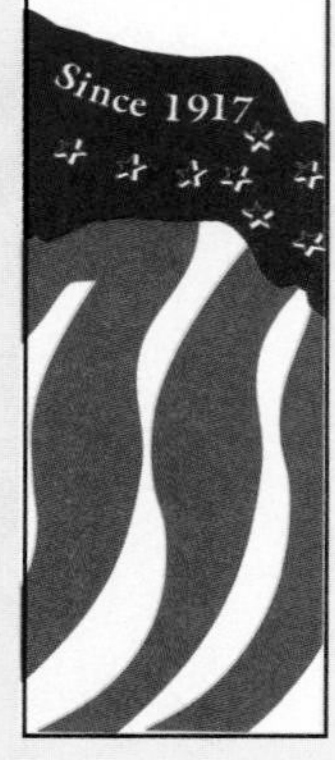

Magruder's American Government: *A Witness to Change* by William A. McClenaghan

For decades in American politics, interest groups were much more commonly called "pressure groups" for the rather obvious reason that these organizations exist to bring group pressures to bear at strategic places in the governing process. In fact, the term *interest group* did not become a part of the general American political vocabulary until the 1960s and it was in that period that the term began to appear in the pages of this book.

In this chapter, we stress the point that interest groups play a number of inevitable and necessary roles in American politics. But we also make the point that these organizations and their activities are not, and never have been held in very high regard by the American people.

The public's less-than-admiring view of interest (*nee* pressure) groups was reflected in pre-1950 editions of this book. Thus, to take but one example, several editions in the 1930s noted Wisconsin's pioneering efforts to regulate lobbyists and castigated those "agents of pressure groups" as being "responsible for much bad legislation" in that State.

United We Stand Local government workers rally in support of their union, the American Federation of State, County, and Municipal Employees. Political activities of labor unions are subject to federal supervision.

1 The Nature of Interest Groups

Find Out:

- What are interest groups?
- What are the positive and negative influences of interest groups in American politics?

Key Terms:

interest group, public policy, public affairs

Do you belong to an interest group? You may not think so. But, as you read this section, you will almost certainly discover that you do.

What Is an Interest Group?

Everyone has certain interests that he or she thinks are important. Joining with others who share those interests is both practical and democratic. Organized efforts to protect group interests are a fundamental part of the democratic process; and the right to do so is protected by the Constitution. Recall, the 1st Amendment guarantees "the right of the people peaceably to assemble, and to petition the government for a redress of grievances."

1.a **Definition** An **interest group** is a private organization that tries to persuade public officials to respond to the shared attitudes of its members. Interest groups are also called pressure groups or special interests. Committees, clubs, associations, unions, federations, leagues—whatever they call themselves—they seek their ends by attempting to influence the making and
1.b the content of public policy. **Public policy** is all those things that a government endeavors to do in order to achieve certain goals. In a democracy, these goals are set by the people.

Because interest groups exist to influence public policy, they operate wherever those policies are made or can be influenced. They function at every level of government—on Capitol Hill and elsewhere in Washington, D.C., in every one of the 50 State capitals, and

SECTION 1
The Nature of Interest Groups

FOCUS

Teacher's Resource File See the Unit 2 File, p. 90, for the Section 1 Outline.

Objectives

9.1 Explain what interest groups are.
9.2 Identify positive and negative influences of interest groups in American politics.

Bellringer Activity Ask students to imagine that the school board has decided to reduce the funds for such school activities as sports, music, theater, and clubs. How would the students who take part in those activities respond? Point out to students that groups that seek to influence policies such as how to use school funds are interest groups.

State the Purpose Tell students that most Americans belong to some interest group—an organization whose members share the same ideas about an issue, along with a desire to influence public action on that issue. In Section 1, students will learn what interest groups are, what they contribute to the political process, and some common criticisms of them.

ABCNEWS INTERACTIVE
The following video segment may be used to highlight aspects of interest groups.

POWERS OF THE CONGRESS GUIDEBOOK
Chapter 18: Interest Groups, p. 94

Vocabulary

Point out "Key Terms" on page 211 to the students. Ask students to predict what the difference is between *public policy* and *public affairs*. Have students refer back to their predictions as they encounter these terms in the text. LEP

Reading Strategy: Relating to Topic

Ask students to think of examples from their school or community of ways in which groups can accomplish more than individuals and ways in which groups can have a powerful negative influence on people. Tell students that as they read this section, applying their basic understanding of the influence of groups will help them understand the nature of interest groups.

INSTRUCT

Explain/Analyze/Discuss
Refer back to the "Bellringer Activity." Ask how many of the students expected the various groups to put pressure on the school board to save their group's interest or side of the issue?

Explain to students that in the society at large, there are many interest groups similar to the groups at school discussed in the "Bellringer Activity." Each group has its own interests, and each tries to fulfill those interests by putting pressure on people who make the decisions of government.

Ask students to analyze the similarities between interest groups and political parties. *(Both consist of people who share a common purpose. However, interest groups are unlike parties in that they do not try to nominate officials and they do not confine their activities to electoral politics.)*

Ask students to discuss the benefits and drawbacks of group activity. Have students analyze the ways in which interest groups represent the democratic ideal. (*Possible answers: They provide citizens a chance to be heard; they enable people to become directly involved with government.*) Also, ask students to consider the ways in which interest groups are dangerous to a democratic society. (*Possible answer: The power of groups can be used to intimidate individuals; groups can appear to be larger, stronger, more representative than they really are.)*

VOICES *on Government*

Ralph Nader, consumer activist and self-described "full-time citizen"

On the Lack of Support for Public Interest Groups

"If [people] watch TV 32 hours a week on the average, how much time are they spending watching city hall or watching Congress or watching their community? . . . If people grew up needing to be fulfilled as citizens, needing to feel psychologically that they count, that they could take on city hall, they could stand up and make a difference, then that would become a psychological need that is fulfilled as a form of human happiness. It's important to connect civic activity with human happiness."

in thousands of city halls and county courthouses and other places at the local level all across the country. In short, as diplomat and historian Lord Bryce put it somewhat indelicately more than a century ago: "Where the body is, there will ten vultures be gathered."[1]

Recall, American society is pluralistic. It is not dominated by a single elite but, instead, consists of a great variety of interests. Increasingly, the members of various ethnic, racial, religious, and other social groups compete for and share in the exercise of political power in this country.

Political Parties and Interest Groups

Interest groups are composed of people who join together for some political purpose. So, too, are political parties. These two types of political organizations necessarily overlap in a number of ways. They differ from one another in three striking ways, however: (1) in the making of nominations, (2) in their primary focus, and (3) in the scope of their interests.[2]

First, parties nominate candidates for public office; interest groups do not. Remember, the making of nominations is a major function of political parties. If an interest group were to nominate candidates, it would, in effect, become a political party.

This is not to say that interest groups do not try to affect the outcomes of primaries and other partisan nominating contests; they often do. However, interest groups do not themselves pick candidates who then run under their labels. It may be widely known that a particular interest group actively supports a candidate, but that candidate seeks votes as a Republican or a Democrat.

The second difference between parties and interest groups is that political parties are chiefly interested in winning elections and controlling government. Interest groups are chiefly concerned with controlling or influencing the *policies* of government. Unlike parties, interest groups do not face the problems involved in trying to appeal to a broad range of people. To put the point another way: Parties are mostly interested in the *who* and interest groups in the *what* of government.

Finally, political parties are necessarily concerned with the whole range of public affairs, with everything of concern to voters. Interest groups almost always concentrate only on those matters that affect the interests of their members.

Recall, too, that interest groups are private organizations. Unlike parties, they are not accountable to the general public. Their members, not the voters, pass judgment on their performance.

[1]James Bryce, *The American Commonwealth* (Chicago: Charles R. Sergel, 1891) American ed., vol. 2, page 153.

[2]Note that this discussion centers on the differences between interest groups and major parties. There are some striking parallels between interest groups and most minor parties—for example, in terms of their scope of interest.

SPOTLIGHT ON: Behind the Scenes

Ralph Nader is probably best-known for his fight for auto safety, which took place during the 1960s. Nader first came to public attention by uncovering evidence that automobile makers were designing cars with little consideration for passenger safety. However, because the accident rate seemed to have no effect on car sales, there was no incentive for car makers to improve safety. Nader maintained that it was the responsibility of the government to protect the safety of citizens, and so he began an active campaign for government safety regulations that included the best-selling book, *Unsafe at Any Speed: The Designed-in Dangers of the American Automobile*. Nader was soon able to persuade Congress to hold hearings on car safety, which resulted in the creation of the National Highway Traffic Safety Administration, and the implementation of safety standards. These reforms are estimated to have saved over two hundred thousand lives from 1966 to 1991, and to have prevented millions of injuries.

Interest Groups: Good or Bad?

Do interest groups pose a threat to the well-being of the American political system? Or, on the contrary, are they a valuable part of that system? The argument over the merit of interest groups goes back to the beginnings of the Republic.

Many have long viewed interest groups with deep suspicion. In 1787, James Madison warned the new nation against the dangers of what he called "factions." He made his view of those groups clear in *The Federalist* No. 10, where he defined a faction as

> "a number of citizens . . . who are united by some common impulse . . . adverse to the rights of other citizens, or to the permanent and aggregate interests of the community."[3]

Madison thought that factions were inevitable in human society, however; and he was opposed to any attempt to abolish them. A society could only eliminate factions, he said, by eliminating freedom. Instead, wrote Madison, it was necessary to moderate the violence of factions with a republican remedy—that is, with the governmental system set out in the proposed Constitution. The functional and territorial separations of power in that governmental arrangement would mean, said Madison, that factions would tend to counteract and balance each others' power and none could become a dominating influence.

Nearly 50 years later, Alexis de Tocqueville was deeply impressed by the vast number of organizations he found in the United States. Tocqueville, a Frenchman who traveled to the United States in the early 1830s, wrote that

> "In no country in the world has the principle of association been more successfully used, or more unsparingly applied to a multitude of different objects, than in America."[4]

In a similar vein, he also observed that

> "Americans of all ages, all conditions, and all descriptions constantly form associations . . . not only commercial and manufacturing . . . but . . . of a thousand different kinds—religious, moral, serious, futile, extensive or restricted, enormous or diminutive."[5]

To determine whether interest groups are "good" or "bad," you must weigh, on the one hand, the functions those groups perform in American politics and, on the other, the several criticisms that are often leveled at them.

Functions First among their several valuable functions, interest groups help to stimulate
1.c interest in **public affairs,** those events and issues that concern the people at large. They do so mostly by developing and pushing those policies they favor and by opposing those policies they see as threats to their interests.

Second, interest groups represent their members on the basis of shared attitudes rather than on the basis of geography—by what their members think as opposed to where they happen to live. Public officials are elected from districts drawn on maps. But many of the issues that concern and unite people today have less to do with *where* they live than with, say, *how* they make a living. A labor union member who lives in Chicago may have much more in common with someone who does the same kind of work in Seattle than he or she does with someone who owns a business in Chicago or runs a farm in another part of Illinois.

Third, organized interests often provide useful, specialized, and detailed information to government—for example, on civilian employment, price levels, or the sales of new and existing homes. These data are important to the making of public policy, and government officials often cannot obtain it from any other source. This process is a two-way street, however; interest groups frequently get information from public agencies and pass it along to their members.

Interest groups are also vehicles for political participation. They are a means through which like-minded citizens can pool their resources and channel their energies into collective

[3]The text of *The Federalist* No. 10 appears in the documents section that begins on page 720.

[4]Alexis de Tocqueville, *Democracy in America*, Henry Reeves, trans. (New York: Schocken Books, 1961), vol. 1, page 216.

[5]*Ibid.*, vol. 2, page 128.

Provide Guided Practice On the board, make a chart with two headings: "Functions of interest groups" and "Criticisms of interest groups." Have students volunteer information from the section to fill in each column. (*Functions: to influence public policy; to represent the interests of their members; to stimulate interest in public affairs, to provide information; to serve as vehicles for participation; to add an element to checks and balances. Criticisms: push their own interests at the expense of others; misrepresent their membership; exert influence out of proportion to their size; occasionally use unethical tactics.*)

Provide Independent Practice

TRF Teacher's Resource File You may wish to assign Section 1 Guided Reading and Review, Unit 2 File, p. 91, to help students master section objective content.

Enrichment

Have students find examples of advertisements placed by interest groups or articles about interest groups in newspapers and magazines. Have students use these gathered materials to develop a presentation—written, oral, or visual—to show how interest groups inform the public and the government and what issues they are seeking to address. (Average)

MONITOR COMPREHENSION

Answers to Section 1 Review
1. "Key Terms" are defined on the following pages:
a. interest group, p. 211
b. public policy, p. 211
c. public affairs, p. 213
2. Wherever policy is influenced. **3.** (1) Parties alone nominate candidates; (2) parties aim to win elections, interest groups influence policies; (3) parties focus on many issues, interest groups focus on one issue. **4.** They stir public interest, represent members, provide information, serve as a vehicle for political participation, provide an element to the checks-and-balance system.**5.** They have too much influence; it is hard to tell who a group represents; they may not represent all their members; some use tactics that are unethical. **6.** Interest groups represent many people, much as elected officials do.

Teacher's Resource File See the Unit 2 File for the Section 1 Quiz on p. 92.

CLOSURE

Remind students that an interest group is any group that tries to influence public policy. Interest groups have the potential to contribute to and detract from the political process. As students read the next section, they will learn about different types of interest groups.

Assignment Assign Section 2, pages 215–220, for the next class period.

political action. One mother concerned about drunk driving cannot accomplish very much acting alone; but thousands of people joined in an organization like MADD (Mothers Against Drunk Driving) certainly can.

Finally, interest groups add an element to the checks-and-balances feature of the political process. When, for example, one interest group makes an unreasonable or blatantly self-serving demand on government, other interest groups will very likely oppose it. Many interest groups also keep fairly close tabs on the behavior of officials in the government and help to make sure that these officials perform their duties responsibly.

Criticisms The "bad" side of interest groups is sometimes all too apparent. Many of these groups push their own special interests which, despite their claims to the contrary, are not always in the best interests of other Americans. Critics often make these more specific charges:

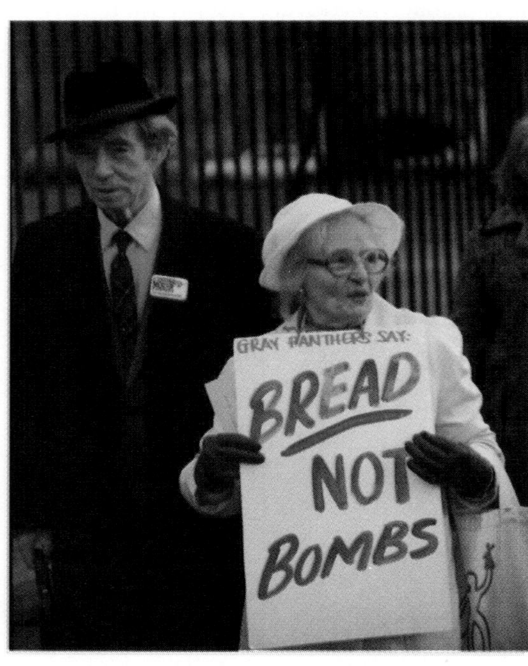

The Gray Panthers As a group of like-minded older Americans, the Gray Panthers have more impact than any one individual would have on calling attention to the special concerns of senior citizens.

First, some interest groups have an influence far out of proportion to their size—or, for that matter, to their importance or contribution to the public good. Thus, the contest over "who gets what, when, and how" is not always a fair fight. The more highly organized and better financed groups often have a decided advantage.

Second, it is sometimes very hard to tell just who or how many people a group really represents. Many groups have titles that suggest that they have thousands—even millions—of dedicated members. Some organizations that call themselves such things as "The American Citizens Committee for . . ." or "People United Against . . ." are, in fact, only "fronts" for a very few persons with very narrow interests.

Third, many groups do not in fact represent the views of all of the people for whom they claim to speak. Very often, both in and out of politics, an organization is dominated by its leaders, by an active minority who conduct its affairs and make its policy decisions.

Finally, some groups use tactics that, if they were to become widespread, would undermine the whole political system. These practices—including bribery and other heavy-handed uses of money, overt threats of revenge, and so on—are not altogether common, but the danger is certainly there.

Section 1 Review

1. Define: interest group, public policy, public affairs
2. Where in the American political system do interest groups operate?
3. What are the three main areas in which political parties and interest groups differ?
4. What are the functions of interest groups in American politics?
5. On what bases are interest groups attacked?

Critical Thinking

6. Distinguishing False from Accurate Images (p. 19) In what sense do interest groups reflect the representative nature of American democracy?

SPOTLIGHT ON: Political Talk

Since his retirement from the Senate in 1987, former Arizona senator and 1964 Republican presidential nominee Barry Goldwater has been a persistent critic of interest groups and the influence they achieve through political action committees. Goldwater's first campaign for the Senate, in 1952, cost $45,000; his last, in 1980, cost $3 million. Says Goldwater: "It's not 'we, the people,' but political action committees and moneyed interests who are setting the nation's political agenda and are influencing the position of the candidates on the important issues of the day."

Reteach

Have students write a television or design a newspaper or magazine advertisement for an interest group. The ad should communicate clearly the group's stand on an issue.

2 Types of Interest Groups

Find Out:

- What are the different types of interest groups?
- On what basis has the largest number of interest groups been founded?

Key Terms:

trade association, labor union, public-interest group

"Everything from A to Z." That expression can be very aptly applied to interest groups in this country. These organizations include, among thousands of others, the American Association of Advertising Agencies, the American Association of Retired Persons, the Association on American Indian Affairs, the Amateur Athletic Union of the United States, Zero Population Growth, the Zionist Organization of America, and the American Association of Zoological Parks and Aquariums. As you will see in this section, all of these thousands of organizations can be more or less readily classified and, so, usefully described as interest groups.

An American Tradition

The United States has often been called "a nation of joiners." Recall what you read about Alexis de Tocqueville's observations in the previous section. Tocqueville's comments, true when he made them, have become even more accurate over time. No one really knows how many associations Americans belong to today. There are thousands upon thousands of them, however—and at every level in society. Each and every one of them, remember, is an interest group whenever it tries to influence the actions of government in order to promote its own goals and special interests.

Interest groups come in all shapes and sizes. They may have thousands or even millions of members, or only a handful. They may be well- or little-known, long-established or new and even temporary, highly structured or quite loose and informal, wealthy or with few resources, and so on. No matter what their characteristics, they are found in every field of human activity in this country.

The largest number of interest groups have been founded on the basis of an economic interest, especially on the bases of business, labor, agricultural, and professional interests. Some groups are grounded in a geographic area, like the South, the Columbia River Basin, or the State of Ohio. Others have been born out of a cause or an idea, such as prohibition of alcohol, environmental protection, or gun control. Still other interest groups exist to promote the welfare of certain groups of people—veterans, senior citizens, a racial minority, the homeless, women, people with disabilities, and so on.

Interest groups often share members. That is, many people belong to a number of them. A car dealer, for example, may be a member of the local Chamber of Commerce, a car dealers' association, the American Legion, a local taxpayers' league, a garden club, a church, the PTA, the American Cancer Society, the National Wildlife Federation, and several other local, regional, or national groups. All of these are, to one degree or another, interest groups, including the church and the garden club, even though the car dealer may never think of them in that light.[6]

Also, many people belong to groups that take conflicting stands on political issues. For example, a program to improve the city's streets may be supported by the local Chamber and the car dealers' association but opposed by the taxpayers' league. The taxpayers' league may endorse a plan to eliminate plantings in traffic islands that has the support of the garden club.

[6]Churches often take stands on such public issues as drinking, curfew ordinances, legalized gambling, and so on; and they often try to influence public policy in those matters. Garden clubs often try to persuade cities to do such things as improve public parks, beautify downtown areas, and the like. Not every group to which people belong can properly be called an interest group, of course. But the point here is that many groups that are not often thought to be interest groups in fact are.

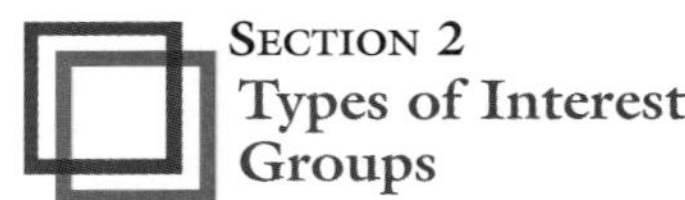

SECTION 2
Types of Interest Groups

FOCUS

Teacher's Resource File See the Unit 2 File, p. 93, for the Section 2 Outline.

Objectives

9.3 Identify different types of interest groups.
9.4 Examine the bases for categorizing interest groups.

Bellringer Activity Give students 30 seconds to brainstorm a list of as many groups as they can name—local, State, or national. At the end of the 30 seconds, ask students to identify which of these groups are interest groups. Then, point out to students that all the groups are interest groups if they try to influence public policy.

State the Purpose It has been observed that there are a staggering number of interest groups in the U.S., representing almost every belief and activity imaginable. In Section 2, students will learn about the most common types of interest groups and some of the bases upon which interest groups can be classified.

ABCNEWS INTERACTIVE
The following video segment may be used to highlight aspects of interest groups.

POWERS OF THE CONGRESS GUIDEBOOK
Chapter 18: Interest Groups, p. 94

Vocabulary

Point out "Key Terms" on page 215. Write the names of the following interest groups on the board: Common Cause, United Mine Workers, and the American Bankers Association. Then ask students to predict which of these groups is a labor union (*United Mine Workers*), which is a trade association (*American Bankers Association*), and which is a public interest group (*Common Cause*).

Reading Strategy: Structured Overview

Write at the top of the board "Kinds of Interest Groups." Beneath that, write the main headings in the section, "Groups Based on Economic Interests" and "The Maze of Other Groups." Ask students to tell you the subheadings under each heading in the text. As you write, have students skim the text under each subheading for examples of interest groups. Discuss how the interest groups are categorized in the resulting list.

INSTRUCT

Discuss/Explain/Analyze Ask students to discuss the statement that the United States is a "nation of joiners." Have students offer their interpretations of this concept, recalling their responses to the "Bellringer Activity."

Explain to students that interest groups exist at all levels of society and for virtually every interest. Point out the various types of groups discussed in the section. Also discuss the point that these groups often have competing interests.

To help initiate a discussion of the role of interest groups in American society, you might ask students to answer the following question: How does the democratic character of the United States encourage citizens to form interest groups? (*Possible answer: In the United States, government is "by the people," so people feel the right and obligation to influence policy.*)

Next, have students observe and discuss the range of interest groups in the United States. Ask students the following question: How does democracy encourage the growth of multiple groups with multiple interests? (*The democratic system gives great power to groups of citizens. Thus, people see that group action can be effective, and they see that it is often necessary to protect their interests in the face of the actions by other interest groups.*)

Groups Based on Economic Interests

Most interest groups are formed on economic interests. That is, they are based on the manner in which people make their livings. Among them, the most active, and certainly the most effective, are those representing business, labor, agriculture, and at least certain professional groups.

Business Groups Business has long looked to government to promote and protect its interests. Recall that merchants, creditors, and property owners were most responsible for the calling of the Constitutional Convention in 1787. The idea of the protective tariff was fought for and won in the early years of the Republic by business interests. Along with organized labor, they continue to work to maintain it.

The United States Brewers' Association is the oldest organized interest group at work in national politics today. It was born in 1862—when Congress first levied a tax on beer—to assure "the brewing trade that its interests be vigorously prosecuted before the legislative and executive departments."

Hundreds of business groups now operate in Washington, D.C., in the 50 State capitals, and at the local level across the country. The two best-known business organizations today are the National Association of Manufacturers (NAM) and the Chamber of Commerce of the United States. Formed in 1895, NAM now represents some 13,000 firms. It generally speaks for "big business" in public affairs. The Chamber of Commerce was founded in 1912. Over the years, it has become a major voice for the nation's thousands of smaller businesses. It has more than 4,000 local chambers and now counts more than 200,000 business and professional firms and some 5 million individuals among its members. Another major group, the Business Roundtable, has also taken a large role in promoting and defending the business community in recent years. Begun in 1972, the Roundtable is composed of the chief executive officers of 200 of the nation's largest, most prestigious, and most influential corporations.

Most segments of the business community also have their own interest groups, often called
1.a **trade associations.** They number in the hundreds—including the American Trucking Association, the Association of American Railroads, the American Bankers Association, the National Association of Retail Grocers, and many more.

Despite a common impression, business groups do not always present a solid front. In fact, they often disagree, and sometimes fight, among themselves. The trucking industry, for example, does its best to get as much federal aid as possible for highway construction. But the railroads are less than happy with what they see as "special favors" for their competition. At the same time, the railroads see federal taxes on gasoline, oil, tires, and other "highway users fees" as legitimate and necessary sources of federal income. The truckers take quite another view, of course.

Labor Groups The strength and the clout of organized labor has ebbed over the past several years. Some 17 million Americans, less than 14 percent of the nation's labor force, belong to
1.b labor unions today. A **labor union** is an organization of workers who share the same type of job or who work in the same industry. Labor unions press for policies that will benefit their members. In the 1940s and 1950s as many as a third of all working Americans were union members; and as recently as 1975 union membership accounted for fully a fourth of the labor force. But in spite of recent declines in union membership, labor unions remain a potent force in American politics.

A host of groups represent the interests of organized labor. The largest, in both size and political power, is the AFL-CIO (the American Federation of Labor-Congress of Industrial Organizations). It is now made up of some 100 separate unions, such as the Retail Clerks International Union, the International Association of Machinists and Aerospace Workers, the American Federation of State, County, and Municipal Employees, and the American Federation of Musicians. With all its unions, the AFL-CIO has about 12 million members. Each union, like the AFL-CIO itself, is organized on a national, State, and local basis.[7]

There are also a number of independent unions—that is, unions not affiliated with the

AFL-CIO. The largest and most powerful of them include such groups as the United Mine Workers, the United Transportation Union, and the International Longshoremen's and Warehousemen's Union.

Organized labor generally speaks with one voice on such social welfare and job-related matters as social security programs, minimum wages, and unemployment. But labor sometimes opposes labor. White-collar and blue-collar workers, for example, do not always share the same economic interests. Then, too, such factors as sectional interests (East-West, North-South, urban-rural, and so on) and production interests (trucks versus railroads versus airplanes, for example) sometimes divide labor's forces.

[7]The AFL was formed in 1886 as a federation of craft unions. A craft union is made up of those workers who have the same craft or skill—for example, a carpenters, plumbers, or electricians union. The growth of mass production industries created a large class of workers not skilled in any particular craft, however. The AFL found it difficult to organize workers in the new mass production industries. Many of its craft unions opposed the admission of unions of unskilled workers to the AFL. After years of bitter fights over craft versus industrial unionism, a group led by John L. Lewis of the United Mine Workers was expelled from the AFL in 1935. They formed the CIO in 1938. The rivalries between these two major national unions eased to the point where a merger, as the AFL-CIO, took place in 1955.

Agricultural Groups Only about five million people—some two percent of the population—live on farms in this country today. Still, farmers' influence on the government's agricultural policies is and has been enormous. Several powerful associations serve the interests of agriculture. They include several broad-based farm groups and a larger number that represent farmers who raise particular commodities.

The most prominent farm groups are the National Grange, the American Farm Bureau Federation, and the National Farmers Union. The Grange, established in 1867, is the oldest and generally the most conservative of them. Over the years, it has been as much a social as a political organization, concerned about the welfare of farm families. Some 400,000 farm families are now members, and much of the Grange's strength is centered in the Northeast and the Mid-Atlantic States.

The Farm Bureau is the largest and generally the most effective of the three. Formed in 1920, it soon developed a close working relationship with the Department of Agriculture.

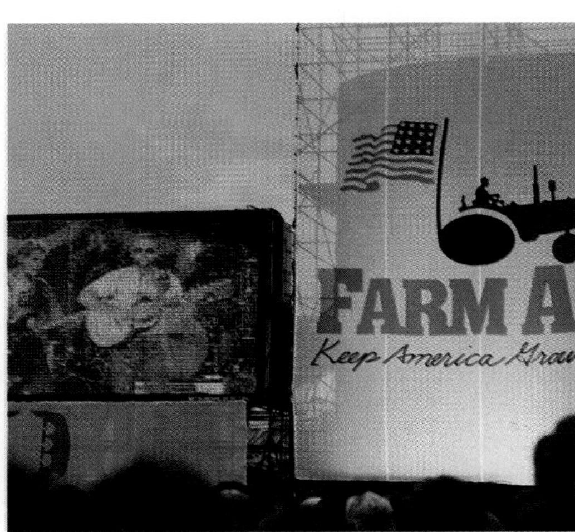

Farm Aid After such events as this "tractor-cade" down Pennsylvania Avenue dramatized the effects of falling prices and high costs on American farmers (left), a group of popular entertainers sponsored a fundraiser to help farmers meet their expenses (right).

SPOTLIGHT ON: Economics
The mid-1980s witnessed a new windfall for the campaign funds of representatives and senators, thanks to an increase of more than 100% in contributions from economic-based interest groups. According to political analyst Philip Stern, the leading corporate, trade association, and professional group political action committees increased their contributions to congressional campaigns from $8.15 million in 1983 to almost $16.7 million in 1987. Likewise, the contributions of the leading labor PACs increased from $6.6 million to almost $13.3 million over the same period.

It has some 3.8 million farm-family members and is especially strong in the Midwest. The Farm Bureau generally supports federal programs to promote agriculture. However, it opposes most government regulation and favors the free market economy.

The smaller Farmers Union draws its strength from smaller and less prosperous farmers. It now has some 250,000 farm-family members, most of them in the upper Midwest and West. The Farmers Union often calls itself the champion of the dirt farmer and often disagrees with the other two major organizations. It generally favors high levels of federal price supports for crops and livestock and other programs to regulate the production and marketing of commodities.

Another group, the National Farmer's Organization, came to the fore in the 1970s. The NFO calls for efforts to withhold produce from the market in order to raise the prices paid to farmers. It has sponsored "tractor-cades" to Washington and other cities to dramatize the farmers' high-costs/low-prices problems.

Many other groups speak for the producers of specific farm commodities—dairy products, grain, fruit, peanuts, livestock, cotton, wool, corn, soybeans, and so on. For example, three major organizations represent dairy farmers: the Associated Milk Producers, Inc., Mid-American Dairies, and Dairymen, Inc. Then, too, there are the National Association of Wheat Growers, the American Meat Institute, the American Cattlemen's Association, the National Wool Growers Association, the National Cotton Council, and many, many others.

Like business and labor groups, farm organizations sometimes find themselves at odds with one another. Thus, dairy, corn, soybean, and cotton groups compete as each of them tries to influence State laws regulating the production and sale of such products as margarine and yogurt. California and Florida citrus growers, each with their own groups, are sometimes pitted against one another, and so on.

Professional Groups The professions—generally defined as those occupations that require extensive and specialized training, such as medicine, law, and teaching—also maintain organizations to protect their interests.

Most professional groups are not nearly so large, well-organized, well-financed, or effective as most business, labor, and farm groups. Three major groups are exceptions, however: the American Medical Association (AMA), the American Bar Association (ABA), and the National Education Association (NEA). Each has a very real impact on public policies—and at every level of government.

There are dozens of less well-known, and less politically active, professional groups—the American Society of Civil Engineers, the American Library Association, the American Political Science Association, and a great many more. Much of their effort centers on such matters as the standards of the profession, the holding of professional meetings, and the publication of scholarly journals. Still, each of them acts in some ways as an interest group, bent on promoting the welfare of the profession and its members.

The Maze of Other Groups

As you have read, most interest groups are based on economic concerns. But hundreds have been formed for other reasons, and many have a good deal of political clout.

Groups that Promote Causes A large number of these other groups exist to promote a cause or an idea. In fact, it would take several pages just to list them here, and so what follows is only a sampling of the more important ones. The Woman's Christian Temperance Union was founded in 1874 and has some 50,000 members today; the WCTU has long sought the prohibition of alcohol. The American Civil Liberties Union was born in 1920; the ACLU now has some 250,000 members and fights in and out of court to protect civil and political rights. Common Cause dates from 1970 and its membership now exceeds 270,000; it calls itself "the citizen's lobby" and works for major reforms in the political process. The League of Women Voters and its many local leagues and now 120,000 members have since 1920 been dedicated to stimulating participation in and greater knowledge about public affairs.

Activity: for Gifted Students

Theme: Leadership Have students consider the leaders of historical artistic movements (such as Impressionism and Post-Modernism) and literary movements (such as Dadaism and Naturalism) as examples of groups or individuals that attempted to influence people's thoughts and feelings. Students can compare this artistic and literary leadership with the leadership provided by business, labor, and agricultural interest groups that attempt to influence public policy. Students may take notes from periodicals, biographies, interviews, documentaries, etc. They may present their findings in the form of a written or oral report.

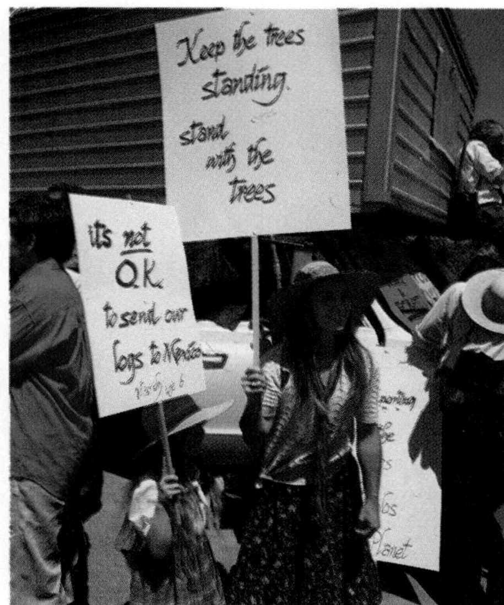

Conflict of Interest Groups that promote causes often find that their causes conflict with other groups' interests. As public sympathy grows for the protection of woodlands and wildlife (right), loggers muster support for protection of their jobs (left).

The list of cause groups goes on and on. Many women's rights groups—such as the National Women's Political Caucus, and several others—carry that banner. Several other groups, including the National Wildlife Federation, the Sierra Club, the Wilderness Society, and Friends of the Earth, are pledged to conservation and environmental protection. The National Right-to-Life Committee, Women Exploited by Abortion, and other groups oppose abortion; they are countered by the National Abortion Rights Action League, Planned Parenthood, and their allies. The National Rifle Association fights gun control legislation; Handgun Control, Inc. works for it. The list is endless.

Organizations that Promote the Welfare of Certain Groups A number of groups seek to promote the welfare of certain segments of the population. Among the best-known and most powerful are the American Legion and the Veterans of Foreign Wars, which work to advance the interests of the country's veterans. Groups like Older American, Inc. and the American Association of Retired Persons are very active in such areas as pensions and medical care for senior citizens. Several organizations—notably the National Association for the Advancement of Colored People (NAACP), the National Urban League, and People United to Save Humanity (PUSH)—are closely concerned with public policies of special interest to African Americans. Then, too, there are such organizations as the Japanese American Citizens League, the Mexican-American Legal Defense Fund, and the National Association of Arab Americans. Again, the list goes on and on.

Religious Organizations Many religious organizations also try to influence public policy in several important areas. Thus, many individual Protestants and their local and national churches do so through the National Council of Churches; and many other Protestants belong to such groups as Christian Voice and the Christian Coalition.

Roman Catholics pursue their interests through the National Catholic Welfare Council; and Jewish communicants, through the American Jewish Congress and B'nai B'rith's Anti-Defamation League. Yet again, the list of these organizations is endless.

Provide Guided Practice Have students give you the names of the basic types of interest groups (*business groups, labor groups, agricultural groups, groups that promote causes, groups that promote the welfare of particular groups, religious groups, public interest groups*) as you write them on the board. Then, skim through the section, name and briefly describe an interest group, and ask to which category the group belongs. For example, you might mention the Grange, an agricultural group. Have students check their answers in the text whenever there is a difference of opinion.

Provide Independent Practice

TRF **Teacher's Resource File** You may wish to assign Section 2 Guided Reading and Review, Unit 2 File, p. 94, to help students master section objective content.

Interpreting Political Cartoons Refer students to the political cartoon on page 220. Ask students what the "great privilege" the speaker on the right is referring to. (*The right not to listen to another person.*)

Caption Answer Interest groups are an example of citizens exercising their right to voice an opinion; others have the right not to listen to those opinions.

Activity: Teaching Heterogeneous Groups

Students may work cooperatively to design and produce a brochure for a new interest group to represent the needs of students. Working in small groups, students should come up with a list of goals and a statement of the policies for the new interest group. Students should also design a symbol that expresses their particular interest group's goals and values. Then each group should work together to produce the brochure. After the brochures are completed, have each team present its brochure to the class.

Spotlight on: Multiculturalism

The oldest and largest civil rights interest group in the United States, the National Association for the Advancement of Colored People (NAACP), has been committed to the "elimination of all barriers to political, educational, social, and economic equality" of African Americans and other minority groups since its founding in 1909. The NAACP has emphasized legal action to combat discrimination and brought many landmark cases before the Supreme Court, with *Brown* v. *Board of Education of Topeka* being perhaps the most important. About half a million Americans belong to the NAACP.

MONITOR COMPREHENSION

Answers to Section 2 Review
1. "Key Terms" are defined on the following pages:
a. trade association, p. 216
b. labor union, p. 216
c. public-interest group, p. 220
2. When it tries to influence public policy. **3.** Economic or occupational interests. **4.** Business, agricultural, labor, and professional. **5.** Groups promoting causes or the welfare of certain groups; religious organizations. **6.** (a) Some might criticize because groups harm others; others might say that it is the people's right to influence policy if they can.
(b) Answers will vary; some might say that in a democracy everyone is free to pursue their interests.

Teacher's Resource File See the Unit 2 File, p. 95, for the Section 2 Quiz. .

CLOSURE

Remind students that interest groups in the United States represent a huge variety of interests. Yet these groups generally fall into one of a few categories. As students read the next section, they will learn more about how interest groups attempt to influence policy and public opinion.

Assignment Assign Section 3, pages 222–227, for the next class period.

Interpreting Political Cartoons How does this cartoon emphasize the nature of interest groups in the United States?

Public-Interest Groups

Recall that interest groups are private groups. As you have read, most of them represent some special interest—business, labor, agriculture, veterans, teachers, and so on. They seek public policies of special benefit to their members, and they work against policies that threaten their own interests.

There are some groups, often called public-interest groups, with a broader goal, however. They work for the "public good." That is, a
1.c **public-interest group** is an interest group that seeks to institute certain public policies of benefit to all or most people in this country, whether they belong to or support that organization or not.[8]

Unlike most interest groups, public-interest groups focus on the roles that all Americans share. That is, they represent people as citizens, as consumers, as breathers of air, as drinkers of water, and so on.

Public-interest groups have become quite visible over the past 20 years. Among the best-known and most active of them today are Common Cause, of which you read on page 218, and the several organizations that make up Ralph Nader's Public Citizen, Inc. Some have existed for a much longer time—for example, the League of Women Voters. Recall that the League has roots that reach deep into the long history of the women's suffrage movement.

[8]Of course, nearly all interest groups claim that they work for the "public good." Thus, the NAM says that lower taxes on business will stimulate the economy and so help everyone. The AFL-CIO says the same thing about spending more public dollars for more public works programs. But, as a general rule, most interest groups support or oppose public policies on a much narrower basis: on what they see to be the best interests of their own members.

Section 2 Review

1. Define: trade association, labor union, public-interest group
2. At what point does an association become an interest group?
3. On what basis are most interest groups founded?
4. What are the major types of economically based interest groups?
5. What kinds of groups constitute the "maze of other groups"?

Critical Thinking

6. Identifying Central Issues (p. 19) Recall what you have read about interest groups in this section. Interest groups are sometimes criticized for pursuing their interests in spite of the welfare of other people. (a) Is this criticism fair? (b) Explain why you do or do not think a democratic society should tolerate such activities.

★

Reteach

Have students write a skit in which representatives from two competing interest groups (e.g., an environmentalist and an industry group) each approaches a member of Congress to discuss his or her side of an issue, such as the building of a new factory. Be sure that both sides of the issue are clearly explained in the skit, and that the congressperson comes to some decision.

Enrichment

Have students interview friends, relatives, other teachers, or anyone they know who is involved with an organized interest group. Have the students ask their subjects what they think the goals of their group are and what benefit they get from being a part of the group. Students can then contact the group to which their subject belongs. (Students can get the phone number or address from the subject or from a library resource such as the *Encyclopedia of Associations.*). Students should ask the group for information on its goals and the benefits it offers its members. Students should present their findings in an oral or written report. (Easy)

Debating Key Issues

Should Federal Projects Be Allowed to Violate the Law?

Tennessee Valley Authority v. *Hill*

In 1967, the Tennessee Valley Authority (TVA) began its construction of the Tellico Dam and Reservoir Project on a stretch of the Little Tennessee River. Congress had already appropriated the initial funding for this project. Six years later, the dam and reservoir was near completion.

At about this same time, after passage of the Endangered Species Act of 1973, the secretary of the interior declared that a small fish known as the snail darter was an endangered species. The secretary determined that the snail darter apparently lived only in that portion of the Little Tennessee River that would be flooded by the creation of the dam. The result would be total destruction of the snail darter's habitat.

According to the act, federal agencies were required to ensure that their actions did not destroy or modify any endangered species' critical habitat, yet the Tellico Project continued. Groups concerned with saving the snail darter brought action against the TVA in U.S. district court in order to forbid completion of the dam. Despite finding that the dam would jeopardize the fish's existence, the district court dismissed the case. On appeal, the U.S. court of appeals determined that the completion of the dam violated the Endangered Species Act and reversed the decision. At this point the TVA appealed to the Supreme Court.

Review the following arguments and evidence presented to the Supreme Court.

Arguments for the Tennessee Valley Authority

1. The district court refused to forbid completion of the dam even though it was well aware of the snail darter problem.

2. Congress had appropriated funds in every year since the starting of the dam, even after 1973. The continuance of appropriations, therefore, implied a repeal of the act in regard to the dam project.

3. The Endangered Species Act did not apply to a project that was completed or substantially completed when its threat to an endangered species was discovered.

Arguments for Hill

1. The completion of the Tellico Dam is clearly in violation of the Endangered Species Act.

2. When voting on appropriations measures, legislators are entitled to assume that the funds will be used for lawful purposes. An appropriations committees' approval does not operate to repeal or modify other existing legislation.

3. When Congress passed the act, it foresaw that it would occasionally require federal agencies to alter projects in progress in order to fulfill the act's goals, whatever the cost.

Getting Involved

1. Identify the grounds upon which each side based its arguments.

2. Debate the opposing viewpoints presented in this case.

3. Predict how you think the Supreme Court ruled in this case and why. Then refer to the Supreme Court glossary that begins on page 764 to read about the decision. Discuss the factors that you think should be considered in a conflict between technology and wildlife preservation.

TEACHING

Debating Key Issues

***Tennessee Valley Authority* v. *Hill:* Should Federal Projects Be Allowed to Violate the Law?**

Objective

Order information to predict the outcome of a court case.

Instruct

Before students read the feature, ask them to answer the question in the title. When students have finished reading, ask them if their answers have changed, and, if so, why.

Next, work through the "Identify" section. Have students briefly summarize each of the grounds for both sides' cases. Then have students compare their own reasoning in the case with those used in support of Hill or TVA.

When students have completed this comparison, debate the question informally as a whole class.

Supreme Court Decision

In order to prevent violation of the Endangered Species Act, the Supreme Court upheld the decision of the U.S. court of appeals, ruling for an injunction against TVA's completion of the nearly finished dam.

TRF **Teacher's Resource File**
See the Supreme Court Case file, p. 7, for an activity that extends coverage of this case.

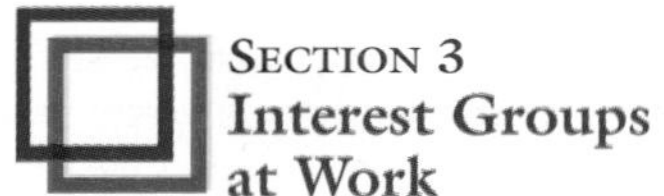

SECTION 3
Interest Groups at Work

FOCUS

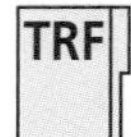

Teacher's Resource File See the Unit 2 File, p. 96, for the Section 3 Outline.

Objectives

9.5 Identify the relationship between interest groups and public opinion.
9.6 Explain the role of interest groups in the election process.
9.7 Describe how interest groups actually apply pressure on the policy-making process.

Bellringer Activity Write the sentence "Is propaganda good or bad?" on the board. Give students a few moments to think about the question, then elicit responses. Be sure students explain their opinions. Lead students to the understanding that although propaganda has taken on negative connotations, it is not inherently "good" or "bad."

State the Purpose In order to achieve their goals of influencing public policy, interest groups seek to influence public opinion, the nomination of candidates, and the making, enforcement, and interpretation of laws. In Section 3, students will learn how interest groups try to achieve their goals

3 Interest Groups at Work

Find Out:

- What is the relationship between interest groups and public opinion?
- What is the role of interest groups in the election process?
- How do interest groups actually apply pressure on the policy-making process?

Key Terms:

propaganda, single-interest group, lobbying, grass roots

Interest groups exist to influence public policies—and so they are fairly good illustrations of why it has been said that politics is all about "who gets what, when, and how."[9] As you will see in this section, interest groups use a wide range of techniques as they (1) try to influence public opinion, (2) work to affect the outcome of elections, and (3) lobby those who make public policy.

[9]The phrase comes from a pioneering study of political behavior, Harold Lasswell, *Politics: Who Gets What, When, How* (New York: McGraw-Hill, 1936).

Interest Groups and Public Opinion

Public opinion is the most significant long-term force in American politics. It is abundantly clear that, over the long run, no public policy can be followed successfully without the support of a goodly portion of the population—and interest groups know this.

Interest groups regularly reach out to the public to accomplish one or all of three major goals:

1. To supply the public with information an organization thinks the people should have. The information is presented to support that group's interests, of course. Thus Handgun Control, Inc. often runs full-page magazine ads keyed to one fact: the number of Americans who are killed by handguns each year.
2. To build a positive image for a group. Thus, the National Rifle Association frequently

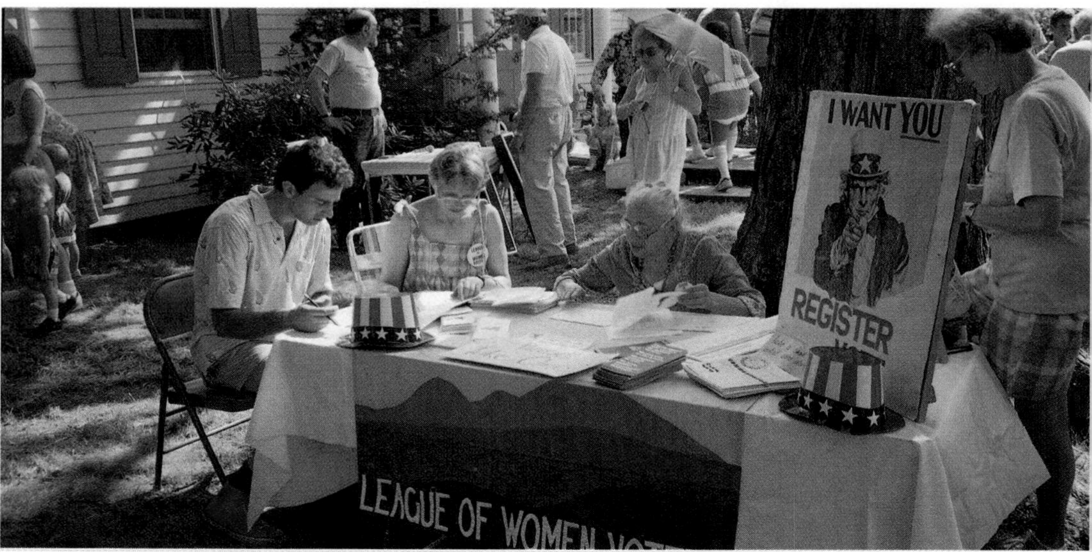

The League of Women Voters Public interest groups exist to respond to the needs of all the people, not just a few. This nonpartisan public-interest group promotes voter registration and dispenses information on election issues.

Reading Strategy: Problem Solving

Ask students to imagine that they are employed by an interest group. There is one key member of Congress who does not vote for the group's position. Have students list possible approaches they can use to influence the member of Congress. (*Examples: threats, promises, persuading with information about the need for more funding.*)

Vocabulary

Point out "Key Terms" on page 222. Have students use dictionaries to provide several variations on the meaning of the word *propaganda*. LEP

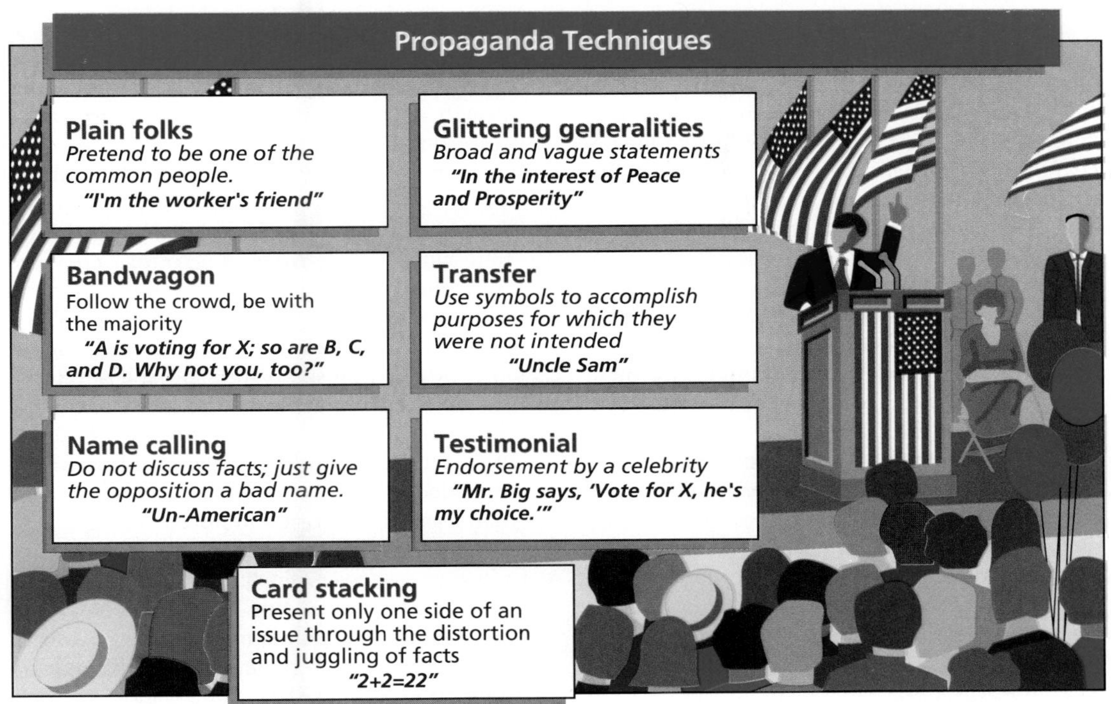
Propaganda Techniques
Plain folks
Pretend to be one of the common people.
"I'm the worker's friend"
Glittering generalities
Broad and vague statements
"In the interest of Peace and Prosperity"
Bandwagon
Follow the crowd, be with the majority
"A is voting for X; so are B, C, and D. Why not you, too?"
Transfer
Use symbols to accomplish purposes for which they were not intended
"Uncle Sam"
Name calling
Do not discuss facts; just give the opposition a bad name.
"Un-American"
Testimonial
Endorsement by a celebrity
"Mr. Big says, 'Vote for X, he's my choice.'"
Card stacking
Present only one side of an issue through the distortion and juggling of facts
"2+2=22"

Interpreting Charts Propaganda is found in every form of mass communication and increases with importance as an issue becomes more controversial. After looking at the chart, list some media where propaganda techniques can be used.

runs ads that feature the NRA's gun-safety programs and the many shooting tournaments it sponsors.

3. To promote a particular public policy. This, of course, is the purpose of most interest groups' efforts.

Propaganda Interest groups try to create the public attitudes they want by using propaganda.[10] **Propaganda** is a technique of persua- 1.a
sion aimed at influencing individual or group behaviors. Its goal is to create a particular popular belief. That belief may be completely true or false, or it may lie somewhere between those extremes. Today, people tend to think of propaganda as a form of lying and deception. As a technique, however, propaganda is neither moral nor immoral; it is amoral.

Propaganda does not use objective logic. Rather it begins with a conclusion and then brings together any evidence that will support that conclusion and disregards information that will not. Propaganda and objective analysis sometimes agree in their conclusions, but their methods are quite different. In short, propagandists are not teachers interested in determining the truth; rather, they are advertisers, persuaders, and brainwashers who are interested in influencing others.

The development of the mass media in this country encouraged the use of propaganda, first in the field of commercial advertising and then in politics. To be successful, propaganda must almost always be presented in simple, interesting, and credible terms. The major techniques that propagandists use are outlined in the chart on this page.

[10]The term comes from the Latin *propagare*—to propagate, to spread, to disseminate. It has been a part of the American political vocabulary since the 1930s.

Interpreting Charts Have students explain how each of the techniques might be effective at influencing people's opinions. *(Possible answers: "Plain folks": helps listener relate to the speaker. "Bandwagon": appeals to people who want to be on the winning side. "Name calling": attaches negative image to opposing person or idea. "Glittering generalities": uses broad and vague statements. "Transfer": associates person or idea with a positive image. "Testimonial": makes people think that a positive view of the person or idea is the "correct" one. "Card stacking": makes evidence against person or idea seem overwhelming.)*

Caption Answer Newspapers, magazines, political rallies, speeches, pamphlets, television, radios, books, billboards, bumper stickers.

ABCNEWS INTERACTIVE

The following video segments may be used to highlight aspects of the political influence of interest groups.

POWERS OF THE CONGRESS GUIDEBOOK
Chapter 58: Committees of the House of Representatives, p. 64
Chapter 59: Committees of the Senate, p. 65

See also Enrichment Questions and Activities, beginning on page 161.

SPOTLIGHT: Political Talk

Not only did the word *propaganda* not always have a negative connotation, it also originally had nothing to do with politics. Interestingly, the word comes to modern English from the Latin *collegium de propaganda,* the name of a committee of Roman Catholic cardinals established in 1627 by Pope Urban VIII. The purpose of the collegium was to train missionaries, who would then go out from Rome to "propagate" the faith.

INSTRUCT

Explain/Discuss Remind students of the definition of an *interest group:* Any private group that attempts to influence public policy. Also review the definition of *public policy:* all those things that government does.

Explain to students that influencing public policy requires that interest groups influence those who make public policy.

Have students discuss the means by which this might be most effectively accomplished. To aid in this discussion, you might want to have students answer the following questions: Why would an interest group want to influence public opinion? (*Because the public can put pressure on policy makers.*) Why might interest groups want to influence elections? (*Because elected officials will be the people who actually make and implement policy.*)

Explain that a *lobbyist* is a representative of an interest group responsible for carrying out the group's goals wherever necessary. Have students discuss the various aspects of a lobbyist's job.

Talented propagandists almost never attack the logic of some policy they oppose. Instead, they often attack it with name-calling; that is, they paint such labels as "communist," "fascist," "ultraliberal," "ultraconservative," "pie-in-the-sky," or "greedy," and so on. Or they try to discredit the policy or person by card-stacking—that is, presenting only material that will make something appear to be what in fact it is not.

Policies that propagandists support receive labels that will produce favorable reactions—such glittering generalities as "American," "sound," "fair," and "just." Symbols are often used to elicit those reactions, too: Uncle Sam and the flag are favorites. So, too, are testimonials—endorsements, or supporting statements, from well-known television stars, professional athletes, and the like. Both the bandwagon and the plain-folks approaches get heavy use, too.

Propaganda is spread through newspapers, radio, television, movies, billboards, books, magazines, pamphlets, posters, speeches—in fact, through every form of mass communication. The more controversial—or the less popular—a group's position may be, the more necessary the propaganda campaign becomes, because competing groups will likely be conducting campaigns of their own.

Interest Groups, Parties, and Elections

As you know, interest groups and political parties are very different creatures. They exist in the same environment, however, and their paths often cross.

For their part, interest groups know that political parties play a central role in selecting those people who make public-policy decisions. They are quite aware, too, of the fact that much of government's policy-making machinery is organized by and through parties. So, interest groups try to influence the behavior of political parties—and they do so in a number of ways. Some groups keep close ties with one or the other of the major parties. Most hope to secure the support of both of them, however. Several urge their members to become active in party affairs and try to win posts in party organizations.

As you have seen, campaigns for public office cost money. Interest groups are quite aware of this fact, too—and they are a major source of campaign funds today. Much of their financial help now goes to parties and their candidates through political action committees (PACs), as you read in Chapter 7.

The number of PACs has grown rapidly in recent years. One particular variety has grown most rapidly, however. These organizations are
1.b often called **single-interest groups**. They are PACs that concentrate their efforts on one issue—for example, abortion, gun control, or nuclear power development. They work for or, more often, against a candidate solely on the basis of that candidate's stand on that one issue. For them, all other considerations—the candidate's record on other questions, his or her party identification or political experience, and so on—are of little or no importance.

An interest group's election tactics often have to involve some very finely tuned decisions. The group must consider how its actions on behalf of or against a candidate might affect its overall goal of influencing policy. If, for example, a group supports the Democratic candidate for a seat in the U.S. Senate, it may not want to help that candidate by attacking the Republican nominee in the race—especially if the Republican has some chance of winning. The interest group might also be concerned that another Republican candidate who wins some other office might be offended by attacks on a party colleague, even if he or she agrees with the group's policy aims. Most interest groups try to remember that their first concern is with the making of public policy. Any part they play in the election process is only secondary to that objective. But, notice, single-interest groups do not follow this rule.

Lobbying

1.c **Lobbying** is usually defined as those activities by which group pressures are brought to bear on legislators and the legislative process. Certainly, it is that, but it is also much more. Realistically, lobbying includes all of the means by which group pressures are brought to bear on all aspects of the public-policy-making process. Lobbying takes place in legislative bodies, of course, and it often has important effects there.

ACTIVITY: Cooperative Learning

Time: One class period **Activity:** Create a poster that uses a technique of propaganda. **Grouping:** Groups of three to four students **Purpose:** Assign one of the major techniques of propaganda to each group. Then have students choose an issue of public concern and design a poster using the assigned technique to influence people's beliefs about the issue. **Roles:** Assign the following roles: manager, recorder, illustrator, spokesperson. **Outcome:** Have the spokesperson present the group's poster. The class may identify the particular technique of propaganda used; have the class discuss each poster's effectiveness.

But it is also often directed at administrative agencies, and sometimes even at the courts.

What happens in a legislative body is often of deep concern to several different, and competing, interests. A bill to regulate the sale of firearms, for example, excites the interest of many persons and groups. Those companies that make guns, those that sell them, and those that produce or sell ammunition, targets, scopes, hunting jackets, sleeping bags, and a host of other related products have a clear stake in that bill's contents and its fate. So, too, do law-enforcement agencies, hunters, wildlife conservationists, such groups as the National Rifle Association and the American Civil Liberties Union, and many others.

But public policy is made by much more than the words in a statute. What happens after a law has been passed is often of real concern to organized interests, too. How is a law interpreted and how vigorously is it applied by the agency that enforces it? What attitude do the courts take if the law is challenged on some legal ground? These questions point up the fact that interest groups often have to carry their lobbying efforts beyond the legislative arena—into one and sometimes several agencies in the executive branch and sometimes into the courts, as well.

Nearly all of the more important organized interests in the country—business groups, labor unions, farm organizations, the professions, veterans, churches, and many more—maintain lobbyists in Washington.[11]

The Work of the Lobbyist Lobbyists themselves often prefer to be known by some

[11]Lobbyists are also stationed in the 50 State capitals, and their number grows whenever the State's legislature is in session. The "lobby" is actually an outer room or main corridor or some other part of a capitol building to which the general public is admitted. The term *lobby-agent* was being used to identify favor-seekers at sessions of the New York State legislature in Albany by the late 1820s. By the 1830s the term had been shortened to *lobbyist* and was in wide use in Washington and elsewhere.

Lobbyists in Action Part of daily life in Congress includes listening to the many lobbyists who wish to persuade members of Congress to support their views. These lobbyists are waiting to see members of the House Ways and Means Committee.

Enrichment

Tell students to imagine that they work on the staff of an interest group that promotes programs to end hunger. Have the students draft a memo to others on the staff in which they outline a strategy for influencing public policy. Tell students to include ideas for reaching the public, candidates, and all levels of government. (Average)

OR

TRF **Teacher's Resource File**
See the Unit 2 File, pp. 100–102, for the Case Study on Contemporary Issues for Chapter 9.

Interpreting Tables Ask students to explain why people's approval of Congress generally might be lower than that of their individual representatives. (*Possible answer: People are less likely to be critical of a representative they elected.*)

Caption Answer A lobbyist might use the information to persuade a member of Congress that the public is unhappy with current policies and that he or she should switch to endorsing the lobbyist's point of view.

Provide Guided Practice On the chalkboard, write "The Public," "The Candidates," and "The Government." Have students write one sentence for each item that explains their significance to interest groups. (*Possible answers: Interest groups are interested in the public because public opinion is a powerful weapon. Candidates are important because they might soon be in a position to influence policy. The government is important because that is where public policy is actually made and implemented.*)

Provide Independent Practice

TRF **Teacher's Resource File** You may wish to assign Section 3 Guided Reading and Review, Unit 2 File, p. 97, to help students master section objective content.

Taking the Public Pulse

Question	Response
Do you approve or disapprove of the job Congress is doing?	*Disapprove: 60%*
Do you approve or disapprove of the job your representative in Congress is doing?	*Approve: 64%*
Do you believe the country is headed in the right direction or is off on the wrong track?	*On the wrong track: 79%* *Heading in the right direction: 19%*
Source: Washington Post/ABC News poll, October 16, 1990.	

Interpreting Tables The table above shows the results of a poll examining people's views of Congress. How might a lobbyist use the information in the poll to influence a member of Congress?

other title—"legislative counsel" or "public representative," for example. Whatever they call themselves, their major task is to work for those matters of benefit to their clients and against those that may harm them.

A lobbyist's effectiveness depends in large part on his or her knowledge of the political system. The competent lobbyist is thoroughly familiar with government and its ways, with the facts of current political life, and with the techniques of "polite" persuasion. Some have been members of Congress or the State legislature. They know the "legislative ropes" and have many close contacts among present-day members. Many others are lawyers, former journalists, or men and women who have come into lobbying from the closely related field of public relations.

Lobbyists at work use a number of techniques as they try to persuade legislators and other policy makers to share their points of view. They see that articles, reports, and all sorts of other information favorable to their causes reach those officeholders. Many testify before legislative committees. If the House Committee on the Judiciary is considering a gun control bill, for example, representatives of all those groups mentioned a moment ago are certain to be invited, or to ask for the opportunity, to present their views. The testimony that lobbyists give is usually "expert," but, of course, it is also couched in terms favorable to the interests they represent.

Most lobbyists also know how to bring
1.d "grass-roots" pressures to bear. **Grass roots** means of or from the "common people," the average voter. The groups they speak for can mount campaigns by letter, phone, and telegram from "the folks back home"—and often on short notice. Favorable news stories, magazine articles, advertisements, radio and television appeals, endorsements by noted personalities—these and the many other weapons of publicity are contained within the arsenal of the good lobbyist.

Several interest groups now publish ratings of members of Congress. Those rankings are based on the votes cast on measures that those groups regard as crucial to their interests. Among the most prominent of the many organizations that now compile and publish such ratings are the Americans for Democratic Action (AFDA), the American Civil Liberties Union (ACLU), the AFL-CIO's Committee on Political Education (COPE), the American Conservative Union (ACU), the National Tax Limitation Committee (NTLC), and the Chamber of Commerce of the United States.

Each of these groups selects a number of key measures and then rates each member on the basis of his or her votes on those bills. In the usual rating scheme, each senator or representative is given a score, a number that reflects how often he or she voted with the interest group.

Interest groups see to it that the mass media publicize these ratings. They also distribute the ratings to the group's membership. Their ultimate objective is twofold: Either to persuade unfriendly legislators to change their voting behavior or to help bring about their defeat in future elections.

The typical lobbyist of today is a far cry from those of an earlier day—and from many

SPOTLIGHT ON: Behind the Scenes
Certain interest groups "target" candidates to receive negative publicity during elections. Between 1972 and 1980, 24 of the 52 representatives whom Environmental Action Incorporated targeted as members of its "dirty dozen" were defeated in the next election. In 1980, the National Conservative Political Action Committee (NCPAC) raised $1.2 million to campaign against the Senate Democrats it found "most distasteful." Nine senators who were targeted by NCPAC were defeated.

of the ficticious ones still found on television and in novels and the movies. The once fairly common practice of bribery and the heavy-handed use of unethical practices are almost unknown. Most present-day lobbyists work in the open, and their major techniques come under the headings of friendliness, persuasion, and helpfulness.

Lobbyists are ready to do such things as buy lunches and dinners, provide information, write speeches, and prepare bills in proper form. The lunch and dinners are good, the information usually quite accurate, the speeches forceful, and the bills well drawn. Most lobbyists know that if they behaved otherwise—gave false information, for example—they would damage, if not destroy, their credibility and so their overall effectiveness.

Lobbyists work hard to influence committee action, floor debate, and the final vote in a legislative body. If they fail in one house, they carry their fight to the other. If they lose there, too, they may turn to the executive branch[12] and, perhaps to the courts, as well.

Lobby Regulation Lobbying abuses do occur now and then, of course. False or misleading testimony, bribery, and other unethical pressures are not common, but they do exist. To try to keep the activities of lobbyists within bounds, Congress passed the Federal Regulation of Lobbying Act in 1946. In addition, each of the States now has a somewhat similar law.

The federal law requires lobbyists to register with the clerk of the house and the secretary of the Senate. More exactly, it requires individuals and groups to register if they collect or spend money for the "principal purpose" of influencing legislation. The Supreme Court narrowed the scope of the law somewhat in 1954. In *United States* v. *Harris*, the Court upheld the law against 1st Amendment attacks on its constitutionality. But the Court also held that its registration provisions apply only to lobbying efforts aimed at Congress, not to those aimed at the public at large.

The law has proved to be quite inadequate since its passage, and Congress has not seen fit to strengthen it. Its vague phrase "principal purpose" is a huge loophole through which many active groups avoid registration. They do so on the grounds that lobbying is only "incidental" to their main objectives or that their monies are spent for "research" and "public information" rather than on lobbying. Most estimates put the number of people who now earn at least part of their living by lobbying Congress at about 20,000. Yet only some 7,000 persons are registered under the law, and that number includes many multiple filings by persons who lobby for several different groups. The law does have penalties for its violation, but it has no enforcement provisions. Also, it does not apply to lobbying aimed at agencies in the executive branch nor does it cover testifying before congressional committees.

[12]Notice that various government agencies often act much like interest groups in their relations with Congress or with a State's legislature—for example, when they seek funds or when they offer testimony for or against a bill in committee.

Section 3 Review

1. Define: propaganda, single-interest group, lobbying, grass roots

2. For what three reasons do interest groups reach out to the public?

3. (a) Identify four of the major techniques of the propagandist. (b) Which technique might involve the endorsement of a celebrity?

4. For what reason must interest groups put pressure on government agencies beyond the legislature?

5. What are some of the key skills of a good lobbyist?

6. (a) What are lobbyists required to do by the Federal Regulation of Lobbying Act of 1946? (b) Why has the law proved to be inadequate?

Critical Thinking

7. Formulating Questions (p. 19) Create a list of five questions you could ask your legislator to determine his or her position on an issue of importance to you.

★

Monitor Comprehension

Answers to Section 3 Review
1. "Key Terms" are defined on the following pages:
a. propaganda, p. 223
b. single-interest group, p. 224
c. lobbying, p. 224
d. grass roots, p. 226
2. To provide information, to promote their image, and to promote policies. **3.** "Plain folks," "bandwagon," "glittering generalities," "card stacking," "transfer," and "testimonial." (b) "testimonial."
4. A law's impact can be affected by administrative or judicial policies. **5.** Lobbyists must provide credible information. They must know government. **6.** (a) Register with the clerk of the House and secretary of the Senate. (b) Some lobbyists insist lobbying is only an "incidental" activity for them, so they do not have to register. **7.** Questions will vary but should be designed to provide specific information.

Closure

Interest groups try to win public opinion through propaganda promoting their policies. Interest groups also try to influence elections, but only to the extent that such actions further their overall policy goals. Lobbyists are employed by interest groups to influence policy by putting pressure on government before and after policy is formed.

In the next chapter, students will learn about the most important policy-making body in this country, the United States Congress.

Assignment Assign Chapter 10, Section 1, pp. 235–238, for the next class period.

Reteach

Have students review the main section headings and then describe the three ways in which interest groups can attempt to influence public policy. (*By influencing public opinion, by influencing the election process, and by lobbying in government.*)

Teacher's Resource File
See the Unit 2 File for the Section 3 Quiz on p. 98.

TEACHING
Critical Thinking

Distinguishing Fact from Opinion

Objective
Evaluate a statement to determine whether it is based on fact or opinion.

INSTRUCT

Ask students to describe the difference between these statements: (1) "You will be successful in your career." and (2) "You have been a successful student with a B average." (*The first is opinion, the second fact.*) Then have students read the selection. When students have completed each step, invite them to share their responses.

Answers 1: (a) Students are getting older; 45 percent are over 25; 6,000 students over 65; 14 percent of students over 35; most popular programs; the shift toward service economy and high tech; research on mental stimulation. (b) All of the above. (c) encyclopedias, reference books on education, etc.
2. (a) Society ought to change its definition of a college student; nontraditional students should not worry about their abilities. (b) "Ought," "predict," "should not," "indicates." (c) With the shift toward a service economy . . . higher education is a necessity.
3. (a) Forty-five percent of students over age 25; nontraditional students will be a majority. (b) Most popular programs are career instruction; the shift toward a service economy.

Critical Thinking

Distinguishing Fact from Opinion

Distinguishing fact from opinion means separating those statements that can be proven to be true from those that reflect a particular viewpoint or opinion. Interest groups use both fact and opinion to influence public opinion. So, in order to draw your own conclusions about the issues or policies they support, you need to be able to separate the facts from the opinions when you consider any information these groups put out. The paragraph below is an adaptation from an article published by the American Association of Retired Persons, an interest group serving the needs of senior citizens. Use the following steps to practice distinguishing fact from opinion.

1. Determine which statements are based on fact. A fact is something that is true. It can be checked against a reliable source and confirmed. A fact does not include what someone thinks, values, or believes. (a) What information in the paragraph below might qualify as a fact? (b) Does the paragraph include information that you could check against another source? (c) If so, what might constitute a reliable source?

2. Determine which statements are opinion. An opinion states a belief or feeling about a subject. Opinions usually cannot be proven. Statements of opinion often begin with phrases such as *I think, I feel, I believe,* and use adjectives such as *best, worst, extraordinary.* Read the paragraph below and answer the following questions: (a) What opinions are expressed in the paragraph? (b) What words or phrases give a signal that the statement is an opinion? (c) Are there any statements in the paragraph that contain both fact and opinion?

3. Separate facts and opinions when you read. Well-written material usually contains both facts and opinions, but an opinion is more forceful when facts are given to support it. (a) What facts in the paragraph below support the first sentence? (b) Write down any facts you can find to support this statement: "Higher education has become a necessity for workers."

On average, college students are getting older. In light of this fact, American society ought to change its definition of a college student. A 1988 study of the College Board found that 45 percent of the nation's undergraduate students are at least 25 years old. Studies such as these have led some observers to predict that so-called nontraditional students will become the majority on college campuses within 10 years. The trend is already underway. The City University of New York already has more than 6,000 students over age 65. At the University of Cincinnati students over age 35 make up 14 percent of the student population. The most popular programs are those emphasizing career instruction. With the shift toward a service economy and today's advanced technology, it appears that higher education has become a necessity for workers seeking to upgrade their careers.

Many older students worry that they will not be able to handle the demands of a college education. However, nontraditional students should not feel this way. Research indicates that it is the amount of mental stimulation and not age that determines a person's mental ability.

TRF **Teacher's Resource File**
See the Unit 2 File, p. 99, for the Skill Application to reinforce this skill lesson.

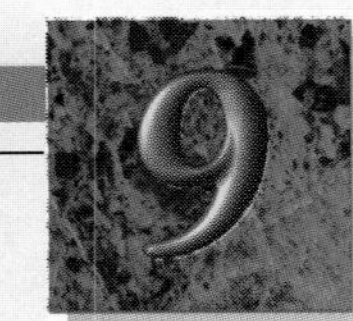

Chapter-in-Brief

Scan all headings, photographs, charts, and other visuals in the chapter before reading the section summaries below.

Section 1 The Nature of Interest Groups (pp. 211–214) Interest groups are private groups that try to persuade public officials to respond to the shared attitudes of their members. Like political parties, interest groups exist to achieve some political purpose. Unlike the major parties, however, interest groups do not nominate candidates; they do not focus on winning elections; and they are not generally concerned with the broad range of issues with which political parties must contend.

Judgment of interest groups is best achieved by weighing their intended function against some of the frequent criticisms. On one hand, interest groups function to: (1) stimulate interest in public affairs; (2) represent members on the basis of shared attitudes; (3) provide information to governments; (4) serve as a vehicle for participation in the political process; and (5) add an element to the system of checks and balances.

On the other hand, interest groups are often criticized for: (1) having influence out of proportion to their size; (2) being hard to define in terms of the size or nature of their membership; (3) misrepresenting their membership; and (4) occasionally using unethical tactics.

Section 2 Types of Interest Groups (pp. 215–220) Interest groups come in all shapes and sizes. Most people belong to several organizations that meet the definition of an interest group, even though those groups may not seem overtly political.

The greatest number of pressure groups exist on the basis of some economic or occupational interest. For example, the business community, labor, and agriculture each have many organizations that serve the peculiar interests of specific professions or industries. Often, the efforts of these groups conflict with one another.

In addition to business, labor, and farm groups, there are many groups devoted to specific political and social causes, to religious interests, and to the welfare of distinct segments of the population.

Most interest groups are private. However, there are groups that work for some aspect of the "public good." These groups are called public-interest groups.

Section 3 Interest Groups at Work (pp. 222–227) Interest groups direct their efforts in three main directions. They aim to: (1) influence public opinion, (2) influence elections, and (3) lobby those who make public policy.

Public opinion is the most significant long-term force in American politics. For this reason, interest groups work hard to capture it. Groups court public opinion by supplying the public with information favorable to the group's cause, working to build a positive image for the group, and promoting their policies. Interest groups frequently use propaganda to achieve their goals.

To the extent that they are interested in influencing policy, interest groups are interested in elections. This is especially true of single-interest groups, which seek their narrow aims largely by promoting the election or defeat of candidates. However, most interest groups are cautious when involving themselves in electoral politics that they do not create unfavorable reactions.

Interest groups also influence policy by lobbying, a practice that takes place wherever policy is made or administered. Lobbyists use a variety of means to exert influence. Most rely on ethical practices. Yet enough abuses have taken place that Congress has passed legislation to regulate lobbyists and their actions.

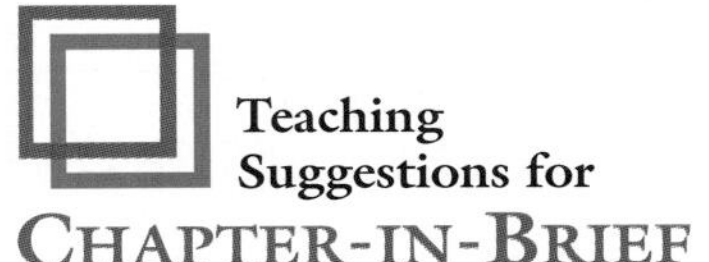

Teaching Suggestions for CHAPTER-IN-BRIEF

Below are some of the possible uses for the Chapter-in-Brief:

To Preview the Chapter You may want to assign the Chapter-in-Brief page and the Section Outlines from the Teacher's Resource File before beginning Chapter 9 to introduce students to the "Key Terms" and concepts in each section.

To Review the Chapter When students have completed Chapter 9, you might want to assign the Chapter-in-Brief as a tool for review, along with the Guided Reading and Reviews from the Teacher's Resource File.

To Omit the Chapter If you wish to skip Chapter 9, it may be helpful to assign the Chapter-in-Brief to students as a review before continuing to another chapter. You may also want to assign the Chapter 9 Test to assess student knowledge of the material. Then specific portions of Chapter 9 may be assigned to students needing reinforcement of "Key Terms" and concepts.

Teacher's Resource File See the Unit 2 File for the following materials:

- Section Outlines, pp. 90, 93, 96.
- Guided Reading and Reviews, pp. 91, 94, 97.
- Chapter 9 Test, pp. 103–105.

ADDITIONAL RESOURCES

A House Divided: Lobbies and Critics. Barr, 1986. Film. Color. 16 min.

Goldfield, Michael. *The Decline of Organized Labor in the United States.* University of Chicago Press, 1989.

Hrebenar, Ronald J. and Ruth K. Scott. *Interest Group Politics in America.* Prentice Hall, 2nd ed., 1990.

Lobbying: A Case History. EBEC, 1977. Film. Color. 18 min.

Mahood, H.R. *Interest Group Politics in America: A New Intensity.* Prentice Hall, 1990.

Richian, W.C. *Lobbying for Social Change.* Haworth Press, 1991.

Vogel, David. *Fluctuating Fortunes: The Political Power of Business in America.* Basic Books, 1989.

Answers to
Chapter 3 Review

Vocabulary and Key Terms

Matching
1. trade association
2. public affairs
3. single-interest group
4. interest group
5. lobbying

True or False
1. False—the correct term is *propaganda.*
2. False—the correct term is *single-interest group.*
3. True.
4. True.

Word relationships
1. grass roots
2. public policy
3. labor union
4. public-interest group

Main Ideas

Section 1
1. They put pressure on the policy-making process and they represent the interests of a special group. **2.** Such groups exist at any level of government where public policy is made or influenced. **3.** They are alike in that they are groups that join together for political purposes. They differ in that only parties nominate candidates; also, parties are interested only in winning elections, whereas interest groups are interested in influencing policy by whatever effective means. They also differ in that political parties have a wider scope of interest than interest groups, which tend to focus on specific fields of interest. **4.** Interest groups have long been criticized because they sought the narrow interest of the few even at the expense of the welfare of the many. Other people, such as Tocqueville, have admired the way that Americans formed so many groups. These people see such groups as a major strength in American democracy.

Section 2
5. Americans have tended to form many associations and groups. Many individuals belong to several groups.
6. Most are based on economic interest. Others include groups that promote causes, groups that promote the welfare of certain groups, religious groups, and others. **7.** Private groups represent the interests of a specific group. Public interest groups seek to achieve benefits for all people.

Section 3
8. (a) Public opinion is the most important force in American politics, which means it is the most effective way to influence public policy. (b) To supply the public with information, to build a positive image for the group and to promote a particular policy. **9.** They are not interested in communicating the truth, per se, or communicating knowledge; rather, they are interested in promoting their cause. **10.** (a) Most groups are interested in elections only to the extent that they have the potential to affect public policy.

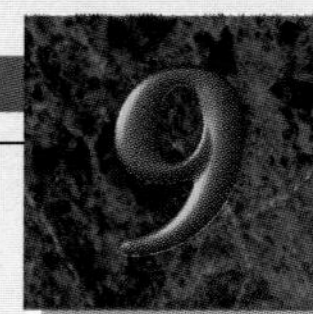

Chapter Review

Vocabulary and Key Terms

interest group (p. 211)
public policy (p. 211)
public affairs (p. 213)
trade association (p. 216)
labor union (p. 216)
public-interest group (p. 220)
propaganda (p. 223)
single-interest group (p. 224)
lobbying (p. 224)
grass roots (p. 226)

Matching: *Review the key terms in the list above. If you are not sure of a term's meaning, look up the term and review its definition. Choose a term from the list above that best matches each description.*

1. a type of interest group representing the interests of a business group
2. those events and issues of concern to all the people of a society
3. political action committees devoted to one issue
4. an organization that works to influence public policy
5. the means by which group pressures are brought to bear on all aspects of the policy-making process

True or False: *Determine whether each statement is true or false. If it is true, write "true." If it is false, change the underlined word or words to make the statement true.*

1. <u>Lobbying</u> is a technique of persuasion aimed at influencing individual or group behaviors.
2. A <u>public-interest group</u> devotes its efforts at defeating or supporting those candidates that support its goals.
3. Interest groups help to stimulate interest in <u>public affairs</u>.
4. As a technique, <u>propaganda</u> is neither moral nor immoral; it is amoral.

Word Relationships: *Replace the underlined definition with the correct term from the list above.*

1. Some interest groups put pressure on lawmakers by launching campaigns that rely on <u>the common people, the average voters</u>.
2. Interest groups exist for the purpose of influencing <u>all the things that a government endeavors to do</u>.
3. In many industries workers have formed <u>organizations of those who share the same type of job or who work in the same industry</u>.
4. One type of interest group is <u>an organization devoted to the interests of all the people</u>.

Main Ideas

Section 1 (pp. 211–214)

1. For what reason are interest groups sometimes called "pressure groups" or "special interests"?
2. At what levels of government can you find interest groups operating?
3. In what ways are interest groups alike and different from political parties?
4. Summarize the nature of the long debate over the role of interest groups in the American political system.

Section 2 (pp. 215–220)

5. For what reason has the United States often been called "a nation of joiners"?

6. Into what categories do most interest groups fall?
7. What is the difference between private and public interest groups?

Section 3 (pp. 222–227)

8. (a) For what reason must interest groups be concerned with public opinion? (b) For what purposes do they appeal to public opinion?
9. For what reason is it correct to say that propagandists are not teachers?
10. (a) To what extent are most interest groups concerned about elections? (b) What is the exception to this rule?
11. (a) At what stage of policy making must lobbyists be involved? (b) Why?

Critical Thinking

1. **Distinguishing Fact from Opinion** (p. 19) Recall the criticism of interest groups that are discussed on page 214 of this chapter. (a) Which of these criticisms are based on fact? (b) Which are based on opinion?
2. **Demonstrating Reasoned Judgment** (p. 19) The text says that forming interest groups is both practical and democratic. (a) Explain your understanding of this statement. (b) Do you agree or disagree?
3. **Making Comparisons** (p. 19) Consider the discussion of the functions and criticisms of interest groups in Section 1. Based on this information, discuss your opinion whether or not interest groups are "good" or "bad."
4. **Drawing Conclusions** (p. 19) The text points out that many people belong to several interest groups, which often work against one another. What does this suggest about the nature of people's participation in interest groups?

Getting Involved

1. **Writing Your Opinion** Write a draft of a bill aimed at regulating the influence of interest groups in government. Begin by reviewing some of the criticisms of interest groups discussed in the chapter. For each criticism, suggest a method that might be used to counteract any harmful effects from interest groups. As you make your suggestions, keep in mind the constitutional guarantees of freedom of association and speech. Begin writing your bill with a statement explaining the purpose of the proposed legislation. Then present each of the provisions you have identified for regulating the activities of interest groups. Revise each provision to ensure that it is precise and clear in its language. Review the bill for errors and make corrections. Draft a final copy.
2. **Class Debate** Hold a class debate on the following topic: *Resolved*, That interest groups should not be allowed to donate money to political candidates. Select teams to argue each side of this issue. The rest of the class can evaluate the presentations of each team.
3. **Gathering Information** You are a member of an interest group that is concerned with protecting the nation's coastline against all forms of environmental damage. Turn to the Government Resources Handbook on page 690, and then answer the following questions. (a) Which sources might you use to find the names of the House members whose congressional districts include stretches of coastline? (b) What sources might you seek to find out how those representatives have tended to vote on environmental issues in the past?

Critical Thinking

1. (a) An example of a fact-based criticism is that some interest groups are better financed than others.
(b) Opinion-based criticisms include the following: that groups do not act in the interest of the American people, or that groups have an influence out of proportion to the good they do.
2. (a) Students might note that interest groups are practical because group action is more effective than individual action. They are democratic in that they enable the people to express themselves and influence the actions of government.
(b) Answers will vary. **3.** Answers will vary. Students might observe that the criticisms of interest groups do not apply to all groups at all times. **4.** Answers will vary. Students might note that many people belong to groups without being concerned with, or aware of all of the policy positions that a group might take. Interest groups offer people benefits beyond their political actions.

Getting Involved

1–3. Answers and results will vary, but students should demonstrate an understanding of the concepts in this chapter.

(b) Special interest groups, which focus entirely on a single issue, are the exceptions.
11. (a) Lobbyists are involved at any stage where they have an opportunity to influence policy, including administrative agencies and courts. (b) They must operate in these realms because even after a policy has been enacted in the form of a law, it is subject to pressure in such areas as its administration and enforcement.

Managing the Unit

You may wish to review the following materials before beginning the unit to help plan your instruction.

Each chapter ends with a Chapter-in-Brief with suggestions for previewing, reviewing, or omitting the chapter.

Unit 3 Outline

Pacing Charts,
pp. T28–T31

Unit 3

Night View of Washington, D.C. This photograph of Washington, D.C., displays the grandeur of the Capitol, the Washington Monument, and the Lincoln Memorial.

Skills and Features

The following skill lessons and features are included in this unit.

Skill Lessons

Citizenship: How to Develop Profiles of Your Members of Congress (p. 254)
Critical Thinking: Recognizing Cause and Effect (p. 278)
Citizenship: How to Work in Groups (p. 308)

Debates/Case Studies

What *You* Can Do: Organizing a Food Bank (p. 248)
Debating Key Issues: Should Discrimination Be Prohibited in Private Facilities? (*Heart of Atlanta Motel, Inc.* v. *U.S.*) (p. 274)
Debating Key Issues: Should Women Be Drafted? (*Rostker* v. *Goldberg*) (p. 295)

The Legislative Branch

In 1847, when Robert C. Winthrop of Massachusetts was chosen to be the new Speaker of the House of Representatives, Winthrop knew that the position entrusted to him was of great importance. It was his job to make sure that the House enacted all the bills needed to keep the government functioning. The position had always commanded the highest respect of the members of the House and Senate. In the very first Congress, in fact, the members had voted to pay the Speaker twelve dollars a day—twice the amount of their own wages! And in those days, when senators and representatives had to share boardinghouse rooms in the nation's capital, the Speaker always got a room to himself. The 30th Congress enacted 109 bills during Winthrop's tenure as Speaker. More than 140 years later, the 101st Congress enacted more than 700 bills into law. As you will see in this unit, the responsibilities of the nation's legislature are greater than ever.

Did You Know That . . .

- During the 100th Congress, 9,588 bills were introduced, compared to 144 during the 1st Congress.
- As of January 1, 1991, the annual salary for the Speaker of the House was $166,200, while the remaining representatives earned $129,500. Senators were paid the same as their counterparts in the House.
- Fifty-seven percent of the male members of Congress were once Boy Scouts.

Unit Focus

Activate Prior Knowledge Ask students if they have ever tried to get a large group of people to agree on when to have a party, what movie to see, or any other issue. Ask students whether this was an easy or difficult task. Tell students that Congress has 535 members and a majority of them must agree in order for a bill to become a law.

Interpreting the Visual Point out the photo of Washington, D.C. in the unit opener. Discuss with students the importance of monuments and memorials, especially in the nation's capital, where our leaders shape the nation's laws.

Did You Know That . . . Direct students to the items under "Did You Know That . . . " Ask students to explain whether these facts seem to them to be positive or negative and why.

Journal Writing A journal may serve as a record of students' impressions, thoughts, and ideas about their course work and related events in the world and in their lives. It is an opportunity for students to be creative; to create political cartoons, songs, poems, and stories as well as editorials and essays. Students should make entries at least once a week, and be sure to date each entry. Although journal writing generally is not graded, you should collect and review the journals at regular intervals. Suggested topics for the third unit include a creative writing piece describing one representative's frustration in moving a bill through Congress or a reaction to a newspaper article on the Congress.

You may also want to utilize **CNN Video-link** to generate ideas for journal writing.

Bulletin Board Idea

Using the Poster Tell students that the members of Congress—senators and representatives—have been called "the servants of the people." Ask the class what they think is meant by this expression. Then, provide one or more dictionaries so students can look up the word *serve*. Students should read the definitions that they find aloud and determine which of the meanings describe the work of the members of Congress. Direct students to read the statement by George Bush on the wall poster titled "Congress: Lawmaking and Representative Government." In light of the definitions of *serve*, ask students what they think Bush meant. Ask students to find the cartoon on the poster that most closely illustrates the same idea. Then, read the quote by George Bernard Shaw. Ask students what they think are the characteristics of a "good" law and what difficulties might be encountered in creating one. You may wish to ask students to write a new law, according to their interpretation of "good", that can be displayed on the bulletin board.

CHAPTER 10 RESOURCES

IN THE TEACHER'S RESOURCE FILE
The following materials are found in the Teacher's Resource File box.

Instructional Support: Unit 3 File

For the Section
Outlines, pp. 2, 5, 8, 11
Guided Reading and Reviews, pp. 3, 6, 9, 12
Quizzes, pp. 4, 7, 10, 13

For the Chapter
Skill Application, p. 14
Case Study on Contemporary Issues, pp. 15–17
Chapter Test, pp. 18–20
Additional Test Questions, pp. 21–23

Enrichment Support Files

Participatory Government Activities, pp. 4–19, 28–39
Simulations and Debates: Term Limitation

Computer Test Bank and Assessment

Transparency Package, pp. 10, 35

Election Kit, p. 38

CHAPTER 10 FOCUS

Introduce the Chapter Tell students that in this chapter they will gain an overview of the structure and duties of the legislative branch of the United States government—the Congress. Read with students the Chapter Preview and the Objectives.

Writing Activity Direct students' attention to "Describe" under "Before you read this chapter." Ask students to write a description of how representative government operates in their school. If students wish, they can describe representative government in their community.

Motivate for Learning Direct students' attention to "Predict" under "Before you read this chapter." Ask students to predict why the Framers of the Constitution chose to make the United States Congress a bicameral body.

Congress

Chapter Preview

"The world's most exclusive club." This is a title that has often been given to none other than the United States Senate, Congress's upper house. The name refers to the fact that, although senators are charged with representing the people, they themselves are hardly a representative cross section of the American population. Indeed, fewer than 6 percent of the members of Congress are women or African Americans, while women make up more than 51 percent and African Americans more than 12 percent of the nation. The disparity for Hispanic and Asian Americans is even greater.

Nevertheless, Congress is the branch of the National Government closest to the people. It is empowered by the Constitution to translate the will of the people into public policy in the form of law. This chapter is about the structure of Congress and the selection, qualifications, and characteristics of its members.

Before you read this chapter:

- **Describe** the way that representative government operates in your school or community.
- **Predict** one major difference between the House and the Senate.

As you read, focus on the main objective for each section. Understand:

1. The place, the role, and the structure of Congress.
2. The structure of the House of Representatives.
3. The structure of the Senate.
4. The general characteristics of members of Congress.

Magruder's American Government: *A Witness to Change* by William A. McClenaghan

The Constitution gives to Congress the power to fix its members' salaries and other compensations—and congressional pay has been a political hot potato for more than 200 years now. Recall that one of the 12 amendments that the 1st Congress sent to the States in 1789 dealt with congressional salaries. That unratified proposal has taken on new life in recent years.

In 1917 when this book was first published, members of Congress were paid $7,500 a year. Their salary increased to $10,000 a year in 1925 and then to $12,500 in 1946. They are now paid ten times that amount.

During the first half of this century, this book described congressional pay as "moderate." That word does not seem very appropriate today. Given inflation, $12,500 a year in 1946 translates to just about $80,000 today—less than two-thirds of what members of Congress now pay themselves. And that says nothing about the many and generous fringe benefits that now go along with the job.

The Elegance of the Office Congressional representatives meet in the Senate Reception Room. In the foreground are Alan K. Simpson (R., Wyoming), Robert Dole (R., Kansas), Robert C. Byrd (D., West Virginia), and Alan Cranston (D., California).

1 The National Legislature

Find Out:

- In what way is the lawmaking function central to democracy?
- What does it mean to say that Congress is bicameral?
- What are the terms and sessions of Congress?

Key Terms:

term, session, special session

You know that you live in a democracy. And you know, too, that in a democracy the people rule. But what does that really mean? You are one of "the people"—and you know that you do not rule. At least you do not in the hands-on sense. You do not make or enforce laws or collect taxes or decide court cases.

You do not do those and all of the other things that government does because you live in a representative democracy. Here, it is the representatives of the people who do the day-to-day work of the government.

Congress stands as a leading example of that fact. It is the legislative branch of the National Government. Its major function is to make law. Congress, then, is charged with the most basic governmental function in a democratic system: that of translating the public will into public policy in the form of law. How profoundly important the Framers thought that function to be can be seen in the fact that the first, and lengthiest, of the articles of the Constitution is devoted to it. Article I, Section 1 reads:

> "All legislative powers herein granted shall be vested in a Congress of the United States, which shall consist of a Senate and House of Representatives."

In this section, you will read about some of the important characteristics of Congress—the role and structure of the Senate and the House of Representatives.

Section 1
The National Legislature

Focus

Teacher's Resource File See the Unit 3 File, p. 2, for the Section 1 Outline.

Objectives

10.1 Determine ways in which the lawmaking function is central to democracy.
10.2 Explain the meaning of *bicameral* as it relates to Congress.
10.3 Analyze the importance of the terms and sessions of Congress.

Bellringer Activity As students enter the room, assign each the name of a State, which they will represent in several classroom votes. Ask the students to discuss how they should best conduct these votes so that the people in the States are fairly represented. How many votes should the larger States get compared to the smaller States?

State the Purpose Congress has the responsibility to turn public will into public policy in a way that respects the rights of each person. In Section 1, students will learn about some of the important characteristics of Congress that enable that body to fulfill its function.

ABCNEWS INTERACTIVE

The following video segment may be used to highlight aspects of the national legislature.

Powers of the Congress Guidebook
Chapter 38: Powers of the House and Senate, p. 42.

Vocabulary

Direct students' attention to "Key Terms" on page 235. Ask students to write down the words along with a definition based on how each term applies to the subject of school and the school year. As they read Section 1, have students write down the definitions of key terms as they relate to Congress. When they have finished their reading, have them compare the two sets of definitions. LEP

Reading Strategy: Question Writing

Have students read the main headings in Section 1. Then have students write each heading in the form of a question. As they read the section, have students look for the answers to the questions they have written. Tell students to write those answers underneath the questions.

Interpreting Tables: Multicultural Awareness Ask students to explain how the United States differs from all other countries in the way it selects its representatives. (*All of its representatives are directly elected.*)

Caption Answer It is (1) the only three-house legislature and (2) racially based.

INSTRUCT

Analyze/Discuss Ask students to analyze and discuss the following statement from the text: "Congress is charged with the most basic governmental function in a democratic system: that of translating the public will into public policy."

To aid in this discussion, you might ask students to respond to these questions: How do laws and other public policies help preserve democracy? (*By ensuring that all people are treated equally and fairly under the law.*) In what sense does Congress represent the public will? (*Congress is made up of elected representatives.*)

Have students discuss how the structure of Congress helps it fulfill its responsibility to democratic ideals. Discuss the historical, practical, and theoretical reasons for bicameralism. To further highlight the importance of the structure of Congress, ask students: Why is it important to have constitutional guidelines for terms and sessions? (*So that Congress is always bound by a set of known rules and procedures.*)

Global Awareness

Legislative Bodies

Country	Type of Legislative Body	Size of Legislative Body	How Elected	Term of Office
United States	Bicameral House of Representatives Senate	 435 members 100 members	 Directly Directly	 2 years 6 years
South Africa	Tricameral House of Assembly House of Representatives House of Delegates	 178(all white) 85 (all coloured*) 45 (all Asian)	 166 directly; 8 indirectly 80 directly; 5 indirectly 40 directly; 5 indirectly	 5 years 5 years 5 years
Egypt	Unicameral People's Assembly Shura Council (consultative body)	 448 members 210 members	 Directly Two-thirds directly; one-third appointed by the president	 5 years
Poland	Bicameral Parliament (Lower House) Senate (Upper House)	 460 members 100 members	 Popularly elected from a list of official candidates Directly	 4 years
Venezuela	Bicameral Senate Chamber of Deputies	 48 members 1 member for every 50,000 inhabitants (1985 population est.: 17,316,740)	 Voting (by proportional representation) is compulsory for men and women over 18 years of age	 5 years 5 years

*"Coloured" is defined as people of mixed racial origin.

Interpreting Tables: Multicultural Awareness America's bicameral legislature is based on the British model. What two factors distinguish South Africa's legislative body from the others?

Bicameralism

As you have just read, the Constitution immediately establishes a bicameral legislature—that is, a legislature made up of two houses. It does so for historical, practical, and theoretical reasons.

Historically, the British Parliament, which the Framers and most other Americans knew quite well, had consisted of two houses since the 1300s. As you may recall from Section 1 of Chapter 2, in 1787 most colonial assemblies and all but two of the new State legislatures were also bicameral.[1]

Practically, the Framers had to create a two-chambered body to settle the conflict between the Virginia and the New Jersey plans at the Constitutional Convention in 1787. Bicameralism is a reflection of federalism. Each State is equally represented in the Senate and in terms of its population in the House.

Theoretically, the Framers favored a bicameral Congress in order that one house might act as a check and balance on the other. A leading constitutional historian reports how one Framer expected this relationship to work:

> "Thomas Jefferson, who possessed great faith in 'the voice of the people,' was in France when the Constitution was framed. Upon his return, while taking breakfast with Washington, he opposed the two-body form of legislature, and was disposed to twit Washington about it. At this time Jefferson poured his coffee from his cup into

[1] Only Georgia and Pennsylvania had unicameral colonial and then State legislatures. Georgia's legislature became bicameral in 1789 and Pennsylvania's in 1790. Today, only Nebraska (since 1937) has a unicameral legislature.

his saucer. Washington asked him why he did so. 'To cool it,' he answered. 'So,' said Washington, 'we will pour legislation into the Senatorial saucer to cool it.'' [2]

Some say that the equal representation of the States in the Senate should be scrapped as undemocratic.[3] Those critics often point to the two extremes to make their case. The State with the least population, Alaska, has fewer than 600,000 residents. The largest State, California, has nearly 30 million. Yet each of these States has two senators.

Those who argue against State equality in the Senate ignore a vital fact. The Senate was purposely created as a body in which the States would be represented as coequal members and partners in the Union. Had the States not been equally represented in the Senate, there might never have been a Constitution.

[2] Max Farrand, *The Framing of the Constitution* (New Haven: Yale University Press, 1913), page 74.

[3] The prospects for any such change are very slim. Article V of the Constitution says that "no State, without its consent, shall be deprived of its equal suffrage in the Senate."

Terms and Sessions of Congress

1.a A **term** is the length of time between elections in Congress. Each term of Congress lasts for two years.[4] Terms are numbered consecutively from the first term, or the 1st Congress, which began on March 4, 1789.

The 20th Amendment of 1933 changed the date for the start of each term. It is now "noon on the 3d day of January" of every odd-numbered year. Thus the two-year term of the 102nd Congress began at noon on January 3, 1991, and it will end at noon on January 3, 1993.

1.b There are two **sessions**—formal meetings in which members perform legislative work—to each term of Congress. Section 2 of the 20th Amendment provides that

> "The Congress shall assemble at least once in every year, and such meeting shall begin at noon on the 3d day of January . . . "

[4] Article I, Section 2, Clause 1.

Interpreting Political Cartoons Many people frequently complain about the performance of Congress. What does the artist suggest that American citizens should do rather than complain?

Interpreting Political Cartoons Direct students' attention to the small figure in the lower left corner of the cartoon that is saying "Use it or lose it." Ask students what they think "it" means in the cartoon. (*The right to express one's opinion about representatives through voting.*)

Caption Answer Citizens should exercise their rights by voting ineffective representatives out of office.

Provide Guided Practice Ask students to respond either "yes" or "no" to the following statements: Representation in the Senate is based on population. (*No*) All States are represented equally in both houses of Congress. (*No*) Congress can choose not to meet in any given year. (*No*)

Ask students to rephrase each statement to make it correct. (*Possible answers: Representation in the House is based on population; States are represented equally in the Senate; Congress must meet at least once every year.*)

Provide Independent Practice

TRF **Teacher's Resource File** You may wish to assign Section 1 Guided Reading and Review, Unit 3 File, p. 3, to help students master section objective content.

Enrichment

Have students create a piece of art, a poem, an essay, or some other image that captures the idea of Congress translating public will into public policy. Students may display their finished work in the classroom. (Easy)

Congress adjourns each regular session as it sees fit. Until World War II, a typical session lasted four or five months. Today, however, Congress remains in session through most of each year. Both houses recess for several short periods during a session.

Neither house may adjourn *sine die*—that is, finally, ending a session—without the consent of the other. Article I, Section 5, Clause 4 provides that

> "Neither House . . . shall, without the consent of the other, adjourn for more than three days, nor to any other place than that in which the two Houses shall be sitting."

1.c Congress can also meet in **special session**—a meeting called by the President to deal with a pressing issue.[5] Only the President may call special sessions and only 26 such sessions have ever been held. President Truman called the last one in 1948, to consider a number of anti-inflation and welfare measures. Of course, the fact that Congress now meets nearly year-round reduces the likelihood of special sessions. That fact also lessens the importance of the President's power to call one.

Section 1 Review

1. **Define:** term, session, special session
2. What is the basic governmental function of Congress?
3. What are the historical, practical, and theoretical reasons for bicameralism in Congress?
4. How has the power to call a special session been diminished?

Critical Thinking

5. **Demonstrating Reasoned Judgment** (p. 19) Would Congress be better able to fulfill its basic function of translating the people's will into public policy if it were a unicameral body?

[5] Article II, Section 3 provides that the President may "convene both Houses, or either of them," in a special session. The Senate has been called into special session alone on 46 occasions to consider treaties and appointments, but not since 1933. The House has never been called alone.

2 The House of Representatives

Find Out:

- How are House members chosen and what are their terms and qualifications?
- How and for what reason is the House reapportioned every 10 years?
- What are congressional districts and what is gerrymandering?
- What are the effects of the "one-person, one-vote" rule on the House and on electoral politics in general?

Key Terms:

apportion, reapportion, single-member district, at-large, gerrymander

Every other autumn, all across the country, hundreds of men and women seek election to the House of Representatives. Most of them try to attract voters with colorful posters, yard signs, billboards, buttons, and other eye-catching campaign materials. Some of them campaign door to door. And nearly all of them make their "pitches" with radio and television spots and in leaflets and newspaper ads.

In this section, you will discover the general shape of the office that all of those candidates pursue so eagerly.

Size and Terms

The exact size of the House—today, 435 members—is not fixed by the Constitution. Rather, it is set by Congress. The Constitution provides that
1.a the total number of seats shall be **apportioned**—that is, distributed—among the States on the basis of their respective populations.[6]

Each State is guaranteed at least one seat in the House, no matter what its population. Today, six States—Alaska, Delaware, North Dakota, South Dakota, Vermont, and Wyoming—have only one representative apiece. Montana is slated to lose

[6] Article I, Section 2, Clause 3.

Monitor Comprehension

Answers to Section 1 Review
1. "Key Terms" are defined on the following pages:
a. term, p. 237
b. session, p. 237
c. special session, p. 238
2. Translating public will into public policy. **3.** Historical: Parliament was bicameral. Practical: Bicameralism settled conflicts that arose at the Constitutional Convention. Theoretical: Bicameralism fulfilled the Framers' concept of checks and balances. **4.** Because Congress now meets nearly year-round, the President has little opportunity to call a special session. **5.** Students might note that a unicameral body might make Congress more efficient. However, depending on the basis for determining representation, it might give too much weight to either the more populous or the smaller States.

Teacher's Resource File
See the Unit 3 File, p. 4, for the Section 1 Quiz.

Closure

Remind students that Congress translates public will into public policy. The structure, terms, and sessions of Congress were written by the Framers to help ensure that Congress fulfilled its function.

In Section 2, students will examine in more detail one of the two houses of Congress, the House of Representatives.

Assignment Assign Section 2, pp. 238–244, for the next class period.

Reteach

Ask students to write letters describing the United States Congress to a person who is unfamiliar with the United States and its government. Students should use the words *bicameral, term, sessions, lawmaking,* and *representative democracy* in their letters.

Spotlight on: Behind the Scenes

Most congressional candidates who are seeking to unseat an incumbent learn the hard way about the difficulty of that challenge. In the three elections between 1986 and 1990, voters returned incumbents to the House at a rate of 98 percent, leading many analysts to conclude that contributions from PACs and other sources have made incumbents nearly impossible to beat. Yet since 1948, well before the growth in interest groups, incumbents in the House have been reelected at a rate of over 90 percent, giving credence to the conventional Washington wisdom that although voters do not think much of Congress as a whole, they still like their own representatives individually.

one of its two seats in 1993 as a result of the 1990 census, and will then join this list. The District of Columbia, Guam, the Virgin Islands, and American Samoa are represented by a delegate, and Puerto Rico by a resident commissioner. However, these officials are not members of the House.

The Constitution provides that "Representatives shall be . . . chosen every second year"—that is, for two-year terms. This rather short term is intended to make the House responsive to popular pressures. House members always know that an election is just around the corner and so are anxious to please the voters. There is no constitutional limit on the number of terms representatives may serve.[7]

[7] Article I, Section 2, Clause 1. Current efforts to persuade Congress to offer an amendment to limit congressional tenure to 12 years mark the strongest attempt yet made to that end.

Reapportionment

Article I of the Constitution directs Congress
1.b to **reapportion**—redistribute—the seats in the House after each decennial census [8] Until a first census could be taken, the Constitution set the size of the House at 65 seats, and there were that many members in the 1st and 2nd Congresses (1789–1793). The census of 1790 showed a national population of 3,929,214 persons, and in 1792 Congress increased the number of House seats by 41, to 106.

As the nation's population grew, and as the number of States increased, so did the size of the House. It went to 142 seats after the census of 1800, to 186 seats 10 years later, and so on [9] By 1912, following the census of 1910 and the

[8] Article I, Section 2, Clause 3.

[9] Once, following the census of 1840, the size of the House was reduced from 242 to 232 seats.

Congressional Apportionment, 1993–2003
GAINED REPRESENTATION
LOST REPRESENTATION
NO CHANGE
+ – Seats gained or lost
5 Number=State's seats in House
This map shows the changes in State representation due to the reapportionment of the House after the 1990 Census, and effective from January 3, 1993 to January 3, 2003. The next apportionment, following the 2000 Census, will occur in 2001 and become efective with the congressional elections in 2002.

▲ **Interpreting Maps** As the map above shows, the enormous State of Alaska has one representative while the tiny State of Rhode Island has two. Why is this the case?

Section 2
The House of Representatives

FOCUS

Teacher's Resource File See the Unit 3 File, p. 5, for the Section 2 Outline.

Objectives

10.4 Determine how the House members are chosen and what their terms and qualifications are.

10.5 Examine the means by which and the reasons why the House is reapportioned each decade.

10.6 Examine Congressional districts and understand gerrymandering.

10.7 Determine the effects of the "one-person, one vote" rule on the House and electoral politics in general.

Bellringer Activity Have students discuss and list what kinds of skills and characteristics their ideal representative would have.

State the Purpose The members of the House represent the citizens of every State. In Section 2, students will learn about the House of Representatives—its terms, size, election process, member qualifications, and the controversies surrounding the apportionment of its seats.

Interpreting Maps Ask students to observe that there is no relationship between the size of a State and its number of representatives.

Caption Answer Because representation is based on population, not geography.

Vocabulary

Direct students' attention to "Key Terms" on page 238. Ask students to write the words *size* and *election* on a piece of paper. As they read Section 2 and understand the meaning of the key terms, have them explain what each word has to do with the size and election of the House of Representatives.

Reading Strategy: Who? What? When? Where? How? Why?

Ask students to list the following questions on a piece of paper: Who? What? When? Where? How? and Why? Tell students to expand these questions so that they relate to the House of Representatives (for example, "How is the size of the House determined?"). As students encounter key concepts in their reading, have them use the information to answer these questions.

INSTRUCT

Discuss/Explain Ask students to recall their responses to the "Bellringer Activity." Have them discuss why it is important for them to have representatives who represent their interests and concerns effectively.

Explain to students that all people in the United States are represented in the House of Representatives and that the voters get to select those representatives every two years. Ask students to discuss why it is important that all people be equally represented in Congress. As part of this discussion, you might have students answer the following questions: Why would it be unfair if one representative represented 1 million people and another represented 500,000? (*The 500,000 people would have more representation per person.*) How has the Constitution sought to prevent this unfairness? (*By requiring reapportionment; the courts have also said that the Constitution requires "one person-one vote" in cases such as Wesberry* v. *Sanders.*)

Explain to students that the Constitution also helps ensure that representatives serve their people well by requiring periodic elections and by ensuring that they meet certain minimum qualifications.

Off-Year Elections

Year	Party in Power	House Seats	Senate Seats
1946	D	-55	-12
1950	D	-29	-6
1954	R	-18	-1
1958	R	-48	-13
1962	D	-4	+3
1966	D	-47	-4
1970	R	-12	+2
1974	R	-48	-5
1978	D	-15	-3
1982	R	-26	0
1986	R	-5	-8
1990	R	-9	-1

Interpreting Tables Congressional elections that occur in nonpresidential years, or between presidential elections, are called the off-year elections. Which party consistently loses seats in the off-year elections—the party in power, or the party in opposition?

admission of Arizona and New Mexico, the House had grown to 435 seats.

With the census of 1920, Congress found itself in a painfully difficult political position. The House had long since grown too large for effective floor action. But, to reapportion without adding more seats to the House itself meant that some States would lose seats if every State were to be represented on the basis of its population.

Congress met the problem by doing nothing. So, despite the Constitution's command, there was no reapportionment on the basis of the 1920 census.

Faced with the 1930 census, Congress moved to avoid repeating its earlier lapse with the Reapportionment Act of 1929. That law, still on the books, sets up what is often called an "automatic reapportionment." It provides for the following:

1. The "permanent" size of the House is 435 members. Of course, that figure is permanent only so long as Congress does not decide to change it. Congress did enlarge the House temporarily in 1959 when Alaska and then Hawaii became States.
2. Following each census, the Census Bureau is to determine the number of seats each State should have.
3. When the bureau's plan is ready, the President must send it to Congress.
4. If, within 60 days of receiving it, neither house rejects the Census Bureau's plan, it becomes effective.

The scheme set out in the 1929 law has worked quite well through seven reapportionments. The law leaves to Congress its constitutional responsibility to reapportion the House, but it gives to the Census Bureau the mechanical chores (and political "heat") that go with that task. Today each of the 435 seats in the House represents an average of some 575,000 persons.

Congressional Elections

According to the Constitution, any person whom a State allows to vote for members of "the most numerous branch" of its own legislature is qualified to vote in congressional elections.[10] The Constitution also provides that

> "The times, places, and manner of holding [congressional] elections . . . shall be prescribed in each State by the legislature thereof; but the Congress may at any time, by law, make or alter such regulations . . ."[11]

Date Congressional elections are held on the same day in every State. Since 1872 Congress has required that those elections be held on the Tuesday following the first Monday in November of each even-numbered year.[12] Congress has made an exception for Alaska, which may hold its election in October. To date, however, Alaskans have chosen to use the November date. In the same law, Congress directed that representatives be chosen by written or printed ballots. The use of voting machines was sanctioned in 1899.

[10] Article I, Section 2, Clause 1.

[11] Article I, Section 4, Clause 1. The Constitution allows only one method for filling a vacancy in the House—by a special election, which may be called only by the governor of the State involved; Article I, Section 2, Clause 4.

[12] On the formula fixing the election date, see Chapter 7, Section 2.

TRF **Teacher's Resource File**
See the Election Kit, p. 38, for materials to support this section.

Off-Year Elections Those congressional elections that occur in the nonpresidential years—that is, between presidential elections—are called the off-year elections. The most recent ones were held in 1990, and the next ones will come in 1994.

Quite consistently, the party in power—the party that holds the presidency—loses seats in the off-year elections. The table on page 240 illustrates that point. It sets out the House and Senate seats gained (+) or lost (–) by the President's party in the off-year elections from 1946 through 1990.

Districts The 435 members of the House are chosen by the voters in 435 separate congressional districts across the country. Recall that seven States will have only one seat in the House following the 1992 election. There will be, then, a total of 428 districts within the other 43 States.

The Constitution makes no mention of congressional districts. For more than half a century, Congress allowed each State to decide whether to elect its members by a general ticket system or on a single-member district basis.

Under the **single-member district** arrangement, 1.c the voters in each district are able to elect one of the State's representatives from among a field of candidates running in that district.

Most States quickly set up single-member districts. Several States used the general ticket system, however. Under that arrangement, all of the State's seats were filled from the State **at-large**—that is, from the State as a whole. 1.d All the voters could vote for all of that State's representatives.

At-large elections proved grossly unfair. A party with a plurality of the votes in a State, no matter how small, could win all of the State's seats in the House. Congress finally did away with the general ticket system in 1842. Thereafter, all of the seats in the House were to be filled from single-member districts in each State.

The 1842 law made each State legislature responsible for the drawing of any congressional districts within its own State. It also required that each congressional district be made up of "contiguous territory," meaning that it must be all one piece. In 1872 Congress added the command that the districts within each State have "as nearly as practicable an equal number of inhabitants." In 1901 it further directed that all the districts be of "compact territory," meaning that they should cover the smallest possible area.

Congressional Redistricting in Indiana

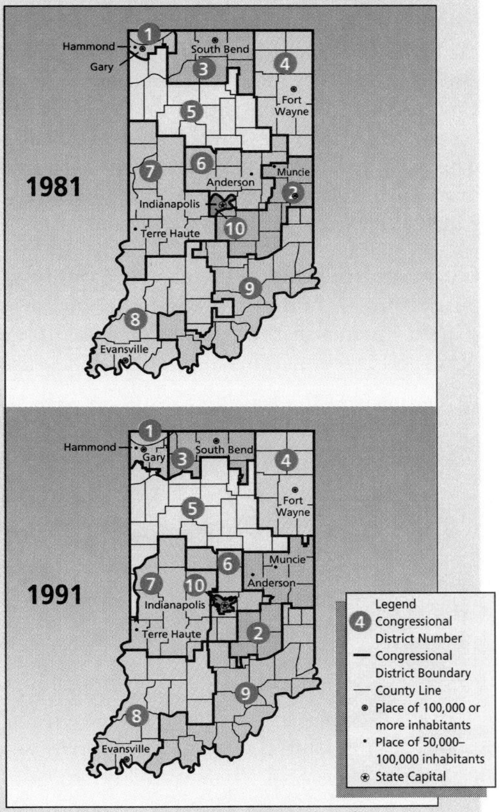

1981

1991

Legend
Congressional District Number
Congressional District Boundary
County Line
Place of 100,000 or more inhabitants
Place of 50,000–100,000 inhabitants
State Capital

Source: Legislative Services Agency, Indianapolis, Indiana; U.S. Bureau of the Census

Interpreting Maps After each census, State legislatures draw new lines for congressional districts. From the map, what demographic factor appeared to play a major part in Indiana's redistricting—and in redistricting across the United States?

Interpreting Tables Ask students to observe that the House generally shows a far more dramatic shift away from the party in power than the Senate.

Caption Answer The party in power consistently loses seats in off-year elections.

Interpreting Maps Ask students to study the map on page 241. Ask them to explain why the different congressional districts vary in size and shape. (*Because the size and shape of each district is determined in part by population, which may be more or less dense in different areas.*)

Caption Answer Large cities, such as Indianapolis or South Bend, because of their populations. Note that there is only one large city per district in Indiana.

ABCNEWS INTERACTIVE

The following video segments may be used to highlight aspects of the House of Representatives.

POWERS OF THE CONGRESS GUIDEBOOK
Chapter 54: Profile of Congress, p. 60.
Chapter 55: Speakers of the House, p. 61

SPOTLIGHT ON: Global Awareness

In contrast to the simple, single-member district scheme used for the U.S. House, seats in Japan's House of Representatives, one of the two houses in the Japanese parliament, are apportioned by a more complex arrangement. The 491 members of Japan's House are elected for two-year terms from 124 different voting districts—which, depending on population, elect three to five members. A party must win two seats from each district to gain a majority in the House. But since each voter can vote for only one candidate, parties guard against running too many candidates in any one district and spreading the vote too thinly among them.

Interpreting Political Cartoons Ask students to consider the image in this cartoon. What does the use of a dragon suggest about the artist's opinion on the tactic of gerrymandering? *(Possible answer: The artist did not like gerrymandering and considered it "creating a monster.")*

These requirements of contiguity, population equality, and compactness were often disregarded by State legislatures, and Congress made no real effort to enforce them. The requirements were left out of the Reapportionment Act of 1929, and in 1932 the Supreme Court held (in *Wood* v. *Broom*) that they had therefore been repealed. Over time, then, and most notably since 1929, the State legislatures have drawn many districts with very peculiar geographic shapes. Moreover, until fairly recently, many districts were also of widely varying populations.

Gerrymandering The maps of congressional districts in a number of States show districts shaped much like the letter Y or a dumbbell or other odd form. Those districts have usually
1.e been **gerrymandered**. That is, they have been drawn to the advantage of the political party or faction that controls the State legislature.

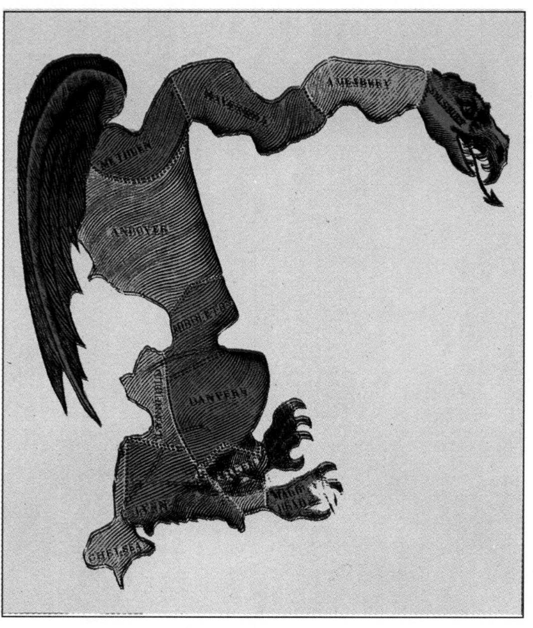

The Gerrymander!
Gerrymandering takes its name from Governor Elbridge Gerry, who in 1812 redrew the State's legislative districts to favor the Democratic-Republicans. It is said that the painter, Gilbert Stuart, added a head, wings, and claws to Essex County on a district map hanging over the desk of a Federalist newspaper editor. "That," he said, "will do for a salamander." "Better say Gerrymander," growled the editor.

The practice of gerrymandering can be found in most places where lines are drawn for the election of public officeholders. Most often gerrymandering takes one of two forms. Either the lines are drawn (1) to concentrate the opposition's voters in one or a few districts, thus leaving the other districts comfortably safe for the dominant party; or (2) to spread the opposition as thinly as possible among several districts, limiting the opposition's ability to win anywhere.

For decades, gerrymandering produced congressional districts of widely different populations. State legislatures were responsible for this situation. A number of them regularly drew district lines on a partisan basis. In fact, that remains the case in several States today.

Historically, however, most States were carved up on a rural vs. urban basis—for, until recently, the typical State legislature was dominated by the less-populated, over-represented rural areas of the State.[13]

Wesberry v. *Sanders*, 1964

Suddenly, and quite dramatically, the longstanding patterns of wide population variation in districts and of rural over-representation came to an end in the late 1960s.

These abrupt changes were the direct result of a historic decision by the Supreme Court in 1964. In *Wesberry* v. *Sanders*, the Court held that the population differences among Georgia's congressional districts were so great as to violate the Constitution.

In reaching its landmark decision, the Supreme Court noted that Article I, Section 2 declares that representatives shall be chosen "by the people of the several States" and shall be

[13] The pattern of rural overrepresentation in the State legislatures has now all but disappeared as a consequence of the Supreme Court's several "one-person, one-vote" decisions of the 1960s and 1970s. In *Reynolds* v. *Sims*, 1964, the Court held that the seats in both houses of a State's legislature must be apportioned on the basis of population equality.

Activity: for Gifted Students

Theme: Interdependence Encourage students to recognize the interdependence between electoral districting and the electoral process. Remind students that strategies such as gerrymandering have enabled political parties to establish a degree of control over the electoral process that is out of proportion to their voter support. Students can compare party registration figures within congressional districts or other electoral units to see how often they favor the party in control of the State legislature. (Have students check the Government Resources Handbook on page 690 for possible sources of information.) Through an oral presentation, students may share their observations about the relationship between party control of a legislature and future electoral success.

CONTEMPORARY AMERICAN REALISM #3
I CALL IT 'REDISTRICTING'
MAGNUSON

©Steve Magnuson

Interpreting Political Cartoons Why would the cartoonist poke fun at the practice of redistricting by drawing a similarity between congressional redistricting maps and abstract art?

"apportioned among the several States . . . according to their respective numbers." These words, the Court held, mean that

> "as nearly as practicable one man's vote in a congressional election is to be worth as much as another's."

And, the Court added that

> "While it may not be possible to draw congressional districts with mathematical precision, that is no excuse for ignoring our Constitution's plain objective of making equal representation for equal numbers of people the fundamental goal of the House of Representatives. That is the high standard of justice and common sense which the Founders set for us."

The importance of *Wesberry* and the Court's later "one-person, one-vote" decisions cannot be overstated. They have had an extraordinary impact on the makeup of the House, on the content of public policy, and on electoral politics in general. The nation's cities and suburbs now speak with a much larger voice in Congress than ever before. But notice, it is quite possible to draw congressional (or any other) district lines in accord with the "one-person, one vote" rule and, at the same time, to gerrymander them.[14]

[14] Except for gerrymandering based on race, a violation of the 14th Amendment's Equal Protection Clause, *Gomillion* v. *Lightfoot,* 1960; see Chapter 6, Section 3. In 1986 the Supreme Court ruled, for the first time, that gerrymanders are subject to constitutional challenge, even if the disputed districts meet the "one-person, one-vote" test. It did so in *Davis* v. *Bandemer,* where it upheld the districting of Indiana's legislature, a districting that heavily favored the State's Republican party.

Interpreting Political Cartoons The cartoonist is attempting to point out a humorous aspect of the redistricting issue. Ask students where they think the humor in this cartoon comes from? (*Possible answer: The humor comes from the comparison of district maps to a piece of art; the use of the word "realism" in the title points out the fact that district maps can in fact look this way.*)

Caption Answer Just as the district gets "redefined," so does the word "realism."

Provide Guided Practice Read aloud to students the "Find Out" questions for Section 2 from page 238. Ask volunteers to answer the questions by citing information from the text.

Provide Independent Practice

TRF **Teacher's Resource File** You may wish to assign Section 2 Guided Reading and Review, Unit 3 File, p. 6, to help students master section objective content.

Enrichment

Have students work cooperatively to research changes in congressional apportionment redistricting for their State since 1900. (Students might consult the Government Resources Handbook on page 690 for possible sources of information.) Have them analyze their findings to determine the reasons why these changes have occurred. When they have completed their research, ask them to present their findings as an oral report. (Challenging)

MONITOR COMPREHENSION

Answers to Section 2 Review
1. "Key Terms" are defined on the following pages:
a. apportioned, p. 238
b. reapportion, p. 239
c. single-member district, p. 241
d. at-large, p. 241
e. gerrymandered, p. 242
2. Two years. **3.** Permanent size of the House is 435; Census Bureau decides each State's representation; President sends plan to Congress; it becomes law unless rejected within 60 days. **4.** State legislatures. **5.** Helped end rural overrepresentation. **6.** Members must be 25, have been citizens for 7 years, and live in State from which elected. **7.** It is the judge of elections, returns, and qualifications of members. **8.** If a district is drawn to include 400 voters and another includes 800, then each of the 400 voters' votes is worth the same as 2 votes from the 800-voter district.

TRF **Teacher's Resource File** See the Unit 3 File, p.7, for the Section 2 Quiz.

CLOSURE

The Constitution and several court decisions help ensure that membership in the House of Representatives accurately represents the people.

In Section 3, students will look closely at the other lawmaking branch of Congress—the Senate.

Assignment Assign Section 3, pp. 245–247, for the next class period.

Qualifications for House Members

According to the Constitution, a member of the House must be at least 25 years of age, must have been a citizen for at least seven years, and must be an inhabitant of the State from which he or she is chosen.[15]

Longstanding custom, not the Constitution, also requires that a representative must live in the district he or she represents. The custom is based on the belief that the legislator should be closely familiar with the locale he or she represents, its people, and its problems. Rarely, then, does a district choose an outsider to represent it.

The Constitution makes the House "the judge of the elections, returns, and qualifications of its own members."[16] Thus, when the right of a member-elect to be seated is challenged, the House has the power to decide the matter. Challenges are rarely successful.

The House may refuse to seat a member-elect by majority vote. It may also "punish its own members for disorderly behavior" by majority vote, and "with the concurrence of two-thirds, expel a member."[17]

Historically, the House viewed its power to judge the qualifications of members-elect as the power to impose additional standards. For example, the House in 1900 refused to seat Brigham H. Roberts of Utah because he was a polygamist—that is, he had more than one wife. In *Powell* v. *McCormack,* 1969, however, the Supreme Court held that the House could not exclude a member-elect who meets the Constitution's standards of age, citizenship, and residence. The House has not excluded a member since.

In nearly 200 years, the House has expelled only four members. Three were ousted in 1861 for their "support of rebellion." More recently, Michael Myers (D., Pa.) was expelled in 1980 for corruption. Myers had been caught up in the Abscam probe, an undercover FBI investigation of corruption.[18]

The House has not often punished a member for "disorderly behavior," but such actions are not nearly so rare as expulsions. Most recently, the House voted to "reprimand" Barney Frank (D., Mass.) in 1990 for conduct stemming from his relationship with a male prostitute. Mr. Frank, an avowed homosexual, was subsequently reelected by the voters in his congressional district. The Speaker of the House left Congress under a cloud in 1989. Jim Wright (D., Tex.) resigned his seat after the House Ethics Committee charged him with a number of violations of House rules. Most of those allegations centered around Mr. Wright's financial dealings with individuals and companies with an interest in legislation before the House.

Section 2 Review

1. Define: apportion, reapportion, single-member district, at-large, gerrymander
2. How long is the term of a representative?
3. What are the major provisions of the Reapportionment Act of 1929?
4. Who draws congressional districts?
5. What is the significance of the Supreme Court decision in *Wesberry* v. *Sanders*?
6. What are the constitutional qualifications for membership in the House?
7. What powers does the House have over the elections and qualifications of its members?

Critical Thinking

8. Expressing Problems Clearly (p. 19) In some cases, courts have found that the drawing of district lines can violate the "one-person, one-vote" standard. Explain how district lines can have this result.

[15] Article I, Section 2, Clause 2. See also Article I, Section 6, Clause 2.
[16] Article I, Section 5, Clause 1.
[17] Article I, Section 5, Clause 2.
[18] A few members have resigned to avoid almost certain expulsion. The most recent, two New York City Democrats: Mario Biaggi in 1988 and Robert Garcia in 1990. Both had been convicted of federal crimes arising out of their relationships with a defense contractor.

Reteach
Have students complete a chart on the House of Representatives that identifies the number of House members, how they are chosen, their terms, and their qualifications. Students may refer to the material in this section as they complete their charts.

3 The Senate

Find Out:

- How is the size (number of seats) of the Senate determined?
- What are the terms and qualifications of its members?

Key Term:

continuous body

You should not be very much surprised by these facts: Nearly a third of the present members of the Senate once served in the House of Representatives; none of the current members of the House has ever served in the Senate. Indeed, many of the men and women who now serve in the House look forward to the day when, they hope, they will sit in the Senate and, perhaps one day, in the Executive Office.

This section should help you understand why these things are so. Or, to put it another way, as you read this section you will come to see very clearly why the Senate is often called the "upper house."

Election and Terms

The Senate is a much smaller body than the House. The Constitution states that it "shall be composed of two senators from each State."[19] The first Senate had 22 members when it first met in 1789, and 26 members by the end of the 1st Congress. Like the House of Representatives, the Senate has grown with the country. Today, 100 senators represent the 50 States.

Until the adoption of the 17th Amendment in 1913, senators were chosen by State legislatures. The legislatures were generally expected to choose wealthy, distinguished men to the Senate. From 1914 on, they have been chosen by the people at the regular November elections.[20]

[19] Article I, Section 3, Clause 1; 17th Amendment.

VOICES on Government

On Being a Woman Senator

Barbara Mikulski, Democratic senator from Maryland

"I feel that within my own party, I'm called upon to represent a kind of at-large constituency for the women of America. . . . I hope I'm the first of many. But for now, this is it. Sure, it's a burden when we're talking about issues, where you think you'll do the most good if you have to pick and choose among priorities. And the burden comes from the letters I get from all over the country. People write to me about their concerns as if I were their Congresswoman. . . . It is an enormous responsibility. When you know that you are the first . . . you have a celebrity status, but you also know that you're casting the mold for those who will participate afterward."

Each senator is elected from the State at-large. The 17th Amendment declares that all persons whom the State allows to vote for members of "the most numerous branch" of its legislature are qualified to vote for candidates for the United States Senate.

[20] Only one senator is elected from a State in any given election, except when the other seat has been vacated by death, resignation, or expulsion. The 17th Amendment gives each State a choice of methods for the filling of a vacancy in the Senate. A State may (1) fill the seat at a special election called by the governor, or (2) allow the governor to appoint someone to serve until the voters fill the vacancy at such a special election or at the next regular (November) election. Most States use the appointment-special election method.

SECTION 3
The Senate

FOCUS

Teacher's Resource File See the Unit 3 File, p. 8, for the Section 3 Outline.

Objectives

10.8 Identify the means by which the size of the Senate is determined.

10.9 Describe the terms and qualifications of Senate members.

Bellringer Activity Write the names of the two U.S. senators from your state on the board. Exclude the title *senator*. Ask students if they know who these people are. If students do know, ask them why they think they might be familiar with these names. If not, explain that they are members of the Senate, the "upper house" of the Congress.

State the Purpose The Senate is made up of two elected officials from each of the 50 states—100 in all. These men and women are highly visible on the national as well as Statewide level. In Section 3, students will learn more about the structure of the Senate and qualifications required of each member.

ABCNEWS INTERACTIVE

The following video segment may be used to highlight aspects of the Senate.

POWERS OF THE CONGRESS GUIDEBOOK
Chapter 38: Powers of the House and Senate, p. 42

Vocabulary

Ask students to look at "Key Terms" on page 245. Ask them if they can predict what the word *continuous body* might mean in relation to the Senate. If they cannot, have them skim the text to get a sense of the meaning.

Reading Strategy: Structured Overview

Have students write "The Senate" at the top of a piece of paper. Below that, have them write "Elections and Terms" and "Qualifications" next to one another. As students read and encounter key concepts, have them write them under the appropriate headings.

Interpreting Charts Ask students why the guidelines in Step 4 are important. (*It is important to treat others with respect.*) Ask them to create a list of "Dos" instead of "Don'ts" for Step 4.

Caption Answer Members of Congress are busy; current and specific information is most useful to them.

INSTRUCT

Discuss/Analyze Ask students to discuss the terms and qualifications for senators. Have them reinforce their points with references in the text.

As they demonstrate an understanding of the Senate, ask students to analyze differences between the members of the House and the members of the Senate. Encourage them to examine such factors as the size of a senator's and a House member's constituency and the frequency of election.

Interpreting Tables
Caption Answer Possible answer: Six-year terms mean less concern over reelection and less pressure from public opinion.

Provide Guided Practice Ask students to properly apply the words *House* or *Senate* to the following: six-year term (*Senate*); subject to gerrymandering (*House*); more national visibility (*Senate*); historical training ground for the presidency (*Senate*).

Provide Independent Practice
TRF **Teacher's Resource File** You may wish to assign Section 3 Guided Reading and Review, Unit 3 File, p. 9, to help students master section objective content.

Early Civil Rights Leader: Multicultural Awareness Hiram Rhodes Revels (R., Mississippi), was the first African-American senator. During the Civil War, he recruited African-American soldiers for the Union army.

How to Write to Your Lawmakers

1. Choose a method. You can write to your representative's local address or to their Washington address. Check your telephone directory's blue pages to find local addresses. Letters can be sent to representatives in Washington at the following addresses:

Representative ______	Senator ______
House Office Building	Senate Office Building
Washington, D.C. 20515	Washington, D.C. 20510

2. Write while your issue is still current. Don't wait until a bill is out of committee or has passed the House (or Senate).

3. Be specific. Identify the bill or issue that prompted you to write, preferably in your first paragraph. Give the bill number or mention its popular title—e.g. the Minimum Wage Bill, the Child Care Bill.

4. Be brief, but give the reasons for your position. Avoid these don'ts:
- Don't make threats or promises.
- Don't berate your lawmaker.
- Don't pretend to wield vast political influence.
- Don't try to instruct your lawmaker on every issue.

Interpreting Charts These guidelines were suggested by former Congressman Morris Udall (D., Arizona). After examining the chart, explain why steps 2 and 3 are important.

Senators serve six-year terms—terms three times the length of those for which members of the House are chosen[21] They may be reelected to any number of terms. The terms are staggered. Only a third of them—33 or 34—expire every two years. The Senate then, can be called
1.a a **continuous body**. That is, all its seats are never up for election at the same time.

The six-year term is intended to make senators less subject to the pressures of public opinion and to the pleas of special interests than are their colleagues in the House. The larger size and the geographic scope of their constituencies—the people and interests the senators represent—are designed to have much the same effect. In other words, senators are supposed to be less concerned with the interests of a specific small locality and more focused on the "big picture" of the national interest. Indeed, senators are in general more likely to be regarded as national political leaders than most House members. In addition, senators are more likely to have more power in their State party organizations. This is due partly to the relatively small size of the Senate, to its easier access to the media, and, no doubt, to the larger staffs that senators have at their disposal. Over the years, far more senators have run for the presidency than have members of the House. The Senate is considered an excellent "training ground" for presidential candidates.

Qualifications for Senators

A senator must meet a higher level of qualifications than those the Constitution sets for a

[21] Article I, Section 3, Clause 1. See note 7, page 239.

SPOTLIGHT ON: Roots of Democracy

The institution of the senate appeared first in ancient Rome, where Romulus established an advisory council comprised of the heads of 100 prominent families. By 500 B.C., the senate had come to represent the patrician—or aristocratic—members of Roman society. Its membership increased to 300 and later to 600 as the aristocracy grew. The principal political institution of the Roman Republic (509–31 B.C.), the senate functioned as the municipal government during the Roman Empire but declined as did other Roman institutions in the 4th and 5th centuries A.D.

Enrichment

Have students think of an issue currently pending in the Senate. They may want to do a little research by reading a newspaper or news magazine from the last week or so. Then invite them to discuss the issue in class. Ask the class to decide on one important issue raised by a classmate. Then have students write to both of their senators to inform him or her about the class's feelings on the issue. Refer to the chart on page 246 for instructions. (Easy) representative. A senator must be at least 30 years of age, must have been a citizen for at least nine years, and must be an inhabitant of the State from which he or she is elected.[22]

The Senate, like the House, judges the qualifications of its members, and it may exclude a member-elect by a majority vote.[23] It may also "punish its members for disorderly behavior" by majority vote and, "with the concurrence of two-thirds, expel a member."[24]

Fifteen members of the Senate have been expelled by that body, one in 1797 and 14 during the Civil War. Senator William Blount of Tennessee was expelled in 1797 for conspiring to lead two Native-American groups, supported by British warships, in attacks on Spanish Florida and Louisiana. The 14 senators ousted in 1861 and 1862 were all from States of the Confederacy and were expelled for supporting secession. In 1982 Senator Harrison Williams (D., N.J.) resigned to avoid expulsion by the Senate. He was convicted of bribery in 1981 in a case related to the Abscam probe. Following his trial, the Senate Ethics Committee unanimously recommended that he be expelled.

The punishing of a senator for "disorderly behavior" has also been rare. In one recent case the Senate voted in 1990 to "denounce" one of its members, David Durenberger (R., Minn.), as a result of charges of financial misconduct lodged against him by the Senate Ethics Committee. Among the several counts, the committee found that Senator Durenberger had "knowingly and willfully" tried to avoid the Senate's limits on members' outside income from such sources as speaking fees; he had falsely reported $95,000 in such fees as book royalties. Durenberger's behavior violated a code of ethics passed by each house of Congress in 1977 and revised in the 1980s. The ethics code was based on the assumption that financial transactions are often associated with improper influence. This is, of course, not always the case.

[22] Article I, Section 3, Clause 3. Under the inhabitant qualification, a senator need not have lived in the State for any prescribed time. Most often, of course, senators have been longtime residents of their States.

[23] Article I, Section 5, Clause 1. As has the House, the Senate has at times refused to seat a member-elect. Presumably, the Court's holding in *Powell* v. *McCormack,* 1969, applies with equal force to the Senate.

[24] Article I, Section 5, Clause 2.

Major Differences Between the House and the Senate

House	Senate
▪ Larger body (435 members)	▪ Smaller body (100 members)
▪ Shorter term (2 years)	▪ Longer term (6 years)
▪ Smaller constituencies (elected from districts within States)	▪ Larger constituencies (elected from entire State)
▪ Younger membership	▪ Older membership
▪ Less prestige	▪ More prestige
▪ Lower visibility in news media	▪ Higher visibility in news media

Interpreting Tables What effect might the difference in the length of terms between representatives and senators have on their performance?

Section 3 Review

1. **Define:** continuous body
2. How many people now serve in the United States Senate?
3. How is that number fixed?
4. What is the term of office for senators?
5. In what way is the Senate a "continuous body"?
6. What are the constitutional qualifications for membership in the Senate?
7. What powers does the Senate have over the election and qualifications of its members?

Critical Thinking

8. **Identifying Assumptions** (p. 19) Senators are elected less frequently than House members, and so are supposed to face less political pressure. What does this arrangement suggest about the Constitution's view of political pressure?

★

Monitor Comprehension

Answers to Section 3 Review
1. The "Key Term" is defined on the following page:
a. continuous body, p. 246
2. 100 **3.** The Constitution states that each State will have two senators. **4.** Six years.
5. Only one-third of its members are up for election at any one time. **6.** A senator must be 30, have been a citizen for nine years, and live in the State from which elected. **7.** Like the House, the Senate is judge of the elections, returns, and qualifications of its members.
8. Students might conclude that political pressure is not an entirely positive force; that is, that there is a benefit to the nation from having senators less subject to electoral concerns.

Teacher's Resource File See the Unit 3 File for the Section 3 Quiz on p. 10.

Closure

The Senate is made up of 100 members. Emphasize for students that these lawmakers differ from House members in that they are elected every 6 years. As a result, senators tend to be less subject to political pressure.

In Section 4, students will read more about the members of Congress, their personal and professional backgrounds, the ways they perform their jobs, and their compensation.

Assignment Assign Section 4, pp. 249–253, for the next class period.

Reteach

Have students refer to material in the section to create a chart that outlines the size, terms, and membership qualifications of the United States Senate. Suggest that students also compare their charts to the charts they made for the "Reteach" activity for Section 2 and note any differences.

TEACHING

What You Can Do

Organizing a Food Bank

Objective

Appreciate the commitment of knowledge, time, and effort that characterizes a person's involvement in civic affairs.

INSTRUCT

Sean Fox demonstrated real commitment to needy people by helping to create a food bank for his community.

Through determination and hard work, he was able to make a difference. Before students read the feature, ask them to identify issues that they are aware of in their community that could inspire such commitment. Ask them to consider what obstacles exist to addressing those issues successfully. After students have read the feature, ask them to discuss the following questions:

- What knowledge and experience did Sean Fox have that inspired him to start a food bank in Toledo, Washington?
- What sacrifices might Sean have had to make in order to realize his goal of creating a food bank?
- What are the rewards of working in your community to make a difference?

What You Can Do

Organizing a Food Bank

Many American citizens think of hunger as a problem only in other parts of the world. Unfortunately, however, about 20 million people suffer from hunger in the United States, the world's wealthiest country.

Costly Cutbacks

During the 1960s and 1970s, Congress appropriated funds to create programs to ease the problems of our country's poor. Among them were Medicaid, Supplemental Security Income (SSI), and Food Stamps. In the early 1980s, however, many programs aimed at fighting poverty and hunger came under attack as being too costly to the American taxpayer, and the government cut back drastically on these programs.

Fortunately, a number of individuals and private organizations picked up where federal programs left off. Sean Fox, from Ethel, Washington, was one of those individuals. At the age of 17, Sean played the leading role in establishing a food bank in Toledo, Washington. Food banks obtain and offer a selection of basic foods to people at no cost. Eligible families may use a food bank for some or all of the food they need. This idea was inspired after he attended a month-long Washington State Governor's School for Leadership. "When I came back," he said, "I wanted to do something."

What Sean did was impress upon his parents and community, civic, and church leaders the need for a food bank in Toledo. Toledo had a high unemployment rate and was the only town in the county that did not have a food bank. Those in need had to drive about 30 miles to another town. Sean felt that the citizens of Toledo should "care for their own."

A Driving Force

After spearheading the initial organizational efforts, he and his committee worked hard for four months. They formed a corporation, dealt with legal concerns, found a good location, and obtained food. One community leader said, The effort to form the Toledo Food Bank was probably 25 percent local endeavor and 75 percent Sean's drive, persistence, and unyielding impatience in achieving success . . . [h]e was the driving force in the formation of the food bank."

The food bank was an immediate success. After one year of operation, the Toledo Food Bank aided more than 80 families each month. And in addition to feeling the satisfaction that comes from taking action, Sean was chosen by the U.S. Department of Justice to receive a Young American Medal for outstanding service to his community.

Getting Involved

1. Identify a need in your community similar to the one addressed in this case.
2. Formulate a plan for how you might organize volunteer efforts to help remedy this problem and identify resources that could be used in your plan.
3. Predict any problems or objections you might encounter in implementing your plan.

TRF **Teacher's Resource File**
See the Participatory Government Activities file, pp. 28–39, for materials to support or extend this feature.

4 The Members of Congress

Find Out:

- Who are the members of Congress and what are their personal and political backgrounds?
- What are the several roles members of Congress play in performing their duties?
- What are members of Congress paid—in money and in various other forms of compensation?

Key Terms:

constituents, oversight function

You have almost certainly seen help wanted ads in your newspaper, and you know that most of those listings include a description of the job, its pay, and so on. Of course, you will not find an ad that reads: "Wanted: Members of Congress . . . " But, as you will discover in this section, those who do become senators and representatives have certain characteristics that help them get their jobs. And you will also see that those jobs carry a number of responsibilities with them—and a number of benefits, as well.

Personal and Political Backgrounds

Whatever else they may be, the 535 members of Congress are *not* a representative cross section of the American people. Rather, the "average" member is a white male in his mid-50s. The median age of the members of the House is just over 53 and of the Senate, 58. Only 31 women sit in Congress: 29 in the House and two—Nancy Landon Kassebaum (R., Kans.) and Barbara Mikulski (D., Md.)—in the Senate. There are only 26 African Americans, 14 Hispanics, and 1 Native American in Congress—and all of them sit in the House of Representatives. Two Asian Americans sit in the Senate and three in the House.

Nearly all members are married, a few are divorced, and they have, on the average, two children. Only a few members say they have no religious affiliation. Nearly two-thirds are Protestants, one-fourth are Roman Catholics, and about eight percent are Jewish.

Well over a third of the members of the House and well over half the senators are lawyers. Most others come from business and banking, education, agriculture, journalism, and public service/politics. Nearly all went to college. More than four out of five have a college degree and a number have several.

Most senators and representatives were born in the States they represent. Only a handful were born outside the United States. Sprinkled among the members of Congress are several millionaires. A surprisingly large number, however, depend on their salaries as their major source of income.

Most members of Congress have had considerable political experience. The average senator is now serving a second term, and the

First Woman in Congress Jeannette Rankin (R., Montana) was first elected in 1916. She voted against entering World War I and was the only member of the House to vote against entering World War II.

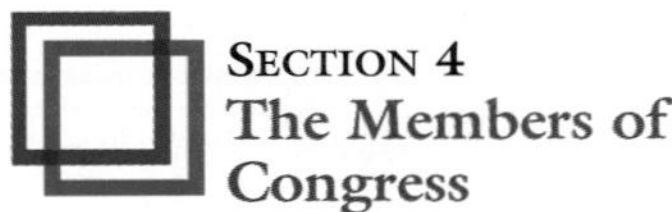

SECTION 4
The Members of Congress

FOCUS

Teacher's Resource File See the Unit 3 File, p. 11, for the Section 4 Outline.

Objectives

10.10 Identify who the members of Congress are and determine what are their political and personal backgrounds.

10.11 Examine the several roles played by members of Congress as they perform their duties.

10.12 Determine how members of Congress are compensated for their service.

Bellringer Activity Ask students to imagine that they are directing a movie in which one of the key characters is a member of Congress. Ask students to discuss what kind of person they would cast for that role. Tell students that in this section, they will read about the individuals who make up the United States Congress and the job that they do.

State the Purpose Congress is made up of 535 individuals. Nevertheless, it is possible to draw up a profile of the members and the way they perform their job. In Section 4, students will learn about the personal and political backgrounds of Congressional members and the various ways in which they represent their constituents.

Vocabulary

Direct students' attention to "Key Terms" on page 249. As students read the text of Section 4, ask them which word they feel represents the more important function of members of Congress—as representatives of their constituents or as agents of their oversight function.

Reading Strategy: Problem Solving

As students read, ask them to consider the question of ethnicity and gender among the members of Congress. Have them pose the problem: How can Congress truly represent the people when it is made up almost entirely of white, educated, middle-aged men? Ask students to consider how the members of Congress could exercise their roles so as to better represent the overall population of the United States.

INSTRUCT

Discuss/Analyze Direct students' attention to the questions in paragraph 2 on page 251 of Section 4: "How do the people's representatives represent the people?" and "On what basis do they cast their votes?"

Ask students whether or not it is accurate to say that Congress represents the people on the basis of race, age, or other personal characteristics. Next have the class analyze the four general ways that members of Congress make decisions. To aid in this discussion, ask the following questions: If a person votes on an issue primarily as a partisan, what oversight might possibly occur? (*They might ignore their constituents' wishes.*) If a member votes as a delegate, does it matter whether or not he or she shares a personal background that is different from most of his or her constituents? Do students think that the current congressional pay package reflects the votes of trustees, delegates, partisans or politicos?

Interpreting Graphs: Multicultural Awareness Lead students in a discussion about whether or not the composition of Congress truly represents the people of the United States. (*Possible answers: No, it fails to truly represent women and minority groups. Others might say that Congress is democratically elected, and so it is as true a representation of the American people as is possible.*)

Caption Answer White, middle-aged males.

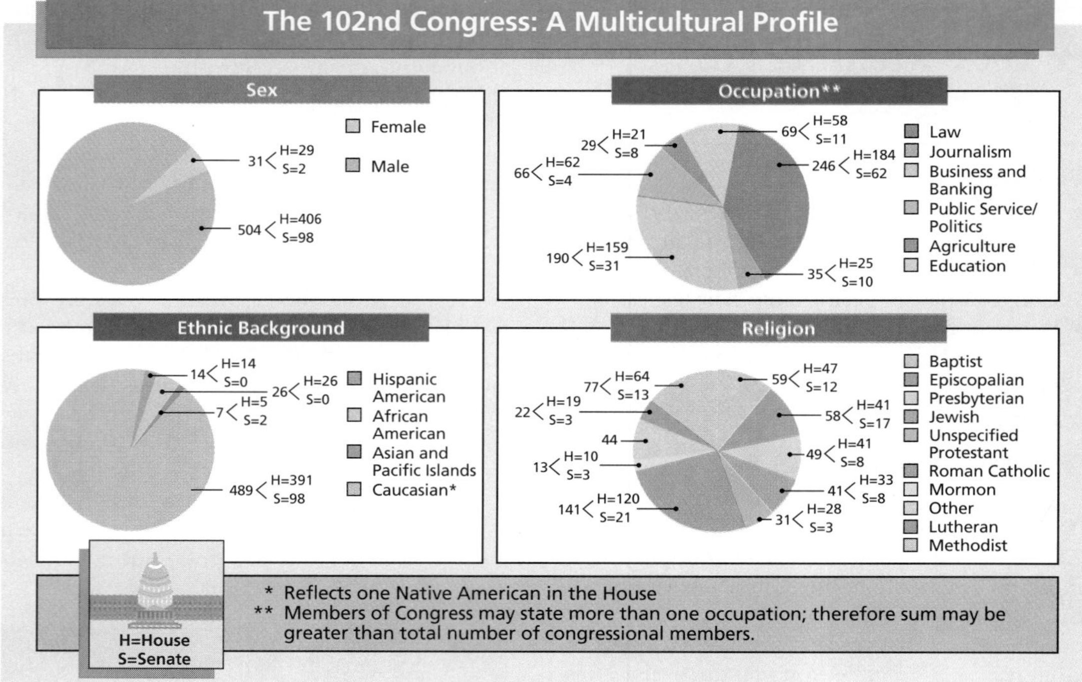

Interpreting Graphs: Multicultural Awareness This graph indicates that Congress does not represent the multicultural richness of American society. Which group dominates Congress?

average representative has served four terms. Nearly a third of the Senate once sat in the House. Several senators are former governors. A few senators have held cabinet seats or other high posts in the executive branch. The House has a large number of former State legislators and prosecuting attorneys among its members.

Again, Congress is not an accurate cross section of the nation's population. Rather, it is made up of upper-middle-class Americans. On the whole, however, most members are quite able and hard-working people.

Duties of the Job

The 535 members of Congress play several closely related and vital roles. Their major job, of course, is to make law. That is, they are (1) legislators. In addition, members of Congress also serve as (2) committee members; (3) representatives of their
1.a **constituents**, the people of their districts; (4) servants of their constituents; and (5) politicians. You have read about some aspects of these roles in this and in earlier chapters, and you will consider other facets of them in the next two chapters. For now, consider the following overview of the roles of a member of Congress.

As committee members, representatives and senators serve on those bodies to which proposed laws (bills) are referred in each house. They must screen those proposals and decide which of them will go on to floor consideration—that is, be considered, debated, and acted upon by the full membership of their respective chambers.

As another and vital part of their committee work, representatives and senators also exercise
1.b the **oversight function**. That is, they check to see that the various agencies in the executive branch are working effectively and are acting in line with the policies that Congress has set by law.

ACTIVITY: Cooperative Learning

Time: One class period **Activity:** List pros and cons of congressional voting options. **Grouping:** Small groups **Purpose:** Assign each group one of the four broad voting options—trustee, delegate, partisan, politico. Have groups work together to identify the pros and cons of their assigned options. Suggest that students pick an imaginary topic and consider how their option would affect a vote on that issue. Remind students to draw upon information presented in earlier chapters to help them develop their lists. **Roles:** Assign the following roles: discussion leader, recorder, spokesperson. **Outcome:** Have the spokesperson present the group's list. Then have the class vote on the option they would like their lawmakers to choose.

As you have read, members of the Senate and the House are elected to represent their constituents. But what does that really mean? Every senator and representative must cast hundreds of votes during each session of Congress. Many of those votes come on relatively unimportant matters—minor bills and so on. But many votes, including some on matters of organization and procedure, are cast on matters of far-reaching importance.

So, no questions about the lawmaking branch can be more vital than these: How do the people's representatives represent the people? On what basis do they cast their votes?

In broad terms, each lawmaker has four voting options. He or she can vote as a trustee, as a delegate, as a partisan, or as a politico.

Trustees These members believe that each question they face must be decided on its merits. Conscience and independent judgment are their guides. Trustees call issues as they see them, regardless of the views held by their constituents or by any of the other groups that seek to influence their decisions.

Delegates These members see themselves as the agents of those who elected them. They believe that they should vote the way they think "the folks back home" would want. These members are willing to suppress their own views, ignore those of their party's leaders, and turn a deaf ear to the arguments of colleagues and of special interests from outside their constituencies.

Partisans The partisans are those lawmakers who owe their first allegiance to their political party. They feel duty-bound to vote in line with the party platform and the wishes of their party's leaders. Most studies of legislators' voting behavior show that partisanship is the leading factor influencing their votes on most important measures.

Politicos Politicos attempt to combine the basic elements of the trustee, delegate, and partisan roles. They try to balance these often conflicting factors: their own views of what is best for their constituents and/or the nation as a whole, the political facts of life, and the peculiar pressures of the moment.

Other Roles Representatives and senators also act as servants of their constituents. They do this particularly as they work to help them solve whatever problems they may have with the federal bureaucracy. Many constituents believe members of Congress are in Washington especially to do favors for them. The average member is swamped with constituent requests from the moment he or she takes office. The range of these requests is almost without limit—everything from help in securing a government contract or an appointment to a military academy, to asking for a free sight-seeing tour of Washington or even a personal loan. Consider this job description offered only half-jokingly by former Representative Luther Patrick of Alabama:

> "A Congressman has become an expanded messenger boy, an employment agency, getter-outer of the Navy, Army, Marines, ward heeler, wound healer, trouble shooter, law explainer, bill finder, issue translator, resolution interpreter, controversy oil pourer, gladhand extender, business promoter, convention goer, civil ills skirmisher, veterans' affairs adjuster, ex-serviceman's champion, watchdog for the underdog, sympathizer with the upper dog, namer and kisser of babies, recoverer of lost luggage, soberer of delegates, adjuster for traffic violators, voters straying into Washington and into toils of the law, binder up of broken hearts, financial wet nurse, Good Samaritan, contributor to good causes—there are so many good causes—cornerstone layer, public building and bridge dedicator, ship christener—to be sure he does get in a little flag waving—and a little constitutional hoisting and spread-eagle work, but it is getting harder every day to find time to properly study legislation—the very business we are primarily here to discharge, and that must be done above all things."

Most members of Congress know that to deny or fail to respond to these requests would mean to lose votes in the next election. This is a key fact, for all of the roles a member of Congress plays—legislator, committee member, constituent representative, constituent servant, and politician—are related, at least in part, to their efforts to win reelection from the voters of their districts.

Compensation

The Constitution gives Congress the power to set its own pay and also provide other

Provide Guided Practice
Write the words "Duties of the Job" on the chalkboard. Ask students to volunteer items to create a list of duties expected of members of Congress. When they are done, create a job description based on the responsibilities students have compiled.

Provide Independent Practice

TRF **Teacher's Resource File**
You may wish to assign Section 4 Guided Reading and Review, Unit 3 File, p. 12, to help students master section objective content.

ABCNEWS INTERACTIVE

The following video segments may be used to highlight aspects of congressional membership.

POWERS OF CONGRESS GUIDEBOOK
Chapter 54: Profile of Congress, p. 60
Chapter 55: Speakers of the House, p. 61

See also Enrichment Questions and Activities beginning on page 161.

Enrichment

Ask students to find out more about their members of Congress. Have them formulate and answer questions such as: What is the cultural and religious background of each member of Congress? What is his or her political background? (Students might consult the Government Resources Handbook on page 690.) Invite students to create an outline that shows the key points about their chosen representative. (Average)

OR

TRF **Teacher's Resource File**
See the Unit 3 File, pp.15–17, for the Case Study on Contemporary Issues for Chapter 10.

ACTIVITY: Teaching Heterogeneous Groups

In order that students understand the concept of representative government, have students create a profile of their ideal representative. Tell students to review the various characteristics of the representatives discussed in the chapter, such as personal information, political background, voting styles, and other characteristics. Make sure students can explain the significance behind each of the features they choose for their representative.

Interpreting Graphs Ask students to compare the increase in pay between 1978 and 1991 to other roughly similar time intervals (such as 1870–1872, 1935–1950, or 1966–1978.) Given these figures, is the rate of increase in recent years significantly greater than in previous times? (*It is much greater than certain eras, but similar to others.*)

Caption Answer Drawbacks include that the public has no direct control over salaries. Advantages include that political pressure works to keep salaries within a reasonable range.

Monitor Comprehension

Answers to Section 4 Review
1. "Key Terms" are defined on the following pages:
a. constituents, p. 250
b. oversight function, p. 250
2. Members of Congress are likely to be white, male, college educated. A significant percentage are lawyers by training. Many had political experience before being elected to their current offices.
3. Members may be legislators, committee members, representatives of their constituents, servants of their constituents, and politicians. They may cast their votes as trustees, delegates, partisans, or politicos. **4.** Congress sets its own salaries. This gives Congress the power to vote itself significant raises, but also applies significant political pressure. **5.** Answers may vary. Students might note that the temptation of setting one's own salary is too great, thus no "good man" would want it. At

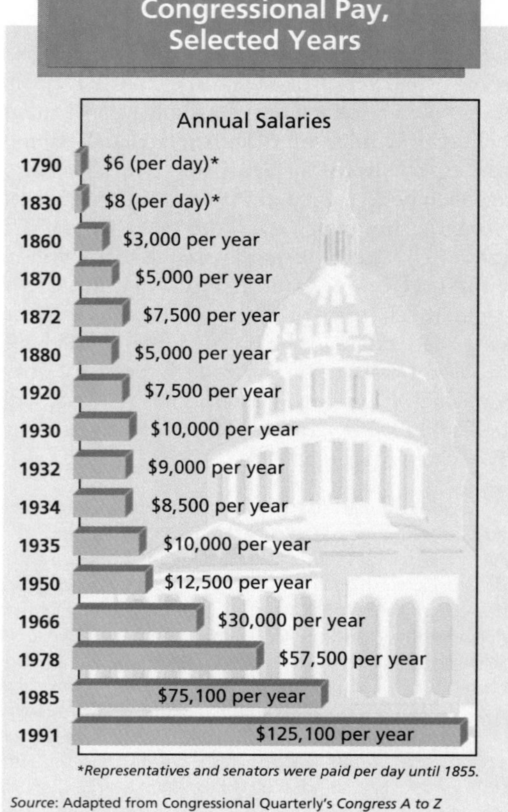

Interpreting Graphs Congress has the constitutionally mandated task of setting its own salary. What might be some drawbacks and some advantages of this arrangement?

compensations for its members.[25] Today, senators and representatives receive $125,100 a year. (The Speaker of the House is paid $155,000 a year—the same salary Congress has set for the Vice President of the United States.)

[25] Article I, Section 6, Clause 1. The pay question has always sparked controversy—both in and out of Congress. Consumer activist Ralph Nader described the most recent (1991) congressional pay raise as "a raid on the Treasury." Senator Robert C. Byrd (D., W.Va.) defended the raise, asking: "How does it enhance good government to make [serving in Congress] a luxury which only the wealthy can afford?"

Nonsalary Compensation Each member also receives a number of "fringe benefits," some of which are quite substantial. For example, each member is allowed a tax deduction to help keep up two residences, one in his or her home district and another in Washington. Travel allowances cover the cost of several round trips between the home State and the capital each year.

Each member pays only small amounts from their salaries for life and health insurance policies. A medical staff offers free care at the Capitol, and full care can be had, at very low rates, at any military hospital. Also, members contribute to a generous pension plan. The plan is based on a member's years of service in Congress and can lead to a retirement income for some members of more than $100,000 a year. Like other Americans, members of Congress are also covered by social security, and they pay the maximum social security tax on their salaries—now more than $3,500 a year.

Each member also has offices in one of the Senate or House office buildings and allowances for offices in the home State or district. Each is allowed funds for hiring staff and for running those offices. All of a member's official mail is sent postage free under what is called the franking privilege.

There is also free printing and distribution of speeches, newsletters, and other material. Radio and television tapes may also be produced and distributed at a sharply reduced cost. Each member has free parking, plants for the office, the research help of the Library of Congress, and still more—including the use of several fine restaurants and two first-rate gymnasiums with swimming pools and saunas. (In 1991, congressional use of these restaurants became the focus of a scandal when it was revealed that several members had run up large, unpaid tabs.) Adding up everything, the compensation of a typical member of Congress now comes to well over $200,000 a year.

The Politics of Pay There are only two real limits on the level of congressional pay. One is the President's veto power. The other and more potent limit is the fear of voter backlash, an angry reaction by constituents at the ballot box. That fear of election-day fallout has always

Spotlight on: Economics

For 1992, the federal budget appropriated $69.2 million for Senate staff salaries and $821 million for staff salaries and office expenses of the House. Political scientists have estimated that the average senator receives $700,000 and the average representative $400,000 to staff and run his or her offices on Capitol Hill and in the home district. Representatives generally employ 15 to 18 staffers, not counting committee staff, and senators often have twice that many. Since Senate rules allocate staff on the basis of population, senators from States such as New York and California may employ as many as 60 staffers!

made most members reluctant to vote to raise their own salaries.

Most often, Congress has tried to skirt the troublesome and politically sensitive pay question by providing for such fringe benefits as a special tax break, a liberal pension plan, more office and travel funds, and other perquisites, or "perks"—items of value that are much less apparent to "the folks back home."

The debate over congressional pay is not likely to end soon—at least not as long as the current method of establishing salaries remains in effect. All sides of the issue present reasonable arguments. And clearly, decent salaries—pay in line with the responsibilities of the job—will not automatically bring the most able men and women to Congress, or to any other public office. But certainly, decent salaries can make public service much more appealing to qualified people.

Membership Privileges

Beyond the matter of their salaries and other compensation, members of Congress enjoy several important privileges. The Constitution commands that senators and representatives

> "shall, in all cases, except treason, felony, and breach of the peace, be privileged from arrest during their attendance at the session of their respective Houses, and in going to, and returning from, the same . . ."[26]

The provision dates from English and colonial practice, when the king's officers often harassed legislators on petty grounds. It has been of little importance in our national history, however.[27]

Another much more important privilege is set out in the same place in the Constitution. The Speech and Debate Clause of Article I, Section 6, Clause 1 declares

> ". . . for any speech or debate in either House, they shall not be questioned in any other place."

The words "any other place" refer to the courts.

The privilege is intended to "throw a cloak of legislative immunity" about members of Congress. The clause protects representatives and senators from suits for libel or slander arising out of their official conduct. The Supreme Court has held that the immunity applies "to things generally done in a session of the House [or Senate] by one of its members in relation to the business before it.'[28] The protection goes, then, beyond floor debate, to include work in committees and all other things generally done by members of Congress in relation to congressional business.

The important and necessary goal of this provision of the Constitution is to protect freedom of legislative debate. Clearly, members must not feel restrained in their vigorous discussion of the sometimes contentious issues of the day. However, this provision is not designed to give members unbridled freedom to attack others verbally or in writing. Thus, a member is not free to defame another person in a public speech, an article, a conversation, or otherwise.

Section 4 Review

1. **Define:** constituents, oversight function
2. What are some of the common features found in the backgrounds of members of Congress?
3. What are the principal roles that a member of Congress plays?
4. (a) Who sets the salary for the members of Congress? (b) How has this fact led to controversy?

Critical Thinking

5. **Identifying Central Issues** (p. 19) Former Senator Russell Long (D., La.) once described Congress's power to set its own pay as a "power no good man would want and a power no bad man should have." What do you think he meant by this?

26 Article I, Section 6, Clause 1.

27 The courts have regularly held that the words "breach of the peace" cover all criminal offenses. So the protection covers only arrest for civil (noncriminal) offenses while engaged in congressional business.

28 The leading case is *Kilburn* v. *Thompson,* 1881. The holding has been affirmed many times since. In *Hutchinson* v. *Proxmire,* 1979, however, the Court held that members of Congress may be sued for libel for statements they make in news releases or in newsletters.

the same time, the power is so great that it should not be left to a "bad man."

Teacher's Resource File See the Unit 3 File, p. 13, for the Section 4 Quiz.

Closure

Though Congress represents the American people, it does not reflect the characteristics of those people. Regardless of their personal backgrounds, however, the members of Congress perform a number of important roles. In doing so, they generally follow four basic decision-making patterns—that of the trustee, delegate, partisan, and politico, among others.

In Chapter 11, students will learn about the constitutionally defined fields within which Congress exercises its powers.

Assignment Assign Chapter 11, Section 1, pp. 259–261, for the next class period.

Reteach

Have students assume the role of a spokesperson for a minority candidate for Congress. Tell students to write a short public announcement explaining why they believe that Congress and the voting public will benefit by electing their candidate. Have the students present their announcements to the class.

TEACHING
Citizenship

How to Develop Profiles of Your Members of Congress

Objective

Analyze information about individual members of Congress.

INSTRUCT

Before you begin the feature, ask students what they already know about their representatives in Congress. Have them write down a few notes and name the sources from which their information came.

As they read through the Citizenship feature, make sure students notice the kind of information that is recommended for inclusion in a profile of a member of Congress.

Answers 1. (a) *The Congressional Directory, The Congressional Record, CQ's Guide to Congress.* (b) Personal and political background, service in Congress and past accomplishments, committees served on. (c) Have students check their library for other possible resources. **3.** Possible answers include: *Almanac of American Politics,* various other almanacs. **4.** (a) *Almanac of American Politics, Congressional Directory.* (b) Some information might be available in the *Government Manual* and various almanacs. **5** and **6.** *Almanac of American Politics, Congressional Directory.*

Citizenship

How to Develop Profiles of Your Members of Congress

Who are your senators and who is your representative in Congress? How well do these people represent you and the people of your State and district? These important questions will become even more vital when you become qualified to vote, for casting an informed ballot is a key responsibility for all citizens.

Fortunately, there is no shortage of information about your representatives in Washington, D. C. Follow the steps below to develop a profile of the men and women who represent you in Congress.

1. Find useful sources of information on your representatives in Congress. As you know, information about the United States government is available from a wide variety of sources. For example, check the Government Resources Handbook that begins on page 690 of your textbook. (a) Which sources are specifically devoted to the United States Congress? (b) What kinds of information would you be able to find in those sources? (c) What additional sources hold information about Congress?

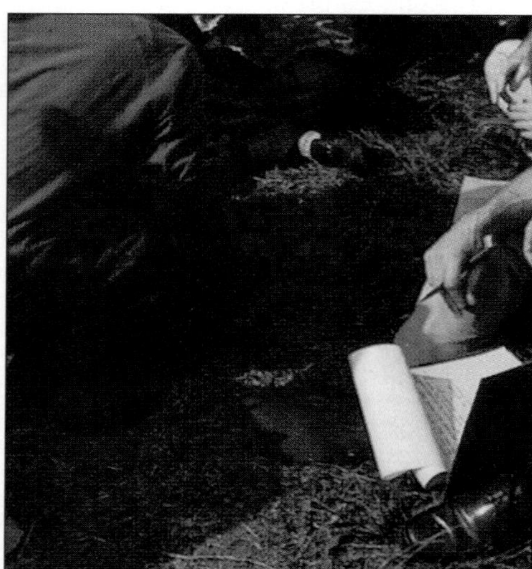

2. Check local sources of information. Local newspapers are an invaluable source of good information about your representatives in Washington. Such sources often include stories about election campaigns and about your representatives.

3. List the personal backgrounds of your representatives. Information such as age, birthplace, home, religion, marital status, education, and occupation are available in published sources. In which of the resources listed in the Government Resources Handbook would you most likely find personal background information?

4. Describe your representatives' political backgrounds. Political background includes data such as party membership, political experience before serving in Congress, years of service in Congress, and nature of constituency. Research committee assignments, leadership positions, and major bills authored and/or sponsored by your members of Congress. Answer these questions: (a) In which resource(s) would this data be most readily available? (b) In what other sources could you find this information?

5. Define your representatives' voting records. It is important to know where your representatives stand on the vital issues of the day. Analyze their positions (votes) on key economic, social, foreign policy, and defense issues. What resource might you use to find this information?

TRF **Teacher's Resource File**
See the Unit 3 File, p. 14, for the Skill Application for this skill lesson. See also the Participatory Government Activities file for reference materials on public and private sources of information.

Chapter-in-Brief

Scan all headings, photographs, charts, and other visuals in the chapter before reading the section summaries below.

Section 1 The National Legislature (pp. 235–238) Because the Framers attached great importance to the legislative branch, they devoted the first and the lengthiest of the articles of the Constitution to it. Article I establishes a bicameral Congress—a two-house body as the national legislature.

Congress is a bicameral body mainly because the Framers (1) were familiar with British, colonial, and early State practice, (2) agreed to bicameralism to settle conflict at the Philadelphia Convention, and (3) hoped that one house would act as a check on the other.

A term of Congress extends over two years. There are two regular sessions during each term, one each year. Only the President can call a special session of Congress—but no special sessions have been held in more than 40 years.

Section 2 The House of Representatives (pp. 238–244) The House of Representatives is the larger of the two chambers. By law, there are 435 seats (members) in the House. The seats are distributed among the States on the basis of their respective populations.

The Constitution provides for a census to be taken every 10 years, and it directs Congress to reapportion (reallocate) the seats in the House on the basis of each census. Following each of the last six censuses, Congress has approved the reapportionment plan recommended to it by the Census Bureau. Each State is entitled to at least one seat in the House.

Voters elect members of the House for two-year terms. They are chosen from districts within the States. The State legislatures draw those congressional districts, and they are often gerrymandered. The Supreme Court has held that congressional districts must be drawn in accord with the "one-person, one vote" rule—that is, in terms of population equality.

Section 3 The Senate (pp. 245–247) The Constitution provides that each State is to have two senators. Thus, the Senate has 100 members today. Senators serve six-year terms.

The Constitution sets higher qualifications for senators than it does for representatives. Members of the Senate must be at least 30 years of age, unlike 25 years of age for representatives. Also, senators must have been citizens for at least nine (instead of seven) years. Members of both houses must be inhabitants of the States they represent.

Section 4 The Members of Congress (pp. 249–253) Members of Congress are not a representative cross section of the American people. Instead, the average member is a white male in his mid-50s. There are only a few women, African Americans, and Hispanic Americans in Congress.

Members of Congress are legislators, of course. They also serve as representatives and servants of their constituents, as committee members, and as politicians. Most members usually adopt one of four styles. They behave and vote as (1) trustees, who base their decisions solely on their best judgments, (2) delegates, who follow the wishes of their constituents, (3) partisans, who feel duty-bound to support their parties' positions, or (4) politicos, who try to balance these roles as situations demand.

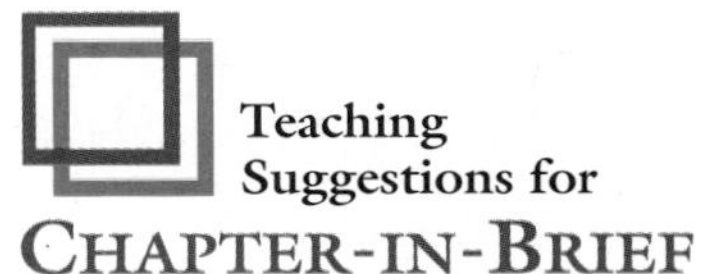

Teaching Suggestions for CHAPTER-IN-BRIEF

Below are some of the possible uses for the Chapter-in-Brief:

To Preview the Chapter You may want to assign the Chapter-in-Brief page and the Section Outlines from the Teacher's Resource File before beginning Chapter 10 to introduce students to "Key Terms" and concepts in each section.

To Review the Chapter When students have completed Chapter 10, you might want to assign the Chapter-in-Brief as a tool for review, along with the Guided Reading and Reviews from the Teacher's Resource File.

To Omit the Chapter If you wish to skip Chapter 10, it may be helpful to assign the Chapter-in-Brief to students as a review before continuing to another chapter. You may also want to assign the Chapter 10 Test to assess student knowledge of the material. Then specific portions of Chapter 10 may be assigned to students needing reinforcement of "Key Terms" and concepts.

Teacher's Resource File See the Unit 3 File for the following materials:

- Section Outlines, pp. 2, 5, 8, 11.
- Guided Reading and Reviews, pp. 3, 6, 9, 12.
- Chapter 10 Test, pp. 18–20.

ADDITIONAL RESOURCES

Baker, Ross K. *House and Senate.* Norton, 1989.

Congress: Reflecting the Public Will. Video. Close Up Foundation, 1984. Color. 30 minutes.

Every Two Years. Film. Barr, 1986. Color. 28 minutes.

Fowler, Linda L. and Robert D. McClure. *Political Ambition: Who Decides to Run for Congress.* Yale University Press, 1989.

Jacobson, Gary C. *The Politics of Congressional Elections.* Little, Brown, 2nd ed., 1987.

Jigsaw Politics: Shaping the House After the 1990 Census. Congressional Quarterly Books, 1990.

Ornstein, Norman, *et al. Vital Statistics on Congress, 1989–1990.* Congressional Quarterly, 1989.

Vogler, David J. *The Politics of Congress.* Wm. C. Brown, 5th ed., 1988.

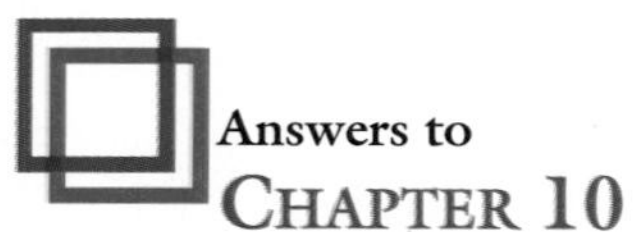

Answers to
CHAPTER 10

Vocabulary and Key Terms

Matching
1. gerrymandered
2. constituents
3. oversight function
4. term
5. reapportion

True or False
1. True.
2. False—the correct term is *special session.*
3. True.
4. False—the correct term is *continuous body.*
5. False—the correct term is *session.*

Word Relationships
1. At-large refers to election of an official from an entire governmental unit; e.g., senators are elected at-large by the entire State. Single-member districts are electoral districts from which a single office-holder is chosen for each office on the ballot; most representatives are chosen in single-member districts.
2. A session is the regular period of time during which Congress meets. A special session is an extraordinary meeting of Congress.
3. Apportioned refers to the distribution of the seats of the House among the States based on their population. Reapportion refers to the process by which apportionment is adjusted every 10 years to reflect changes in population.

Main Ideas

Section 1
1. The Framers created a bicameral Congress partly because their British heritage made them familiar with it. Also, bicameralism resolved many of the conflicts at the Constitutional Convention; and it augmented the Framers' concept of checks and balances.
2. Each State is represented equally in the Senate; each State is represented by population in the House.
3. Terms used to begin in March—the 20th Amendment changed the date for the start of each term to "noon on the 3rd day of January." Also, sessions of Congress today last nearly all year.

Section 2
4. The seats in the House are supposed to reflect the population in the States. So, the Constitution directs Congress to reapportion the seats as needed by changes in population. The census, which takes place every 10 years, provides Congress with the information they need to decide which States should have how many seats. **5.** States have often gerrymandered districts. This has been done to enhance the political power of certain groups or political parties. **6.** A House member must be 25, must have been a citizen for 7 years, and must be a resident of the State from which he

Chapter Review

Vocabulary and Key Terms

term (p. 237)
session (p. 237)
special session (p. 238)
apportioned (p. 238)
reapportion (p. 239)
single-member district (p. 241)
at-large (p. 241)
gerrymandered (p. 242)
continuous body (p. 246)
constituents (p. 250)
oversight function (p. 250)

Matching: *Review the key terms in the list above. If you are not sure of a term's meaning, look up the term and review its definition. Choose a term from the list above that best matches each description.*

1. how you might describe an electoral district that has been drawn by a legislator in a very odd shape
2. what a senator considers every citizen of his or her state
3. what function Congress is performing when it checks on the programs of the executive branch
4. the period of time for which a representative serves in Congress before coming up for reelection
5. what happens to the seats of Congress every decade

True or False: *Determine whether each statement is true or false. If it is true, write "true." If it is false, change the underlined word or words to make the statement true.*

1. The Constitution says that the seats of the House of Representatives must be apportioned among the States based on population.
2. The President has the power to call a session of Congress.
3. A member of Congress represents his or her constituents.
4. Because the entire membership of the Senate is never up for election at the same time, the upper house is called a single-member district.
5. Congress performs its formal legislative work during a special session.

Word Relationships: *Distinguish between words in each pair.*

1. at-large/single-member district
2. session/special session
3. apportioned/reapportion

Main Ideas

Section 1 (pp. 235–238)

1. What factors explain why the United States Congress is bicameral?
2. How does bicameralism reflect the principle of federalism?
3. How have the terms and sessions of Congress changed over the course of United States history?

Section 2 (pp. 238–244)

4. For what reasons must Congress be reapportioned every 10 years?
5. In what way has the reapportionment of House seats been used for the political gain of certain groups and parties in the various States?
6. What are the constitutional qualifications that all members of the House must meet?

Section 3 (pp. 245–247)

7. How does the Senate differ from the House in terms of size and the election of its members?

8. What is the purpose of the differences between the House of Representatives and the Senate?
9. What are the qualifications that all senators must meet?

Section 4 (pp. 249-253)

10. (a) For what reasons is it untrue to say that the members of Congress represent a cross section of the American people? (b) Describe the typical member.
11. What are the different ways in which members of Congress may view their function?
12. (a) How are members of Congress compensated for their work? (b) What is the controversy surrounding congressional pay?

Critical Thinking

1. **Identifying Alternatives** (p. 19) In *The Federalist* No. 10, Madison warns that ". . . representatives must be raised to a certain number to guard against the cabals of a few; and that however large it may be, they must be limited to a certain number, in order to guard against the confusion of a multitude." In light of this statement, discuss whether or not you think Congress today—with 535 seats—is too large or too small.
2. **Distinguishing False from Accurate Images** (p. 19) Congress is frequently blamed for many of the problems of the National Government. Yet the text says that the members of Congress are on the whole hard-working and able people. How can you explain the existence of these two opposing viewpoints?
3. **Expressing Problems Clearly** (p. 19) Recall what you have read about the differences between the House and Senate. (a) What are the benefits and drawbacks of having senators serve six-year terms? (b) What might happen if they had shorter or longer terms?
4. **Recognizing Ideologies** (p. 19) The saying "to the victor goes the spoils" has a long tradition in the American political system. (a) What do you think this saying means? (b) How might this saying help explain the practice of gerrymandering?

Getting Involved

1. **Writing Your Opinion** Write a newspaper editorial about your views on what the qualifications of a member of Congress should be. To start, list the current constitutional qualifications that members must meet. In addition, be sure to consider the standards of behavior discussed in the chapter. Then write down your ideas for any modifications or additions to the list. Begin your first draft with a statement about why firm standards and qualifications are necessary for members of Congress. Then give your own ideas for amending or adding onto the current qualifications. For each idea, explain how you think your idea will make the United States Congress a better institution. Read your draft for clarity and revise. Then proofread and draft a final copy.
2. **Class Debate** Hold a class debate on one of the following topics: (a) *Resolved,* That the minimum age for representatives in the House be 18 years of age; (b) *Resolved,* That no member of either house of Congress be allowed to serve more than 12 years in office. Select one team to debate in favor of the statement and another to argue against it. The rest of the class should evaluate each team's presentation.
3. **Creating a Poster** Consider what you have read in Chapter 10 about the roles of members of Congress. Make a poster that illustrates your idea of what it means to be a member of Congress. You can use a combination of words and images in your poster.

or she is chosen. In addition, House members are subject to certain standards imposed by the House itself.

Section 3

7. The Senate includes only 100 members, each of whom is elected at large for a six-year term. 8. These differences are supposed to make the Senate less subject to the pressures of election and thus free to focus on issues of national concern.
9. A senator must be 30 years old, must have been a citizen for 9 years, and must be a resident of the State from which he or she is elected. In addition, senators are subject to certain standards imposed by the Senate itself.

Section 4

10. (a) It does not include a representative sample of racial or ethnic populations, or an equal number of males and females, or an accurate representation of the economic classes. (b) The typical member would be a white male lawyer.
11. Members can perform their jobs according to several roles. They may seek first and foremost to please their constituents or their parties, or they may vote by their own consciences, or they may try to balance each of these interests at the same time. 12. (a) In addition to their salary, members receive a number of valuable benefits that makes their total compensation package worth well over \$200,000 a year. (b) Congress sets its own salary, and thus must give itself raises.

Critical Thinking

1. Answers will vary. Students can consider the size of the first Congress in relation to population, and the size of Congress in relation to the population today. Encourage students to incorporate their personal views of the effectiveness and responsiveness of Congress.
2. Answers will vary. Students might consider the many roles members of Congress must fill, and speculate on the difficulty of being "all things to all people."
3. Answers will vary. (a) Students should consider the fact that senators are supposed to be less subject to political pressures than members of Congress, but that they are consequently less responsive to the will of the voters. (b) Answers will vary. Ensure that students explain their reasoning.
4. (a) The winner of a contest deserves to benefit from his or her victory. (b) Those parties that manage to gain a majority of legislative seats ought to be able to take advantage of their victory by gerrymandering.

Getting Involved

1–3. Answers and results will vary, but students should demonstrate an understanding of the concepts in this chapter.

Chapter 11 Resources

In the Teacher's Resource File
The following materials are found in the Teacher's Resource File box.

Instructional Support: Unit 3 File

For the Section
Outlines, pp. 24, 27, 30, 33
Guided Reading and Reviews, pp. 25, 28, 31, 34
Quizzes, pp. 26, 29, 32, 35

For the Chapter
Skill Application, p. 36
Case Study on Contemporary Issues, pp. 37–39
Chapter Test, pp. 40–42
Additional Test Questions, pp. 43–45

Enrichment Support Files

Supreme Court Cases, pp. 8, 20–21, 22–23
Participatory Government Activities, pp. 4–19
Historical and Legal Documents, pp. 45, 46
Simulations and Debates: The War Powers Resolution, p. 49

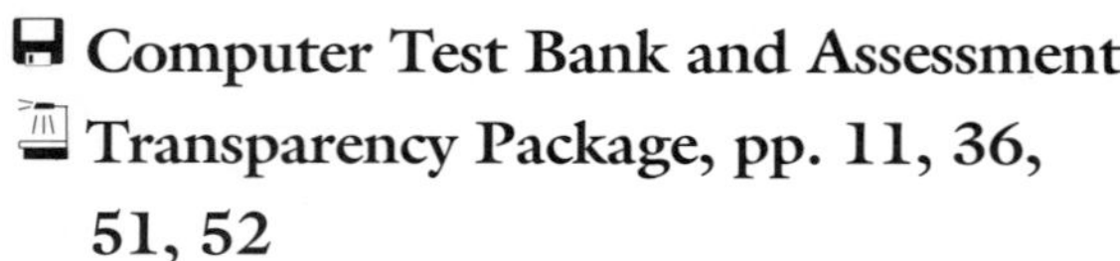

Computer Test Bank and Assessment
Transparency Package, pp. 11, 36, 51, 52

Chapter 11 Focus

Introduce the Chapter Tell students that in Chapter 11 they will read about the legislative branch of the United States government—Congress. Read with students the Chapter Preview and Objectives.

Writing Activity Direct students' attention to "Describe." Ask students to write a list of steps they could follow to create and maintain a budget. Discuss some of the difficulties of maintaining a budget.

Motivate for Learning Direct students' attention to "Predict." Ask students to discuss what would happen were they to consistently borrow money from a friend without paying it back. Then have them predict the possible consequences of government's unlimited borrowing of money.

Powers of Congress

Chapter Preview

"If only I had as much money as I need." This thought has crossed the mind of almost anyone who is responsible for sticking to a budget—stretching the money that is available far enough to cover expenses. Like an individual or a business, the Federal Government creates a budget that describes the government's financial plan. Unlike individuals or businesses, however, the government has the legislative power to acquire as much money as it needs.

The powers that concern budget making are among the many powers given to Congress by the Constitution. This chapter is about the two basic categories of constitutional power held and exercised by Congress: those that form the base on which Congress can and does make the law and those functions that are closely related to its role as the lawmaking branch of the National Government.

Before you read this chapter:

- **Describe** how you or your family creates a budget.
- **Predict** one possible consequence of the government's unlimited borrowing of money.

As you read, focus on the main objective for each section. Understand:

1. The scope of the powers of Congress in a governmental system that is both limited and federal in character.
2. The concepts of the expressed powers.
3. The concepts of the implied powers.
4. The nonlegislative powers of Congress.

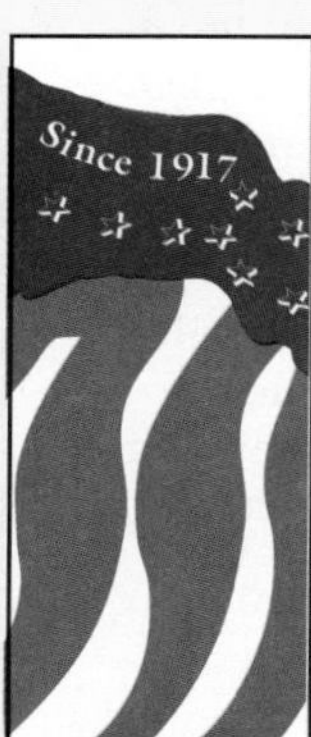

Magruder's American Government: *A Witness to Change* by William A. McClenaghan

The scope, the reach of the powers and functions of the Federal Government have increased enormously over the past two centuries. Another way of saying that is to note that the powers that the Constitution gives to Congress have expanded remarkably over the past 200 years.

The largest single spurt in the growth of federal power occurred in the era of the Great Depression, which began in 1929 and brought Franklin Roosevelt and the New Deal to power in 1933. It is both fascinating and instructive to look back at the successive annual editions of this book in those years. Their pages are a barometer of that dramatic change. For example, the 1932 edition of *American Government* dealt with the powers of Congress in only 17 pages. By 1938, the space devoted to the discussion of what the Federal Government can and does do had tripled, to just over 50 pages.

War Powers In 1990, Congress vigorously debated what action the United States should take following the invasion of Kuwait. The President is commander in chief of the armed forces, but only Congress may declare war.

1 The Scope of Congressional Powers

Find Out:

- How does the Constitution and the federal system itself affect the powers that Congress exercises?
- How has the controversy over strict versus liberal construction of the Constitution affected American government?

Key Terms:

strict constructionist, liberal constructionist

A look at a typical day in Congress might suggest that there is no limit to what Congress can do. Thus, on any given day, the House might consider bills dealing with such varied matters as the space shuttle program, aid to a famine-stricken country, the regulation of cable TV, and the fate of some tiny endangered fish. Meanwhile, the Senate might be debating such matters as the reorganization of the nation's banking system, veterans' benefits, and dairy price supports. And the upper house might also be considering the President's nomination of a new Supreme Court justice.

Congress is not all-powerful, of course. The United States government is, as you know, both limited and federal in nature. And in this section you will see how both of those basic features shape and limit the powers of Congress.

Congressional Power

The Constitution places many restrictions on Congress, as it does on the Federal Government as a whole. Large areas of power are denied to Congress because of what the Constitution says, what it does not say, and because of the federal system itself.

In other words, Congress has only those powers delegated to it—and not specifically

SECTION 1
The Scope of Congressional Powers

FOCUS

TRF **Teacher's Resource File** See the Unit 3 File, p. 24, for the Section 1 Outline.

Objectives

11.1 Examine how the Constitution and the federal system affect the power that Congress exercises.

11.2 Determine how the controversy of strict versus liberal construction of the Constitution has affected the United States government.

Bellringer Activity Write on the chalkboard: "Rule: Students must be in class when the bell rings." Ask students to discuss the many possible interpretations of this rule. For example, does the rule mean that students must be seated? Tell students that Congress is also subject to certain rules, and that these rules are also subject to interpretation.

State the Purpose Congress has considerable power, but those powers are limited. In Section 1, students will learn about the powers of Congress and about the debate over the strict versus liberal interpretations of those powers.

ABCNEWS INTERACTIVE

The following video segment may be used to highlight aspects of the powers of Congress.

POWERS OF THE CONGRESS GUIDEBOOK
Chapter 7: Constitutional Powers of Congress, p. 10

Vocabulary

Point out "Key Terms" on page 259. Explain that these terms have to do with interpreting the Constitution. Invite students to discuss their understanding of the words *strict* and *liberal*. Have students predict how these words might apply to the meaning of the Constitution. LEP

Reading Strategy:Relating to Topic

Students will be reading about strict and liberal constructionism of the Constitution in Section 1. Have them relate the concept of strict and liberal to their own lives. For example, ask students to think of various rules and guidelines to which they are subject in school. Ask students to discuss the benefits and drawbacks of strict enforcement of rules and of liberal—not as strict, broad—enforcement of rules.

INSTRUCT

Explain Tell students that Congress operates under a set of guidelines, which are set out in the Constitution and imposed by the nature of federalism. Debate over a liberal versus a strict construction of the Constitution's limits has been an ongoing theme in political history.

Interpreting Political Cartoons Caption Answer Congress has become less accountable.

Provide Guided Practice Direct students' attention to the questions under "Find Out" on page 259. Have students write answers to the questions.

Provide Independent Practice You may wish to assign Section 1 Guided Reading and Review, Unit 3 File, p. 25.

MONITOR COMPREHENSION

Answers to Section 1 Review
1. Limited government, federalism. **2.** (a) Wanted to limit the powers of Congress. (b) Favored a broader reading. (c) Liberal. **3.** As the country grew, the complexity of government concern also grew.

CLOSURE

The powers of Congress have long been the subject of debate. Today, Congress exercises its power based on a liberal constructionist interpretation of the Constitution. In Section 2, students will examine the expressed powers of Congress.

Assignment Assign Section 2, pp. 261–271, for the next class.

VOICES *on Government*

Norman Y. Mineta,
Democratic representative from California

On Being a Public Servant

"There is no great secret to performing a public service. There is no magical laundry list of I's to dot or T's to cross before a particular act of selflessness may be officially proclaimed as a public service. But whether you act on your own or in concert with others, there is always one common denominator: the sense of community that says, 'This is my home, and I want to help make it better. I care not only about myself, but about my neighbors, about where I live."

denied to it—by the Constitution. Thus, it cannot create a national public school system, require that all eligible citizens vote, or insist that all persons attend religious services. Congress cannot do these and many other things because it has not been given the power to do them in the Constitution.

Of course, Congress does have the power to do many things. As you saw in Chapter 4, the Constitution delegates a number of specific powers to Congress in three different ways: (1) expressly, in so many words—the expressed powers; (2) by reasonable deduction from the expressed powers—the implied powers; and (3) by creating a National Government for the United States—the inherent powers.

Strict Versus Liberal Construction

The Framers of the Constitution intended to create a strong National Government. As you know, the ratification of their plan was opposed by many. That opposition was not stilled by the adoption of the Constitution. Rather, the conflict between the Federalists and Anti-Federalists continued into the early years of the Republic. That conflict centered on the extent of the powers granted to Congress.

The **strict constructionists**, led by Thomas Jefferson, continued to argue the Anti-Federalist position from the ratification period: That Congress should be able to exercise only (a) its expressed powers and (b) those implied powers absolutely necessary to carry out those expressed powers. They wanted the States to keep as much power as possible. They agreed with Jefferson that "that government is best which governs least."

The **liberal constructionists**, led by Alexander Hamilton, had led the fight to adopt the

▲ **Interpreting Political Cartoons** This cartoon depicts a fictitious member of Congress at a press conference. What statement is the cartoonist making on the accountability of Congress to the public?

TRF **Teacher's Resource File**
See the Unit 3 File, p. 26, for the Section 1 Quiz.

Reteach

Ask students to create an outline based on the material they learned in Section 1. One way to begin would be to create an outline based on the major headings found in the text. Ask them to include in their outlines the key points found under each major heading.

Enrichment

Direct students' attention to Article I, Section 8 of the Constitution. Ask them to discuss each clause and to think of how it could be interpreted strictly or liberally. (Challenging)

Constitution. Now they favored a liberal interpretation of the Constitution, a broad construction of the powers given to Congress. The liberal constructionists won that conflict, as you will see. As a result, the powers of the Federal Government have grown to a point that none of the Framers could have imagined.

Several factors, working together with the liberal construction of the Constitution, have been responsible for that marked growth in national power. Wars, economic crises, and other national emergencies have been major causes. Spectacular advances, especially in transportation and communication, have also had a real impact on the size and the scope of government. Equally important have been the demands of the people themselves for more and more services from government.

Congress has been led by these and other factors to view its powers in broader and broader terms. Most Presidents have regarded their powers in similar fashion. The Supreme Court has generally taken a like position in its decisions in cases involving the powers of the National Government. Moreover, the American people have generally agreed with a liberal interpretation of the Constitution. This consensus has prevailed even though American political history has been marked, and still is, by controversies over the proper limits of national power.

Section 1 Review

1. What two features of the American system of government have an impact on the scope of the powers of Congress?
2. (a) What position did the strict constructionists take in the early years under the Constitution? (b) The liberal constructionists? (c) Which group's view prevailed?

Critical Thinking

3. Recognizing Cause and Effect (p. 19) Explain how the growth and change of the nation might have influenced people's views on the expansion of the powers of Congress.

★

2 The Expressed Powers

Find Out:

- For what purposes was Congress given each of its several expressed powers?
- How does Congress exercise its expressed powers?
- How have the expressed powers granted to Congress changed over time?

Key Terms:

direct tax, indirect tax, commerce power, legal tender, bankruptcy, copyright, patent, eminent domain

Most, but not all, of the expressed powers of Congress are found in Article I, Section 8 of the Constitution. There, in 18 separate clauses, 27 different powers are explicitly given to Congress.[1]

These grants of power are brief. What they do and do not allow Congress to do often cannot be discovered by merely reading the few words involved. Rather, their meaning is found in the ways in which Congress has exercised its powers since 1789—and, too, in scores of Supreme Court cases arising out of the actions taken by Congress.

As a case in point, take the Commerce Clause. Article I, Section 8, Clause 3 gives to Congress the power

> "To regulate commerce with foreign nations, and among the several States, and with the Indian tribes."

Its wording is both brief and broad. Congress and the Court have had to answer hundreds of questions about its scope and content. Here are

[1]Several of the expressed powers of Congress are set out elsewhere in the Constitution. Thus, Article IV, Section 3 grants it the power to admit new States to the Union (Clause 1) and to manage and dispose of federal territory and other property (Clause 2). The 16th Amendment gives Congress the power to levy an income tax. The 13th, 14th, 15th, 19th, 24th, and 26th amendments each vest in Congress the "power to enforce" their provisions "by appropriate legislation."

SECTION 2
The Expressed Powers

FOCUS

Teacher's Resource File See the Unit 3 File, p. 27, for the Section 2 Outline.

Objectives

11.3 Determine the purposes for which Congress was granted each of its expressed powers.
11.4 Examine the ways in which Congress exercises its expressed powers.
11.5 Explain the ways in which expressed powers have changed over time.

Bellringer Activity Hold up a dollar bill, quarter, or some other piece of currency. Ask students if they can think of a connection between the money and Congress. Explain to students that it is Congress that coins and prints money, and it is Congress that regulates many of the activities in which money is earned. Tell students that the power to print and coin money is an expressed power of Congress.

State the Purpose The Constitution explicitly grants a number of powers to Congress. These powers are called *expressed powers.* Through the years, the meaning of these powers has changed to meet the needs of the American people. In Section 2, students will learn about the specific powers granted to Congress under the Constitution.

Vocabulary

Direct students' attention to "Key Terms" on page 261. Explain that each of these terms refers to the expressed powers of Congress. Have students make a list of these terms and, as they read, write how each term relates to the expressed powers of Congress.

Reading Strategy: Question Writing

Tell students that each of the main headings in the section refer to expressed powers. Ask students to write down each main heading in the form of a question. As they read, have them write down notes that answer the questions they have written.

INSTRUCT

Explain/Discuss Review with students the meaning of the term *expressed power.* Explain to students that most of the expressed powers are outlined in Article I, Section 8 of the Constitution. To begin students' discussion of these powers, you may want to direct them to the table on page 270, which will help them remember the powers and their sources in the Constitution.

Invite students to discuss the purposes for each of the expressed powers. Why is it important for Congress to exercise these powers? How would economic or social life in this country be different if Congress did not exercise its authority in these fields? (*Possible answers: Economic chaos might result if, for example, each State had its own currency or if Congress could not tax or borrow money to perform governmental functions.*)

As a conclusion, ask students to examine and explain the ways in which the expressed powers have changed over time. You may want to ask students to think of specific examples of the expressed powers that highlight the debate over strict versus liberal construction. (*Possible answers: The debate over the extent over the commerce power; the debate over whether the power to "coin" money also included the power to print money.*)

but a few examples: Does "commerce" include persons entering or leaving the country or crossing State lines? Radio and television broadcasts? Air transportation? Does the Commerce Clause give Congress the power to fix a minimum wage? Does it allow Congress to prohibit shipment of certain goods? To regulate banks? To prohibit discrimination?

In answering these and hundreds of other questions on this one brief provision, Congress and the Court have spelled out, and are still spelling out, the meaning of the Commerce Clause.

So it is with most of the other provisions that grant power to Congress[2] In this section, you will read about these provisions and their evolution over the course of this nation's history.

The Power to Tax

Article I, Section 8, Clause 1 gives Congress the power

"To lay and collect taxes, duties, imposts, and excises, to pay the debts, and provide for the common defense and general welfare of the United States . . ."

Recall, the Articles of Confederation had not given Congress the power to tax. Without it, the government was powerless; and the lack of that power was a leading cause for the coming of the Constitution.

The Federal Government will take in some $1.3 trillion in fiscal year 1992, and an even larger sum in fiscal 1993. Over 90 percent of that money will come from the various taxes levied by Congress.

A tax is a charge levied by government on persons or property to meet public needs. But, notice, taxes are sometimes imposed for other purposes. The protective tariff is perhaps the oldest example of the point. Although it does bring in revenue, its real goal is to "protect" domestic industry against foreign competition by increasing the cost of foreign goods.

Taxes are also sometimes levied to protect the public health and safety. The Federal Government's regulation of narcotics is a case in point. Only those who have a proper federal license may legally manufacture, sell, or deal in those drugs—and licensing is a form of taxation.

But, recall, the power to tax is not unlimited. As with all other powers, it must be used in accord with all other provisions of the Constitution. Thus, Congress cannot lay a tax on church services. Such a tax would violate the 1st Amendment protection of the free exercise of religion.

More specifically, the Constitution places four explicit limitations on the taxing power. First, Congress may tax only for public purposes, not for private benefit. Article I, Section 8, Clause 1 says that taxes may be levied only

"to pay the debts, and provide for the common defense and general welfare of the United States . . ."

Second, Congress may not tax exports. Article I, Section 9, Clause 5 declares

"No duty or tax shall be laid on any article exported from any State."

Thus, customs duties or tariffs, which are taxes, may be placed only on imports.

Third, direct taxes must be apportioned among the States, according to their populations. Article I, Section 9, Clause 4 declares

"No capitation, or other direct tax, shall be laid, unless in proportion to the census or enumeration herein before directed to be taken."

1.a A **direct tax** is one that must be paid by the person on whom it is imposed—for example, a tax on the ownership of land or buildings, or a capitation (head or poll) tax.

An income tax is a direct tax. But, notice, it may be laid without regard to population because of the 16th Amendment:

"The Congress shall have power to lay and collect taxes on incomes, from whatever source derived, with-

---

[2]But, notice, a few of the expressed powers are of little importance today. Thus, Congress has the power to grant letters of marque and reprisal, Article I, Section 8, Clause 11; and the States are denied the power to issue them, Article I, Section 10, Clause 1. Letters of marque and reprisal are relics of the past. They are commissions, written grants of power authorizing private persons to fit out vessels to capture and destroy the enemy in time of war. In effect, they authorize a form of legalized piracy. Letters of marque and reprisal are forbidden by international law by the Declaration of Paris, 1856, and the United States honors the rule in practice.

TRF **Teacher's Resource File**
See the Historical and Legal Documents file, pp. 45 and 46, for materials to support this section.

ACTIVITY: Teaching Heterogeneous Groups
To help students understand the concepts introduced in this chapter, especially the expressed and implied powers of Congress, call on students at various points in the discussion. Ask selected students to formulate one question about the material they have been reading. Then tell the student to select another student in the class to try to answer the question. If the second student cannot answer the question, invite volunteers from the rest of the class to attempt an answer.

How the Federal Government Spent an Average Family's Tax Dollar in Fiscal Year 1991

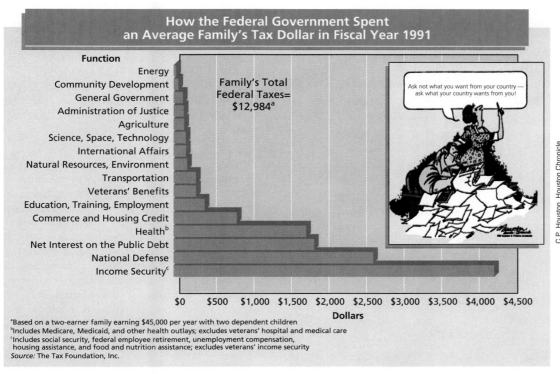

Function
Energy
Community Development
General Government
Administration of Justice
Agriculture
Science, Space, Technology
International Affairs
Natural Resources, Environment
Transportation
Veterans' Benefits
Education, Training, Employment
Commerce and Housing Credit
Health[b]
Net Interest on the Public Debt
National Defense
Income Security[c]

Family's Total Federal Taxes= $12,984[a]

Ask not what you want from your country — ask what your country wants from you!

C.P. Houston, Houston Chronicle

$0 $500 $1,000 $1,500 $2,000 $2,500 $3,000 $3,500 $4,000 $4,500

Dollars

[a]Based on a two-earner family earning $45,000 per year with two dependent children
[b]Includes Medicare, Medicaid, and other health outlays; excludes veterans' hospital and medical care
[c]Includes social security, federal employee retirement, unemployment compensation, housing assistance, and food and nutrition assistance; excludes veterans' income security
Source: The Tax Foundation, Inc.

Interpreting Graphs and Political Cartoons What percent of this family's taxes was spent on deficit financing (the public debt) in 1991? What does the cartoon say about taxes?

out apportionment among the several States, and without regard to any census or enumeration.”

Finally, Article I, Section 8, Clause 1 provides that

“all duties, imposts, and excises, shall be uniform throughout the United States.”

That is, all indirect taxes must be levied at the same rate in all parts of the country.

Whether a tax is direct or indirect is, in practical terms, decided by Congress and the Supreme Court. As a general rule, however, an **indirect tax** is one first paid by one person 1.b
but then passed on to another. It is indirectly paid by that second person. Take, for example, the federal tax on cigarettes. It is paid to the Treasury by the tobacco company that makes the cigarettes. But that company then passes the tax on to the person who finally buys the cigarettes.

The Power to Borrow

Congress has the power “to borrow money on the credit of the United States.”[3] That power permits the government to finance projects that cannot be paid for out of current revenues.

There is no constitutional limit on the amount that Congress can borrow. Congress has put a statutory ceiling on the public debt—that is, on the total amount the government has borrowed and not yet repaid, plus accrued interest. But that limit is little more than a political gesture. Congress adjusts the ceiling whenever it needs to borrow beyond that limit.

The Federal Government regularly practices deficit financing. That is, it spends more than it takes in each year, and it borrows to make up the difference. The government's

[3]Article I, Section 8, Clause 2.

Interpreting Graphs and Political Cartoons Ask students their opinion of the average family tax total and examine the ways in which an average family's tax dollar was spent in 1991. Have them discuss how they would recommend prioritizing national spending if they were a member of Congress. Then ask students if they know upon what source the cartoon is based. Explain that it comes from President John F. Kennedy's 1961 inaugural speech—“Ask not what your country can do for you, ask what you can do for your country.”

Caption Answer Approximately 14%—$1,750 out of $12,984. By paraphrasing Kennedy's famous statement, the cartoonist implies that paying more taxes is what a person can do for his or her country.

ABCNEWS INTERACTIVE

The following video segments may be used to highlight aspects of the expressed powers of Congress.

POWERS OF THE CONGRESS GUIDEBOOK
Chapter 16: Provide for the Common Defense, p. 20
Chapter 21: Collecting Revenues, p. 25
Chapter 25: Money & Foreign Currency, p. 29
Chapter 27: Interstate Commerce, p. 31

SPOTLIGHT ON: Economics

After the ratification of the 16th Amendment, Congress enacted the first-ever U.S. income tax when it passed the Underwood Tariff Act in 1913. This act lowered the tariff on imports but imposed an income tax to make up for lost government revenues. The act set a graduated tax rate—meaning the more one earned, the more one paid. Individual incomes under $3,000 were exempt; individuals and corporations earning from $3,000 to $20,000 paid a one percent tax, and the rate increased gradually to a seven percent ceiling on annual earnings over $500,000.

Interpreting Graphs Ask students to consider the meaning of GNP—Gross National Product—as explained on the graph. Have students observe the range of share of GNP taken in taxes that is demonstrated by different countries.

Caption Answer Possible answer: U.S. GNP is higher, thus a lower percentage of it is required to provide basic services; the U.S. government offers fewer costly services than some other countries.

Global Awareness

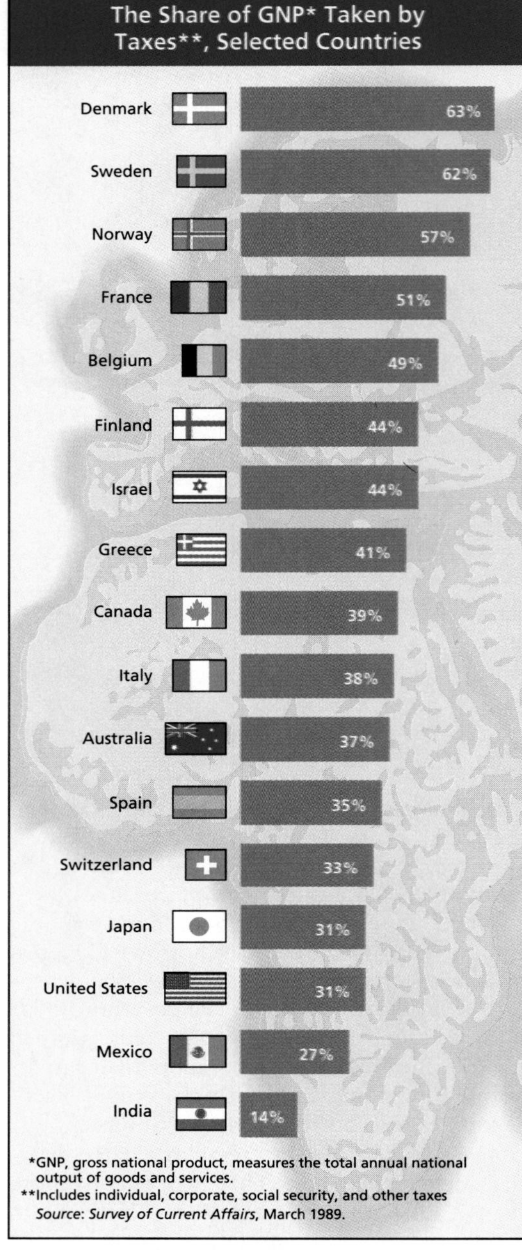

Interpreting Graphs The U.S. tax rate is much lower than in some other industrialized countries. What factors might account for this?

financial books have not shown a surplus (more income than outgo) in more than 20 years. As a result of this deficit financing, the public debt had risen to more than $3.6 trillion at the beginning of fiscal year 1992.

The power to borrow is absolutely vital to the function of Congress. This power also plays an important role in the field of federal finance, which you will read about in Chapter 16.

The Commerce Power

1.c The **commerce power**—the power of Congress to regulate interstate and foreign trade—is as vital to the welfare of the nation as the taxing power. As you know, the commerce power played a major role in the formation of the Union. The weak Congress created under the Articles had no power to regulate interstate trade and only very little authority over foreign commerce. The Critical Period of the 1780s was marked by intense commercial rivalries and bickering among the States. High trade barriers and spiteful State laws created chaos and confusion in much of the country.

Consequently, the Framers wrote the Commerce Clause, Article I, Section 8, Clause 3. It gives Congress the power

> "To regulate commerce with foreign nations, and among the several states, and with the Indian tribes."

Together with the taxing power, the commerce power has contributed to the vast growth in the authority of the National Government and the emergence of a strong union.

The first case to reach the Supreme Court involving the Commerce Clause was *Gibbons* v. *Ogden*, decided in 1824. The case arose out of a clash over the regulation of steam vessels by the State of New York, on the one hand, and the Federal Government, on the other. In 1807 Robert Fulton's steamboat, the *Clermont*, had made its first successful run up the Hudson River, from New York City to Albany. The State legislature then gave Fulton an exclusive, long-term grant to navigate the waters of the State by steamboat. Fulton's monopoly then gave Aaron Ogden a permit for steamboat navigation between New York City and New Jersey.

TRF **Teacher's Resource File**
See the Supreme Court Cases file, pp. 22–23, for material that supports this section

Activity: Cooperative Learning
Time: Two Class Periods. **Activity:** Write a "matching" quiz for Chapter 11. **Grouping:** Four to six students. **Purpose:** Have students work together to compile a list of 25–30 terms discussed in the chapter. Then have group members divide the list and work independantly to write a definition for each term. **Roles:** All group members will write definitions. Appoint one member of each group to act as recorder. **Outcome:** Have the recorder prepare the final quiz, listing all the group's definitions in a "matching" format. Then have group members prepare an answer key. Duplicate quizzes and have groups exchange and complete them.

Thomas Gibbons, operating with a coasting license from the Federal Government, began to carry passengers on a line that competed with Ogden. Ogden sued him, and the New York courts held that Gibbons could not sail by steam in New York waters.

Gibbons appealed that ruling to the Supreme Court. He claimed that the New York grant conflicted with the congressional power to regulate commerce. The Court agreed. It rejected Ogden's argument that "commerce" should be defined narrowly, as simply "traffic" or the mere buying and selling of goods. Instead, it read the Commerce Clause in broad terms. Wrote Chief Justice John Marshall:

> "Commerce undoubtedly is traffic, but it is something more—it is intercourse. It describes the commercial intercourse between nations, and parts of nations, in all its branches, and is regulated by prescribing rules for carrying on that intercourse."

The Court's ruling was widely popular at the time because it dealt a death blow to steamboat monopolies. Freed from restrictive State regulation, steam navigation developed rapidly. Within a few years, the railroads, similarly freed, revolutionized domestic transportation.

Over the decades, the Court's sweeping definition of commerce has brought an extension of federal authority into many areas of American life—a reach of federal power beyond anything the Framers could possibly have imagined.

As another of the many examples of the point, note this: It is on the basis of the commerce power that the Civil Rights Act of 1964 prohibits discrimination in access to or service in hotels, motels, theaters, restaurants, and in other public accommodations on grounds of race, color, religion, or national origin [4]

Based on the expressed powers to regulate commerce and to tax, Congress and the courts have built nearly all of the implied powers. Most of what the Federal Government does, day to day and year to year, it does as the result of legislation passed by Congress in the exercise of these two powers.

Interstate Navigation The passage of this freighter on the Delaware River is regulated by the commerce power.

The commerce power is not unlimited. It, too, must be used in accord with all other provisions in the Constitution. Thus, Congress could not say that only companies that employ only native-born citizens can do business in more than one State. Such an arbitrary regulation would violate the 5th Amendment's Due Process Clause.

Specifically, the Constitution also places four explicit limitations on the use of the commerce power. First, as you have read, Article I, Section 9, Clause 5 forbids Congress the power to tax exports. Second, Article I, Section 9, Clause 6 prevents Congress from favoring the ports of one State over those of any other in the regulation of trade. Third, the same provision forbids Congress to require that "vessels bound to, or from, one State, be obliged to enter, clear, or pay duties in another." The fourth limitation is the curious "slave trade compromise" found in Article I, Section 9, Clause 1. That clause has been obsolete for more than 180 years now.

[4]The Supreme Court considered this use of the commerce power in *Heart of Atlanta Motel, Inc.* v. *United States*, 1964. You will read about this case on page 274 of this chapter.

Spotlight on: Multiculturalism

With the passage of the Civil Rights Act of 1991, Congress addressed a long-standing criticism that it abused its congressional prerogatives. Because of certain expressed protections granted to Congress in the Constitution, House and Senate congressional leaders had long maintained that Congress did not have to obey the regulations it passed under the commerce clause—including regulations for minimum wages, worker health and safety, and affirmative action in hiring. The 1991 Civil Rights Act expressly applies to Congress, however, and provides for enforcement by the federal courts.

The Currency Power

The Constitution gives Congress the power "to coin money [and] regulate the value thereof."[5] The States are forbidden that power.[6]

Until the Revolution, the English money system, built on the shilling and the pound, was in general use in the colonies. With independence, that stable currency system collapsed, however. The Second Continental Congress and then the Congress under the Articles issued paper money. But without sound backing, and with no taxing power behind it, the money was practically worthless. Each of the 13 States also issued its own currency. In several States, this amounted to little more than the State's printing its name on paper and calling it money. Adding to the confusion, people still used English coins, and Spanish money circulated freely in the southern States.

Nearly all the Framers agreed on the need for a single, national system of "hard" money. So the Constitution gave the currency power to Congress, and it all but excluded the States from that field. From 1789 on, among the most important of all of the many tasks performed by the government has been that of providing the nation with a uniform, stable monetary system.

From the beginning, the United States has issued coins—in gold (until 1933), silver, and other metals. Congress chartered the First Bank of the United States in 1791 and gave it the power to issue bank notes—paper money. But those notes were not legal tender. **Legal tender** 1.d is any kind of money that a creditor must by law accept in payment for debts. Congress did not create a national paper currency, and make it legal tender, until 1863.

At first, the new national notes, known as greenbacks, could not be redeemed for gold or silver coin at the Treasury. Their worth fell to less than half of their face value. Then, in 1870, the Supreme Court held their issuance to be unconstitutional. In *Hepburn* v. *Griswold* it said "to coin" meant to stamp metal and that the Constitution did not authorize paper money.

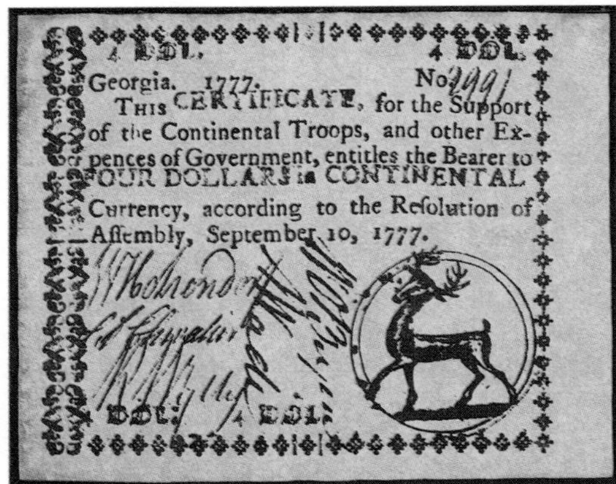

▲ **Currency Power** State currency, like the banknote issued by Georgia in 1777 (top), was common during the Revolution. After about 1780, the value of these "continentals" had fallen dramatically, and the expression "not worth a continental" was born. Today, the Federal Government is the only source of paper money (bottom).

The Court soon changed its mind, however, in the *Legal Tender Cases* in 1871 and again in *Juliard* v. *Greenman* in 1884. In both cases it held the issuing of paper money as legal tender to be a proper use of the currency power and a power properly implied from the borrowing and the war powers.

Bankruptcy

Congress has the power "to establish . . . uniform laws on the subject of bankruptcies,

---

[5]Article I, Section 8, Clause 5.
[6]Article I, Section 10, Clause 1.

Enrichment

Ask students to examine the information that appears in footnote 1 on page 261. Have students find the powers discussed in the footnote in the Constitution that begins on page 726 of their text. Tell students to write brief explanations of the powers and purposes of these additional powers. (Easy)

OR

TRF **Teacher's Resource File**
See the Unit 3 File, pp. 37–39 for the Case Study on Contemporary Issues for Chapter 11.

throughout the United States."[7] A bankrupt individual is one whom a court has found to be insolvent—that is, unable to pay his or her debts in full. **Bankruptcy** is the legal proceeding in which the bankrupt's assets are distributed among those to whom a debt is owed. That proceeding frees the bankrupt from legal responsibility for debts acquired before bankruptcy. 1.e

Both the States and the National Government have the power to regulate bankruptcy. It is, then, a concurrent power. In 1898, however, Congress passed a general bankruptcy law, and today that law is so broad that it all but excludes the States from the field. Most bankruptcy cases are heard in the federal district courts; only a very few are handled by State courts today.

Foreign Relations and War Powers

The Constitution gives Congress several important responsibilities in the country's dealings with foreign states.

[7]Article I, Section 8, Clause 4.

Foreign Relations Powers The National Government has greater powers in the field of foreign affairs than it has in any other. Congress shares power in this field with the President, who is primarily responsible for the conduct of relations with other nations. Because the States in the Union are not sovereign, they have no standing in international law. The Constitution does not allow them to take part in foreign relations.[8]

Congressional authority in the field of foreign relations comes from two sources: (1) from various expressed powers—including, especially, the several war powers and the power to regulate foreign commerce and (2) from the fact that the United States is a sovereign state in the world community. As the nation's lawmaking body, Congress has the inherent power to act on matters affecting the security of the nation. You will explore this subject at much greater length in Chapter 17.

[8]Article I, Section 10, Clauses 1 and 3.

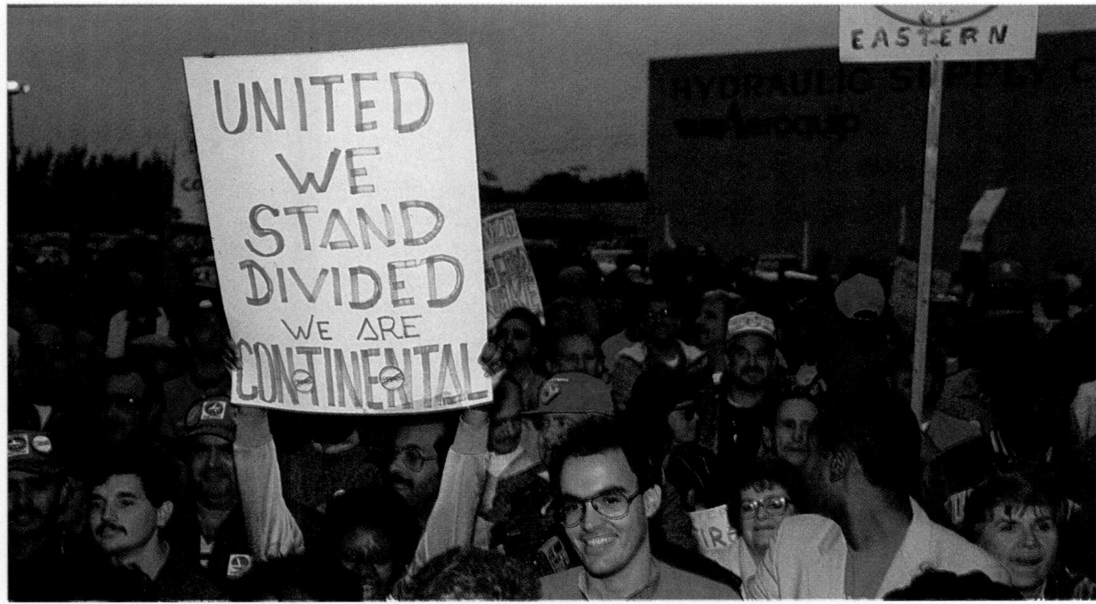

Bankruptcy Power Employees of Eastern Airlines picket in Miami, Florida, in an attempt to forestall the company's bankruptcy proceedings. Most bankruptcy hearings fall under federal jurisdiction.

Provide Guided Practice
Write the words "expressed powers" on the chalkboard. Ask students to look ahead to the table on page 270. After they have studied the chart briefly, have them close their books. Ask students to list as many powers as they can think of and the reasons for each. Have them check their answers against the table. Then have them provide the purposes for each of the powers that they failed to identify earlier.

Provide Independent Practice
TRF **Teacher's Resource File**
You may wish to assign the Section 2 Guided Reading and Review from the Unit 3 File, p. 28, to help students master section objective content.

War Powers Eight of the expressed powers given to Congress in Article I, Section 8 deal with war and national defense.[9] Here, too, Congress shares power with the chief executive. The Constitution makes the President the commander in chief of the nation's armed forces,[10] and, as such, the President dominates the field.

The congressional war powers, however, are extensive and substantial. Only Congress may declare war. It has the power to raise and support armies, to provide and maintain a navy, and to make rules pertaining to governing the land and naval forces. Congress also has the power to provide for "calling forth the militia," and for the organizing, arming, and disciplining of it. And Congress has the power to grant letters of marque and reprisal and make rules concerning captures on land and water.

With the passage of the War Powers Resolution of 1973, Congress claimed the power to restrict the use of American forces in combat in areas where a state of war does not exist; see Chapter 14, Section 3.

Additional Powers of Congress

The Constitution grants Congress a number of other specific powers.

Naturalization Naturalization is the process by which citizens of one country become citizens of another. Article I, Section 8, Clause 4 gives Congress the exclusive power "to establish an uniform rule of naturalization." You will read more about the naturalization process in Chapter 21.

The Postal Power Congress has the exclusive power "to establish post offices and post roads."[11] That power covers the authority to protect the mails and to ensure their quick and efficient distribution. Congress is also empowered to prevent the use of the mails for fraud or for the carrying of outlawed materials.

Congress has established a number of crimes based on the postal power. Thus, it is a federal crime for any person to obstruct the mails, to use the mails to commit any fraud, or to use them as a part of any other criminal act.

Articles prohibited by a State's laws, such as firecrackers or switchblade knives, cannot be sent into that State through the mails. A great many other items, including alcoholic beverages, lottery tickets, and obscene materials, are also barred from the mails.

The States cannot interfere with the mails unreasonably. Nor can they require a license for vehicles owned by the Postal Service or tax the gas they use. The States cannot tax the post offices or any other property of the United States Postal Service.

Copyrights and Patents Congress has the power

> "To promote the progress of science and useful arts, by securing, for limited times, to authors and inventors, the exclusive right to their respective writings and discoveries."[12]

1.f A **copyright** is the exclusive right of an author to reproduce, publish, and sell his or her creative work. That right may be assigned—transferred by contract—to another, as to a publishing firm by mutual agreement between the author and the other party.

Copyrights are registered by the Copyright Office in the Library of Congress. Under present law they are good for the life of the author plus 50 years. They cover a wide range of creative efforts: books, magazines, newspapers, musical compositions and lyrics, dramatic works, paintings, sculptures, cartoons, maps, photographs, motion pictures, sound recordings, and much else.[13]

---

[9]The war powers of Congress are set out in clauses 11 through 16.

[10]Article II, Section 2, Clause 1.

[11]Article I, Section 8, Clause 7. Post roads are all postal routes, including railroads, airways, and waters within the United States, during the time that mail is being carried on them.

[12]Article I, Section 8, Clause 8.

[13]Not all publications can be protected by copyright, however. Thus, the Supreme Court has recently held that such "factual compilations" as telephone directories "lack the requisite originality" for copyright protection, *Feist Publications, Inc.* v. *Rural Telephone Service Co.*, 1991.

TRF **Teacher's Resource File**
See the Simulations and Debates file, for the debate "The War Powers Act."

William Gropper, *The Senate* (1935).

Interpreting Political Art This 1935 painting by artist William Gropper depicts Congress in session. The content of this unit suggests that the work of lawmakers involves heavy responsibilities and hard work. Would Gropper be likely to agree? Why or why not?

A **patent** grants a person the sole right to 1.g manufacture, use, or sell "any new and useful art, machine, manufacture, or composition of matter, or any new and useful improvement thereof." A patent is good for a varying number of years—today, 17 years on the patent of an invention. The term of a patent may be extended only by a special act of Congress. The Patent and Trademark Office in the Department of Commerce administers patent laws [14]

[14]The power to protect trademarks is an implied power, drawn from the commerce power. A trademark is some distinctive word, name, symbol, or device used by a manufacturer or merchant to identify his goods or services and distinguish them from those made or sold by others. A trademark need not be original, merely distinctive. The registration of a trademark carries the right to its exclusive use in interstate commerce for 10 years. The right may be renewed an unlimited number of times.

Weights and Measures The Constitution gives Congress the power to "fix the standards of weights and measures" throughout the United States.[15] The power reflects the absolute need for and usage of accurate, uniform gauges of time, distance, area, weight, volume, and the like.

In 1838 Congress set the English system of pound, ounce, mile, foot, gallon, quart, and so on, as the legal standards of weights and measures in this country. In 1866 Congress also legalized the use of the metric system.

The National Institute of Standards and Technology in the Commerce Department keeps the original standards for the United States. It is these standards by which all other measures in the United States are tested and corrected.

[15]Article I, Section 8, Clause 5.

Interpreting Political Art Ask students to discuss what they have learned about the job of a representative or senator. Based on their impression of those jobs, does this painting seem realistic to them? (*Possible answers: No, the members would have to be much more busy to perform all of their duties; yes, service in the Congress seems like it might be tedious and tiring.*)

Caption Answer No. He shows Congress (as represented by the speaker) as pompous and (as represented by the other figures) as lazy and disinterested.

Interpreting Tables Refer students to the table of expressed powers on page 270. Point out to students how many of the expressed powers deal with issues of money and the national economy.

Caption Answer They allow government to collect the funds needed to operate.

SPOTLIGHT ON: Global Awareness

The United States is one of the few countries in the world in which the metric system of weights and measures is not the national standard. The metric system was devised for geometrical precision, with larger units standing in relation to smaller units by multiples of ten. (For example, 10 millimeters is a centimeter; 100 centimeters is a meter.) France embraced the metric system in 1800, and 35 countries had followed suit by 1900. The metric system was adopted as the standard international system in 1960. But despite periodic efforts to encourage its use in the United States, metric units are commonly used only in the scientific and other specialized communities.

Monitor Comprehension

Answers to Section 2 Review
1. "Key Terms" are defined on the following pages:
- **a.** direct tax, p. 262
- **b.** indirect tax, p. 263
- **c.** commerce power, p. 264
- **d.** legal tender, p. 266
- **e.** bankruptcy, p. 267
- **f.** copyright, p. 268
- **g.** patent, p. 269
- **h.** eminent domain, p. 270

2. Article I, Section 8; few appear elsewhere. **3.** (a) To raise revenues. (b) To finance projects that revenues will not pay for. **4.** To ensure a stable money supply. **5.** Interstate and foreign. **6.** (a) Expressed powers and the fact that the U.S. is a sovereign state. (b) The President. **7.** Declare war, raise and support armies; provide and maintain a navy; make rules regarding land, naval forces; call forth, organize, arm, and discipline militia; issue letters of marque and reprisal; make rules concerning captures on land and water. **8.** Examples: the use of commerce power to prohibit discrimination in public accommodations; printing of currency under the power to coin money.

Closure

The expressed powers of Congress leave room for interpretation. Over time, the interpretations have changed. In Section 3, students will read about another set of powers granted to Congress—the implied powers.

Assignment Assign Section 3, pp. 271–273, for the next class.

The Expressed Powers Vested in Congress by Article I, Section 8 of the Constitution

Peace Powers	
Clause 1.	To lay taxes. a. Direct (not used since the War Between the States, except income tax). b. Indirect (customs [tariffs], excise for internal revenue).
Clause 2.	To borrow money.
Clause 3.	To regulate foreign and interstate commerce.
Clause 4.	To establish naturalization and bankruptcy laws.
Clause 5.	To coin money and regulate its value; to regulate weights and measures.
Clause 6.	To punish counterfeiters of federal money and securities.
Clause 7.	To establish post offices and post roads.
Clause 8.	To grant patents and copyrights.
Clause 9.	To create courts inferior to the Supreme Court.
Clause 10.	To define and punish piracies and felonies on the high seas; to define and punish offenses against the law of nations.
Clause 17.	To exercise exclusive jurisdiction over the District of Columbia; to exercise exclusive jurisdiction over forts, dockyards, national parks, federal buildings, and the like.
War Powers	
Clause 11.	To declare war; to grant letters of marque and reprisal; to make rules concerning captures on land and water.
Clause 12.	To raise and support armies.
Clause 13.	To provide and maintain a navy.
Clause 14.	To make laws governing land and naval forces.
Clause 15.	To provide for calling forth the militia to execute federal laws, suppress insurrections, and repel invasions.
Clause 16.	To provide for organizing, arming, and disciplining the militia, and for its governing when in the service of the Union.

Interpreting Tables This table lists the powers expressly granted to Congress by the Constitution. Why are the commerce and other money powers of primary importance to the Federal Government?

Power Over Territories and Other Areas Congress has the power to acquire, manage, and dispose of various federal areas.[16] That power relates to the District of Columbia and to the several federal territories, including Puerto Rico, Guam, and the Virgin Islands. It also covers hundreds of military and naval installations, arsenals, dockyards, post offices, prison facilities, park and forest preserves, and many other federal holdings throughout the country.

The Federal Government may acquire property by purchase or gift. It may do so, too, through the exercise of **eminent domain**—the 1.h inherent power to take private property for public use.[17] Territory may also be acquired from a foreign state based on the power to admit new States, the war powers, and the President's treaty-making power.[18] Under international law, any sovereign state may acquire unclaimed territory by discovery.

Judicial Powers As an important part of the principle of checks and balances,

[16]Article I, Section 8, Clause 17; Article IV, Section 3, Clause 2.

[17]The 5th Amendment restricts the government's use of the power with these words: "nor shall private property be taken for public use, without just compensation." Each of the State constitutions has a similar provision.

[18]Article IV, Section 3, Clause 1; Article I, Section 8, Clauses 11–16; Article II, Section 2, Clauses 1 and 2.

Teacher's Resource File
See the Unit 3 File, p. 29, for the Section 2 Quiz.

Reteach

Ask students to review the table that appears on page 270. Have them illustrate each of the expressed powers by creating a symbol that communicates the purpose of the power. For example, for the expressed power to coin money, students could create a symbol showing a small printing press printing dollar bills.

Congress has several judicial powers. These include the expressed power to create all of the federal courts in the federal judiciary below the Supreme Court and to provide for the organization and composition of the federal judiciary.[19] (You will read more about the federal judiciary in Chapter 18.)Congress also has the power to define federal crimes and provide for the punishment of those who violate federal law.[20]

Section 2 Review

1. Define: direct tax, indirect tax, commerce power, legal tender, bankruptcy, copyright, patent, eminent domain
2. Where are the expressed powers of Congress set out in the Constitution?
3. (a) What is the purpose of the power to tax? (b) To borrow money?
4. For what reason does the Constitution grant the National Government the power to make coins and currency?
5. What kind of trade does the Constitution give Congress the power to regulate?
6. (a) From what two sources does Congress draw its powers in foreign affairs? (b) With whom does it share power in that field?
7. Identify the several war powers that the Constitution gives Congress.

Critical Thinking

8. Demonstrating Reasoned Judgment (p. 19) Explain how Congress' exercise of the expressed powers has reflected the liberal constructionist viewpoint. Cite examples from the text.

[19]Article I, Section 8, Clause 9; Article III, Section 1. Also, recall, the President's power to appoint all federal judges is subject to Senate confirmation, Article II, Section 2, Clause 2.

[20]The Constitution mentions only four types of federal crimes: counterfeiting, piracies and felonies committed on the high seas, offenses against the law of nations (in Article I, Section 8, Clauses 6 and 10), and treason (in Article III, Section 3). But Congress has the implied power to define many other offenses and provide for their punishment.

3 The Implied Powers

Find Out:

- For what reason did the Framers include the Necessary and Proper Clause in the Constitution?
- For what reason is *McCulloch* v. *Maryland* one of the most important cases ever decided by the Supreme Court?
- What impact does the Necessary and Proper Clause have today?

Key Term:
Necessary and Proper Clause

As you have just seen, the Constitution grants a number of very important expressed powers to Congress. In addition to those powers, recall the Constitution also gives Congress a large number of other powers that are not specifically mentioned in the document: the implied powers.

The Necessary and Proper Clause

1.a The **Necessary and Proper Clause** is a dramatically important part of the Constitution. It is from that provision that the implied powers flow. The Necessary and Proper Clause gives to Congress the power

> "To make all laws which shall be necessary and proper for carrying into execution the foregoing powers, and all other powers vested by this Constitution in the Government of the United States, or in any department or officer thereof."

Much of the vitality and adaptability of the United States Constitution can be traced directly to the Necessary and Proper Clause. It can also be related to the manner in which both Congress and the Supreme Court have interpreted and applied it over the years. For good reason, the Necessary and Proper Clause—found in Article I, Section 8, Clause 18—has often been called the "Elastic Clause" because it has allowed the Federal Government to stretch its powers.

SECTION 3
The Implied Powers

FOCUS

Teacher's Resource File See the Unit 3 File, p. 30, for the Section 3 Outline.

Objectives

11.6 Examine the reasons why the Framers included the Necessary and Proper Clause in the Constitution.
11.7 Explain why *McCulloch* v. *Maryland* is a landmark Supreme Court case.
11.8 Determine the impact of the Necessary and Proper Clause today.

Bellringer Activity Present students with the following situation: A teacher has told them "get your homework done—no matter what it takes." What, exactly, does it mean to do "whatever it takes"? Next tell students that Congress faces a similar dilemma as it interprets the Necessary and Proper Clause.

State the Purpose The Constitution directs Congress to do whatever is "necessary and proper" to carry out its expressed powers. In Section 3, students will learn about the powers implied by this instruction and about the Supreme Court case that helped define "necessary and proper."

ABCNEWS INTERACTIVE

The following video segment may be used to highlight aspects of the Necessary and Proper Clause.

POWERS OF THE CONGRESS GUIDEBOOK
Chapter 9: The Elastic Clause, p. 12

Vocabulary

Point out "Key Term" on page 271. Tell students that the term is the key to understanding the implied powers of Congress. Tell students to consider the meaning of the words *necessary and proper* and to keep these two words in mind as they read about the debate over the extent of the powers of Congress. LEP

Reading Strategy: Who? What? When? Where? How? Why?

Ask students to write the following questions on a piece of paper: Who? What? When? Where? How? and Why? As they read through Section 3, ask them to answer these questions as they relate to the implied powers of Congress.

INSTRUCT

Discuss/Explain Explain that the Necessary and Proper Clause (also called the Elastic Clause) of the Constitution presents complicated questions with regard to the powers of Congress. Tell students that as Congress and the courts have answered these questions, they have helped create a vast range of implied powers.

Ask students to discuss the development of the Necessary and Proper Clause. You might ask students to discuss the meaning of the term *implied powers. (The term suggests that the powers are not stated explicitly, but indirectly.)* Remind students to include an analysis of *McCulloch* v. *Maryland. (It gave sweeping approval to the concept of implied powers.)*

Provide Guided Practice Write the following on the board: *Jefferson, Hamilton, Maryland, Marshall.* Have students explain how these names relate to the issue of implied powers. (*Jefferson favored a strict construction; Hamilton favored liberal construction; Maryland argued a strict constructionist view in* McCulloch *v.* Maryland; *Marshall wrote the opinion that gave sweeping approval to the concept of implied powers.*)

Provide Independent Practice

TRF **Teacher's Resource File** You may wish to assign the Section 3 Guided Reading and Review, Unit 3 File, p. 31, to help students master section objective content.

The Battle Over Implied Powers

The Constitution had barely come into force when the meaning of Clause 18 was called into question. In 1790 Alexander Hamilton, as Secretary of the Treasury, urged Congress to set up a national bank. That proposal touched off one of the most important disputes in all of American political history.

The opponents of Hamilton's plan insisted that nowhere did the Constitution give to Congress the power to establish such a bank. As you read in Section 1, these strict constructionists, led by Thomas Jefferson, believed that the new government had only (1) those powers expressly granted to it by the Constitution and (2) those powers absolutely necessary to carrying out those expressed powers.

Hamilton and other liberal constructionists looked to the Necessary and Proper Clause. They said that it gave Congress the power to do anything that was reasonably related to the exercise of the expressed powers. As for the national bank, they argued that it was necessary and proper to the execution of the taxing, borrowing, commerce, and currency powers. Strict constructionists rejected the "implied powers" argument. To do otherwise, they said, would be to give the new government almost unlimited authority and all but destroy the reserved powers of the States.[21]

Reason and practical necessity carried the day for Hamilton and his side. Congress established the Bank of the United States in 1791. Its charter—the act creating it—was to expire in 1811. Over those 20 years, the constitutionality of both the bank and the concept of implied powers went unchallenged in the courts.

[21]In 1801 a bill was introduced in Congress to incorporate a company to mine copper. As Vice President, Jefferson ridiculed that measure with this comment: "Congress is authorized to defend the nation. Ships are necessary for defense; copper is necessary for ships; mines necessary for copper; a company necessary to work the mines; and who can doubt this reasoning who has ever played at 'This Is the House that Jack Built'?" While Jefferson himself was President (1801–1809), he and his party were many times forced to reverse their earlier stand. Thus, for example, it was only on the basis of the implied powers doctrine that the Louisiana Purchase in 1803 and the embargo on foreign trade in 1807 could be justified.

***McCulloch* v. *Maryland*, 1819** In 1816 Congress created the Second Bank of the United States. Its charter came only after another hard-fought battle over the extent of the powers of Congress.

Having lost in Congress, opponents of the new bank now tried to persuade several State legislatures to cripple its operations. In 1818 Maryland placed a tax on all notes issued by any bank doing business in the State but not chartered by the State legislature. The tax was aimed directly at the Second Bank's branch in Baltimore. James McCulloch, the bank's cashier, purposely issued notes on which no tax had been paid. The State won a judgment against him in its own courts. Acting for McCulloch, the United States then appealed to the Supreme Court.

Maryland took the strict-construction position before the Supreme Court. It argued that the creation of the bank had been an unconstitutional act. In reply, the United States defended the concept of implied powers, and it also argued that no State could lawfully place a tax on any agency of the Federal Government.

In one of its most important and far-reaching decisions, the Court unanimously reversed the Maryland courts. It held that it was not necessary that the Constitution expressly empower Congress to create a bank. In short, the Court gave sweeping approval to the concept of implied powers.[22]

Chief Justice John Marshall wrote the Court's opinion in the case. For the Court, he said:

> "We admit, as all must admit, that the powers of the government are limited, and that its limits are not to be transcended. But we think the sound construction of the Constitution must allow to the national legislature that discretion, with respect to the means by which the powers it confers are to be carried into execution, which will enable that body to perform the high duties assigned to it, in the manner most beneficial to the people. Let the end be legitimate, let it be within the scope of the Constitution, and all means which are appropriate, which are not prohibited, but consist with

[22]The Court also invalidated the Maryland tax. Because, said the Court, "the power to tax involves the power to destroy," no State may tax the United States or any of its agencies or functions.

Enrichment

Organize a class debate on the benefits and drawbacks of following a liberal construction of the Constitution. Create two teams to argue each side of the issue. Each member of the team should help prepare the arguments for the debate. Assign members of the group to be spokespersons. (Average)

Teacher's Resource File
See the Supreme Court Cases file, pp. 20–21, for material to support this section.

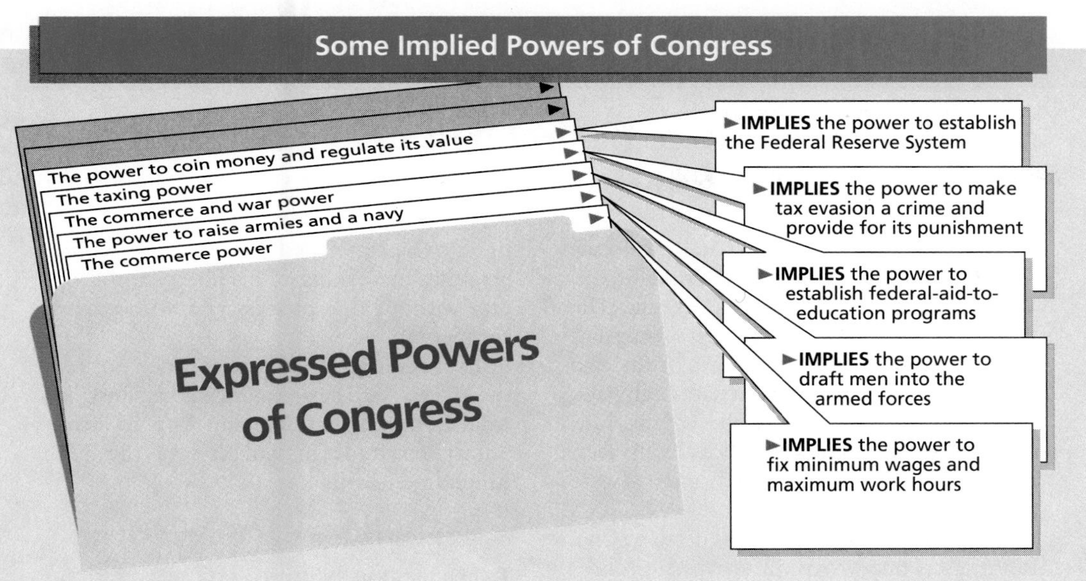
Some Implied Powers of Congress
The power to coin money and regulate its value
The taxing power
The commerce and war power
The power to raise armies and a navy
The commerce power
Expressed Powers of Congress
►IMPLIES the power to establish the Federal Reserve System
►IMPLIES the power to make tax evasion a crime and provide for its punishment
►IMPLIES the power to establish federal-aid-to-education programs
►IMPLIES the power to draft men into the armed forces
►IMPLIES the power to fix minimum wages and maximum work hours

Interpreting Graphs Congress often exercises broad interpretation of its powers. In the late 1950s, in order to compete with the Soviet space program, it granted aid to education under its commerce and war powers.

the letter and spirit of the Constitution, are constitutional.”

This broad interpretation of the constitutional powers granted to Congress has become firmly fixed in America's constitutional system. Indeed, it is impossible to see how the United States could have developed as it has under the Constitution without it.

The Doctrine in Practice There are an almost uncountable number of examples of the application of the doctrine of implied powers. Both the way Congress has looked at and used its powers and the supporting decisions of the Supreme Court have made Article I, Section 8, Clause 18 truly the Elastic Clause. Today the words "necessary and proper" really read "convenient and useful." This is most especially true when applied to the power to regulate interstate commerce and the power to tax.

Yet, there is a real limit to how far the Federal Government can push the doctrine of implied powers. Neither Congress nor any other element of the Federal Government has the blanket authority to do anything that may seem desirable or that may seem to be for the "general welfare" or in the "public interest." As the chart above shows, the basis for any implied power must always be found among the expressed powers. The implied powers are those that may be reasonably drawn from the expressed powers.

Section 3 Review

1. **Define:** Necessary and Proper Clause
2. For what reason is the Necessary and Proper Clause of the Constitution also called the Elastic Clause?
3. What is the doctrine of implied powers?
4. What is the significance of *McCulloch* v. *Maryland*?
5. What is the fundamental limitation on the doctrine of implied powers?

Critical Thinking

6. **Predicting Consequences** (p. 19) What might have happened had Jefferson and his supporters won the early debate over implied powers?

★

Interpreting Graphs As students study the graph, ask them to discuss how the implied powers have influenced the role of government in people's lives today. (*The implied powers have given government a direct role in the lives of many Americans.*)

Monitor Comprehension

Answers to Section 3 Review
1. The "Key Term" is defined on the following page:
a. Necessary and Proper Clause, p. 271.
2. It has enabled Congress to stretch its powers. **3.** Congress has any power reasonably related to the exercise of the expressed powers. **4.** It declared constitutional the concept of implied powers. **5.** Implied power must be based on an expressed power. **6.** Students might conclude that strict views might have led to a weak central government. Or students might suggest that States would have assumed many powers.

Closure

The debate over what is necessary and proper to the execution of the expressed powers helped establish the concept of implied powers. This concept has enabled Congress to assume a vast range of powers. In Section 4, students will read about another category of powers of Congress—the nonlegislative powers.

Assignment Assign Section 4, pp. 275–277, for the next class period.

TRF **Teacher's Resource File**
See the Unit 3 File, p. 32, for the Section 3 Quiz.

Reteach

Tell students that they are reporters covering the case *McCulloch* v. *Maryland*. Have students write a brief "newspaper" report summarizing the key events and issues in the case, including its outcome. Student reports should conclude with a prediction about how the decision will affect the country in the future. Tell students that they may dramatize their reports if they wish.

TEACHING
Debating Key Issues

Heart of Atlanta Motel, Inc. v. *United States:*
Should Discrimination be Prohibited in Private Facilities?

Objective

Analyze, synthesize, and evaluate information.

INSTRUCT

Before they read, have students predict what issues relating to the powers of Congress might be raised by the question: "Should discrimination be prohibited in private facilities?" As they begin their discussion of the case, encourage students to think about the powers of Congress to regulate commerce. Then ask them to identify their own points of view about the case and present them to the class.

SUPREME COURT DECISION

The Court upheld the Civil Rights Act of 1964, saying "if it is interstate commerce that feels the pinch, it does not matter how 'local' the operation which applies the squeeze." ". . . [T]he power of Congress to promote interstate commerce also includes the power to regulate the local incidents thereof, including local activities. . . which have a substantial and harmful effect upon that commerce." Segregation by race of private facilities engaged in interstate commerce was therefore held to be unconstitutional.

Should Discrimination Be Prohibited in Private Facilities?

Heart of Atlanta Motel, Inc. v. *United States*

The Heart of Atlanta Hotel was located two blocks from Peachtree Street, in downtown Atlanta, Georgia. The hotel had 216 rooms available to transient guests and was easily accessible from two State highways and two interstate highways. The hotel solicited patrons through various magazines that circulated nationally. In fact, 75 percent of its registered guests were from out of State.

In 1964, Congress passed the Civil Rights Act, one provision of which prohibited racial discrimination or segregation in certain public accommodations. Title II of the act listed four classes of public accommodations that were subject to the act, including "any inn, hotel, motel, or other establishment which provides lodging to transient guests . . . if its operations affect commerce. . . . "

Before the passage of the Civil Rights Act, the Heart of Atlanta Motel had followed a practice of refusing to rent rooms to African Americans. In an effort to continue this policy of racial discrimination, the owner and operator of the hotel filed a suit in which he claimed that Title II of the Civil Rights Act was unconstitutional.

Review the following evidence and arguments presented to the U.S. Supreme Court.

Arguments for Heart of Atlanta Hotel

1. In passing the Civil Rights Act of 1964, Congress exceeded its power to regulate commerce under the Commerce Clause of the Constitution.
2. The act violates the 5th Amendment because the hotel owner is deprived of the right to operate his business as he wishes, resulting in a taking of his liberty and property without due process and without just compensation.
3. By requiring the hotel owner to rent rooms to African Americans against his will, Congress is subjecting him to involuntary servitude in violation of the 13th Amendment.

Arguments for the United States

1. The unavailability to African Americans of adequate accommodations interferes significantly with interstate travel, and Congress, under the Commerce Clause, has the power to remove such obstructions.
2. The 5th Amendment does not forbid reasonable regulation. Such regulation does not constitute a "taking of liberty" within the meaning of that amendment.
3. It is entirely frivolous to claim that forcing a hotel owner to be subject to the act against his will is in violation of the 13th Amendment.

Getting Involved

1. Identify the constitutional grounds on which each side based its arguments in this case.
2. Debate the opposing viewpoints presented in this case.
3. Predict how you think the Supreme Court ruled in this case and why. Now turn to page 764 in the Supreme Court Glossary to read the decision. What types of businesses, if any, do you think the Federal Government has the right to regulate?

TRF **Teacher's Resource File**
See the Supreme Court Cases file, p. 8, for an activity that extends coverage of this case.

4 The Nonlegislative Powers

Find Out:

- For what purposes does the Constitution give several nonlegislative powers to Congress?
- How does Congress exercise those powers?

Key Term:

impeach

As you know, Congress is a legislative body. Its major function, therefore, is to make law. But the Constitution gives it a number of other chores, as well. This section explores those other chores, the nonlegislative powers and duties of Congress.

Constitutional Amendments

You have read how Congress plays a key role in the process of constitutional amendment.[23] It may propose an amendment to the Constitution by a two-thirds vote in each house—and it has done so 33 times to this point.

Congress may also call a national convention to propose an amendment, but it may do so only if that step has been requested by at least two-thirds of the State legislatures. In recent years Congress has received petitions for a convention to propose amendments to permit states to encourage prayer in public schools, to reverse Supreme Court decisions relating to abortions, and to deal with school busing. The most active campaign for a convention has been sponsored by the National Taxpayers Union in behalf of a Balanced Budget Amendment. Thirty-two State legislatures have petitioned Congress on this issue. To this point, no such convention has been called.

Electoral Duties

The Constitution gives certain electoral duties to Congress, but they are to be exercised only in very unusual circumstances.

[23]Article V; see Chapter 3, Section 2.

The Power to Impeach Some officeholders have resigned under the threat of Congress's impeachment power, as did President Nixon when, in 1974, the House Judiciary Committee (shown above) began impeachment proceedings after the Watergate scandal.

The House of Representatives may be called on to elect a President. If no candidate receives a majority of the electoral votes for President, the House of Representatives, voting by States, must decide the issue. In that situation, it must choose from among the three highest contenders in the electoral college balloting. Each State has but one vote to cast, and a majority of the States is necessary for election.[24]

Similarly, the Senate must choose a Vice President when no candidate wins a majority of the electoral votes for that office. In that situation, the vote is not by States but by individual senators, with a majority of the full Senate necessary for election.[25]

The House of Representatives has had to choose a President only twice: Thomas Jefferson in 1801 and John Quincy Adams in 1825.

[24]12th Amendment.

[25]12th Amendment. Note that these provisions make possible a situation in which the President would be of one party and the Vice President of another. The 12th Amendment also provides that the final, official count of the electoral votes cast for President and for Vice President every four years is to be made by the president of the Senate at a joint session of Congress.

SECTION 4
The Nonlegislative Powers

FOCUS

Teacher's Resource File See the Unit 3 File, p. 33, for the Section 4 Outline.

Objectives

11.9 Analyze why the Constitution gives nonlegislative power to Congress.

11.10 Determine the ways in which Congress exercises nonlegislative powers.

Bellringer Activity Write "August 9, 1974" on the board. Challenge students to identify the historical importance of this date. (*On that date Richard Nixon became the first and only President to resign from office.*) Explain that Nixon's resignation was a direct result of investigations by Congress—an example of nonlegislative power.

State the Purpose In addition to expressed and implied powers, Congress exercises a number of significant nonlegislative powers. In Section 4, students will examine the purpose and the scope of these nonlegislative powers of Congress.

ABCNEWS INTERACTIVE

The following video segments may be used to highlight aspects of the nonlegislative powers of Congress.

POWERS OF THE CONGRESS GUIDEBOOK
Chapter 39: Impeachment, p. 43
Chapter 43: Presidential Appointments, p. 49

Vocabulary

Direct students' attention to "Key Term" on page 275. Direct students to the "Impeachment" heading on page 276. Tell students to scan the text that follows the heading, and write down the grounds on which an official can be impeached and the different roles of the House and Senate in the impeachment process.

Reading Strategy: Structured Overview

Have students create a graphic organizer such as the one below. As they read, have them fill in details from the section under each heading.

Nonlegislative Powers

Impeach	Executive	Legislative

INSTRUCT

Discuss Ask students to discuss the nonlegislative powers and how Congress exercises them. To aid in the discussion, ask students the following questions: What might happen if Congress did not have these powers; that is, what if these powers were held by some other branch? (*Possible answers: The amendment process would involve a branch that does not include representation from each State; electoral disputes would have to be decided by judges or the outgoing executive; without impeachment there would be no recourse in the event of corrupt judges, and corrupt Presidents would be free to exercise their enormous powers; a President could appoint officials without regard to the wishes of the public.*)

Provide Guided Practice Write the phrase "nonlegislative powers" on the chalkboard. Ask students to come forward and write the five examples of nonlegislative powers on the board. Ask other volunteers to describe what these powers are and why they are important to the system of government.

Provide Independent Practice

TRF **Teacher's Resource File** You may wish to assign the Section 4 Guided Reading and Review, Unit 3 File, p. 34, to help students master section objective content.

The Senate chose Richard M. Johnson as Vice President in 1837.

Remember, too, that the 25th Amendment provides for the filling of a vacancy in the vice presidency. When one occurs, the President nominates a successor, subject to a majority vote in both houses of Congress. That process has been used twice: Gerald Ford was confirmed as Vice President in 1973 and Nelson Rockefeller in 1974.

Impeachment

The Constitution provides that the President, Vice President, and all civil officers of the United States may "be removed from office on impeachment for, and conviction of, treason, bribery, or other high crimes and misdemeanors."[26] The House has the sole power to **impeach**—bring 1.a
charges—and the Senate the sole power to judge—sit as a court—in impeachment cases.[27]

The House may impeach by a majority vote. A two-thirds vote of the senators present is needed for conviction. The chief justice must preside over the Senate when a President is tried. The penalty for conviction is removal from office. The Senate may add a prohibition against the person ever holding federal office again. In addition, a person who has been impeached and convicted can also be indicted, tried, convicted, and punished in the regular courts.[28]

To date, the House of Representatives has impeached only 16 persons. Of that number, the Senate has convicted seven.[29] Perhaps the most noteworthy impeachment occurred in 1868, when the House impeached President Andrew Johnson. The Senate, however, failed by a single vote to convict him.

A few officeholders have resigned in the face of certain impeachment—most notably Richard Nixon, who resigned the presidency in 1974 after the Watergate scandal. Although the House Judiciary Committee recommended three articles of impeachment against him, the House did not press the matter further after his resignation.

Executive Powers

The Constitution gives two "executive powers" to the Senate. One of those powers has to do with appointments and the other with treaties made by the President [30]

All major appointments made by the President must be confirmed by the Senate by majority vote. Each nomination is referred to the appropriate standing committee of the Senate. That committee may then hold hearings to decide whether or not to make a favorable recommendation to full Senate for that appointment. A recent example of such hearings were the Judiciary Committee's hearings to confirm or reject Clarence Thomas—President Bush's nominee to the U.S. Supreme Court. (Thomas, of course, was ultimately confirmed.) When that committee's recommendation is brought to the floor of the Senate, it may be, but seldom is, considered in executive (secret) session.

The appointment of a cabinet officer or of some other top member of the President's "official family" is rarely turned down by the Senate. [31] But the unwritten rule of "senatorial courtesy" comes into play with the President's appointment of federal officers who serve in the various States—for example, U.S. attorneys and federal marshals. The Senate will turn down such a presidential appointment if it is opposed by a senator of the President's party from the State involved.

The President makes treaties "by and with the advice and consent of the Senate, . . . provided two-thirds of the senators present concur.' [32] For a time after the adoption of the Constitution, the President asked the advice of the Senate when a treaty was being prepared. Now the President most often consults the members of the Senate Foreign Relations Committee and

---

[26]Article II, Section 4. Military officers are not "civil officers" and may be removed by court-martial. Nor are members of Congress. When the House impeached Senator William Blount of Tennessee in 1798, the Senate refused to try the case on grounds that it had the power to expel one of its own members if it chose to do so. Blount was then expelled. The precedent set in that instance has been followed ever since.

[27]Article I, Section 2, Clause 5; Section 3, Clause 6.

[28]Article I, Section 3, Clause 6 and Clause 7.

[29]All seven persons impeached by the House and then convicted by the Senate were federal judges. Four other federal judges were impeached by the House but later acquitted by the Senate; and two federal judges impeached by the House resigned before the Senate could act in their cases; see Chapter 18, Section 1.

SPOTLIGHT ON: Behind the Scenes

Although the House has chosen a President only twice (1800 and 1824), representatives did intervene to settle an election dispute in 1876. In spite of the fact that Democrat Samuel Tilden had won the popular vote, several States produced conflicting sets of electoral votes. One set made Republican Rutherford B. Hayes the winner, 185–184. However, powerful Southern House Democrats agreed to accept the electoral vote that gave Hayes the victory after Republicans promised that Hayes would remove all federal troops from the former Confederacy and appoint a Southerner to his cabinet.

Activity: For Gifted Students

Theme: Power Remind students that one of the executive powers of Congress is the Senate's power to confirm or reject presidential appointments. Ask students to research the debate over the Senate's exercise of this power. Students may wish to focus on such recent confirmation battles as Ronald Reagan's appointment of Robert Bork to the Supreme Court or George Bush's appointment of Clarence Thomas to the Court or John Tower to the cabinet. Have students present their findings in the form of a written or oral report.

other influential senators of both parties.

The Senate may accept or reject a treaty as it stands, or it may offer amendments, reservations, or understandings to it. Treaties are sometimes considered in executive session. Because the House has a hold on the public purse strings, influential members of that body are often consulted in the treaty-making process, too.

Investigatory Power

Congress has the power to investigate any matter that falls within the scope of its legislative powers. Congress exercises this authority through its standing committees, and subcommittees, and by its special committees; see Chapter 12, Section 2. Congress may choose to conduct investigations for several reasons. Most often, those inquiries are held to (1) gather information useful to Congress in the making of some legislation; (2) oversee the operations of various executive branch agencies; (3) focus public attention on a particular subject; (4) expose the questionable activities of public officials or private persons; and/or (5) promote the interests of some members of Congress. Congressional exercise of its investigatory powers have resulted in some of the more dramatic moments in American political history. One recent example was the hearings surrounding the Iran-Contra scandal. For months during the summer of 1987, a joint congressional committee questioned Lieutenant Colonel Oliver North and others about White House involvement in evading congressional limits on action in Nicaragua. Although he was initially found guilty of wrongdoing, all charges against Lieutenant Colonel North were dismissed in 1991.

Iran-Contra Lt. Colonel Oliver North testifies before the committee that probed the Reagan administration's secret foreign policy initiatives in Iran and Nicaragua.

[30]Article II, Section 2, Clause 2.

[31]All told, only 12 of the now more than 600 cabinet appointments have been rejected by the Senate. The first was Roger B. Taney, Andrew Jackson's choice for secretary of the treasury. Two years later President Jackson named Taney to succeed John Marshall as chief justice. The Senate confirmed him, and he served until his death in 1863. The most recent rejection came in 1989 when the Senate refused to approve President Bush's nomination of John Tower as secretary of defense. On the other rejections, see Chapter 14, Section 5.

[32]Article II, Section 2, Clause 2. It is often said that the Senate "ratifies" a treaty. It does not. The Senate may give or withhold its "advice and consent" to a treaty made by the President. Once the Senate has consented to a treaty, the President then ratifies it by exchanging the "instruments of ratification" with the other party or parties to the agreement.

Section 4 Review

1. **Define:** impeach
2. What roles does Congress play in the constitutional amendment process?
3. Who makes the choice if the electoral college fails to elect a President?
4. How is a vice-presidential vacancy now filled?
5. (a) Which chamber of Congress has the power to impeach? (b) The power to try those who are impeached?
6. What two "executive powers" are held by the Senate?

Critical Thinking

7. **Testing Conclusions** (p. 19) Cite examples of the fact that Congress has powers that check and balance the judicial and executive branches.

★

Monitor Comprehension

Answers to Section 4 Review
1. The "Key Term" is defined on the following page:
a. impeach, p. 276
2. Congress can propose amendments by two-thirds vote or call a national convention upon the request of two-thirds of the State legislatures. **3.** The House. The Senate chooses the Vice President if the electoral college cannot. **4.** The President nominates a successor, who must be approved by a majority of both houses. **5.** (a) The House. (b) The Senate. **6.** It confirms presidential appointments and offers advice and consent on treaties. **7.** Congress checks and balances the judicial branch through impeachment and its power to confirm or reject appointments of judges. It checks and balances the executive through impeachment and the Senate's power to confirm or reject appointments and offer advice and consent on treaties.

Teacher's Resource File See the Unit 3 File, p. 35, for the Section 4 Quiz.

Closure

Congress possesses five nonlegislative powers in the fields of 1) amendments, 2) electoral duties, 3) impeachment, 4) executive powers, such as confirmation of presidential appointments and advice and consent, and 5) investigatory powers. In the next chapter, students will learn how Congress actually uses its powers.

Assignment Assign Chapter 12, pp. 283–290, for the next class period.

Reteach

Write the words "expressed," "implied" and "inherent" on the chalkboard. Ask students to come forward and write down examples of each way that Congress exercises its legislative and nonlegislative powers.

Enrichment

Ask students to recall what they have learned about the system of checks and balances of the United States government. (If necessary, have students review Chapter 3, Section 1.) Then tell students to create a brief report of how the nonlegislative powers help to strengthen the system of checks and balances. Invite students to present their reports to class orally or in writing. (Average)

TEACHING
Critical Thinking

Recognizing Cause and Effect

Objective

Determine the relationship between cause and effect.

INSTRUCT

Before they read the feature, ask students to define the words *cause* and *effect.* Have students predict how they are related to one another.

As they read the feature, have students discuss why it is important to know how events relate to one another. (*Possible answer: So they can predict how one set of actions will influence others; or so that they can trace the source of a problem back to an earlier decision.*)

Answers: **1.** (a) A and B. (b) A: The cause is "because the federal budget . . ." The effect is "Congress . . . voted to approve . . ." B: The cause is "For years, Congress was unable . . ." The effect is "As a result, Gramm, Rudman, and Hollings opted . . ." D: See answers to questions 2 and 3. **2.** (a) In D, the effect "Congress adopting Gramm-Rudman-Hollings" has two causes. (b) In D, the cause "passage of Gramm-Rudman-Hollings" has two effects. **3.** Answers could include: Budget problems and inability of Congress causes/passage of Gramm-Rudman-Hollings, which causes/limited ability of Congress to perform its function.

Critical Thinking

Recognizing Cause and Effect

Recognizing cause and effect means to examine how one event or idea causes other events or ideas to occur. Understanding cause and effect is a key skill in problem solving. If you can see how events or ideas relate to and affect each other, you can see where problems begin. Then, you can begin to formulate solutions. Follow the steps below to practice recognizing cause and effect.

1. Identify the two parts of a cause-effect relationship. A cause is an event or an action that brings about an effect. Writers sometimes indicate a cause-effect relationship by using words such as *so, thus, because,* and *as a result.* Read statements A through C below and answer the following questions: (a) Which statements contain both a cause and an effect? (b) Which is the cause and which is the effect in each cause-effect statement? (c) What words, if any, indicate the presence of a cause-effect statement?

2. Remember that an event can have more than one cause and more than one effect. Several causes can combine to create one event. In the same way, a single cause can have several effects. Read paragraph D below. (a) Find an example of an effect that has more than one cause. (b) Find an example of a cause that has more than one effect.

3. Understand that an event can be both a cause and an effect. A cause can lead to an effect, which in turn can become the cause of another event. In this way, causes and effects can form a chain of related events. You can diagram such a chain as follows:

- Government borrows to pay for current expenditures. This causes:
- interest rates to rise. This causes:
- fewer people and businesses to borrow money. This causes:
- a drop in purchasing and in the growth of businesses. This causes:
- an economic slump.

Read paragraph D below and draw a diagram of the chain of events formed by causes and effects as shown in the example.

Statements

A Because the federal budget process was not working well, the Congress, with White House support, voted to approve the Balanced Budget and Emergency Reduction Act of 1985.

B For years, Congress was unable to cure the problem of deficit spending. As a result, Senators Gramm, Rudman, and Hollings opted for what many considered to be radical measures.

C The plan set annual limits on the budget deficit. These limits require that the deficit be cut to zero by 1993.

D Ongoing budget problems and the inability of Congress to come up with any better solutions led Congress to adopt the Gramm-Rudman-Hollings measure. Since its passage many people have criticized the measure. In the long run, the Gramm-Rudman-Hollings approach to budgeting appears to limit Congress's ability to perform some of its critical policy clarification function. It also forces Congress to yield some of its authority to the executive in hopes of resolving our deficit problem. In the end, Congress and the White House will doubtless have to make further cuts in spending as well as raise new revenues.

Teacher's Resource File
See the Unit 1 File, p. 36, for the Skill Application to reinforce this skill lesson.

Chapter-in-Brief

Scan all headings, photographs, charts, and other visuals in the chapter before reading the section summaries below.

Section 1 The Scope of Congressional Powers (pp. 259–261) The Constitution places strict limits on what Congress can and cannot do. However, the Constitution does grant to Congress a number of powers.

The extent of the powers of Congress has long been a subject of debate. Early in the nation's history, this debate was fought between strict constructionists, led by Thomas Jefferson, and liberal constructionists, led by Alexander Hamilton. The liberal constructionists won the early battles. In addition, the viewpoint they represented has been generally supported by Congress, Presidents, the courts, and the American people throughout American history.

Section 2 The Expressed Powers (pp. 261–271) The Constitution grants to Congress a large number of specific powers. Most of these expressed powers appear in Article I, Section 8.

The expressed powers are brief and broad, and their full meanings have evolved over time. Congress and the courts have addressed hundreds of questions about the the expressed powers. They have tended to interpret them broadly, thus expanding the powers of Congress.

The Constitution grants Congress the power to tax, to regulate commerce, to coin and borrow money, and to create laws on bankruptcy. The ability of Congress to regulate commerce and to tax have been key to the growth and success of the nation.

Another important realm of congressional power is foreign relations and defense.

Other powers of Congress include the power to naturalize citizens, to create a postal system, to govern copyrights and patents, and to set standards for weights and measures. Congress may add and administer new territories. Congress also has certain judicial responsibilities, including the power to establish courts.

Section 3 The Implied Powers (pp. 271–273) Besides those powers specifically mentioned in the Constitution, Congress has the power to make whatever laws it deems "necessary and proper." The Necessary and Proper Clause is the basis of what are called implied powers. The extent of the implied powers has long been debated.

A key moment in this debate occurred in 1819, when the Supreme Court decided *McCulloch* v. *Maryland*. In that case, the Court embraced a broad view of implied powers. Ever since, Congress has steadily expanded its powers.

Section 4 The Nonlegislative Powers (pp. 275–277) Congress has many nonlegislative functions. These include its key role in the process of amending the Constitution. Also, in certain unusual circumstances, the House may be called upon to select a President and the Senate to choose a Vice President.

The House has the power to impeach federal officers, and the Senate to try them. Also, the Senate must confirm the President's major appointments and accept or reject treaties.

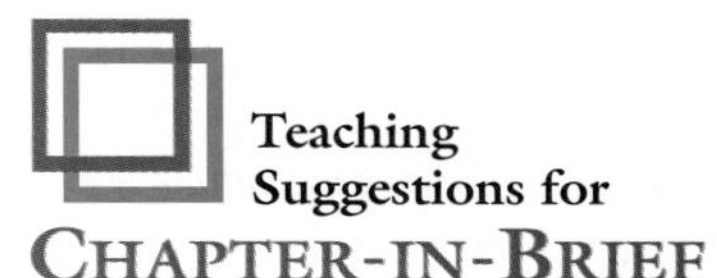

Teaching Suggestions for CHAPTER-IN-BRIEF

Below are some of the possible uses for the Chapter-in-Brief:

To Preview the Chapter You may want to assign the Chapter-in-Brief page and the Section Outlines from the Teacher's Resource File before beginning Chapter 11 to introduce students to "Key Terms" and concepts in each section.

To Review the Chapter When students have completed Chapter 11, you might want to assign the Chapter-in-Brief as a tool for review, along with the Guided Reading and Reviews from the Teacher's Resource File.

To Omit the Chapter If you wish to skip Chapter 11, it may be helpful to assign the Chapter-in-Brief to students as a review before continuing to another chapter. You may also want to assign the Chapter 11 Test to assess student knowledge of the material. Then specific portions of Chapter 11 may be assigned to students needing reinforcement of "Key Terms" and concepts.

Teacher's Resource File See the Unit 3 File for the following materials:

- Section Outlines, pp. 24, 27, 30, 33.
- Guided Reading and Reviews, pp. 25, 28, 31, 34.
- Chapter 11 Test, pp. 40–42.

ADDITIONAL RESOURCES

Cochran, Charles E., *et al. American Public Policy.* St. Martin's Press, 3rd ed., 1990.

The Congress. Video. PBS Video. Color. 60 minutes.

Congress: How It Works—and Sometimes Doesn't. Video. Guidance Associates, 1989. 59 minutes.

Conlan, Timothy J., *et al. Taxing Choices: The Politics of Tax Reform.* CQ Press, 1989.

Fisher, Louise. *The Politics of Shared Power: Congress and the Executive.* CQ Press, 2nd ed., 1987.

Kozak, David C. and John D.McCartney (eds.). *Congress and Public Policy: A Source Book of Documents and Readings.* Dorsey, 2nd ed., 1987.

Mezey, Michael L. *Congress, the President, and Public Policy.* Westview Press, 1989.

Warmuth, Francis D. and Edwin B. Fumage. *To Chain the Dog of War: The War Powers of Congress.* University of Illinois Press, 2nd ed., 1989.

Answers to
CHAPTER 11 REVIEW

Vocabulary and Key Terms

Matching
1. eminent domain
2. Necessary and Proper Clause
3. legal tender
4. commerce power
5. impeach

True or False
1. True.
2. False—the correct term is *Necessary and Proper Clause.*
3. True.
4. False—the correct term is *copyright.*
5. False—the correct term is *liberal constructionist.*

Word Relationships
1. *Strict constructionists* promote a narrow interpretation of the Constitution's provisions, particularly those that grant powers to the government. *Liberal constructionists* advocate a broad reading of the Constitution's provisions.
2. A *direct tax* is one that is paid by the person on whom it is levied. An *indirect tax* is levied on one person or business but passed on to someone else for actual payment.
3. A *copyright* is the exclusive right of an author to reproduce, publish, or sell his or her literary, musical, or artistic creations. A *patent* grants a person a sole right to make, use, or sell any machine or other useful composition of matter.

Main Ideas

Section 1
1. The Constitution limits Congress by what it says and by what it does not say. The federal system, which reserves many powers for the States, also limits the powers that Congress can exercise. **2.** Strict constructionists argued for a narrow interpretation of the powers of the National Government. Liberal constructionists favored an interpretation that gave the National Government broader powers to act beyond the expressed powers. **3.** Factors include the success of the liberal constructionists in the debate over the government's power. National emergencies such as war and economic crises have also led the National Government to expand its powers. Also, advances in technology have influenced the size and scope of government.

Section 2
4. The brevity of the expressed powers means that Congress has had to interpret their meanings. Supreme Court rulings have also helped interpret the powers and set limits on them. **5.** The Articles did not grant the National Government the power to tax, which rendered it powerless. The Articles also failed to allow regulation of commerce, and the result was chaos in the young nation. These failures of the Articles helped lead to the creation of the Constitution, including its grant to Congress of the power to tax and regulate commerce. **6.** Congress shares these powers with the President, who plays the

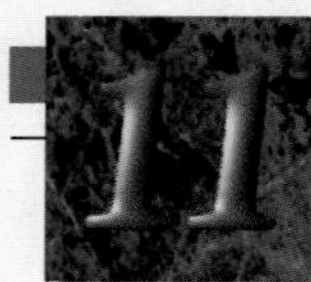

Chapter Review

Vocabulary and Key Terms

strict constructionist (p. 260)
liberal constructionist (p. 260)
direct tax (p. 262)
indirect tax (p. 263)
commerce power (p. 264)
legal tender (p. 266)
bankruptcy (p. 267)
copyright (p. 268)
patent (p. 269)
eminent domain (p. 270)
Necessary and Proper Clause (p. 271)
impeach (p. 276)

Matching: *Review the key terms in the list above. If you are not sure of a term's meaning, look up the term and review its definition. Choose a term from the list above that best matches each description.*

1. the power of a government to take private property for public use
2. a part of the Constitution from which the implied powers flow
3. what a creditor must accept in return for a debt
4. the expressed power by which Congress regulates interstate and foreign trade
5. to formally charge a public official for the purpose of removing him or her from office

True or False: *Determine whether each statement is true or false. If it is true, write "true." If it is false, change the underlined word or words to make the statement true.*

1. <u>Bankruptcy</u> is a legal proceeding in which a person who cannot pay his or her debts has his or her assets distributed among the creditors.
2. The <u>commerce power</u> is sometimes referred to as the "Elastic Clause."
3. An example of an <u>indirect tax</u> is the tax on cigarettes, which is passed on to the consumer.
4. An author of a new book would seek a <u>patent</u> on his or her work.
5. A <u>strict constructionist</u> would have approved of the Supreme Court's decision in *McCulloch* v. *Maryland*.

Word Relationships: *Distinguish between the words in each pair.*

1. strict constructionist/liberal constructionist
2. direct tax/indirect tax
3. copyright/patent

Main Ideas

Section 1 (pp. 259–261)

1. Describe the several ways in which the Constitution and the American system of government limit the powers of Congress.
2. Describe the basic features of the debate over the proper extent of the Federal Government's power in the early years of the United States.
3. What forces have led to the growth in national power since the first days of the National Government?

Section 2 (pp. 261–271)

4. What is the significance of the fact that the expressed powers are brief?
5. How did the power to tax and the commerce power address weaknesses in the Articles of Confederation?
6. With whom does Congress share its powers in the areas of foreign policy and war?

Section 3 (pp. 271–273)

7. What is the relationship between the Necessary and Proper Clause and the implied powers?
8. How has the Necessary and Proper Clause contributed to the vitality of the Constitution over the course of American history?
9. What role did *McCulloch* v. *Maryland* play in the development of the concept of implied powers?

Section 4 (pp. 275–277)

10. What are the functions that the Constitution gives Congress beyond its basic lawmaking function?
11. How do certain of the nonlegislative powers help preserve the system of checks and balances?
12. In what sense does the practice of "senatorial courtesy" dictate certain presidential appointments?

Critical Thinking

1. **Demonstrating Reasoned Judgment** (p. 19) The Supreme Court found in *McCulloch* v. *Maryland* that "the power to tax involves the power to destroy." How does this statement explain the constitutional limit on the power of Congress to tax?
2. **Formulating Questions** (p. 19) The American people have long debated the extent of the Necessary and Proper Clause. Write a list of questions that could be applied to any proposed act of Congress to judge whether or not it is necessary and proper.
3. **Recognizing Cause and Effect** (p. 19) Review what you have read in this chapter about the debate over the extent of the powers granted to Congress. How might the short length of the Constitution have influenced the debate over a strict vs. a liberal construction of the Constitution?

Getting Involved

1. **Writing Your Opinion** The year is 1790. Alexander Hamilton has just made his proposal that Congress set up a national bank. Write a speech in which you argue in favor of either a strict or a liberal interpretation of the Constitution. Before you write, review the facts of the debate between the strict and liberal constructionists. Identify three points that you will use to make your argument. Begin the speech by summarizing the overall debate, explaining why you think it should be of concern to the American people. Then spell out your arguments, devoting one paragraph to each idea. Conclude with a prediction of what will happen if the nation makes the "wrong" decision. Revise your speech to make sure that each paragraph is stated as persuasively as possible. Check for errors, and then make a final draft.
2. **Cooperative Activity** Work as a class to create an illustrated diagram of the powers of Congress. The diagram should clearly show the powers and explain and illustrate their meaning. Begin by dividing the class into three groups. One group should work together to list and define the powers of Congress. Another group should decide on and sketch a design for the diagram. The design should clearly show the organization of the powers of Congress and include suggested illustrations for each of the powers. The third group will actually create the diagram. Some students can draw the illustrations while others construct and letter the diagram itself.
3. **Creating a Political Cartoon** Design and draw a political cartoon that illustrates the concept of the Elastic Clause. Recall that you can use both words and pictures in your cartoon.

leading role in these fields.

Section 3

7. The Necessary and Proper Clause is the part of the Constitution from which the implied powers flow. **8.** It has enabled the Constitution to be flexible and adaptable to the changing needs of the nation. **9.** This decision provided the Supreme Court's approval of the concept of implied powers.

Section 4

10. Congress plays a key role in amending the Constitution. It can, under certain circumstances, play a part in the electoral process. Congress has the power to remove civil officers of the United States through impeachment. Congress also has certain executive powers, as well as the power to investigate the executive branch. **11.** Congress has powers to check and balance the executive branch through its executive and investigatory powers and its power to impeach. Congress has a check over the judicial branch through its power to impeach, and through its power to confirm or reject presidential appointments. **12.** The practice of senatorial courtesy ensures that certain appointments will be turned down by the Senate. Thus, in such situations a President would face a practical limitation on his or her choice for appointment.

Critical Thinking

1. Students might observe that because the power to tax is so powerful, the Constitution placed limits on Congress. These limits ensure that Congress does not "destroy" people or property by taxing them. **2.** Answers will vary. Students might formulate questions such as: From what expressed power does the proposed legislation stem? In what sense is this proposed act necessary? What will be the result if this act is not passed? **3.** Answers will vary. Students might suggest that the short length of the Constitution left many questions about congressional power unanswered. When Congress addressed these questions, it often found answers that had the effect of broadening its powers.

Getting Involved

1–4. Answers and results will vary, but students should demonstrate an understanding of the concepts in this chapter.

Chapter 12 Resources

In the Teacher's Resource File
The following materials are found in the Teacher's Resource File box.

Instructional Support: Unit 3 File

For the Section
Outlines, pp. 46, 49, 52, 55
Guided Reading and Reviews, pp. 47, 50, 53, 56
Quizzes, pp. 48, 51, 54, 57

For the Chapter
Skill Application, p. 58
Case Study on Contemporary Issues, pp. 59–61
Chapter Test, pp. 62–64
Additional Test Questions, pp. 65–67

Enrichment Support Files

Participatory Government Activities, pp. 4–19
Supreme Court Cases, p. 9
Simulations and Debates: Senate Debate
Historical and Legal Documents, p. 22

Computer Test Bank and Assessment
Transparency Package, pp. 12, 37

Chapter 12 Focus

Introduce the Chapter Tell students that in Chapter 12 they will read about Congress in action. They will learn about the organization and operation of both houses of Congress. Read with students the Chapter Preview and Objectives.

Writing Activity Direct students' attention to "Describe." Ask students to write a description of a recent action of any congressional committee. For a list of House and Senate standing committees, refer students to the graphic on page 291.

Motivate for Learning Direct students' attention to "Predict." Discuss what would happen if students were allowed to establish rules for the entire school. Then have them predict the number of bills introduced in Congress that actually become laws.

Chapter 12 Congress in Action

Chapter Preview

Figures run back and forth in the landscape beneath the streets. Subway cars emerge from tunnels to swallow them up, only to deposit them at another location where they start to run again. Who are these people in a perpetual state of motion? They are the senators and representatives who use the maze of subway tunnels beneath Capitol Hill to negotiate the distances between their offices and the House or Senate.

Six office buildings sit adjacent to the Capitol building. In these offices and inside the Capitol building is where most of the complicated legislative work of the country takes place. What happens in this setting? How does Congress perform its lawmaking functions? This chapter answers these questions—by describing Congress in action.

Before you read this chapter:

- **Describe** any recent action of a congressional committee with which you are familiar.
- **Predict** the percentage of bills introduced in Congress that actually become law.

As you read, focus on the main objective for each section. Understand:

1. The organizational structure of both houses of Congress.
2. The committee system and the types of committees in both houses of Congress.
3. The legislative process in the House of Representatives.
4. The handling of bills in the Senate and the final stages in the legislative process.

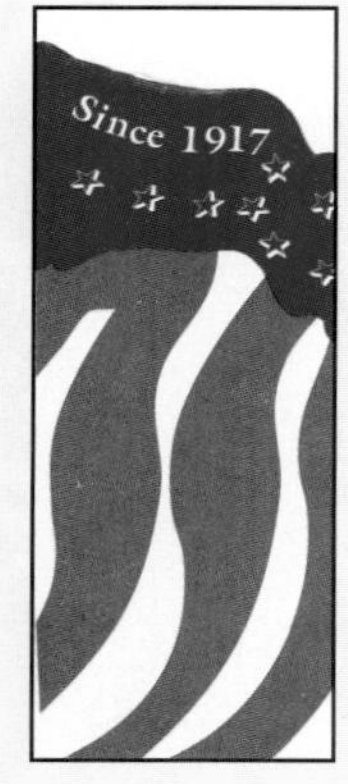

Magruder's American Government: *A Witness to Change* by William A. McClenaghan

The Senate first adopted its Cloture Rule, Rule 22, in 1917; therefore, that change in Senate procedures was not noted until the second edition of *American Government.* Its discussion of the filibuster and the new rule closed with this statement: "Thus, the old abuse of 'talking a bill to death' . . . may be prevented if two-thirds of the members desire to do so."

That sentence lived, intact, for decades—in fact, until the 1956 edition. However, it really should not have survived—at least not without some emphasis on the words "may be."

The Senate first voted cloture to end debate on the Versailles Treaty in 1919. It did so again on the issue of joining the World Court in 1926, and on a banking bill and then a prohibition measure in 1927. But over the next 35 years, from 1927 to 1962, every attempt to choke off a filibuster failed. Two-thirds of the members did not "desire to do so." In fact, the odds on invoking cloture even today (with a relaxed rule) run only about one in three.

Grass Roots Campaigning Representative Richard A. Gephardt (D., Missouri) discusses issues with voters at an informal gathering in the home of a constituent.

1 Congress Organizes

Find Out:

- How do the House and Senate begin new terms?
- What are the contrasts between the roles of the Speaker of the House and the president of the Senate?
- Who are the floor leaders in Congress and where does their power come from?
- How are committee chairmen chosen and what is their role in the legislative process?

Key Terms:

Speaker of the House, president of the Senate, president *pro tempore*, floor leaders, whip, party caucus, committee chairman, seniority rule

What do you think when you see or hear the word *Congress*? Maybe you picture the Capitol, or perhaps the senators and representatives you see on the evening news. Of course, you know that the nation's legislature is much more than that. Congress is in fact a very complex enterprise; and it is a much larger one than most people realize. More than 37,000 men and women work for the legislative branch; and Congress has appropriated more than \$2.3 billion to finance its operations this year.[1]

In this section, you will see just how complex Congress is and how it has organized itself to conduct its business.

Congress Convenes

Congress convenes, that is, begins a new term, every two years—on January 3 of every odd-numbered year, following the general elections in November.

[1]More than 19,000 of the men and women who work in the legislative branch have jobs in the House or Senate—in members' offices, as committee staff, or in some part of the administrative organization in one or the other of the two houses. The other 18,000 or so employees work in the several other agencies Congress has over time established in the legislative branch.

Section 1
Congress Organizes

Focus

Teacher's Resource File See the Unit 3 File, p. 46, for the Section 1 Outline.

Objectives

12.1 Explain how the House and Senate begin new terms.
12.2 Contrast the roles of the Speaker of the House and the president of the Senate.
12.3 Identify the floor leaders in Congress and the source of their powers.
12.4 Explain how committee chairs are chosen and their role in the legislative process.

Bellringer Activity Ask students to imagine they are forming a new school club. How would they go about organizing their club? Would they have a president? Who would preside over meetings?

State the Purpose Students will learn how the House and Senate begin new terms, the roles of the leadership positions in Congress and the source of their power. Students also will learn about committee chairs and the seniority rule.

Vocabulary

Point out to students the list of "Key Terms" on page 283. Explain that *party caucus* means "a closed meeting of the members of each party in each house." Tell students that the word *caucus* probably derived from the Caucus Club, an eighteenth-century social and political club.

Reading Strategy: Question Writing

As a preparation for reading, have students read the section's main headings. Then ask students to write down a question about each heading, and look for the answers to their questions as they read.

Opening Day in the House

When the 435 men and women who have been elected to the House come together at the Capitol to begin a new term, they are, in effect, just so many representatives-elect. Because all 435 of its seats are filled by people elected every two years, the House technically has no sworn members, no rules, and no organization until its opening-day ceremonies are held.

The clerk of the House in the preceding term presides, chairs, at the beginning of the first day's session [2] The clerk calls the chamber to order and checks the roll of representatives-elect. Those members-to-be then choose a Speaker as their permanent presiding officer. By custom, the Speaker is a long-standing member of the majority party, and election on the floor is only a formality. The majority party's caucus—the conference of party members in the House—has settled the matter beforehand.

The Speaker then takes the oath of office. It is administered by the Dean of the House, the member-elect with the longest record of service in the House of Representatives [3] With that accomplished, the Speaker swears in the rest of the members as a body. The Democrats take their seats to the right of the center aisle; the Republicans, to the left.

Next, the House elects its clerk, sergeant at arms, doorkeeper, postmaster, and chaplain. These elections are also a formality. The majority party's caucus has already decided who these nonmember officers will be.

Then, the House adopts the rules that will govern its proceedings through the term. The rules of the House have been developing for over 200 years now, and they are contained in a volume of about 400 pages. They are readopted, most often with little or no change, at the beginning of each term.

Finally, members of the 22 permanent committees of the House are appointed by a floor vote, and with that the House is organized.

[2]The clerk is a nonmember officer, chosen by the House, who serves as that body's chief administrative officer.

[3]Today, Jamie L. Whitten (D., Miss.), a member of the House since November 4, 1941.

Opening Day in the Senate

The Senate is a continuous body. It has been organized without interruption since its first session in 1789. Recall that only one-third of the seats are up for election every two years. From one term to the next, two-thirds of the Senate's membership is carried over. As a result, the Senate does not face large organizational problems at the beginning of a term. Its first-day session is nearly always short and routine, even when the elections have brought a change in the party having the majority of seats. Newly elected and reelected members must be sworn in, vacancies in Senate organization and on committees must be filled, and a few other details attended to.

The President's State of the Union Message

When the Senate is notified that the House is organized, a joint committee of the two is appointed and instructed

> "... to wait upon the President of the United States and inform him that a quorum of each House is assembled and that the Congress is ready to receive any communication he may be pleased to make."

Within a few weeks, the President delivers the annual State of the Union message to a joint session of Congress. The President's speech is a major political event based on this constitutional command:

> "He shall from time to time give to the Congress information of the state of the Union, and recommend to their consideration such measures as he shall judge necessary and expedient ..."[4]

The members of both houses, together with the members of the cabinet, the justices of the Supreme Court, the foreign diplomatic corps, and other dignitaries assemble in the House chamber to listen.

In his address, the President reports on the state of the nation as he sees it, in both domestic and foreign policy terms. The message is televised live, and it is followed very closely, both here and abroad. In it, the President lays out the broad shape of the policies his administration will follow and the course he has charted

[4]Article II, Section 3.

INSTRUCT

Model/Discuss Lead students in a short, 15-minute simulated exercise in which the class reenacts opening day in the House. As students come into class, stand at the door and hand out slips of paper to two students that say *clerk of the House* and *Dean of the House.* Divide the class into two groups, the Democrats and the Republicans, and ask them to sit on opposite sides of the room, with one aisle between the desks separating the two sides of the room. (You may wish to set the room up in this manner before students enter class.) Have students read the description of the opening day in the House on page 284, and then have them reenact the process, referring back to the book as necessary.

Have students discuss the differences between how the House and the Senate are organized. Ask: Why is opening day in the Senate largely routine? How is the presiding officer of the House different from the Senate's presiding officer? Would students rather be Speaker of the House or president of the Senate?

ABCNEWS INTERACTIVE

The following video segments may be used to highlight aspects of congressional organization.

POWERS OF THE CONGRESS GUIDEBOOK
Chapter 24: Congress Convenes, p. 100
Chapter 25: Congressional Leadership, p. 101
Chapter 26: Speaker of the House, p. 102
Chapter 27: Vice President (President of the Senate), p. 103

SPOTLIGHT ON: Behind the Scenes

At age 82, Representative Jamie Whitten (D., Mississippi) is the oldest member of the current House—but historically he is not the oldest person to be elected to Congress. Representative James Bowler, a Chicago Democrat, won a special election for a seat left vacant by Representative Al Sabath's death. Long before that event, Bowler and Sabath served on the city council together. The council reached a deadlock over which of the two men should run for the congressional seat. Finally, the two men tossed a coin. Sabath won, with Bowler agreeing to fill the seat when Sabath left it. Fifty-two years later, he did. Bowler was sworn into Congress for his first term in the late 1940s at the age of 86.

for the nation. He also may include specific legislative recommendations.

With the conclusion of the President's speech, the joint session is adjourned, and each house returns to the mass of legislative business before it.

The Presiding Officers

The Constitution provides for the presiding officers of each house. The Speaker of the House is by far the most important and influential member of the House of Representatives. The Constitution commands that the post be filled by a vote of the House at the beginning of each of its two-year terms. In fact, the Speaker is the leader of the majority party in the House and is chosen by the members of that party.

Although neither the Constitution nor its own rules require it, the House has always chosen the Speaker from among its own members. Usually, the Speaker is a longtime member who has risen in stature and influence through years of service.

Today, Representative Thomas S. Foley (D., Wash.) is the Speaker of the House. He was first elected to Congress in 1964 and became Speaker in 1989.[5]

Basically, the great power held by the Speaker arises from this fact: The **Speaker of the** 1.a
House is both the elected presiding officer of the House *and* the acknowledged leader of its majority party. Speakers are expected to preside in a fair and judicious manner. They are also expected to aid the fortunes of their own parties and their legislative goals.

Nearly all the Speaker's specific powers revolve around two duties: to preside and to keep order. The Speaker presides over all sessions of the House, or appoints a temporary presiding officer. No member may speak until recognized by the Speaker. The Speaker interprets and applies the rules, refers bills to the standing committees, rules on points of order (questions of procedure raised by members), puts questions to a vote, and decides the outcome of most of the votes taken. The Speaker also names the members of all select and conference committees and signs all bills and resolutions passed by the House.

As a member, the Speaker may debate and vote on any matter before the House. But if he chooses to do so, he must appoint a temporary presiding officer (the Speaker *pro tempore*), and that member then occupies the Speaker's chair. The Speaker does not often vote, and the House rules say that he *must* vote only to break a tie. Notice then, because a tie vote defeats a question, the Speaker can vote to cause a tie and so defeat a proposal.

Presidential Tradition Since 1913 Every President since Woodrow Wilson (inset) has personally delivered the State of the Union address to Congress. President Bush (above) is shown delivering his 1990 address.

[5]Article I, Section 2, Clause 5. Speaker Foley is the 49th person to serve in the post. He succeeded James C. (Jim) Wright, Jr. (D., Tex.). The first Speaker, elected at the first session in 1789, was Frederick A. C. Muhlenburg, a Federalist from Pennsylvania. Sam Rayburn (D., Tex.) held the office for a record 17 years, 62 days.

Analyze/Discuss Explore with students the importance of the position of Speaker of the House. What makes the Speaker so powerful? Explain to students that such powers as the ability to defeat a proposal by causing a tie, pass a proposal by breaking a tie, or to prevent members from speaking unless recognized by the Speaker, make this a very powerful position. Ask students if they can find other evidence in the section of the Speaker's influence.

SPOTLIGHT ON: Behind the Scenes

Although both Washington and Adams addressed Congress in person, Thomas Jefferson broke with that tradition and instead sent his addresses in writing. He said he did not want to act like a king addressing Parliament from a throne, but it is widely believed that this might have been an excuse, for Jefferson was uncomfortable speaking before crowds. It was not until 1913, when Woodrow Wilson chose to deliver his State of the Union message to Congress in person, that the tradition begun by Jefferson was broken. From Wilson to Bush, all Presidents, except Herbert Hoover, have stood before Congress to deliver their State of the Union messages.

INSTRUCT

Analyze Ask students to consider what qualifications and personal characteristics an effective floor leader would possess? Would they need to have strong decision-making ability? Delegating ability? Would they need to be forceful? Persuasive? Students also can list the important qualifications and personal characteristics for party whips.

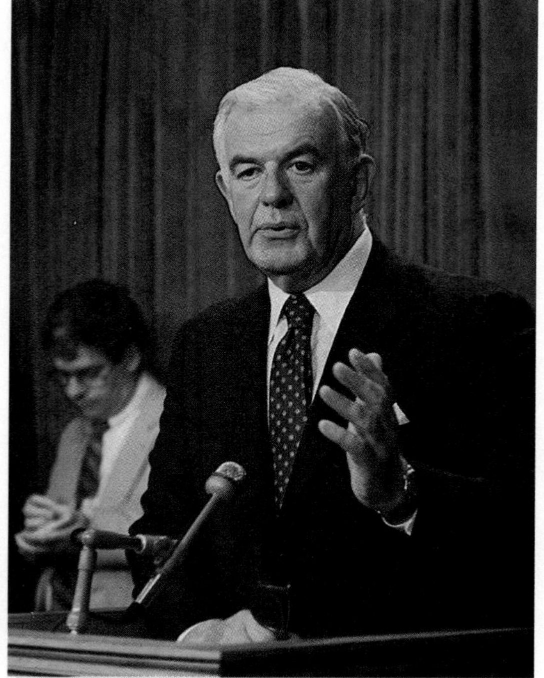

An Influential Post Speaker of the House Thomas Foley, known for his ability to consider all sides of an issue, speaks at a press briefing on Capitol Hill.

The Speaker of the House follows the Vice President in the line of succession to the presidency—a considerable testimony to the power and importance of the office.

The **president of the Senate**, the presiding officer in that body, is not a member of the Senate. Instead, the Constitution assigns the office to the Vice President of the United States.[6] Largely for this reason, the president of the Senate occupies a much less powerful chair than the Speaker's in the House. The Vice President does not become the Senate's presiding officer as a direct result of long service in that body. In fact, the president of the Senate is sometimes not even a member of the party with a majority of seats in the upper house.

The president of the Senate does have the usual powers of a presiding officer—to recognize members, put questions to a vote, and so on. However, the Vice President cannot take the floor to speak or debate and may vote *only* to break a tie.

Any influence a Vice President may have in the Senate is largely the result of personal abilities and relationships. Several of the more recent Vice Presidents came to that office from the Senate: Harry Truman, Alben Barkley, Richard Nixon, Lyndon Johnson, Hubert Humphrey, Walter Mondale, and J. Danforth Quayle. Each of them was able to build at least some power into the position out of that earlier experience.

The Senate does have another presiding offi-
1.b cer, the **president *pro tempore***, who serves in the Vice President's absence. The president *pro tem* is elected by the Senate itself and is always a leading member of the majority party. Senator Robert C. Byrd (D., W.Va.) has been the Senate's president *pro tem* since 1989. Other members of the Senate also preside over the chamber, on a temporary basis. Newly elected senators are regularly given this honor early in their terms.

The president *pro tem* is an important office. But as you will read, it is not the most powerful post to which senators can rise.

Floor Leaders and Other Party Officers

Congress is a political body. This is so for two leading reasons: (1) because Congress is the nation's central policy-making body and, (2) because of its partisan makeup. Reflecting its political complexion, both houses are organized along party lines. This organization creates some powerful positions.

The Floor Leaders Next to the Speaker, the most important officers in Congress are the majority and minority floor leaders in the House and Senate. They do not hold official positions in either chamber. Rather, they are party officers, picked for their posts by their party colleagues.

The **floor leaders** are legislative strategists. They try to carry out the decisions of their parties' caucuses and steer floor action to their

[6]Article I, Section 3, Clause 4.

parties' benefit. All of that calls for political skills of a high order.

The majority leader's post is the more powerful in each house, for the obvious reason that the majority party has more seats—that is, more votes—than the other party has. Together with the presiding officer and the minority leader, the majority leader plans the order of business on the floor.

The two floor leaders in each house are assisted by party whips—a majority whip and a minority whip. They are, in effect, assistant floor leaders. Each of them is chosen by the party caucus, almost always on the floor leader's recommendation. There are a number of assistant whips in the House, and both floor leaders in each house have a paid staff.

The job of a **whip** is to check with party members and advise the floor leader of the number of votes that can be counted on in any particular matter. Whips attempt to see that members of their parties are present for important votes and that they vote with the party leadership. If a member must be absent for some reason, the whip sees that that member is paired with a member of the other party who will also be absent or who agrees not to vote on certain measures. In this way, one nonvote cancels out another.

The Party Caucus The **party caucus** is a 1.c
closed meeting of the members of each party in each house. It meets just before Congress convenes in January and occasionally during a session. In recent years the Republicans have called their caucus in each house the party conference, and the Democrats now use this term in the Senate, too.

The caucus deals mostly with matters of party organization, such as the selection of the party's floor leaders and questions of committee membership. It sometimes takes stands on

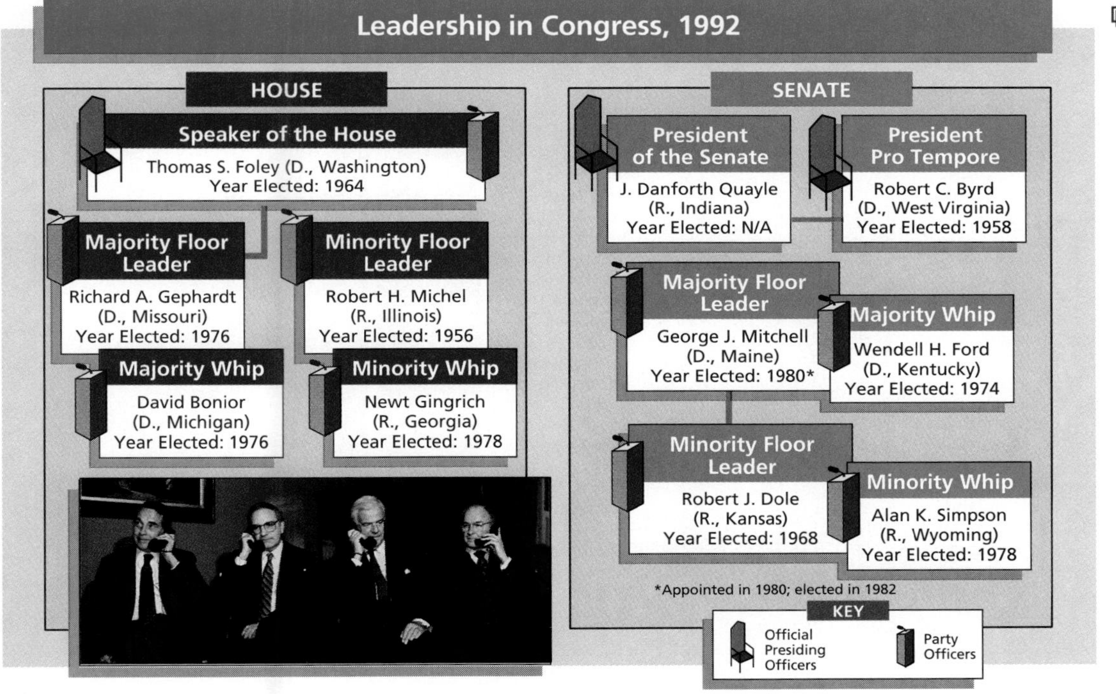

Interpreting Charts Who are the most important officers in Congress after the Speaker? The photograph shows party leaders for the 101st Congress informing the President of their appointments.

Interpreting Charts Ask students to state the relationship between political party and majority and minority leadership. *(Majority and minority floor leaders are party officers, picked for their posts by their party colleagues. They try to steer the actions of Congress in the direction that benefits their party.)*

Caption Answer The majority and minority floor leaders in both the House and Senate.

ACTIVITY: For Gifted Students

Theme: Power After students have studied the chart on page 287, have them choose a particular year in history in which they are interested and do research to determine who the leaders in Congress were that year. Then have students write a paper describing one of these leaders in particular and how much control they had over legislative matters.

SPOTLIGHT ON: Multiculturalism

The two major parties form the major, but not the only, caucuses in Congress. Other groups also convene caucuses, of which the Congressional Black Caucus, established in 1971, is one of the most widely known. The Congressional Black Caucus provides a forum for discussing and formulating positions on important legislative issues of interest to African Americans.

Interpreting Charts Point out to students that the chart uses both symbols (the donkey and the elephant) and colors are used to denote party affiliation. Have students locate their state under "Representation by State." Using this information, have students form hypotheses about the party preference of their State.

Caption Answer The Democratic party.

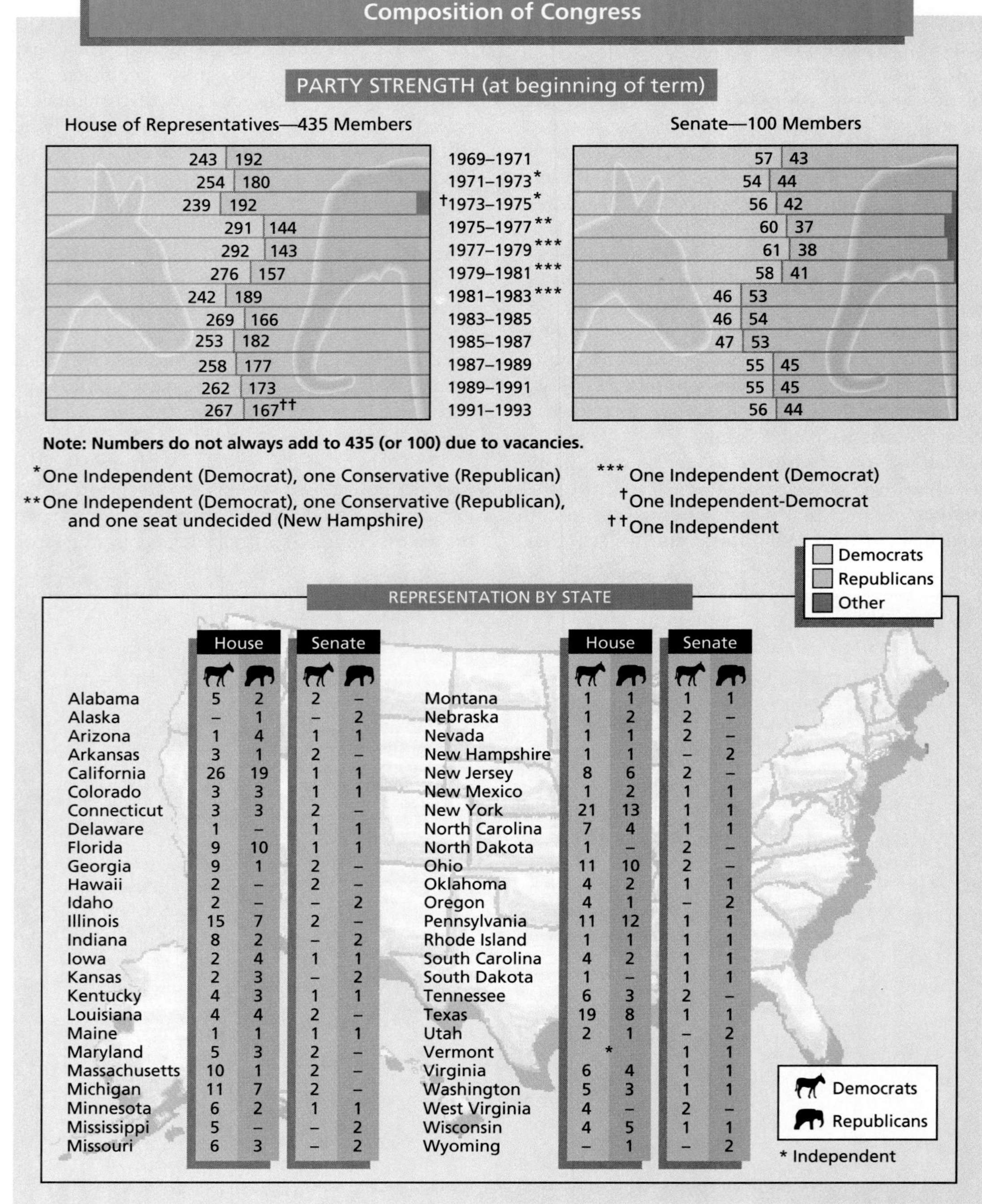

Composition of Congress

PARTY STRENGTH (at beginning of term)

House of Representatives—435 Members (Democrats)	House of Representatives—435 Members (Republicans)	Term	Senate—100 Members (Democrats)	Senate—100 Members (Republicans)
243	192	1969–1971	57	43
254	180	1971–1973*	54	44
239	192	†1973–1975*	56	42
291	144	1975–1977**	60	37
292	143	1977–1979***	61	38
276	157	1979–1981***	58	41
242	189	1981–1983***	46	53
269	166	1983–1985	46	54
253	182	1985–1987	47	53
258	177	1987–1989	55	45
262	173	1989–1991	55	45
267	167††	1991–1993	56	44

Note: Numbers do not always add to 435 (or 100) due to vacancies.

*One Independent (Democrat), one Conservative (Republican)

**One Independent (Democrat), one Conservative (Republican), and one seat undecided (New Hampshire)

*** One Independent (Democrat)

†One Independent-Democrat

††One Independent

Democrats / Republicans / Other

REPRESENTATION BY STATE

State	House Democrats	House Republicans	Senate Democrats	Senate Republicans
Alabama	5	2	2	–
Alaska	–	1	–	2
Arizona	1	4	1	1
Arkansas	3	1	2	–
California	26	19	1	1
Colorado	3	3	1	1
Connecticut	3	3	2	–
Delaware	1	–	1	1
Florida	9	10	1	1
Georgia	9	1	2	–
Hawaii	2	–	2	–
Idaho	2	–	–	2
Illinois	15	7	2	–
Indiana	8	2	–	2
Iowa	2	4	1	1
Kansas	2	3	–	2
Kentucky	4	3	1	1
Louisiana	4	4	2	–
Maine	1	1	1	1
Maryland	5	3	2	–
Massachusetts	10	1	2	–
Michigan	11	7	2	–
Minnesota	6	2	1	1
Mississippi	5	–	–	2
Missouri	6	3	–	2
Montana	1	1	1	1
Nebraska	1	2	2	–
Nevada	1	1	2	–
New Hampshire	1	1	–	2
New Jersey	8	6	2	–
New Mexico	1	2	1	1
New York	21	13	1	1
North Carolina	7	4	1	1
North Dakota	1	–	2	–
Ohio	11	10	2	–
Oklahoma	4	2	1	1
Oregon	4	1	–	2
Pennsylvania	11	12	1	1
Rhode Island	1	1	1	1
South Carolina	4	2	1	1
South Dakota	1	–	1	1
Tennessee	6	3	2	–
Texas	19	8	1	1
Utah	2	1	–	2
Vermont	*		1	1
Virginia	6	4	1	1
Washington	5	3	1	1
West Virginia	4	–	2	–
Wisconsin	4	5	1	1
Wyoming	–	1	–	2

Democrats / Republicans

* Independent

Interpreting Charts This chart shows party strength in Congress. Which party has dominated Congress since 1969?

particular bills, but neither party tries to force its members to follow its caucus decisions, nor can it.[7]

The policy committee, composed of the party's top leadership, acts as an executive committee for the caucus.

In strict fact, that body is known as the policy committee in each party's structure in the Senate and in the Republicans' organization in the House. However, it is called the policy and steering committee by the Democrats in the lower chamber.

Committee Chairmen

The bulk of the work of Congress, especially in the House, is really done in committee. Thus, each **committee chairman**[8]—those members who head the standing committees in each chamber—also hold strategic posts. The chairman of each of these permanent committees is chosen from the majority party by the majority party caucus. Committee chairmen decide when their committees will meet, which bills they will take up, whether they will hold public hearings, and what witnesses the committee should call. When a committee's bill has been reported to the floor, the chairman usually manages the debate and tries to steer it to final passage.

You will read more about committees, and return to the role of their chairmen, in a moment. But first, you will read about the seniority rule.

[7]There are a number of informal groupings of members of Congress who meet to discuss matters of mutual interest. Some are partisan, others bipartisan, and several use the word *caucus* in their titles. These groups include the Congressional Black Caucus, the Democratic Study Group, the House Republican Study Committee, the Northeast-Midwest Congressional Coalition, the Pro-Life Caucus, and the Congressional Hispanic Caucus.

[8]The title *chairman*, rather than *chairperson*, is used advisedly. First, because this is the form used in both houses of Congress, both officially and informally; and second, no woman now chairs a standing committee in either house. Only three women have ever done so; the most recent, Leonor K. Sullivan (D., Mo.), chaired the House Merchant Marine and Fisheries Committee from 1973 until her retirement from the House in 1977.

Seniority Rule The seniority rule is, in fact, an unwritten custom. It dates from the late 1800s, and is still closely followed in both houses today. The **seniority rule** provides that the most important posts, in both the formal and the party organization in each chamber, will be held by its ranking members—those party members with the longest records of service in Congress.

The rule is applied most strictly to the choice of committee chairmen. The head of each committee is almost always that majority party member who has served the longest time on that committee.

Criticism of Seniority Rule Critics of the rule are many, and they do make a strong case. They insist that the seniority system ignores ability and discourages younger members. Critics

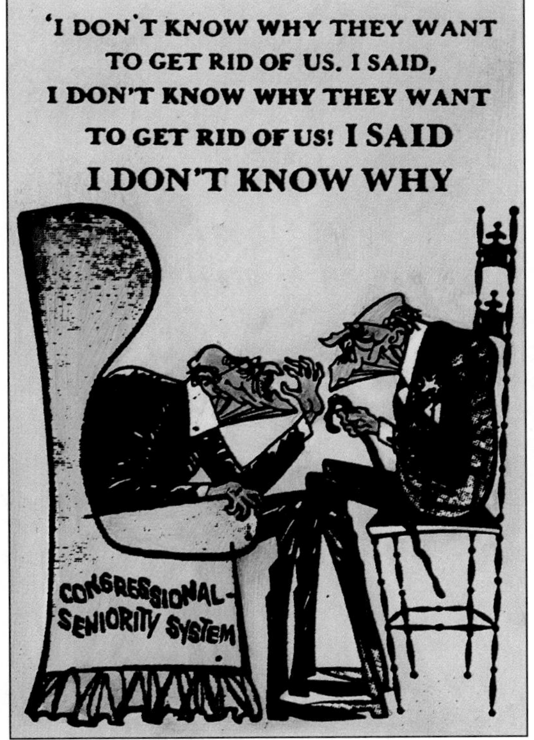
'I DON'T KNOW WHY THEY WANT
TO GET RID OF US. I SAID,
I DON'T KNOW WHY THEY WANT
TO GET RID OF US! I SAID
I DON'T KNOW WHY
CONGRESSIONAL-
SENIORITY SYSTEM

Interpreting Political Cartoons
How is the seniority rule, subject to much criticism because it ignores ability, viewed by this cartoonist?

Interpreting Political Cartoons Ask students to predict the average age of members of Congress *(mid-fifties)* and then point out that only eight percent of the 101st Congress were freshmen.

Caption Answer Negatively, implying that the age of senior committee members is a handicap.

Provide Guided Practice On the board write: *Speaker of the House, president of the Senate, president pro tempore, floor leaders, whip,* and *committee chairs.* Provide clues about each position and ask students to indicate what position the clue describes. Examples include: "assistant floor leaders," and "serves in the absence of the Vice President." Then ask volunteers to summarize the responsibilities for each leadership position and identify persons currently holding these positions.

Provide Independent Practice
TRF **Teacher's Resource File** You may wish to assign Section 1 Guided Reading and Review, Unit 3 File, p. 47, to help students master section objective content.

ACTIVITY: Cooperative Learning
Time: Two class periods **Activity:** Write a "matching" quiz for Chapter 12. **Grouping:** Groups of four to six students **Purpose:** Have students work together to compile a list of 25–30 terms and their definitions from the chapter. **Roles:** All group members will write definitions. Appoint one member of each group to act as recorder. **Outcome:** Have the recorder prepare a final quiz, listing all the group's terms and definitions in random order in a "matching" format. Have groups exchange quizzes, complete the matching, and correct each other's quizzes.

MONITOR COMPREHENSION

Answers to Section 1 Review
1. "Key Terms" are defined on the following pages:
a. Speaker of the House, p. 285
b. president *pro tempore,* p. 286
c. party caucus, p. 287
2. The House requires reorganization, but the Senate continues from its last term. **3.** (a) The Speaker of the House. (b) By the party caucus of the majority party. **4.** (a) To preside over the Senate. (b) The office is filled by the Vice President. **5.** (a) Both are chosen by their party caucuses. (b) To ensure that their party's goals are met; the whip assists the floor leader. **6.** (a) From the majority party by party caucus. (b) The chair usually goes to the longest serving committee member. **7.** The Speaker controls much of what goes on at the party and the legislative level; the president of the Senate has relatively little power, because the Senate has few rules to enforce.

Teacher's Resource File
See the Unit 3 File, p. 48, for the Section 1 Quiz.

CLOSURE

Remind students that within Congress, constitutional officers and party leadership play important roles. In the next section, students will learn how the committee system is organized and how it functions.

Assignment Assign Section 2, pp. 290–294, for the next class period.

also note that the rule means that a committee head often comes from a "safe" constituency—a State or district in which, election after election, one party regularly wins. With no play of fresh and conflicting forces in those places, critics claim, the chairman of a committee is often out of touch with current public opinion.

Defenders of the seniority rule argue that it ensures that a powerful and experienced member will head each committee, that the rule is easy to apply, and that it very nearly eliminates the possibility of fights within the party.

Opponents of the rule have gained some ground in recent years. Thus, the House Republican Conference (caucus) now picks several GOP members of House committees by secret ballot. House Democrats use secret ballots to choose a committee chairman whenever 20 percent of their caucus requests that procedure. The House Democrats did overcome the seniority rule and oust three long-tenured committee chairmen in 1975, another one in 1985, and two in 1991.

Whatever the arguments against the rule, there is little chance that it will be eliminated. Those members with the real power to abolish the seniority rule are the ones who benefit most from it.

Section 1 Review

1. Define: Speaker of the House, president *pro tempore*, party caucus
2. How does opening day in the House contrast with opening day in the Senate?
3. (a) Who presides over the House? (b) How is that officer chosen?
4. (a) What is the function of the president of the Senate? (b) How is that officer chosen?
5. (a) Who selects the floor leaders in each house? The whips? (b) What are their functions?
6. (a) How are committee chairmen chosen? (b) What is the seniority rule?

Critical Thinking

7. Making Comparisons (p. 19) Compare the roles and power of the party officials and presiding officers in both houses of Congress.

★

2 Committees in Congress

Find Out:

- Why is the committee system necessary?
- What are the different kinds of committees in Congress?
- What is the key role of the House Rules Committee?
- Why is the congressional investigative power important?

Key Terms:

standing committee, select committee, joint committee, conference committee

Do you know the phrase "a division of labor"? Roughly explained, it means dividing up the work to be done, assigning the several parts of the overall task to various members of the group.

The House and the Senate are both so large, and the business they each face is so great, that both chambers must rely on a division of labor. That is to say, much of the work that Congress does is in fact done by committees. Indeed, Representative Clem Miller (D., Calif.) once described Congress as "a collection of committees that comes together periodically to approve one another's actions."

As you will see, this section is devoted to the vital role committees play in the work of Congress.

Standing Committees

In 1789 the House and Senate each adopted the practice of naming a special committee to consider each bill as it was introduced. By 1794 there were more than 300 committees in each chamber. Each house then began to set up permanent groups, known as **standing committees**, to which all similar bills could be sent.

The number of these committees has varied over the years. The graphic on page 291 lists the current 22 standing committees in the

Reteach

Choose one leadership position in Congress, such as the president *pro tempore.* Write one sentence about this position on a piece of paper, e.g., *The president* pro tempore *is a presiding officer in the Senate.* Hand the paper to a student and ask them to add one sentence about the post. That student should then hand the paper to another student, who adds a sentence, and so on. When all the information has been accounted for, have one student read the paragraph aloud. You may wish to repeat this exercise for other leadership positions in Congress.

Enrichment

Using the description in the text, have students create imaginary journal entries for either a historical or a current Speaker of the House. Journal entries need only be two or three paragraphs long. Students might focus on the tension involved in being both presiding officer and party leader, or a decision to vote on a particularly important issue, etc. (Average)

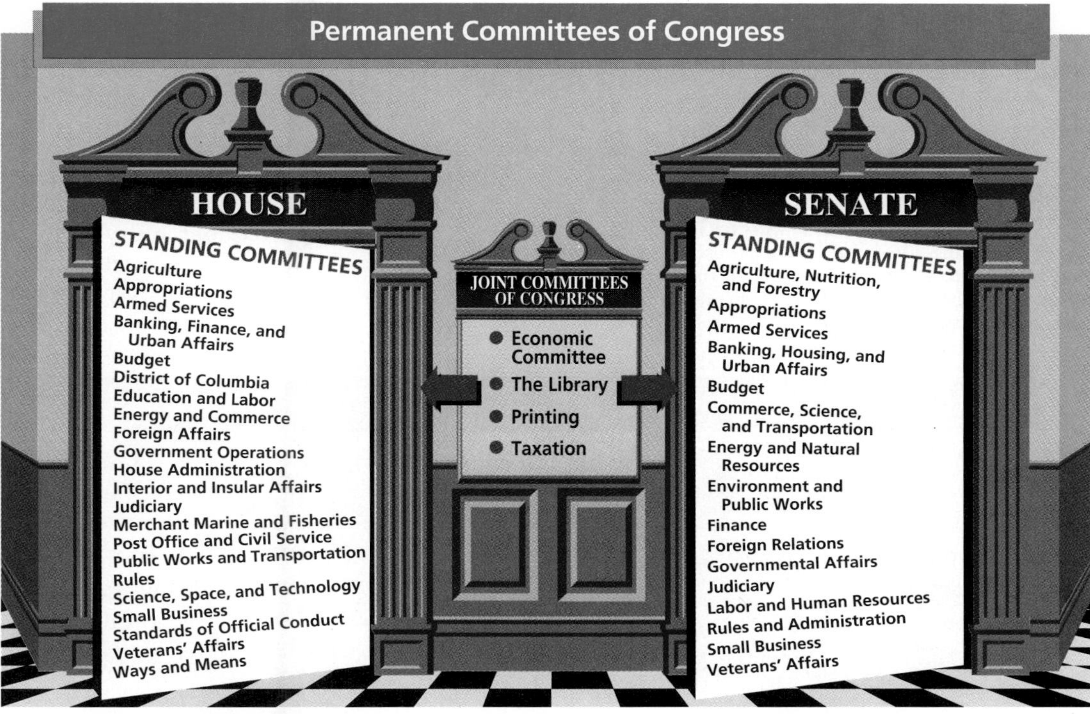

Permanent Committees of Congress
HOUSE
STANDING COMMITTEES
Agriculture
Appropriations
Armed Services
Banking, Finance, and Urban Affairs
Budget
District of Columbia
Education and Labor
Energy and Commerce
Foreign Affairs
Government Operations
House Administration
Interior and Insular Affairs
Judiciary
Merchant Marine and Fisheries
Post Office and Civil Service
Public Works and Transportation
Rules
Science, Space, and Technology
Small Business
Standards of Official Conduct
Veterans' Affairs
Ways and Means
JOINT COMMITTEES OF CONGRESS
Economic Committee
The Library
Printing
Taxation
SENATE
STANDING COMMITTEES
Agriculture, Nutrition, and Forestry
Appropriations
Armed Services
Banking, Housing, and Urban Affairs
Budget
Commerce, Science, and Transportation
Energy and Natural Resources
Environment and Public Works
Finance
Foreign Relations
Governmental Affairs
Judiciary
Labor and Human Resources
Rules and Administration
Small Business
Veterans' Affairs

Interpreting Graphics Most legislation is considered in standing committees, and party politics shape these committees. Why might a legislator favor participation on one committee over another?

House and 16 in the Senate. Each House committee has from 12 to 57 members, and each Senate committee has from 11 to 29. The rules of the House limit representatives to service on one major committee, and the Senate allows its members to serve on two.

You may also notice from the graphic that most of the standing committees handle bills dealing with particular policy matters, such as veterans' affairs or foreign relations. Three standing committees do not operate as subject-matter bodies, however: in the House the Rules Committee and the Committee on Standards of Official Conduct, and in the Senate the Committee on Rules and Administration.

When a bill is introduced in either house, the Speaker or the president of the Senate refers the measure to the appropriate standing committee. Thus, the Speaker sends all tax measures to the House Ways and Means Committee; in the Senate tax measures go to the Finance Committee. A bill dealing with the Army, Navy, Air Force, or Marines is sent to the Armed Services Committee in either chamber, and so on.

You have read how the chairman of each of the standing committees is chosen according to the seniority rule. Indeed, look at the tables on pages 292 and 293 and notice that most committee chairmen have served in Congress for at least 20 years. The seniority rule is also applied closely in each house when it elects the other members of each of its committees.[9]

[9]In form, the members of each standing committee are elected by a floor vote at the beginning of each term of Congress. In fact, each party draws up its own committee roster, and those party decisions are then ratified on the floor.

Section 2 Committees in Congress

Focus

Teacher's Resource File See the Unit 3 File, p. 49, for the Section 2 Outline.

Objectives

12.5 Explain why the committee system is necessary.
12.6 Identify the different kinds of committees in Congress.
12.7 Determine the key role of the House Rules Committee.
12.8 Analyze the importance of congressional investigative powers.

Bellringer Activity Tell students that the class has been asked to implement a school recycling policy. How would students go about implementing the plan? Would they act as an entire body or assign a team to carry out various steps?

State the Purpose In Section 2, students will learn why the committee system is necessary, the kinds of committees in Congress, and the importance of congressional investigative power.

Interpreting Graphics Have students list the committees that exist in one house of Congress but not the other. Are there any committees on their lists which they think should be permanent in both houses?

Caption Answer Committee preference would relate to the needs of the constituency; e.g., an Iowa representative would choose the agriculture committee.

Vocabulary

Point out to students the list of "Key Terms" on page 290. Discuss with students the concept of committees in relation to the work of Congress. Why is such division of labor necessary to accomplish the work of Congress?

Reading Strategy: Structured Overview/Graphic Organizer

Put the list of "Key Terms" on page 290 on one side of the board. On the other side of the board place the following committees: *Agriculture, Budget, Veterans' Affairs, Watergate, Iran-Contra,* and *Library of Congress.* Have students indicate into which category each of these would fit.

ABCNEWS INTERACTIVE

The following video segments may be used to highlight aspects of congressional committees.

POWERS OF THE CONGRESS GUIDEBOOK
Chapter 28: Congressional Committees, p. 104
Chapter 58: Committees of the House of Representatives, p. 64
Chapter 59: Committees of the Senate, p. 65

Interpreting Tables Ask students to find the three highest ranking House committee chairs in terms of seniority. *(Whitten, Brooks, and Fascell.)* How many years has each served in the House? *(51 years, 39 years, 38 years.)*

Caption Answer All were elected before 1980; all belong to the majority party—Democratic. California has five representatives serving as chairs, indicating that the state has a good deal of political clout.

Interpreting Tables Ask students whether, judging by the committee chairs, these Senate committees are geographically balanced. *(The committees seem fairly well balanced geographically.)*

The majority party always holds a majority of the seats on each committee.[10] The other party is well represented, however. Party membership on each committee is more or less in proportion to party strength in each house.

[10]The only exception is the House Committee on Standards of Official Conduct, with six Democrats and six Republicans. Often called the House Ethics Committee, it investigates allegations of misconduct by House members. In the Senate, a six-member bipartisan Select Committee on Ethics plays a similar role.

The House Rules Committee

The House Committee on Rules is sometimes called the "traffic cop" in the lower house.

So many measures are introduced in the House each term that some sort of screening is necessary. Most bills die in the committees to which they are referred. Still, several hundred bills are reported out every year. So, before most of these bills can reach the floor of the House, they must also clear the Rules Committee.

House Committee Chairmen, 1992

Position	Name	Age*	Year Elected to House	Party Affiliation and State
Agriculture	E (Kika) de la Garza	65	1964	D., Texas
Appropriations	Jamie L. Whitten	82	1941	D., Mississippi
Armed Services	Les Aspin	54	1970	D., Wisconsin
Banking, Finance and Urban Affairs	Henry B. Gonzalez	76	1961	D., Texas
Budget	Leon Panetta	54	1976	D., California
District of Columbia	Ronald V. Dellums	57	1970	D., California
Education and Labor	William D. Ford	65	1964	D., Michigan
Energy and Commerce	John D. Dingell	80	1955	D., Michigan
Foreign Affairs	Dante Fascell	75	1954	D., Florida
Government Operations	John Conyers, Jr.	63	1964	D., Michigan
House Administration	Charles Rose	58	1972	D., North Carolina
Interior and Insular Affairs	George Miller	47	1974	D., California
Judiciary	Jack Brooks	70	1953	D., Texas
Merchant Marine and Fisheries	Walter B. Jones	79	1966	D., North Carolina
Post Office and Civil Service	William Clay	61	1968	D., Missouri
Public Works and Transportation	Robert A. Roe	68	1969	D., New Jersey
Rules	Joe Moakley	65	1973	D., Massachusetts
Science, Space, and Technology	George E. Brown, Jr.	72	1972	D., California
Small Business	John J. LaFalce	53	1975	D., New York
Standards of Official Conduct	Julian C. Dixon	58	1979	D., California
Veterans' Affairs	Gillespie V. Montgomery	71	1967	D., Mississippi
Ways and Means	Dan Rostenkowski	64	1959	D., Illinois

*As of birthdate in 1992.
Sources: Congressional Directory, with additional data from the clerk of the House and *Almanac of American Politics*.

Interpreting Tables After examining the table, name two things the chairmen have in common and two things that can be learned about California from the table.

Senate Committee Chairmen, 1992

Position	Name	Age[a]	Year Elected to Senate[b]	Party Affiliation and State
Agriculture, Nutrition, and Forestry	Patrick J. Leahy	52	1974	D., Vermont
Appropriations	Robert C. Byrd	74	1958 (1953)	D., West Virginia
Armed Services	Sam Nunn	54	1972	D., Georgia
Banking, Housing, and Urban Affairs	Donald W. Riegle, Jr.	54	1976 (1967)	D., Michigan
Budget	James R. Sasser	56	1976	D., Tennessee
Commerce, Science, and Transportation	Ernest F. Hollings	70	1966	D., South Carolina
Energy and Natural Resources	J. Bennett Johnston	60	1972	D., Louisiana
Environment and Public Works	Quentin W. Burdick	84	1960	D., North Dakota
Finance	Lloyd Bentsen	71	1970	D., Texas
Foreign Relations	Claiborne Pell	74	1960	D., Rhode Island
Governmental Affairs	John Glenn	71	1974	D., Ohio
Judiciary	Joseph R. Biden, Jr.	48	1972	D., Delaware
Labor and Human Resources	Edward M. Kennedy	60	1962	D., Massachusetts
Rules and Administration	Wendell H. Ford	68	1974	D., Kentucky
Small Business	Dale Bumpers	67	1974	D., Arkansas
Veterans' Affairs	Alan Cranston	78	1968	D., California

a As of birthdate in 1992.
b Date in parentheses indicates first year of prior service in House of Representatives.
Source: Congressional Directory, with additional data from the secretary of the Senate.

Interpreting Tables Appropriations is one of the most powerful committees in the Senate. How can this be detected from examining the table?

This powerful 13-member committee manages the flow of bills for action by the full House. Normally, a bill cannot be brought to the floor unless it has been granted a rule—that is, scheduled for consideration—by the Rules Committee. That committee decides whether or not and under what conditions a bill will be taken up. To state it briefly, the Rules Committee can speed, delay, or even prevent House consideration of a measure.

In the Senate, where the process is not so closely regulated, the majority floor leader controls the appearance of bills on the floor.

Select Committees

At times, each house finds need for a **select committee**—a special group set up for some specific purpose and, most often, for a limited time. The Speaker of the House or the president of the Senate appoints the members of these special committees with the advice of the majority and minority leaders.

Most select committees are formed to investigate a current matter. The congressional power to investigate is an essential part of the lawmaking function. Congress must decide on the need for new laws and the adequacy of laws it has already passed. And it must exercise its oversight function to ensure that executive agencies are working according to the policies Congress has set by law. Also, Congress sometimes conducts an investigation in order to focus public attention on some topic.

Most congressional investigations are conducted by standing committees or by their subcommittees. Select committees sometimes perform

Caption Answer Because the chair, Robert C. Byrd, is the longest serving *(since 1958)* senator listed.

INSTRUCT

Discuss/Analyze Ask students which standing committee they would be interested in serving on and why. Are there any new standing committees students would like to see formed? If so, what are they? Students can refer to the graphic on page 291 as they discuss these issues.

Examine with students the difference between a select committee and a standing committee. Why might a select committee receive more publicity than, say, the House Administration Committee?

Provide Guided Practice Have students write three clues to various types of committees on a piece of paper. For example, a clue may be "This committee is the traffic cop in the House of Representatives." The answer would be "the House Rules Committee." Divide the class into groups of three or four students and have students take turns trying to stump the others. Students' clues should cover standing committees, select committees, and joint and conference committees.

Provide Independent Practice

TRF **Teacher's Resource File** You may wish to assign Section 2 Guided Reading and Review, Unit 3 File, p. 50, to help students master section objective content.

Enrichment

Have students clip newspaper and magazine articles that illustrate work being done by committees in Congress. Students should then answer the following questions: What are the committee's areas of concern? What type of work are they accomplishing? You may wish to have students write to one committee and request an example of a report they have published. (Easy)

Monitor Comprehension

Answers to Section 2 Review
1. "Key Terms" are defined on the following pages:
a. joint committee, p. 294
b. conference committee, p. 294
2. (a) The regular, permanent committees of each house that deal with bills introduced to Congress. (b) Each committee deals with a specific subject matter or area. **3.** Chairs and members are chosen by seniority rule. The majority party holds the majority of seats on each committee. **4.** It helps govern the process by which bills appear before the House for consideration. **5.** A special committee set up for a specific time and purpose. **6.** Congress must be able to investigate in order to make laws and to exercise its oversight function. **7.** Answers will vary. Students might note that most of the actual work and decision-making of Congress takes place in committees or in subcommittees.

Teacher's Resource File See the Unit 3 File, p. 51, for the Section 2 Quiz.

Closure

Remind students why much of the work of Congress is done by committees. (standing, select, joint, and conference) In the next section, students will learn how a bill becomes a law and how committees act in the legislative process.

Assignment Assign Section 3, pp. 296–302, for the next class period.

that work, however. Thus, over the past several years, each house has created a Select Committee on Aging. They hold hearings in Washington and around the country, issue committee reports, and otherwise try to bring greater public and governmental attention to those problems.

At times, a select committee becomes a spectacularly important body. This happened, for example, to the Senate's Select Committee on Presidential Campaign Activities, popularly known as the Senate Watergate Committee. As the Watergate scandal began to unfold in 1973, the Senate created that committee. Chaired by Senator Sam Ervin (D., N.C.), its job was to investigate "the extent, if any, to which illegal, improper, or unethical activities were engaged in by any persons . . . in the presidential election of 1972." Its sensational hearings fascinated the nation for months.

Two select panels commanded the public's attention through much of 1987: the Senate's Select Committee on Secret Military Assistance to Iran and the Nicaraguan Opposition, and the House Select Committee to Investigate Covert Arms Transactions with Iran. These twin committees, most often called the Iran-Contra Committees, worked closely with one another, probing the Reagan administration's conduct of two highly secret foreign policy initiatives. Their dramatic inquiries focused on the covert sale of arms to the Khomeini regime in Teheran and on clandestine efforts to give military aid to the Contra rebels fighting the Sandanista government in Nicaragua. The Iran initiative was intended, at least in part, as an arms-for-hostages maneuver, and it failed. The Contra aid effort was in part financed with money from the Iranian arms sales, and it was carried out despite an act of Congress prohibiting such aid by the United States.

Most congressional investigations are not nearly so visible, nor are they very often so historic. Their more usual shape can be seen when, for example, the House Committee on Agriculture looks at some problem in the farm price-support system.

Joint and Conference Committees

1.a A **joint committee** is one composed of members from both houses. You may recall seeing some of these committees listed on the chart on page 291. Some are select committees set up to serve some temporary purpose. Most are permanent groups that serve on a regular basis.

Some joint committees are investigative in nature and issue periodic reports to the House and Senate—for example, the Joint Economic Committee. Most joint committees have housekeeping duties, however—for example, the Joint Committee on Printing and the Joint Committee on the Library of Congress.

Because the standing committees of the two houses often needlessly duplicate one another's work, many have long urged that Congress make much greater use of the joint committee device.

Before a bill may be sent to the President, it must be passed in identical form by each house. Sometimes, the two houses pass differing versions of a measure, and the first house will not agree to the changes the other has made. When this hap-
1.b pens a **conference committee**—a temporary, joint body—is created to iron out the differences in the bill. Its job is to produce a compromise bill, one that both houses will accept. You will read more about the strategic role of conference committees later in this chapter.

Section 2 Review

1. Define: joint committee, conference committee
2. (a) What is a standing committee? (b) Why are such committees called "subject-matter" committees?
3. How are the members of the standing committees chosen?
4. What is the role of the Rules Committee?
5. What is a select committee?
6. For what reason is the investigative power so important to Congress?

Critical Thinking

7. Identifying Central Issues (p. 19) Woodrow Wilson once noted that "Congress in its committee rooms is Congress at work." Explain what you think is the meaning of this statement.

★

Reteach

Have students assume the role of a member of Congress. They have received a letter from a high school student in their constituency asking why the committee system is used, how it is organized, how it functions, and whether the senator or representative believes it is the best system possible. Have students write a letter from the member of Congress responding to these questions.

Debating Key Issues

Should Women Be Drafted?

Rostker v. *Goldberg*

During the 1970s, American women gradually began to participate more and more in the armed services. In 1972 women were allowed to become navy pilots. Four years later, they were accepted at the military service academies. By 1981, 8.4 percent of the nation's 2 million armed services personnel were women.

Although women were making clear gains, some people believed that the military discriminated against them. For example, women were still ineligible for certain benefits and were not part of the draft. Many men in the military believed that the exemption of women from registration violated their own 5th Amendment due process rights.

Three men originally filed *Rostker* v. *Goldberg* in 1971 to protest U.S. involvement in Vietnam. But when the military draft was suspended in 1973, the case was not pursued. Then, when the Soviet Union invaded Afghanistan in 1980, President Carter requested that Congress allocate funds to reinstate registration for the draft, recommending conscription for both men and women. Congress approved funds for a men-only draft registration program. At this time, the American Civil Liberties Union (ACLU), backed by many women's rights advocates, revived *Rostker* v. *Goldberg*.

The Federal District Court of Eastern Pennsylvania decided that the congressional draft act violated the 5th Amendment through its gender-based discrimination. The Federal Government appealed directly to the Supreme Court.

Review the following evidence and arguments presented to the U.S. Supreme Court.

Arguments for Rostker (Director of Selective Service)

1. Congress acted within its powers when it authorized the registration of men only.
2. Since women are excluded from combat by statute or military policy, it is not necessary to require them to register for the draft.
3. The decision not to require registration for women was based on military need and not on a traditional view of women's roles in society.

Arguments for Goldberg

1. There is no legal support for Congress's exclusion of, and bias against, women. It violates the 5th Amendment.
2. Large numbers of women already serve in the armed forces, demonstrating extensive expertise and commitment. If women are denied draft eligibility, the government will be losing a pool of skilled personnel that could be critical in an emergency.
3. Barring women from required registration perpetuates outdated ideas that women are weaker and less able than men.

Getting Involved

1. Identify the constitutional grounds upon which each side based its arguments.
2. Debate the opposing viewpoints presented in this case.
3. Predict how you think the Supreme Court ruled in this case and why. Then refer to the Supreme Court Glossary on page 764 to read about the decision. Discuss the impact of the Court's decision on the current and future state of gender equality in the United States.

TEACHING

Debating Key Issues

Rostker v. *Goldberg*:
Should Women Be Drafted?

Objective

Analyze and evaluate evidence.

Instruct

Before reading the feature, you may wish to ask students for their opinions on whether women should be drafted. After students read the feature, have them analyze both sides of the argument, evaluate the evidence, and try to predict the decision of the Court. Since this case was decided in 1981, ask students: If a similar case were to be brought before the Court today, might it be decided differently?

Supreme Court Decision

The Court did not support the challenge, observing that "the purpose of the registration is to develop a pool of potential combat troops . . ." and that ". . . Congress and the Executive have decided that women should not serve in combat." Since the matter of using women in combat had received considerable attention in Congress, with debates, hearings and committee actions, the Court agreed that Congress did not act unthinkingly.

TRF **Teacher's Resource File**
See the Supreme Court Case File for an activity that extends coverage of this case.

3 How a Bill Becomes a Law: The House

Find Out:

- What is the overall shape of the lawmaking process in both houses?
- What are the several different kinds of measures involved in that process?
- What are the many steps in the lawmaking process in the House of Representatives?

Key Terms:

bill, joint resolution, concurrent resolution, resolution, rider, discharge petition, subcommittee, Committee of the Whole, quorum

These numbers may surprise you: As many as 10,000 bills—proposed laws—are introduced in the House and Senate during a term of Congress. Fewer than 10 percent ever become law. Where do all those measures come from? Why are so few of them passed? By what process does Congress make law?

In this section, you will see in some detail how the legislative process works in the House. Then, because bills follow a quite similar route in the Senate, the major differences to be found in the upper chamber will be noted.

Creating and Introducing Bills

Most bills introduced in either house do *not* originate with members of Congress themselves. Instead, most bills—the important as well as the routine—are born somewhere in the executive branch. Business, labor, agriculture, and other pressure groups often draft measures as well. Some bills, or at least the ideas for them, come from private citizens who think "there ought to be a law . . ." And many are born in the standing committees of Congress.

According to the Constitution:

> "All bills for raising revenue shall originate in the House of Representatives, but the Senate may propose or concur with amendments as on other bills."[11]

Measures dealing with any other matter may be introduced in either chamber. Only members can introduce bills in the House, and they do so by dropping them into the "hopper"[12]—a box hanging on the edge of the clerk's desk.

[11] Article I, Section 7, Clause 1.

[12] Puerto Rico's resident commissioner and the delegates from the District of Columbia, Guam, the Virgin Islands, and American Samoa also may introduce measures in the House. Only a senator may introduce a measure in the upper house. He or she does so by addressing the chair.

101ST CONGRESS
1ST SESSION

H. R. 4

To amend the Clean Air Act to control hazardous air pollutants.

IN THE HOUSE OF REPRESENTATIVES

JANUARY 3, 1989

Mr. DINGELL introduced the following bill; which was referred to the Committee on Energy and Commerce

A BILL

To amend the Clean Air Act to control hazardous air pollutants.

Be it enacted by the Senate and House of Representatives of the United States of America in Congress assembled,

SECTION 1. SHORT TITLE

This Act may be cited as the "Clean Air Act Amend-

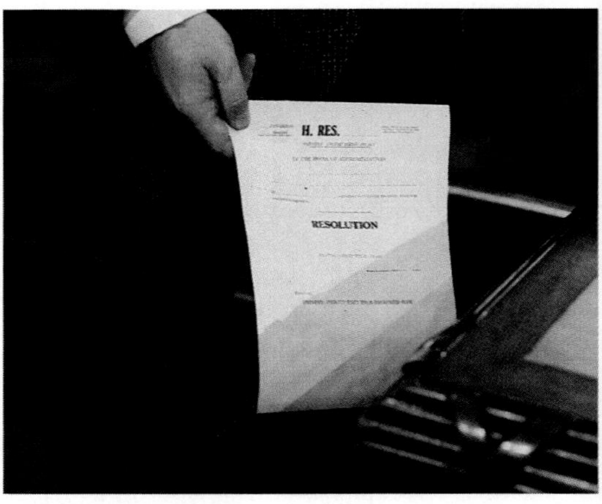

First Steps to Passage of a Bill The hopper is a large box hanging at the edge of the clerk's desk (right). Only a very small number—fewer than 10 percent—of all the bills dropped into the hopper ever become law.

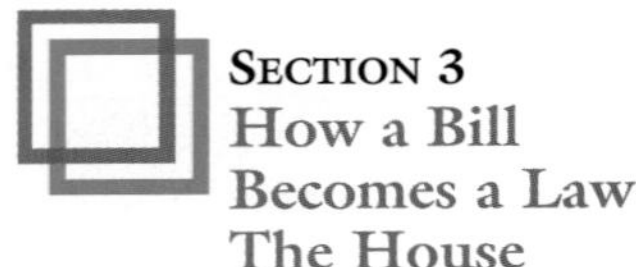

SECTION 3
How a Bill Becomes a Law: The House

FOCUS

Teacher's Resource File
See the Unit 3 File, p. 52, for the Section 3 Outline.

Objectives

12.8 Describe the lawmaking process in both houses of Congress.

12.9 Identify the kinds of measures involved in the lawmaking process.

12.10 Describe the steps in the lawmaking process in the House of Representatives.

Bellringer Activity Ask students to write down one school procedure that they would like to change, the reasons why, and their proposal for change. Then tell students that in order to see their proposal enacted they must win others over to their viewpoint, make public speeches supporting the proposal, and convince the principal that the proposal is necessary. Does this influence their decision about the worthiness of their proposal?

State the Purpose The text points out that fewer than 10 percent of all bills become law. In Section 3, students will learn about the laborious process of how a bill becomes a law in the House of Representatives.

Reading Strategy: Problem Solving

Invite students to generate answers to the following: "You are a senator from an area of the country where a large employer has closed a plant and announced that their overseas plants will take over production. You are concerned about this growing trend in a number of U.S. companies. How might you solve this problem? How will you go about promoting a solution to this problem in Congress?"

Vocabulary

Point out to students the list of "Key Terms" on page 296. Below are some additional words whose meanings may help students understand the section content.

—jurisdiction: power or authority
—concurrent: occurring at the same time
LEP

Types of Bills and Resolutions

The thousands of measures—bills and resolutions— Congress considers at each session take several forms.

Bills are proposed laws, or drafts of laws, 1.a
presented to the House or Senate for enactment. There are two types of bills: public bills and private bills.

Public bills are measures applying to the nation as a whole—for example, a tax measure, an amendment to the copyright laws, or an appropriation of funds for the Navy.

Private bills are those measures that apply to certain persons or places rather than to the nation generally. As an example: Congress recently passed an act to give an Idaho sheep rancher $85,000 for his losses resulting from attacks by grizzly bears, which had been moved from Yellowstone National Park onto nearby public lands on which he grazed his flock.

Joint resolutions are little different from 1.b
bills, and when passed have the force of law. Joint resolutions most often deal with unusual or temporary matters. For example, they may be used to appropriate money for the presidential inauguration ceremonies or correct an error in a statute already passed. Recall that joint resolutions also are used to propose constitutional amendments, and they have been used for territorial annexations.

Concurrent resolutions deal with matters 1.c
in which the House and Senate must act jointly. However, they do not have the force of law and do not require the President's signature. Concurrent resolutions are used most often by Congress to state a position on some matter—for example, in foreign affairs.

Resolutions deal with matters concerning 1.d
either house alone and are taken up only by that house. They are regularly used for such things as the adoption of a new rule of procedure or the amendment of some existing rule. Like concurrent resolutions, a resolution does not have the force of law and is not sent to the President for approval.

A bill or resolution usually deals with a single subject, but sometimes a rider dealing with an unrelated matter is included. A **rider** is a provi- 1.e
sion not likely to pass on its own merit that is attached to an important measure certain to pass. Its sponsors hope that it will "ride" through the legislative process on the strength of the other measure. Most riders are tacked onto appropriations measures—those in which Congress provides the money to pay for something. In fact, some money bills are hung with so many of them that they are called "Christmas trees." The opponents of those "decorations" and the President are almost always forced to accept them if they want the bill's major provisions to become law.

The First Reading

The clerk of the House numbers each bill as it is introduced. Thus, H.R. 3410 would be the 3,410th measure introduced in the House during the congressional term [13] The clerk also gives each bill a short title—a very brief summary of its principal contents.

Having received its number and short title, the bill is then entered in the House *Journal* and in the *Congressional Record* for the day [14]

With these actions the bill has received its first reading. Each bill that is finally passed in either house is given three readings along the legislative route. In the House, second reading comes during floor consideration if the measure gets that far. Third reading takes place just before the final vote on the measure. Each reading is usually by title only: "H.R. 3410, A bill to provide . . ." However, the more impor-

[13]Bills originating in the Senate receive the prefix *S.*—such as S. 210. Resolutions are similarly identified in each house in order of their introduction. Thus, H.J. Res. 12 would be the 12th joint resolution introduced in the House during the term, and, similarly in the Senate, S.J. Res. 19. Concurrent resolutions are identified as H. Con. Res. 16 or S. Con. Res. 4, and simple resolutions as H. Res. 198 or S. Res. 166.

[14]The *Journal* contains the minutes, the official record, of the daily proceedings in the House (Senate). The *Congressional Record* is a voluminous account of the daily proceedings (speeches, debates, other comments, votes, motions, etc.) in each house. The *Record* is not quite a word-for-word account, however. Members have five days in which to make changes in each temporary edition. They often insert speeches that were in fact never made, reconstruct "debates," and revise thoughtless or inaccurate remarks.

INSTRUCT

Discuss Examine with students the process of creating and introducing a bill in the House of Representatives. You may wish to use an imaginary example, such as a draft of a bill establishing a national test for all seniors to assess their knowledge of the U.S. political system. Introduce the bill by number and title. Discuss with students the referral of the bill to committee, identifying the likely sequence of events for such a bill. Have students draw a flowchart of the steps through which the bill would have to pass before becoming law. You may wish to direct students to page 305 and ask them to compare their flowchart with the one in the text, correcting any errors they may have made.

ABCNEWS INTERACTIVE

The following video segments may be used to highlight aspects of the legislative process.

POWERS OF THE CONGRESS GUIDEBOOK
Chapter 8: Making Laws, p. 11
Chapter 12: Method of Voting, p. 16

TRF **Teacher's Resource File**
See the Historical and Legal Documents file, p. 225, for material to support this section.

INSTRUCT

Model Explain to students that many bills are pigeonholed by the standing committees, but that they can be forced out by a discharge petition. Ask students to draw a cartoon that illustrates the concept of the discharge petition.

United States of America

Congressional Record

PROCEEDINGS AND DEBATES OF THE 102^d^ CONGRESS, FIRST SESSION

Vol. 137 WASHINGTON, TUESDAY, MAY 21, 1991 No. 77

House of Representatives

The House met at 10 a.m.

The Chaplain, Rev. James David Ford, D.D., offered the following prayer:

Our prayers cry out this day O gracious God, for those people who are confined without cause and who do not share the liberties we enjoy. We remember especially the hostages who have been separated from their lands

commercial motor vehicles, and for other purposes.

SALUTE TO THE FAIRNESS NETWORK

(Mr. MAZZOLI asked and was given permission to address the House for 1 minute and to revise and extend his remarks.)

Mr. MAZZOLI. Mr. Speaker, a year

been cut. If there were any doubts as to the utility of stealth technology, our recent experience in the Persian Gulf should make anyone a believer in stealth.

How important was stealth technology in the gulf war? The F-117 was able to penetrate and destroy the most formidable Iraqi defenses without loss or damage to a single aircraft. With

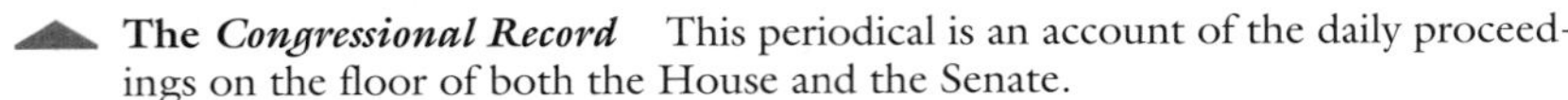

The *Congressional Record* This periodical is an account of the daily proceedings on the floor of both the House and the Senate.

tant or controversial bills are read in full and taken up line by line, section by section, at second reading.[15]

After first reading, the Speaker refers the bill to the appropriate standing committee—that is, the committee with jurisdiction over the bill's subject matter.

The Bill in Committee

The standing committees have been described as sieves, sifting out most bills and considering and reporting only those they judge to be worthwhile.

Most bills die in committee. They are pigeonholed[16]—simply put away, never to be acted upon—and most deserve that fate. At times, however, a committee pigeonholes a measure that a majority of the House wishes to consider. When that happens, the bill can be blasted out
1.f of the committee with a **discharge petition**. This device enables members to force a bill that has been in committee 30 days (7 in the Rules Committee) onto the floor for consideration.[17] But this maneuver is not often tried and is seldom successful.

Those bills that a committee, or at least its chairman, does wish to consider are discussed at times chosen by the chairman. Today, most committees do most of their work through their
1.g several **subcommittees**—divisions of existing committees formed to address specific issues. There are now some 140 of these committees within committees in the House, and nearly 90 in the Senate. Where an important or controversial bill is involved, a committee, or more often one of its subcommittees, holds public hearings on the measure. Interested persons,

[15]All bills introduced are immediately printed and distributed to the members. The three readings, an ancient parliamentary practice, are not very significant today. But they were quite important in the days when some members of Congress could not read.

[16]The term comes from the old-fashioned rolltop desks with pigeonholes into which papers were put and often soon forgotten.

[17]Any member may file a discharge motion. If that motion is signed by a majority (218) of House members, the committee has seven days to report the bill. If it does not, any member who signed the motion may, on the second and fourth Mondays of each month, move that the committee be discharged—relieved—of the bill. If the motion carries, the House considers the bill at once.

special interest groups, and government officials are invited to testify at these information-gathering sessions.[18] If necessary, a committee can force a witness to testify under threat of imprisonment.

Occasionally, a subcommittee will make a junket (trip) to locations affected by a measure. Thus, members of the National Parks and Public Lands Subcommittee of the House Committee on Interior and Insular Affairs may take a firsthand look at a number of national parks. Or, the Water and Power Subcommittee of the Senate Energy and Natural Resources Committee may visit the Pacific Northwest to gather information on a public power bill.

These junkets are made at public expense, and members of Congress are sometimes criticized for taking them. Some junkets deserve criticism. But an on-the-spot investigation often proves to be the best way a committee can inform itself.

When a subcommittee has completed its work on a bill, the measure goes to the full committee. That body may choose one of several courses of action. It may:

1. Report the bill favorably, with a "do pass" recommendation. It is then the chairman's job to steer the bill through debate on the floor.
2. Refuse to report the bill—that is, pigeonhole it. Again, this is the fate suffered by most measures in both houses.
3. Report the bill in amended form. Many bills are changed in committee, and several bills on the same subject may be combined into a single measure.
4. Report the bill with an unfavorable recommendation. This does not often happen. But sometimes a committee feels that the full House should have a chance to consider a bill or does not want to take the responsibility for killing it.

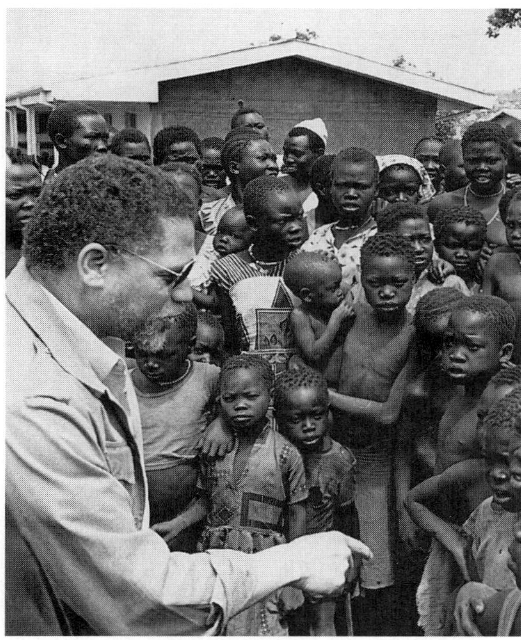

Fact-Finding Mission Mickey Leland (D., Texas), visited many famine-plagued areas in Africa as chairman of the House Select Committee on Hunger. Leland died in a plane crash in 1989.

5. Report a committee bill. This is an entirely new bill that the committee has substituted for one or several bills referred to it.

Rules and Calendars

Before it goes to the floor for consideration, a bill reported by a standing committee is placed on one of several calendars. A calendar is a schedule of the order in which bills will be taken up on the floor. There are five of these calendars in the House:

1. The Calendar of the Committee of the Whole House on the State of the Union, commonly known as the Union Calendar, for all bills having to do with revenues, appropriations, or government property.
2. The House Calendar for all other public bills.
3. The Calendar of the Committee of the Whole House, commonly called the Private Calendar, for all private bills.

[18] If necessary, a committee may subpoena witnesses. A subpoena is an order compelling one to appear. Failure to obey a subpoena may lead the House or Senate to pass a resolution citing the offender for contempt of Congress—a federal crime punishable by fine and/or imprisonment.

Discuss Explain to students that the standing committee has five actions available to it when a measure is reported from a subcommittee. Outline these five actions on the board, pointing out that pigeonholing is the most common action taken and that reporting the bill with an unfavorable recommendation is the least common action taken.

Spotlight on: Economics

Congress will spend over half a billion dollars on several agencies it established to perform investigations. The General Accounting Office, which monitors and audits how federal agencies spend the money Congress appropriates, is the largest of these agencies, with a budget of almost $490 million for 1992. Congress will spend an additional $61 million for the Congressional Research Service, an agency of the Library of Congress that conducts policy analysis, information gathering, and other administrative support for the members.

Provide Guided Practice Put the following list on the board: Create a bill, final vote on the bill, introduce a bill, the bill on the floor, first reading of the bill, the bill in committee. Work with students to place these steps in the correct sequence. Then ask students to place the following terms under the step in the process to which they most directly relate: ***discharge petition, subcommittees, quorum, debate,*** and ***engrossed.***

Provide Independent Practice

TRF **Teacher's Resource File** You may wish to assign Section 3 Guided Reading and Review, Unit 3 File, p. 53, to help students master section objective content.

VOICES *on Government*

On the Duties of a Congressman

Sam Rayburn, Speaker of the House for nearly 17 years, explains his views on the nation and its lawmakers.

"I have always dreamed of a country which I should believe this should and will be, and that is one in which the citizenship is an educated and patriotic people, not swayed by passion and prejudice, and a country that shall know no East, no West, no North, no South, but inhabited by a people liberty loving, patriotic, happy and prosperous, with its lawmakers having no other purpose than to write such just laws as shall in the years to come be of service to human kind yet unborn."

4. The Consent Calendar for all bills from the Union or House Calendar taken out of order by unanimous consent of the House of Representatives. These are most often minor bills to which there is no opposition.
5. The Discharge Calendar for petitions to discharge bills from committee.

Under the rules of the House, bills are taken from each of these calendars for consideration on a regularly scheduled basis. For example, bills from the Consent Calendar are considered on the first and third Mondays of each month. Measures relating to the District of Columbia are to be taken up on the second and fourth Mondays, and private bills every Friday. On "Calendar Wednesdays" the various committee chairmen may each call up one bill that has cleared their committees.

None of these arrangements is followed too closely, however. What often happens is even more complicated. First, remember that the Rules Committee plays a critical role in the legislative process of the House. It must grant a rule before most billls can in fact reach the floor. That is, before most measures can be taken from a calendar, the Rules Committee must approve that step and set a time for its appearance on the floor.

By not granting a rule for a bill, the Rules Committee can effectively kill it. Or, when the Rules Committee does grant a rule, it may be a special rule—one setting conditions under which the measure will be considered by the members of the House. A special rule regularly sets a time limit on floor debate. It may even prohibit amendments to certain or even to any of the bill's provisions.

Then, too, certain bills are privileged—that is, they may be called up at almost any time, ahead of any other business before the House. The most highly privileged measures include major appropriations (spending) and general revenue (tax) bills, conference committee reports, and special rules from the Rules Committee.

On certain days, usually the first and third Mondays and Tuesdays, the House may suspend its rules. A motion to that effect must be approved by a two-thirds vote of the members present. When that happens, as it sometimes does, the House moves so far away from its established operating procedures that a measure can go through all the many steps necessary to enactment in a single day.

All of these—the calendars, the role of the Rules Committee, and the other complex procedures—have developed over time and for several reasons. In major part, they have developed because of the large size of the House and the sheer number and variety of bills its members introduce. In their own ways, the calendars, rules, and other complex procedures have developed to help members of the House manage their heavy workload. Without such help, no one member could possibly know the contents, let alone the merits, of every bill on which he or she has to vote.

Enrichment

Have students use newspapers and magazines to identify key issues that face the current Congress. Then have students write letters to representatives asking them their opinion on the issues and how they intend to vote. Students should create a bulletin board display identifying the bills likely to be considered and including the responses they get from representatives. (Average)

The Bill on the Floor

If a bill finally reaches the floor, it receives its second reading in the House.

Many bills the House passes are minor ones, with little or no opposition. Most minor bills are called from the Consent Calendar, get their second reading by title only, and are quickly disposed of.

Nearly all the more important measures are dealt with in a much different manner, however. They are considered in the Committee of the Whole, an old parliamentary device for speeding business on the floor.

The **Committee of the Whole** is the House sitting not as itself but as one large committee of itself. Its rules are much less strict than the rules of the House, and floor action moves along at a faster pace. For example, a **quorum**—majority[1.h] of the full membership, 218—must be present in order for the House to do business. However, only 100 members need be present in the Committee of the Whole.

When the House resolves itself into the Committee of the Whole, the Speaker steps down because the full House of Representatives is no longer in session. Another member presides.

General debate begins, and the bill receives its second reading, section by section. As each section is read, amendments may be offered. Under the five-minute rule supporters and opponents of each amendment have just that long to make their cases. Votes are taken on each section and its amendment as the reading proceeds.

When the bill has been gone through—and many run to dozens and sometimes hundreds of pages—the Committee of the Whole has completed its work. It then rises—that is, dissolves itself. The House is now back in session. The Speaker resumes the chair, and the House formally adopts the committee's work.

Debate Its large size has long since forced the House to impose severe limits on floor debate. A rule first adopted in 1841 forbids any member from holding the floor for more than one hour without unanimous consent. Since 1880 the Speaker has had the power to force any member who strays from the subject at hand to give up the floor.

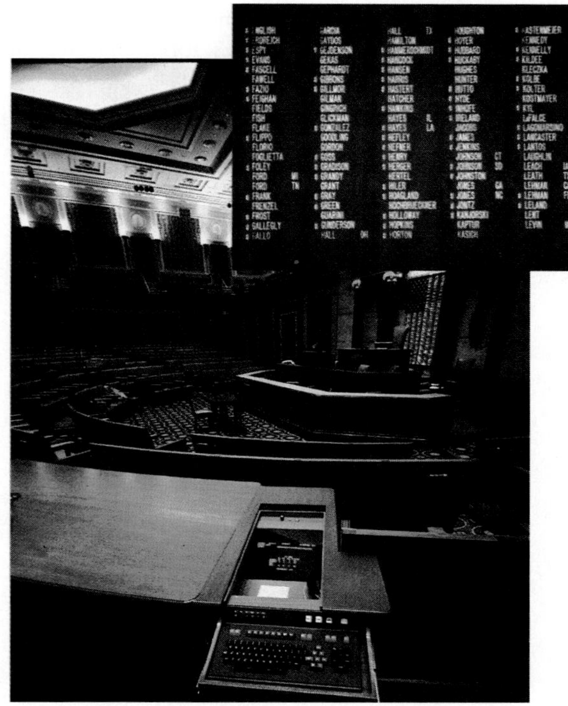

Recording House Votes A computerized voting system saves a large amount of time in each session. Progress of the bill on the floor is monitored on a summary board (top).

The majority and minority floor leaders generally decide in advance how they will split the time to be spent on a bill. But at any time, any member may "move the previous question." That is, any member may demand a vote on the issue before the House. If that motion passes, only 40 minutes of further debate are allowed before a vote is taken. This device is the only motion that can be used in the House to close (end) debate, but it can be a very effective one.

Voting A bill may be the subject of several votes on the floor. If amendments are offered, as they frequently are, members must vote on each of them. Then, too, a number of procedural motions may be offered—for example, one to table the bill (lay it aside), another for the previous question, and so on. The members must vote on each of these motions. These several other votes can be a better guide to a bill's

---

TRF **Teacher's Resource File**
See the Simulations and Debates file, pp. 18–25, for material to support this section.

SPOTLIGHT ON: Behind the Scenes
In their book *Congress and Its Members,* Roger Davidson and Walter Oleszek point out the following factors among those influencing members of Congress as they vote on particular bills: member's policy and philosophical convictions; member's perception of the State's or district's needs; constituent opinion; committee leaders; other members of Congress; congressional staff members; interest groups; ideological or ethnic caucuses; President's position; party leaders; political action committees; congressional research; and national editorial and public opinion

Monitor Comprehension

Answers to Section 3 Review
1. "Key Terms" are defined on the following pages:
a. bill, p. 297
b. joint resolution, p. 297
c. concurrent resolution, p. 297
d. resolution, p. 297
e. rider, p. 297
f. discharge petition, p. 298
g. subcommittee, p. 298
h. quorum, p. 301
2. The executive branch, pressure groups, private citizens, and standing committees. **3.** (a) Only members. (b) Senators. **4.** To allow the public to offer information about important matters. **5.** Report the bill favorably or unfavorably; pigeonhole it; report it in amended form; create an entirely new bill based on the old one. **6.** The entire House sitting as a committee of itself. **7.** Governs the "traffic" on the floor of the House; sets the time for the bill's appearance and governs the debate of the bill. **8.** The volume of bills would likely overwhelm the Congress.

Teacher's Resource File See the Unit 3 File, p. 54, for the Section 3 Quiz.

Closure

Remind students that most bills proposed in Congress never become laws. In the next section, students will learn about the lawmaking process in the Senate.

Assignment Assign Section 4, pp. 303–307, for the next class period.

friends and foes than is the final vote itself. Sometimes, a member votes for a bill that is now certain to pass, even though he or she supported amendments to it that would have scuttled the measure.

The House uses four different methods for the taking of floor votes:

1. Voice votes are the most common. The Speaker calls for the "ayes" and then the "noes," the members answer in chorus, and the Speaker announces the result.
2. If any member thinks the Speaker has erred in judging a voice vote, he or she may demand a standing vote, also known as a division of the House. All in favor, and then all opposed, stand and are counted by the clerk.
3. One-fifth of a quorum (44 members in the House or 20 in the Committee of the Whole) can demand a teller vote. When this procedure is used, the Speaker names two tellers, one from each party. The members pass between them and are counted, for and against. Teller votes are rare today. The practice has been replaced by electronic voting; see below.
4. A roll-call vote, also known as a record vote, may be demanded by one-fifth of the members present.[19]

In 1973, the House installed a computerized voting system for all quorum calls and record votes to replace the roll call by the clerk. Members now vote at any of the 48 stations on the floor by inserting a personalized plastic card in a box and then pushing one of three buttons—"Yea," "Nay," or "Present."[20] A large master board above the Speaker's chair shows instantly how each member has voted. The House rules allow the members 15 minutes to answer quorum calls or cast record votes. Voting ends when the Speaker pushes a button to lock the electronic system, producing a permanent record of the vote at the same time. Under the former roll-call process, it took the clerk up to 45 minutes to call each member's name and record his or her vote. Before 1973, roll calls took up about three months of House floor time each session.

Voting procedures are much the same in the Senate. The upper house uses voice, standing, and roll-call votes, but does not take teller votes or use an electronic voting process. Only six or seven minutes are needed for a roll-call vote in the upper chamber.

Final Steps

Once a bill has been approved at second reading, it is engrossed—that is, printed in its final form. Then it is read a third time, by title, and a final vote is taken. If the bill is approved at third reading, it is signed by the Speaker. A page—a legislative aide—then carries it to the Senate and places it on the Senate president's desk.

Section 3 Review

1. Define: bill, joint resolution, concurrent resolution, resolution, rider, discharge petition, subcommittee, quorum
2. From what main sources do drafts of bills originate?
3. (a) Who may introduce a bill in the House? (b) In the Senate?
4. What is the purpose of public subcommittee hearings?
5. What options does a full committee have when acting on a bill?
6. What is the Committee of the Whole?
7. What is the role of the Rules Committee?

Critical Thinking

8. Predicting Consequences (p. 19) What might happen if the House were required to consider each one of the bills introduced by its members?

★

[19]The Constitution (Article I, Section 7, Clause 2) requires a record vote on the question of overriding a presidential veto. No record votes are taken in the Committee of the Whole.

[20]The "Present" button is most often used for a quorum call—a check to make sure that a quorum of the members is in fact present. Otherwise, it is used when a member does not wish to vote on a question but still wants to be recorded as present. A "present" vote is not allowed on some questions—for example, a vote to override a veto.

Reteach

Choose the part of the lawmaking process that seems to cause the most difficulty in understanding for students. Then have the class act out that part of the process in small groups and then before the class.

4 The Bill in the Senate and the Final Stages

Find Out:

- How does the legislative process in the Senate differ from that in the House?
- Why are conference committees sometimes called the "third house"?
- What is a filibuster and how can cloture be imposed?
- What are the options open to the President after both houses have passed a bill?

Key Terms:

filibuster, cloture, veto, pocket veto

As you can see in the chart on page 305, the basic steps in the lawmaking process are much the same in the House and the Senate. There are notable differences, however. Given the many similarities, there is no need here to trace a bill step-by-step through the Senate. However, it is important to consider some of the unique characteristics of the Senate's treatment of bills. It is also important to look at what happens to bills once they have passed in each house.

Introducing the Bill in the Senate

Bills are introduced by senators, who are formally recognized for that purpose. A measure is then given a number and short title, read twice, and referred to committee, where bills are dealt with much as they are in the House.

All in all, the Senate's proceedings are less formal and its rules less strict than those of the much larger House. For example, the Senate has only one calendar for all bills reported out by its committees. Bills are called to the floor at the discretion of the majority floor leader.[21]

[21]The Senate does have another, nonlegislative calendar, the Executive Calendar, for treaties and appointments made by the President and awaiting Senate approval or, rarely, rejection. The majority leader controls that schedule, too.

Behind the Scenes Before the Senate debate on the 1991 budget bill, Republican leader Robert Dole (right) meets with Democratic leader George Mitchell to discuss their tally of expected votes.

The Senate's Rules for Debate

The major differences in House and Senate procedures involve debate. Floor debate is strictly limited in the House, but almost unrestrained in the Senate. Most senators are intensely proud of belonging to what has often been called "the greatest deliberative body in the world."

As a general matter, senators may speak on the floor for as long as they please. There is no rule that they speak only to the measure under consideration. Unlike the House, the Senate's rules do not allow the moving of the previous question.

The Senate's consideration of most bills is brought to a close by unanimous consent agreements. That is, discussion ends and the senators vote at a time previously agreed to by the majority and minority leaders. But if any senator

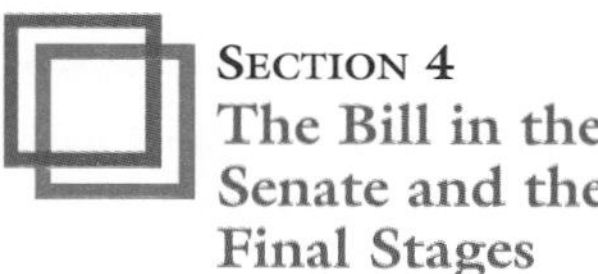

Section 4
The Bill in the Senate and the Final Stages

Focus

Teacher's Resource File See the Unit 3 File, p. 55, for the Section 4 Outline.

Objectives

12.11 Compare the lawmaking process in both houses.

12.12 Explain why conference committees are sometimes called the "third house."

12.13 Define filibuster and identify how cloture can be imposed.

12.14 Analyze the President's options after both houses have passed a bill.

Bellringer Activity Ask students if they have ever been in a dance marathon or other type of marathon. Ask one student who has participated in such an event to describe the event and its purpose. Students will probably say that the purpose is to reach a particular goal, e.g., to raise money. Explain that senators sometimes undertake a "talking marathon." Their goal is to prevent a bill from becoming law.

State the Purpose In Section 4, students will focus on the final stages of the lawmaking process, specifically on the process in the Senate. The Senate tactics of filibuster and cloture will be discussed, as well as the President's options after both houses have passed a bill.

Vocabulary

Point out "Key Terms" on page 303. Ask students to hypothesize as to what the term *pocket veto* might mean. LEP

Reading Strategy: Relating to Topic

Have students review the path of a bill through the House of Representatives. Then have students skim the section and write down the ways in which the path in the Senate differs from the path in the House of Representatives.

INSTRUCT

Discuss/Analyze Explore with students the differences in the legislative process in the Senate and the House. Explain how one of those differences, the use of the filibuster in the Senate, has made it difficult to pass legislation. Ask students if they can think of any other factors that might make the passage of a bill difficult. Remind students of the discussion of interest groups in Chapter 9 and explain that interest groups often block the passage of a bill.

Model The process of a bill becoming a law includes many possible delays or outright rejection. To illustrate, ask students to personify a bill. Students should choose a specific bill, either an imaginary one or one currently pending in the Senate, and write a brief narrative in which the bill describes its path to passage or rejection.

ABCNEWS INTERACTIVE

The following segments may be used to highlight aspects of lawmaking in the Senate.

POWERS OF THE CONGRESS GUIDEBOOK
Chapter 8: Making Laws, p. 11
Chapter 11: Enactment in the House and Senate, p. 14

The Filibuster Rule Senators rest on cots set up in the old Supreme Court Chamber during the filibuster that attempted to prevent passage of the Civil Rights Act of 1957.

objects—prevents unanimous consent—the device fails.[22]

The Senate's dedication to freedom of debate is almost unique among modern legislative bodies. That freedom is intended to encourage the fullest possible discussion of matters on the floor. The great latitude it allows, however, can be abused by the filibuster.

The Filibuster Essentially, a **filibuster** is an attempt to "talk a bill to death." It is a stalling tactic, a process in which a minority of senators seeks to delay or prevent Senate action on a measure. The filibusterers try to so monopolize the Senate floor and its time that the Senate must either drop the bill or change it in some manner acceptable to the minority. 1.a

Talk—and more talk—is the filibusterers' major weapon. But senators may also use time-killing motions, quorum calls, and other parliamentary maneuvers.

Among the many better known filibusterers, Senator Huey Long (D., La.) spoke for more than 15 hours in 1935. He stalled by reading from the Washington telephone directory and gave his colleagues his recipes for "pot-likker," corn bread, and turnip greens. In 1947, Glen Taylor (D., Idaho) used more than eight hours of floor time talking of his children, Wall Street, baptism, and fishing. The current filibuster record was set by Senator Strom Thurmond (R., S.C.). He held the floor for 24 hours and 18 minutes in an unsuccessful, one-person effort against what later became the Civil Rights Act of 1957.

No later efforts have come close to matching that one. Still, the practice is often used and to great effect in the Senate. Over the past century and more, well over 200 measures have been killed by filibusters. Just the *threat* of a filibuster alone has resulted in the Senate's failure to consider a number of bills and the amending of many more.

The Senate often tries to beat off a filibuster with lengthy, even day-and-night, sessions to wear down the participants. At times, some little-observed rules are quite strictly enforced. Among them is the requirement that senators stand—not sit, lean on their desks, or walk about—as they speak and that they not use "unparliamentary language." But these countermeasures seldom work.

[22]The Senate does have a "two-speech rule." Under it, no senator may speak more than twice on a given question on the same legislative day. By recessing—temporarily interrupting—rather than adjourning a day's session, the Senate can prolong a "legislative day" indefinitely. Thus, the two-speech rule does have some limiting effect on the amount of time the Senate spends on some matters on its agenda.

SPOTLIGHT ON: Political Talk

Senator Henry Cabot Lodge, one of the most powerful members of Congress in the 1910s and 1920s, traced the Senate's tradition of freedom of debate back to the founding of that body, where "twenty-two gentlemen . . . sat together in one not very large room and talked over matters with an informality and familiarity which have never entirely departed. . . . This small body of men, sitting in this way very private, . . . did not require anything very elaborate in the way of rules. Business was largely transacted by general assent and with much regard for the convenience of each Senator, habits which have survived unchanged to the present time."

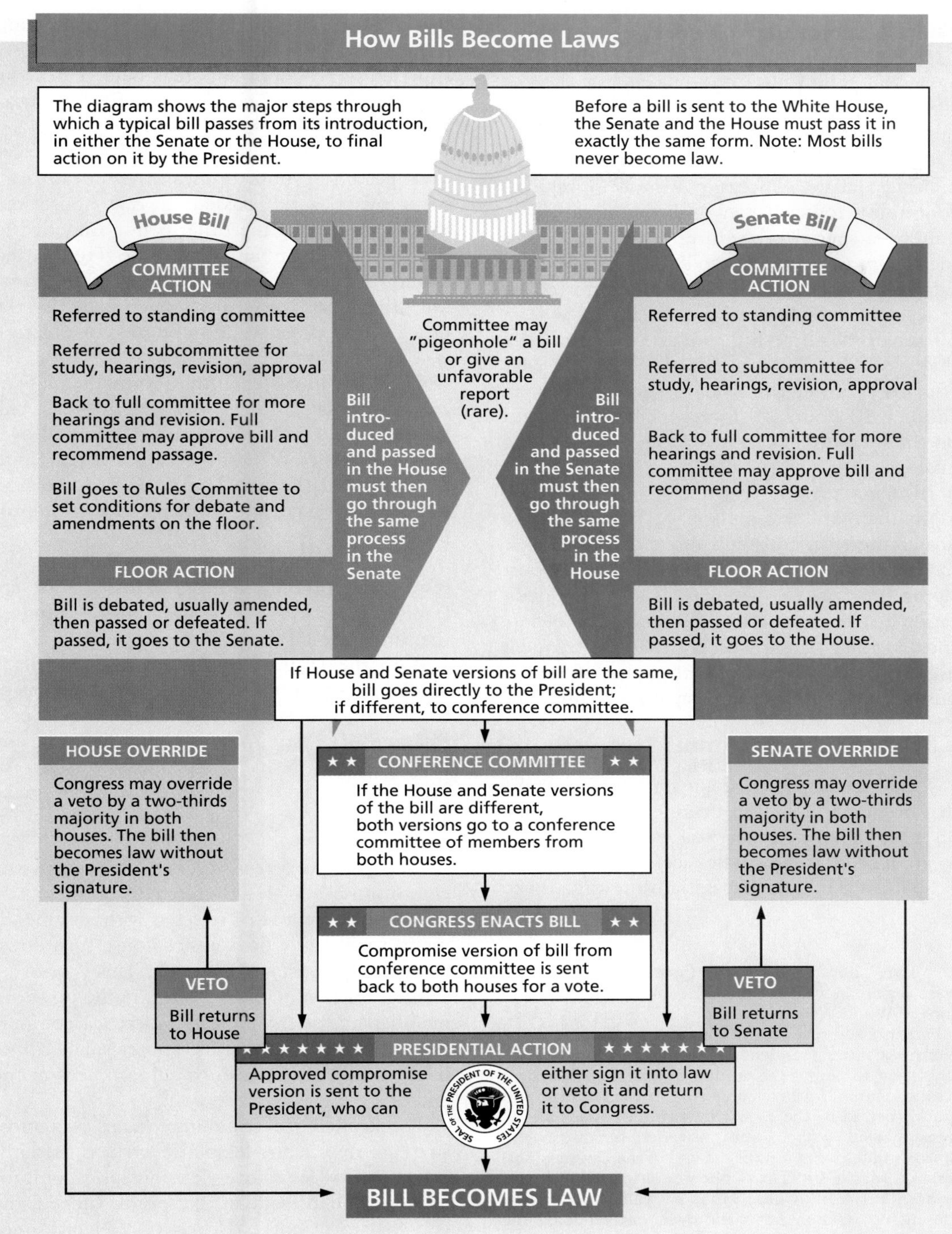
How Bills Become Laws
The diagram shows the major steps through which a typical bill passes from its introduction, in either the Senate or the House, to final action on it by the President.
Before a bill is sent to the White House, the Senate and the House must pass it in exactly the same form. Note: Most bills never become law.
House Bill
COMMITTEE ACTION
Referred to standing committee
Referred to subcommittee for study, hearings, revision, approval
Back to full committee for more hearings and revision. Full committee may approve bill and recommend passage.
Bill goes to Rules Committee to set conditions for debate and amendments on the floor.
FLOOR ACTION
Bill is debated, usually amended, then passed or defeated. If passed, it goes to the Senate.
Bill introduced and passed in the House must then go through the same process in the Senate
Committee may "pigeonhole" a bill or give an unfavorable report (rare).
Bill introduced and passed in the Senate must then go through the same process in the House
Senate Bill
COMMITTEE ACTION
Referred to standing committee
Referred to subcommittee for study, hearings, revision, approval
Back to full committee for more hearings and revision. Full committee may approve bill and recommend passage.
FLOOR ACTION
Bill is debated, usually amended, then passed or defeated. If passed, it goes to the House.
If House and Senate versions of bill are the same, bill goes directly to the President; if different, to conference committee.
HOUSE OVERRIDE
Congress may override a veto by a two-thirds majority in both houses. The bill then becomes law without the President's signature.
CONFERENCE COMMITTEE
If the House and Senate versions of the bill are different, both versions go to a conference committee of members from both houses.
SENATE OVERRIDE
Congress may override a veto by a two-thirds majority in both houses. The bill then becomes law without the President's signature.
CONGRESS ENACTS BILL
Compromise version of bill from conference committee is sent back to both houses for a vote.
VETO
Bill returns to House
VETO
Bill returns to Senate
PRESIDENTIAL ACTION
Approved compromise version is sent to the President, who can
either sign it into law or veto it and return it to Congress.
SEAL OF THE PRESIDENT OF THE UNITED STATES
BILL BECOMES LAW

Interpreting Charts Ask students: When must a bill go to conference committee? *(When both houses of Congress pass a different version of the same bill.)*

Provide Guided Practice On the board, list steps in the process of a bill becoming a law. The list could include "referred to standing committee," "unlimited debate on the floor," and "bill goes to the Rules committee." Have students indicate whether each action refers to the House, the Senate, or both.

Provide Independent Practice

TRF **Teacher's Resource File** You may wish to assign Section 4 Guided Reading and Review, Unit 3 File, p. 56, to help students master section objective content.

Enrichment

Have students research the historical use of the filibuster. Students should identify an example in which the filibuster was used, successfully or unsuccessfully, and prepare a news segment that might have aired on the evening news at the time that describes the filibuster. Students should present their news broadcast to the class. (Challenging)

Interpreting Graphs Using the figures provided in the graph, have students estimate the percentage of proposed bills that become laws. *(6.5%)*

Caption Answer With so many stages, opponents of a bill have numerous opportunities to kill the bill.

MONITOR COMPREHENSION

Answers to Section 4 Review
1. "Key Terms" are defined on the following pages:
- **a.** filibuster, p. 304
- **b.** cloture, p. 306
- **c.** veto, p. 307
- **d.** pocket veto, p. 307

2. The Senate has fewer rules because of its smaller size. **3.** (a) Cloture. (b) By a three-fifths vote of the Senate. **4.** When each house passes a different version of the same bill; it is usually necessary in order to come up with a form of the bill that is acceptable to all. **5.** Made up of key members; Congress usually is anxious to resolve its business at the end of its session, which is when most conference committee reports come out. **6.** Sign it into law; veto it; allow it to become law without signing it; reject it by a pocket veto. **7.** In each case, the President can achieve a certain effect by not taking action. This might provide him some political protection in some cases.

TRF **Teacher's Resource File** See the Unit 3 File, p. 57, for the Section 4 Quiz.

The Cloture Rule The Senate's real check on the filibuster is its Cloture Rule, Rule XXII in the Standing Rules of the Senate. It was first adopted in 1917, after one of the most notable of all filibusters in Senate history.[23]

Rule XXII provides for **cloture**—that is, 1.b
limiting debate. The rule is not in regular, continuing force; it can be brought into play only by a special procedure. A vote to invoke the rule must be taken two days after a petition calling for that action has been submitted by at least 16 members of the Senate. If at least 60 senators—three-fifths of the full Senate—then vote for the motion, the rule becomes effective. From that point, no more than another 30 hours of floor time may be spent on the measure. Then it *must* be brought to a final vote.

Invoking the rule is no easy matter. So far, more than 300 attempts have been made to invoke the rule, and only about one-third have succeeded. Many senators hesitate to support cloture motions for two reasons: (1) their dedication to the Senate's tradition of free debate and (2) their practical worry that the frequent use of cloture will undercut the value of the filibuster that they may some day want to use.

The Conference Committees

If you have ever watched a marathon, you know that no matter how well a runner covers the first 25 miles or so, he or she still has some distance to go in order to finish the race.

So it is for bills in the legislative process. Even those that survive the long route through committees and rules and the floor in both houses still face some important steps before they can finally become law. Some of those final steps can be very difficult ones.

Any measure enacted by Congress *must* have been passed by both houses in identical form. Most often, a bill passed by one house and then approved by the other is not amended in the second chamber. When the House and Senate do pass different versions of the same bill, the first house usually concurs in the other's amendments, and congressional action is completed.

There are times when the House or the Senate will not accept the other's version of a bill. When this happens, the measure is turned over to a conference committee—a temporary joint committee of the two houses. It seeks to iron out the differences and come up with a compromise bill.

The conferees, managers, are named by the respective presiding officers. Mostly, they are leading members of the standing committee that first handled the measure in each house.

Both the House and Senate rules restrict a conference committee to the consideration of those points in a bill on which the two houses disagree. The committee cannot include any new material in its compromise version. In practice, however, the conferees often make changes that were not even considered in either house.

Once the conferees agree, their report—the compromise bill—is submitted to both houses. It must be accepted or rejected without amendment. Only rarely does either house turn down a conference committee's work. This is not surprising, for two major reasons: (1) the powerful membership of the typical conference committee and (2) the fact that its report usually comes in the midst of the rush to adjournment at the end of a congressional session.

The conference committee stage is a most strategic step in the legislative process. A number of major legislative decisions and compromises are often made at that point. Indeed, the late Senator George Norris (R., Nebr.) once quite aptly described conference committees as "the third house of Congress."

[23]That filibuster lasted for three weeks, and took place less than two months before the United States entered World War I on April 6, 1917. Because German submarines had renewed their attacks on shipping in the North Atlantic, President Wilson asked Congress for legislation to permit the arming of American merchant vessels. The bill, widely supported in the country, was quickly passed by the House by a vote of 403–12. The measure died in the Senate, however, because twelve senators filibustered it until the end of the congressional term on March 4th. The public was outraged. President Wilson declared: "A little group of willful men, representing no opinion but their own, has rendered the great Government of the United States helpless and contemptible." The Cloture Rule was passed by the Senate at its next session, later that same year.

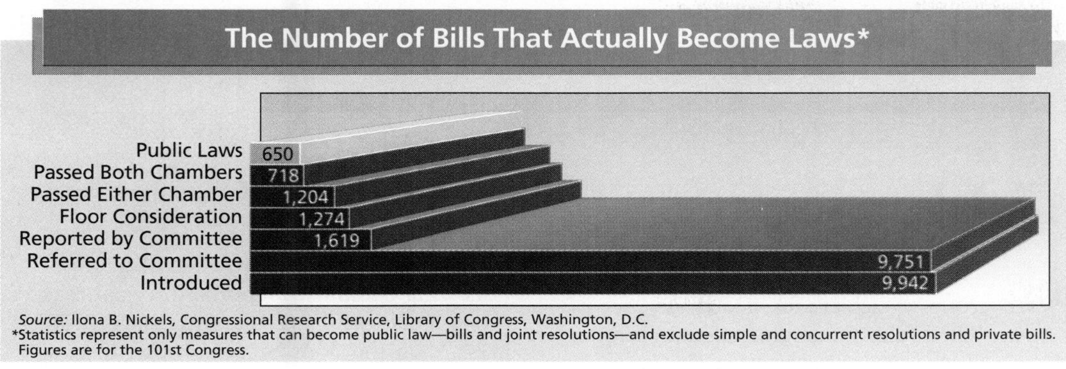

Interpreting Graphs The left-hand column simplifies the many stages through which a bill must pass before it becomes law. Why do so few bills actually become laws?

The President Acts

You have followed the long, difficult path of a bill moving through Congress. Still, a measure that survives the legislative process in both houses has yet one more major hurdle to face. The Constitution requires that

> "Every bill which shall have passed the House of Representatives and the Senate . . . [and] every order, resolution, or vote, to which the concurrence of the Senate and House of Representatives may be necessary (except on a question of adjournment) shall be presented to the President. . . ."[24]

The Constitution presents the President with four options at this point:

1. The President may sign the bill, and it then becomes law.
2. The President may **veto**—refuse to sign—the bill. The measure must then be returned to the house in which it originated, together with the President's objections (a veto message). Although it seldom does, Congress may then pass the bill over the President's veto, by a two-thirds vote of the members present in each house. 1.c
3. The President may allow the bill to become law without signing it—by not acting on it within 10 days, not counting Sundays, of receiving it.
4. The fourth option is a variation of the third called the **pocket veto**. If Congress adjourns its session within 10 days of submitting a bill to the President, and the President does not act, the measure dies. 1.d

You will read more about the President's veto power and his other legislative powers in Chapter 14.

[24]Article I, Section 7, Clauses 2 and 3.

Section 4 Review

1. **Define:** filibuster, cloture, veto, pocket veto
2. What is the major difference between floor debate in the Senate and House?
3. (a) What is the Senate's check on the filibuster? (b) How is this procedure invoked?
4. When is a conference committee formed and why is its job so important?
5. Why is a conference committee's report seldom rejected by either house?
6. What four options does the President have on receiving a measure passed by both houses of Congress?

Critical Thinking

7. **Drawing Conclusions** (p. 19) (a) If you were the President, under what circumstances might you use a pocket veto? (b) Why might you let a bill become law without signing it?

★

Closure

Remind students that when Congress passes a bill, the President may reject that bill by exercising the constitutional power to veto legislation. In the next chapter, students will learn about the veto power and other powers of the President.

Assignment Assign Section 1 of Chapter 13, pp. 315–321, for the next class period.

Activity: Teaching Heterogeneous Groups

Have students work in cooperative groups to develop a bill they want to be enacted into law. First, students within each group should arrive at a consensus as to the bill that they want to submit to the class for approval. The class then debates and votes on the bill; if it is approved, you can either sign it into law or veto it. If the law is vetoed, the class must obtain a two-thirds vote to override the veto. If the class does not approve the bill, it returns to the group to be amended for reconsideration by the class.

Reteach

Draw students' attention to the chart on page 305. Ask students to verbally indicate the various points in the process at which a bill can be killed.

TEACHING
Citizenship

How to Work in Groups

Objective

Work as a group to make decisions.

INSTRUCT

Tell students that they have been asked by the principal to choose a new school song. Record students' ideas of songs on the board. After they have read through the feature, have students hold a mock meeting, using the list of songs on the board and following the steps in the feature. Afterwards, ask students how they managed to choose a song and if the meeting was conducted in a democratic fashion.

Answers 1. So the opinions of the majority of people are heard and a decision is not made by a few people. **2.** Reminds members of the issues discussed at the last meeting and gives them a chance to correct any errors or omissions. **3.** Otherwise it would be too difficult to accomplish the many tasks a group faces, also each committee can devote more time to an issue if it isn't concerned with all the issues concerning the larger group. **4.** (a) The chance to speak in front of the group. (b) Rights of both majority and minority groups, equal rights for everyone, impartiality of the presiding officer. **5.** The meeting might adjourn before all business was discussed.

How to Work in Groups

When people form a group to work together—whether it is the local school committee or the United States Congress—an orderly procedure helps the group to achieve its goals. One set of established rules for conducting a meeting in an orderly manner has been in use for more than three centuries. This set of rules is called parliamentary procedure. *Robert's Rules of Order*, written in 1876 by Major Henry M. Robert, is the most popular guide to parliamentary procedure used in the United States. Use the following steps for parliamentary procedure when working in a group.

1. Call the meeting to order. The presiding officer, or chair, officially begins the meeting by calling the group to order. He or she does this when a quorum is present. A quorum is the agreed-upon minimum number of members that must be present in order to conduct business. In most cases, a simple majority constitutes a quorum. Why do you think it is necessary to require a quorum in order to discuss business?

2. Read and approve the minutes. The group's secretary keeps a record, called the minutes, of all business matters that the group discusses, the actions proposed, and the actions taken. After the secretary reads the minutes of the previous meeting, the chair asks whether any member wants to make any additions or corrections. Each addition or correction must be voted on. The chair then asks for a vote to approve the minutes. What purpose(s) does the keeping of minutes serve?

3. Hear committee reports. Much of the work of large groups, such as Congress, is carried out in committees. Committee reports are handled in much the same way as the reading of the minutes. Why do you think it is advantageous for groups to form committees to perform work?

4. Discuss unfinished and new business. Following committee reports, the chair asks if members wish to discuss unfinished business. Then the floor becomes open to new business. In general, the conduct of business is based on the following principles:

- The majority rules.
- The minority will be heard.
- All members have equal rights and responsibilities.
- Only one subject can be debated at a time.
- The presiding officer must remain objective on all matters.

(a) What is the meaning of "floor" as it pertains to parliamentary procedure?
(b) What basic democratic rights are ensured by parliamentary procedure?

5. Adjourn the meeting. When the group has no more business to discuss, the chair makes a motion to adjourn. If the motion is seconded, the whole group votes on the measure. What might happen if a member could move for a vote without having the motion seconded?

TRF **Teacher's Resource File**
See the Participatory Government Activities File for reference materials on public and private sources of information.

Chapter-in-Brief

Scan all headings, photographs, charts, and other visuals in the chapter before reading the section summaries below.

Section 1 Congress Organizes (pp. 283–290) Congress convenes each new term on January 3 of every odd-numbered year. Opening day in the House is filled with organizing tasks. A Speaker must be chosen, all members sworn in, rules adopted, and committee and other organization posts filled. The Senate's first day is a much simpler one, for the upper house is a continuous body.

Soon after both chambers are organized, the President delivers the State of the Union message to a joint session.

The Speaker of the House presides over the lower chamber. The Speaker is always a member of the majority party and is the dominant figure in the House. The Constitution makes the Vice President the president of the Senate. The Senate selects an alternate presiding officer, its president *pro tem*.

In both houses, the parties' organizations are headed by floor leaders who are assisted by whips; whips manage their party's programs on the floor. Each party's caucus is composed of the party's members in that chamber.

Section 2 Committees in Congress (pp. 290–294) Congress does much of its work in its committees. Standing committees are the permanent committees in both houses. The Senate has 16 standing committees and the House has 22. Most of them are subject-matter bodies and are dominated by chairpersons chosen under the seniority rule. Both houses may also have select committees, which are special, often temporary bodies. Joint committees, made up of members of both houses, are usually permanent bodies. Conference committees are temporary joint committees formed to iron out the differences in Senate- and House-passed measures.

Section 3 How a Bill Becomes a Law: The House (pp. 296–302) Only a member can introduce a bill in either house. Many important measures actually originate elsewhere, however—often in the executive branch. Bills are referred to standing committees, where most die. Those that survive usually receive their closest study in subcommittees.

Bills reported out of committee are placed on a calendar. Also, the Rules Committee must ordinarily approve bills before they can reach the floor. Strict rules govern floor consideration in the House of Representative. Measures that do win House approval are then sent to the Senate.

Section 4 The Bill in the Senate and the Final Stages (pp. 303–307) The basic steps in the lawmaking process are much the same in the House and Senate. The Senate's rules are much less strict than those of the House, however.

A key difference lies in debate. Floor debate is strictly limited in the House but largely unrestricted in the Senate. The Senate's dedication to free debate gives rise to the filibuster—the tactic of "talking a bill to death." Senators can end a filibuster by cloture, but senators are often reluctant to do so.

The two houses approve some measures in different form. Before a bill can become law, the differences must be reconciled. Conference committees perform this task. These committees try to forge compromises acceptable to both chambers.

After both houses approve a bill in identical form, it is sent to the President. The President can sign the bill, allow it to become law without his signature, veto it, or, in some cases, apply a pocket veto.

Teaching Suggestions for Chapter-in-Brief

Below are some of the possible uses for the Chapter-in-Brief:

To Preview the Chapter You may want to assign the Chapter-in-Brief page and the Section Outlines from the Teacher's Resource File before beginning Chapter 12 to introduce students to "Key Terms" and concepts in each section.

To Review the Chapter When students have completed Chapter 12, you might want to assign the Chapter-in-Brief as a tool for review, along with the Guided Reading and Reviews from the Teacher's Resource File.

To Omit the Chapter If you wish to skip Chapter 12, it may be helpful to assign the Chapter-in-Brief to students as a review before continuing to another chapter. You may also want to assign the Chapter 12 Test to assess student knowledge of the material. Then specific portions of Chapter 12 may be assigned to students needing reinforcement of "Key Terms" and concepts.

Teacher's Resource File See the Unit 3 File for the following materials:

- Section Outlines, pp. 46, 49, 52, 55.
- Guided Reading and Reviews, pp. 47, 50, 53, 56.
- Chapter 12 Test, pp. 62–64.

Additional Resources

Fiorino, Morris P. *Congress: Keystone of the Washington Establishment.* Yale University Press, 2nd ed., 1989.

Hardeman, D.B. and Donald C. Bacon. *Rayburn: A Biography.* Texas Monthly Press, 1987.

Industry Location and Public Policy. University of Tennessee Press, 1991.

The Legislative Branch. 16mm film. National Geographic, 1982. Color. 22 min.

McCubbins, Mathew D. and Terry Sullivan (eds.). *Congress: Structure and Policy.* Cambridge University Press, 1987.

Oleszek, Walter J. *Congressional Procedures and the Policy Process.* CQ Press, 3rd ed., 1988.

O'Neill, Thomas P., with William Novak. *Man of the House: The Life and Political Memoirs of Speaker Tip O'Neill.* Random House, 1987.

Power in Congress: Who Has It, How They Got It, How They Use It. Congressional Quarterly, 1987.

Smith, Steven S. Call to Order: *Floor Politics in the House and Senate.* Brookings, 1989.

The United States Congress. Film. EBEC, 1972. Color. 26 minutes.

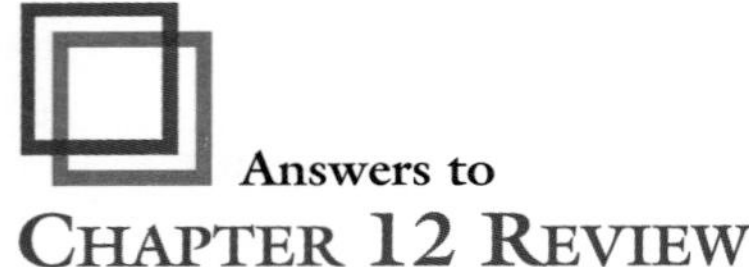

Answers to CHAPTER 12 REVIEW

Vocabulary and Key Terms

Matching
1. party caucus
2. discharge petition
3. quorum
4. conference committee
5. select committee

True or False
1. False—the correct term is *joint resolution.*
2. True.
3. False—the correct term is *standing committees.*
4. False—the correct term is *pocket veto.*
5. True.

Word Relationships
1. Resolution does not belong. Resolution does not relate to issues of selecting committee leaders or other posts. A resolution is a measure passed by Congress.
2. *Whip* does not belong. Items *a, c,* and *d* are techniques and measures in Congress to affect the handling of bills. A whip is a party officer whose job is to ensure party unity on votes.
3. *Committee chairman* does not belong. Items *a, b,* and *c* are all presiding officers in Congress. Committee chairs do not preside over Congress.
4. *Discharge petition* does not belong. Items *b, c,* and *d* are types of measures that Congress considers part of its legislative function. A discharge petition is a device by which a bill can be forced onto the floor.

Main Ideas

Section 1
1. All members of the House must be sworn in. Presiding officers and other officials are elected. The Senate has little to do on opening day since only one-third of its members are new. **2.** In the House, the Speaker of the House controls much of the activity and is also the majority party's party leader, and so holds much influence. The president of the Senate is not a senator; that function is largely ceremonial. **3.** In each house, the party officers seek to ensure party unity on important votes.

Section 2
4. Committees perform most of the actual legislative work of Congress, studying bills and performing investigations.
5. (a) and (b) Bills first go to a standing committee, which has responsibility for a specific area. Select committees are set up for a specific purpose and usually for a limited time. Joint committees include members of both houses and are often select committees. Conference committees meet to hammer out differences between versions of the same bill passed by each house. **6.** (a) In the House, the Rules Committee acts as a "traffic cop" for the handling of thousands of bills. (b) In the Senate, the majority floor leader performs this function.

Chapter Review

Vocabulary and Key Terms

Speaker of the House (p. 285)
president of the Senate (p. 286)
president *pro tempore* (p. 286)
floor leader (p. 286)
whip (p. 287)
party caucus (p. 287)
committee chairman (p. 289)
seniority rule (p. 289)
standing committee (p. 290)
select committee (p. 293)
joint committee (p. 294)
conference committee (p. 294)
bill (p. 297)
joint resolution (p. 297)
concurrent resolution (p. 297)
resolution (p. 297)
rider (p. 297)
discharge petition (p. 298)
subcommittee (p. 298)
Committee of the Whole (p. 301)
quorum (p. 301)
filibuster (p. 304)
cloture (p. 306)
veto (p. 307)
pocket veto (p. 307)

Matching: *Review the key terms in the list above. If you are not sure of a term's meaning, look up the term and review its meaning. Choose a term from the list above that best matches each description.*

1. selects the party's leaders in each house of Congress
2. can force a committee to bring a bill to the floor of the House or Senate
3. the minimum number of legislators needed to perform official business
4. where a bill goes that has passed each house in different versions
5. a legislative committee created for a limited time and specific purpose

True or False: *Determine whether each statement is true or false. If it is true, write "true." If it is false, change the underlined word or words to make the statement true.*

1. A rider is quite similar to a bill, has the force of law, and usually deals with unusual or temporary matters.
2. Floor leaders are party officers selected by their partisan colleagues.
3. When a bill comes before Congress, it is assigned to one of the subcommittees.
4. The President only applies a veto in situations where the Congress has adjourned.
5. It only requires 100 members to form the Committee of the Whole in the House of Representatives.

Word Relationships: *Three of the terms in each of the following sets of terms are related. Choose the term that does not belong and explain why it does not belong.*

1. (a) committee chairman (b) seniority rule (c) party caucus (d) resolution
2. (a) filibuster (b) whip (c) cloture (d) discharge petition
3. (a) Speaker of the House (b) president of the Senate (c) president *pro tempore* (d) committee chairman
4. (a) discharge petition (b) resolution (c) bill (d) concurrent resolution

Main Ideas

Section 1 (pp. 283–290)

1. (a) What happens at the opening sessions in the House and the Senate? (b) What makes those events different in the two houses?

310

2. What are the functions of the presiding officers in the House and Senate?
3. What are the roles of the party officers in the House and Senate?

Section 2 (pp. 290–294)

4. What is the role of the committee in the function of Congress?
5. (a) What are the different types of committees? (b) What are their functions?
6. (a) What is the role of the Rules Committee in the House? (b) How is that role filled in the Senate?

Section 3 (pp. 296–302)

7. What are the sources of the bills introduced into Congress?
8. What are the different types of bills?
9. What happens to a bill once it enters the House?

Section 4 (pp. 303–307)

10. For what reasons are the Senate's rules less strict than those of the House?
11. (a) What is the unique role of the filibuster in the legislative process of the Senate? (b) For what reason are senators often unwilling to end filibusters?
12. What role does the conference committee play in the legislative process?
13. After a bill has survived the House, Senate, and conference committee, what might happen to it?

Critical Thinking

1. **Identifying Assumptions** (p. 19) Consider what you have read about the seniority rule. What assumption about qualifications for leadership underlie the seniority rule?
2. **Predicting Consequences** (p. 19) What do you think would happen to the legislative process in the Senate if the Senate were to no longer allow unlimited debate?
3. **Formulating Questions** (p. 19) Write a list of questions that would enable you to find an answer to this question: Should it be easier or more difficult to override a presidential veto?

Getting Involved

1. **Writing Your Opinion** You have just been selected as the Speaker of the House. Write a letter to a friend in which you tell of your new job and your expectations for the future. Before you begin writing, list the powers and functions of the Speaker of the House. Review the legislative process in the House, where you will be presiding. Also review the other individuals who will take part in the leadership of the House. Begin your letter with an announcement of your selection. Then describe in order what you see as the most important aspects of your job. Also predict three challenges you might face as Speaker. Conclude your letter by stating what you hope to accomplish as Speaker. Proofread and revise to correct errors. Then draft a final copy.
2. **Class Debate** Hold a class debate on the following topic: *Resolved*, That the seniority rule should be abolished. Select one team to argue in favor of this statement and one to argue against it. The rest of the class should evaluate each team's presentation.
3. **Gathering Information** Using the Government Resources Handbook that begins on page 690, identify sources you could use to find the following information: (a) the subject of a bill recently debated in the Senate; (b) a House member's vote on a measure; (c) the members of a standing committee of Congress.

Section 3

7. Most come from the executive branch. Pressure groups, private citizens, and the committees of Congress also draft many measures. **8.** Bills may be public—dealing with the nation as a whole—or private—dealing with specific persons or places. **9.** When a bill enters the House, it is assigned to a committee. Then the bill goes to a subcommittee, where most of the work is performed. If a bill survives this process, it must be placed on a calender and pass through the Rules Committee. Then the bill is considered on the floor of the House.

Section 4

10. The Senate has fewer members, therefore there is less need for rules to govern its procedures. **11.** (a) The Senate has no rule limiting debate. Therefore, senators can hinder consideration of a bill by talking endlessly. Senators can only stop a filibuster with the Cloture Rule. (b) Senators are reluctant to use cloture because doing so weakens one of their most potent weapons. Senators also deeply cherish the Senate's tradition of free debate. **12.** When the two houses pass different versions of the same bill, the versions go to conference committee, which includes members of both houses. It resolves the differences between the two houses' versions. **13.** A President may sign a bill and make it law. Or, he may veto it. A President may also choose not to sign a bill; after ten days it becomes a law automatically. However, if Congress adjourns during those ten days, the President's failure to sign it effectively vetoes the bill. This is called the pocket veto.

Critical Thinking

1. The assumption that experience is a necessary qualification for leadership. **2.** Answers will vary, but students should realize that the tradition of debate is closely linked to freedom of speech. **3.** Answers will vary, but students should demonstrate an understanding of the American system of checks and balances, the lawmaking process, and demonstrate an ability to formulate effective questions.

Getting Involved

1–3. Answers and results will vary, but students should demonstrate an understanding of the concepts in this chapter.

Managing the Unit

You may wish to review the following materials before beginning the unit to help plan your instruction.

Each chapter ends with a Chapter-in-Brief with suggestions for previewing, reviewing, or omitting the chapter.

Unit 4 Outline

Pacing Charts,
pp. T28–T31

Unit 4

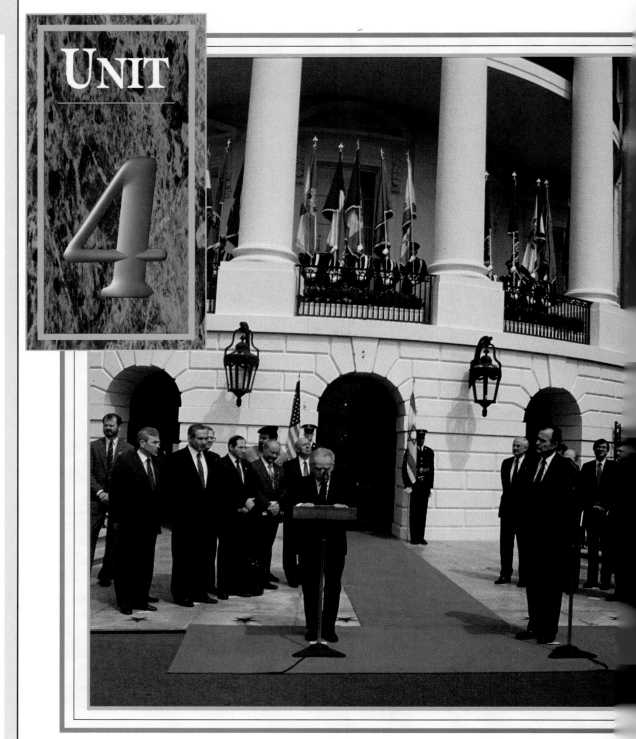

The President's Many Roles Hosting visits from heads of state, such as Israeli prime minister Yitzhak Shamir (left), is part of President Bush's official duties as head of the executive branch.

Skills and Features

The following skill lessons and features are included in this unit.

Skill Lessons

Critical Thinking: Testing Conclusions (p. 348)
Critical Thinking: Making Comparisons (p. 376)
Citizenship: How to File a Consumer Complaint (p. 400)
Citizenship: How to File a Tax Return (p. 420)
Critical Thinking: Identifying Alternatives (p. 454)

Debates/Case Studies

Debating Key Issues: Should the President's Executive Privilege Be Absolute? (*United States* v. *Nixon*) (p. 322)
Debating Key Issues: Should the Government Limit Individual Liberties During Wartime? (*Korematsu* v. *U.S.*) (p. 369)
What *You* Can Do: Realizing a Dream, (p. 394)
Debating Key Issues: Should the Government Subsidize Private School Education? (*Mueller* v. *Allen*) (p. 415)
What *You* Can Do: Helping Victims of Natural Disasters (p. 439)

The Executive Branch

If you were visiting Washington, D.C., in the mid-1800s and wished to meet the President of the United States, you could simply walk into the White House and shake Grover Cleveland's hand. At one o'clock each day, on his way to the private dining room, President Cleveland passed through the East Room and shook the hand of every person gathered there. This routine was typical for Presidents in an era when every American felt he or she had a right to walk into the White House to see firsthand that the President was doing his job. No longer is the President so accessible. Many layers of aides, advisers, assistants, and security guards form an impenetrable barrier between the nation's people and the chief executive. But, even without seeing for themselves, most Americans are confident that the President is doing his job. The President's job—and the Executive Branch the President heads—is the topic of the five chapters in this unit.

Did You Know That . . .

- In 1992, the President's annual salary was $200,000, plus $150,000 for expenses.
- Of the approximately $146 billion paid in salaries to federal workers in 1990, nearly half went to Department of Defense personnel, 25 percent went to Postal Service employees, and the remainder to all other federal employees.
- Revenue from alcoholic beverage and tobacco taxes made up 8 percent of all tax collections in 1970. In 1989 revenue from these sources totaled only 3 percent.

Unit Focus

Activate Prior Knowledge Ask students to think of the last photograph, television news story, or other image they have of the President. Then ask them to identify the event or purpose related to the President's appearance. Gradually bring students to realize that in every public appearance the President makes, he or she is fulfilling a presidential role. They will read about these roles in Unit 4.

Interpreting the Visual Point out the photo of President Bush meeting with the Israeli prime minister. Ask students to assess the importance of the President's role as chief diplomat in comparison to his or her other duties.

Did You Know That . . . Direct students to the items under "Did You Know That . . . ." Ask students what clues these items give them about the makeup of the executive branch.

Journal Writing Suggested topics for the fourth unit include a song or poem about past Presidents, a comment on a recent current event involving the President, or a personal statement about why the students would or would not want to be the President.

You may also want to utilize **CNN Video-link** to generate ideas for journal writing.

Bulletin Board Idea

Using the Poster Tell the class the following story: President Dwight Eisenhower once told the newly elected President Kennedy that he would rarely face any simple decisions. If a problem was simple, Eisenhower said, it would be solved long before it reached the presidential level. Have students examine the wall poster titled "The Executive Branch: Powers and Responsibilities" and find the cartoon that best illustrates this story. Point out that the responsibilities and powers of the executive branch of government are very far-reaching. After students have an opportunity to examine all the cartoons and quotes on the poster, ask them to name some of the responsibilities of the executive branch that are illustrated, as well as any others they may know about. Throughout the study of this unit, students should locate additional political cartoons that illustrate the workings of the executive branch, to display on the bulletin board.

Chapter 13 Resources

In the Teacher's Resource File
The following materials are found in the Teacher's Resource File box.

Instructional Support: Unit 4 File

For the Section
Outlines, pp. 2, 5, 8, 11, 14, 17
Guided Reading and Reviews, pp. 3, 6, 9, 12, 15, 18
Quizzes, pp. 4, 7, 10, 13, 16, 19

For the Chapter
Skill Application, p. 20
Case Study on Contemporary Issues, pp. 21–23
Chapter Test, pp. 24–26
Additional Test Questions, pp. 27–29

Enrichment Support Files

Supreme Court Cases, p. 10
Participatory Government Activities, pp. 4–19
Simulations and Debates, Reforming the Electoral College
Historical and Legal Documents, p. 34

Computer Test Bank and Assessment

Transparency Package, pp. 13, 38

Election Kit, pp. 7, 8, 9–10, 13, 30–31, 32–33, 34, 35–37, 39

Chapter 13 Focus

Introduce the Chapter Tell students that in this chapter they will learn about presidential qualifications and the path to becoming President. Read with students the Chapter Preview and Objectives.

Writing Activity Direct students' attention to "Describe." Have students list words that come to mind when they hear the word *President.* Ask students to associate an idea with each word; e.g., if the word was *depression*, the idea might be "New Deal."

Motivate for Learning Direct students' attention to "Predict." Have students suggest which government leader they think would be best suited to take over the responsibilities of the presidency, and why.

The Presidency

Chapter Preview

A barrage of six shots ripped through the air. Several men fell to the street as others used their bodies to shield them. Still others hurried to tackle the assailant—one young man with a gun. Among the victims of this March 30, 1981, shooting was President Ronald Reagan, who was shot in the chest. He underwent surgery that night and returned to the White House after twelve days.

Several of this country's Presidents have been shot at with guns. Four—including Abraham Lincoln and John Kennedy—have been killed while in office. Who takes over if a President dies in office or is too ill to perform his duties? As you read this chapter about the presidency and about the electoral process, you will find the answers to this question.

Before you read this chapter:

- **Describe** three issues that the President was involved with last week.
- **Predict** what might occur if both the President and Vice President became unable to fulfill their duties.

As you read, focus on the main objective for each section. Understand:

1. The interrelated roles of the presidency.
2. The process of presidential succession.
3. The qualifications, tenure, and compensation of the office.
4. The roles of primaries, caucuses, and conventions as parts of the nominating process.
5. How the national conventions operate.
6. The presidential campaign and the role of the electoral college.

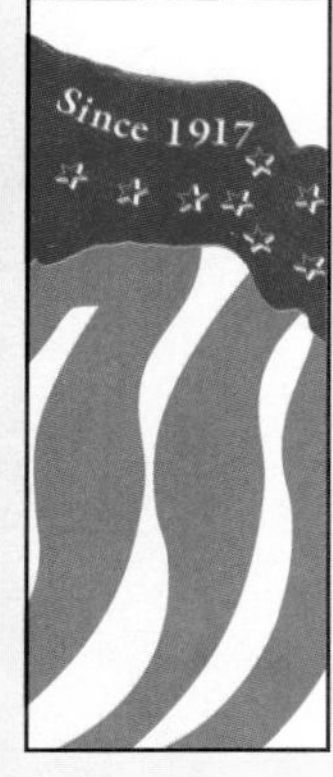

Magruder's American Government: *A Witness to Change* by William A. McClenaghan

Woodrow Wilson was in the White House when the first edition of *American Government* appeared in 1917. Through all the editions since then, this book has chronicled the growth of the presidential office to its position as, as John Kennedy described it, "the vital center of our whole scheme of government."

The next presidential term will begin on January 20. But when this book was first published, the President was inaugurated on the 4th of March every fourth year. The date for the beginning of each presidential term was changed by the 20th Amendment, which was added to the Constitution in 1933. As the 1937 edition of *American Government* reported, Franklin Roosevelt became the first Chief Executive to take the oath of office on the new date—he was inaugurated for the second time on January 20th, not March 4th, 1937.

Inaugural Pageantry George Bush becomes the nation's 41st President amidst the traditional splendor of the inaugural ceremonies.

1 The President's Job Description

Find Out:

- What are the many roles a President must play?
- In what ways are those roles interrelated?
- What are the constitutional guidelines for qualifications and terms?
- What is the President's compensation?

Key Terms:

chief of state, chief executive, chief administrator, chief diplomat, commander in chief, chief legislator, chief of party, chief citizen

Forty men have held the office of President of the United States; yet, George Bush is regularly identified as the 41st President. How can this fact be true? Do you know who was the youngest person ever to be the President? The oldest? Who held the presidency for the longest time? The shortest?

You will find the answers to these questions in this section, which lays out the overall shape of the presidential office.

The President's Roles

At any given time, of course, only one person is President of the United States. The office, with all of its powers and duties, belongs to that one individual. Whoever that person may be, he—and likely someday she[1]—must fill a number of different roles, and all of them at the same time. The President is, simultaneously, (1) chief of state, (2) chief executive, (3) chief administrator, (4) chief diplomat, (5) commander in chief, (6) chief legislator, (7) party chief, and (8) chief citizen.

[1]To this point all of the Presidents have been men, but nothing in the Constitution prevents the selection of a woman to that office.

SECTION 1
The President's Job Description

FOCUS

TRF **Teacher's Resource File** See the Unit 4 File, p. 2, for the Section 1 Outline.

Objectives

13.1 Describe the many roles a President must play.
13.2 Explain how the President's roles are interrelated.
13.3 Outline the guidelines for presidential qualifications and terms.
13.4 Quantify the compensation of the President.

Bellringer Activity Ask students to consider the many roles they are expected to fill, for example: son or daughter, student, brother or sister, team member, etc. Have students list as many roles for themselves as they can. Point out that students must play all of these roles simultaneously.

State the Purpose The office of President demands that many interrelated roles be filled simultaneously. In Section 1, students will learn about the roles a President plays, the guidelines that define the presidency, and the changes those laws have undergone.

ABCNEWS INTERACTIVE

The following video segments may be used to highlight aspects of presidential roles.

POWERS OF THE PRESIDENT GUIDEBOOK
Chapter 3: Constitution and the President, p. 4
Chapter 16: Constitutional Roles of the President, p. 22

Vocabulary

Point out the list of "Key Terms" on page 315. Tell students that these are terms for various presidential roles. Ask students to rank these terms in order of descending importance. After students read the section, you may wish to refer them back to their lists to see if they would still rank the items in the same order.

Reading Strategy: Relating to Topic

Tell students to imagine that they have been asked to serve on a national committee searching for the ideal presidential candidate. What factors would students consider in their search? Put the list of factors on the board and bring it to students' attention after they read the section. Would they add or delete any items?

INSTRUCT

Discuss/Analyze Remind students of their responses to the "Bellringer Activity." Explain that, in a similar way, the President is required to fill many roles. In addition to the roles a President fills in his or her personal life, he or she is expected to fill a wide array of roles in the official capacity as President.

Divide the class into groups of four or five students. Ask each group to look through their textbooks and locate photographs that illustrate the various roles of the President. For example, the opening photograph on page 312 is an illustration of the President as chief of state. Give students five minutes to look for photographs and then have each group present the photographs they found to the class.

The President in Action To be effective in his many roles, President Bush must maintain a close working relationship with Congress.

CHIEF OF STATE To begin with, the President is
1.a **chief of state**, the ceremonial head of the government of the United States, the symbol of all the people of the nation—in President William Howard Taft's words, "the personal embodiment and representative of their dignity and majesty."

In many countries, the chief of state reigns but does not rule. That is certainly true of the queens of England and of Denmark, the emperor of Japan, the kings of Norway and of Sweden, and the presidents of Italy and of Germany. It is most certainly not true of the President of the United States, who both reigns and rules.

CHIEF EXECUTIVE The President is the
1.b nation's **chief executive**, vested by the Constitution with "the executive power of the United States." As you will see, that power is immensely broad in both domestic and foreign affairs. Indeed, the presidency is often described as "the most powerful office in the world."

CHIEF ADMINISTRATOR The President is also
1.c the **chief administrator** of the Federal Government, heading one of the largest governmental machines the world has known. Today, the President directs an administration that employs nearly three million civilians and spends something on the order of $1.5 trillion a year.

CHIEF DIPLOMAT The President is also the
1.d nation's **chief diplomat**, the main architect of American foreign policy and the nation's chief spokesperson to the rest of the world. "I make foreign policy," President Harry Truman once said—and he did. What the President says and does is carefully followed in this country and abroad.

COMMANDER IN CHIEF In close concert with the President's role in foreign affairs, the Constitution also makes the President the **commander**
1.e **in chief** of the nation's armed forces. Nearly two million men and women in uniform and all the power in the nation's military arsenal are subject to the President's direct and immediate control.

CHIEF LEGISLATOR The President is also the
1.f nation's **chief legislator**, the main architect of its public policies. It is the President who sets the overall shape of the congressional agenda—initiating, suggesting, requesting, supporting, insisting, and demanding that Congress enact much of the major legislation that it does.

These six presidential roles all come directly from the Constitution. Yet they do not complete the list. The President must fill other vital roles.

CHIEF OF PARTY The President acts as the
1.g **chief of party**—the acknowledged leader of the political party that controls the executive branch. As you know, parties are not mentioned in the Constitution, yet they play a vital role in the function of American government. Thus, much of the real power and influence wielded by the President depends on the manner in which he or she plays this critical role.

CHIEF CITIZEN The office also automatically
1.h makes of its occupant the nation's **chief citizen.** The President is expected to be "the representative of all the people," the one to work for and represent the public interest against the many private interests. "The presidency," said Franklin Roosevelt, "is not merely an administrative

Activity: Cooperative Learning

Time: Two class periods **Activity:** Research and report on the roles of the President. **Grouping:** Groups of three to four students. **Purpose:** Assign the name of a former President of the United States to each group. Have students use outside resources to prepare a report on how that President fulfilled all of the roles mentioned in the text. Explain that the report is to include specific examples and should also note the roles in which the President excelled and those in which he was weak. **Roles:** Have students assign the following roles: manager, researcher(s), recorder, spokesperson. **Outcome:** Have each spokesperson present the group's report to the class. Invite the class to discuss each group's conclusions about this particular President.

office. That is the least of it. It is preeminently a place of moral leadership."

Interrelated Nature of Presidential Roles

Each of these presidential roles is played simultaneously and is inseparable from the others. None of them can be performed in isolation. The manner in which a President plays any one role can have a powerful effect on his or her ability to play the others.

As two illustrations, take the experiences of Presidents Lyndon Johnson and Richard Nixon. Each was a strong and a relatively effective President during his first years in office. But the agonizing and increasingly unpopular war in Vietnam persuaded Mr. Johnson not to run for reelection in 1968. In effect, the manner in which he acted as commander in chief during that conflict seriously damaged his effectiveness in the White House.

The many-sided, sordid Watergate scandal and the manner in which Nixon filled the roles of party leader and chief citizen so destroyed Nixon's presidency that he was forced to leave office in disgrace in 1974.

Radio Days Each President has reinterpreted his role. President Roosevelt's fireside chats not only gained support for his New Deal program, but also established a personal rapport with the public.

Formal Qualifications for the Presidency

The Constitution[2] says that the President must:

1. Be "a natural-born citizen." Under the doctrine of *jus sanguinis* (Chapter 21, Section 4), it is apparently possible for a person born abroad as a United States citizen to become President. Some dispute that view; and the real shape of this requirement cannot be known until someone born a citizen, but born abroad, does in fact become President.[3]
2. Be at least 35 years of age. As the table on the following page shows, John F. Kennedy, at 43, was the youngest person ever to be elected to the presidency. Theodore Roosevelt reached it by succession at age 42. Ronald Reagan, who was 69 when he was first elected in 1980, is the oldest man ever elected. And, when he completed his second term eight years later, he was the oldest person ever to hold the office. George Bush was 64 years old when he became President in 1989.
3. Have lived in the United States for at least 14 years.[4]

While these formal qualifications do have some importance, they are really not very difficult to meet. In fact, there are more than 100 million people in this country today who do so.

Clearly, there are other and much more telling informal qualifications for the presidency—as you will see shortly.

[2]Article II, Section 1, Clause 5.

[3]Martin Van Buren, who was born December 5, 1782, was the first President actually born in the United States. His seven predecessors were each born before the Revolution. But notice that the Constitution anticipated that situation with these words: "or a citizen of the United States at the time of the adoption of this Constitution."

[4]Given Herbert Hoover's election in 1928 and Dwight Eisenhower's in 1952, the 14-year requirement means any 14 years in a person's life. Both Hoover and Eisenhower spent several years before election outside the United States.

Discuss Review the three constitutional qualifications for President with students. Ask if students are surprised that the Constitution set forth so few qualifications for the office of President. Why do students think this is so? Ask students to think of people they know who meet these qualifications. Can they imagine any of these people as President? Based on their answers, bring students to the realization that the informal qualifications for the presidency are highly significant.

Activity: For Gifted Students

Theme: Leadership Review with students the eight roles filled by the President. Form small groups of students, and assign each a presidential role. Students should research quotations from Presidents which allude to that role; for example, Harry Truman's comment, "I make foreign policy." Each group's list can be displayed on a bulletin board.

Interpreting Tables: Multicultural Awareness Ask students what factors may account for the overwhelming tendency of Presidents to belong to a Christian faith and have British ancestry. Students' answers may include the fact that early colonial leaders were British. Discuss the part played by xenophobia, sexism, anti-semitism, and racism in keeping most other groups away from the presidency.

Caption Answer Answers will vary. Some students will identify this as a negative phenomenon, since the President does not accurately represent the American public. Others may think the religion, ancestry, and gender of the President are of no consequence as long as he or she strives to represent all the people.

Presidents of the United States

Name	Party	State[a]	Entered Office	Age on Taking Office	Religion
George Washington (1732-1799)	Federalist	Virginia	1789	57	Anglican
John Adams (1735-1826)	Federalist	Massachusetts	1797	61	Unitarian
Thomas Jefferson (1743-1826)	Dem-Rep[b]	Virginia	1801	57	———
James Madison (1751-1836)	Dem-Rep	Virginia	1809	57	Episcopal
James Monroe (1758-1831)	Dem-Rep	Virginia	1817	58	Episcopal
John Q. Adams (1767-1848)	Dem-Rep	Massachusetts	1767	57	Unitarian
Andrew Jackson (1767-1845)	Democrat	Tennessee (SC)	1829	61	Presbyterian
Martin Van Buren (1782-1862)	Democrat	New York	1837	54	Dutch Reformed
William H. Harrison (1773-1841)	Whig	Ohio (VA)	1841	68	Episcopal
John Tyler (1790-1862)	Democrat	Virginia	1841	51	Episcopal
James K. Polk (1795-1849)	Democrat	Tennessee (NC)	1845	49	Presbyterian
Zachary Taylor (1784-1850)	Whig	Louisiana (VA)	1849	64	Episcopal
Millard Fillmore (1800-1874)	Whig	New York	1850	50	Unitarian
Franklin Pierce (1804-1869)	Democrat	New Hampshire	1853	48	Episcopal
James Buchanan (1791-1868)	Democrat	Pennsylvania	1857	65	Presbyterian
Abraham Lincoln (1809-1865)	Republican	Illinois (KY)	1861	52	———
Andrew Johnson (1808-1875)	Democrat[c]	Tennessee (NC)	1865	56	———
Ulysses S. Grant (1822-1885)	Republican	Illinois (OH)	1869	46	Methodist
Rutherford B. Hayes (1822-1893)	Republican	Ohio	1877	54	———
James A. Garfield (1831-1881)	Republican	Ohio	1881	49	Disciples of Christ
Chester A. Arthur (1830-1886)	Republican	New York (VT)	1881	50	Episcopal
Grover Cleveland (1837-1908)	Democrat	New York (NJ)	1885	47	Presbyterian
Benjamin Harrison (1833-1901)	Republican	Indiana (OH)	1889	55	Presbyterian
Grover Cleveland (1837-1908)	Democrat	New York (NJ)	1893	55	Presbyterian
William McKinley (1843-1901)	Republican	Ohio	1897	54	Methodist
Theodore Roosevelt (1858-1919)	Republican	New York	1901	42	Dutch Reformed
William H. Taft (1857-1930)	Republican	Ohio	1909	51	Unitarian
Woodrow Wilson (1856-1924)	Democrat	New Jersey (VA)	1913	56	Presbyterian
Warren G. Harding (1865-1923)	Republican	Ohio	1921	55	Baptist
Calvin Coolidge (1872-1933)	Republican	Massachusetts (VT)	1923	51	Congregationalist
Herbert Hoover (1874-1964)	Republican	California (IA)	1929	54	Quaker
Franklin Roosevelt (1882-1945)	Democrat	New York	1933	51	Episcopal
Harry S Truman (1884-1972)	Democrat	Missouri	1945	60	Baptist
Dwight D. Eisenhower (1890-1969)	Republican	NY-PA (TX)	1953	62	Presbyterian
John F. Kennedy (1917-1963)	Democrat	Massachusetts	1961	43	Roman Catholic
Lyndon B. Johnson (1908-1973)	Democrat	Texas	1963	55	Disciples of Christ
Richard M. Nixon (1913-)	Republican	New York (CA)	1969	55	Quaker
Gerald R. Ford (1913-)	Republican	Michigan (NE)	1974	61	Episcopal
James E. Carter (1924-)	Democrat	Georgia	1977	52	Baptist
Ronald W. Reagan (1911-)	Republican	California (IL)	1981	69	Christian Church
George W. Bush (1924-)	Republican	Texas (MA)	1989	64	Episcopal

Interpreting Tables: Multicultural Awareness Most Presidents have shared similar backgrounds, although the Constitution sets no qualification regarding the religion, ancestry, or gender of the President. Do you see this as a positive or a negative phenomenon? Shown at right are Presidents Andrew Jackson (7th), Theodore Roosevelt (26th), Harry Truman (33rd), and George Bush (41st).

Ancestry	Vice Presidents
English	John Adams
English	Thomas Jefferson
Welsh	Aaron Burr/George Clinton
English	George Clinton/Elbridge Gerry
Scots	Daniel D. Tompkins
English	John C. Calhoun
Scots-Irish	John C. Calhoun/Martin Van Buren
Dutch	Richard M. Johnson
English	John Tyler
English	. . . .
Scots-Irish	George M. Dallas
English	Millard Fillmore
English	. . . .
English	William R. King
Scots-Irish	John C. Breckinridge
English	Hannibal Hamlin/Andrew Johnson
Scots-Irish, English	. . . .
English, Scots	Schuyler Colfax/Henry Wilson
English	William A. Wheeler
English, French	Chester A. Arthur
Scots-Irish, English	. . . .
Irish, English	Thomas A. Hendricks
English, Scots	Levi P. Morton
Irish, English	Adlai E. Stevenson
Scots-Irish, English	Garret A. Hobart/Theodore Roosevelt
Dutch, Scots, English, Huguenot	. . . . /Charles W. Fairbanks
English, Scots-Irish	James S. Sherman
Scots-Irish	Thomas R. Marshall
English, Scots-Irish	Calvin Coolidge
English	. . . . /Charles G. Dawes
Swiss-German	Charles Curtis
Dutch	John N. Garner/Henry A. Wallace/ Harry S Truman
Scots-English	. . . . /Alben W. Barkley
Swiss-German	Richard M. Nixon
Irish	Lyndon B. Johnson
English	. . . . /Hubert H. Humphrey
English, Scots-Irish	Spiro T. Agnew[d]/Gerald R. Ford[e]
English	Nelson A. Rockefeller[f]
English	Walter F. Mondale
English-Scots-Irish	George H.W. Bush
English	J. Danforth Quayle

[a]State of residence when elected; if born in another State that State in parentheses.
[b]Democratic-Republican.
[c]Johnson, a War Democrat, was elected Vice President on the coalition Union Party ticket.
[d]Resigned October 10, 1973.
[e]Nominated by Nixon, confirmed by Congress on December 6, 1973.
[f]Nominated by Ford, confirmed by Congress on December 19, 1974.

Provide Guided Practice On the board, draw a stick figure to represent the President. Then draw a stack of eight large hats around the President's head. Ask students to provide the various presidential roles and write their responses inside each hat.

Point out that the President's job requires all the "hats" to be worn at the same time. Then ask students to think of a pictorial image to add to the stick figure to illustrate the formal qualifications of the presidency. For example, a flag might be drawn in the figure's hand to illustrate that the President must be a natural-born citizen.

Provide Independent Practice

TRF **Teacher's Resource File** You may wish to assign Section 1 Guided Reading and Review, Unit 4 File, p. 3, to help students master section objective content.

Enrichment

Have students identify the best (and, if desired, the worst) of the last ten Presidents with respect to each of the eight roles a President must fill. This task will be accomplished most effectively if students use encyclopedias, almanacs, and other reference materials. Have students give a brief evaluation of each President they name. Students might present their work in an "Academy Awards" format—for example, "Best President as Diplomat: Nixon, for his visits to China and the Soviet Union." (Average)

OR

Teacher's Resource File
See the Unit 4 File, pp. 21–23, for the Case Study on Contemporary Issues for Chapter 13.

Interpreting Tables: Multicultural Awareness Ask students which head of state in the table has been in office the longest. What does this fact, in combination with the other information in the table, tell you about that country?

Caption Answer Saudi Arabia is a monarchy; Nigeria is probably a military dictatorship.

The President's Term

The Framers considered a number of different limits on the length of the presidential term. Most of their debate centered on a four-year term, with the President to be eligible for reelection, versus a single six-year or seven-year term. They finally settled on a four-year term [5] They agreed, as Alexander Hamilton wrote in *The Federalist* No. 71, that that was a long enough period for a President to have gained experience, demonstrated his abilities, and established stable policies.

Until 1951, the Constitution placed no limit on the number of terms a President might serve. Several Presidents, beginning with George Washington, refused to seek more than two terms, however. Soon, the "no-third-term tradition" became an unwritten rule in presidential politics.

After Franklin D. Roosevelt broke the tradition by winning a third term in 1940, and then a fourth in 1944, the unwritten custom limiting presidential terms became a part of the written Constitution. The 22nd Amendment, adopted in 1951, reads in part:

> "No person shall be elected to the office of the President more than twice, and no person who has held the office of President, or acted as President, for more than two years of a term to which some other person was elected President shall be elected to the office of the President more than once."

[5]Article II, Section 1, Clause 1.

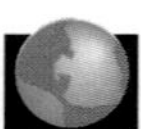

Global Awareness

Former Professions/Titles of Heads of State, Selected Countries

Country	Title	Name	Length of time in office	Previous profession/title
Philippines	President	Corazon Aquino	Inaugurated February 25, 1986	Political activist
Saudi Arabia	King	Fahd IBN AL-AZIZ AS-SAUD	Acceded to the throne June 13, 1982	Crown prince
Nicaragua	President	Violeta Barrios de Chamorro	Took office April 25, 1990	Newspaper owner and political activist
Hungary	President of the Republic	Árpád Göncz	Elected August 3, 1990	Writer
Ireland	President	Mary Robinson	Assumed office December 3, 1990	Lawyer
Nigeria	President and Commander in Chief	Gen. Ibrahim Babangida	Took power August 27, 1985	Army chief of staff
Peru	President	Alberto Fujimori	Sworn in December 29, 1989	Agronomist (Agriculturist)
Czechoslovakia	President of the Republic	Vaclav Havel	Re-elected July 5, 1990	Playwright
Poland	President	Lech Walesa	Sworn in December 22, 1990	Leader of Solidarity (Poland's labor union)
United States	President	George Herbert Walker Bush	Inaugurated January 20, 1989	Ambassador/Vice President

Interpreting Tables: Multicultural Awareness The previous occupation of a head of state can often suggest information about the political structure of that country. What does the table tell you about the governments of Saudi Arabia and Nigeria?

As a general rule, then, each President may now serve a maximum of two full terms—eight years—in office. *But* a President who has succeeded to the office beyond the midpoint in a term to which another person was originally elected could possibly serve for more than eight years. In that circumstance, the President may finish out the predecessor's term and then seek two full terms of his or her own. However, no President may now serve more than 10 years in the office.

Many people, including Presidents Truman, Eisenhower, and Reagan, have called for the repeal of the 22nd Amendment and its limit on presidential service. They argue that it is undemocratic because it places an arbitrary limit on the right of the people to decide who should be President. Some critics also say that the amendment undercuts the authority of a two-term President, especially in the latter part of his second term. Supporters of the amendment defend it as a reasonable safeguard against "executive tyranny."

Several Presidents, most recently Lyndon Johnson and Jimmy Carter, have urged a single six-year term. They, and others, have argued that a single, nonrenewable term would free a President from the pressures of a campaign for a second term, allowing him or her to focus on the pressing duties and/or responsibilities of the office.

Pay and Benefits

The President's salary is fixed by Congress, and it can neither be increased nor decreased during a term.[6]

The salary was first set at $25,000 a year in 1789. Congress put the figure at its present level—$200,000—in 1969. Since 1949 the President has also received a $50,000-a-year expense account. This sum is taxable as income and, in effect, it is a part of the President's pay above and beyond the salary.

The Constitution forbids the President "any other emolument from the United States, or any of them." But this clause does not prevent the President from being provided with a great many benefits, including the White House, a magnificent 132-room mansion set on an 18.3-acre estate in the heart of the nation's capital; a sizable suite of offices and a large staff; a yacht, a fleet of automobiles, a lavishly fitted Air Force One, and several other planes and helicopters; Camp David, the resort hideaway in the Catoctin Mountains in Maryland; the finest medical, dental, and other health care available; generous travel and entertainment funds; and many other fringe benefits.

Since 1958 each former President has received a lifetime pension, now $99,500 a year, and each presidential widow is entitled to a pension of $20,000 a year.

[6]Article II, Section 1, Clause 7. At Philadelphia, Benjamin Franklin argued that, as money and power might corrupt a man, the President ought to receive nothing beyond his expenses; his suggestion was not put to a vote at the Convention, however. The present salary was set in the first measure passed by Congress in 1969. It was signed by President Johnson on January 17, three days before the new presidential term, President Nixon's first, began.

Section 1 Review

1. Define: chief of state, chief executive, chief administrator, chief diplomat, commander in chief, chief legislator, chief of party, chief citizen

2. (a) What roles must a President play, and (b) how must he fulfill them?

3. What are the formal qualifications for the presidency?

4. (a) According to the 22nd Amendment, to how many terms may a President be elected? (b) What is the maximum length of time any person may serve as President?

5. (a) Who fixes the President's pay? (b) How much is it today?

Critical Thinking

6. Distinguishing Fact from Opinion (p. 19) Admiral George Dewey once said, "The office of President is not such a very difficult one to fill, his duties being mainly to execute the laws of Congress." Do you agree or disagree with this statement? Explain.

★

Monitor Comprehension

Answers to Section 1 Review
1. "Key Terms" are defined on the following pages:
a. chief of state, p. 316
b. chief executive, p. 316
c. chief administrator, p. 316
d. chief diplomat, p. 316
e. commander in chief, p. 316
f. chief legislator, p. 316
g. chief of party, p. 316
h. chief citizen, p. 316
2. The President must fill each of the above roles simultaneously and effectively. **3.** Must be a natural-born citizen of at least 35 years of age and have lived in the United States for at least 14 years. **4.** (a) Two terms. (b) Maximum service of 10 years. **5.** (a) Congress fixes the salary. (b) $200,000 per year. **6.** Students might answer that the many different roles of the President require great skill and flexibility; filling them all at the same time is a difficult job.

Teacher's Resource File See the Unit 4 File, p. 4, for the Section 1 Quiz.

Closure

Remind students that the President serves in eight capacities which, while distinct, are also interrelated. As students read the next section, they will learn about presidential succession and the status of the Vice President.

Assignment Assign Section 2, pp. 323–326, for the next class period.

Reteach

Have students write an advertisement for the job of President of the United States, to run in the employment section of the Sunday newspaper. In addition to responsibilities, qualifications, and pay and benefits, students should describe special knowledge and qualities it would be desirable for the President to have.

Spotlight on: Economics

According to the federal budget for fiscal year 1992, total outlays for running the vast operations of the White House Office—including the salaries for legions of administrative, domestic, and security staff, and expenses for office supplies and equipment, car rentals, utilities, official entertainment, and other expenses—will total almost $35 million. Another $8.3 million will be spent to maintain the executive residence, for such things as groundskeeping and restorations to the exterior.

TEACHING

Debating Key Issues

United States v. *Nixon:* **Should the President's Executive Privilege Be Absolute?**

Objective

Evaluate evidence.

INSTRUCT

Before students read the feature, you may wish to assess their comprehension of the title question. Ask students to see if reading the selection tells them the meaning of "executive privilege." Appoint two interested students to debate the question and others to play the roles of justices on the Supreme Court. After the debaters have made their opening arguments, the justices will ask them questions and then decide the case by a vote. One justice for the majority opinion and one for the dissenting opinion should then give their reasons for deciding the case as they did.

SUPREME COURT DECISION

The Court overruled the President and ordered him to surrender the tapes. The President's "generalized interest in confidentiality . . . " was subordinate to "the fundamental demands of due process of law in the fair administration of criminal justice."

TRF **Teacher's Resource File** See the Supreme Court Cases file, p. 10, for an activity that extends coverage of this case.

Debating Key Issues

Should the President's Executive Privilege Be Absolute?

United States v. *Nixon*

In June 1972, seven men armed with cameras and electronic bugging equipment were arrested while breaking into the Democratic National Committee headquarters located in the Watergate building in Washington, D.C. Investigators soon discovered that two of them were members of the Committee to Reelect the President (Richard M. Nixon).

The White House and Nixon's campaign chairman promptly denied any involvement in or knowledge of the incident. At the conclusion of the trial in United States district court, however, all seven burglars were found guilty. Soon afterwards, the presiding judge received a letter from one of the convicted men. The letter spoke of payoffs to the burglars in return for their silence; they had perjured themselves to protect others who were involved in the break-in.

A Senate select committee began to investigate, and it became increasingly clear that prominent members of the Nixon administration were involved in the cover-up of the break-in. The President himself fell under considerable suspicion.

The Senate committee learned that the President had installed microphones in the White House to record all presidential conversations. The special prosecutor subpoenaed the tapes from this recording system. Nixon, however, refused to turn them over, citing the power of executive privilege.

In the ensuing months, Nixon at first refused but later turned in nine of the tapes amid public outcry and rumors of impeachment. Mysteriously, some portions of the tapes had been deleted. The courts continued to pressure Nixon to release the remaining tapes, but he refused, appealing the case all the way to the Supreme Court in 1974.

Review the following evidence and arguments presented to the U.S. Supreme Court:

Arguments for Nixon

1. The constitutional provision for separation of powers grants the President the privilege to withhold information from other branches of the government.
2. The President's privilege of confidentiality is absolute and vital when high-level communications are concerned.
3. This dispute should be dealt with within the Justice Department of the executive branch, not the courts.

Arguments for the United States

1. It is the constitutional function of the courts to uphold justice in criminal prosecutions. Evidence is necessary for deciding criminal cases.
2. Executive privilege may not deny the court its right to secure evidence in a criminal proceeding.
3. This dispute falls well under the jurisdiction of the judiciary branch.

Getting Involved

1. Identify the constitutional grounds on which each side based its arguments.
2. Debate the opposing viewpoints presented in this case.
3. Predict how you think the Supreme Court ruled in this case and why. Then refer to the Supreme Court Glossary on page 764 to read about the decision. Discuss some possible future consequences of the Court's decision on presidential power.

2 Presidential Succession and the Vice Presidency

Find Out:

- What are the constitutional provisions for succession to the presidency?
- How is presidential disability determined and dealt with?
- What is the status of the vice presidency, in history and today?

Key Term:

presidential succession

Consider these facts: Forty-four men[7] have served in the vice presidency. Nine of them, one in five, became President by succession. Altogether, 13 Vice Presidents, nearly one in three, later reached the White House—most recently, George Bush. Indeed, four of our last six Presidents were at some point Vice President.

Clearly, these facts tell a very significant story. And they point up the importance of the main topics of this section: presidential succession and the vice presidency.

The Constitution and Succession

If a President dies, or resigns, or is removed from office by impeachment, the Vice President automatically succeeds to the office.

Originally, the Constitution did not provide for the succession of the Vice President, however. Rather, it declared that "the powers and duties" of the office, not the office itself, were to "devolve on the Vice President."[8]

The practice, however, begun by John Tyler in 1841, had been that should the office become vacant, the Vice President succeeded to it. That informal amendment became a part of the written Constitution with the adoption of the 25th Amendment in 1967. Section 1 of the amendment provides:

> “In case of the removal of the President from office or of his death or resignation, the Vice President shall become President.”

Congress fixes the order of succession following the Vice President.[9] The present law on the matter is the Presidential Succession Act of 1947. By its terms, the Speaker of the House and then the president *pro tem* of the Senate are next in line. They are followed, in turn, by the secretary of state and then by each of the other 13 heads of the cabinet departments, in order of precedence, as shown on the table at the top of this page.[10]

[7]No woman has yet held the office, but nothing in the Constitution bars that possibility. To 1992, at least, only one woman has ever run as a major party's vice-presidential nominee: Geraldine Ferraro, the unsuccessful Democratic candidate in 1984.

[8]Article II, Section 1, Clause 6.

[9]Article II, Section 1, Clause 6. On removal of the President by impeachment, see Article I, Section 2, Clause 5; Article I, Section 3, Clauses 6 and 7; Article II, Section 4, and Chapter 11, Section 4.

[10]Article II, Section 1, Clause 6.

Presidential Succession

1	Vice President
2	Speaker of the House
3	President *pro tempore* of the Senate
4	Secretary of State
5	Secretary of the Treasury
6	Secretary of Defense
7	Attorney General
8	Secretary of the Interior
9	Secretary of Agriculture
10	Secretary of Commerce
11	Secretary of Labor
12	Secretary of Health and Human Services
13	Secretary of Housing and Urban Development
14	Secretary of Transportation
15	Secretary of Energy
16	Secretary of Education

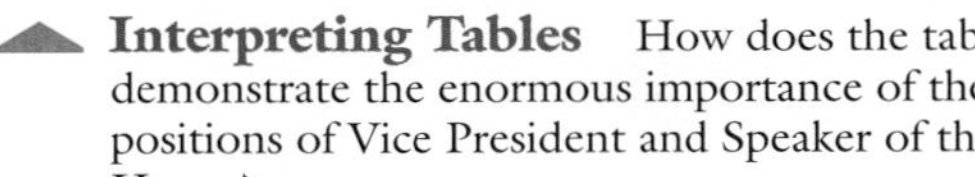

Interpreting Tables How does the table demonstrate the enormous importance of the positions of Vice President and Speaker of the House?

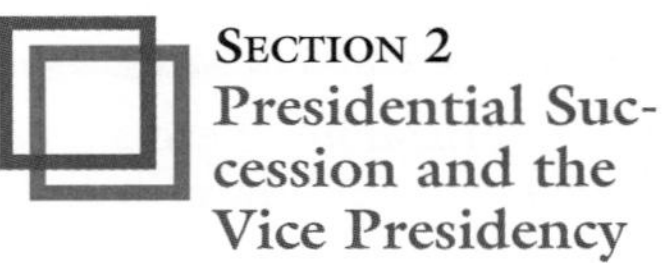

SECTION 2
Presidential Succession and the Vice Presidency

FOCUS

Teacher's Resource File See the Unit 4 File, p. 5, for the Section 2 Outline.

Objectives

13.5 State the provisions for presidential succession.

13.6 Explain how presidential disability is determined and dealt with.

13.7 Describe the status of the vice presidency, in history and today.

Bellringer Activity Ask students to imagine that they will be participating in an important concert, play, game, or religious ceremony. Have students list a succession of people who would lead the event if the current leader could not be present. Point out that a similar succession occurs with respect to the office of the President.

State the Purpose If the President dies, leaves office, or is disabled, the Vice President assumes the presidency. In Section 2, students will learn that the most significant roles of the Vice President have been to help win the election of the President and to be prepared to take over the presidency if necessary.

Interpreting Tables Point out that Congress has gone to great lengths to assure that the presidency is never vacant. What does this imply about the importance of the post?

Caption Answer By indicating that these positions are first and second in the line of succession.

Vocabulary
Point out "Key Term" on page 323 to students. Tell students that the word *succession* comes from the Latin verb *succedere,* meaning "to follow after." LEP

Reading Strategy: Who? What? When? Where? How? Why?
As students read Section 2, have them write and answer six focus questions using Who?, What?, When?, Where?, How?, and Why? to determine facts about presidential succession and the vice presidency.

INSTRUCT

Discuss/Examine Lead a class discussion about how presidential disability is determined. Then examine the text on page 325 that states that the Vice President and a majority of the cabinet, with approval by the Congress, can challenge the President's assertion that he or she is capable of resuming office. How does the 25th Amendment illustrate the American system of checks and balances?

Bring to class some recent newspaper or magazine articles that deal with the debate over whether the current Vice President is qualified to assume the presidency should the President become incapacitated. Divide the class into groups, giving each group one article to read. Then ask the groups to skim Section 2 for an answer to this question: Why might the President have chosen a Vice President whose credentials could ever be called into question?

ABCNEWS INTERACTIVE

The following video segment may be used to highlight aspects of presidential roles.

POWERS OF THE PRESIDENT GUIDEBOOK
Chapter 15: Presidential Vacancy, p. 20

The Law of Succession When Vice President Calvin Coolidge heard of President Harding's death in 1923, his father, a justice of the peace, administered the oath of office, as depicted in this painting.

Presidential Disability

Before the passage of the 25th Amendment, there were serious gaps in the arrangement for **presi-**
1.a **dential succession**—the plan by which a vacancy in the presidency would be filled. Neither the Constitution nor Congress had made any provision for deciding when a President was disabled. Nor was there anything to indicate by whom such a decision was to be made.

For nearly 180 years, then, the nation played with fate. President Eisenhower suffered three serious but temporary illnesses while in office: a heart attack in 1955, ileitis in 1956, and a mild stroke in 1957. Two other Presidents were disabled for much longer periods of time. James Garfield lingered for 80 days before he died from an assassin's bullet in 1881. Woodrow Wilson suffered a paralytic stroke in 1919 and was an invalid for the rest of his second term. He was so ill that he could not meet with his cabinet for seven months after his stroke.

Sections 3 and 4 of the 25th Amendment fill the disability gap, and in detail. The Vice President is to become Acting President if (1) the President informs Congress, in writing, "that he is unable to discharge the powers and duties of his office" or (2) the Vice President and a majority of the members of the cabinet inform Congress, in writing, that the President is so incapacitated.[11]

In either case, the President may resume the powers and duties of the office by informing Congress that no inability exists. However, the

[11]The 25th Amendment gives this authority to the Vice President and the cabinet or to "such other body as Congress may by law provide." To date, no "such other body" has been established.

SPOTLIGHT ON: Behind the Scenes

While no woman has yet been elected President, historians suggest that one woman has nonetheless controlled the office. Edith Bolling Galt Wilson, the wife of President Woodrow Wilson, was thrust into the role of major decision maker in the Wilson administration after her husband's stroke in October 1919.

While the President is believed to have regained his mental faculties within a month of the ordeal, Mrs. Wilson and the President's doctor, Colonel Cary Grayson, kept a tight circle around the stricken President and functioned as his chief advisers on foreign and domestic affairs for as long as seven months.

Vice President and a majority of the cabinet may challenge the President on this score. Congress then has 21 days in which to decide the matter.

To this point, the disability provisions of the 25th Amendment have come into play only once and then only for a few hours. On July 13, 1985, surgeons removed a malignant tumor from President Reagan's large intestine. Just before surgery, Mr. Reagan transferred the powers of the presidency to Vice President Bush. He reclaimed those powers immediately after he awoke, seven hours and 54 minutes later.

The Vice Presidency

"I am Vice President. In this I am nothing, but I may be everything." So said John Adams, the nation's first Vice President. Those words could have been repeated, very appropriately, by each of the 43 Vice Presidents who have followed him in that office.

The Constitution pays little attention to the office. It assigns the Vice President only two formal duties: (1) to preside over the Senate[12] and (2) to help decide the question of presidential disability.[13] Beyond those duties, the Constitution makes the Vice President a "President-in-waiting."

Through much of this nation's history, the vice presidency has been treated as an office of little real consequence and, often, as the butt of jokes. Many Vice Presidents themselves have had a hand in this. John Adams described his post as "the most insignificant office that ever the invention of man contrived or his imagination conceived." Thomas Jefferson, who followed him, found the office "honorable and easy" and "tranquil and unoffending."

Theodore Roosevelt, who had come to the White House from the vice presidency, was annoyed by the tinkling of the prisms of a chandelier in the presidential study. He ordered it removed, saying: "Take it to the office of the Vice President. He doesn't have anything to do. It will keep him awake." The fixture has been in the Vice President's office ever since.

John Nance Garner, who served for two terms as Franklin Roosevelt's Vice President, once said: "The vice presidency isn't worth a warm pitcher of spit." And Alben Barkley, who served during Harry Truman's second term, often told the story of a woman who had two sons. One of them, Barkley said, went away to sea and the other one became Vice President, "and neither of them was ever heard from again."

Vice Presidents Who Succeeded to the Presidency

John Tyler—on the death (pneumonia) of William Henry Harrison, April 4, 1841.

Millard Fillmore—on the death (gastroenteritis) of Zachary Taylor, July 9, 1850.

Andrew Johnson—on the death (assassination) of Abraham Lincoln, April 13, 1865.

Chester A. Arthur—on the death (assassination) of James A. Garfield, September 19, 1881.

Theodore Roosevelt—on the death (assassination) of William McKinley, September 14, 1901.

Calvin Coolidge—on the death (undisclosed illness) of Warren G. Harding, August 2, 1923.

Harry S Truman—on the death (cerebral hemorrhage) of Franklin D. Roosevelt, April 12, 1945.

Lyndon B. Johnson—on the death (assassination) of John F. Kennedy, November 22, 1963.

Gerald R. Ford—on the resignation of Richard M. Nixon, August 9, 1974.

Interpreting Tables From what you have read, what situation, other than the death or resignation of the President, may lead to a Vice President succeeding to the presidency?

Importance of the Office

Despite these and a great many other unkind comments, the office is clearly an important one. Its occupant is literally "only a heartbeat away from the presidency." Remember, eight Presidents have died in office, and one, Richard M. Nixon, was forced to resign. So, clearly, the office has great significance.

[12]Article I, Section 3, Clause 4; see Chapter 12, Section 1.

[13]25th Amendment, Sections 3 and 4. The 12th Amendment says the Vice President must meet the same qualifications as those set out for the presidency.

Interpreting Tables Discuss with students their perceptions regarding the number of times a Vice President succeeded to the presidency. Did this event occur more or less often than they had realized?

Caption Answer The incapacity of a President or the impeachment of a President.

Provide Guided Practice Draw a table on the board with two columns: *Causes* and *Effect.* Under the *Effect* column write: "Vice President becomes President." Then ask students to provide the various causes that would result in this effect.

Provide Independent Practice

TRF **Teacher's Resource File** You may wish to assign Section 2 Guided Reading and Review, Unit 4 File, p. 6, to help students master section objective content.

Enrichment

Have students look through old magazines and newspapers to locate as many political cartoons as they can find about the office of the Vice President. Bring all the cartoons together into a book entitled *Cartoonists' Views of the Vice Presidency.* Have students write a brief statement describing whether or not the cartoons support the information in the text about the importance of the office of the Vice President. (Easy)

MONITOR COMPREHENSION

Answers to Section 2 Review
1. The "Key Term" is defined on the following page:
a. presidential succession, p. 324
2. The 25th Amendment.
3. The Speaker of the House.
4. (a) The President can inform Congress in writing that he cannot perform his duties, or (b) the Vice President and a majority of the cabinet inform Congress that the President is incapacitated. **5.** The Vice President presides over the Senate and helps decide presidential disability. **6.** One reason is the manner of vice-presidential nomination, which places emphasis on the ability of the nominee to balance the ticket. **7.** What is the likelihood of the Vice President ascending to the presidency? What is the reputation of most Vice Presidents?

Teacher's Resource File See the Unit 4 File , p. 7, for the Section 2 Quiz.

CLOSURE

Remind students that the fact that the Vice President can succeed to the presidency is one of the most important aspects of that office. As students read the next section, they will learn how the Framers intended the President to be selected, and how that selection process has changed.

Assignment Assign Section 3, pages 327–329, for the next class period.

Some blame for the low status of the vice presidency in modern times may stem from the way in which the two major parties nominate their candidates for the office. Each convention names the hand-picked choice of its just-nominated presidential candidate. Usually the presidential candidate picks someone who will "balance the ticket." That is, the presidential candidate chooses a running mate who can improve his electoral chances. In short, fate and the vice presidency do not have a very high priority in the vice-presidential selection process.

The vice presidency has been vacant 18 times thus far—nine times by succession to the presidency, twice by resignation, and seven times by death[14] Yet, not until 1967 and the 25th Amendment did the Constitution deal with the matter. Section 2 provides:

> "Whenever there is a vacancy in the office of the Vice President, the President shall nominate a Vice President who shall take office upon confirmation by a majority vote of both houses of Congress."

The provision was first implemented in 1973, when President Nixon selected and Congress confirmed Gerald Ford to succeed Spiro Agnew as Vice President. It came into play again in 1974, when President Ford named and Congress approved Nelson Rockefeller.

Many have long urged that the Vice President be given a larger role in the executive branch. The more recent Presidents, from Eisenhower to Bush, have in fact made greater use of their Vice Presidents. Today, Vice President Quayle takes part in cabinet meetings, chairs the National Space Council, and is a member of the critically important National Security Council. He also performs a variety of political and diplomatic chores for the President.

So far, however, no President has upgraded the Vice President to the role of a true "assistant president." The major reason: Of all the President's official family, only the Vice President is not subject to the ultimate discipline of removal from office by the President. No matter what the circumstances, the President cannot fire the Vice President.

[14]John C. Calhoun resigned to become a senator from South Carolina in 1832. Spiro T. Agnew resigned in 1973, after a conviction for income tax evasion and in the face of charges of corruption dating from his service as a county executive and then governor of Maryland. The seven who died in office were: George Clinton 1812), Elbridge Gerry (1814), William R. King (1853), Henry Wilson (1875), Thomas A. Hendricks (1885), Garret A. Hobart (1899), and James S. Sherman (1912).

A Heartbeat Away J. Danforth Quayle was serving a second term in the Senate when he became Vice President.

Section 2 Review

1. **Define:** presidential succession
2. Which amendment states that if the presidency becomes vacant, the Vice President succeeds to that office?
3. Who follows the Vice President in the line of presidential succession?
4. How is presidential disability determined?
5. What official duties does the Constitution grant the Vice President?
6. For what reasons is the vice presidency so lightly regarded?

Critical Thinking

7. **Formulating Questions** (p. 19) Imagine you are a politician who has just been offered the vice-presidential nomination. Make a list of questions that will help you decide whether to accept or reject the offer.

★

Reteach

Ask students: If the pitcher is injured during a baseball game, is t season cancelled? If the star of a musical gets laryngitis before op ing night, is the performance cancelled? Explain that, in a similar if the President is injured or disabled, the country must not ceas function. Thus, the Constitution provides for the Vice President assume the duties of the presidency.

3 Presidential Selection: The Framers' Plan

Find Out:

- What did the Framers intend the electoral college to be?
- What factors helped transform the presidential selection process?

Key Terms:

presidential electors, electoral college

In formal terms, the President is chosen according to the provisions of the Constitution.[15] In practice, however, the President is elected through an altogether extraordinary process that is not very well understood by most of the American people. That process is a combination of constitutional provisions, a few State and federal laws, and, in largest measure, a number of practices born of the nation's political parties.

To make sense of that very complex matter, you must first understand the subject of this section: what the Framers had in mind when they designed the presidential election process.

Original Constitutional Provisions

The Framers of the Constitution gave more time to the method for choosing the President than to any other matter. It was, said James Wilson of Pennsylvania, "the most difficult of all on which we have had to decide." It was difficult largely because most of the Framers were against selecting the President by either of the obvious ways: by Congress or by a direct vote of the people.

Early in the Convention, most of the delegates favored selection by Congress. Later, nearly all delegates came to the view that congressional selection would, as Hamilton said, put the President "too much under the legislative thumb."

[15]The Constitution deals with the process of presidential selection in several places: Article II, Section 1, Clauses 2 and 4, and the 12th, 20th, and 23rd amendments.

Only a few of the Framers favored choosing the President by popular vote. Nearly all agreed that that would lead "to tumult and disorder." Most delegates felt, too, that the people, scattered over so wide an area, could not possibly know enough about the available candidates to make wise, informed choices. George Mason of Virginia spoke for most of his colleagues at the convention: "The extent of the country renders it impossible that the people can have the requisite capacity to judge the respective contentions of the candidates."

After weeks of debate, the Framers finally agreed on a plan first put forward by Hamilton. Under it, the President was to be chosen by a special body of electors. In detail, the plan provided:

1. Each of the several States would have as
1.a many **presidential electors** as it has senators and representatives in Congress.
2. These electors would be chosen in each State in a manner the State legislature directed.
3. The electors, meeting in their own States, would each cast two votes—each for a different person for President.
4. The electoral votes from the States would be opened and counted before a joint session of Congress.
5. The person receiving the largest number of electoral votes, provided that total was a majority of all the electors, would become President.
6. The person with the second highest number of electoral votes would become Vice President.
7. If a tie occurred, or if no one received the votes of a majority of the electors, the President would be chosen by the House of Representatives, voting by States.
8. If a tie occurred for the second spot, the Vice President would be chosen by the Senate.[16]

[16]Remember, these were the original provisions, in Article II, Sections 2 and 4; they were modified by the 12th Amendment, as you will see. As curious as it may seem today, the electoral college system was one of the few major features of the Constitution to escape widespread criticism in the struggle over the ratification.

SECTION 3 Presidential Selection: The Framers' Plan

FOCUS

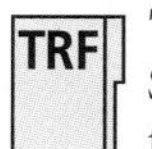

Teacher's Resource File See the Unit 4 File, p. 8, for the Section 3 Outline.

Objectives

13.8 Describe what the Framers intended the electoral college to be.

13.9 Name the factors that helped transform the presidential election process.

Bellringer Activity Ask students: What would you think if the President of the United States were not popularly elected by the American people? Then tell students that, in fact, the President is elected by presidential electors from each State, who are not bound to vote for the winner of the popular election.

State the Purpose The Framers of the Constitution sought a means of choosing a qualified President who would not be controlled by Congress. In Section 3, students will learn about the complex selection process designed by the Framers, and why that process was subverted almost completely within twelve years.

ABCNEWS INTERACTIVE

The following video segments may be used to highlight aspects of presidential roles.

POWERS OF THE PRESIDENT GUIDEBOOK
Chapter 6: Elected by the People, p. 7
Chapter 13: Electing a President, p. 17

Vocabulary

Point out "Key Terms" on page 327 to students. Below are some additional words whose meaning may help students understand the section content.

—**deliberate:** to think about or discuss
—**fiasco:** a complete failure

Reading Strategy: Problem Solving

As a way to master section content, have students jot down whatever questions come to mind as they skim the section. Then, as they read, have students write the answers to those questions. If the answers cannot be found in the section, have students raise their questions in class for general discussion.

Interpreting Tables and Political Cartoons Ask students if they would change any of the ratings of the Presidents. Why or why not?

Caption Answer Yes; more information and changing social mores change public opinion of historical figures. The cartoon character says that ranking Presidents is unimportant and arbitrary.

INSTRUCT

Analyze With students, write an outline on the board of the main ideas of the Framers' plan for presidential election. Then, looking at the remainder of the section, have students point out those elements in the plan that changed or did not change with time. Then ask: Was the Framers' plan sound? What happened to change the original plan? Do students think the Framers' concerns regarding popular election of the President are valid today? How might the presence of the mass media affect at least one of their concerns?

Provide Guided Practice Remind students of their responses to the question posed in the "Bellringer." Do they still have the same opinion after reading the rationale for this method of electing the President? Have students write a few sentences stating the specific points from the chapter that either reinforced their opinion or caused them to change their minds.

Provide Independent Practice

TRF **Teacher's Resource File** You may wish to assign Section 3 Guided Reading and Review, Unit 4 File, p. 9, to help students master section objective content.

The Framers intended the electors to be "the most enlightened and respectable citizens" from each State. They were to be "free agents" who would "deliberate freely" in choosing the persons best qualified to fill the nation's two highest offices.

The Impact of the Rise of Parties

1.b The original version of the **electoral college** worked as the Framers intended only for as long as George Washington was willing to seek and hold the presidency. He was twice, and unanimously, elected President. That is, in 1789 and again in 1792, each elector cast one of his two ballots for the great Virginian.

Flaws began to appear in the system in 1796, however. By then, political parties had begun to form. John Adams, the Federalist candidate, was elected to the presidency. Thomas Jefferson, an arch-rival and Democratic-Republican, who lost to Adams by just three votes in the electoral balloting, became his Vice President.

The Election of 1800 The system broke down in the election of 1800. By then there were two well-defined parties: the Federalists, led by Adams and Hamilton, and the Democratic-Republicans, headed by Jefferson. Each of these parties nominated presidential and vice-presidential candidates. They also nominated candidates to serve as presidential electors in the several States. Those elector-candidates were picked with the clear understanding that, if elected, they would then vote for their party's presidential and vice-presidential nominees.

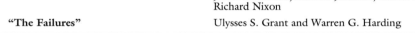

Rating the Presidents

"The Great Presidents"	George Washington, Thomas Jefferson, Abraham Lincoln, Franklin D. Roosevelt
"The Near Great Presidents"	Andrew Jackson, Theodore Roosevelt, Woodrow Wilson, Harry Truman
"The Above Average Presidents"	John Adams, James Madison, James Monroe, John Quincy Adams, James K. Polk, Grover Cleveland, Dwight Eisenhower, John F. Kennedy, Lyndon Johnson
"The Average Presidents"	Martin Van Buren, Rutherford B. Hayes, Chester A. Arthur, Benjamin Harrison, William McKinley, William Howard Taft, Herbert Hoover, Gerald R. Ford, Jimmy Carter
"The Below Average Presidents"	John Tyler, Zachary Taylor, Millard Fillmore, Franklin Pierce, James Buchanan, Andrew Johnson, Calvin Coolidge, Richard Nixon
"The Failures"	Ulysses S. Grant and Warren G. Harding

Interpreting Tables and Political Cartoons This is how a recent survey rated the Presidents. Do you think the passage of time changes such ratings? Why? What value does the cartoon place upon such polls?

Enrichment

Refer students to the table on page 328. Have students poll people to see if they agree with the ratings in the table. Students should try to poll at least two individuals from each of the following age brackets: 18–24 years, 25–32 years, 33–40 years, 41–50 years, 60 years and over. Have students bring their results to class. Discuss the results, comparing them to the table on page 328 and comparing different age brackets. (Average)

Each of the 73 Democratic-Republicans who won posts as electors voted for his party's nominees: Jefferson and Aaron Burr. In doing so, they produced a tie for the presidency. Remember the Constitution gave each elector two votes, each to be cast for a different person, but each to be cast for someone as President. Popular opinion clearly favored Jefferson for the presidency, and the party had intended Burr for the vice presidency. Still, the House of Representatives had to take 36 separate ballots before it finally chose Jefferson.

The spectacular election of 1800 left a lasting imprint on the presidential election process. It marked the introduction of three new elements into the process of selecting a President: (1) party nominations for the presidency and vice presidency, (2) the nomination of candidates for presidential electors pledged to vote for their party's presidential ticket, and (3) the automatic casting of the electoral votes in line with those pledges. Gone forever was the notion that the electors would be "free agents" who would deliberate in the selection of a President to lead the nation.

The 12th Amendment The election of 1800 produced another notable result. The 12th Amendment was added to the Constitution in 1804, to make certain there would never be another such fiasco. The amendment is a lengthy one, but it made only one major change in the electoral college system. It separated the presidential and vice-presidential elections: "The Electors . . . shall name in their ballots the person voted for as President, and in distinct ballots the person voted for as Vice President."[17]

With the appearance of parties, the elections of 1800, and then the 12th Amendment, the constitutional setting was laid for the presidential selection system as it exists today. That system is, indeed, a far cry from what was agreed on in 1787—as you will see in the sections ahead.

[17]Not only does the amendment mean there cannot be a tie, it almost certainly guarantees that the President and Vice President will be of the same party.

Party Impact John Adams served as the nation's second President. With his defeat for reelection, the Federalists never again gained control of either the presidency or Congress.

Section 3 Review

1. **Define:** presidential electors, electoral college
2. (a) Why were most of the Framers opposed to choosing the President by popular vote? (b) To selection by Congress?
3. (a) Outline the original provisions for the electoral college. (b) How did the Framers expect electors to vote?
4. What three events combined to change the intent of the original electoral college system?
5. What major change did the 12th Amendment make in the electoral college system?

Critical Thinking

6. **Recognizing Ideologies** (p. 19) The Framers intended the presidential electors to be "the most enlightened and respectable citizens" in each State. What does this suggest about their definition of good citizenship?

★

Monitor Comprehension

Answers to Section 3 Review
1. "Key Terms" are defined on the following pages:
a. presidential electors, p. 327
b. electoral college, p. 328
2. (a) People could not learn enough about the candidates. (b) Feared congressional control of President. **3.** State has as many electors as representatives and senators. State legislatures outline method of choosing electors. Electors would cast two votes for President. Electors were expected to choose based on their own judgment. **4.** Party nominations for presidency and vice presidency; nomination by parties of presidential electors; and casting of electoral votes along party lines. **5.** Separated elections for President and Vice President. **6.** It reveals that Framers saw only the most educated, upstanding citizens as worthy of choosing national leaders.

Closure

The Framers developed a system for electing a President that did not foresee the rise of political parties. Political parties, along with a complex system, undermined the Framers' plan. In Section 4, students will explore the first stage in the selection of the President: party nomination.

Assignment Assign Section 4, pp. 330–335, for the next class period.

TRF **Teacher's Resource File**
See the Unit 4 File, p. 10, for the Section 3 Quiz.

Reteach

Ask students: How did the rise of political parties in the United States change the Framers' original plan for the electoral college?

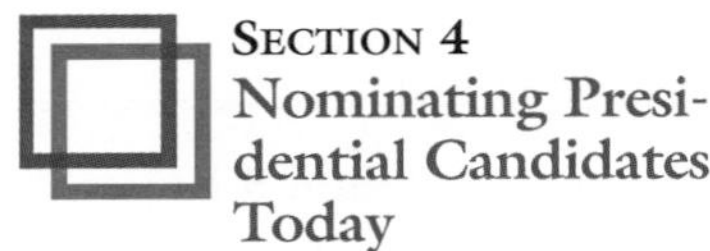

SECTION 4
Nominating Presidential Candidates Today

FOCUS

Teacher's Resource File See the Unit 4 File, p. 11, for the Section 4 Outline.

Objectives

13.10 Understand the features that make the presidential nominating process complicated.

13.11 Explain the roles that primaries, caucuses, and conventions play in the nominating process.

Bellringer Activity Ask students to consider what it would be like if every class in the school had its own rules about when the school year begins and ends, its own grading system, and its own rules for governing student behavior. Explain that this situation is similar to that of the States: each State has its own primary rules and policies.

State the Purpose The Constitution does not address the issues of political parties or candidate nomination. In Section 4, students will learn the general outlines of the presidential nominating process and how it varies from State to State.

ABCNEWS INTERACTIVE

The following video segments may be used to highlight aspects of presidential roles.

POWERS OF THE PRESIDENT GUIDEBOOK
Chapter 9: Primaries and Caucuses, p. 11
Chapter 10: Nominating a Candidate, p. 13

4 Nominating Presidential Candidates Today

Find Out:

- What features make the presidential nominating process so complicated?
- What roles do primaries, caucuses, and conventions play in that process?

Key Terms:

presidential primary, winner-take-all

The Constitution makes no provision for the nomination of candidates for the presidency. Rather, as you have just seen, the Framers designed a system in which presidential electors would, out of their own knowledge, select the "wisest and best man" as President. But, as you have also seen, the rise of parties altered that system drastically.

In this section, you will examine what emerged from that historic revision of the Framers' original plan: the modern-day presidential nominating process.

The Role of Conventions

The first method the parties developed to nominate presidential candidates was the congressional caucus. As you read in Chapter 7, that method was regularly used in the elections of 1800 to 1824. But, as you know, its closed character led to its downfall in the mid-1820s. For the election of 1832, both major parties turned to the national convention as their nominating device. It has continued to serve them ever since.

Extent of Control by Law As a result of the convention process, the final selection of the President is, for all practical purposes, narrowed to one of two persons: the Republican or the Democratic nominee. Yet in spite of its important role in the American political system, there is almost no legal control over the convention process.

The Constitution is silent on the subject of presidential nominations. There is, as well, almost no statutory law on the matter. The only provisions in federal law have to do with the financing of conventions; see Chapter 7, Section 3. Also, only a very small body of State law deals with a few aspects of convention organization and procedure—for example, the choosing of delegates and the manner in which they may cast their votes, which you will read about in the coming pages. In short, the convention is largely a creation and responsibility of the political parties themselves.

Convention Arrangements In both parties the national committee makes the arrangements for the national convention. A year or more before it is held, the committee meets, usually in Washington, D.C., to set the time and place for the convention. Over recent years, the party out of power has held its convention first, sometime in July; the President's party has met a month later, in August.

Where the party holds its convention is a matter of prime importance. There must be an adequate convention hall, sufficient hotel accommodations, plentiful entertainment outlets, and convenient transportation facilities. Political considerations are also key. A city in a doubtful State—one that might vote either way—or in a supportive State is usually picked, in the hope of swaying the election outcome.

Many of the nation's larger cities bid for the honor—and the financial return to local business—of hosting a national convention. The Democrats decided to meet in New York in July for their 1992 meeting, and the Republicans chose to meet in Houston in August.

The Democrats held each of their first six conventions, from 1832 through 1852, in Baltimore. Since 1856—when the Republicans held their first convention in Philadelphia, and the Democrats moved to Cincinnati—the two parties have met in the cities listed in the table on page 331.

The Apportionment of Delegates With the date and the location set, the national committee issues its "call" for the convention. That formal announcement names the time and place and also tells the party's organization in each State how many delegates it may send to the national meeting. It is the delegates who

Reading Strategy: Question Writing

As a preparation for reading, have students turn the section's main headings and subheadings into questions. Then have students skim the text to find the answers to these questions.

Vocabulary

Point out "Key Terms" on page 330. Have students hypothesize as to the meaning of *winner-take-all* with regard to presidential nomination. After reading the section, refer students back to their hypotheses to determine how accurate they were.

will actually cast the votes that will nominate the party's presidential candidate.

Traditionally, both parties give each State organization a number of convention votes based on that State's electoral votes. Over the past several conventions, however, both parties have developed complicated formulas that award bonus delegates to those States that have supported the party's candidates in recent elections.

For 1988, the Republicans' apportionment formula produced a convention of 2,277 delegates, and the Democrats' more complicated plan, 5,374.[18] Those numbers will be about the same in 1992—and, from them, it should be fairly clear that neither party's convention can really be called a "deliberative body."

Selection of Delegates There are really two campaigns for the presidency every four years. One is the contest between the Republican and the Democratic nominees, of course. The other, earlier and quite different one, takes place within each of the parties: the struggle for convention delegates.

State laws and/or party rules fix the procedures for picking the delegates in each State. That fact is a reflection of federalism, and it has produced a crazy-quilt pattern of presidential primaries, conventions, and caucuses among the 50 States.[19]

[18]The conventions of both parties include delegates from the District of Columbia, Puerto Rico, the Virgin Islands, Guam, and American Samoa.

The Democratic convention also includes a number of "superdelegates"—mostly top party officers and Democrats who hold major elective public offices. They are automatically members of their respective State delegations. There were more than 750 superdelegates to the Democrats' 1992 convention; their number included all 413 members of the Democratic National Committee, the governors of 27 States, and 260 members of Congress (46 senators and 214 representatives).

[19]To a very large extent, the GOP leaves the matter of selecting national convention delegates to its State party organizations and to State law.

The Democrats have added several rules in recent years that have in effect nationalized much of the delegate-selection process. Most of these rules are aimed at prompting broader involvement in the choosing of delegates (especially by the young, African Americans, other minority groups, and women) and at making other aspects of convention organization and procedure more democratic.

National Convention Sites Since 1856

City	Republicans	Democrats
Atlanta		1988
Atlantic City		1964
Baltimore	1864	1860, 1872, 1912
Chicago	1860, 1868, 1880, 1884, 1888, 1904, 1908, 1912, 1916, 1920, 1932, 1944, 1952, 1960	1864, 1884, 1892, 1896, 1932, 1940, 1944, 1952, 1956, 1968
Cincinnati	1876	1856, 1880
Cleveland	1924, 1936	
Dallas	1984	
Detroit	1980	
Denver		1908
Houston	1992	1928
Kansas City, Mo.	1928, 1976	1900
Los Angeles		1960
Miami Beach	1968, 1972	1972
Minneapolis	1892	
New Orleans	1988	
New York		1868, 1924, 1976, 1980, 1992
Philadelphia	1856, 1872, 1900, 1940, 1948	1936, 1948
St. Louis	1896	1876, 1888, 1904, 1916
San Francisco	1956, 1964	1920, 1984

Interpreting Tables Politics plays as large a part in choosing a convention site as does location. Why do you think the most popular choice is Chicago?

Presidential Primaries

More than three-fourths of all the delegates to both conventions now come from States that hold presidential primaries. Several of those primaries are major media events, and serious contenders in both parties must make the best possible showing in most of them.

A **presidential primary** is one or both of two things. Depending on the State, it is a process in which those who vote in a party's primary (1) elect some or all of a State party 1.a

Interpreting Tables Ask students: Should the convention be held where support is strong? Or will the presence of the convention garner support in an area where party support is weak?

Caption Answer Because of its central midwest location and because Illinois is seen as a pivotal State in a presidential election.

INSTRUCT

Discuss Explain to students that the presidential primary can be one or both of two things: a delegate selection process or a "preference" election, in which voters express a preference for a particular candidate.

Explain that there are two main methods of achieving these purposes: the presidential primary and the caucus-convention.

Analyze Guide students through an examination of what is meant by a "crazy-quilt pattern" of State laws governing primaries and selection of delegates. Invite students to propose political reasons for holding State primaries on different dates. Elicit the idea that doing so enables the field of candidates to be sifted gradually: voters can rethink their choices on the basis of whether the candidate they were supporting appears to have a chance.

Divide the class into four groups and have each group research one of the following questions about the primary in your State: Who may vote in a primary? How are delegates selected? When is the primary held? What rules govern its operation? Each group should elect a spokesperson to present its findings to the class.

TRF **Teacher's Resource File**
See the Election Kit, p. 8, for material to support the section.

Interpreting Tables Help students interpret this table by explaining that those polled picked these characteristics as desirable in a presidential candidate from a list of many choices. One person may have picked all six qualities. More people picked "Honest" than any other quality.

Caption Answer Possible answers: Trust in government has to come from the top; an honest President has the country in safe hands.

Qualities Desired in a Presidential Candidate

Quality	Percent
Honesty	94%
Intelligence	87
Ability to communicate	74
Political experience	52
Political philosophy	33
Political party	23

Source: US News and World Report—CNN poll of 1,000 adults, 1986.

Interpreting Tables According to this poll, honesty is the highest quality required of a presidential candidate. Explain why you think this is so.

organization's delegates to the national convention, and/or (2) express a preference among the various contenders for that party's presidential nomination.

History The presidential primary first appeared in the early 1900s. It was part of the reform movement aimed at the boss-dominated convention system. Wisconsin passed the first presidential primary law in 1905, providing for the popular election of national convention delegates. Several States soon followed that lead, and Oregon added the preference feature in 1910.

By 1916 nearly half the States had adopted presidential primary laws. But many States later dropped the device. By 1968 it was found in only 16 States and the District of Columbia.

Efforts to reform the national convention process, especially in the Democratic party, reversed that downward trend in the 1970s, however. For 1992, some form of the presidential primary was in place in 39 of the States[20] and also in the District of Columbia and Puerto Rico.

[20]In Alabama, Arkansas, California, Colorado, Connecticut, Florida, Georgia, Illinois, Indiana, Kentucky, Louisiana, Maryland, Massachusetts, Michigan, Minnesota, Mississippi, Missouri, Montana, Nebraska, New Hampshire, New Jersey, New Mexico, New York, North Carolina, Ohio, Oregon, Oklahoma, Pennsylvania, Rhode Island, South Carolina, South Dakota, Tennessee, Texas, Utah, Virginia, Washington, West Virginia, Wisconsin. In some of those States, the law permits but does not require a major party to hold a primary.

Primaries Today Again, a presidential primary is either or both of two things: a delegate-selection process and/or an election to determine the voters' choice among the actual candidates seeking the nomination. Once that much has been said, the device becomes very hard to describe, except on a State-by-State basis.

The difficulty comes largely from two sources: (1) the fact that in each State the details of the delegate-selection process are determined by that State's own law—and those details vary from one State to the next, and (2) the ongoing reform efforts in the Democratic party. Since 1968, when the Democrats were shattered by disputes over Vietnam and civil rights policies, the Democratic National Committee has written and rewritten the party's rules to prompt greater grassroots participation in the delegate-selection process. Those new rules have prompted many changes in most States' election laws.

Even a matter that seems so simple as the date for the primary shows the crazy-quilt pattern of State laws. New Hampshire holds the first of the presidential primaries every four years. For 1992, it scheduled its primary on February 18, and all of the other presidential primaries were set for various dates over the next four months.

Most States prefer a date early in the primary season, and so the schedule has become "front-loaded." Many primaries—and most of the larger States' contests—are held in March and early April. But the largest State, California, holds one of the last primaries, in June. Often by that time, and usually in both parties, some candidate has won enough delegate support in other States' contests as to virtually guarantee nomination at the convention.

Until fairly recently, most primaries were both delegate-selection and preference exercises. Several primaries were also **winner-take-all** contests. That is, the candidate who won the preference vote automatically won the support of all delegates chosen at the primary.

1.b

Winner-take-all primaries have all but disappeared, however. The Democratic party rules now prohibit them. Instead the Democrats have a complex "proportional representation" rule. Any aspirant who wins at least 15 percent of the votes cast in a primary gets the number of that State's Democratic convention delegates that

SPOTLIGHT ON: Behind the Scenes

National conventions usually are occasions for great celebration, but they also have been the scenes of tremendous controversy. The 1968 Democratic Convention was held in Chicago at the height of the war in Vietnam. Inside the convention the Democratic nominee Hubert Humphrey pledged to continue the war, while outside the building young supporters of antiwar candidates took to the streets to protest the party's position. Before a national television audience, protesters clashed with Chicago police, projecting an image of the Democratic party as hopelessly divided.

corresponds to his or her share of that primary vote. Take, as an example, a State that has 40 convention delegates. If Senator Bob Kerrey won 45 percent of the primary vote, he automatically won the support of at least 18 of the delegates.

Most States had to change their primary laws to account for the Democrats' proportional representation rule—and so in many States, Republican delegates are also chosen on a share-of-the-vote basis. But some States still permit winner-take-all primaries and the Republicans hold them where they can. The Democrats' proportional representation rule had yet another major impact on the shape of these primaries. It led several States—among them both Oregon and Wisconsin, the States that pioneered the presidential primary idea—to give up the popular selection of delegates.

More than half of the presidential primary States now hold only a preference primary. The delegates themselves are chosen later, at party conventions [21] Most of the preference contests are also "all-candidate" primaries: contests in which all generally recognized contenders for a party's presidential nomination are (must be) listed on that party's preference ballot.

Evaluation of the Presidential Primary

No one who surveys the presidential primary system needs to be told that it is complicated, nor that it is filled with a number of confusing variations.

Nevertheless, these primaries are vital. Over recent years they have played the major part in deciding the presidential nominating contests in both parties—and especially in the party out of power.

Presidential primaries tend to democratize the delegate-selection process. And, importantly, they force would-be nominees to test their candidacies in actual political combat.

Hard-fought contests occur but are not common in the party in power. This tends to be true either because the President (1) is himself seeking reelection or (2) has given his backing to someone he favors for the nomination. In either case the President almost always gets his way.

Both 1976 and 1980 were exceptions to that rule. In 1976 Ronald Reagan made a stiff run at President Ford in the Republican party. Senator Edward Kennedy gave President Carter a real fight in the Democratic party in 1980. But, notice, in the end the incumbent President did win his party's nomination.

For the party out of power, the primaries are often "knock-down, drag-out" battles. Without the unifying force of the President as party leader, the several leaders and factions in the party vie with one another, vigorously, for the presidential nomination. Here, one of the presidential primaries' key functions can be seen: the screening out of the lesser possibilities to the point where only a few contenders for the presidential nomination remain.

The recent explosion in the number of presidential primaries places great demands on

"Dairy State" Delegate A Wisconsin Democrat shows her approval of presidential nominee Michael Dukakis, and his support of the Equal Rights Amendment, at the 1988 national convention.

[21]In most of these States, the delegates must be picked in line with the results of the preference primary—for example, for the Democrats in 1992, so many delegates for Jerry Brown, so many for Tom Harkin, and so on. In some, however, the preference vote does not govern the choice of the delegates; in those States, the preference primary is often called a "beauty contest."

Provide Guided Practice
Draw a two-column chart on the board. Label one column *Primary* and the other *Caucus-Convention.* Ask students to outline the points made in the text about each type of delegate selection/preference election.

Provide Independent Practice
TRF **Teacher's Resource File**
You may wish to assign Section 4 Guided Reading and Review, Unit 4 File, p. 12, to help students master section objective content.

Enrichment

Have students bring scraps of material and safety pins to class. Assign each student one or two States and ask them to use periodicals to determine when those States held their presidential primaries or caucuses in 1992. Have students indicate each State and the date of its primary or caucus on a different scrap of material. Connect the scraps with safety pins to illustrate the "crazy-quilt" pattern of primaries. (Average)

Interpreting Political Cartoons Ask students what this cartoon says about the emphasis placed on primaries by the media.

Caption Answer Because these States hold an early caucus and primary, an immense amount of attention is focused on them.

MONITOR COMPREHENSION

Answers to Section 4 Review
1. "Key Terms" are defined on the following pages:
a. presidential primary, p. 331
b. winner-take-all, p. 332
2. (a) Regulates the financing of conventions. (b) Deals with convention organization and procedure. **3.** A crazy-quilt pattern of primaries, conventions, and caucuses. **4.** A delegate-selection process and/or a preference election. **5.** In power: the President usually wins, either by seeking reelection or backing someone else. Out of power: without a unifying force like the President, factions within the party battle for the nomination. **6.** It promotes compromise and thus party unity. **7.** A caucus-convention process. **8.** To win some candidates will indulge in such things as negative campaigning or empty campaign promises.

CLOSURE

The presidential nomination process is complex because the parties and the States establish procedures on a State-by-State basis. In the next section, students will learn about the national conventions.

Assignment Assign Section 5, pp. 335–339, for the next class period.

candidates in terms of time, effort, money, scheduling, and fatigue. They also test the public's endurance. Adlai Stevenson once said, in a day when there were many fewer primaries, "The hardest thing about any political campaign is how to win without proving that you are unworthy of winning."

Many critics think that each of the major parties should hold a single, nationwide presidential primary. Some critics would have both parties nominate their presidential candidates in those contests. They would do away with the conventions, except perhaps to pick vice-presidential nominees or to write platforms.

Other critics see a national primary as the best way for the parties either (1) to select all of their convention delegates or (2) to allow their voters to express their candidate preferences, which would then bind their delegates.

Still other critics favor a series of regional primaries, held at two- or three-week intervals in groups of States across the country.

Hope for any of these plans is dim at best. Each plan would require joint action by Congress, the States, and both major parties. Beyond that hurdle, recall this point from Chapter 7: However it is conducted, the nominating process can have a very divisive effect on a party; and the primary magnifies that ever-present possibility. In short, neither major party has ever expressed any interest in abandoning its national convention. Both parties see the convention as a device to promote compromise and, out of it, party unity.

Caucuses and Conventions

In those States that do not hold presidential primaries, delegates to the national conventions are chosen in a system of caucuses and conventions.[22] Here, too, the details of the process are different from State to State. However, it works pretty much as described on pages 158–160.

The party's voters meet in local caucuses, generally at the precinct level. There they choose delegates to a local or district convention where delegates to the State convention are picked. At the State level, and sometimes in the district conventions, delegates to the national convention are chosen.

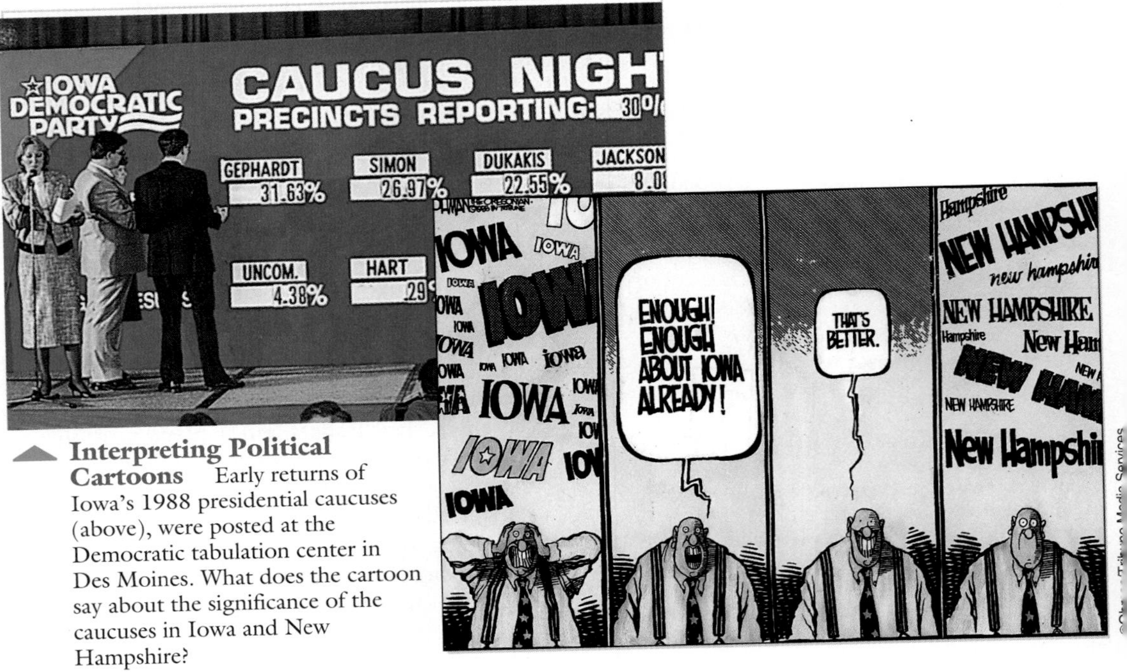

Interpreting Political Cartoons Early returns of Iowa's 1988 presidential caucuses (above), were posted at the Democratic tabulation center in Des Moines. What does the cartoon say about the significance of the caucuses in Iowa and New Hampshire?

TRF **Teacher's Resource File**
See the Unit 4 File, p. 13, for the Section 4 Quiz.

Reteach

Have students imagine that they are doing a special documentary on the primary process in the United States. Have students scan the text for key ideas and terms, while you write each one on the board. Then ask students to write a brief explanation of the process to be read by a narrator in the documentary.

The caucus-convention process is the oldest method for picking national convention delegates. But, notice, in 1992 less than a quarter of all delegates to either party's convention came from those States that still use the caucus-convention process. The Iowa caucuses generally get the most attention, largely because they are now the first delegate-selection event held in every presidential election season.

Section 4 Review

1. Define: presidential primary, winner-take-all
2. (a) To what extent does federal law deal with the national conventions? (b) State law?
3. What effect do the different State laws have upon the nominating process?
4. A presidential primary is one or both of what two things?
5. For what reasons are hard-fought presidential primaries fairly common in the party out of power and rather rare for the President's party?
6. For what reason have the two major parties continued to rely on the national convention to nominate candidates?
7. By what other processes are convention delegates chosen?

Critical Thinking

8. Demonstrating Reasoned Judgment (p. 19) This observation by Adlai Stevenson appears earlier in the section: "The hardest thing about any political campaign is how to win without proving that you are unworthy of winning." What do you think he meant?

[22]Delegates were chosen, in one or both parties by the caucus-convention method in 16 States in 1992. Both parties chose delegates that way in Alaska, Arizona, Delaware, Hawaii, Iowa, Kansas, Maine, Nevada, Utah, Vermont, and Wyoming. The Republicans (but not the Democrats) held caucuses in South Carolina; Democrats (alone) in Idaho and North Dakota. In Texas the Democrats selected some of their national convention delegates by caucuses and conventions and some of them in a presidential primary. The caucus-convention process was also used by both parties in Guam, the Virgin Islands, and American Samoa.

5 At the National Convention

Find Out:

- What are the purposes of the national conventions?
- What takes place at the different sessions?

Key Terms:

keynote address, platform

The national conventions have never been very much admired. In fact, they are roundly criticized every four years—by radio and television commentators, newspaper editors, syndicated columnists, late-night talk show hosts, and a great many others.

All of this is nothing new. In 1908 a foreign observer who had just attended both parties' conventions called them "a colossal travesty of popular institutions." He went on to describe the convention participants as: "A greedy crowd of office-holders, or of office-seekers, disguised as delegates of the people . . . "

Despite their many detractors, the conventions do play an important role in the American political system. As you will see in this section, they are held every four years to do three main things: (1) adopt the party's platform, (2) pick its presidential and vice-presidential nominees, and (3) unify the party behind those candidates and for the upcoming campaign.

The Convention Setting

Each party's national convention meets in a huge auditorium hung with flags, bunting, and various party symbols. Portraits of great figures from the party's past adorn the hall. The front of the hall is dominated by a large platform and the speaker's rostrum. The floor itself is jammed with row upon row of chairs. Standards and placards mark the seating reserved for each State's group of delegates. There are extensive facilities for the army of reporters, commentators, camera operators, technicians, and all their equipment. The galleries seat

SECTION 5
At the National Convention

FOCUS

Teacher's Resource File See the Unit 4 File, p. 14, for the Section 5 Outline.

Objectives

13.12 State the purposes of the national conventions.
13.13 Describe what takes place at the different sessions.

Bellringer Activity Direct students' attention to the photographs on pages 315, 333, 336, 337, and 339. Point out that the images shown on pages 333 through 339 are steps toward what is portrayed on page 315. Then, as a prelude to the section, have the quote from Mencken on page 336 read aloud.

State the Purpose National conventions are used to nominate each party's candidate for the presidency. In Section 5, students will learn about the sequence of events at a national convention and how those events serve to unify and focus the party for the upcoming election.

ABCNEWS INTERACTIVE

The following video segment may be used to highlight aspects of presidential roles.

POWERS OF THE PRESIDENT GUIDEBOOK
Chapter 10: Nominating a Candidate, p. 13

Vocabulary

Point out "Key Terms" on page 335 to the students. Brainstorm with students as many qualities and characteristics of a *platform* as you can. Then invite students to share ideas about what a platform may have to do with a national convention. Tell students that in this section they will learn what a platform and Jell-O have in common. LEP

Reading Strategy: Problem Solving

Have students think about the problems of mobilizing any organization—a team, a band, the cast and crew of a play, a service organization—for the upcoming season, production, or project. Ask students to list activities, from speeches to pep rallies, that help to kick off the activity and ensure that everyone involved is unified and enthusiastic.

INSTRUCT

Discuss Read again to students Mencken's comment about party national conventions. Based on the information in this section, discuss what is meaningful and what may seem ridiculous in a convention. For example, the nominations of candidates who either will not or cannot win the final nomination may seem a waste of time, while what the nominee says in his or her acceptance speech may be very important to Americans. Point out to students that the three purposes of the convention are extremely important in American politics.

Have students read Goldwater's comment about platforms on page 337. Ask: Why do parties bother with a platform if they are really so meaningless? Have students brainstorm five current topics that both major parties could not avoid having in their platforms.

Examine Write in a column on one side of the board *platform, keynote address, credential committee, balloting, nominating, "Star Spangled Banner," committee on permanent organization,* and *acceptance speech.* Then ask students to name the main events at the national convention as you list them on the other side of the board. Finally, ask students to indicate to which event each of the items on the left relates. Draw a line to indicate that, for example, the platform relates to the second and third sessions.

thousands of people who come from all over the country to see a spectacle H. L. Mencken once described this way:

> "[T]here is something about a national convention that makes it as fascinating as a revival or a hanging. It is vulgar, it is ugly, it is stupid, it is tedious, it's hard upon both the cerebral centers and the gluteus maximus, and yet it is somehow charming. One sits through long sessions wishing heartily that all the delegates were dead and in hell—and then suddenly there comes a show so gaudy and hilarious, so melodramatic and obscene, so unimaginably exhilarating and preposterous that one lives a gorgeous year in an hour."

The Opening Session

Each party's convention generally runs four days, with one and sometimes two sessions held each day. The order of business is much the same in both conventions.

The opening session is very largely devoted to two matters: organizing the convention and delivering rousing speeches. The delegates are called to order by the chairperson of the party's national committee. The "Star Spangled Banner" is sung, the official call is read, prayer is offered, and the temporary roll of delegates is called. The national chairperson and party dignitaries make welcoming speeches.

Keynote Address At the 1988 Democratic Convention, the honor of making this mood-setting speech went to Ann Richards. She became governor of Texas in 1991.

The chairperson then announces a slate of temporary officers for the convention—all of them picked by the national committee. The delegates promptly elect them.

1.a The **keynote address** is almost always the high point of the first session. That speech is usually delivered by one of the party's most dynamic orators. It is intended to spur the delegates and set the tone for the convention and the campaign to come. The keynoter's remarks, and nearly all of the many other speeches made during the convention, follow a predictable pattern: They glorify the party, its leaders, and its programs, condemn the opposition, urge party unity, and predict a smashing victory for November.

The opening session winds down with the routine election of the convention's standing committees. There are four major committees at every convention: rules and order of business, permanent organization, credentials, and platform and resolutions. Each State delegation now has two of its members, a man and a woman, on each of them.

The Second and Third Sessions

The next two or three, and sometimes four, sessions of the convention are given over to more speeches by leading party figures and to committee reports.

Typically, the committee on rules and order of business reports first. It regularly recommends the adoption of the rules of the last convention, with perhaps a few changes. Its report, which also presents an agenda for the rest of the convention, is generally accepted with little or no dissent.

The credentials committee prepares the permanent roll of delegates entitled to seats and votes in the convention. Occasionally, there are disputes over the right of particular delegates and even whole delegations to be seated, and the credentials committee must decide those disputes. Its decisions may be appealed, but the floor almost always adopts its report unchanged.

The committee on permanent organization nominates a slate of permanent convention officers. Their selection, and especially the naming of the permanent chairperson, can be a major

SPOTLIGHT ON: Behind the Scenes

The party symbols of the Republican elephant and the Democratic donkey are common sights at the national conventions. The donkey was adopted as the Democratic symbol by Andrew Jackson during the 1828 election. Jackson chose the donkey in response to the off color characterization of him by his opponents. The Republican elephant was created by cartoonist Thomas Nast in 1874 to symbolize the great power of the Republican vote; it quickly came to stand for the party itself. Nast was responsible for popularizing both symbols through his political cartoons.

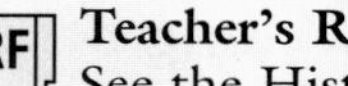

Teacher's Resource File
See the Historical and Legal Documents file, p. 34, and the Election Kit pp. 13, 30–31, for materials to support the section.

test of strength within the party. Those officers run the remaining sessions of the convention.

The report of the committee on platform and resolutions, in the form of a proposed platform, usually reaches the floor by the third session.

The party's platform emerges from a draft drawn up by the party's leadership before the convention meets. Its more controversial planks often prompt heated disputes within the committee, and those struggles may spill over to the convention floor.

Platform-writing is a fine art. A **platform** is 1.b
supposed to be a basic statement of the party's principles and its stands on major policy matters. It is also a campaign statement, aimed at appealing to as many people and winning as many votes as possible. So, both parties tend to produce somewhat generalized comments on many of the hard questions of the day. Neither wishes to alienate large blocks of voters but, necessarily, both end up alienating some voters because of stands on controversial issues.

Some party platforms are regularly criticized for their apparent blandness. Listen to Senator Barry Goldwater, the Republicans' presidential nominee in 1964: "Platforms are written to be ignored and forgotten . . . Like Jell-O shimmering on a dessert plate, there is usually little substance and nothing you can get your teeth into."

Still, the platforms are important. They usually do set out a number of hard and fast policy positions advocated by the two parties. At the same time, they reflect the compromise nature of both American politics and the two major parties.

The Final Sessions

By its fourth, sometimes fifth session, the convention at last comes to its chief task: the nomination of the party's candidate for the presidency.

The names of any number of contenders may be offered to the delegates [23] For each contender, a nominating speech and then several seconding speeches are made. They are lavish hymns of praise, extolling the virtues of "The person who. . . " The "who" is well known before the nominator begins to speak, but tradition has it that the speaker only hint at that person's name until the very end of the speech. Its final announcement sets off a lengthy, wild, noisy demonstration on the floor of the convention hall. These "spontaneous" demonstrations—supposed to show widespread and enthusiastic support for the aspirant—are carefully planned, of course.

Republican National Convention In a tradition called "the greatest political show on earth," a 1988 delegate unabashedly shows his loyalty to the Grand Old Party.

After all the nominating speeches and their seconds have been made, the balloting finally begins. The secretary calls the names of the States alphabetically, and each State chairperson announces the vote of his or her delegation or may pass. Each complete roll call is known as a ballot. Balloting goes on until a candidate achieves a majority of the delegate's votes and is thus nominated.

Most often, the results of the first ballot produce a choice. In the 23 conventions held by each party between 1900 and 1988, the Republicans

[23]Some candidates offered to a convention have no real chance of becoming the party's presidential nominee, but are put forward for some other reason. Thus, a "candidate" may be offered because a State delegation wants to honor one of its own.

Discuss In their discussion of whom the party nominates, raise to students the issue of the withdrawal of L. Douglas Wilder, the governor of Virginia, from the 1992 presidential race. Why might Wilder have withdrawn, other than his stated reason of fulfilling his first responsibility to the State of Virginia?

TRF **Teacher's Resource File**
See the Election Kit pp. 32–33, for material to support the section.

Provide Guided Practice
Have students draw flow charts showing what happens in the opening session, the second and third sessions, and the final session of a national convention.

Provide Independent Practice
TRF **Teacher's Resource File** You may wish to assign Section 5 Guided Reading and Review, Unit 4 File, p. 15, to help students master section objective content.

have made a first ballot nomination 19 times and the Democrats, 18 times.[24]

Once the convention has chosen the presidential nominee, the choice of a running mate often comes as an anticlimax. The vice-presidential nominee is almost invariably the choice of the just-nominated presidential candidate; see Section 2.

With its candidates named, the convention comes to the last major item on its agenda: the presidential candidate's acceptance speech. And, as that speech comes to an end, the delegates—all of them superpatriots of the party—nearly tear the convention hall apart in wild celebration.

Whom Does the Party Nominate?

If an incumbent President wants another term, the convention's choice of a nominee is easy. The President is almost certain to get the nomination, and usually with no real opposition from within the party. Indeed, in this century, each time the incumbent has sought the nomination, he has received it. The President's advantages are immense: the majesty and publicity of the office and close control of the party's machinery.[25]

When the President is not in the field, up to a dozen or so contenders surface in the preconvention period. At most, two or three of them may survive to contest the prize at the convention.

Who among them will win the nomination? The record argues this answer: the one who is, in the jargon of politics, the most available—the one who is the most nominatable and electable. Conventions want to pick candidates who can win, candidates with the broadest possible appeal within the party and to the electorate.

Most presidential candidates have come to their nominations with substantial and well-known records in public office. But those records have to be free of controversies that could have antagonized important elements within the party or among the voting public. Generally, presidential candidates have served in elective office, where they have shown vote-getting ability. Seldom does a candidate step from the business world or from the military directly into the role of candidate, as did Wendell Willkie in 1940 or Dwight Eisenhower in 1952.

Historically, the governorships of larger States have produced the largest number of presidential candidacies. Eleven of the 20 men nominated by the two major parties between 1900 and 1956 were either then serving or had once served as a governor. Note that governors can claim experience as chief executives of a government.

For a time, however, the Senate became the prime source. In the four elections from 1960 through 1972, each major party nominee had been a senator. None had ever been a governor.

But the old pattern has been restored. Jimmy Carter, the former governor of Georgia, was nominated by the Democrats in 1976 and 1980. Ronald Reagan, former governor of California, was the GOP choice in 1980 and again in 1984. And the Democrats chose Michael Dukakis, the governor of Massachusetts, in 1988.

With a few exceptions, notably Democrats Alfred E. Smith in 1928, John F. Kennedy in 1960, and Michael Dukakis in 1988, most leading contenders for presidential nominations have been Protestants. Most have also come from the larger and doubtful States. Thus, candidates from such pivotal States as New York, Ohio, Illinois, and California are more available than those from smaller States. From this standpoint, the nominations of Senator Barry

[24]A convention can become deadlocked—that is, find itself unable to make a choice between the top two, or sometimes three, contenders for the nomination. In that event, a "dark horse" (someone who did not appear to be a likely choice before the convention) may finally be nominated. The most spectacular deadlock occurred at the Democratic convention in New York in 1924. The convention took 123 separate ballots, over a period of nine days, before John W. Davis became the party's candidate.

[25]In fact, only four sitting Presidents have ever been denied nomination: John Tyler, by the Whigs in 1844; Millard Fillmore, by the Whigs in 1852; Franklin Pierce, by the Democrats in 1856; and Chester Arthur, by the Republicans in 1884.

Enrichment

Have students do research comparing and contrasting the Democratic National Convention in 1912 with the Democratic National Convention of 1964. How did these conventions differ in their final sessions? (*In 1912 the nomination was very much up in the air, while in 1964 Lyndon Johnson was nearly undisputed.*) Have students write brief comparisons of the two elections. (Challenging)

Presidential and Vice-Presidential Nominees George Bush (left) and his vice-presidential nominee, J. Danforth Quayle, enjoy acclaim at New Orleans in 1988. At right, Michael Dukakis and his running mate, Lloyd Bentsen, are joined by their wives as they accept the cheers of delegates at the 1988 Democratic Convention.

Goldwater of Arizona by the Republicans in 1964 and Senator George McGovern of South Dakota by the Democrats in 1972 were more than just a little exceptional. So, too, was the Democratic nomination of Jimmy Carter from Georgia in 1976.

Neither party has, to this point, seriously considered a woman as its candidate for the presidency—or, until 1984 and the Democratic party's nomination of Geraldine Ferraro, for the vice presidency. Nor has either party yet nominated a member of any minority group for either role. Jesse Jackson, an African American, did show significant strength in the 1988 pre-convention race, eventually losing the Democratic presidential nomination to Michael Dukakis of Massachusetts.

The candidates usually have a pleasant and healthy appearance, seem to be happily married, and have a happy (and exploitable) family. Adlai Stevenson, the Democratic nominee in 1952 and 1956, and Ronald Reagan, the GOP candidate in 1980 and 1984, are the only nominees of one of the major parties ever to have been divorced.

A well-developed speaking ability has always been a major factor of availability in American politics. Of course, being able to project well over television and in other media has become a must in recent decades.

Section 5 Review

1. **Define:** keynote address, platform
2. (a) What happens at a national convention? (b) What is the major event?
3. What is the general tone of a party platform?
4. Why are incumbent Presidents almost certain to win their party's nomination if they choose to pursue it?

Critical Thinking

5. **Recognizing Bias** (p. 19) Consider the concept of availability in presidential politics. (a) In what ways are women and minorities unavailable as candidates? (b) What does this suggest about American politics and voters?

Monitor Comprehension

Answers to Section 5 Review
1. "Key Terms" are defined on the following pages:
a. keynote address, p. 336
b. platform, p. 337
2. (a) Party committees give reports, the party platform is written, and the presidential candidate is nominated. (b) The nomination of the party's presidential candidate. **3.** Party platforms are generalized comments on the issues. **4.** The incumbent President has the publicity of the office and close control of his party's machinery to his or her advantage. **5.** (a) Students may suggest that women and minorities have been allowed to gain positions of great political importance only within the last few decades. (b) Politics and voters tend to stay with the tradition of a white, male presidential candidate who has a long history of political experience.

Closure

Remind students that national conventions are the subject of much criticism, but they provide the public with important information about a candidate. As students read the next section, they will learn how one of the people nominated at the national convention is chosen to be President, what the criticisms of that process are, and some ideas as to how it might be revised.

Assignment Assign Section 6, pp. 340–347, for the next class period.

TRF **Teacher's Resource File**
See the Unit 4 File, p. 16, for the Section 5 Quiz.

Reteach

To help students understand what takes place at a convention, make one set of index cards with the words *Opening Session, Second and Third Sessions,* and *Final Sessions.* Make a second set with the words *Election of Standing Committees, Selection of Permanent Convention Officers, Keynote Address, Platform, Nominating Speeches,* and *Acceptance Speech.* Give one card from each set to various students, so that each student has two cards. Have students group together according to the sessions written on their cards, and then by trading, collect all the cards for activities that take place during their sessions.

SECTION 6
The Election

FOCUS

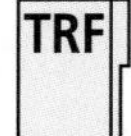

Teacher's Resource File See the Unit 4 File, p. 17, for the Section 6 Outline.

Objectives

13.14 Explain how the electoral college works today.
13.15 Describe the major criticisms of the electoral college.
13.16 Identify some of the proposals to revise the presidential selection process.

Bellringer Activity Present this scenario to the class: Joe Smith and Susan Jones are the Democratic and Republican candidates for President. Susan Jones wins the popular vote by a landslide. Yet Joe Smith is the new President of the United States. Tell students that, with the present system of electing the President, this scenario is possible.

State the Purpose The President is chosen by the electoral college, which usually reflects the popular vote. Nothing, however, prevents the electoral college from rejecting the popular vote entirely. In Section 6, students will learn how the electoral college functions, its weaknesses, and what changes have been suggested.

ABCNEWS INTERACTIVE

The following video segment may be used to highlight aspects of presidential roles.

POWERS OF THE PRESIDENT GUIDEBOOK
Chapter 14: The Electoral College, p. 18

6 The Election

Find Out:

- How does the electoral college work today?
- What are the major criticisms of the electoral college?
- What are some of the proposals to revise the presidential selection process?

Key Term:
electorate

The presidential campaign, the all-out effort to win the votes of the people, begins soon after the conventions. Both candidates' campaign organizations work to present them in the best possible light. Radio and television speeches; "whistle-stop" tours; press conferences and press releases; public rallies; party dinners; newspaper, radio, and television advertisements; stickers and buttons; placards and pamphlets; billboards and matchcovers—all bombard the voters. The candidates pose for hundreds of photographs and shake thousands of hands as each of them tries to convince the people that he is best for the country.

The presidential campaign ends on election day. Millions of voters go to the polls in all 50 States and the District of Columbia. But the President, whoever that is to be, is not actually elected until the presidential electors cast their votes, several weeks later.

In this section, you will focus on the present-day workings of the electoral college, and on several major proposals for its reform.

The Electoral College Today

Here you come to one of the least understood parts of the American political process. As the people vote in the presidential election, they do not cast a vote directly for one of the contenders for the presidency. Indeed, they vote to elect presidential electors.

Remember, the Constitution provides for the election of the President by the electoral college, in which each State has as many electors as it has members of Congress. The Framers expected that the electors would use their own judgment in selecting a President. The electors, once chosen, are really just "rubber stamps." They are expected to vote, automatically, for their party's candidates for President and Vice President.

In short, the electors go through the form set out in the Constitution, in order to meet the letter of the Constitution—but their behavior is a far cry from its original intent.

The electors are chosen by popular vote in every State[26] and on the same day everywhere, the Tuesday after the first Monday in November every fourth year. So, in 1992 the presidential election takes place on November 3.

The electors are chosen at-large in every State except Maine.[27] That is, they are chosen on a winner-take-all basis. The presidential candidate—technically, the slate of elector-candidates nominated by his party—receiving the largest popular vote in a State wins all of that State's electoral votes. Today, the names of the individual elector-candidates appear on the ballot in less than a fourth of the States. In most, only the names of the presidential and vice-presidential candidates are listed. They stand as "shorthand" for the elector slates.

The electors meet at their State capitol on the date set by Congress, now the Monday after the

[26]The Constitution (Article II, Section 1, Clause 2) says that the electors are to be chosen in each State "in such manner as the legislature thereof may direct." In several States the legislatures themselves chose the electors in the first several elections. By 1832, however, every State except South Carolina had provided for popular election. The electors were picked by the legislature in South Carolina through the elections of 1860. Since then, all presidential electors have been chosen by popular vote in every State, with two exceptions. The State legislatures chose the electors in Florida in 1868 and in Colorado in 1876.

[27]Beginning with the 1972 election, Maine has used the "district plan." Two of that State's four electors are chosen from the State at-large and the other two from each of the State's congressional districts. The district plan was used by several States in the first several presidential elections, but every State except South Carolina had provided for the choice of the electors from the State at-large by 1832. Since then, the district plan has been used only by Michigan in 1892 and by Maine in the last five elections.

Reading Strategy: Problem Solving

Have students imagine they are voting for a committee that will select either a class trip to Orlando, Florida, or one to Morro Bay, California. Have students state advantages of voting for electors if the students themselves know nothing about either place, and the disadvantages of voting for electors if they know their preference.

Vocabulary

Point out "Key Term" on page 340. Tell students that *electorate* means "the voters." Explain that, in the electoral college system, the electorate that chooses the President is the electoral college. LEP

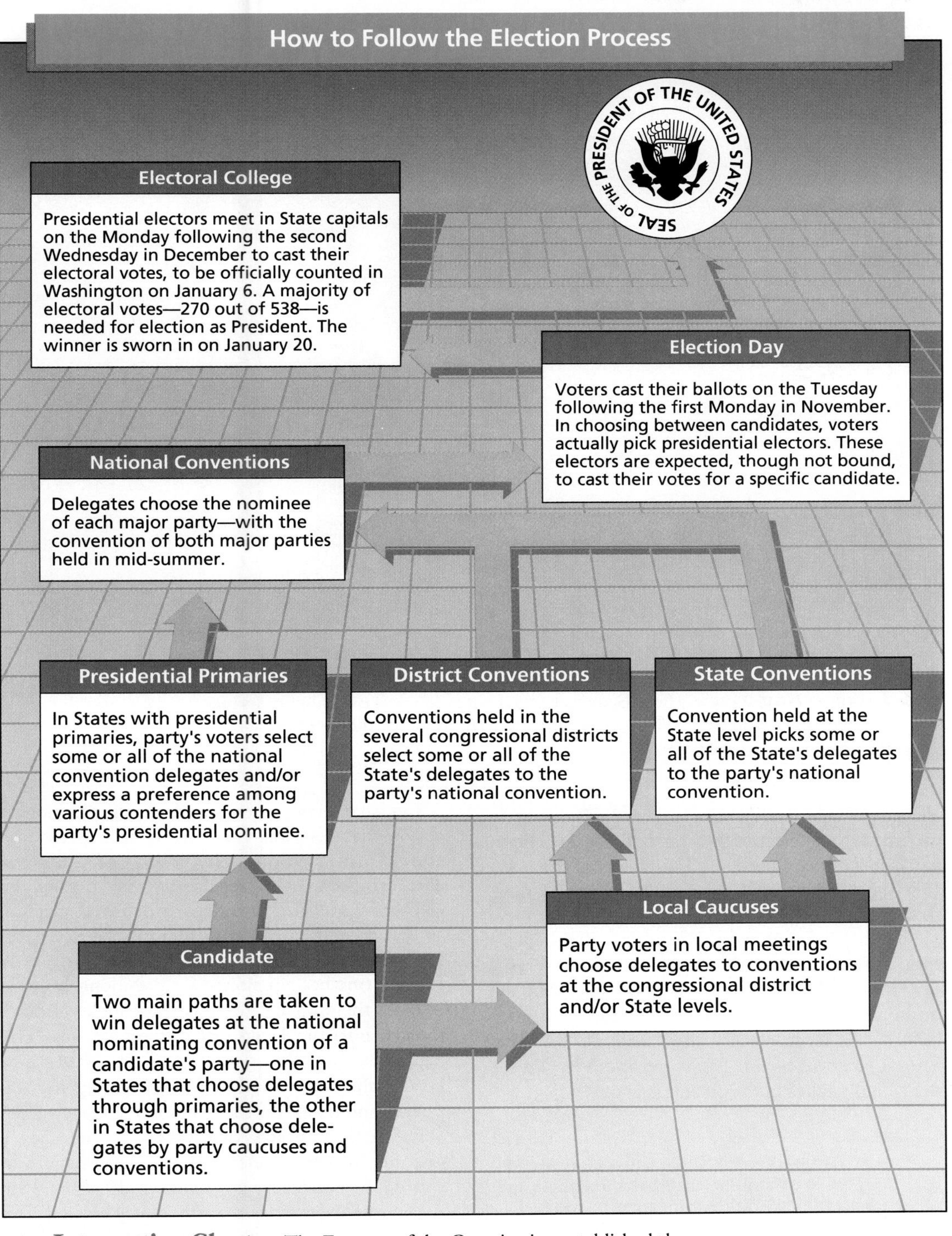

How to Follow the Election Process
SEAL OF THE PRESIDENT OF THE UNITED STATES
Electoral College
Presidential electors meet in State capitals on the Monday following the second Wednesday in December to cast their electoral votes, to be officially counted in Washington on January 6. A majority of electoral votes—270 out of 538—is needed for election as President. The winner is sworn in on January 20.
Election Day
Voters cast their ballots on the Tuesday following the first Monday in November. In choosing between candidates, voters actually pick presidential electors. These electors are expected, though not bound, to cast their votes for a specific candidate.
National Conventions
Delegates choose the nominee of each major party—with the convention of both major parties held in mid-summer.
Presidential Primaries
In States with presidential primaries, party's voters select some or all of the national convention delegates and/or express a preference among various contenders for the party's presidential nominee.
District Conventions
Conventions held in the several congressional districts select some or all of the State's delegates to the party's national convention.
State Conventions
Convention held at the State level picks some or all of the State's delegates to the party's national convention.
Local Caucuses
Party voters in local meetings choose delegates to conventions at the congressional district and/or State levels.
Candidate
Two main paths are taken to win delegates at the national nominating convention of a candidate's party—one in States that choose delegates through primaries, the other in States that choose delegates by party caucuses and conventions.

Interpreting Charts The Framers of the Constitution established the electoral college to allow the most capable citizens in each State to select the President. Is this how the electoral college operates today? Why or why not?

Interpreting Charts Ask students: According to the chart, how many electoral votes does a candidate need to win the presidential election? *(270)*

Caption Answer No, because the electors now act as rubber stamps for the popular vote taken in their State.

Interpreting Maps Ask students to explain how a candidate could win 50.1% of the popular vote and still win every single electoral vote. *(Because whoever wins the popular vote in each State wins all of that State's electoral votes.)*

Caption Answer California, Texas, and New York are important because they carry so many electoral votes.

INSTRUCT

Discuss/Analyze Tell students that, in some ways, political parties actually serve some of the functions of the Framers' electors. Have students imagine that there were no political parties, no electors, and no candidates for President; that every four years people were simply asked to vote for someone to be President. It is conceivable that hundreds, even thousands of people would receive votes, and the winner could be someone who had no desire to be President. One solution is to vote for electors; another is to have knowledgeable people begin by selecting candidates, which is what political parties do.

Explore the first major defect in the electoral system by analyzing an election in which the United States consists only of Ohio, Illinois, Pennsylvania, and Texas, with 23, 24, 25, and 29 electoral votes respectively. A candidate loses the popular vote by a margin of 60% to 40% overall, carrying Ohio and Texas but losing in Illinois and Pennsylvania. This would result in the candidate winning the presidency even though he or she lost the popular vote.

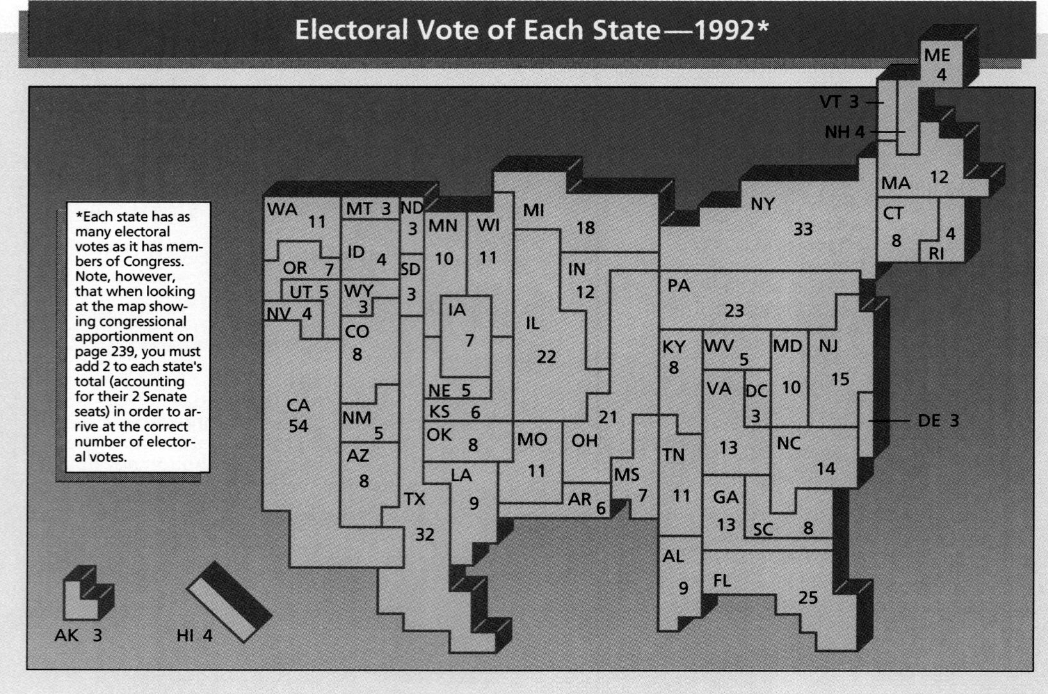

Interpreting Maps Each State's electoral votes equals the number of its representatives in Congress. Which States are important ones for the 1992 presidential candidates to carry? Why?

second Wednesday in December.[28] There they each cast their electoral votes, one for President and one for Vice President. The ballots of the electors, signed and sealed, are sent by registered mail to the President of the Senate in Washington.

Which party has won a majority of the electoral votes, and who then will be the next President of the United States, is usually known by midnight of election day, more than a month before the electors cast their ballots. But the formal election of the President and Vice President finally takes place on January 6.[29]

On that date, the President of the Senate opens the electoral votes from each State and counts them before a joint session of Congress. The candidate who receives a majority of the electors' votes for President is declared elected, as is the candidate with a majority of the votes for Vice President.

If no one has a majority for President—at least 270 of the 538 electoral votes—the election is thrown into the House of Representatives. This happened in 1800, and again in 1824. The House chooses a President from among the top three candidates in the electoral college. Each State delegation has one vote, and it takes a majority of 26 to elect. If the House fails to choose a President by January 20, the 20th Amendment provides that the newly elected Vice President shall act as President until it does.[30]

If no person receives a majority for Vice President, the Senate decides between the top two

[28]Article II, Section I, Clause 4 provides that the date Congress sets "shall be the same throughout the United States." The 12th Amendment provides that the electors "shall meet in their respective States."

[29]Unless that day falls on a Sunday, as it did most recently in 1985 (but will not again until 2013). Then, the ballot-counting is held the following day.

candidates. It takes a majority of the whole Senate to elect. The Senate has had to choose a Vice President only once. It elected Richard M. Johnson in 1837.

Flaws in the Electoral College

A number of defects exist in the structure and operation of the electoral college.

The First Major Defect There is the ever-present threat that the winner of the popular vote will not win the presidency. This continuing threat is largely the result of two factors. The most important is the winner-take-all feature of the electoral college system. In each State the winning candidate customarily receives all that State's electoral votes. In 1988, for example, George Bush won 50.7 percent of the popular vote in Illinois and so all of that State's 24 electoral votes. Even though 2,310,939 people—nearly half the voters in Illinois—marked their ballots for Michael Dukakis, he did not win any of that State's electoral votes.

The other major culprit here is the way the electoral votes are distributed among the States. Remember, each State has two electors because of its Senate seats, regardless of its population. Because of them, the distribution of electoral votes does not match the facts of population and voter distribution.

Take the extreme case to illustrate this situation: California, the largest State, now has 54 electoral votes, or one for each 551,112 persons, based on its 1990 population of 29,760,021. Alaska has three electoral votes, or one for each 183,348 persons, with its 1990 population of 550,043.

The popular vote winner has, in fact, failed to win the presidency three times: 1824, 1876, and 1888. In 1824, Andrew Jackson won the largest share (a plurality, but not a majority) of the popular votes: 151,174, or 40.3 percent of the total. Jackson's nearest rival, John Quincy Adams, received 113,122 votes, or 30.9 percent. Ninety-nine of the 261 electors then voted for Jackson, again more than any other candidate but far short of a majority. The election thus went to the House and, early in 1825, it elected Adams to the presidency.[31]

In the election of 1876, Republican candidate Rutherford B. Hayes received 4,034,311 popular votes and his Democratic opponent, Samuel J. Tilden, won 4,288,548. Tilden received 184 electoral votes; Hayes won 185 electoral votes and so became President.[32]

In 1888 President Grover Cleveland won 5,534,488 popular votes, 90,596 more than his Republican opponent, Benjamin Harrison. But Harrison received 233 electoral votes to Cleveland's 168, and so became the 23rd President.[33]

The system has not misfired since 1888, but it could have several times—most recently in 1976. As the table on page 344 shows, Jimmy Carter defeated Republican Gerald Ford by only a bare majority of the popular vote. If only a handful of voters in a few States had voted for Ford instead of Carter, Ford would have had a majority of the electoral votes and so kept the

[30]The 20th Amendment further provides that "the Congress may by law provide for the case wherein neither a President-elect nor a Vice President-elect shall have qualified" by inauguration day. Congress has done so in the Succession Act of 1947; see Section 2. The Speaker of the House would "act as President . . . until a President or Vice President shall have qualified."

[31]These figures, as most of the popular vote results cited in this book, are drawn from the authoritative *Guide to U.S. Elections*, Congressional Quarterly, Inc., 2nd ed., 1985, and updates of that volume.

[32]The election of 1876 is often called "the Stolen Election." Two conflicting sets of electoral votes were received from Florida (4 votes), Louisiana (8 votes), and South Carolina (7 votes), and the validity of one vote from Oregon was disputed. Congress set up an Electoral Commission with five Senators, five Representatives, and five Supreme Court Justices—to decide the matter. The Commissioners, eight Republicans and seven Democrats, voted on strict party lines, awarding all of the disputed votes, and so the presidency, to Hayes.

[33]To this point, 13 Presidents have been elected although they did not win a majority of the popular vote. You have already read about John Quincy Adams, Hayes, and Benjamin Harrison. The other 10 all were elected with a plurality, but not a majority, of the popular vote. These "minority Presidents": James K. Polk (1844), Zachary Taylor (1848), James Buchanan (1856), Abraham Lincoln (1860), James A. Garfield (1880), Grover Cleveland (1884 and 1892), Woodrow Wilson (1912 and 1916), Harry Truman (1948), John F. Kennedy (1960), Richard Nixon (1968).

Analyze Ask students to describe what sort of situation would have to be present in order for the second flaw in the electoral college to occur: i.e., the electoral vote would have to be fairly close.

Ask students what the third major flaw of the electoral college system is. Then ask what three reasons the text gives to support the idea that this would be a negative phenomenon. Discuss with students whether they feel that the first two proposed reforms are really plausible, since they do not eliminate the possibility that the candidate who wins in the popular vote might lose the election. Have students point out what is positive in these reforms—i.e., that they tie the electoral vote more closely to the popular vote.

Interpreting Tables Ask students how the results of the electoral vote in 1976 compare with the results of the popular vote. How are the results of the 1976 electoral vote misleading? *(They imply that the race was not as close as it really was.)*

Caption Answer Because if only a few voters had voted for Ford rather than Carter, Ford would have received a majority of electoral votes and thus won the election, although Carter had actually won the popular vote.

Interpreting Tables Point out that the 1988 electoral vote implies that Bush received four times as many votes as Dukakis, whereas in reality, Bush received only 7.8 percent more of the popular vote. Ask students how these results are possible. *(Due to the winner-take-all phenomenon.)*

Caption Answer Because the winning candidate in each State customarily receives all of that State's electoral votes, many of the popular votes that Dukakis received had no impact on the electoral vote.

presidency. Different combinations of several States can be used to play this game, but the simplest one involves Ohio and Hawaii. If only 4,667 of the 2,009,959 Carter votes in Ohio (25 electoral votes) and only 3,687 of the 147,376 Carter votes in Hawaii (4 electoral votes) had gone to Ford instead, Ford would have received 270 electoral votes and won the election.

Several other presidential elections can be used to illustrate the point, as well. In short, the "winner-take-all" factor produces an electoral vote result that is, at best, a distorted reflection of the popular vote. You can see the gap between the percentages of popular and electoral votes in the 1988 figures shown in the table below right.

The Second Major Defect Nothing in the Constitution, nor in any federal statute, requires the electors to vote for the candidate favored by the popular vote in their States. Several States do have such laws, but they are of doubtful constitutionality, and none has ever been enforced.

The electors are expected to vote for the candidate who carries their State, and as loyal members of their parties, they almost always do. Thus far, electors have "broken their pledges"—voted for someone other than their party's presidential nominee—on only nine occasions: in 1796, 1820, 1948, 1956, 1960, 1968, 1972, 1976, and 1988. In the most recent case, a West Virginia elector turned her party's ticket upside down; she voted for Lloyd Bentsen for President and Michael Dukakis for Vice President. Bentsen was the Democrats' candidate for Vice President.

In no case has the vote of a "faithless elector" had a bearing on the outcome of a presidential election—but the potential is certainly there.

The Third Major Defect In any presidential election, it is possible that the contest will be decided in the House of Representatives. This has happened only twice, as you know, and not since 1824. But in several other elections—especially in 1912, 1924, 1948, and 1968—a strong third-party bid has threatened to make it impossible for either major party candidate to win a majority in the electoral college. Look at the 1968 results in the table on page 345.

George Wallace, the American Independent party candidate, won five States and 46 electoral votes, as the map on page 345 shows. If Democrat Hubert Humphrey had carried Alaska, Delaware, Missouri, Nevada, and Wisconsin—States where Richard Nixon's margin was thin and in which Wallace had a substantial vote—Nixon's electoral vote would have been 268 and Humphrey's 224. Neither would have had a majority. The House would then have had to choose among Humphrey, Nixon, and Wallace.

Three serious objections can be raised to election by the House. First, the voting in such cases is by States, not by individual members. A small State, such as Alaska or Nevada, would have as much weight as even the most populous States. Second, if the Representatives from a State were so divided that no candidate was favored by a majority of them, the State would lose its vote. Third, the Constitution requires a majority of the States for election in the House—today 26.

Popular Vote vs. Electoral Vote, 1976

1976	Popular Vote	%	Electoral Vote	%
Carter	40,825,839	50.03	297	55.2
Ford	39,147,770	47.97	240	44.6
Others	1,629,737	2.00	1	0.2

▲ **Interpreting Tables** How does the election of 1976 reflect a possible defect of our present electoral college system?

Popular Vote vs. Electoral Vote, 1988

1988	Popular Vote	%	Electoral Vote	%
Bush	48,881,278	53.4	426	79.2
Dukakis	41,805,374	45.6	111	20.6
Others	898,168	1.0	1	0.2

▲ **Interpreting Tables** Why is this table a good example of the "winner-take-all" factor in presidential elections?

If a strong third-party candidate were involved, there is a real possibility that the House could not make a decision by inauguration day.[34]

Proposed Reforms

Observers have long recognized the defects in the electoral college system. Constitutional amendments to change the process have been introduced in every term of Congress since 1789. Most of the reforms people have offered fall under three headings: the district plan, the proportional plan, and direct popular election.

The District Plan Over time, many have proposed that the electors be chosen in each State as are members of Congress. That is, two electors would be chosen from the State at-large, and they would cast their electoral votes in line with the statewide popular vote result. The other electors would be elected, separately, in each of the State's congressional districts. Their votes would be cast in accord with the popular vote result in their district.[35]

The district plan would do away with the winner-take-all problem in the present system. Its supporters have argued that it would make the electoral vote a more accurate reflection of the popular returns.

The strongest argument against the plan is that it would not eliminate the possibility that the loser of the popular vote could still win the electoral vote. In fact, had it been in effect in 1960, Richard Nixon would have received 278 electoral votes, and he, not John Kennedy, would have won the presidency.

[34]In such a case, Section 3 of the 20th Amendment states that "the Vice President-elect shall act as President until a President shall have qualified." If no Vice President-elect is available, the Presidential Succession Act would come into play. Notice that it is even mathematically possible for the minority party in the House to have control of a majority of the individual State delegations. That party could then elect its candidate, even though he or she may have run second or even third in both the popular and the electoral vote contests.

[35]Maine now uses the district plan, as noted earlier. Any other State could do so, but it would take a constitutional amendment to make its use mandatory in all States.

Popular Vote vs. Electoral Vote, 1968

1968	Popular Vote	%	Electoral Vote	%
Nixon	31,785,148	43.4	301	55.9
Humphrey	31,274,503	42.7	191	35.5
Wallace	9,901,151	13.5	46	8.6
Others	242,568		—	—

Interpreting Tables Third party power was a real threat to the Democratic and Republican candidates in 1968. How is this shown by the table?

Further, the results under the district plan would depend very much on how the congressional districts were drawn in each State. Its use would be yet another motive for gerrymandering.

The Proportional Plan Under this arrangement, each presidential candidate would receive the same share of a State's electoral vote as he or she received in the State's popular vote. Thus, if a candidate won 40 percent of the votes cast in a State with 20 electoral votes, he or she would get eight of that State's electoral votes.

Clearly, this plan would cure the winner-take-all problem and eliminate faithless electors. And it would yield an electoral vote count more nearly in line with the popular vote, at least for each State.

The proportional plan would not, however, necessarily produce the same result nationally. Because each of the smaller States is overweighted by its two Senate-based electors, the proportional plan would still make it possible for the loser of the popular vote to win the presidency in the electoral vote. In fact, this would have happened in 1896. William Jennings Bryan would have defeated William McKinley even though McKinley had a comfortable popular vote margin of 596,985 (5.1 percent).[36]

[36]In the closest of all the presidential elections, Winfield S. Hancock would have defeated James A. Garfield in 1880, even though Garfield had a popular plurality of only 1,898 votes, 0.0213 percent. On the other hand, there would have been no "Stolen Election" in 1876, and Cleveland would have defeated Harrison in 1888.

Interpreting Tables Ask students: Since Wallace was a conservative and a Democrat, is it more likely that his votes would have gone to Nixon, a conservative, or to Humphrey, a relatively liberal Democrat? Or would his votes have been split evenly between Nixon and Humphrey?

Caption Answer By the strength of the Wallace vote.

Teacher's Resource File
See the Simulations and Debates file, pp. 35–70, and the Election Kit file, p. 39, for materials to support the chapter.

SPOTLIGHT ON: Constitutional Issues
As the Constitution mandates, seats in the electoral college were reapportioned after the 1990 census. As a result of shifts in the population, electoral college votes for the largest States now are: California with 54 votes, followed by New York with 33 and Texas with 32. Florida casts 25 electoral votes, Pennsylvania 23 and Illinois 22, followed by Ohio with 21; Michigan with 18; New Jersey with 15; and Georgia and North Carolina with 14 votes each. New Hampshire, Maine, Rhode Island, Nevada, Idaho, and Hawaii each cast 4 votes, while Alaska, Delaware, Montana, the Dakotas, Vermont, Wyoming and Washington, D.C. each cast 3.

Provide Guided Practice To guide students through the major criticisms and proposed reforms of the electoral college, make a two-column chart on the board, headed *Criticisms/Defects* and *Proposed Reforms.* Invite students to provide information from the text for the chart as you write it on the board. Then have student volunteers tell you how the information in the chart should be arranged so that each proposed reform answers a criticism or defect.

Provide Independent Practice

TRF **Teacher's Resource File** You may wish to assign Section 6 Guided Reading and Review, Unit 4 File, p. 18, to help students master section objective content.

Many critics of the plan worry about its effect on the two-party system. Certainly, its adoption would bring an increase in the number and vigor of minor parties. They would no longer need to win entire States in order to get electoral votes. Their candidates would regularly win at least some share of the electoral vote—and the odds that a presidential election would have to go to the House would be increased.[37]

Direct Popular Election The most common and widely supported proposal is the most obvious one: Do away with the electoral college system altogether and allow direct popular election of the President.

The arguments for direct election seem overpowering. The strongest one is that it would support the democratic ideal: Each vote would count equally in the national result. The winner would always be the majority or plurality choice. The dangers and confusions of the present system would be eliminated, replaced by a simple and easily understood process.

Several "practical" obstacles stand in the way of this proposal, however. Because of them, there seems little real chance of its adoption any time soon.[38]

The constitutional amendment process itself is a major stumbling block. First, there are three built-in minority vetoes in the amendment process. Two of them are in Congress, where one-third plus one of the members of either house can block the proposal of an amendment. And, one-fourth plus one of the State legislatures or conventions can defeat an amendment once it is proposed.

Second, the smaller States are greatly over-represented in the electoral college. They would lose that advantage in a direct election—so, likely, enough Senators, Representatives, or small States would oppose a direct election amendment to kill it.

Some opponents of direct election argue that it would weaken federalism, because the States, as States, would lose their role in the choice of a President.

Others believe that direct election would put too great a load on the election process. They say that because every vote cast in each State would count in the national result, the candidates would have to campaign strenuously in every State. The impact that would have on campaign time, effort, and finance would be huge and, opponents argue, probably unmanageable.[39]

Some say that direct election would spur ballot-box stuffing and other forms of vote fraud. And that, they predict, would lead to lengthy, bitter, highly explosive post-election challenges.

In many States, a State-wide election often hangs on the behavior of some specific group in the **electorate**—the mass of people who actually cast votes in an election. The result depends on how those voters cast their ballots or, even more importantly, on how heavily they do or do not turn out to vote. Thus, for example, the African American vote in Chicago is often decisive in the presidential election in Illinois. But in a direct election these groups would not hold the balance of power, the clout, they now have—so many of them oppose the direct election plan.

Given all this, there seems little real chance that direct election will come to pass any time soon—unless, that is, the electoral college system malfunctions in another presidential election. Then, a direct election amendment would likely be adopted, and quickly.

The National Bonus Plan Another and very different plan has recently surfaced. It is the national bonus plan. At first glance, the plan seems quite complicated and "off the wall." In fact, it is neither.

[37]Most of the plan's backers agree that an increase in minor party clout would mean that the popular vote winner would often fail to gain a clear majority of the electoral vote; see the table on page 345. Hence, they would lower the present requirement of a majority of the electoral votes to a plurality of at least 40 percent. If no candidate won 40 percent of the electoral votes, the two frontrunners would face one another in a runoff election.

[38]The House of Representatives did approve a direct election amendment by the necessary two-thirds vote in 1969. The measure was killed by a Senate filibuster in 1970. President Carter championed a similar proposal, but it was rejected by a Senate floor vote in 1979.

[39]In fact, it is possible for a candidate to win the presidency by carrying only the 11 largest States, because they now have a total of 270 electoral votes, exactly the minimum number to win the presidency.

Enrichment

Have students write letters to the editor of a local newspaper, advocating their point of view on the electoral college. (Easy)

The national bonus plan would keep much of the electoral college system, especially its winner-take-all feature. It would weight that feature in favor of the winner of the popular vote, however.

Under the plan, a national pool of 102 electoral votes would be awarded, automatically, to the winner of the popular vote contest. That is, that bloc of electoral votes would be added to the electoral votes that candidate won in the election. If all those votes added up to a majority of the electoral college—at least 321—that candidate would be declared the winner of the presidency. In the unlikely event that they did not, a runoff election between the two front-runners in the popular vote would then be held.

The advocates of this plan see the electors themselves as unnecessary to it, and so would do away with them. They say that their plan meets all of the major objections to the present system and all of those raised against the other proposals for its reform. They also claim their plan would almost guarantee that the winner of the popular vote would always be the winner of the electoral vote.

To date, the national bonus plan has not attracted much public attention—let alone understanding, interest, or support.

A Final Word Their case is not often heard, but the present electoral college system does have its defenders. They react to the several proposed reforms by raising the various objections to them you have just read. Beyond that they argue that critics exaggerate the "dangers" in the system. Only two elections have ever gone to the House of Representatives and none in nearly 170 years. True, the loser of the popular vote has three times won the presidency, but that has not happened in more than a century.

They also say that the arrangement, whatever its warts, has two major strengths:

(1) It is a known process. Each of the proposed, but untried, reforms may very well have defects that could not be known until they appeared in practice.

(2) It identifies the winner of the presidential election, and it does so quickly and certainly. Even in a close election, the nation does not have to wait for weeks or months to know the outcome.

VOICES *on Government*

On the Presidential Electoral Process

Jimmy Carter, 39th President of the United States

"The present system is satisfactory. To abbreviate the [presidential election] season, some evolutionary trend toward regional primaries would be good and is already taking place. The long ordeal sometimes endured by candidates can be beneficial in two ways: It ensures a broader and deeper knowledge of our country, including the smaller states, and it provides a mental, political and physical test of the various would-be Presidents in full view of the American people."

Section 6 Review

1. **Define:** electorate
2. (a) How many electors does each state have, and (b) how are they chosen?
3. What happens if no candidate gets a majority of the electoral vote?
4. What are the three major weaknesses in the electoral college system?
5. Which plan for reform of the electoral college is most widely supported?
6. On what grounds do some defend the present electoral college system?

Critical Thinking

7. **Identifying Alternatives** (p. 19) What should be the major goal of the presidential election system? Choose one of the methods discussed in this section, or make up your own.

★

Monitor Comprehension

Answers to Section 6 Review
1. The "Key Term" is defined on the following page:
a. electorate, p. 346
2. (a) As many electors as it has members of Congress. (b) By popular vote on a winner-take-all basis. **3.** The election is thrown into the House of Representatives. **4.** The three major weaknesses are (a) the winner of the popular vote may not win the presidency, (b) nothing requires the electors to vote for the candidate who wins the popular vote in their State, and (c) it is possible that the election will be decided in the House of Representatives. **5.** Abolish the electoral college system altogether and allow the President to be elected by direct popular vote. **6.** On the grounds that it is a known process and identifies the winner of the election quickly and certainly. **7.** Answers will vary but students should demonstrate an understanding of the current system.

Teacher's Resource File See the Unit 4 File, p. 19, for the Section 6 Quiz .

Closure

Remind students that, although flawed, the electoral college system identifies the winning candidate quickly and certainly. As students read the next chapter, they will learn about the responsibilities of the presidency.

Assignment Assign Chapter 14, Section 1, pp. 353–355, for the next class period.

Activity: Teaching Heterogeneous Groups

Have students develop an outline to show how a person becomes President of the United States. Suggest that they include three major headings in their outlines: *Nominations, National Convention,* and *Election.* Have them review Sections 4, 5, and 6 to find important ideas pertaining to each of these topics. Encourage students to use their own words as they add subheadings and details to their outlines.

Reteach

Have students write a letter to a member of Congress from your district arguing for one of the proposed reforms or for keeping the present system. Students' letters should identify the defects in the present system, how the reform would cure those defects (or why the defects are not significant), and also answer criticisms of the reforms.

Testing Conclusions

Objective

Analyze information to test a conclusion.

INSTRUCT

Ask students how they would evaluate this conclusion: "Saving in a bank does not guarantee the safety of your money." Ask what information students would look for to evaluate this statement. Students should understand that they would need to look for specific examples of people losing money by saving in a bank.

When students have completed each step in the feature, invite them to share their responses, as you list them on the board. Discuss the importance of testing conclusions before making decisions based on those conclusions.

Answers 1. (a) One flaw of the electoral college system. (b) A study of every presidential election to determine how often the will of the majority has been subverted. **2.** (a) Yes. (b) All sets can be used. **3.** Set "A" indicates that the Constitution does not require electors to vote according to the popular vote. Sets "B" and "C" show that on one occasion, the winner of the popular vote did not win the presidency. More information is needed to reach this conclusion, however, than one case in American history.

Testing Conclusions

Testing conclusions means examining a conclusion and determining whether or not it is supported by known facts. As you make the many decisions required of a citizen in a democracy, you will need to test the validity of the conclusions on which those decisions are based. Follow the steps below to practice testing conclusions.

1. Identify what kind of data you will need to test your conclusion. In order to test a conclusion, you need facts on which to base your test. Read the conclusion below. (a) What is the subject of the conclusion? (b) What kind of information might enable you to test this conclusion?

2. Decide what source of information you will use to test your conclusion. Once you have determined what kind of information you need to test your conclusion, you will need to find an "answer key." Look at information sets A, B, and C in the box below. (a) Will any set provide an answer to the test? (b) Can you use more than one information set?

3. Test the conclusion by comparing it to the selected information. Once you have selected your answer key or keys, you can test the conclusion. (a) Does the information set or sets you have chosen support the conclusion? (b) Is more information necessary? (c) Give reasons for each of your answers.

Conclusion: The electoral college system fails to ensure that the choice for President accurately reflects the will of the majority of voters.

A

Article II, Section 2, Clause 2: "Each State shall appoint, in such manner as the legislature thereof may direct, a number of Electors, equal to the whole number of Senators and Representatives, to which the State may be entitled in Congress . . . "

12th Amendment: "The Electors shall meet in their respective States, and vote by ballot for President and Vice President . . . . the person having the greatest number of [electoral] votes for President shall be the President, if such number be a majority of the whole number of Electors appointed . . ."

B

Electoral Vote for President (Selected Years)

Year	President Elected and Electoral Vote		Opponents and Electoral Vote	
1824	John Quincy Adams	84	Andrew Jackson Henry Clay William H. Crawford	99 37 41
1876	Rutherford B. Hayes	185	Samuel J. Tilden	184
1888	Benjamin Harrison	233	Grover Cleveland	168

C

Popular Vote for President (Selected Years)

Year	President Elected and Popular Vote		Opponents and Popular Vote	
1824	John Quincy Adams	113,122	Andrew Jackson Henry Clay William H. Crawford	151,174 46,587 44,282
1876	Rutherford B. Hayes	4,034,311	Samuel J. Tilden	4,288,548
1888	Benjamin Harrison	5,443,892	Grover Cleveland	5,534,488

TRF **Teacher's Resource File**
See the Unit 4 File, p. 20, for the Skill Application to reinforce the skill lesson.

Chapter-in-Brief

Scan all headings, photographs, charts, and other visuals in the chapter before reading the section summaries below.

Section 1 The President's Job Description (pp. 315–321) American Presidents must serve as the nation's (1) chief of state, (2) chief executive, (3) chief administrator, (4) chief diplomat, (5) commander in chief, (6) chief legislator, (7) chief of party, and (8) chief citizen. These roles must be played simultaneously, and a failure in any one of them can cripple a Presidency.

In addition, a President must meet several basic constitutional qualifications. The President is paid an annual salary of $200,000 and receives a great many other benefits, as well.

Section 2 Presidential Succession and the Vice Presidency (pp. 323–326) Originally, the Constitution was vague about what was to happen if a vacancy in the presidency occured. The 25th Amendment formalized the practice of making the Vice President the President on the death, resignation, or removal of the President.

Even though the Vice President is "only a heartbeat away from the presidency," the office has long been treated as one of little consequence. No President has ever granted a Vice President any real power.

Section 3 Presidential Selection: The Framers' Plan (pp. 327–329) The Framers did not believe that the people were qualified to select a President. So, they developed the complicated electoral college to perform this function.

Electors were supposed to choose the President based on their own best judgment. But the rise of political parties, among other factors, changed the electoral college. Parties began choosing electors, who then acted as "rubber stamps" for the parties' candidates.

Section 4 Nominating Presidential Candidates Today (pp. 330–335) In 1832, parties began using national conventions to nominate presidential candidates. At the conventions, delegates from each State's party organizations chose a ticket for the upcoming election.

Today, the selection of delegates for the conventions is a long process. Many States choose their delegates in presidential primaries. Some States also use caucuses and conventions to select delegates for the national conventions.

Section 5 At the National Convention (pp. 335–339) Conventions are grand events full of speeches and displays of party enthusiasm. The keynote address is one highlight wherein a renowned speaker seeks to whip up enthusiasm in support of a party's goals.

Another key event is the adoption of the party platform—a political statement outlining a party's policies and beliefs.

The high point of each convention is the nomination of a party's presidential candidate. Ideally, this person is someone who can carry the large and the uncommitted States in the November election.

Section 6 The Election (pp. 340–347) Voters finally cast presidential ballots in November. However, their votes do not actually elect the President. They select electors, who in turn select the President.

The electoral college system is not perfect. For example, it is possible that the loser of the popular vote will nonetheless win the presidency.

A number of plans to reform the electoral college system have been offered and debated over the past 200 years. Even the most widely supported of those proposals, direct popular vote, will not likely be adopted in the foreseeable future.

Teaching Suggestions for CHAPTER-IN-BRIEF

Below are some of the possible uses for the Chapter-in-Brief:

To Preview the Chapter You may want to assign the Chapter-in-Brief page and the Section Outlines from the Teacher Resource File before beginning Chapter 13 to introduce students to "Key Terms" and concepts in each section.

To Review the Chapter When students have completed Chapter 13, you might want to assign the Chapter-in-Brief as a tool for review, along with the Guided Reading and Reviews from the Teacher's Resource File.

To Omit the Chapter If you wish to skip Chapter 13, it may be helpful to assign the Chapter-in-Brief to students as a review before continuing to another chapter. You may also want to assign the Chapter 13 Test to assess student knowledge of the material. Then specific portions of Chapter 13 may be assigned to students needing reinforcement of "Key Terms" and concepts.

Teacher's Resource File See the Unit 4 File for the following materials:

- Section Outlines, pp. 2, 5, 8, 11, 14, 17.
- Guided Reading and Reviews, pp. 3, 6, 9, 12, 15, 18.
- Chapter 13 Test, pp. 24–26.

ADDITIONAL RESOURCES

Abramson, Paul R., *et al.Change and Continuity in the 1988 Elections.* CQ Press, 1990.

DiClerico, Robert E. *The American President.* Prentice Hall, 3rd ed., 1990.

Diller, Daniel C. and Stephen L. Robertson. *The Presidents, First Ladies, and Vice Presidents.* CQ Press, 1989.

Dunham, P. *Electoral Behavior in the United States.* Prentice Hall, 1991.

Electing the President. Film. EBDC, 1983. Color. 29 min.

Geer, John G. *Nominating Presidents: An Evaluation of Voters and Primaries.* Praeger, 1989.

Heard, Alexander. *Made in America: The Nomination and Election of Presidents.* HarperCollins, 1991.

Meet the Presidents. Computer software. Versa Computing, Inc., 1984. Apple II/II+, 48K.

Ordeal of Power: The President and the Presidency. Video. Guidance Associates, 1990. Color. 56 minutes.

The Possible President: VP's and Third Parties. 16mm film. Lucerne Films, 1976. Color. 50 min.

The Two Presidencies. Nelson-Hall, 1991.

Whitney, David C. and Robin V. Whitney. *The American Presidents: Biographies of the Chief Executives from Washington Through Bush.* Prentice Hall, 7th ed., 1990.

Answers to
CHAPTER 13 REVIEW

Vocabulary and Key Terms

Matching
1. electoral college
2. chief of party
3. chief legislator
4. presidential primary
5. electorate
6. chief of state
7. chief executive

True or False
1. False—the correct term is *chief diplomat.*
2. False—the correct term is *commander in chief.*
3. False—the correct term is *presidential electors.*
4. True.
5. True.

Word Relationships
1. winner-take-all
2. chief citizen
3. chief administrator
4. platform

Main Ideas

Section 1
1. So that he or she can successfully run the government. **2.** The Framers decided on a single four-year term with the possibility for reelection. An informal two-term limit was established, until broken by FDR. The Constitution was then amended to include the two-term limit. **3.** (a) $200,000 per year. (b) An expense account, the use of the White House, transportation and entertainment funds, a pension, and more.

Section 2
4. The Constitution states the order of succession. The Constitution also states the procedures for determining presidential disability. **5.** The 25th Amendment changed the Constitution to read that the Vice President assumes the presidency in the event of a vacancy in the office. The 25th Amendment also addressed the question of presidential disability. **6.** (a) The Constitution says little about the office, granting it only two duties. (b) The office is often regarded as of little real consequence. **7.** Vice-presidential nominees are selected largely on the basis of their ability to help get the presidential nominee elected.

Section 3
8. The Framers intended that presidential electors would make the selection of the President based on reasoned judgment and debate. They were to be selected in each State in a manner of each State legislature's choosing. Each State was to have a number of electors equal to the State's number of senators and representatives. The electors' first choice became President, their second became Vice President. **9.** Parties soon began to nominate slates of electors who bound themselves to vote for their parties' candidates. The electors became rubber stamps for their parties' chosen candidates. **10.** The 12th Amendment separated the election of President and Vice President.

Section 4
11. Parties are the exclusive nominators of candidates. Delegates to a national party convention are selected through a series of primary elections, caucuses, and conventions held within the party. The delegates then attend the national convention, where they select their party's nominee. **12.** Depend-

Chapter Review

Vocabulary and Key Terms

chief of state (p. 316)	chief of party (p. 316)	winner-take-all (p. 332)
chief executive (p. 316)	chief citizen (p. 316)	keynote address (p. 336)
chief administrator (p. 316)	presidential succession (p. 324)	platform (p. 337)
chief diplomat (p. 316)	presidential elector (p. 327)	electorate (p. 346)
commander in chief (p. 316)	electoral college (p. 328)	
chief legislator (p. 316)	presidential primary (p. 331)	

Matching: *Review the key terms in the list above. If you are not sure of a term's meaning, look up the term and review its definition. Choose a term from the list above that best matches each description.*

1. the group chosen every four years to make the formal selection of the President and Vice President
2. the role in which the President exercises leadership over his or her political party
3. the role in which the President acts as the main architect of the nation's public policies
4. an election at which a party's voters choose delegates to the party's national convention and/or express a preference for candidates for the party's nomination
5. all the people entitled to vote in a given election
6. the role in which the President acts as the head of the government
7. the role in which the President exercises the executive power of the United States

True or False: *Determine whether each statement is true or false. If it is true, write "true." If it is false, change the underlined word or words to make the statement true.*

1. As chief executive, the President is the primary architect of the nation's foreign policy.
2. As the chief of state, the President is the leader of the nation's armed forces.
3. In actuality, the electorate casts the votes that officially select the President of the United States.
4. The keynote address is usually delivered by one of the party's best orators and is one of the highlights of a national convention.
5. According to the arrangement for presidential succession, the Vice President is first in line to fill a vacancy in the presidency.

Word Relationships: *Replace the underlined definition with the correct term from the list above.*

1. In the past, some presidential primaries were contests in which the winner of the preference vote won the support of all the delegates.
2. As the representative of all the people, the President speaks for the people of the nation and offers important moral leadership.
3. As the head of a large organization that employs nearly three million people, the President leads one of the world's largest governmental machines.
4. The written declaration of the principles and policy decisions of a party is an important product of each national convention.

Main Ideas

Section 1 (pp. 315–321)

1. For what reason is it important that the President fulfill each presidential role?

2. Describe the historical development of the guidelines for the length of a President's term.
3. (a) How much is the President paid? (b) What additional forms of compensation does the President receive?

Section 2 (pp. 323–326)

4. How does the Constitution ensure a smooth transition of power in the event of presidential disability or vacancy?
5. How has the Constitution been changed over the course of history to ensure a smooth arrangement for presidential succession in all situations?
6. (a) What does the Constitution say about the role of the Vice President? (b) How does this fact relate to the reputation of the office?
7. What factors count most in the selection of a Vice President today?

Section 3 (pp. 327–329)

8. Describe the Framers' original plan and intent for the selection of the nation's President.
9. How did the rise of parties affect the functioning of the plan developed by the Framers?
10. How did the 12th Amendment change the way Presidents and Vice Presidents are selected?

Section 4 (pp. 330–335)

11. What role do political parties play in the nominating process today?
12. What are the major purposes of presidential primaries in the nominating process?
13. What factors make the current presidential nominating process confusing?

Section 5 (pp. 335–339)

14. For what major purposes do parties hold national conventions?
15. What kind of image does a convention hope to present to the voters?
16. What factors are most important to a party in the selection of a candidate?

Section 6 (pp. 340–347)

17. How does the way that electors cast their votes today differ from the intent of the Framers?
18. On what grounds is the electoral college system criticized?
19. What attempts have been made to address these criticisms?

Critical Thinking

1. **Testing Conclusions** (p. 19) What kind of information might enable you to test the accuracy of the following conclusion? Conclusion: The presidential nominating process is an important demonstration of this nation's continuing commitment to its basic principles of popular sovereignty and limited government.
2. **Checking Consistency** (p. 19) The vice presidency is regarded as both highly important and insignificant. Summarize the reasons for these conflicting viewpoints.

Getting Involved

1. **Writing Your Opinion** Write a letter to an official of one of the major parties urging him or her to nominate a woman or a minority candidate for the presidency and/or vice presidency. In your letter, explain why you believe such a nomination would be good for the nation. Also explain why such a nomination would be good for the party. After you have completed your first draft, review your arguments to ensure that they are as persuasive as possible. Correct any errors and draft a final copy.
2. **Gathering Information** If you wanted to study the relationship of popular vote to electoral vote throughout the history of United States' presidential elections, what sources might you use? Check the Government Resources Handbook on page 690 to find possible answers.

ing on the State, the primary is a process in which those who vote in a party's primary (1) elect some or all of a State's delegates to that party's convention and/or (2) express their preference for the candidates for the party's nomination. **13.** The delegate selection process differs widely from one State to the next. In addition, the rules for delegate selection tend to change frequently.

Section 5

14. To nominate presidential and vice-presidential candidates, to put forward a party platform, and to unite the party for the upcoming elections. **15.** An image of unity, confidence, and patriotism. **16.** Each party seeks to nominate a candidate who can win. He or she should have the broadest possible appeal among the party and the voters in general.

Section 6

17. Electors are almost universally "rubber stamps" for their parties. The electoral college engages in none of the deliberation that the Framers intended. **18.** Because it makes possible a situation in which the loser of the popular vote could win the presidency; because the distribution of electoral votes is such that each electoral vote does not represent the same number of voters; because situations can arise in which the electoral college is unable to select a winner in an election and the choice would be forced into the House of Representatives. **19.** Some seek to choose one elector from each district, and two electors elected at-large. Other plans would distribute electors in each State based on the proportion of votes cast for the candidates in the State. Others propose direct popular election of candidates. Another plan, the National Bonus Plan, automatically gives the winner of the popular vote a large block of electoral votes.

Critical Thinking

1. Students may suggest that they need to find out how much one person's vote still counts, i.e., how many elections have resulted in the loser having the majority of the popular vote. When this happens, popular sovereignty is not being upheld. **2.** Students might observe that the office of the Vice President is important because he or she is "a heartbeat away" from becoming President. The office is sometimes considered insignificant because the Vice President has very few official duties.

Getting Involved

1–2. Answers and results will vary, but students should demonstrate an understanding of the concepts in this chapter.

Chapter 14 Resources

In the Teacher's Resource File
The following materials are found in the Teacher's Resource File box.

Instructional Support: Unit 4 File

For the Section
Outlines, pp. 30, 33, 36, 39, 42
Guided Reading and Reviews, pp. 31, 34, 37, 40, 43
Quizzes, pp. 32, 35, 38, 41, 44

For the Chapter
Skill Application, p. 45
Case Study on Contemporary Issues, pp. 46–48
Chapter Test, pp. 49–51
Additional Test Questions, pp. 52–54

Enrichment Support Files

Supreme Court Cases, p. 11
Participatory Government Activities, pp. 4–19
Simulations and Debates: The War Powers Act
Historical and Legal Documents, p. 29
Comparative Government: A Multicultural View, pp. 12–13

Computer Test Bank and Assessment
Transparency Package, pp. 14, 39

Chapter 14 Focus

Introduce the Chapter Tell students that in this chapter they will learn about presidential powers and how different Presidents have exercised those powers. Read with students the Chapter Preview and Objectives.

Writing Activity Direct students' attention to "Describe." Have students brainstorm a list of various jobs and duties of the President. Then ask students to write a job description for the office of President based on their lists.

Motivate for Learning Direct students' attention to "Predict." Ask students to predict the significance of President Truman's sign. Discuss why it is important that the President be the one to "stop the buck" in the American system of government.

The Presidency in Action

Chapter Preview

One of President Bush's key advisors described Air Force One, the presidential jet, as an extension of the Oval Office, where the President works, and a mobile East Wing, where he sleeps. The airplane features 85 telephones, four computers, two copying machines, a conference room, a pressroom with TV monitors, and a television system that can receive eight channels at the same time.

Even when traveling six miles above the earth, the President is never out of touch. Perhaps it was this characteristic of the office that prompted Lyndon B. Johnson to write, "No one can experience with the President of the United States the glory and agony of his office. . . . No one can share the burden of his decisions or the scope of his duties." This chapter is about the scope and growth of those duties and the ways in which they are exercised.

Before you read this chapter:

- **Describe** several of the President's many jobs and duties.
- **Predict** why President Truman displayed a sign on his desk reading, "The buck stops here."

As you read, focus on the main objective for each section. Understand:

1. The historic and ongoing debate over the scope of presidential power.
2. The nature and extent of the executive power of the President.
3. The President's diplomatic and military powers.
4. The President's legislative and judicial powers.
5. The functions of the executive agencies and the role of the cabinet.

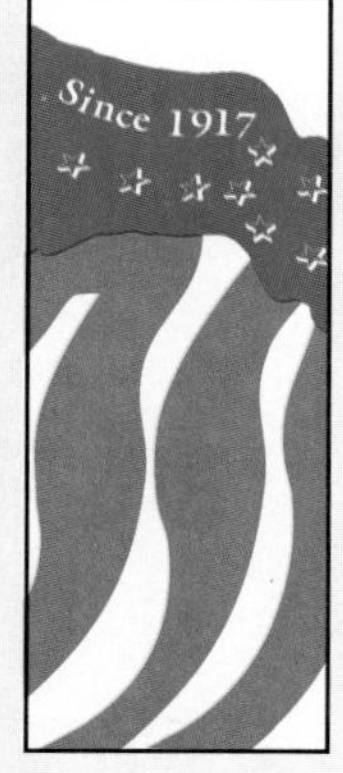

Magruder's American Government: *A Witness to Change* by William A. McClenaghan

Reading past editions of this book inevitably brings to mind Alphonse Karr's oft-quoted maxim: "The more things change, the more they are the same."

But that point can be carried only so far, of course. The American system of government is extraordinarily dynamic, and change is a basic element of its character. Examples of that fact can be found in every chapter of every edition of *American Government.*

As but one of the many examples of change found in this chapter, take our discussion of the Executive Office of the President. The 1940 edition of *American Government* noted, "To assist the President in his strenuous duties, he appoints three Secretaries and six Administrative Assistants at $10,000 a year each." This passage had to be revised for this edition, as it has had to be revised through every edition since 1940.

"**Great American Workout**" The President's many duties include promoting the general welfare of the American people. Here, the President and the First Lady show their support for physical health and fitness.

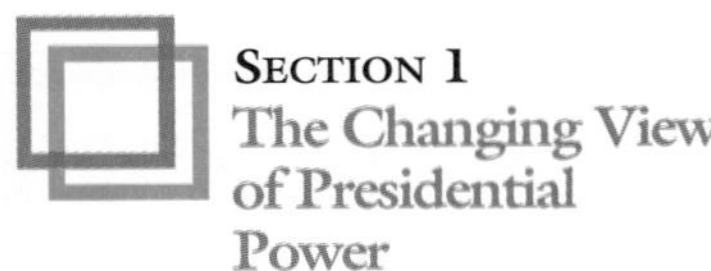

Section 1
The Changing View of Presidential Power

Focus

Teacher's Resource File See the Unit 4 File, p. 30, for the Section 1 Outline.

Objectives

14.1 Examine the historical and ongoing debate over the proper scope of presidential power.

14.2 Analyze the ways in which presidential power has grown over time.

Bellringer Activity Ask students to quickly name the five strongest United States Presidents. Write their responses on the board. Then ask students to explain their answers.

State the Purpose The definition of the presidency and of presidential power has grown since 1787 when the Framers outlined presidential duties in the Constitution. In Section 1, students will examine the history of the office of President, and they will look at ways presidential power has grown throughout history.

ABCNEWS INTERACTIVE

The following video segments may be used to highlight aspects of the powers of the presidency.

Powers of the President Guidebook
Chapter 3: Constitution and the President, p. 4
Chapter 40: Historical Figures, p. 48
Chapter 42: Presidents of the United States, p. 50

1 The Changing View of Presidential Power

Find Out

- What is the historic and ongoing debate over the proper scope of presidential power?
- In what ways has the power grown over time?

Key Term:
media

The presidency is often called "the most powerful office in the world." But is this what the Framers had in mind when they created the post in 1787? At Philadelphia, they purposely created a single executive with broad powers. But they also agreed with Thomas Jefferson, who wrote in the Declaration of Independence that "a Tyrant is unfit to be the ruler of a free people." And, so, just as purposely, they constructed a "checked" presidency.

In this section, you will consider the forces that have shaped the growth of presidential power over the past 200 years.

Article II of the Constitution begins in the following way:

> "The executive power shall be vested in a President of the United States of America."

With those few words, the Framers established the presidency. With them, they laid the basis for the vast power and influence the nation's chief executive has today.

The Constitution does set out several other, and somewhat more specific, grants of presidential power. Thus, as you have read at various points in the book, the President is given the power to command the armed forces, to make treaties, to approve or veto acts of Congress, to send and receive diplomatic representatives, to grant pardons and reprieves, and "to take care that the laws be faithfully executed."[1]

But, notice that the Constitution deals with the powers of the presidency in very sketchy fashion. Article II reads almost as an outline. It has been called "the most loosely drawn chapter" in

[1] Most of the specific grants of presidential power are found in Article II, Sections 2 and 3. A few are elsewhere in the Constitution, however, such as the veto power, in Article I, Section 7, Clause 2.

Vocabulary

Direct students' attention to "Key Terms" on page 353. Ask them to discuss the power of television, radio, and the newspapers, and how a President's use of the media might enable him to achieve greater power.

Reading Strategy: Predicting Content

Before they begin the selection, have students read the major headings in Section 1. Point out that the headings form a brief outline of the content. Then invite students to write a prediction of the content.

INSTRUCT

Explain/Analyze Explain to students that the presidency is perhaps the most loosely defined component of the government created by the Constitution.

Ask students to analyze the historical growth of the presidency. As part of this analysis, you might ask students to consider the following questions: In what ways has the United States changed since 1789? (*Possible answers: It has more people and territory. It has been through wars and economic crises.*) How might these changes have affected the presidency? (*They have tended to increase the responsibilities of the office.*)

Interpreting Political Cartoons Ask students to comment on the role of Congress in the cartoon. (*Congress is giving the President greater authority.*)

Caption Answer Congress.

Provide Guided Practice Write the following on the board: "Debate over presidential power" and "Reasons for growth in presidential power." Ask students to identify the main ideas in the text that address these two points.

Provide Independent Practice

TRF **Teacher's Resource File** You may wish to assign Section 1 Guided Reading and Review, Unit 4 File, p. 31, to help students master section objective content.

the nation's fundamental law.[2] It does not define "the executive power." The other grants of presidential authority are put in equally broad terms.

Much of the story of the development of the American system of government can be told in terms of the growth of presidential power. A large part of our political history has revolved around a continuing struggle over the meaning of the constitutional phrase "executive power." That struggle has pitted those who have argued for a weaker presidency, subordinate to Congress, against those who have pressed for a stronger, independent chief executive.

That never-ending contest began at the Philadelphia Convention in 1787. At that time, several Framers agreed with Roger Sherman of Connecticut who, according to James Madison's *Notes*

> "considered the executive magistracy as nothing more than an institution for carrying the will of the legislature into effect, and that the person or persons [occupying the presidency] ought to be appointed by and accountable to the legislature only, which was the depository of the supreme will of the Society."

[2] Edward S. Corwin, *The President: Office and Powers* (New York: New York University Press, 1957), 4th ed., page 3.

KINDA PINCHES ACROSS THE TOES – GIMME A SIZE LARGER.
CONGRESS
VAST PRESIDENTIAL AUTHORITY
Chicago Historical Society

Interpreting Political Cartoons The cartoon above comments on the growth of presidential power through the years. Who does the cartoonist blame for allowing this expansion to occur?

As you have seen, those who argued for a stronger executive—led by Alexander Hamilton, James Wilson, and James Madison—carried the day. They persuaded the convention to establish a single executive, chosen independently of Congress and with its own distinct field of powers.

Why Presidential Power Has Grown

Over the course of American history, the champions of a stronger presidency have almost always prevailed. One of the leading reasons they have is the "unity" of the presidency. The office and its powers are held by one person. The President is the single, commanding head of the executive branch. On the other hand, Congress consists of two houses. Both of them must agree on a matter before the Congress can do anything. Moreover, one of those two houses is made up of 100 separately elected members, and the other has 435 members.

Several other factors have worked to strengthen the role and the powers of the presidency. One highly important one has been referred to a number of times: the influence the Presidents themselves have had on the office.

Yet another influence has been pressures from the increasingly complex nature of the nation's social and economic life. As the United States has become more industrialized and technologically centered, the people have demanded that the Federal Government play a larger role in a long list of areas of public concern, such as transportation, labor-management relations, civil rights, health, welfare, communications, education, and environmental protection. And it has been to the presidency that they have most often looked for leadership in these matters.

Another of these closely related factors has been the frequent need for extraordinary and decisive action in times of national emergency—most notably in times of war. The ability of the President—the single, commanding chief executive—to act in such situations has done much to strengthen the executive power.

Congress itself has had a major hand in strengthening the presidency, especially as it has passed the thousands of laws that have been an essential part of the historic growth of

Enrichment

Ask students to write a letter to either Theodore Roosevelt or William Howard Taft in response to their quotes on page 355. Students may write a favorable or a negative response to either president's views. (Average)

SPOTLIGHT ON: Economics

One period of growth in the powers of the presidency took place during the administrations of Franklin D. Roosevelt in the 1930s and 1940s. That fact is illustrated by the increase in the federal budget during FDR's tenure. Roosevelt's New Deal programs boosted the federal budget from $3 billion in 1929 to $9.5 billion a decade later. That $9.5 billion budget included a deficit as large as the entire 1929 budget. World War II, however, ushered in a truly massive federal budget expansion, and the budget skyrocketed to $95.2 billion in 1945, the last year of the war.

the Federal Government. Congress has neither the time nor the technical knowledge to do much more than provide the basic outlines of public policy. It has been forced to delegate substantial authority to the executive branch.

A number of other factors have also fed the growth of the executive power. Among them have been the President's roles as chief legislator, party leader, and chief citizen. Another is the huge amount of staff support a President has. Still another is the unique position from which the President can attract and hold the public's attention, and so gather support for policies and actions. Every recent President, from Franklin Roosevelt to George Bush, has purposely used the **media**—means of communi- 1.a cating with people, such as the press, radio, and television—to that end.

How Presidents Have Viewed Their Power

What the presidency is at any given time depends, in no small part, on the manner in which the President views the office and exercises its several powers.

Historically, Presidents have held one of two general and contrasting views. The stronger and the more effective of them have taken a broad view of their powers. Theodore Roosevelt defined this position in what he called the stewardship theory:

> "My view was that every executive officer . . . in high position, was a steward of the people bound actively and affirmatively to do all he could for the people. . . . I declined to adopt the view that what was imperatively necessary for the Nation could not be done by the President unless he could find some specific authorization to do it. My belief was that it was not only [a President's] right but his duty to do anything that the needs of the Nation demanded unless such action was forbidden by the Constitution or by the laws. . . . I did not usurp power, but I did greatly broaden the use of executive power. In other words, I acted for the public welfare, I acted for the common well-being of all our people, whenever and in whatever manner was necessary, unless prevented by direct constitutional or legislative prohibition."[3]

Ironically, the strongest presidential statement of the opposing view came from Roosevelt's handpicked successor in the office, William Howard Taft. Looking back upon his presidency, Taft had this to say about Roosevelt's view:

> "My judgment is that the view of Mr. Roosevelt, ascribing an undefined residuum of power to the President, is an unsafe doctrine. . . . The true view of the executive function is, as I conceive it, that the President can exercise no power which cannot be fairly and reasonably traced to some specific grant of power or justly implied and included within such express grant . . . Such specific grant must be either in the Federal Constitution or in an act of Congress passed in pursuance thereof. There is no undefined residuum of power which he can exercise because it seems to be in the public interest."[4]

Recall this point, from Section 1 of the last chapter: The President plays a number of different roles. As you will see in the sections ahead, the presidency can also be described in another quite useful way—by grouping the specific powers of the office under five main headings: the President's executive, diplomatic, military, legislative, and judicial powers.

Section 1 Review

1. **Define:** media
2. Around what two competing views of "the executive power" can much of the nation's political history be written?
3. What are three reasons for the historical growth of presidential power?
4. Describe the two major and contrasting views of the presidency.

Critical Thinking

5. **Identifying Assumptions** (p. 19) Read the statement by Theodore Roosevelt on this page. What does Roosevelt assume about the "needs of the nation"? Explain why you agree or disagree with this assumption.

★

[3] *Theodore Roosevelt: An Autobiography* (New York: Macmillan, 1913), page 389.

[4] *Our Chief Magistrate and His Powers* (New York: Columbia University Press, 1916), pages 139–140, 144.

Monitor Comprehension

Answers to Section 1 Review
1. The "Key Term" is defined on the following page:
a. media, p. 355
2. Those who want a weaker presidency and those who favor a more independent President.
3. (1) The influence of individual Presidents. (2) The growing complexity of social and economic life, which has led to a demand for expanded leadership. (3) The need for strong leadership in times of national emergency. **4.** One view holds that the President can act in whatever manner necessary for the common good. The other view holds that the President must use only those powers that have been specifically granted to the office. **5.** Roosevelt assumes that he could accurately interpret "the needs of the nation." Reactions to Roosevelt's assumption will vary.

Closure

The extent of the powers of the presidency has long been the subject of debate. Over the course of U.S. history, those favoring a stronger President have generally prevailed. Their arguments have been aided by such factors as the nature of the office itself and the growing complexity of economic and social life. In Section 2, students will examine some specific executive powers of the President.

Assignment Assign Section 2, pp. 356–360, for the next class period.

Teacher's Resource File
See the Unit 4 File, p. 32, for the Section 1 Quiz.

Reteach

Tell students to read the long quote by Madison that appears on page 354. Ask students to discuss whether or not they agree with this quote and why. Also tell students to explain how the view conveyed in this quote has fared over the course of United States history. How would that view be received today?

Activity: Cooperative Learning

Time: Two class periods. **Activity:** Debate Theodore Roosevelt's view of the presidency versus that of William Howard Taft. **Grouping:** Teams of four students. **Purpose:** Refer to the quoted material on page 355. Assign Roosevelt's statement about the presidency to half the teams and Taft's statement to the remaining teams. Explain that teams are to analyze the assigned statement and to prepare a list of arguments supporting that view. **Roles:** Assign the following roles: team leader, recorder. **Outcome:** Invite two volunteer teams to debate the issue for the class. Have the class evaluate the arguments of each team and vote on the winning team.

SECTION 2
The President's Executive Powers

FOCUS

Teacher's Resource File See the Unit 4 File, p. 33, for the Section 2 Outline.

Objectives

14.3 Examine the scope of the President's executive powers.

14.4 Determine the ways in which the President exercises executive powers.

Bellringer Activity Ask students to quickly generate a list of current events or activities that they have read or heard about involving the President. For each example, ask students if they can identify or define the nature of the presidential role the President is fulfilling by the action.

State the Purpose The President of the United States has a number of important roles and responsibilities. Among the President's primary responsibilities is the execution of the law. The President is equipped with several powers with which he or she can carry out this responsibility. Students will read about these powers in Section 2.

ABCNEWS INTERACTIVE

The following video segments may be used to highlight aspects of the President's executive powers.

POWERS OF THE PRESIDENT GUIDEBOOK

Chapter 22: Carrying Out Laws, p. 29

Chapter 19: Supreme Court Nominations, p. 25

Chapter 20: Cabinet Nominations, p. 26

2 The President's Executive Powers

Find Out:

- What is the scope of the President's executive powers?
- How does the President exercise these powers?

Key Term:

executive order

Thomas Jefferson wrote this to a friend in 1789: "The execution of the laws is more important than the making of them." Whether Jefferson was altogether right about that or not, in this section you will see that the President's power to execute the law endows him with an enormous amount of power.

Executing the Law

As chief executive, the President executes—enforces, administers, carries out—the provisions of federal law. The power to do so rests on two brief constitutional provisions. The first of them is the oath of office the President must take:

> "I do solemnly swear (or affirm) that I will faithfully execute the office of President of the United States, and will, to the best of my ability, preserve, protect, and defend the Constitution of the United States."[5]

The other provision is the Constitution's command that "he shall take care that the laws be faithfully executed."[6]

The President's power to execute the law covers all federal laws. Their number, and the different subject matters they cover, nearly boggle the mind. The armed forces, social security, civil rights, housing, taxes, environmental pollution, collective bargaining, farm price supports, public health, and immigration—these only begin the list; there are scores of others.

[5]Article II, Section 1, Clause 8.

[6]Article II, Section 3; this provision gives the President what is often called the take care power.

The President and the President's subordinates have much to say about the meaning of the law, just as do Congress and the courts. In executing and enforcing law, the executive branch also interprets it. The Constitution requires the President to execute *all* federal laws no matter what the chief executive's own views of any of them may be. But the President may, and does, use some discretion as to how vigorously and in what particular way any given law will be applied in practice.

To look at the point more closely: Many laws that Congress passes are written in fairly broad terms. Congress sets out the basic policies and standards. The specific details, much of the fine print, necessary to the actual, day-to-day administration of the law, are usually left to be worked out in the executive branch.

For example, the immigration laws require that all immigrants seeking permanent admission to this country must be able to "read and understand some dialect or language." But what does this literacy requirement mean in everyday practice? How well must an alien be able to read and write? What words in some language must he or she know, and how many of them? The law does not say. Rather, such answers come from within the executive branch—in this case, from the Immigration and Naturalization Service in the Department of Justice.

The Ordinance Power

From what has just been said, the President clearly deserves the title of chief administrator as well as chief executive. The job of administering and applying most federal law is the day-to-day work of all of the many departments, bureaus, offices, boards, commissions, councils, and other agencies that make up the huge executive branch of the Federal Government. All of the some three million men and women who staff those agencies are subject to the President's control and direction.

The President has the power to issue execu-
1.a tive orders. An **executive order** is a directive, rule, or regulation that has the effect of law. The power to issue these orders, the ordinance power, arises from two sources: the Constitution and acts of Congress.

Reading Strategy: Problem Solving

Tell students to imagine that they are President. They have just learned that their own head of the Environmental Protection Agency has instructed EPA officials to go easy on enforcement of certain antipollution laws. You are unhappy with this action and want to reverse it. What's more, this is just the latest in a string of conflicts you have had with this official. Tell students to look for ways to solve these problems as they read the section.

Vocabulary

Point out "Key Term" on page 356. Provide students with an example, such as an executive order directing the military forces to desegregate. Reinforce the point that these orders have the effect of law.

Appointing Power President Bush introduces several high-level appointees to his first administration. Department of Transportation head Sam Skinner (third from left) replaced John Sununu as chief of staff in late 1991.

The Constitution does not mention the ordinance power in so many words, but that power is clearly intended. In granting certain powers to the President, the Constitution obviously anticipates their use. In order to exercise those powers, the President must have the power to issue the necessary orders, as well as the power to implement them. The President must also have the power to authorize his subordinates to issue such orders.[7]

As the number, the scope, and the complexity of governmental problems have grown, Congress has found it necessary to delegate more and more discretion to the President and to presidential subordinates to spell out the policies and programs it has passed. Members of Congress are not, and cannot be expected to be, experts in all of the fields in which they must legislate.

The Appointing Power

A President cannot hope to succeed without loyal subordinates who support the policies of the President's administration.

The Constitution provides that the President

> "by and with the advice and consent of the Senate . . . shall appoint ambassadors, other public ministers, and consuls, judges of the Supreme Court, and all other officers of the United States whose appointments are not otherwise herein provided for . . . but the Congress may by law vest the appointment of such inferior officers, as they think proper, in the President alone, in the courts of law, or in the heads of departments."[8]

Acting alone, the President names only a handful of the nearly three million federal civilian employees. Many of that handful fill the top spots in the White House Office, as you will read.

With Senate consent, the President names most of the top-ranking officers of the Federal Government. Among them are ambassadors and

---

[7]All executive orders are published in the *Federal Register*, which appears five times a week. At least annually, all orders currently in force are published in the *Code of Federal Regulations*. Both of these publications are issued by the National Archives and Records Administration.

[8]Article II, Section 2, Clause 2. Those whose appointments are "otherwise provided for" are the Vice President, senators, representatives, and presidential electors.

INSTRUCT

Explain/Discuss Point out the quote by Jefferson at the beginning of the section. Ask students to explain what Jefferson meant. (*Possible answer: It does not matter what a law says if it is not carried out properly.*)

Explain to students that the President has several powers with which to execute the law. Ask students to identify these powers as they are discussed in the section. (*Ordinance, appointing, and removal.*) Next have students discuss these powers. You might ask students to react to the idea that the President can issue orders that have the effect of law. Ask students whether or not they think this gives the President too much power. Should Congress restrain this power by making the laws it passes less subject to interpretation? What might happen if the President did not have the ordinance power? (*Possible answer: The President would be unable to execute any of his or her ideas.*)

Next, consider the appointment and removal power. Ask students to discuss the importance of having loyal subordinates. (*Possible answer: The President can be certain that his or her policies are being carried out properly.*) Then ask students to discuss the question of whether the President should be required to obtain Senate consent in order to remove officials appointed with Senate consent.

SPOTLIGHT ON: Multiculturalism

The ordinance power permits the President to take independent initiatives that may not be popular with other branches of government. One good example of this point is President Truman's integration of the U.S. armed forces, instituted by Executive Order 9981 in 1948. While other civil rights reforms promoted by Truman's administration failed in Congress, the ordinance power gave the President a means to make a substantive civil rights reform in spite of congressional and court opposition. United States forces served in integrated units for the first time during the Korean War.

VOICES *on Government*

Lyndon B. Johnson,
36th President of the United States

On Working with Congress to Execute the Law

"[A] President must be willing to bypass the Congress and take the issue to the people. By instinct and experience, I preferred to work from within, knowing that good legislation is the product not of public rhetoric but of private negotiations and compromise. But sometimes a President has to put Congress' feet to the fire. . . . Sometimes it seemed that the only way to reach the papers and the people was to pick a fight with the Congress, to say mean words and show my temper."

other diplomats; cabinet members and their top aides; the heads of such independent agencies as the Environmental Protection Agency and the National Aeronautics and Space Administration; all federal judges, attorneys, and marshals; and all officers in the armed forces.

When the President makes one of these appointments, the nomination is sent to the Senate where the support of a majority of the senators present and voting is needed for confirmation. As you may recall, the unwritten rule of senatorial courtesy plays an important part in this process. As noted in Chapter 11, Section 4, that rule applies to the choice of those federal officers who serve within a State—a federal district judge or a federal marshal, for example. The rule holds that the Senate will approve only those federal appointees acceptable to the senator or senators of the President's party from the State involved.

The practical effect of this custom, which is closely followed in the Senate, is to place a meaningful part of the President's appointing power in the hands of particular senators.

Of course, not all executive branch employees are chosen by the President and Senate. Well over half of all the federal civilian work force is selected on the basis of competitive civil service examinations. Today, the Office of Personnel Management examines applicants for some two million positions.

The Removal Power

The power to remove is the other side of the appointment coin, and it is as critically important to presidential success as the power to appoint. Except for mention of the little-used impeachment process,[9] however, the Constitution does not say how or by whom appointed officers may be dismissed, whether for incompetence, for opposition to presidential policies, or for any other cause.

The Historical Debate The question was hotly debated in the first session of Congress in 1789. Several members argued that for those offices for which appointment required Senate approval, Senate consent should also be required for removal. They insisted that this restriction on presidential authority was essential to congressional supervision (oversight) of the executive branch. But others argued that the President could not "take care that the laws be faithfully executed" without a free hand to dismiss those who were incompetent or otherwise undesirable.

The latter view prevailed. The 1st Congress gave to the President the power to remove any officer he appointed, except federal judges. Over the years since then, Congress has sometimes tried, with little success, to restrict the President's freedom to dismiss.

One notable instance came in 1867. Locked with Andrew Johnson in the fight over Reconstruction, Congress passed the Tenure of Office Act. The law's plain purpose was to prevent

[9] Article II, Section 4; see Chapter 11, Section 4.

Enrichment

Ask students to assume the role of an advocate of either a weak or a strong presidency. Have them write a brief set of guidelines about how a President ought to exercise each of the executive powers. (Easy)

Teacher's Resource File
See the Unit 4 File, pp. 46–48, for the Case Study on Contemporary Issues for Chapter 14.

President Johnson from removing several top officers in his administration, especially the secretary of war, Edwin M. Stanton. The law provided that any person holding an office by presidential appointment with Senate consent should remain in that office until a successor had been confirmed by the Senate. The President vetoed the bill, charging that it was an unconstitutional invasion of executive authority. The veto, which was overridden, and Stanton's removal sparked the move for Johnson's impeachment. Nevertheless, the law was ignored in practice. It was finally repealed in 1887.

Removal and the Supreme Court The question of the President's removal power did not reach the Supreme Court until *Myers* v. *United States*, 1926. In 1876, Congress had passed a law requiring Senate consent before the President could dismiss any first-, second-, or third-class postmaster.

In 1920, without consulting the Senate, President Woodrow Wilson removed Frank Myers as the postmaster at Portland, Oregon. Myers then sued for the salary for the rest of his four-year term. He based his claim on the point that he had been removed in violation of the 1876 law. The Court found the law unconstitutional, however. Its opinion was written by Chief Justice William Howard Taft, himself a former President. The Court held that the power of removal was an essential part of the executive power, clearly necessary to the faithful execution of the laws.

The Supreme Court did place some limit on the President's removal power in 1935, in *Humphrey's Executor* v. *United States*. President Herbert Hoover had appointed William Humphrey to a seven-year term on the Federal Trade Commission (FTC) in 1931. When Franklin D. Roosevelt entered office in 1933, he found Humphrey in sharp disagreement with many of his policies. He asked Humphrey to resign, saying that his administration would be better served with someone else on the FTC. When Humphrey refused, Roosevelt removed him. Humphrey soon died, but his heirs filed a suit for back salary.

The Supreme Court upheld the heirs' claim. It based its decision on the act creating the FTC.

Presidents on the Presidency

"[The presidency is] a place of splendid misery."
–*Thomas Jefferson*

"The four most miserable years of my life were my four years in the presidency."
–*John Quincy Adams*

"Nobody ever left the presidency with less regret."
–*Rutherford B. Hayes*

"What is there in this place that a man should ever want to get into it!"
–*James A. Garfield*

"I have had enough of it, Heaven knows! I have had all the honor there is in this place, and have had responsibilities enough to kill any man."
–*William McKinley*

"I'm glad to be going– this is the loneliest place in the world."
–*William H. Taft*

"[The presidency is] a prison."
–*Warren G. Harding*

"The first twelve years are the hardest."
–*Franklin D. Roosevelt*

"There is no exaltation in the office of the President of the United States—sorrow is the proper word."
–*Harry S Truman*

"No one can experience with the President of the United States the glory and agony of his office."
–*Lyndon B. Johnson*

Interpreting Charts This chart shows that many Presidents have viewed the presidency as a bittersweet experience. What common theme runs through these quotations?

Interpreting Charts Ask students to think about the challenge of serving as President according to the quotes presented in the chart. Have them speculate about whether or not they would like to become President. Tell students to explain the reasons for their decisions.

Caption Answer Isolation, lack of appreciation, frustration.

Provide Guided Practice Ask volunteers to write the President's executive powers on the board. (*Take care, ordinance, appointment, and removal powers.*) Have students copy this information on a sheet of paper and then list the following examples under the proper power: Issuing an order that requires firms doing business with the Federal Government to hire more minority employees (*ordinance power*); nominating an ambassador to Kuwait (*appointment power*); ensuring that civil rights legislation is being followed (*take care power*); seeking the resignation of a cabinet official (*removal power*).

Provide Independent Practice

TRF **Teacher's Resource File** You may wish to assign Section 2 Guided Reading and Review, Unit 4 File, p. 34, to help students master section objective content.

Monitor Comprehension

Answers to Section 2 Review
1. The "Key Term" is defined on the following page:
a. executive order, p. 356
2. It is up to the executive branch to work out the specific details of the day-to-day administration of many laws. **3.** All of the agencies that administer federal law are under the authority of the President. **4.** It gives the President power to manage the executive branch and enables him or her to execute the law. **5.** (a) Ambassadors and diplomats; cabinet members and their top aides; heads of certain independent agencies; federal judges, attorneys, and marshals; officers in the armed forces. (b) The Senate offers advice and consent. Senators confirm or reject appointments by majority vote. **6.** Some may disagree, saying that senatorial courtesy falls within the Senate's right to offer advice and consent. Others may agree, saying that it enables one or two senators to influence the appointment process.

Closure

The President has executive powers with which he or she performs the duties of the office. These are the take care power, the ordinance power, and the power to appoint and remove subordinates. In Section 3, students will read about the President's powers in the fields of diplomacy and the military.

Assignment Assign Section 3, pp. 361–365, for the next class period.

Lonely at the Top The enormous responsibility shouldered by the chief executive is evident in this famous photograph of President John F. Kennedy alone in the Oval Office.

That law provides that a member of the commission may be removed only for "inefficiency, neglect of duty, or malfeasance in office."[10] The President had given none of these reasons when he removed Humphrey.

The Court further held that Congress does have the power to set the conditions under which a member of the FTC and other such agencies might be removed by the President. It did so because those agencies, the independent regulatory commissions, are not purely executive agencies. You will read more about such agencies in Chapter 15, Section 2.

As a general rule, however, the President may remove those whom the President appoints. Occasionally, the President does have to remove someone; most often, however, what was in fact a dismissal is called a "resignation."

[10] *Malfeasance* is wrongful conduct, especially by a public officeholder.

Section 2 Review

1. **Define:** executive order
2. In what way can the executive branch affect the meaning of a particular law?
3. How is the President the chief administrator as well as the chief executive?
4. In what way does the ordinance power enable the President to exercise the executive powers?
5. (a) What officers does the President appoint? (b) What is the Senate's role in the appointment process?

Critical Thinking

6. **Demonstrating Reasoned Judgment** (p. 19) Explain why you agree or disagree with this statement: The unwritten rule of senatorial courtesy contradicts the principle of separation of powers.

★

Teacher's Resource File
See the Unit 4 File, p. 35, for the Section 2 Quiz.

Reteach

Have students list each of the executive powers discussed in the section. Then have students review the section and write explanations of each of the powers. Encourage students to use examples from the text where appropriate.

3 The Diplomatic and Military Powers

Find Out:

- What is the scope of the President's diplomatic powers? How does the President exercise these powers?
- What is the scope of the President's military powers? How does the President exercise these powers?

Key Terms:

treaty, executive agreement, recognition

President John F. Kennedy once described the pressures of the presidency in these words:

> "When I ran for the presidency . . . I knew the country faced serious challenges, but I could not realize—nor could any man who does not bear the burdens of this office—how heavy and constant would be those burdens."

When Kennedy made that comment, he had in mind, particularly, the subject of this section: the President's awesome responsibilities as chief diplomat and as commander in chief.

The Power to Make Treaties

A **treaty** is a formal agreement between two or 1.a
more sovereign states. The President, usually acting through the secretary of state, negotiates these international agreements. The Senate must give its approval, by a two-thirds vote of the members present, before a treaty made by the President can become effective.[11] Recall, the Constitution makes treaties a part of the "supreme law of the land."

The Framers considered the Senate—with, originally, only 26 members—a suitable council to advise the President in foreign affairs. Secrecy was thought to be necessary and was seen as an impossibility in a body as large as the House.

The two-thirds rule creates the possibility that a relatively small minority in the Senate can kill a treaty. To take one example: In 1919 the Senate rejected the Versailles Treaty, the general peace agreement to end World War I. The treaty included provisions for the League of Nations. Forty-nine senators voted for the pact and 35 against, but the vote was 7 short of the necessary two-thirds. More than once a President has been forced to bow to the views of a few senators in order to get a treaty approved, even when this has meant making concessions opposed by the majority.

At times, a President has had to turn to roundabout methods in order to achieve his goals. When a Senate minority defeated a treaty to annex Texas, President Tyler was able to bring about annexation in 1845 by encouraging passage of a joint resolution—a move that required only a majority vote in each house. In 1898 President McKinley used the same tactic to annex Hawaii, again after a treaty his administration had negotiated had failed to achieve the necessary two-thirds vote in the Senate.

Executive Agreements

More and more, international agreements, especially the routine ones, are made as executive
1.b agreements. **Executive agreements** are pacts between the President and the heads of foreign states, or their subordinates. Unlike treaties, executive agreements do not require Senate consent.

Most executive agreements either flow out of legislation already passed by Congress or out of treaties to which the Senate has agreed. The President can make these executive agreements

---

[11]Contrary to popular belief, the Senate does not ratify treaties. The Constitution requires the Senate's "advice and consent" to a treaty made by the President. Once the Senate has approved a treaty, the President ratifies it by the exchange of formal notifications with the other party or parties to the agreement.

Treaties have the same legal standing as do acts passed by Congress. Congress may repeal (abrogate) a treaty by passing a law contrary to its provisions, and an existing law may be repealed by the terms of a treaty. When a treaty and a statute conflict, the courts consider the latest enacted to be the law (*The Head Money Cases*, 1884). The terms of a treaty cannot conflict with the higher law of the Constitution (*Missouri* v. *Holland*, 1920), but the Supreme Court has never found a treaty provision to be unconstitutional.

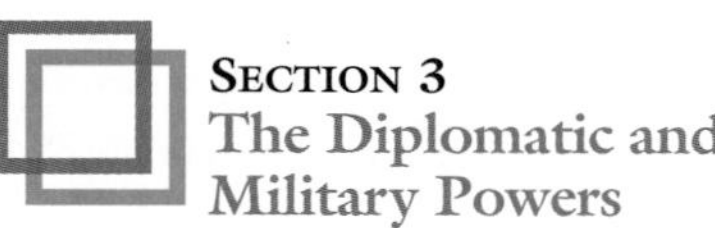

SECTION 3
The Diplomatic and Military Powers

FOCUS

Teacher's Resource File See the Unit 4 File, p. 36, for the Section 3 Outline.

Objectives

14.5 Analyze the scope and exercise of the President's diplomatic powers.

14.6 Analyze the scope and exercise of the President's military powers.

Bellringer Activity Have students imagine that they are President. Country Y has invaded a close ally. As President, they must decide quickly how to respond. How do they feel about the idea of sending hundreds of thousands of young men and women halfway around the world to fight a war? Explain to students that this is the kind of a decision that Presidents must be prepared to make.

State the Purpose Decisions about war and peace are among the many difficult choices facing the President. It is the President's job to oversee this country's relations with the other countries of the world. In Section 3, students will examine the role of President as diplomat and as military chief.

Vocabulary

Direct students' attention to "Key Terms" on page 361. As they read the text in Section 3, tell students to notice the differences between a treaty and an executive agreement. Ask students how executive agreements help make Presidents more powerful than Congress in diplomatic affairs. *(A President makes executive agreements without the consent of the Senate.)*

Reading Strategy: Question Writing

Have students read the major headings in Section 3. Ask students to convert each of these headings into questions. As they read through the text, have students write down answers to the questions they created.

INSTRUCT

Analyze Have students analyze the enormous power of the President in the diplomatic field. For example, you could ask students to describe the several options the President has for making diplomatic agreements. (*Treaties, joint resolutions, executive agreements.*) Have students discuss the importance of the power to recognize countries. You might cite recent examples such as President Bush's recognition of several former Soviet republics in 1991.

Next, explain that like the diplomatic powers, the military powers are quite broad. Have students compare the options of the President in this field with those in the diplomatic field. (*In both cases, the President has several means by which he or she can circumvent the checks and balances of Congress. For example, although only Congress can declare war, the President can simply send troops off to battle without a declaration of war.*) Have students discuss their feelings about the war powers resolution.

ABCNEWS INTERACTIVE

The following video segments may be used to highlight aspects of the President's diplomatic and military powers.

POWERS OF THE PRESIDENT GUIDEBOOK
Chapter 29: Making Treaties, p. 37
Chapter 31: Receiving Ambassadors, p. 39
Chapter 33: Waging War, p. 41

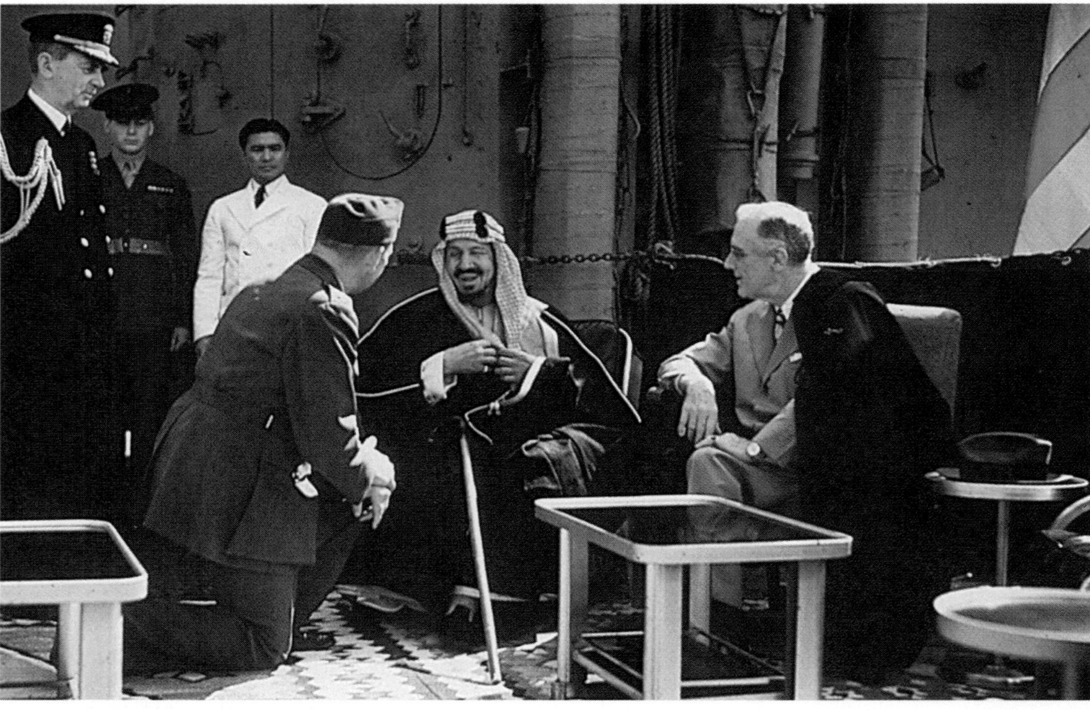

The Art of Diplomacy In 1945 President Roosevelt met with King Ibn Saud aboard a cruiser to establish closer relations between Saudi Arabia and the United States. Such negotiations typify a crucial role played by the President.

without any congressional action or approval, however.[12]

Dozens of routine executive agreements are made each year. At times, though, they are extraordinary. For example, in the "Destroyer-Bases Deal" of 1940, the United States gave the British 50 "over-age" destroyers in return for 99-year leases to several island bases extending from Newfoundland to the Caribbean.

The Power of Recognition

When the President receives the diplomatic representatives of another sovereign state, the President exercises the power of **recognition**. That 1.c is, the President, acting for the United States, acknowledges the legal existence of that country and its government. The President indicates that the United States accepts that country as an equal in the family of nations.[13]

Recognition does not mean that one government approves of the character and conduct of another. The United States recognizes several governments about which it has serious misgivings—among the most notable examples of the point today, the People's Republic of China. The facts of life in world politics make relations with these governments necessary.

[12]The Supreme Court has held executive agreements to be as binding as treaties and a part of the supreme law of the land, *United States* v. *Belmont*, 1937; *Pink* v. *United States*, 1942.

[13]Sovereign states generally recognize one another through the exchange of diplomatic representatives. Recognition may be carried out in any of several other ways, however. For example, it may be accomplished by proposing to negotiate a treaty, since under international law only sovereign states can make such agreements.

Teacher's Resource File
See Comparative Government: A Multicultural View, pp. 12–13, for materials to support this section.

Recognition is often used as a weapon in foreign relations, too. Prompt recognition of a new state or government may do much to guarantee its life. In the same way, the withholding of recognition may seriously affect its continued existence.

President Theodore Roosevelt's quick recognition of the Republic of Panama in 1903 is one of the classic examples of American use of the power as a diplomatic weapon. He recognized the new state less than three days after the Panamanians had begun an American-supported revolt against Colombia, of which Panama had been a part. Roosevelt's quick action guaranteed their success. Similarly, President Truman's recognition of Israel, within 24 hours of its creation in 1948, helped that new state to survive its turbulent beginnings.

The President may show the United States' displeasure with the conduct of another country by asking for the recall of that nation's ambassador or other diplomatic representatives in this country. The official recalled is declared to be *persona non grata*—an unwelcome person. A similar message can be sent by the recalling of an American diplomat from a post in another country. The withdrawal of recognition is the sharpest diplomatic rebuke one government may give to another and has often been a step on the way to war.

The President's Dominant Role in Military Affairs

The Constitution makes the President the commander in chief of the nation's armed forces.[14] Even though Congress shares the war powers,[15] the President's position in military affairs is as dominant as it is in the field of foreign affairs. In fact, it does not stretch the matter too far to say that the President's powers as commander in chief are almost without limit.

Consider this illustration of the point: In 1907 Theodore Roosevelt sent the Great White Fleet around the world. Several members of Congress objected to the cost and threatened to block the bill to fund the President's project. To which Roosevelt replied: "Very well, the existing appropriation will carry the Navy halfway around the world and if Congress chooses to leave it on the other side, all right." Congress was forced to give in.

Presidents almost always delegate much of their command authority to military subordinates. They are not required to do so, however. George Washington actually took command of federal troops and led them into Pennsylvania during the Whiskey Rebellion of 1794. Abraham Lincoln often visited the Army of the Potomac and instructed his generals in the field during the Civil War.

Most Presidents have not become so directly involved in military operations. Still, the President always has the final authority over and responsibility for any and all military matters. The most critical decisions are invariably made by the commander in chief. Thus, it was President

Powers of Recognition Many republics, incorporated into the Soviet Union from 1922 to 1940, broke away from it in the early 1990s. The newly independent republics hope for official recognition from the United States.

[14]Article II, Section 2, Clause 1; see also Chapter 17.
[15]Article I, Section 8, Clauses 11–17; see also Chapter 11, Section 2.

Provide Guided Practice
Write the words *Exercising Diplomatic Powers* and *Exercising Military Powers* on the board. Ask volunteers to name the formal powers of the President. (*Diplomatic: making treaties, executive agreements; recognizing foreign countries. Military: commander in chief; calling up militia.*) Next, have students identify the other means by which Presidents achieve diplomatic and military goals. (*Diplomatic: recommending joint resolutions. Military: sending troops into combat without a declaration of war.*)

Provide Independent Practice
TRF **Teacher's Resource File**
You may wish to assign Section 3 Guided Reading and Review, Unit 4 File, p. 37, to help students master section objective content.

Enrichment

Have students use magazine and newspaper articles to identify President Bush's use of diplomatic and military powers as the events in the Persian Gulf unfolded from August 1990 to February 1991. (Average)

SPOTLIGHT ON: Behind the Scenes

Lyndon B. Johnson's close supervision of the bombing of North Vietnam is one of the rare examples of a President's becoming actively involved in military operations. Whereas most wartime Presidents—including President Bush during the Gulf War—generally limit their participation to broad, strategic considerations, Johnson and his cabinet were intimately involved in even the smallest tactical decisions, such as the selection of specific targets to be bombed. Military analysts often cite Johnson's compulsive micromanagement as one of the recurrent problems in the Vietnam war effort.

Monitor Comprehension

Answers to Section 3 Review
1. "Key Terms" are defined on the following pages:
a. treaty, p. 361
b. executive agreement, p. 361
c. recognition, p. 362
2. The power to make treaties and executive agreements, the power of recognition, and certain military powers as commander in chief. **3.** (a) By receiving diplomatic representatives. (b) Quick recognition can show United States support for the country and thus guarantee its survival. Or, recognition can be removed as a major rebuke of a country. **4.** (a) The power of the commander in chief. The President can thus commit troops even without a declaration of war. (b) Congress must declare war and pay for the maintenance of military forces. Also, Congress has passed the War Powers Resolution, which attempts to limit the President's ability to wage undeclared war. **5.** (a) It places limits on the President's war-making powers. (b) The constitutionality of the law is in question. **6.** The resolution seeks to ensure that the decision to commit troops to a major war is made by both the Congress and the President, not by one acting alone.

TRF **Teacher's Resource File**
See the Unit 4 File, p. 38, for the Section 3 Quiz.

Harry Truman who made the fateful decision to use nuclear weapons against Japan in 1945 and so bring World War II to a close.

Making Undeclared War Several Presidents have used the armed forces abroad, in combat, without a declaration of war by Congress. In fact, most Presidents have done so, and on no fewer than 200 occasions.

John Adams was the first to do so, in 1798. At his command, the Navy fought and won a number of battles with French warships harassing American merchantmen in the Atlantic and the Caribbean. Thomas Jefferson and then James Madison followed that precedent in the war against the Barbary Coast pirates of North Africa in the early 1800s. Many other foreign adventures occurred throughout the last century and into the present one. The long military conflicts in Korea (from 1950 to 1953) and in Vietnam (from 1965 to 1973) were the largest of those "undeclared wars."

More recently, President Reagan used the armed forces in four combat situations. At his command, elements of the Marines and Navy were part of an international peace-keeping force in strife-torn Beirut, Lebanon, from 1982 to 1984. The invasion of Grenada in late 1983 was a joint exercise involving the Army, Navy, and Air Force. The Air Force bombed military targets in Libya in 1986 to punish that nation for its role in international terrorism. And, prompted by Iran's attacks on shipping in the Persian Gulf, the President ordered the Navy to provide escort protection to oil tankers plying those waters in 1987 and 1988.

President Bush sent the armed forces into battle in Panama and then in Kuwait and Iraq. He ordered the invasion of Panama in late 1989. That brief but bloody operation involved some 25,000 Army, Navy, Marine, and Air Force personnel. It was mounted to oust the dictatorship of General Manuel Noriega and to safeguard the Panama Canal.

The President ordered the armed forces to the Persian Gulf in August of 1990. The next several months saw the largest deployment of American military might since the war in Vietnam. Bush acted in response to Iraq's invasion of Kuwait on August 2nd and to protect this country's vital interests in the oil-rich Middle East.

As the American military buildup continued, Iraqi dictator Saddam Hussein ignored the repeated demands of the United States and the United Nations Security Council that Iraq withdraw from Kuwait. Nearly all of the world community joined in support of those demands.

Finally, on January 16, 1991, American warplanes began a sustained bombing of Iraqi positions in Kuwait and of targets in Iraq itself. British, French, Saudi Arabian, and other air forces also took part in that devastating attack. Then, on February 24th, a massive land offensive was launched, led by American ground forces.

Ground fighting in the Gulf War lasted less than 100 hours. Iraqi troops were driven from Kuwait, and much of southern Iraq was occupied by American and other allied troops.

Altogether, more than 500,000 Americans saw duty in the Gulf War. Several thousand remain stationed in the region several months after the conflict—most of them in Saudi Arabia. Though there was no declaration of war, Congress did pass a joint resolution authorizing the use of American military forces in the Gulf.

Wartime Powers The President's powers as commander in chief are far greater during a war than they are in more normal times. In fact, presidential wartime authority goes far beyond the traditional military field. Thus, in World War II, for example, Congress gave the President the power to do such things as ration food and gasoline, control wages and prices, and seize and operate certain private industries.

The President may also use the armed forces to keep the domestic peace, as you saw in Chapter 4.[16] When necessary, the President also has the power to call any State's militia, or all of them, into federal service.[17]

The War Powers Resolution In today's world, no one can doubt that the President must be able to respond rapidly and effectively to threats to this nation's security. Still, many have long warned of the dangers inherent in the President's power to involve the nation in undeclared wars. They insist that

[16]Article IV, Section 4.
[17]Article I, Section 8, Clause 15; Article II, Section 2, Clause 1.

Reteach

Have students create two side-by-side charts, one for the diplomatic powers discussed in this section, another for the military powers. In each chart, have them make two columns. In one column, ask them to list the various powers. In the second column, have them provide examples from the section or from current events. Ask students to identify which they think is the greatest—diplomatic or military power.

Teacher's Resource File
See the Simulations and Debates file, pp. 35–70, for activities to support and extend this section.

Power During Crisis Thomas Jefferson issued Mediterranean passports, or "sea letters" (inset), in the early 1800s to safeguard American ships from pirates. In 1990 Congress supported President Bush's decision to use force to drive the invading Iraqi forces out of Kuwait.

the Constitution never intended the President to have such power.

The nation's frustrations and growing anguish over the war in Vietnam finally moved Congress to pass the War Powers Resolution of 1973. The  act is designed to place close limits on the President's war-making powers. President Nixon vetoed the measure, calling it "both unconstitutional and dangerous to the best interest of our nation." Congress overrode the veto.

The resolution's central provisions require that:

1. Within 48 hours after committing American forces to combat abroad, the President must report to Congress, detailing the circumstances and the scope of his actions.
2. That combat commitment must end within 60 days, unless Congress authorizes a longer period. That 60-day deadline may be extended for as much as 30 days, however, to allow for the safe withdrawal of the American forces involved.
3. Congress may bring an end to the combat commitment at any time, by passing a concurrent resolution to that effect.

The constitutionality of the War Powers Resolution remains in dispute. A determination of the question must await a situation in which Congress demands that its provisions be obeyed but the President refuses to do so.

Section 3 Review

1. Define: treaty, executive agreement, recognition

2. What powers does the President have in foreign affairs?

3. (a) How does the President usually exercise the power of recognition? (b) How can the power of recognition be used as a weapon?

4. (a) What is the President's major military power? (b) What limits are placed on that power?

5. (a) For what purpose was the War Powers Resolution designed? (b) What is the controversy surrounding the resolution?

Critical Thinking

6. Determining Relevance (p. 19) Framer George Mason said, "The purse and the sword must never be in the same hands." How is this idea reflected in the War Powers Resolution?

★

Closure

In addition to the domestic duties of the office, the presidency also includes several diplomatic and military powers. The President is the country's chief diplomat and its commander in chief, and he or she enjoys enormous power in these fields. In Section 4, students will learn about the legislative and judicial powers of the President.

Assignment Assign Section 4, pp. 366–368, for the next class period.

Activity: For Gifted Students

Theme: Power As a part of their study of presidential powers, have students critically examine how the growth in presidential power has affected the system of checks and balances, and the separation of powers as outlined by the Framers of the Constitution. Invite students to draw on examples from history and current events to state their arguments. Students can present their findings in the form of a written or oral report.

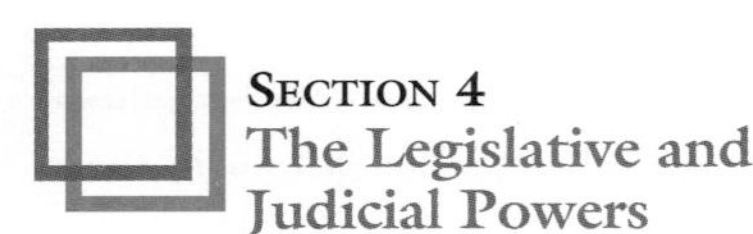

SECTION 4
The Legislative and Judicial Powers

FOCUS

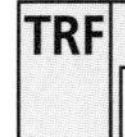

Teacher's Resource File
See the Unit 4 File, p. 39, for the Section 4 Outline.

Objectives

14.7 Examine the scope of the President's legislative and judicial powers.

14.8 Determine the ways in which the President exercises legislative and judicial powers.

Bellringer Activity Ask students to imagine having the power to overrule school rules and regulations single-handedly. How would they use their power?

State the Purpose The President possesses certain powers over the lawmaking and judicial branches of government. In Section 4, students will examine the legislative and judicial roles of the President.

ABCNEWS INTERACTIVE

The following video segments may be used to highlight aspects of the President's legislative and judicial powers.

POWERS OF THE PRESIDENT GUIDEBOOK
Chapter 21: Presidential Pardons, p. 28
Chapter 25: Call for Legislation, p. 33
Chapter 26: Proposing Laws, p. 34
Chapter 28: Vetoing Legislation, p. 36

4 The Legislative and Judicial Powers

Find Out:

- What is the scope of the President's legislative and judicial powers?
- How does the President exercise these powers?

Key Terms:

reprieve, pardon, commutation, amnesty

As you know, the Federal Government is built on the principles of the separation of powers and checks and balances. Each branch has formal powers with which it can check, delay, or block actions by the other branches. In this section you will consider the President's constitutional powers in the legislative and the judicial domains.

The President in the Legislative Field

With his legislative powers—and the skillful playing of his roles as chief of party and chief citizen—the President can have a considerable influence on Congress. The President is in effect, then, the nation's chief legislator.

Power to Recommend Legislation The Constitution says that the President

> ". . . shall, from time to time, give to the Congress information of the state of the Union, and recommend to their consideration such measures as he shall judge necessary and expedient. . . ."[18]

Soon after the beginning of each congressional session, the President delivers his State of the Union message to Congress. This is followed by the proposed budget and the annual Economic Report. At times, the President also submits special messages on certain subjects to Congress. In all of them the legislators are called on to enact those laws the President thinks are necessary to the welfare of the nation. Many recommendations are shared with the public.

[18]Article II, Section 3; see also Chapter 12, Section 1.

The Veto Power The Constitution says that "every bill" and "every order, resolution, or vote to which the concurrence of the Senate and House of Representatives may be necessary (except on a question of adjournment) shall be presented to the President."[19]

As noted in Chapter 12, the Constitution presents the President with four options when the Congress passes a measure: First, the President may sign the bill, thus making it law. Second, the President may veto[20] the bill.

As a third option, the President may allow the bill to become law by not acting on it, neither signing nor vetoing it, within 10 days (not counting Sundays). This rarely happens.

The fourth option, the pocket veto, can be used only at the end of a congressional session. If Congress adjourns within 10 days of sending a bill to the President and the chief executive does not act on it, the measure dies.

The veto power allows the President, the only representative of all the people, to act as a check on Congress. Often, just the threat of a veto is enough to defeat a bill or to bring about changes in the measure.

The historical record of presidential vetoes, and the fact that they are rarely overridden, can be seen in the table on page 367.

Bills must be vetoed in their entirety. The President has no "item veto," as do most State governors; see Chapter 24, Section 2. With that power, specific items can be eliminated from an appropriations measure or an objectionable provision removed from a bill the President might otherwise wish to become law.

On the other hand, some observers worry that the power could be used as a weapon to punish or pressure the President's opponents in Congress by specifically targeting parts of legislation that directly affect them. Nevertheless, every President since Woodrow Wilson has favored a constitutional amendment to add the item veto to the President's arsenal of legislative powers.

[19]Article I, Section 7, Clauses 2 and 3. Notice that in practice, joint resolutions proposing constitutional amendments and concurrent resolutions, which do not have the force of law, are not sent to the President.

[20]*Veto,* from the Latin, "I forbid."

Reading Strategy: Structured Overview

Before students read the section, have them write the major headings—*The President in the Legislative Field* and *Judicial Powers*—on a sheet of paper. Then have the students scan each section and write specific examples from each section beneath each heading.

Vocabulary

Direct students' attention to "Key Terms" on page 366. As they read the text in Section 4, ask students to consider how these terms help define the judicial powers of the President

Presidential Vetoes

President	Regular Vetoes	Pocket Vetoes	Total	Vetoes Overridden
Washington (1789–97)	2	–	2	–
Madison (1809–17)	5	2	7	–
Monroe (1817–25)	1	–	1	–
Jackson (1829–37)	5	7	12	–
Van Buren (1837–41)	–	1	1	–
Tyler (1841–45)	6	4	10	1
Polk (1845–49)	2	1	3	–
Pierce (1853–57)	9	–	9	5
Buchanan (1857–61)	4	3	7	–
Lincoln (1861–65)	2	5	7	–
Johnson (1865–69)	21	8	29	15
Grant (1869–77)	45	48	93	4
Hayes (1877–81)	12	1	13	1
Arthur (1881–85)	4	8	12	1
Cleveland (1885–89)	304	110	414	2
Harrison (1889–93)	19	25	44	1
Cleveland (1893–97)	42	128	170	5
McKinley (1897–01)	6	36	42	–
Roosevelt (1901–09)	42	40	82	1
Taft (1909–13)	30	9	39	1
Wilson (1913–21)	33	11	44	6
Harding (1921–23)	5	1	6	–
Coolidge (1923–29)	20	30	50	4
Hoover (1929–33)	21	16	37	3
Roosevelt (1933–45)	372	263	635	9
Truman (1945–53)	180	70	250	12
Eisenhower (1953–61)	73	108	181	2
Kennedy (1961–63)	12	9	21	–
Johnson (1963–69)	16	14	30	–
Nixon (1969–74)	26	17	43	5
Ford (1974–77)	48	18	66	12
Carter (1977–81)	13	18	31	2
Reagan (1981–89)	39	39	78	9
Bush (1989)	14	8	22	–
	1,433	**1,058**	**2,491**	**101**

Source: Congressional Research Service, Library of Congress. The Presidents not listed vetoed no measures.

Interpreting Tables Why is the veto power an effective tool in the American system of checks and balances?

Other Legislative Powers Only the President has the authority to call special sessions of Congress, as you read in Chapter 10, Section 1. The President also has the power to adjourn (prorogue) Congress when the Senate and House cannot agree together on an adjournment date—something that has never happened.

Judicial Powers

The President has the constitutional power to

“. . . grant reprieves and pardons for offenses against the United States, except in cases of impeachment.”[21]

[21]Article II, Section 2, Clause 1.

Interpreting Tables Ask students to consider why vetoes are rarely overridden. *(Possible answers: It is difficult for two-thirds of Congress to agree on any subject; overriding a veto is a risky political maneuver.)*

Caption Answer Because the veto enables the President to check and balance the Congress.

INSTRUCT

Explain/Discuss Explain to students that the President helps to maintain the system of checks and balances by using his legislative and executive powers.

Ask students to discuss the ways in which the President directly and indirectly affects the legislative process. (*A direct effect is a veto; an indirect effect occurs when the President recommends legislation.*)

Next, ask students to consider what checks exist on the President's use of judicial powers. (*Possible answer: The only restraint is the threat of political repercussions.*)

Provide Guided Practice Have students identify the power that might be used in the following situations: The President disapproves of a bill passed by Congress. (*Veto.*) The President wishes to forgive all who disobeyed a certain law. (*Amnesty.*) The President proposes five anticrime measures. (*Recommend legislation.*)

Provide Independent Practice

TRF **Teacher's Resource File** You may wish to assign Section 4 Guided Reading and Review, Unit 4 File, p. 40, to help students master section objective content.

Enrichment

Ask students to compare the legislative and judicial powers of the President with those powers that are held by the governor of their State. Suggest that students examine a copy of the State constitution to learn about the various legislative and judicial powers of the governor. (Challenging)

Monitor Comprehension

Answers to Section 4 Review
1. "Key Terms" are defined on the following pages:
a. pardon, p. 368
b. amnesty, p. 368
c. reprieve, p. 368
d. commutation, p. 368
2. (a) So that the President can influence Congress. (b) The power to recommend legislation, to veto, and to call special sessions. **3.** (a) Two-thirds in each house. (b) It may be enough to defeat or lead to changes in a bill. **4.** When a federal law has been broken, except in cases of impeachment. **5.** An item veto enables an executive (not the President) to veto specific items in a bill. A pocket veto is a form of veto in which the entire measure is vetoed. **6.** (a) A President might say no, that such a power would just make the legislative process more efficient. (b) A member of Congress might say yes because it would enable the President to create his or her own legislation.

Closure

The President has legislative and judicial powers that enable him or her to influence legislation and to affect the punishment of those who have violated federal laws. In Section 5, students will read about two governmental units that help the President perform his or her duties.

Assignment Assign Section 5, pp. 370–375, for the next class period.

A **reprieve** is the postponement of the execu- 1.c
tion of a sentence. A **pardon** is legal forgiveness 1.a
of a crime.

The President's power to grant reprieves and pardons is absolute—except in cases of impeachment, where they may never be granted. These powers of clemency—of mercy, leniency—may be used only in cases involving federal offenses, however. The President has no such authority with regard to those who violate State law. As you will read in Chapter 24, Section 2, each State governor generally possesses the powers of clemency.

Presidential pardons are usually granted after a person has been convicted in court. The President may pardon a federal offender before that person is tried, however. In fact, a pardon may be issued even before that person has been formally charged.

Pardons in advance of a trial or charge are rare. The most noteworthy pardon, by far, was granted in 1974. In that year, President Gerald Ford gave "a full, free and absolute pardon unto Richard Nixon for all offenses against the United States which he . . . has committed or may have committed or taken part in during the period from January 20, 1969, through August 9, 1974." Of course, Ford's pardon referred to the series of events that are known today as the Watergate scandal.

Judicial Power of Pardon Gerald Ford felt it necessary to grant a presidential pardon to Richard Nixon following his resignation from office.

To be effective, a pardon must be accepted by the person to whom it is granted. When one is granted before charge or conviction, as in Mr. Nixon's case, its acceptance is regularly seen as an admission of guilt by the person to whom it is given.

The pardoning power includes the power to
grant conditional pardons if the conditions are
1.d reasonable. It also includes the power of **com-**
mutation—that is, the power to commute
(reduce) the length of a sentence or a fine
imposed by a court.

The pardoning power also includes the power
1.b of **amnesty**—in effect, a general pardon offered
to a group of law violators. Thus, in 1889 President Benjamin Harrison issued a proclamation of amnesty forgiving all Mormons who had violated the antipolygamy laws in the federal territories. And in 1977 President Jimmy Carter granted a blanket pardon to Vietnam War draft evaders.

Section 4 Review

1. Define: pardon, amnesty, reprieve, commutation
2. (a) Why does the Constitution give certain legislative powers to the President? (b) What are they?
3. (a) What vote is required for Congress to override a presidential veto? (b) In what way is the threat of a veto at times an important presidential tool?
4. Under what circumstances may a President pardon someone?
5. What is the difference between a pocket veto and an item veto?

Critical Thinking

6. Predicting Consequences (p. 19) How might (a) the President and (b) a member of Congress answer this question: Would giving the President the item veto have any significant effect on the separation of powers between the two branches?

★

TRF **Teacher's Resource File**
See the Unit 4 File, p. 41, for the Section 4 Quiz.

Reteach

Have students write a brief instruction manual for future Presidents, explaining the various legislative and judicial powers of the office.

Debating Key Issues

Should the Government Limit Individual Liberties During Wartime?

Korematsu v. *United States*

After the Japanese bombing of Pearl Harbor, Hawaii, on December 7, 1941, and after Japanese conquests in the Pacific, near-hysteria gripped the West Coast of the United States. Many people feared that Japan would attack the region. In addition, many became suspicious and fearful of Japanese people who lived in the United States. At the time, approximately 112,000 people of Japanese descent lived in the states bordering the Pacific Ocean. Of these, about 70,000 were American citizens.

In February 1942, President Franklin D. Roosevelt issued Executive Order 9066. This order authorized the secretary of war and certain military officers to exclude anyone they deemed necessary from designated military areas. The order was made to protect the country from possible espionage and sabotage. The following month, the commander of the West Coast Defense Area designated the entire West Coast, up to 40 miles inland, as Military Area I. He ordered the exclusion of all persons of Japanese descent from the area. These people, whether American citizens or not, were to report for "relocation" to designated centers outside Military Area I.

Toyosaburo Korematsu was a law-abiding American citizen living in the San Francisco area who saw no reason for leaving his home. He refused to report for relocation and was later arrested. At his trial in federal court he was convicted for violation of the military order. Korematsu appealed to the United States Court of Appeals, which upheld the decision of the lower court. At this point Korematsu appealed to the United States Supreme Court.

Review the following evidence and arguments presented to the U.S. Supreme Court:

Arguments for Korematsu

1. Because Executive Order 9066 denied Korematsu liberty without due process, it was in violation of his 5th Amendment rights.
2. The exclusion order was based purely on a racial classification, which is forbidden by the Constitution.
3. Martial law was not declared in the area. Therefore, the President illegally delegated power governing civilians to the military.

Arguments for the United States

1. The danger of sabotage and espionage justified the denial of liberty to American citizens.
2. Because the United States had been attacked by Japan, it was logical that people of Japanese ancestry would be suspect. This was not racial prejudice.
3. War had been declared. The President, as commander in chief, had the right to issue such orders to military personnel.

Getting Involved

1. Identify the constitutional grounds on which each side based its arguments.
2. Debate the opposing viewpoints presented in this case.
3. Predict how you think the Supreme Court ruled in this case and why. Refer to the Supreme Court Glossary that begins on page 764 to read about the decision. Discuss the impact of the Court's decision on the right of American citizens to equal protection.

TEACHING *Debating Key Issues*

***Korematsu* v. *United States*: Should the Government Limit Individual Liberties During Wartime?**

Objective
Analyze and evaluate evidence.

INSTRUCT

Before students read the feature, ask them to answer the question in the title. Then, after students have read the feature, ask them if their answers have changed, and if so, why. Then work through the three activities in the "Getting Involved" section.

Following the class debate (Activity 2), ask students to explain which arguments they found most effective. Then have students predict the Supreme Court's decision in the case. Ask students to explain clearly the reasons for their predictions.

SUPREME COURT DECISION

The Court upheld the military order, noting that ". . . pressing public necessity (World War II) may sometimes justify the existence of restrictions . . . which curtail the civil rights of a single racial group . . ." but added that "racial antagonism never can . . . (justify such restrictions)." Only Japanese Americans were interned during World War II, while hundreds of thousands of Italian and German Americans were not.

TRF **Teacher's Resource File**
See the Supreme Court Case File, p. 11, for an activity that extends coverage of this case.

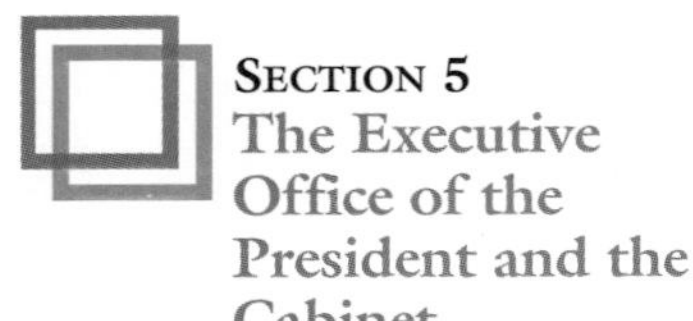

Section 5
The Executive Office of the President and the Cabinet

Focus

Teacher's Resource File See the Unit 4 File, p. 42, for the Section 5 Outline.

Objectives

14.9 Examine why the Executive Office is described as umbrella-like.
14.10 Identify some of the key components of the Executive Office.
14.11 Analyze the ways in which the cabinet and its current role have evolved.
14.12 Determine the way in which cabinet members are selected.

Bellringer Activity Ask students what they do if they have a difficult question. Do they seek the advice of others? Point out that Presidents also have a number of key people who help them.

State the Purpose Many people assist the President, including the members of the Executive Office and the cabinet. In Section 5, students will examine the roles of the people who support the President in his job as chief executive.

ABCNEWS INTERACTIVE

The following video segments may be used to highlight aspects of the President's administration.

Powers of the President Guidebook
Chapter 5: The White House, p. 6
Chapter 45: Executive Departments, p. 53

5 The Executive Office of the President and the Cabinet

Find Out:

- For what reason is the Executive Office of the President described as umbrella-like?
- What are some of the key components of the Executive Office?
- How has the cabinet and its current role evolved?
- How are cabinet members selected?

Key Terms:
federal budget, cabinet

Why did Harry Truman say that being President "is like riding a tiger"? And why did he have a small sign on his desk that read "The buck stops here"? Lyndon Johnson also commented on what it is like to sit in the White House:

> "No one can experience with the President of the United States the glory and agony of his office. No one can share the majestic view from his pinnacle of power. No one can share the burden of his decisions or the scope of his duties. A Cabinet officer, no matter how broad his mandate, has a limited responsibility. A Senator, no matter how varied his interests, has a limited constituency. But the President represents all the people and must face up to all the problems. He must be responsible, as he sees it, for the welfare of every citizen and must be sensitive to the will of every group. He cannot pick and choose the issues. They all come with the job."[22]

You will examine the federal bureaucracy, that huge complex of agencies that make up the bulk of the executive branch, in the next chapter. But first, in this section, you will take a look at the two agencies that are specially designed to help the President meet the immense responsibilities of his office: the Executive Office of the President and the cabinet.

[22]Lyndon Johnson, *The Vantage Point* (New York: Holt, Rinehart and Winston, 1971), page 2.

The Executive Office of the President

The Executive Office of the President has been called the President's "right arm." It is an umbrella agency: a complex of several separate offices, staffed by most of the President's closest advisers and assistants.

Created by Congress in 1939, the Executive Office has been reorganized in every administration since then, including the Bush administration.

The "nerve center" of the Executive Office of the President—in fact, of the entire executive branch—is the White House Office. It houses the President's key personal and political staff. Most of them have offices in one of the two wings on either side of the White House. They occupy most of the crowded West Wing, which the public seldom sees and where the legendary Oval Office and the Cabinet Room are located. Some of them work in the East Wing, where public tours of the White House begin.

In recent years, the chief of staff of the White House Office has been among the most influential of these presidential aides. The chief of staff is usually one of the President's closest advisers and directs the operations of the whole presidential staff. A number of other top officials in the office, assistants and special assistants to the President, aid the chief executive in such vital

Size of the Executive Office of the President, 1970–1988

Year	Employees
1970	4,742
1975	1,918
1980	1,886
1984	1,595
1985	1,526
1986	1,492
1987	1,553
1988	1,554

Source: Statistical Abstract of the United States: 1990

Shrinking of the Executive Office The dramatic decrease in employees from 1970 to 1975 resulted from the termination of the Office of Economic Opportunity, which had employed roughly 2,600 people.

Reading Strategy: Who? What? When? Where? How? Why?

Ask students to write the following questions on a sheet of paper or in their notebooks: Who? What? When? Where? How? Why? As they read through the information in Section 5, have them answer these questions as they relate to the two governmental bodies that support the President.

Vocabulary

Have students look at "Key Terms" on page 370. Ask them to predict what these terms might have to do with the office of the President. When they have finished reading the section, have them review their predictions and compare them with the actual meanings of the terms.

areas as foreign policy, defense, the economy, political affairs, congressional relations, and contacts with the news media and the public.

The White House staff also includes the counsel to the President, the press secretary, the President's physician, and a deputy assistant to the President who serves as chief of staff to the First Lady. Altogether, the White House staff now numbers more than 350 men and women who, in a very real sense, work for the President.

The National Security Council

Most of the President's major steps in foreign affairs are taken in close consultation with the National Security Council (NSC). It meets at the President's call, often on short notice, to advise him in all domestic, foreign, and military matters that bear on the nation's security.

The President chairs the Council. Its other members are the Vice President and the secretaries of state and defense. The director of the Central Intelligence Agency (CIA) and the chairman of the Joint Chiefs of Staff also attend its meetings.

The NSC has a small staff of foreign and military policy experts. They work under the direction of the President's assistant for national security affairs, who is often called the President's national security adviser.

The super-secret Central Intelligence Agency does much of its work at the direction of the NSC.

The National Security Council is a staff agency. That is, its job is to advise the President in all matters affecting the nation's security. However, during the Reagan administration in the 1980s, the NSC's staff actually conducted a number of secret operations. The most spectacular of them involved the sale of arms to Iran and the use of some of the proceeds from those sales to aid the Contra rebels in Nicaragua. Congress had prohibited military aid to the Contras, and the disclosure of the NSC's activities produced the Iran-Contra scandal of 1986–1987.

The Office of Management and Budget

The Office of Management and Budget (OMB) is the largest and, after the White House Office, the most influential unit in the Executive Office. The OMB is headed by a director who is appointed by the President and confirmed by the Senate. The OMB's major task is the preparation of the federal budget, which the President must submit to Congress in January each year.

The budget-making function is far more than a routine bookkeeping chore. It is the preparation of an annual statement of the public policies of the United States expressed as dollars and cents.

1.a The **federal budget** is a financial document, a detailed estimate of federal income and outgo during the coming fiscal year[23] More than that, the federal budget is a carefully drawn work plan for the conduct of government and the execution of public policy.

The many steps by which each fiscal year's budget is built is a lengthy process. In fact, it begins more than a year before the start of the fiscal year for which the budget is intended. In its first stages, each federal agency prepares detailed estimates of its spending needs for the upcoming 12-month period. Those proposals are reviewed by the OMB, usually in a series of budget hearings at which agency officials defend their requests. Following that review, the revised—and usually lowered—spending estimates are fitted into the President's overall program. They become a part of the budget document the chief executive presents to Congress.

The OMB is much more than a budget-making agency. It also monitors the spending of the funds Congress appropriates. That is, it oversees the execution of the budget. The President's close control over the preparation and execution of the budget is a major factor in the President's ability to command the huge executive branch.

Beyond its budget chores, the OMB is a sort of presidential odd-job agency. It makes studies of the organization and management of the executive branch and keeps the President up to date on the work of all its agencies. The OMB checks and clears agency stands on all legislative matters

[23]A fiscal year is the 12-month period used by a government and the business world for its record-keeping, budgeting, revenue-collecting, and other financial management purposes. The Federal Government's fiscal year now runs from October 1 through the following September 30.

INSTRUCT

Explain/Discuss The President is the foremost leadership figure in the United States. Ask students to discuss the awesome responsibility of this position. Suggest that students brainstorm a list of the many areas of economic and social life the President is looked to for leadership. Then ask students to discuss why it is important for the President to have assistance in performing the duties of the job.

Next, have students describe the many departments and offices assisting the President, including components of the Executive Office of the President and the cabinet departments. You might suggest that students consult the Government Resources Handbook on page 690 to look for sources of additional information on these agencies. Ask students to discuss why it is important for the President to have support in each of the various subject areas represented by these units. (*Possible answer: No one person could be expected to have a thorough knowledge of each of these fields.*) Also, have students consider why it is important for the President to have people in those posts with whom he is comfortable. As part of this discussion, ask students whether they agree that such appointments should be subject to approval by the Senate. (*Possible answers: Yes; these posts entail great responsibility and therefore should be subject to Senate advice and consent. No; the President should be free to choose whomever he or she pleases to support him or her.*)

to be certain that they agree with the President's own positions. It also helps the President prepare the hundreds of executive orders he must issue and the veto messages he occasionally sends to Congress and does much more to live up to the word *management* in its title.

The Office of National Drug Control Policy

The Office of National Drug Control Policy is the newest of the major units within the Executive Office. It was established in 1989, and its existence dramatizes the nation's concern over drugs. The office is headed by a director who is appointed by the President, subject to the approval of the Senate.

The news media regularly identify the director as "the nation's drug czar." To this point, at least, the office has two major responsibilities: (1) to prepare an annual national drug control strategy, which the President sends on to Congress; and (2) to coordinate the efforts of the more than 50 federal agencies participating in the war on drugs.

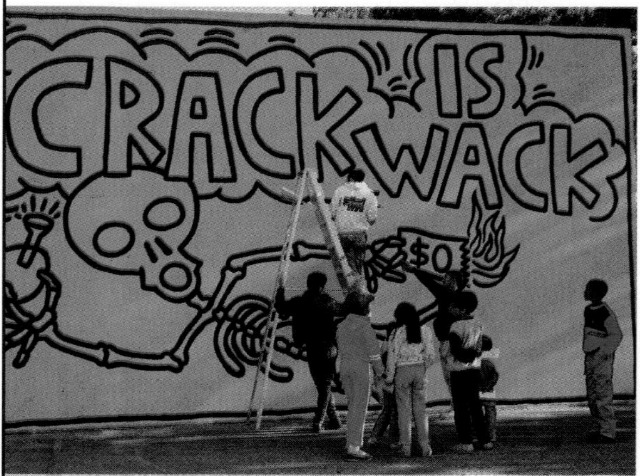

The War on Drugs The campaign against illicit drug use in the United States was supported by the Office of National Drug Control Policy. This street mural by artist Keith Haring graphically communicates its antidrug message.

The Council of Economic Advisers

Three of the country's leading economists, chosen by the President with the consent of the Senate, make up the Council of Economic Advisers. It is the chief executive's major source of information and advice on the state of the nation's economy.

The Council also helps the President prepare his annual Economic Report to Congress. That report, together with a presidential message, goes to Capitol Hill in late January or early February each year.

Other Units in the Executive Office

Several other agencies in the Executive Office house key presidential aides who give the President the assistance he must have in order to meet his many and wide-ranging responsibilities.

THE OFFICE OF POLICY DEVELOPMENT. This unit advises the President in all matters of domestic concern. It is headed by the deputy assistant to the President for domestic policy.

THE NATIONAL SPACE COUNCIL. This group advises the President on the nation's civil and military efforts in outer space. The Vice President chairs the council, and its other members include the secretaries of state, defense, commerce, and transportation; the administrator of the National Aeronautics and Space Administration; and the directors of the CIA and OMB.

THE COUNCIL ON ENVIRONMENTAL QUALITY. The council aids the President in all environmental policy matters and in the writing of the annual "state of the environment" report to Congress. The council's three members are named by the President, with the Senate's consent. They work closely with the Environmental Protection Agency and various agencies in the Departments of the Interior, Agriculture, and Energy.

THE OFFICE OF UNITED STATES TRADE REPRESENTATIVE. This agency advises the chief executive in all matters of foreign trade. The trade representative, appointed by the President and confirmed by the Senate, carries the rank of ambassador and represents the President in foreign trade negotiations.

SPOTLIGHT ON: Global Awareness

Government plays a far more active part in the conduct of business in the world's other major industrial powers than it does in the United States. Nowhere is this more true than in Japan, where the Ministry of International Trade and Industry (MITI) sets industrial policies that govern Japanese business. A government agency, MITI regulates business on a variety of fronts, ranging from controls on prices, output, imports and exports, to tax policy, special lending programs, and government subsidies. United States business regulation, by contrast, is much less centralized, reflecting the American belief in market forces as the best regulator of business.

THE NATIONAL CRITICAL MATERIALS COUNCIL. This group is composed of three members appointed by the President with the consent of the Senate. They advise the chief executive on policies relating to such "critical materials" as oil, natural gas, copper, aluminum, titanium essential to the nation's security and well-being.

THE OFFICE OF SCIENCE AND TECHNOLOGY POLICY. The President's major adviser in all scientific, engineering, and other technological matters bearing on national policies and programs is the Office of Science and Technology Policy. Its director, who is chosen by the President and confirmed by the Senate, is drawn from the nation's scientific community.

THE OFFICE OF ADMINISTRATION. This is the general housekeeping agency for all the other units in the Executive Office. It provides them with the many support services they must have in order to do their jobs. The list of those things is almost endless: clerical help, data processing, library services, transportation, and much more.

The Cabinet

The **cabinet** is an informal advisory body 1.b
brought together by the President to serve his needs. The Constitution makes no mention of it,[24] nor did Congress create it. Instead, the cabinet is the product of custom and usage.

At its first session in 1789, Congress established four executive posts: secretary of state, secretary of the treasury, secretary of war, and attorney general. By his second term, Washington was regularly seeking the advice of the four outstanding people he had named to those offices: Thomas Jefferson in the Department of State, Alexander Hamilton at the Treasury, Henry Knox in the War Department, and Edmund Randolph, the attorney general. So the cabinet was born.

The First Cabinet The nation's first cabinet included President George Washington (right); Secretary of State Thomas Jefferson (second left); and Secretary of the Treasury Alexander Hamilton (second right).

By tradition, the heads of the now 14 executive departments form the cabinet. In the Bush administration, the director of the OMB, the counsel on Domestic Policy, and the United States trade representative also have cabinet rank. In addition, every Vice President since Alben Barkley, who served under Truman, has been a regular participant at cabinet meetings. A number of other aides are usually there, as well—in particular, the White House chief of staff.

Choosing Cabinet Members The President appoints the head of each of the 14 executive departments. Each of these appointments is subject to confirmation by the Senate, but rejections have been exceedingly rare. The Senate generally respects the personal choice of the President. You may recall from Chapter 11, Section 4 that of the more than 600 presidential

[24]The closest approach to it is in Article II, Section 2, Clause 1, where the President is given the power to "require the opinion, in writing, of the principal officer in each of the executive departments, upon any subject relating to the duties of their respective offices." The cabinet was first mentioned in an act of Congress in 1907, well over a century after its birth.

Provide Guided Practice Have students volunteer the names of the components of the Executive Office and the cabinet. Then provide students with examples of responsibilities and ask them to match those examples with the appropriate office or department. Examples could include: Advise the President on the budget (*OMB*); advise the President on events unfolding in China (*NSC or Department of State*); coordinate an antidrug message (*Office of National Drug Control Policy*); advise the President on the recession (*Council of Economic Advisors*); update the President on the activities of the executive departments (*the cabinet*).

Provide Independent Practice

TRF **Teacher's Resource File** You may wish to assign Section 5 Guided Reading and Review, Unit 4 File, p. 43, to help students master section objective content.

Enrichment

Have students imagine that they are the newly elected President. Ask them to write a help-wanted ad for openings in the Executive Office and the cabinet. Student advertisements should indicate the professional and personal qualifications each candidate should have. (Easy)

Interpreting Charts Tell students to look at the chart and the dates on which each department was created. What conclusions can students draw from these dates? (*Possible answer: The needs of the nation have changed over time. For example, the energy crisis of the 1970s helped create the need for a cabinet department that did not exist before.*)

Caption Answer Succession to the presidency follows the same order.

MONITOR COMPREHENSION

Answers to Section 5 Review
1. "Key Terms" are defined on the following pages:
 a. federal budget, p. 371
 b. cabinet, p. 373
2. Because its various offices, departments, and agencies help the President oversee the conduct of his or her administration. **3.** The National Security Council advises the President in matters of national security; the Office of Management and Budget prepares and oversees the execution of the federal budget. The Office of National Drug Control Policy plans drug control strategies; the Council of Economic Advisors, the Office of Policy Development, the National Space Council, the Council on Environmental Quality, the Office of United States Trade Representative, the National Critical Materials Council, and the Office of Science and Technology Policy operate as advisors in their various areas of expertise. The Office of Administration provides support for all

appointments made since 1789, only 12 have been turned down by the Senate.[25]

Many factors influence these presidential choices. Republican Presidents do not often pick Democrats, and vice versa. One or more of a new President's appointees usually come from among those who played a major role in the recent presidential campaign.

Of course, professional qualifications and practical experience are also taken into account in the selection of cabinet secretaries. Geography also plays a part. In broad terms, each President tries to give some sectional balance to the cabinet. Thus, the secretary of the interior often comes from the West, where most of the department's work is carried out.

Many interest groups care about who are appointed to head certain departments, and these groups influence some of the choices. Thus, the secretary of agriculture almost always has a background closely related to agriculture. The secretary of the treasury usually comes from the financial community, the secretary of commerce from the ranks of business, and so on.

Considerations of sex and race, an appointee's stand on the "hot" issues of the day, management abilities and experience, and other personal characteristics—these and a host of other factors play a part of the decision mix in selecting cabinet members.

Women and Minorities in the Cabinet

To date, only ten women, five African Americans, and two Hispanics have served in the cabinet. Franklin Roosevelt appointed the first woman, Frances T. Perkins, secretary of labor from 1933 to 1945. Lyndon Johnson named the first African American, Robert C. Weaver, as the first secretary of housing and urban development (HUD) in 1966. The Ford cabinet was the first to include both a woman (Carla Hills, secretary of HUD) and an African American (William T. Coleman, secretary of transportation); both were appointed in 1975. Jimmy Carter appointed the first (and so far only) African American woman to the cabinet; Patricia Roberts Harris was named secretary of HUD in 1977 and then secretary of health and human services (HHS) in 1979. Ronald Reagan appointed the first Hispanic cabinet member; Lauro F. Cavazos became secretary of education in 1988.

To 1992, the Bush cabinet has included one African American (Louis Sullivan, secretary of HHS), two women (Elizabeth Dole, secretary of labor, 1989–1991, and her successor, Lynn

[25]The most recent rejection occurred in 1989, when the Senate refused to confirm President Bush's selection of John Tower as secretary of defense.

The President's Cabinet

Cabinet Post* (Year Created)
Secretary of State (established 1789)
Secretary of the Treasury (established 1789)
Secretary of Defense (established 1947)[a]
Attorney General (established 1789)
Secretary of the Interior (established 1849)
Secretary of Agriculture (established 1889)
Secretary of Commerce (established 1903)[b]
Secretary of Labor (established 1913)
Secretary of Health and Human Services (established 1953)[c]
Secretary of Housing and Urban Development (established 1965)
Secretary of Transportation (established 1967)
Secretary of Energy (established 1977)
Secretary of Education (established 1979)
Secretary of Veterans Affairs (established 1989)

*The cabinet posts are listed in the order in which each was established. This ranking is followed for formal and ceremonial purposes (protocol) and also is the order in which the cabinet officers rank in the line of presidential succession; see page 323. Note: The Postmaster General, who headed the cabinet-level Post Office Department, was a member of the cabinet from 1829 until Congress replaced the department with an independent agency, the United States Postal Service, in 1971.

[a]Congress created the National Military Establishment as an executive department in 1947. It was renamed the Department of Defense in 1949. Since 1947 it has included the former cabinet-level Departments of War (1789), and the Navy (1798), and the Department of the Air Force (1947). The secretaries of Army, Navy, and Air Force do not hold cabinet rank.

[b]The secretary of commerce was originally the secretary of commerce and labor. The Department of Commerce and Labor, created in 1903, was replaced by the separate Departments of Commerce and of Labor in 1913.

[c]The secretary of health and human services was originally the secretary of health, education, and welfare. The Department of Health, Education, and Welfare was created in 1953. HEW's education functions were transferred to a separate Department of Education in 1979, and HEW was renamed at that time.

Interpreting Charts Cabinet posts are listed in the order in which they were established. What does this order tell you about presidential succession?

Martin), and two Hispanics (Lauro Cavazos, secretary of education, 1989–1991, and Manuel Lujan, secretary of the interior).

The Cabinet's Role

Cabinet members have two major jobs. Individually, each is the administrative head of one of the executive departments. Together, they are advisers to the President.

How the President uses the cabinet is something for each President to decide. A number of Presidents have given great weight to the cabinet and to its advice; others have given it only a secondary role. The Bush cabinet wields more power and apparently has more influence with the President than any cabinet since the Eisenhower presidency in the 1950s. On the other hand, John Kennedy described his cabinet meetings as "a waste of time."

Kennedy's view notwithstanding, most Presidents have held regular cabinet meetings—where reports are made and discussed, and advice is offered to the chief executive. That advice need not be taken, of course. Abraham Lincoln once laid a proposition he favored before his cabinet. Each member opposed it, whereupon Lincoln declared: "Seven nays, one aye: the ayes have it."

William Howard Taft put the role of the cabinet in its proper light years ago:

> "The Constitution . . . contains no suggestion of a meeting of all of the department heads in consultation over general governmental matters. The Cabinet is a mere creation of the President's will. It exists only by custom. If the President desired to dispense with it, he could do so."[26]

No President has ever gone so far as to suggest eliminating the cabinet. However, several Presidents have leaned on other, unofficial advisory groups, and sometimes more heavily than on the cabinet. Andrew Jackson began the practice when he became President in 1829. Several of his close friends often met with him in the kitchen at the White House and, inevitably, came to be known as the Kitchen Cabinet. Franklin Roosevelt's Brain Trust of the 1930s and Harry Truman's cronies in the late 1940s were in the same mold.

Secretary of the Interior: Multicultural Awareness The work of Manuel Lujan, one of two Hispanic members of the Bush Cabinet, often takes him away from his desk.

[26] *Our Chief Magistrate and His Powers* (New York: Columbia University Press, 1916), pages 29–30.

Section 5 Review

1. **Define:** federal budget, cabinet
2. In what way is the Executive Office of the President an umbrella agency?
3. Name the different components of the Executive Office of the President and their roles.
4. (a) How was the cabinet created? (b) Who are its members?
5. What two major jobs do the cabinet members have?

Critical Thinking

6. **Identifying Central Issues** (p. 19) In what ways is the budget-making power a major administrative tool for the President?

★

the other offices. **4.** (a) The 1st Congress created four executive departments. Washington named the heads of these departments, and he came to rely on them as an advisory body. (b) The heads of the 14 executive departments. In addition, the Vice President now regularly sits in on meetings, as do various other administration officials. **5.** Each cabinet member is the head of an executive department and an adviser to the President. **6.** It is the means by which the President can lay out and provide for his or her plan for the public policies of the Federal Government. It establishes priorities.

Teacher's Resource File See the Unit 4 File, p. 44, for the Section 5 Quiz.

Closure

The scope of presidential power and duties is huge. Without the help of a strong support staff, the work of the President would be impossible. Two governmental units in particular, the Executive Office and the cabinet, help the President to carry out the duties of office. In Chapter 15, students will read more about the various departments, agencies, and offices of the Federal Government.

Assignment Assign Chapter 15, Section 1, pp. 381–385, for the next class period.

Activity: Teaching Heterogeneous Groups

In order that students understand all the roles of a modern President, have them work in small groups to review and describe the many powers designated to the President, including the executive powers, diplomatic and military powers, and the legislative and judicial powers. Then have students show how the current President is fulfilling these roles through a discussion of current events. Suggest that students discuss current issues and presidential activities to determine which power(s) are being executed. Invite students to bring in stories from newspapers or magazines, or to discuss news reports from television or radio.

Reteach

Ask students to create a chart that shows the organization and major components of the governmental units that support the President. Explain to students that these charts should have separate branches for the Executive Office and the cabinet. Have students explain the different roles of these units.

TEACHING
Critical Thinking

Making Comparisons

Objective
Analyze the process of making comparisons between different sets of information and ideas.

INSTRUCT

Before students read the feature, brainstorm a list of reasons why it is important to be able to make good comparisons. Explain that making comparisons is the foundation of any decision.

As students complete each step on the page, invite them to share their responses. Discuss the importance of making comparisons when making any type of selection, whether it is what to eat for dinner or whom to vote for in an upcoming election.

Answers 1. (a) Public opinion and presidential decision making. (b) How the President responds to public opinion.
2. (a) Yes, Truman's and Roosevelt's. (b) Both advocated making decisions without regard for public opinion.
3. Truman said that Presidents must make decisions in spite of public opinion; Roosevelt advocated making decisions first, then changing public opinion. Wilson felt that the President should get a grasp on public thinking and work from there.
4. (a) Truman and Roosevelt felt that Presidents should not be constrained by public opinion; Wilson worked with public opinion in order to win the public trust. (b) Wilson.

Making Comparisons

Making comparisons means identifying how different ideas, objects, people, or situations are alike and/or different. Mastering this skill is key to the process of decision making. The decisions you make as a citizen—such as the ones you make in a voting booth, for instance—are among the most important decisions you will make in your life.

For example, making comparisons between different presidential leadership styles can help you decide what kind of leader you want for your President. As you know, the ability to lead is a critically important quality in a President. If a President cannot lead the people and the Congress, his or her administration will be crippled. Follow the steps below to practice making comparisons.

1. Identify the basis on which you will make the comparison. Have you ever heard the expression "comparing apples to oranges"? It refers to the impossibility of comparing items that are fundamentally different. Making a comparison is possible only on the basis of a concept or characteristic that each item shares in common. Read each of the statements below. (a) What is the subject of each statement? (b) On what basis can you compare the differing views of each President?

2. Determine the ways in which each item is alike. Making comparisons includes finding ways in which two items are the same. (a) Are any of the statements below similar in their views on public opinion? (b) If so, in what ways are they similar?

3. Determine the ways in which each item is different. Of course, the other purpose of making comparisons is to identify differences between items. In what ways do each of the statements below differ from one another?

4. Summarize the comparison between the items. Once you have identified the similarities and differences between the items, you can complete the comparison. (a) How do the three Presidents quoted below compare in their views of popular opinion and the presidency? (b) In your opinion, which President has the view that is most unlike the others?

Presidential Leadership Styles

Harry Truman	Theodore Roosevelt	Woodrow Wilson
"A man who is influenced by the polls or is afraid to make decisions which may make him unpopular is not a man to represent the welfare of the country."	"I did not 'divine' how the people were going to think; I simply made up my mind what they ought to think, and then did my best to get them to think it."	"If he rightly interprets the national thought and boldly insists upon it, he is irresistible; and the country never feels the zest of action so much as when its President is of such insight and calibre."

Teacher's Resource File
See the Unit 4 File, p. 45, for the Skill Application for this lesson.

Chapter-in-Brief

Scan all headings, photographs, charts, and other visuals in the chapter before reading the section summaries below.

Section 1 The Changing View of Presidential Power (pp. 353–355) The powers of the President have grown since 1789. The fact that the presidency consists of one person has given the office great stature—and power. Also, as American economic and social life has become more complex, people have looked to the President for more and more leadership.

Historically, the actions of those Presidents who favored a stronger presidential role have helped expand the powers of the office.

Section 2 The President's Executive Powers (pp. 356–360) The President is responsible for executing federal laws. But the meaning of many laws is vague, and enforcing them is a matter of interpretation. So, the President enjoys some special powers to help him execute and enforce laws.

The President can issue executive orders, which have the force of law. And the President may appoint subordinates—and dismiss those whom he no longer wants.

Section 3 The Diplomatic and Military Powers (pp. 361–365) The President presides over relations with other countries. This duty requires that the President possess certain powers. Thus, only the President may negotiate treaties, and only the President may recognize the existence of foreign countries. The President alone may appoint ambassadors and other diplomatic officers.

Though Congress shares some powers in military affairs, the President is the undisputed leader. For example, though Congress can declare war, a President can—and on 200 occasions has—carried out military action without the consent of Congress. Congress has tried to contain the President's power through the War Powers Resolution, but its success has been limited.

Section 4 The Legislative and Judicial Powers (pp. 366–368) As part of the system of checks and balances, the President holds several legislative and judicial powers.

The President may recommend legislation, and he may veto bills passed by Congress. Congress may override a veto, but rarely does so.

In the judicial field, a President may delay the carrying out of a sentence (a reprieve), legally forgive a convicted person (a pardon), lessen a convicted person's sentence (commutation), or offer a general pardon to a group of law violators (amnesty).

Section 5 The Executive Office of the President and the Cabinet (pp. 370–375) As the President performs his vital responsibilities, he relies on the assistance and guidance of key advisors and agencies.

The Executive Office of the President acts as the President's "right arm." It includes the White House Office. A key member of this office is the Chief of Staff. Other offices of the Executive Office support the President's foreign policy efforts, the administration of the budget, and numerous other endeavors.

The cabinet is not mentioned in the Constitution. Yet it has played an important role in every administration.

The cabinet has two major roles. Each cabinet member serves as head of an executive department, such as Defense or the Treasury. Collectively, the cabinet serves as an advisory body to the President.

Teaching Suggestions for CHAPTER-IN-BRIEF

Below are some of the possible uses for the Chapter-in-Brief:

To Preview the Chapter You may want to assign the Chapter-in-Brief page and the Section Outlines from the Teacher's Resource File before beginning Chapter 14 to introduce students to "Key Terms" and concepts in each section.

To Review the Chapter When students have completed Chapter 14, you might want to assign the Chapter-in-Brief as a tool for review, along with the Guided Reading and Reviews from the Teacher's Resource File.

To Omit the Chapter If you wish to skip Chapter 14, it may be helpful to assign the Chapter-in-Brief to students as a review before continuing to another chapter. You may also want to assign the Chapter 14 Test to assess student knowledge of the material. Then, specific portions of Chapter 14 may be assigned to students needing reinforcement of "Key Terms" and concepts.

Teacher's Resource File See the Unit 4 File for the following materials:

- Section Outlines, pp. 30, 33, 36, 39, 42.
- Guided Reading and Reviews, pp. 31, 34, 37, 40, 43.
- Chapter 14 Test, pp. 49–51.

ADDITIONAL RESOURCES

Bailey, Harry A. and Jay M. Shafritz (eds.). *The American Presidency: Historical and Contemporary Perspectives.* Dorsey, 1988.

Barnet, Richard J. *The Rockets' Red Glare: When America Goes to War—The Presidents and the People.* Simon and Schuster, 1990.

Bond, John R. and Richard Fleisher. *The President of the Legislative Arena.* University of Chicago Press, 1990.

Crabb, Cecil V. and Kevin V. Mulcahy. *American National Security: A Presidential Perspective.* Brooks/Cole, 1991.

The Executive Branch. Video or film. National Geographic, 1982. Color. 22 min.

Five Presidents on the Presidency. 16mm film. BFA, 1974. Color. 24 min.

Kellerman, Barbara and Ryan J. Barilleaux. *The President as World Leader.* St. Martin's Press, 1990.

Mann, Thomas E. (ed.). *A Question of Balance: The President, the Congress, and Foreign Policy.* Brookings, 1990.

Answers to CHAPTER 14 REVIEW

Vocabulary and Key Terms

Matching
1. media
2. executive order
3. reprieve
4. commutation
5. treaty

True or False
1. True.
2. False—the correct term is *amnesty.*
3. True.
4. False—the correct term is *executive agreement.*

Word Relationships
1. cabinet
2. treaty
3. federal budget
4. recognition

Main Ideas

Section 1
1. There was debate among the Framers over whether the presidency should be strong or weak. **2.** Those who favored a strong presidency carried the day. The reasons include the unity of the office, the influence of strong Presidents, the pressures brought by the growing complexity of American society and economy, the actions of Presidents in emergencies, and the willingness of Congress to grant the President more power. The President has a huge staff and a unique position from which to appeal to the people and thus increase the stature of the office. **3.** Some Presidents have favored a broad view while others have argued for a more narrow view.

Section 2
4. In executing the law, the President must often interpret the law and make decisions about how to enforce laws. **5.** Executing all the laws is an enormous task. In order to do this, the President must preside over a vast administration. **6.** The President appoints all the top officials—ambassadors and diplomats; cabinet members and their top aids; the heads of independent agencies; federal judges, attorneys, and marshals; and officers in the armed forces. All these appointments must be approved by the Senate. As a general rule, Presidents can also remove appointees, except federal judges. **7.** The President must have this power in order to carry out the other constitutional powers of the presidency.

Section 3
8. The President can make treaties (which must be approved by the Senate). The President can also make executive agreements with heads of foreign states or their subordinates. Presidents can also request that Congress pass joint resolutions to achieve foreign policy goals. **9.** It is the power to recognize the sovereignty of a foreign state. Presidents can use it as a weapon; prompt recognition (or denial of recognition) of a government can ensure (or seriously threaten) its

Chapter Review

Vocabulary and Key Terms

media (p. 355)
executive order (p. 356)
treaty (p. 361)
executive agreement (p. 361)
recognition (p. 362)
reprieve (p. 368)
pardon (p. 368)
commutation (p. 368)
amnesty (p. 368)
federal budget (p. 371)
cabinet (p. 373)

Matching: *Review the key terms in the list above. If you are not sure of a term's meaning, look up the term and review its definition. Choose a term from the list above that best matches each description.*

1. the collective term for the press, radio, and television; a powerful tool through which the President attracts and holds public attention
2. a directive, rule, or regulation made by a President and/or the President's subordinates that has the force of law
3. the official postponement of the execution of a sentence in a crime
4. the power to reduce the length of a sentence in a crime
5. a formal agreement made between or among sovereign states

True or False: *Determine whether each statement is true or false. If it is true, write "true." If it is false, change the underlined word or words to make the statement true.*

1. A pardon enables the President to release a person from the punishment or legal consequences of a crime.
2. A reprieve is a general pardon issued to a group of law-breakers.
3. An executive agreement has the force of law but does not require the approval of the Senate.
4. An executive order is a pact between the President and the head of a foreign state or the President's subordinates.

Word Relationships: *Replace the underlined definition with the correct term from the list above.*

1. Different Presidents have relied on the presidential advisory body composed of heads of the executive departments for different purposes.
2. A formal agreement made between or among sovereign states requires the approval of the Senate.
3. A financial document, a detailed estimate of federal income and outgo in the coming fiscal year, is a carefully drawn plan for the conduct of government.
4. By exercising the exclusive power of the President to establish formal diplomatic relations with foreign states, the President accepts a country as an equal in the family of nations.

Main Ideas

Section 1 (pp. 353–355)

1. What were the differing views of the presidency held by the Framers?
2. Which view has prevailed and for what reasons?
3. How have Presidents themselves viewed their powers?

Section 2 (pp. 356–360)

4. For what reason does the presidential power to execute the law grant the President such power?
5. How do the President's executive responsibilities relate to administrative responsibilities?

6. What is the extent of the President's control over the personnel of the President's administration?
7. For what reason does the President have the ordinance power?

Section 3 **(pp. 361–365)**

8. Through what means can the President make agreements on behalf of the country with foreign states?
9. What is the power of recognition and how can the President use it as a diplomatic tool?
10. Describe the President's role in the military affairs of the country.

Section 4 **(pp. 366–368)**

11. How do the President's legislative and judicial powers serve the principle of separation of powers?
12. What are the President's primary legislative powers?
13. What are the President's primary judicial powers?

Section 5 **(pp. 370–375)**

14. What agencies work directly with the President to give assistance and advice?
15. What responsibilities does the cabinet have that the Executive Office of the President does not?
16. How have Presidents differed in their reliance on the cabinet?

Critical Thinking

1. **Making Comparisons** (p. 19) Compare the cabinet of today with the first cabinet under President Washington. (a) How are the two alike? (b) How are they different? (c) Why do you think cabinet membership has grown since Washington's first term of office?
2. **Identifying Central Issues** (p. 19) Article II of the Constitution, which covers the powers of the executive, has been called the most loosely drawn chapter in the Constitution. Why might the Framers have created Article II in this way?
3. **Drawing Conclusions** (p. 19) The text cites the unity of the presidency as a key reason for the growth of presidential power. Assuming this is true, what does that fact suggest about the American people's view of political leadership?
4. **Demonstrating Reasoned Judgment** (p. 19) The text states that the President's powers in the field of military affairs is nearly without limit. What are the benefits and drawbacks of this fact?

Getting Involved

1. **Writing Your Opinion** You have just been elected President of the United States. Write a diary entry in which you explain how you intend to lead the nation in the four years ahead. Open with a statement in which you summarize your beliefs about the proper role of the President in the American political system. Then, explain how you intend to fulfill this role. Write one paragraph each on such topics as your cabinet and Executive Office, your constitutional powers, and your overall view of presidential power. Conclude by expressing what you predict will be your greatest challenge in office. Revise to correct for errors, and draft a final copy.
2. **Class Debate** Hold a class debate on the following topic: *Resolved*, That the Constitution be amended to forbid the President to use the armed forces in combat without a declaration of war by Congress. Choose teams to debate each side of the topic. The rest of the class should evaluate each team's presentation.
3. **Gathering Information** (a) What sources might you consult to learn about how different Presidents have viewed their use of military power? (b) What sources might you use to learn about the historical view of Congress on this issue? Use the Government Resources Handbook on page 690 to identify possible sources.

existence; and removal of recognition can show a President's disapproval of a state. **10.** The President is commander in chief. Though the President shares military powers with Congress, the President is the undisputed leader. For example, the President has numerous means by which to circumvent the constitutional requirement that Congress declare war.

Section 4

11. They enable the President to check and balance the power of the legislative branch and the judicial branch. **12.** The President can recommend legislation; he or she can exercise influence on Congress through the role of chief of party and chief citizen; he or she can veto legislation passed by Congress; he or she can call a special session of Congress. **13.** The President can grant reprieves and pardons. The President can commute sentences and offer amnesty to groups of law violators.

Section 5

14. The Executive Office of the President and the cabinet advise and assist the President. **15.** The cabinet not only advises the President, its members are each responsible for running one of the executive departments. **16.** Some Presidents have relied heavily on their cabinets. Others have held their cabinets in lower regard. Some Presidents have developed their own informal network of advisers outside of the cabinet.

Critical Thinking

1. (a) Cabinet members still run executive departments and advise the President. (b) There are now fourteen cabinet members, as opposed to the original four. (c) Growth of the country has created the need for new cabinet departments. **2.** Answers will vary. Some students might suggest that the Framers wanted to create a presidency in which the office-holder was free to respond to the particular needs of the time. Others might say that the Framers simply could not agree on the proper limits and definition of the chief executive. **3.** Answers will vary. Students might respond that the fact suggests that individual characteristics such as personality play a large role in determining the strength of political leadership in the eyes of the American people. **4.** Answers will vary. Students might say that the benefits are that the country can respond quickly and decisively in a conflict. Others might suggest that such broad powers in the hands of one person invite abuse and disaster.

Getting Involved

1–2. Answers and results will vary, but students should demonstrate an understanding of the concepts of this chapter. **3.** Possible answers include: (a) *CQ's Guide to the Presidency* and the *Weekly Compilation of Presidential Documents,* (b) *CQ's Guide to Congress*, and the *Congressional Record.*

Chapter 15 Resources

In the Teacher's Resource File
The following materials are found in the Teacher's Resource File box.

Instructional Support: Unit 4 File

For the Section	For the Chapter
Outlines, pp. 55, 58, 61	Skill Application, p. 64
Guided Reading and Reviews, pp. 56, 59, 62	Case Study on Contemporary Issues, pp. 65–67
Quizzes, pp. 57, 60, 63	Chapter Test, pp. 68–70
	Additional Test Questions, pp. 71–73

Enrichment Support Files

Participatory Government Activities, pp. 28–39
Simulations and Debates: National Energy Plan

Computer Test Bank and Assessment

Transparency Package, pp. 15, 40

Chapter 15 Focus

Introduce the Chapter Tell students that in this chapter they will learn about the many different components of the executive branch of the Federal Government, their functions, and their staffing. Read with students the Chapter Preview and Objectives.

Writing Activity Direct students' attention to "Describe." Have students write down any general impressions they have about the people who work for the Federal Government. Ask students to comment on the sources of their impressions.

Motivate for Learning Direct students' attention to "Predict." Discuss ways in which people ought to be rewarded for doing a good job. Ask students to imagine they worked in an organization that did not reward its top performers. What affect might that situation have on them? How might it affect the organization involved?

Government at Work: The Bureaucracy

Chapter Preview

Bureaucracy. The word is used most often in a critical way by those who see government and its workers as too powerful, always tangled in red tape, unresponsive, overpaid and underworked, or all of those things. Whatever its other good or bad characteristics, the federal bureaucracy is huge.

In 1991, the government employed just under three million civilian employees and paid them about $129 billion. What do all those people do? Journalist Kenneth Walsh once wrote that they perform: " . . . an endless variety of tasks that reach into nearly every corner of national life—from collecting taxes to measuring air pollution, from enforcing civil-rights laws to investigating airplane crashes, from granting television-station licenses to approving new medical devices for pulverizing kidney stones." This chapter is about the federal bureaucracy—the machinery and the personnel through which the executive branch of the Federal Government operates.

Before you read this chapter:

- **Describe** two jobs in your community that are part of the federal bureaucracy.
- **Predict** what is meant by the "merit system."

As you read, focus on the main objective for each section. Understand:

1. The need for and growth of the federal bureaucracy.
2. The organization and functions of the executive departments and the independent agencies.
3. The development of the federal civil service.

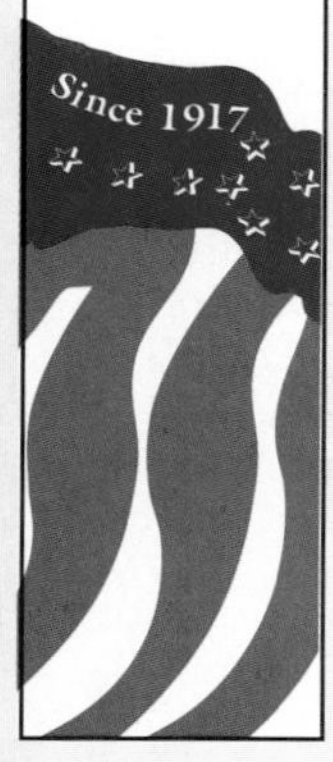

Magruder's American Government: *A Witness to Change* by William A. McClenaghan

In editions from the late 1940s and into the mid-1950s, *American Government's* consideration of the federal civil service system began with this statement: "We hear many complaints of the rising costs of government; but it is really not a question of how much we pay, but whether we get our money's worth: and that depends on whom we employ to run the government."

That observation was followed by these remarks, clearly aimed at the high school students of that era: "To build an efficient government service it must be made a career. Young people of education and ability should be chosen. . . . Older people who succeed in private industry are not likely to shift to the government; and those who have not succeeded are not likely to be an asset to the government. Outstanding young people will be attracted to government service if there is reasonable assurance of permanent tenure, promotion according to merit, and well-paid positions as the reward for success."

Three Million Strong Over three million Americans work as part of our federal bureaucracy—the maze of agencies, departments, commissions, administrations, and bureaus that perform the everyday work of the government.

1 The Federal Bureaucracy

Find Out:

- In what sense is the Federal Government a bureaucracy?
- What are the various titles given to administrative units?
- How do staff and line agencies differ?

Key Terms:

bureaucracy, bureaucrat, administration

Think about this for a moment. It is impossible for you to live through a single day without somehow encountering the federal bureaucracy. Federal bureaucrats deliver the mail, collect federal taxes, regulate business practices, manage the national forests, conduct American foreign policy, administer social security programs—the list goes on and on.

In this section you will consider the nature and the overall shape of the federal bureaucracy.

What Is a Bureaucracy?

People often use the word *bureaucracy* to identify any large and complex administrative body.[1]
1.a In dictionary terms, a **bureaucracy** is an organization built on three principles.

1. Hierarchical authority. The organization is like a pyramid in structure. Officials and units at the top of the organization have control over those in the middle, who in turn direct those at the bottom.
2. Job specialization. Each person who works
1.b for the organization—each **bureaucrat**—has defined duties and responsibilities. There is a precise division of labor.

[1]The term is a combination of the French word *bureau*, which originally referred to a desk of a government official and later to the place where an official worked, and the suffix *-cracy*, signifying a type of government.

SECTION 1
The Federal Bureaucracy

FOCUS

Teacher's Resource File See the Unit 4 File, p. 55, for the Section 1 Outline.

Objectives

15.1 Examine the ways in which the Federal Government meets the definition of a bureaucracy.
15.2 Identify the various titles given to administrative units.
15.3 Distinguish between staff and line agencies.

Bellringer Activity List the following initials on the board: NASA, FBI, CIA. Ask students if they know the full names represented by these initials. *(National Aeronautics and Space Administration, Federal Bureau of Investigation, Central Intelligence Agency.)* Ask students to describe what they think these organizations do.

State the Purpose Point out to students that the organizations described in the "Bellringer Activity" are all part of the federal bureaucracy, which they will be reading about in this section.

In Section 1, students will learn about some of the characteristics of a bureaucracy, the main elements of the bureaucracy in the executive branch, and the differences among its components.

Vocabulary

Point out "Key Terms" on page 381. Refer students to footnote 1 on page 381. Have students compare the literal meaning of the word *bureaucracy* as translated from the French with the definition given in the chapter.
LEP

Reading Strategy: Relating to Topic

Refer students to the three-part definition of the Key Term, *bureaucracy*, given on pages 381–382. Have students name as many different school departments, offices, and programs in the school as they can. After they have read the chapter, ask students to compare the bureaucracy in their school to the federal bureaucracy.

INSTRUCT

Explain/Analyze Help students to recognize that the federal bureaucracy evolved as the government set up various organizations to carry out its programs and policies. Ask students to analyze how the growth of the nation might have contributed to the growth of this enormous bureaucracy. (*The introduction of new services and programs made necessary by expanding territory and growing population led to the introduction of new components and layers to the bureaucracy.*)

Ask students to consider the confusion in the manner in which government units are named. Have students speculate how this confusion might contribute to the negative views of the bureaucracy referred to in footnote 2 on page 382. (*Possible answer: People perceive a lack of order and structure in the bureaucracy.*)

Finally, focus student attention on the distinction between staff and line agencies. Ask students to discuss the idea that a significant portion of the bureaucracy exists primarily to support the bureaucracy.

ABCNEWS INTERACTIVE

The following video segment may be used to highlight aspects of the bureaucracy in the executive branch.

POWERS OF THE PRESIDENT GUIDEBOOK
Chapter 45: Executive Departments, p. 53

3. Formal rules. The organization conducts its operations according to established regulations and procedures.

In short, a bureaucracy is a way of organizing people to do work.[2] Bureaucracies are found in the public and private sectors. For example, the United States Army, your school, McDonald's, the Department of Agriculture, and the Roman Catholic Church are all bureaucracies.

Major Elements of the Federal Bureaucracy

The federal bureaucracy is all of the agencies, people, and procedures through which the Federal Government operates. It is the means by which the government makes and administers public policy—the sum of its decisions and actions. As the chart on the next page shows, nearly all of that bureaucracy is in the executive branch.

The Constitution says little about the organization of the executive branch. It does make the President its chief administrator by giving him the power to "take care that the laws be faithfully executed."[3] But the Constitution makes only the barest mention of the administrative machinery through which the President is to exercise that power.

Article II does suggest the existence of executive departments by giving to the President the power to "require the opinion, in writing, of the principal officers in each of the executive departments."[4] The Constitution also suggests the existence of two departments in particular, for military and for foreign affairs, by making the President the "commander in chief of the army and navy," and by giving him the power to make treaties and to appoint "ambassadors, other public ministers, and consuls."[5]

Beyond those references, the Constitution is silent on the organization of the executive branch. However, the Framers certainly intended for administrative agencies to be created. They understood that no matter how wise the President and the Congress, their decisions still had to be acted upon to be effective. Without
1.c an **administration**—the government's many administrators and agencies—even the best policies would amount to so many words.

As the chart on page 383 shows, the executive branch is now made up of three major groups of administrative agencies: (1) the Executive Office of the President, (2) the 14 cabinet Departments, and (3) a large number of independent agencies.[6] You read about the Executive Office and its several agencies in Chapter 14. You will look at the other groups shortly.

The Name Game

The titles given to the many units that make up the executive branch vary a great deal. The name *department* is reserved for agencies of cabinet rank. Beyond that, however, there is little standardized use of titles.

The term *agency* is often used to refer to any governmental body. It is sometimes used to identify a major unit headed by a single administrator of near-cabinet status, such as the Environmental Protection Agency. But the same is true of the title *administration*; for example, the National Aeronautics and Space Administration.

The name *commission* is usually given to agencies charged with the regulation of business activities, such as the Interstate Commerce Commission and the Securities and Exchange Commission. These units are composed of varying numbers of top-ranking officers called commissioners. The same title, however, is given to

[2]Some use the words *bureaucracy* and *bureaucrat* in another, less than complimentary sense. To them, government ("the bureaucracy") and its bureaucrats are too powerful, or inefficient, or mired in red tape, or filled with an inflated sense of self-importance, or overpaid and underworked, or all of those things. Big government has never been popular in this country and, to many Americans, *bureaucracy* is simply another way of saying big government.

[3]Article II, Section 3.

[4]Article II, Section 2, Clause 1. There is also a reference to "heads of departments" in Clause 2, and to "any department or officer" of the government in Article I, Section 8, Clause 18.

[5]Article II, Section 2, Clauses 1 and 2.

[6]The chart is adapted from the current edition of the *United States Government Manual.*

ACTIVITY: For Gifted Students

Theme: Systems While studying the organization and function of the federal bureaucracy, you may wish to remind students that a bureaucracy is an organizational system. Have students create a diagram to represent the bureaucracy as a system. Students should describe the layers of hierarchical organization and give examples of the kinds of duties and responsibilities of different organizations at several layers of the system. To extend this focus, students may be introduced to the concept that systems exist in both artificial and natural settings—for example, a computer system or a weather system.

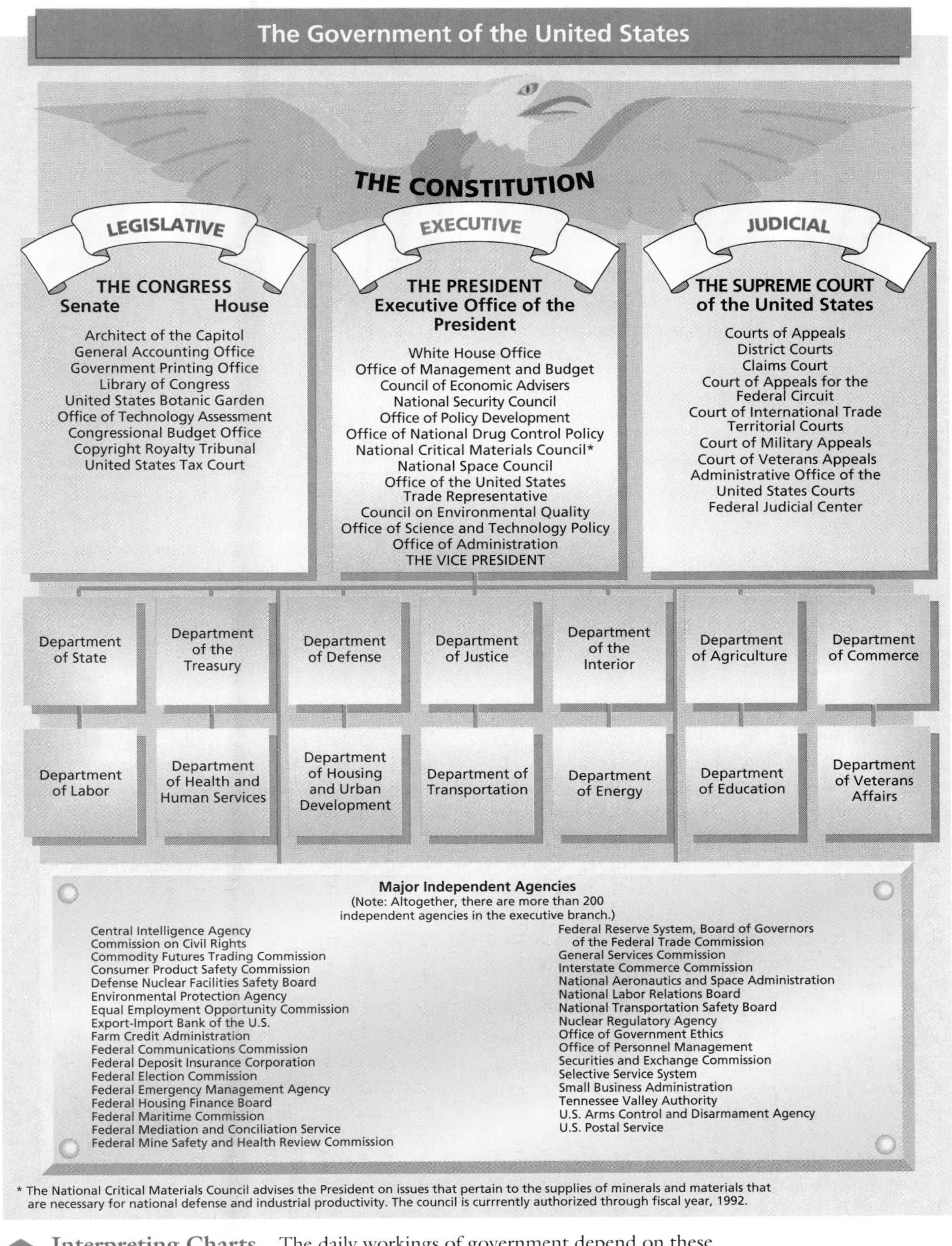

Interpreting Charts The daily workings of government depend on these departments and agencies, which are staffed by nonelected employees. According to this chart, which branch makes up the largest share of the federal bureaucracy?

Interpreting Charts Be sure students notice the lines connecting the various parts of the chart, which indicate that most of the agencies shown are part of the executive branch of government. Point out that those in the middle, all named *department,* are the cabinet departments. Remind students that some 3 million people work for the federal bureaucracy.

Caption Answer The executive branch.

Provide Guided Practice Write the following questions on the board: What is a bureaucracy? How does the Constitution imply the creation of a federal bureaucracy? What is the name game? What are staff and line agencies? Ask volunteers to write answers to these questions on the board. Then have volunteers revise or refine the definitions as needed.

Provide Independent Practice

TRF **Teacher's Resource File** You may wish to assign Section 1 Guided Reading and Review, Unit 4 File, p. 56, to help students master section objective content.

Enrichment

Using the definition of bureaucracy on pages 381–382, have students think of examples of non-governmental bureaucracies. How does each meet the requirements for a bureaucracy? Then have them think of other "organizations" that are not bureaucracies. (Average)

Interpreting Tables and Political Cartoons Ask students how government could change features that employees dislike. Have students react to the cartoon caption.

Caption Answer Bureaucrats are too powerful and are not elected to their positions.

Monitor Comprehension

Answers to Section 1 Review
1. "Key Terms" are defined on the following pages:
- **a.** bureaucracy, p. 381
- **b.** bureaucrat, p. 381
- **c.** administration, p. 382

2. The executive branch. **3.** (a) Makes President chief administrator, suggests existence of executive departments. (b) It implies the creation of agencies and departments. **4.** (a) Examples: Department, agency, administration, commission. (b) The use of names is not systematic. **5.** (a) Staff agencies offer support to line agencies. (b) Line agencies perform the tasks for which the organization exists. **6.** Job specialization helps efficiency; formal rules create "red tape."

Closure

The Federal Government is but one example of a bureaucracy. Most of this bureaucracy is part of the executive branch. In Section 2, students will read about some major components of the bureaucracy.

Assignment Assign Section 2, pp. 385–394, for the next class period.

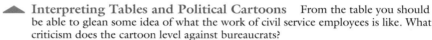

What Top Federal Career Employees Like Least and Most About Their Work

Like Least
Inability to take personnel actions that should be a manager's prerogative (e.g., hiring and discipline)
Inadequate resources (e.g., personnel, budget)
Personal financial sacrifice
"Red tape"
Frustrations in dealing with interest groups and Congress

Like Most
Challenging assignments
Opportunity to have an impact on policy programs
Opportunity for public service
Opportunity to use and expand one's knowledge and skills
Caliber of colleagues

"Think of it. Presidents come and go, but WE go on forever!"

 **Interpreting Tables and Political Cartoons** From the table you should be able to glean some idea of what the work of civil service employees is like. What criticism does the cartoon level against bureaucrats?

some investigative, advisory, and reporting bodies, including the Civil Rights Commission and the Federal Election Commission.

Either *corporation* or *authority* is the title most often given to agencies headed by a board and a manager, and that conduct business-like activities—for example, the Federal Deposit Insurance Corporation and the Tennessee Valley Authority.

Within each major agency, the same confusing lack of uniformity in the use of names is common. *Bureau* is the name often given to the major elements in a department, but *service*, *administration*, *office*, *branch*, and *division* are often used for the same purpose. This lack of uniformity in agency names can be clearly seen in the chart on page 383.

Many federal agencies are often referred to by their initials. The EPA, IRS, FBI, CIA, FCC, and TVA are but a few of the dozens of familiar examples.[7] A few of the federal agencies are also known by nicknames. For example, the Federal National Mortgage Association is often called "Fannie Mae" and the National Railroad Passenger Corporation is better known as Amtrak.

Staff and Line

The several units that make up any administrative organization can be classified as either staff or line agencies. Staff agencies serve in a support capacity. They aid the chief executive and other administrators by furnishing advice and other assistance in the management of the organization. Line agencies, on the other hand, actually perform the tasks for which the organization exists.

Two illustrations of this distinction are the several agencies that make up the Executive Office of the President and, in contrast, the Environmental Protection Agency. The agencies

[7]The use of acronyms can sometimes cause problems. When the old Bureau of the Budget was reorganized in 1970, it was also renamed. It is now the Office of Management and Budget (OMB). However, it was for a time slated to be known as the Bureau of Management and Budget (BOMB).

Reteach

Have students prepare a glossary defining the following terms: *bureaucracy, administration, department, staff agency,* and *line agency.* Then have students use each of these terms to formulate a response in support of the following statement: "The federal bureaucracy has grown steadily since the framing of the Constitution."

 **Teacher's Resource File**
See the Unit 4 File, p. 57, for the Section 1 Quiz.

Spotlight on: Behind the Scenes

The bewildering use of initials to represent the names of federal agencies can create an "alphabet soup" capable of confusing the most experienced bureaucrat. One famous story involves Harold Ickes, secretary of the interior during World War II. At a press conference a reporter asked Ickes about the newly formed Office of Petroleum Coordination, the OPC. "I can't speak for the OPC," Ickes said. After a long pause an aide reminded Ickes that Ickes himself was director of the new agency. "I'm all balled up on these initials," an embarrassed Ickes told the press.

that make up the Executive Office—the White House Office, the National Security Council, and so on—each exist as staff support to the President. Their primary mission is to assist the President in the exercise of the executive power and in the overall management of the executive branch. They are not operating agencies. That is, they do not actually operate—administer—public programs.

The Environmental Protection Agency (EPA), on the other hand, has a different mission. It is responsible for the day-to-day enforcement of the several federal antipollution laws. The EPA operates "on the line," where "the action" is.

This difference between staff agencies and line agencies can help you find your way through the complexities of the federal bureaucracy. But remember, the distinction between the two can be oversimplified. For example, most line agencies do have staff units to aid them in their line operations. Thus, the EPA's Office of Civil Rights is a staff unit established to insure that the agency's personnel practices do not violate the Federal Government's antidiscrimination policies.

Section 1 Review

1. Define: bureaucracy, bureaucrat, administration
2. In which branch of the government is most of the federal bureaucracy located?
3. (a) What does the Constitution say about the organization of the executive branch? (b) How did those words contribute to the creation of the federal bureaucracy?
4. (a) What terms are most often used in the titles of federal agencies? (b) How does the use of those terms create confusion?
5. (a) What are staff agencies and functions? (b) Line agencies and functions?

Critical Thinking

6. Demonstrating Reasoned Judgment (p. 19) Explain how the characteristics of a bureaucracy both help and hurt the effective and efficient administration of government.

2 The Executive Departments and the Independent Agencies

Find Out:

- What are the responsibilities of each of the 14 executive departments?
- For what reasons are the departments composed of so many subagencies?
- What are the three types of independent agencies and what do they do?

Key Terms:

independent agencies, quasi-legislative, quasi-judicial

Governor Mario Cuomo of New York said, "Democracy is not meant to be efficient, it is meant to be fair." How do you react to that comment? Does the demand for fairness offer any possible explanation for why public bureaucracies are sometimes less efficient than private ones?

In this section, you will read about the major components of the federal bureaucracy.

The Cabinet

Most federal bureaucrats work in one of the 14 cabinet departments. The cabinet departments are also called the executive departments. They are the traditional units of the federal administration, and each is built around a broad field of activity.

The 1st Congress set up three of these departments in 1789: State, Treasury, and War. As the size and the workload of the Federal Government grew, Congress added new departments. Some of the newer departments took over various duties originally assigned to older departments, and they gradually assumed new functions, as well. The Congress also created, and later abolished, a few departments.

The head of each department is known as the secretary, except for the attorney general, who directs the work of the Justice Department. The President names each department head, subject to confirmation by the Senate.

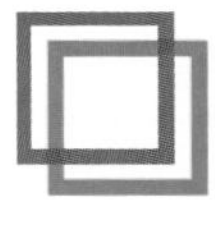

SECTION 2
The Executive Departments and the Independent Agencies

FOCUS

Teacher's Resource File See the Unit 4 File, p. 58, for the Section 2 Outline.

Objectives

15.4 Identify the responsibilities of each of the 14 executive departments.
15.5 Analyze why the executive departments are composed of so many subagencies.
15.6 Define the three types of independent agencies and their functions.

Bellringer Activity Ask students to explain what they think it means to be "independent." Is independence a positive or negative characteristic? Tell students that they will be reading about the independent agencies of the federal bureaucracy.

State the Purpose The federal bureaucracy contains many executive departments and independent agencies that perform specialized tasks. In Section 2, students will learn about the responsibilities of the executive departments and about the missions of the various independent agencies.

ABCNEWS INTERACTIVE

The following video segment may be used to highlight aspects of the bureaucracy in the executive branch.

POWERS OF THE PRESIDENT GUIDEBOOK
Chapter 20: Cabinet Nominations, p. 26

Vocabulary

Point out to students the list of "Key Terms" on page 385. Direct students' attention to footnote 9 on page 391. Students might consult several different dictionaries to find additional examples of words formed with the prefix *quasi*.
LEP

Reading Strategy: Question Writing

Before students read the section, have them read the major headings and convert each of them into a question. Tell students to write these questions on a piece of paper and write answers to them as they read the section.

Caption Answer That census data is gathered in a careless and unsystematic manner.

INSTRUCT

Explain/Analyze Tell students that there are two main categories into which the bureaucracy of the executive branch is divided: the executive departments, or the cabinet, and the independent agencies.

Remind students that the cabinet departments are the traditional units of administration. That fact defines one of the major differences between the cabinet and the independent agencies. Ask students to identify the two responsibilities of cabinet secretaries. (*Running their departments and advising the President.*)

Have students review the chart on page 383 and observe that each department is built around a broad field of activity, such as transportation or agriculture. Ask students why the broad scope of these departments might lead to the growth of subagencies. (*Possible answer: There are many specific activities going on within each cabinet department. For example, there are many different kinds of transportation, thus the need for many subagencies.*)

Census-Taking The Census Bureau is one part of the Department of Commerce. This collage shows the bureau gathering population data in the mid-1800s (top), 1940, and 1990. The cartoon comments on the 1990 census, which was estimated to have been miscounted by several hundred thousand people. What comment does the cartoon make on how census data is gathered?

Together, the department secretaries serve as the members of the President's cabinet, as you saw in the last chapter. Their duties as the chief officers of their own departments generally take most of their time, however. Each of them is the primary link between presidential policy and his or her own department. Of equal importance are each department head's efforts to promote and protect that department with the President, congressional committees, the rest of the bureaucracy, and the public.

An under secretary or deputy secretary and several assistant secretaries aid the secretary in his or her multidimensional role. These officials are also named by the President and confirmed by the Senate. Staff support for the secretary comes from assistants and aides with a wide range of titles in such areas as personnel, planning, legal advice, budgeting, and public relations.

Each department is made up of a number of subunits, both staff and line. As noted earlier, these agencies are known as bureaus, offices, services, divisions, and so on. Each of these agencies is usually further divided into smaller working units. Thus, the Criminal Division in the Department of Justice is composed of 12 sections—

SPOTLIGHT ON: Economics

Among the executive departments, the largest single item of the 1992 federal budget is the $351 billion social security program, controlled by the Department of Health and Human Services. That department's budget, excluding Social Security, ranks third among the executive departments at $167 billion—behind the Treasury Department's $300 billion budget and the Defense Department's $292 billion figure. Agriculture ranks fourth at $62 billion, followed by Veterans Affairs at $33 billion; Education at $29 billion; Housing and Urban Development at $25.5 billion, and Energy at $16 billion. Justice, Transportation, Labor, Interior, State, and Commerce budgets descend from $10 to $2 billion.

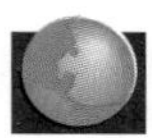

Global Awareness

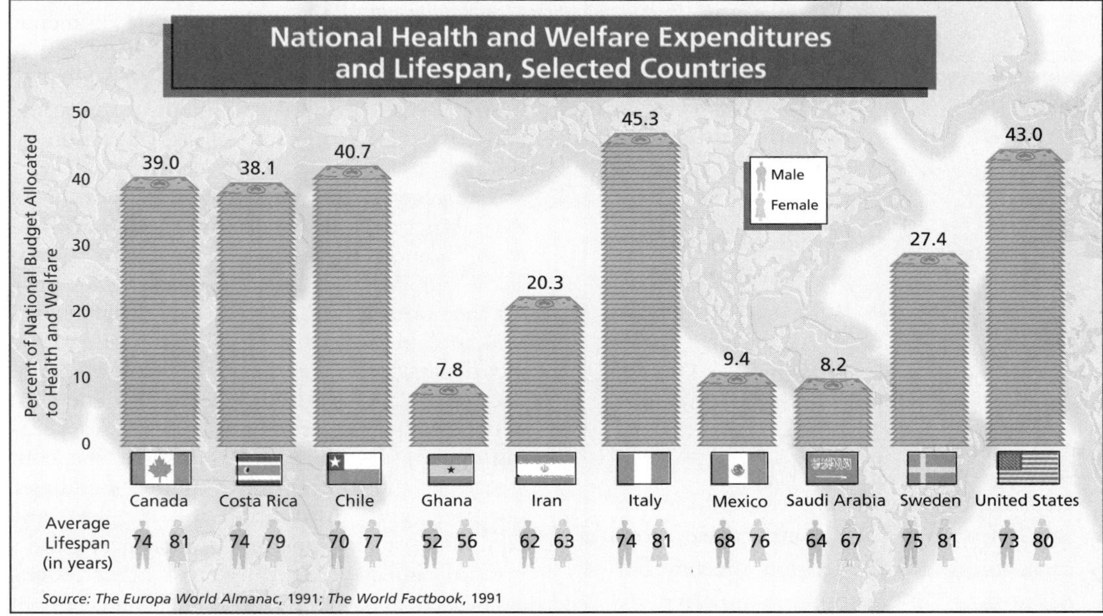

Interpreting Graphs The Department of Health and Human Services is responsible for dispensing health and social security services to the public. How does this graph show the essential relationship between national health budgets and public welfare?

including, for example, the Narcotics and Dangerous Drugs Section and the Fraud Section. About 80 percent of the bureau and office chiefs are career people, not political appointees.

The internal structure of most of the departments is arranged on a geographic basis. That is, each department conducts many of its activities through regional offices that direct the work of agency employees in the field. For example, the Treasury Department's Internal Revenue Service (IRS) is headquartered in Washington. Yet, the IRS carries out most of its tax collection and enforcement work through 7 regional offices, 64 district offices, and some 200 local offices. Altogether, nearly 90 percent of all federal civilian employees work outside the nation's capital.

The 14 executive departments that exist today are listed here followed by the year each was created: the State Department (1789); Department of the Treasury (1789); Department of Defense (1949); Department of Justice (1870); Department of the Interior (1849); Department of Agriculture (1889); Department of Commerce (1903); Department of Labor (1913); Department of Health and Human Services (1953); Department of Housing and Urban Development (1965); Department of Transportation (1967); Department of Energy (1977); Department of Education (1979); and Department of Veterans Affairs (1989).

You will find summaries of the work and functions of the executive departments on pages 697–709. The Departments of State and Defense are discussed in further detail in Chapter 17.

What Are Independent Agencies?

Until the 1880s, nearly all that the Federal Government did was done through the cabinet departments. Since then, however, Congress has

Interpreting Graphs Have students review the graph. Ask them if they can see a direct relationship between percentage of budget spent on health and welfare and life expectancy. (*Possible answers: No—Sweden has the highest life expectancy rates and spends far less than many other countries. Yes—notwithstanding the example of Sweden, those countries that spend a higher percentage have longer-lived populations.*)

Caption Answer By comparing average life spans with percentages of selected countries' budgets spent on health and welfare.

ACTIVITY: Teaching Heterogeneous Groups

In order for students to understand more clearly one of the components of the federal bureaucracy, have them investigate the workings of the cabinet departments. Refer students to the chart on page 383. Review the different departments of the cabinet with students. Then, acting as the President, make appointments to your cabinet. Have each appointed "secretary" work with one or two partners to research the workings of his or her department and prepare a report for the class. Students should include information about the current secretary, responsibilities, and interesting facts about their departments. Student reports can take the form of an illustrated chart or diagram. LEP

INSTRUCT

Analyze Have students identify the three different types of independent agencies. (*Independent executive agencies, regulatory commissions, and government corporations.*) Ask students to analyze the history of these agencies and the main reasons why they exist outside of the cabinet departments. (*For example: To protect them from the politics of the cabinet departments; or as a result of accident or inefficiency.*)

Finally, have students discuss the benefits and drawbacks of having the additional bureaucratic layer of the independent agencies. (*Possible answers: Benefits: They can regulate, be critical of, and operate independently of the politicized executive branch. Drawback: They duplicate many functions of the cabinet departments; they are not as accountable to the people.*)

VOICES *on Government*

Patricia F. Saiki, head of the Small Business Administration

On the Importance of the SBA, an Independent Agency

"[I]t behooves us to encourage the growth and development of small business in order to retain our nation's prosperity. . . . I do feel the small-business community should be heard, not only in the administration, but in all government agencies and in Congress. I think small-business concerns underlie every decision affecting our economy. Unless those concerns are addressed, we are not going to be offering encouragement to the very base of our economy—small business."

created a large number of additional agencies—
1.a the **independent agencies** located outside of the departments. Today, they number more than 200. Most of the more important independent agencies are listed in the chart on page 383.

Several independent agencies administer programs that cannot be easily distinguished from those of the cabinet departments. The work of the National Aeronautics and Space Administration (NASA), for example, is similar to that of a number of agencies in the Defense Department; and NASA's responsibilities are not very far removed from those of the Department of Transportation.

Neither the size of an independent agency's budget nor the number of its employees provides a good way to distinguish between many of these agencies and the executive departments. Thus, NASA's budget for fiscal year 1992 is just over $15 billion—about the same as the total for the Energy Department, and substantially more than the monies to be spent by four other cabinet departments: Commerce, Interior, Justice, and State. The space agency now employs more persons (more than 23,000) than do the departments of Housing and Urban Development, Labor, Education, or Energy.

The reasons these agencies exist outside of the cabinet departments are nearly as numerous as the agencies themselves. A few major reasons stand out, however. Some agencies have been set up outside of the regular departmental structure because they do not fit well within any department. The General Services Administration (GSA) is a leading example. The GSA is the Federal Government's major housekeeping agency. Its main chores include the construction and operation of public buildings, purchase and distribution of supplies and equipment, management of real property, and a host of similar services to most other federal agencies. The Office of Personnel Management (OPM) is another example. It is the hiring agency for nearly all other federal agencies, as you will soon see.

Congress has given some of these agencies an independent status to protect them from the influence of both partisan and pressure politics. The OPM is an example of just such an agency, as are the Civil Rights Commission and the Federal Election Commission. The point can be turned on its head, also; some agencies are located outside the cabinet departments because that is exactly where certain pressure groups want them. Other federal agencies were born as independents largely by accident. In short, no thought was given to the problems of administrative confusion when they were created. Finally, some agencies are independent because of the peculiar and sensitive nature of their functions. This is especially true of the independent regulatory commissions.

The label *independent agency* is a catchall. Most of these agencies are independent only in the sense that they are not located within any of the 14 cabinet departments. They are not independent of the President and the executive branch. Some are independent in a much more

TRF **Teacher's Resource File**
See the Simulations and Debates file, pp. 35–70, for material to support or extend this section.

concrete way, however. For most purposes, they do lie outside the executive branch and are largely free of presidential control.

Perhaps the best way to understand all of these independent agencies is to divide them into three main groups: (1) the independent executive agencies, (2) the independent regulatory commissions, and (3) the government corporations.

The Independent Executive Agencies

This group includes most of the independent agencies. Some are large, with thousands of employees, multimillion-dollar or even billion-dollar budgets, and extremely important public tasks to perform. The GSA, NASA, and the EPA are three examples of larger, independent executive agencies. They are organized much like the cabinet departments—that is, they are headed by a single administrator with subunits operating on a regional basis, and so on. The most important difference between the independent executive agencies and the 14 executive departments is simply that they do not have cabinet status.

Some of the agencies in this group are not administrative and policy giants. They do important work, however, and sometimes attract public notice. The Civil Rights Commission, the Peace Corps, the Federal Election Commission, and the Small Business Administration all fall into this category.

Most independent executive agencies operate far from the limelight. They have few employees, small budgets, and almost never attract any attention. The American Battle Monuments Commission, the Institute of Museum Services, and the Migratory Bird Conservation Commission are typical of the dozens of these seldom seen or heard public bodies.

The Independent Regulatory Commissions

The independent regulatory commissions stand out among the independent agencies because they are largely beyond the reach of presidential direction and control. There are 11 of these agencies today, each created to regulate, or police, important aspects of the nation's economy. The vital statistics of the 11 independent regulatory commissions appear in the table on page 390.

Peace Corps Volunteer This Honduran child is learning English from a member of the Peace Corps, an independent agency that was originally part of the State Department.

The independent regulatory commissions' large measure of independence from the White House comes mainly from the way in which Congress has structured them. Each is headed by a board or commission made up of from five to seven members appointed by the President with Senate consent. However, those officials have terms of such length that it is unlikely a President will gain control over any of these agencies through the appointment process, at least not in a single presidential term.

Several other features of these boards and commissions put them beyond the reach of presidential control. No more than a bare majority of the members of each board or commission may belong to the same political party. Thus, several of those officers must belong to the party out of power. Moreover, the appointed terms of

Activity: Cooperative Learning

Time: One class period **Activity:** Create a "help wanted" ad for a federal agency. **Grouping**: Partners **Purpose:** Have students work in pairs to write an ad for a job in one of the federal agencies described in the chapter. The ad should include information about the job responsibilities as well as information that would make the job sound attractive. Students should look at "help wanted" ads from newspapers for examples of ads. **Roles:** Have students assign the following roles: recorder, spokesperson. **Outcome:** Have the spokesperson read the ad to the class. Invite comments and discussion.

Interpreting Tables Ask students to carefully consider the major functions of the independent regulatory commissions. Have students discuss the vital importance of such tasks as ensuring product safety, supervising the banking system, and others. Encourage students to include discussion of such current events as the savings and loan bailout, nuclear safety, or other issues in the context of this table.

Caption Answer Examination of their functions reveals their powers to make rules and decide disputes, much as legislative and judicial bodies do.

The Independent Regulatory Commissions

Agency, Date Established	Term of Members	Major Functions
Interstate Commerce Commission (ICC), 1887	5 years	Licenses, fixes rates, and regulates other aspects of commercial transportation by railroad, highway, and domestic waterway.
Board of Governors, Federal Reserve System (the Fed), 1913	14 years	Supervises banking system, practices; regulates money supply, use of credit in economy.
Federal Trade Commission (FTC), 1914	7 years	Enforces antitrust, other laws prohibiting unfair competition, price-fixing, false advertising, other unfair business practices.
Securities and Exchange Commission (SEC), 1934	5 years	Regulates securities, other financial markets, investment companies, brokers; enforces laws prohibiting fraud, other dishonest investment practices.
Federal Communications Commission (FCC), 1934	5 years	Regulates radio and television broadcasting, telephone, telegraph, and cable television operations, two-way radio and radio operators, and satellite communications.
National Labor Relations Board (NLRB), 1935	5 years	Administers federal labor-management relations laws; holds collective bargaining elections; prevents, remedies unfair labor practices.
Federal Maritime Commission (FMC), 1936	5 years	Regulates waterborne foreign, domestic off-shore commerce of the United States; supervises rates, services.
Consumer Product Safety Commission (CPSC), 1972	7 years	Sets, enforces safety standards for consumer products; directs recall of unsafe products; conducts safety research, information programs.
Nuclear Regulatory Commission (NRC), 1974	5 years	Licenses, regulates all civilian nuclear facilities, all civilian uses of nuclear materials.[a]
Commodity Futures Trading Commission (CFTC), 1974	5 years	Regulates commodity exchanges, brokers, futures trading in agricultural, metal, other commodities.
Federal Energy Regulatory Commission (FERC), 1977	4 years	Regulates, fixes rates for transportation, sale of natural gas, transportation of oil by pipelines, interstate transmission, sale of electricity.[b]

[a]These functions performed by the Atomic Energy Commission from 1946 to 1974 (when AEC was abolished); other AEC functions now performed by agencies in the Energy Department.
[b]These functions performed by the Federal Power Commission (created in 1930) until FPC was abolished in 1977. FERC is within the Energy Department, but only for administrative purposes; otherwise is independent (except Energy Secretary may set reasonable deadlines for FERC action in any matter before it). Under terms of National Energy Act of 1978, FERC's authority to regulate natural gas prices ended in 1985.

Interpreting Tables These commissions are independent of all three branches of government, and thus are exceptions to the separation of powers rule. How do the functions listed on the table show the unique role of the commissions as quasi-judicial and quasi-legislative agencies?

the members are staggered so that the term of only one member on each board or commission expires in any one year. Finally, the President can remove most of these officers only for those causes Congress has specified.[8]

As with the other independent agencies, the regulatory commissions are executive bodies. That is, Congress has given them the power to administer the programs for which they were created. However, unlike those other independent agencies, the regulatory commissions are

[8]Recall this point from Chapter 14. The members of five of these bodies (the SEC, FCC, CPSC, NRC, and CFTFC) are exceptions. Congress has provided that any of them may be removed at the President's discretion.

quasi-legislative and **quasi-judicial** bodies.[9] 1.b
That is, Congress has given them certain legisla- 1.c
tive-like and judicial-like powers.

These agencies exercise their quasi-legislative powers when they make rules and regulations. Those rules and regulations have the force of law. They explain the details of the laws Congress has directed these regulatory bodies to enforce. For example, Congress has said the railroads must offer "reasonable service" to the public and charge only "just and reasonable" rates for that service. The Interstate Commerce Commission (ICC) implements those requirements—directs how the railroads are to meet them—by issuing detailed rules and regulations.

The regulatory commissions exercise their quasi-judicial powers when they decide disputes in those fields in which Congress has given them their policing authority. For example, if a railroad asks the ICC for permission to raise its rates for carrying goods between two points, that request is likely to be opposed by the companies that ship those goods. The ICC holds a hearing to determine the merits of each side of the argument. It then makes a decision, much as a court would do. The decisions made by the ICC, and by the other independent regulatory bodies, can be appealed to the United States courts of appeals, as you will see in Chapter 18.

In a sense, Congress has created these agencies to act in its place. Congress could hold hearings and set freight rates, license radio and TV stations and nuclear reactors, check on business practices, and do the many other things it has directed the regulatory commissions to do. But these activities are complex and time-consuming, and they demand constant and expert attention. If Congress did all of this work it would then have no time for its important legislative work.

Note that these regulatory bodies possess all three of the basic governmental powers: executive, legislative, and judicial. They are exceptions to the principle of separation of powers. They should not be grouped with the other independent agencies, as they are in the chart on page 383. Instead, they should somehow be located somewhere between the executive and legislative branches, and between the executive and judicial branches, too.

Several authorities, and most recent Presidents, have urged that at least the administrative functions of the independent regulatory commissions be given to cabinet department agencies. Other serious questions have arisen about these agencies and have prompted proposals to abolish or redesign them. The most troubling questions are these: Have some of the independent regulatory commissions been captured by the special interests they are expected to regulate? Are all of the many and detailed rules made by these agencies really needed? Do some of them have the effect of stifling legitimate competition in the free enterprise system? Do some of them add unreasonably to the costs of doing business and therefore to the prices that consumers must pay?[10]

The regulatory authority of some of these agencies has been decreased in recent years. Ronald Reagan campaigned for the presidency in 1980 promising to cut most federal domestic programs—and, in particular, to reduce the government's regulation of the business community. Indeed, the 1980s came to be known as "the era of deregulation."[11] The Reagan administration pushed hard for a general deregulation of the nation's economic life, and the Bush administration has taken the same position.

---

[9]The prefix *quasi* is from the Latin, meaning "in a certain sense, resembling, seemingly."

[10]Because Congress sets the basic policies of these regulatory bodies, the major responsibility for answering these questions lies with Congress. It has responded to some of them in recent years. In particular, and especially at the urging of the Reagan administration in the 1980s, it has deregulated much of the nation's transportation industry, giving airlines, truckers, bus companies, railroads, and so on much greater freedom to operate.

[11]Deregulation had in fact begun before Mr. Reagan's first election. In several statutes, Congress had given the nation's transportation industry much greater freedom to operate in the late 1970s; for example, the Airlines Deregulation Act of 1978. That law all but eliminated the power of the Civil Aeronautics Board (CAB) to regulate commercial airlines. Instead, the CAB's mission became the promotion of competition in the air transport industry. The law also provided that the CAB was to be abolished by 1985, and it was.

Provide Guided Practice Have students make a chart that lists and explains the similarities and differences between the cabinet departments and the independent agencies.

Provide Independent Practice

TRF **Teacher's Resource File** You may wish to assign Section 2 Guided Reading and Review, Unit 4 File, p. 59, to help students master section objective content.

Enrichment

Have students find examples from the chart on page 383 of independent agencies and cabinet departments that share subject areas. Ask students to do research to compare and contrast the functions of these units. (Average)

OR

Teacher's Resource File
See the Unit 4 File for the Case Study on Contemporary Issues for Chapter 15.

Interpreting Political Art Ask students to comment on the techniques used in the painting to communicate the idea of uniformity and lack of humanity. (*Possible answers: The bureaucrats are faceless; the people all look the same.*)

Caption Answer Bureaucracies are portrayed as lacking in human characteristics such as individuality and warmth.

Monitor Comprehension

Answers to Section 2 Review
1. "Key Terms" are defined on the following pages:
  a. independent agencies, p. 388
  b. quasi-legislative, p. 391
  c. quasi-judicial, p. 391
2. They are the chief officers of their own departments and they are members of the cabinet. **3.** The cabinet departments. **4.** (a) Some agencies do not fit within any department; others need to be apart from the influence of partisan and pressure politics; in some cases, it appears as if the agencies are "independent" as a result of accident or lack of planning. (b) Most are independent simply in the sense that they do not reside within a cabinet department. **5.** They are beyond the reach of presidential direction and control. **6.** Flexibility. They are free from the controls of regular departmental organization. **7.** Cuomo suggests that government must be fair and accountable, therefore it must sacrifice a degree of efficiency. Advocates of corporation see the increased efficiency alone as justification for their existence.

Interpreting Political Art *Government Bureau* is the title of this eerie painting by George Tooker, which is displayed in the Metropolitan Museum of Art. How does the artist view bureaucracies?

The S&L scandal demonstrates that deregulation has not been altogether successful. When Congress ended restrictions on how savings and loan (S&L) institutions could invest their depositors' savings, many of them put billions of dollars into high-risk business ventures. Bad investments and fraud brought the failure of more than 1,000 S&Ls in the late 1980s and early 1990s.

The Government Corporations

Several of the independent agencies are government corporations. Like most of the other independent agencies, they are within the executive branch and subject to the President's direction and control. Unlike the other agencies, however, Congress created these agencies to carry out certain business-like activities.

Congress established the first government corporation when it chartered the First Bank of the United States in 1791. Yet government corporations were little used until World War I and the Depression. In both periods Congress set up dozens of corporations to carry out crash programs. Several still exist—among them, the Federal Deposit Insurance Corporation (FDIC), which insures bank deposits, and the Export-Import Bank of the United States (Eximbank), which makes loans to help the export and sale of American goods abroad.

There are over 60 of these government corporations today. Examples of the operations they perform include mail service (the United States Postal Service); the insurance of bank deposits (the FDIC); the management of the assets and liabilities of failed savings and loan institutions (the FDIC and the Resolution Trust Corporation); and the protection of pension benefits (the Pension Benefit Guaranty Corporation).[12]

[12] State and local governments maintain many of their own government corporations, most often called *authorities*, to operate airports, turnpikes, seaports, power plants, liquor stores, housing developments, and to conduct many other corporate activities. Of them all, the Port of New York Authority is probably the best known.

Spotlight on: Political Talk

Statements of the Presidents often reflect popular opinion of government in the United States. These opinions change over time, as the following examples suggest. Franklin D. Roosevelt wrote in 1944 that "as new conditions and problems arise beyond the power of men and women to meet as individuals, it becomes the duty of Government itself to find new remedies with which to meet them." Thirty-seven years later, Republican President Ronald Reagan revealed a change in the prevailing popular attitude about government, saying "Government is not the solution to the problem. Government is the problem."

Reteach

Present examples of different agencies and departments from the text. Ask volunteers to identify the unit as a cabinet department or an independent agency.

The typical government corporation is set up much like a corporation in the private sector. It is run by a board of directors, with a general manager who directs the corporation's operations in line with the policies established by that board. Most government corporations produce income that is plowed back into the business.

There are several striking differences between government and private corporations, however. Congress decides the purpose for which the public agencies exist and the functions they can perform. Their officers are public officers; in fact, all who work for these corporations are public employees. The President selects most of the top officers of government corporations with Senate confirmation. These public agencies get their financing from public monies appropriated by Congress, not from private investors. The Federal Government owns the stock.

The advantage most often claimed for the use of government corporations is their flexibility. It is said that the government corporation, freed from the controls of regular departmental organization, can carry on its activities with the incentive, efficiency, and ability to experiment that make many private concerns successful. Whether or not that claim is valid is open to question. At the very least, it raises this complex issue: Is a public corporation's need for flexibility in its operations compatible with democratic government's requirement that all public agencies be held responsible and accountable to the people?

The degree of independence and flexibility government corporations have varies considerably. In fact, some corporations are not independent at all. They are attached to an executive department. The Commodity Credit Corporation, for example, is the government's major crop-loan and farm-subsidy agency. It is located within the Department of Agriculture, and the secretary of agriculture chairs its seven-member board. The Commodity Credit Corporation carries out most of its functions through a line agency in the Department of Agriculture—the Agricultural Stabilization and Conservation Service—which is also subject to the direct control of the secretary.

Some corporations do have considerable independence, however. The Tennessee Valley Authority (TVA) is a case in point. It operates under a statute in which Congress has given it considerable discretion over its policies and programs. Although its budget is subject to review by the OMB, the President, and then Congress, the TVA has a large say in the uses of the income its several operations produce. It even has its own civil service system.[13]

Section 2 Review

1. **Define:** independent agencies, quasi-legislative, quasi-judicial
2. What are the main responsibilities of the department secretaries?
3. What agencies performed the activities of the independent agencies prior to the 1880s?
4. (a) For what reasons has Congress created many independent agencies in the executive branch? (b) In what sense are they independent?
5. In what ways are the independent regulatory commissions most strikingly different from other independent agencies?
6. What major advantage is claimed for the creation of government corporations?

Critical Thinking

7. **Making Comparisons** (p. 19) Compare the view put forth by Mario Cuomo in the quote at the beginning of the section with the views of those who support the use of government corporations.

★

[13]The TVA is one of the major illustrations of government in business. It was established by Congress, after years of controversy, in the Tennessee Valley Authority Act of 1933. The act called for the coordinated development and use of the natural resources of a huge area that today includes large parts of Tennessee, Kentucky, Virginia, North Carolina, Georgia, Alabama, and Mississippi.

The TVA has had an extraordinary impact on the Tennessee River Valley and its approximately four million residents. Its operations include electric power development, flood control and navigation work, reforestation, soil conservation, fertilizer production, agricultural research, recreational facilities, and the promotion of industrial growth in the Tennessee River Valley. The TVA's power program is self-supporting. Much of the support for its other activities comes from Congress. Still, it generates considerable revenues from sales of electricity and fertilizer and from its power to issue bonds.

TRF **Teacher's Resource File** See the Unit 4 File, p. 60, for the Section 2 Quiz.

Closure

The cabinet departments are the traditional units of federal administration. Since the late 1800s, however, independent agencies have become an important part of the federal bureaucracy. Cabinet departments and certain independent agencies look very much alike in terms of size, function, and organization. However, other independent agencies are quite unique in their form and function.

In the next section, students will read about many of the people who work in the federal bureaucracy.

Assignment Assign Section 3, pp. 395–399, for the next class period.

TEACHING
What You Can Do

Realizing a Dream

Objective

Determine that time and effort are required in order to make a difference in government.

INSTRUCT

Before students begin reading the feature, ask them if there is any group or individual from their community or the country whom they would like to honor. Tell students that they are going to read about a group of students who wanted to honor Martin Luther King, Jr., and how they went about doing so. Students may be surprised to learn of all the hard work and commitment required in making a difference in government. They may also be inspired by the rewards of success.

Below are some possible questions for postreading discussion:

- How can a person draw attention to his or her cause?
- What resources are necessary to "make a difference" and effectively influence government?
- What kinds of issues might motivate students to commit themselves to get involved and make a difference?

What You Can Do

Realizing a Dream

Each year, countless citizens from all over the United States and around the world visit Washington, D.C. The Capitol building, the Lincoln Memorial, and the Vietnam Veterans Memorial are only a few of the sights that inspire feelings of patriotism and awe. They serve as a reminder of the high ideals—and individual effort and sacrifice—that have made this country great.

In 1989, six high school students from Scottsdale, Arizona, were among the many visitors to the nation's capital. Seeing the Lincoln Memorial reminded them that it was the site where Martin Luther King, Jr., delivered his "I Have a Dream" speech in 1963, at the height of the civil rights movement. In that public demonstration for racial equality, more than 200,000 people gathered before the Lincoln Memorial and listened as King spoke about his dream: a United States where all people are equal. After seeing the memorial and recalling the drama of that day in 1963, the students thought of a way to commemorate King's speech—and they presented their idea before Congress.

The students proposed installing a commemorative plaque to mark the spot where King delivered his now-famous speech. Congress, however, informed the students that an ordinance prohibits the placement of a memorial on the site of another memorial.

Rather than drop the idea, the students adapted it. With the help of their history teacher, they decided to propose a First Amendment Museum in a room to the left of the Lincoln statue.

The group quickly went to work promoting their new idea. They sent out information packets and wrote letters to the appropriate officials that outlined their proposal for a museum illustrating the ways that Abraham Lincoln inspired King and others to work for freedom and individual rights. The students received encouraging support from local politicians, civic groups, and the press.

On a second trip to Washington, the group approached the National Park Service and the National Parks and Public Lands House Subcommittee with their plan for the First Amendment Museum. To the students' delight, their plan was approved. The museum should be completed in 1993.

Like many teenagers around the country, the Scottsdale students saw the chance to make an impact and took action. As a result, they made a difference in government long before they were eligible to cast their first vote. As one of the students put it, "If you're not involved, you'll never make a change. You can talk about it, but it's just talk."

Getting Involved

1. Identify a need in your school or community that is similar to the one addressed in this case.

2. Formulate a plan for ways that you could convince government officials to listen to your ideas, and identify resources that could be used in your plan.

3. Predict any problems or objections you might encounter in putting your plan into action.

TRF **Teacher's Resource File**
See the Participatory Government Activities file, pp. 28–39, for material to support and extend this feature.

3 The Civil Service

Find Out:

- How did the civil service system begin?
- How did the spoils system work?
- How does the civil service operate today?

Key Terms:

spoils system, patronage, register

Some 2.9 million men and women work for the Federal Government today.[14] Only about 300,000 of those federal bureaucrats live and work in the Washington area. Nearly 90 percent of all career federal employees have jobs in regional, field, and local offices scattered throughout the country and around the world.

The President appoints the people who hold the highest ranking jobs in the executive branch. There are only about 2,500 of those positions at the top levels of the Executive Office, the cabinet departments, the independent agencies, and in American embassies and other diplomatic stations.

All of the other jobs in the federal bureaucracy are covered, as you will see in this section, by some aspect of the civil service system.

Development of the Civil Service

The Constitution says very little about the staffing of the federal bureaucracy. In fact, its only direct reference is in Article II, Section 2, Clause 2. There the Constitution says that the President

"... shall nominate, and, by and with the advice and consent of the Senate, shall appoint ambassadors, other public ministers, and consuls, judges of the Supreme Court, and all other officers of the United States whose appointments are not herein otherwise provided for, and which shall be established by law; but the Congress may by law vest the appointment of such inferior officers, as they think proper, in the President alone, in the courts of law, or in the heads of departments."

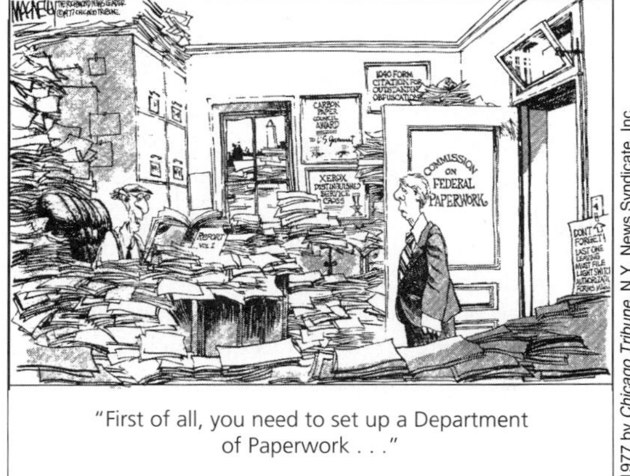

"First of all, you need to set up a Department of Paperwork . . ."

Interpreting Political Cartoons What comment does this cartoon make about the federal bureaucracy?

The Beginnings When he became President in 1789, George Washington knew that the success of the new government would depend in large part on those whom he appointed to office. Those to be chosen, he said, would be "such persons alone . . . as shall be the best qualified." Still, he favored members of his own party, the Federalists. So did his successor, John Adams.

In 1801 Thomas Jefferson found most federal posts filled by men politically and personally opposed to him. He agreed with Washington's standard of fitness for office, but he combined it with another: political acceptability. Jefferson had several hundred Federalists dismissed and replaced by Democratic-Republicans.

The Spoils System By the late 1820s, the number of federal employees had risen above 10,000. When Andrew Jackson became President in 1829, he dismissed over 200 presidential appointees and nearly 2,000 other officeholders. They were replaced by Jacksonian Democrats.

Ever since, Andrew Jackson has been called the
1.a father of the **spoils system**—a reference to the the practice of giving offices and other favors of

[14] Another 2 million men and women serve in the armed forces; see Chapter 17. Altogether, there are now some 18.5 million civilian public employees in this country. Nearly 4.3 million work for the States, and another 11.3 million work for local governments (including 6.2 million persons employed by school districts). About 2.5 million of those who work for State and local governments are employed on a part-time basis.

SECTION 3
The Civil Service

FOCUS

Teacher's Resource File See the Unit 4 File, p. 61, for the Section 3 Outline.

Objectives

15.7 Identify the origins of the civil service system.
15.8 Analyze the operation of the spoils system.
15.9 Describe the operation of the civil service today.

Bellringer Activity Have students imagine they were just elected mayor or governor of their community or State. Now they must hire 100 new people to fill positions in their administration. Have students discuss what standards they would use and why. Tell students that they will read about the hiring practices of the Federal Government.

State the Purpose The federal government employs nearly 3 million men and women. About 90 percent of these jobs are part of the government's civil service system. In Section 3, students will learn about the historical development and current characteristics of the civil service system.

Interpreting Political Cartoons Ask students to comment on the irony of the caption. (*A Department of Paperwork would simply add more paperwork.*)

Caption Answer It points out the inordinate amount of paperwork and "red tape" of the bureaucracy.

Vocabulary

Point out "Key Terms" on page 395. Direct students to footnote 15 on page 396. Ask students to discuss how the quotation in the note helps clarify the meaning of the term *spoils system*.

Reading Strategy: Problem Solving

Refer students to the "Bellringer Activity." Have them consider what problems and issues might be involved in hiring the many people who work for the hundreds of governmental agencies. For example, should the government give preference to certain groups? Should this preference take precedence over merit? Have students brainstorm a list of guidelines for hiring people to work in government.

ABCNEWS INTERACTIVE

The following video segment may be used to highlight aspects of the bureaucracy in the executive branch.

POWERS OF THE PRESIDENT GUIDEBOOK
Chapter 20: Cabinet Nominations, p. 26

Interpreting Political Cartoons Ask students to give possible explanations for the meaning of the pig in the cartoon at left. (*Possible answers: The pig symbolizes the political gluttony of Jackson. Jackson is riding the pig as he would a horse, part of a satirical comparison of Jackson to the victor in a military campaign.*)

Caption Answer The main figure is besieged by supporters demanding a piece of the governmental cake, which symbolizes government jobs.

INSTRUCT

Discuss/Analyze Tell students to analyze the development of the civil service over the first few administrations. As a part of this analysis, have students discuss Washington's and Jefferson's formulas for filling government posts. Ask students whether or not they agree with Jefferson that a President should have politically acceptable people in office.

Next have students critically examine the spoils system as practiced by Andrew Jackson. Direct students' attention to the four arguments used by Jackson in defense of his policies. Ask them to discuss ways in which they agree or disagree with these ideas. Ask students how

government to political supporters and friends.[15] This title is not altogether fair, however. The practice of giving jobs to supporters and friends,
1.b also known as **patronage**, was in wide use in politics long before Jackson's presidency.

Jackson saw his appointing policy as democratic. In his first message to Congress, he explained and defended it on four grounds: (1) Since the duties of public office are basically simple, any normally intelligent person can fill such office. (2) There should be a "rotation in office" so that a large number of people can have the privilege of serving in government. (3) Long service in office by any person can lead to both tyranny and inefficiency. (4) The people are entitled to have the party they have placed in power in control of all offices of government, top to bottom.

Whatever Jackson's view, many saw the spoils system as a way to build and hold power. For the next half-century, every change of administration brought a new round of rewards and punishments. Many posts were filled by political hacks who were ill-equipped for their jobs and interested mainly in enriching themselves or their friends. Inefficiency and even corruption became the order of the day.

[15]The phrase comes from a statement made on the floor of the Senate in 1832. Senator William Learned Marcy of New York, defending Jackson's appointment of an ambassador, declared: "To the victor belongs the spoils of the enemy."

The Movement to Reform Able people, in and out of government, pressed for reforms. Congress did create a Civil Service Commission in 1871. But that effort soon died, mainly because Congress failed to give the Commission enough money to do a proper job.

A tragedy at last brought about fundamental changes in the hiring and other staffing practices of the Federal Government. In 1881, a deranged and disappointed office-seeker assassinated President James Garfield. The nation was outraged. Congress, pushed hard by Garfield's successor, Chester Arthur, passed the Pendleton Act—the Civil Service Act of 1883.[16]

The Pendleton Act The 1883 law laid the foundation of the present federal civil service. The act's main purpose was to make merit the basis for hiring, promotion, and other personnel actions in the federal work force.

The Pendleton Act set up two categories of employment in the executive branch: the classified

Interpreting Political Cartoons These cartoons comment on the spoils system, or patronage practices of the kind used by Andrew Jackson. How does the 1872 cartoon (right) illustrate this practice?

and the unclassified service. The act gave the President the key power to decide into which of these categories most federal agencies and their personnel were to be placed. All hiring for the classified service was to be based on merit, determined by "practical" examinations given by an independent agency called the Civil Service Commission.

The Pendleton Act forbade classified employees to take any part in partisan politics. But two of the law's other provisions undercut the law's emphasis on merit, at least to a degree. One provision required that the federal work force was to be made up of men and women from every State, and the number from each State had to bear a close relationship to that State's share of the total population. The other provision was the veterans' preference: All veterans, especially disabled veterans and veterans' widows, received preferred ranking in federal hiring.

At first only about 10 percent of the Federal Government's then 130,000 employees were placed into the classified service. However, the merit system began to grow rapidly when Theodore Roosevelt became President. When Roosevelt left office in 1909, the classified umbrella covered two-thirds of the federal work force, which by then had climbed to 365,000. Today, nearly 90 percent of all the men and women who work for executive branch agencies are in the classified service.[17]

Civil Service Today

The first goal of civil service reform—doing away with the spoils system—was largely reached in the early part of this century. Gradually, a newer goal emerged: recruiting and keeping the best available people in the federal work force.

On the whole, efforts to reach that goal have succeeded. Most federal employees are hired through competitive examinations; they are paid and promoted on the basis of evaluations by their superiors; and they are largely protected from dismissal for partisan reasons.

Still, the civil service has never been perfect. Critics often claim that not enough attention has been paid to merit in the merit system.

President Jimmy Carter put it this way in 1978:

> "The Pendleton Act, . . . the Civil Service Commission and the merit system . . . have served our nation well in fostering the development of a federal work force which is basically honest, competent, and dedicated.
>
> But the system has serious defects. It has become a bureaucratic maze which neglects merit, tolerates poor performance, and mires every personnel action in red tape, delay, and confusion.
>
> Most civil service employees perform with spirit and integrity. Nevertheless, the public suspects that there are too many government workers, that they are underworked, overpaid, and insulated from the consequences of incompetence.
>
> Such sweeping criticisms are unfair; but we must recognize that the only way to restore public confidence in the vast majority who work well is to deal effectively with the few who do not."

Reorganization At President Carter's urging, Congress passed the Civil Service Reform Act of 1978. That law made major changes in the civil service system. The Civil Service Commission was replaced by two new independent agencies—the Office of Personnel Management (OPM) and the Merit Systems Protection Board.

The Office of Personnel Management is now the Government's central personnel agency. The OPM is headed by a single director appointed by the President and Senate. The OPM examines and recruits most new federal employees, carries on extensive training programs for career civil

[16]The 1880 Republican convention was sharply divided by the civil service question. Its nominee, Garfield, was a strong supporter of reform. To balance the ticket, the Republicans chose Arthur, a leader of the antireform faction, as his running mate. President Garfield was shot by Charles J. Guiteau at Washington's Union Station on July 2, 1881; he died 80 days later, on September 19. Garfield had refused Guiteau's request that he be appointed American ambassador to Austria. Garfield's assassination brought a complete change in Arthur's stand; as President he became the leading champion of reform.

[17]That is, 90 percent not counting the United States Postal Service and a few other federal agencies. The Postal Service, with almost 820,200 employees, is the largest agency not covered by the civil service system. It is the only federal agency in which employment policies are set by collective bargaining and labor union contracts. The other major agencies not counted in fixing that 90 percent figure are the FBI, CIA, and TVA; each of those agencies has its own merit system.

the practice of ***patronage*** led to abuse and corruption. (*Possible answers: Political posts were filled not with qualified, skilled people, but with opportunists who used their power to enrich themselves and their friends.*)

Next have students discuss the civil service system. Ask them their opinion of the merit system of today. In what way is this system preferable to a patronage system? (*It ensures the quality of the work force by basing many decisions on objective qualification standards.*)

Provide Guided Practice Have students create a time line marking key events in the development of the civil service as discussed in the section. Tell students to annotate each of the dates on the time line to explain their significance to the discussion.

Provide Independent Practice

TRF **Teacher's Resource File** You may wish to assign Section 3 Guided Reading and Review, Unit 4 File, p. 62, to help students master section objective content.

SPOTLIGHT ON: Multiculturalism

To enforce federal regulations against discrimination in the work place, the Federal Government established the Equal Opportunity Employment Commission (EEOC) in 1964. The EEOC resolves charges filed against employers alleged to engage in discriminatory work and hiring practices in violation of the Civil Rights Act of 1964, the Equal Pay Act, the Age Discrimination in Employment Act, and the Americans with Disabilities Act of 1990. In 1991, EEOC heard some 43,500 complaints of alleged discrimination on the basis of race and gender, 14,500 on the basis of age, and 1,227 alleging discriminatory pay.

Enrichment

Have students do further research about the history of patronage, its critics and defenders, in the past 100 years. Some students may look into the benefits patronage was said to offer immigrants. Others may explore the long history of patronage in cities such as Chicago. (Challenging)

Interpreting Graphs: Multicultural Awareness Point out that the top pie chart does not represent all federal civil service employees, but only those of minority group background. Ask students whether or not they are surprised by the information in the graphs.

Caption Answer 72.8%.

Interpreting Charts After reviewing the steps in the chart on page 399, ask students to explain how these steps help ensure a qualified, quality work force. (*Possible answer: By requiring that all applicants are judged on the same basis rather than their relationships with powerful people.*)

Caption Answer Possible answers: High school diploma; literacy in English; completion of the civil service examination.

MONITOR COMPREHENSION

Answers to Section 3 Review
1. "Key Terms" are defined on the following pages:
a. spoils system, p. 395
b. patronage, p. 396
c. register, p. 398
2. He chose those who were best qualified, favoring members of his own party. **3.** (a) Anyone can fill a public office; (b) Gives more people a chance to serve in government; (c) holding a position for a long time can result in tyranny and inefficiency; and (d) the people chose the party in power, so that party should have control of all government offices. **4.** It divided government employment into classified and unclassified service; classified employment was

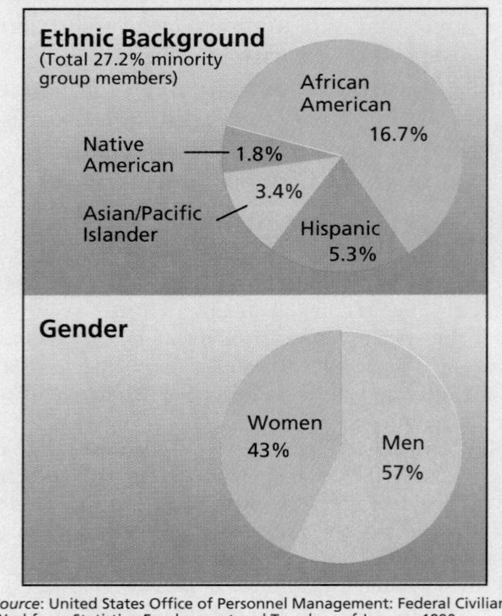

Interpreting Graphs: Multicultural Awareness The Civil Service must be nondiscriminatory in its hiring practices. What percentage of its workers are white?

servants, sets position classifications, and manages the salary and other job benefits for some 2.2 million of the people who work for Uncle Sam.

The Merit Systems Protection Board handles the rest of the work once done by the Civil Service Commission. A bipartisan three-member panel picked by the President and Senate, it is the agency that polices and protects the merit principle in the federal bureaucracy[18]

The Office of Personnel Management can best be described as the central clearinghouse in the federal recruiting, examining, and hiring process. It advertises for employees, gives exam-
1.c inations, and keeps **registers**—lists of those persons who pass its tests.

When there is a job opening in some agency, OPM usually sends it the names of the top three persons on its register for that type of position[19] If the agency turns down all three, it asks OPM for another set. Many jobs can also be filled by promotion from within an agency or by transfer from another agency. The OPM supervises those processes, too.

Federal Employees and Party Activists

Federal employees may not strike. Strikes and similar work stoppages are outlawed by the Labor-Management Relations (Taft-Hartley) Act of 1947. Within that framework, federal employees can join any of several labor unions and other groups that promote the interests of government employees.

Federal employees' political activities are also subject to limit. The major statute here is the Hatch Act of 1939. In essence, that law says that classified employees cannot be party activists. However, they can register and vote as they choose. They can belong to a party, make voluntary campaign contributions, take part in—but not organize or lead—partisan rallies. They can also put bumper stickers on their own cars and wear campaign buttons when off duty. And they can take an active part in nonpartisan politics and even be elected to nonpartisan local offices.

But they cannot do such things as run for a partisan office, become an officer in a political organization or a delegate to a party convention, or raise funds for a political party or any of its candidates.

Many see these limits as both unnecessary and unjustifiable limits on their political and civil rights[20] Those who support the limits say that they prevent: the use of federal workers in presidential and congressional campaigns and the possibility that employees' job security might come to depend on party loyalty.

[18]Another independent agency, the Federal Labor Relations Authority, now handles labor-management relationships in federal employment. It, too, is a bipartisan three-member body appointed by the President and Senate.

[19]The place each applicant for a federal job has on a register is fixed by three factors: (1) time of application, (2) OPM test scores, and (3) veterans' preference points, if any. Nearly half of all federal jobs are now held by veterans, wives of disabled veterans, and unremarried widows of veterans. Some jobs, such as guards and messengers, are reserved especially for veterans.

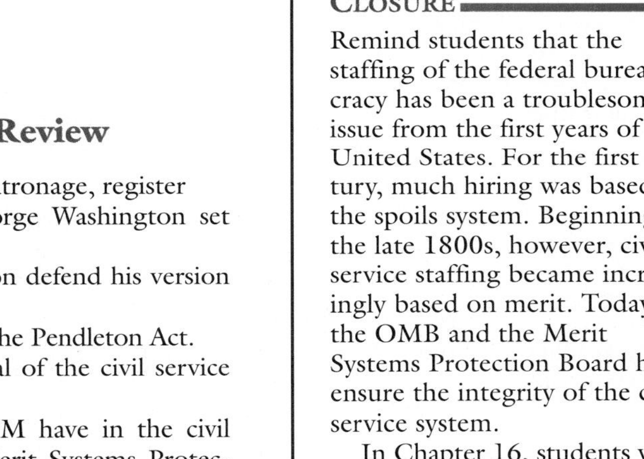

How to Get a Government Job
1. Determine what positions are available. Contact the Federal Job Information Center or the State Employment Security Office serving the area in which you are seeking federal employment to determine what positions are available. You can locate this telephone number in a telephone directory or by calling the Job Information Center in Washington D.C. at (202) 606-2700. You may also check the newspapers, post office, or library for this information.
2. Determine whether you are qualified for the available position in which you are interested. The Federal Job Information Center will tell you the specific qualifications required for the position, as well as its grade level (salary) and location. Only qualified applicants are considered, so evaluate your standing carefully. Most civil service jobs require a high school diploma.
3. Complete the appropriate application form. The Federal Job Information Center will provide you with the correct form. Application forms vary from position to position, so be sure your application is for the position in which you are interested.
4. Take the civil service examination. Some positions require that you take this written exam. The Federal Job Information Center will advise you if this is true in your case. If you pass the exam, your name is included on a list of qualified applicants.
5. Wait for notification that you will be interviewed. When a position opens, the top three applicants on the list will be interviewed. Those applicants will be notified by mail. If you are not hired, your name will remain on the list of qualified applicants in the event of a future opening.

Interpreting Charts The standard steps to getting a job with the government are listed above. After examining these steps, list three probable requirements for a government position.

Pay and Benefit Issues Equal opportunities for career advancement remains a problem in the federal bureaucracy. Although minority groups and women are well represented in most agencies, they tend to be concentrated in lower-level positions. Women, for example, now hold nearly half of all white-collar federal jobs; but they hold less than 10 percent of the highest paid positions.

Congress sets the pay and other job conditions for everyone who works for the Federal Government.[21] At the lower and middle levels, civil service pay compares fairly well with salaries paid in the private sector. Government can never hope to compete dollar for dollar with private industry at the upper levels, however.

[20]The Supreme Court has upheld them, however, as reasonable restrictions on 1st Amendment rights. The leading case is *Civil Service Commission* v. *National Association of Letter Carriers, AFL-CIO*, 1973.

[21]Except postal workers; see page 397, note 17.

Section 3 Review

1. **Define:** spoils system, patronage, register
2. What standard did George Washington set for federal employment?
3. How did Andrew Jackson defend his version of the spoils system?
4. Describe the features of the Pendleton Act.
5. What is the primary goal of the civil service today?
6. (a) What role does OPM have in the civil service system? (b) The Merit Systems Protection Board?
7. What kinds of political activity are federal workers prohibited from participating in?

Critical Thinking

8. **Recognizing Cause and Effect** (p. 19) Summarize how the spoils system led to corruption in the government.

based on merit; hiring preference was given to veterans and veterans' widows. **5.** Getting and keeping the best available people in the federal work force. **6.** (a) The OPM recruits new employees, trains them, sets job classifications, and manages salary and benefits. (b) It protects and polices the merit principle. **7.** Federal workers cannot be party activists, run for a partisan office, be a convention delegate, be an officer in a political organization, or raise funds for a party or candidate. **8.** Positions became rewards in exchange for support. People could obtain powerful and lucrative government positions without being qualified by bribing people, offering favors, and other unethical means.

Closure

Remind students that the staffing of the federal bureaucracy has been a troublesome issue from the first years of the United States. For the first century, much hiring was based on the spoils system. Beginning in the late 1800s, however, civil service staffing became increasingly based on merit. Today, the OMB and the Merit Systems Protection Board help ensure the integrity of the civil service system.

In Chapter 16, students will read about the financing of the Federal Government.

Assignment Assign Chapter 16, Section 1, pp. 405–411, for the next class period.

TRF **Teacher's Resource File**
See the Unit 4 File, p. 63, for the Section 3 Quiz.

Reteach

Have students write a description of a civil servant from the mid-1800s and a civil servant of today. Tell students to include as many details as possible about how the two imaginary employees got their jobs. Ask students to identify which one they feel is most likely qualified for his or her job.

TEACHING
Citizenship

How to File a Consumer Complaint

Objective

Determine the steps involved in filing a consumer complaint.

INSTRUCT

Before students read the "Citizenship" feature, ask them to think of various ways in which they can respond if they are dissatisfied with a product or service. *(Possible answers: They could demand a refund; they could go straight to the court; they could go talk to the merchant or service provider.)* Then have students read the feature and ask them to think of a product with which they have been dissatisfied in the past and compare their response with the steps in the skill feature.

Answers **1.** Answers to a, b, and c will vary depending upon the situation. **2.** (a) Answer should be "yes." (b) Answer should be "yes." (c) Answer should be "yes."

TRF **Teacher's Resource File** See the Unit 4 File, p. 64, for the Skill Application for this lesson.

Citizenship

How to File a Consumer Complaint

You have just read about the federal bureaucracy and its role in the lives of the American people. Of course, each State has its own bureaucracy, as well. One area in which you can observe your State bureaucracy at work is in the field of consumer affairs.

State governments have become increasingly involved in ensuring the health, safety, and satisfaction of the State's consumers. If you ever lodge a formal complaint against a supplier of a product or service, there is a good chance that you will encounter your State's bureaucracy. Follow the steps below to learn how to file a consumer complaint.

1. Identify the specific problem you have. Before you can lodge a complaint, you have to identify specifically the nature of the problem. Ask yourself the following questions: (a) What exactly did you expect the business to supply? (b) How did the business fail to provide that good or service? (c) What do you expect the business to do to solve the problem?

2. Before making the complaint, make sure that you cannot get satisfaction from the business. Filing a formal complaint should not be your first step when you experience problems as a consumer. Often, you can receive satisfaction simply by clearly stating your problem and expectations with the appropriate person at the business. Before filing a complaint, make sure you can answer each of the following questions with a "yes": (a) Have you exhausted all your options with that business? For example, have you spoken with a manager or a customer-relations representative? (b) Have you presented your problem calmly and reasonably? (c) Have you made your request in writing (and saved a copy)?

3. If you are certain that the business will not respond, contact the appropriate consumer agency. For the most part, individual consumer problems are handled at the State level. To find out where to seek information about lodging a complaint in your State, look in the front section of your telephone book or under your State's name in the white pages. There you will find information about where to call for information about consumer complaints.

4. Follow the instructions you receive for filing a complaint. Once you have reached the appropriate organization for your complaint, follow exactly their instructions for filing the complaint. (a) Ask questions about when to expect a response from the agency. (b) Make copies of any letters or paperwork you complete.

5. Follow up—but give the agency a chance to do its work. After you file your complaint, give the agency time to do its work. If the agency has not responded in the expected time, follow up with a short letter requesting the status of your complaint. Include a telephone number in your letter to help speed communication.

CONSUMER PROBLEMS (cont)

Consumer Protection/Consumer Info

Atty Gen Ofc	Bos **727-2200**
Consumer Action Center	Bos **482-5772**
Exec Ofc Consumer Affairs	Bos **727-7780**

Credit Counseling

Consumer Credit Counseling Svc of Eastern MA	Bos **426-6644**

Credit Harassment

Div Banks & Loans	Bos **727-2102**

Chapter-in-Brief

Scan all headings, photographs, charts, and other visuals in the chapter before reading the section summaries below.

Section 1 The Federal Bureaucracy (pp. 381–385) The Federal Government is a bureaucracy; that is, its organization includes hierarchical authority, job specialization, and formalized rules. The federal bureaucracy is the machinery through which the Federal Government makes and administers its public policy.

The bureaucracy consists of numerous administrative agencies. Most of these agencies are in the executive branch and fall into one of three groups: (1) the Executive Office of the President, (2) the 14 cabinet departments, and (3) a large number of independent agencies.

The lack of a uniform system for naming administrative agencies creates confusion. The title department is used exclusively at the cabinet level, but the use of other designations—bureau, service, and so on—follows no consistent pattern.

All administrative organizations are made up of both staff and line units. Staff agencies serve in a support capacity. Line agencies do the work the organization was created to perform.

Section 2 The Executive Departments and the Independent Agencies (pp. 385–393) Cabinet departments are the traditional units of federal administration. Today, there are 14 cabinet departments. The head of each department is known as the secretary, except for the attorney general, who heads the Justice Department.

Cabinet secretaries direct the efforts of their departments in line with the policies of the President. A secretary also promotes the department and its programs with Congress, the public, the bureaucracy, and the President.

Each department has a number of staff and line units. In addition, most departments have regional offices outside of Washington.

Until the 1880s, cabinet departments performed most of the work of the Federal Government. Since then, Congress has created numerous independent agencies to perform many administrative functions.

Most independent agencies are independent only in the sense that they are not part of a cabinet department. Some do enjoy significant independence from the executive branch and the President.

Each independent agency falls into one of three groups: (1) the independent executive agencies, (2) the independent regulatory commissions, and (3) the government corporations.

Section 3 The Civil Service (pp. 395–399) Today, the federal bureaucracy includes nearly 3 million employees. Yet the Constitution says little about how these jobs are to be filled. Throughout much of the 1800s, most government posts were filled according to the spoils system. The result was inefficiency and corruption in government.

In 1883, the Pendleton Act laid the foundation for the civil service, the system by which much of the bureaucracy is staffed today. This system attempts to ensure that personnel decisions are based largely on merit.

Today, the civil service system is administered by the Office of Personnel Management, which acts as the government's central personnel agency, and the Merit Systems Protection Board, which polices the merit principle in the federal bureaucracy.

Federal employees cannot strike. And though they are permitted to support, belong to, and make contributions to political parties, they cannot take an active role in party politics. Equal opportunities for career advancement remains a challenge to the federal bureaucracy.

401

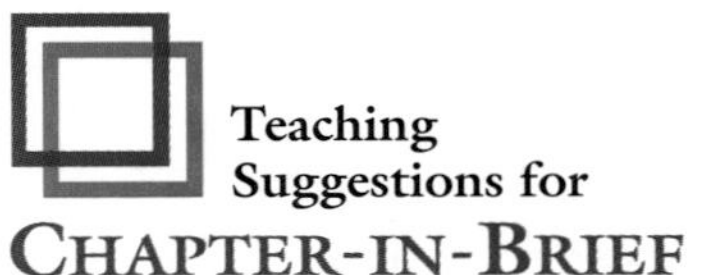

Teaching Suggestions for CHAPTER-IN-BRIEF

Below are some of the possible uses for the Chapter-in-Brief:

To Preview the Chapter You may want to assign the Chapter-in-Brief page and the Section Outlines from the Teacher's Resource File before beginning Chapter 15 to introduce students to the "Key Terms" and concepts in each section.

To Review the Chapter When students have completed Chapter 15, you might want to assign the Chapter-in-Brief as a tool for review, along with the Guided Reading and Reviews from the Teacher's Resource File.

To Omit the Chapter If you wish to skip Chapter 15, it may be helpful to assign the Chapter-in-Brief to students as a review before continuing to another chapter. You may also want to assign the Chapter 15 Test to assess student knowledge of the material. Then specific portions of Chapter 15 may be assigned to students needing reinforcement of "Key Terms" and concepts.

Teacher's Resource File See the Unit 4 File for the following materials:

- Section Outlines, pp. 55, 58, 61.
- Guided Reading and Reviews, pp. 56, 59, 62.
- Chapter 15 Test, pp. 68–70.

ADDITIONAL RESOURCES

The Capital Source: Who's Who, What, Where in Washington. The National Journal, annual.

Cochran, Clarke C., *et al. American Public Policy.* St. Martin's Press, 3rd ed., 1989.

Fisher, Louis. *The Politics of Shared Power: Congress and the Executive.* CQ Press, 2nd ed., 1987.

Hart, John. *The Presidential Branch.* Pergamon, 1987.

Kelman, Stephen. *Making Public Policy: A Hopeful View of American Government.* Basic Books, 1987.

Kozak, David C. and Macarthey (eds.). *Congress and Public Policy: A Short Book of Documents and Readings.* Dorsey, 2nd ed., 1987.

Levine, Charles H., *et al. Public Administration: Challenges, Choices, and Consequences.* Scott, Foresman, 1990.

Rosenbloom, David H. and Deborah D. Goldman. *Public Administration: Understanding Management, Politics, and Law in the Public Sector.* Random House, 1986.

Strausman, Jeffrey D. *Public Administration.* Longman, 2nd ed., 1990.

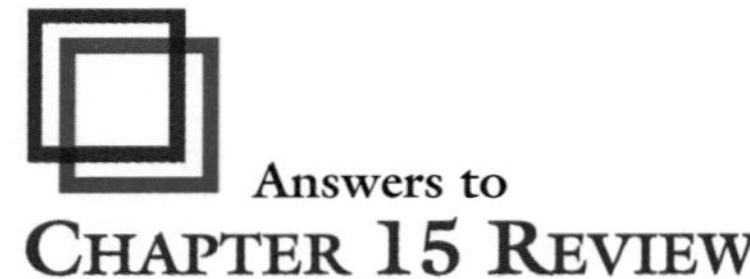

Answers to
CHAPTER 15 REVIEW

Vocabulary and Key Terms

Matching
1. administration
2. patronage
3. registers
4. independent agencies
5. bureaucracy

True or False
1. True.
2. True.
3. False—the correct term is *independent agencies.*
4. False—the correct term is *quasi-legislative*.

Word Relationships
1. *Bureaucracy* is a term that describes any large organization with hierarchical authority, job specialization, and formalized rules. *Administration* refers to the people and agencies serving a President.
2. Both words have similar meanings—the giving of jobs to political supporters and friends.
3. *Quasi-legislative* refers to the rule-making power of some agencies. *Quasi-judicial* refers to the power of some agencies to decide disputes.

Main Ideas

Section 1
1. Some are suggested by the language of the Constitution. Others developed as a result of a clear intent of the Framers that agencies would be created to carry out the functions of government. **2.** (a) It refers to the idiosyncratic way that the bureaucratic agencies are named. (b) It is a game in the sense that there is little consistency in the use of names. **3.** Line units perform the work of the governmental unit; staff units support the efforts of the unit. **4.** Many agencies require staff units to support the execution of their line functions.

Section 2
5. They were the first agencies, set up by Congress beginning in 1789. They carried out the functions of the bureaucracy until the 1800s, when Congress began creating independent agencies. **6.** Each has a number of subunits, staff and line. They are also structured geographically, with many activities carried on at regional offices. **7.** There are several reasons that vary depending upon the individual agency. Some are independent agencies: because they do not fit well within a cabinet department; to protect them from partisan politics; by accident or lack of planning; because of their peculiar and sensitive nature. **8.** (a) Independent executive agencies, independent regulatory commissions, and government corporations. (b) Executive agencies perform a variety of functions, many indistinguishable from those of certain cabinet departments. Regulatory commissions regulate some important aspects of the economy. Government corporations carry on business-like activities.

Section 3
9. Washington held the standard of "fitness for office,"though he did favor members of his own

Chapter Review

Vocabulary and Key Terms

bureaucracy (p. 381)	independent agencies (p. 388)	spoils system (p. 395)
bureaucrat (p. 381)	quasi-legislative (p. 391)	patronage (p. 396)
administration (p. 382)	quasi-judicial (p. 391)	registers (p. 398)

Matching: *Review the key terms in the list above. If you are not sure of a term's meaning, look up the term and review its definition. Choose a term from the list above that best matches each description.*

1. a government's many administrators and administrative agencies
2. the practice of giving offices and other favors of government to political supporters and friends
3. the lists of the persons who have passed the tests given by the Office of Personnel Management
4. agencies located outside any of the executive departments
5. the term that describes an organization that is built on the principles of hierarchical authority, job specialization, and formalized rules

True or False: *Determine whether each statement is true or false. If it is true, write "true." If it is false, change the underlined word or words to make the statement true.*

1. Each person who works in a bureaucracy is known as a bureaucrat.
2. The giving of jobs by officeholders to political supporters and friends is known as patronage.
3. A register is the name given to a governmental agency that is not part of a cabinet department.
4. Agencies in the executive branch exercise their quasi-judicial function when they formulate regulations.

Word Relationships: *Distinguish between words in each pair.*

1. bureaucracy/administration
2. spoils system/patronage
3. quasi-legislative/quasi-judicial

Main Ideas

Section 1 (pp. 381–385)

1. How did the different components of the bureaucracy in the Federal Government's executive branch develop?
2. (a) What is the "name game" in the context of the federal bureaucracy? (b) In what sense is it a game?
3. What is the difference between a staff unit and a line unit?
4. Why do many departments have both staff and line units?

Section 2 (pp. 385–393)

5. In what sense are the cabinet departments of the executive branch the traditional units of federal administration ?
6. How are the cabinet departments organized and structured?
7. For what major reasons do the independent agencies exist apart from the cabinet-level departments?

8. (a) What are the three types of independent agencies? (b) What are their functions?

Section 3 (pp. 395–399)

9. Briefly describe the standards for staffing the federal bureaucracy that were held by Presidents George Washington and Thomas Jefferson.
10. (a) What was the spoils system? (b) What was its effect on the quality of administration of government?
11. What was the primary objective of the efforts to reform the country's civil service in the late 1800s?
12. (a) What steps do current civil service laws take to ensure that the public work force is free from political influences? (b) What is the controversy over these rules?

Critical Thinking

1. **Identifying Central Issues** (p. 19) (a) Is an efficient government always an effective government? (b) What is the proper relationship between efficiency and effectiveness in government? Give support for your answer.

2. **Identifying Assumptions** (p. 19) Consider the characteristics and role of the independent regulatory agencies that are discussed in Section 2. What is the assumption about the executive branch that underlies the existence of these agencies?

3. **Recognizing Ideologies** (p. 19) Thomas Jefferson once said, "When a man accepts a public trust, he should consider himself a public property." (a) What do you think this statement means? (b) Do you agree or disagree with this statement? (c) What values underlie this statement?

Getting Involved

1. **Writing Your Opinion** You are a citizen living in the United States in the 1830s. Write a letter to President Andrew Jackson offering your views on the spoils system. Before you start your letter, determine whether you will argue in favor of or against the spoils system. To what extent does it promote or hinder the deomcratic process and the smooth operation of government? Identify three reasons why you think the system is good or bad for government. Begin the letter by stating your purpose in writing, including your overall opinion of the spoils system. Then, devote one paragraph each to the three reasons you identified to support your argument. Revise the letter, making sure that each paragraph clearly, persuasively, and respectfully presents your case. Correct any errors and draft a final copy.
2. **Class Debate** Hold a class debate on one of the following topics: *Resolved,* That the use of government corporations be expanded; *Resolved,* That veterans of the armed forces and their relatives should be denied preference for federal employment in the interest of governmental quality; *Resolved,* That the spoils system practiced by Andrew Jackson fulfilled the principle of representative democracy. Select teams to debate in favor of each side of the issue. The rest of the class should evaluate each team's debate presentation.
3. **Creating a Political Cartoon** Consider what you have read in Chapter 15 about the federal bureaucracy. Make a political cartoon that illustrates your understanding of the concept of bureaucracy. For example, you might focus on the following ideas: independent regulatory agencies, government corporations, or the name game.

party. Jefferson added to Washington's standard the standard of "political acceptability," which included greater consideration of party affiliation. **10.** (a) It was the practice of giving jobs and favors to political supporters and friends. (b) It was blamed for leading to widespread corruption in government. **11.** The Pendleton Act sought to make merit the basis for hiring, promotion, and other personnel actions. **12.** (a) The OPM acts as the central personnel agency for many federal jobs. The Merit Systems Protection Board polices and protects the merit system in the bureaucracy. Workers are limited to some extent in their ability to take part in party politics. (b) The rules are seen as unnecessary and unjustifiable limits on the political and civil rights of the employees.

Critical Thinking

1. Answers will vary. Students might suggest that efficiency will in all cases help the government provide more services for more people. Others will suggest that efficiency should be secondary to a government's commitment to fairness, that government should be expected to sacrifice some efficiency in its efforts to be fair. **2.** Answers will vary. Students might suggest that such agencies suggest that the executive cannot be relied on to adequately regulate certain segments of society. **3.** (a) Students might suggest that the statement reflects the need for the public to trust its government and the responsibility of government workers to be worthy of that trust. (b) Answers will vary. (c) Students may identify such values as honesty, trust, and public responsibility.

Getting Involved

1–3. Answers and results will vary, but students should demonstrate an understanding of the concepts in this chapter.

Chapter 16 Resources

In the Teacher's Resource File
The following materials are found in the Teacher's Resource File box.

Instructional Support: Unit 4 File

For the Section
Outlines, pp. 74, 77, 80
Guided Reading and Reviews, pp. 75, 78, 81
Quizzes, pp. 76, 79, 82

For the Chapter
Skill Application, p. 83
Case Study on Contemporary Issues, pp. 84–86
Chapter Test, pp. 87–89
Additional Test Questions, pp. 89–91

Enrichment Support Files

Supreme Court Cases, pp. 12, 20–21
Historical and Legal Documents, pp. 45, 46
Comparative Government: A Multicultural View, pp. 22–23

Computer Test Bank and Assessment

Transparency Package, pp. 16, 41, 51, 52

Chapter 16 Focus

Introduce the Chapter Tell students that in this chapter they will learn about the financing of the Federal Government—where the money comes from and how it is spent. Read with students the Chapter Preview and Objectives.

Writing Activity Direct students' attention to "Describe." Have students list three types of taxes with which they are familiar. Then have each student write a brief description of each tax, including what it applies to and who pays it.

Motivate for Learning Direct students' attention to "Predict." Lead students in a discussion of the reasons that taxes are levied, including defending the nation and providing services. Have students suggest what would happen if there were no taxes.

Chapter 16 Financing Government

Chapter Preview

Have you ever celebrated Tax Freedom Day? That is the day on which American taxpayers have earned enough money to pay their total tax debt for the year. The day on which this "holiday" falls varies somewhat from State to State and from year to year. In 1990, taxpayers in Washington, D.C., for example, didn't celebrate Tax Freedom Day until May 23, while residents of South Dakota earned enough to pay all their taxes by April 19. All across the country, people worked three to four months of the year just to pay their taxes!

No wonder everyone complains. People with high incomes grumble because they pay the highest taxes. Low-income earners point out that even a low tax rate is too much to bear. People in the middle consider their situation the worst of all—their incomes aren't high but their taxes are. In this chapter you will read about financing the Federal Government—where more than a trillion dollars comes from and where it all goes.

Before you read this chapter:

- **Describe** three types of taxes that you are familiar with.
- **Predict** why most Americans would complain if there were no taxes.

As you read, focus on the main objective for each section. Understand:

1. How the Federal Government raises money.
2. Borrowing as a source of government revenue.
3. How the Federal Government spends money and the complex process of preparing the federal budget.

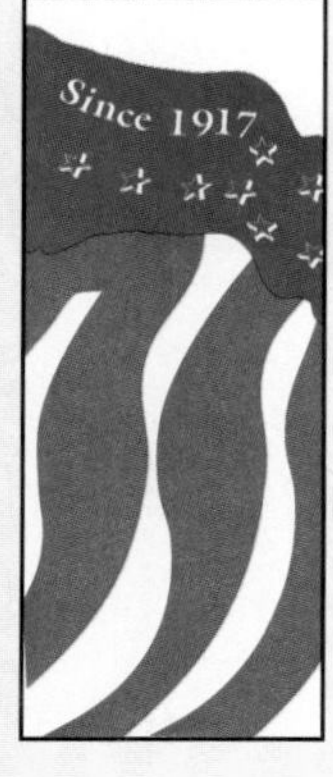

Magruder's American Government: *A Witness to Change* by William A. McClenaghan

In editions through the 1960s, this book observed that the Federal Government "has discovered that the art of taxation, like that of picking geese, is to get the most feathers with the fewest squawks. So it picks part of its revenue from the wealthy 10 percent of the population in the form of the direct income tax which brings no squawk from the 90 percent in the form of indirect taxes in such a way that they are hardly conscious of being picked."

During one year in that period (1935), the federal income tax brought in $527.1 million. That tax was, in fact, paid by fewer than two million persons, or about 1.5 percent of the total population.

Today, the federal income tax produces 1000 times more revenue than it did in 1935. Income tax is now paid by more than 100 million Americans, or more than 40 percent of all the people in this country. And generally, nearly every last one of us squawks!

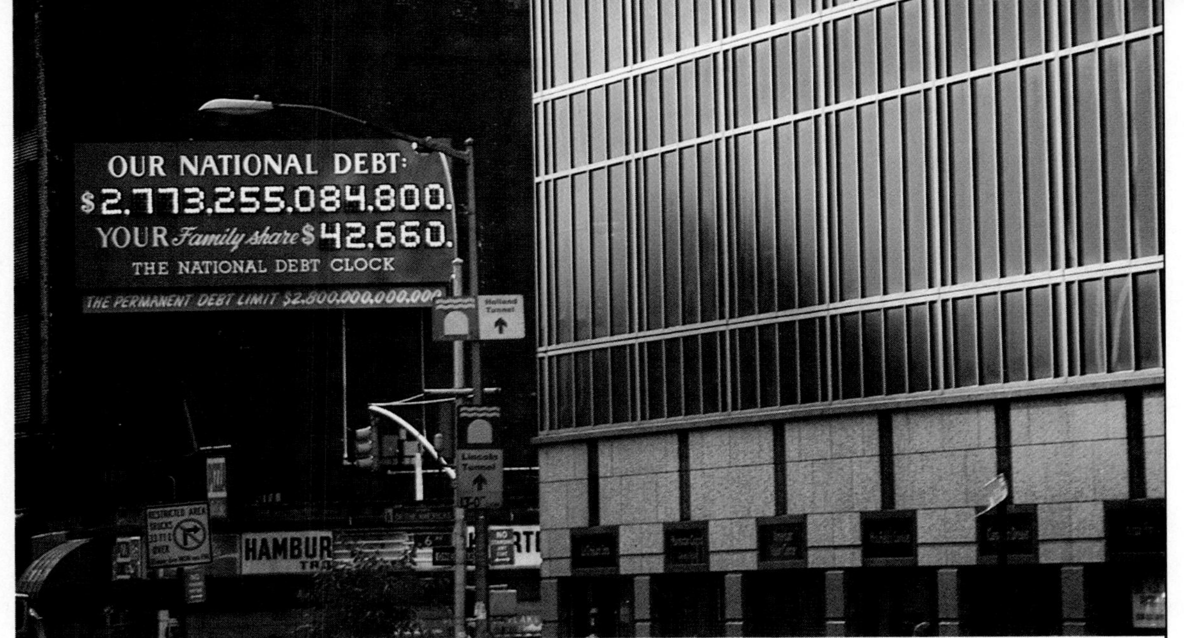

The National Debt Clock Continues to Tick This clock in New York City gives the public up-to-date figures on the total amount of the national debt. By the end of fiscal year 1992, the figure should reach $4 trillion, according to the Office of Management and Budget.

1 Where the Money Comes From: Taxes

Find Out:

- What is the Federal Government's power to tax?
- What kinds of taxes does the Federal Government levy?
- For what purposes may the Federal Government levy taxes?

Key Terms:

progressive tax, tax return, payroll tax, regressive tax, excise tax, estate tax, gift tax, custom duty

According to Benjamin Franklin's oft-quoted assertion, "in this world nothing is certain but death and taxes." In this section, you will consider the second of Franklin's certainties, taxes—and more specifically, those taxes levied by the Federal Government.[1]

For fiscal year 1993—the 12-month period beginning October 1, 1992, and ending September 30, 1993—the Federal Government expects to collect more than $1.3 trillion. And, as you will see, it will almost certainly spend more than that stupendous sum.

Those mind-boggling numbers tell you that it now costs every man, woman, and child more than $5,000 on average a year to support the Federal Government. And that fact should tell you how important the subject of governmental finance is.

The Power to Tax

The Constitution underscores the cardinal importance of the power to tax by listing it first among the many powers granted to Congress. In Article I, Section 8, Clause 1, the Constitution gives to Congress the power:

> "To lay and collect taxes, imposts and excises, to pay the debts, and provide for the common defense and general welfare of the United States . . . "

First and foremost, Congress exercises the taxing power in order to raise money to finance

[1]On State and local taxes, see Chapter 25.

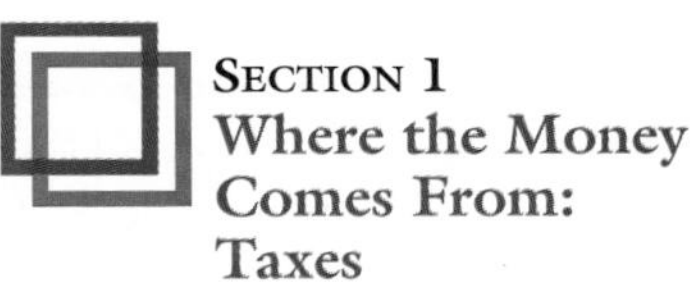

SECTION 1
Where the Money Comes From: Taxes

FOCUS

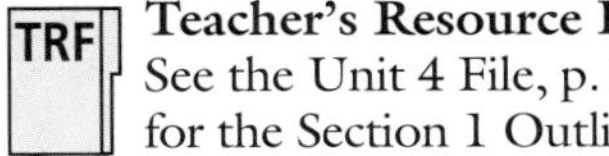

Teacher's Resource File See the Unit 4 File, p. 74, for the Section 1 Outline.

Objectives

16.1 Explain the Federal Government's power to tax.
16.2 Identify the kinds of Federal Government taxes.
16.3 Analyze the Federal Government's reasons for levying taxes.

Bellringer Activity Put the figure $1,300,000,000,000 ($1.3 trillion) on the board. Ask students how many millions this figure equals. *(1,300,000 millions)* Ask students how many $100 bills would equal $1.3 trillion. *(13 billion)* Invite students to create ways of visualizing this amount of money or number of objects.

State the Purpose The figure $1.3 trillion represents the amount of money the Federal Government expects to spend in fiscal year 1993. In this section, students will learn about the ways by which the Federal Government raises the money it spends, especially the many taxes used to generate revenue.

ABCNEWS INTERACTIVE

The following video segment may be used to highlight aspects of financing the Federal Government.

POWERS OF THE CONGRESS GUIDEBOOK
Chapter 21: Collecting Revenues, p. 25

Vocabulary

Direct students' attention to "Key Terms" on page 405. Ask students to look up the words *regressive* and *progressive* in a dictionary and compare the dictionary meaning of these words with their meaning in the context of taxes. How are the meanings similar, and how are they different? LEP

Reading Strategy: Predicting Content

Tell students to read the boldfaced headings in the section. Point out that these headings form an outline of the section content. Have students write a one- or two-sentence prediction of the section content based on their preview of the section headings.

INSTRUCT

Explain/Discuss Have students recall the $1.3 trillion figure discussed in the "Bellringer Activity," and remind them that this is the amount of money the government expects to spend in fiscal year 1993. Explain to students that the Constitution authorizes the government to levy taxes in order to raise the revenue needed to "pay the debts, and provide for the common defense and general welfare of the United States. . . ." Ask students to discuss how that power to tax is limited by the Constitution. Direct students to the table on page 408, and have them observe that the tax that generates the greatest amount of revenue today (the income tax) was not permitted under the Constitution prior to the 16th Amendment.

Next, have students discuss the various types of federal taxes. Ask students who are currently employed or who have worked summer jobs to recall whether or not any money was withheld from their checks for federal taxes. Ask students to recall what those taxes were and how they felt about their being withheld. Would students rather have money withheld from their checks, or would they rather pay their entire tax bill for the year on April 15 when they file their tax returns?

Finally, have students discuss the use of taxes to regulate certain activities. Ask them to consider whether or not using taxes for this purpose meets the constitutional requirement that taxes be used to "provide for the common defense and general welfare of the United States."

at least most of what it costs to operate the Federal Government. But Congress also levies some taxes for nonrevenue purposes.

Constitutional Limitations The power to tax is not an unlimited one. Like all of its other powers, Congress must exercise the taxing power in accord with the Constitution. Thus, for example, Congress cannot levy a tax on church services—for such a levy would violate the provisions of the 1st Amendment.

In more specific terms, the Constitution puts four expressed limits and one very significant implied limit on the power of Congress to tax.

First, taxes must be for public purposes only. That is, the Constitution says that Congress may levy taxes only for public purposes, not for the benefit of some private interest.

The second expressed limit is that export taxes are prohibited. Article I, Section 9, Clause 5 declares that "No tax or duty shall be laid on articles exported from any State." Thus, customs duties can be applied only to imports—on goods brought into the United States. This restriction was written into the Constitution as a part of the Commerce Compromise made by the Framers at Philadelphia in 1787 (see Chapter 2, Section 4).

While Congress cannot tax exports, it can and does prohibit the export of certain items—usually for reasons of national security and acting under its expressed power to regulate foreign commerce.

The third expressed limit is that direct taxes must be equally apportioned. Article I, Section 9, Clause 4 provides that:

> "No capitation, or other direct tax, shall be laid, unless in proportion to the census or enumeration hereinbefore directed to be taken."

This restriction was a part of the Three-Fifths Compromise the Framers made at the Philadelphia Convention (see Chapter 2, Section 4). In effect, delegates from the northern States insisted that if slaves were to be counted in the populations of the southern States, then those States would have to pay for them.

Recall that a direct tax is one that must be borne by the person upon whom it is levied—as, for example, a tax on land or buildings, which must be paid by the owner of the property; or a capitation tax—a head or poll tax—laid on each person. Other taxes are indirect taxes. That is, they are levies that may be shifted to another for payment—as, for example, the federal tax on liquor. That tax, placed initially on the distiller, is ultimately paid by the person who buys the liquor.

The direct tax restriction means, in effect, that any direct tax that Congress levies must be apportioned among the States according to their populations. Thus, a direct tax that raised $1 billion would have to produce just about $120 million in California and $10 million in Kansas—because California has just about 12 percent of the nation's population and Kansas 1 percent.

Wealth is not evenly distributed among the States, of course. So, a direct tax laid in proportion to population would be grossly unfair; the tax would fall more heavily on the residents of some States than it would on others. As a result, Congress has not imposed a direct tax—except for the income tax—outside the District of Columbia since 1861.

An income tax is a direct tax. But, recall, it may be laid without regard to population because of the 16th Amendment:

> "The Congress shall have power to lay and collect taxes on incomes, from whatever source derived, without apportionment among the several States, and without regard to any census or enumeration."

Congress first levied an income tax in 1861, to help finance the Civil War. The tax, which expired in 1873, was later upheld by the Supreme Court, in *Springer* v. *United States*, 1881. A unanimous Court found that income tax to be an indirect rather than a direct tax. But a later income tax law, enacted in 1894, was declared unconstitutional in *Pollack* v. *Farmers' Loan and Trust Co.*, in 1895. There, the Court held that the 1894 law imposed a direct tax that Congress should have apportioned among the several States.

The impossibility of taxing incomes fairly in accord with any plan of apportionment led to the adoption of the 16th Amendment in 1913.

ACTIVITY: For Gifted Students

Theme: Systems The power to tax is exercised by the Federal Government in many different ways. Have students compare taxation in another industrialized country to taxation in the United States. Students should compare such features as the range of items and activities taxed, the rates of various taxes, and the amount of the average person's income that goes to taxes. Students can present their findings in the form of an oral or written report or a series of graphs and tables.

Teacher's Resource File
See the Supreme Court Cases file, pp. 20–21, for material that extends coverage of this section.

The fourth expressed limitation on the taxing power is that indirect taxes must be uniform. This is stated in Article I, Section 8, Clause 1.

The limitation imposed here means that all indirect taxes must be levied at the same rate in all parts of the country. Thus, the federal excise tax on gasoline or beer or firearms must be the same in New York as it is in New Mexico.

The Implied Limitation The Federal Government cannot tax the States or any of their local governments in the exercise of their governmental functions. That is, federal taxes cannot be imposed on those governments when they are doing such things as providing public education, furnishing health care, or building streets and highways. Recall, the Supreme Court laid down that rule in *McCulloch* v. *Maryland* in 1819, when it declared that "the power to tax involves the power to destroy." If the Federal Government could tax the governmental activities of the States or their local units, it could conceivably tax them out of existence and so destroy the federal system.

The Federal Government can and does tax those State and local activities that are of a nongovernmental character, however. Thus, in 1893, South Carolina created a State monopoly to sell liquor, and it claimed that each of its liquor stores was exempt from the federal saloon license tax. But, in *South Carolina* v. *United States*, 1905, the Supreme Court held that the State was liable for the tax—because the sale of liquor is not a necessary or usual governmental activity.

Current Federal Taxes

Oliver Wendell Holmes once described taxes as "what we pay for civilized society."[2] Society does not appear to be much more civilized today than it was when Justice Holmes made that observation in 1927. But "what we pay" has certainly gone up. In 1927, the Federal Government's tax collections totaled, altogether, $3.364 billion. Compare that figure with the figures in the table on page 408.

The Income Tax The income tax is the largest source of federal revenue today. It first became the major source in 1917 and 1918. Except for a few years during the Depression of the 1930s, it has remained so.

Several features suit the income tax to its dominant role. It is a flexible tax; its rates can be adjusted to produce whatever amount of money Congress thinks is necessary. The tax is easily adapted to the principle of ability to pay. It is a **progressive tax**—that is, the higher the income and the ability to pay, the higher the tax rate.

Ever since 1913, the income tax has been levied on the incomes of both individuals and corporations.

The Individual Income Tax The tax on individuals' incomes regularly produces the largest amount of federal revenue. For fiscal year 1992, the individual income tax is expected to provide more than $500 billion.

The tax is levied on each person's taxable income—one's total income in the previous year

Interpreting Political Cartoons Filing taxes often requires following complicated instructions. According to this cartoon, how effective was the Tax Reform Bill of 1986 in simplifying tax form preparation?

[2]In a dissenting opinion in an insurance tax case, *Compania General de Tabacos de Filipinas* v. *Collector of Internal Revenue*, 1927.

Interpreting Political Cartoons Ask students to identify the irony communicated by this cartoon. *(The "simplification" of the tax laws has created great confusion.)*

Caption Answer According to this cartoon, the bill was not effective. Even though the tax reform bill was aimed at simplifying the tax collection process, most people still have to read through pages of directions, fill out several different forms, and interpret complicated tables in order to file their taxes.

Enrichment
Have students do an investigative report on the income taxes paid by people with the highest incomes in the United States. Their report can take the form of a simulated news report, a written article, or a cartoon. (Challenging)

SPOTLIGHT ON: Behind the Scenes
The United States is unusual among industrialized nations for the amount of revenues it gets from income taxes. Thirty-seven percent of the federal budget for 1992 comes from income taxes. Only Sweden derives more revenue from income taxes than does the United States. Japan, Germany, Italy, and the United Kingdom collect between 25 and 30 percent of their revenues from income taxes, while France gets only 13 percent from income taxes. In these countries, federal income comes largely from taxes on goods and services. On the whole, however, Americans pay fewer taxes than citizens in those nations.

Interpreting Tables Point out to students that the two major revenue producers for the Federal Government did not exist just 80 years ago. Have students determine the percentage of 1992 revenue represented by the top two taxes. *(82 percent)*

Caption Answer Revenue from social insurance taxes has increased the most.

The Federal Government's Income (by major source for selected fiscal years, in billions of dollars)

	1970	1975	1980	1985	1990	1992 (est.)
Individual income taxes	$90.4	$122.4	$244.1	$334.6	$468.9	$529.5
Corporation income taxes	32.8	40.6	64.6	61.3	93.5	101.9
Social insurance taxes and contributions	45.3	84.5	157.8	265.2	380.0	429.4
Excise taxes	15.7	16.6	24.3	36.0	35.3	47.8
Estate and gift taxes	3.6	4.6	6.4	6.4	11.5	13.3
Customs duties	2.4	3.7	7.2	12.1	16.7	19.3
Miscellaneous receipts	3.4	6.7	12.7	18.5	25.6	23.9
Total receipts	$193.6	$279.1	$517.1	$734.1	$1,031.5	$1,165.1

Source: Office of Management and Budget

Interpreting Tables This table reveals that individual income and social insurance taxes account for the largest sources of the government's income. Revenue from which type of tax has increased most dramatically since 1970?

minus exemptions and deductions. For 1992, each taxpayer had a personal exemption of $2,300, plus another exemption of that amount for each dependent.[3] Deductions are allowed for a number of things, including the costs of some medical care, most State and local taxes (except for sales taxes), interest paid on home mortgages, and contributions to charitable organizations.

By April 15, all persons who earned taxable income in the preceding calendar year must file
1.a **tax returns**—declarations of that income and of the exemptions and deductions claimed. Those returns are filed with the Internal Revenue Service, the IRS. A husband and wife can file a joint return, even if one of them had no income in the previous year. All taxable income received in 1991 was taxed at one of three rates—at 15 or 28 or 31 percent. Couples who filed joint returns paid 15 percent on income up to $32,450; 28 percent on income up to $78,400; and 31 percent on anything over that amount. Single taxpayers paid 15 percent on income up to $19,450; 28 percent up to $47,050; and the top rate on anything higher.

Most of those who pay income taxes do so through withholding—a pay-as-you-go plan. Employers are required to withhold a certain amount from each employee's paycheck and send that money to the IRS. When the employee files a tax return, he or she will receive a refund if more than the tax due has been withheld; or he or she must pay an additional amount if not enough has been withheld. Those persons who have income from sources not subject to withholding must estimate the income tax they will owe and make quarterly payments on that amount through the year.

The Corporation Income Tax

Each corporation must pay a tax on its net income—that is, on all of its earnings above the costs of doing business. The corporate tax has been called the most complicated of all federal taxes because of the many deductions allowed. Nonprofit organizations such as churches and charitable foundations are not subject to the corporation income tax.

[3]The personal exemption is adjusted for inflation each year. From 1991 on, the personal exemption amount is reduced for those with higher incomes. For single taxpayers, it begins to decline on taxable income over $100,000, and it disappears altogether on taxable income over $200,000. For married couples who file joint returns, the exemption is phased down on taxable incomes over $150,000 and disappears at $275,000.

SPOTLIGHT ON: Roots of Democracy

Taxes are as old as government and have existed in various forms for thousands of years. One early record of the collection of a tax is found in the New Testament, which tells us that during the reign of Caesar Augustus (27 B.C. to 14 A.D.), Mary and Joseph returned to Bethlehem to be taxed—"And it came to pass in those days, that there went out a decree from Caesar Augustus, that all the world should be taxed. . . . And all went to be taxed, every one into his own city." (Luke 2:1, 2:3)

"Small Society" by Brickman. Washington Star Syndicate, Inc.

Interpreting Political Cartoons The Internal Revenue Service is responsible for collecting income tax from both individuals and corporations. What does this cartoon reveal about the feedback that the IRS receives?

For 1992, the corporate tax rates run from 15 percent on the first $50,000 of taxable earnings up to a top rate of 34 percent on taxable incomes of more than $135,000.

Social Insurance Taxes The Federal Government collects huge sums to finance three major social welfare programs: (1) the Old-Age, Survivors, and Disability Insurance (OASDI) program—the basic social security program, established by the Social Security Act of 1935; (2) Medicare—health care for the elderly, added to the social security program in 1965; and (3) the unemployment compensation program—benefits paid to jobless workers, a program also established by the Social Security Act in 1935.

OASDI and Medicare are supported by taxes imposed on nearly all employers and their employees, and on self-employed persons. These levies are often called **payroll taxes** 1.b because the amounts owed by employees are withheld from their paychecks. To finance OASDI, employees must now (1992) pay a 6.2 percent tax on the first $55,500 of their yearly salaries or wages. Employers must match the OASDI tax paid by each employee. Those persons who are self-employed pay a 12.4 percent tax on the first $55,500 of their annual income.

For Medicare, employees now pay a 1.45 percent tax on the first $125,000 of their annual pay. Employers must pay an amount equal to that withheld from their employees' pay. The self-employed are taxed 2.9 percent of their annual incomes, up to the limit of $125,000.

The unemployment insurance program is a joint federal-State operation, to make payments to workers who lose their jobs for reasons beyond their control. The program now covers most workers in this country. Each State and the District of Columbia, Puerto Rico, and the Virgin Islands has its own unemployment compensation law; and the amount of a worker's weekly benefits, and their duration, is determined by State law.

The unemployment compensation program is financed by a combination of federal and State taxes. The federal tax is now 6.2 percent of the first $7,000 an employer pays to each employee in a year. Each employer is given a credit of up to 5.4 percent against that tax for the unemployment taxes that employer pays to the State—so, usually, the federal tax really amounts to 0.8 percent on the taxable wages.

Notice that these social insurance taxes for OASDI, Medicare, and unemployment compensation are not progressive taxes. They are, instead, **regressive taxes**—taxes levied at a flat rate, without regard to the level of a taxpayer's income or his or her ability to pay them.

The IRS collects the social insurance taxes. The money is then credited to trust accounts maintained by the Treasury, and Congress

Interpreting Political Cartoons Ask students to comment on what this cartoon reveals about public perception of taxes and government spending. *(Possible answer: The public feels that they contribute too much toward taxes, and that what they give is squandered and not used wisely.)*

Caption Answer Many citizens hold the IRS responsible for the frustration they feel over taxes.

Provide Guided Practice Write on the board the words *Constitutional Limitations on Taxes* and ask students to identify the four expressed and one implied constitutional limits on the power of Congress to tax. *(Expressed: taxes must be for public purposes; export taxes are prohibited; direct taxes must be apportioned; direct taxes must be uniform. Implied: the Federal Government cannot tax States or local governments in the exercise of governmental functions.)*

Then ask students to generate a list of current federal taxes. Ask them to describe characteristics of each tax. *(Possible answers: Income tax is individual and corporate, is progressive, was made possible by the 16th Amendment. Social insurance taxes are regressive and are often payroll taxes. Excise taxes are called "sin" taxes and are indirect. Estate and gift taxes are indirect taxes. Custom duties are also called tariffs.)*

Provide Independent Practice

TRF **Teacher's Resource File** You may wish to assign Section 1 Guided Reading and Review, Unit 4 File, p. 75, to help students master section objective content.

Monitor Comprehension

Answers to Section 1 Review
1. "Key Terms" are defined on the following pages:
a. tax return, p. 408
b. payroll tax, p. 409
c. excise tax, p. 410
d. estate tax, p. 410
e. gift tax, p. 410
f. custom duty, p. 410
2. Income taxes, which were made possible in their present form by the 16th Amendment. **3.** The individual income tax and the social insurance taxes. **4.** Progressive taxes are based on a person's ability to pay. Regressive taxes fall at the same rate on all people in all situations. **5.** Individuals on a payroll have half of their social insurance taxes paid by their employer in the form of matching contributions. Self-employed individuals pay the full tax themselves. **6.** The government must obey the Constitution. For example, it can't use taxes in such a way as to force individuals to provide incriminating evidence against themselves. **7.** Answers will vary. Students might suggest that popular opinion would generally work to limit taxes. Congress would be discouraged from adding new taxes or increasing tax rates for fear of angering voters.

Both Large and Small Contributors Tax revenues in the United States come from both individuals (inset) and huge corporations, such as CNN, the Cable TV Network (above).

appropriates funds for the social insurance programs as they are needed.

1.c **Excise Taxes** An **excise tax** is a tax laid on the manufacture, sale, or consumption of goods and/or the performance of services. The Federal Government has imposed and collected them since Congress acquired its taxing power in 1789.

Today, federal excise taxes are imposed on a long list of things, including gasoline, oil, tires, tobacco, liquor, wine, beer, firearms, telephone services, airline tickets, and more. Many excise taxes are often called hidden taxes because they are collected from producers who then figure them into the price that the retail customer finally pays. Some are called luxury taxes because they are levied on goods not usually considered to be necessities. And some excise taxes are known as sin taxes, in particular, those laid on tobacco products, beer, wine, liquor, and gambling.

1.d **Estate and Gift Taxes** An **estate tax** is a levy imposed on the assets (the estate) of one
1.e who dies.[4] A **gift tax** is one imposed on the making of a gift by a living person. Congress first provided for the estate tax in 1916. It added the gift tax in 1924 to plug a loophole in the estate tax—the giving of money or other property before death to avoid the estate tax.

The first $600,000 of an estate is exempt from the federal tax. So, in fact, most estates are not subject to the federal levy. Deductions are allowed for such things as State death taxes and bequests to religious and charitable groups. Anything a husband or wife leaves to the other is taxed, if at all, only when the surviving spouse dies.

Any person may make up to $10,000 in tax-free gifts to any other person in any one year. Gifts that husbands/wives make to one another are not taxed, regardless of value.

The estate and gift taxes are separate federal taxes, but both are levied at the same rates. For 1992, those rates ranged from a minimum of 18 percent on an estate or a gift with a net value of less than $10,000, on up to a maximum of 55 percent on an estate or gift worth more than $3 million.

1.f **Custom Duties** A **custom duty** is a tax laid on goods brought into the United States from abroad. They are also known as tariffs, import duties, or imposts. Congress decides which imports will be dutied and at what rates.[5] Most imports, some 30,000 different items, are dutied; but some are not—for example, Bibles, coffee, bananas, and up to $300 of a tourist's purchases abroad.

[4]An inheritance tax is another form of the so-called death tax. It is not levied on the entire net estate but, instead, on each portion inherited by each heir. Most States impose inheritance, not estate, taxes; most States also levy gift taxes.

[5]Since 1922, Congress has authorized the President to raise or lower any tariff by as much as 50 percent. The President can do so by an executive order, issued on the basis of recommendations made by the United States International Trade Commission, which studies the effect of tariffs and imports on the economy.

TRF **Teacher's Resource File**
See the Unit 4 File, p. 76, for the Section 1 Quiz.

Custom duties were the major source of income for the Federal Government for more than a century. Now, they produce less than 2 percent of the money the government takes in.

Taxing for Nonrevenue Purposes

Remember, the power to tax can be, and often is, used for purposes other than the raising of revenue. Usually, that other purpose is to regulate some activity that Congress thinks is harmful or dangerous to the public.

Thus, much of the Federal Government's regulation of narcotics is based on the taxing power. Federal law provides that only those who hold a valid license may legally manufacture, sell, or otherwise deal in those drugs—and licensing is a form of taxation. The government also regulates a number of other things by licensing, including, for example, certain firearms, prospecting on public lands, and the hunting of migratory birds. The federal excise tax on gas-guzzling cars is intended to discourage their purchase.

The Supreme Court first upheld the use of the taxing power for other than revenue purposes in *Veazie Bank* v. *Fenno* in 1869. Congress had established a national paper money system in the midst of the Civil War in 1863. It did so to provide a single, sound currency for the country. Private bank notes, which were also used as paper money, soon interfered with the circulation of the government's new "greenbacks." So, in 1865, Congress composed a 10 percent tax on the issuing of those private notes, and they soon disappeared. In upholding the tax, the Court declared:

> "Having, in the exercise of undisputed constitutional powers, undertaken to provide a currency for the whole country, it cannot be questioned that Congress may, constitutionally, secure the benefits of it to the people by appropriate legislation."

In 1912, Congress used its taxing power to destroy a segment of the domestic match industry. It levied a tax of two cents per hundred on matches made with white or yellow phosphorous—highly poisonous substances that caused serious harm to the workers who produced the matches. Matches made from other substances commonly sold for a penny a hundred, and the two-cent tax drove the phosphorous matches from the market. But Congress cannot use its taxing power in any manner it chooses. As in all other matters, Congress is bound by all of the other provisions of the Constitution.

To illustrate that point, consider several provisions of a 1951 tax law that was aimed at professional gamblers. The law imposed a $50-a-year license tax on bookies, levied other taxes on their activities, and required them to register with and submit detailed reports to the IRS. The law did produce a small amount of income. But its real purpose was to force gamblers into the open and to the attention of State and local police and prosecutors, and to set a federal tax evasion trap for those who failed to comply with the law.

The Supreme Court held the antigambling provisions unconstitutional in *Marchetti* v. *United States*, 1968. The Court did not hold that the taxes had been imposed for some improper purpose. Rather, it held that the tax, registration, and reporting provisions forced gamblers to furnish evidence against themselves—in violation of the 5th Amendment's guarantee against self-incrimination.

Section 1 Review

1. Define: tax return, payroll tax, excise tax, estate tax, gift tax, custom duty
2. What is the major exception to the requirement that direct taxes be levied in proportion to each State's population?
3. What are the two largest income producers for the federal government?
4. What is the difference between a progressive and a regressive tax?
5. What is the difference between the rate paid for social insurance taxes by those on payrolls and by those who are self-employed?
6. What limits exist on the power to tax for purposes other than raising revenue?

Critical Thinking

7. Determining Relevance (p. 19) Explain how you think public opinion might affect and place limits on the government's power to tax.

★

Closure

In order to raise the revenue it needs to operate and provide services to its citizens, the Federal Government has the constitutional power to levy a variety of different taxes. In Section 2, students will learn of other sources of revenue for the United States government.

Assignment Assign Section 2, pp. 412–414, for the next class period.

Reteach

Have students create a pie chart showing the Federal Government's sources of income and the percentages generated by each source. Students can use the information provided in the table on page 408 and throughout the section. The pie chart should be labeled with a caption that describes the Federal Government's power to levy taxes.

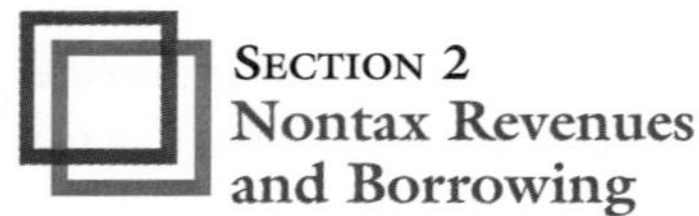

SECTION 2
Nontax Revenues and Borrowing

FOCUS

Teacher's Resource File See the Unit 4 File, p. 77, for the Section 2 Outline.

Objectives

16.4 Identify the major sources of nontax revenues for the United States Government.
16.5 Explain the historical purpose of the power to borrow.
16.6 Determine the purpose of current borrowing.

Bellringer Activity Before beginning this section, ask students to recall a time they needed money for something they wanted to buy or do. What were their legal options for obtaining that money?

State the Purpose The United States Government frequently experiences a need for money above and beyond what it is able to raise through taxes. In this chapter students will learn how the Federal Government meets this need through nontax revenue and borrowing.

ABCNEWS INTERACTIVE

The following video segments may be used to highlight aspects of financing the Federal Government.

POWERS OF THE CONGRESS GUIDEBOOK
Chapter 22: Paying the Nation's Debts, p. 26
Chapter 23: Borrowing on Credit, p. 27

2 Nontax Revenues and Borrowing

Find Out:

- What are the major sources of nontax revenues in the United States?
- What is the historical purpose of the power to borrow?
- What is the purpose of much of the current borrowing?

Key Terms:
deficit, public debt

In *Hamlet*, Shakespeare writes: "Neither a borrower, nor a lender be." That may be good advice in some situations. As you will see in this section, however, it certainly has not been followed by the government of the United States.

Nontax Revenues

Large sums of money reach the federal treasury from a multitude of nontax sources. As you can see from the table on page 408, these miscellaneous receipts now come to well over $20 billion a year.

These monies come from dozens of places. A large portion comes from the earnings of the Federal Reserve System, mostly in interest charges. The interest on loans made by several other federal agencies, canal tolls, and fees for such items as passports, copyrights, patents, and trademarks also generate large sums. So do the premiums on veterans' life insurance policies, the sale or lease of public lands, the sale of surplus property, and such other things as the fines imposed by the federal courts.

The Treasury Department maintains what it calls the conscience fund for all the money, several thousand dollars a year, that people send in to ease their minds over their past tax-paying mistakes. Another little-known source of nontax money is seigniorage, the profit the United States Mint makes in the production of coins. That profit is the difference between the value of the metals used and the other costs of production and the monetary value of the minted coins. It is a tidy little sum, more than $500 million in most years. The Philatelic Sales Branch of the United States Postal Service sells more than $100 million in mint stamps to collectors each year; and stamp collectors spend untold millions more at local post offices. Most of the stamps they buy are never used on mail.

Managing the Country's Money Supply Pictured here is a Federal Reserve building in Washington, D.C. There are twelve Federal Reserve banks in this country that supply money to banks throughout the nation.

Borrowing

Congress has the power "to borrow money on the credit of the United States."[6] Historically, the power to borrow has been viewed as a power that makes it possible for the government to (1) meet the costs of short- and long-term crisis situations and (2) finance large-scale

[6]Article I, Section 8, Clause 2.

Reading Strategy: Relating to the Topic

Ask students to consider the question, "What happens when I do not have enough money to buy what I want?" After students have identified their options, have them read the section to see how the Federal Government responds in such a situation.

Vocabulary

Point out to students "Key Terms" on page 412. Have them examine the term *public debt*. Ask students to define each word separately to help them understand the meaning of the term. LEP projects that would not be paid for out of current income. Thus, the Federal Government borrowed huge sums when the United States entered World War I, to combat the Depression of the 1930s, and again during World War II.

In recent decades, the Federal Government has borrowed for yet another reason: deficit financing. Over these years, the government has regularly spent more than it has taken in. That is, it has run up an annual **deficit**—the yearly shortfall 1.a
between income and outgo; and it has borrowed to make up the difference. Indeed, the Federal Government's financial books have not shown a surplus, more income that outgo, since fiscal year 1969.[7] As the graph on page 414 shows, deficit financing—often called deficit spending—became especially pronounced in the 1980s, and it has continued at a hefty rate in the 1990s.

Congress must authorize any and all federal borrowing. The borrowing itself is done by the Treasury Department, which issues various kinds of securities to investors, principally individuals and banks, investment companies, and other financial institutions. These securities usually take the form of Treasury notes or bills—T-bills—issued for short-term borrowings, or bonds for long-term purposes. They are, in effect, IOUs, promissory notes in which the government agrees to repay a certain sum, with interest, at a certain time.

The government is able to borrow money at lower rates of interest than those paid by private borrowers. This is true largely because investors can find no safer securities than those issued by the United States; if the United States could not pay its debts, no one else would be able to, either. Federal securities are also attractive because the interest they generate cannot be taxed by the States or their local governments.

The Public Debt

Borrowing produces a debt, of course. The public debt is the result of the Federal Government's borrowing over time. More precisely, the **public debt** is the government's outstanding 1.b
indebtedness, all of the money borrowed and not yet repaid, plus the accrued interest.[8]

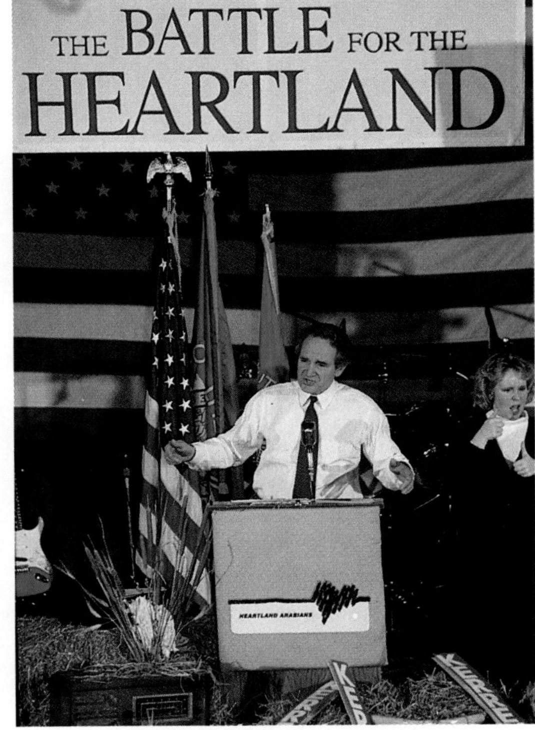

Campaigning on the Budget Issue Democratic presidential candidate Tom Harkin of Iowa promised to address the deficit problem if elected in 1992.

The Federal Government has built up a huge debt over time. As you can see in the table on page 414, the nation's debt doubled in the years 1981 through 1985 because of deficit financing; and it had quadrupled by 1992.

The amounts involved here are absolutely mind-boggling. In 1981, when the debt was approaching $1 trillion, President Ronald Reagan said that he found "such a figure—a trillion dollars—incomprehensible." He then drew this verbal picture: "[I]f you had a stack of $1,000 bills in your hand only four inches high, you would be a millionaire. A trillion dollars would be a stack

[7]In fact, since 1930, the Federal Government has ended only seven fiscal years "in the black"—that is, with a surplus: fiscal years 1947, 1948, 1951, 1956, 1957, 1960, and 1969.

[8]The public debt, often called the national debt, is frequently confused with the government's annual deficits. Notice, however, that each of those deficits amounts to an annual increase in the total of the public debt.

Instruct

Explain/Discuss Point out to students that the Federal Government obtains its operating funds from sources other than the taxes it levies. Ask students to identify some of these nontax sources of revenue. *(Examples include: interest charged by the Federal Reserve System; the conscience fund; fees for passports and visas; and seigniorage.)*

Next, ask students to discuss how the purpose of borrowing by the Federal Government has changed over time. *(It began as a way to meet crisis situations and to finance large-scale projects. It became a way of financing government from year to year.)* Have students discuss their opinions about deficit financing.

Provide Guided Practice Write the words *Nontax Revenues, Deficit,* and *Public Debt* on the board. Ask students to identify and explain the significance of these terms in the context of financing the Federal Government. *(*Nontax revenues *are sources of income in addition to taxes.* Deficit *is the shortfall between revenue and spending, which must be covered by borrowing.* Public Debt *refers to the accumulated deficits that have not been paid off.)*

Provide Independent Practice

TRF **Teacher's Resource File** You may wish to assign Section 2 Guided Reading and Review, Unit 4 File, p. 78, to help students master section objective content.

Enrichment

Have students create a collage of pictures, words, and/or artifacts that describe events or items that have contributed to the public debt. Students can find information on the public debt by reading newspaper and magazine articles. (Average)

Spotlight on: Global Awareness

Until the 1960s, nearly all of the Federal Government's debt was held by American creditors. But as the Federal Government's borrowing has increased, so has the amount of the debt held by foreign governments, banks, and individual foreign investors. By the end of the 1960s, international creditors held $10 billion of a $343.7 billion United States debt—about 3 percent. By 1990, however, international creditors held $404 billion of the $2.4 trillion debt, a total of 17 percent. Foreign central banks and other institutional investors hold 67 percent of this portion. United States government debt accounts for one-fifth of the foreign-owned assets in the United States.

Interpreting Tables and Graphs Ask students to compare the development of the public debt in the last 10 years with other 10-year periods.

Caption Answer a) The year 1980 to the present. b) Reluctance to raise taxes, large increases in uncontrollable spending.

MONITOR COMPREHENSION

Answers to Section 2 Review
1. "Key Terms" are defined on the following pages:
a. deficit, p. 413
b. public debt, p. 413
2. Over $20 billion yearly in recent years. **3.** It issues treasury bills for short-term borrowing and bonds for long-term borrowing. **4.** Investment in the Federal Government is very safe and the interest earned is not taxed by State or local governments. **5.** (a) and (b) Students should recognize that this could be done either by increasing revenues or decreasing spending. Students' assessments of effects and reactions of voters should range from negative in the short term to positive in the long term.

CLOSURE

The Federal Government raises money through nontax sources and by borrowing. In recent years, deficit financing has led to enormous growth in the public debt. In Section 3, students will learn how the Federal Government spends money and about the importance of the federal budget.

Assignment Assign Section 3, pp. 416–419, for the next class period.

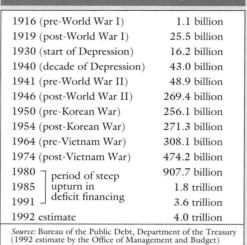

The Public Debt (at end of selected fiscal years)

1916 (pre-World War I)	1.1 billion
1919 (post-World War I)	25.5 billion
1930 (start of Depression)	16.2 billion
1940 (decade of Depression)	43.0 billion
1941 (pre-World War II)	48.9 billion
1946 (post-World War II)	269.4 billion
1950 (pre-Korean War)	256.1 billion
1954 (post-Korean War)	271.3 billion
1964 (pre-Vietnam War)	308.1 billion
1974 (post-Vietnam War)	474.2 billion
1980 (period of steep upturn in deficit financing)	907.7 billion
1985	1.8 trillion
1991	3.6 trillion
1992 estimate	4.0 trillion

Source: Bureau of the Public Debt, Department of the Treasury (1992 estimate by the Office of Management and Budget)

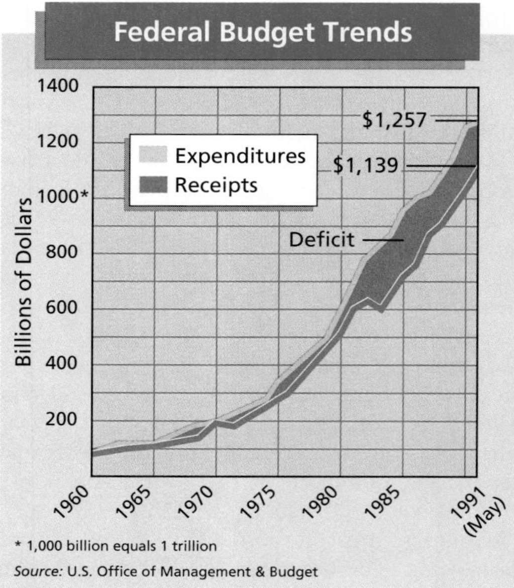

Interpreting Tables and Graphs The public debt can be affected by national and world events, as shown in the table at left. Which recent period saw the greatest growth in deficit spending and the public debt? Can you think of any explanation for this growth?

67 miles high." Mr. Reagan's stack would have to be more than 250 miles high to equal the national debt today!

There is no constitutional limit on the amount that may be borrowed, and so there is no constitutional limit on the public debt. Congress has put a statutory ceiling on the debt. But Congress simply adjusts the ceiling upward whenever fiscal realities seem to call for it.

The debt has always been the subject of much controversy; and its rapid rise in recent years has fueled the fire. The annual interest on the debt—the amount that must be paid each year to those from whom the government has borrowed—came to more than $286 billion in 1991; and that figure will be well over $300 billion in 1992. That means that about one in five dollars the Federal Government now spends goes just to service the debt.

Most of those who are most concerned about the size of the debt are worried about its impact on future generations of Americans. In short, they believe that today's deficit financing—that is, today's borrowing to pay for yesterday's and today's spending—is being done at the expense of tomorrow's taxpayers.

Section 2 Review

1. **Define:** deficit, public debt
2. How much revenue does the government raise through nontax sources?
3. Describe the mechanism by which the Federal Government borrows money.
4. Why is the Federal Government able to borrow money at lower rates of interest than private borrowers?

Critical Thinking

5. **Predicting Consequences** (p. 19) (a) What would be the possible effects if the Congress decided to cease its habit of deficit spending? (b) How do you expect the voters of the United States would respond?

★

TRF **Teacher's Resource File**
See the Unit 4 File, p. 79, for the Section 2 Quiz.

Reteach

Have students write a brief summary of this section. The summary should include the following headings: *Nontax Revenues, Borrowing,* and *The Public Debt.*

Debating Key Issues

Should the Government Subsidize Private School Education?

Mueller v. *Allen*

Although public schools have been the cornerstone of the United States educational system, many parents choose to send their children to private schools at their own expense. Yet a portion of these individuals' taxes still go to support public education. This system is designed to provide an equal opportunity for an education to all, while keeping church and State separate.

In 1983, a group of Minnesota taxpayers, Mueller et al., challenged a State law that allowed parents to deduct up to $700 a year from their income in order to pay for their children's school tuition and expenses. Because parents of children in public schools paid so little for these items, the law benefitted parents who utilized private schools. Furthermore, the taxpayers felt that because the majority of private schools in Minnesota had religious affiliations, the law was using public funds to advance religion.

The parents brought the case before the U.S. District Court of Minnesota, arguing that the tax deduction violated the 1st Amendment clause commanding the separation of church and State. The court ruled against the parents. After this ruling was affirmed in the State court of appeals, the parents appealed to the Supreme Court.

Review the following evidence and arguments presented to the United States Supreme Court:

Arguments for Mueller

1. The statute violates the 1st Amendment's establishment of religion clause. The deduction provided to parents of public-school children is unequal to that given to parents of private-school children.
2. The law indirectly funds private education by permitting parents to pay for private schools with public tax money.
3. The statute weakens the public educational system by robbing it of needed funds. Thus, the public schools lose resources and the quality of education suffers.

Arguments for Allen

1. The statute does not seek to advance any particular religion. Because it provides tax deductions for parents of both public and private school children, it does not favor any specific group.
2. All education benefits the public. Thus, private as well as public schools should get taxpayer support.
3. Parents who send their children to private schools should not have to pay equal taxes to support the public schools. By utilizing private schools, these parents remove the financial burden of their children from the public schools, and deserve to be compensated.

Getting Involved

1. Identify the constitutional grounds on which each side based its arguments.
2. Debate the opposing viewpoints presented in this case.
3. Predict how you think the Supreme Court ruled in this case and why. Then refer to the Supreme Court Glossary on page 764 to read about the decision in this case. Discuss the impact of the Court's decision on the future of public education.

TEACHING
Debating Key Issues

***Mueller* v. *Allen*:**
Should the Government Subsidize Private School Education?

Objective
Explore the issue of public funding for private schools.

Instruct

Before reading the feature, you may want to elicit student answers to the question in the title. When they have finished reading, ask them if their answers have changed, and if so, why. Then work through the "Getting Involved" section.

Following the class debate (Activity 2), encourage students to explain which arguments they found to be most compelling and why. Then have students predict the Supreme Court's decision in the case. After students have read the Court's decision from the Supreme Court Glossary, have students discuss their reactions.

Supreme Court Decision

The Court upheld the law, stating that it met the Lemon test (*Lemon* v. *Kurtzman*, 1971), and that the deduction was available to all parents with children in school. Although it was of greater benefit to parents of children in private schools, each parent had the choice of which school their children attended.

Teacher's Resource File
See the Supreme Court Cases file, p. 12, for an activity that extends coverage of this case.

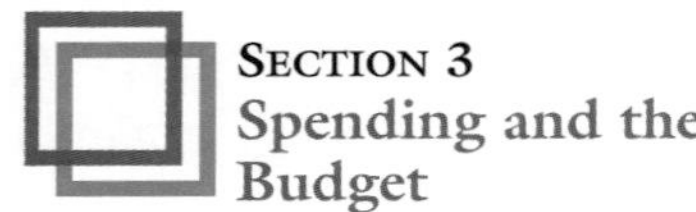

SECTION 3
Spending and the Budget

FOCUS

Teacher's Resource File See the Unit 4 File, p. 80, for the Section 3 Outline.

Objectives

16.7 Determine what the Federal Government does with revenue it collects.
16.8 Explain the importance of the federal budget.
16.9 Identify how the budget process works.

Bellringer Activity Ask students to imagine that they had a part-time job at which they earned $25 a week. Have students create a budget for their weekly income and expenses. Students should carefully allocate certain amounts of money to such line items as food, entertainment, transportation, and any other items they can think of. Ask students to discuss how they arrived at the decisions for their budgets.

State the Purpose The Federal Government spends a vast amount of money each fiscal year. The government determines its spending priorities through its federal budget.

ABCNEWS INTERACTIVE

The following video segment may be used to highlight aspects of financing the Federal Government.

POWERS OF THE PRESIDENT GUIDEBOOK
Chapter 10: Manager of the Economy, p. 70

3 Spending and the Budget

Find Out:

- What does the Federal Government do with the revenue it collects?
- What is the importance of the federal budget?
- How does the budget process work?

Key Terms:
entitlement, continuing resolution

The Federal Government will spend about $1.5 trillion in fiscal year 1992. If you placed 1.5 trillion dollar bills end to end, they would stretch about 140 million miles, just about the distance from the earth to the sun and halfway back.

Decrease in Military Spending National budget priorities have changed over the last few years. With the end of the cold war, the build-up in military armaments has slowed.

In this section, you will see how the government spends all that money, and how it plans for that spending, through the budget process.

Federal Spending

Look at the table on page 417. As shown, the largest amount of money is spent by the Health and Human Services Department—largely for social security and other entitlement programs.
1.a **Entitlements** are benefits that federal law says must be paid to all those who meet the eligibility requirements. OASDI is the largest federal entitlement program today. Others include Medicare, Medicaid, food stamps, unemployment compensation, and veterans' pensions. In effect, those who receive the benefits paid under these programs are entitled to them.

Defense is the second largest object of current federal spending, and it has consumed a substantial part of the federal budget every year for more than 50 years now. Note that the amount shown in the table on page 417 as the Defense Department's spending for 1991 is somewhat misleading. That figure does not account for some $40 billion of Persian Gulf War expenditures that were then offset by contributions from Germany, Japan, Saudi Arabia, and several other countries. Nor does that figure include the defense-related spending by other federal agencies—for example, the extensive nuclear weapons research and development work of the Department of Energy.

Interest in the public debt now rivals defense spending. In fact, interest payments, stoked by deficit financing, will likely surpass defense spending and rank as the second largest category of federal expenditures in fiscal year 1992.

Controllable and Uncontrollable Spending What the Federal Government spends can be described in terms of controllable and uncontrollable spending. Most specific items in the federal budget are controllable. That is, Congress and the President decide how much will be spent each year on many of the individual expenditures the government makes—for example, on farm subsidies, military equipment, aid to education, and so on. Some spending is uncontrollable, however, such as interest on the

Reading Strategy: Problem Solving

Ask students to consider the following situation: As President of the United States, you want to stay within the national budget and still ensure that your programs are put into effect. How will you accomplish this goal? Have students compare their responses to the information presented in the section.

Vocabulary

Point out to students "Key Terms" on page 416. Have students use their prior knowledge of the word *entitled* to predict the meaning of this term. If students are unfamiliar with the word, have them look it up in a dictionary. Then have students check their prediction against the definition given in the text.

Federal Spending, Fiscal Years 1988-1992 (by agency, in billions of dollars)

Agency	1988	1989	1990	1991	1992 (est.)
Legislative Branch	1.9	2.1	2.2	2.3	3.0
Judicial Branch	1.3	1.5	1.6	2.0	2.3
Executive Office of the President	0.1	0.1	0.2	0.2	0.2
Funds appropriated to the President (Mostly for foreign economic/military aid)	7.3	4.3	10.1	11.7	12.0
Department of Agriculture	44.0	48.3	46.0	54.1	55.7
Department of Commerce	2.3	2.6	3.7	2.6	2.8
Department of Defense—Military	281.9	294.9	289.8	261.9	283.0
Department of Defense—Civil	22.0	23.4	25.0	26.5	28.2
Department of Education	18.2	21.6	23.1	25.3	27.5
Department of Energy	11.2	11.4	12.0	12.5	14.9
Department of Health and Human Services	373.6	399.8	438.7	484.4	525.3
Department of Housing and Urban Development	18.9	19.7	20.2	22.8	24.3
Department of the Interior	5.1	5.2	5.8	6.1	6.5
Department of Justice	5.4	6.2	6.5	8.2	10.0
Department of Labor	21.9	22.7	25.3	34.0	34.8
Department of State	3.4	3.7	4.0	4.3	4.5
Department of Transportation	26.4	26.6	28.6	30.5	31.9
Department of the Treasury	202.4	230.6	255.3	276.9	298.6
Department of Veterans Affairs	29.3	30.0	29.0	31.2	32.8
Environmental Protection Agency	4.9	4.9	5.1	5.8	5.9
National Aeronautics and Space Administration	9.1	11.0	12.4	13.9	14.7
Office of Personnel Management	29.2	29.1	32.0	34.8	37.0
Small Business Administration	-0.5	0.8	0.7	0.6	0.3
Other Independent Agencies	23.5	33.9	73.7	80.5	102.1
Deductions (undistributed offsetting receipts)	-78.9	-89.1	-99.0	-110.6	-118.0
Total Outlays	**1,064.1**	**1,144.1**	**1,251.8**	**1,323.0**	**1,445.9**
Deficit (Outlays greater than receipts)	-155.1	-153.4	-220.4	-268.8	-280.9

Source: Financial Management Service, Department of the Treasury

Interpreting Tables Examine the table above. Which agency has seen a decrease in spending since 1989?

debt. That interest is a fixed charge; once the money is borrowed, the interest must be paid when it comes due and at the rate the government promised to pay.

Social security benefits, food stamps, and most other entitlements are also largely uncontrollable because, once Congress has set the standards of eligibility for those programs, it has no control over how many people will then meet those standards. Thus, Congress cannot determine how many people covered by social security will become eligible for retirement benefits. Those expenditures are not completely uncontrollable, however. Congress could redefine eligibility standards, or it could reduce the amount of money each beneficiary is to receive. But, clearly, those actions would be politically difficult.

The Office of Management and Budget estimates that the uncontrollable items in the budget total nearly 80 percent of all current federal spending.

INSTRUCT

Analyze/Discuss Ask students to analyze the table on page 417. Have students discuss their reactions to the spending priorities revealed in that budget. To aid in this discussion, suggest that students read more about these departments in the Government Resources Handbook on page 690.

Have students discuss the concepts of controllable and uncontrollable spending. Ask students to explain in what sense uncontrollable spending is in fact uncontrollable. *(It is uncontrollable in the sense that the government cannot control who is eligible for certain entitlement programs. It is controllable in that the government could change the guidelines for eligibility.)*

Next, ask students why they think that the budget is described as a "political document." *(Possible answer: It reflects politically determined priorities for program spending.)* How might decisions made in the budgeting process impact on the President and Congress politically? *(Setting spending priorities may benefit or harm certain groups, who may have the power to punish or reward politicians.)*

Interpreting Tables Have students identify the departments that have the largest budgets. Ask students if they are surprised by the ranking of major items in the budget.

Caption Answer Small Business Administration.

ACTIVITY: Cooperative Learning

Time: One class period **Activity:** Write a letter to the President regarding deficit financing. **Grouping:** Partners **Purpose:** Have partners compose a letter to the President expressing their feelings about deficit financing and the impact it may have on their future. Explain that students are responsible for correct spelling, punctuation, capitalization, sentence structure, and letter format. **Roles:** Have students assign the following roles: recorder, spokesperson. **Outcome:** After revisions and corrections have been made, have the spokesperson read the letter to the class. Encourage students to mail their letters.

SPOTLIGHT ON: Economics

Given the continual upward trend in uncontrollable spending, many government officials believe that reductions in uncontrollable spending will soon be necessary, despite political difficulties. For example, social security payments in 1992 totaled $290 billion—nearly 20 percent of the budget and up from from a figure of 15 percent in 1970. What is more, these payments will increase sharply in the 21st century as the baby boom generation reaches retirement age. Medicare payments have also skyrocketed, from $7.5 billion in 1970 to $37 billion (or 6.3 percent of the budget) in 1980. These payments are expected to reach $130 billion in 1992—or 9 percent of the federal budget.

Provide Guided Practice Have students work in small groups or individually to create a diagram that outlines the federal spending and budget processes. The diagram should include coverage of such concepts as controllable and uncontrollable spending.

Provide Independent Practice

TRF **Teacher's Resource File** You may wish to assign Section 3 Guided Reading and Review, Unit 4 File, p. 81, to help students master section objective content.

The Federal Budget

Recall, the Constitution declares that

"No money shall be drawn from the treasury, but in consequence of appropriations made by law. . . ."[9]

Thus, only Congress can provide the money upon which the Federal Government must depend. But it is the President who initiates the spending process by submitting a budget at the beginning of each congressional session.[10] The budget is a hugely important political document. It is the President's work plan for the conduct of government and the execution of public policy.

[9]Article I, Section 9, Clause 7. [10]The word *budget* comes from the French *bougette*, meaning a small pouch or bag with its contents. Originally, the budget was the bag in which in the 18th century the British Chancellor of the Exchequer carried financial documents.

VOICES *on Government*

George Bush,
41st President of the United States

On the Thrust of His Proposed Budget

"The budget proposal that we sent up there to Capitol Hill has been well received. I'm not saying that we don't have any critics—but when you look back over your shoulder, I think it's fair to say this one has been well received. It includes a record $76 billion for research and development, one of the most important investments we can make in the long-term economic and military strength of our nation. . . . This isn't an investment in machines, it's an investment in people—in the scientists, the engineers and the educators who will produce the advances of the 21st century."

The Budget Process The budgeting process is a joint effort of the President and Congress. The President prepares the budget and submits (proposes) it to Congress. Congress then reacts to the President's proposals, over a period of several months. It usually enacts most of them, usually in some altered form, in appropriate measures.

The President and the Budget The process of building the budget is a lengthy one. In fact, that process begins some 18 months before the start of the fiscal year for which it is intended. First, each federal agency prepares detailed estimates of its spending needs for that 12-month period. Each agency submits its spending plans to the Office of Management and Budget, the President's budget-making agency (see Chapter 14, Section 5).

The OMB reviews all of the many agency proposals, often in budget hearings at which agency officials must defend their dollar requests. Following the OMB's review, revised and usually lowered spending plans for all of the agencies in the executive branch are fitted into the President's overall program. They become a part of the budget document the President sends to Capitol Hill.[11]

Congress and the Budget Remember that Congress depends upon and works through its standing committees. The President's budget is referred to the Budget Committee in each chamber. There, in both committees, the budget is studied and dissected with the help of the Congressional Budget Office. The CBO is a staff agency, created by Congress in 1974. It provides both houses of Congress and their committees with basic budget and other economic data and analyses. The information that the CBO supplies is independent of the information provided by the OMB, which, recall, is the President's budget agency.

[11]Congress makes and enacts its own budget. The spending requests for the judicial branch, prepared by the Administrative Office of the United States Courts, are included in the President's budget without OMB review.

Enrichment
Have students trace the development of a recent year's federal budget, from the version proposed by the President through the version passed by Congress. Have students use the Government Resources Handbook on page 690 to find sources of information. (Challenging)

OR

TRF **Teacher's Resource File**
See the Unit 4 File, pp. 84–86, for the Case Study in Contemporary Issues for Chapter 16.

THE WIZARD OF ID

Interpreting Political Cartoons Mayors, governors, and Presidents strive to balance their budgets. According to this cartoon, what is sometimes required to accomplish this task?

The President's budget is also sent to the House and Senate Appropriations Committees.[12] Their subcommittees hold extensive hearings in which they examine agency requests, quiz agency officials, and take testimony from a wide range of interested parties. The two Appropriations Committees fashion measures that later are reported to the floor of each house. Those measures are the bills that actually appropriate the funds on which the government will operate.

The two Budget Committees propose a concurrent resolution on the budget to their respective chambers. That measure, which must be passed by both houses by May 15, sets overall targets for federal receipts and spending in the upcoming fiscal year. The estimates are intended to guide the committees in both houses as they continue to work on the budget.

The two Budget Committees propose a second budget resolution in early September. Congress must pass that resolution by September 15, just two weeks before the beginning of the next fiscal year; it sets binding spending limits for all federal agencies in that upcoming year. No appropriations measure can provide for any spending that exceeds those limits.

Congress passes 13 major appropriations bills each year. Recall, each of these measures must go to the White House for the President's action. Every year, Congress hopes to pass all 13 of the appropriations measures by October 1—that is, by the beginning of the fiscal year. It seldom does so, however, and Congress must then pass emergency spending legislation to avoid a shutdown of those agencies for which appropriations have not yet been signed into law. That legislation takes the form
1.b of a **continuing resolution**, a measure that, when signed by the President, allows the affected agencies to continue to function on the basis of the previous year's appropriations.

[12] If the budget includes any tax proposals, they are referred to the House Ways and Means Committee and to the Senate's Finance Committee.

Section 3 Review

1. **Define:** entitlement, continuing resolution
2. What are the three most expensive items for which the Federal Government spends money?
3. What is the President's role in the budget-making process?
4. What is the role of the Congress in the budget-making process?
5. (a) Why must Congress pass its appropriations measures by October 1? (b) What happens if it does not?

Critical Thinking

6. **Drawing Conclusions** (p. 19) What does the text mean when it says that redefining the eligibility standards for certain entitlement programs would be politically difficult?

Interpreting Political Cartoons Ask students to explain why the king's budget is not really "balanced." (A pound, in fact, equals only 16 ounces.)

Caption Answer The value of the monetary unit itself must change.

Monitor Comprehension

Answers to Section 3 Review
1. "Key Terms" are defined on the following pages:
a. entitlement, p. 416
b. continuing resolution, p. 419
2. Entitlements, defense, and interest on debt. **3.** With the help of the executive agencies and the OMB, the President proposes a budget to Congress. **4.** Congress studies and revises the budget. Then it passes a budget and appropriates the funds. **5.** (a) The previous year's appropriations run out on September 30. (b) Congress must pass a continuing resolution. **6.** Some benefits would be eliminated, which might prevent re-election of legislators or the President.

Closure

The process by which Congress and the executive departments establish the federal budget determines spending priorities. In the next chapter, students will learn more about one of the most important fields of governmental activity—foreign policy and national defense.

Assignment Assign Chapter 17, Section 1, pp. 424–427, for the next class period.

Activity: Teaching Heterogeneous Groups

Have students work in small groups to create an illustrated diagram that covers the topic of the chapter, Financing Government. The diagram should cover the process by which the Federal Government raises revenues and spends money. Encourage students to include such concepts as deficit financing and the public debt in their diagrams. Also, encourage students to be as creative as possible in the drawing of their diagrams. For example, tell students to use a combination of words and symbols and to use the diagram to express their own opinions on such topics as taxation, the deficit, entitlements, and other issues. Have each group present their diagrams to the class.

Teacher's Resource File
See the Unit 4 File, p. 82, for the Section 3 Quiz.

Reteach

Write a letter to Alexander Hamilton describing what has happened to the Federal Government budget since he was the first secretary of the treasury. Be sure to include a description of how the Federal Government now spends its revenue and how important the budget is. Also, describe the budget process itself.

TEACHING Citizenship

How to File a Tax Return

Objective

Identify and organize the information needed to complete a tax return.

INSTRUCT

Before students read the Citizenship feature, point out how the Federal Government depends on the support of its taxpayers to fund its programs, and that a tax return is the way by which the Federal Government ensures that each person is paying the proper amount. Ask students to discuss why it would be unfair for some persons to file tax returns while others did not. *(If some were not filling out tax returns and paying the proper amount of taxes, the burden on those who do would increase.)* Also, help students understand that filing a tax return is the only way to obtain from the government any money they are owed due to the withholding of too much income.

You may wish to provide students with sample returns and an instruction booklet. After students have reviewed the forms and the booklet, you may wish to have students offer their opinions on the simplicity or complexity of the forms. Ask students to comment on how the Federal Government could simplify the filing of tax returns.

How to File a Tax Return

As you know, the Federal Government requires huge sums of money in order to operate. In addition, State and local governments also require money in order to provide the many services they offer. Governments obtain much of this money by taxing citizens. One important tax that many individuals pay is an income tax. The Federal Government, most States, and many cities require people to pay this type of tax. For this reason, wage earners must file by April 15 a tax return on which they report their incomes from the previous year. This process is called filing a tax return. The steps for filing a federal tax return are outlined below.

1. Obtain the proper tax forms. If you have filed a tax return in previous years, you should receive your tax forms in the mail. If you have never filed a return before, you can obtain the forms and instructions at local offices of the Internal Revenue Service, most post offices, and many banks. (a) Look in the phone book under the United States government for the local office of the Internal Revenue Service. (b) Look under your State's and your local government's name to get any State or local forms you need.

Form **1040EZ**
Department of the Treasury - Internal Revenue Service
Income Tax Return for Single Filers With No Dependents (0) **1990**

Name & address — Use IRS label (see page 9). If you don't have one, please print.
Please print your numbers like this: 9876543210
Your social security number

Please see instructions on the back. Also, see the Form 1040EZ booklet.

Presidential Election Campaign (see page 9) Do you want $1 to go to this fund? — Yes No

Dollars Cents

Report your income
Attach Copy B of Form(s) W-2 here. Attach tax payment on top of Form(s) W-2.

1 Total wages, salaries, and tips. This should be shown in Box 10 of your W-2 form(s). (Attach your W-2 form(s).) 1

2 Taxable interest income of $400 or less. If the total is more than $400, you cannot use Form 1040EZ. 2

3 Add line 1 and line 2. This is your **adjusted gross income.** 3

4 Can your parents (or someone else) claim you on their return?
Note: You must check Yes or No.
☐ **Yes.** Do worksheet on back; enter amount from line E here.
☐ **No.** Enter 5,300.00. This is the total of your standard deduction and personal exemption. 4

5 Subtract line 4 from line 3. If line 4 is larger than line 3, enter 0. This is your **taxable income.** 5

Figure your tax

6 Enter your Federal income tax withheld from Box 9 of your W-2 form(s). 6

7 **Tax.** Use the amount on **line 5** to find your tax in the tax table on pages 14–16 of the booklet. Enter the tax from the table on this line. 7

Refund or amount you owe

8 If line 6 is larger than line 7, subtract line 7 from line 6. This is your **refund.** 8

9 If line 7 is larger than line 6, subtract line 6 from line 7. This is the **amount you owe.** Attach your payment for full amount payable to "Internal Revenue Service." Write your name, address, social security number, daytime phone number, and "1990 Form 1040EZ" on it. 9

Sign your return
Keep a copy of this form for your records.

I have read this return. Under penalties of perjury, I declare that to the best of my knowledge and belief, the return is true, correct, and complete.

Your signature Date
X

For Privacy Act and Paperwork Reduction Act Notice, see page 4 in the booklet. Form 1040EZ (1990)

2. Read the instruction booklets. The booklets that come with the tax forms will answer many of your questions about paying income taxes. They will also help you determine which tax form you will need to fill out. (a) Read the instructions and follow them carefully. (b) Follow the directions for getting help in the instruction booklet.

3. Collect your W-2 forms. Each January, you will receive reports from your employer(s) stating the amount of money you earned during the previous year. Usually, these reports are W-2 forms. W-2's report what you were paid, as well as how much money was withheld from your earnings to pay federal, State, and local taxes. W-2's also list FICA withholdings—your contribution to the social security system. The withholdings on your W-2's represent income taxes that you have already paid.

4. Collect other earnings information. You may also receive other statements of income. For example, any bank where you earned interest will report those earnings to you. You must also gather information about any income you made, such as tips and cash payments you received, that does not appear on a W-2 form. Remember that no money has been withheld on these earnings.

5. Complete the form according to the instructions. (a) Check your arithmetic to be sure you have paid enough tax. (b) Be sure to make copies of your tax return before sending it back to the appropriate agency.

TRF **Teacher's Resource File**
See the Unit 4 File, p. 83, for the Skill Application for this lesson.

Chapter-in-Brief

Scan all headings, photographs, charts, and other visuals in the chapter before reading the section summaries below.

Section 1 Where the Money Comes From: Taxes (pp. 405–411) The power to tax is granted to Congress by the Constitution but that power is not unlimited. Congress may levy taxes only for public purposes, not to benefit any private interest. No tax may be applied to any exported articles. Direct taxes must be apportioned among the States according to their populations. Indirect taxes must be uniform in every State. The Federal Government may not tax any governmental function of either State or local governments.

Income taxes levied on individuals and corporations are progressive taxes and are the largest source of federal revenue. Most individuals pay income taxes through withholding from their paychecks. Nonprofit organizations such as churches are not subject to an income tax. Social insurance taxes (payroll taxes) are regressive and pay for three major social welfare programs: Old-Age, Survivors, and Disability Insurance; Medicare; and unemployment compensation. Excise taxes, estate and gift taxes, and customs duties also contribute to federal revenues. Some taxes are used for nonrevenue purposes. Licensing is used for both regulatory purposes and revenue.

Section 2 Nontax Revenues and Borrowing (pp. 412–414) Many nontax sources contribute to the federal treasury: interest on loans made by federal agencies, the "conscience fund," the profit the U.S. Mint makes in the production of coins, and the sale of mint stamps to collectors by the U.S. Postal Service, for example.

The Constitution gives Congress the power to borrow money on the credit of the United States for crisis situations such as war or for large-scale projects. The Federal Government also borrows for deficit financing and has built up a huge public debt. The public debt is estimated to reach $4 trillion in 1992. No constitutional limit exists on the amount that may be borrowed. Congress has put a statutory ceiling on the public debt, however, which may be raised whenever the need arises. The current debt will have to be paid by future taxpayers and has always been the subject of much controversy.

Section 3 Spending and the Budget (pp. 416–419) The Federal Government will spend nearly $1.5 trillion in 1992, mostly for social security and other entitlement programs. Defense is the second largest government expense, followed by interest on the public debt. Nearly 80 percent of federal spending is uncontrollable—it cannot be reduced.

The executive branch initiates the spending process by submitting a budget to Congress each year. Each federal agency submits a detailed spending plan to the Office of Management and Budget. These become a part of the budget document sent to Congress by the President. In Congress, it is referred to the Budget Committee and the Appropriations Committee in each chamber. Congress reviews the budget, holds hearings, and makes appropriations. Funds cannot be spent until appropriated by Congress. Congress passes 13 major appropriations bills every year, each covering a broad slice of federal spending. Each of these measures must go to the President for approval. Congress must often pass emergency legislation in the form of a continuing resolution. This allows the affected agencies to continue to function on last year's appropriations.

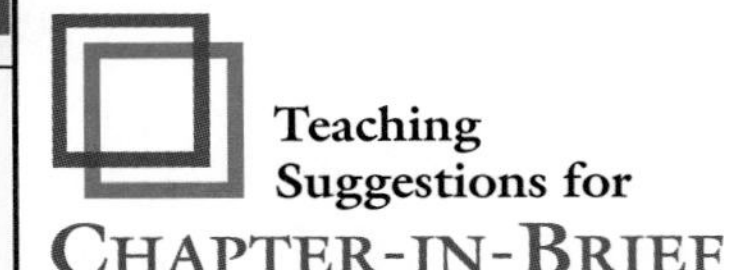

Teaching Suggestions for Chapter-in-Brief

Below are some of the possible uses for the Chapter-in-Brief:

To Preview the Chapter You may want to assign the Chapter-in-Brief page and the Section Outlines from the Teacher's Resource File before beginning Chapter 16 to introduce students to the "Key Terms" and concepts in each section.

To Review the Chapter When students have completed Chapter 16, you might want to assign the Chapter-in-Brief as a tool for review, along with the Guided Reading and Reviews from the Teacher's Resource File.

To Omit the Chapter If you wish to skip Chapter 16, it may be helpful to assign the Chapter-in-Brief to students as a review before continuing to another chapter. You may also want to assign the Chapter 16 Test to assess student knowledge of the material. Then, specific portions of Chapter 16 may be assigned to students needing reinforcement of "Key Terms" and concepts.

Teacher's Resource File See the Unit 4 File for the following materials:

- Section Outlines, pp. 74, 77, 80.
- Guided Reading and Reviews, pp. 75, 78, 81.
- Chapter 16 Test, pp. 87–89.

Additional Resources

Burnham, David. *A Law Unto Itself: Power, Politics, and the IRS.* Random House, 1990.

Collander, Stanley E. *The Guide to the Federal Budget: Fiscal 1989.* Urban Institute, 1988.

Decisions, Decisions: The Budget Process. Computer software. Tom Snyder Productions. Apple II/Mac/IBM.

Heilbroner, Robert and Peter Bernstein. *The Debt and the Deficit: False Alarms/Real Possibilities.* Norton, 1989.

Peterson, W.C. *Transfer Spending, Taxes, and the American Welfare State.* Kluwer Acad. Pubs. Group, 1991.

Shuman, Howard E. *Politics and the Budget: The Struggle Between the President and the Congress.* Prentice Hall, 1988.

Tax Foundation. *Facts and Figures on Government Finance.* Biennial.

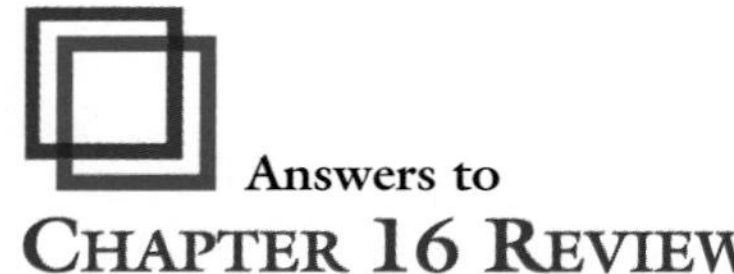

Answers to

Chapter 16 Review

Vocabulary and Key Terms

Matching

1. estate tax
2. progressive tax
3. public debt
4. entitlement
5. customs duty

True or False

1. False—the correct term is *regressive tax.*
2. False—the correct term is *gift tax.*
3. False—the correct term is *deficit.*
4. True.

Word Relationships

1. continuing resolution
2. excise taxes
3. customs duties
4. tax return

Main Ideas

Section 1

1. Taxes can be used only for public purposes, and export taxes are prohibited. Direct taxes must be equally apportioned, and indirect taxes must be uniform. **2.** The implied limitation is that the Federal Government cannot tax State and local governments in the exercise of their governmental functions. **3.** The income tax (individual and corporate), social insurance taxes, excise taxes, estate and gift taxes, and customs duties. **4.** Government can use taxes to control or suppress some activity that Congress thinks is harmful or dangerous to the public.

Section 2

5. Possible answers: Interest earnings from the Federal Reserve System and interest from loans made by several other agencies. Tolls, fees, premiums on insurance, sale of public lands and property, and fines imposed by courts are other sources. The conscience fund is another non-tax revenue source, as is seigniorage. **6.** Historically, borrowing was used only for crisis situations and to fund large-scale projects. Today, deficit financing is used in virtually every annual budget. **7.** The public debt has grown to about four times its 1980 size. **8.** The cost of servicing the debt is rising rapidly and will continue to do so.

Section 3

9. Entitlement programs.

10. (a) Uncontrollable spending is that which the Federal Government cannot change—at least not without some political difficulty. Controllable spending is decided upon by the President and Congress. (b) Most individual budget items are controllable, but only about 20 percent of total spending is controllable.

11. The President prepares the budget, which the Congress then dissects, alters, and ultimately passes in its own form. The President must sign it before it goes into effect.
12. The Budget Committees in each house consider and, if necessary, amend the budget submitted by the President. They

Chapter Review

Vocabulary and Key Terms

progressive tax (p. 407)	excise tax (p. 410)	deficit (p. 413)
tax return (p. 408)	estate tax (p. 410)	public debt (p. 413)
payroll tax (p. 409)	gift tax (p. 410)	entitlement (p. 416)
regressive tax (p. 409)	customs duty (p. 410)	continuing resolution (p. 419)

Matching: *Review the key terms in the list above. If you are not sure of a term's meaning, look up the term and review its definition. Choose a term from the list above that best matches each description.*

1. imposed on the assets of one who dies
2. a tax that falls most heavily on those who are most able to pay
3. the total amount of money owed by the United States, plus all accrued interest
4. payments that federal law says must be paid to all those who meet the eligibility requirements
5. sometimes called tariffs, import duties, or imposts

True or False: *Determine whether each statement is true or false. If it is true, write "true." If it is false, change the underlined word or words to make the statement true.*

1. Certain taxes that fall most heavily on those who are least able to pay them are sometimes referred to as <u>progressive taxes</u>.
2. If you were to receive $20,000 as a present from a relative, you would have to pay an <u>estate tax</u>.
3. In recent decades, the United States has been consistently unable to spend less than it takes in; thus, the country runs a yearly <u>public debt</u>.
4. A <u>payroll tax</u> is one in which the amount owed by the individual is withheld from the person's paycheck.

Word Relationships: *Replace the underlined definition with the correct term from the list above.*

1. When Congress fails to pass the necessary appropriations by October 1st, they pass a <u>measure that allows affected agencies to continue functioning on the basis of the last year's appropriations</u>.
2. These <u>taxes laid on the manufacture, sale, or consumption of goods and/or the performance of services</u> are sometimes called, luxury, sin, or hidden taxes.
3. Certain items such as bananas and Bibles are exempt from <u>taxes laid on goods brought into the United States from abroad</u>.
4. Wage earners in the United States must file annual <u>declarations of income and exemptions or deductions claimed</u>.

Main Ideas

Section 1 (pp. 405–411)

1. What are the four expressed limitations on the Federal Government's power to tax?
2. What is the implied limitation on that power?
3. What are the different taxes by which the Federal Government raises revenue?

4. For what purposes besides raising revenue can the Federal Government use its power to levy taxes?

Section 2 **(pp. 412–414)**

5. List five of the nontax sources of revenue utilized by the Federal Government.
6. How does the historical use of borrowing differ from the practice of governmental borrowing in recent decades?
7. How has the public debt changed since the 1980s?
8. What is the significance of the public debt for future taxpayers?

Section 3 **(pp. 416–419)**

9. What is the largest item on which the Federal Government spends the money it raises?
10. (a) What is the difference between uncontrollable and controllable spending? (b) About what percentage of the annual budget is controllable?
11. In what sense is the budget-making process a joint effort of the President and Congress?
12. What are the roles of the Budget Committees and the Appropriations Committees?

Critical Thinking

1. **Checking Consistency** (p. 19) Consider the discussion of the purposes for which Congress can levy taxes. Do you think that the Constitution intends for Congress to use its power to tax certain activities as a means of regulating or destroying that activity? Explain your answer.
2. **Predicting Consequences** (p. 19) (a) In your opinion, should the United States seek an amendment to the Constitution requiring a balanced budget? (b) What might be the result of such an amendment?
3. **Testing Conclusions** (p. 19) The text states that "the federal budget is a hugely important political document." Use evidence from the chapter to support and/or explain this statement.

Getting Involved

1. **Writing Your Opinion** Write a questionnaire you could use to determine people's views on the issue of federal taxes. To begin with, identify what you hope to learn from the survey, and write a statement that explains why you are conducting it. Then, create a list of questions that you hope will produce the kind of information you are looking for. Remember, the questions in your survey must be carefully worded to avoid influencing people's responses. Review each question to ensure that it is presented in a straightforward and unbiased manner. Once you have refined your questions, reread them, correct any errors, and make a final draft.
2. **Cooperative Activity** As a class, consider the table on federal spending on page 417. Work together to create a new budget that reflects the shared priorities of the class. To begin with, list each of the cabinet-level departments that appear on the table. Then, as a group, prioritize these budget items, placing them in order of descending importance. Continue the discussion until a majority of the class agrees on a list. Repeat the process, this time distributing specific funds for each department.
3. **Gathering Information** You are interested in obtaining some information about government finance. Using the Government Resources Handbook that begins on page 690, identify possible sources you could use to (a) find the amount of money the government raised from various revenue sources; (b) read about the budget submitted to Congress by the President; and (c) examine certain figures presented in the two congressional budget committees' May 15th budgets.

prepare resolutions, first setting targets for government receipts and spending, and then setting firm guidelines. The Appropriations Committees also examine the President's budget, amend it if necessary, and authorize spending. Their authorizations cannot exceed the limits set by the Budget Committees.

Critical Thinking

1. Answers will vary. Students might suggest that regulating or destroying certain activities falls within the constitutionally acceptable guideline that taxes be used to provide for the general welfare. Others might say that this use of taxation does not fit this constitutional guideline. **2.** (a) Answers will vary. (b) Students may suggest that entitlement programs and other services would have to be cut. Others will point to the long-term benefit of lower interest payments that ultimately make more money available for government services. **3.** Possible answer: The National budget sets guidelines and priorities for all of the government's spending. The decisions made by the President and Congress regarding the budget have the potential to benefit or harm certain constituencies. These groups will ensure—to the best of their abilities—that Congress and the President are aware of the political risks and benefits of certain actions.

Getting Involved

1–2. Answers and results will vary, but students should demonstrate an understanding of the concepts in this chapter. **3.** Possible answers: (a) *Statistical Abstract of the United States*; (b) *The Weekly Compilation of Presidential Documents*; (c) *The Congressional Record.*

Chapter 17 Resources

In the Teacher's Resource File
The following materials are found in the Teacher's Resource File box.

Instructional Support: Unit 4 File

For the Section
Outlines, pp. 93, 96, 99, 102, 105
Guided Reading and Reviews, pp. 94, 97, 100, 103, 106
Quizzes, pp. 95, 98, 101, 104, 107

For the Chapter
Skill Application, p. 108
Case Study on Contemporary Issues, pp. 109–111
Chapter Test, pp. 112–114
Additional Test Questions, pp. 115–117

Enrichment Support Files

Participatory Government Activities, pp. 28–39
Simulations and Debates: The Draft
Historical and Legal Documents, pp. 20, 26, 28, 47
Comparative Government: A Multicultural View, pp. 2–2, 8–9, 12–13, 22–23

Computer Test Bank and Assessment

Transparency Package, pp. 17, 42, 55

Chapter 17 Focus

Introduce the Chapter Tell students that in this chapter they will learn about U.S. foreign policy and national defense, and the role of the executive branch in conducting foreign and defense policies. Read with students the Chapter Preview and Objectives.

Writing Activity Direct students' attention to "Describe." Have students write an explanation of the comparison of the U.S. to the caliph. Then have students write their own metaphors for the role they see the U.S. playing in world affairs.

Motivate for Learning Direct students' attention to "Predict." Discuss with students the primary goal of U.S. foreign policy. Have students read the quotation from Colin Powell (p. 447). Ask: How does this quotation seem to characterize U.S. foreign policy goals?

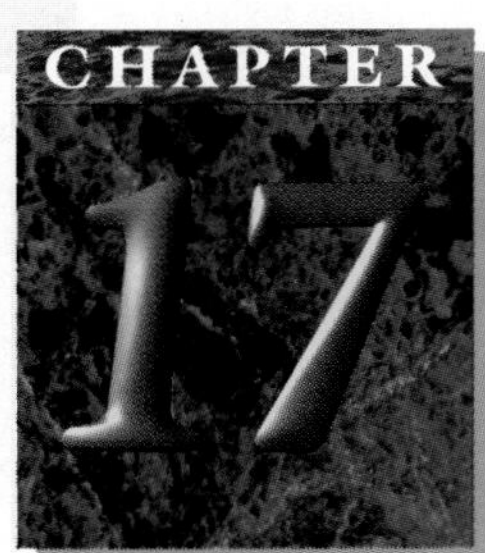

Foreign Policy and National Defense

Chapter Preview

In November 1991, President Bush met with leaders from the Mideast to urge Israel and the Arab states to put aside longstanding feuds and create a peaceful future. A Palestinian delegate compared President Bush's role at the conference to an old Arab folktale.

A caliph, or Islamic ruler, discovers a poor woman boiling a pot of stones. She explains that she hopes her children will fall asleep before she has to tell them that there is no food. The tale ends happily as the caliph bestows plenty of food on the woman and her children. "We hope," the Palestinian said, "that America will be the caliph." Is this the role of the United States in foreign affairs? This chapter is about the character of our country's foreign policy and its relation to national security.

Before you read this chapter:

- **Describe** your reaction to the comparison of the United States to the caliph in the tale above.
- **Predict** the primary goal of United States foreign policy.

As you read, focus on the main objective of each section. Understand:

1. The historic and continuing goal of America's foreign and defense policies.
2. The process of setting a foreign and defense policy.
3. The role of other federal agencies in making and carrying out foreign and defense policies.
4. Major features of American foreign policy, past and present.
5. The purposes of American foreign aid and defense alliances and the role of the United Nations.

Magruder's American Government: *A Witness to Change* by William A. McClenaghan

As we note at several points in this chapter and elsewhere, World War II brought a profound change in the role of the United States in world affairs. That titanic conflict produced the dramatic shift from this nation's historic posture of isolationism to our present-day policy of internationalism. As we note on page 443, "America hoped to force a world community in which all or at least most nations would agree to act together against any nation that threatened the peace."

A plea for that reordering of America's priorities ran through successive editions of *American Government* in the years between the two World Wars. For example, editions through the 1920s and '30s cited the many, ongoing, and tragic costs of World War I, and described those costs as "a strong argument for better cooperation among nations!" And by the mid-1930s, several years before the United States finally emerged from its isolationism, this book was arguing that it had long since become "impossible for any nation to isolate itself from the rest of the world."

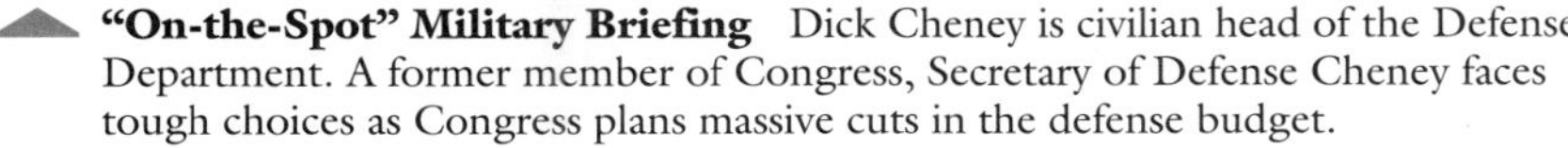

"On-the-Spot" Military Briefing Dick Cheney is civilian head of the Defense Department. A former member of Congress, Secretary of Defense Cheney faces tough choices as Congress plans massive cuts in the defense budget.

1 Foreign and Defense Policy: An Overview

Find Out:

- Why must the United States have a policy for its relationship with the rest of the world?
- What makes up a nation's foreign policy?
- Which officials are primarily responsible for United States foreign policy?

Key Terms:

isolationism, foreign policy

Do you know where your shoes were made? The odds are that they are not American-made, that they came instead from Mexico or Korea or Italy or somewhere else abroad. What about your shirt or blouse and your pants or skirt? Where were they made? And what about your stereo, compact disc player, television set, watch, umbrella, baseball glove, bicycle?

Those questions, and their answers, ought to begin to suggest to you why the topic of this section is so vitally important to you.

From Isolationism to Internationalism

Through much of this nation's history, American politics turned largely on questions of domestic concern. For more than 150 years, the American people were chiefly interested in what was happening at home. For most Americans, foreign affairs were matters of little or no concern to them. This country's relationships with countries abroad were largely shaped by a
1.a policy of **isolationism**—a purposeful refusal to become generally involved in the affairs of the rest of the world.

The past 50 years have been marked by a profound change in the place of the United States in world affairs, however. That historic shift from isolationism to internationalism brought major changes in American foreign and defense policies. World War II finally convinced the

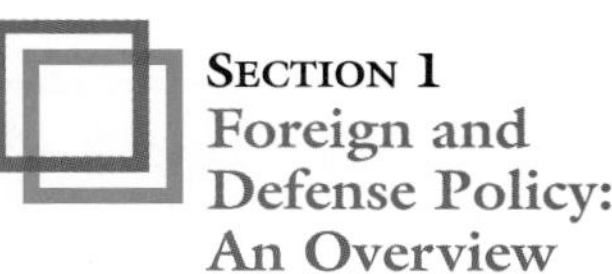

SECTION 1
Foreign and Defense Policy: An Overview

FOCUS

Teacher's Resource File See the Unit 4 File, p. 93, for the Section 1 Outline.

Objectives

17.1 Explain why the United States must have a policy for its relationship with the rest of the world.
17.2 Describe what makes up a nation's foreign policy.
17.3 Identify the officials primarily responsible for U.S. foreign policy.

Bellringer Activity Ask students to inspect their shoes, shirts, or other personal items. Ask: How many items were made in America? In another country? Point out that trade links the U.S. closely with many other countries.

State the Purpose In Section 1, students will learn how American policies evolved from isolationism to internationalism, what foreign policy is, and the President's foreign policy responsibilities.

ABCNEWS INTERACTIVE

The following video segment may be used to highlight aspects of presidential roles.

POWERS OF THE PRESIDENT GUIDEBOOK
Chapter 34: Controlling the Military, page 42

Vocabulary

Point out "Key Terms" on page 425 to the students. Tell students that in some ways these words are opposites of each other. Ask students which word they think would better describe the United States today.

Reading Strategy: Structured Overview

Write the section title, "Foreign and Defense Policy: An Overview," on the board. Then list the three main headings across the board, underneath the title. Have students skim the section for details to write under the three column headings.

INSTRUCT

Discuss Analyze the appeal of isolationism. Ask students what might happen if the U.S. adopted an isolationist position today.

Have students devise a graph using the following information on U.S. military active duty personnel: 1991—2,000,000 people; 1992—1,900,000 people. Projected figures are: 1993—1,800,000; 1994—1,700,000; 1995—1,600,500. Ask students to write a brief explanation for how these figures reflect that we live in "one world."

Explain to students that three factors influence all foreign policy: politics, economics, and geography. Have students examine the specific examples given in the chapter to identify how each of these factors influenced U.S. foreign policy.

Provide Guided Practice Write *Foreign Policy* on the board and draw a large circle around it. Have students suggest the many different policy matters that make up foreign policy. Write these items inside the circle. Ask students to identify the three elements that influence foreign policy: *politics, economics,* and *geography.* Draw these outside the circle and draw arrows from them to the circle.

Provide Independent Practice
TRF **Teacher's Resource File** You may wish to assign Section 1 Guided Reading and Review, Unit 4 File, p. 94, to help students master section objective content.

American people that neither they nor anyone else can live in isolation, that, like it or not, the world of today is indeed "one world."

You can see that this is one world, that this nation's peace and security are intimately bound up with the peace and security of the rest of the world, in any number of ways. This nation is inextricably linked with others in a global community. The realities of ultra-rapid travel and of instantaneous worldwide communications make that point abundantly clear.

Wars and other political upheavals anywhere on the globe have a decided impact on the interests of the United States—and on the daily lives of every American. Five times in this century the United States has become involved in major wars thousands of miles from its shores; and in several other instances in the last 100 years this nation has committed its forces to lesser, but still significant, battles abroad. The nation's security has also been threatened by other events elsewhere on the globe—by the acts of terrorists in Europe and Asia, by racial strife in South Africa, by revolutions in Latin America, Arab-Israeli conflicts in the Middle East, and by many others.

Foreign Policy in Action: 1979 President Jimmy Carter congratulates Egypt's President Sadat (left) and Israeli Prime Minister Begin (right) on the signing of the Camp David Accord. The agreement, initiated by President Carter, ended more than 30 years of armed hostilities between Egypt and Israel.

Economic conditions elsewhere also have a direct effect on and in this country. Japanese automobiles, European steel, Arab oil, Brazilian coffee, Italian shoes, and all of the many other things that Americans buy from abroad make that fact an obvious one, every day.

The world of the 1990s cannot be described as "one world" in all respects, however. Relations between the United States and its former adversary, the Soviet Union, have improved remarkably over the past few years, yes: but as you have read, the world remains a dangerous place. Iraq's 1990 invasion of Kuwait and the subsequent Gulf War in 1991 is major proof of that fact. So, too, is the unrest that has followed the collapse of communism in the former Soviet Union and Eastern Europe, continuing Arab-Israeli enmities in the Middle East, civil wars in Afghanistan, Morocco, Sri Lanka, and other places, and much more.

Most Americans agree that in such a divided world it is only through policies that are designed to promote and protect the security and well-being of all nations that the security and well-being of the United States can be assured. As President Bush has put it, America's goal is

> ". . . a world where the rule of law supplants the rule of the jungle, a world in which nations recognize the shared responsibility for freedom and justice, a world where the strong respect the rights of the weak."

Foreign Policy: What It Is

1.b Every nation's **foreign policy** is actually many different policies on many different topics. It is made up of all of the stands and actions that a nation takes in every aspect of its relationships with other countries—diplomatic, military, commercial, and all others. To put the point another way, a nation's foreign policy is made up of all of its many foreign policies.

Thus, American foreign policy consists of all of the Federal Government's official statements and all of its actions as it conducts this nation's foreign relations. It involves such matters as treaties and alliances, international trade, the defense budget, foreign economic and military aid, the United Nations, nuclear weapons testing, and disarmament negotiations. It also

Enrichment
Have students look through newspapers and magazines in the library to locate as many articles as possible pertaining to American foreign policy. Students should note the subject of the article, the date of the article, and how much the President seems to be involved in the issue. (Easy)

includes the American position on oil imports, grain exports, immigration, space exploration, fishing rights in the Atlantic and Pacific oceans, cultural exchange programs, economic sanctions, computer technology exports, and a great many other matters.

Some foreign policies remain largely unchanged over time. For example, an insistence on freedom of the seas has been a basic part of American policy from the very earliest years of American history. Other policies are more flexible, subject to change as circumstances change. Thus, only a very few years ago, resisting the ambitions of the Soviet Union was a basic part of American foreign policy. Today, the United States and many of the states that once made up the Soviet Union are seeking and building ever closer political, military, and economic ties with one another.

At times the United States can take the lead in world affairs. It can launch new policies and take initiatives that seek to gain support and heighten America's power and prestige abroad. It has done so on a number of occasions, as you will see later in this chapter—including, for example, the Open Door policy in China at the turn of the last century, with the Marshall Plan after World War II, and the forging of the coalition of nations that defeated Iraq in the Persian Gulf War in 1991.

Very often, American policy must be defensive in nature. Leaders must adjust it to meet the actions of some other country. Thus, containment—resisting the spread of Soviet influence—became a basic part of United States foreign policy soon after World War II.

As you will read, this policy of containment began with the Truman Doctrine in 1947, in direct response to the Soviet Union's policy of aggressive expansion in the immediate postwar years; and it was to remain a basic part of American policy until the collapse of the Soviet Union and its communist empire in the late 1980s and early 1990s.

The President's Responsibilities

The President is both the nation's chief diplomat and the commander in chief of its armed forces. As you have seen, Congress also has significant powers in the fields of foreign and military affairs, especially with its power of the purse, its power to declare war, and in the Senate's role in the treaty-making and the appointment processes.[1] But, as you have also seen, it is the President who dominates those policy fields. Both constitutionally and by tradition, the President bears the major responsibility for both the making and conduct of foreign policy.[2]

The President depends on a number of officials and agencies to meet the immense responsibilities that come with his role as chief diplomat and commander in chief. Recall, you considered the National Security Council, in the Executive Office of the President, in Chapter 14, Section 5. Here, you will look at the other elements of what is often called the foreign policy bureaucracy. You will begin with the Departments of State and Defense, and then encounter several others.

Section 1 Review

1. Identify: isolationism, foreign policy
2. Why can the foreign and defense policies of the United States be properly called this country's national security policy?
3. (a) In what ways does this nation exist in "one world"? (b) In what ways does it not?
4. Of what does a nation's foreign policy consist?
5. Who is the commander in chief of the nation's armed forces?

Critical Thinking

6. Distinguishing Fact from Opinion (p. 19) The text says the world remains a dangerous place. (a) Do you agree with this statement? (b) Why or why not?

★

[1]See, especially, Chapter 11, Section 2.
[2]See Chapter 14, Section 3. Recall, the Constitution forbids to the States any role in foreign relations, Article I, Section 10, Clauses 1 and 3.

Monitor Comprehension

Answers to Section 1 Review
1. "Key Terms" are defined on the following pages:
a. isolationism, p. 425
b. foreign policy, p. 426
2. The nation's security depends on how it conducts foreign affairs and defense issues with other nations. **3.** (a) The events and actions in other nations affect the lives of American people. (b) The world is divided by conflicts between nations. **4.** All the policies that impact its relations with other nations, including military, commercial, and diplomatic policies. **5.** The President. **6.** (a) Answers will vary. (b) Some students might note continued conflict as evidence of danger. Others might say the declining tension between the superpowers makes the world safer.

Teacher's Resource File See the Unit 4 File, p. 95, for the Section 1 Quiz.

Closure

Remind students that foreign policy can be classified as isolationist or internationalist, that isolationist positions are not realistic in today's world, that foreign policy is the sum of many policies, and that foreign policy is conducted largely by the President. In the next section, students will learn about the State and Defense departments, the heads of which are appointed by, report to, and are accountable to the President.

Assignment Assign Section 2, pages 428–434, for the next class period.

Reteach

Ask students how difficult they think it would be to contact a particular person or company in another country. Then explain to students that, just as it is a relatively simple matter for them to communicate quickly with people thousands of miles away, it is also a simple matter for heads of state and government leaders from different countries to communicate. Reinforce the fact that the entire world is now "neighbor" to the United States.

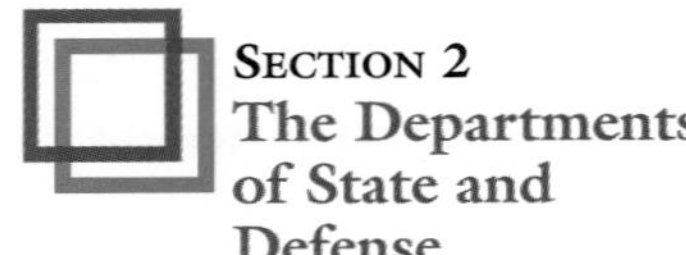

SECTION 2
The Departments of State and Defense

FOCUS

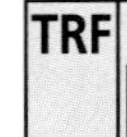

Teacher's Resource File See the Unit 4 File, p. 96, for the Section 2 Outline.

Objectives

17.4 Describe the secretary of state's key role in foreign policy.
17.5 Explain how the State Department is organized.
17.6 Describe the key role of the secretary of defense in national security policy.
17.7 Explain how the Department of Defense is organized.

Bellringer Activity Ask students to offer ideas as to how the President can be kept aware of events of possible significance to the U.S. in some 150 sovereign countries, as far as 12,000 miles away. Tell students that two departments, State and Defense, assist the President in monitoring and dealing with other countries.

State the Purpose The Departments of State and Defense are responsible for knowing what is happening worldwide and for being prepared to respond to any threat to American security. In Section 2, students will learn how two of the President's cabinet members direct these huge organizations that gather, process, and respond to information about world events.

2 The Departments of State and Defense

Find Out:

- What is the secretary of state's key role in the making and conduct of foreign policy?
- How is the State Department organized?
- What is the key role of the secretary of defense in the making and conduct of national security policy?
- How is the Department of Defense organized?

Key Terms:

right of legation, ambassador, passport, visa, diplomatic immunity

As Alexander Hamilton noted in *The Federalist* No. 72, the Framers expected that "the actual conduct" of the nation's foreign affairs would be in the hands of "the assistants and deputies of the Chief Magistrate."

As you will see in this section, many of the President's "assistants and deputies" in the field of foreign affairs are in the State Department. In addition, the Department of Defense assists the President in the conduct of military affairs.

Secretary of State James Baker (right, front), the highest ranking official in the Bush cabinet, visited China in November 1991. The amount of influence that the secretary of state has on foreign policy is decided by the President.

The State Department

The State Department, headed by the secretary of state, is the President's right arm in foreign affairs. The secretary is named by the President, subject to confirmation by the Senate. It is to the secretary and to the Department of State that the President looks for advice in both the formulation and conduct of the nation's foreign policy.

The secretary of state ranks first among the members of the President's cabinet. This is true in part because of the importance of the office, but it is especially the case because the Department of State was the first of the now 14 executive departments created by Congress.

The Department of Foreign Affairs, which had first been created in 1781 under the Articles of Confederation, was re-created by Congress in 1789 as the first major unit in the executive branch under the Constitution. Later that same year, its name was changed to the Department of State, and President Washington appointed Thomas Jefferson as the nation's first secretary of state. For 200 years now, 59 other men, many of them quite distinguished, have held that important post.

The duties of the secretary relate almost solely to foreign affairs today: to the making and conduct of policy and to managing the work of the department, its many overseas posts, and its more than 25,000 employees.[3]

Some Presidents have relied heavily on the secretary of state; others have chosen to keep foreign policy more tightly in their own hands. In either case, the secretary has been an important and influential officer in every administration.

Organization and Key Components

The department is organized along both geographic and functional lines. Some of its

[3]The secretary does have some domestic responsibilities. Thus, when Richard Nixon resigned the presidency on August 9, 1974, his formal, legal announcement of that fact had to be submitted to Secretary of State Henry Kissinger. Over the years, the secretary and the department have had (and been relieved of) various domestic functions—including, for example, publishing the nation's laws, issuing patents, and supervising the decennial census.

Reading Strategy: Problem Solving

Have students imagine that they are traveling in a foreign capital. Quite unexpectedly, they are stopped by the police at dusk one evening, told that they are in violation of a curfew, and ordered back to their hotel room. Ask what role the United States' Departments of State and Defense could conceivably play in this scenario.

Vocabulary

Point out "Key Terms" on page 428. Below are some additional words whose meanings may help students understand the section content.

—**sovereign:** independent of all others
—**persona non grata:** a person who is unacceptable or unwelcome

agencies, such as the Bureau of African Affairs and the Bureau of Near Eastern and South Asian Affairs, deal with matters involving certain countries or regions of the world. Other agencies have more broadly defined responsibilities, such as the Bureau of Economic and Business Affairs and the Bureau for Refugee Programs. Most of these bureaus are headed by an assistant secretary and include several "offices"—for example, the Passport Office and the Visa Office in the Bureau of Consular Affairs.

The Foreign Service More than 4,200 men and women now represent the United States abroad as members of the Foreign Service.

Under international law[4] every nation has the **right of legation**—the right to send and 1.a
receive diplomatic representatives. An ancient practice, its roots can be traced back to the Egyptian civilization of 6,000 years ago.

The Second Continental Congress named this nation's first foreign service officer in 1778, when it chose Benjamin Franklin to be America's minister to France.

Ambassadors Today the United States is represented by an ambassador stationed at the capital of each state the United States recognizes.[5] American embassies are found in more than 150 countries around the world today.

The President appoints ambassadors, with Senate consent, and they serve at the President's pleasure. Some of their posts are much desired political plums, and whenever a new President moves into the White House, he typically makes many new appointments. Too often, Presidents have appointed people to ambassadorships and other major diplomatic posts as reward for their support—financial and otherwise—of the President's election to office.

America Abroad Foreign Service officials represent the United States government in other countries. American ambassador Shirley Temple Black maintains official communications between Czechoslovakia and the United States.

President Truman named the first woman as an ambassador, to Denmark, in 1949. President Johnson appointed the first African American (also a woman), as ambassador to Luxembourg in 1965. Today, several women, African Americans, and other minority persons hold high rank in the Foreign Service.

1.b Each American **ambassador** is the personal representative of the President of the United States, and he or she reports to the President through the secretary of state. Each of them must keep the President fully informed of events in the host country, negotiate diplomatic agreements, protect the rights of American citizens abroad, and do whatever else is in the best interests of the United States.[6]

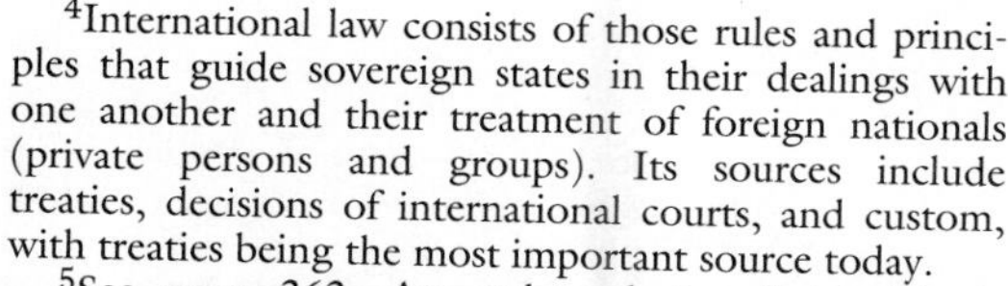

[4]International law consists of those rules and principles that guide sovereign states in their dealings with one another and their treatment of foreign nationals (private persons and groups). Its sources include treaties, decisions of international courts, and custom, with treaties being the most important source today.

[5]See page 362. An ambassador's official title is *Ambassador Extraordinary and Plenipotentiary*. When the office is vacant or the ambassador is absent, the post is usually filled by a next-ranking Foreign Service officer in the embassy. That officer, temporarily in charge of embassy affairs, is known as the *chargé d'affaires*.

[6]The United States also has some 120 consular offices abroad. There, Foreign Service officers promote American interests in a multitude of ways—e.g., encouraging trade, gathering intelligence data, advising persons who seek to enter this country, and aiding American citizens who are abroad and in need of legal advice or other help.

ABCNEWS INTERACTIVE

The following video segment may be used to highlight aspects of presidential roles.

POWERS OF THE PRESIDENT GUIDEBOOK
Chapter 30: Appointing Ambassadors, p. 38

INSTRUCT

Discuss/Analyze Discuss with students the importance of the State Department and the secretary of state in the formulation and implementation of U.S. foreign policy. Have students list the primary responsibilities of the secretary of state.

Explore with students the importance of civilian control of the military. Ask students to think of examples of countries in which this policy is not followed. What problems have resulted? Tell students that civilian control of the military is ensured by three constitutional provisions: the elected leader (President) of the country is the commander in chief of the armed forces; other elected representatives (Congress) have wide military powers; the secretary of defense can not have been in active military service for ten years.

Analyze with students the reasons why there are three major branches of the armed services. Have students find details in the text that help distinguish the different roles of the branches of the armed forces.

Write *secretary of state* and *secretary of defense* on the board. Ask students to identify the duties of each office as you write them on the board.

Enrichment

Divide the class into two groups and have each group role play a day in the life of the secretary of state and the secretary of defense. Students' dramatizations should incorporate details from the text. (Challenging)

OR

Teacher's Resource File
See the Unit 4 File, pp. 109–111, for the Case Study on Contemporary Issues for Chapter 17.

To carry out these duties effectively, an ambassador must have the closest possible contacts with the leaders of the host country as well as with its people. A well-grounded knowledge of the language, history, customs, and culture of that country is an almost indispensable qualification for the job. To help with their duties, ambassadors have the assistance of a number of skilled advisors.

Special Diplomats Those persons whom the President names to certain other top diplomatic posts also carry the rank of ambassador—for example, the United States representative to the UN and the American member of the North Atlantic Treaty Council; see Section 5. The President also gives the personal rank of ambassador to those who take on special assignments abroad—for example, representing the United States at an international conference on arms limitations.

Passports A **passport** is a certificate issued 1.c
by a government to its citizens who travel or live abroad. Passports entitle their holders to the privileges accorded to them by international custom and treaties. Few states will admit persons who do not hold valid passports. Legally, no American citizen may leave the United States without a passport, except for trips to Canada, Mexico, and a few other nearby places.

The State Department's Passport Office now issues some four million passports to American citizens each year. Passports are not the same as visas. A **visa** is a permit to enter another state 1.d
and must be obtained from the country one wishes to enter. Most visas to enter this country are issued at American consulates abroad.

Diplomatic Immunity

In international law, every sovereign state is supreme within its own boundaries, and all persons or things found within its territory are subject to its jurisdiction.

As a major exception to that rule of international law, ambassadors are regularly granted **diplomatic immunity**. That is, they are not sub- 1.e
ject to the laws of the state to which they are accredited. They cannot be arrested, sued, or taxed. Their official residences (embassies) cannot be entered or searched without their consent, and their official communications, papers, and other properties are protected in the same way. All other embassy personnel and their families normally receive this same immunity.

Diplomatic immunity is essential to the ability of every nation to conduct its foreign relations. The practice assumes that diplomats will not abuse their privileged status. If a host government finds a diplomat's conduct unacceptable, that official may be declared *persona non grata* and expelled from the country. The mistreatment of diplomats is a major breach of international law.

Diplomatic immunity is a generally accepted practice. But there are exceptions. The most serious breach in modern times occurred in Iran in late 1979. Militant followers of the Ayatollah Khomeini seized the American embassy in Teheran on November 4 of that year; 52 Americans were taken hostage and held for 444 days. The Iranians finally released the hostages moments after Ronald Reagan became President on January 20, 1981.

The Defense Department

A nation's military policies are an integral part of its foreign policy. Karl von Clausewitz, the Prussian general and military philosopher, put that point in these oft-quoted words more than 150 years ago: "War is the continuation of political relations by other means."

Moral Support Secretary of Defense Dick Cheney (foreground) visits United States troops stationed in Saudi Arabia in August 1990.

SPOTLIGHT ON: Political Talk

When the rights of U.S. citizens traveling in foreign countries are violated without reason, the U.S. government will intervene on the citizens' behalf. But most citizens do not get the kind of personal treatment from the President that Theodore Roosevelt delivered in one memorable case in 1903. Roosevelt authorized Secretary of State Hay to send a rather undiplomatic message via telegram to Morocco, where one Ahmed ibn-Muhammed Raisuli had kidnapped a Greek-born United States citizen, Ion Perdicaris, and his British stepson. The message was brief: "We want Perdicaris alive or Raisuli dead." Perdicaris and his stepson were freed, unharmed.

Congress established what is today called the Defense Department in the National Security Act of 1947. It is the present-day successor to two historic cabinet-level agencies: the War Department, created by Congress in 1789, and the Navy Department, created in 1798.[7]

Civil Control of the Military The authors of the Constitution understood, absolutely, the importance of the nation's defense. They emphasized that fact clearly in the Preamble, and they underscored it in the body of the Constitution by mentioning defense more frequently than any other governmental function.

The Framers also saw the dangers inherent in military power. They knew that its very existence can pose a threat to free government. For that reason, the Constitution is studded with provisions to keep the military always subject to the control of the nation's civilian authorities.

Thus, the Constitution makes the elected President the commander in chief of the armed forces. To the same end, it gives wide military powers to Congress—that is, to the elected representatives of the people.[8]

The United States has obeyed the principle of civilian control throughout its history. That principle has been a major factor in the making of defense policy, and in the creation and the staffing of the various agencies responsible for the execution of that policy. The point is clearly illustrated by this fact: The National Security Act of 1947 provides that the secretary of defense cannot have served on active duty in any of the armed forces for at least 10 years before being named to that post.

"No, no. When I say this new secret weapon can slip past their defenses undetected, I'm not referring to the Russians, I'm referring to Congress."

Drawing by Stevenson; ©1986 The New Yorker Magazine, Inc.

Interpreting Political Cartoons The system of checks and balances ensures that the military remains subject to civilian control. How does this cartoonist convey the opinion that this check on the military is necessary?

The Secretary of Defense The Defense Department is headed by the secretary of defense, who is appointed by the President subject to Senate confirmation. The secretary, who serves at the President's pleasure, has two major responsibilities: (1) as the President's chief aide and adviser in making and carrying out defense policy; and (2) as the operating head of the Defense Department, with its more than two million men and women in uniform and more than one million civilian employees.

The secretary's huge domain is often called the Pentagon—because of its massive five-sided headquarters building on the Virginia side of the Potomac River, across from the Capitol. Year in and year out, its operations take a large slice of the federal budget—today, in fact, 25 percent of all federal spending. The end of the

---

[7]Congress created the Defense Department in order to unify the nation's armed forces—that is, to bring the then-separate army (including the air force) and the navy under the control of a single cabinet department. The new department was first called the National Military Establishment; Congress gave it its present name in 1949. The secretary of defense has been known by that title from 1947 on.

[8]Recall that the Constitution makes defense a national function and practically excludes the States from that field. Each State does have a militia, which it may use to keep the peace within its own borders. Today the organized portion of the militia is the National Guard. Congress has the power (Article I, Section 8, Clauses 15 and 16) to "provide for calling forth the militia" and to provide for organizing, arming, and disciplining it.

Congress first delegated to the President the power to call the militia into federal service in 1795, and the commander in chief has had that authority ever since. Today the governor of each State is the commander in chief of that State's units of the Army and the Air National Guard, except when the President has ordered those units into federal service.

Interpreting Political Cartoons Have students read the cartoon caption. Ask students what the caption implies about the military's opinion of Congress's powers in military matters.

Caption Answer The cartoonist implies that the military would try to mislead Congress and the public if not checked.

ACTIVITY: Teaching Heterogeneous Groups
In order to help students understand the responsibilities of and the relationship between the State Department and the Department of Defense, have them identify the key members of each department and describe the responsibilities of these members. Students should include the secretaries of each department and their principal deputies, as well as members of the Foreign Service, ambassadors, special diplomats, chief military aides, and members of the military departments.

Provide Guided Practice Provide the following clues to students and ask students to identify whether they describe the secretary of state, the secretary of defense, or both: Works at the Pentagon; appointed by the President; highest ranking member of President's cabinet; chairs the Armed Forces Policy Council; Thomas Jefferson was the first; appointment by the President must be confirmed by the Senate; carries out foreign policy; carries out defense policy.

Provide Independent Practice

TRF **Teacher's Resource File** You may wish to assign Section 2 Guided Reading and Review, Unit 4 File, p. 97, to help students master section objective content.

Across the River from the Capitol The Pentagon, which houses the Department of Defense, covers 29 acres and is one of the largest office buildings in the world.

cold war has brought some slight reductions in military spending; still, total outlays for the nation's defense will be about $300 billion in fiscal year 1992.

Chief Civilian Aides The secretary's chief assistant, the deputy secretary, directs the day-to-day operations of the department. There are a number of other civilians at the top levels of the Pentagon. The most important of them are the two under secretaries, one for policy and the other for acquisitions; the several assistant secretaries of defense, often referred to as ASDs; and the secretaries of the army, the navy, and the air force. All of them are appointed by the President with Senate consent.

Chief Military Aides The five members of the Joint Chiefs of Staff serve as the principal military advisers to the secretary, and to the President and the National Security Council, as well. They are the highest ranking uniformed officers in the armed services: the chairman of the Joint Chiefs, the army chief of staff, the chief of naval operations, the commandant of the Marine Corps, and the air force chief of staff. Each of them is also named by the President, subject to Senate approval.

The Armed Forces Policy Council is the department's major planning and decision-making body. The secretary of defense chairs its meetings. Its other members are the deputy secretary; the two under secretaries; the secretaries of the army, the navy, and the air force; and the members of the Joint Chiefs of Staff.

The Military Departments

The three military departments—the Departments of the Army, the Navy, and the Air Force—are major units (sub-cabinet departments) within the Department of Defense. Each is headed by a civilian secretary, named by the President and directly responsible to the secretary of defense. The nation's armed forces—the army, the navy, and the air force—operate within that unified structure.[9]

The Department of the Army The army is the largest of the armed services, and also the oldest. The American Continental Army, now the United States Army, was established by the Second Continental Congress on June 14, 1775—more than a year before the Declaration of Independence.

The army is essentially responsible for military operations on land. The army must be ready (1) to defeat any attack on the United States itself and (2) to take swift and forceful action to protect American interests in any other part of the world. It must organize, train, and equip its active duty forces—the Regular Army—and its reserve units—the Army National Guard and the Army Reserve—for those purposes. All of its forces are under the direct command of the army's highest ranking officer, the chief of staff.

The Regular Army is the nation's standing army, the heart of its land forces. There are now some 630,000 men and 70,000 women on active duty in the army—officers and enlisted

[9]The United States Marine Corps is a separate branch of the armed forces, but, for organizational purposes, it is located within the Navy Department.

The Coast Guard is also a branch of the armed forces. It is organized as a military service, with a present strength of some 37,000 commissioned officers and enlisted personnel. Since 1967, the Coast Guard has been located in the Department of Transportation. At the President's direction, the Coast Guard becomes a part of the United States Navy.

personnel, professional soldiers, and volunteers. The United States is downsizing the army in the post-cold war environment of the 1990s; its authorized strength is scheduled to drop to 618,000 in 1993. Women now serve in all of the Regular Army's units; by law, however, they are barred from direct combat roles—in the army, as well as in each of the other armed services.

The army's combat units are made up of soldiers trained and equipped to fight enemy forces. The infantry takes, holds, and defends land areas. The artillery supports the infantry, seeks to destroy enemy concentrations with its heavier guns, and gives antiaircraft cover. The armored cavalry also supports the infantry, using armored vehicles and helicopters to spearhead assaults and oppose enemy counteroffensives.

The other units of the army provide the many services and supplies for the soldiers in those combat organizations. They could not fight without the help of those other troops: the soldiers of the engineer, quartermaster, signal, ordnance, transportation, chemical, military police, finance, and medical corps.

The Department of the Navy The United States Navy was first formed as the Continental Navy—a fledgling naval force formed by the Second Continental Congress on October 13, 1775. From that day to this, its major responsibility has been sea warfare and defense.

The chief of naval operations (CNO) is the navy's highest ranking officer and is responsible for its preparations and readiness for war and for

Interpreting Graphs In light of world events in the early 1990s, what do students expect the figures on these graphs to do? (*Students should expect military expenditures to decrease.*)

Caption Answer Military spending grew much more quickly in the 1980s. Procurement; aircraft, ships, missiles, guns, vehicles, electronic equipment.

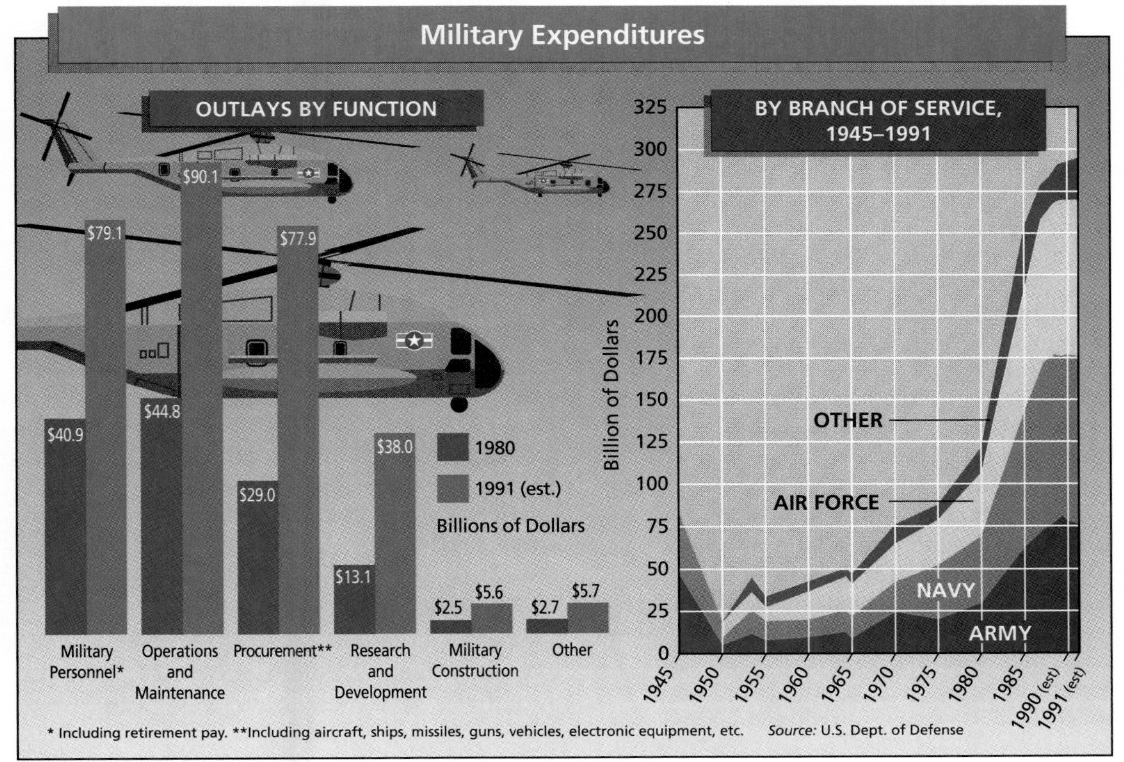

Interpreting Graphs How does the growth in military spending in the 1980s compare with its growth in other decades? After examining outlays by function, determine what area of military spending has increased the most since 1980. On what was the increase spent?

Spotlight on: Economics

The cost supplying our armed services is enormous. In 1992 alone, the U.S. government will spend over $63 billion on weapons systems and supplies for our armed forces and the defense agencies. If Pentagon procurement were a cabinet agency, it would rank fourth, $1 billion ahead of the Department of Agriculture. Navy procurement ($27 billion) is slightly less than the budget for the Department of Education ($29 billion). Air Force procurement is about equal to the budget for the Department of Housing and Urban Development ($25 billion).

Monitor Comprehension

Answers to Section 2 Review
1. "Key Terms" are defined on the following pages:
- **a.** right of legation, p. 429
- **b.** ambassador, p. 429
- **c.** passport, p. 430
- **d.** visa, p. 430
- **e.** diplomatic immunity, p. 430

2. To help the President conduct foreign policy. **3.** (a) State Department branch that represents the U.S. abroad. (b) Act as the President's personal representative in other nations, negotiate diplomatic agreements, protect the rights of American citizens abroad. **4.** The military can pose a threat to democracy. **5.** The President's chief advisor in conducting defense policy; head of the Defense Department. **6.** Army—largest branch, responsible for land operations. Navy—sea warfare, includes the Marine Corps. Air Force—first line of defense. **7.** Students might observe that this suggests a belief that women are not capable of combat or that women are to be protected from harm.

TRF Teacher's Resource File See the Unit 4 File, p. 98, for the Section 2 Quiz.

Closure

Remind students that the Departments of State and Defense have key roles in conducting foreign and defense policy.

Assignment Assign Section 3, pages 435–438, for the next class period.

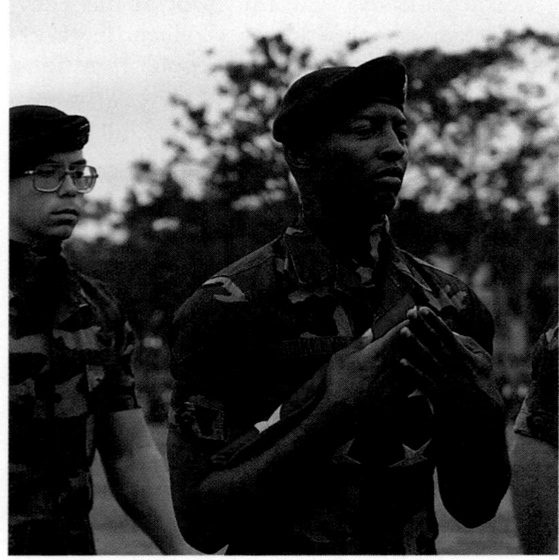

Toward Peace in Our Time The 1991 closing of Clark Air Force Base in the Philippines followed a volcano eruption that caused damage to much of the base.

its use in combat. Some 550,000 officers and enlisted personnel, including nearly 50,000 women, serve in the navy today; their number is slated to drop to 536,000 in 1993.

The United States Marine Corps was established by the Second Continental Congress on November 10, 1775. Today it operates as a separate armed service, within the Navy Department but not under the control of the chief of naval operations. Its commandant answers directly to the secretary of the navy for the efficiency, readiness, and performance of the corps.

The marines are essentially a combat-ready land force for the navy. They have two major combat missions: (1) to seize or defend land bases from which the ships of the fleet and the navy and marine air arms can operate and (2) to carry out other land operations essential to a naval campaign. Today some 180,000 men and nearly 10,000 women serve in the USMC.

The Department of the Air Force The air force is the youngest of the military services. Congress established the United States Air Force and made it a separate branch of the armed forces in the National Security Act of 1947. However, its history dates back to 1907, when the army assigned an officer and two enlisted men to a new unit, the Aeronautical Division of the army's Signal Corps. They were ordered to take "charge of all matters pertaining to military ballooning, air machines and all kindred subjects."

Today the USAF is the nation's first line of defense. It has primary responsibility for military air and aerospace operations. In time of war, its major duties are to defend the United States, attack and defeat enemy air, ground, and sea forces, strike military and other war-related targets in enemy territory, and provide transport and combat support for land and naval operations. The air force played a major role in the swift defeat of Iraq during the Persian Gulf War.

The air force now has about 500,000 officers and enlisted personnel, including more than 60,000 women—all under the direct command of the chief of staff of the air force. The authorized strength of the USAF is now set at 458,000 for 1993.

Section 2 Review

1. Define: right of legation, ambassador, passport, visa, diplomatic immunity
2. What is the secretary of state's first responsibility?
3. (a) What is the Foreign Service? (b) What are the principal duties of an ambassador?
4. For what reason does the Constitution provide for civilian control of the military?
5. What are the two major roles of the secretary of defense?
6. Briefly describe the basic military components of the Defense Department.

Critical Thinking

7. Identifying Assumptions (p. 19) Consider the fact that women are not allowed to engage in combat. What does this fact suggest about attitudes toward women in the military and in society at large?

★

Reteach

Have students imagine that they are career counselors and, either orally or in writing, explain to a person seeking help some of the positions and offices in which one might work in the Departments of State and Defense. Have students explain as much as they know or can find in the text about the duties of each office or position.

3 Other Foreign/Defense Policy Agencies

Find Out:

- What federal agencies, in addition to the Departments of State and Defense, are involved in making and carrying out foreign and defense policies?
- What roles do these departments play?

Key Term:
draft

How many federal agencies, in addition to the Departments of State and Defense, are involved with the nation's foreign affairs? Dozens of them. The Immigration and Naturalization Service deals with those who come here from abroad. The Customs Service combats international smuggling operations. The Public Health Service works with the United Nations and foreign governments to conquer diseases and meet other health problems in many parts of the world. The Coast Guard keeps an iceberg patrol in the North Atlantic to protect the shipping of all nations . . .

A recitation of this sort could go on and on. But, as you will see, this section deals with those other agencies that are most directly involved in the foreign and defense policy fields.

The Central Intelligence Agency

The CIA is a key part of the foreign policy establishment. Created by Congress in 1947, the CIA works under the direction of the National Security Council. The "agency," as it is often called, is headed by a director appointed by the President and confirmed by the Senate.

On paper, the CIA has three major tasks: (1) to coordinate the information-gathering activities of all State, Defense, and other federal agencies involved in the areas of foreign affairs and national defense, (2) to analyze and evaluate all data collected by those agencies, and (3) to brief the President and the National Security Council—that is, keep them fully informed of all of that intelligence.

The CIA is far more than a coordinating and reporting body, however. It also conducts its own worldwide intelligence operations. In fact, it is a major "cloak-and-dagger" agency. Much of the information it gathers comes from such more or less open sources as foreign newspapers and other publications, radio broadcasts, travelers, satellite photos, and the like. But a large share of information comes from its own secret, covert activities. Those operations cover the full range of espionage.

The CIA's work is regularly shrouded in deepest secrecy. Even Congress has generally shied away from more than a surface check on its activities. Indeed, the agency's operating funds are disguised in several places in the federal budget each year.

When Congress established the CIA it recognized the need for such an organization in a trouble-filled world—and most agree that that need continues today. But Congress also saw the dangers inherent in a supersecret intelligence agency that operates outside the realm of public scrutiny and knowledge. Therefore, the National Security Act of 1947 expressly denies the CIA the authority to conduct any investigative, surveillance, or other clandestine activities within the United States. The agency has not always obeyed that command, however.

The United States Information Agency

The United States Information Agency (USIA) is basically a propaganda unit. Its mission is to promote the image of the United States and to sell its policies and its way of life abroad.

The USIA works to sell the United States in a number of ways: by making radio and television broadcasts; distributing publications; producing films and tapes; sponsoring academic exchange programs; organizing cultural exchanges for athletes, artists, and leaders in professional fields such as medicine and politics; and using various other channels. It operates more than 200 libraries, film centers, and other posts in some 130 foreign countries.

Section 3
Other Foreign/Defense Policy Agencies

Focus

Teacher's Resource File
See the Unit 4 File, p. 99, for the Section 3 Outline.

Objectives

17.8 Identify federal agencies, in addition to the Departments of State and Defense, that are involved in making and carrying out foreign and defense policies.

17.9 Describe the roles these departments play.

Bellringer Activity Ask students to name any movies involving the CIA that they have seen in the last two years. Then tell students that such "cloak and dagger" operations are a real part of American foreign and defense policies. Many other agencies besides the CIA also are involved with the nation's foreign affairs.

State the Purpose Dozens of agencies besides the Departments of State and Defense are involved in some way with defense and foreign policy. In Section 3, students will learn about five additional organizations that have significant impact in those two areas.

ABCNEWS INTERACTIVE

The following video segment may be used to highlight aspects of presidential roles.

POWERS OF THE PRESIDENT GUIDEBOOK
Chapter 37: Reserve Call-Up, p. 45

[Voc]abulary
[Poin]t out the "Key Term" on page 435. Tell [stud]ents that *conscription* is a synonym for "draft." LEP

Reading Strategy: Relating to Topic
Ask students to describe the benefits of the following items to any project (1) obtaining information, (2) having others on your side, (3) possessing technical know-how, and (4) having others obligated to help you. Explain that the Federal Government uses these advantages in defense and foreign policy.

INSTRUCT

Analyze/Discuss Explore with students the CIA's two distinctly different types of information-gathering activities. Explain the dichotomy between secret intelligence services and democracy. Ask: Why does this secrecy go against the principles of a democracy? Is it necessary?

Analyze the role of the USIA by comparing its activities with those of the CIA. (*The CIA gathers information from other countries, while the USIA distributes information in other countries.*) Explore NASA's role in defense. Ask whether NASA has a role in foreign policy that is different from its role in defense. Ask students whether and how they think space exploration can benefit "all humankind." Finally, discuss the goals of the U.S. Arms Control and Disarmament Agency and the Selective Service System. Discuss whether these two entities reinforce or contradict each other.

Question Have students write down one question about a part of the section that was unclear to them. Divide the class into groups of three or four to answer each student's question. Review questions and answers as a class, including any questions that the group could not answer.

The USIA is best known for the Voice of America. The VOA's round-the-clock radio programs are beamed in more than 40 languages to audiences all over the world.

The National Aeronautics and Space Administration

The modern space age is only some 35 years old. It began on October 4, 1957, when the Soviet Union put its first satellite, *Sputnik I*, in space. The first American satellite, *Explorer I*, was fired into orbit a few months later, on January 31, 1958. From that point on, a great number of space vehicles have been thrust into the heavens by both of the superpowers.

NASA is an independent agency created by Congress in 1958 to handle this nation's space programs. Today, the scope of those programs is truly extraordinary. NASA's work now ranges from basic research that focuses on the origin, evolution, and structure of the universe to explorations of outer space and the development of a permanently occupied space station to be deployed sometime in the latter 1990s.

Outer Space *Atlantis* lifts off from the Kennedy Space Center, Florida, in November 1991. NASA's space shuttle program carries out publicly and privately funded projects and top-secret military missions.

The military importance of NASA's work can hardly be exaggerated, but Congress has ordered the space agency to bend its efforts "to peaceful purposes for the benefit of all humankind," as well. NASA's research and development efforts have opened new frontiers in several fields: in astronomy, physics, and the environmental sciences, in communications, medicine, and weather forecasting, and in many more.

NASA conducts its operations at a number of flight centers, laboratories, and other installations throughout the country. Among the best known are the Kennedy Space Center, at Cape Canaveral in Florida; the Johnson Space Center, near Houston, Texas; the Ames Research Center and the Jet Propulsion Laboratory, both in California; and the Goddard Space Flight Center, at Greenbelt, Maryland.

Over the years, NASA's accomplishments were so many, its programs so successful, that space flights and space probes seemed to become almost routine. Tragedy struck on January 28, 1986, however. The space shuttle *Challenger* exploded moments after liftoff from Cape Canaveral, and all of its seven-member crew died.

NASA appears to have recovered from the disaster to the point where it now tries to launch as many as 10 space vehicles each year, some of them with secret military payloads. A new *Challenger* is expected to begin flying in 1992.

The United States Arms Control and Disarmament Agency

The USACDA is responsible for American participation in arms limitations and disarmament negotiations with other nuclear powers. Its director also serves as the principal adviser to the President, the National Security Council, and the secretaries of state and defense in all matters dealing with those policy areas.

Much of the agency's work has centered on nuclear test ban and arms limitations talks with the former Soviet Union. Those discussions

Enrichment

Divide the class into four groups and assign each group one of the following: the CIA, the USIA, NASA, and USACDA. One subgroup should locate the United States Government Manual and write down the address of the agency. A second subgroup should write a letter to the agency requesting information. A third subgroup should arrange the materials received for display on a bulletin board. (Average) were held periodically since the late 1950s, most often in Geneva, Switzerland. American-Soviet relations were at best unfriendly and most often hostile well into the late 1980s. Even so, the two superpowers managed to conclude several agreements.

The most recent major U.S.-Soviet arms agreement, the Strategic Arms Reduction Treaty (START), was signed by Presidents Bush and Gorbachev at a summit meeting in Moscow in 1991. That pact obligated both nations to destroy up to half of all their intercontinental ballistic missiles (ICBMs) over the ensuing seven years. The treaty was intended to be a step toward the eventual elimination of all missiles capable of delivering nuclear warheads over long distances.

The United States and the Soviet Union ratified the Intermediate Range Nuclear Force (INF) Treaty in 1988. That agreement called on both nations to eliminate *all* intermediate range missiles—those capable of delivering warheads 300 to 3,400 miles—and this goal had been achieved by 1992.

The successes of the 1980s and early 1990s assumed added importance with the breakup of the Soviet Union in late 1991 and the resulting potential for political turmoil in that region.

The Selective Service System

Through most of American history, the armed forces have depended on voluntary enlistments to fill their ranks. But from 1940 to 1973, the
1.a **draft**—conscription, compulsory military service—was a major source of military manpower. At present, the draft, which is administered by the Selective Service System, exists only on a standby basis.

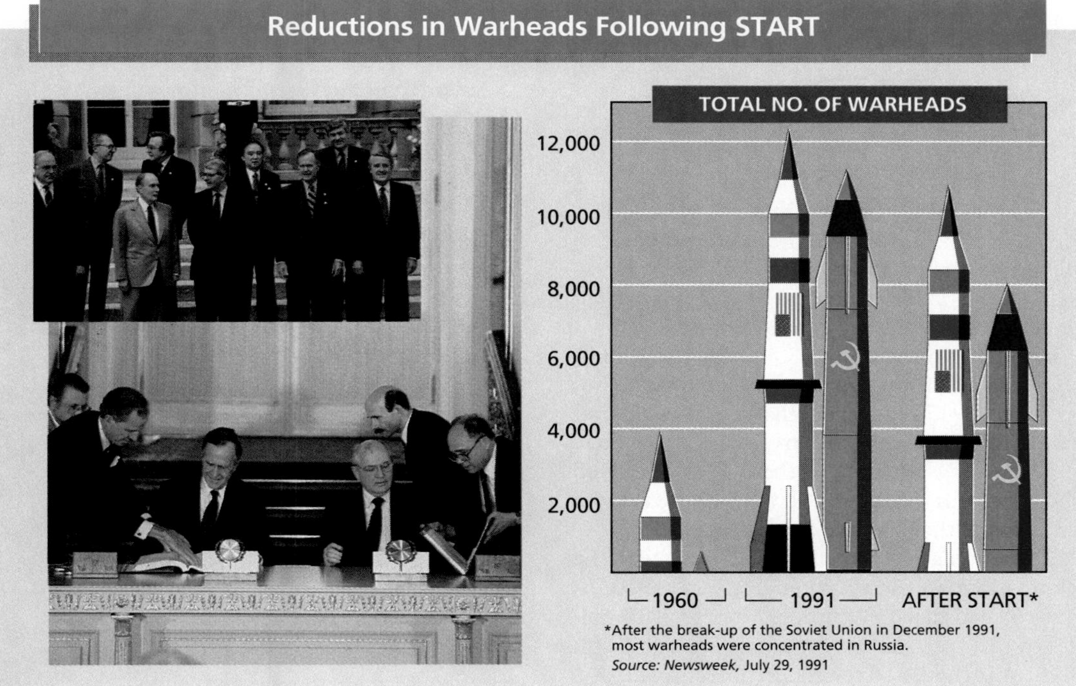

Interpreting Graphs START, ratified by President Bush and then Soviet President Gorbachev in July 1991, is an ambitious plan to phase out both countries' stocks of intercontinental ballistic missiles. World leaders (inset) were briefed on START when Bush visited London the same month. What does the graph show about the build-up of United States/Soviet warheads since 1960?

Interpreting Graphs Based on the information about START in the text, do students expect the number of warheads to increase, decrease, or stay the same in the 1990s? (*Decrease.*)

Caption Answer In 1960 the U.S. had 4,000 warheads, but the Soviet stock had just gotten off the ground; from 1960–1991, competition raised the U.S. stock to over 12,000 with the Soviets not far behind with about 11,000 warheads.

Provide Guided Practice
Make a list of key words such as espionage, Sputnik, Voice of America, START, and the draft. Write a word on the board and invite a student volunteer to identify the agency associated with that word and explain the association. After one round, have students find other key words in the text to present as clues to others.

Provide Independent Practice
TRF **Teacher's Resource File** You may wish to assign Section 3 Guided Reading and Review, Unit 4 File, p. 100, to help students master section objective content.

Teacher's Resource File
See Simulations and Debates: The Draft; Historical and Legal Documents, p. 47; and Comparative Government: A Multicultural View, pp. 8–9 for material to support this section.

Interpreting Charts Ask students: Do they think an all-volunteer army sufficient to defend the nation in times of war?

Caption Answer Females.

MONITOR COMPREHENSION

Answers to Section 3 Review
1. The "Key Term" is defined on the following page:
a. draft, p. 437
2. Many other agencies participate in foreign policy. **3.** (a) To communicate to the world America's official view of itself. (b) U.S. space programs, both military and civilian applications. (c) Participate in arms limitation and disarmament talks. **4.** Males 18 years old must register. **5.** Some students will insist upon complete openness. Others might say that the CIA is necessary to protect U.S. interests.

Teacher's Resource File See the Unit 4 File, p. 101, for the Section 3 Quiz.

CLOSURE

Remind students that many federal agencies are involved in foreign and defense policy. Besides the Departments of State and Defense, the CIA, USIA, NASA, USACDA, and the Selective Service are the agencies most directly involved in foreign policy and defense.

Assignment Assign Section 4, pages 440–447, for the next class period.

How to Register for the Draft

In 1980 the Selective Service System was reinstated. All eligible males must register for military service.

1. Determine whether you must register. All male citizens and aliens must register within 30 days after their 18th birthday. Exceptions include those already on active duty with the armed forces and nonimmigrant aliens.

2. Determine where you should go to register. You can register for the draft at any United States post office.

3. Complete a registration form. The form will ask for such information as your name, address, sex, date of birth, social security number, and current telephone number.

4. Date and sign the form in the presence of a clerk at the post office. Be sure to use ink on the form.

Interpreting Charts This chart goes through the steps necessary to register for military service. Which major segment of the population is not included in the draft?

Conscription has a long history in this country. Several colonies and later nine States required all able-bodied males to serve in their militia. However, in the 1790s Congress rejected proposals for national compulsory military service.

Both the North and the South did use a limited conscription program in the Civil War. It was not until 1917, however, that a national draft was first used in this country, even in wartime. More than 2.8 million of the 4.7 million men who served in World War I were drafted under the terms of the Selective Service Act of 1917.

The nation's first peacetime draft came with the Selective Service and Training Act of 1940, as World War II raged in Europe. More than 10 million of the 16.3 million Americans in uniform in World War II entered the service under that law.

The World War II draft was ended in 1947. The crises of the postwar period, however, quickly moved Congress to revive the draft with the Selective Service Act of 1948. From 1948 to 1973, nearly 5 million young men were drafted.

Mounting criticisms of compulsory military service, fed by opposition to Vietnam policy, led many Americans to call for an end to the draft in the late 1960s. Fewer than 30,000 men were drafted in 1972, and selective service was suspended in 1973. The draft law is still on the books, however.

The draft law places a military obligation on all males in the United States between the ages of 18 1/2 and 26. Over the years in which the draft operated, it was largely conducted through hundreds of local selective service boards. All young men had to register for service at age 18. The local boards then selected those who were to enter the armed forces.

As of 1980, the registration requirement was back in place. President Carter reactivated it, and his executive order is still in force. All young males are required to sign up soon after they reach their 18th birthday.[10]

Section 3 Review

1. Identify: draft
2. Why is it incorrect to view national security policy only in terms of the President and the State and Defense departments?
3. What is the primary function of each of these governmental agencies: (a) the USIA? (b) NASA? (c) USACDA?
4. What is the status of the selective service system today?

Critical Thinking

5. Checking Consistency (p. 19) Is the concept of an intelligence agency whose actions can be kept secret from the people consistent with the principle of popular sovereignty?

[10]The President's power to order the induction of men into the armed forces expired on June 30, 1973. If the draft is ever to be reactivated, Congress must first renew that presidential authority. Recall that the Supreme Court first upheld the constitutionality of the draft in the *Selective Draft Law Cases* in 1918. The Court also found its all-male features constitutional in *Rotsker* v. *Goldberg* in 1981; see pages 521, 555.

Reteach
Have students write riddles in the first person as the representative of one of the five agencies discussed in the section. Each riddle should convey the purpose and one or more activities of the agency. Have students exchange papers and guess the answers to each other's riddles.

SPOTLIGHT ON: Multiculturalism
The Vietnam experience also demonstrated the racial and class inequalities of the draft. Deferments were often granted based on college attendance, which resulted in more deferments for white, middle-class youths. Assignments once in the service were made in part on the basis of education. Thus, minorities were vastly over-represented among frontline troops and suffered almost 50% of all U.S. ground casualties. African Americans made up 12% of the troops in Vietnam but accounted for 20% of all combat deaths. Hispanic losses were even higher: one of every two Hispanics in Vietnam saw combat; one in five Hispanics in Vietnam was killed; and one in every in three was wounded.

Helping Victims of Natural Disasters

On December 7, 1988, a devastating earthquake struck the Soviet Republic of Armenia. In the days following, aftershocks continued to terrify the local population. The official death toll was estimated to be about 40,000; as many as 400,000 Armenian men, women, and children were left homeless amid the twisted rubble of crumbled buildings. The only possible good that could be gleaned from this massive tragedy was the selfless outpouring of aid that flooded into the Soviet Union from around the world.

International Relief Efforts

As the United States government responded immediately with offers of medicine, medical equipment, doctors, and trained rescue teams, United States citizens of all ages amassed money, clothing, and other supplies under the auspices of the American Red Cross. The Red Cross is an organization whose goal is to relieve human suffering. It has chapters in the United States and in more than 135 countries around the world. Based in Washington, D.C., the work of the American Red Cross depends on more than 10 million volunteers, including students, veterans, and senior citizens. In Glendale, California, a relief group collected $7 million in pledges. Equally significant, students of a school in California sent $800—the money for their school lunches. Relief aid also poured in from churches, synagogues, and colleges, as well as many private organizations.

A New Era

Two months after the earthquake, an article by Soviet citizen Anna Lerina appeared in *Soviet Life*. Through this medium, she expressed some thoughts and feelings concerning the help that came from American citizens: "For the first time since the Second World War, the Soviet Union accepted humanitarian aid from the government of the United States. The unprecedented bridge of relief aid to Armenia that has spanned thousands of miles and many years of mistrust serves as another confirmation that the United States and the Soviet Union can live in peace and friendship."

By the end of 1991 the Soviet Republic of Armenia was an independent nation. The optimism and words of friendship expressed by the Soviet woman in *Soviet Life* were reinforced when the United States was prompt in officially recognizing Armenian independence. It is one of seven new republics that marked the demise of the Soviet Union and the beginning of a new world order.

Getting Involved

1. Identify a need in your global or local community similar to the one addressed in this case. Or, identify an organization in your global or local community that helps victims of natural disasters.
2. Formulate a plan for organizing volunteer efforts to help remedy this problem and identify resources which could be used in your plan. Or, formulate a plan for the organization you have chosen to help.
3. Predict any problems or objections you might encounter in implementing your plan.

TEACHING

What You Can Do

Helping Victims of Natural Disasters

Objective

Identify a need in the local or global community and determine what can be done to help.

INSTRUCT

Ask if any students have ever been or known someone who was a victim of a natural disaster. If not, ask if they have read or heard about any natural disaster occurring in recent months. Ask students to brainstorm ways in which to help these victims. Then tell students that they will read about a natural disaster halfway around the world and how American citizens were able to help.

Below are some possible questions for post-reading discussion:

- What would it take for students to get involved in a disaster relief program?
- What kind of fundraisers could the school hold to raise money for disaster relief?
- How could students raise awareness about an area in need of relief?

TRF **Teacher's Resource File**
See Participatory Government Activities, pp. 28–39, for materials to support this section.

SECTION 4
American Foreign Policy: Past and Present

FOCUS

Teacher's Resource File
See the Unit 4 File, p. 102, for the Section 4 Outline.

Objectives

17.10 Describe U.S. foreign policy for its first 150 years.
17.11 Identify the basic elements of American foreign policy today.
17.12 Explain the impact of the cold war on American foreign policy.

Bellringer Activity Ask students to imagine that a friend of theirs has been consistently bullied by another class member. What should they do? If their answer is to defend their friend, then they have made the same decision made by the United States government in response to Soviet aggression.

State the Purpose Until World War I, American foreign policy was largely concerned with protecting the economic interests and security of the United States. Soviet aggression after World War II prompted a shift to internationalism. In Section 4, students will learn how the cold war changed the face of American foreign policy.

ABCNEWS INTERACTIVE

The following video segment may be used to highlight aspects of presidential roles.

POWERS OF THE PRESIDENT GUIDEBOOK
Chapter 29: Making Treaties, p. 37

4 American Foreign Policy: Past and Present

Find Out:

- What was United States foreign policy for its first 150 years?
- What are the basic elements of American foreign policy today?
- What was the impact of the cold war on American foreign policy?

Key Terms:

collective security, deterrence, containment

Why should you know as much as you can about history? Let a leading historian answer the question: "History is our social memory. Our memories tell us who we are, where we belong, what has worked and what has not worked, and where we seem to be going."[11]

A complete history of America's foreign relations cannot be told in these pages, of course. But you will find a review of the major themes and highlights of that history here.

Foreign Policy from Independence Through WWI

As you read in Section 1, American foreign policy was largely built on a policy of isolationism for its first 150 years. At the time, isolationism seemed a wise policy to most Americans. The United States had a great many problems of its own, a huge continent to explore and settle, and two oceans to separate it from the rest of the world. That policy did not demand a complete separation, however. From the first, the United States developed economic and diplomatic ties abroad. In fact, isolationism was, over time, more a statement of America's desire for noninvolvement outside the Western Hemisphere than within it.

[11]Robert Kelly, *The Shaping of the American Past* (Englewood Cliffs, New Jersey: Prentice Hall, 1978) 2nd ed., page xxxiii.

The Monroe Doctrine James Monroe gave the policy of isolationism a wider shape in 1823. In an historic message to Congress, he proclaimed what has been known ever since as the Monroe Doctrine. In his message, President Monroe restated America's intentions to stay out of the affairs of Europe. He also warned the nations of Europe—including Russia, then in control of Alaska—to stay out of the affairs of North and South America. He declared that the United States would look on

> "any attempt on their part to extend their system to any portion of this hemisphere as dangerous to our peace and safety."

At first, most Latin Americans took little notice of the doctrine. They knew that it was really the Royal Navy and British interest in their trade that protected them from European domination. Later, as the United States became more powerful, many Latin Americans came to view the doctrine as a selfish policy designed to protect American interests, not their independence.

Continental Expansion By the Treaty of Paris, which officially ended the Revolutionary War in 1783, the United States held title to all of the territory from the Great Lakes in the north to Spanish Florida in the south and from the Atlantic coast westward to the Mississippi.

The United States began to fill out the continent almost at once. President Jefferson negotiated the Louisiana Purchase in 1803, and at a single stroke, the nation's size was doubled. With the Florida Purchase in 1819, the nation completed its expansion to the south.

Through the second quarter of the 19th century, the United States pursued what most Americans believed was this nation's "Manifest Destiny": the expansion of its boundaries to the Pacific Ocean. Texas was annexed in 1845. The United States obtained the Oregon Country by treaty with Great Britain in 1846. Mexico ceded what today makes up most of the southwestern quarter of the lower 48 states after its defeat in the Mexican War of 1846–1848. The southwestern limits of the United States were rounded out by the Gadsden Purchase in 1853. In 1867 the United States bought Alaska from Russia and so became a colonial power.

Reading Strategy: Reinforcing Key Ideas

Have students write down the "Key Terms" on page 440. As they read Section 4, ask students to explain how these terms reflect American foreign policy from World War II to the present.

Vocabulary

Point out "Key Terms" on page 440 to the students. Many students may think of the word *contain* in *containment* as meaning "hold or include." Ask students what *containment* might mean if the word *contain* is taken to mean "hold back" or "hold in," and how the word then might be relevant to foreign policy. LEP

The United States, a World Power The United States emerged as a first-class power in world politics with the Spanish-American War in 1898. With Spain's decisive defeat, America gained the Philippines and Guam in the Pacific and Puerto Rico in the Caribbean. Cuba became independent, under American protection. Hawaii was also annexed in 1898.

By 1900, the United States had become a colonial power with interests extending across the continent, to Alaska, to the tip of Latin America, and across the Pacific to the Philippines.

The Good Neighbor Policy The threat of European intervention, which gave rise to the Monroe Doctrine, declined in the last half of the 19th century. That threat was replaced by problems within the hemisphere. Political instability, revolutions, unpaid foreign debts, and injuries to citizens and property of other countries plagued Central and South America.

Under what came to be known as the Roosevelt Corollary to the Monroe Doctrine, the United States began to police Latin America in the early 1900s. Several times, the marines were used to quell revolutions and other unrest in Nicaragua, Haiti, Cuba, and elsewhere.

In 1903 Panama revolted and became independent of Colombia, with American blessings. In the same year, the United States gained the right to build a canal across the isthmus. In 1917 the Virgin Islands were purchased from Denmark to help guard the canal. These and other steps were resented by many in Latin America. They complained of "the Colossus of the North," of "Yankee imperialism," and of "dollar diplomacy" (and many still do).

This country's Latin American policies took an important turn in the 1930s. Theodore Roosevelt's Corollary was replaced by Franklin Roosevelt's Good Neighbor Policy, a conscious attempt to win friends to the south.

The central provision of the Monroe Doctrine—the warning against foreign encroachments—is now set out in the Inter-American Treaty of Reciprocal Assistance (the Rio Pact) of 1947. Still, the United States is, without question, the dominant power in the Western Hemisphere, and the Monroe Doctrine is still a vital part of American foreign policy. The American invasions of Grenada in 1983 and of Panama in 1989 underscored that point.

"Yankee Imperialism" The Panama Canal, built by the United States as a shorter trade route to the Pacific, opened in 1914. Many Latin American nations resented the presence of the United States in the region.

The Open Door in China Historically, American foreign policy interests have centered on Europe and on Latin America. America's involvements in the Far East reach back to the mid-1800s, however. Forty-five years before the United States acquired territory in the far Pacific, the navy's Commodore Matthew Perry had opened Japan to American trade.

By the latter years of the 19th century, America's thriving trade in Asia was seriously threatened. The British, French, Germans, and Japanese were each ready to take slices of the Chinese coast as their own exclusive trading preserves. In 1899 Secretary of State John Hay announced this country's insistence on an Open Door Policy. That doctrine promoted equal trade access for all nations and a demand that China's independence and sovereignty over its own territory be preserved.

INSTRUCT

Explore Explore reasons for the Monroe Doctrine, and whether or not students think the Monroe Doctrine went against Washington's and Jefferson's warnings against alliances. Also have students summarize the reactions of Latin American countries to the Monroe Doctrine.

Discuss Discuss the territorial expansion of the United States by having students make time lines showing the dates when various territories were acquired by the United States.

Discuss the sequence of policies including the Monroe Doctrine, Roosevelt Corollary, Good Neighbor Policy, and the policies of collective security, containment, and deterrence by having students summarize each policy. You might wish to make up two sets of index cards, one set with the names of foreign policies, the other with a brief statement of the threat those policies were intended to counter. Have students match the names of the policies with the threats or problems with which they are associated.

Analyze with students the significance of wars with respect to changes in foreign policy. Have students compare the United States' reasons for entering the Spanish-American War and World Wars I and II, and the foreign policy that followed those wars.

TRF **Teacher's Resource File**
See Historical and Legal Documents, pp. 20, 26; and Comparative Government: A Multicultural View, pp. 12–13, for materials to support this section.

Interpreting Poster Art Caption Answer This poster preys on the sense of gratitude and obligation felt by recent immigrants to the country.

The other major powers came to accept the American position, however reluctantly. Relations between the United States and Japan worsened from that point on until the climax at Pearl Harbor in 1941. Over the same period, the United States built increasingly strong ties with China; but those ties were cut when communists won control of the Chinese mainland in 1949. For nearly 30 years, the United States and the People's Republic of China refused to recognize one another.

The realities of world politics finally forced a reshaping of American-Chinese relations in the 1970s. President Nixon made an historic visit to Beijing in 1972, and full-fledged diplomatic ties were reestablished in 1979.

Still, the People's Republic is a totalitarian state, and American policy reflects that fact—though many argue that it does not do so strongly enough. The Chinese government's brutal response to prodemocracy demonstrations by thousands of students in Beijing's Tiananmen Square in 1989 will likely color American-Chinese relations for years to come.

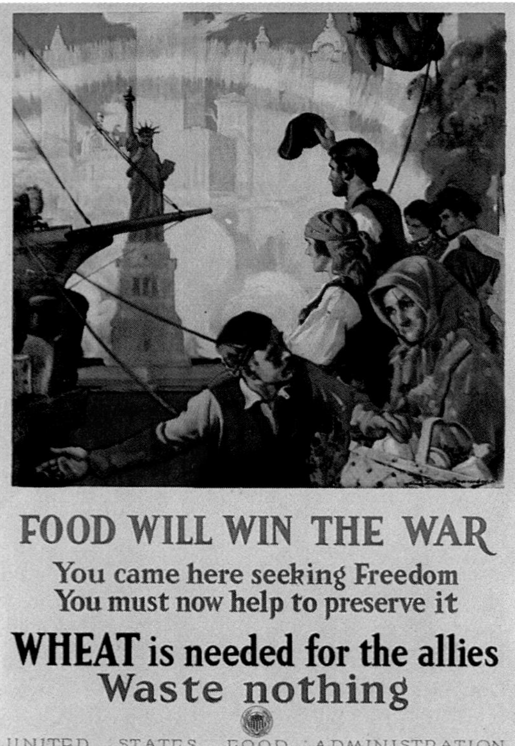
FOOD WILL WIN THE WAR
You came here seeking Freedom
You must now help to preserve it
WHEAT is needed for the allies
Waste nothing
UNITED STATES FOOD ADMINISTRATION

Poster Art World War I launched the era of the propaganda poster. What technique does this poster use to convince Americans to save for the war effort?

The Two World Wars

Germany's submarine campaign against American shipping in the North Atlantic forced the United States out of its isolationist cocoon in 1917. America entered World War I "to make the world safe for democracy."

With the defeat of Germany and the Central Powers, however, this nation pulled back from the involvements brought on by the war. The United States refused to join the League of Nations, which had been conceived by President Woodrow Wilson. Briefly, the nation returned to its historical isolationism.

America's commitment to isolationism was finally ended by World War II. The United States became directly involved in the war when the Japanese suddenly attacked Pearl Harbor on December 7, 1941. From that point on, together with the British, the Soviets, the Chinese, and other allies, this country waged an all-out effort to defeat the Axis Powers (Germany, Italy, and Japan). America supplied most of the materials that were essential to victory. Within a short time, the United States was transformed into the world's mightiest military power.

Foreign Policy from 1945 to Today

World War II led to an historic shift from a position of isolationism to one of internationalism. This nation's foreign policy has been cast in that newer direction for nearly 50 years now. Even so, the overall objective of that policy remains what it has always been: the protection of the security of the United States. The major features of current American foreign policy are all, as you will see, reflections of that overriding goal.

Peace Through Collective Security The United States, and most of the rest of a war-weary world, looked to the principle of

ACTIVITY: Cooperative Learning
Time: Two class periods **Activity:** Create a chart of major events in the diplomatic history of the United States. **Grouping:** Groups of four to six students **Purpose:** Using information in the chapter, have students develop a chart summarizing, in chronological order, the important events in the history of America's foreign relations. **Roles:** Have students assign the following roles: manager, recorder. **Outcome:** Have groups refer to their chart as you lead the class in a discussion of the important consequences of each event described in the chapter.

collective security to keep international 1.a peace and order after World War II. That is, America hoped to forge a world community in which all or at least most nations would agree to act together against any nation that threatened the peace.

To that end, the United States took the lead in creating the United Nations in 1945. The organization's charter declares that the UN was formed to promote international cooperation and so "to save succeeding generations from the scourge of war . . . and to maintain international peace and security"; see pages 450–453.

It soon became clear that the future of the world would not be shaped in the UN alone, however. Rather, international security would depend largely on the nature of the relations between the two superpowers, the United States and the Soviet Union. These relations, never very close, quickly deteriorated—and for the next 40 years American foreign policy was built around that fact.

Relations between the superpowers have improved dramatically in recent years. Still, collective security remains a cornerstone of American policy. The United States has supported the United Nations and other efforts to further international cooperation. And, because the UN did not immediately fulfill the dreams on which it was founded, the United States soon took another path to collective security—a network of regional alliances, as you will see.

The principle of collective security was at work in the 1991 Persian Gulf War, too. The United States led the diplomatic and then the military effort to force Iraq to withdraw from Kuwait—an effort supported by the United Nations and nearly all of its member states.

Deterrence The policy of deterrence is another major plank of current American foreign policy. It was begun under President Truman, as the antagonisms between the United States and the Soviet Union grew after World War II. Every President since has maintained it. **Deterrence** is the policy of making the country 1.b and its allies so militarily strong that its very strength will deter (discourage, prevent) any attack. As President Bush has said, "Weakness tempts aggressors. Strength stops them."

Resisting Soviet Aggression

One cannot hope to understand either recent or current American foreign policy without a grounding in the long years of the cold war—the more than 40 years in which relations between the two superpowers were at least tense and, more often than not, distinctly hostile.

The United States had planned to work with the Soviet Union, particularly through the UN, to build international cooperation and keep the peace in the postwar world. Those plans were quickly dashed, however.

At the Yalta Conference in early 1945, Soviet Premier Josef Stalin had agreed with President Franklin Roosevelt and British Prime Minister Winston Churchill that "democratic governments" would be established by "free elections" in the liberated countries of Eastern Europe. Instead, the Soviets imposed communist governments on those countries.

As they devoured Eastern Europe, the Soviets also attempted to take over the oil fields of Iran, to the south. At the same time, the Soviets supported communist guerrillas in a civil war in Greece. And, pursuing the historic Russian dream of a "window to the sea," they demanded military and naval bases in Turkey.

The Truman Doctrine and Containment

The United States began to counter the Soviet Union's aggressive actions in the early months of 1947. The Truman Doctrine marked the first step in that long-standing process. Both Greece and Turkey were in danger of falling under the Soviet Union's control. At President Harry Truman's urgent request, Congress approved a massive program of economic and military aid, and both countries were saved. In his message to Congress, the President declared that it was now

> "the policy of the United States to support free peoples who are resisting subjugation by armed minorities or outside pressures."

The Truman Doctrine soon became part of a broader American plan for dealing with the Soviet Union. From mid-1947 on through the 1980s the United States followed the policy of
1.c **containment**. That policy was rooted in the

INSTRUCT

Compare Explore with students the impact of the end of the cold war on American foreign policy. Have students compare and contrast the policy of *détente* with the policy of isolationism. Ask students: How has the role of the United States in the world community changed since the early 1800s?

TRF **Teacher's Resource File**
See Historical and Legal Documents, p. 28, for materials to support this section.

belief that if communism could be contained within its existing boundaries it would collapse under the weight of its internal weaknesses.

The United States and the Soviet Union confronted one another often during the cold war years. Two of those confrontations were of major, near-war proportions: in Berlin in 1948–1949 and in Cuba in 1962. And, during that same time, the United States fought two wars against communist forces in Asia.

The Berlin Blockade At the end of World War II, the city of Berlin, surrounded by Soviet-occupied East Germany, was divided into four sectors. One sector, East Berlin, was controlled by the Soviet Union. The other three sectors, comprising West Berlin, were occupied by the United States, Britain, and France.

In 1948 the Soviets tried to force their former allies to withdraw from West Berlin. They clamped a land blockade around the city, stopping the shipment of food and supplies to the western sectors. The United States mounted a massive airlift that kept the city alive until the blockade was lifted, a year and a half after it had begun.

Executive Action: 1962 Shortly after he ordered the removal of Soviet missiles from Cuba, President Kennedy inspected military installations at Key West, off the Florida coast.

The Cuban Missile Crisis The United States and the Soviet Union came perilously close to a nuclear conflict during the Cuban missile crisis in 1962.

Cuba had slipped into the Soviet orbit soon after Fidel Castro gained power there in 1959. By mid-1962, huge quantities of Soviet arms and thousands of Soviet "technicians" had been sent to Cuba. Suddenly, in October, the build-up became unmistakably offensive in character. Aerial photographs revealed the presence of several Soviet missiles capable of nuclear strikes against this country and much of Latin America.

Immediately, President Kennedy ordered a naval blockade of Cuba to prevent the delivery of any more missiles. Cuba and the Soviet Union were warned that the United States would attack Cuba unless the existing Soviet missiles were removed.

After several tense days, the Soviets backed down. Rather than risk all so far from home, they returned the weapons to the Soviet Union.

The Korean War The Korean War began on June 25, 1950. South Korea (the UN-sponsored Republic of Korea) was attacked by communist North Korea (the People's Democratic Republic of Korea). Immediately, the UN's Security Council called on all UN members to help South Korea repel the invasion.

The war lasted for more than three years. It pitted the United Nations Command, largely made up of American and South Korean forces, against Soviet-trained and -equipped North Korean and communist Chinese troops. A cease-fire agreement was signed in July 1951, but fighting continued until an armistice was signed on July 27, 1953. Final peace terms have never been agreed to.

The long and bitter Korean conflict did not end in a clear-cut UN victory. The war cost the United States 157,530 casualties, including 33,629 combat dead, and more than $20 billion. South Korea's military and civilian casualties ran into the hundreds of thousands, and much of Korea, north and south, was laid to waste.

Still, the invasion was turned back, and the Republic of Korea was saved. Perhaps more importantly, for the first time in history, armed forces fought under an international flag against aggression. There is no telling how far that

SPOTLIGHT ON: Behind the Scenes

During the height of the Cuban missile crisis, President Kennedy put the chance of nuclear war between the United States and the Soviet Union at "between one-in-three and fifty-fifty." Teetering on the brink of confrontation gave pause to both sides, and the missile crisis resulted in the cold war's first strategic arms limitation treaty, the Atmospheric Test Ban. Both sides agreed to cease testing nuclear weapons above ground, thus limiting nuclear fallout. A "hot line" linking the White House and Kremlin by telephone was set up so that the leaders would be able to speak directly to one another in the event of a crisis.

aggression might have carried had the United States not come to the aid of South Korea.

The War in Vietnam In the years following World War II, a Vietnamese nationalist movement, seeking independence from France and made up mostly of communist forces led by Ho Chi Minh, fought and defeated the French in a lengthy conflict. Under truce agreements signed at Geneva in 1954, what had been French Indochina was divided into two zones: a communist-dominated North Vietnam, with its capital in Hanoi, and an anticommunist South Vietnam, based in Saigon.

Almost at once, communist guerrillas (the Viet Cong), supported by North Vietnamese, began a civil war in South Vietnam. The Eisenhower administration responded with economic and then military aid to Saigon. This aid was increased by President Kennedy. But, even with stepped-up U.S. support to South Vietnam, the Viet Cong—and growing numbers of North Vietnamese supplied with mostly Soviet and some Chinese weapons—continued to make major gains.

It was President Johnson who, in early 1965, committed the United States to full-scale war. By 1968, more than 540,000 Americans were involved in a fierce ground and air conflict.

In 1969, President Nixon began what he called the "Vietnamization" of the war. Over the next four years, American troops were pulled out of combat. Finally, a cease-fire agreement was signed in early 1973, and the last American units were withdrawn. (In spite of the cease-fire, the war between North and South Vietnam went on. By 1975, South Vietnam had been overrun, and the two Vietnams became the Socialist Republic of Vietnam.)

The ill-fated war in Vietnam cost the United States a staggering $200 billion and, irreplaceably, more than 57,000 American lives. In addition, the war caused many to lose faith in the workings of the American political system.

Détente and the Return to Containment

As the United States withdrew from Vietnam, the Nixon administration embarked on a policy of *détente*. The term is French, meaning "a relaxation of tensions." The policy included a purposeful attempt to improve relations with the Soviet Union and, separately, with China.

Lest We Forget Americans were deeply divided by the war in Vietnam. This granite memorial in Washington, D.C., is meant to be a national symbol of healing and forgiveness.

Provide Guided Practice
Draw a time line on the board including the following dates: 1823, 1898, 1899, 1903, 1917, 1941, 1945, 1947, 1948, 1949, 1950, 1962, 1965, 1968, 1969, 1972, 1979, 1983, 1985, 1987 1989, and 1991. Then, using the text, ask students to indicate the importance of each of these dates as you write their responses on the board. Invite student volunteers to point out on a wall map areas of the world that have been the focus of United States foreign policy, beginning with the Monroe Doctrine.

Provide Independent Practice
TRF **Teacher's Resource File** You may wish to assign Section 4 Guided Reading and Review, Unit 4 File, p. 103, to help students master section objective content.

Enrichment

Have students choose one of the leaders mentioned in the section. Then ask them to write a speech that may have been given by that leader on one of the dates from the "Provide Guided Practice" activity. The speech might be made by an American or foreign leader and should in some way address foreign policy issues. (Challenging)

Interpreting Graphs Point out that funds may be allocated to defense spending without appearing in a country's budget.

Caption Answer No. Example: Brazil, with the lowest percentage, was until recently under military dictatorship.

Monitor Comprehension

Answers to Section 4 Review
1. "Key Terms" are defined on the following pages:
- **a.** collective security, p. 443
- **b.** deterrence, p. 443
- **c.** containment, p. 443

2. The nation was not strong. **3.** Monroe Doctrine demanded Western Hemisphere be free of European intervention. Roosevelt Corollary expanded U.S. role to police force for the region. FDR's Good Neighbor Policy aimed for better relations. **4.** Ended America's isolationist impulses; established the U.S. as a world power; saw introduction of collective security; beginning of cold war. **5.** Soviet takeover of Eastern Europe, Berlin Blockade, Korean War, Vietnam War, détente, return to cooler relations. **6.** U.S. has friendlier relations with former Soviet nations.

Closure

World War II made it clear that the United States could not exist in isolation. As students read the next section, they will focus on three important aspects of present-day United States foreign policy.

Assignment Assign Section 5, pages 447–453, for the next class period.

Global Awareness

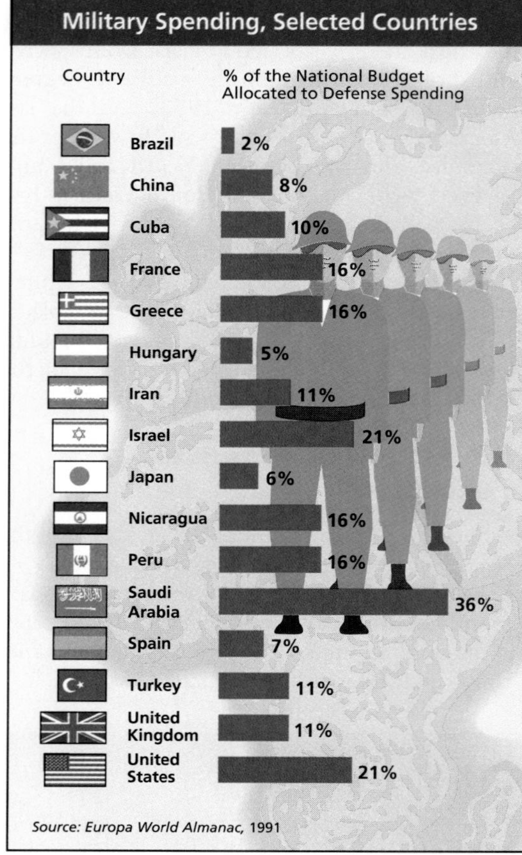

Interpreting Graphs This graph shows the percentage of the national budget allocated to defense spending in various countries. Since the chart lacks political and economic information, can you safely conclude that nations that spend the most for defense are the most militaristic? Why, or why not?

President Nixon flew to Beijing in 1972 to begin a new era in American-Chinese relations. His visit paved the way to further contacts and, finally, to formal diplomatic ties between the United States and the People's Republic.

Less than three months later, Nixon journeyed to Moscow. There, he and Soviet Premier Leonid Brezhnev signed the first Strategic Arms Limitations Talks agreement, SALT. It was a five-year pact in which both sides agreed to a measure of control over their nuclear weapons.

Relations with mainland China have improved fairly steadily since the 1970s. Efforts at détente with the Soviets, however, proved less successful. Moscow continued to apply its expansionist pressures and provided economic and military aid to revolutionary movements around the world.

The short-lived period of détente ended altogether when the Soviets invaded Afghanistan in 1979. From that point, first the Carter and then the Reagan administration placed a renewed emphasis on containing Soviet power.

The End of the Cold War

Relations between the United States and the Soviet Union improved remarkably after Mikhail Gorbachev gained power in Moscow in 1985. By the 1990s, the cold war had ended.

Presidents Reagan and Gorbachev paved the way to the end of the cold war at four summit conferences. They met first in Geneva in 1985, and then in Reykjavik, Iceland, in 1986, in Washington in 1987, and in Moscow in 1988. Those meetings helped ease longstanding tensions, and they produced a major disarmament pact, the INF Treaty in 1987.

President Bush met with the Soviet leader at Malta in late 1989, in Washington in 1990, and in Washington, London, and Moscow in 1991. Those meetings reaffirmed the friendlier American-Soviet environment. They also produced commitments from both sides to eliminate a portion of their long-range nuclear missiles, to cut stockpiles of chemical weapons, and to reduce the levels of conventional forces.

Clearly, Mikhail Gorbachev deserves a large share of the credit for the fundamental change in the Soviets' approach to world affairs. However, another key factor has been the economic and political chaos that ultimately brought the collapse of the Soviet Union itself in 1991. You will read more about these critical developments in chapters 22 and 23.

The historic fact that the cold war is at long last over can and should be seen in this light: The American policy of containment, first put in place in 1947, finally realized its goal.

TRF **Teacher's Resource File**
See the Unit 4 File, p. 104, for the Section 4 Quiz.

Reteach

Have students draw a political cartoon or write a slogan to represent each stage or component of United States foreign policy, from the Monroe Doctrine through the end of the cold war.

VOICES *on Government*

General Colin L. Powell, chairman of the Joint Chiefs of Staff in the Bush administration

On United States Foreign Policy in a Changing World

"Now the task is keeping democracy alive, not fighting and containing communism. Now the task is helping the dozens of democracies that are just being born. Now the task is teaching the basics of government of the people, by the people, and for the people—to the people. Now the task, in the words of the playwright–turned-president [of Czechoslovakia] Vaclav Havel, is to continue 'approaching democracy'—to do so with hundreds of thousands of new recruits."

Section 4 Review

1. Define: collective security, deterrence, containment

2. Why did the policy of isolationism make sense to the United States in its early years?

3. Briefly trace this nation's policy toward Latin America and the Western Hemisphere.

4. What decisive impact did World War II have on the shape of American foreign policy?

5. Briefly describe the major political and military events of the cold war.

Critical Thinking

6. Testing Conclusions (p. 19) The text states that "the American policy of containment . . . finally realized its goal." What evidence can you find to support this statement?

★

5 Foreign Aid, Defense Alliances, and the United Nations

Find Out:

- What are the purposes of foreign aid?
- Why does the United States maintain a network of regional security alliances?
- Why was the United Nations created?
- What are the UN's purposes, organization, and membership?

Key Terms:

foreign aid, regional security alliance, UN Security Council

Do you know this ancient saying: "Those who help others help themselves"? You will see that that maxim underlies two other and basic elements of present-day American foreign policy: foreign aid and security alliances.

Foreign Aid

1.a **Foreign aid**—economic and military aid to other countries—has been a basic feature of American foreign policy for more than 50 years now. It began with the Lend-Lease program of the early 1940s, in which the United States gave nearly $50 billion in food, munitions, and other supplies to its allies in World War II. Since then, American aid has totalled over $400 billion to more than 100 countries.

Foreign aid became a part of the containment policy with American aid to Greece and Turkey in 1947. Under the Marshall Plan, named for its author, Secretary of State George C. Marshall, the United States poured some $17 billion into 16 nations in Western Europe between 1948 and 1952.

Foreign aid policy has taken several directions over time. Immediately after World War II, American aid was primarily economic in form. Over the years since then, however, military assistance has assumed a large role in aid policy. Until the mid-1950s, Europe received the lion's share of American help. Since then,

Section 5
Foreign Aid, Defense Alliances, and the United Nations

Focus

Teacher's Resource File
See the Unit 4 File, p. 105, for the Section 5 Outline.

Objectives

17.13 State the purposes of foreign aid.
17.14 Explain why the United States maintains a network of regional security alliances.
17.15 Explain why the United Nations was created.
17.16 Describe the UN's purposes, organization, and membership.

Bellringer Activity Ask students whether they might donate money and time to help people in a nearby town that has been flooded. Ask whether it is then fair to expect something in return. Tell students that such interdependence and cooperation can be fostered among people as well as nations.

State the Purpose World War II and its aftermath saw the birth of three essential components of United States foreign policy: foreign aid, regional alliances, and the United Nations. In Section 5, students will learn the nature of these three foreign policy components and how they work.

Vocabulary

Point out "Key Terms" on page 447 to the students. Discuss the meaning of the word *security* as it applies to nations and ask students what might be the relationship between foreign policy and security.

Reading Strategy: Relating to Topic

Point out to students the ancient saying quoted on page 447: "Those who help others help themselves." As they read, have students jot down how American foreign aid and security alliances help the United States.

INSTRUCT

Discuss/Analyze Discuss the meaning of "internationalism" with students. Point out that an internationalist foreign policy is based on the belief that the security and economic well-being of the United States is closely tied to the security, stability, and prosperity of other nations. Therefore, we help ourselves by helping others.

Review with students the two types of foreign aid—i.e., economic and military aid. Draw students' attention to the fact that foreign aid went from primarily economic aid (to Europe under the Marshall Plan) toward an emphasis on military aid to Asia, Latin America, and the Middle East.

Discuss with students why the United States benefits directly from the foreign aid it gives. Be sure students understand from the text that most foreign aid money is used to purchase American products.

Discuss with students why the Middle East has posed particularly difficult problems for American foreign policy. You might wish to list events in the Middle East noted in the text on a time line on the board. Discuss with students why these events indicate a degree of unpredictability in that area.

Discuss the UN charter with students and review the organization of the United Nations. Invite students to find the names of the six principal organs of the UN and identify them as you list them on the board.

the largest amounts have gone to nations in Asia and Latin America.

On balance, most aid has been sent to those countries regarded as the most critical to the realization of this country's foreign policy objectives. Over the past 25 years, South Vietnam, Israel, and Taiwan have been the major recipients of military aid. India has received the most in economic assistance.

Most foreign aid money must be used to buy American goods and services. So, most of the billions spent for that aid amount to a substantial subsidy to both business and labor in this country. Most of the economic aid programs are administered by the independent Agency for International Development (AID), in close cooperation with the Departments of State and Agriculture. Most military aid is channeled through the Defense Department.

Security Through Alliances

Over the past four decades, the United States has constructed a network of **regional security** 1.b
alliances built on mutual defense treaties. In each of those treaties, the United States and the other countries involved have agreed to take collective action to meet aggression in a particular part of the world.

The North Atlantic Treaty, signed in 1949, established NATO, the 16-member North Atlantic Treaty Organization. The alliance was formed to promote the collective defense of Western Europe, particularly against the threat of Soviet aggression. Each member country has agreed that "an armed attack against one or more of them in Europe or in North America shall be considered an attack against them all."[12]

NATO was originally composed of the United States and 11 other countries: Canada, Great Britain, France, Italy, Portugal, the Netherlands, Belgium, Luxembourg, Denmark, Norway, and Iceland. Greece and Turkey joined the alliance in 1952, West Germany in 1955, and Spain in 1982. When East and West Germany united in 1990, that new state joined NATO.

NATO has been the cornerstone of American foreign policy in Europe ever since its creation. The end of the cold war has not diminished NATO's role. In 1991 the NATO Council reiterated the organization's mission in these words: "To deter and defend against any threat of aggression against the territory of any member state."

Other Alliances The Rio Pact, the Inter-American Treaty of Reciprocal Assistance, was signed in 1947. In it, the United States, Canada, and now 32 Latin American countries have agreed "that an armed attack by any state against an American state shall be considered as an attack against all the American states." The treaty pledges those countries to the mutual peaceful settlement of all disputes. In effect, the Rio Pact is a restatement of the Monroe Doctrine.

In addition to NATO and the Rio Pact, the United States is involved with a number of regional security alliances. For example, the ANZUS Pact of 1951 unites Australia, New Zealand, and the United States.

The Japanese Pact also dates from 1951. After six years of American military occupation, the allies of World War II (but not the Soviet Union) signed a peace treaty with Japan. At the same time, the United States and Japan signed a mutual defense treaty. In return for American protection, the United States is permitted to maintain land, sea, and air forces in and about Japan.

The Philippines Pact was also signed in 1951. The pact provides for a continuing American military presence in the Philippines, to guarantee that country's independence; but the terms of the agreement are now (1992) being redrawn. The Philippines Pact was followed in 1953 by the Korean Pact, which pledges this country to come to the aid of South Korea should it be attacked again.

The Taiwan Pact was in effect between the United States and Nationalist China from 1954 to 1980. The United States and the People's Republic of China established full diplomatic relations in 1979. At that time, the United States withdrew recognition of the Nationalist

[12]In answer to NATO, the Soviets formed the Warsaw Treaty Organization (the Warsaw Pact) in 1955. The Pact created a Moscow-based mutual defense alliance among Albania, Bulgaria, Czechoslovakia, East Germany, Hungary, Poland, Romania, and the Soviet Union. The Warsaw Pact did not survive the collapse of communism in the Soviet Union and Eastern Europe; it was formally dissolved in 1991.

TRF **Teacher's Resource File**
See Comparative Government: A Multicultural View, pp. 2–3, for materials to support this section.

SPOTLIGHT ON: Economics

The Rio Pact also left the U.S. the dominant power in the Hemisphere, and U.S. policymakers acted quickly to stifle perceived threats to U.S. interests in the region. For example, in 1952, elected President of Guatemala Jacobo Arbenz proposed land reforms including nationalization of some 400,000 acres of the United Fruit Company, a U.S. firm and the largest landholder in Guatemala. The company protested to Washington and, in 1953, the CIA recruited an opposition leader and small army to topple the Arbenz regime.

Chinese government; it also served the one-year notice required by the 1954 treaty to abrogate (end) that agreement.

The United States and the Middle East

The American network of regional alliances is far-reaching. It does not cover all of the globe, however—and most notably today, not the Middle East.

The Middle East is both oil-rich and conflict-ridden. America's foreign policy interests in the region have, for decades, been torn in two quite opposite directions: by its long-standing support of Israel, and by the critical importance of Arab oil.

Israel was established as an independent state by the United Nations in 1948. Carved out of what had been British-controlled Palestine, Israel has been in continuous conflict with its Arab neighbors. Some Arab nations and the Palestine Liberation Organization (PLO) have been committed to the destruction of Israel.

In spite of its support for Israel, the United States has made considerable efforts to promote friendly relations with most Arab states in the region.

With the active involvement of President Carter, Israel and Egypt negotiated a peace treaty, which became effective in 1979. That agreement, the Camp David Accord, ended more than 30 years of hostilities between those two countries. But no other Arab state would join that peace-building effort.

A new attempt to bring peace to the region was mounted by Secretary of State James Baker in 1991, and the Soviet Union joined the United

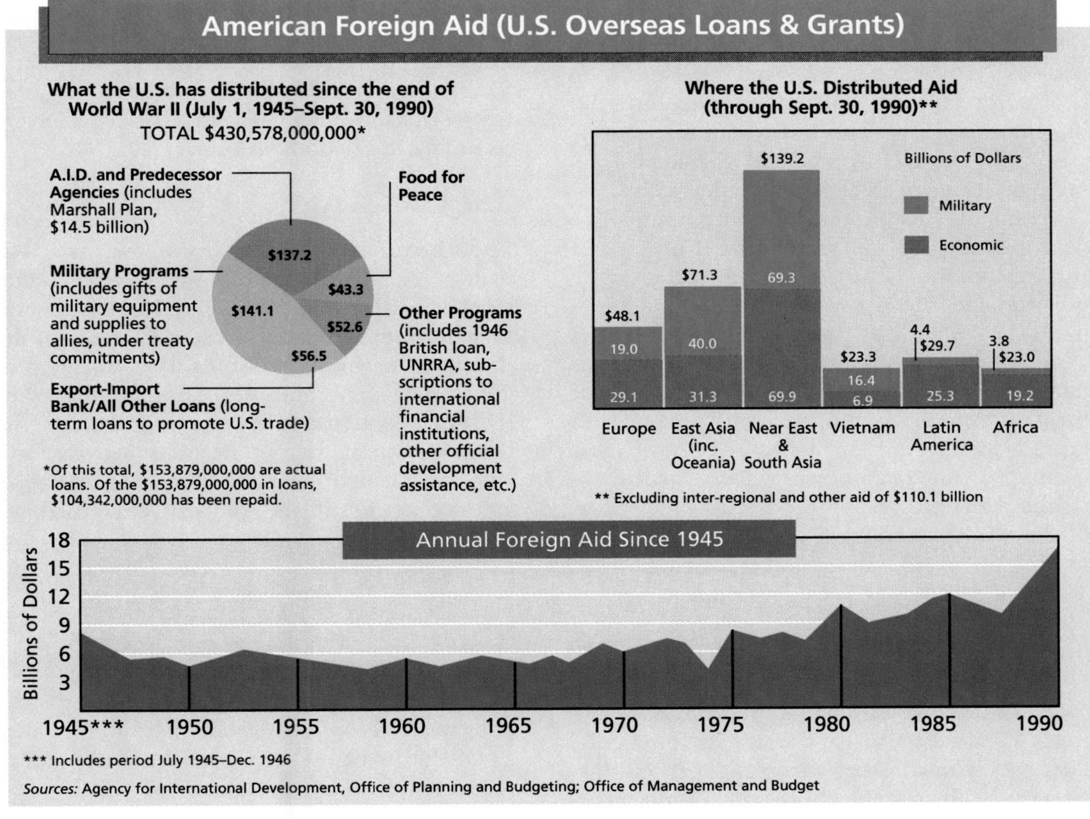

Interpreting Graphs According to the bar graphs above, which region(s) has (have) received the largest share of American foreign aid?

ABCNEWS INTERACTIVE

The following video segment may be used to highlight aspects of presidential roles.

POWERS OF THE PRESIDENT GUIDEBOOK
Chapter 11: Protector of the Peace, p. 71

Interpreting Graphs How does the graph support the text statement that "military assistance has assumed a large role in aid policy"? (*In the pie graph, "military programs" makes up the largest portion of aid.*)

Caption Answer Near East and South Asia.

INSTRUCT

Illustrate To demonstrate to students the striking change in American foreign policy during and after World War II, draw an outline that represents the United Nations on the board. To the left of the outline, write *Isolationism*. To the right of the outline, write *Internationalism*. Tell students that one evidence of the change in American foreign policy is this country's participation in the United Nations. Ask students why they think participation in the UN indicates a foreign policy of internationalism.

Debate Point out to students the five permanent members of the UN Security Council: the United States, Britain, France, Russia, and China. Remind students that, because of their individual veto power over resolutions of the council, these five countries bear the main responsibility for maintaining international peace. Ask students: Are these five nations representative of all of the countries of the world? Which regions of the world are not represented? What sort of conflicts or problems might this cause?

States in sponsoring what is hoped will be a continuing series of Arab-Israeli negotiations.

Since the late 1970s, many of America's problems in the Middle East have involved a non-Arab country, Iran. Iran has been fiercely anti-Western, and especially anti-American for more than a decade now. Iranian militants seized the American embassy in Teheran in late 1979, and 52 Americans were held hostage for more than a year. Through the 1980s the government of the Ayatollah Ruhollah Khomeini was quite apparently involved in several acts of terrorism in the Middle East and Europe. The Iranians were also implicated in the taking of several Americans and others as hostages in Lebanon.

In 1988, a UN-sponsored cease-fire halted the Iran–Iraq war. That conflict had begun in 1980, when Iraq's President Saddam Hussein ordered the Iraqi military to attack Iran. The long and bitter struggle threatened world access to Middle East oil—and prompted President Reagan to order the navy to escort oil tankers plying the perilous Persian Gulf in 1987 and 1988.

Saddam Hussein launched another invasion in August of 1990. This time, Iraqi forces overran small, oil-rich Kuwait and threatened the security of America's close ally, Saudi Arabia.

President Bush demanded the immediate withdrawal of Iraqi forces from Kuwait and the restoration of that country's legitimate government. He also ordered a huge deployment of American military might to the Persian Gulf region. That operation was code-named Desert Shield. By early 1991 it brought American troop strength in the Gulf region to more than 500,000—the largest massing of American power since Vietnam.

The American response was backed by most of the world community. A multinational (but mostly American) military force was established. The United Nations Security Council imposed economic sanctions on Iraq, hoping to bring a peaceful resolution to the crisis.

Iraq refused to withdraw from Kuwait, however; and its continued stubbornness finally triggered the Persian Gulf War. That brief conflict, code-named Desert Storm, began in mid-January with sustained air attacks on Iraqi positions. On February 24th, American, British, Saudi, and other allied forces commenced a massive ground attack that in just 100 hours drove Iraq's troops from Kuwait.

The United Nations

The decisive change in American foreign policy that occurred during and immediately after World War II is strikingly illustrated by this country's participation in the United Nations.

The United Nations was formed at the UN Conference on International Organization, which met in San Francisco from April 25 to June 26, 1945. There, the representatives of 51 nations—the victorious allies of World War II—drafted the United Nations Charter. The charter is a treaty among all of the UN's member-states, and it serves as the body's constitution.

The United States became the first nation to ratify the UN Charter. The Senate approved it by an overwhelming vote, 89–2, on July 24, 1945. The charter was then ratified in quick order by the other states that had taken part in the San Francisco Conference. The charter went into force on October 24, 1945, and the UN held its first formal meeting, a session of the General Assembly, in London, on January 10, 1946.

The UN Charter

The charter is a lengthy document. It opens with an eloquent preamble, which declares that the UN was created "to save succeeding generations from the scourge of war." The body of the document begins in Article I with a statement of the organization's purposes. They are the maintenance of international peace and security, the development of friendly relations between and among all nations, and the promotion of justice and cooperation in the solution of international problems.

Membership Today the UN has 166 members. Under the charter, membership is open to those "peace-loving states" that accept the obligations of the charter and are, in the UN's judgment, able and willing to carry out those obligations. New members may be admitted by a two-thirds vote of the General Assembly, upon recommendation by the Security Council.

Basic Organization The charter sets forth the complicated structure of the UN, built

ACTIVITY: For Gifted Students

Theme: Interdependence Because environmental issues are global and reflect the interdependence of our world, the United Nations Conference on Environment and Development (UNCED) has developed an "Earth Charter"—an outline for ecologically sound economic development. Have students develop a plan for the U.S. Environmental Security Agency using periodicals, interviews, scientific studies, etc. as resources to support their plan. These should include the agency organization, its goals, and strategies for work with other nations on interdependent environmental issues. Students may present an exhibit in the school library or a video presentation.

Teacher's Resource File
See Comparative Government: A Multicultural View, pp. 22–23, for materials to support this section.

around six "principal organs": the General Assembly, the Security Council, the Economic and Social Council, the Trusteeship Council, the International Court of Justice, and the Secretariat.

The General Assembly

The General Assembly has been called "the town meeting of the world." Each of the UN's members has a seat and a vote in the assembly.

The General Assembly meets once a year, normally in September. Most of its sessions are held at the UN's permanent headquarters in New York. Special sessions may be called by the secretary-general, either at the request of the Security Council or a majority of the UN members.

The assembly may take up and debate any matter within the scope of the charter,[13] and it may make whatever recommendation it chooses to the Security Council, the other UN organs, and any member-state. The recommendations it makes to UN members are not legally binding on them. Yet they do carry weight because they have been approved by a significant number of the governments of the world.

The assembly elects the 10 nonpermanent members of the Security Council, the 54 members of the Economic and Social Council, and the elective members of the Trusteeship Council. With the Security Council, the assembly also selects the secretary-general and the 15 judges of the International Court of Justice. The assembly also shares with the Security Council the power to admit, suspend, or expel members. It alone may propose amendments to the charter.

The Security Council

The **UN Security Council** is made up of 15 members. Five of them—the United States, Britain, France, Russia (the Soviet Union's old seat), and China—are permanent members.[14] The 10 nonpermanent members are chosen by the General Assembly for two-year terms; they 1.c

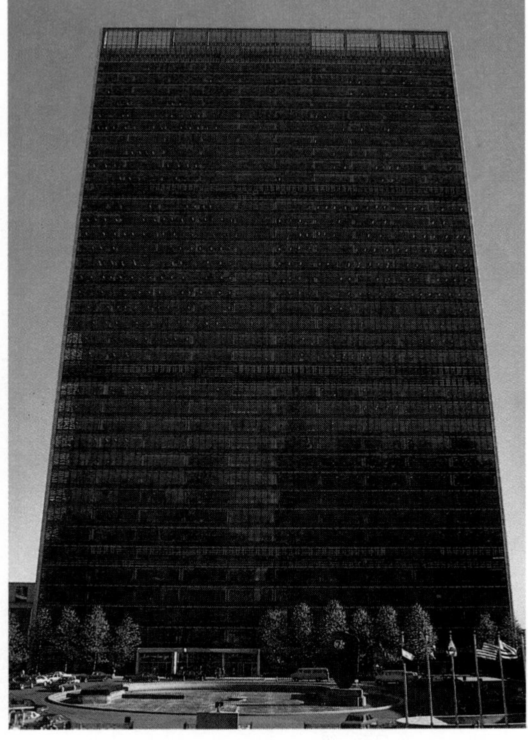

United Nations The UN headquarters has been in New York City since 1945, when the organization was formed to work for a more peaceful and secure world for all people.

cannot be immediately reelected. The council meets in continuous session.

The Security Council bears the UN's major responsibility for maintaining international peace. It may take up any matter involving a threat to or a breach of that peace. It may adopt measures ranging from calling on the parties to settle their differences peacefully to placing economic and/or military sanctions on an offending nation. The only time the Security Council has undertaken a military operation against an aggressor came in Korea in 1950. It has provided UN peace-keeping forces in several trouble spots, however—most notably in the Middle East.

On procedural questions—routine matters—decisions of the Security Council can be made by the affirmative vote of any nine members. On the more important matters—substantive

[13]Except those matters currently under consideration by the Security Council.

[14]In 1971 the People's Republic of China replaced the Nationalist Chinese regime on Taiwan as a permanent member of the Security Council and acquired China's membership in the UN in all other respects.

Provide Guided Practice Distribute to students a black and white outline map of the world. As a class, have students identify and label the countries mentioned in Section 5 on their maps. Then have students color code the various countries with regard to which security alliances they belong.

Provide Independent Practice

TRF **Teacher's Resource File** You may wish to assign Section 5 Guided Reading and Review, Unit 4 File, p. 106, to help students master section objective content.

Spotlight on: Global Awareness

The decline of tensions across the globe has sparked what many diplomatic observers see as a "renaissance" at the United Nations. While the UN undertook a total of 13 peacekeeping missions between 1945 and 1987, between 1988 and 1991 alone it launched nine. In that time, the UN was a vital player in shaping the Gulf War coalition, inspecting Iraqi weapon capability, and aiding Kurdish refugees after the war. The UN also recently helped Namibia achieve independence, mediated civil strife in Angola, Nicaragua, El Salvador, and Yugoslavia, and helped secure the release of U.S. hostages from Lebanon.

Interpreting Charts Ask students to identify the six most important bodies in the United Nations and give examples of the type of problem each might handle.

Caption Answer The General Assembly.

Monitor Comprehension

Answers to Section 5 Review
1. "Key Terms" are defined on the following pages:
a. foreign aid, p. 447
b. regional security alliance, p. 448
c. UN Security Council, p. 451
2. The United States generally grants such aid to nations that are deemed important to the achievement of United States' foreign policy objectives. **3.** NATO covers the United States and Canada, Great Britain, France, Italy, Portugal, the Netherlands, Belgium, Luxembourg, Denmark, Norway, Iceland, Greece Turkey, Germany, and Spain; Rio Pact covers the United States, Canada, and Latin America; ANZUS covers Australia, New Zealand, and the United States **4.** The Middle East presents the United States with a conflict over its support for Israel and the importance of Arab oil. **5.** The UN charter was formed at the UN Conference on International Organization, which met in San Francisco in 1945. Fifty-one nations, the victorious allies of World War II, drafted the charter. **6.** (a) The General Assembly, the Security Council, the Economic and Social Council, the Trusteeship

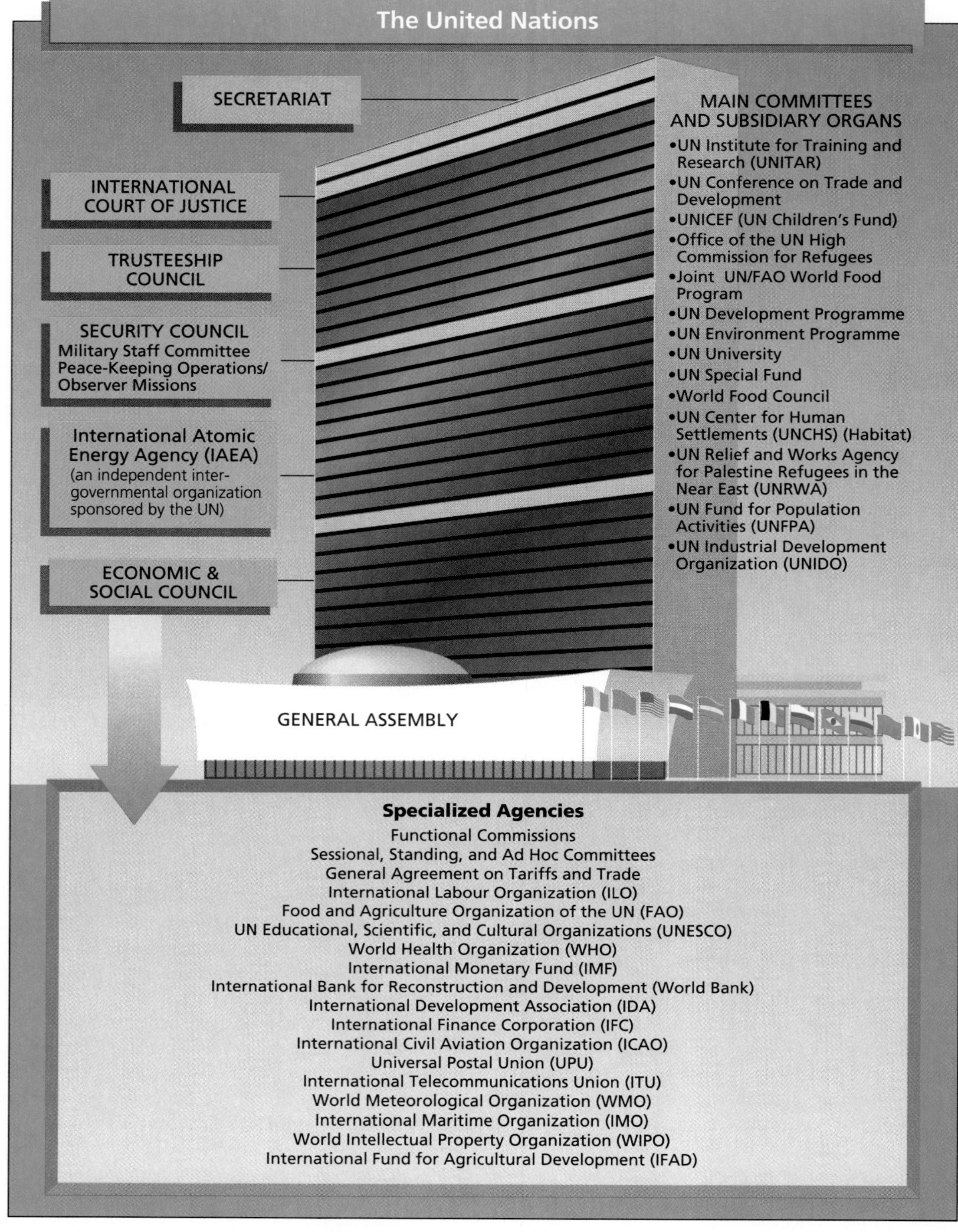

Interpreting Charts This chart shows the principal organs and agencies of the United Nations. The Secretariat, with some 18,000 employees, is the administrative body of the organization. From what you have read, which body within the United Nations has the most power?

Enrichment

Have students choose one of the main committees or specialized agencies of the United Nations listed on page 452. Ask students to research this committee and report to the class on its functions and programs. (Average) questions—at least nine affirmative votes are also needed. But a negative vote by any one of the permanent members is enough to kill any substantive resolution.[15] Because of that veto power, the Security Council is effective only when and if the permanent members are willing to cooperate with one another.

Other Important UN Bodies

In addition to the General Assembly and Security Council, the UN has several important bodies.

The Economic and Social Council The Economic and Social Council is made up of 54 members elected by the General Assembly to three-year terms. The council is responsible to the assembly for carrying out the UN's many economic, cultural, educational, health, and related activities.

The Trusteeship Council The UN Charter requires each member to promote the interests and well-being of the peoples of all "non-self-governing territories" as a "sacred trust." The Trusteeship Council sets guidelines for the government of all dependent areas and makes rules for the administration of all UN trust territories.[16]

The International Court of Justice The International Court of Justice (ICJ) is the UN's judicial arm.

All members of the UN are automatically parties to the ICJ Statute. Under certain conditions the services of the court are also available to nonmember states. A UN member may agree to accept the court's jurisdiction over cases in which it may be involved either unconditionally or with certain reservations (exceptions that may not conflict with the ICJ Statute).

The ICJ is made up of 15 judges selected for nine-year terms by the General Assembly and the Security Council. It sits in permanent session at The Hague, in the Netherlands. It handles cases brought to it voluntarily by both members and nonmembers of the UN. The ICJ also advises the other UN organs on legal questions arising out of their activities. If any party to a dispute fails to obey a judgment of the court, the other party may take that matter to the Security Council.

The Secretariat The Secretariat is the civil service branch of the UN. It is headed by the secretary-general, who is chosen to a five-year term by the General Assembly on the recommendation of the Security Council.

Dr. Boutros Boutros Ghali, an Egyptian, is now the secretary-general. He became the UN's top administrative officer in 1992. In addition to his housekeeping chores, the charter gives him a very important power. He may bring before the Security Council any matter he believes poses a threat to international peace and security.

Section 5 Review

1. **Define:** foreign aid, regional security alliance, UN Security Council
2. What kind of country is generally the recipient of United States foreign aid?
3. What regions do the NATO, Rio, and ANZUS pacts cover?
4. The United States' interests in the Middle East are torn by what two considerations?
5. When, where, and by whom was the UN Charter drafted?
6. (a) What are the UN's principal organs? (b) What are the major functions of the General Assembly and the Security Council?

Critical Thinking

7. **Making Comparisons** (p. 19) Consider the subject of international alliances. (a) Compare the attitudes of early Americans and the foreign policy makers of today. (b) What factors might have led to this shift in attitude?

★

[15]The veto does not come into play in a situation in which one or more of the permanent members abstains (does not cast a vote). When, on June 25, 1950, the Security Council called on all UN members to aid South Korea to repel the North Korean invasion, the Soviet delegate was boycotting sessions of the Security Council and so was not present to veto that action.

[16]There were 11 of those territories originally—most of them former possessions of the defeated Axis Powers of World War II. There are no trust territories today.

Council, the International Court of Justice, and the Secretariat. (b) The General Assembly is the meeting of all member states at which any matter under the charter can be discussed. The Security Council bears the UN's major responsibility for maintaining international peace. 7. (a) Students should observe that early Americans like Washington and Jefferson feared "entangling alliances," whereas the United States today sees security in such alliances. (b) Possible answers include: the two world wars; the growth of the United States as a world power; developments in technology and communications, which have made nations more interdependent.

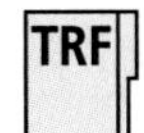

Teacher's Resource File See the Unit 4 File, p. 107, for the Section 5 Quiz.

Closure

Point out to students that our foreign policy has always been and continues to be conducted to serve what we believe are our country's best interests. In this vein, foreign aid, regional alliances, and participation in the United Nations all are intended to contribute directly or indirectly to our national security.

Assignment Assign Chapter 18, Section 1, pp. 461–466, for the next class period.

Reteach

Ask students whether they feel more secure alone or when in a group. Then point out that the United States has chosen both to show strength alone in its defensive capabilities as well as to foster regional security alliances.

TEACHING
Critical Thinking

Identifying Alternatives

Objective
Identify and evaluate defense alternatives.

INSTRUCT

Remind students that many situations will present them with various alternatives. Intelligent decisions require careful evaluation of these. As students complete each step on the page, invite them to share responses. List the alternatives identified and discuss their viability.

Answers 1. (a) To ensure the country's ability to protect itself and its interests. (b) Possible answers include: How does the end of the cold war affect the U.S.? Is there a possibility of another incident like the Persian Gulf War? **2.** (a) The Soviet Union is no longer a threat, so defense spending should be used for other purposes. (b) The world is still very dangerous, and the U.S. needs to protect itself and its interests. **3.** Answers will vary. Students may suggest making lists of the various U.S. interests and the cost of keeping them secure. **4.** Students should answer these questions based on their lists of alternatives.

TRF **Teacher's Resource File**
See the Unit 4 File, p. 108, for the Skill Application for this lesson.

Identifying Alternatives

As a citizen in a democratic society, you will have to make and evaluate a great number and variety of decisions. Some will be simple. Many, however, will be quite complicated. In order to find the best solutions to such problems you must be able to identify alternatives. Mastering this skill will enable you to (1) identify one or more methods to achieve a goal or to solve a problem and (2) recognize the possibility of other goals. Follow the steps below to practice identifying alternatives.

1. Identify the nature of the problem. Before you can identify possible solutions to a problem, you must understand exactly what the problem is. Read the paragraph below, describing a foreign policy question faced by the United States. (a) What is the ultimate goal of the United States regarding its military spending? (b) What challenges and questions does the nation face in achieving that goal?

2. Identify the interests that must be satisfied and/or conditions that must be met. In any conflict or disagreement, a solution must be acceptable to all sides. Read the passage below again. (a) What is the position of those who favor a cut in military spending? (b) What is the view of those who favor a continuation of military spending at levels similar to those during the cold war?

3. Identify possible alternatives. A common technique for identifying alternatives is brainstorming. In a brainstorming session, participants volunteer all sorts of ideas, which are then collected and analyzed. At first some of the ideas may seem odd, and many turn out to be of little value. However, the process often yields unexpected and effective alternatives. Brainstorm ways in which the United States can determine the appropriate level of defense spending. What are some of your ideas?

4. Test your ideas. Once you have generated a list of possible alternatives, you should try to eliminate those that will not work. Examine each idea that you brainstormed by answering the following questions: (a) Is this idea likely to accomplish the goal of providing a strong defense for the United States? Why or why not? (b) Will all parties involved in the debate be satisfied? Why or why not?

With the apparent end of the cold war, the United States faces a reevaluation of its defense needs. Most American leaders agree that the United States needs a strong defense in order to remain secure. However, there is disagreement about how much money the nation must spend in order to build this defense. A number of policymakers want to take advantage of the diminished threat from the Soviet Union to lower dramatically the nation's defense budget. The resulting so-called peace dividend could then be used to lower the budget deficit and provide more domestic services to the American people. Other analysts insist that in spite of the great changes in the alignment of world military power, the world remains a dangerous place. These leaders point to the Persian Gulf War of 1991 as an example. They insist that the nation continue to invest in its military near the levels of the past in order to ensure the continued ability of the United States to protect its interests around the world.

Chapter-in-Brief

Scan all headings, photographs, charts, and other visuals in the chapter before reading the section summaries below.

Section 1 Foreign and Defense Policies: An Overview (pp. 425–427) Throughout much of American history, relations with other countries were shaped largely by the policy of isolationism. Today, however, the United States understands that its security is directly linked with that of other nations.

For this reason, governmental leaders carefully shape American foreign policy. The President, as chief diplomat and commander in chief, plays the leading role in foreign and military affairs.

Section 2 The Departments of State and Defense (pp. 428–434) The State Department is the President's right arm in the field of foreign policy. The department is headed by the secretary of state, and it is organized along geographic and functional lines. The department includes the Foreign Service and ambassadors who represent the United States around the world. The State Department also issues passports to American citizens.

The Defense Department assists the President in making and conducting military policy. Its secretary must be a civilian, in keeping with the principle of civilian control of the military.

Section 3 Other Foreign/Defense Policy Agencies (pp. 435–438) Besides the Departments of State and Defense, several agencies are closely involved with foreign policy.

The CIA coordinates the government's intelligence gathering. It also analyzes that data. The United States Information Agency promotes American policy and way of life around the world.

The United States Arms Control and Disarmament Agency is responsible for American participation in arms limitation and disarmament talks. The Selective Service System oversees the draft, which presently exists on a standby basis.

Section 4 American Foreign Policy, Past and Present (pp. 441–447) Isolationism guided American foreign policy for its first 150 years. During that time, the nation expanded; it also promoted such foreign policies as the Monroe Doctrine and the Open Door.

World War I led to a renewed spirit of isolationism in the 1920s and 1930s. World War II put an end to that policy; the war's aftermath saw the beginning of the cold war and the commitment to collective security and deterrence.

During the cold war, the United States pursued containment of communism, particularly through armed conflict in Korea and Vietnam. A period of détente in the 1970s led to better relations with the Soviets and China.

Section 5 Foreign Aid, Defense Alliances, and the United Nations (pp. 447–453) The United States began practicing foreign aid during World War II. Early aid was economic, but military aid has become increasingly important.

Since World War II, the United States has forged a number of regional security alliances. NATO is one example; others include the Rio Pact, ANZUS, the Japanese Pact, the Philippines Pact, the Korean Pact, and the Taiwan Pact.

The United Nations is perhaps the best example of America's full-scale involvement in world affairs. The UN seeks to maintain peace and security, develop friendly relations among nations, and promote justice and cooperation in the solution of international problems.

455

Teaching Suggestions for Chapter-in-Brief

Below are some of the possible uses for the Chapter-in-Brief:

To Preview the Chapter You may want to assign the Chapter-in-Brief page and the Section Outlines from the Teacher's Resource File before beginning Chapter 17 to introduce students to the "Key Terms" and concepts in each section.

To Review the Chapter When students have completed Chapter 17, you might want to assign the Chapter-in-Brief as a tool for review, along with the Guided Reading and Reviews from the Teacher's Resource File.

To Omit the Chapter If you wish to skip Chapter 17, it may be helpful to assign the Chapter-in-Brief to students as a review before continuing to another chapter. You may also want to assign the Chapter 17 Test to assess student knowledge of the material. Then specific portions of Chapter 17 may be assigned to students needing reinforcement of "Key Terms" and concepts.

Teacher's Resource File See the Unit 4 File for the following materials:

- Section Outlines, pp. 93, 96, 99, 102, 105.
- Guided Reading and Reviews, pp. 94, 97, 100, 103, 106.
- Chapter 17 Test, pp. 112–114.

Additional Resources

Craig, Gordon A. and Alexander L. George. *Force and Statecraft: Diplomatic Problems of Our Time.* Oxford, 1989.

Decisions, Decisions: Foreign Policy. Software. Tom Snyder Productions, 1991. Apple II, Macintosh, IBM.

Hastedt, Glenn P. *American Foreign Policy: Past, Present, Future.* Prentice Hall, 2nd ed., 1991.

History of the U.S. Foreign Relations, Part 3: The Reluctant World Power. 16mm film. U.S. Dept. of State, 1973. Color. 29 min.

Hughes, Barry B. *Continuity and Change in World Politics.* Prentice Hall, 1991.

McNamara, Robert S. *Out of the Cold: New Thinking for American Foreign and Defense Policy in the 21st Century.* Simon and Schuster, 1989.

Profiles in Democracy: The U.S. Foreign Service. Video. PBS Video. 60 min.

Schultzinger, Robert D. *American Diplomacy in the Twentieth Century.* Oxford, 2nd ed., 1990.

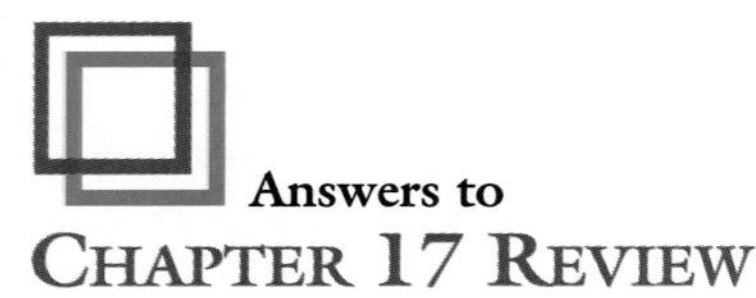

Answers to CHAPTER 17 REVIEW

Vocabulary and Key Terms

Matching
1. right of legation
2. diplomatic immunity
3. collective security
4. passport
5. foreign aid

True or False
1. False—the correct term is *draft.*
2. True.
3. False—the correct term is *isolationism.*
4. True.

Word Relationships
1. A passport is a certificate issued by a government that identifies a person as a citizen and authorizes him/her to travel abroad. A visa is a permit for a person to enter a country, issued by the country one wishes to visit.
2. Foreign policy is all the actions taken by a country with respect to other countries. Foreign aid is a foreign policy of military and economic aid to foreign countries.
3. Deterrence maintains that keeping a massive military will discourage others from attacking. Containment is the resistance to Soviet expansion.
4. Collective security is the principle that security can be achieved by forging a worldwide community. Regional security refers to mutual agreements between the United States and other countries.

Main Ideas

Section 1
1. With the exception of trade, the U.S. avoided commitments to other countries. That attitude shifted during and after World War II to one of internationalism. **2.** Events and actions elsewhere in the world have a direct and powerful impact on events in the U.S. **3.** The President, as commander in chief, plays the leading role. Congress also has significant powers in this field.

Chapter Review

Vocabulary and Key Terms

isolationism (p. 425)
foreign policy (p. 426)
right of legation (p. 429)
ambassador (p. 429)
passport (p. 430)
visa (p. 430)
diplomatic immunity (p. 430)
draft (p. 438)
collective security (p. 443)
deterrence (p. 443)
containment (p. 444)
foreign aid (p. 447)
regional security alliance (p. 448)
UN Security Council (p. 452)

Matching: *Review the key terms in the list above. If you are not sure of a term's meaning, look up the term and review its definition. Choose a term from the list above that best matches each description.*

1. the right to send and receive diplomatic representatives
2. the rule by which ambassadors are not held subject to the laws of the state to which they are accredited
3. a foreign policy principle based on a worldwide system of security
4. a certificate issued by a government identifying a person as a citizen of a country
5. economic and military aid to foreign countries

True or False: *Determine whether each statement is true or false. If it is true, write "true." If it is false, change the underlined word or words to make the statement true.*

1. The right of legation is the means by which the Federal Government requires young men to serve in the military.
2. The personal representative of the United States in foreign states is the ambassador.
3. For its first 150 years, American foreign policy was largely one of diplomatic immunity.
4. The UN Security Council bears a major responsibility for maintaining international peace.

Word Relationships: *Distinguish between words in each pair.*

1. passport/visa
2. foreign policy/foreign aid
3. deterrence/containment
4. collective security/regional security alliance

Main Ideas

Section 1 (pp. 425–427)

1. Briefly describe the historical attitudes of the United States toward foreign affairs.
2. For what reasons must the United States be concerned about events elsewhere in the world?
3. Which individuals and organizations play major roles in the conduct of foreign policy?

Section 2 (pp. 428–434)

4. Which two cabinet-level departments are most responsible for the making and conduct of foreign policy?
5. (a) What are the key components of the State Department in the field of foreign policy? (b) What are their functions?
6. What is the main function of the Department of Defense?

Section 3 (pp. 435–438)

7. List three agencies besides the State Department and the Department of Defense involved with making and/or conducting foreign policy.

456

Section 2
4. The Departments of State and Defense. **5.** (a) The Foreign Service, including ambassadors, counsels, and special diplomats. (b) To represent the United States abroad. **6.** The Department of Defense is the main agency for helping carry out the nation's defense and military policies.

Section 3
7. Possible answers include the CIA, the USIA, NASA, and the USACDA. The Immigration and Naturalization Service, the Public Health Service, and the Coast Guard also are such departments. **8.** (a) To coordinate the information-gathering activities of different agencies, to analyze and evaluate data collected by those agencies, and to brief the President and others on all intelligence. (b) The USIA distributes information about the U.S. to other countries. **9.** (a) NASA is responsible for all aspects of the nation's space program. (b) The USACDA conducts American

8. (a) What is the function of the Central Intelligence Agency? (b) The United States Information Agency?
9. (a) What is the function of the National Aeronautics and Space Administration? (b) The United States Arms Control and Disarmament Agency?
10. Briefly describe the history of the draft in the United States.

Section 4 (pp. 441–447)

11. Explain the significance of the Monroe Doctrine.
12. Describe two key foreign policy developments of the late 1800s.
13. What two terms describe the broad goals of American foreign policy in the post-World War II era?
14. (a) What was the cold war? (b) What is its status today?

Section 5 (pp. 447–453)

15. Briefly trace the history of the United States policy of foreign aid.
16. What is the function of the several regional security alliances to which the United States is a party?
17. What, according to the UN charter, are the UN's basic purposes?
18. How does the veto power of the UN's Security Council affect its ability to make policy?

Critical Thinking

1. **Identifying Alternatives** (p. 19) (a) In your opinion, what should be the overall goal of American foreign policy? (b) Which of the principles discussed in this chapter seem most likely to help the United States achieve this goal? Explain your answer.
2. **Recognizing Ideologies** (p. 19) President Dwight Eisenhower once said, " Americans, indeed all free men, remember that in the final choice a soldier's pack is not so heavy a burden as a prisoner's chains." What do you think Eisenhower meant by this comment?
3. **Predicting Consequences** (p. 19) Consider the concept of isolationism discussed in Sections 1 and 3. What would you predict might happen if the United States were again to shape its foreign policy around this principle?

Getting Involved

1. **Writing Your Opinion** You are a candidate for President of the United States. Write a speech in which you explain to the voters your view of United States foreign policy. Prepare for your speech by reviewing the foreign policy history of the United States. Select those policies and principles that you feel best serve the interests of the country. Begin the speech by stating why you believe the country must have a clearly defined foreign policy. Then, carefully explain each of the principles and policies that you advocate. Remember, the purpose of your speech is to convince voters to support you in the election. So, explain how you believe your policies will benefit the nation. Revise the speech to correct errors, then draft a final copy.
2. **Class Debate** Hold a class debate on one of the following topics: (a) *Resolved,* That the United States should reinstitute compulsory military service for young men and women. (b) *Resolved,* That the United States favor the abolition of the veto power of the permanent members of the United Nations Security Council. Select teams to debate each side of the selected issue. The rest of the class should evaluate each team's presentation.
3. **Creating a Poster** Create a poster to illustrate your understanding of national security. Remember, your poster can include a combination of words and images to communicate your ideas.

participation in arms limitation and disarmament negotiations. **10.** No national conscription existed until the Civil War. Conscription also was used in WW I. The first peacetime draft came in 1940, and it continued, with only a brief interruption, until 1973. Since 1980, all males have been required to register at age 18, but the armed services are all-volunteer.

Section 4

11. The Monroe Doctrine declared that foreign powers would not be allowed to meddle in the affairs of the Western Hemisphere. **12.** The Spanish-American War demonstrated the U.S. role as a world power. The Open Door policy in China revealed the expanding influence of the United States **13.** Collective security and deterrence. **14.** (a) Period of tension and hostility between the United States and the Communist world in the decades following World War II. (b) Cold war is over.

Section 5

15. The policy began with the Lend-Lease program of the early 1940s. It became part of the United States containment policy, and was exemplified by the Marshall Plan. In the immediate postwar years, foreign aid was primarily economic; more recently, military aid has been the focus. **16.** They ensure that each participating nation will support the other in the event of a threat from an outside power. **17.** The maintenance of international peace and security, the development of friendly relations between and among nations, and the promotion of justice and cooperation in the solution of international problems. **18.** Cooperation among the permanent members is needed for the Security Council to be effective.

Critical Thinking

1. (a) Answers will vary, but might include security and peace for the U.S., security for its allies. (b) Answers will vary. Ensure that students are able to explain how their proposed foreign policy will achieve the goal they identified in part A. **2.** Students should observe that the quotation suggests that war is preferable to enslavement. **3.** Answers will vary. Students might observe that the U.S. is now inextricably integrated in a world community. America depends on other nations for economic and military security. Others might suggest that American strength and wealth would be enough to ensure United States security.

Getting Involved

1–3. Answers and results will vary, but students should demonstrate an understanding of the concepts in this chapter.

Managing the Unit

You may wish to review the following materials before beginning the unit to help plan your instruction.

Each chapter ends with a Chapter-in-Brief with suggestions for previewing, reviewing, or omitting the chapter.

Unit 5 Outline

Unit 5

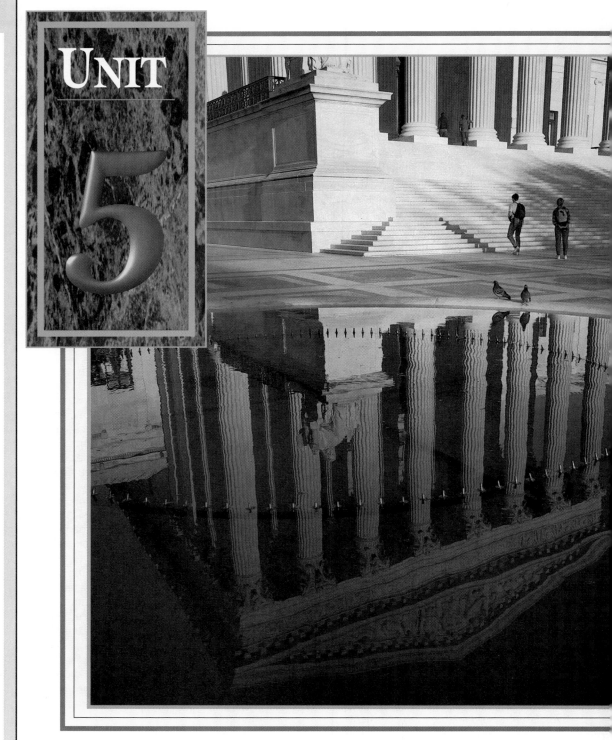

▲ **Constitutionally Mandated** The Constitution requires the existence of a Supreme Court in order to maintain uniform interpretation of national legislation.

Skills and Features

The following skill lessons and features are included in this unit.

Skill Lessons

Critical Thinking: Identifying Assumptions (p. 480)
Critical Thinking: Predicting Consequences (p. 512)
Critical Thinking: Formulating Questions (p. 540)
Critical Thinking: Demonstrating Reasoned Judgment (p. 568)

Debates/Case Studies

Debating Key Issues: Should School Officials Have the Right to Search Your Property? (*New Jersey* v. *TLO*) (p. 467)
Debating Key Issues: Should Public Schools Ban Political Protests? (*Tinker* v. *Des Moines*) (p. 498)
Debating Key Issues: Should Defendants Have the Right to Appointed Counsel? (*Gideon* v. *Wainwright*) (p. 527)
Debating Key Issues: Should Universities Have the Right to Use Admissions Quotas? (*Regents of the University of California* v. *Bakke*) (p. 560)

The Judicial Branch

It was the first session of the Supreme Court, and the day was going badly. Early on February 1, 1790, Chief Justice John Jay and two associate justices arrived at the Exchange Building in New York City and waited for the three remaining justices to arrive. They never showed up. The next day a fourth justice joined the original three. Within a short time it was clear that the court had little business to conduct. No cases were presented for argument and after ten days the court adjourned. By contrast, the Supreme Court today schedules to hear about 150 cases of the more than 5,000 petitions that are submitted to it each year. In spite of this and many other changes, tradition dominates the Supreme Court. The marshals still make sure that proper behavior is maintained at all times. Recently, a reporter sitting in the press section draped his arm over the brass rail next to him. A marshal was quickly at his side with the firm but polite request, "No body parts on the brass rail." The room with the brass rail—contained inside the imposing building shown at left—is the meeting place of the topmost level of the judicial branch, which you will study in this unit.

Did You Know That . . .

- It was not until 1935 that the Supreme Court had its own building. In its early history, the Supreme Court spent a full year convening in a Washington tavern.
- From 1980 through 1990, the prison population in the United States increased by nearly 90 percent.
- Ninety-nine percent of Americans think it is an important obligation of citizenship for a person to report a crime that he or she has witnessed.

Unit Focus

Activate Prior Knowledge Ask students whether they can imagine a time when African-American students were not allowed in the same classrooms as white students. Tell students that it was the Supreme Court that struck down this form of racial discrimination. Ask: Can you think of any other areas in which the decision of the Supreme Court has had a major impact on the nation?

Interpreting the Visual Point out the photo of the Supreme Court building in the unit opener. Tell students that, like many government buildings, this building was designed in the Greco-Roman style. Explain that many aspects of American democracy have their roots in Greco-Roman principles.

Did You Know That . . . Direct students to the items under "Did You Know That . . . ." What impact do students think some of these statistics might have on the American judicial system in the future?

Journal Writing A journal may serve as a record of students' impressions and ideas about their courses and related events in the world and their lives. It is an opportunity for students to create political cartoons, songs, poems, and stories as well as editorials and essays. Students should make entries at least once a week, and be sure to date each entry. Although journal writing generally is not graded, you should collect and review the journals at regular intervals. Suggested topics for the fifth unit include opinions about affirmative action or the value of citizenship, or an imaginary circumstance in which a person must decide whether or not to report a crime to the police.

You may also want to utilize **CNN Video-link** to generate ideas for journal writing.

Bulletin Board Idea

Using the Poster Read aloud to the class the statement of Chief Justice William Rehnquist on the wall poster titled "Individual Rights: Toward Justice for All." Discuss whether students agree or disagree that majority rule and individual rights are on opposite sides of the judicial scale. Explain that providing equal rights for all is a goal of the American judicial system. Ask students to explain what Clarence Darrow meant when he said, "There is no such thing as justice—in or out of court." Tell the class that Clarence Darrow practiced law in the early twentieth century. Ask students to give examples that refute his statement as well as examples that support it. Do they think that Darrow, if alive today, would hold to his statement? Ask students to write a paragraph or short poem about the state of equal rights today, and display it on the bulletin board.

Chapter 18 Resources

In the Teacher's Resource File
The following materials are found in the Teacher's Resource File box.

Instructional Support: Unit 5 File

For the Section
Outlines, pp. 2, 5, 8, 11
Guided Reading and Reviews, pp. 3, 6, 9, 12
Quizzes, pp. 4, 7, 10, 13

For the Chapter
Skill Application, p. 14
Case Study on Contemporary Issues, pp. 15–17
Chapter Test, pp. 18–20
Additional Test Questions, pp. 21–23

Enrichment Support Files

Supreme Court Cases, p. 13
Participatory Government Activities, pp. 4–15, 20–27

Computer Test Bank and Assessment

Transparency Package, pp. 18, 43

Chapter 18 Focus

Introduce the Chapter Tell students that in this chapter they will read about the role of the judicial branch of government as well as the various types of federal courts and their jurisdictions. Read with students the Chapter Preview and Objectives.

Writing Activity Direct students' attention to "Describe." Define the word *justice* for the class. Then ask students to finish this sentence: "In a system of justice, the most important thing is. . . ."

Motivate for Learning Direct students' attention to "Predict." Ask students to imagine what it would be like in the classroom if there were no rules or if there were no teacher to arbitrate disagreements about the interpretation of the rules. Lead students in a discussion of what society would be like without laws and the court system.

The Federal Court System

Chapter Preview

Homicide, robbery, assault, tax fraud, embezzlement—these are just a few of the most common criminal and civil cases heard in the United States district courts each year. While the Framers of the Constitution may never have imagined all of the types of cases these courts would hear, they did realize that government would be impossible to manage without law—and so they added Article III to the Constitution. It established the Supreme Court and gave Congress the power to create other, lower federal courts. It is the prime function of the legislative branch, therefore, to make the law, and of the judicial branch—the system of federal courts and federal judges—to interpret and apply the law. This chapter is about the structure and work of all parts of the federal court system.

Before you read this chapter:

- **Describe** what the concept of justice means to you.
- **Predict** what might occur if the laws and the court system did not exist.

As you read, focus on the main objective for each section. Understand:

1. The basic role of the judiciary in the governmental process.
2. The structure and function of the constitutional courts in the federal court system.
3. The role of the Supreme Court as the nation's highest court, and the significance of judicial review in the American governmental system.
4. The role and jurisdiction of special courts in the federal court system.

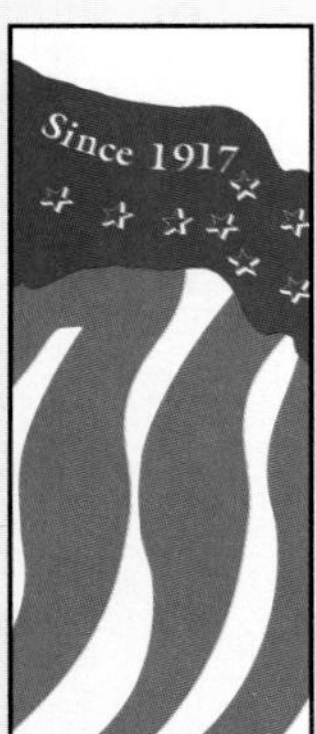

Magruder's American Government: *A Witness to Change* by William A. McClenaghan

The Supreme Court struck down several key pieces of New Deal legislation in a number of cases in 1935 and 1936. The Court's decisions in those cases prompted critics to characterize the members of the Court as "the Nine Old Men"; and President Franklin Roosevelt vowed to use his appointing power to bring the Court out of what he called "the horse and buggy age." At the same time (1936), the average age of the nine members of the Court was 71.

The 1938 edition of American Government quoted Henry Ford's response to the Court's critics: "Elderly persons are not as slow in taking up new things as young folks sometimes suppose. They are only a little more careful not to be fooled again by old fallacies that are masquerading as new truths."

As you can see in the table on page 475, the average age of the members of the High Court today is just under 65—even with the recent appointments of camparatively young Justices Scalia, Kennedy, Souter, and Thomas.

Richmond, Virginia, Courthouse Cases that involve federal or constitutional laws are brought before a federal court rather than a State court.

Section 1
The National Judiciary

Focus

Teacher's Resource File See the Unit 5 File, p. 2, for the Section 1 Outline.

Objectives

18.1 Examine the reasons why the national court system was established.

18.2 Determine the two bases upon which federal courts hear and decide cases.

18.3 Explain jurisdiction and examine the kinds of jurisdiction held by federal courts.

18.4 Determine ways in which federal judges are selected and compensated, and see who helps judges perform their jobs.

Bellringer Activity Have students consider the idea of jurisdiction, using the following activity. Ask them to imagine this situation: You are watching television at home with other members of your household. An argument breaks out over what you all will watch. Then, your next-door neighbor comes in and makes a pronouncement, deciding the issue for you. What is your reaction?

State the Purpose The United States judicial system is divided into two systems: the national judiciary and the States' courts. In Section 1, students will learn about the national judiciary—its formation, its jurisdiction, its judges, and the people who support them.

1 The National Judiciary

Find Out:

- For what reasons was the national court system established?
- On what two bases can the federal courts hear and decide cases?
- What is jurisdiction, and what kinds of jurisdiction do the various federal courts have?
- How are federal judges selected and compensated, and who helps them perform their jobs?

Key Terms:

jurisdiction, exclusive jurisdiction, concurrent jurisdiction, plaintiff, defendant, original jurisdiction, appellate jurisdiction

What do you think your life would be like if there were no courts to enforce laws in our society? How would the United States function without a system of national courts? Not efficiently, you might well answer. As you will see, this was just the case during about eight years of America's early history. You will read about the problems caused by this situation, and then about the federal court system as it exists today.

The Creation of a National Judiciary

Over the years the Articles of Confederation were in force (1781–1789), there were no national courts, no national judiciary. The laws of the United States were interpreted and applied in the States as each of them chose to do so, and sometimes not at all. Disputes between States and between persons who lived in different States were decided, if at all, by the

Vocabulary

Direct students' attention to "Key Terms" on page 461. Ask them to make a list of all of the terms that have to do with *jurisdiction.* As they read, students may compare the meanings of *exclusive jurisdiction, concurrent jurisdiction, original jurisdiction,* and *appellate jurisdiction.* Explain that knowing these words will help them differentiate among courts in the national judiciary.

Reading Strategy: Reinforcing Key Ideas

To help students understand the often complex systems of courts within the national judiciary, have them write down the main headings in Section 1. As they read, have them make notes that reinforce the key ideas under each heading.

INSTRUCT

Discuss Use the example from the "Bellringer Activity" to initiate a discussion on jurisdiction and the need for a higher authority in settling arguments. Point out the two neighbors are like two States. One State has no right to settle disputes within the other State's domain. However, if two States do have an argument between themselves, a higher authority is needed to judge the matter.

Ask students to explain why it was important to establish a national court system. Then invite them to describe the national judiciary and its structures and functions. Brainstorm certain kinds of cases that would fall under the domain of constitutional and special court jurisdiction. Be sure that students include an explanation of the two bases upon which jurisdiction is determined: subject matter and parties.

To further the discussion, you may want to ask students how the national judiciary affects the U.S. system of government and why it is so important to the daily workings of the government. (*It plays a critical role in the system of checks and balances.*)

ABCNEWS INTERACTIVE

The following video segment may be used to highlight discussion of the federal courts.

POWERS OF THE SUPREME COURT GUIDEBOOK
Chapter 3: Constitution and the Court, p. 4

courts in one of the States involved. Often, decisions by the courts in one State were ignored by the courts in the other States.

Alexander Hamilton spoke to the point in *The Federalist* No. 78. He described "the want of a national judiciary" as a "circumstance that crowns the defects of the Confederation." Arguing the need for a national court system he added:

> "Laws are dead letters without courts to expound and define their true meaning and operation."

To meet the need, the Framers wrote Article III into the Constitution. It created the national judiciary in a single sentence:

> "The judicial power of the United States shall be vested in one Supreme Court, and in such inferior courts as the Congress may from time to time ordain and establish."[1]

A Dual Court System Keep this important point in mind: There are *two* separate court systems in the United States.[2] On one hand, the national judiciary spans the country, with its more than 100 courts. On the other hand, each of the 50 States has its own system of courts. Their numbers run well into the thousands. These State courts hear most of the cases in this country. You will take a look at the States' court systems in Chapter 25.

Two Kinds of Courts The Constitution creates the Supreme Court and leaves to Congress the creation of the inferior courts—the lower federal courts, those beneath the Supreme Court. Over the years, Congress has created two distinct types of federal courts: (1) constitutional courts and (2) special courts.

CONSTITUTIONAL COURTS The constitutional courts are the federal courts that Congress has formed under Article III to exercise "the judicial power of the United States." Together with the Supreme Court, they now include the courts of appeals, the district courts, and the Court of International Trade. The constitutional courts are sometimes called the regular courts, and sometimes Article III courts.

SPECIAL COURTS The special courts do not exercise the broad "judicial power of the United States." Rather, they have been created by Congress to hear cases arising out of some of the expressed powers given to Congress in Article I. The special courts hear a much narrower range of cases than those that may come before the constitutional courts.

These special courts are sometimes called the legislative courts. Today, they include the Court of Military Appeals, the Court of Veterans Appeals, the Claims Court, the Tax Court, the various territorial courts, and the courts of the District of Columbia. You will read about the unique features of these courts in Section 4. First, you will be reading about jurisdiction—the meaning of the term and the kinds of jurisdiction of the various federal courts.

Jurisdiction in the Federal Courts

The constitutional courts hear most of the cases tried in the federal courts. That is, those courts have jurisdiction over most federal cases.

1.a The word **jurisdiction** is defined as the authority of a court to hear and decide a case. The term means, literally, the power "to say the law."

The Constitution gives the federal courts jurisdiction over certain cases. Article III, Section 2 provides that the federal courts may hear a case either because of (1) the subject matter or (2) the parties involved in the case.

Subject Matter In terms of subject matter, the federal courts may hear a case if it deals with:

1. the interpretation and application of a provision in the Constitution or in any federal statute or treaty; or
2. a question of admiralty (matters that arise on the high seas or navigable waters of the United States) or a question of maritime law (matters arising on land but directly relating to the

[1] Article III, Section 1. Article I, Section 8, Clause 9 also grants Congress the expressed power "to constitute tribunals inferior to the Supreme Court."

[2] Federalism does not require two separate court systems. Article III provides that Congress "may" establish lower federal courts. At its first session, in 1789, Congress decided to construct a complete set of federal courts to parallel those of the States. In most of the world's other federal systems, the principal courts are those of the states or provinces; typically, the only significant federal court is a national court of last resort, often called the supreme court.

ACTIVITY: For Gifted Students

Theme: Justice As students begin their study of our national judiciary, they may choose to consider this ancient law of justice found in the Code of Hammurabi—"an eye for an eye." Students can find the Code of Hammurabi on page 743 of their text. Through the use of library resources, periodicals, interviews, documentaries, etc., students may research the history of the United States' penal system to analyze the ways in which the contemporary judicial system might reflect an earlier view of justice. Students may present their findings in the form of an oral or written report.

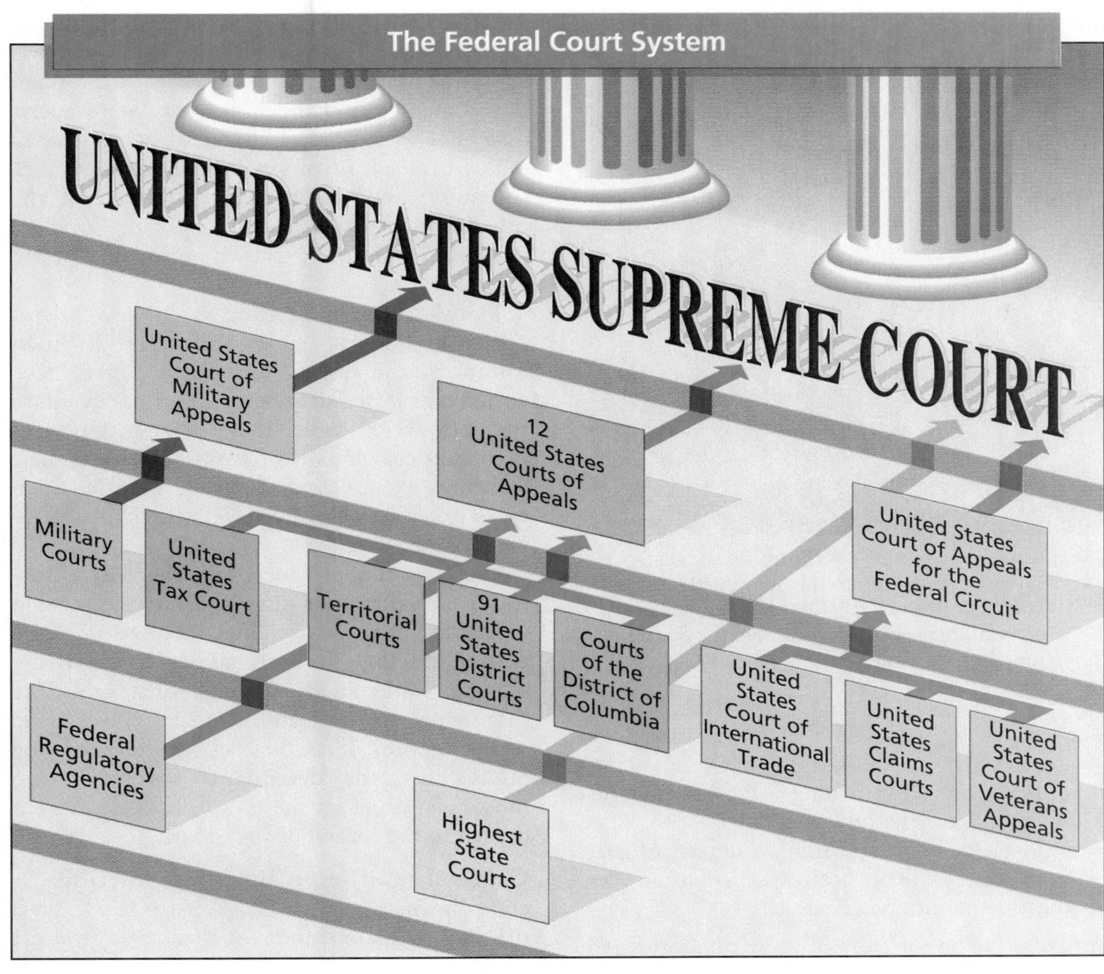

Interpreting Charts Cases involving the highest State courts bypass all lower courts and appeal directly to the United States Supreme Court. To which court do cases from the Federal Regulatory Agencies first appeal?

water—for example, a contract to deliver a ship's supplies at dockside).[3]

Parties A case comes within the jurisdiction of the federal courts if any of the parties in the case is:

1. the United States or one of its officers or agencies;
2. an ambassador, consul, or other official representative of a foreign government;
3. a State suing another State, or a citizen of another State, or a foreign government or one of its subjects;[4]

[3]The Framers gave the federal courts exclusive jurisdiction in such cases to ensure national supremacy in the regulation of all waterborne commerce.

[4]Note that the 11th Amendment says that a State may not be sued in the federal courts by a citizen of another State or of a foreign state. A State may be sued without its consent in the federal courts only by the United States, another State, or a foreign state. If a citizen of a State (or of another State or of a foreign state) wants to sue a State, he or she may do so only with that State's consent and only in that State's own courts.

Interpreting Charts Ask students to study the chart. Then have them discuss the structure of the federal court system in the United States. Why do they think it is important to have several tiers in the court system? (*So that different courts can handle matters relating to different jurisdictions.*)

Caption Answer Cases from the federal regulatory agencies appeal to the courts of appeals.

Appointee in the Spotlight Clarence Thomas, appointed to the Supreme Court by President Bush in 1991, is seen here during his confirmation hearings before the Senate Judiciary Committee.

4. a citizen of one State suing a citizen of another State;
5. an American citizen suing a foreign government or one of its subjects;
6. a citizen of one State suing a citizen of that same State where both claim land under grants from different States.

Any case falling into any of these categories can be brought in the proper federal court. If a case does not fit into one of these categories, it cannot be heard in a federal court. Remember, most of the cases heard by courts in this country are State, not federal cases.

All of this may seem quite complicated, and it is. But notice that federal jurisdiction is a reflection of federalism and of the dual system of courts in this country. Stating the whole point of federal court jurisdiction in another way: All cases that are not heard by the federal courts are within the jurisdiction of the States' courts.

Exclusive and Concurrent Jurisdiction In several of the categories of cases just listed, the federal courts have **exclusive jurisdiction**. 1.b That is, those cases can be heard only in the federal courts. For example, a case involving an ambassador or some other official of a foreign government cannot be heard in a State court. The trial of a person charged with a federal crime, or a suit involving the infringement of a patent or a copyright, or a case involving any other matter arising out of an act of Congress also falls within the exclusive jurisdiction of the federal courts.

Many cases may be tried in either a federal court or a State court, however. In such instances, the federal and State courts have
1.c **concurrent jurisdiction**; that is, they share the power to hear those cases. Disputes involving citizens of different States are fairly common examples of this type of case. Such cases are known in the law as cases in diverse citizenship.[5]

Congress has provided that the federal district courts may hear cases in diverse citizenship only if the amount of money involved in a case
1.d is over $50,000. In such cases the **plaintiff**—the one who initiates the suit—may bring the case in the proper State or federal court, as he or she chooses. If the case is brought before the
1.e State court, the **defendant**—the party who must defend against the complaint—may have it moved to the federal district court.

Original and Appellate Jurisdiction A court in which a case is heard first is said to have
1.f **original jurisdiction** over that case. A court that hears a case on appeal from a lower court
1.g has **appellate jurisdiction** over that case. The higher court—the appellate court—may uphold, overrule, or in some way modify the decision appealed from the lower court.[6]

In the federal court system, the district courts have only original jurisdiction and the courts of appeals have only appellate jurisdiction.

[5]The major reason that cases in diverse citizenship may be heard in federal courts is to provide a neutral forum to settle the disputes involved. That reason reflects an early fear that State courts (and their juries) might be prejudiced against "foreigners," residents of other States. There seems little real likelihood of such bias today.

[6]The term appellate comes from the Latin *appellare,* meaning "to speak to, to call upon, to appeal to."

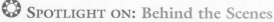

SPOTLIGHT ON: Behind the Scenes

In 1991 President Bush chose Clarence Thomas to succeed retired Justice Thurgood Marshall on the Supreme Court. Amid great controversy, the Senate confirmed the nomination by a 52–48 vote. A graduate of Holy Cross College (1971) and Yale Law School (1974), Justice Thomas passed the Missouri bar in 1974 and served as assistant attorney general there until 1977, when he joined the staff of Senator John Danforth (R-MO). He was appointed to the U.S. Court of Appeals, Washington, D.C., in 1990 after serving as an assistant secretary of education and as chairman of the Equal Employment Opportunity Commission, 1982 to 1990.

Appointment of Judges

The manner in which federal judges are chosen, the terms for which they serve, and even the salaries they are paid play a vital part in maintaining the independence of the judicial branch. The Constitution declares that the President

> "shall nominate, and, by and with the advice and consent of the Senate, shall appoint . . . judges of the Supreme Court."[7]

Congress has provided the same procedure for the selection of all other federal judges. So, the President is free to name to the federal bench anyone the Senate will confirm. Recall the very real impact of the unwritten rule of senatorial courtesy here; see Chapter 11, Section 4.

Most federal judges are drawn from the ranks of leading attorneys, legal scholars and law school professors, former members of Congress, and from the State courts. A President's judicial selections are shaped by the same sorts of political considerations as other exercises of the chief executive's appointing power you read about in Chapter 14.

Since George Washington's day, Presidents have looked to their own political party in making judicial appointments. Republican Presidents regularly choose Republicans; Democrats usually pick Democrats.

Every President knows that most of the judges he or she appoints will serve for decades. So, Presidents also regularly look for judges who share their own legal and political outlook—the President's ideology.

The President and his closest political and legal aides, especially the attorney general take the leading role in selecting judges, of course. But other contributors to the selection process include influential senators, most of all those from the nominee's home State; the legal profession, especially the American Bar Association's Committee on the Federal Judiciary; and various other important personalities in the President's political party.

[7]Article II, Section 2, Clause 2.

Terms and Pay of Judges

Article III, Section 1 reads, in part:

> "The judges, both of the Supreme and inferior courts, shall hold their offices during good behavior . . . "

The judges of the constitutional courts are appointed for life—until they resign, retire, or die in office. They may be removed only through the impeachment process. Only 13 federal judges have ever been impeached. Of them, seven were convicted and removed by the Senate, including three in the past few years.[8]

The Constitution's grant of what amounts to life tenure for most judges is intended, and works, to ensure the independence of the federal judiciary.

A few federal judges are not appointed for life. The judges of the Claims Court, the Court of Military Appeals, and the Court of Veterans Appeals are appointed for 15-year terms, and those of the Tax Court for 12 years. Territorial court judges are appointed to 10-year terms. In the District of Columbia, Superior Court judges are chosen for four-year terms; those who sit on the court of appeals are chosen for a period of eight years.

Article III, Section 1 also declares that federal judges in the constitutional courts

> "shall, at stated times, receive for their services a compensation which shall not be diminished during their continuance in office."

Congress sets the salaries of all federal judges. For their salaries today, see page 478.

[8]The judges removed from office were John Pickering of the district court in New Hampshire, for judicial misconduct and drunkenness, in 1804; West H. Humphreys of the district court in Tennessee, for disloyalty, in 1862; Robert W. Archibald of the old Commerce Court, for improper relations with litigants, in 1913; Halsted L. Ritter of the district court in Florida, on several counts of judicial misconduct, in 1936; Harry E. Clairborne of the district court in Nevada, for filing false income tax returns, in 1986; Alcee Hastings of the district court in Florida, on charges of bribery and false testimony, in 1989; and Walter Nixon of the district court in Mississippi, for perjury, in 1989.

Four judges, impeached by the House, were acquitted in the Senate. Two other district court judges, impeached by the House, resigned and so avoided a Senate trial.

Provide Guided Practice
Write the words *constitutional courts* and *special courts* on the chalkboard. Ask students to come forward and write a sentence or phrase that describes the function of each type of federal court. Then lead them in a discussion that explains the jurisdiction of the federal court system.

Provide Independent Practice

TRF **Teacher's Resource File**
You may wish to assign Section 1 Guided Reading and Review, Unit 5 File, p. 3, to help students master section objective content.

Spotlight on: Behind the Scenes

Several Presidents have discovered that the person they thought they were appointing to the Supreme Court was not the person they got. When Dwight Eisenhower appointed California Governor Earl Warren chief justice of the Supreme Court in 1953, for example, Ike assumed that the Republican Warren shared his conservative views. But Warren turned out to be a most liberal chief justice, and his tenure was marked by landmark decisions extending civil rights and the rights of the accused. In private Eisenhower groused that the appointment was "the biggest . . . mistake I ever made."

Enrichment

Using magazines and newspapers, have students choose a federal court case that is in the news. Have them write a statement about the kind of court and its jurisdiction, then cite examples from the case that outline the court's authority, activities, and the roles of its officers. (Average)

Monitor Comprehension

Answers to Section 1 Review
1. "Key Terms" are defined on the following pages:
- **a.** jurisdiction, p. 462
- **b.** exclusive jurisdiction, p. 464
- **c.** concurrent jurisdiction, p. 464
- **d.** plaintiff, p. 464
- **e.** defendant, p. 464
- **f.** original jurisdiction, p. 464
- **g.** appellate jurisdiction, p. 464

2. To provide a means of interpreting and applying federal laws. **3.** The Federal and State governments each have their own court systems. **4.** Subject matter and parties involved. **5.** The President. Life. **6.** Impeachment. **7.** Clerks keep court seal and a record of proceedings. Magistrates issue warrants, decide whether there is a need for a grand jury, set bail. Bankruptcy judges handle bankruptcy cases. Attorneys prosecute. Marshals make federal arrests, keep accused people in custody, serve legal papers. **8.** Students may suggest experience, integrity, knowledge.

Closure

Point out to students that the United States has a dual court system that includes State and federal courts. Federal courts have jurisdiction in cases involving certain subject matter and certain parties. In Section 2, students will read more about federal courts, specifically the inferior courts.

Assignment Assign Section 2, pages 468–470, for the next class period.

Congress has provided a generous retirement arrangement for federal judges. They may retire at age 70, and if they have served for at least 10 years, receive full salary for the rest of their lives. Or, they may retire at full salary at age 65, after at least 15 years of service. The chief justice may call any retired judge back to temporary duty in a lower federal court at any time.

Court Officers

Today, federal judges are little involved in the day-to-day administrative operations of the courts over which they preside. Their primary mission is to hear and decide cases. Other judicial personnel provide the support services necessary to permit the federal judges to perform that basic task.

Each federal court appoints a clerk who has custody of the seal of the court and keeps a record of the court's proceedings. Deputy clerks, stenographers, bailiffs, and others assist the clerk.

Each of the 91 federal district courts now appoints at least one United States magistrate, an officer of the court who handles a number of legal matters once dealt with by the judges themselves. Federal magistrates serve eight-year terms. They issue warrants of arrest and often hear evidence to decide whether or not a person who has been arrested on a federal charge should be held for action by the grand jury. They also set bail in federal criminal cases, and even have the power to try those who are charged with certain minor offenses.

Each federal judicial district also has at least one bankruptcy judge. These court officers handle bankruptcy cases at the direction of the district court to which they are assigned.[9] There are now altogether 291 bankruptcy judges; they are appointed to 14-year terms by the judges of each of the federal courts of appeals.

The President appoints, subject to Senate confirmation, a United States attorney for each federal judicial district. The U.S. attorneys and their assistants are responsible for the prosecution of all persons charged with federal crimes and they represent the United States in all civil actions brought by or against the government in their district.

The President and Senate also appoint a United States marshal to serve each district court. Each federal marshal and the marshal's deputies carry out duties much like those handled by a county sheriff and the sheriff's deputies. They make arrests in federal criminal cases, keep accused persons in custody, secure jurors, serve legal papers, keep order in the courtroom, and execute court orders and decisions.

United States attorneys and marshals are each appointed to four-year terms. Although they are officers of the court, they serve under the direction of the attorney general and are officials of the Department of Justice.

[9]Recall that bankruptcy is a legal proceeding in which a debtor's assets are distributed among those to whom the bankrupt person, business firm, or other organization owes money. Although some bankruptcy cases are heard in State courts, nearly all of them fall within the jurisdiction of the federal district courts.

Section 1 Review

1. Define: jurisdiction, exclusive jurisdiction, concurrent jurisdiction, plaintiff, defendant, original jurisdiction, appellate jurisdiction

2. For what reasons did the Framers provide for a national judiciary?

3. What is meant by the phrase "a dual system of courts"?

4. What are the two general principles that determine if the federal courts have jurisdiction over cases?

5. Who appoints federal judges and for what terms?

6. How may federal judges be removed from office?

7. Describe the functions of the officers who assist the judges in the administrative operations of the federal courts.

Critical Thinking

8. Drawing Conclusions (p. 19) In your opinion, what are the most important qualifications a President should consider in appointing a Supreme Court justice?

★

Teacher's Resource File
See the Unit 5 File, p. 4, for the Section 1 Quiz.

Reteach

Write the word *jurisdiction* on the board and ask students to describe its meaning. When they have fully explored the word, have students discuss the various jurisdictions found in the federal court system.

Should School Officials Have the Right to Search Your Property?

New Jersey v. *T.L.O.*

In 1980, at Piscataway High School in New Jersey, a teacher caught two students smoking cigarettes in the girls' restroom. One of these students was T.L.O., aged 14. In the vice-principal's office T.L.O. denied that she was smoking, but the other student admitted it. The vice-principal asked to inspect the contents of T.L.O.'s purse and found cigarette-rolling papers. Because the vice-principal thought that he might also find marijuana, he searched further. T.L.O.'s purse contained a small amount of marijuana, several empty plastic bags, and a pipe.

The police and T.L.O.'s mother were notified, and T.L.O. was taken to police headquarters where she confessed to selling marijuana at the high school. In juvenile court, T.L.O. was declared a delinquent. She received a year's probation as punishment.

T.L.O. appealed her case to the superior court of New Jersey. Her lawyer cited the 4th Amendment, which states that a warrant must be obtained before searching personal property. Furthermore, the exclusionary rule states that illegally obtained evidence is not admissible in court. The superior court of New Jersey upheld the lower court's ruling. T.L.O. then appealed to the Supreme Court of New Jersey, which reversed the lower court's decision. At this point, the State of New Jersey appealed to the U.S. Supreme Court.

Review the following evidence and arguments presented to the U.S. Supreme Court:

Arguments for New Jersey

1. School officials are acting for the parents of the students. Therefore, like parents, they do not need a search warrant.
2. The exclusionary rule of the 4th Amendment does not apply because searching T.L.O.'s purse was not illegal.
3. To protect students, school officials must have broad disciplinary powers, including the right to conduct searches.
4. School officials found that the students had broken a school rule. This fact gave the teacher "reasonable" cause for the search.

Arguments for T.L.O.

1. Students are entitled to expect a right to personal privacy in school.
2. The exclusionary rule does apply and it has been violated. Students are entitled to the protection of the 4th Amendment.
3. Public school officials are employees of the State, not representatives of parents; they do not have the right to act as parents.
4. The school official did not have "reasonable" cause to search T.L.O. Therefore, anything that he found should not be used as evidence against her.

Getting Involved

1. Identify the constitutional grounds upon which each side based its arguments.
2. Debate the opposing viewpoints presented in this case.
3. Predict how you think the Supreme Court ruled in this case and why. Then refer to the Supreme Court Glossary on page 764 to read about the decision. Discuss the impact of the Court's ruling on a student's right to privacy.

467

TEACHING
Debating Key Issues

New Jersey v. *T.L.O.*: **Should School Officials Have the Right to Search Your Property?**

Objective
Determine whether the constitutional protections against unreasonable searches apply to students.

INSTRUCT

Before reading the feature, you may want elicit student responses to the question in the title. Once they have read the feature, ask them if they have changed their minds and if so, why. Begin working through the "Getting Involved" section, starting with identifying the constitutional issues involved.

Have students read the Supreme Court's decision. Ask students to write a reaction to the decision explaining whether they agree or disagree with the decision.

SUPREME COURT DECISION

The Court set a new standard for searches in schools in this case, stating that the school had a "legitimate need to maintain an environment in which learning can take place," and that to do this ". . . requires some easing of the restrictions to which searches by public authorities are ordinarily subject. . . ." The Court thus created a "reasonable suspicion rule" for school searches, a change from the "probable cause" requirement in the wider society.

TRF **Teacher's Resource File**
See the Supreme Court Case File, p. 13, for an activity that extends coverage of this case.

SECTION 2
The Inferior Courts

FOCUS

Teacher's Resource File
See the Unit 5 File, p. 5, for the Section 2 Outline.

Objectives

18.5 Determine where most federal cases are heard.
18.6 Examine the jurisdiction of the federal district courts and the court of appeals.

Bellringer Activity Use the following activity to help students understand the concept of "appeal." Ask students how they would react if they felt that they had been improperly penalized on a quiz or test. Guide them to conclude that they would "appeal" to you to change the grade, and if that did not work, they might choose to appeal to a higher authority.

State the Purpose The courts of appeals represent one of the groups of courts in the federal judicial system. That system also includes the district courts, which hear the largest share of federal cases, the courts of appeals, the Court of International Trade, and the Court of Appeals for the Federal Circuit. In this section, students will read about these courts.

ABCNEWS INTERACTIVE

The following video segment may be used to highlight discussion of the inferior courts.

POWERS OF THE SUPREME COURT GUIDEBOOK
Chapter 3: Constitution and the Court, p. 4

2 The Inferior Courts

Find Out:

- Where are most federal cases heard?
- What is the jurisdiction of the federal district court and the courts of appeals?

You know and use a great many words that have more than one meaning. The particular meaning of any of them depends on the context, or the setting, in which you use it. Thus, *pitch* can either be a baseball or a musical term; or it can be used to refer to the setting up of a tent, or to a high-pressure sales talk, or to a number of other things.

So it is with the word *inferior.* Here it describes the lower federal courts, those beneath the Supreme Court.

As you will see in this section, those very important courts handle nearly all of the cases tried in the federal courts.

The District Courts

The United States district courts are the federal trial courts. Their 649 judges handle some 250,000 cases a year, some 80 percent of the federal caseload.

The district courts were created by Congress in the Judiciary Act of 1789. There are now 91 of them. The 50 States are divided into 89 judicial districts, with one court in each district. There is also a district court in the District of Columbia and another in Puerto Rico. The map on page 470 shows how these districts are distributed across the country.

Each State forms at least one federal judicial district, no matter what that State's size or population. The larger, more populous States are divided into two or more districts. At least two judges are assigned to each district, but many have several. Thus, the populous state of New York is divided into four judicial districts; and one of those districts, the United States Judicial District for Southern New York, now has 27 judges.

Cases tried in the district courts are most often heard by a single judge. However, certain cases may be heard by a three-judge panel.[10]

Jurisdiction The district courts have original jurisdiction over most cases that are heard in the federal courts.[11] That amounts to another way of saying that these district courts are the principal trial courts in the federal court system.

The district courts hear a wide range of both criminal cases and civil cases.[12] They try cases ranging from bank robbery, kidnapping, and mail fraud to counterfeiting, tax evasion, and narcotics violations. They hear civil cases arising under the bankruptcy, postal, tax, labor relations, public lands, civil rights, and other laws of the United States.

The district courts are the only federal courts that regularly use grand juries to indict defendants and petit juries to try defendants. (You will read about grand and petit juries in more detail in Chapter 20. You will also read about grand and petit juries in the State court system in Chapter 25.)

Most of the decisions made in the 91 federal district courts are final and proceed no further in the judicial system. However, some cases are appealed to the court of appeals in that judicial circuit or, in a few instances, directly to the Supreme Court.

[10]Congress has directed that three-judge panels hear certain cases. Chiefly, these are cases that involve congressional districting or State legislative apportionment questions, those arising under the Civil Rights Act of 1964 or the Voting Rights Acts of 1965, 1970, 1975, and 1982, and certain antitrust actions.

[11]The district courts have original jurisdiction over all federal cases except: (1) those few cases that fall within the original jurisdiction of the United States Supreme Court and (2) those cases that are heard by the Court of International Trade or by one of the special courts (see Section 4).

[12]In the federal courts, a criminal case is one in which a defendant is tried for committing some action that Congress has declared by law to be a federal crime, a wrong against the public. A federal civil case involves some noncriminal matter, such as a dispute between two parties over the terms of a contract or a claim of patent infringement.

Reading Strategy: Who? What? When? Where? How? Why?

As students read Section 2, have them write short answers to the questions: who? what? when? where? how? and why? to help them sort out the differences among the various inferior courts.

Vocabulary

There are no "Key Terms" listed in Section 2. Instead, ask students to review the words from Section 1, specifically *jurisdiction* and *appellate.* As they read through Section 2, check students' understanding of the words *district* and *circuit.*

The Courts of Appeals

The courts of appeals were created by Congress in 1891. They were established as "gatekeepers" to relieve the Supreme Court of much of the burden of hearing appeals from the district courts.[13] Those appeals had become so numerous that the Supreme Court was then three years behind its docket—its list of cases to be heard.

There are now 12 courts of appeals in the judicial system. The United States is divided into 11 judicial circuits, with one court of appeals for each of those circuits; there is also one in the District of Columbia. Again, the map on page 470 shows the extent of the federal judicial circuits.

Altogether, 179 circuit judges sit on these appellate courts. In addition, a justice of the Supreme Court is assigned to each of them. For example, the Fifth Circuit of the United States Court of Appeals covers three States: Louisiana, Mississippi, and Texas. Its court of appeals has 18 judges, and Associate Justice Byron White is also assigned to the circuit. The court sits in a number of different cities within the circuit.

Each of the courts of appeals usually sits in panels of three judges. However, occasionally, to hear an important case a court will sit *en banc*—that is, with all of the judges for that circuit participating.

Jurisdiction The courts of appeals have only appellate jurisdiction. They hear cases on appeal from the lower federal courts. Most often, those appeals come from the district courts within their circuits. But some do come from the United States Tax Court and from the several territorial courts. The courts of appeals also hear appeals from the decisions of several federal regulatory agencies—from such quasi-judicial agencies as the Interstate Commerce Commission, the Nuclear Regulatory Commission, and the Federal Trade Commission.[14]

[13]These tribunals were originally known as the circuit courts of appeals. Before 1891, Supreme Court justices "rode circuit" to hear appeals from the district courts. Congress renamed these courts in 1948, but they still are often called the circuit courts.

[14]Recall that the several independent regulatory commissions have both quasi-legislative (rule-making) and quasi-judicial (decision-making) powers; see Chapter 15, Section 2.

Interpreting Political Cartoons What does this cartoon reveal about the need for the creation of the courts of appeals in 1891?

The courts of appeals now handle about 40,000 cases a year. Their decisions are final, unless the Supreme Court chooses to hear appeals taken from them.

Two Other Constitutional Courts

The Court of International Trade and the Court of Appeals for the Federal Circuit are also constitutional courts.

The Court of International Trade The Trade Court was originally created as the Board of United States General Appraisers in 1890. That body became the Court of Customs in 1926, and Congress restructured and renamed that court in 1980.

The Trade Court now has nine judges, one of whom is its chief judge. It hears civil cases arising out of the tariff and other trade-related laws. The judges of the Trade Court sit in panels of three and often hold trials at such major ports as New Orleans, San Francisco, Boston, and New York.

Appeals from decisions of the Trade Court are taken to the Court of Appeals for the Federal Circuit.

The Court of Appeals for the Federal Circuit Congress created the Court of Appeals for  the Federal Circuit in 1982. It established the new tribunal to centralize, and so speed up, the handling of appeals in certain kinds of civil cases.

INSTRUCT

Explain/Discuss The inferior courts are so-called because they are the *lower* federal courts, those beneath the Supreme Court. Among the courts that are called inferior are district courts, the courts of appeals, the Court of International Trade, and the Court of Appeals for the Federal Circuit.

Direct students' attention to the statement that the district courts are the trial courts in the federal system and hear the large majority of the federal caseload. Then ask students to consider the role of the courts of appeals. Have students discuss why the courts were created.

Interpreting Political Cartoons Ask students what image this artist used to communicate the idea of the problems facing the Supreme Court. (*Many disorganized papers.*)

Caption Answer The Supreme Court justices appear to be overloaded with cases from the lower courts.

Provide Guided Practice Write on the chalkboard the words *Inferior Courts.* Ask volunteers to identify the four types of inferior courts discussed in this section. Then ask students to fill in information under each heading that explains the function and jurisdiction of each court.

Provide Independent Practice
TRF **Teacher's Resource File** You may wish to assign the Section 2 Guided Reading and Review, Unit 5 File, p. 6, to help students master section objective content.

Enrichment
Have students generate imaginary examples of cases that would fall under the jurisdiction of each of the inferior courts discussed in this section. (Average)

SPOTLIGHT ON: Economics
The U.S. district courts and the courts of appeals consume the vast majority of the judiciary's annual budget, accounting for $2.54 billion of the judicial branch's $2.57 billion budget in 1992. About $2 billion of that amount goes to pay the salaries of justices, clerks, administrators, custodians, and other permanent employees of the district and appeals courts. The budget for security alone in these courts ($85 million) is over three times the amount paid to run the entire Supreme Court ($25 million). The lower federal courts paid some $70 million in juror fees alone in 1992.

Interpreting Maps Ask students to describe the difference between the sizes and shapes of judicial districts and circuits. (*Circuits are large and consist of several States. Districts are smaller—at least one per State.*)

Caption Answer Population is a factor in the division of judicial districts.

Monitor Comprehension

Answers to Section 2 Review
1. (a) 91. (b) 649. **2.** All federal cases except those in the original jurisdiction of the Supreme Court or those heard by the Court of International Trade or the special courts. **3.** To relieve the Supreme Court. **4.** District courts, Tax Court, territorial courts, and appeals from regulatory agencies. **5.** (a) Cases involving tariffs or trade-related laws. (b) Appeals in civil cases from the Court of International Trade and other courts. **6.** Need to provide opportunities to review decisions involving the law.

Closure

In the federal judicial system, the inferior courts hear most of the caseload. The district courts are the principal trial courts, and the courts of appeals hear most of the appeals. Other courts hear specific types of cases. In Section 3, students will read about the Supreme Court, the highest court in the land.

Assignment Assign Section 3, pages 471–476, for the next class period.

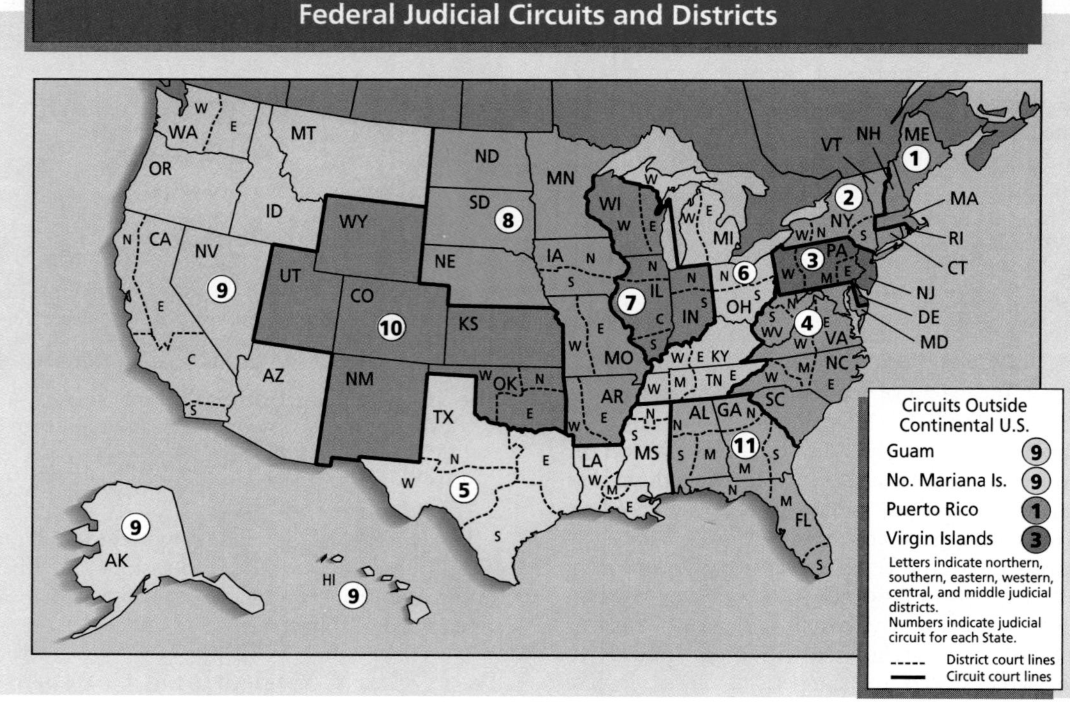

Interpreting Maps Examine the outlines of the judicial circuits and districts on the map above. How do you think the division of judicial districts was determined?

This court, unlike the 12 other federal courts of appeals, hears cases from all across the country. That is, has a nationwide jurisdiction.

The Court of Appeals for the Federal Circuit hears appeals from several different courts. Many of its cases come from the Trade Court, and others from the Claims Court and the Court of Veterans Appeals, two special courts. It also hears appeals in certain cases—those involving patents, trademarks, or copyrights—decided by any of the 91 district courts around the country. Then, too, it takes cases that arise out of the administrative rulings made by the International Trade Commission, the Patent and Trademark Office in the Department of Commerce, and the Merit Systems Protection Board.

The Court of Appeals for the Federal Circuit has 12 judges. Appeals from their decisions are occasionally carried to the United States Supreme Court.

Section 2 Review

1. (a) How many federal district courts are there? (b) How many district court judges?
2. Over what cases do the district courts have jurisdiction?
3. Why were the courts of appeals created?
4. Where do cases that reach the courts of appeals originate?
5. (a) Over what type of cases does the Court of International Trade have jurisdiction? (b) The Court of Appeals for the Federal Circuit?

Critical Thinking

6. Drawing Conclusions (p. 19) A significant portion of the federal court system is set up to hear appeals. What does this fact suggest about the nature of law and judicial proceedings?

★

TRF **Teacher's Resource File**
See the Unit 5 File, p. 7, for the Section 2 Quiz.

Reteach

Have students look at the objectives for Section 2 and write them down on a sheet of paper. Then ask them to write out the answers to each of the objectives, filling in as much detail as they can from their reading.

3 The Supreme Court

Find Out:

- For what reasons is the Supreme Court of the United States often called the High Court?
- Why is judicial review such a key feature of the American system of government?

Key Terms:

writ of certiorari, certificate, majority opinion, concurring opinion, dissenting opinion

The eagle, the flag, Uncle Sam—you almost certainly recognize these symbols. They are widely used to represent the United States. You probably also know the symbol for justice—the blindfolded woman holding a balanced scale. She represents what is perhaps this nation's highest goal: equal justice for all. Indeed, those words are chiseled into the marble above the entrance to the Supreme Court building in Washington, D.C.

The Supreme Court of the United States is the only court specifically created in the Constitution.[15] It is made up of the chief justice of the United States, whose office is also established by the Constitution,[16] and eight associate justices.[17] The Framers quite purposely placed the Court on an equal plane with the President and Congress and designed it as the apex, the highest point, of the nation's judicial system. As the highest court in the land, the Supreme Court stands as the court of last resort in all questions of federal law. That is, it is the final authority in any case involving any question arising under the Constitution, an act of Congress, or a treaty of the United States.

[15]Article III, Section 1.

[16]Article I, Section 3, Clause 6.

[17]Congress sets the number of associate justices and thus the size of the Supreme Court. The Judiciary Act of 1789 created a Court of six justices, including the chief justice. Its size was reduced to five members in 1801, but increased to seven in 1807, to nine in 1837, and to 10 in 1863. It was reduced to seven in 1866 and raised to its present size in 1869.

VOICES *on Government*

On the Function of the Supreme Court

Sandra Day O'Connor, Associate Justice of the Supreme Court

"[O]ne of the Supreme Court's most important functions—perhaps the most important function—is to oversee the system-wide elaboration of federal law, with an eye toward creating and preserving uniformity of interpretation. Today, this function is uppermost in the minds of the Justices in exercising the discretion to take cases for review. Indeed, the most commonly enunciated reason for granting review on a case is the need to resolve conflicts among other courts over the interpretation of federal law."

Judicial Review

As you read in Chapter 3 and elsewhere, most courts in this country, both federal and State, may exercise the critically important power of judicial review. They have the extraordinary power to decide the constitutionality of an act of government, whether executive, legislative, or judicial. The ultimate exercise of that power rests with the Supreme Court of the United States. That single fact makes the Supreme Court the final authority on the meaning of the Constitution.

The Constitution does not in so many words provide for the power of judicial review. Still, there is little room for doubt that the Framers intended that the federal courts—and,

Section 3
The Supreme Court

Focus

Teacher's Resource File See the Unit 5 File, p. 8, for the Section 3 Outline.

Objectives

18.7 Examine the reasons why the Supreme Court is often called the High Court.

18.8 Determine the reasons why judicial review is a key feature in the American system of government.

Bellringer Activity Ask students to express their opinion on one or all of the following issues: the death penalty, affirmative action, discrimination against women and minority groups, or abortion. Encourage students to identify both sides of the debate over these issues and to appreciate the difficulty of making laws and decisions about these issues that satisfy all people.

State the Purpose The Supreme Court is the highest court in the United States judicial system, and it is often called upon to decide the most troublesome and divisive questions facing the country. In addition, the Court has the key power of judicial review. In Section 3, students will read in detail about the Supreme Court and its role within the United States judicial system.

Vocabulary

Have students keep a list of "Key Terms" found on page 471. As they read through Section 3, ask them to fill in the definition of each term and to jot down notes about what each term has to do with the Supreme Court.

Reading Strategy: Problem Solving

Ask students to consider the following: Congress has passed a law prohibiting the burning of the American flag. The law has stirred great debate among the American people. Some argue that the law violates the Constitution, others say that it is constitutional. How would you propose resolving this dispute? Who should decide what is and is not permissible under the Constitution?

INSTRUCT

Explain/Analyze Discuss with students the concept of judicial review. Tell students that this power of the Supreme Court gives the judicial branch the power to check and balance the other two branches of government. Have students explain why this is essential to the American system of government. (*Checks and balances help ensure that no individual or branch obtains too much power over government and the people.*) In light of the power of judicial review, ask students to speculate on why the Supreme Court is called the High Court. (*It is the top authority on matters of the Constitution and federal law.*) Also, ask students to discuss how the manner in which cases reach the Court reflect the preeminent role of the Court. (*The Court generally hears only those few questions that it feels raise profound constitutional questions.*)

To have students understand the role of the Supreme Court, conduct a role play based on a topic introduced in the "Bellringer." Before class, prepare two briefs that outline the opposing arguments. (If time permits, you may want to assign small groups of students to do this.)

Assign two students to play the roles of the lawyers who present the different arguments. Have the rest of the class pretend that they are justices of the Supreme Court. They must listen to the arguments, then discuss the case as though they were meeting in conference. Ask two volunteers to present the majority and dissenting opinions.

in particular, the Supreme Court—should have the power.[18] In *The Federalist* No. 78 Alexander Hamilton wrote:

> "The interpretation of the laws is the proper and peculiar province of the courts. A constitution is, in fact, and must be regarded by the judges, as a fundamental law. It therefore belongs to them to ascertain its meaning, as well as the meaning of any particular act proceeding from the legislative body. If there should happen to be an irreconcilable variance between the two, that which has the superior obligation and validity ought, of course, to be preferred; or, in other words, the Constitution ought to be preferred to the statute, the intention of the people to the intention of their agents."

The Court first asserted its power of judicial review in the classic case of *Marbury* v. *Madison* in 1803.[19] The case arose in the aftermath of the stormy elections of 1800. Thomas Jefferson and his Anti-Federalists had won the presidency and control of both houses of Congress. The outgoing Federalists, stung by their defeat, then tried to pack the judiciary with loyal party members. Congress created several new federal judgeships in the early weeks of 1801; President John Adams quickly filled those judgeships with Federalists.

William Marbury had been appointed a justice of the peace for the District of Columbia. The Senate had confirmed his appointment and, late the night of March 3, 1801, the soon-to-be outgoing President Adams had signed his and a number of other new judges' commissions of office. The next day Jefferson became the President—and learned that Marbury's commission, and several others, had not yet been delivered.

Angered by the Federalists' court-packing, Jefferson at once told James Madison, the new secretary of state, not to deliver those commissions to the "midnight justices." William Marbury then went to the Supreme Court, seeking a *writ of mandamus*[20] to force delivery.

Marbury based his suit on a provision of the Judiciary Act of 1789, in which Congress had created the federal court system. That law gave the Supreme Court the right to hear such suits in its *original* jurisdiction (not on appeal from a lower court).

In a unanimous opinion written by Chief Justice John Marshall, the Court refused Marbury's request.[21] It did so because it found the section of the judiciary act on which Marbury had based his case in conflict with the Constitution and, therefore, void. Specifically, it found the statute in conflict with Article III, Section 2, Clause 2, which reads in part:

> "In all cases affecting ambassadors, other public ministers and consuls, and those in which a State shall be a party, the Supreme Court shall have original jurisdiction. In all other cases before mentioned, the Supreme Court shall have appellate jurisdiction . . . "

The impact of the Court's decision goes far beyond the fate of an obscure individual named William Marbury. In this decision, Chief Justice Marshall claimed for the Court the right to declare acts of Congress unconstitutional, and so laid the foundation for the judicial branch's key role in the development of the American system of government.

Marshall's powerful opinion was based on three propositions. First, the Constitution is, by its own terms, *the* supreme law of the land. Second, all legislative enactments, and all other actions of government, are subordinate to and cannot be allowed to conflict with the supreme law. Third, judges are sworn to enforce the provisions of the Constitution and therefore must refuse to enforce any governmental action they find to be in conflict with it.

[18]See Article III, Section 2, setting out the Court's jurisdiction, and Article VI, Section 2, the Supremacy Clause.

[19]It is often mistakenly said that the Court first exercised the power in this case, but, in fact, the Court did so at least as early as *Hylton* v. *United States* in 1798. In that case it upheld the constitutionality of a tax Congress had laid on carriages.

[20]A court order compelling an officer of government to perform an act which that officer has a clear legal duty to perform.

[21]Marshall was appointed chief justice by President John Adams, and he took office on January 31, 1801. He served in the post for 34 years, until his death on July 6, 1835. He also served as Adams's secretary of state from May 13, 1800 to March 4, 1801. Thus, he served as secretary of state and as chief justice for more than a month at the end of the Adams administration. What is more, he was the secretary of state who had failed to deliver Marbury's commission in a timely fashion.

Activity: Cooperative Learning

Time: One class period **Activity:** Create scenarios of federal court cases. **Grouping:** Groups of three to four students **Purpose:** Have each group create two hypothetical cases that would be tried in the federal court system. Cases may involve criminal or civil matters, and each scenario should describe the subject matter of the case, the plaintiff, and the defendant. Encourage students to create scenarios for different courts in the federal system. **Roles:** Assign the following roles: discussion leader, recorder, spokesperson. **Outcome:** Have spokespersons describe to the class the subject matter and the parties in each group's scenarios. The class may then identify the case as criminal or civil, and determine the courts that would have original and appellate jurisdiction.

The Justices of the Supreme Court From left to right, Byron R. White, Chief Justice William H. Rehnquist, Antonin Scalia, Sandra Day O'Connor, David Souter, Thurgood Marshall (retired, 1991; replaced by Clarence Thomas, not pictured here), Anthony M. Kennedy, Harry A. Blackmun, and John Paul Stevens.

As you have seen, the Court has used its power of judicial review in thousands of cases since 1803. Usually it has upheld the constitutionality of federal and State actions.

The dramatic and often far-reaching effects of the Supreme Court's exercise of the power of judicial review tends to overshadow much of its other work. Each year it hears dozens of cases in which questions of constitutionality are not raised, but in which federal law still is interpreted and applied. Thus, many of the more important statutes that Congress has passed have been brought to the Supreme Court time and again for decision. So, too, have many of the lesser ones. In interpreting those laws and applying them to specific situations, the Court has had a real impact on both their meaning and their effect.

Remember, too, that the Court has a very large role as the umpire in the federal system, as noted in Chapter 4. It decides those legal disputes that arise between the National Government and the States and those that arise between or among the States.

Jurisdiction

The Supreme Court has both original and appellate jurisdiction. But most of its cases come on appeal—from the lower federal courts and from the State supreme courts.

Article III, Section 2 of the Constitution spells out two classes of cases that may be heard by the High Court in its original jurisdiction: (1) those to which a State is a party and (2) those affecting ambassadors, other public ministers, and consuls.

Congress cannot enlarge on this constitutional grant of original jurisdiction. If Congress could do so, it would in effect be amending the Constitution. But Congress can implement the constitutional provision, and it has done so. It has provided that the Court shall have original *and* exclusive jurisdiction over (1) all controversies between two or more States and (2) all cases brought against ambassadors or other public ministers, but not consuls. The Court may, if it chooses to do so, take original jurisdiction over any other case covered by the

ABCNEWS INTERACTIVE

The following video segments may be used to highlight discussion of the Supreme Court.

POWERS OF THE SUPREME COURT GUIDEBOOK
Chapter 3: A Typical Day, p. 62
Chapter 5: U.S. Supreme Court, p. 6
Chapter 14: Granting "Certiorari," p. 76
Chapter 20: Judicial Review, p. 83

See also Enrichment Questions and Activities.

SPOTLIGHT ON: Multiculturalism

After 178 years of imparting "equal justice under law," the color line on the Supreme Court was finally broken in 1967 when President Lyndon Johnson appointed Justice Thurgood Marshall to the nation's highest court. Marshall, a celebrated attorney who argued several landmark civil rights cases in the 1950s, was the first African American to serve on the Supreme Court. Fourteen years later, in the Court's 192nd year, Sandra Day O'Connor, a justice on the Arizona Court of Appeals, was appointed by President Ronald Reagan as an associate justice, the first and, so far, only woman to hold that position.

Interpreting Tables As students study the chart on page 474, ask them to consider the ages of the chief justices. What does this suggest about the job of chief justice? (*Long experience in the court system is critical to the job.*)

Caption Answer Oliver Ellsworth (4 years) and Harlan F. Stone (5 years). Also, John Rutledge, who was not confirmed, served but a few months. As of 1993, Rehnquist will have served the same amount of time as Fred M. Vinson.

broad wording in Article III, Section 2 of the Constitution. But, almost always, those cases are tried in the lower courts. The Supreme Court hears only a very small number of cases in its original jurisdiction—in fact, only a case or two each term.

Article III, Section 2 of the Constitution also gives to Congress the power to set the Court's appellate jurisdiction. Until 1925 the High Court had little control over its caseload; since then, however, Congress has given it an increasingly broad authority to choose the cases it will review. Today, that authority is practically complete.

How Cases Reach the Court

Some 4,500 to 5,000 cases are now appealed to the Supreme Court each year. Of these, the Court accepts only a few hundred for decision. The Court selects those cases it will hear according to "the rule of four": at least four of its nine justices must agree that a case should be put on the Court's docket.

More than half the cases decided by the Court are disposed of in brief orders. For example, an order may remand (return) a case to a lower court for reconsideration in the light of some other recent and related case decided by the High Court. All told, the Court decides, after hearing arguments and with full opinions, only about 120 cases a year.

1.a Most cases reach the Supreme Court by **writ of certiorari** (from the Latin, "to be made more certain"). This writ is an order by the Court directing a lower court to send up the record in a given case for its review.

Either party to a case can petition the Court to issue a writ. But, again, "cert" is granted in only a limited number of instances—typically, only when a petition raises some important constitutional question or a serious problem of statutory interpretation.

When certiorari is denied, the decision of the lower court stands in that particular case. But the denial of cert is not a decision on the merits of a case. All that a denial means is that, for

Chief Justices of the United States

Name and Years of Service	State From Which Appointed	President By Whom Appointed	Salary (Last Year of Service)	Age When Appointed
John Jay (1789–1795)	New York	Washington	$ 4,000	44
John Rutledge (1795)*	South Carolina	Washington	$ 4,000	55
Oliver Ellsworth (1796–1800)	Connecticut	Washington	$ 4,000	51
John Marshall (1801–1835)	Virginia	John Adams	$ 5,000	46
Roger B. Taney (1836–1864)	Maryland	Jackson	$ 6,500	59
Salmon P. Chase (1864–1873)	Ohio	Lincoln	$ 8,500	56
Morrison R. Waite (1874–1888)	Ohio	Grant	$ 10,500	58
Melville W. Fuller (1888–1910)	Illinois	Cleveland	$ 13,000	55
Edward D. White (1910–1921)	Louisiana	Taft	$ 15,000	65
William Howard Taft (1921–1930)	Connecticut	Harding	$ 20,500	64
Charles Evans Hughes (1930–1941)	New York	Hoover	$ 20,500	68
Harlan F. Stone (1941–1946)	New York	F. D. Roosevelt	$ 20,500	69
Fred M. Vinson (1946–1953)	Kentucky	Truman	$ 25,500	56
Earl Warren (1953–1969)	California	Eisenhower	$ 40,000	62
Warren E. Burger (1969–1986)	Washington, D.C.	Nixon	$ 108,400	61
William H. Rehnquist (1986–)	Arizona	Reagan	$ 160,600	62

*Rutledge was appointed chief justice on July 1, 1795, while Congress was not in session. He presided over the August 1795 term of the Supreme Court, but the Senate rejected his appointment on December 15, 1795.

Interpreting Tables Length of terms of service on the Supreme Court vary widely. Chief Justice Rehnquist already has served on the Court longer than which three former chief justices?

Justices of the Supreme Court

Name	State From Which Appointed	President By Whom Appointed	Year of Birth	Year When Appointed
Chief Justice:				
William H. Rehnquist	Arizona	Reagan	1924	1986*
Associate Justices:				
Byron R. White	Colorado	Kennedy	1918	1962
Harry A. Blackmun	Minnesota	Nixon	1908	1970
John Paul Stevens	Illinois	Ford	1916	1975
Sandra Day O'Connor	Arizona	Reagan	1930	1981
Antonin Scalia	Washington, D.C.	Reagan	1936	1986
Anthony M. Kennedy	California	Reagan	1935	1988
David H. Souter	New Hampshire	Bush	1939	1990
Clarence Thomas	Washington, D.C.	Bush	1948	1991

*Originally appointed as an Associate Justice by President Nixon in 1971.

Interpreting Tables Some Presidents have the opportunity to appoint more than one Supreme Court justice. From the table, how did former President Reagan use his appointments to diversify the Court?

whatever reason, four or more justices could not agree that the Supreme Court should accept that case for review.

A few cases do reach the Court in yet another way, by **certificate**. This process is used when a 1.b lower court is not clear about the procedure or the rule of law that should apply in a case. The lower court asks the Supreme Court to certify the answer to a specific question in the matter.

Most cases that reach the Court do so from the highest State courts and the federal courts of appeal. A few do come, however, from the federal district courts and a very few from the Court of Military Appeals.

The Supreme Court at Work

The Court sits from the first Monday in October to sometime the following June or July. Each term is identified by the year in which it began. Thus, the 1992 term begins on October 5, 1992.

Oral Arguments Once the Supreme Court accepts a case, it sets a date on which lawyers on both sides will present oral arguments.

As a rule, the justices consider cases in two-week cycles, from October to early May. They hear oral arguments in several cases for two weeks; then the justices recess for two weeks, to consider those cases and handle other Court business.

While the Supreme Court is hearing oral arguments, it convenes at 10 A.M. on Mondays, Tuesdays, Wednesdays, and sometimes Thursdays. At those public sessions, the lawyers make their oral arguments. Their presentations are almost always limited to 30 minutes.[22] Most lawyers try to use that half hour to emphasize the major points they made in their written briefs.

Briefs Briefs are written documents filed with the Court before oral argument. They are detailed statements that support one side of a case and are largely built of relevant facts and the citation of previous cases. Many run to hundreds of pages.

The Court may also receive ***amicus curiae*** (friend of the court) briefs. These are briefs filed by persons or groups who are not actual parties to a case but who nonetheless have a substantial

[22]The justices usually listen closely to the lawyers' oral arguments and sometimes interrupt them with questions or requests for information. After 25 minutes of a lawyer's time, a white light comes on at the lectern from which he or she addresses the Court; five minutes later a red light signals the end of that lawyer's presentation, even if he or she is in midsentence.

Interpreting Tables Ask students to look at the list of current Supreme Court justices on page 475. Ask students to comment on whether or not they think it is a positive development that the two recent Presidents have been able to name so many active justices. (*Possible answers: Yes, voters select Presidents knowing that they have the power to select justices, therefore it is the people's will that the Court be so composed. No, the Supreme Court is not meant to be influenced by party politics, and the predominance of justices chosen by Reagan and Bush too clearly politicizes the Court.*)

Caption Answer Reagan appointed the first woman ever to serve on the Supreme Court.

Provide Guided Practice Write the words *Constitution, Other Court,* and *The Executive and Legislative Branches* on the chalkboard. Ask students to volunteer information about how the Supreme Court relates to each of these terms.

Provide Independent Practice
TRF **Teacher's Resource File** You may wish to assign the Section 3 Guided Reading and Review, Unit 5 File, p. 9, to help students master section objective content.

Enrichment

Have students create a poster or a political cartoon that illustrates and explains the role of the Supreme Court in the American system of government. The poster or cartoon should include such concepts as judicial review and opinions. (Easy)

Monitor Comprehension

Answers to Section 3 Review
1. "Key Terms" are defined on the following pages:
- **a.** writ of certiorari, p. 474
- **b.** certificate, p. 475
- **c.** majority opinion, p. 476
- **d.** concurring opinion, p. 476
- **e.** dissenting opinion, p. 476

2. (a) Supreme Court. (b) Chief justice. **3.** A court's power to determine the constitutionality of an act of government. **4.** The Constitution grants original and exclusive jurisdiction to cases involving controversies between two or more States, cases against ambassadors or other public ministers, and any other case covered by the broad wording of Article III, Section 2. **5.** Highest State courts, federal courts of appeals, federal district courts, and the Court of Military Appeals. **6.** The Court stands as the final authority in interpreting and applying the Constitution. Therefore, the Court focuses only on those cases that present the most difficult questions.

Closure

Point out that the Supreme Court is the highest court in the land, which means that it has final authority over other State and federal courts concerning questions of constitutionality and federal law. In Section 4, students will learn one final class of federal courts, the special courts.

Assignment Assign Section 4, pages 477–479, for the next class period.

interest in its outcome. Thus, for example, cases involving such highly charged matters as abortion or affirmative action regularly attract a large number of *amicus* briefs. But, notice, these briefs can be filed only with the Court's permission, or at its request.

The Solicitor General The solicitor general, a principal officer in the Department of Justice, is often called the Federal Government's chief lawyer. The solicitor general represents the United States in all cases to which it is a party in the Supreme Court,[23] and may appear in any federal or State court. He or she decides which cases the government should ask the Supreme Court to review and, also, what position the United States should take in cases before the High Court. The solicitor general often files *amicus* briefs, urging the Federal Government's views in those cases.

The Conference On most Fridays through a term, the justices meet in conference. There, in closest secrecy, they consider the cases in which they have heard oral arguments.[24]

The chief justice presides over the conference. He or she speaks first on each case to be considered, and usually indicates how he or she intends to vote. Then each associate justice summarizes his or her views. Those presentations are made in order of seniority—with the justice most recently named to the Court speaking last. After the justices are "polled," they usually debate the case.

About a third of all the Court's decisions are unanimous, but most find the Court divided. The High Court is sometimes criticized for its split decisions. But, notice, its cases pose very difficult questions. And many also present questions on which lower courts have disagreed. In short, most of the Court's cases are the difficult ones; the easy cases seldom get that far.

Opinions If the chief justice is in the majority on a case, he or she assigns the writing of the Court's opinion. When the chief justice is in the minority, the assignment is handled by the senior associate justice on the majority side.

The Court's opinion is often called the
1.c **majority opinion**; officially, it is the Opinion of the Court. It announces the Court's decision in a case and sets out the reasoning on which it is based.[25] Often, one or more of the justices who agree with the Court's decision may write a **con-**
1.d **curring opinion**—to make or emphasize a point that was not made in the majority opinion.
1.e One or more **dissenting opinions** are often written, too, by those justices who do not agree with the Court's majority decision.

The Court's written opinions are exceedingly valuable. The majority opinions stand as precedents to be followed in similar cases as they arise in the lower courts or reach the Supreme Court. The concurring opinions may bring the Supreme Court to modify its present stand in future cases. Chief Justice Hughes once described dissenting opinions as "an appeal to the brooding spirit of the law, to the intelligence of a future day." On rare occasion, the Supreme Court does reverse itself; the minority opinion of today could become the Court's majority position in the future.

Section 3 Review

1. Define: writ of certiorari, certificate, majority opinion, concurring opinion, dissenting opinion
2. (a) Which is the only court created in the Constitution? (b) The only judicial office?
3. What is the power of judicial review?
4. (a) Over what cases does the Court have original jurisdiction? (b) Exclusive jurisdiction?
5. From what courts are cases appealed to the Supreme Court?

Critical Thinking

6. Demonstrating Reasoned Judgment (p. 19) The chapter says that "easy" cases do not reach the Supreme Court. For what reason do you think this is so?

★

[23]The attorney general may argue the government's position before the Supreme Court but rarely does.

[24]At conference, the justices also decide which new cases they will accept for decision.

[25]Most majority opinions, and many concurring and dissenting opinions, run to dozens of pages. Some decisions are accompanied by very brief and unsigned opinions, however. These *per curiam*, or for the court, opinions seldom run more than a paragraph or two and usually dispose of relatively uncomplicated cases.

Spotlight on: Constitutional Issues

The relatively obscure post of solicitor general became the center of a controversy over executive privilege in 1973, when Solicitor General Robert Bork fired Watergate special prosecutor Archibald Cox under orders from President Nixon. Cox, appointed by Attorney General Elliott Richardson to investigate an alleged cover-up of Nixon's involvement in the affair, sued for access to private White House tapes. Nixon ordered Richardson to fire the special prosecutor. But in what became known as the "Saturday night massacre," Richardson and his deputy resigned, leaving the firing of Cox to Bork, the number three official at the Department of Justice.

Teacher's Resource File
See the Unit 5 File, p. 10, for the Section 3 Quiz.

Reteach

Ask students to write the major section headings on a sheet of paper. Then have students review the chapter and fill in details about the content under each heading.

4 The Special Courts

Find Out:

- In what ways do the special courts differ from the constitutional courts?

Key Term:

redress

Every field has its specialists. In medicine, some doctors build their entire careers around treating a single disease. In law, some attorneys handle only criminal cases, some only accident cases, others only divorce cases, and so on. In sports, too, players have specialized roles.

In a sense, the special courts are also specialists. They are federal courts Congress has created to hear only certain cases—cases that involve only certain of the many subjects covered by the expressed powers of Congress.

These courts, also known as legislative courts, were not established under Article III, so they do not exercise the broad "judicial power of the United States." Rather, as you will see in this section, each of them has a very narrow jurisdiction.

The United States Claims Court

The United States cannot be sued—by anyone, in any court, for any reason—without its consent. It may be taken to court only in those cases in which Congress has declared that the government is open to suit.[26]

[26]The government is shielded from suit by the doctrine of sovereign immunity. It comes from an ancient principle of English public law summed up by the phrase: "The King can do no wrong." The rule is not intended to protect public officials from charges of corruption or any other wrongdoing. Rather, it is intended to prevent government from being ineffective in its own courts. Congress has long since agreed to a long list of legitimate court actions against the government.

Noriega on Trial After his capture by the American military, Panama's General Manuel Noriega is brought to court in the United States to face narcotics charges.

SECTION 4
The Special Courts

FOCUS

Teacher's Resource File See the Unit 5 File, p. 11, for the Section 4 Outline.

Objective

18.9 Determine the ways in which the special courts differ from the constitutional courts.

Bellringer Activity Ask students to look at the title of the section. Then have students offer predictions on what a special court is in the federal court system.

State the Purpose As their name suggests, the special courts serve a specialized function within the federal judicial system. They are set up by Congress to deal with subjects that are related to the expressed powers of Congress. In Section 4, students will examine the role of special courts in the U.S. federal court system.

ABCNEWS INTERACTIVE

The following video segments may be used to highlight discussion of the special courts.

POWERS OF THE SUPREME COURT GUIDEBOOK
Chapter 3: Constitution and the Court, p. 5

POWERS OF THE CONGRESS GUIDEBOOK
Chapter 19: Governing the Military, p. 22

Vocabulary

Direct students' attention to "Key Term" *redress* on page 477. Tell students to consult several dictionaries to observe the different meanings of the word. LEP

Reading Strategy: Question Writing

As students prepare to read Section 4, have them skim the headings found in the section. Ask them to turn these headings into questions such as "What is the United States Claims Court and how does it function?" As they read, have students jot down the answers to the questions they have created.

INSTRUCT

Explain/Discuss Ask students to recall what they have read about the expressed powers of Congress. (*Specifically granted to Congress in the Constitution.*) Using the example of the Claims Court, tell students that the special courts are designed to hear cases related to those powers.

Ask students to compare special courts with the constitutional courts. In what ways are they similar? (*Both are federal courts.*) In what ways do they differ? (*Constitutional courts exercise the "broad judicial power." Special courts hear a narrow range of cases.*)

Interpreting Tables Ask students to observe that judges in the constitutional courts serve for life, while special court judges serve fixed terms. Why is this so? (*The Constitution mandates life terms for judges of the constitutional courts.*)

Caption Answer The President appoints judges to these courts, but the Senate must confirm those appointments.

Provide Guided Practice Write the names of each special court on the board. Invite students to come forward and write a phrase that describes the function of each court and the expressed power of Congress on which it is based.

Provide Independent Practice

TRF **Teacher's Resource File** You may wish to assign Section 4 Guided Reading and Review, Unit 5 File, p. 12, to help students master section objective content.

The National Judiciary

Court	Created	Number of Courts	Number of Judges	Term of Judges	Judges Appointed by[a]	Salary of Judges
District Court	1789	91	563	Life	President	$125,100
Court of Appeals	1891	12	156	Life	President	$132,700
Supreme Court	1789	1	9	Life	President	$153,600[b]
Trade Court	1926	1	9	Life	President	$125,100
Court of Appeals for the Federal Circuit	1982	1	12	Life	President	$132,700
Claims Court	1982	1	16	15 years	President	$125,100
Court of Military Appeals	1950	1	3	15 years	President	$132,700
Court of Veterans Appeals	1988	1	6	15 years	President	$125,100
Tax Court	1969	1	19	12 years	President	$125,100

[a]With Senate confirmation [b]Chief justice receives $160,600.

Interpreting Tables In this table listing information about the federal courts, how is the American system of checks and balances illustrated?

Originally, a person with a claim against the
1.a United States could secure **redress**—satisfaction of the claim, payment—only by an act of Congress. In 1855, however, Congress set up the Court of Claims to hear these pleas.[27] Congress restructured the Court of Claims as the United States Claims Court in 1982.

The Claims Court is composed of 16 judges appointed by the President and Senate for 15-year terms. They hold trials—hear claims for damages against the government—throughout the country.[28] Those claims they uphold cannot in fact be paid until Congress appropriates the money, which it does almost as a matter of standard procedure. Appeals from the court's decisions may be carried to the Court of Appeals for the Federal Circuit.

Occasionally, those who lose in the Claims Court still manage to win some compensation. Some years ago, for example, a Puget Sound mink rancher lost a case in which he claimed that low-flying Navy planes had frightened his animals and caused several of the females to become sterile. He asked $100 per mink. (Even though the rancher lost the case, his congressman introduced a private bill that eventually paid him $10 for each animal.)

The Territorial Courts

Acting under its power to "make all needful rules and regulations respecting the territory . . . belonging to the United States,"[29] Congress has created courts for the nation's territories. Today these territorial courts sit in the Virgin Islands, Guam, and the Northern Marianas. These courts function much as do the local courts in each of the 50 States.

The Courts of the District of Columbia

Acting under its power "to exercise exclusive legislation in all cases whatsoever, over such District . . .

[27]Congress acted under its expressed power to pay the debts of the United States, Article I, Section 8, Clause 1.

[28]Under the Federal Tort Claims Act of 1946, the district courts also have jurisdiction over many claims cases, but only where the amount sought is not more than $10,000. The same statute also gives executive branch agencies the authority to settle claims under $1,000.

[29]Article IV, Section 3, Clause 2. Two judges hear cases in the territorial court in the Virgin Islands, one in Guam, and one in the Northern Marianas.

Enrichment

Have students select one of the special courts and prepare a report on why that court exists apart from the constitutional courts. Students might wish to write to the special court they select to find more information on its function. (Challenging) as may . . . become the seat of the government of the United States,"[30] Congress has set up a judicial system for the nation's capital. Both the District Court and the Court of Appeals for the District of Columbia hear many local cases as well as those they try as constitutional courts. Congress has also established two local courts, much like the courts in the States: a superior court, which is the general trial court, and a court of appeals.

The Court of Military Appeals

Acting under its power "to make rules for the government and regulation of the land and naval forces,"[31] Congress created the United States Court of Military Appeals in 1950. The court is a civilian tribunal. Its chief judge and two associate judges are *not* members of the armed forces; they are appointed by the President and Senate to 15-year terms.

The Court of Military Appeals has been called the GI Supreme Court. It reviews the more serious court-martial convictions of members of the armed forces. Appeals from its decisions can be, but almost never are, heard by the Supreme Court. The Court of Military Appeals is, then, the court of last resort in most cases involving offenses against military law.

The Court of Veterans Appeals

Acting under its power to "constitute tribunals inferior to the Supreme Court,"[32] Congress created the United States Court of Veterans Appeals in 1988. This newest court in the federal judiciary is composed of a chief judge and six associate judges, all appointed by the President and Senate to 15-year terms.

[30]Article I, Section 8, Clause 17.

[31]Article I, Section 8, Clause 14. This provision, and the 5th Amendment, allows Congress to regulate the conduct of members of the armed forces under a separate, noncivilian code of military law. The present-day system of military justice has developed over a period of more than 200 years, since the Revolutionary War. Today, the Uniform Code of Military Justice, passed by Congress in 1950, and the military justice acts of 1968 and of 1983 are the major statutes designed to meet the special disciplinary needs of the armed forces.

[32]Article I, Section 8, Clause 9.

The court has the power to hear appeals from the decisions of an administrative agency, the Board of Veterans Appeals in the Department of Veterans Affairs. Thus, this court hears cases in which individuals claim that the VA has denied or otherwise mishandled valid claims for veterans' benefits. Appeals from the decisions of the Court of Veterans Appeals can be taken to the Court of Appeals for the Federal Circuit.

The United States Tax Court

Acting under its constitutionally granted power to tax, Congress established the Tax Court in 1969.[33] The Tax Court has 19 judges, one of whom serves as chief judge. Each of these 19 judges is named by the President and the Senate for a 12-year term.

The Tax Court hears civil, but not criminal, cases involving disputes over the application of the tax laws. Most of its cases, then, are generated by the Internal Revenue Service and other Treasury Department agencies. Its decisions may be appealed to the federal courts of  appeals.

Section 4 Review

1. **Define:** redress
2. Which are the special courts in the national judiciary?
3. (a) Over what types of cases do the territorial courts have jurisdiction? (b) The Claims Court? (c) The Court of Veterans Appeals?
4. In what sense is the Court of Military Appeals the court of last resort for most cases involving military law?

Critical Thinking

5. **Checking Consistency** (p. 19) Congress has extended its powers over the years. It has also expanded the number of courts it has established. How are these two facts related?

★

[33]Article I, Section 8, Clause 1.

Monitor Comprehension

Answers to Section 4 Review
1. "Key Term" is defined on the following page:
a. redress, p. 478
2. U.S. Claims Court, territorial courts, Courts of the District of Columbia, Court of Military Appeals, Court of Veterans Appeals, U.S. Tax Court.
3. (a) Cases in the nation's territories. (b) Cases in which the Congress has declared the United States open to suit.
(c) Appeals from the Board of Veterans Appeals in the Department of Veterans Affairs.
4. Appeals from its decisions are almost never heard by the Supreme Court. **5.** As Congress has broadened the scope of its powers, it may have experienced a need to set up courts to sort out disputes arising from the exercise of those powers.

TRF **Teacher's Resource File** See the Unit 5 File, p. 13, for the Section 4 Quiz.

Closure

The special courts were established to hear cases arising out of the exercise by Congress of its expressed powers. Among the special courts are the Court of Military Appeals, the Court of Veterans Appeals, the U.S. Tax Court, and the territorial courts. In Chapter 19, students will read about the civil rights and liberties held by the American people.

Assignment Assign Chapter 19, Section 1, pages 485–489, for the next class period.

Reteach

Ask students to imagine a type of case that might be heard in one of the special courts. Have students explain why that case would not be heard in one of the constitutional courts. (*Possible answer: An appeal of a court martial would be heard in the Court of Military Appeals. This case would not be heard in a constitutional court because Congress has the expressed power to make rules governing the armed forces. Thus, Congress established a special court apart from the constitutional courts to hear those cases.*)

Activity: Teaching Heterogeneous Groups

Have students create a pyramid chart to illustrate the different levels of the federal court system. Students should label the apex of the pyramid "Supreme Court" and add the appropriate inferior court labels to the lower levels. Students should indicate the jurisdictions for the courts at each level. Have students compare their pyramid charts and make corrections as necessary.

TEACHING
Critical Thinking

Identifying Assumptions

Objective
Evaluate an article and determine whether it is based on fact or opinion.

INSTRUCT

Before students read the feature, discuss with them the word *assumption*. Ask a volunteer to explain the difference between an assumption and a fact. Then have students work their way through the feature.

Discuss with students why it is important to know when a statement or an article is based on an assumption. Point out that assumptions may or may not be valid, but they are not the same as facts.

Answers 1. (a) The retirement of Justice Brennan and how it will affect the Court.
(b) Replacing Brennan must be done carefully. **2.** Bush should replace Brennan with a justice similar to Brennan in temperament and philosophy. This opinion stems from the following: Brennan was an outstanding justice; the Court has become increasingly conservative. Brennan's voice helped modify the Court. **3.** (a) Justice Brennan is retiring; he served 34 years.
(b) None of the main points in the piece are supported by facts. **4.** Possible answers: "At stake is the finely tuned balance . . ."—unsupported by facts. "The addition of a strong conservative could ignite radical change"—unsupported by facts.

Identifying Assumptions

Identifying assumptions means recognizing unstated beliefs that may underlie a statement, action, or event. An assumption is an idea that a person assumes to be true. In reality, an assumption may prove to be either true or false. But before you can determine the accuracy of an assumption, you must be able to identify it.

Newspaper editorial and opinion pieces, such as the one below, frequently contain many assumptions. Follow the steps below to practice identifying assumptions.

1. Read the selection carefully to determine its topic. Identify the subject matter of the editorial in question. Answer the following questions: (a) What is the subject of the editorial below? (b) What is the editorial's overall message?

2. Define the author's opinion and the arguments used to defend it. Summarize the author's opinion on the subject and the way in which he or she states the argument. Answer the following question: On what grounds does the author base his or her opinions?

3. Look for facts that support the author's opinion. An author will often use factual information to support his or her opinions. Factual information can include statistical data, direct quotations, and any other information that everyone accepts as correct. Answer the following questions: (a) What factual information, if any, does the writer cite in the editorial? (b) Which of the writer's points are supported by facts?

4. Identify any assumptions used in the author's argument. When an author presents an opinion as a fact without valid factual information to support it, the author has made an assumption. For each of the arguments presented in the editorial, ask: Is there any factual information to support the opinion?

The *New York Times*
July 22, 1990

Only moments after Justice William Brennan's retirement, the politicians and interest groups began churning with speculation. Will the Supreme Court, teetering on its center, veer sharply right? How will President Bush exploit his first chance to nominate a justice? Must we brace for a confirmation fight that could dwarf the Senate's 1987 brawl over Robert Bork?

Before getting caught up in future politics, there's time for perspective. A great judge, an influential shaper of the Constitution, is leaving the scene after 34 years at the center of the nation's legal storms. One who, though increasingly outvoted by justices of a different philosophy, rose above single issues and managed to the end to proclaim a dominant constitutional vision. . . .

At stake in appointing the successor to the man who framed these rulings is the finely tuned balance on the Court. Now, in many critical cases, change is made slowly by narrow majorities. The addition of a strong conservative could ignite radical rather than careful change.

At stake as well is the balance in American politics, now divided between a Republican President and a Democratic Congress. A radical Court could go well beyond political tolerance. If President Bush recognizes these enormous stakes, he will appoint someone who approaches the stature and vision of Justice William Brennan.

Teacher's Resource File
See the Unit 5 File, p. 14, for the Skill Application for this lesson.

Chapter-in-Brief

Scan all headings, photographs, charts, and other visuals in the chapter before reading the section summaries below.

Section 1 The National Judiciary (pp. 461–466) In reaction to a major flaw in the Articles of Confederation, the Framers included a judiciary in the Constitution. Article III calls for the establishment of a Supreme Court and gives Congress power to set up other courts. These federal courts work alongside the court systems of the 50 States.

The federal system sets up two types of courts: special courts, which hear a narrow range of cases related to the expressed powers of Congress; and constitutional courts. These include the Supreme Court, district courts, courts of appeals, and several others.

The national judicial system has jurisdiction, or the authority to hear, only certain cases. Jurisdiction is determined by the subject matter of a case and the parties involved. Most cases do not fall under the jurisdiction of the federal courts.

Judges in the federal courts are appointed by the President and confirmed by the Senate. Judges are appointed for life (though they can be impeached).

Section 2 The Inferior Courts (pp. 468–470) The inferior courts include all constitutional courts below the Supreme Court. The district courts are the federal trial courts and hear about 80 percent of the federal caseload. There are 91 of these courts spread across the country, with at least one in each state. District courts have original jurisdiction over most cases in the federal system.

The courts of appeals have only appellate jurisdiction. This means they can only hear cases on appeal from another court. There are 12 courts of appeals, with 179 judges. Each court is also assigned one of the Supreme Court justices.

There are two other inferior courts: the Court of International Trade and the Court of Appeals for the Federal Circuit.

Section 3 The Supreme Court (pp. 471–476) The Supreme Court has the final word on the constitutionality of any issue. The key to the Court's power is its power of judicial review. This means that the Court can declare unconstitutional any act of government. The Supreme Court claimed this power in the landmark case *Marbury* v. *Madison*.

The Court has appellate jurisdiction and original jurisdiction over specific types of cases. In reality, the Court hears only those few hundred cases that pose complicated or important constitutional questions.

After hearing oral arguments from lawyers in the case and reading their briefs, the justices render opinions. The majority opinion states the majority decision of the court. Justices who agree with the overall decision but wish to state other or additional reasons issue concurrent opinions. Justices who disagree issue a dissenting opinion.

Section 4 The Special Courts (pp. 477–479) Special courts are sometimes called legislative courts. Their job is to hear cases that arise from the exercise by Congress of its expressed powers.

For example, Congress established the territorial courts to regulate U.S. territories.

There are also the United States Claims Court, the courts of the District of Columbia, a Court of Military Appeals, a Court of Veterans Affairs, and a United States Tax Court. These courts were established by Congress to fulfill their power to regulate in these areas.

Teaching Suggestions for CHAPTER-IN-BRIEF

Below are some of the possible uses for the Chapter-in-Brief:

To Preview the Chapter You may want to assign the Chapter-in-Brief page and the Section Outlines from the Teacher's Resource File before beginning Chapter 18 to introduce students to "Key Terms" and concepts in each section.

To Review the Chapter When students have completed Chapter 18, you might want to assign the Chapter-in-Brief as a tool for review, along with the Guided Reading and Reviews from the Teacher's Resource File.

To Omit the Chapter If you wish to skip Chapter 18, it may be helpful to assign the Chapter-in-Brief to students as a review before continuing to another chapter. You may also want to assign the Chapter 18 Test to assess student knowledge of the material. Then specific portions of Chapter 18 may be assigned to students needing reinforcement of "Key Terms" and concepts.

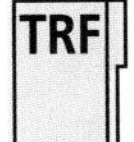

Teacher's Resource File See the Unit 5 File for the following materials:

- Section Outlines, pp. 2, 5, 8, 11.
- Guided Reading and Reviews, pp. 3, 6, 9, 12.
- Chapter 18 Test, pp. 18–20.

ADDITIONAL RESOURCES

Abraham, Henry J. *The Judicial Process.* Oxford, 5th ed., 1986.

Baum, Lawrence. *American Courts: Process and Policy.* Houghton Mifflin, 2nd ed., 1990.

Carp, Robert A. and Ronald Stidham. *Judicial Process in America.* CQ Press, 1989.

Cox, Archibald. *The Court and the Constitution.* Houghton Mifflin, 1987.

Equal Justice Under the Law: 1803 Marbury v. Madison. 16mm film. National Audiovisual Center, 1977. Color. 36 min.

Gates, John B. and Charles A. Johnson. *American Courts: A Critical Assessment.* CQ Press, 1990.

The Judicial System of the United States. Sound filmstrip. National Geographic, 1983. Color. 2 parts, 16–18 min.

Louthan, William C. *The United States Supreme Court: Lawmaking in the Third Branch of Government.* Prentice Hall, 1991.

Wheeler, Russell B. and Cynthia Harrison. *Creating the Federal Judicial System.* Federal Judicial Center, 1989.

Witt, Elder (ed.). *Guide to the U.S. Supreme Court.* CQ Press, 2nd ed., 1990.

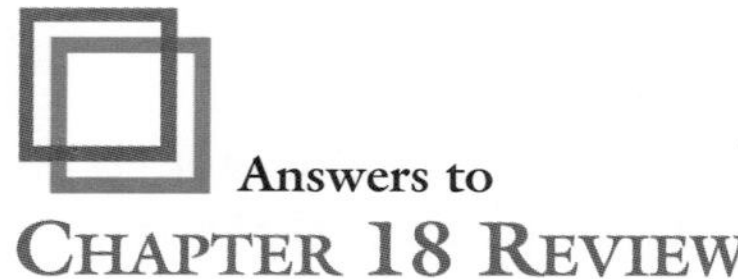

Answers to CHAPTER 18 REVIEW

Vocabulary and Key Terms

Matching
1. redress
2. jurisdiction
3. majority opinion
4. writ of certiorari
5. appellate jurisdiction

True or False
1. True.
2. False—the correct term is *dissenting opinion.*
3. True.
4. False—the correct term is *writ of certiorari.*

Word Relationships
1. Exclusive jurisdiction is jurisdiction that belongs to only one court or type of court. Concurrent jurisdiction is shared by more than one court; i.e. State and federal courts.
2. A plaintiff is the person who brings legal action. The party against whom the legal action is brought is the defendant.
3. A writ of certiorari is an order by the Supreme Court to have a lower court send up a case's record for review. It is the most common way for a case to reach the Supreme Court. Certificate is used when a lower court wishes to have the Supreme Court certify the answer to a specific question. It is another way that a case can reach the Supreme Court.

Main Ideas

Section 1
1. The national judiciary enabled the National Government to enforce its laws in a uniform way across the nation. This addressed a major weakness of the Articles of Confederation. **2.** When certain subject matter is involved, such as federal law; questions of admiralty and maritime law; and when certain parties are involved—for example, the United States or its officers or agencies, or official representatives of foreign governments. **3.** Judges are appointed for life terms and are paid a salary that cannot be reduced. This helps ensure that judges can be free to act without fear of political recrimination.

Section 2
4. Inferior courts are the federal courts that are below the Supreme Court. They include the district courts, the courts of appeals, the Court of International Trade, and the Court of Appeals for the Federal Circuit. **5.** The inferior courts hear the large majority of federal cases. District court are the major trial courts; courts of appeals hear appeals from district courts and several other sources. The Court of International Trade and the Court of Appeals for the Federal Circuit hear specific types of federal cases. **6.** District courts have original jurisdiction over most cases in the federal system.

Section 3
7. The Supreme Court is the final authority on questions of federal law and the Constitution. Therefore, the Supreme Court

Chapter Review

Vocabulary and Key Terms

jurisdiction (p. 462)
exclusive jurisdiction (p. 464)
concurrent jurisdiction (p. 464)
plaintiff (p. 464)
defendant (p. 464)
original jurisdiction (p. 464)
appellate jurisdiction (p. 464)
writ of certiorari (p. 474)
certificate (p. 475)
majority opinion (p. 476)
concurring opinion (p. 476)
dissenting opinion (p. 476)
redress (p. 478)

Matching: *Review the key terms in the list above. If you are not sure of a term's meaning, look up the term and review its definition. Choose a term from the list above that best matches each description.*

1. the satisfaction of a claim
2. the power of a court to hear a case
3. the written statement by more than half the judges on a court supporting the court's decision
4. the order of the Supreme Court directing a lower court to send the Court the record of a certain case
5. the authority of a court to review the decisions of lower courts

True or False: *Determine whether each statement is true or false. If it is true, write "true." If it is false, change the underlined word or words to make the statement true.*

1. A court in which a case is heard for the first time is said to have original jurisdiction over the case.
2. A concurring opinion expresses a judge or judges' disagreement with a court's majority decision.
3. A plaintiff is the person who brings a suit against another party.
4. Certificate is the most common way by which a case reaches the United States Supreme Court.

Word Relationships: *Distinguish between the words in each pair.*

1. exclusive jurisdiction/concurrent jurisdiction
2. plaintiff/defendant
3. writ of certiorari/certificate

Main Ideas

Section 1 (pp. 461–466)

1. For what reasons were the national judiciary created?
2. Under what circumstances do federal courts have jurisdiction in a case?
3. In what ways does the method of selection, terms, and salaries of judges play a role in preserving the independence of the judicial branch?

Section 2 (pp. 468–470)

4. What are the inferior courts?
5. What is the role of the inferior courts in the national judiciary?
6. In what sense are the United States district courts the principal trial courts in the federal judiciary?

Section 3 (pp. 471–476)

7. What is the Supreme Court's role in the process of judicial review, and how did the Court secure that role?
8. What kinds of cases does the Supreme Court hear, and by what means do they get there?

482

9. What are the Court's opinions and what makes them so important?

Section 4 **(pp. 477–479)**

10. What role do the special courts play in the federal court system?
11. What does it mean to say that these courts have a very narrow jurisdiction?
12. In which court might a civil case involve the Internal Revenue Service?

Critical Thinking

1. **Identifying Alternatives** (p. 19) Federal judges are always appointed for life. (a) In your opinion, is this the best way to achieve a judiciary that is free from political pressures? (b) What other methods of achieving an independent judiciary can you think of?
2. **Checking Consistency** (p. 19) Consider the principles of popular sovereignty and majority rule discussed in earlier chapters.Explain why you do or do not think the principle of judicial review is consistent with these concepts.
3. **Testing Conclusions** (p. 19) Woodrow Wilson once described the Supreme Court as "a constitutional convention in continuous session." Find evidence in the chapter to support this view.
4. **Identifying Assumptions** (p. 19) Chief Justice Warren Burger once suggested that a new level of appellate courts be created just below the Supreme Court to relieve its caseload. What assumption do you think this idea is making about the cases that reach the Supreme Court?

Getting Involved

1. **Writing Your Opinion** You are a newspaper editor in the year 1803. The Supreme Court has just issued its opinion in *Marbury* v. *Madison*. Write a newspaper editorial in which you respond to this decision. Review the case and its outcome by reading page 472. Begin your editorial by telling readers briefly about the facts of the case and explaining the significance of the decision. Then, explain the reasons why you agree or disagree with the decision. Devote one well-written paragraph to each of your ideas. Then, review your first draft to ensure that your editorial forcefully and clearly argues your point. Finally, correct any errors and draft a final copy.
2. **Class Debate** Hold a debate on the following topic: *Resolved*, That federal judges should be popularly elected instead of appointed. Select teams to debate each side of the issue. The rest of the class can evaluate each team's presentation and vote to determine the "winning" side.
3. **Class Activity** Create a bulletin board display devoted to the judicial branch and its activities. Ask each class member to bring in newspaper or magazine articles, political cartoons, or other materials that communicate information about the judicial system. Create separate categories for the Supreme Court, other federal courts, State courts, and local courts.
4. **Creating a Political Cartoon** Create a political cartoon that illustrates the concept of justice. To get ideas for your cartoon, review what you have read in the chapter about the role of the courts in the American system of government. Recall, your cartoon may use words and pictures to communicate your message.
5. **Creating a Poster** Create a poster that is a "help wanted" advertisement for a federal judge. Describe the characteristics that you think should be requirements for the position. State the term of office and salary offered.

can make the final determination of whether or not a law or action is constitutional. The Court asserted this power for itself in *Marbury* v. *Madison*. **8.** The Supreme Court has original jurisdiction over certain cases (those in which a State is a party and which affect ambassadors, public ministers and consuls). It can claim original jurisdiction over a broad range of cases covered by the wording of Article III, Section 2. Most cases come from the highest State courts and from the federal courts of appeals by writ of certiorari or, less often, by certificate. **9.** The Court's opinions come in three forms: *Majority*, which is the official opinion of the Court; *concurring*, which agrees with the Court's holding but wishes to emphasize some additional point; or *dissenting*, which expresses the reasoning of justices who do not agree with the majority. The majority opinion serves as precedent for all other courts. The other decisions express careful legal thought and may influence future decisions.

Section 4

10. The special courts do not exercise the broad judicial power of the United States. Instead, they address cases that involve certain expressed powers of Congress. **11.** Each of the special courts is set up to hear only those cases that arise out of the exercise of one of the expressed powers of Congress. **12.** The case would be heard in the United States Tax Court.

Critical Thinking

1. (a) Answers will vary. Students might say that lifetime tenure frees judges from political pressures. (b) Students might suggest such ideas as long but limited terms, such as of 10 years; appointment of judges by both houses of Congress. **2.** Answers will vary. Some students might suggest that the power of such a small group to determine the meaning of the Constitution gives that group too much power. Others might say that the Court is a a sort of representative body: It is a small group that makes decisions for the larger whole; and, because it is appointed by politicians who are responsible to the people, there is an adequate amount of indirect political pressure on the body.
3. Answers will vary. Some students might point to cases such as *Marbury* v. *Madison* to demonstrate how the Court has interpreted—and in some people's view, altered—the words and meaning of the Constitution.
4. Answers will vary. Students may suggest that this idea assumes that not all of the cases in the Supreme Court's caseload are critical enough to be heard by the Court; they could be handled by one of these new-level courts.

Getting Involved

1–5. Answers and results will vary, but students should demonstrate an understanding of the concepts in this chapter.

Chapter 19 Resources

In the Teacher's Resource File
The following materials are found in the Teacher's Resource File box.

Instructional Support: Unit 5 File

For the Section	For the Chapter
Outlines, pp. 24, 27, 30, 33, 36	Skill Application, p. 39
Guided Reading and Reviews, pp. 25, 28, 31, 34, 37	Case Study on Contemporary Issues, pp. 40–42
Quizzes, pp. 26, 29, 32, 35, 38	Chapter Test, pp. 43–45
	Additional Test Questions, pp. 46–48

Enrichment Support File

Supreme Court Case, pp. 14, 36–37, 38, 39, 46–47, 48–49, 58–59, 62–63, 70–71, 76–77, 78–79, 82–83, 86–87, 92–93, 100–101, 112–113, 114–115
Participatory Government Activities, pp. 20–27
Simulations and Debates: Flag Burning; Prayer in the Schools

Computer Test Bank and Assessment

Transparency Package, pp. 19, 44

Chapter 19 Focus

Introduce the Chapter Tell students that in this chapter they will learn about the various types of freedom of expression protected by the First Amendment to the Constitution. Read with students the Chapter Preview and Objectives.

Writing Activity Direct students' attention to "Describe." Ask students to complete the following sentence: The use of warning labels for recordings . . ." Tell students to write at least three points in completing the sentence.

Motivate for Learning Direct students' attention to "Predict." Lead students in a discussion about why it is sometimes necessary to limit people's expression.

Civil Liberties: First Amendment Freedoms

Chapter Preview

Along with the arrival of rock-and-roll music came efforts to censor it. In 1985, as just one example, a group called Parents' Music Resource Center convinced the record industry to adopt the use of warning labels for recordings that contain so-called explicit lyrics. Some critics of rock music believe that labeling alone does not go far enough. Other people, however, call such labeling an infringement on the freedom of speech.

The 1st Amendment guarantee of freedom of speech grants all persons the right to speak, publish, and otherwise express their views. Yet this freedom, like all other civil rights and liberties, may be exercised only in light of the rights of all other persons, as this chapter describes. This chapter also examines the many other civil rights and liberties held by the American people.

Before you read this chapter:

- **Describe** your feelings about record warning labels.
- **Predict** what might occur if no limits on free speech existed.

As you read, focus on the main objective for each section. Understand:

1. The relationship of civil rights and liberties to the concept of limited government.
2. The importance of religious freedom in the United States.
3. The scope of and limits on free speech and free press.
4. The relationship of the protection of civil rights and liberties to national security.
5. The limits on the freedoms of assembly and petition.

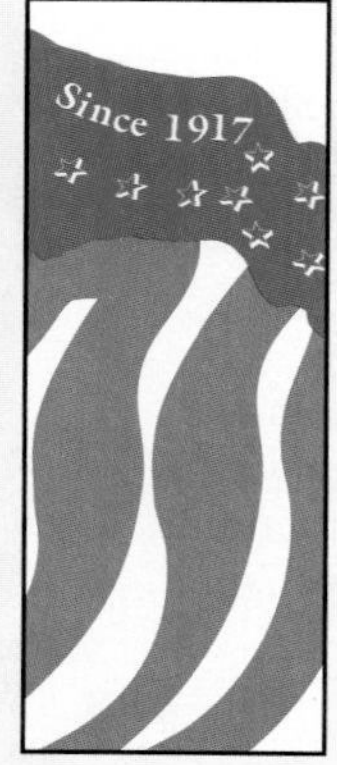

Magruder's American Government: *A Witness to Change* by William A. McClenaghan

The Constitution's protections of individual rights have been a matter of great importance throughout United States history. But, clearly, those protections have assumed more significance and inspired greater controversy in recent decades than ever before. This book has been something of a barometer of that development.

From 1917 through the early 1970s, *Magruder's* devoted a single chapter to the subject of individual rights. That one chapter, originally entitled "Civil Rights," grew in length from edition to edition, until in 1973 it finally grew to two chapters. In one of those chapters we dealt with the 1st Amendment freedoms; in the other we covered all the remaining rights held by the American people.

The growth in the law of individual rights continued through the 1970s, 1980s, and into the 1990s. This ongoing expansion of the constitutional protections of rights and liberties has led us to increase our coverage to the *three* chapters you find in this edition.

Freedom of Religion Among other rights, every citizen of the United States has the right to worship according to his or her beliefs, without fear of interference from the government.

1 The Unalienable Rights

Find Out:

- For what reasons were individual rights included in the Constitution?
- What factors limit individual rights?
- For what reasons is the Due Process Clause of the 14th Amendment so important?

Key Terms:

Bill of Rights, civil liberties, civil rights, alien, Due Process Clause

Have you ever heard of Walter Barnette? Probably not. How about Toyosaburo Korematsu? Dollree Mapp? Clarence Earl Gideon? Almost certainly, the same answer: No.

Walter Barnette was a Jehovah's Witness who told his children not to salute the flag or recite the Pledge of Allegiance. Toyosaburo Korematsu was a citizen of the United States interned by the Federal Government during World War II. Dollree Mapp was fined $25 for possessing "lewd and lascivious books." And Clarence Earl Gideon was sentenced to prison for breaking into and entering a poolroom.

You will encounter their names again over the next few pages, for each of them played an important part in the building and protecting of the rights that all Americans hold.

Rights and Liberties in American Political Thought

As you read in Chapter 2, American commitment to personal freedom is deeply rooted in colonial history. The concept of individual liberties had been developing for centuries in other

Section 1
The Unalienable Rights

Focus

Teacher's Resource File
See the Unit 5 File, p. 24, for the Section 1 Outline.

Objectives

19.1 Explain why the Constitution includes guarantees of individual rights.
19.2 Analyze the factors that limit individual rights in this country.
19.3 Define the importance of the Due Process Clause of the 14th Amendment.

Bellringer Activity Ask students to offer their opinions on the President of the United States. Encourage people to be unrestrained in their criticism and praise. Then point out to students that in many parts of the world, citizens might not be able to have such a conversation about their political leader without risking their freedom or safety.

State the Purpose The United States was founded on a commitment to individual freedom, including the freedom to hold critical views of the government. In the view of the nation's founders, the main purpose of government was to protect individual rights and liberties. In Section 1, students will study the concepts of rights and liberties and the ways in which our government guarantees them.

Vocabulary

Point out to students "Key Terms" on page 485. Direct students to read the Bill of Rights— the first 10 amendments to the Constitution—that appears on page 726 of their texts. Suggest that students read the annotations that go along with each amendment.

Reading Strategy: Who? What? When? Where? How? Why?

Tell students to write each of the main section headings on a sheet of paper. As students read the text under each of the main headings, have them write brief answers to each of the six questions above.

INSTRUCT

Discuss/Analyze Tell students that the Bill of Rights is one of the clearest expressions of individual rights and liberties in the American system of government. Have students discuss how the individual rights guaranteed in the Constitution help fulfill the principle of limited government. (*The people rule in a limited government. Individual rights help ensure that they remain free and capable of expressing their feelings about and exerting their control over government.*)

Next, have students examine the challenges of preserving individual rights. Direct students to Justice Holmes' quote on page 487. Have students discuss why falsely shouting "Fire!" in a theater would be unacceptable. How would this impact on others? (*It might cause them harm in the resulting panic to flee the theater.*) Direct students to the text coverage of *Sheppard* v. *Maxwell* as an example of how one person's or group's behavior cannot be protected if it denies another person his or her rights.

Next, make sure that students understand the complicated impact of federalism on the individual rights guarantees. Explain that the Bill of Rights only guarantees individuals rights against what the Federal Government might do. However, the Supreme Court has interpreted the 14th Amendment so that many of the Bill of Rights guarantees are guaranteed against State actions. Ask students to explain why this is a vital fact? (*Ensures that people will be protected against actions by all governments.*)

parts of the world. The early colonists brought to North America a firm dedication to freedom.

Their commitment took root here, and it flourished. The Revolutionary War was fought to preserve and expand the rights of the individual against government. In proclaiming the independence of the new United States, the founders of this country declared:

> "We hold these truths to be self-evident, that all men are created equal, that they are endowed by their Creator with certain unalienable rights, that among these are Life, Liberty and the pursuit of Happiness. . . . to secure these rights, Governments are instituted among Men."

The Framers of the Constitution repeated that justification for the existence of government in the Preamble to the Constitution.

The Constitution, as it was written at Philadelphia, contained a number of important guarantees—notably in Article I, Sections 9 and 10 and in Article III. Unlike many of the first State constitutions, however, it did not include a general listing of the rights of the people.

The outcry that that omission raised was so strong that several States ratified the Constitution only with the understanding that such a listing be immediately added. The first session of the new Congress met that demand with a series of proposed amendments. Ten of them,
1.a the **Bill of Rights**, were ratified by the States and became a part of the Constitution on December 15, 1791. Later amendments, especially the 13th and the 14th, have added to the Constitution's guarantees of personal freedom.

The Constitution guarantees many rights and liberties to the American people. However, there are several points you must understand about the overall shape of those guarantees.

Civil Rights and Civil Liberties The distinction between civil rights and civil liberties is at best murky. Legal scholars often disagree on the matter, and the two terms are quite often used interchangeably. In general, however,
1.b **civil liberties** are protections against government. They are guarantees of the safety of persons, opinions, and property from the arbitrary acts of government. Examples of civil liberties include freedom of religion, freedom of speech and press, and the guarantees of fair trial.

1.c The term **civil rights** is sometimes reserved for those positive acts of government that seek to make constitutional guarantees a reality for all people. From this perspective, examples of civil rights would include the prohibitions of discrimination on the basis of race or sex set out in the Civil Rights Act of 1964.

Individual Rights and the Principle of Limited Government

As you know, government in the United States is limited government. It can do only those things the sovereign people have given it the power to do. The Constitution is filled with examples of this fact. Chief among them are its many guarantees of personal freedom. Each one of those guarantees is either an outright prohibition or a restriction on the power of government to do something.

All governments have and use authority over individuals. The all-important difference between a democratic government and a dictatorial one lies in the extent of that authority. In a dictatorial regime, the government's powers are practically unlimited. The government regularly suppresses dissent, often harshly. In the United States, however, governmental authority is closely limited. As Justice Robert H. Jackson once wrote:

> "If there is any fixed star in our constitutional constellation, it is that no official, high or petty, can prescribe what shall be orthodox in politics, nationalism, religion, or any other matter of opinion or force citizens to confess by word or act their faith therein."[1]

Relativity of Individual Rights

The Constitution guarantees a number of rights. But no one has the right to do as he or she pleases. Rather, all persons have the right to do as they please as long as they do not infringe on the rights of others. Each person's rights are relative to the rights of every other person.

To illustrate the point, everyone in the United States has a right of free speech, but no one enjoys absolute freedom of speech. A person

[1] In *West Virginia Board of Education* v. *Barnette*, 1943; see page 497.

found guilty of using obscene language can be punished by a court. So, too, can someone who uses words in a way that causes another person to commit a crime—for example, to riot or to desert the armed forces.

Justice Oliver Wendell Holmes once put the relative nature of each person's rights this way:

> "The most stringent protection of free speech would not protect a man in falsely shouting fire in a theatre and causing a panic."[2]

When Rights Conflict

People usually think of individual rights guarantees in ways that suggest that each of them are to be observed all of the time. In fact, there are many situations in which different rights conflict with one another. Take this celebrated, but not uncommon, example of rights in conflict: free press versus fair trial.

Dr. Samuel Sheppard of Cleveland, Ohio, had been convicted of murdering his wife. His lengthy trial was widely covered in the national media. On appeal, Sheppard claimed that the highly sensational coverage had denied him a fair trial. The Supreme Court agreed. It rejected the free press argument, overturned his conviction, and ordered a new trial, *Sheppard* v. *Maxwell*, 1966.

Persons to Whom Rights Are Guaranteed

Most constitutional rights are extended to all persons. The Supreme Court has held that the Constitution's word "persons" covers **aliens**—foreign-born residents, noncitizens—as well as citizens. 1.d

Not all rights are given to aliens, however. Thus, the right to travel freely throughout the country is guaranteed to all citizens by the Constitution's two Privileges and Immunities clauses.[3] But aliens can be restricted in this regard.

Civil Liberties Which constitutional right is State Senator Ted Lyon (D., Texas) upholding when he speaks at a labor union rally for worker's compensation insurance reform?

Early in World War II, the United States government evacuated—forcibly moved—all persons of Japanese descent living on the Pacific Coast. The government sent some 120,000 persons, two-thirds of them native-born American citizens, to "war relocation camps" set up and run by the Federal Government. In 1944 the Supreme Court reluctantly upheld the forced evacuation as a reasonable wartime emergency measure.[4] Many people have strongly criticized the action ever since.

In 1988, the Federal Government admitted that the wartime relocation was unnecessary and unjust. Congress voted to pay $20,000 to each of the internees still alive. It also declared: "On behalf of the nation, the Congress apologizes."

[2]In *Schenck* v. *United States*, 1919; see page 506.

[3]Article IV, Section 2, Clause 1 and the 14th Amendment; see page 91. The guarantee does not extend to citizens in jail, on bail, committed to a mental institution, etc.

[4]*Korematsu* v. *United States*, 1944; however, on the same day the Court held in *Ex parte Endo* that once the loyalty of any citizen internee had been established, no restriction could be placed on that person's freedom to travel that was not legally imposed on all other citizens.

ABCNEWS INTERACTIVE

The following video segment may be used to highlight aspects of individual rights and liberties.

POWERS OF THE SUPREME COURT GUIDEBOOK
Chapter 8: Amendment 1 (1791), Freedom of Speech, p. 11

Provide Guided Practice Have students work in small groups. Ask students to prepare a one-page flyer that promotes awareness of individual rights in the United States. Make sure student flyers cover such topics as: the source of these rights (*The Bill of Rights*); the limits of these rights (*People cannot exercise their rights in such a way as to deny others their rights.*); how these rights relate to actions by State and local governments.

Provide Independent Practice

TRF **Teacher's Resource File** You may wish to assign Section 1 Guided Reading and Review, Unit 5 File, p. 25, to help students master section objective content.

Caption Answer Freedom of speech.

SPOTLIGHT ON: Multiculturalism

The word *persons* of course also applies to foreign-born citizens. But since many laws were written without this interpretation in mind, these citizens have often had to challenge laws to obtain their rights. For example, in 1967, Genoveva Castro, a Mexican American who could read the Constitution only in Spanish, sued the State of California for a clause in its Constitution reading: "No person who shall not be able to read the Constitution in English ... shall ever exercise the privileges of an elector in this state." This form of discrimination against a citizen came to an end when the California Supreme Court ruled in favor of Castro in 1970.

Teacher's Resource File
See the Supreme Court Cases file pp. 70–71, for material to support the section.

Enrichment

Have students study the ideas of the French Revolution of 1789 and identify similarities to American ideas of freedom as expressed in the Bill of Rights. (Challenging)

Monitor Comprehension

Answers to Section 1 Review
1. "Key Terms" are defined on the following pages:
a. Bill of Rights, p. 486
b. civil liberties, p. 486
c. civil rights, p. 486
d. alien, p. 487
e. Due Process Clause, p. 488
2. Governments exist to secure certain rights for people, such as life, liberty, and the pursuit of happiness. **3.** Each guarantee is a prohibition or restriction on the power of government.
4. Each person has the right to do as he or she pleases as long as he or she does not infringe on the rights of others. **5.** The Court holds that most of the Bill of Rights' protections apply against the States. **6.** The 9th Amendment indicates that there are rights beyond those set down in words. **7.** Answers will vary. Students may suggest the consequences in the event that Sheppard's rights are denied are more severe, for he would possibly suffer unjust punishment. The press would merely suffer a delay in their right to exercise freedom of the press.

TRF **Teacher's Resource File**
See the Unit 5 File, p. 26, for the Section 1 Quiz.

Federalism and Individual Rights

Federalism produces this complex pattern of individual rights guarantees:

1. Some rights are guaranteed against the National Government only.
2. Some rights are guaranteed against the States and their local governments only.
3. A great many rights are guaranteed against both the National Government and the States and their local governments.
4. Some rights guaranteed against a State and its local governments arise from the National Constitution while others arise from that State's own constitution.

Over time, the Supreme Court has modified (lessened) some of the impact of federalism here, especially in a long series of decisions involving the 14th Amendment's Due Process Clause. Before you can understand that complicated matter, however, you must grasp this point: The provisions of the Bill of Rights apply against the National Government only—not the States.

The Scope of the Bill of Rights Remember, the first 10 amendments were originally intended as restrictions on the new National Government, not on the already existing States. They continue to function that way today.[5]

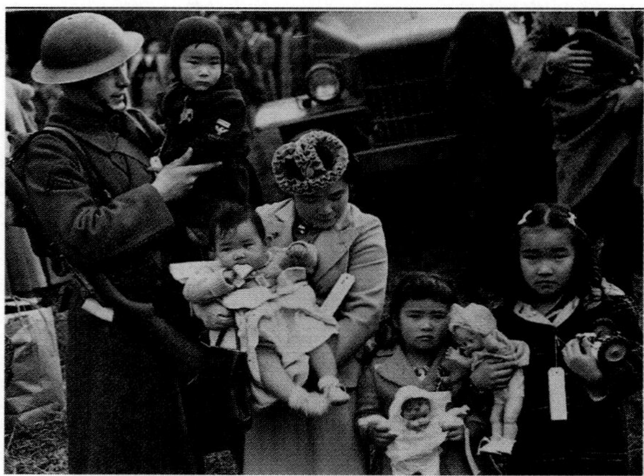

Internment Camps "They say: 'We did it for your protection.' When you protect somebody, you don't aim a gun at the guy you're protecting." The words of a Japanese internee.

Take the 2nd Amendment to make the point here. It reads:

> "A well-regulated militia being necessary to the security of a free state, the right of the people to keep and bear arms shall not be infringed."

This restriction applies only to the National Government. The States can and do limit the right to keep and bear arms. They can require the registration of all or of certain guns, forbid the carrying of concealed weapons, and so on.

The Modifying Effect of the 14th Amendment Again, the provisions of the Bill of Rights apply against the National Government only. This does *not* mean, however, that the States can deny people their rights.

In part, the States cannot do that because each of their own constitutions contains a bill of rights. Also, they cannot because of the 14th
1.e Amendment's **Due Process Clause**. It says:

> "No State shall . . . deprive any person of life, liberty, or property, without due process of law. . . ."

The Supreme Court has often held that this provision means that no State can deny to any person any right that is "basic or essential to the American concept of ordered liberty."

But what rights are "basic or essential"? In a long series of cases, the Court has ruled that most of the protections set out in the Bill of Rights are also within the meaning of the 14th Amendment, and so are applicable against the States.

This complicated matter can be stated this way: The Supreme Court has "nationalized" the Bill of Rights by holding that most of its protections apply against the States, as a part of the meaning of the 14th Amendment's Due Process Clause.

The Court began this historic process in *Gitlow* v. *New York*, in 1925. That landmark case involved Benjamin Gitlow, a communist, who had been convicted in the State courts of criminal anarchy. On appeal, the Supreme Court

[5]The Supreme Court first held that the provisions of the Bill of Rights restrict only the National Government in *Barron* v. *Baltimore*, 1833.

Teacher's Resource File
See the Supreme Court Cases file, pp. 38–39, for material to support the section.

upheld Gitlow's conviction and the State law under which he had been tried. In deciding the case, however, the Court made this crucial point: Freedom of speech and press, which the 1st Amendment says cannot be denied by the National Government, are also "among the fundamental personal rights and liberties protected by the Due Process Clause of the 14th Amendment from impairment by the States."

Soon after *Gitlow*, the Court held each of the 1st Amendment's guarantees to be covered by the 14th Amendment. It struck down State laws involving speech (*Fiske* v. *Kansas*, 1927; *Stromberg* v. *California*, 1931), the press (*Near* v. *Minnesota*, 1931), assembly and petition (*DeJonge* v. *Oregon*, 1937), and religion (*Cantwell* v. *Connecticut*, 1940). In each of those cases, the Court declared a State law unconstitutional as a violation of the 14th Amendment's Due Process Clause.

The Court extended the scope of the 14th Amendment's Due Process Clause even further in several cases in the 1960s—to the point where, today, it covers nearly all of the guarantees set out in the Bill of Rights.

Thus, in *Mapp* v. *Ohio*, 1961, the Court held that the 14th Amendment's Due Process Clause prohibits unreasonable searches and seizures by State and local police. The clause also forbids State and local police the use of evidence gained by such illegal actions.

In later cases, the Court gave the same 14th Amendment coverage to:

—the 8th Amendment's ban on cruel and unusual punishment, in *Robinson* v. *California*, 1962;
—the 6th Amendment's right to counsel, in *Gideon* v. *Wainwright*, 1963;
—the 5th Amendment's ban on self-incrimination, in *Malloy* v. *Hogan*, 1964;
—the 6th Amendment's right of persons accused of crime to confront the witnesses against them, in *Pointer* v. *Texas*, 1965;
—the 6th Amendment's right of persons accused of crime to compel witnesses to testify in their behalf, in *Washington* v. *Texas*, 1967;
—the 6th Amendment's guarantee of a speedy trial, in *Klopfer* v. *North Carolina*, 1967;
—the 6th Amendment's guarantee of trial by jury, in *Duncan* v. *Louisiana*, 1968; and
—the 5th Amendment's ban of double jeopardy, in *Benton* v. *Maryland*, 1969.

The Role of the 9th Amendment

As you know, the Constitution contains many guarantees of individual rights. But nowhere in the Constitution—and, indeed, nowhere else—will you find a complete catalog of all of the rights held by the American people.

The little-noted 9th Amendment declares that there are rights beyond those set out in so many words in the Constitution:

> "The enumeration in the Constitution of certain rights shall not be construed to deny or disparage others retained by the people."

Over the years, the Supreme Court has found that there are, in fact, a number of other rights "retained by the people." For example: The right of a person charged with a crime not to be tried on the basis of evidence gained by an unlawful search or seizure; and the right of a woman to have an abortion without undue interference by government.

Section 1 Review

1. Define: Bill of Rights, civil liberties, civil rights, alien, Due Process Clause
2. According to the Declaration of Independence, governments exist for what reason?
3. How do individual rights guarantees illustrate the principle of limited government?
4. In what sense are individual rights relative to each other?
5. In what sense has the Supreme Court "nationalized" most of the civil rights protections set out in the Bill of Rights?
6. For what reason is it impossible to list all of the rights guaranteed by the Constitution?

Critical Thinking

7. Identifying Assumptions (p. 19) For what reason do you think the Supreme Court found that the right to a fair trial suppressed the freedom of the press in *Sheppard*? Do you agree with this decision?

★

CLOSURE

This country was founded on the values of individual rights and liberties. The Bill of Rights is perhaps the clearest expression of those rights. The individual rights guaranteed in those 10 amendments are limited only by the rights of other individuals. The Supreme Court has held that they also apply against the States and their local governments.

In the next section, students will learn about the 1st Amendment guarantees of freedom of religion.

Assignment Assign Section 2, pp. 490–497, for the next class period.

SPOTLIGHT ON: Constitutional Issues

The "freedom of religion" in various States before 1868 attests to the need for the Due Process Clause of the 14th Amendment. In New Hampshire Protestant churches were tax-supported, but Catholics could not vote in the Granite State until 1851, and non-Protestants were barred from holding office until 1868. In New Jersey, non-Protestants did not receive full civil rights until 1844. Georgia barred non-Protestants from office, and in Connecticut and Massachusetts, taxpayers were forced to support community churches. Only in New York, Rhode Island, and Virginia granted full religious freedom from the earliest days of the United States.

Reteach

Write the following words on the board: *Bill of Rights, "Fire!" in a crowded theater, the 14th Amendment.* Have students explain the significance of these terms. (*Bill of Rights enumerates many individual rights and liberties. "Fire!" . . . is an example of the limits of individual rights. The 14th Amendment nationalizes many of those rights.*)

SECTION 2
Freedom of Religion

FOCUS

Teacher's Resource File
See the Unit 5 File, p. 27, for the Section 2 Outline.

Objectives

19.4 Explain why freedom of expression is vital to democracy.
19.5 Analyze the extent to which the Constitution prohibits the establishment of religion by government.
19.6 Define the extent to which Americans enjoy free exercise of religion.

Bellringer Activity Write the words *In God We Trust* on the board. Lead students to recognize that this motto appears on United States currency. Ask students if they can determine what might be considered controversial about this motto.

State the Purpose Tell students that freedom of religion is one of the central concepts in the American democracy and a major component of the freedom of expression. Section 2 explores the two features of this freedom, the separation of church and state and the free exercise of religion.

ABCNEWS INTERACTIVE

The following video segment may be used to highlight aspects of individual rights and liberties.

POWERS OF THE SUPREME COURT GUIDEBOOK
Chapter 7: Amendment 1 (1791)
Freedom of Religion, p. 10

2 Freedom of Religion

Find Out:

- For what reason is freedom of expression vital to democracy?
- To what extent does the Constitution prohibit government establishment of religion?
- To what extent do Americans enjoy free exercise of religion?

Key Terms:

Establishment Clause, Free Exercise Clause

A century and a half ago, Alexis de Tocqueville came to the United States from France to observe life in the young nation. When he was finished, Tocqueville wrote that he had searched for the key to the greatness of America in many places: in its large harbors and deep rivers; in its fertile fields and boundless forests; in its rich mines and vast world commerce; in its public schools, its democratic legislature, and matchless Constitution. Yet, not until he went into the churches of America, Tocqueville said, did he understand the genius and power of this country.

In this section, you will read about the important—and often controversial—guarantees of religious freedom found in the Constitution.

Religion and the Bill of Rights

The right to freedom of expression is indispensable to the idea of democracy. Without it—without what has been called a "free trade in ideas"—a free society simply cannot exist.

Freedom of expression is protected against actions by the Federal Government in the 1st Amendment:

> "Congress shall make no law respecting an establishment of religion, or prohibiting the free exercise thereof; or abridging the freedom of speech or of the press; or the right of the people peaceably to assemble, and to petition the government for a redress of grievances."

And, as you know, the 14th Amendment's Due Process Clause protects these freedoms from the arbitrary acts of States or their local governments.

It is not surprising that the Bill of Rights provides first for the protection of religious liberty. Religion has always played a large and important role in American life. Many of the early colonists, and many later immigrants, came here to escape persecution for their religious beliefs.

The 1st and 14th amendments set out two guarantees of religious freedom. They prohibit (1) an "establishment of religion" (the Establishment Clause) and (2) any arbitrary interference by government in "the free exercise" of religion (the Free Exercise Clause).[6]

Separation of Church and State

1.a The **Establishment Clause** sets up, in Thomas Jefferson's words, "a wall of separation between church and state." But just how high is that wall? That question remains a matter of continuing and often heated controversy.

Government has done much to encourage churches and religion in this country. Thus, nearly all property of and contributions to churches and religious sects are free from federal, State, and local taxes. Most public officials take an oath of office in the name of God. Sessions of Congress and of most State legislatures and many city councils open with prayer. The nation's anthem and its coins and currency make reference to God. Clearly, the limits of the Establishment Clause cannot be described in precise terms.

The Supreme Court did not hear its first Establishment Clause case until 1947. A few earlier cases did involve government and religion, but none of them involved a direct consideration of the "wall of separation."

The most important of those earlier cases was *Pierce* v. *Society of Sisters*, 1925. There, the Court held an Oregon compulsory school attendance law unconstitutional. That law required parents to send their children to public schools. In destroying the law, the Court did not reach the Establishment Clause question. Instead, it found

[6]Also, Article VI, Section 3 provides that ". . . no religious test shall ever be required as a qualification to any office or public trust under the United States." In *Torcaso* v. *Watkins*, 1961, the Supreme Court held that the 14th Amendment puts the same restriction on the States.

Reading Strategy: Problem Solving

Have students imagine that they are one of the first Americans in the year 1788. You want to ensure that everyone will be free to think and believe what they wish, especially in the field of religion. How might you suggest amending the Constitution to ensure that you will be able to pursue your own religious beliefs free from government interference?

Vocabulary

Point out "Key Terms" on page 490. Have students predict the meanings of these terms based on their knowledge of the section content. Then have students compare their predictions to the text definitions given on pages 490 and 496.

the law to be an unreasonable interference with the liberty of parents to direct the upbringing of their children, and, so, in conflict with the Due Process Clause of the 14th Amendment.

The first direct ruling on the Establishment Clause came in *Everson* v. *Board of Education*, a 1947 case often called the *New Jersey School Bus Case*. There the Court upheld a State law that provided for the public, tax-supported busing of students attending any school in the State, including parochial (church-related) schools. Critics attacked the law as a support of religion in that it relieved parochial schools of the need to pay for busing and so freed their money for religious purposes. The Court disagreed; it found the law to be a safety measure intended to benefit children, no matter what schools they might attend.

Since that decision, the largest number of the Court's Establishment Clause cases have involved religion and education.

Released Time Two of those cases involved "released time" programs in public schools. Such programs allow schools to release students from school time to attend religious classes.

In *McCollum* v. *Board of Education*, 1948, the Court struck down the released time program in Champaign, Illinois, because the program used public facilities for religious purposes. In *Zorach* v. *Clauson*, 1952, however, the Court upheld New York City's released time program because that program required that the religious classes be held in private places.

Prayers and the Bible Two later key decisions dealt with the recitation of prayers and the reading of the Bible in public schools.

In *Engel* v. *Vitale*, 1962, the Court outlawed the use, even on a voluntary basis, of a prayer written by the New York State Board of Regents. The "Regents' prayer" read:

> "Almighty God, we acknowledge our dependence upon Thee, and we beg Thy blessings upon us, our parents, our teachers, and our country."

The Supreme Court held that

> "The constitutional prohibition against laws respecting an establishment of religion must at least mean that in this country it is no part of the business of government to compose official prayers for any group of the American people to recite as part of a religious program carried on by government."

The Court twice extended that holding in 1963. In *Abington School District* v. *Schempp*, the Court struck down a Pennsylvania law that required that each school day begin with readings from the Bible and a recitation of the Lord's Prayer. In *Murray* v. *Curlett*, the Court erased a similar rule in the city of Baltimore. In both cases the Court found violations of

> "the command of the 1st Amendment that the government maintain strict neutrality, neither aiding nor opposing religion."

The Court found Alabama's "moment of silence" law unconstitutional, in *Wallace* v. *Jaffree*, 1985. That law provided for a one-minute period of silence, for "meditation or voluntary prayer," at the beginning of each school day. The Court held that the law's specific reference to "voluntary prayer" made it constitutionally unacceptable. The Court did not strike down all "moment of silence" laws here. Nearly half the States have passed such statutes, and most of them make no mention of prayer. Their constitutionality remains an open question.

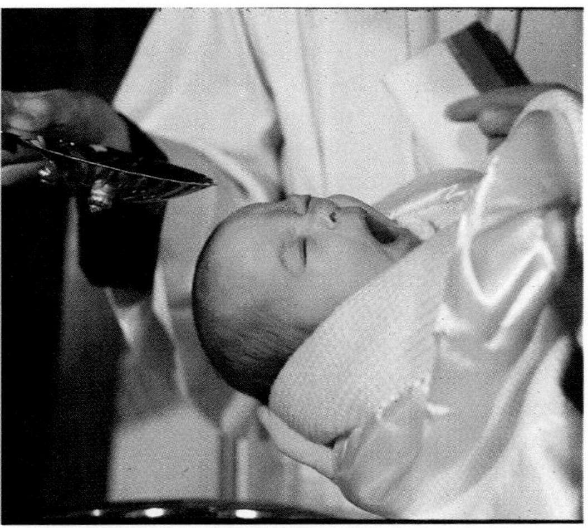

Freedom of Expression Which specific 1st Amendment right is being exercised by the participants in this Catholic baptismal ceremony?

INSTRUCT

Explain/Discuss Discuss with students the two key components of the freedom of religion, the Establishment Clause and the Free Exercise Clause. Ask students to discuss the importance of forbidding government from establishing religion. What might happen if government did endorse a particular religion? (*Such an endorsement might be used to encourage one religion or discourage others.*) Have students choose cases from the section and discuss whether or not they feel the Court correctly ruled on whether or not a particular action constituted establishment of religion. For each case, have students consider how society might change if the ruling were different, and how they would feel if they practiced a religion other than the one involved in the case.

Now have students discuss the Free Exercise Clause. Have students identify the point at which people are no longer free to exercise their religion. (*When their actions violate laws, offend public morals, or threaten the health, welfare or safety of the community.*) Have students compare this limitation to Justice Holmes' prohibition against yelling "fire" in a crowded theater. (*Both limits seek to ensure that one person's actions do not infringe on another's rights.*)

Caption Answer Freedom of Religion.

TRF **Teacher's Resource File**
See the Supreme Court Cases file, pp. 46–47, 58–59, 62–63, 100–101, and the Simulations and Debates file, pp. 35–70, for materials to support the section.

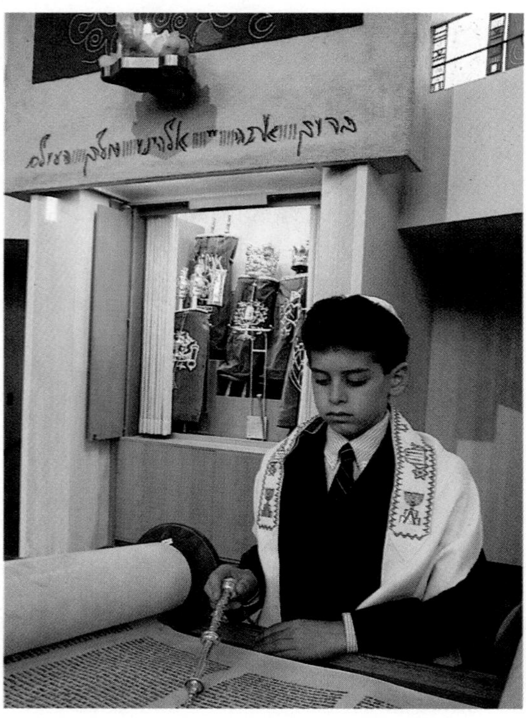

Bar Mitzvah The right of Americans to practice religion in their own way is being exercised in this ceremony, which initiates boys into the Jewish religion.

To sum up these rulings, the Court has held that public schools cannot sponsor religious exercises. But it has not held that individuals cannot pray, when and as they choose, in schools, or in any other place. Nor has it held that students cannot study the Bible in a literary or historic frame in the schools.

These rulings have stirred strong criticism. Many individuals and groups have long proposed that the Constitution be amended to allow voluntary prayer in the public schools.

Despite the several decisions here, both organized prayer and Bible readings are found in a great many public school classrooms today.

Student Religious Groups Congress has dealt with the matter of prayer in public schools in only one law, the Equal Access Act of 1984. That statute declares that any public high school that receives federal funds—nearly all do—must allow student religious groups to meet in the school on the same terms that it sets for other student organizations.

The Supreme Court upheld the law in *Westside Community Schools* v. *Mergens* in 1990. The case arose at Westside High School in Omaha, Nebraska, in 1985. Bridget Mergens and several other students asked school officials for permission to form a Christian Club at Westside High. They said that membership in their group would be voluntary and open to all students. The Christian Club's main purposes were to permit students to read and discuss the Bible, have fellowship, and pray together.

School officials denied the students' request, mainly on Establishment Clause grounds. The students then took their case to the federal courts, where they finally won their point.

Justice Sandra Day O'Connor delivered the Court's opinion upholding the Equal Access Act. At the core of that opinion, she wrote:

> "Although a school itself may not lead or direct a religious club, a school that permits a student-initiated and student-led religious club to meet after school, just as it permits any other student group to do, does not convey a message of State approval or endorsement of the particular religion."

Evolution In *Epperson* v. *Arkansas*, 1968, the Court struck down a State law forbidding the teaching of the scientific theory of evolution. The Court held that the Constitution

> "forbids alike the preference of a religious doctrine or the prohibition of theory which is deemed antagonistic to a particular dogma. . . . The State has no legitimate interest in protecting any or all religions from views distasteful to them."

The Court found a similar law to be unconstitutional in 1987. In *Edwards* v. *Aguillard*, it voided a 1962 Louisiana law that provided that whenever teachers taught the theory of evolution, they also had to offer instruction in "creation science." The Court held that the law violated the Establishment Clause because its "primary purpose [was] to endorse a particular religious doctrine."

Seasonal Displays Many public bodies sponsor celebrations of the holiday season with street

TRF

Teacher's Resource File
See the Supreme Court Cases file, pp. 114–115, for material to support the section.

How to Express Your Opinion

1. Decide what you think and why. Your opinion should be clearly thought out and supported by evidence. This may involve doing some research, both to help you form an opinion and to help support that opinion with facts.

2. Know your constitutional rights. It is important for you to know that you have a right to express your opinion on public policy matters to public officials. You should also research the rights you have with regard to the particular issue about which you are concerned; this information will help you support your opinion with facts.

3. Choose a form of expression. You can express your opinion in many ways. You must decide which form would be most effective, and how much time you can commit to the issue. Some forms of expression include: forming a group, writing letters to or calling public officials, testifying at a school board hearing, and preparing an editorial for local newspaper, television, or radio.

4. Offer constructive suggestions. When expressing your opinion, be careful not to criticize others; show sympathy for their position and offer alternative proposals for dealing with a situation. End with a summary of your position.

5. Determine which public official can do something about the issue. For the best response to your concerns, aim your efforts at the most appropriate targets—those officials who are directly responsible for dealing with your concerns.

Interpreting Charts Read the steps outlined in the chart. Then explain why it is important to a democratic society for all people to express their opinions effectively.

Interpreting Charts Ask students to select an issue that they are concerned about. Then have them express their opinion on the subject using the steps in the chart.

Caption Answer Possible answer: Democratic society depends on a free exchange of ideas and opinions.

decorations, programs in public schools, and the like. Can these publicly sponsored observances properly include expressions of religious belief?

In *Lynch* v. *Donnelly*, 1984, the Court held that the city of Pawtucket, Rhode Island, could include the Christian nativity scene in its seasonal display, which also featured nonreligious objects such as candy canes and Santa's sleigh and reindeer. But that ruling left open this question: What about a public display made up *only* of a religious symbol?

The Court faced that question in 1989. In *Allegheny County* v. *ACLU* it held that the county's seasonal display "endorsed Christian doctrine," and so violated the 1st and 14th amendments. The county had placed a large display celebrating the birth of Jesus on the grand stairway in the county courthouse, with a banner proclaiming "Glory to God in the Highest."

At the same time, however, the Court upheld another holiday display in *Pittsburgh* v. *ACLU.* The city's display consisted of a large Christmas tree, an 18-foot menorah, and a sign declaring the city's dedication to freedom.

Chaplains in Congress and the State Legislatures Daily sessions of both houses of Congress and most of the State legislatures begin with prayer. In Congress, and in many States, a chaplain paid with public funds offers the opening prayer.

The Supreme Court has ruled that this practice, unlike prayers in the public schools, is constitutionally permissible—in a case involving Nebraska's one-house legislature, *Marsh* v. *Chambers*, 1983. The Court rested its distinction between school prayers and legislative prayers on two points. First, prayers have been offered in the nation's legislative bodies "from colonial times through the founding of the Republic and ever since." Second, legislators, unlike schoolchildren, are not "susceptible to religious indoctrination or peer pressure."

Tax Exemptions Every State exempts property of religious organizations used for religious purposes from State and local taxation. The Supreme Court has upheld this practice, *Walz* v. *New York City Tax Commission*, 1970. 

TRF **Teacher's Resource File**
See the Supreme Court Cases file, pp. 76–77, for material to support the section.

SPOTLIGHT ON: Economics
Taxes on religious institutions constitute a violation of 1st Amendment liberties, so religious institutions continue to be exempt. But, as in all things, abuses of this exemption do occur, as in the case of the wayward Christian Brothers winery in California. The brothers claimed a tax exemption as members of a monastery making wine for communion. But their wine and brandy were also being sold in supermarkets and liquor stores across the country. The State government sued in 1950 to end that particular exemption, leaving the brothers owing the State government $3.5 million in back taxes.

Separation of Church and State Parochial, or religion-affiliated schools are entitled to federal aid for only secular, or nonreligious, purposes.

A citizen named Walz had challenged the exemption of houses of worship from local property taxes. He argued that these exemptions made property tax bills higher than they would otherwise be, and that the exemptions amounted to a public support of religion.

The Court turned down Walz's plea. It found that those exemptions are evidence only of a State's "benevolent neutrality" toward religion, not support of it. Said the Court, the exemptions "create only a minimal and remote," and therefore permissible, "involvement between church and state."

But the Court has ruled that church-related schools that discriminate on the basis of race can be denied a tax-exempt status under federal law, *Bob Jones University* v. *United States* and *Goldsboro Christian Schools* v. *United States*, 1983. The schools involved in these 1983 cases argued that their racial policies reflected their sincerely held religious beliefs. The Supreme Court granted that point. It said, nevertheless, that the nation's interest in eradicating racial discrimination in education "substantially outweighs whatever burden denial of tax benefits places on [those schools in the] exercise of their religious beliefs."

State Aid to Parochial Schools Most recent Establishment Clause cases have centered on this highly controversial question: What forms of State aid to parochial schools are constitutional?

Several States give help to private schools—including those related to church organizations—for transportation, textbooks, laboratory equipment, standardized testing, and much else.

Those who support that aid argue that parochial schools enroll large numbers of students who would otherwise have to be educated at public expense. They also point to the fact that the Supreme Court has held that parents have a legal right to send their children to those schools (*Pierce* v. *Society of Sisters*). To give that right real meaning, they say, the State must give some aid to parochial schools—to relieve parents of some of the double burden they carry because they must pay taxes to support the public schools their children do not attend. Many advocates also insist that schools run by religious organizations pose no real church-state problems, because, they say, those schools devote most of their time to secular (nonreligious) subjects rather than to sectarian (religious) ones.

Opponents of aid to parochial schools argue that those parents who choose to send children to parochial schools should accept the financial consequences of that choice. Many of them also insist that it is impossible to draw clear lines between secular and sectarian courses in parochial schools. They say that religious beliefs are bound to have an effect on the teaching of nonreligious subjects in church-run schools.

The *Lemon* Test The Supreme Court has been picking its way through cases involving State aid laws for several years. In most of them, it now applies a three-pronged standard, the *Lemon* test: (1) The purpose of the aid must be clearly secular, not religious, (2) its primary effect must neither advance nor inhibit religion, and (3) it must avoid an "excessive entanglement of government with religion."

The test stems from *Lemon* v. *Kurtzman*, 1971. There, the Supreme Court held that the Establishment Clause is designed to prevent three main evils: "sponsorship, financial support, and active involvement of the sovereign in religious activity."

TRF

Teacher's Resource File

See the Supreme Court Cases file, pp. 92–93 and 78–79, for materials to support the section.

ACTIVITY: For Gifted Students

Theme: Systems Have students select five nations that differ from the United States in size and political structure. Once students have identified the countries they would like to investigate, have them research the official and unofficial role of religion in their selected countries. Students might consider such issues as whether a country has a state religion, whether religious freedom is permitted, and what different faiths are widely practiced by the people. Have students organize their findings in a table and share their tables with the rest of the class.

In *Lemon*, the Court struck down a Pennsylvania law that provided for reimbursements—financial payments—to private schools to cover their costs for teachers' salaries, textbooks, and other teaching materials in nonreligious courses.

The Court held that the State program was of direct benefit to the parochial schools, and so to the churches sponsoring them. It also found that the program required such close State supervision that it produced an excessive entanglement of government with religion.

A number of State aid programs have passed the *Lemon* test over the past 20 years, and others have failed it. Thus, for example, the Court has allowed the use of public funds to loan textbooks to students in parochial schools, in a case from Pennsylvania, *Meek* v. *Pittinger*, 1975. And it has held that a State can pay church-related schools what it costs them to administer the State's standardized tests, in a New York case, *Committee for Public Education* v. *Regan*, 1980. Both textbooks and standardized tests can be evaluated to be sure that they do not promote religion.

But public funds cannot be used to pay for such things as field trips for students at parochial schools, *Wollman* v. *Walter*, 1977. In that Ohio case, the Court said that field trips managed by parochial school teachers present "an unacceptable risk of fostering of religion." Nor can tax monies be used to pay any part of the salaries of parochial school teachers, including those who teach only secular courses, *Grand Rapids School District* v. *Ball*, 1985. The Court said in that Michigan case that while the contents of a book can be checked easily, the way a teacher handles a course cannot.

The Supreme Court struck down a New York law that provided for direct cash payments to parents to reimburse them for the tuition they paid to schools operated by religious organizations, *Committee for Public Education* v. *Nyquist*, 1973. But the Court has upheld a Minnesota tax law that accomplishes the same end, *Mueller* v. *Allen*, 1983. That law gives parents a State income tax deduction for the costs of tuition, textbooks, and transportation. Parents can claim the tax break no matter what schools their children attend. Most public school parents pay little or nothing for these items. Hence, the law is of particular benefit to parents with children in private, mostly parochial, schools. The Court found that the law meets the *Lemon* test, and it also leaned on this point: The deduction is available to all parents with children in school, and they are free to decide which type of school their children attend.

The Reagan and Bush administrations have supported a similar program at the federal level.

The Court has taken a different view in cases involving public aid to church-related colleges and universities. Thus, in *Tilton* v. *Richardson*, 1971, it upheld federal grants for the construction of academic buildings to be used for nonreligious purposes. The Court could find no excessive entanglement in these "one-shot" grants.[7]

In *Bowen* v. *Kendrick*, 1988, the Court took a more tolerant view of government aid to religion than it has in most recent cases. There, it upheld a controversial federal statute, the Adolescent Family Life Act of 1981. That law provides for grants to both public and private agencies dealing with the problems of adolescent sex and pregnancy. Some of the grants were made to religious groups that oppose abortion, prompting the argument that those groups use federal money to teach religious doctrine. However, the Supreme Court found the law's purpose—curbing "the social and economic problems caused by teenage sexuality, pregnancy, and parenthood"—to be a legitimate one. That some grants pay for counseling that "happens to coincide with the religious views" of some groups does not by itself mean that the federal funds are being used with "a primary effect of advancing religion."

Still, the Court was enough troubled by the church-state question to send the case back to the lower court, to determine how widespread violations have been and how to remedy them. Certainly, the court's future holds many additional "parochial" cases.

---

[7]In *Tilton* the Court held one section of the Higher Education Facilities Act of 1963 unconstitutional. That section limited to 20 years a college's obligation not to use a federally financed building for religious instruction or worship. The Court ruled that such buildings may never be used for those purposes.

Provide Guided Practice

Write the words *Establishment Clause* and *Free Exercise Clause* on the board. Present students with the following situations, and have them identify which clause might be involved in such a situation: Government employees are required to swear out an oath of loyalty to God and country. (*Establishment.*) Government workers are prohibited from voluntarily kneeling and praying on their coffee breaks. (*Free Exercise.*) Government workers receive a "Christmas bonus." (*Establishment.*) Members of an unpopular religious cult are denied the right to use a public park for group meetings. (*Free Exercise.*)

Have students invent their own scenarios that might involve questions about the Free Exercise Clause and the Establishment Clause.

Provide Independent Practice

TRF **Teacher's Resource File**
You may wish to assign Section 2 Guided Reading and Review, Unit 5 File, p. 28, to help students master section objective content.

Enrichment

Have students conduct a survey of students in school about their feelings on issues of the Free Exercise and Establishment clauses. Suggest that students use examples from the section, such as school prayer, or have students create their own situations. (Easy/Average)

MONITOR COMPREHENSION

Answers to Section 2 Review
1. "Key Terms" are defined on the following pages:
a. Establishment Clause, p. 490
b. Free Exercise Clause, p. 496
2. It is unclear what actions or policies violate the concept of separation of church and state. **3.** Education. **4.** The Free Exercise Clause gives people the right to believe whatever they choose in religious matters, but not necessarily to act as they choose. **5.** Some students may say that the decisions limit people's right to pray and thus limit free exercise. Others will say the decisions do not limit people's right to pray, simply their right to pray as part of an official, school activity; thus, those rulings do not limit free exercise unreasonably.

Teacher's Resource File See the Unit 5 File, p. 29, for the Section 2 Quiz.

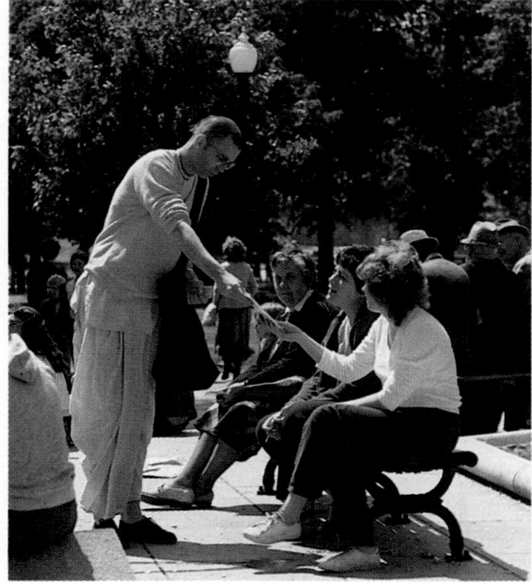

The Free Exercise Clause This clause upholds the right to freedom of religion; but the law can require Hare Krishna members to limit public handouts of their literature.

The Free Exercise of Religion

The second part of the constitutional guarantee of religious freedom is set out in the Con-
1.b stitution's **Free Exercise Clause**. That clause guarantees to each person the right to believe whatever that person chooses to believe in matters of religion. It is protected by the 1st and the 14th amendments.

No person has an absolute right to act as he or she chooses, however. The Free Exercise Clause does *not* give one the right to violate the criminal laws, offend public morals, or otherwise threaten the health, welfare, or safety of the community.

The Supreme Court laid down the basic shape of the Free Exercise Clause in the first case it heard on the point, *Reynolds* v. *United States*, 1879. Reynolds, a Mormon, had two wives. That practice—polygamy—was allowed by the teachings of his church; but it was prohibited by a federal law.

Reynolds was tried and convicted under the law. On appeal, he argued that the law violated his constitutional right to the free exercise of his religious beliefs. The Supreme Court disagreed, however. It held that the 1st Amendment does not forbid Congress the power to punish those actions that are "violations of social duties or subversive of good order." To hold otherwise, said the Court

> "would be to make the professed doctrines of religious belief superior to the law of the land, and in effect permit every citizen to become a law unto himself."

Over the years, the Court has approved many regulations of human conduct in the face of free exercise challenges. For example, it has upheld laws that require the vaccination of school children, *Jacobson* v. *Massachusetts*, 1905; that forbid the use of poisonous snakes in religious rites, *Bunn* v. *North Carolina*, 1949; and so-called blue laws that require businesses to be closed on Sundays, *McGowan* v. *Maryland*, 1961.

A State can require religious groups to have a permit to hold a parade on the public streets, *Cox* v. *New Hampshire*, 1940; and organizations that enlist children to sell religious literature must obey child labor laws, *Prince* v. *Massachusetts*, 1944. The Federal Government can draft those who have religious objections to military service, *Welsh* v. *United States*, 1970.[8] The Air Force can forbid an Orthodox Jew the right to wear his yarmulke—skull cap—while on active duty, *Goldman* v. *Weinberger*, 1986. The U.S. Forest Service can allow private companies to build roads and cut timber in national forests that Native Americans have traditionally used for religious purposes, *Lyng* v. *Northwest Indian Cemetery Protective Association*, 1988. And a State can deny unemployment benefits to a man fired by a private drug counseling group because he used peyote in violation of the State's drug laws—even though he ingested the hallucinogenic drug as part of a ceremony of his Native American Church, *Oregon* v. *Smith*, 1990.

But, over time, the Court has also found many actions by governments to be contrary to

---

[8]The Court has made this ruling many times. *Welsh* is the leading case from the Vietnam War period. There, the Court held that the only persons who could not be drafted were those "whose consciences . . . would give them no rest if they allowed themselves to become part of an instrument of war."

the Free Exercise guarantee. The Court did so for the first time in one of the landmark Due Process cases cited earlier in this chapter, *Cantwell* v. *Connecticut*, 1940. There, the Court struck down a law requiring a license before any person could solicit money for a religious cause.

There are many other cases in that line. Thus, Amish children cannot be forced to attend school beyond the 8th grade, because that sect's centuries-old "self-sufficient agrarian lifestyle essential to their religious faith is threatened by modern education," *Wisconsin* v. *Yoder*, 1972. But the Amish, who take care of their own people, must pay social security taxes, as all other employers do, *United States* v. *Lee*, 1982.

A State cannot forbid ministers to hold elected public offices, *McDaniel* v. *Paty*, 1978. Nor can it deny unemployment compensation benefits to a worker who quit a job because it involved some conflict with his or her religious beliefs, *Sherbert* v. *Verner*, 1963; *Thomas* v. *Indiana*, 1981; *Hobbie* v. *Florida*, 1987; *Frazee* v. *Illinois*, 1989.[9]

The Court has often held that "only those beliefs rooted in religion are protected by the Free Exercise Clause" (*Sherbert* v. *Verner*, 1963). But that rule begs this thorny question: Which beliefs are those "rooted in religion?" Clearly, religions that seem strange or even bizarre to most Americans are as entitled to constitutional protection as are the more traditional ones. "[R]eligious beliefs need not be acceptable, logical, consistent, or comprehensible to others to merit 1st Amendment protection," *Thomas* v. *Indiana*, 1981.

[9]Typically, State unemployment compensation laws bar such benefits to those who leave jobs voluntarily and "without good cause in connection with the work." Some bar benefits to those who are fired. In *Sherbert*, to take one example of these cases, a Seventh Day Adventist lost her job in a South Carolina textile mill when she refused to work on Saturdays, her Sabbath. In *Thomas*, a Jehovah's Witness who worked for a machinery company quit after he was transferred from one section of the company that was being closed down to another where gun turrets for tanks were made. He left because, he said, his religious beliefs would not allow him to work on war materials. Note this distinction between these two cases and *Oregon* v. *Smith*, 1990: Smith's conduct involved the violation of a State law.

The Jehovah's Witnesses have carried several important religious freedom cases to the Supreme Court. Perhaps the stormiest of the controversies that sect has stirred arose out of the Witnesses' refusal to salute the flag.

The Witnesses refuse to salute the flag because they see such conduct as a violation of the Bible's commandment against idolatry. In *Minersville School District* v. *Gobitis*, 1940, the Court upheld a Pennsylvania school board regulation requiring students to salute the flag at the beginning of each school day. Gobitis instructed his children not to do so, and the school expelled them. He went to court, basing his case on the constitutional guarantee. He finally lost in the Supreme Court, however. The Court declared that the board's rule was not an infringement of religious liberty. Rather, the Court held that the rule was a lawful attempt to promote patriotism and national unity.

Three years later, the Court reversed that decision. In *West Virginia Board of Education* v. *Barnette*, 1943, it held a compulsory flag-salute law unconstitutional. Justice Robert H. Jackson's words on page 486 are from the Court's powerful opinion in that case. So are these:

> "To believe that patriotism will not flourish if patriotic ceremonies are voluntary and spontaneous instead of a compulsory routine is to make an unflattering estimate of the appeal of our institutions to free minds."

Section 2 Review

1. Define: Establishment Clause, Free Exercise Clause
2. What does it mean to say that it is unclear how high the wall between Church and State is?
3. Over what subjects have most Establishment Clause cases been fought?
4. What is the basic shape of the rights guaranteed by the Free Exercise Clause?

Critical Thinking

5. Identifying Central Issues (p. 19) Some observers feel that Supreme Court decisions such as *Engle* v. *Vitale* and *Murray* v. *Curlett* limit people's free exercise of religion. Do you agree or disagree?

★

Closure

Remind students that the freedom of religion is a central part of this country's dedication to freedom of expression. In order to ensure a free exercise of religion, the 1st Amendment includes the Establishment Clause, which requires a separation of church and state, and the Free Exercise Clause, which protects people's right to believe whatever they wish in the field of religion.

In Section 3, students will read about other key 1st Amendment freedoms, freedom of speech and the press.

Assignment Assign Section 3, pp. 499–505, for the next class period.

Reteach

Have students complete the following sentences:

- The Establishment Clause ensures freedom of religion by . . .
- The Free Exercise Clause ensures freedom of religion by . . .

Teacher's Resource File
See the Supreme Court Cases file, pp. 82–83, for material to support the section.

TEACHING
Debating Key Issues

Tinker v. *Des Moines:*
Should Public Schools Ban Political Protests?

Objective

Determine whether or not a person's rights have been violated.

INSTRUCT

Before reading the feature, elicit student responses to the title question. When students have finished reading the feature, have them work through the "Getting Involved" section, beginning with the identification of the constitutional issues involved.

Following class debate, have students reconsider their opinions on the case. Then have them read the Supreme Court's decision to find out if they agree with the Court. You may wish to ask students to write one or two paragraphs about how they would feel if they were denied the right to peacefully express themselves as Mary Beth and John Tinker did.

SUPREME COURT DECISION

The Court agreed with the Tinkers, noting that "students do not abandon their civil rights at the school house door. . ." and that "the wearing of black arm bands (was) peaceful expression of political opinion. . ." Schools would need to show evidence of the possibility of "substantial disturbance" before free speech could be limited at school.

Debating Key Issues

Should Public Schools Ban Political Protests?

Tinker v. *Des Moines*

In the 1960s, political protests against United States involvement in Vietnam occurred daily on college campuses. The protests included peace marches, sit-ins, and mass burnings of draft cards. Some demonstrations turned violent.

In Des Moines, Iowa, a group of local citizens decided to demonstrate silently their opposition to the war by wearing black armbands bearing white peace signs. Their protest began on December 16 and was to run until New Year's Day.

When the principals of the local school district heard of the plan, they informed the public of a new policy: Any student who wore an armband would be asked to remove it. If the student refused, he or she would be suspended from school.

On December 16, despite the school's regulation, a number of students, including Mary Beth and John Tinker and two of their friends, decided to wear the black armbands to school. The students were instructed not to return to school until they were willing to appear without the black armbands. They did not return until after the school holiday, when the silent protest period had ended.

Believing that their childrens' constitutional right to free speech had been violated, the students' parents and the Iowa Civil Liberties Union filed a petition in the U.S. district court on the students' behalf. The court decided in favor of the school officials. On appeal, the lower court ruling was allowed to stand. At this point, the American Civil Liberties Union petitioned the Supreme Court to hear the case.

Review the following evidence and arguments presented to the Supreme Court:

Arguments for Des Moines School District

1. Students can be denied their right to free speech with just cause, in this case to avoid a disruption of school discipline.
2. The no armband rule was made to avoid a disruption of school discipline.
3. The disciplined atmosphere of the classroom, not the right to wear armbands, is entitled to the protection of the law.
4. Schools are not places for demonstrations. Controversial issues should be confined to classroom discussions, where students' right to free speech is protected.

Arguments for Tinker

1. No general ban existed against all controversial symbols, only black armbands. Such a selective ban was unconstitutional.
2. By banning armbands, the school district had denied students freedom of speech.
3. School officials did not have the right to deny students their 1st Amendment rights.
4. Students wearing armbands had not in fact disrupted school discipline.

Getting Involved

1. Identify the constitutional grounds upon which each side based its arguments.
2. Debate the opposing viewpoints presented in this case.
3. Predict how you think the Supreme Court ruled in this case and why. Then refer to the Supreme Court Glossary on page 764 to read about the decision. Discuss whether students' freedom of speech may be denied under any circumstances.

TRF **Teacher's Resource File**
See the Supreme Court Cases file, p. 14, for an activity that extends coverage of this case.

3 Freedom of Speech and Press

Find Out:

- What is the breadth of the guarantees of free speech and free press?
- What are the limits on the guarantees of free speech and free press?

Key Terms:

libel, slander, shield law, symbolic speech, picketing

Think about this children's verse for a moment: "Sticks and stones may break my bones, but names will never hurt me." That rhyme says, in effect, that acts and words are separate things and that acts can do harm but words cannot.

Is that really true? Certainly not. You know that words can and do have consequences—sometimes powerful consequences. Words, spoken or written, can make you happy, sad, bored, informed, or entertained. They can also expose you to danger, deny you a job, or lead to other serious consequences.

In this section you will read about the Constitution's protection of the vitally important freedom expression and how the meaning of those freedoms has developed over the course of American history.

Democracy and Freedom of Expression

The 1st and 14th amendment's protections of free speech and a free press serve two fundamentally important purposes:

1. To guarantee to each person a right of free expression—in the spoken and the written word, and by all other means of communication, as well.
2. To ensure to all persons a full, wide-ranging discussion of public affairs.

That is, the 1st and 14th amendments give to all people the right to have their say and to hear what others have to say. Most often, people think of these great freedoms in terms of that first purpose. The second one is just as important, however.

The American system of government depends on the ability of the people to make sound, reasoned judgments on matters of public concern. Clearly, people can best make such judgments when they know all of the facts in a given matter, *and* can hear all the available interpretations of those facts.

Justice Oliver Wendell Holmes once underscored the importance of that second purpose in these words:

> "Persecution for the expression of opinions seems to me perfectly logical. If you have no doubt of your premises and want a certain result with all your heart, you naturally express your wishes in law and sweep away all opposition. . . . But when men have realized that time has upset many fighting faiths, they may come to believe even more than they believe the very foundations of their own conduct that the ultimate good desired is better reached by free trade in ideas—that the best test of truth is the power of the thought to get itself accepted in the competition of the market. . . . That at any rate is the theory of our Constitution."[10]

As you examine the Constitution's 1st and 14th amendments here, keep two other key points in mind:

First, the guarantees of free speech and press are intended to protect the expression of unpopular views. That is because the opinions of the majority need, after all, little or no constitutional protection.

Second, some forms of expression are not protected by the Constitution. No person has an unbridled right of free speech or free press. Many reasonable restrictions can be placed on those rights.

You will see a number of illustrations of this point over the next several pages. For now, recall Justice Holmes's comment about the right to shout "Fire!" in a crowded theater. Or, note this restriction: No person has the right to libel or
slander another. **Libel** is the false and malicious 1.a
use of printed words; **slander** is such use of spo- 1.b
ken words. Similarly, the law prohibits the use of

[10]Dissenting in *Abrams* v. *United States*, 1919.

SECTION 3
Freedom of Speech and Press

FOCUS

Teacher's Resource File See the Unit 5 File, p. 30, for the Section 3 Outline.

Objectives

19.7 Examine the breadth of the guarantees of free speech and free press.
19.8 Define the limits on the guarantees of free speech and free press.

Bellringer Activity Ask students whether or not they think groups such as the Ku Klux Klan or a communist group should be allowed to say whatever they want in public? At what point can they be rightfully silenced? Who decides such questions and when—before or after they express their views?

State the Purpose The 1st Amendment guarantees the freedoms of speech and press. These freedoms, like the freedom of religion, are central to the American democracy. However, these rights are not absolute, and the debate over what speech is protected is ongoing. Students will read about that debate in this section.

ABCNEWS INTERACTIVE

The following video segments may be used to highlight aspects of individual rights and liberties.

POWERS OF THE SUPREME COURT GUIDEBOOK
Chapter 8: Amendment 1 (1791), Freedom of Speech, p. 11
Chapter 9: Amendment 1 (1791), Freedom of the Press, p. 13

Vocabulary

Direct students' attention to "Key Terms" on page 499. Review the term *symbolic speech* and have students suggest specific examples of it. Ask which they think would or would not be legally protected.

Reading Strategy: Relating to Topic

Have students think about a time when something someone said has hurt or offended them. Discuss whether people should be permitted to use such language. Tell students that they will be reading about how the American system of government has wrestled with issues of free speech and free press.

INSTRUCT

Explain/Discuss The free speech and free press guaranteed by the 1st and 14th amendments secure each person's right to free expression. They also protect the right to a wide-ranging discussion of public affairs. Ask students to discuss why such public discussion is so vital to a democracy? (*It allows people to hear and evaluate competing ideas.*) Have students read and respond to Justice Holmes' statement on page 499.

While the courts have repeatedly confirmed the rights of free speech and free press, they have restricted them in certain cases. Ask students to discuss the limits on libel, slander, and obscenity. Have students discuss whether or not they think these limits threaten in any meaningful way the free trade in ideas?

Have students consider the concept of prior restraint. Ask students to identify the reasons why prior restraint is so rarely allowed? (*Because it could deprive the "marketplace of ideas" of valuable ideas.*) Have students discuss situations in which it would be necessary to prohibit speech before it occurs rather than waiting until after the speech is uttered.

obscene words, the printing and distributing of obscene materials, and false advertising. You will rsead about these prohibitions in the pages ahead.[11]

Obscenity

The 1st and 14th amendments do not protect obscenity, but in recent years the Court has had to wrestle several times with these questions: What language in printed matter, films, and other materials are, in fact, obscene? What restrictions can be properly placed on such materials?[12]

Today, the leading case is *Miller* v. *California*, 1973. There the Court laid down a three-part test to determine what material is obscene.

A piece of material is legally obscene if (1) "the average person applying contemporary [local] community standards" finds that the work, taken as a whole, "appeals to the prurient interest"—that is, tends to excite lust; (2) "the work depicts or describes, in a patently offensive way," a form of sexual conduct specifically dealt with in an antiobscenity law; and (3) "the work, taken as a whole, lacks serious literary, artistic, political, or scientific value."

That the problem is a knotty one is evident from several cases. In *Stanley* v. *Georgia*, 1969, the Court ruled that a State cannot make it a crime for a person to possess obscene materials for his or her own use at home.[13] Yet, in two 1971 cases, the Court upheld laws that punish those who send obscene materials in interstate commerce or through the mails or import them from abroad, *United States* v. *Thirty-Seven Photographs*; *United States* v. *Reidel*.[14]

Sexually explicit material about or aimed at minors does not enjoy constitutional protection. In *Osborne* v. *Ohio*, 1990, it said that the State has a compelling interest in protecting the well-being of minors and also in the destruction of the market in which minors are abused.

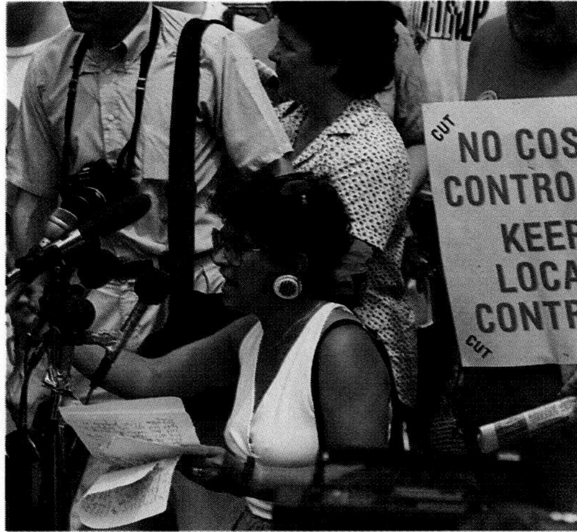

Freedoms of Speech and Assembly Minority rights to freedom of expression are protected under the 1st and 14th amendments.

[11]Libel and slander involve the use of words, maliciously—with vicious purpose—to injure a person's character or reputation or expose that person to public contempt, ridicule, or hatred. Truth is generally an absolute defense against a libel or slander claim. The law is less protective of public officials, however. In *New York Times* v. *Sullivan*, 1964, the Supreme Court held that public officials cannot recover damages for a published criticism, even if exaggerated or false, unless "the statement was made with actual malice—that is with knowledge that it was false or with reckless disregard of whether it was false or not." Several later decisions have extended that ruling to cover "public figures" and even private individuals who have become involved in newsworthy events. Those public figures cannot win damages even for an "intentional infliction of emotional distress," *Hustler Magazine* v. *Falwell*, 1988.

[12]Congress passed the first of a series of laws to keep obscene matter from the mails in 1872. The current law was upheld by the Court in *Roth* v. *United States*, 1957. The law excludes "every obscene, lewd, lascivious, or filthy" piece of material. The Court found the law a proper exercise of the postal power (Article I, Section 8, Clause 7).

[13]Films were involved in the case. Said the Court: "If the 1st Amendment means anything, it means that the State has no business telling a man, sitting alone in his own home, what books he may read or what films he may watch." But, in *United States* v. *Orito*, 1973, it held that the "zone of privacy" protected by *Stanley* does not go beyond one's own home.

[14]The 1st Amendment does not forbid a city to regulate the location of "adult entertainment establishments" through its zoning ordinances, *Young* v. *American Mini Theatres*, 1976. The Court has also ruled that a State law that bans totally nude dancing at adult entertainment establishments does not violate the Constitution, *Barnes* v. *Glen Theatre, Inc.*, 1991.

SPOTLIGHT ON: Constitutional Issues

Most people know what they like, what offends them and what does not. But the difficulty of establishing a clear, precise, usable standard for judging the obscenity of a book or film has long troubled judges and justices. In the 1964 case *Jacobellis* v. *Ohio,* Justice Potter Stewart expressed the frustration of many when he wrote in a concurring opinion, "Perhaps I could never succeed in intelligibly [creating a definition of hard core pornography]. But I know it when I see it. . . ."

Teacher's Resource File
See the Supreme Court Cases file, pp. 86–87, for material to support the chapter.

Businesses that offer "dial-a-porn" services have sprung up around the country in the past few years. Congress and several State legislatures have moved against these services.

The federal law, passed in 1988, made it a crime for any person to use a telephone to send any "obscene or indecent" communication for a commercial purpose. The Supreme Court destroyed the statute, however, in *Sable Communications* v. *FCC* in 1989. A unanimous Court held that only "obscene" calls—and not those that are merely "indecent"—can be outlawed under the 1st Amendment.

Prior Restraint

The Constitution allows government to punish some utterances, *after* they are made. But, with almost no exceptions, government cannot place any prior restraint on spoken or written words. That is, except in the most extreme situations, government cannot curb ideas before they are expressed.

Near v. *Minnesota*, 1931, is a leading case in point. The Supreme Court struck down a State law that prohibited the publication of any "malicious, scandalous, and defamatory" periodical. Acting under that law, a local court had issued an order forbidding the publication of The *Saturday Press*. The paper had printed several articles charging public corruption and attacking "grafters" and "Jewish gangsters" in that city. The Court held that the guarantee of a free press does not allow a prior restraint on publication, except in such extreme cases as wartime, or when a publication is obscene or incites readers to violence. The Court said that even "miscreant purveyors of scandal" and anti-Semitism have a constitutional protection against prior restraint.

The Constitution does not forbid any and all forms of prior censorship, but "a prior restraint on expression comes to this Court with a 'heavy presumption' against its constitutionality," *Nebraska Press Association* v. *Stuart*, 1976.[15] The Court has used that general rule several times—for example, in the famous Pentagon Papers Case, *New York Times* v. *United States*, 1971.

In that case, several newspapers had obtained copies of a set of classified documents. The documents, widely known as the Pentagon Papers, were officially titled *History of U.S. Decision-Making Process on Viet Nam Policy*. They had been stolen from the Defense Department and then leaked to the press. The government sought a court order to bar their publication, but the Court held that the government had not shown that printing the documents would endanger the nation's security, and so had not overcome the "heavy presumption" against prior censorship.

The few prior restraints the Court has approved include regulations prohibiting the distribution of political literature on military bases without the approval of military authorities, *Greer* v. *Spock*, 1976; a CIA rule that agents must agree never to publish anything about the agency without the CIA's permission, *Snepp* v. *United States*, 1980; a federal prison rule that allows officials to prevent an inmate from receiving publications considered "detrimental to the security, good order, or discipline" of the prison *Thornburgh* v. *Abbott*, 1989.

The Court has recently said that public school officials have a broad power to censor school newspapers, plays, and other "school-sponsored expressive activities." In *Hazelwood School District* v. *Kuhlmeier*, 1988, it held that "educators do not offend the 1st Amendment by exercising editorial control over the style and content of student speech in school-sponsored expressive activities so long as their actions are reasonably related to legitimate pedagogical [teaching] concerns."

Confidentiality

Can news reporters be forced to testify before a grand jury, in court, or before a legislative committee, and there be required to name their sources and reveal other confidential information?

Many reporters and news organizations insist that they must have the right to refuse to testify, the right to protect their sources. They argue that without this right they cannot assure confidentiality to their sources. Unless they can

[15]In this case a judge had ordered the media not to report certain details of a murder trial. The Court held the judge's gag order to be unconstitutional.

Have students discuss the power of the media to communicate the ideas that must be communicated in a vital democracy. To demonstrate, ask students their opinion on an important topic of the day, such as an election, a scandal, or some other issue with which most students are familiar. Then ask students where they and other citizens got their information. Given the power of the media, tell students to discuss the responsibility of government to keep it free—and to keep it free of harmful and dangerous information such as false advertising.

Introduce the idea of symbolic speech. Ask students to discuss whether or not they think symbolic speech deserves the same protection as spoken or written words. (*Students might suggest that symbolic speech must be limited in the same way other actions are limited; that is, symbolic speech cannot be used as a license to do whatever a person wants.*) Students might wish to discuss here the case of *Tinker* v. *Des Moines* from the "Debating Key Issues" feature on page 498.

Federally Regulated Television and radio are subject to more federal regulation than other media, on the grounds that the airwaves they use are public property.

do that, reporters say, many sources will not give them information they need to keep the public informed.

Both State and federal courts have generally rejected the news media argument. In recent years several reporters have refused to obey court orders directing them to give information. As a consequence, a number of reporters have gone to jail, testifying to the importance of these issues.

In the leading case, *Branzburg* v. *Hayes*, 1972, the Supreme Court held that reporters, "like other citizens, [must] respond to relevant questions put to them in the course of a valid grand jury investigation or criminal trial." If the media are to receive any special exemptions, said the Court, the exemptions must come from Congress and the State legislatures.

To date, Congress has not acted on the Court's suggestion. However, some 30 States have passed so-called **shield laws**. These laws 1.c give reporters some protection against having to disclose their sources or reveal other confidential information in legal proceedings in those States.

Motion Pictures

The Supreme Court took its first look at motion pictures early in the history of the movie industry. In 1915, in *Mutual Film Corporation* v. *Ohio*, the Court upheld a State law that barred the showing of any film that was not of a "moral, educational, or harmless and amusing character." The Court declared that "the exhibition of moving pictures is a business, pure and simple," and "not . . . part of the press of the country." With that decision, nearly every State and thousands of communities set up movie review—really movie censorship—programs.

The Court reversed itself in 1952, however. In *Burstyn* v. *Wilson*, a New York censorship case, it found that "liberty of expression by means of motion pictures is guaranteed by the 1st and 14th amendments."

Movie censorship is not necessarily unconstitutional, however. A State or local government can ban an obscene film, but only under a law that provides for a prompt judicial hearing. At that hearing that government must show that the picture in question is in fact obscene, *Teitel Film Corporation* v. *Cusack*, 1968.

Very few of the once common local movie review boards still exist. Most movie-goers now depend on the film industry's own rating system and on the comments of movie critics on television and in newspapers and magazines.

Radio and Television

Both radio and television broadcasting are subject to extensive federal regulation. Most of this regulation is based on the often-amended Federal Communications Act of 1934, which is administered by the Federal Communications Commission. As the Supreme Court has described the situation: "Of all forms of communication, it is broadcasting that has received the most limited 1st Amendment protection," *Red Lion Broadcasting Co.* v. *FCC*, 1969.

The Court has several times upheld this wide-ranging federal regulation as a proper exercise

Spotlight on: Global Awareness

While listeners' and viewers' rights are indeed the primary goal of government regulation, the Federal Government has also been careful to protect the media's right to free speech since the founding of the FCC in 1934. The rise of Hitler's propaganda machine—the Ministry of Propaganda and Popular Enlightenment—offered a prime example to government officials of the damage that could result from centralized control of the media. German radio, which, as elsewhere in Europe, was under the control of the state, was simply taken over by the Nazis when they came to power in 1933. The Third Reich used the medium to devastating effect, spreading disinformation, stirring hysteria, and limiting public debate.

of the commerce power. Unlike newspapers and other print media, radio and television use the public's property—the public airwaves—to broadcast their materials. They have no right to do so without the public's permission—that is, without a proper license, *National Broadcasting Co.* v. *United States*, 1942.

The Court has regularly rejected the argument that the 1st Amendment prohibits such regulations. Instead, it has taken the view that that regulation implements the constitutional guarantee. It has held that there is no "unabridgeable 1st Amendment right to broadcast comparable to the right of every individual to speak, write, or publish." However, "this is not to say that the 1st Amendment is irrelevant to broadcasting. But . . . it is the right of the viewers and the listeners, not the right of the broadcasters, which is paramount."[16]

Congress has forbidden the FCC to censor the content of programs before they are broadcast. But the FCC can prohibit the use of indecent language, and it can take violations of the ban into account when a station applies for the renewal of its operating license, *FCC* v. *Pacifica Foundation*, 1978. The FCC has refused applications for renewal of licenses due to past use of objectionable practices. And Congress itself cannot prohibit the broadcasting of editorials by public radio and television stations, *FCC* v. *League of Women Voters of California*, 1984.

In several recent decisions, the Supreme Court has given the growing cable television industry broader 1st Amendment freedoms than those enjoyed by traditional television. A 1987 case, *Wilkinson* v. *Jones*, is fairly typical. There, the Court held that the States cannot regulate "indecent" cable programming. It reached that decision by striking down a Utah law that prohibited the cable broadcast of any sexually explicit or other "indecent material" between the hours of 7 A.M. and midnight.

VOICES *on Government*

To the Press, on Freedom of the Press

Mario M. Cuomo,
governor of New York

"The press . . . has the power to inform, but that implies the power to distort. You have the power to instruct, but that implies the power to mislead. . . . You can lead our society toward a more mature and discriminating understanding of the process by which we choose our leaders, make our rules, and construct our values. Or you can encourage people to despise our systems and avoid participating in them. You can teach our children a taste for violence, encourage a fascination with perversity and inflicted pain. Or you can show them a beauty they have not known. . . . You can make us all wiser, fuller, surer, sweeter than we are. Or you can do less. And worse. And one of the miracles of this democracy is that you are free to make all the choices."

Symbolic Speech

People also communicate ideas by conduct—by the way a person does some particular thing. Thus, a person can say something with a facial expression or a shrug of the shoulders, or by carrying a sign or wearing an arm band. This mode of expression—expression by conduct—is
1.d known as **symbolic speech**.

[16]*Red Lion Broadcasting Co.* v. *FCC*, 1969, in which the Court upheld the fairness doctrine, an FCC rule in effect until its repeal by the commission in 1987. The rule provided that broadcasters had to air opposing viewpoints, not just one side, on important issues.

The FCC still enforces the equal time doctrine, set out in the Communications Act. The law's equal time provision means that if, for example, a television network makes air time available to one candidate for a public office, it must offer equal time to all other candidates for that office. Most of those who have opposed the fairness doctrine also oppose this rule and urge Congress to repeal it.

Provide Guided Practice
Write the following on the board: *obscenity, prior restraint, confidentiality, motion pictures, radio and television, symbolic speech,* and *commercial speech.* Ask students to volunteer explanations of how the constitutional protections of free speech and press relate to these terms. (*Possible answers: Truly obscene material is not protected by the 1st and 14th amendments; prior restraint is allowed only in extreme circumstances; confidentiality is generally not guaranteed; motion pictures are now protected by the 1st and 14th amendments; radio and television are regulated by the government and receive the most limited 1st amendment protection; symbolic speech is protected just as speech is, but such protection does not give people the right to act in any manner in the name of freedom of expression; commercial speech can be limited, but not in an arbitrary way.*)

Provide Independent Practice
TRF **Teacher's Resource File**
You may wish to assign Section 3 Guided Reading and Review Unit 5 file, p. 31, to help students master section objective content.

Enrichment
Hold a class debate on the following topic: *Prior restraint should never be allowed.* Form two teams of three or four students. The rest of the class can evaluate each team's presentation. (Easy)

Monitor Comprehension

Answers to Section 3 Review
1. "Key Terms" are defined on the following pages:
a. libel, p. 499
b. slander, p. 499
c. shield law, p. 502
d. symbolic speech, p. 503
e. picketing, p. 504
2. So people can have their say and hear what others are saying. By being able to hear all this information, people can make sound, reasoned judgments.
3. Unpopular views. **4.** Only in extreme situations, for example, during wartime. **5.** No. However, to be judged obscene, material must meet strict standards. **6.** Many States have shield laws, which protect reporters against having to disclose sources or other confidential information. **7.** Today government regulation of movies is minimal, while regulation of radio and television is extensive. **8.** (a) The Court generally regards symbolic speech as it does spoken speech, though people are not free to do whatever they wish in the name of free speech. (b) It is generally protected, though the government prohibits false and misleading advertisements, the advertising of illegal goods, and certain other kinds of advertising. **9.** Some students may say that the expression of such views causes pain and anguish out of proportion to whatever benefit they bring; others may say that by being able to hear such views, people have been able to consider them and reject them in many cases.

Clearly, not all conduct amounts to symbolic speech. If it did, murder or robbery or any other crime could be excused on grounds that the person who committed the act meant to say something by doing so.

But, just as clearly, some conduct does express opinion. Take picketing in a labor dispute as an
1.e example. **Picketing** involves patrolling of a business site by workers who are on strike. By their conduct, picketers attempt to inform the public of the controversy, and to persuade others not to deal with the firm involved. Picketing is, then, a form of expression. If peaceful, it is protected by the 1st and 14th amendments.[17]

Generally, the Supreme Court has been sympathetic to the symbolic speech argument. But it has not given blanket 1st Amendment protection to that means of expression. As a sampling, note these cases:

United States v. *O'Brien*, 1968, involved four young men who had burned their draft cards to protest the war in Vietnam. A court convicted them of violating a federal law that makes that act a crime. O'Brien appealed, arguing that the 1st Amendment protects "all modes of communication of ideas by conduct." The Supreme Court disagreed. Said the Court: "We cannot accept the view that an apparently limitless variety of conduct can be labeled 'speech' whenever the person engaging in the conduct intends thereby to express an idea."

The Court also held that acts of dissent by conduct can be punished if: (1) the object of the protest—here, the war and the draft—is within the constitutional powers of the government; (2) whatever restriction is placed on expression is no greater than necessary in the circumstances; and (3) the government's real interest in the matter is not to squelch dissent.

Using that test, the court has denied some claims of symbolic speech. Thus, for example, it held that a policeman does not have a constitutional right to protest a department dress code by growing long hair—even if he believes that to be "a means of expressing his attitude and lifestyle"—because a government has a reasonable stake in requiring a "similarity of garb and appearance" among its police officers, *Kelley* v. *Johnson*, 1976. And the Court upheld a National Park Service regulation under which a group of protesters was not allowed to sleep overnight in Lafayette Park near the White House, *Clark* v. *Community for Creative Non-Violence*, 1984.

Tinker v. *Des Moines School District*, 1969, on the other hand, is one of several cases in which the Court has come down on the side of symbolic speech. A small group of students in the Des Moines public schools had worn black armbands to publicize their opposition to the war in Vietnam. The school suspended them for it. The Court ruled that school officials had overstepped their authority and violated the Constitution. Said the Court: "It can hardly be argued that either students or teachers shed their constitutional rights to freedom of speech or expression at the schoolhouse gate."[18]

Campaign contributions are "a symbolic expression of support" for candidates, so the making of those contributions is entitled to constitutional protection, *Buckley* v. *Valeo*, 1976. Both federal and State laws regulate campaign contributions, but the fact that in politics "money is speech" greatly complicates that whole matter of campaign finance regulation (see Chapter 7).

Burning the American flag as an act of political protest is expressive conduct protected by the 1st and 14th amendments—so a sharply divided Court has twice held. In *Texas* v. *Johnson*, 1989, a 5–4 majority ruled that State authorities had violated a protester's rights when they prosecuted him under a law that forbids the "desecration of a venerated object." Johnson had set fire to

[17]The leading case on the point is *Thornhill* v. *Arizona*, 1940. There, the Court struck down a State law that made it a crime for one to loiter about or picket a place of business in order to influence others not to trade or work there. But picketing that is "set in a background of violence" can be prevented. Even peaceful picketing can be restricted if it is conducted for some illegal purpose, for example, to force someone to do something that is itself illegal.

[18]Do not read too much into this, however, for the Court added, it "has repeatedly affirmed the comprehensive authority of the States and of school authorities, consistent with fundamental constitutional safeguards, to prescribe and control conduct in the schools." The fact that in *Tinker* the students' conduct did not produce any substantial disruption of normal school activities was an important factor in the Court's decision.

Activity: Cooperative Learning

Time: One class period **Activity:** Write interview questions for Supreme Court justices. **Grouping:** Small groups **Purpose:** Assign one of the following cases described in Chapter 19 to each group of students: (1) *Everson* v. *Board of Education*, 1947; (2) *Engel* v. *Vitale*, 1962; (3) *Wallace* v. *Jaffrey*, 1985; (4) *Epperson* v. *Arkansas*, 1968; (5) *Edwards* v. *Aguillard*, 1987; (6) *Lemon* v. *Kurtzman*, 1971; (7) *West Virginia Board of Education* v. *Barnette*, 1943; (8) *Branzburg* v. *Hayes*, 1972; (9) *United States* v. *O'Brien*, 1968; (10) *Texas* v. *Johnson*, 1989. Have group members work together to compose four questions they would like to ask the justices of the Supreme Court about their decision in the assigned case. **Roles:** Have students assign the following roles: discussion leader, recorder, spokesperson. **Outcome:** Have the spokesperson identify the group's case and its subject matter, and read the interview questions to the class.

TRF **Teacher's Resource File**
See the Supreme Court Cases file, pp. 112–113, and the Simulations and Debates file, pp. 35–70, for materials to support the section.

an American flag during an anti-Reagan demonstration at the Republican National Convention in Dallas in 1984. Said the Court:

> "If there is a bedrock principle underlying the 1st Amendment, it is that the government may not prohibit the expression of an idea simply because society finds the idea itself offensive. . . . We do not consecrate the flag by punishing its desecration, for in doing so we dilute the freedom that this cherished emblem represents."

The Court's decision in *Johnson* set off a firestorm of criticism around the country and prompted Congress to pass the Flag Protection Act of 1989. It, too, was struck down by the Court, 5 to 4, in *United States* v. *Eichman* in 1990—on the same grounds as those set out a year earlier in *Johnson.*

Commercial Speech

Commercial speech is speech for business purposes—mostly, advertising. Until fairly recently, it was generally thought that the 1st and 14th amendments did not protect such speech. In *Bigelow* v. *Virginia*, 1975, however, the Supreme Court held unconstitutional a State law that prohibited the newspaper advertising of abortion services. And in 1976 it struck down another Virginia law forbidding the advertisement of prescription drug prices, *Virginia State Board of Pharmacy* v. *Virginia Citizens Consumer Council.*

Not all commercial speech is protected, however. Thus, government can and does prohibit false and misleading advertisements, and the advertising of illegal goods or services.

In fact, government can even forbid advertising that is neither false nor misleading. Thus, in *Posadas de Puerto Rico* v. *Tourism Company of Puerto Rico*, 1986, the Court held that Puerto Rico can outlaw advertising of casino gambling on the island even though such gambling is legal there. In the same vein, Congress banned cigarette ads on radio and television in 1970; and in 1986 it extended the ban to include chewing tobacco and snuff. The tobacco industry did not challenge the constitutionality of either of those actions.

In most of its commercial speech cases the Court has struck down some arbitrary restriction on advertising. For example, in *Carey* v. *Population Services International*, 1977, it voided a New York law forbidding the advertisement of contraceptives. A more recent case involved advertising and targeted mailing. In *Shapero* v. *Kentucky Bar Association*, 1988, the Court said that a State cannot forbid a lawyer to seek clients by sending letters to persons who are known to have particular legal problems.

One of the Court's first commercial speech cases had a peculiar twist to it. In *Wooley* v. *Maynard*, 1977, the Court held that a State cannot force its citizens to act as "mobile billboards"—not, at least, when the words used conflict with their religious or moral beliefs. The Maynards, who were Jehovah's Witnesses, objected to the New Hampshire State motto on their automobile license plates. The words *Live Free or Die* clashed with their belief in everlasting life, and so they covered those words with tape. For this, Maynard was arrested three times. On appeal, the Supreme Court sided with Maynard.

Section 3 Review

1. Define: libel, slander, shield law, symbolic speech, picketing
2. For what reason does the Constitution guarantee freedom of expression?
3. The rights of free speech and press are especially intended to protect the expression of what views?
4. When can government impose a prior restraint on expression?
5. Is obscenity entitled to constitutional protections?
6. What special protections of freedom of expression do many news reporters enjoy?
7. What is the extent of government regulation of movies, radio, and television?
8. What are the constitutional protections of (a) symbolic speech? (b) commercial speech?

Critical Thinking

9. Identifying Central Issues (p. 19) Is American society better or worse off for allowing even those who promote racist and sexist views to express their beliefs?

★

Teacher's Resource File
See the Unit 5 File, p. 32, for the Section 3 Quiz.

CLOSURE

In this section, students have explored the guarantees and restrictions placed on free speech and free press in the areas of obscenity, prior restraint, confidentiality, radio, television, movies, symbolic speech, and commercial speech. In the next section, students will read about the conflict between national security and the protection of individual rights.

Assignment Assign Section 4, pp. 506–508, for the next class period.

Reteach

Have students imagine they are representatives for a newspaper from a foreign country wishing to sell its paper in the United States. Have students write a set of guidelines that the newspaper will need to follow in order to comply with constitutional standards of freedom of expression.

ACTIVITY: Teaching Heterogeneous Groups

Have students skim and scan Section 3, *Freedom of Speech and Press.* When students understand the principles of the 1st and 14th amendments in regard to freedom of speech and press, have them conduct a mock debate. Pose a question for the group, such as: Do news reporters have a constitutional right to withhold certain information from government? Divide students into teams and allow them ample time to prepare their arguments. Encourage them to support their opinions with convincing arguments and specific examples.

Section 4
Freedom of Expression and National Security

Focus

Teacher's Resource File
See the Unit 5 File, p. 33, for the Section 4 Outline.

Objectives

19.9 Explain how the protection of civil rights and the demands of national security conflict.

19.10 Describe the ways in which government has tried to settle that conflict.

Bellringer Activity Ask students whether or not they believe that it is wrong for people to be critical of the Federal Government. Do they think it is acceptable for people to advocate the overthrow of the United States government? Why or why not?

State the Purpose While freedom of expression is guaranteed in the Bill of Rights, the government may limit that freedom to protect itself against threats to its own security. Section 4 analyzes the historical conflict between the freedom of expression and the nation's security.

ABCNEWS INTERACTIVE

The following video segment may be used to highlight aspects of the debate over freedom of expression and national security.

POWERS OF THE SUPREME COURT GUIDEBOOK
Chapter 8: Amendment 1 (1791), Freedom of Speech, p. 11

4 Freedom of Expression and National Security

Find Out:

- How do protection of civil rights and the demands of national security conflict?
- How has government tried to settle that conflict?

Key Terms:

espionage, sabotage, treason, sedition

For several years in the early 1950s, Senator Joseph McCarthy waged an intense battle to rid the United States government of what he claimed was communist infiltration. McCarthy found no real evidence of subversion. However, his smear tactics and wild accusations did manage to destroy the reputations and lives of dozens of innocent people.

Eventually, McCarthy was exposed and denounced for his actions. His story, however, touches on an important dilemma facing the American political system: Government has a right to protect itself against domestic threats to the nation's security. But how far can government go when it tries to accomplish that goal? In this section, you will focus on that dilemma.

Punishable Acts

Clearly, government can punish espionage,
sabotage, and treason. These are forms of con-
1.a duct. **Espionage** is the practice of spying for a
1.b foreign power. **Sabotage** involves an act of
destruction intended to hinder a nation's war
1.c or defense effort. **Treason** is defined in the
Constitution in Article III, Section 3. It can
consist only in levying war against the nation
or supporting its enemies.

Sedition presents a much more delicate problem, for it involves the use of spoken or written
1.d words. **Sedition** is the incitement of resistance to
lawful authority. It does not necessarily involve
acts of violence or betrayal.

The Alien and Sedition Acts

Congress first acted to curb opposition to government in the Alien and Sedition Acts of 1798.[19] Those laws gave the President power to deport undesirable aliens and made "any false, scandalous, and malicious" criticism of the government a crime. The acts were intended to stifle the opponents of John Adams and the Federalists.

The Alien and Sedition Acts were undoubtedly unconstitutional, but they were never tested in the courts. Some 25 persons paid fines or went to jail for violating them. In 1801 President Jefferson pardoned those sentenced under the acts, and Congress soon repealed them.

Seditious Acts in Wartime

Congress passed another sedition law during World War I, as part of the Espionage Act of 1917. That law made it a crime to encourage disloyalty, interfere with the draft, obstruct recruiting, incite insubordination in the armed forces, or hinder the sale of government bonds. The act also made it a crime to "willfully utter, print, write, or publish any disloyal, profane, scurrilous, or abusive language about the form of government of the United States."

More than 2,000 persons were convicted for violating the Espionage Act. The constitutionality of the law was tested and upheld several times. The most important of those tests came in *Schenck* v. *United States*, 1919.

Charles Schenck, an officer of the Socialist party, had been found guilty of obstructing the war effort. He had sent fiery leaflets to some 15,000 men who had been drafted, urging them to resist the call to military service.

The Supreme Court upheld Schenck's conviction. The case is particularly noteworthy because the Court's opinion, written by Justice

[19]This is the collective title given to a number of different laws passed by Congress at the time. Violations were punishable by a maximum fine of $2,000 and two years in prison. The first person convicted under the acts was Matthew Lyon, a member of Congress from Vermont. He had accused President Adams of "a continual grasp for power—an unbounded thirst for ridiculous pomp, foolish adulation and selfish avarice."

Reading Strategy: Predicting Content

Before they have read the section, have students scan the section and read the boldfaced headings. Tell students that these headings form an outline of the section. Have students predict the content of the section based on these boldfaced headings.

Vocabulary

Point out "Key Terms" on page 506. Have students use each of these terms in a sentence or sentences.

Oliver Wendell Holmes, established the "clear and present danger" rule.

> "Words can be weapons. . . . The question in every case is whether the words used are used in such circumstances and are of such nature as to create a clear and present danger that they will bring about the substantive evils that Congress has a right to prevent."

In short, the rule says that words can be outlawed, and those who utter them can be punished when the words they use trigger an immediate danger that criminal acts will follow.

Sedition in Peacetime

In 1940, however, Congress passed a new sedition law, the Smith Act, and made it applicable in peacetime. Congress later passed two other such statutes: the Internal Security (McCarran) Act of 1950 and the Communist Control Act of 1954.

The Smith Act makes it unlawful for any person to teach or advocate the violent overthrow of government in the United States or to organize or knowingly be a member of any group with such an aim. It also forbids conspiring with others to commit any of those acts.

The Court first upheld the Smith Act in *Dennis* v. *United States* in 1951. Eleven leaders of the Communist party had been convicted of advocating the overthrow of the Federal Government. On appeal, they argued that the law violated the 1st Amendment's guarantees of freedom of speech and press. They also claimed that no act of theirs constituted a clear and present danger to this country. The Court disagreed, and modified Justice Holmes's doctrine as it did so:

> "An attempt to overthrow the government by force, even though doomed from the outset because of inadequate numbers or power of the revolutionists, is a sufficient evil for Congress to prevent. . . ."

The Court modified that holding in several later cases, however. In *Yates* v. *United States*, 1957, for example, the Court overturned the Smith Act convictions of several party leaders. It held: Merely to urge someone to *believe* something, in contrast to urging that person to *do* something, cannot be made illegal.

The result of *Yates* and other Smith Act cases was this: The Court upheld the constitutionality of the law, but construed its provisions so that enforcement was practically impossible.

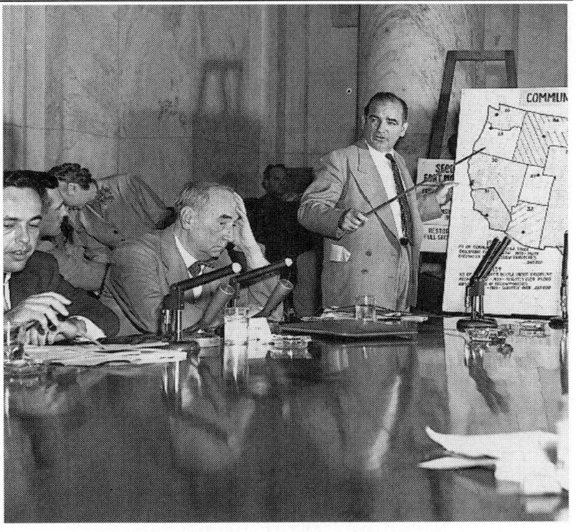

Trial by Accusation In the 1950s Senator Joseph McCarthy's unjust accusations of "un-American" beliefs or activities created a climate of fear across the country.

The McCarran Act proved to be an even less effective sedition law. It required every "communist-front" and "communist-action" organization to register with the attorney general. The act also created the Subversive Activities Control Board to decide which groups were subject to the law.

The Board first ordered the Communist party to register in 1953, and the Supreme Court held that it could be forced to do so, *Communist Party* v. *SACB*, 1961. It never actually did, however, largely because any person who came forward to register the party could then be charged as a "knowing member" under the Smith Act. In 1965 the Court held that to force someone into this position would contradict the 5th Amendment's guarantee against self-incrimination, *Albertson* v. *SACB*, 1965.[20]

The Court further limited the effectiveness of the McCarran Act by holding other parts of it to be unconstitutional. The net effect of the Court's response was to leave it a hollow shell.

---

[20] The decision left the SACB with no real functions to perform. It finally passed out of existence when Congress stopped funding it in 1973.

INSTRUCT

Explain/Analyze Espionage, sabotage, and treason are acts that clearly and directly undermine national security. Sedition, however, is a much more indirect and ambiguous threat to national security, since it involves speech rather than a direct act.

Ask students to analyze the development of the concept of sedition over the course of United States history. Ask students to consider how the historical eras of the 1790s, WWI, and the 1950s might have influenced the government's thinking about the definition of *sedition*. (*Each era was characterized by international stress and conflict. The nation faced what it perceived to be extraordinary threats to its security.*) How do students expect current developments in the former Soviet Union to influence governmental concern over issues of internal security? (*The threat from the Soviet Union is greatly diminished; the concern over internal subversion will continue to lessen.*)

Provide Guided Practice Have students recall the predictions they made at the beginning of the lesson under "Reading Strategy." Ask volunteers to read their predictions aloud. Have the rest of the class respond to those predictions, identifying where they are correct and where they are incorrect.

Provide Independent Practice

TRF **Teacher's Resource File** You may wish to assign Section 4 Guided Reading and Review, Unit 5 File, p. 34, to help students master section objective content.

Enrichment

Have students research the McCarthy hearings and present to the class a brief dramatization of a typical hearing. (Challenging)

TRF **Teacher's Resource File**
See the Supreme Court Cases file, pp.48–49, for material to support the section.

MONITOR COMPREHENSION

Answers to Section 4 Review
1. "Key Terms" are defined on the following pages:
- **a.** espionage, p. 506
- **b.** sabotage, p. 506
- **c.** treason, p. 506
- **d.** sedition, p. 506

2. Passed in 1798, they gave the President the power to deport aliens and made criticism of the government a crime. Jefferson pardoned those sentenced under the acts in 1801, and Congress soon repealed them. **3.** Certain words can be made illegal and those who use them can be punished if the words trigger an immediate danger that criminal acts will follow. **4.** They were rendered nearly impossible to enforce. **5.** Some students may say that the United States has the responsibility to protect the people's government from rule by a few. Others may say that the United States should recognize the legitimacy of people's revolutionary goals.

CLOSURE

The Federal Government has the right to bar speech that threatens its own existence. Over the course of its history, the United States has periodically made efforts to combat what it saw as dangerous internal threats to its security.

In the next section, students will read about another 1st Amendment freedom—the freedom of assembly and petition.

Assignment Assign Section 5, pp. 508–511, for the next class period.

The Communist Control Act declares the Communist party in this country to be "a conspiracy to overthrow the Government of the United States." The act's goal was to outlaw the party and keep its candidates off the ballot in any election. The law was never enforced.

Two factors have made the matter of internal subversion much less prominent today than it was a few years ago. One is the overall ineffectiveness of the sedition laws. The other is that U.S.-Soviet relations are today remarkably different from what they were in the cold war period.

Not all applications of the clear and present danger rule have centered on members of the Communist party. Take *Brandenburg* v. *Ohio*, 1969, as a leading case in point.

Clarence Brandenburg, a Ku Klux Klan leader in Ohio, had been punished for violating the State's criminal syndicalism law. He had organized a rally where, standing in front of a burning cross, he had addressed a group of men, most of them hooded and some of them armed. Brandenburg shouted: "We are not a revengent organization, but if our President, our Congress, our Supreme Court continues to suppress the white, Caucasian race, it's possible that there might have to be some revengence taken." For those remarks an Ohio court sentenced Brandenburg to ten years in prison.

The Supreme Court reversed that conviction. It held that although Brandenburg had urged others to break the law, his remarks had produced no likelihood of "imminent lawless action."

Section 4 Review

1. Define: espionage, sabotage, treason, sedition
2. What were the Alien and Sedition Acts, and what became of them?
3. What is the clear and present danger rule?
4. What became of the Smith Act, McCarran Act, and the Communist Control Act?

Critical Thinking

5. Checking Consistency (p. 19) Should American society limit those who seek revolution, given the revolutionary history of this country?

★

5 Freedom of Assembly and Petition

Find Out:
- For what reasons are there limits on the freedoms of assembly and of petition?

A noisy street demonstration by gay rights activists, or by neo-Nazis, or by any number of other groups; a candlelight vigil of opponents of the death penalty; the prolife faithful singing hymns as they picket an abortion clinic; prochoice partisans gathered on the steps of the State capitol . . . These are commonplace events today, and they are also everyday manifestations of freedom of assembly and petition.

In this section, you will examine the shape of that freedom and its importance to you and to all Americans.

The Constitution's Guarantees

The 1st Amendment guarantees

"... the right of the people peaceably to assemble, and to petition government for a redress of grievances."

The 14th Amendment's Due Process Clause also protects those rights of assembly and petition against actions by the States or their local governments. The Supreme Court first made that holding in *DeJonge* v. *Oregon*, 1937.

A court in Oregon had found Dirk DeJonge guilty of violating Oregon's criminal syndicalism law. The statute prohibited "any unlawful acts" that were intended to bring about "industrial or political change or revolution." DeJonge had helped organize and had spoken at a meeting of the Communist party. For that behavior, a State court sentenced him to seven years in prison.[21]

The Supreme Court reversed DeJonge's conviction, declaring: "Peaceable assembly for lawful discussion cannot be made a crime."

[21]Note the close similarities between *DeJonge* and *Brandenburg* v. *Ohio*.

Teacher's Resource File
See the Unit 5 File, p. 35, for the Section 4 Quiz.

Reteach
Have students create a time line on which to chart the development of the concept of sedition. Student time lines should begin in 1798 and continue to the present. Time lines should include key dates discussed in the section along with explanations of their significance.

The Constitution protects the right of the people to assemble—to gather with one another—to express their views on public matters. It protects their right to organize—in political parties, pressure groups, and other organizations—to influence public policy. It also protects the people's right to bring their views to the attention of public officials by such varied means as written petitions, letters, or advertisements; lobbying; or parades, marches, or other demonstrations.

But, notice, the 1st and 14th amendments protect the rights of peaceable assembly and petition. The Constitution does not give people the right to incite others to violence, to block a public street, close a school, or otherwise to endanger life, property, or public order.

Time–Place–Manner Regulations

Government can make and enforce reasonable rules covering the time, place, and manner of assemblies. Thus, the Supreme Court has upheld a city ordinance that prohibits making a noise or causing any other diversion near a school if that action disrupts school activities, *Grayend* v. *City of Rockford*, 1972. It has also upheld a State law that forbids parades near a courthouse when they are intended to influence court proceedings, *Cox* v. *Louisiana*, 1965.

But rules for keeping the public peace must be more than reasonable. They must also be precisely drawn and fairly administered. In *Coates* v. *Cincinnati*, 1971, the Court struck down a city ordinance that made it a crime for "three or more persons to assemble" on a sidewalk or street corner "and there conduct themselves in a manner annoying to persons passing by, or to occupants of adjacent buildings." The Court found the ordinance too vague. It was so loosely drawn that it contained "an obvious invitation to discriminatory enforcement against those whose association together is 'annoying' because their ideas, their lifestyle, or their physical appearance is resented by the majority."

Government's rules must be content neutral. That is, while government can regulate assemblies on the basis of time, place, and manner, it cannot regulate them on the basis of what might be said there. Thus, in *Police Department of the City of Chicago* v. *Mosely*, 1972, the Court threw out a city ordinance that banned all picketing within 150 feet of a school. The law did allow one exception, however—the peaceful picketing of a school involved in a labor dispute. The Court held that the ordinance was not content neutral because it permitted picketing in a labor dispute but prohibited it for any other lawful purpose.

The responsibility of public officials to control traffic or to keep a demonstration from growing into a riot can be, and sometimes is, used as an excuse to prevent speech. The line between crowd control and thought control can be a very thin one, indeed.

Demonstrations on Public Property

Over the past several years, most of the Court's freedom of assembly cases have involved organized demonstrations. Demonstrations are, of course, assemblies.

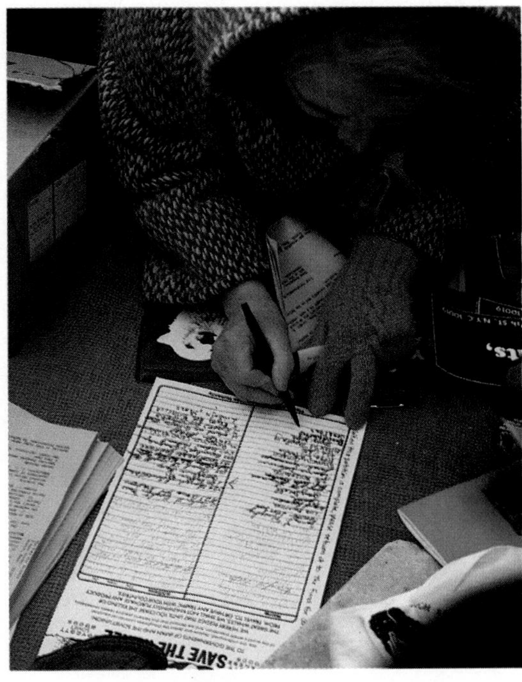

Freedom of Petition When persons publicly solicit signatures or conduct opinion polls, they are exercising rights guaranteed under the 14th Amendment.

SECTION 5
Freedom of Assembly and Petition

FOCUS

Teacher's Resource File See the Unit 5 File, p. 36, for the Section 5 Outline.

Objective

19.11 Explain why there are limits on the freedom of assembly and petition.

Bellringer Activity Pose this hypothetical situation: A white supremacist group is planning a rally on a college campus. Several students have begun recruiting others to disrupt the rally and prevent it from taking place. Should the college allow the students to organize in this way? Should the college allow the white supremacist group to rally? Does the college have the right to stop either group? Why or why not?

State the Purpose The rights of assembly and petition are important aspects of the 1st Amendment's guarantee of freedom of expression. In this section, students will examine the legal restraints that have been put on these rights.

ABCNEWS INTERACTIVE

The following video segment may be used to highlight aspects of individual rights and liberties.

POWERS OF THE SUPREME COURT GUIDEBOOK
Chapter 10: Amendment 1 (1791), Rights of Assembly and Petition, p. 15

Vocabulary

Below are some words the meanings of which may help students understand the section content:

—**petition**: bring one's views to the attention of public officials

—**association**: a collection of people who voluntarily join together, such as those who meet to promote political, economic, or social causes

Reading Strategy: Question Writing

Have students scan the section and note the boldfaced headings. Then have students convert each heading into a question. As students read the section, have them find information under each heading that will enable them to answer the questions.

INSTRUCT

Discuss Ask students to consider why freedom of expression should include the rights of assembly and petition. How does this protection help preserve a free exchange of ideas? (*People working together facilitate free trade in ideas.*)

Have students identify the point at which the right to assemble is no longer protected. (*When the assembly incites others to violence or to act in such a way as to threaten or deny people's rights.*) How is this limit similar to those on other 1st Amendment freedoms? (*People are protected by this and other 1st Amendment freedoms so long as the exercise of the freedom does not directly threaten or infringe on the rights of others.*) Do students agree with the Court's ruling in *Gregory* v. *Chicago?* Should Gregory and his group have been held responsible in any way for the actions of those who witnessed their demonstration?

Provide Guided Practice Ask students to volunteer a definition of the freedom of assembly and petition. Then ask them to volunteer answers about the circumstances under which a government can restrict such a right.

Provide Independent Practice

TRF **Teacher's Resource File** You may wish to assign Section 5 Guided Reading and Review, Unit 5 File, p. 37, to help students master section objective content.

Most demonstrations take place in public places—on streets and sidewalks, in parks or public buildings, and so on. Demonstrations take place in these locations because it is the public the demonstrators want to reach.

Demonstrations almost always involve some degree of conflict. Mostly, they are held to protest something, and so a clash of ideas is present. Many times there is also a conflict with the normal use of streets or other public facilities. It is hardly surprising, then, that the tension generated can sometimes rise to a serious level.

Given all this, the Supreme Court has often upheld laws that require advance notice and permits for demonstrations in public places. In an early leading case, *Cox* v. *New Hampshire*, 1941,[22] it unanimously approved such a law:

> "The authority of a municipality to impose regulations in order to assure the safety and convenience of the people in the use of public highways has never been regarded as inconsistent with civil liberties but rather as one of the means of safeguarding the good order on which they ultimately depend. . . . The question in a particular case is whether the control is exercised so as to deny . . . the right of assembly and the opportunity for the communication of thought and the discussion of public questions."

Right-to-demonstrate cases raise many basic and thorny questions. How and to what extent can government regulate demonstrators and their demonstrations? Does the Constitution require that police officers allow an unpopular group to continue to demonstrate when its activities have excited others to violence? When, in the name of public peace and safety, can police properly order demonstrators to disband?

Among these cases, *Gregory* v. *Chicago*, 1969, remains typical. While under police protection, Dick Gregory and others had marched—singing, chanting, and carrying placards—from city hall to the mayor's home some five miles away. Marching in the streets around the mayor's house, they demanded the firing of the city's school superintendent and an end to de facto segregation in the city's schools.

A crowd of several hundred people, including many residents of the all-white neighborhood quickly gathered. Soon, the bystanders began throwing insults and threats, rocks, eggs, and other objects. The police tried to keep order, but after about an hour, they decided that serious violence was about to break out. At that point, they ordered the demonstrators to leave the area. When Gregory and the others failed to do so, the police arrested them and charged them with disorderly conduct.

The convictions of the demonstrators were unanimously overturned by the High Court. The Court noted that the marchers had done no more than exercise their constitutional rights of assembly and petition. Neighborhood residents and others, not the demonstrators, had caused the disorder. No matter how reasonable the police order, or how laudable the police motives, so long as the demonstrators acted peacefully, they could not be punished for disorderly conduct.

The Supreme Court has recently upheld an ordinance that forbids demonstrations that target a specific private residence. It did so in *Frisby* v. *Schultz*, 1988, where it ruled that a local government can legitimately protect residential privacy. Prolife demonstrators had several times paraded around the home of a doctor who reportedly performed abortions. Their picketing sparked controversy, and the town board responded this way: "It is unlawful for any person to engage in picketing before or about the residence of any individual in the Town of Brookfield."

Right of Assembly and Private Property

What of demonstrations on private property—for example, at shopping centers? The Court has heard only a few cases raising this question. However, at least this much can be said: The rights of assembly and petition do not give people a right to trespass on private property, even if they wish to express political views.

Privately owned shopping centers are not public streets, sidewalks, parks, and other "places of public assembly." Thus, no one has a constitutional right to do such things as hand

[22]This is one of the several Jehovah's Witness cases referred to on page 496. Cox and several other Witnesses had violated a State law that required a license to hold a parade or procession on the public streets.

Enrichment

Have students imagine that they are officials in a community that has been asked to allow a rally by an objectionable hate group. Tell students to write a letter to the group explaining and justifying the restrictions the community is placing on them. (Easy)

out political leaflets or ask people to sign petitions in those places.

These comments are based on the leading case here, *Lloyd Corporation* v. *Tanner*, 1972. However, since that case the Court has held this: A State supreme court may interpret the provisions of that State's own constitution in such a way as to require the owners of shopping centers to allow the reasonable exercise of the right of petition on their private property. In that event, there is no violation of the property owners' rights under any provision in the federal Constitution, *PruneYard Shopping Center* v. *Robins*, 1980. In that case, several California high school students had set up a card table in the shopping center, passed out pro-Israeli pamphlets, and asked passersby to sign petitions to be sent to the President and Congress.

Freedom of Association

The guarantees of freedom of assembly and petition include a guarantee of association. That is, those guarantees include the right to associate with others to promote political, economic, and other social causes. That right is not set out in so many words in the Constitution, but the Supreme Court has said "it is beyond doubt that freedom to engage in association for the advancement of beliefs and ideas is an inseparable aspect" of the Constitution's guarantees of free expression, *National Association for the Advancement of Colored People* v. *Alabama*, 1958. Of course, there is no right to gather to pursue illegal ends.

The case just cited is one of the early right to associate cases. There, a State law required the Alabama branch of the NAACP to disclose the names of all its members in that State. When the organization refused a court's order that it do so, it was found in contempt of court and fined $100,000.

The Supreme Court overturned the contempt conviction. It said that it could find no legitimate reason why the State should have the NAACP's membership list.

You have seen some illustration of the guarantee of freedom of expression at work in earlier chapters. Recall, for example, *Tashjian* v. *Republican Party of Connecticut*, a 1986 case noted on page 162. In that case the Supreme Court held that a State's election laws cannot forbid a political party to allow independents to vote in that party's primary if the party wants to do so.

You will see other illustrations later on. Thus, in Chapter 21 you will consider such cases as *Roberts* v. *United States Jaycees*, 1984 and *Board of Directors of Rotary International* v. *Rotary Club of Duarte*, 1987. In both cases the Supreme Court rejected attempts by an all-male organization to invoke freedom of association as a shield against the admission of women to the club.

"I DON'T WANT YOU PLAYING WITH THAT LITTLE JONES BOY.... WHY, HIS FAMILY DOESN'T EVEN COMPOST!"

Interpreting Political Cartoons What bias is guiding this parent's decision to limit her son's freedom of association?

Section 5 Review

1. What does the guarantee of freedom of assembly and petition intend to protect?
2. On what basis can government regulate the rights of assembly and petition?
3. What factors make the right to demonstrate such a thorny issue?
4. For what reason is the right to associate protected by the Constitution?

Critical Thinking

5. **Identifying Alternatives** (p. 19) What might be an acceptable response to the announcement that a neo-Nazi group was planning a demonstration in your community?

★

Interpreting Political Cartoons How does the cartoon view this mother's restriction on her child's choice of playmates? (*It makes her look unfair.*)

Caption Answer While Americans are supposed to be free to associate, children are restricted by adults.

Monitor Comprehension

Answers to Section 5 Review
1. The rights of the people to express their views and to organize. **2.** Government can make time-place-manner restrictions. Also, demonstrations that incite people to violence or that otherwise endanger life, property, or public order are not protected. **3.** The extent to which government can regulate demonstrations, and when police have the right to break up a demonstration. **4.** Considered an unwritten part of the guarantees of freedom of assembly and petition. **5.** Students may suggest a counter-demonstration.

Closure

As part of the 1st Amendment guarantee of freedom of expression, people have the right to assemble peaceably and petition the government for a redress of grievances. In the next chapter, students will read about the rights of people under several other amendments of the Bill of Rights.

Assignment Assign Section 1 of Chapter 20, pp. 517–520, for the next class period.

TRF **Teacher's Resource File**
See the Unit 5 File, p. 38, for the Section 5 Quiz.

Reteach

Have students write a pamphlet that a community could use as a guidebook for groups wishing to hold public demonstrations in that community. The pamphlet should explain what the rights of people are and what government can constitutionally do to limit those rights.

TEACHING

Critical Thinking

Predicting Consequences

Objective

Evaluate given information to predict the possible consequences of an event or decision.

INSTRUCT

Before you introduce the lesson, explain to students that predicting consequences involves evaluating given information and combining it with what they already know to make an informed prediction.

When students have completed each step on the page, invite them to share their responses before continuing to the next step. Discuss the importance of being able to evaluate a situation and predict the possible consequences of an event or decision. You might use an example such as the recent breakup of the Soviet Union. What might be the possible consequences of this event?

Answers 1. (a) Free exercise of religion. (b) Free exercise cannot be infringed. **2.** (a) The Court could allow the practice based on the Free Exercise Clause, or the Court could find that the clause does not protect this kind of action. (b) Answers will vary. **3.** (a) The Court has curtailed certain religious practices in the past. (b) Answers will vary. **4.** (a) He or she might say that the Constitution does not allow infringement of the free exercise of religion. (b) It would probably disagree.

Critical Thinking

Predicting Consequences

When you predict consequences, you determine the likely effect of an event or action on the outcome of future events or actions. Predicting consequences is an important skill that enables you to make decisions and choices that are likely to be effective. Of course, no one can be certain about what will happen in the future. However, there are ways to foresee how one set of actions will influence future events or actions. Follow the steps below to practice your skill at predicting consequences.

1. Have a clear and accurate understanding of the event or action in question. Your predictions can only be as valid as the information upon which you base them. Read the information below, and answer the following questions: (a) What is the nature of the legal conflict in this hypothetical case? (b) What does the Constitution say about the subject?

2. Identify and evaluate all possible consequences. Study the facts below and answer the following questions: (a) What are the possible consequences of the hypothetical case given below? (b) How likely is it that any of these consequences will occur?

3. Use your knowledge of history. The pattern of events in the past can be helpful in predicting future outcomes, particularly when strong parallels exist. Read the information about a past Supreme Court decision on this topic. Answer the following questions: (a) How has the Supreme Court ruled in the past on the subject of free exercise of religion? (b) What other facts do you know about this subject and how the courts have responded in the past?

4. Predict the consequences. Combine your knowledge of history with your evaluation of the possible consequences to predict the consequences of the hypothetical case below. Answer the following question: (a) How do you expect the sect leader to argue his or her case? (b) How do you expect the courts to respond to the sect leader's arguments?

Hypothetical Case

The leader of a small religious sect is convicted under a State law that outlaws the inhumane treatment of animals. The incident in question occurred during one of the sect's religious observances, which involves the ritual sacrifice of animals.

Constitutional Background

The 1st Amendment: "Congress shall make no law respecting an establishment of religion, or prohibiting the free exercise thereof, or abridging the freedom of speech, or of the press; or the right of the people peaceably to assemble, and to petition the government for a redress of grievances."

Past Supreme Court Action

"Laws are made for the government of actions, and while they cannot interfere with mere religious belief and opinions, they may with practices. Suppose one believed that human sacrifices were a necessary part of religious worship, would it be seriously contended that the civil government could not interfere to prevent a sacrifice?"—from *Reynolds* v. *United States,* 1878.

TRF **Teacher's Resource File**

See the Unit 5 File, p. 39, for the Skill Application for this lesson.

Chapter-in-Brief

Scan all headings, photographs, charts, and other visuals in the chapter before reading the section summaries below.

Section 1 The Unalienable Rights (pp. 485–489) The Constitution, especially its Bill of Rights, guarantees many rights and liberties to the American people. These guarantees reflect the principle of limited government.

An individual's rights can be exercised only to the extent that they do not limit the rights of others. In cases where individual rights conflict, one right must take precedence.

The Bill of Rights restricts only the National Government. Each State constitution, however, contains its own bill of rights. Also, the 14th Amendment's Due Process Clause "nationalizes" most of the protections of the Bill of Rights.

Section 2 Freedom of Religion (pp. 490–497) Freedom of expression is vital to democracy. One key component of this freedom is the freedom of religion.

Freedom of religion is guaranteed in part by the Establishment Clause. Still, the nature of the wall between church and state has been the subject of many court decisions.

Freedom of religion is also guaranteed by the Free Exercise Clause. This clause protects people's right to believe—though not necessarily to do—whatever they wish regarding religion.

Section 3 Freedom of Speech and Press (pp. 499–505) The 1st and 14th amendments' guarantee of free speech and free press protect people's right to speak and their right to be heard.

There are limits to these rights. Obscene material is not protected, nor is slanderous and libelous speech. Freedom of the press does not allow reporters to withhold certain information from government. Movies and electronic media are also subject to regulation. In most cases, government cannot exercise prior restraint.

Symbolic and commercial speech also enjoy constitutional protection. Yet, government can limit both under certain circumstances.

Section 4 Freedom of Expression and National Security (pp. 506–508) Government must protect itself from internal subversion. Therefore, government can regulate some expression in the interest of national security.

Historically, some government attempts to regulate opposition to the government have proven unworkable. For example, the Alien and Sedition Acts of 1798 and several anti-communist efforts of the cold war era were largely ineffective. However, the Supreme Court has held that government has a right to control speech that creates "a clear and present danger" of violence or harm to public order or national security.

Section 5 Freedom of Assembly and Petition (pp. 508–511) The 1st Amendment guarantees the right to assemble peaceably and to petition for redress of grievances. Government can reasonably regulate the time, place, and manner of such expression. Those regulations must, however, be "content neutral."

The Court has held that demonstrations targeted at specific private residences can be outlawed. Also, citizens do not generally enjoy the right to assemble on private property.

Freedom of assembly and petition includes a guarantee of association. This means that people are free to to associate with others in order to promote causes of mutual concern.

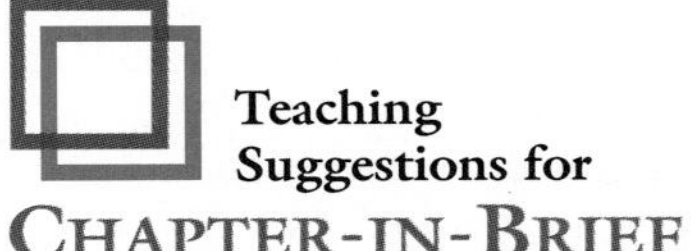

Teaching Suggestions for CHAPTER-IN-BRIEF

Below are some of the possible uses for the Chapter-in-Brief:

To Preview the Chapter You may want to assign the Chapter-in-Brief page and the Section Outlines from the Teacher's Resource File before beginning Chapter 19 to introduce students to "Key Terms" and concepts in each section.

To Review the Chapter When students have completed Chapter 19, you might want to assign the Chapter-in-Brief as a tool for review, along with the Guided Reading and Reviews from the Teacher's Resource File.

To Omit the Chapter If you wish to skip Chapter 19, it may be helpful to assign the Chapter-in-Brief to students as a review before continuing to another chapter. You may also want to assign the Chapter 19 Test to assess student knowledge of the material. Then, specific portions of Chapter 19 may be assigned to students needing reinforcement of "Key Terms" and concepts.

Teacher's Resource File See the Unit 5 File for the following materials:

- Section Outlines, pp. 24, 27, 30, 33, 36.
- Guided Reading and Reviews, pp. 25, 28, 31, 34, 37.
- Chapter 19 Test, pp. 43–45.

ADDITIONAL RESOURCES

Barnett, Randy E. *The Rights Retained by the People: The History and Meaning of the Ninth Amendment.* Cato Institute, 1989.

Canedy, Susan. *America's Nazis: A Democratic Dilemma.* Markgraf, 1990.

Fenwick, Lyndon B. *Should the Children Pray? A Historical, Judicial, and Political Examination of Public School Prayer.* Baylor University Press, 1990.

Irons, Peter. *The Courage of Their Convictions: Sixteen Americans Who Fought Their Way to the Supreme Court.* Free Press, 1989.

Leahy, J.E. *The First Amendment, 1791–1991.* McFarland & Co., 1991.

Levine, Herbert M. and Jean Edward Smith. *Civil Liberties and Civil Rights Debated.* Prentice Hall, 1988.

Powe, Lucas A. *American Broadcasting and the 1st Amendment.* University of California Press, 1987.

Protecting Your Rights. Sound filmstrip. Produced by Globe Filmstrips, distributed by Coronet Media, 1979. Color. 6 parts, 9 min. each.

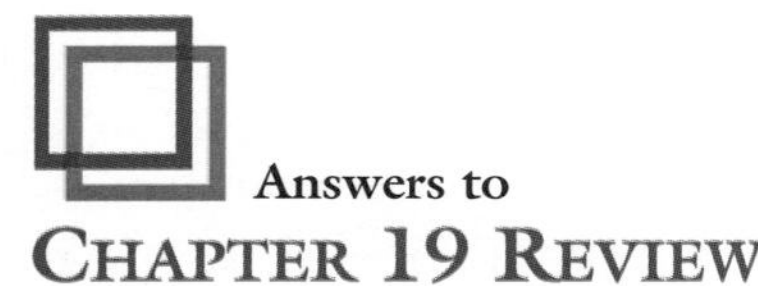

Answers to
CHAPTER 19 REVIEW

Vocabulary and Key Terms

Matching
1. Due Process Clause
2. shield law
3. picketing
4. Bill of Rights
5. treason

True or False
1. True.
2. True.
3. False—the correct term is *picketing*.
4. False—the correct term is *Bill of Rights*.

Word Relationships
1. *Libel* is written speech that wrongfully damages another. *Slander* is spoken speech that wrongfully damages another. **2.** The Establishment Clause prohibits the government's establishment of religion and sets up a wall of separation between church and state. The Free Exercise Clause guarantees people the right to believe whatever they want to believe in matters of religion. **3.** *Treason* is disloyalty against the United States—a crime that can be committed only in wartime. *Sedition* is speech that promotes resistance to lawful authority. **4.** *Espionage* is spying for a foreign power. *Sabotage* is a destructive act intended to hinder a nation's defense effort. **5.** *Civil liberties* are protections against government, such as guarantees of security of the person against arbitrary acts of government. *Civil rights* are those positive acts of government designed to make constitutional guarantees a reality for all people; for example, prohibitions against discrimination.

Main Ideas

Section 1
1. The founders of the nation were motivated in large part by their love of freedom. They based the government on the principle of individual freedom. **2.** The exercise of an individual's right cannot infringe upon the rights of another. Thus each person's rights are relative to another's. **3.** The 14th Amendment, in a sense, nationalizes the Bill of Rights.

Section 2
4. It prohibits government actions that might promote or hinder any religion. The clause helps ensure that all religious ideas are free to circulate among people. **5.** It ensures that all people have the freedom to believe whatever they wish with regard to religion. It helps ensure that people will be exposed to many ideas. **6.** A person may believe whatever he or she wishes, but government can limit the way a person acts.

Section 3
7. In order to have a knowledgeable citizenry, people need to be able to say what they think and to hear a wide range of ideas. **8.** Possible answers include: libelous or slanderous speech, obscene materials, certain radio and television broadcasts, and certain commercial

Chapter Review

Vocabulary and Key Terms

Bill of Rights (p. 486)
civil liberties (p. 486)
civil rights (p. 486)
aliens (p. 487)
Due Process Clause (p. 488)
Establishment Clause (p. 490)
Free Exercise Clause (p. 496)
libel (p. 499)
slander (p. 499)
shield laws (p. 502)
symbolic speech (p. 503)
picketing (p. 504)
espionage (p. 506)
sabotage (p. 506)
treason (p. 506)
sedition (p. 506)

Matching: *Review the key terms in the list above. If you are not sure of a term's meaning, look up the term and review its definition. Choose a term from the list above that best matches each description.*

1. the part of the Constitution that ensures that no State can deny any right that is "basic or essential to the American concept of ordered liberty"
2. designed to protect reporters in the media from having to reveal their confidential news sources
3. what striking workers do when they patrol outside a business
4. what the first 10 amendments to the Constitution are called
5. the crime of levying war against the United States or giving aid and comfort to the enemy

True or False: *Determine whether each statement is true or false. If it is true, write "true." If it is false, change the underlined word or words to make the statement true.*

1. Symbolic speech is the expression of beliefs or ideas by conduct.
2. An alien is one who is not a citizen of the state in which he or she lives.
3. When workers who are on strike patrol a business, they are engaged in a practice called sabotage.
4. That part of the Constitution in which many civil rights and liberties are spelled out is the Free Exercise Clause.

Word Relationships: *Distinguish between words in each pair.*

1. libel/slander
2. Free Exercise Clause/Establishment Clause
3. treason/sedition
4. espionage/sabotage
5. civil rights/civil liberties

Main Ideas

Section 1 (pp. 485–489)

1. What does it mean to say that the concept of individual freedom is rooted in American colonial history?
2. What does it mean to say that individual rights guaranteed in the Constitution are relative and not absolute?
3. What is the relationship between the 14th Amendment and the Bill of Rights?

Section 2 (pp. 490–497)

4. Summarize the meaning and impact of the Establishment Clause. How does this clause help guarantee "a free trade in ideas"?
5. Summarize the meaning and impact of the Free Exercise Clause. How does this clause help guarantee a "free trade in ideas"?

6. At what point can the government limit a person's exercise of religion?

Section 3 **(pp. 499-505)**

7. Why does the Constitution seek to guarantee the right of people both to speak and to hear?
8. Give three examples of circumstances in which the freedom of speech is not protected under the Constitution.
9. What kinds of actions are protected as "speech"?

Section 4 **(pp. 506–508)**

10. Summarize the conflict between the need for national security and the need for individual rights.
11. What is the significance of the "clear and present danger" rule?
12. What has been the overall result of the United States' efforts to prevent internal subversion?

Section 5 **(pp. 508–511)**

13. At what point do people cease to enjoy the right to assemble and petition?
14. Briefly describe the nature of the limits a government can place upon assemblies.
15. (a) What is the freedom of association? (b) What is the limit on that freedom?

Critical Thinking

1. **Checking Consistency** (p. 19) The American government places the highest possible value on individual rights. Yet it also protects the rights of the many against the actions of the few. Are these statements consistent? If so, how?
2. **Identifying Assumptions** (p. 19) Consider the concept of "the free marketplace of ideas." (a) What do you think this concept really means? (b) What does this concept suggest about the role and responsibility of citizens in the American democratic society?
3. **Predicting Consequences** (p. 19) (a) Why is it so important that the Constitution guarantee the rights of people to assemble and associate. (b) What might happen if people could not enjoy this right? (c) How might this right be increased?

Getting Involved

1. **Writing Your Opinion** You are a Supreme Court justice sitting on a case involving the free exercise of religion. Write an opinion in which you create a test for determining at what point a government can constitutionally restrict a person's free exercise of religion. Begin your opinion by stating the test you have established. Then, explain the reasoning on which you have based the test. Devote one paragraph to each idea that supports your reasoning. Review the paragraphs to be sure they logically and clearly explain why you think your ideas are supported by the Constitution. Revise to correct any errors. Then make a final copy.
2. **Class Debate** Hold a class debate on the following topic: *Resolved*, That the Federal and State governments should be allowed to provide financial assistance to parents with children in parochial schools. Select teams to debate each side of the issue. The rest of the class can evaluate each team's arguments.
3. **Gathering Information** Suppose you were researching the development of the concept of individual rights in American political history. (a) What source might you be able to use to identify the names and citation numbers of some important Supreme Court cases? (b) How might you find the text of the decisions once you have found their citations? Use the Government Resources Handbook that appears on page 690 of your textbook to identify possible sources of this information.

presentations; also, symbolic speech that endangers others. **9.** Actions that express opinions, such as picketing and that do not threaten the safety or rights of others are protected.

Section 4

10. The nation has a legitimate interest to protect itself against internal threats. However, a government's pursuit of this goal has often raised questions about the lengths to which government can limit people's rights to hold and express political views. **11.** The rule enables society to protect itself against dangers resulting from a person's expression. The "clear–and–present–danger" rule says that words can be outlawed, and that those who utter them can be punished when those words trigger an immediate danger that criminal acts will follow. **12.** Many of the laws Congress has passed aimed at stopping sedition have been ineffective.

Section 5

13. People lose this right when they incite others to violence or when their actions otherwise endanger life, property, or public order. **14.** Government can put time, place, and manner restrictions on the right of assembly. **15.** (a) It allows people to join together with others to promote their political, economic, or other causes. (b) People are not protected from associating for the purposes of pursuing illegal ends.

Critical Thinking

1. Answers will vary. Students should observe that American society can honor individual rights without granting individuals the unbridled right to injure others. **2.** (a) Students might say this concept means that people should be able to consider competing ideas and make their own decisions about what they want to believe. (b) Citizens must critically evaluate competing ideas and be counted on to make good choices about those competing ideas. **3.** Answers will vary. Students might respond: (a) People can accomplish more in groups than they can individually. (b) Political participation by citizens would become much less effective. (c) Answers will vary.

Getting Involved

1–2. Answers and results will vary, but students should demonstrate an understanding of the concepts in this chapter. **3.** Possible answers include: (a) sources such as *Summaries of Leading Cases on the Constitution*, (b) *The Supreme Court Reporter* or the *United States Reports*.

Chapter 20 Resources

In the Teacher's Resource File
The following materials are found in the Teacher's Resource File box.

Instructional Support: Unit 5 File

For the Section
Outlines, pp. 49, 52, 55, 58
Guided Reading and Reviews, pp. 50, 53, 56, 59
Quizzes, pp. 51, 54, 57, 60

For the Chapter
Skill Application, p. 61
Case Study on Contemporary Issues, pp. 62–64
Chapter Test, pp. 65–67
Additional Test Questions, pp. 68–70

Enrichment Support Files

Supreme Court Cases, pp. 15, 26–27, 30–31, 34–35, 40–41, 54–55, 64–65, 68–69, 70–71, 74–75, 80–81, 84–85, 96–97, 98–99, 106–107, 108–109, 110–111
Participatory Government Activities, pp. 20–27
Simulations and Debates: Drug Testing, Gun Control
Historical and Legal Documents, pp. 39, 40, 42

Computer Test Bank and Assessment

Transparency Package, pp. 20, 45, 59, 60

Chapter 20 Focus

Introduce the Chapter Tell students that in this chapter they will read about the Constitution's guarantees of due process, of freedom and security of persons, and of the rights of the accused. Read with students the Chapter Preview and the Objectives.

Writing Activity Direct students' attention to "Describe." Ask students to write a paragraph outlining what they believe constitutes justice.

Motivate for Learning Direct students' attention to "Predict." Lead students in a discussion about what rights, if any, a person who is accused of a crime should be entitled to. Ask students to discuss the idea, "innocent until proven guilty."

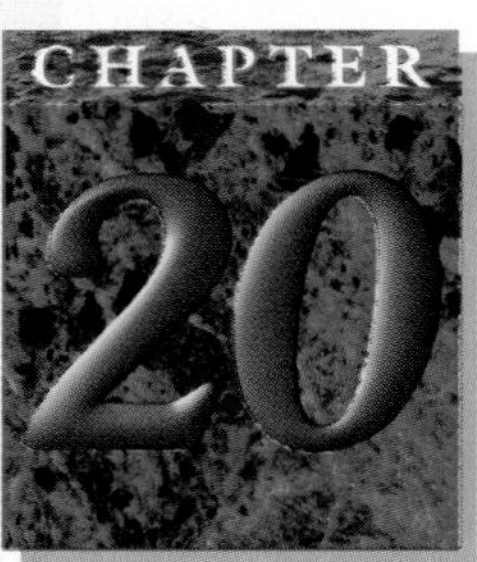

Civil Liberties: Protecting Individual Freedoms

Chapter Preview

In 1991, five years after being convicted of crimes stemming from his role in the Iran-Contra affair, all charges against Lieutenant Colonel Oliver North were dismissed. The dismissal was granted in spite of the fact that North had admitted wrongdoing—illegally selling arms to Iran and diverting funds to Nicaraguan freedom fighters. The reason, simply, was because one witness testified that his crucial testimony had been influenced by remarks he had heard about the scandal on television. The trial, therefore, was unfair.

If guilty people go free, is justice served? Because the Constitution provides for protection against unfair criminal procedures, the answer is "yes." This chapter is about those constitutional guarantees related to fair treatment of the accused and freedom and the security of all persons.

Before you read this chapter:

- **Describe** your definition of justice.
- **Predict** what might occur if safeguards for people accused of crimes did not exist.

As you read, focus on the main objective for each section. Understand:

1. The concept of due process of law.
2. The rights to freedom and security of the person.
3. The rights of the accused to a fair trial.
4. The constitutional limits on punishments for crime.

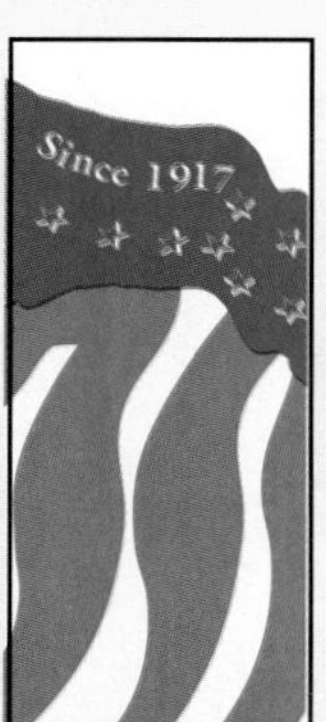

Magruder's American Government: *A Witness to Change* by William A. McClenaghan

"Congress may not take away any of the liberties set forth in these amendments [the Bill of Rights], *but the States may deprive their citizens of many of these liberties without violating the Constitution of the United States."*

That statement appeared in the first edition of this book in 1917. It continued to appear in substantially the same form into the 1950s. The Supreme Court began to undermine its accuracy in *Gitlow* v. *New York* in 1925, when it held that the 14th Amendment's Due Process Clause required States to guarantee the freedoms of speech and the press. Still, the word "many" saved the 1917 statement for many years—until the advent of Chief Justice Earl Warren and the series of Supreme Court decisions that began with *Mapp* v. *Ohio* in 1961.

High school students may not realize it, but they already have at least some knowledge of many Bill of Rights freedoms and of the ways they are applied against the States. They have this knowledge because of television crime shows that focus on topics such as search warrants, the right to counsel, the Miranda Rule, and so on.

Symbol of Justice The system of federal courts helps ensure that, in all that it does, the government acts fairly and in accord with established rules in order that individual freedoms are protected.

1 Due Process of Law

Find Out:

- For what reason is there no exact definition of the due process guarantees?
- What is the difference between procedural and substantive due process?

Key Terms:

due process, police power, search warrant

In Argentina they are called the *desaparecidos*—the disappeared. They are the thousands of Argentinians, most of them young, who were secretly abducted, tortured, and killed by the military in the 1970s and early 1980s. Their crime? They had criticized the government.

Could such a nightmare occur in this country? No? Why not? Because of the deep-rooted American commitment to the concept of due process.

The Constitution includes two Due Process clauses. The 5th Amendment declares that the Federal Government cannot deprive any person of "life, liberty, or property, without due process of law." The 14th Amendment places that same restriction on the States.

Procedural and Substantive Due Process

It is impossible to define the two due process guarantees in exact and complete terms. Over the years, the Supreme Court has consistently refused to give them an exact definition. Instead, it has relied on finding the meaning of due process on a case-by-case basis. Fundamen-
1.a tally, the constitutional guarantees of **due process** mean this: Government must act fairly and in accord with established rules.

The concept of due process began and developed in English and then in American law as a procedural concept. That is, it developed as a requirement that government must act fairly, using fair procedures.

Fair procedures are of little value, however, if they are used to administer unfair laws. The Supreme Court recognized this fact toward the end of the last century. It began to hold that

SECTION 1
Due Process of Law

FOCUS

Teacher's Resource File See the Unit 5 File, p. 49, for the Section 1 Outline.

Objectives

20.1 Explain why there is no exact definition of due process guarantees.

20.2 Analyze the differences between procedural and substantive due process.

Bellringer Activity Present the following situation to the class: Your friend has been charged by the police with speeding. Your friend swears that he or she was not driving too fast, yet the police want to take away his or her driver's license for two years. What procedures does the class think should be followed before the license is suspended?

State the Purpose The Constitution's two Due Process guarantees each aim to ensure that government acts fairly and in accordance with established rules. In Section 1, students will learn about these due process guarantees and how the Supreme Court has helped clarify their meaning over the course of United States history.

ABCNEWS INTERACTIVE

The following video segments may be used to highlight aspects of due process.

POWERS OF THE SUPREME COURT GUIDEBOOK
Chapter 16: Amendment 5 (1791), Due Process, p. 25
Chapter 21: Amendment 14 (1868), Civil Rights, p. 33

Vocabulary

Point out "Key Terms" on page 517. After students have reviewed the meaning of these terms in the text, have them write a two- or three-sentence paragraph in which they use all three of these terms.

Reading Strategy: Question Writing

Tell students to page through the chapter and write down each of the main headings in the form of a question. Then have students fill in answers to these questions as they read the material under each heading.

INSTRUCT

Discuss Ask students to provide imaginary examples of laws or actions that would violate procedural and substantive due process guarantees. (*Possible answers: A procedural due process violation might include searching a person's apartment without a warrant. A substantive due process violation might include a law that punishes people for criticizing the government.*)

Discuss with students the due process questions that arise out of each State's exercise of its police power. Ask students to summarize the tension between the rights of individuals and the responsibility of government to protect all people. (*Though individuals have due process rights, government often seeks to limit individuals' rights in order to guarantee the welfare of all.*) Ask students to discuss how a society can determine the point at which the general welfare becomes more important than individual rights. This question can be used to enter into a discussion of the right of privacy. Ask students whether or not they think that an individual's actions in private can threaten the welfare of the public and so warrant regulation by the State. (*Possible answers: Yes, private actions can threaten the fabric of a society and thus be subject to regulation; no, private actions do not affect others in the way that drunk driving or polluting can, and therefore should not be regulated by government.*)

VOICES *on Government*

Thurgood Marshall, former associate justice of the Supreme Court of the United States

On the Supreme Court and Civil Liberties

“Paraphrasing [President] Kennedy, those who wish to assure the continued protection of important civil rights should 'ask not what the Supreme Court alone can do for civil rights; ask what you can do to help the cause of civil rights.' Today, the answer to that question lies in bringing pressure to bear on all branches of Federal and State governmental units, including the Court, and urging them to undertake the battles for civil liberties that remain to be won. With that goal as our guide, we can go forward together to advance civil rights and liberty rights with the fervor we have shown in the past.”

due process requires that both the ways in which government acts *and* the laws under which it acts must be fair. Thus, the Court added the idea of substantive due process to the original notion of procedural due process.

Examples of Procedural and Substantive Due Process Any number of cases illustrate these elements of due process. Consider *Rochin* v. *California*, 1952, as an illustration of procedural due process.

Rochin was a suspected narcotics pusher. Acting on a tip, three Los Angeles County deputy sheriffs went to his rooming house. They forced their way into Rochin's room. There the deputies found him sitting on a bed and spotted two capsules on a nightstand. When one of the deputies asked, “Whose stuff is this?” Rochin popped the capsules into his mouth, and although all three officers jumped him, managed to swallow them.

The deputies took Rochin to a hospital, where his stomach was pumped. The capsules were recovered and found to contain morphine. The State then prosecuted and convicted Rochin for violating the State's narcotics laws.

The Supreme Court held that the deputies had violated the 14th Amendment's guarantee of procedural due process. Said the Court:

> “This is conduct that shocks the conscience. Illegally breaking into the privacy of the petitioner, the struggle to open his mouth and remove what was there, the forcible extraction of his stomach's contents—this course of proceeding by agents of government to obtain evidence is bound to offend even hardened sensibilities. They are methods too close to the rack and the screw. . . .”

As an example of substantive due process, take a case considered earlier, *Pierce* v. *Society of Sisters*, 1925. In 1922 Oregon voters had adopted a new compulsory school-attendance law. It required that all persons between the ages of 8 and 16 who had not completed the eighth grade had to attend public schools.

A Roman Catholic order challenged the constitutionality of the law. The Supreme Court ruled that the law violated the 14th Amendment's Due Process Clause.

Note that the Court did not find that the State had enforced the law unfairly. Rather, the Court found fault with the law itself.

The 14th Amendment and the Bill of Rights Recall this crucial point from the last chapter: The provisions of the Bill of Rights apply only to actions of the Federal Government. As you read on page 489, the Supreme Court has held that most of those rights are also protected against the actions by the States through the 14th Amendment's Due Process Clause.[1]

Understanding this nationalization of rights is crucial to an understanding of the 14th Amendment's Due Process Clause and the meaning of individual rights in this country.

[1] The key 1st Amendment cases were discussed in Chapter 19. You will look at those involving the 4th through the 8th amendments over the next several pages.

Due Process and the Police Power

In the federal system, the reserved powers of the States include the broad and important **police power**—the power of each State to act 1.b to protect and promote the public health, safety, morals, and general welfare.

What a State and its local governments can and cannot do in the exercise of their police power is decided by the courts. They must strike a balance between the needs of society and the rights of individuals to due process.

Any number of cases can illustrate the conflict between the use of a State's police power and the rights of individuals. Take, as an example, a matter often involved in drunk-driving cases.

Every State's laws allow the use of one or more tests to determine whether a person arrested and charged with drunk driving was in fact drunk at the time of the incident.

Does the requirement that a person submit to such a test violate his or her rights under the 14th Amendment? Does the test involve an unconstitutional search for and seizure of evidence? Does it amount to forcing a person to testify against himself or herself—unconstitutional compulsory self-incrimination? Or is the requirement a proper use of the police power?

Time after time, State and federal courts have upheld the right of society to protect itself against drunk drivers and rejected the individual rights' argument.

The leading case is *Schmerber* v. *California*, 1966. The Court found no objection to a situation in which a police officer had directed a doctor to draw blood from a drunk-driving suspect. The Court stressed these points: The blood sample was drawn in accord with accepted medical practice. The officer had reasonable grounds to believe that the suspect was drunk. Further, had the officer taken time to secure a **search warrant**—a court 1.c order authorizing a search—the evidence could have disappeared from the suspect's system.

Legislators and judges have often found the public's health, safety, morals, and/or welfare to be of overriding importance. For example:

—To promote health: States can limit the sale of alcoholic beverages and tobacco, make laws to combat pollution, and require the vaccination of school children.

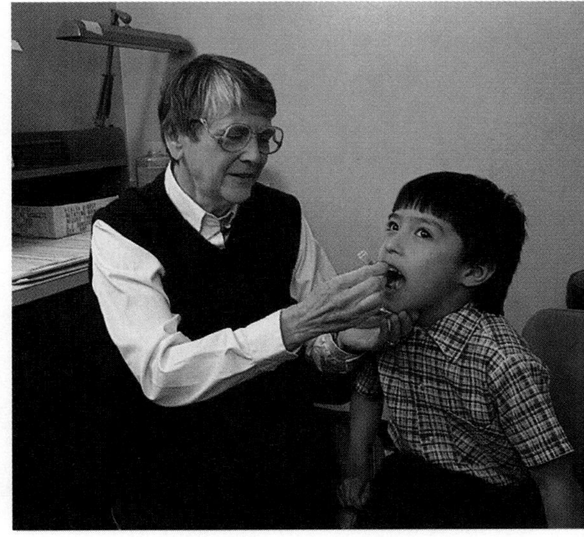

Proper Use of the Police Power States can require the vaccination of school children. This is just one example of the proper use of police power.

—To promote safety: States can forbid concealed weapons, require the use of seatbelts, and punish drunk drivers.

—To promote morals: States can outlaw gambling, the sale of obscene materials, and the practice of prostitution.

—To promote the general welfare: States can enact compulsory education laws, provide help to the medically needy, and limit the profits of public utilities.

Clearly, no government can use the police power in any unreasonable or unfair way. In short, they cannot violate the 14th Amendment's Due Process Clause. Thus, police officers may not use unnecessary force as they enforce the criminal law. No State may prohibit the operation of private schools. And a city may not ban a street demonstration simply because the mayor opposes the demonstrators' cause.

Right of Privacy

The constitutional guarantees of due process create a right of privacy. As the Supreme Court defined it in *Stanley* v. *Georgia*, in 1969, the right of privacy is "the right to be free, except in

Provide Guided Practice

Write the following words on the board: *Procedural and substantive due process; police power; right of privacy.* Ask students to identify these concepts and explain their significance in relation to due process of law. (*Procedural and substantive due process are two dimensions of the Constitution's due process guarantees. Procedural due process is the requirement that laws must be applied fairly, and substantive due process is the requirement that laws themselves be fair. Police power is the power of each State to act to protect and promote the public health, safety, morals, and general welfare. Exercise of police power sometimes creates conflicts with the rights of individuals. The right of privacy is the right to be free, except in very limited circumstances, from governmental intrusions into one's privacy. Though it does not exist in the Constitution, the Supreme Court has held that it stems from the Due Process Clause.*)

Provide Independent Practice

TRF **Teacher's Resource File** You may wish to assign Section 1 Guided Reading and Review, Unit 5 File, p. 50, to help students master section objective content.

Enrichment

Have students form two teams to debate one or both of the following topics: Individual rights should take precedence over the general welfare; or, the Constitution does not guarantee the right to privacy. (Easy)

Teacher's Resource File
See the Historical and Legal Documents file, p. 40, for material to support the section.

MONITOR COMPREHENSION

Answers to Section 1 Review
1. "Key Terms" are defined on the following pages:
- **a.** due process, p. 517
- **b.** police power, p. 519
- **c.** search warrant, p. 519

2. Procedural requires that government acts be fair; substantive requires that laws be fair. **3.** The 14th Amendment makes the Bill of Rights protections applicable to the States. **4.** Power of each State to protect and promote the public health, safety, morals, and general welfare. **5.** Freedom from unwanted government intrusion into one's privacy; Due Process Clause of the 14th Amendment. **6.** Yes: Protection of morals falls within the State's police powers. No: Right of privacy limits the right of government to deem actions immoral.

Teacher's Resource File See the Unit 5 File, p. 51, for the Section 1 Quiz.

CLOSURE

The two Due Process clauses are a key to the American concept of justice. Courts have held that due process must be procedural and substantive. Yet courts have also held that States can exercise their police power in the interest of the public good even at the expense of individual rights. In Section 2, students will read about individual freedoms and security of the person as guaranteed in the Constitution.

Assignment Assign Section 2, pp. 521–526, for the next class period.

very limited circumstances, from unwanted governmental intrusions into one's privacy."[2]

The Constitution makes no specific mention of the right, but the Supreme Court declared its existence in *Griswold* v. *Connecticut* in 1965. ✪ That case centered on a State law that outlawed birth-control counseling and prohibited all use of birth-control devices. The Court held the law to be a violation of the 14th Amendment's Due Process Clause, and noted that the State had no business policing the marital bedroom.

Abortion The most controversial applications of the right of privacy have come in cases that raise this question: To what extent can a State limit a woman's right to an abortion?

The leading case is *Roe* v. *Wade*, 1973. There, the Supreme Court struck down a Texas law that made abortion a crime except when necessary to save the life of the mother.

In *Roe*, the Court held that the 14th Amendment's right of privacy "encompass[es] a woman's decision whether or not to terminate her pregnancy." More specifically, the Court ruled that (1) during the first trimester of pregnancy (about three months) a State must recognize a woman's right to choose an abortion and cannot interfere with medical judgments in that matter; (2) during the second trimester a State, acting in the interest of women who undergo abortions, can make reasonable regulations about how, when, and where abortions can be performed, but cannot prohibit the procedure; and (3) during the final trimester a State, acting to protect the unborn child, can choose to prohibit all abortions except those necessary to preserve the life or health of the mother.

In several later cases the Court rejected a number of challenges to its basic holding in *Roe*. But as the composition of the Court has changed, so has the Court's position on abortion.

Thus, the Court has recently upheld additional restrictions on the right in *Webster* v. *Reproductive Health Services*, in 1989. There, a divided Court upheld two key parts of a Missouri law. Those provisions prohibit abortions, except those to preserve the mother's life or health, (1) in any public hospital or clinic in that State and (2) in any case where the mother is 20 or more weeks pregnant and tests show that the fetus is viable—capable of life outside the mother's body.

In *Webster*, the Court did not overrule *Roe* v. *Wade*. But, clearly, it did make it possible for State legislatures to adopt stricter regulations.

Since *Webster*, the Court has upheld two State laws that require a minor (1) to inform at least one parent before she can obtain an abortion, *Ohio* v. *Akron Center for Reproductive Health*, 1990, and (2) to tell both parents of her plans, except in cases where a judge gives permission for an abortion without parental knowledge, *Minnesota* v. *Hodgson*, 1990.

The Court's only major recent abortion decision, *Rust* v. *Sullivan*, 1991, involved federal regulations. The Court held that the Department of Health and Human Services could issue rules that forbid the staff of federally financed family planning clinics to engage in any discussion of abortion with patients. The Court rejected arguments that the rules violated the free speech rights of clinic personnel or the abortion rights of patients.

[2]Recall, *Stanley* involved the possession of obscene materials in one's own home; see page 500. More recently, the Court upheld a Georgia law that provides for the punishment of homosexual conduct in the privacy of one's home, *Bowers* v. *Hardwick*, 1986.

Section 1 Review

1. Define: due process, police power, search warrant
2. What is the difference between procedural and substantive due process?
3. What is the relationship between the Bill of Rights and the 14th Amendment's Due Process Clause?
4. What is a State's police power?
5. What is the right to privacy, and from where in the Constitution does it come?

Critical Thinking

6. Checking Consistency (p. 19) Considering the constitutional right to privacy, do you think it is proper for a State to use its police power to promote morals among its citizens?

★

✪ SPOTLIGHT ON: Constitutional Issues

On the *Griswold* decision and the privacy due to married couples, Justice William O. Douglas wrote the following: "We deal with a right of privacy older than the Bill of Rights—older than our political parties, older than our school system. Marriage is a coming together for better or for worse, hopefully enduring, and intimate to the degree of being sacred. It is an association that promotes a way of life, not causes; a harmony in living, not political faiths; a bilateral loyalty, not commercial or social projects. Yet it is an association for as noble a purpose as any involved in our prior decisions." *Griswold* later served as a precedent for the 1973 *Roe* v. *Wade* decision permitting abortion.

Reteach

Have students create a section glossary that includes the following terms and their definitions: Due Process, Procedural Due Process, Substantive Due Process, Police Power, and Right of Privacy.

Teacher's Resource File See the Supreme Court Cases file, pp. 84–85, 110–111, for materials to support the section.

2 Freedom and Security of the Person

Find Out:
- How does the Constitution protect the freedom and security of the person?
- What is the extent of those protections?

Key Terms:
probable cause, exclusionary rule

Few people realize how many different rights the Constitution guarantees to the American people. More than three dozen individual liberties are protected by that document.

As you will see in this section, several of those guarantees protect the right of each person to be free from physical restraint and to be reasonably secure in his or her person and home.

Slavery and Involuntary Servitude: The 13th Amendment

The 13th Amendment was added to the Constitution in 1865, ending over 200 years of slavery in this country. Section 1 of the amendment declares, "Neither slavery nor involuntary servitude . . . shall exist within the United States, or any place subject to their jurisdiction." Importantly, Section 2 of this amendment gives Congress the expressed power "to enforce this article by appropriate legislation."

Until 1865, each State could decide for itself whether or not to allow slavery. With the 13th Amendment, that power was denied to them, and to the National Government, as well.

Section 1 As a widespread practice, slavery disappeared more than 125 years ago. There are still occasional cases of it, however. As recently as 1986, in fact, three men were sentenced to prison in Texas for the crime. They had been convicted of holding four drifters at an isolated ranch.

Most cases that have arisen under Section 1 have turned on the question of "involuntary servitude"—that is, forced labor. The Antipeonage Act of 1867 makes it a federal crime for any person to hold another in peonage—a condition in which a person is bound to work for another in order to fulfill a contract or satisfy a debt.

Several times, the Supreme Court has struck down State laws making it a crime for any person to fail to work after having received money or other benefits by promising to do so.[3]

The 13th Amendment does not forbid *all* forms of involuntary servitude, however. Thus, in 1918 the Court drew a distinction between "involuntary servitude" and "duty" in upholding the constitutionality of the selective service system—the draft.[4] And, those who are convicted of crimes can be forced to work.

Section 2 Shortly after the Civil War, Congress passed several civil rights laws, based on the 13th Amendment. But in several cases, especially the *Civil Rights Cases*, 1883, the Supreme Court sharply narrowed the scope of federal authority. In effect, the Court held that racial discrimination against African Americans by *private* persons did not place the "badge of slavery" on them nor keep them in servitude.

---

[3]But note, the fact that a person cannot be forced to work in order to satisfy a debt does not relieve that person of the legal obligation to pay the debt.

[4]*Selective Draft Law Cases* (*Arver* v. *United States*), 1918.

This position will be responsible for designing, developing and implementing business curriculum in support of the company's strategic plans. This individual will need to support all levels of management and staff at the Chicago Tribune Company.

In return, we offer a challenging, progressive and fast-paced work environment and a competitive salary and benefits package. Please send resume to:

Chicago Tribune Company
435 North Michigan Avenue, 3rd Floor
Human Resources (Trainer)
Chicago, IL 60611

equal opportunity employer
We have a non-smoking environment

Equal Opportunity in Employment This right makes it illegal for employers to discriminate on the basis of race, color, sex, religion, or national origin.

SECTION 2
Freedom and Security of the Person

FOCUS

Teacher's Resource File
See the Unit 5 File, p. 52, for the Section 2 Outline.

Objectives

20.3 Analyze how the Constitution protects the freedom and security of the person.

20.4 Identify the scope and limits of the protections of the person.

Bellringer Activity Before students read the section, ask them to discuss whether or not they feel it is right for school and law-enforcement officials to search randomly student lockers. Have students explain their feelings on this subject.

State the Purpose The Constitution guarantees many individual rights and liberties. In Section 2, students will learn about several constitutional protections insuring people a reasonable degree of security in their persons and their homes.

ABCNEWS INTERACTIVE

The following video segments may be used to highlight aspects of the freedom and security of the person.

POWERS OF THE SUPREME COURT GUIDEBOOK
Chapter 20: Amendment 13 (1865), Abolition of Slavery, p. 32
Chapter 11: Amendment 2 (1791), Right to Bear Arms, p. 17
Chapter 13: Amendment 4 (1791), Search and Arrest Warrants, p. 20

Vocabulary

Direct students' attention to "Key Terms" on page 521. Have students scan the content of the section and then predict the meaning of each term. As students read the section, have them compare their predictions with the actual definitions.

Reading Strategy: Relating to the Topic

Before students read the section, ask them to consider the following question: When is it permissible for school officials or law-enforcement officers to search the jacket pocket of a 17-year-old high-school student? Have students create and consider a variety of scenarios that might lead them to different answers to the question.

INSTRUCT

Explain/Analyze Ask students to recall their responses to the "Bellringer Activity" at the beginning of the section. Tell students that at the heart of that discussion was the individual's right to freedom, privacy, and security of the person.

Ask students to explain how the 13th and 2nd amendments help to ensure the freedom and security of the person. (*The 13th Amendment makes the ultimate infringement of freedom—slavery—unconstitutional. It also has been used to attack many forms of discrimination. The 2nd Amendment is aimed at helping States maintain their security by keeping an armed militia.*)

Next, have students analyze the importance and meaning of the 4th Amendment. Ask students to summarize the basic message of the amendment. (*Government cannot arbitrarily search and/or seize a person or that person's property, but must have a warrant or exception to the warrant clause to do so.*) Have students attempt to design guidelines to help determine what constitutes an unreasonable search and what kind of activity or behavior rates as probable cause.

Finally, ask students to consider how the exclusionary rule "puts teeth" into the 4th Amendment. (*It helps ensure that evidence gained as the result of actions that violate the 4th Amendment will not be used in court against the person whose rights were violated.*) Have students respond to recent court decisions, such as *United States* v. *Leon* and *Maryland* v. *Garrison*.

Congress soon repealed most of those laws based on the 13th Amendment. Federal enforcement of the few that remained was, at best, unimpressive.

In *Jones* v. *Mayer*, 1968, however, the Supreme Court breathed new life into the 13th Amendment. The case centered on one of the post-Civil War acts Congress had not repealed. Passed in 1866, that almost-forgotten law provided in part:

> "All citizens of the United States shall have the same right in every State and Territory, as is enjoyed by white citizens thereof, to inherit, purchase, lease, sell, hold, and convey real and personal property."

Jones, an African American, had sued because Mayer had refused to sell him a home, solely because of his race. Mayer contended that the 1866 law was unconstitutional, as it sought to prohibit private racial discrimination.

The Court upheld the law, declaring that the 13th Amendment abolished slavery and gave to Congress the power to abolish "the badges and the incidents of slavery." Said the Court:

> "At the very least, the freedom that Congress is empowered to secure under the 13th Amendment includes the freedom to buy whatever a white man can buy, the right to live wherever a white man can live."

The Court affirmed that decision in several later cases.[5] For example, in *Runyon* v. *McRary*, 1976, two private schools had refused to admit two African Americans. The Court found that the schools had violated another provision of the 1866 law:

> "All persons . . . shall have the same right in every State and Territory to make and enforce contracts . . . as is enjoyed by white citizens."

The Court has also ruled that the Civil Rights Act of 1966 protects all "identifiable groups who are subject to intentional discrimination solely because of their ancestry or ethnic characteristics"—for example, Jews, *Shaare Tefila Congregation* v. *Cobb*, 1987; and Arabs, *St. Francis College* v. *Al-Khazraji*, 1987.

[5] While *Jones* v. *Mayer* was before the Court, Congress enacted the Civil Rights (Open Housing) Act of 1968; see Chapter 21, Section 2.

Most recently, however, the Court has backed off a bit. In *Patterson* v. *McLean Credit Union*, 1989, it declared that while the 1866 law does prohibit race discrimination in a contract of employment, any on-the-job discrimination should be handled in accord with the Civil Rights Act of 1964—which is treated in Chapter 21, Section 2.

Still, note this critical point: The Court has now several times held that the 13th Amendment gives Congress significant power to attack "the badges and incidents of slavery."

Right to Keep and Bear Arms

The 2nd Amendment reads this way:

> "A well-regulated militia being necessary to the security of a free state, the right of the people to keep and bear arms shall not be infringed."

The 2nd Amendment is widely misunderstood. It was added to the Constitution to protect the right of each State to keep a militia. Its aim was to preserve the concept of the citizen-soldier. It does not guarantee a right to keep and bear arms free from restriction by government.

The only important 2nd Amendment case is *United States* v. *Miller*, 1939. There, the Court upheld a section of the National Firearms Act of 1934. That section makes it a crime to ship sawed-off shotguns, machine guns, or silencers across State lines unless the shipper has registered the weapons with the Treasury Department and paid a $200 tax. The Court said that it could find no reasonable link between the sawed-off shotgun and "the preservation . . . of a well-regulated militia."

The Court has never found the 2nd Amendment to be within the meaning of the 14th Amendment's Due Process Clause. Thus, each of the States can limit the right to keep and bear arms—and all of them do, in various ways.

Security of Home and Person

In several provisions, the Constitution insists that government cannot arbitrarily violate the home or the person of any American citizen.

The 3rd Amendment This Amendment forbids the quartering of soldiers in private

TRF Teacher's Resource File
See the Simulations and Debates file, pp. 35–70, for material to support the section.

homes in time of peace. It also prohibits the practice in time of war except "in a manner to be prescribed by law." The guarantee was added to prevent what had been British practice in colonial days.

The amendment has had almost no importance since its adoption, however. It has never been the subject of a Supreme Court case.

The 4th Amendment The 4th Amendment also grew out of colonial practice. It was designed to prevent the use of writs of assistance—blanket search warrants with which British customs officials had invaded private homes to search for smuggled goods.

Unlike the 3rd Amendment, the 4th has proved a highly important guarantee. It reads:

> "The right of the people to be secure in their persons, houses, papers, and effects, against unreasonable searches and seizures, shall not be violated, and no warrants shall issue, but upon probable cause, supported by oath or affirmation, and particularly describing the place to be searched, and the persons or things to be seized."

Each State constitution has a similar provision. The guarantee also applies to the States through the 14th Amendment's Due Process Clause.

The general rule laid down by the 4th Amendment is this: Police officers have no general right to search for evidence or to seize either evidence or persons. Except in particular circumstances, they must have a proper warrant obtained with **probable cause**—that is, reason- 1.a
able grounds.

The Supreme Court has often said that police need a search warrant whenever the person targeted by the search has "a reasonable expectation of privacy." The particular place is not that important, for the Constitution "protects people—and not simply 'areas'—against unreasonable searches and seizures." The Court first made that important point in *Katz* v. *United States*, 1969.

Again, there are many situations in which police do not need a warrant. They do not, for example, when evidence is "in plain view." Thus, the Court recently upheld a search in which officers, equipped with a warrant to search a home for stolen jewelry, found illegal weapons in plain view and seized them, *Horton* v. *California*, 1990. As one more example: The Court recently endorsed the warrantless search of plastic garbage bags left at the curb, in *California* v. *Greenwood*, 1988. There is, said the Court, no "reasonable expectation of privacy" in the garbage one puts out to be hauled away.

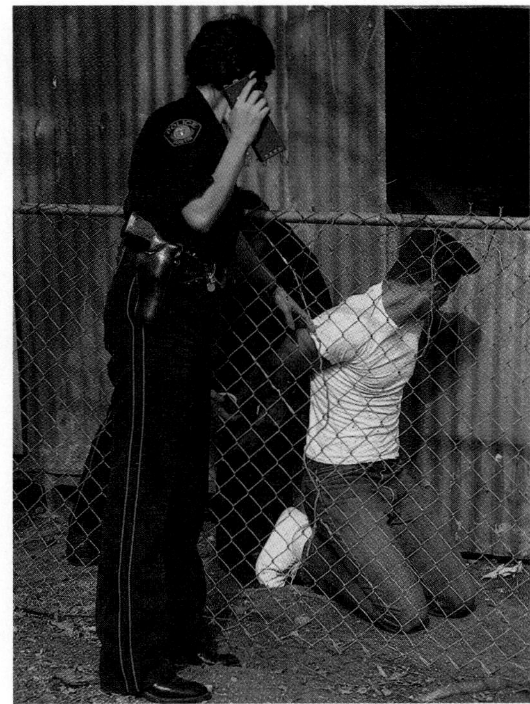

Probable Cause Police can arrest a person in a public place without a warrant provided they have probable cause to believe that person is about to commit or has committed a crime.

Take a widely noted case to illustrate the line between warrantless searches that are lawful and those that are not. In *Michigan* v. *Tyler*, 1978, the Court set aside the arson convictions of two furniture dealers. Much of the evidence against them had come from two separate sets of warrantless searches. The first searches were made as the fire department fought a blaze in their store and immediately thereafter. The other searches were conducted some weeks later.

The Court found that a burning building presents an emergency situation, one in which a warrantless entry is clearly reasonable. But the

TRF **Teacher's Resource File**
See the Supreme Court Cases file, pp. 106–107, for material to support the section.

Provide Guided Practice
Write the following on the board: *2nd Amendment, 3rd Amendment, 4th Amendment, 13th Amendment.* Have students volunteer to tell how each of these amendments help to ensure the freedom and security of the person. (*Second Amendment: Enables States to maintain well-regulated militias by protecting the right to keep and bear arms. Third Amendment: Has little relevance today; relates to a practice in colonial times. Fourth Amendment: Seeks to prevent government from engaging in unreasonable searches and seizures. Thirteenth Amendment: Outlaws slavery and the "badges and incidents of slavery."*)

Provide Independent Practice
TRF **Teacher's Resource File**
You may wish to assign Section 2 Guided Reading and Review, Unit 5 File, p. 53, to help students master section objective content.

Court also held that the later searches, made well after the emergency, and also made without warrants, violated the 4th and 14th amendments.

An arrest is the seizure of a person. When officers make a lawful arrest of a person, they do not need a warrant to search "the area within which he might gain possession of a weapon or destructible evidence."[6]

In fact, most arrests take place without a warrant. Police can arrest a person in a public place without one, provided they have probable cause to believe that that person has committed or is about to commit a crime.[7]

When, exactly, does the 4th Amendment protection come into play? The Court has several times held that that point is reached "only when the officer, by means of physical force or show of authority, has in some way restrained the liberty of a citizen," *Terry* v. *Ohio*, 1968. Thus, the driver of a stolen car was "seized" when deputies blocked his escape by placing an 18-wheel tractor-trailer across both lanes of a two-lane highway, *Brower* v. *Inyo County*, 1989.

Automobiles The Court has long had difficulty applying the 4th Amendment to automobiles. It has several times held that an officer needs no warrant to search an automobile, a boat, an airplane, or some other vehicle when there is probable cause to believe that it is involved in illegal activities—because such a "movable scene of crime" could disappear while a warrant was being sought.[8] The Court has also recently held that police can stop automobiles at roadside checkpoints to examine drivers and passengers for signs of intoxication—even when they have no evidence to indicate that the occupants of a particular car have been drinking, *Michigan* v. *Sitz*, 1990.

The court overturned a long string of automobile-search cases in 1991. Prior to that date, it had held in several cases that a warrant was generally needed to search a glove compartment, a paper bag, a piece of luggage, or other "closed container" in an automobile. But in *California* v. *Acevedo*, 1991, the Court set out what it called "one clear-cut rule to govern automobile searches": Whenever police lawfully stop a car, they do not need a warrant to search anything in that vehicle that they have reason to believe holds evidence of a crime.

The Exclusionary Rule If an unlawful search or seizure does occur, what use can be made of the evidence that is found? If that "tainted evidence" can be used in court, then the 4th Amendment offers no real protection to a person accused of crime.

To meet that problem posed by that issue, the Supreme Court adopted, and is still refining, the
1.b **exclusionary rule**. At base, the rule is this: Evidence gained as the result of an illegal act by police cannot be used against the person from whom it was seized.

The rule was first laid down in *Weeks* v. *United States*, 1914. The Court held that evidence obtained illegally by federal officers cannot be used in the federal courts.

The exclusionary rule was extended to cover the States by the Supreme Court's historic decision in *Mapp* v. *Ohio*, 1961 (see page 489). There, police officers had entered Mapp's home without a warrant. They said they were looking for evidence of illegal gambling. They found no gambling evidence, but their very thorough search did turn up some dirty books. Mapp was convicted of possession of obscene materials and sentenced to jail. The Supreme Court found that the evidence against her had been found and seized without a proper warrant.

The exclusionary rule was intended to put teeth into the 4th Amendment, and it has. The rule says to police: As you enforce the law, obey the law. Critics of the rule note that the rule enables some persons who are clearly guilty to go free. Why, they often ask, should criminals be able "to beat the rap" on "a technicality"?

---

[6]The present rule, quoted here, was first laid down in *Chimel* v. *California*, 1969.

[7]A person arrested without a warrant must be brought promptly before a judge for a probable cause hearing. In *County of Riverside* v. *McLaughin*, 1991, the Court held that "promptly" means within 48 hours.

[8]In an early leading case on the point, *Carroll* v. *United States*, 1925, the Court emphasized that "where the securing of a warrant is reasonably practicable it must be used. . . . In cases where seizure is impossible except without a warrant, the seizing officer acts unlawfully and at his peril unless he can show the court probable cause."

Enrichment

Have students work in small groups to create four political cartoons to represent each of the amendments discussed in this section. (Average)

TRF **Teacher's Resource File**
See the Supreme Court Cases file, pp. 34–35, 54–55, for material to support the section.

OR

TRF **Teacher's Resource File**
See the Unit 5 File, pp. 62–64, for the Case Study on Contemporary Issues for Chapter 20.

Of late, the High Court has been narrowing the scope of the rule.[9] It has done so most notably in three recent cases. First, it found an "inevitable discovery" exception to the rule, in *Nix* v. *Williams* in 1984. There the Court held that tainted evidence can be used if that evidence "ultimately or inevitably would have been discovered by lawful means."

Then, in another 1984 case, *United States* v. *Leon*, the Court found a "good faith" exception to the rule. There, federal agents in Los Angeles had used what they thought was a proper warrant to seize illicit drugs. Their warrant was later shown to be faulty, however. The Court upheld their actions nonetheless. It said: "When an officer acting with objective good faith has obtained a search warrant . . . and acted within its scope . . . there is nothing to deter."

The Court has also given police room for "honest mistakes." In *Maryland* v. *Garrison*, 1987, it allowed the use of evidence seized in the mistaken search of an apartment in Baltimore. Officers had a warrant to search for drugs in an apartment on the third floor of a building. Not realizing that there were two apartments there, they entered, searched, and found drugs in the apartment for which they did not have a warrant.

The Federal Government's drug testing programs involve searches of persons, and so they are covered by the 4th Amendment. To date, the Court has upheld two of those programs. In both instances it found that carefully drawn tests are a reasonable response to the drug problem, and they can be conducted without either warrants or even any indication of drug use by those who must take them. The first case, *Skinner* v. *Railway Labor Executives Association*, 1989, involved the Federal Railway Administration's requirement that workers take drug tests after a major accident. The other case, *National Treasury Employees Union* v. *Von Raab*, 1989, centered on a Customs Service rule mandating drug tests for all employees who carry firearms.

Interpreting Political Art An untitled painting by Hank Virgona shows a court in session. What impression of a courtroom does this painting give you?

Wiretapping Law-enforcement agents now frequently use wiretapping and other sophisticated means of "bugging."

In its first wiretapping case, in 1928, the Supreme Court held that intercepting telephone conversations without a warrant was not an unreasonable search or seizure. In 1967 it reversed that decision, however.

The earlier case, *Olmstead* v. *United States*, 1928, involved a large ring of bootleggers. Federal agents had tapped Olmstead's telephone calls over several months. That bugging produced a mass of evidence that authorities presented in court to convict him and others in the ring. The Supreme Court upheld their convictions. It found that there had been no "actual physical invasion"

[9]For example, the Court has held that the rule does not apply to federal grand jury proceedings, *United States* v. *Calandra,* 1974. Thus, tainted evidence that cannot be used at a person's trial could nonetheless be presented to the grand jury—the body that indicted that person and so caused the trial. The Court has also held that evidence against a defendant that was gained by an illegal search of another person's property can be used in a criminal trial, *United States* v. *Payner*, 1980.

Interpreting Political Art Ask students to identify the techniques that the artist has used to communicate his message in this painting. (*Possible answer: The judge appears weary and the other people in the courtroom appear passive and disinterested.*)

Caption Answer The impression that the system moves very slowly and the participants in the system are apathetic.

TRF **Teacher's Resource File**
See the Supreme Court Cases file, pp. 40–41, 96–97, 98–99, and the Simulations and Debates file, pp. 35–70, for materials to support the section.

Monitor Comprehension

Answers to Section 2 Review
1. "Key Terms" are defined on the following pages:
a. probable cause, p. 523
b. exclusionary rule, p. 524
2. Individuals can be held in involuntary servitude as punishment for a crime. People can be constitutionally drafted. **3.** Gave Congress power to attack the "badges and incidents of slavery." **4.** Protect the right of each State to keep a militia. **5.** Never been the subject of a Supreme Court case. **6.** Ensures the security of persons against unreasonable searches and seizures. **7.** (a) Evidence that is gained illegally cannot be used against the person from whom it is seized. (b) Found "inevitable discovery" and "good faith" exceptions to the rule. **8.** Yes: If constitutional protections are to have meaning, government cannot violate them. No: Those who have clearly violated the law must be punished.

Closure

The Constitution offers several protections of freedom and security of the person. The 13th Amendment prohibits slavery and involuntary servitude, the 2nd Amendment ensures the right to bear arms, and the 4th Amendment protects against unreasonable searches and seizures. As students read the next section they will learn about the rights of persons accused of a crime.

Assignment Assign Section 3, pp. 528–535, for the next class period.

of Olmstead's home or office; the agents had tapped the lines outside those places.[10]

The Supreme Court expressly overruled *Olmstead* in *Katz* v. *United States*, 1967. Katz had been found guilty of transmitting betting information across State lines from a public phone booth in Los Angeles to his contacts in Boston and Miami. Much of the evidence against him came from an electronic bug FBI agents had placed on the outside of the booth. The Supreme Court reversed the conviction and overruled *Olmstead*. It held that the 4th Amendment protects persons and not just places. Though Katz was in a public, glass-enclosed booth, he was entitled to make a private call. Said the Court:

> "What a person knowingly exposes to the public, even in his own home or office, is not a subject of 4th Amendment protection. . . . But what he seeks to preserve as private, even in an area accessible to the public, may be constitutionally protected."

The Court went on to say, however, that the 4th Amendment could be satisfied in such situations if police officers have a proper warrant before they install a listening device.

Congress reacted to *Katz* in a number of sections in the Omnibus Crime Control Act of 1968. They make it illegal for any unauthorized person to tap telephone wires or use electronic bugging devices or sell those devices in interstate commerce.

The 1968 law does allow federal and State police agencies to search for and seize evidence by electronic means under close court control. If officers can show probable cause, a federal or State judge can issue a warrant for a bugging operation.[11]

When it passed the 1968 law, Congress carefully avoided this knotty question: Does the President, acting under the inherent power to protect the nation against foreign attack and internal subversion, have the power to order the bugging of suspected foreign agents or domestic subversives without a warrant? For many years, several Presidents had used the FBI, the CIA, and other federal police agencies in just that way.

The Supreme Court has since ruled that the President has no such power in cases of domestic subversion, *United States* v. *United States District Court*, 1972. In the Foreign Intelligence Surveillance Act of 1978, Congress, for the first time, required a warrant even for the wiretapping or other electronic bugging of foreign agents in this country.[12]

Section 2 Review

1. Define: probable cause, exclusionary rule
2. For what reason does the 13th Amendment not forbid all forms of involuntary servitude?
3. In what sense has the Supreme Court "breathed new life" into the 13th Amendment?
4. What is the true purpose of the 2nd Amendment?
5. In what sense is the 3rd Amendment of so little importance?
6. What is the basic purpose of the 4th Amendment?
7. (a) What is the exclusionary rule? (b) In what ways has the Supreme Court been narrowing the rule in recent years?

Critical Thinking

8. Expressing Problems Clearly (p. 19) Discuss whether or not you feel that people who have clearly committed crimes should be able to go free if their rights are violated during arrest or trial.

★

[10]In a vigorous dissent, Justice Oliver Wendell Holmes was strongly critical of "such dirty business"—federal agents acting without a warrant. He wrote: "For my part I think it is a less evil that some criminals should escape than that the government should play such an ignoble part."

[11]In certain "emergency" situations, especially those involving national security or organized crime, the attorney general can authorize bugging operations by federal agents for up to 48 hours without a judge's approval—that is, without a warrant. Agents must seek a warrant during that period, however.

[12]The 1978 law set up a special federal court, the Foreign Intelligence Surveillance Court, with the power to issue such warrants.

The law allows only one exception to its warrant requirement: The National Security Agency, the Defense Department's top-secret code-making and code-breaking agency, does not need a warrant to eavesdrop on the electronic communications of foreign governments.

Teacher's Resource File
See the Unit 5 File, p. 54, for the Section 2 Quiz.

Teacher's Resource File
See the Supreme Court Cases file, pp. 74–75, for material to support the section.

Reteach

Have students write a letter to an imaginary or real acquaintance outside this country in which they explain how the Constitution has historically sought to protect the security of the person. Students' letters should contain references to the prohibition of slavery, the right to keep and bear arms, and the guarantees against unreasonable searches and seizures.

Debating Key Issues

Should Defendants Have the Right to Appointed Counsel?

Gideon v. *Wainwright*

Clarence Earl Gideon was a destitute man living in Florida. One night, Gideon was arrested for breaking into a pool room and charged with burglary. He pleaded innocent to the felony charges.

In court, Gideon requested that an attorney be appointed to represent him. His request was denied. The judge explained that such appointments were only made for those accused of capital crimes—those crimes that were punishable by death. Gideon had no choice but to defend himself. The jury convicted Gideon and sentenced him to five years in the State penitentiary.

Gideon wrote an appeal to the Supreme Court of Florida, which was denied. He then filed a petition with the U.S. Supreme Court, maintaining that his constitutional rights had been violated because he had been denied counsel at his trial. In 1963, the justices of the Supreme Court agreed to try the case and appointed a lawyer to argue Gideon's case.

The Supreme Court agreed to hear Gideon's case, in part because it wished to review its 1942 decision in *Betts* v. *Brady.* In that decision, the Court held that the Due Process Clause of the 14th Amendment did not require the State to invoke the 6th Amendment's guarantee of counsel in non-capital cases unless "special circumstances" revealed a trial to be "a denial of fundamental fairness shocking to the universal sense of justice."

Wainwright, named by Gideon as defendant in this case, was the head of the Florida Department of Corrections.

Review the following evidence and arguments presented to the U.S. Supreme Court:

Arguments for Gideon

1. The appointment of an attorney to those who otherwise could not afford counsel is central to the right guaranteed by the 6th Amendment.
2. The right of the indigent to appointment of counsel is implicit in the 14th Amendment's Due Process and Equal Protection clauses.
3. *Betts* v. *Brady* should be overruled. A layman is not familiar with the mechanics of preparing a defense, and must be guided by counsel.

Arguments for Wainwright

1. Gideon received a fair trial, and no "special circumstances'" were present that would warrant court-appointed counsel.
2. Neither the 6th nor the 14th amendments intended that the State should provide and fund counsel for every person accused of a relatively insignificant crime.
3. *Betts* v. *Brady* must not be overruled. To do so would require the State to furnish counsel in every case.

Getting Involved

1. Identify the constitutional grounds on which each side based its arguments.
2. Debate the opposing viewpoints presented in this case.
3. Predict how you think the Supreme Court ruled in this case and why. Then refer to the Supreme Court Glossary on page 764 to read about the decision in the case. Discuss the impact of the Court's decision on the judicial system, the rights of the accused, and the individual States.

TEACHING
Debating Key Issues

***Gideon* v. *Wainwright*: Should Defendants Have the Right to Appointed Counsel?**

Objective
Determine whether a defendant always has the right to legal representation.

INSTRUCT

Before students read the feature, you may want to elicit students' responses to the question in the title. After they read the feature, ask them if they have changed their point of view, and if so, why. Then have students work through the "Getting Involved" section, starting with Step 1, identifying the constitutional issues involved.

Following class debate, have each student explain whether his or her opinion has changed and identify which of the arguments used in the debate were most effective. Then have students read and discuss the Supreme Court's decision.

Supreme Court Decision
Gideon won a new trial and was found not guilty with the help of a court-appointed attorney. The "Gideon Rule," requiring counsel for all poor persons facing a felony charge in State courts, was a further "incorporation" of Bill of Rights guarantees into State constitutions.

TRF Teacher's Resource File
See the Supreme Court Cases File, p. 15, for an activity that extends coverage of this case.

SECTION 3
Rights of the Accused

FOCUS

Teacher's Resource File See the Unit 5 File, p. 55, for the Section 3 Outline.

Objectives

20.5 Identify the Constitutional protections for persons accused of a crime.

20.6 Explain what constitutes a fair trial.

Bellringer Activity Write the following statement on the board: *A person is presumed innocent until proven guilty.* Ask students to discuss their understanding of this statement. Do they truly believe in this principle?

State the Purpose In the American system of justice, a person is presumed innocent until proven guilty. Thus, the Constitution takes several measures to protect those accused of a crime. In Section 3, students will learn about some of those protections.

Interpreting Charts Ask students to imagine examples of situations that would constitute violations of the protections listed in the chart.

Caption Answer No excessive fine, no cruel or unusual punishment, and the right to appeal.

3 Rights of the Accused

Find Out:

- What protections does the Constitution set out for persons accused of crime?
- What constitutes a fair trial?

Key Terms:

writ of habeas corpus, bill of attainder, ex post facto law, grand jury, indictment, presentment, information, double jeopardy, bench trial, Miranda Rule

Think about this statement for a moment: "It is better that ten guilty persons go free than that one innocent person be punished." That maxim expresses one of the bedrock principles of the American legal system.

Of course, society *must* punish criminals in order to preserve itself. However, the law intends that any person who is suspected or accused of a crime must be presumed to be innocent—until that person is proved guilty by fair and lawful means.

Habeas Corpus

The **writ of habeas corpus**, sometimes called the writ of liberty, is intended to prevent unjust arrests and imprisonments.[13] It is a court order directed to an officer holding a prisoner. It commands that the prisoner be brought before the court and that the officer show cause—explain, with good reason—why the prisoner should not be released. 1.a

The right to seek a writ of habeas corpus is protected against the National Government in Article I, Section 9 of the Constitution. That right is guaranteed against the States in each of their own constitutions.

The right to the writ cannot be suspended, says the Constitution, "unless when in cases of rebellion or invasion the public safety may

[13]The phrase *habeas corpus* comes from the Latin, meaning "you should have the body," and those are the opening words of the writ.

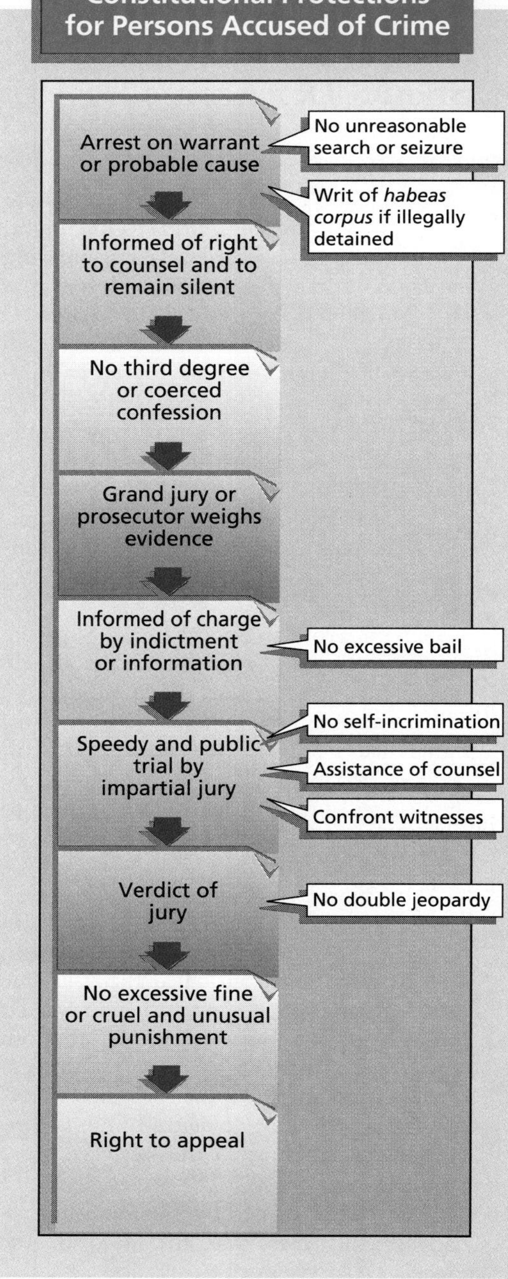

Interpreting Charts Any person accused of a crime is presumed innocent until proven guilty. What protections does the Constitution extend to those who are convicted of a crime?

Reading Strategy: Predicting Content

On the board, write the title of this section, *Rights of the Accused.* Next, have students read the boldfaced headings throughout the section. Remind students that these headings form an outline of the section. Based on their preview of this outline, have students write a two- or three-sentence prediction of the content of the section.

Vocabulary

Point out "Key Terms" on page 528. Discuss with students the terms *writ of habeas corpus* and *ex post facto law.* Direct students' attention to the direct translations of these terms contained in footnotes 13 (page 528) and 16 (page 529). Ask students to explain whether or not the literal translations help clarify the meaning of the terms. LEP require it." In *Ex parte Milligan*, 1866, the Supreme Court ruled that neither the President nor Congress can legally suspend the writ in those places where there is no actual fighting nor the likelihood of any.[14]

The right to the writ has been suspended only once since the Civil War, in Hawaii during World War II; and the Supreme Court later ruled that action illegal.

Bills of Attainder

A **bill of attainder** is a legislative act that inflicts punishment without a court trial. Neither Congress nor the States can pass such measures.[15]

The ban on bills of attainder is both a protection of individual freedom and a part of the system of separation of powers. A legislative body can pass laws that define crime and set the penalties for violation of those laws. But it cannot decide that a person is guilty of a crime and then impose a punishment on that person.

The Supreme Court has held that the prohibition is aimed at all legislative acts that apply "to named individuals or to easily ascertainable members of a group in such a way as to inflict punishment on them without a judicial trial," *United States* v. *Lovett*, 1946. The "punishment" may include the loss of a privilege.

United States v. *Brown*, 1965, is one of the few cases in which the Court has struck down a law as a bill of attainder. There it overturned a provision of the Landrum-Griffin Act of 1959 that made it a federal crime for a member of the Communist party to serve as an officer of a labor union.

[14]President Lincoln suspended the writ in 1861. His order covered various parts of the country, including several areas in which war was not then being waged. Chief Justice Roger B. Taney, sitting as a circuit judge, held Lincoln's action unconstitutional. Congress then passed the Habeas Corpus Act of 1863, giving the President the power to suspend the writ when and where, in his judgment, that action was necessary. Note that *Ex parte Milligan* arose after the enactment of the 1863 law.

[15]Article I, Sections 9 and 10.

Ex Post Facto Laws

1.c An **ex post facto law** has three features. It is (1) a criminal law, one defining a crime or providing for its punishment; (2) applied to an act committed before its passage; and (3) a law that works to the disadvantage of the accused. Neither Congress nor the State legislatures may pass such laws.[16]

For example, a law making it a crime to sell marijuana cannot be applied to one who sold it before that law was passed. Or, a law that
1.b changed the penalty for murder from life in prison to death could not be applied to a person who committed a murder before the punishment was changed.

Retroactive civil laws are *not* forbidden. Thus, a law raising income tax rates could be passed in November and applied to income earned through the whole year.

Grand Jury

The 5th Amendment also provides that:

"No person shall be held to answer for a capital, or otherwise infamous, crime, unless on a presentment or indictment of a grand jury. . . ."

1.d The **grand jury** is the formal device by which a person can be accused of a serious crime.[17] In federal cases, it is a body of from 16 to 23 persons drawn from the area of the federal district court that it serves. The votes of at least 12 of the grand jurors are needed to return an indict-
1.e ment or to make a presentment. An **indictment** is a formal complaint laid before a grand jury by the prosecutor. It charges the accused with one or more crimes. If the grand jury finds that there is enough evidence for a trial, it returns a "true bill of indictment." The accused is then held for prosecution. If the grand jury does not make such a finding, the charge is dropped.

[16]Article I, Sections 9 and 10. The phrase *ex post facto* is from the Latin, meaning "after the fact."

[17]The 5th Amendment provides that the guarantee of grand jury does not extend "to cases arising in the land or naval forces." The conduct of members of the armed forces is regulated under a code of military law enacted by Congress.

Instruct

Discuss/Analyze Ask students to recall their discussion in the "Bellringer Activity" about the principle, "innocent until proven guilty." Explain that the Constitution includes several safeguards of that principle.

Have students examine the various protections of the accused included in each section. To aid in this analysis, you might ask students to discuss how each protection, prohibition, and guarantee helps protect the accused. (*Possible answers: The prohibition on bills of attainder helps ensure that the accused will have a hearing, not the summary judgment of a legislature. A grand jury ensures that the accused will not be hastily subjected to a public trial without good evidence. The right to an adequate defense prevents one-sided proceedings.*)

Encourage students to debate and discuss whether or not they think these rights make it too likely that guilty people will escape punishment. Refer students to the opening statement: "It is better that ten guilty persons go free than that one innocent person be punished." Do they agree or disagree?

ABCNEWS INTERACTIVE

The following video segments may be used to highlight aspects of the rights of the accused.

Powers of the Supreme Court Guidebook
Chapter 15: Amendment 5 (1791), The Fifth Amendment, p. 23
Chapter 18: Amendment 6 (1791), Right to a Fair Trial, p. 28
Chapter 23: *Miranda* v. *Arizona* (1966), p. 89

Teacher's Resource File
See the Supreme Court Cases file, pp. 26–27, for material to support the section.

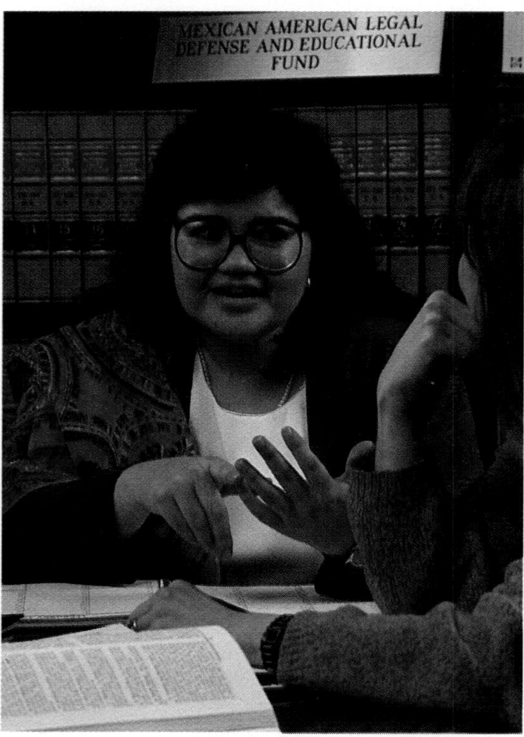

The Right to Counsel The right to be represented by a lawyer—covered under the 6th Amendment— is a fundamental part of the right to a fair trial.

A **presentment** is a formal accusation 1.f
brought by the grand jury on its own motion, rather than that of the prosecutor. It is little used in federal courts.

A grand jury's proceedings are not a trial, and since unfair harm could come if they were public, its sessions are secret. They are also one-sided—in the law, *ex parte*. That is, only the prosecution, not the defense, is present.

The 5th Amendment's grand jury provision is the only part of the Bill of Rights relating to criminal prosecution that the Supreme Court has not brought within the coverage of the 14th Amendment's Due Process Clause.

The right to grand jury is intended as a protection against overzealous prosecutors. Its critics say that it is too time-consuming, too expensive, and too likely to follow the dictates of the prosecutor. In most States today, most criminal charges are not brought by grand jury indictment. They are brought,
1.g instead, by an **information**—an affidavit in which the prosecutor swears that there is enough evidence to justify a trial; see Chapter 25, Section 3.

In addition to the rights of the accused you have just read about, the Bill of Rights sets out several guarantees of fair trial in the federal courts.[18] Fair trial is guaranteed in the State courts by a State's own constitution and by the 14th Amendment's Due Process Clause.

Double Jeopardy

The 5th Amendment says in part that no person can be "twice put in jeopardy of life or limb." Today, this prohibition against **double**
1.h **jeopardy** means that once a person has been tried for a crime, he or she cannot be tried again for that same crime.

A person can violate both a federal *and* a State law in a single act—for example, by selling narcotics. That person can then be tried for the federal crime in a federal court and for the State crime in a State court. A single act can also result in the commission of several crimes. A person who breaks into a store, steals liquor, and sells it, can be tried for illegal entry, theft, and selling liquor without a license.

In a trial in which a jury cannot agree on a verdict, there is no jeopardy. It is as though no trial had been held, and the accused can be tried again. Nor is double jeopardy involved when a case is appealed to a higher court.[19] Recall that the Supreme Court has held that the 5th Amendment's ban on double jeopardy applies against the States through the 14th Amendment, *Benton* v. *Maryland*, 1969.

---

[18] See the 5th, 6th, 7th, and 8th amendments and also Article III, Section 2, Clause 3. The practice of excluding evidence obtained in violation of the 4th Amendment is also intended to guarantee a fair trial.

[19] The Organized Crime Control Act of 1970 allows federal prosecutors to appeal sentences they believe to be too lenient. The Supreme Court has held that such appeals do not violate the double jeopardy guarantee, *United States* v. *Di Francesco*, 1980.

Activity: Teaching Heterogeneous Groups

Refer students to the quote on page 528, "It is better that ten guilty persons go free than one innocent person be punished." Have students form small groups to write and perform a skit based on the plight of an individual who is wrongly convicted of a crime. Or, students can create their skit about the consequences of guilty individuals going free as a result of constitutional protections of the rights of the accused. Regardless of which point of view each team selects, encourage students to examine the cost and/or benefit to society in pursuing the principle expressed by the quote.

Speedy and Public Trial

The 6th Amendment commands:

"In all criminal prosecutions, the accused shall enjoy the right to a speedy and public trial . . . ."

Speedy Trial The guarantee of a speedy trial is meant to ensure that government will try a person accused of crime in a reasonable time, without undue delay. But how long a delay is too long? The Supreme Court has long recognized that no two cases are the same, and each must be looked at on its own merits.

The Speedy Trial Act of 1974 says that the time between a person's arrest and the beginning of his or her federal criminal trial cannot be more than 100 days. The law does allow for some exceptions, however—in a case where the defendant must undergo extensive mental tests, for example, or when the defendant or a key witness is ill.

Public Trial The 6th Amendment says that a speedy trial must also be a public trial. The right to be tried in public is also part of the 14th Amendment's guarantee of procedural due process.

A trial must not be *too* speedy or *too* public, however. The Supreme Court threw out an Arkansas murder conviction in 1923 on just those grounds. The trial had taken only 45 minutes, and it had been held in a courtroom packed by a threatening mob.

Within reason, a judge can limit both the number and the kinds of spectators who may be present at a trial. Those who seek to disrupt a courtroom can be barred from it. A judge can order a courtroom cleared when the expected testimony may be embarrassing to a witness or to someone else not a party to the case.

Many of the questions about how public a trial should be involve the media. As noted in Chapter 19, the guarantees of fair trial and of free press often come into conflict in the courts. On the one hand: "A trial courtroom is a public place where the people generally—and representatives of the media—have a right to be present," *Richmond Newspapers, Inc.* v. *Virginia*, 1980. On the other hand, the Court has ruled, "Trial judges must take strong measures to ensure that the balance is never weighted against the accused," *Sheppard* v. *Maxwell*, 1966.

Champions of the public's right to know hold that the courts must allow the broadest possible press coverage. The Supreme Court has often held, however, that the media have only the same right as the general public to be present in a courtroom. The right to a public trial belongs to the defendant, not to the news media.

What of televised trials? Television cameras were barred from federal courtrooms until recently.[20] Most do allow some form of in-court television. Does the televising of a criminal trial violate a defendant's rights?

An early major case on the point was *Estes* v. *Texas*, 1965. The Court held that the radio and television reporting of Estes' case, which had been allowed from within the courtroom and over his objections, had been so disruptive that it denied Estes his constitutional rights to a fair trial.

Most recently, the Court held in *Chandler* v. *Florida*, 1981, that there is nothing in the Constitution to prevent a State from allowing the televising of a criminal trial—so long as steps are taken to avoid too much publicity and protect the defendant's rights.

Trial by Jury

The 6th Amendment also says that a person accused of a federal crime must be tried "by an impartial jury."[21] This guarantee reinforces an earlier one set out in the Constitution, in Article III, Section 2. The right to trial by jury is also

[20] A three-year experimental program, begun in 1991, permits television cameras to record and broadcast some civil proceedings in a few federal courtrooms.

[21] The amendment adds that the members of the jury must be drawn from "the State and district wherein the crime shall have been committed, which district shall have been previously ascertained by law." This clause gives the defendant any benefit there might be in having a court and jury familiar with the people and problems of the area. A defendant may ask to be tried in another place—seek a "change of venue"—on grounds that the people of the locality are so prejudiced in the case that an impartial jury cannot be drawn. The judge must decide whether or not a change of venue is justified.

Provide Guided Practice
Have students write an imaginary guidebook for federal prosecutors about the rights of the accused. Ask students to include each of the rights and prohibitions included in this section. The guidebook should explain how each right is to be protected and how far that right extends.

Provide Independent Practice
TRF **Teacher's Resource File**
You may wish to assign Section 3 Guided Reading and Review, Unit 5 File, p. 56, to help students master section objective content.

Enrichment

Have students create and conduct a survey in which they ask other students in their school about their feelings concerning the rights of the accused discussed in this section. (Average)

Teacher's Resource File
See the Supreme Court Cases file, pp. 70–71, for material to support the section.

Interpreting Charts Have students read carefully the instructions given to jurors. Ask students whether or not they think it is realistic to expect jurors to disregard their sympathies and keep an open mind until all the evidence is in. (*Possible answers: Yes, people can be encouraged to approach the evidence in such a way as to keep an open mind. No, it is impossible to control an individual's feelings simply by telling him or her how to react.*)

Caption Answer Articles or news reports may reflect incomplete information, faulty conclusions, or information that makes it difficult for the juror to remain open-minded and impartial.

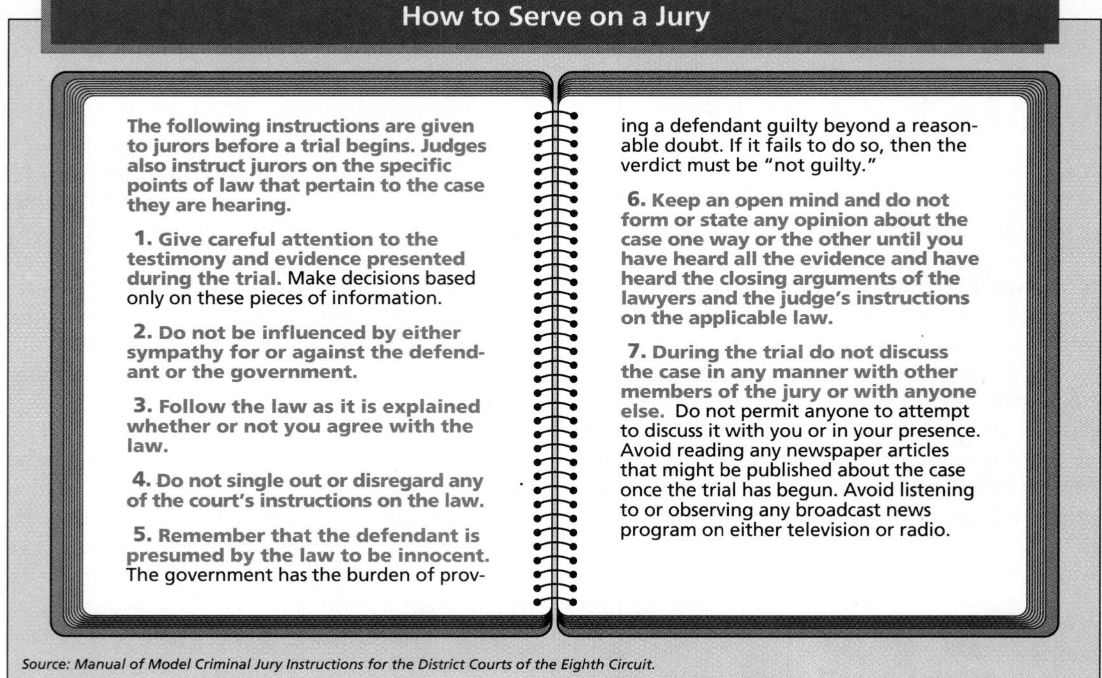

How to Serve on a Jury

The following instructions are given to jurors before a trial begins. Judges also instruct jurors on the specific points of law that pertain to the case they are hearing.

1. Give careful attention to the testimony and evidence presented during the trial. Make decisions based only on these pieces of information.

2. Do not be influenced by either sympathy for or against the defendant or the government.

3. Follow the law as it is explained whether or not you agree with the law.

4. Do not single out or disregard any of the court's instructions on the law.

5. Remember that the defendant is presumed by the law to be innocent. The government has the burden of proving a defendant guilty beyond a reasonable doubt. If it fails to do so, then the verdict must be "not guilty."

6. Keep an open mind and do not form or state any opinion about the case one way or the other until you have heard all the evidence and have heard the closing arguments of the lawyers and the judge's instructions on the applicable law.

7. During the trial do not discuss the case in any manner with other members of the jury or with anyone else. Do not permit anyone to attempt to discuss it with you or in your presence. Avoid reading any newspaper articles that might be published about the case once the trial has begun. Avoid listening to or observing any broadcast news program on either television or radio.

Source: Manual of Model Criminal Jury Instructions for the District Courts of the Eighth Circuit.

Interpreting Charts Why do you think jurors are told not to read newspaper articles or listen to or watch any news programs once the trial has begun?

binding on the States through the 14th Amendment's Due Process Clause, *Duncan* v. *Louisiana*, 1968.[22]

The trial jury is often called the petit jury—*petit*, from the French word for small. You will read more about the trial jury in the State judicial systems in Chapter 25. For now, however, note these points.

A defendant may waive the right to a jury trial. But he or she can do that only if the judge is satisfied that the defendant is fully aware of his or her rights and understands what that action means. In fact, a judge can order a jury trial even when a defendant does not want one, *One Lot Emerald Cut Stones and One Ring* v. *United States*, 1972. If a defendant waives the
1.i right, a **bench trial** is held. That is, a judge alone hears the case.

In federal practice a jury is made up of 12 persons. Several States now provide for smaller juries, however, often with six members. A federal jury can convict only by unanimous vote. Most of the States follow the same rule.[23]

In a long series of cases, dating from *Strauder* v. *West Virginia*, 1880, the Supreme Court has held that a jury must be "drawn from a fair

[22]More precisely, in *Duncan* the Court held that the 14th Amendment's Due Process Clause guarantees trial by jury for those persons accused of "serious" crimes; in *Baldwin* v. *New York*, 1970, it defined those crimes as offenses for which imprisonment for more than six months is possible.

[23]The 14th Amendment does not say that there cannot be juries of fewer than 12 persons, *Williams* v. *Florida*, 1970, but it does not allow juries of less than six members, *Ballew* v. *Georgia*, 1978. Nor does it prevent a State from providing for a conviction on a less than unanimous jury vote, *Apadaca* v. *Oregon*, 1972. But if a jury has only six members, it may convict only by a unanimous vote, *Burch* v. *Louisiana*, 1979.

SPOTLIGHT ON: Roots of Democracy

Where did the Western jury system come from? Although other cultures had a jury system, the American system probably evolved from the juries that the Norman conquerors brought to England in 1066. Their juries consisted of witnesses to the crime who judged what they had seen. Thus, the jury did not simply decide; rather, it presented evidence and testimony for and against the accused. Not until the Middle Ages did the jury's role become one of simply handing down a verdict of guilt or innocence by making judgments on testimony that others presented in a court presided over by a judge.

the small society
by Bill Yates
TRIAL BY JURY IS ONE THING EVERY AMERICAN BELIEVES IN!
UNTIL WE'RE ASKED TO SERVE ON THE JURY
10-9

Interpreting Political Cartoons Jury service is an obligation of citizenship everywhere in the United States. What comment does the cartoon make about this obligation?

cross section of the community." A person is denied the right to an impartial jury if he or she is tried by a jury from which members of any groups "playing major roles in the community" have been excluded, *Taylor* v. *Louisiana*, 1975.

In short, no person can be kept off a jury on such grounds as race, color, religion, national origin, or sex. Incredibly, the Court did not forbid the States to exclude women from jury service until as recently as 1975, in the Louisiana case just cited.

Right to an Adequate Defense

Every person accused of crime has the right to offer the best possible defense that circumstances will allow. The 6th Amendment says that a defendant has the right (1) "to be informed of the nature and cause of the accusation," (2) "to be confronted with the witnesses against him" and question them in open court, (3) "to have compulsory process for obtaining witnesses in his favor," and (4) "to have the assistance of counsel for his defence."

These key safeguards apply in the federal courts. Still, if a State fails to honor any of them, the accused can appeal a conviction on grounds that the 14th Amendment's Due Process Clause has been violated. Recall from page 489, the Supreme Court protected the right to counsel in *Gideon* v. *Wainwright,* 1963; the right of confrontation in *Pointer* v. *Texas,* 1965; and the right to call witnesses in *Washington* v. *Texas,* 1967.

These guarantees are intended to prevent the cards from being stacked in favor of the prosecution. One of the leading right-to-counsel cases, *Escobedo* v. *Illinois*, 1964, illustrates this point.

Danny Escobedo was picked up by Chicago police for questioning in the death of his brother-in-law. On the way to the police station, and then while he was being questioned there, he asked several times to see his lawyer. The police denied these requests—even though his lawyer was in the station and was tring to see him, and the police knew he was there. Through a long night of questioning by the police, Escobedo made several damaging statements. Prosecutors later used those statements in court as a major part of the evidence that led to his conviction for murder.

The Supreme Court ordered Escobedo freed from prison four years later. It held that he had been improperly denied his right to counsel.

In *Gideon* v. *Wainwright*, 1963, the Court held that an attorney must be furnished to a defendant who cannot afford one. In many places, a judge still assigns a lawyer from the local community, or a private legal aid association provides counsel. Since *Gideon*, however, a growing number of States, and many local governments, have established tax-supported public defender offices. In 1970 Congress authorized the appointment of federal public defenders or, as an alternative, the creation of community legal service organizations financed by federal grants.

Interpreting Political Cartoons Have students look at the cartoon on page 553. If given the opportunity, ask students how they would feel if they were called for jury duty.

Caption Answer That people generally agree with the concept of juries but don't like to serve as jurors.

TRF **Teacher's Resource File**
See the Supreme Court Cases file, pp. 64–65, and the Historical and Legal Documents file, p. 42, for materials to support the section.

Reading of Rights to the Accused

Before asking you any questions, it is my duty to advise you of your rights:

1. You have the right to remain silent;
2. If you choose to speak, anything you say may be used against you in a court of law or other proceeding;
3. You have the right to consult with a lawyer before answering any questions and you may have a lawyer present with you during questioning;
4. If you cannot afford a lawyer and you want one, a lawyer will be provided for you by the Commonwealth without cost to you;
5. Do you understand what I have told you?
6. You may also waive the right to counsel and your right to remain silent and you may answer any question or make any statement you wish. If you decide to answer questions you may stop at any time to consult with a lawyer.

"You Have the Right to Remain Silent" In 1989, the Supreme Court ruled that there is no exact form in which a Miranda warning must be given, but police must "reasonably convey" the rights of persons they arrest or want to question.

Self-Incrimination

The guarantee against self-incrimination is among the protections set out in the 5th Amendment—which declares that no person can be

"compelled in any criminal case to be a witness against himself."

People must receive this protection in both the federal and State courts, *Malloy* v. *Hogan*, 1964.

In a criminal case, the burden of proof is always on the prosecution. The defendant does not have to prove his or her innocence. The ban on self-incrimination prevents the prosecution from shifting the burden of proof to the defendant.

The language of the 5th Amendment suggests that the guarantee applies only to criminal cases. In fact, it covers *any* governmental proceeding in which a person is legally compelled to answer any question that could lead to a criminal charge.

The courts, not the individuals who claim it, decide when the right can be properly invoked. If the plea of self-incrimination is pushed too far, a person can be held in contempt of court.

The privilege against self-incrimination is a personal right.[24] A person *can* be forced to "rat" on another. Nor can it be used to protect such "artificial persons" as a corporation or a partnership.

The privilege does not protect a person from being fingerprinted or photographed, submitting a handwriting sample, or appearing in a police lineup, or taking a blood test. And the slurred nature of the answers a drunk-driving suspect gave to questions asked by the arresting

[24] With this major exception: A husband cannot be forced to testify against his wife, or a wife against her husband, *Trammel* v. *United States*, 1980.

Teacher's Resource File
See the Supreme Court Cases file, pp. 68–69, and the Historical and Legal Documents file, p. 39, for materials to support the section.

officer can properly be used as evidence at the suspect's trial, *Pennsylvania* v. *Muniz*, 1990.

A person cannot be forced to confess to a crime under duress—that is, as a result of torture or other physical or psychological pressure. In *Ashcraft* v. *Tennessee*, 1944, for example, the Supreme Court threw out the conviction of a man accused of hiring another to murder his wife. The confession on which his conviction rested had been secured only after some 36 hours of continuous, threatening interrogation. The questioning was conducted by officers who worked in shifts because, they said, they became so tired they had to rest.

The gulf between what the Constitution says and what goes on in some police stations can be wide, indeed. For that reason, the Supreme Court has come down hard in many cases involving the protection against self-incrimination and the right to counsel.

Recall, for example, the Court's decision in *Escobedo* v. *Illinois*. In a truly historic decision two years later, *Miranda* v. *Arizona*, 1966, the Court refined that holding. A mentally retarded man, Ernesto Miranda, had been convicted of kidnapping and rape. Ten days after the crime, the victim picked him out of a police lineup. After two hours of questioning, during which the police did not tell him of his rights, he confessed. The Supreme Court struck down his conviction. More importantly, the Court said that, from that point on, it would not uphold convictions in any cases in which suspects had not been told of their constitutional rights before police questioning. It thus laid down what has since come to be called the **Miranda Rule**. Under the rule, before police 1.j
may question suspects, those persons must be read the rights that appear next to the photo on the previous page.

The Miranda Rule has been in force for more than 25 years now, and the Supreme Court is still refining it, case by case. Most often, the rule has been strictly enforced.

There are a very few situations to which, reasonably, the rule does not apply. For example, in *Illinois* v. *Perkins*, 1990, the Supreme Court held that an undercover police officer, posing as a prisoner in a jail, did not have to give his cellmate a Miranda warning before prompting him to talk about a murder.[25]

Many police officials, and others, criticize the Miranda Rule. They see it as a serious obstacle to effective law enforcement. Many of them say that it "puts criminals back on the streets." Others applaud it, however. They hold that criminal law enforcement is most effective when it depends on independently secured evidence.

Section 3 Review

1. Define: writ of habeas corpus, bill of attainder, ex post facto law, grand jury, indictment, presentment, information, double jeopardy, bench trial, Miranda Rule
2. Under what circumstances can the right to a writ of habeas corpus be suspended?
3. On what two bases are bills of attainder forbidden?
4. What is the basic function of a grand jury?
5. What are the limits on the Constitution's guarantee of a speedy and public trial?
6. What guarantees does the Constitution make about the make-up of juries in federal trials?
7. What are the 6th Amendment guarantees of the right to an adequate defense?
8. For what reason is compulsory self-incrimination forbidden?

Critical Thinking

9. Identifying Assumptions (p. 19) Consider the statement, "It is better that ten guilty persons go free than one innocent person be punished." What does this statement suggest about the relationship between individual rights and society?

[25]In *Berkemer* v. *McCarty*, 1984, the Court held that the rule does not apply to routine traffic stops, where a motorist "most likely will be allowed to continue on his way." But once a person is placed "in custody," the rule must be observed "regardless of the nature or severity of the offense" involved.

Monitor Comprehension

Answers to Section 3 Review
1. "Key Terms" are defined on the following pages:
- **a.** writ of habeas corpus, p. 528
- **b.** bill of attainder, p. 529
- **c.** ex post facto law, p. 529
- **d.** grand jury, p. 529
- **e.** indictment, p. 529
- **f.** presentment, p. 530
- **g.** information, p. 530
- **h.** double jeopardy, p. 530
- **i.** bench trial, p. 532
- **j.** Miranda Rule, p. 535

2. In cases of rebellion or invasion. **3.** Protect individual freedom; part of the system of separation of powers. **4.** Formal means of accusing a person of a serious crime. **5.** The definition of a reasonable length of time is debatable; possible for a trial to become too public, jeopardizing the accused's right to a fair trial. **6.** Guarantees an impartial jury. **7.** Defendants have the right to know what they are accused of and who the witnesses against them are, to get witnesses in their own behalf, and to obtain a lawyer. **8.** Protection set out in the 5th Amendment. **9.** The rights of the individual should take precedence over the needs of society.

Closure

The Constitution includes safeguards to protect the rights of those accused of a crime. These safeguards take the form of protections against government actions or of specific guarantees.

As students read the next section they will learn what the Constitution requires to insure a fair trial.

Assignment Assign Section 4, pp. 536–539, for the next class.

Activity: Cooperative Learning

Time: One class period **Activity:** Write editorials about controversial topics. **Grouping:** Partners **Purpose:** Begin this activity by reading to the class a few newspaper editorials and discussing the nature of the writing in each. Then assign one of the following issues to each pair of students and have partners write opposing viewpoint editorials about the topic assigned: (1) Federal Government drug testing programs; (2) the exclusionary rule; (3) limits on the right to bear arms; (4) the televising of criminal trials; (5) the Miranda rule. **Roles:** Have students decide who will write in favor of the topic and who will write in opposition to it. **Outcome:** Have partners read their opposing viewpoint editorials to the class.

Teacher's Resource File
See the Unit 5 File, p. 57, for the Section 3 Quiz.

Reteach

Have students create an illustrated glossary of the "Key Terms" in this section. Where possible, include specific examples of a practical application of the term.

SECTION 4
Rights of the Accused: Punishment

FOCUS

Teacher's Resource File See the Unit 5 File, p. 58, for the Section 4 Quiz.

Objectives

20.7 Explain how the Constitution sets limits on punishment for a crime.

20.8 Identify the reason why the Constitution defines the crime of treason.

Bellringer Activity Write the following on the chalkboard: *The Constitution prohibits cruel and unusual punishment.* Then ask students to discuss their understanding of the phrase "cruel and unusual." Make sure students are able to explain the reasons for their arguments.

State the Purpose The Constitution establishes several general limits on the punishment of those convicted of a crime. In Section 4, students will examine these limits as established both by the Constitution and by Supreme Court interpretations. They will also learn why the Constitution defines the crime of treason.

ABCNEWS INTERACTIVE

The following video segment may be used to highlight aspects of the constitutional limitations on punishment.

POWERS OF THE SUPREME COURT GUIDEBOOK
Chapter 19: Amendment 8 (1791), Bails, Fines, and Punishments p. 30

4 Rights of the Accused: Punishment

Find Out:

- How does the Constitution set limits on punishments for crime?
- For what reason does the Constitution define the crime of treason?

Key Term:
bail

Once more, think about the statement, "It is better that ten guilty persons go free than one innocent person be punished." Now how do you feel about it?

What about those persons who are guilty and are convicted, and so do not go free? How should they be treated? As you see in this section, the Constitution provides its most specific answers to that question in the 8th Amendment. And here you will also look at treason, at the nature of that singular crime and its punishment.

Excessive Bail, Fines

The 8th Amendment says, in part:

> "Excessive bail shall not be required, nor excessive fines imposed. . . ."

Each of the State constitutions sets out similar restrictions. The general rule here is that the bail or fine in a case must bear a reasonable relationship to the seriousness of the crime involved.

Bail is a sum of money that the accused may be required to post (deposit with the court) as a guarantee that he or she will appear in court at the proper time. The use of bail is justified on two grounds: (1) A person should not be jailed until his or her guilt is established; and (2) a defendant is better able to prepare for trial outside of a jail. 1.a

But, note, the Constitution does not say that all persons accused of crime are automatically entitled to bail. Rather, the guarantee is that, in those cases where bail is set, the amount of that bail will not be excessive.[26]

The leading case on bail in the federal courts is *Stack* v. *Boyle*, 1951. There the Court ruled that "bail set at a figure higher than the amount reasonably calculated" to insure a defendant's appearance at a trial "is 'excessive' under the 8th Amendment."

Preventive Detention In 1984 Congress provided for the "preventive detention" of some persons accused of committing federal crimes. Under the law, federal judges can order the holding of an accused felon without bail if, after a hearing, the judge finds that "no condition or combination of conditions will reasonably assure the appearance" of the accused in court and also protect others and the community from harm by that person.

Critics of the law claim that preventive detention really amounts to punishment before trial; and, they say, it undercuts the presumption of innocence to which all defendants in this country are entitled.

The Supreme Court upheld the 1984 law, 6–3, in *United States* v. *Salerno*, 1987. More than half the States have recently adopted preventive detention laws.

Cruel and Unusual Punishment

The 8th Amendment also forbids "cruel and unusual punishment." The 14th Amendment extends that prohibition against the States, *Robinson* v. *California,* 1962. Each State constitution contains a similar provision.

The Supreme Court decided its first cruel and unusual case over 100 years ago. In *Wilkerson* v. *Utah,* 1879, a territorial court had sentenced a convicted murderer to death by a firing squad. The Court held that that punishment was not forbidden by the Constitution. The

[26]A defendant can appeal the denial of release on bail or the amount of the bail. Bail is usually set in accord with the charge and the reputation and resources of the accused. Those with little or no income often have trouble raising bail; so, the federal and most State courts release many defendants "on their own recognizance," *i.e.*, on their honor. Failure to appear for trial, "jumping bail," is itself a punishable crime.

Reading Strategy: Question Writing

As a preparation for reading, have students read the section's main headings. Then ask students to write a question based on each of the headings, and to look for the answers to their questions as they read.

Vocabulary

Point out the "Key Term" on page 536. Below are some additional terms whose meanings may help students to understand the section content.

—**capital punishment:** the death penalty
—**treason:** (1) waging war against the United States, or (2) adhering to its enemies; giving them aid and comfort LEP

kinds of penalties the Constitution intended to prevent, said the Court, were such barbaric tortures as burning at the stake, crucifixion, drawing and quartering, "and all others in the same line of unnecessary cruelty."

Since then, the Court has heard only a handful of cruel and unusual cases—except for those relating to capital punishment, as you will see. More often than not, the Court has rejected the cruel and unusual punishment claim.[27]

Louisiana v. *Resweber*, 1947, is typical. There the Court found that it was not unconstitutional to subject a convicted murderer to a second electrocution after the chair had failed to work properly on the first occasion.

Rummel v. *Estelle*, 1980, is another example. There a Texas court had imposed a mandatory life sentence on a "three-time loser"—even though the three crimes of which the individual had been convicted were all petty and nonviolent, and had altogether involved a small amount of money—less than $230.

However, the Court has held some punishments to be cruel and unusual. Thus, in *Robinson* v. *California*, 1962, the Supreme Court held that a State law that defined narcotics addiction as a crime to be punished, rather than an illness to be treated, violated the 8th and 14th amendments.[28] And, to take another example, in *Estelle* v. *Gamble*, 1976, it ruled that a Texas prison

[27]The prohibition of cruel and unusual punishment is limited to criminal matters. It does not forbid paddling or similar punishments in the public schools, *Ingraham* v. *Wright*, 1977.

[28]But, notice, that does not mean that buying, selling, or possessing narcotics cannot be made a crime. Such criminal laws are designed to punish persons for their behavior, not for being ill.

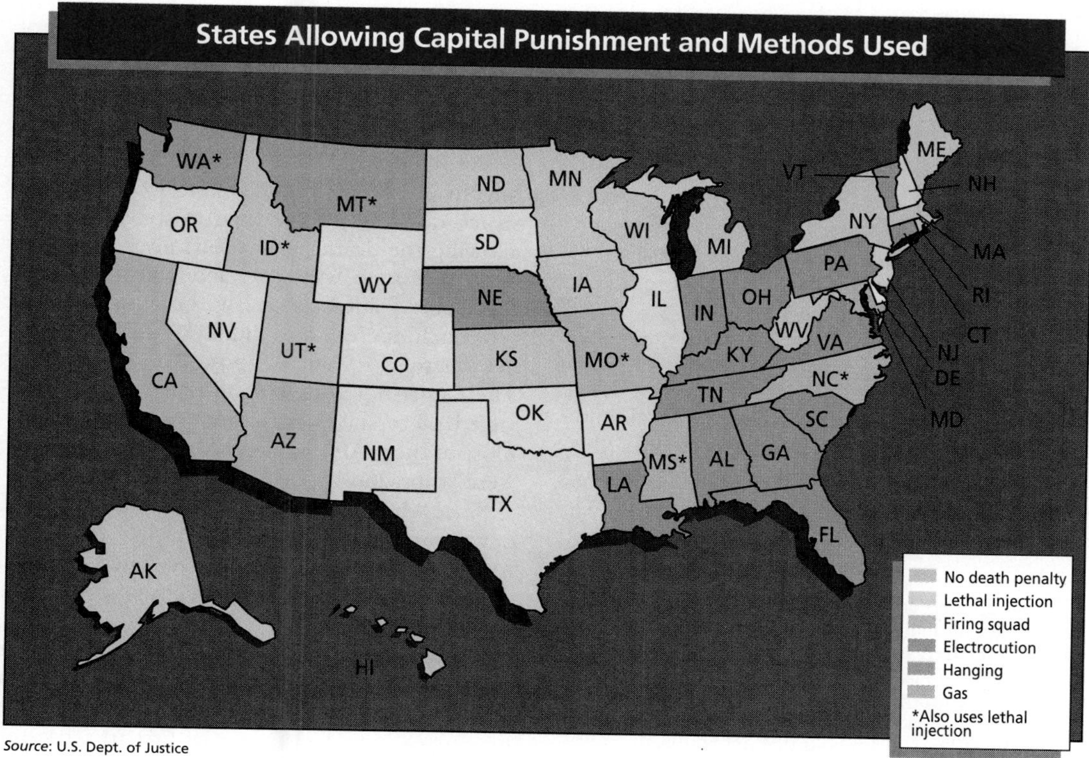

Interpreting Maps Most States allow the use of capital punishment. Why do you think some States, such as Nevada, Illinois, and Texas, use lethal injection rather than one of the other methods?

Interpreting Maps Ask students whether they see a common characteristic among the States that do not have a death penalty. (*All the States are in the northern part of the country.*)

Caption Answer Possible answer: Lethal injection is regarded as a more humane method of execution.

INSTRUCT

Explain/Discuss Have students discuss the idea of bail and preventive detention. How do these ideas fit within the concept of "innocent until proven guilty"? (*Students may say that they are reasonable protections; others might say that they imply guilt and punish before conviction.*) Should people who cannot afford bail be denied its advantages?

Next have students discuss their understanding of the concept, "cruel and unusual punishment." Do they agree with the Court decisions mentioned in the text? Ask students to arrive at a general definition of *cruel and unusual.* Use this discussion to introduce the topic of the death penalty. Have students apply their definitions to the death penalty. Then have students discuss how the Supreme Court has ruled on this subject. Do students' definitions of *cruel and unusual* yield different results from those of the Supreme Court?

Finally, discuss with students the constitutional treatment of treason. Ask students to explain how treason might be used as a "weapon in the hands of tyrants."(*Tyrants might label as traitors all those who merely disagree with them.*)

SPOTLIGHT ON: Behind the Scenes

For some people, certain methods of capital punishment are more cruel and unusual than others. An 18th-century Frenchman, Joseph I. Guillotin, had a special sensitivity to that fact. He devised the guillotine to execute criminals more humanely by quickly and relatively painlessly chopping off their heads! Though popular in England among 19th-century opponents of hanging, the guillotine was never adopted in the United States. Today, methods of execution practiced by the various States that have a death penalty include lethal injection or lethal gas, electrocution, hanging, and firing squad.

Interpreting Charts: Multicultural Awareness Ask students to compare the number of executions in the United States with those in other countries. What possible explanations for the difference can student identify? (*Possible answers: higher population, thus more crime; greater public support for capital punishment.*)

Caption Answer According to the chart, not all States impose capital punishment.

Provide Guided Practice Create two teams to conduct a debate on the issue of the death penalty. Have each side frame the debate in terms of the constitutional prohibition of cruel and unusual punishment. Also, ask students to include references to appropriate Supreme Court cases to make their arguments. Those students not on one of the teams should critique each side's presentation by citing information from the text.

Provide Independent Practice

TRF **Teacher's Resource File** You may wish to assign Section 4 Guided Reading and Review, Unit 5 File, p. 59, to help students master section objective content.

Global Awareness

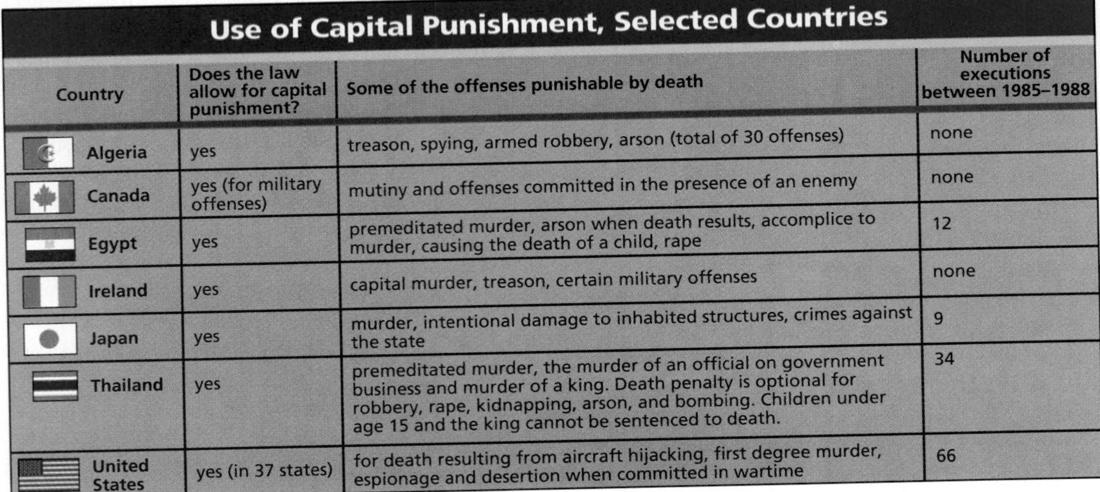

Use of Capital Punishment, Selected Countries

Country	Does the law allow for capital punishment?	Some of the offenses punishable by death	Number of executions between 1985–1988
Algeria	yes	treason, spying, armed robbery, arson (total of 30 offenses)	none
Canada	yes (for military offenses)	mutiny and offenses committed in the presence of an enemy	none
Egypt	yes	premeditated murder, arson when death results, accomplice to murder, causing the death of a child, rape	12
Ireland	yes	capital murder, treason, certain military offenses	none
Japan	yes	murder, intentional damage to inhabited structures, crimes against the state	9
Thailand	yes	premeditated murder, the murder of an official on government business and murder of a king. Death penalty is optional for robbery, rape, kidnapping, arson, and bombing. Children under age 15 and the king cannot be sentenced to death.	34
United States	yes (in 37 states)	for death resulting from aircraft hijacking, first degree murder, espionage and desertion when committed in wartime	66

Source: Amnesty International

Interpreting Charts: Multicultural Awareness Capital punishment can be imposed in the United States for the federal crime of treason. How can you tell by the chart that capital punishment is also imposed by the States?

inmate could not properly be denied needed medical care.

But again most cases have gone the other way. Thus, in *Rhodes* v. *Chapman*, 1981, the Court held that putting two prisoners in a cell built for one is not cruel and unusual.

Capital Punishment

Is the death penalty cruel and unusual and therefore unconstitutional? For years the Supreme Court was reluctant to face that highly charged issue. In fact, it did not give a direct answer to that question until 1976.[29]

The Court did meet the issue more or less directly in *Furman* v. *Georgia*, 1972. There it struck down all of the then existing State laws allowing the death penalty, but *not* because that penalty as such was cruel and unusual. Rather, the Court voided those laws because they gave too much discretion to judges or juries in deciding whether or not to impose the death penalty. The Court noted that of all those persons convicted of capital crimes, only "a random few," most of them African American or poor or both, were "capriciously selected" for execution.

Since that decision, 37 States have passed new capital punishment laws. At first, those laws took one of two forms: Several States removed all discretion from the sentencing process. They made the death penalty mandatory for certain crimes, such as the killing of a police officer or murder done while committing rape, kidnap, or arson. Other States provided for a two-stage process in capital cases: a trial first to settle the issue of guilt or innocence; then a second hearing to decide whether the circumstances justify a sentence of death.

[29]The phrase "capital punishment" comes from the Latin *caput*, meaning "head"; in many cultures, the historically preferred method for executing criminals was beheading (decapitation).

The Court avoided a direct ruling on the constitutionality of capital punishment laws in several cases before 1972. Thus, it did hold that neither death by firing squad (*Wilkerson* v. *Utah*) nor by a second electrocution (*Louisiana* v. *Resweber*) is unconstitutional. But in neither of those cases, nor in others, did it deal with the question of the death penalty as such.

Enrichment

Have students write a poem or short story in which they express the importance of imposing punishment in a fair manner. Students' work should invoke the importance of spiritual or societal values such as fairness and humanity. (Easy)

Teacher's Resource File
See the Supreme Court Cases file, pp. 86–87, for material to support the section.

Activity: For Gifted Students

Theme: Justice Have students research and report on the history of the death penalty in the United States, tracing the development of capital punishment from colonial times to the present day. Encourage students to evaluate past practices in light of current standards of justice and fairness as expressed in Supreme Court opinions such as *Furman* v. *Georgia*, *Ford* v. *Wainwright*, and *Thompson* v. *Oklahoma*. Students can present their findings in the form of an oral or written report. Or, they may create an illustrated and annotated timeline.

The Supreme Court has considered scores of challenges to those newer laws. It found the mandatory death penalty laws to be unconstitutional. They were "unduly harsh and rigidly unworkable," and simply attempts to "paper over" the decision in *Furman*, said the Court in *Woodson* v. *North Carolina*, 1976. But the two-stage approach to capital punishment is constitutional. In *Gregg* v. *Georgia*, 1976, the Court held, for the first time, that the "punishment of death does not invariably violate the Constitution." It ruled that well-drawn two-stage laws can practically eliminate "the risk that [the death penalty] will be inflicted in an arbitrary or capricious manner."

A State can impose the death penalty only for "crimes resulting in the death of the victim," *Coker* v. *Georgia*, 1977; and a capital punishment law "must allow for whatever mitigating circumstances" may be present in a case, *Roberts* v. *Louisiana*, 1977.

Opponents of the death penalty continue to appeal cases to the Court, but to no real avail. The sum of the Court's many decisions in those cases over the past fifteen years is this: The death penalty, fairly applied, is acceptable under the Constitution.

Death penalty cases raise many difficult questions. That point can be seen in these recent cases, each of them decided by a divided Court. In *Ford* v. *Wainwright*, 1986, it ruled that a person who is insane at the time set for his execution cannot be put to death. In *Thompson* v. *Oklahoma*, 1988, the Court held that the 8th and 14th amendments prohibit the execution of a man for a murder he committed when he was 15 years old. But, a year later, the Court allowed the execution of a man for a murder he had committed at age 16, *Wilkins* v. *Missouri*, 1989; and it came to the same decision in *Stanford* v. *Kentucky*, 1989, where the murderer's age was 17.

Most recently, the Court has ruled that, in deciding whether a death penalty should be imposed or not, a jury can consider the impact the murderer's crime has had on the victim's family, *Payne* v. *Tennessee*, 1991.

Treason

Treason against the United States is the only crime that is defined in the Constitution. The ❂ Framers provided a specific definition of the crime because they knew that the charge of treason is a favorite weapon in the hands of tyrants.

Treason, says Article III, Section 3, can consist of only two things: either (1) levying war against the United States or (2) "adhering to their enemies, giving them aid and comfort." No person can be convicted of the crime "unless on the testimony of two witnesses to the same overt act, or on confession in open court."

The law of treason covers all American citizens, at home or abroad, and all permanent resident aliens. Congress has established the death penalty as the maximum penalty for treason against the United States, but no person has ever been executed for the crime.

Note that a person can commit treason only in wartime. But Congress has also made it a crime, in either peace- or wartime, to commit espionage or sabotage, to attempt to overthrow the government by force, or to conspire to do any of these things.

Most of the State constitutions also provide for treason. John Brown was hanged as a traitor to Virginia after his raid on Harpers Ferry in 1859. He is believed to be the only person ever to be executed for treason against a State.

Section 4 Review

1. **Define:** bail
2. What constitutes "excessive" bail?
3. (a) What punishments does the Constitution prohibit? (b) What is the Supreme Court's view of capital punishment?
4. For what reason is treason specifically defined by the Constitution?

Critical Thinking

5. **Demonstrating Reasoned Judgment** (p. 19) Based on what you have read, what is the point at which a punishment becomes "unnecessarily" cruel?

★

Monitor Comprehension

Answers to Section 4 Review
1. The "Key Term" is defined on the following page:
a. bail, p. 536
2. When the bail amount is higher than the amount calculated to ensure a defendant's appearance. **3.** (a) Cruel and unusual punishment. (b) It is constitutional if applied fairly, not arbitrarily or capriciously. It is also prohibited for people of a certain age and mental state.
4. To prevent it from being used as a weapon against those who disagree with government.
5. Answers will vary. Students may suggest that a punishment that goes beyond the point of deterring the criminal or others from committing a crime is unnecessarily cruel.

Teacher's Resource File See the Unit 5 File, p. 60, for the Section 4 Quiz.

Closure

Remind students that the Constitution's 8th Amendment protects the accused in their punishment. The amendment prohibits excessive fines and bail and cruel and unusual punishment. The Supreme Court has held that the death penalty, if administered fairly, is constitutional. The only crime defined in the Constitution is treason. In the next chapter, students will learn about the constitutional guarantees of civil rights.

Assignment Assign Section 1 of Chapter 21, pp. 545–549, for the next class period.

❂ Spotlight on: Global Awareness

The charge of treason is less carefully defined in other countries, and it is often used as a means of political repression. During the Cultural Revolution in China, anyone with "old customs, old habits, old culture," or "old thinking" became a target of the Red Guard as an enemy of the People's Republic. Those so suspected had their homes ransacked and were publicly humiliated. Some were beaten to death or imprisoned for years. Similar abuses of the charge of treason during the past few decades were common in Uganda, Argentina, Cambodia, and the former Soviet bloc nations.

Reteach

Write *bail, cruel and unusual, capital punishment, and treason* on the board. Have students explain the significance of these words in the context of rights of the accused. *(1) Imposed to ensure that defendants appear in court; frees defendants to prepare their cases. Constitution prohibits excessive bail. (2) Level of punishment prohibited by the Constitution. (3) The death penalty, which the Supreme Court has held to be constitutional if applied fairly. (4) Only crime defined in the Constitution; an accusation of treason could be used as a political weapon.*

TEACHING

Critical Thinking

Formulating Questions

Objective

Evaluate given information and use it to formulate questions to gain additional information.

INSTRUCT

Before students begin, ask them to explain why people ask questions. (*To get information.*) Next, have students read the selection.

As students complete each step, invite them to share their responses. Discuss the importance of knowing how to ask questions in order to make an informed decision. You may wish to have each student choose one of the groups in the selection to interview. Have students write five questions that they would like to ask the side of their choice.

Answers 1. (a) A gun control ordinance. (b) The proordinance side feels that the law will reduce violent crime; the antiordinance side feels that owning a gun is a constitutional right and that denying it to people will leave them helpless. **2.** (a) Both sides cite crime statistics. (b) Pro: The ordinance would lower crime. Con: People, not guns, kill; the ordinance will not disarm criminals. **3.** These questions can be used to clarify each side's position. **4.** (a) What do they propose to do about preventing criminals from getting guns? (b) Do they have any better suggestion to lower the crime rate?

Formulating Questions

Experts on creativity maintain that the quality of one's creativity depends on the quality of one's questions. The same can be said about the quality of thinking critically.

Formulating questions means creating questions that lead to a deeper understanding of an issue. Being able to formulate good questions enables you to discover new information through inquiry. Good questions also can help you sharpen your understanding of a topic—even questions you might fear will be dismissed as not being worth asking. Follow these steps to practice formulating good questions.

1. Identify the topic. Try to identify the main idea of the piece of information you are considering. By finding the main idea, you can narrow down your area of inquiry and formulate questions that get at the heart of the matter. Read the selection below and answer the following questions: (a) What is the topic of the dispute described below? (b) What are the two opposing views?

2. Locate the important details. Consider information that you already have on the subject. Then you will be able to identify the questions you will need to ask. Answer the following questions: (a) What factual information does each side use to support its argument? (b) What opinions does each side use to support its argument?

3. Keep in mind these basic questions: Who? What? When? Where? Why? How? These six questions serve as the foundation of any inquiry into a topic. How can you use these questions to gain a deeper understanding of the information below?

4. Determine what else you need to know about the topic, and formulate your questions. Once you understand the topic, you can formulate the questions that will enable you to gather more information. Answer the following questions: (a) What would you want to know about the ordinance supporters' argument before you supported gun control? (b) What would you want to know about the opponents before you supported their view?

Local officials have introduced an ordinance that outlaws the private possession, use, or sale of all handguns in the city. The only exception would be those handguns kept in gun collections or used only for target-shooting purposes.

Most people who support the ordinance have argued that its adoption would help to reduce violent crime in the city. They have built much of their case on the FBI's crime reports, which show that firearms are now used to commit more than 11,000 murders, 200,000 aggravated assaults, and 180,000 robberies in this country every year. Supporters also point to thousands of accidental deaths and injuries that occur every year because of the careless handling of firearms.

Opponents of the ordinance cite the Constitution's 2nd Amendment and what they insist is the Constitution's guarantee of their right to keep and bear arms. Opponents also insist that the ordinance aims at the wrong target. Guns don't kill people, they say, people do. They also point out that criminals will always be able to get guns, and that outlawing handguns will only make it more difficult for innocent people to defend themselves. The opponents also make use of FBI statistics, pointing out that the average person can expect to live well over 20,000 years before being murdered.

Teacher's Resource File
See the Unit 5 File, p. 61, for the Skill Application for this lesson.

Chapter-in-Brief

Scan all headings, photographs, charts, and other visuals in the chapter before reading the section summaries below.

Section 1 Due Process of Law (pp. 517–520) The 5th and 14th amendments guarantee that government cannot deprive a person of "life, liberty, or property, without due process of law." The meaning of due process has developed along two lines: procedural and substantive. Procedural due process means that government must act according to fair procedures. Substantive due process means that laws and policies must be fair.

The government does have the power to protect and promote public health, safety, morals, and general welfare. The exercise of this police power can lead to conflicts with the rights of individuals.

The guarantee of due process has led to the creation of a right of privacy. The most controversial applications of the right of privacy have come in cases involving the question of abortion.

Section 2 Freedom and Security of the Person (pp. 521–526) The Constitution guarantees more than three dozen individual liberties. Among them are those intended to guarantee security of the person.

The 13th Amendment was added to the Constitution in 1865 in order to end slavery. This amendment has also enabled Congress and the Courts to destroy the "badges and incidents of slavery," as well.

The 3rd and 4th amendments aim to make people "secure in their persons, houses, papers, and effects." This includes the guarantee against unreasonable searches and seizures.

The 2nd Amendment guarantees people the right to keep and bear arms. However, government does have the power to restrict the right.

Section 3 Rights of the Accused (pp. 528–535) The Constitution sets out several guarantees for persons accused of crime. These include the right to seek a writ of habeas corpus, which aims at preventing unjust arrests and imprisonments. The Constitution also prohibits bills of attainder, which are legislative acts that inflict punishment without court trials. In addition, Congress and the States are prohibited from passing ex post facto laws.

The Federal and State governments guarantee all who are accused of crime a fair trial. No person, for example, can be exposed to double jeopardy.

The Federal Government guarantees that those accused of a serious federal crime will not face charges unless indicted by a grand jury. This right, however, is not guaranteed against the States by the 14th Amendment.

Accused persons are guaranteed the right to a speedy and public trial. The accused also have the right to a trial by jury. And, they have the right to an adequate defense. This means that the accused must be allowed access to a lawyer. In addition, the accused cannot be made to testify against themselves.

Section 4 Rights of the Accused: Punishment (pp. 536–539) According to the federal and State constitutions, the accused must not face excessive bail or fines. This prohibition is based on the concept that the accused are innocent until proven guilty.

The Constitution also includes a prohibition against cruel and unusual punishment. The Supreme Court, however, has consistently held that the death penalty is constitutional if it is fairly applied.

Treason is the only crime specifically defined in the Constitution because the Constitution wanted to prevent tyrants from using the charge of treason to punish political opponents.

541

Teaching Suggestions for CHAPTER-IN-BRIEF

Below are some of the possible uses for the Chapter-in-Brief:

To Preview the Chapter You may want to assign the Chapter-in-Brief page and the Section Outlines from the Teacher's Resource File before beginning Chapter 20 to introduce students to "Key Terms" and concepts in each section.

To Review the Chapter When students have completed Chapter 20, you might want to assign the Chapter-in-Brief as a tool for review, along with the Guided Reading and Reviews from the Teacher's Resource File.

To Omit the Chapter If you wish to skip Chapter 20, it may be helpful to assign the Chapter-in-Brief to students as a review before continuing to another chapter. You may also want to assign the Chapter 20 Test to assess students' knowledge of the material. Then, specific portions of Chapter 20 may be assigned to students needing reinforcement of "Key Terms" and concepts.

Teacher's Resource File See the Unit 5 File for the following materials:

- Section Outlines, pp. 49, 52, 55, 58.
- Guided Reading and Reviews, pp. 50, 53, 56, 59.
- Chapter 20 Test, pp. 65–67.

ADDITIONAL RESOURCES

1987 v. *The Constitution*. Video. PBS Video. 60 min.
Barron, J.A. *Constitutional Law*. West, 3rd ed., 1991.
Corwin, E.S. *Corwin and Peltason's Understanding the Constitution*. Harcourt Brace Jovanovich, 12th ed., 1991.
Faux, Marian. *Roe v. Wade: The Untold Story of the Landmark Supreme Court Decision*. MacMillan, 1988, New American Library, 1989.
Keenan, Joseph. *The Constitution of the United States: Origins, Documents, and Interpretations*. Dorsey, 2nd ed., 1988.
Klotter, J.C. *Constitutional Law*. Anderson, 6th ed., 1991.
Protecting Your Rights. Sound filmstrip. Produced by Globe Filmstrips, distributed by Coronet Media, 1979. Color. 6 parts, 9 min. each.

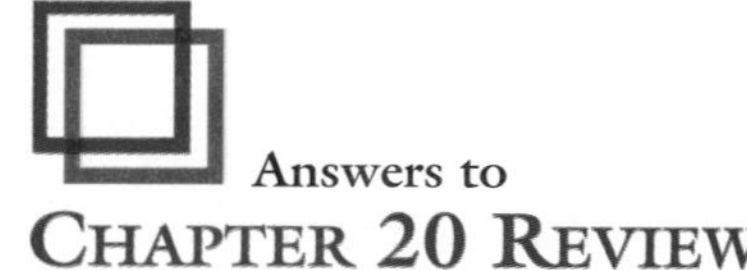

Answers to CHAPTER 20 REVIEW

Vocabulary and Key Terms

Matching
1. grand jury
2. due process
3. double jeopardy
4. police power
5. bench trial

True or False
1. True.
2. False—the correct term is *bill of attainder*.
3. False—the correct term is *Miranda Rule*.
4. True.
5. True.
6. True.

Word Relationships
1. *Writ of habeas corpus* (a) does not belong. The other items are all prohibited by the Constitution.
2. *Miranda rule* (d) does not belong. The other items involve means by which individuals may be accused of crimes.
3. *Police power* (d) does not belong. The other items deal with issues of individual rights and due process, while police power refers to a government's power to act to protect the public.

Main Ideas

Section 1
1. *Procedural,* which means the way a law is applied, and *substantive,* which involves the content of a law. **2.** Even laws that are fair and just in content are worthless if applied unfairly. **3.** The exercise of police power sometimes leads to conflict with the rights of individuals. Generally, courts have permitted the exercise of police power in cases of conflict. **4.** The Constitution's due process guarantees create this right.

Section 2
5. (a) To end slavery. (b) Congress and the Courts have in recent years expanded their view of what constitutes the "badges and incidences of slavery." **6.** The amendment does not, as widely argued, guarantee people the right to bear arms free of restriction by government. **7.** To protect people from unreasonable searches and seizures; to ensure that people are secure in their persons and property. **8.** It ensures that evidence gathered as a result of an unreasonable search or seizure cannot be used against them.

Section 3
9. (a) Crimes are legal wrongs against the public. (b) They must be punished so that a society can preserve itself. **10.** (a) Because of the basic concept that people are presumed innocent until proven guilty. (b) By protecting the right to seek a writ of habeas corpus; prohibiting bills of attainder and ex post facto laws; ensuring that no one shall be held answerable for a crime without indictment by a grand jury; ensuring against double jeopardy; guaranteeing a speedy, public trial, trial by jury, and the right to an adequate defense; prohibiting forced self-incrimination. **11.** Trials must be speedy and public, and they must

Chapter Review

Vocabulary and Key Terms

due process (p. 517)
police power (p. 519)
search warrant (p. 519)
probable cause (p. 523)
exclusionary rule (p. 524)
writ of habeas corpus (p. 528)
bill of attainder (p. 529)
ex post facto law (p. 529)
grand jury (p. 529)
indictment (p. 529)
presentment (p. 530)
information (p. 530)
double jeopardy (p. 530)
bench trial (p. 532)
Miranda Rule (p. 535)

Matching: *Review the key terms in the list above. If you are not sure of a term's meaning, look up the term and review its definition. Choose a term from the list above that best matches each description.*

1. a group convened by a court to determine whether or not there is enough evidence against a person to justify a trial
2. a constitutional guarantee that a government will not deprive any person of life, liberty, or property by any unfair, arbitrary, or unreasonable action
3. trial a second time for a crime of which the accused was acquitted in the first trial
4. the power of a government to act to ensure the overall welfare of a society
5. a trial without a jury

True or False: *Determine whether each statement is true or false. If it is true, write "true." If it is false, change the underlined word or words to make the statement true.*

1. An ex post facto law is one applied to acts performed before the law was passed.
2. A legislative act that inflicts punishment upon a person or group without a trial is a Miranda Rule.
3. A listing of the rights of which suspects must be advised before police questioning is called information.
4. When a person is tried twice for the same crime, he or she may have been exposed to double jeopardy.
5. An indictment is a formal finding by a grand jury that there is sufficient evidence to warrant a trial.
6. Police generally need a search warrant in order to search someone's house.

Word Relationships: *Three of the terms in each of the following sets of terms are related. Choose the term that does not belong and explain why it does not belong.*

1. (a) writ of habeas corpus (b) excessive bail (c) ex post facto law (d) bill of attainder
2. (a) indictment (b) presentment (c) information (d) Miranda Rule
3. (a) search warrant (b) exclusionary rule (c) Miranda Rule (d) police power

Main Ideas

Section 1 (pp. 517–520)

1. Along what two lines has the Supreme Court developed the meaning of due process?
2. For what reasons is it necessary to have both substantive and procedural due process?
3. Describe the relationship between the States' police power and due process of law.
4. From what part of the Constitution does the right of privacy stem?

Section 2 (pp. 521–526)

5. (a) What was the aim of the 13th Amendment? (b) How have Congress and the courts changed in their view of this amendment in the last 25 years?
6. In what sense is the 2nd Amendment misunderstood?
7. What is the aim of the 4th Amendment?
8. How does the exclusionary rule help protect citizens?

Section 3 (pp. 528–535)

9. (a) What are crimes? (b) Why must they be punished?
10. (a) For what reason does the Constitution protect the rights of those accused of crime? (b) In what ways does the Constitution protect the rights of those accused of crime?
11. What are the key constitutional guarantees of a fair trial?
12. (a) What guarantees and rules exist to ensure the accused the right not to incriminate themselves? (b) What guarantees exist to ensure the accused an adequate defense?

Section 4 (pp. 536–539)

13. What are the key constitutional guarantees regarding punishment of the guilty?
14. Under what circumstances has the Supreme Court found death penalty laws to be unconstitutional?
15. For what reason is treason the only crime defined in the Constitution?

Critical Thinking

1. **Recognizing Ideologies** (p. 19) Summarize the belief that underlies the power of the States to exercise their police power, even at the expense of certain individual rights.
2. **Identifying Assumptions** (p. 19) What assumptions underlie the existence of the Miranda Rule and the specific provisions included in it?
3. **Checking Consistency** (p. 19) Recall that Congress passed a law by which the accused can be held without bail when there is reason to believe the person will commit a crime. In your opinion, does this law violate the principle of presumed innocence until proven guilty?

Getting Involved

1. **Writing Your Opinion** Create a survey designed to gauge citizens' opinions of the Constitution's civil liberties protections. Begin by listing the different rights discussed in this chapter; for example, due process and the right against self-incrimination. Next, note some of the more controversial aspects of these rights; for example, the fact that evidence gathered illegally cannot be used against a person. Write an introduction to your survey explaining why you are interested in people's opinions on this topic. Then create a list of questions designed to gather those opinions. Revise your questions to ensure that they do not convey your own bias on the issues under consideration. Correct any errors, then make a final draft.
2. **Cooperative Activity** Work as a class to create a quiz game called "Civil Rights and Liberties." Have each member of the class write a list of five questions and answers involving some aspect of civil rights and liberties. For example, one question could ask whether or not it is constitutional for police to stop cars randomly to check for drunk drivers. Then, decide as a class on the rules for the game. Encourage students to add more questions to the game as ideas occur to them.
3. **Creating a Political Advertisement** Create an advertisement that illustrates your view of one of the issues discussed in this chapter. Your ad can express support or opposition to your chosen constitutional principle or interpretation.

Critical Thinking

1. Students should suggest that the exercise of police power reflects the idea that the interests of the many are more important than the interests of the few. **2.** Students might observe that the Miranda Rule implies that many people do not know their rights. **3.** Answers will vary. Students should question on what basis a person who is technically innocent can be considered a danger and have the potential to commit a crime.

Getting Involved

1–3. Answers and results will vary, but students should demonstrate an understanding of the concepts in the chapter.

involve a jury—unless this right is waived by the defendant. Also, the accused cannot be exposed to double jeopardy. **12.** (a) The 5th Amendment protects people against self-incrimination. The Miranda Rule ensures that the accused are warned of their rights to remain silent and to have counsel. (b) The accused must be informed of the accusation, be allowed to confront witnesses, be allowed to obtain witnesses for his or her defense, and to have counsel.

Section 4

13. No excessive bail or fines are allowed, and punishment cannot be cruel or unusual. **14.** Death penalty laws in which the subjects are "capriciously and arbitrarily selected" have been found unconstitutional. Also, those that were "unduly harsh and rigidly unworkable" were struck down. 15. The Framers knew that a charge of treason was a favorite weapon of tyrants who wanted to do away with political enemies.

Chapter 21 Resources

In the Teacher's Resource File
The following materials are found in the Teacher's Resource File box.

Instructional Support: Unit 5 File

For the Section
Outlines, pp. 71, 74, 77, 80
Guided Reading and Reviews, pp. 72, 75, 78, 81
Quizzes, pp. 73, 76, 79, 82

For the Chapter
Skill Application, p. 83
Case Study on Contemporary Issues, pp. 84–86
Chapter Test, pp. 87–89
Additional Test Questions, pp. 90–92

Enrichment Support Files

Participatory Government Activities, pp. 20–27
Supreme Court Cases, pp. 16, 32–33, 50–51, 88–89
Historical and Legal Documents, pp. 30, 31, 36, 52, 53

Computer Test Bank and Assessment
Transparency Package, pp. 21, 46, 56

Chapter 21 Focus

Introduce the Chapter Tell students that in this chapter they will learn about past discrimination and the federal laws which now work to guarantee the fair and equal treatment of all Americans. Read with students the Chapter Preview and Objectives.

Writing Activity Direct students' attention to "Describe." Have students write a description of an instance of discrimination from their personal experience or one which they may have heard about, read about, or seen on television.

Motivate for Learning Direct students' attention to "Predict. Lead students in a discussion of what they think "equal justice under the law" means. Ask students to give examples of what they think constitutes "equal justice."

Civil Rights: Equal Justice Under Law

Chapter Preview

A tall, well-dressed man stood outside of the suburban post office. While reading his mail, he was confronted by a throng of police officers who forced him at gunpoint to lie face down on the pavement. Was he, as suspected, the gunman who robbed a local bank three days before?

The man in this true story was Dee Brown—a Boston Celtics rookie guard who is African American. The suburb was mostly-white Wellesley, Massachusetts. It turned out that the only characteristic Brown had in common with the bank robber was the color of his skin. Brown, who has since accepted the apologies of Wellesley police and residents, believes the only reason the incident was newsworthy was not that it was unique, but that it happened to a professional athlete. As you can see from this example, the American democratic system has not yet succeeded in extending the guarantees of fair and equal treatment to all persons in the United States. This chapter is about equality as a continuing goal in that democratic ideal.

Before you read this chapter:

- **Describe** two actions or policies that you think are discriminatory.
- **Predict** the meaning of "equal justice under the law."

As you read, focus on the main objective for each section. Understand:

1. The multicultural character of the United States' population.
2. The constitutional guarantees of equality before the law.
3. The civil rights laws passed by Congress over 30 years.
4. How American citizenship is acquired.

Magruder's American Government: *A Witness to Change* by William A. McClenaghan

The popular understanding of the term *civil rights* has changed significantly over the 75 years of *Magruder's American Government*. For example, the 1948 edition defined civil rights in the following way: "To vote and to hold office are political rights. All other rights are civil rights." The 1948 text then proceeds to discuss the specific constitutional guarantees belonging to the American people.

Of course, the 1948 text was correct to locate the meaning of civil rights entirely within the Constitution. This edition of Magruder's does the same. However, the new text also reflects the more popular conception of civil rights—that is, our government's ongoing, positive efforts to secure individual rights and liberties for all citizens, and to remedy the effects of past injustice. This chapter enables us to take a more in-depth look at the struggles and triumphs of this country's minorities—and of the American system of government itself.

Freedom of Expression Demonstrators march on the Capitol. The Constitution protects the rights of citizens to assemble, organize, and bring their views to the attention of public officials.

1 Diversity and Discrimination in American Society

Find Out:

- How has the makeup of the American population changed over the course of its history?
- What is the historical record of the United States' treatment of minority groups?
- What is the historical record of the United States' treatment of women?

Key Terms:

reservation, refugee

Do you know the word *heterogeneous*? It is a compound of two Greek words: *heteros*, meaning other or different, and *genos*, meaning race, family, or kind. As any good dictionary will tell you, something that is heterogeneous is made up of a mix of several ingredients.

As you will see in this section, "We the People of the United States" are a heterogeneous lot—and are becoming more so, year to year.

A Heterogeneous Population

The population of the United States is predominantly white. It is today and, as you can see in the table on page 547, it has been historically. The first census in 1790 reported that there were 3.929 million people living in this country and that four out of every five of them were white. As the nation's population grew over the decades, so, too, did the proportion of the American people who were white—that is, until recently.

Today, the ethnic composition of the population is strikingly different from what it was only a generation ago. Immigrants have arrived in near-record numbers every year since the mid-1960s; and, over that period, the nation's African-American, Hispanic-American, and Asian-American populations have grown at rates several times that of whites.

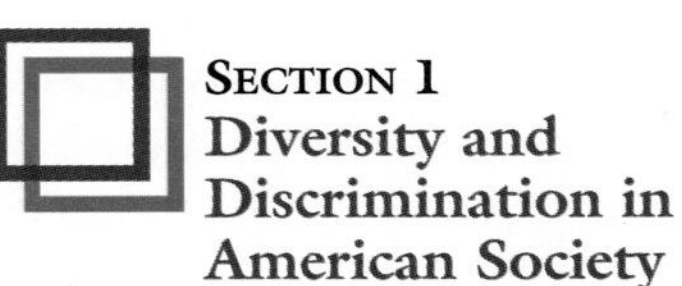

Section 1
Diversity and Discrimination in American Society

Focus

Teacher's Resource File See the Unit 5 File, p. 71, for the Section 1 Outline.

Objectives

21.1 Describe how the makeup of the American population has changed over the course of its history.

21.2 Analyze the historical record of the United States' treatment of minority groups.

21.3 Outline the historical record of the United States' treatment of women.

Bellringer Activity Ask students to imagine 100 people who represent the population of the United States standing in line for tickets to an event. Have students estimate the number of males, females, and members of each ethnic group there might be. Use responses as the basis of a discussion of diversity and discrimination.

State the Purpose In this section, students will learn how the United States has incorporated into its population large minority groups who have been discriminated against. Students also will learn that women, who in fact comprise the majority of the population, have also been victims of discrimination.

Vocabulary

Point out "Key Terms" on page 545 to students. Ask students how the terms *refugee* and *reservation* are related. Guide students to realize that a reservation is a place set aside for people who are refugees in their own land.

Reading Strategy: Relating to the Topic?

Read students this quotation from Molefi Asante, chairman of the department of African-American studies at Temple University: "Once America was a microcosm of European nationalities. Today America is a microcosm of the world." Explain that microcosm means "little world." As they read, ask students to write facts that support or refute this statement.

INSTRUCT

Explain/Discuss Review the history of immigration throughout American history, highlighting recent trends. Discuss the advantages to Americans of living in a multicultural society.

Point out to students that most reference books until very recently have tended to overlook the contributions of minority groups and women to American society. Discuss with students the various groups—African American, Native American, Asian American, Hispanic American, and women—who have been discriminated against in American society.

Illustrate Have students make two collages by cutting images from magazines, one that shows the position of minorities and women in society a hundred years ago and another that demonstrates the current diversity of American society. Those who are artistically inclined might draw posters to demonstrate the same themes.

Interpreting Graphs: Multicultural Awareness Have students study the graph and note which ethnic population grew the fastest from 1980 to 1990. *(Asian/Pacific Islander.)*

Caption Answer This suggests that at some point in the future, people of backgrounds other than white European may be the majority in the country.

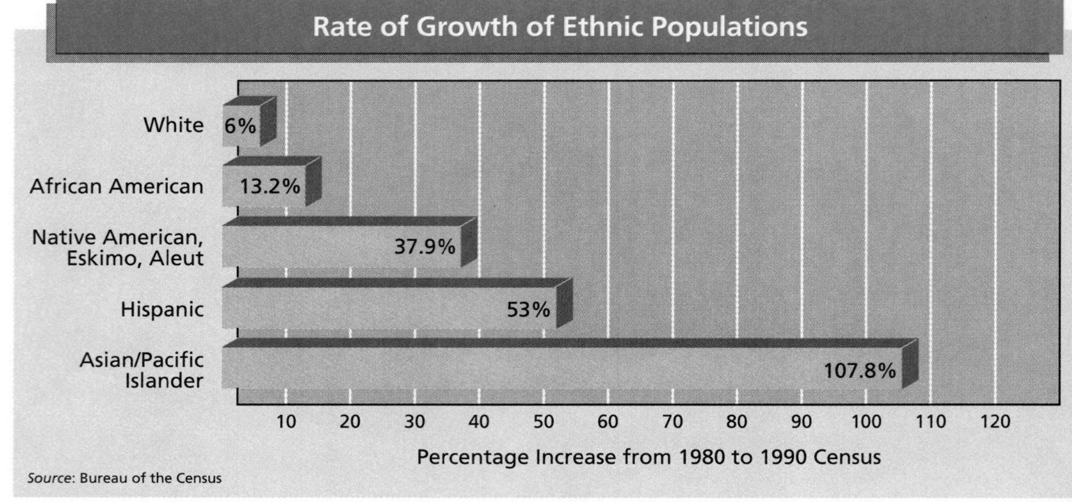

Interpreting Graphs: Multicultural Awareness While the population in the United States remains predominantly white, this table shows that the rate of growth of that group is by far the slowest. What does this suggest about the future population of the United States?

Females are more numerous in the population than males—and they have been for nearly half a century now.

As a result of these changes in the American population, the United States is more heterogeneous than ever before in its history. That fact is likely to have a profound effect on the American social, political, and economic landscape.

Discrimination

As you will see in this chapter, white Americans have been historically reluctant to yield to nonwhite Americans a full and equal place in the social, economic, and political life of this nation. Over time, the principal targets of that ethnic prejudice have been African Americans, Native Americans, Asian Americans, and Hispanic Americans. The white-male-dominated power structure has also been slow to recognize the claims of women to a full and equal place in American society.

African Americans Much of what you will read in these pages focuses on discrimination against African Americans for three reasons:

(1) African Americans constitute by far the largest minority group in the United States. They number more than 30 million today—more than 12 percent of all the American people.

(2) African Americans have been the victims of consistently and deliberately unjust treatment for a longer period of time than perhaps any other group of Americans.[1] It took a civil war to end more than 200 years of slavery in this country. As you have read, slavery was finally abolished by the 13th Amendment in 1865, but the Civil War and the ratification of that amendment did not bring an end to widespread racial discrimination in the United States.

(3) Most of the gains that the nation has made in translating the Constitution's guarantees of equality into a reality for all persons have come out of efforts made by and on behalf of African Americans. You have already encountered a number of illustrations of this point. Recall, for example, the struggles of Martin Luther King, Jr. and others that resulted in the

[1] Slavery began in what was to become the United States in 1619; in June of that year, 20 Africans were sold to white settlers at Jamestown.

ACTIVITY: For Gifted Students

Theme: Change Many methods were used by civil rights activists to bring about change in the treatment of African Americans, including boycotts, protest marches, sit-ins, and "freedom rides." Have students research these methods of nonviolent protest and then write a first-person narrative from the point of view of someone who participated in them.

Teacher's Resource File
See the Historical and Legal Documents file, p. 30, for materials to support this section.

The Ethnic Composition of the Population, 1790-1990 (in thousands)

Census	Race							
	White	%	African American	%	Native American[1]	Asian American[2]	Hispanic Origin[3]	%
1790	3,172	80.7	757	19.3	*	*	*	*
1800	4,306	81.0	1,002	19.0	*	*	*	*
1850	19,553	84.3	3,639	15.7	*	*	*	*
1890	55,101	87.5	7,489	11.9	248	110	*	*
1900	66,809	87.9	8,834	11.6	237	114	*	*
1940	118,215	89.8	12,866	9.8	334	204	*	*
1950	135,150	89.3	15,045	9.9	343	259	*	*
1960	158,832	88.6	18,872	10.5	524	702	*	*
1970	178,098	87.6	22,581	11.1	793	1,026	*	*
1980	194,713	85.9	26,683	11.8	1,420	3,729	14,609	6.4
1990	209,491	84.3	29,986	12.1	1,959	7,274	22,354	9.0

*Not Available.
[1]Includes Alaska Natives, 1960 and later.
[2]Includes Pacific Islanders.
[3]Persons of Hispanic origin may be of any race.
Source: Bureau of the Census

Interpreting Tables: Multicultural Awareness This table shows that minority populations are increasing at higher rates than the majority population. According to the table, which group is growing the fastest?

Civil Rights Act of 1964 and then the Voting Rights Act of 1965; see Chapter 6, Section 3.

Of course this is not to say that other groups of Americans have not also suffered the effects of discrimination. Clearly, they have.

Native Americans White settlers first began to arrive in America in large numbers in the early middle years of the 17th century. At the time, some one million Native Americans were living in territory that was to become the United States.[2] By 1900, however, their number had fallen to less than 250,000. Diseases brought by white settlers had decimated those first Americans. So, too, did the succession of military campaigns that accompanied the westward expansion of the United States. To quote one historian, "'The only good Indian is a dead Indian' is not simply a hackneyed expression from cowboy movies. It was part of the strategy of westward expansion, as settlers and U. S. troops alike mercilessly drove the eastern Indians from their ancestral lands to the Great Plains, then took those lands too."[3] Today, nearly two million Native Americans live in this country, about a third of them on or near
1.a **reservations**—areas of public land set aside by a government for use by a Native-American group.

Like African Americans, Native Americans have been the victims of overbearing discrimination. The consequences of that bias have been truly appalling, and they remain all too evident today. The life expectancy of the more than 600,000 Native Americans living on reservations in the 1990s is 10 years less than the national average, and their infant mortality rate is three times that for white Americans.

[2]Most authorities estimate that there were some 8 to 10 million Native Americans living in all of North and South America in the mid-1600s.

[3]Thomas E. Patterson, *The American Democracy* (New York: McGraw Hill, 1990), page 153.

SPOTLIGHT ON: Global Awareness

The diseases European sailors and settlers carried to this continent resulted in a loss of Native American life on a scale that nearly defies comprehension. Small pox, measles, influenza, and viruses common in Europe ravaged Mexico and Guatemala, where 10 to 20 million Native American inhabitants lacked immunity to these diseases. No more than 3 million are believed to have survived after epidemics in 1521, 1545, and 1575. In the area that would become colonial America, disease decimated the Native American population, killing more than half of the 300,000 natives between 1500 and 1600.

ABCNEWS INTERACTIVE

The following video segment may be used to highlight aspects of civil rights legislation.

POWERS OF THE SUPREME COURT GUIDEBOOK
Chapter 21: Amendment 14 (1868) Civil Rights, p. 33

Interpreting Tables: Multicultural Awareness
Point out to students that the figures on the table are in thousands. Thus the number of Asian Americans in the population in 1990, for example, was over seven million people.

Caption Answer Hispanics.

Provide Guided Practice On the board write *1790, 1940,* and *1990.* Then, referring students to the table on page 547 and using different colors of chalk for each race shown, have students guide you in drawing a curve for each race that represents their fluctuating presence in America.

Provide Independent Practice

TRF **Teacher's Resource File** You may wish to assign Section 1 Guided Reading and Review, Unit 5 File, p. 72, to help students master section objective content.

MONITOR COMPREHENSION

Answers to Section 1 Review

1. "Key Terms" are defined on the following pages:

a. reservation, p. 547
b. refugee, p. 549

2. Predominantly white at the first census, growing more predominantly white over the course of its history. The last four decades, however, have seen a significant growth in minority populations. **3.** White males. **4.** African Americans, Native Americans, Asian Americans, Hispanic Americans, and women. **5.** They constitute a majority of the population. **6.** Students might suggest that the facts suggest the failure of American society to live up to its ideals. Others might suggest that the numbers of people who continue to come to this nation suggest that America does provide a relatively safe and desirable place to live.

Asian Americans The story of white America's mistreatment of Asians is a lengthy one, too. Chinese laborers were the first Asians to come to the United States in large numbers. They were brought here in the 1850s to 1860s as contract laborers to work in the mines and build railroads in the West. Many white Americans, both native-born and immigrants, resented the competition of "coolie labor," and their resentments were frequently expressed in violence toward Asians.

As you will see on page 565, Congress passed the Chinese Exclusion Act in 1882; as a result of this and other government actions, only a very small number of Chinese, Japanese, and other Asians were permitted to enter the United States for more than 80 years. Early in World War II, the Federal Government ordered the evacuation of all persons of Japanese descent from the Pacific Coast. Some 120,000 people, two-thirds of them native-born American citizens, were forcibly removed to inland "war relocation camps"; see Chapter 19, Section 1.

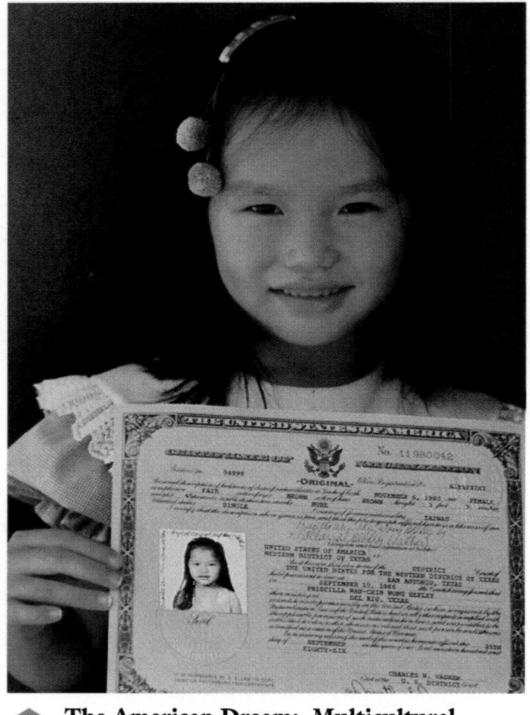

The American Dream: Multicultural Awareness One of the largest groups of new immigrants to the United States is the Vietnamese—represented here by this proud new citizen.

Congress made dramatic changes in American immigration policies in 1965 and, since then, more than three million Asian immigrants have come to this country—mostly from the Philippines, China, Korea, Vietnam, and India.

Today, the Asian-American population approaches 7.5 million; and, as you can see in the table on page 546, it is one of the nation's fastest growing minority groups. By the year 2000, the Asian-American component of the population will likely exceed 12 million. Most Asian Americans now live on the West Coast.

Hispanic Americans Hispanic Americans are those nearly 23 million people in this country who have a Spanish-speaking background; many prefer to be called Latinos. Hispanics may be of any race; they "are among the world's most complex groupings of human beings. [The largest number] are white, millions . . . are mestizo, nearly half a million in the United States are black or mulatto.'[4] Hispanics now constitute the second largest minority group of Americans, and they could replace African Americans as the largest such group by the year 2000.

Hispanic Americans can generally be divided into four main groups:

(1) MEXICAN AMERICANS More than half of all Hispanics in the United States, at least 12 million persons, were either born in Mexico or trace their ancestry there. Those who were born in this country of Mexican parents are often called Chicanos.

(2) PUERTO RICANS Another large group of Hispanics have come to the mainland from their native Puerto Rico. There are now some three million Puerto Ricans in the population.

(3) CUBAN AMERICANS The Hispanic population also includes approximately one million

[4]The Bilateral Commission on the Future of United States–Mexican Relations, *The Challenge of Interdependence* (Bethesda: University Press of America, 1989), page 99. A mestizo is a person with both Spanish or Portuguese and Native-American ancestry. A mulatto is a person with African and white ancestry.

Enrichment

Divide the class into four groups and have each group conduct a poll of either the freshman, sophomore, junior, or senior class in which they determine the ethnic composition of each class. Then have each group create a pie graph to illustrate its findings. Display the graphs on a bulletin board. Compare your school's composition with that of the United States. (Easy)

Cuban Americans. They are mostly persons who fled the Castro dictatorship in Cuba and their descendants.

(4) CENTRAL AND SOUTH AMERICANS The fourth major subgroup of Hispanic Americans came here from Central and South America, most as refugees. A **refugee** is one who leaves his 1.b or her home to seek refuge from war, persecution, or some other danger. More than three million persons have emigrated to the United States from countries south of Mexico over the past 25 years; they have come in the largest numbers from Nicaragua, El Salvador, and Chile.

Discrimination Against Women

Unlike the several ethnic groups described here, women are not a minority in the United States. They are, in fact, a majority group. Still, traditionally in American law and public policy, women have not enjoyed the same rights as men—including, in many instances, men who were themselves the target of virulent discrimination. Women have, instead, been treated as less than equal in a great many matters—including, for example, property rights, education, and employment opportunities.

Those who fought and finally won the long struggle for women's suffrage believed that, with the vote, women would soon achieve other basic rights. That assumption proved to be false. Although more than 51 percent of the population is female, women have held only a fraction of one percent of the nation's top public offices since 1789. Even today, women hold only five percent (29) of the 535 seats in Congress and only 18 percent (some 1,350) of the 7,461 seats in the 50 State legislatures; and only three of the 50 State governors today are female. To the same point, fewer than 20 percent of the nation's doctors, lawyers, and college professors are women.

It is illegal to pay women less than men for the same work. The Equal Pay Act of 1963 requires employers to pay men and women the same wages if they perform the same jobs in the same establishment under the same working conditions. The Civil Rights Act of 1964 also prohibits job discrimination based on sex. Yet, nearly 30 years after Congress passed those laws, working women earn, on the average, only about 70 cents for every dollar earned by working men. See the table on page 555.

Women earn less than men for a number of reasons—including the fact that the male work force is, over all, better educated and has more job experience than the female work force. (Note that these factors themselves can often be traced to discrimination.) But the primary reason is that until quite recently only a fairly narrow range of jobs were open to most women. Even now, more than three-fourths of all jobs held by women are in low-paying clerical and service occupations. The Bureau of Labor Statistics reports that 99 percent of all secretaries today are women; so too are 98 percent of all child-care workers, 96 percent of all nurses, 88 percent of all waiters, 87 percent of all health technicians, and 81 percent of all bank tellers. Efforts in behalf of equal rights for women have gained significant ground in recent years, as you will see. But, recall, that ground has not included the passage of an Equal Rights Amendment to the Constitution.

Section 1 Review

1. **Define:** reservation, refugee
2. In what way has the composition of the American population changed over the course of United States history?
3. Which group has dominated political and social life in the United States since its beginnings?
4. Who have been the traditional targets of prejudice in America?
5. In what sense are women an unusual group among those who have suffered discrimination?

Critical Thinking

6. **Checking Consistency** (p. 19) Consider what you have read about minority groups in this country. How do these facts measure up to the ideals for human freedom expressed in documents such as the Declaration of Independence and the Constitution?

Teacher's Resource File
See the Unit 5 File, p. 73, for the Section 1 Quiz.

CLOSURE

The population of the United States consists of many ethnic groups. Many groups have suffered discrimination throughout American history. The ethnic group that has suffered the most aggressive and unrelenting discrimination has been African Americans. Women, who comprise a majority of the population, also have been deliberately denied the rights of citizens. As students read the next section, they will learn how government may and may not legally distinguish between different groups of people.

Assignment Assign Section 2, pp. 550–555, for the next class period.

Reteach

Have students list the ethnic groups named in the section that have been victims of discrimination. Next to the name of each group, have students indicate how and when they have been discriminated against.

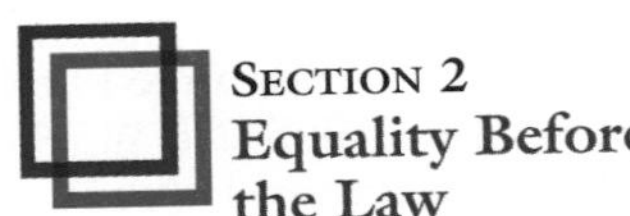

SECTION 2
Equality Before the Law

FOCUS

Teacher's Resource File
See the Unit 5 File, p. 74, for the Section 2 Outline.

Objectives

21.4 Explain in what sense the Constitution guarantees equality of all persons.
21.5 Identify the grounds on which government can draw distinctions among groups of people.
21.6 Identify the grounds on which government is forbidden from drawing distinctions among groups of people.

Bellringer Activity Ask students if they think age limits on drinking, smoking, voting, and driving, or mandatory school attendance constitute discrimination. Ask: Do these laws achieve a proper governmental purpose? Does a compelling governmental interest justify these distinctions based on age? Tell students that the Supreme Court uses these measures to determine whether a law is discriminatory.

State the Purpose Although the Declaration of Independence states that "all men are created equal," the Constitution never makes such a statement. In Section 2, students will learn how the Constitution has been used to evaluate a variety of laws that have discriminated among specific groups of people.

2 Equality Before the Law

Find Out:

- In what sense does the Constitution guarantee equality of all persons?
- On what grounds can government draw distinctions between groups of people?
- On what grounds is government forbidden from drawing distinctions between groups?

Key Terms:
segregation, Jim Crow law, separate-but-equal doctrine, de jure segregation, de facto segregation

Have you read George Orwell's classic, *Animal Farm*? Even if you have not, you may have heard its most celebrated line: "All animals are equal, but some animals are more equal than others." In this section, you will examine the Constitution's guarantees of equality—and, as you do, you might keep that Orwellian aphorism in mind.

VOICES on Government

Larry Echohawk,
attorney general of the State of Idaho

On Equal Protection Under the Law

"At 14, my father—a Pawnee Indian—was taken from his family's Oklahoma reservation and sent to boarding school. There he was forced . . . [to shun] his native language, disavow his culture. For people of color sixty years ago, equal protection was a largely empty promise. For me, it's been more. I went to school, succeeded in law, entered public service—while maintaining my cultural heritage. But . . . as long as our legal system is less than color-blind, 'equal protection' will be less than a reality."

The Equal Protection Clause

Nothing can make people equal in a literal sense. Individuals differ in strength, intelligence, height, and countless other ways. But the democratic ideal demands that, insofar as government is concerned, all persons must be treated alike.

The equality of all persons—so boldly set out in the Declaration of Independence—is not proclaimed in so many words in the Constitution. Still, that concept pervades the document.

The closest approach to a literal statement of equality is to be found in the 14th Amendment's Equal Protection Clause. It declares:

"No State shall . . . deny to any person within its jurisdiction the equal protection of the laws."

The clause was originally intended to benefit those individuals newly freed from slavery. Over time, it has acquired a broader meaning. Today, the Due Process Clause forbids States and their local governments to draw unreasonable distinctions between classes of persons. The Supreme Court has often held that the 5th Amendment's Due Process Clause puts the same restriction on the Federal Government.

Reasonable Classification Government must have the power to draw distinctions between persons and groups. That is, the States can and do discriminate. Thus, those who rob banks fall into a special class and are subject to special treatment by the law. Or, the State can prohibit marriage by those under a certain age. These are reasonable discriminations.

The States cannot discriminate unreasonably. For example, every State now levies a sales tax on cigarettes—and so taxes smokers. But no State can tax only blonde smokers. Nor, for example, may a State make women eligible for alimony in divorce actions but provide that men are not, *Orr* v. *Orr*, in 1979.

Over time, the Supreme Court has rejected many equal protection challenges to the actions of State and local governments. More often

Reading Strategy: Structured Overview
List the headings and subheadings from the section on the board. Have students skim the section for key words and phrases to write under each heading or subheading. Write students' suggestions in the appropriate columns.

Vocabulary
Direct students' attention to "Key Terms" on page 550. Draw a classification diagram on the board. As you discuss the "Key Terms" with students, fill in the diagram to show two types of *segregation* (*de facto* and *de jure*), with *separate-but-equal doctrine* and *Jim Crow law* under de *jure segregation.*

than not, it has found that what those governments have done is, in fact, constitutional.[5] The Court's most recent Equal Protection Clause case provides an example. In *Gregory* v. *Ashcroft*, 1991, the Court upheld a provision in the Missouri constitution that sets a mandatory retirement age for State judges but not for other top officeholders.

The Rational Basis Test The Supreme Court most often decides equal protection cases by applying a standard known as the rational basis test. This test asks: Does the classification in question bear a reasonable relationship to the achievement of some proper governmental purpose?

A California case, *Michael M.* v. *Superior Court*, 1981, illustrates that test. California law says that a man who has sexual relations with a girl under 18 to whom he is not married can be prosecuted for statutory rape; but the girl cannot be charged with that crime, even if she is a willing partner. The Court found the law to bear a reasonable relationship to the achievement of a proper public end: preventing teenage pregnancies.

The Strict Scrutiny Test The Supreme Court imposes a more demanding standard in some equal protection cases, however. This is especially true when a law or some other action deals with (1) such "fundamental rights" as the right to vote, the right to travel between the States, or the rights guaranteed in the 1st Amendment; or (2) such "suspect classifications" as those based on race, sex, or national origins.

In these instances, the Court has said that a law must meet a higher standard than the rational basis test. This standard is called the strict scrutiny test. The State must be able to show that some "compelling governmental interest" justifies the distinctions it has drawn between classes of people. The alimony case cited a moment ago, *Orr* v. *Orr*, involved the use of that stricter test. The Alabama law that made only women eligible for alimony was held

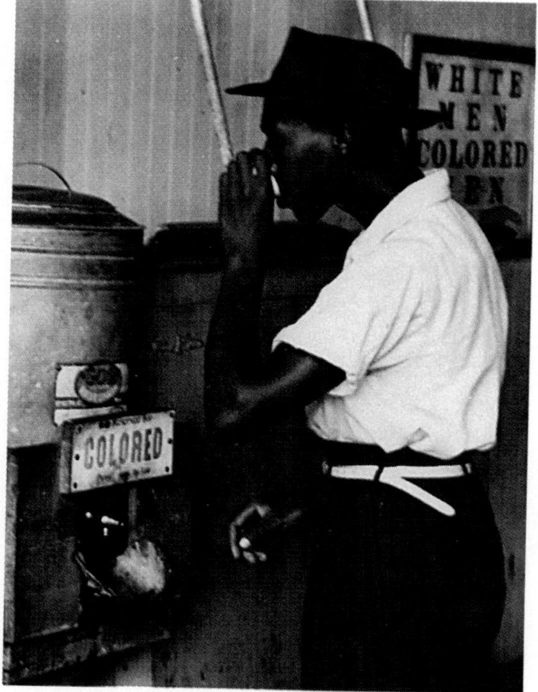

Separate, But Not Equal The goal of the civil rights movement of the 1960s was to show the need for legislation that made racial segregation and discrimination unlawful in public places, employment, housing, and voting.

unconstitutional, as a denial of equal protection, because the law's distinction between men and women did not serve a compelling governmental interest.

Segregation in America

Beginning in the late 1800s, nearly half of the
States passed a number of racial segregation
1.a laws. **Segregation** means the isolation and separation of one group from another. Most of
1.b those were **Jim Crow laws** aimed at African
Americans. Some of them were drawn to affect other groups, as well—especially Mexican Americans, people of Asian descent, and Native Americans. These laws required segregation by race in the use of both public and private facilities: streetcars, schools, parks and playgrounds, hotels and restaurants, even public drinking fountains.

[5]The Court has voided a number of those actions, however—for example, too-lengthy residence requirements for voting purposes; see pages 132–133.

INSTRUCT

Discuss/Analyze Review with students the Equal Protection Clause. Have students tell you where it comes from (*the 14th Amendment*), and which amendment (*5th*) has been invoked in a similar way in discrimination cases. Ask students to explain the meaning of the Equal Protection Clause, citing examples given in the rest of the section.

Analyze the difference between the rational basis test and the strict scrutiny test. Discuss the meaning of a "governmental purpose" as providing a criterion for the rational basis test.

Explain that "Jim Crow" was a derogatory term for African Americans from the name of a stereotypical person portrayed in minstrel shows in the 1800s. Also explain that Jim Crow laws do not pass the rational basis test or the strict scrutiny test. While an attempt was made to validate those laws by associating them with the separate-but-equal doctrine, they were little more than prejudicial reactions against control exerted by the North during Reconstruction.

Distinguish Discuss with students the challenge to the separate-but-equal doctrine that began with the 1938 case of *Missouri ex rel. Gaines* v. *Canada*. Ask students to compare that decision to the decision rendered in *Brown* v. *Topeka Board of Education*. Explain that in the former case the Court left it to the State to decide whether it was practical to provide a separate-but-equal facility and in the latter case the Court stated that it was impossible to establish separate-but-equal facilities.

ABCNEWS INTERACTIVE

The following video segment may be used to highlight aspects of civil rights legislation.

POWERS OF THE SUPREME COURT GUIDEBOOK
Chapter 22: *Brown* v. *Board of Education of Topeka* (KS) (1954), p. 87

Interpreting Political Art Ask students to consider this question, raised by artist Ernest Crichlow: "How can society remove the fence so that everyone has the same opportunities regardless of race?"

Interpreting Political Art *The White Fence* by Ernest Crichlow symbolizes the barriers of prejudice that separate African-American children from opportunities that are available to white children. The flowers surrounding the white child represent those opportunities.

The Separate-but-Equal Doctrine In 1896, the Supreme Court provided a constitutional basis for these many segregation laws: the
1.c **separate-but-equal doctrine**. In *Plessy* v. *Ferguson* it upheld a Louisiana law requiring the segregation of whites and African Americans in rail coaches. It held that the law did not violate the Equal Protection Clause because the separate facilities for African Americans were equal to those for whites.

The separate-but-equal doctrine stood for nearly 60 years. Indeed, until the late 1930s, little real effort was made by the courts or any other arm of government even to see that the separate accommodations for African Americans were, in fact, equal to those reserved to whites.

***Brown* v. *Board of Education of Topeka*, 1954** The Supreme Court began to chip away at the separate-but-equal doctrine in the late 1930s and the 1940s. It did so for the first time in *Missouri ex rel. Gaines* v. *Canada* in 1938. Lloyd Gaines, an African American, was denied admission to the law school at the all-white University of Missouri. Gaines was fully qualified for admission—except that he was an African American. However, the State did offer to pay his tuition at a public law school in any of four neighboring States.

The Supreme Court held that the separate-but-equal doctrine left the State of Missouri with but two choices here: It could either (1) admit Gaines to the State's law school or (2) establish a separate-but-equal one for him. The State gave in and admitted Gaines rather than build a separate-but-equal law school.

Over the next several years the Supreme Court took an increasingly stern attitude toward the doctrine's requirement of equal facilities. In a number of cases it insisted on equality in fact—that is, in terms of quality—between separate facilities. Finally, in an historic decision in 1954, the Court reversed *Plessy* v. *Ferguson*. In *Brown* v. *Board of Education of Topeka*, it struck down the laws of four States requiring or allowing separate public schools for white and African-American students.[6]

Unanimously, the Supreme Court held that segregation by race in public education is unconstitutional:

> "Does segregation of children in public schools solely on the basis of race, even though the physical facilities and other "tangible" factors may be equal, deprive the children of the minority group of equal educational opportunities? We believe that it does.
>
> . . . To separate them from others of similar age and qualifications solely because of their race generates a feeling of inferiority as to their status in the community that may affect their hearts and minds in a way unlikely ever to be undone. . . . We conclude that in the field of public education the doctrine of "separate but equal" has no place. Separate educational facilities are inherently unequal."

[6]Kansas, Delaware, South Carolina, and Virginia. On the same day, it also struck down racially segregated public schools in the District of Columbia, under the 5th Amendment, *Bolling* v. *Sharpe*, 1954.

TRF **Teacher's Resource File**
See the Supreme Court Cases file, pp. 32–33, 50–51, for material to support the section.

ACTIVITY: Cooperative Learning
Time: Two class periods **Activity:** Create graffiti boards. **Grouping:** Groups of four to six students **Purpose:** Divide chalkboards in the classroom so that each group has its own space. Have students use chalk to create graffiti boards illustrating their opinions about discrimination. **Roles:** All group members are encouraged to add to their board. **Outcome:** Groups may compare and discuss boards.

The Court in 1955 directed the States to make "a prompt and reasonable start" and to end segregation "with all deliberate speed."

A "reasonable start" was made in several places: Baltimore, Louisville, St. Louis, Washington, D.C., and elsewhere. In most of the Deep South, however, what came to be known as "massive resistance" soon developed. State legislatures passed laws to block integration. Most were clearly unconstitutional; but the process of attacking them in the federal courts was costly and slow. Many school boards also worked to bar progress.

The pace of desegregation quickened after Congress passed the Civil Rights Act of 1964. That act forbids the use of federal funds to aid any State or local activity in which racial segregation is practiced. It directed the Justice Department to file suits to prompt desegregation actions.

The Supreme Court itself pushed that pace along in 1969. In a case from Mississippi, *Alexander* v. *Holmes County Board of Education*, it ruled that, after 15 years, the time for "all deliberate speed" had finally run out. Said a unanimous Court: "The continued operation of segregated schools under a standard allowing for 'all deliberate speed' . . . is no longer constitutionally permissible."

De Jure and De Facto Segregation By fall 1970, school systems with **de jure segregation**—segregation by law, with legal sanction—had been abolished. That is not to say that desegregation itself had been fully accomplished. The process of achieving a complete integration of the country's schools still continues more than 35 years after the Court's decision in *Brown*.[7]

Many recent integration controversies have come in places where the schools have never been segregated by law. They have occurred, instead, in communities in which de facto segregation has long been present, and continues.

"I Have A Dream" Thousands marched on the Capitol in 1963 to support Martin Luther King, Jr.'s plea for stronger civil rights laws.

De facto segregation is segregation in fact, even though no law requires it. Housing patterns have most often been its major cause. The concentration of African Americans in certain sections of cities inevitably led to local school systems in which some schools are largely African American. That condition is apparent in many northern as well as southern communities.

Efforts to desegregate those school systems have taken several forms. School district lines have been redrawn, pupil assignment programs have been put in place, and the busing of students out of racially segregated neighborhoods has been tried. These efforts have often brought strong protests in many places and violence in some.

[7]Some States, several school districts, and many parents and private groups have sought to avoid integrated schools through established or, often, newly created private schools. See the Court's rulings in two 1983 cases, *Bob Jones University* v. *United States* and *Goldsboro Christian Schools* v. *United States* (page 494) and *Runyan* v. *McCrary*, 1976 (page 522).

INSTRUCT

Analyze/Discuss Compare with students the terms *de jure* and *de facto segregation*. Ask students to suppose that a community deliberately draws school district boundaries to coincide with racial housing patterns. Ask: Is this a case of de facto or de jure segregation? Ask if school segregation resulting from illegal housing discrimination is de facto or de jure segregation.

Discuss ways in which people are and have been classified by sex. Impress upon students that the Supreme Court did not find any sex-based classification to be unconstitutional until 1971.

Illustrate Provide students with the following 1989 Census Bureau statistics on the educational attainment of the population. Ask students to use these figures to draw a graph similar to the one on page 555: Percentage of persons with four years of high school or more—male: 77.2%; female: 76.6%. Percentage of persons with one or more years of college—male: 41.0%; female: 35.3%. Percentage of persons with four or more years of college—male: 24.5%; female: 18.1%. After students have created their graphs, discuss these figures with them in light of the section content regarding classification by sex.

SPOTLIGHT ON: Multiculturalism

At times activists, impatient with the slow pace of legal appeal, challenged segregation outside the courtroom. Mrs. Rosa Parks, a middle-aged African-American woman, was arrested by Montgomery, Alabama, police in December 1955 for refusing to give up her seat on a bus to a white passenger as the law required. Community activists, among them a young reverend, Dr. Martin Luther King, Jr., organized a boycott of the city's bus lines until segregation ended. In December 1956, Montgomery's bus lines were desegregated.

Provide Guided Practice
Invite students to list four or five cases discussed in the section. For each, have students explain how the Equal Protection Clause applies to the case as well as the Court's decision in the case.

Provide Independent Practice
TRF **Teacher's Resource File**
You may wish to assign Section 2 Guided Reading and Review, Unit 5 File, p. 75, to help students master section objective content.

The Supreme Court first sanctioned busing in a North Carolina case, *Swann* v. *Charlotte-Mecklenburg Board of Education*, 1971. There it held that "desegregation plans cannot be limited to walk-in schools." Since then, busing has been used to try to increase the racial mix in many school districts across the country—in some by court order, in others voluntarily.

Segregation in Other Fields This nation has not yet achieved a complete integration of the public schools. Legally enforced racial segregation in all other areas of life has been eliminated, however. Governments and courts have repealed and struck down many discriminatory State laws and local ordinances.

The Supreme Court has found segregation by race to be as unconstitutional in other areas as it is in public education. Thus, for example, it has held that the Equal Protection Clause forbids segregated public swimming pools or other recreational facilities, *Dawson* v. *Baltimore*, 1955. It has made the same holding with regard to such things as local transportation, *Gayle* v. *Browder*, 1956, and State prisons and local jails, *Lee* v. *Washington*, 1968. The High Court struck down all State miscegenation laws—laws that forbid interracial marriages—in *Loving* v. *Virginia*, 1967. Most recently, it has held that race cannot be the basis upon which a child custody decision is based, *Palmore* v. *Sidoti*, 1984.

Classification by Sex

In its many civil rights provisions, the Constitution speaks of "the people," "persons," and "citizens." Nowhere does it make its guarantees only to "men" or separately to "women." The only reference to sex is in the 19th Amendment, which forbids denial of the right to vote "on account of sex."

Gender has long been used as a basis of classification in the law, however. Most often, society and the courts viewed those laws that treated men and women differently as necessary to the protection of "the weaker sex." Over the years, the Supreme Court read that view into the 14th Amendment. It did not find *any* sex-based classification to be unconstitutional until as recently as 1971.

In the first case to challenge sex discrimination, *Bradwell* v. *Illinois*, 1873, the Court upheld a State law barring women from the practice of law. In that case, Justice Joseph P. Bradley wrote:

> "The civil law, as well as nature itself, has always recognized a wide difference in the respective spheres and destinies of man and woman. Man is, or should be, woman's protector and defender. The natural and proper timidity and delicacy of the female sex evidently unfits it for many of the occupations of civil life."

Even as late as 1961, in *Hoyt* v. *Florida*, the Court could find no constitutional fault with a law that required men to serve on juries but gave women the choice of serving or not.

Matters are far different today. As you have read, the Court now takes a very close look at cases involving claims of sex discrimination. Thus, in 1971, in *Reed* v. *Reed*, it struck down an Idaho law that gave fathers preference over mothers in the administration of their children's estates.

Since then, the Supreme Court has found a number of sex-based distinctions to be unconstitutional. You have already encountered some of them—for example, *Taylor* v. *Louisiana*, 1975, holding that the Equal Protection Clause forbids the States to exclude women from jury service; see Chapter 20, Section 3. As other examples, it has also struck down: an Oklahoma law that prohibited the sale of beer to males under 21 and to females under 18, *Craig* v. *Boren*, 1976; an Arizona rule permitting public employee retirement plans providing for smaller pensions for women than for men who paid the same premiums during their working years, *Arizona Governing Committee* v. *Norris*, 1983.

In the same vein, the Supreme Court has upheld a California law that prohibits community service clubs from excluding women from membership, *Rotary International* v. *Rotary Club of Duarte*, 1987, and a New York City ordinance that forbids sex discrimination in any place of public accommodation, including large private membership clubs used by their members for business purposes, *New York State Club Association, Inc.* v. *City of New York*, 1988.

The Court's present attitude was put this way by Justice William Brennan in *Frontiero* v. *Richardson*, 1973:

Enrichment

Have students interview as many women as possible, including family members, teachers, neighbors, and so forth. Students should ask: Do you feel that you have ever been discriminated against? Can you describe a specific occurrence? Students should tape record or videotape the interviews and play them back for the class. (Average)

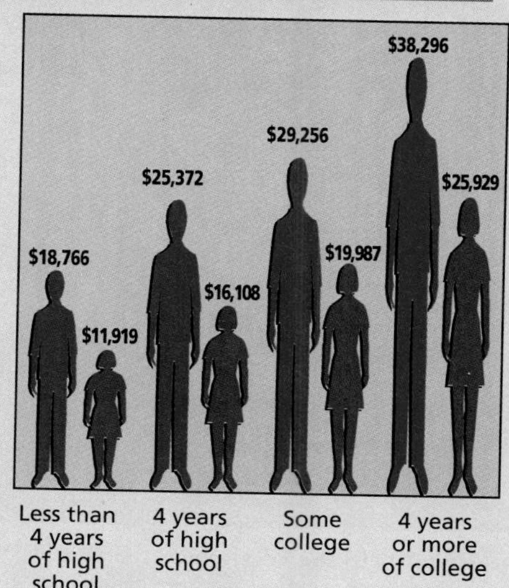

Interpreting Graphs What does this graph show about equality in the workplace a full one hundred years after the women's suffrage movement began?

"There can be no doubt that our nation has had a long and unfortunate history of sex discrimination. Traditionally, such discrimination was rationalized by an attitude of 'romantic paternalism' which, in practical effect, put women, not on a pedestal, but in a cage."[8]

But not all sex-based distinctions are unconstitutional. The Supreme Court has upheld some of them in several cases. You saw one example of this in *Michael M.* v. *Superior Court*, 1981. And the court has held there was no denial of equal protection in:

—a Florida law that gives an extra property tax exemption to widows, but not to widowers, *Kahn* v. *Shevin*, 1974.

—an Alabama law forbidding women to serve as prison guards in all-male penitentiaries, *Dothard* v. *Rawlinson*, 1977.

—the federal selective service law that requires only men to register for the draft, and also its provisions that exclude women from any future draft, *Rostker* v. *Goldberg*, 1981.

In effect, these cases say this: Classification by sex is not in and of itself unconstitutional. However, laws that treat men and women differently will not be upheld by the courts unless (1) they are intended to serve an "important governmental objective" and (2) they are "substantially related" to achieving that goal.

Thus, in upholding the all-male draft, the Court found that Congress did in fact have such an important governmental objective: to raise and support armies and, if necessary, to do so by "a draft of combat troops." "Since women are excluded from combat," said the Supreme Court, they may properly be excluded from the draft.

[8]In this case the Court for the first time struck down a federal law providing for sex-based discrimination, as a violation of the 5th Amendment's Due Process Clause. That law gave various housing, medical, and other allowances to a serviceman for his wife and other dependents, but it made those same allowances available to a servicewoman only if her husband was dependent on her for more than half of his support.

Section 2 Review

1. **Define:** segregation, Jim Crow law, separate-but-equal doctrine
2. The Equal Protection Clause forbids what kinds of discrimination by the States?
3. What was the significance of the Supreme Court's decision in *Plessy* v. *Ferguson*?
4. What did the Court hold in *Brown* v. *Topeka Board of Education*?
5. What is the difference between de jure and de facto segregation?
6. Does the Constitution forbid laws that treat men and women differently?

Critical Thinking

7. **Drawing Conclusions** (p. 19) (a) In your opinion, which would be harder to combat, de facto or de jure segregation? (b) Why?

★

Interpreting Graphs Ask students: How might the government help eliminate these discrepancies?

Caption Answer Whatever their level of education, women still lag behind men in earnings.

Monitor Comprehension

Answers to Section 2 Review
1. "Key Terms" are defined on the following pages:
a. segregation, p. 551
b. Jim Crow law, p. 551
c. separate-but-equal doctrine, p. 552
2. Unreasonable or unfair distinctions. **3.** Allowed for the establishment of separate but equal facilities. **4.** Separate facilities were inherently unequal. **5.** De jure: segregation by law; de facto: segregation in fact. **6.** No, but laws that make such distinctions must pass the strict scrutiny test. **7.** (a) De facto segregation. (b) It requires a change in behavior, which often is more difficult.

Closure

Remind students that equality in the United States means that laws which distinguish between different groups of people must serve a governmental purpose and may not deprive the members of any group of fundamental rights. As students read the next section, they will see how the government has attempted to ensure civil rights.

Assignment Assign Section 3, pp. 556–559, for the next class period.

TRF **Teacher's Resource File**
See the Unit 5 File, p. 76, for the Section 2 Quiz.

Reteach

Ask students to list as many reasons as they can for the federal law that prohibits child labor. Then ask students to read again the information in the section on the rational basis and the strict scrutiny tests and to see whether any of the items on their list answer the questions posed by these tests.

SECTION 3
Federal Civil Rights Laws

FOCUS

Teacher's Resource File See the Unit 5 File, p. 77, for the Section 3 Outline.

Objectives

21.7 Describe what Congress did to ensure civil rights between the 1870s and 1950s and in the last 30 years.
21.9 Explain how the Federal Government has sought to overcome past discrimination.
21.10 Describe how the Supreme Court has responded to affirmative action.

Bellringer Activity Take a poll in class using the question from the table on page 558. Write the response on the board and then have students turn to page 558 to compare their answers with the survey.

State the Purpose From the 1870s until 1957, Congress did nothing to help ensure the civil rights of African Americans. In Section 3, students will learn about legislation since 1957 and will explore questions pertaining to affirmative action and quotas.

ABCNEWS INTERACTIVE

The following video segment may be used to highlight aspects of civil rights legislation.

POWERS OF THE SUPREME COURT GUIDEBOOK
Chapter 28: Poll Taxes, p. 44

3 Federal Civil Rights Laws

Find Out

- What did Congress do to ensure civil rights between the 1870s and 1950s? What has Congress done in the last 30 years?
- How has the Federal Government sought to overcome the effects of past discrimination?
- How has the Supreme Court responded to affirmative action?

Key Terms:
affirmative action, quota, reverse discrimination

You may have heard this oft-made argument: "You can't legislate morality." That is, racism, sexism, and other forms of discrimination cannot be eliminated merely with laws.

Martin Luther King, Jr., replied to that contention this way: "Laws," he said, "may not change the heart, but they can restrain the heartless."

As you will see, Congress has several times agreed with Dr. King—as it has enacted a number of civil rights laws over the past 30 years.

Civil Rights: Reconstruction to Today

From the 1870s to the late 1950s, Congress did not pass a single piece of meaningful civil rights legislation. There were several reasons for that sorry fact. First, through that period the nation's predominantly white population was generally unaware and little concerned with the plight of African Americans, Native Americans, or other nonwhites in this country. Secondly, southern white Democrats, bolstered by such devices as the seniority system and the filibuster, held many of the most strategic posts in Congress.

That historic logjam was broken in 1957—very largely as a result of the pressures brought to bear by the civil rights movement led by Dr. King.[9] Beginning in that year, Congress has passed a number of civil rights laws—notably, the Civil Rights Acts of 1957, 1960, 1964, and 1968 and the Voting Rights Acts of 1965, 1970, 1975, and 1982. The 1957 and 1960 laws set up modest safeguards for the right to vote.[10] In Chapter 6 you considered those two statutes, together with the related provisions of the Civil Rights Act of 1964 and the much stronger Voting Rights Act of 1965.

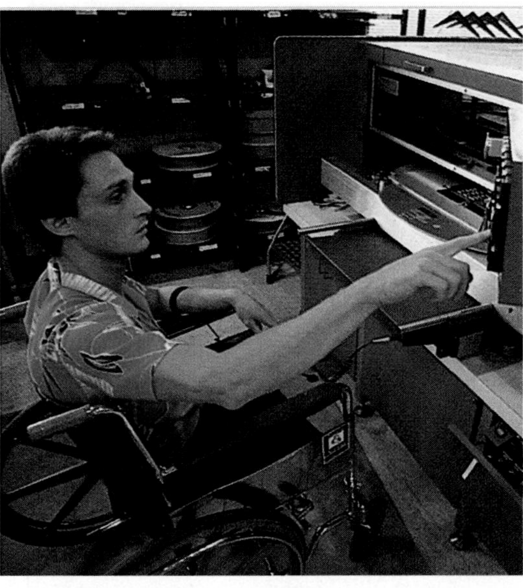

Equality in the Workplace Gradually, hiring practices that discriminate against physically impaired persons are being addressed in the courts.

The Civil Rights Act of 1964

The 1964 law is the most far-reaching of these statutes. It passed after the longest debate in the Senate's history (83 days), and only after the Senate had invoked cloture to kill a filibuster.

Beyond its voting rights provisions, the 1964 law outlaws discrimination in a number of areas of American life. With its several later amendments, the law's major sections now:

[9]See Chapter 6, Section 3.

[10]The 1957 law created the U.S. Civil Rights Commission. The commission is an independent eight-member agency that is supposed to monitor the enforcement of the various civil rights laws, investigate cases of alleged discrimination and report its findings to the President, Congress, and the public. The commission was very active in the 1960s and 1970s.

Reading Strategy: Problem Solving

Have students respond to the following problem: "A very good African-American friend of yours grew up in an inner city and attended an inferior public school at which teachers were inexperienced and materials were scarce. Though extremely intelligent, she now works at unskilled jobs and studies subjects on her own. She wants to attend college." Have students consider whether and why she might be admitted to a college in place of an equally qualified white person.

Vocabulary

Point out "Key Terms" on page 556. Ask students to hypothesize as to what the term *reverse discrimination* might mean.

(1) provide that no person may be denied access to or refused service in various "public accommodations" because of race, color, religion, or national origin (Title II).[11]

(2) prohibit discrimination against any person on grounds of race, color, religion, national origin, sex, or physical disability in any program that receives any federal funding; require the cut-off of federal funds to any program that practices such discrimination (Title VI).

(3) forbid employers and labor unions to discriminate against any person on grounds of race, color, religion, sex, physical disability, or age (40 to 65) in job-related matters (Title VII).[12]

The Civil Rights Act of 1968 The Civil Rights Act of 1968 is often called the Open Housing Act. With minor exceptions, it forbids anyone to refuse to sell or rent a dwelling to any person on grounds of race, color, religion, national origin, sex, or disability, or to a family with children. Until Congress amended the law, the major burden for its enforcement was placed on those persons who claimed to be the victims of housing discrimination. Congress finally strengthened the law in 1988, by allowing the Justice Department to bring criminal charges against those who violate its terms.

Affirmative Action

These several civil rights statutes all come down to this: Discriminatory practices based on such factors as race, color, national origin, or sex are illegal. But what about the present and continuing effects of past discrimination? Consider, for example, the African American who, for no reason of his or her own making, did not get a decent education and so today cannot get a decent job. Of what real help to that person are all of those laws that make illegal today what was done years ago?

So far, the Federal Government's chief answer to this troubling question has been a policy of **affirmative action**. That policy 1.a requires that most employers take positive steps (affirmative action) to remedy the effects of past discriminations.

[11]Congress based this section of the law on its commerce power; see Chapter 11, Section 2. Title II covers those places in which lodgings are offered to transient guests and those where a significant portion of the items sold have moved in interstate commerce. The Supreme Court upheld Title II and the use of the Commerce Clause as a basis for civil rights legislation in *Heart of Atlanta Motel, Inc.* v. *United States*, 1964.

[12]The 1964 law also created the Equal Employment Opportunity Commission. The five-member EEOC's major charge is the enforcement of Title VII.

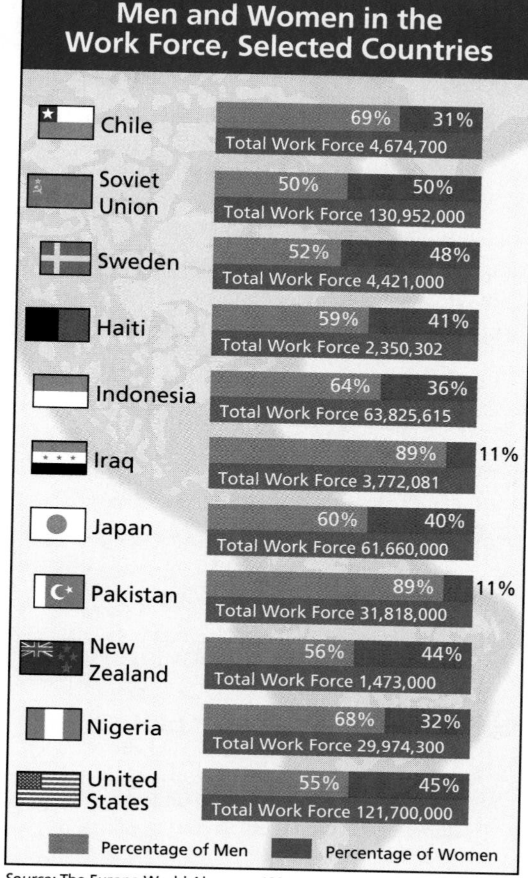

Source: The Europa World Almanac, 1991

Interpreting Graphs: Multicultural Awareness This graph gives statistics on the percentage of men and women in the work force in selected countries. Which two countries employ the lowest percentages of women? The highest?

Interpreting Graphs: Multicultural Awareness Ask students to suggest possible reasons why countries like Iraq and Pakistan have fewer women in the work force than do countries such as Sweden and the former Soviet Union.

Caption Answer Of the countries shown, Iraq and Pakistan; the Soviet Union.

INSTRUCT

Discuss/Analyze Explore with students the possible reasons for the lack of civil rights legislation prior to the 1950s. Discuss the important provisions of civil rights legislation from 1957 to 1968. Have students identify the provisions in the text as you write them on the board.

Divide the class into small groups and have students research, write, and perform a simulated documentary. Tell students to imagine that they are journalists who intend to present a documentary film entitled "The 1960s: A Decade of Change." Their documentaries should include narrative about the civil rights legislation of the decade as well as simulated interviews with people whose lives have been affected by the legislation.

Explain Remind students of the purpose of affirmative action, i.e., to remedy the effects of past discriminations. Discuss the controversy surrounding this policy and the concept of reverse discrimination. Have students look again at their responses to the question asked in the "Bellringer." Do they have the same opinion after reading this section?

SPOTLIGHT ON: Behind the Scenes

Although the tide for civil rights was rising in the 1960s, both the Civil Rights Act of 1964 and of 1968 faced stiff opposition. An appeal to the legacies of two fallen leaders may well have been the only spur to their passage. Lyndon Johnson used the idealistic legacy of recently assassinated President Kennedy to spur passage of the 1964 act, the single most important piece of civil rights legislation since Reconstruction. And, in 1968, the assassination of the Rev. Martin Luther King, Jr. guaranteed passage of a bill that otherwise would have been hotly contested.

Teacher's Resource File
See the Historical and Legal Documents file, p. 31, for material to support the section.

Interpreting Tables: Multicultural Awareness Have students note that a higher percentage of African Americans favor affirmative action. What does this suggest about their views on discrimination? (*Suggests that past discrimination has had an enormous negative impact on their lives and that action is needed to remedy these discriminations.*)

Caption Answer Possible answers: Promote more African Americans to positions of influence in the workplace; encourage more dialogue with African Americans on their concerns; look for other alternatives.

Provide Guided Practice Have students compile chronologies of the civil rights legislation and the Supreme Court cases discussed in this section. For each entry in their chronologies, have students (1) briefly summarize the contents of the legislation or the Court's decision and (2) find photographs in the text that illustrate the event.

Provide Independent Practice

TRF **Teacher's Resource File** You may wish to assign Section 3 Guided Reading and Review, Unit 5 File, p. 78, to help students master section objective content.

Measuring the National Mood on Race-Related Questions

Do you believe that because of past discrimination against African-American people, qualified African Americans should receive preference over equally qualified white Americans in such matters as getting into college or getting jobs?

	African Americans	White Americans
Should	48%	19%
Should not	42%	72%

Can fairness in education, hiring, and promotion be accomplished without quotas?

	African Americans	White Americans
Yes	26%	59%
No	61%	29%

Which categories apply to you?

	African Americans	White Americans
Worked with many members of another race	84%	51%
Worked for a boss of another race	92%	47%

Source: The Newsweek Poll ©1991, *Newsweek*, Inc.

Interpreting Tables: Multicultural Awareness After comparing the ways African and white Americans view their positions today, suggest two possible ways to improve racial equality in America.

The policy applies to all the agencies of the Federal Government, to all the States and their local governments, and to all those private employers who sell goods or services to any agency of the Federal Government.[13]

To illustrate the policy, take the case of a company that does business with the Federal Government. That private business must adopt an affirmative action plan designed to make its work force reflect the general makeup of the population in its locale. The company's program must also include steps to correct or prevent inequalities in such matters as pay, promotions, and fringe benefits. For many employers this has meant that they must hire and/or promote more workers with minority backgrounds and more females. Such rules requiring certain numbers of jobs or promo-
1.b tions for certain groups are called **quotas**.

Reverse Discrimination? Affirmative action programs necessarily involve race-based and/or sex-based classifications. Are programs such as these constitutional?

Critics of the policy say that affirmative action
1.c amounts to **reverse discrimination**—discrimination against the majority group. It demands that preference be given to females and/or nonwhites, solely on the basis of sex or race. Critics insist that the Constitution requires that all public policies be "color blind."

The Bakke Case The Supreme Court has been wrestling with affirmative action cases for more than a dozen years now. The Court's first major case, *Regents of the University of California* v. *Bakke*, was decided in 1979. Alan Bakke, a white male, had been denied admission to the university's medical school at Davis. The school had set aside 16 of the 100 seats in each year's entering class for nonwhite students. He sued, charging the university with reverse discrimination and, so, a violation of the 14th Amendment's Equal Protection Clause. By a 5–4 majority the Court held that Bakke had been denied equal protection and should be admitted to the medical school.

A differently composed 5–4 majority made the really important ruling in the case, however: Although the Constitution does not allow race to be used as the *only* factor in the making of affirmative action decisions, both the Constitution and the 1964 Civil Rights Act do allow its use as one among several factors in such situations.

The Weber Case The Court has upheld quotas in some cases, especially where longstanding and flagrant discrimination was involved.

In *United Steelworkers* v. *Weber*, 1979, the Kaiser Aluminum Company had created train-

[13]The Federal Government began to demand the adoption of affirmative action programs in 1965. Some programs are simply plans that call for the wide advertisement of job openings. Most, however, establish guidelines and timetables to overcome past discriminations.

Affirmative action programs were very actively supported and enforced by the Federal Government from the early 1960s to 1981. The Federal Government's efforts have been much less aggressive over the past several years.

Enrichment

Read to students the following quotation from the journal of African American Charlotte L. Forten (1838–1914): "With what scorn must that government be regarded, which cowardly assembles thousands of soldiers to satisfy the demands of slave holders. . . ." Have students create an imaginary journal entry written upon the passage of the Civil Rights Act of 1968. (Easy)

OR

Teacher's Resource File
You may wish to assign Section 3 Guided Reading and Review, Unit 5

ing programs, intended especially to increase the number of skilled African Americans in its work force. Trainees were chosen on the basis of race and seniority. Brian Weber, a white worker, was rejected for training three times. Each time, however, a number of African Americans with less seniority were picked.

Weber went to court. The Court found that the training programs, although built on quotas, did not violate the 1964 law—which, it said, Congress had purposely designed to "overcome manifest racial imbalances."

Fullilove v. *Klutznick*, 1980, was another case in which the Court upheld quotas. That case centered on a law Congress had passed that provided $4 billion in grants to State and local governments for public works projects. It also contained a "minority set-aside" provision, requiring that at least 10 percent of each grant had to be set aside for minority-owned businesses.

A white contractor challenged the set-asides. He argued that they were quotas and therefore unconstitutional—because they did not give white contractors an equal chance to compete for all of the available funds.

The Court held the law to be a permissible attempt to overcome the effects of blatant and longstanding bias in the construction industry.

Note, however, that quotas can be used in only the most extreme situations. Thus, the Court rejected a city's minority set-aside policy in *Richmond* v. *Croson*, 1989. There the Court held, 6–3, that the city of Richmond, Virginia, had not shown that its ordinance was justified by past discrimination. Therefore, it had denied white contractors their right to equal protection.

Johnson v. *Transportation Agency of Santa Clara County*, 1987, marked the first time the Court decided a case of preferential treatment on the basis of sex. By a 6–3 vote, the justices held that neither the Equal Protection Clause nor Title VII of the 1964 law forbids the promotion of a woman rather than a man, even though he had scored higher on a qualifying interview than she did. The case arose in California, when a woman was promoted to a job that until then had always been held by a man.

Recent Developments The current Supreme Court's increasingly conservative bent is evident in some of its more recent affirmative action decisions. Thus, for example, in *Wards Cove Packing Co.* v. *Atonio*, 1989, the Court made it more difficult for those who charge discrimination to prove their point. There, a group of nonwhite cannery workers in Alaska produced statistical evidence showing a longstanding pattern of employment practices by which their cannery company channeled nonwhites into low-paying jobs while whites received the much more desirable positions.

But the Court ruled against them. It held, 5–4, that such statistical evidence was not an adequate proof of race discrimination. Instead, said the majority, Title VII requires that those who claim discrimination in employment must be able to show that the conditions they challenge are not the result of some legitimate "business necessity."

The Court's holding in *Wards Cove* was pointedly rejected by an act of Congress in 1991. In effect, Congress said that the Court had misread Title VII. The new law declares that Title VII means this: Any business practice that results in the unequal treatment of female or minority employees is permissible only if the employer can show that that practice is based on some legitimate business necessity. Note that in *Wards Cove* it was the employees' responsibility to show that the action did not serve a legitimate business necessity.

Section 3 Review

1. Define: affirmative action, quota, reverse discrimination
2. During what time period was most of the nation's civil rights legislation passed?
3. What are the major provisions of the Civil Rights Act of 1964?
4. What is the significance of the *Bakke* case?
5. Under what circumstances has the Supreme Court allowed quotas?

Critical Thinking

6. Identifying Central Issues (p. 19) In your opinion, is it society's responsibility to rectify the harm suffered by a group of people as a result of discrimination in the past?

★

Monitor Comprehension

Answers to Section 3 Review
1. "Key Terms" are defined on the following pages:
- **a.** affirmative action, p. 557
- **b.** quota, p. 558
- **c.** reverse discrimination, p. 558

2. Since 1957. **3.** No one can be denied service at public accommodations based on race, color, religion, or national origin; prohibits discrimination in programs receiving federal funding; prohibits employers and unions from discriminating. **4.** First major reverse discrimination case. The Court ruled that race may be used as only one factor in making affirmative action decisions. **5.** In cases where there has been longstanding and flagrant discrimination in the past. **6.** Some might argue that society must remedy damage caused by earlier government action or inaction; others that government cannot do anything more than to prevent future harm.

Teacher's Resource File
See the Unit 5 File, p. 79, for the Section 3 Quiz.

Closure

Civil rights legislation was intended to eliminate discrimination. Affirmative action policies are intended to overcome the effects of past discrimination. In Section 4, students will read about diversity in relation to questions of citizenship and immigration.

Assignment Assign Section 4, pp. 561–567, for the next class period.

Reteach

Divide the class into groups of ten or twelve students. Have one student in each group write on a sheet of paper a sentence about civil rights legislation, affirmative action, or reverse discrimination. This student should then pass the paper to another student in the group, who should add a sentence on one of these topics, and pass the paper on to the next student, and so on. Have a spokesperson from each group read the resulting document aloud.

Debating Key Issues

TEACHING
Debating Key Issues

Regents of the University of California v. *Bakke:*
Should Universities Have the Right to Use Admissions Quotas?

Objective
Identify the federal laws that guarantee citizens "equal protection."

INSTRUCT

Before reading the feature, you may want to elicit student responses to the question in the title. Then have them read the feature and work through the "Getting Involved" section, beginning by identifying the constitutional issues involved.

Following class debate, have students read the Supreme Court's decision to find out if the Court agreed with their views. After discussing with the class the various effects of this case on the future of minority rights, you may wish to discuss with students how they would feel if they were in Bakke's position, or a minority applicant who was denied a place in the class because of the *Bakke* decision.

Supreme Court Decision
The Court ruled narrowly, providing an admission for Bakke, but not overturning "affirmative action," preferring to take discrimination questions on a case-by-case basis.

TRF **Teacher's Resource File**
See the Supreme Court Cases File, p. 16, for an activity that extends coverage of this case.

Should Universities Have the Right to Use Admissions Quotas?

Regents of the University of California v. *Bakke*

Allan Bakke was in his thirties when he decided that he wanted to become a doctor. He already held a respected and well-paid job as a NASA engineer. But Bakke decided to give up his career in order to attend medical school.

Allan Bakke applied to the University of California Medical School at Davis in 1973, but he was rejected. Bakke reapplied to the university in 1974, but this attempt at admission also ended in failure. While trying to discover the reasons for his repeated rejection, Bakke learned that his grades and test scores were higher than those of several applicants who had been admitted to the school.

Bakke also learned that the medical school had a special admissions program that reserved 16 of 100 places in each year's class for disadvantaged individuals that were members of several minority ethnic groups. Members of any race could be considered for the remaining 84 places in the class. Bakke, who was white, believed the system was unfair. He sued the university on the grounds that he had been rejected because of racial discrimination.

In the superior court of California, Bakke was denied an order for admission to the university. Upon appeal, the California Supreme Court reversed the decision and mandated that Bakke be admitted to the university's next class. At this point, the Regents of the University of California appealed to the United States Supreme Court.

Review the following evidence and arguments presented to the United States Supreme Court.

Arguments for Bakke

1. The refusal to admit Allan Bakke is a clear case of reverse discrimination and a violation of the 14th Amendment, which provides for equal protection.

2. The university's policy violates the Civil Rights Act of 1964, which states that "No person in the United States shall, on the ground of race, color, or national origin, be excluded from participation in, be denied the benefits of, or be subjected to discrimination under any program or activity receiving federal financial assistance."

Arguments for Regents of the University of California

1. People of certain minority ethnic backgrounds are disadvantaged from the day they are born. They rarely receive equal education and therefore must be afforded greater protection under the 14th Amendment.

2. The intent of the Civil Rights Act of 1964 was to support the healing of past societal discrimination and should protect those minority students who might otherwise be unfairly displaced by whites.

Getting Involved

1. Identify the constitutional grounds on which each side based its arguments.

2. Debate the opposing viewpoints presented in this case. Predict how you think the Supreme Court ruled in this case and why. Then refer to the Supreme Court Glossary that begins on page 764 to read about the decision in this case.

3. Discuss the impact of the Court's decision in this case on minority rights and advancement in the future.

4 American Citizenship

Find Out:

- How can American citizenship be acquired?
- What is the immigration policy of the United States?
- What is the undocumented alien problem?

Key Terms:

citizen, jus soli, jus sanguinis, naturalization, alien, expatriation, denaturalization, deportation

Are you an American **citizen**—one who 1.a
owes allegiance to the state and is entitled to its protection? Very likely you are; more than 90 percent of all the people who live in this country are citizens of the United States. In addition, many of those who are not citizens are actively seeking citizenship.

In this section, you will examine the issue of United States citizenship—what it is, how it is acquired, and who may acquire it.

The Question of Citizenship

As it was originally written, the Constitution mentioned both "citizens of the United States" and "citizens of the States." It did not define either of those phrases, however. Through much of America's early history it was generally agreed that national citizenship followed that of the States.

The coming of the Civil War and the adoption of the 13th Amendment in 1865 raised the need for a constitutional definition, however.[14] That need was finally met by the 14th Amendment in 1868. The amendment begins with these words:

> "All persons born or naturalized in the United States, and subject to the jurisdiction thereof, are citizens of the United States and of the State wherein they reside."

[14]In the *Dred Scott* case (*Scott* v. *Sanford*) in 1857, the Supreme Court had ruled that neither the States nor the National Government had the power to confer citizenship on African Americans—slave or free. The dispute over that issue was one of the several causes of the Civil War.

Thus, the 14th Amendment declares that a person can become an American citizen either by birth or by naturalization. The chart on page 563 summarizes the means of acquiring American citizenship.

Citizenship by Birth

More than 225 million Americans—more than 90 percent of all of us—are American citizens because we were born in the United States. Another several million are also citizens by birth, even though they were born abroad. Citizenship by birth is determined by either (1) **jus** 1.b
soli—the law of the soil, where born, or (2) **jus** 1.c
sanguinis—the law of the blood, to whom born.

Jus Soli The 14th Amendment confers citizenship according to the location of a person's birth: "All persons born . . . in the United States . . . " By law, Congress has defined the United States to include, for purposes of citizenship, the 50 States, the District of Columbia, Puerto Rico, Guam, the Virgin Islands, and the Northern Mariana Islands. It includes, as well, all American embassies and all American public vessels anywhere in the world.[15]

Jus Sanguinis A child born abroad can become an American citizen at birth under certain circumstances. The child must be born to at least one parent who is a citizen and who has at some time lived in the United States.

The 14th Amendment does not provide for jus sanguinis, but Congress has included it as a part of American citizenship law since 1790. The constitutionality of the rule has never been challenged. But if it were, it would almost certainly be upheld—if for no other reason than because of its longstanding history.

[15]United States embassies are, in effect, parts of the United States. A public vessel is any ship or aircraft operated by any agency of the government.

Until 1924, Native Americans born to tribal members living on reservations were not considered citizens. They were instead wards, persons under the legal guardianship, of the government. In that year, however, Congress granted citizenship to all Native Americans who did not already possess it.

Section 4
American Citizenship

Focus

Teacher's Resource File
See the Unit 5 File, p. 80, for the Section 4 Outline.

Objectives

21.11 Explain how American citizenship can be acquired.

21.12 Explain the immigration policy of the United States.

21.13 Describe the undocumented alien problem.

Bellringer Activity Tell students that, whatever their social status, they are all privileged members of American society. Explain that, as American citizens, they have rights and privileges that are not extended to those who merely live and work in the United States but who are not citizens.

State the Purpose The United States is a nation of immigrants. Until 1882 immigration was virtually unrestricted. Then, due partly to a saturated labor market and partly to prejudice, Congress began restricting immigration. In Section 4, students will learn how a person can become a citizen of the United States and how and why people come here illegally.

ABCNEWS INTERACTIVE

The following video segments may be used to highlight aspects of American citizenship.

Powers of the Congress Guidebook
Chapter 48: Citizenship, p. 125
Chapter 49: Becoming a U.S. Citizen, p. 126

Vocabulary

Point out "Key Terms" on page 561. Draw a cluster or flow diagram on the board showing that three of the terms—*jus solis, jus sanguinis,* and *naturalization*—denote ways of becoming a citizen; that two of the terms—*naturalization* and *deportation*—denote three things that can happen to an alien; and two terms—*expatriation* and *denaturalization*—denote things that can happen to a citizen.

Reading Strategy: Question Writing

As a preparation for reading, have students write one question for each of the headings and subheadings in the section. Ask students to skim the section to find the answers to their questions.

Interpreting Charts As students look at the chart, ask them why they think prospective citizens must take an oath of allegiance. (*As an indication that they have relinquished any allegiance to a foreign country.*)

Caption Answer In an oral interview, understanding of the English language can be better tested.

INSTRUCT

Discuss/Analyze Explain to students the two ways in which one can be a citizen by birth. Have students develop an example of jus sanguinis citizenship. For example, an American teacher, born in the United States, goes to teach in Nicaragua after college graduation, marries, and has a daughter there. The daughter is an American citizen. If the child spends her life in Nicaragua and never lives in the United States, then she will not be an American citizen by jus sanguinis.

Have students compare individual naturalization and collective naturalization. Ask students in which case a person has any control over whether or not he or she becomes a citizen. (*Individual naturalization*). Ask in which case a person who does not speak English can become a citizen. (*Collective naturalization*).

Illustrate Give each student an index card and ask them to create a situation that typifies one of the paths to citizenship. Read the situations to the class one by one, asking volunteers to name the means of acquiring citizenship that is described.

How to Apply for Naturalization

1. File an Application. You must be 18 years of age and have lived in the United States for at least five continuous years to file an application for naturalization. The application consists of Application Form N-400, a fingerprint card, and a Biographic Information form. These materials can be acquired at your nearest office of the Immigration and Naturalization Service or from a social service agency in your community. Fill out these forms according to the instructions, then file them with the office of the Immigration and Naturalization Service with jurisdiction over your residence. Three unsigned photographs (described in the application form) must also be submitted.

2. Take the Examination on the Application. You will be informed by the Immigration and Naturalization Service when and where to appear for the examination. During this examination, the examiner will ask questions pertaining to United States history and government. If found eligible by the examiner, you then will be assisted in filing the legal petition for naturalization. At this time, you will be requested to pay a fee to the clerk of the naturalization court.

3. Appear Before the Court for the Final Hearing. At this hearing, the naturalization examiner will inform the judge that you have been found qualified and should be made a citizen. If you have been notified that you are not eligible for naturalization, you may appear at the final hearing, with or without an attorney, and request naturalization before the judge. The judge will listen to your arguments regarding your fitness for citizenship and decide whether to grant citizenship. When the court decides that you should be made a citizen, you will take an oath of allegiance to the United States. In doing so, you give up allegiance to any foreign country and promise to support and defend the Constitution and laws of the United States.

Interpreting Charts This chart outlines the qualifications necessary to become a citizen of the United States. Why do you think the examination is oral, rather than written?

Citizenship by Naturalization

Naturalization is the legal process by which a person becomes a citizen of another country at some time after birth. Congress has the exclusive power to grant naturalization. No State may do so.[16] The naturalization process may be either an individual or a collective one.

Individual Naturalization The process is most often an individual one, conducted by a court. More than 250,000 **aliens**—citizens or nationals of a foreign state living in this country—now become naturalized American citizens each year.

As a general rule, any person who has come to the United States as an immigrant, that is, an alien legally admitted as a permanent resident, can be naturalized. More specifically, current law provides that a person who wants to become a naturalized citizen must:

—have entered the United States legally, lived here for at least five years and in some State for at least three months, and be at least 18 years old.[17]
—file a petition for naturalization with the clerk of a federal district court or of a state court of record.
—be literate in the English language.
—be "of good moral character," "attached to the principles of the Constitution," and "well disposed to the good order and happiness of the United States."
—have "a knowledge and understanding of the fundamentals of the history, and the principles and form of government, of the United States."

[16]Article I, Section 8, Clause 4.

[17]The residence requirements are eased somewhat for the alien husbands, wives, and children of citizens and for present and former members of the armed forces. Also, the naturalization of both parents—one parent, if the other is dead or divorced—automatically naturalizes their children under 16 years of age if the children are living permanently in the United States.

ACTIVITY: Cooperative Learning

Time: Two class periods **Activity:** Research and report on the native country of an immigrant group. **Grouping:** Groups of four to six students **Purpose:** Have each group choose a native country of an immigrant group and prepare a report on life in that country. Explain that the report should describe the standard of living, the political situation, and other factors influencing the lives of the people. **Roles:** Assign the following roles: manager, researcher(s), recorder, spokesperson. **Outcome:** Have the spokesperson present the group's report to the class. Based on the information presented, the class may discuss possible reasons why people leave this homeland to come to the United States.

Teacher's Resource File
See the Historical and Legal Documents file, p. 53, for materials to support the section.

—take an oath or affirmation in which he or she absolutely renounces any allegiance to any foreign power and promises to "support and defend the Constitution and laws of the United States against all enemies, foreign and domestic."[18]

The Immigration and Naturalization Service (INS) in the Department of Justice investigates each applicant. An INS examiner then reports to the judge of the court in which the petition for naturalization was filed. If the judge is satisfied, the oath or affirmation is administered in open court, and the new citizen receives a certificate of naturalization.

Collective Naturalization At various times in American history an entire group of persons has been naturalized en masse. This has most often happened when the United States has acquired new territory. As the table on this page indicates, those living in the areas involved were naturalized by a treaty or by an act or a joint resolution passed by Congress. The largest single instance of collective naturalization came with the ratification of the 14th Amendment, however. The most recent instance occurred in 1977, when Congress gave citizenship to the more than 16,000 native-born residents of the Northern Mariana Islands.

[18]In an oath a person swears to something and binds that pledge with the words "so help me God." Those whose beliefs will not allow them to invoke a supreme being in that way may instead make an affirmation (a legally binding pledge that does not refer to a supreme being).

In the oath or affirmation the citizen-to-be also promises to "bear arms in behalf of the United States" if required to do so by law. However, those whose religious beliefs will not allow them to do so may promise to serve as noncombatants in the armed forces or perform some work of national importance under civilian direction.

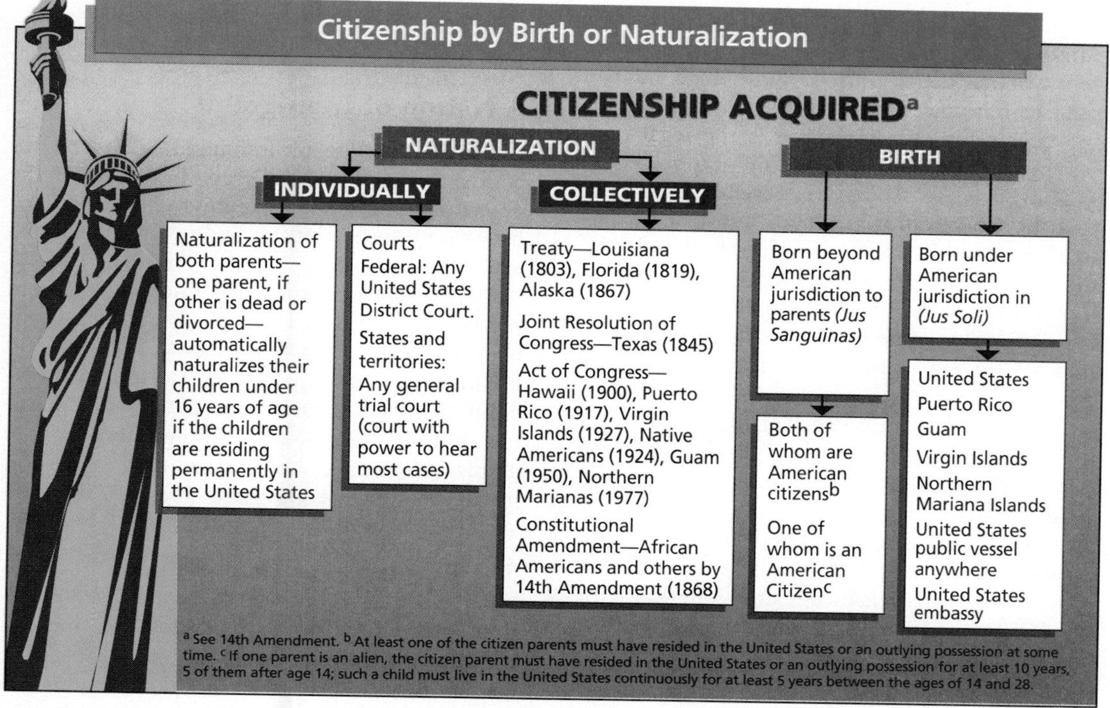

Citizenship by Birth or Naturalization
CITIZENSHIP ACQUIRED[a]
NATURALIZATION
BIRTH
INDIVIDUALLY
COLLECTIVELY
Naturalization of both parents—one parent, if other is dead or divorced—automatically naturalizes their children under 16 years of age if the children are residing permanently in the United States
Courts
Federal: Any United States District Court.
States and territories: Any general trial court (court with power to hear most cases)
Treaty—Louisiana (1803), Florida (1819), Alaska (1867)
Joint Resolution of Congress—Texas (1845)
Act of Congress—Hawaii (1900), Puerto Rico (1917), Virgin Islands (1927), Native Americans (1924), Guam (1950), Northern Marianas (1977)
Constitutional Amendment—African Americans and others by 14th Amendment (1868)
Born beyond American jurisdiction to parents (Jus Sanguinas)
Both of whom are American citizens[b]
One of whom is an American Citizen[c]
Born under American jurisdiction in (Jus Soli)
United States
Puerto Rico
Guam
Virgin Islands
Northern Mariana Islands
United States public vessel anywhere
United States embassy
[a] See 14th Amendment. [b] At least one of the citizen parents must have resided in the United States or an outlying possession at some time. [c] If one parent is an alien, the citizen parent must have resided in the United States or an outlying possession for at least 10 years, 5 of them after age 14; such a child must live in the United States continuously for at least 5 years between the ages of 14 and 28.

Interpreting Charts: Multicultural Awareness Most Americans acquire citizenship by birth. After examining the chart, name at least two other means of acquiring citizenship.

Interpreting Charts: Multicultural Awareness Ask students why the citizens of the areas listed in the collective naturalization box were naturalized in this manner rather than individually? (*The areas involved were acquired territories of the United States.*)

Caption Answer Possible answers: through the naturalization of both parents; through the courts by naturalization; collectively by treaty, act of Congress, or constitutional amendment.

Teacher's Resource File
See the Historical and Legal Documents file, p. 36, for material to support the section.

 **SPOTLIGHT ON: Economics**

The Immigration and Naturalization Service will spend about $1.4 billion in 1992. That money supports INS activities from border patrol and deportation to examination, inspection, and immigrant legalization. The largest share of the budget goes toward enforcement of existing laws. In 1991 the INS inspected 425.7 million persons and apprehended some 1,182,000 people trying to cross the United States border illegally. The agency expects some 450 million inspections in 1992.

Interpreting Graphs: Multicultural Awareness Ask students why immigration fluctuated at certain times, for example, why it was so low from 1931 to 1940. (*The Immigration Acts of 1921 and 1924 and the National Origins Act of 1929.*)

Caption Answer Asians and North Americans.

INSTRUCT

Analyze/Discuss Examine the criteria that must be met for expatriation and denaturalization to occur. Have students explain the circumstances under which a citizen can lose his or her citizenship involuntarily.

Analyze with students why immigration was not regulated before the Chinese Exclusion Act and why immigration has been regulated to some extent ever since. Ask students to explain changes in the ways in which immigration has been limited since the late 1800s.

Discuss with students the categories of aliens in the United States, including immigrants, refugees, temporary residents, and undocumented aliens. Have students define each category.

Discuss what an undocumented alien is, how aliens come to the United States illegally, and what the consequences are, or can be by law, both to undocumented aliens and to their employers in the United States. Discuss with students how effective they think restrictions on immigration are.

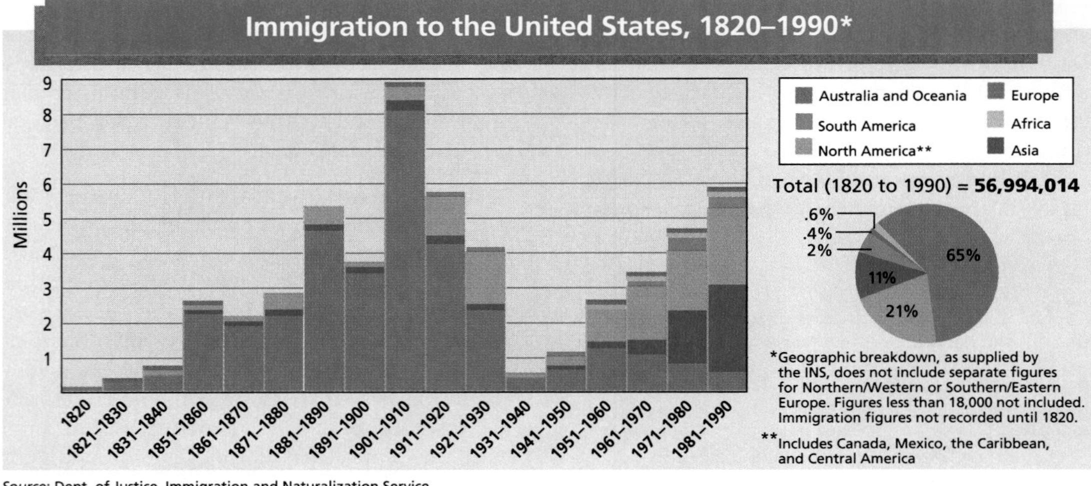

Source: Dept. of Justice, Immigration and Naturalization Service

Interpreting Graphs: Multicultural Awareness The graph shows that, until the 1970s, Europeans dominated United States immigration figures. Which two groups are the largest now?

Loss of Citizenship

Although it rarely happens, every American citizen, whether native-born or naturalized, has the right to renounce—voluntarily abandon—his or her citizenship. **Expatriation** is the legal pro- 1.f
cess by which a loss of citizenship occurs.

The Supreme Court has several times held that the Constitution prohibits automatic expatriation. That is, Congress cannot provide for the involuntary loss of a person's citizenship for something he or she has done—for example, committing a crime, voting in a foreign election, or serving in the armed forces of another country.[19]

Naturalized citizens can lose their citizenship involuntarily, however. That is, they can be denaturalized. But this process—**denaturaliza- 1.g
tion**—can occur only by court order and only after it has been shown that the person became a citizen by fraud or deception.

A person cannot gain nor lose American citizenship by marriage. The only significant effect that marriage has on the matter is to shorten the time required for the naturalization of an alien who marries an American citizen.

A Nation of Immigrants

We are a nation of immigrants. Except for Native Americans—and even they may be the descendants of earlier immigrants—all of us have come here from abroad or are descended from those who did.

There were only some 2.5 million persons in the United States in 1776. Since then, the population has grown a hundredfold, to over 250 million people today. That extraordinary population growth has come from two sources: natural increase—births—and immigration. As the graph on this page shows, more than 55 million immigrants have come here since 1820, when such figures were first recorded.

The Regulation of Immigration Congress has the exclusive power to regulate immigration—that is, the power to decide who may be admitted to the United States and under what conditions.[20]

The United States made no serious attempt to regulate immigration for more than a century after independence. As long as land was plenti-

[19]A person convicted of a federal or a State crime may lose some of the privileges of citizenship, however, either temporarily or permanently—for example, the right to travel freely or to vote or hold public office.

ACTIVITY: Teaching Heterogeneous Groups
In order to represent graphically immigration patterns on a small scale, have students learn the country of origin of their ancestors. You might want to use a world map to highlight the countries of origin and the number of families coming from each. On a broader scale, have each student poll ten people to determine where their ancestors originated.

ful and rapidly expanding industry demanded more and more workers, immigration was encouraged.

By 1890, however, the open frontier was a thing of the past, and labor was no longer in short supply. Then, too, the major source of immigration had shifted. Until the 1880s most immigrants had come from the countries of northern and western Europe. The "new immigration" from the 1880s onward came mostly from southern and eastern Europe—and included peoples against whom there was considerable prejudice.

Congress placed the first major restrictions on immigration with the passage of the Chinese Exclusion Act in 1882. At the same time, it barred the entry of convicts, "lunatics," paupers, and others likely to become public charges. Over the next several years a long list of "undesirables" was added to the law. Thus, contract laborers were excluded in 1885, immoral persons and anarchists in 1903, and illiterates in 1917. By 1920 more than 30 groups were denied admission on grounds of various personal traits.

The tide of newcomers continued to mount, however. In the 10 years from 1905 through 1914 an average of more than a million persons—most of them from southern and eastern Europe—came to this country.

Congress responded to the many pressures for tighter regulation by adding quantitative limits (numerical ceilings) to the qualitative restrictions (personal characteristics) already in place. The Immigration Acts of 1921 and 1924 and the National Origins Act of 1929 established a national origins quota system. Each

By Don Wright, © 1980: Miami News. New York Times Syndicate.

Interpreting Political Cartoons: Multicultural Awareness Newcomers are greeted with suspicion by most cultures. Why is this cartoon particularly pointed?

country in Europe was assigned a quota—a limit on the number of immigrants who could enter the United States from that country each year. The quotas were purposely drawn to favor northern and western Europe. The quota system was not applied to the Western Hemisphere, but immigration from Asia, Africa, and elsewhere was generally prohibited.

In 1952 Congress passed yet another basic law, the Immigration and Nationality Act. That statute modified the quota system to cover every country outside the Western Hemisphere.

Congress finally eliminated the country-based quota system in the Immigration Act of 1965. That law provided that as many as 270,000 immigrants could enter the United States each year—without regard to race, nationality, or country of origin. The 1965 law did establish a special preference for one group of immigrants in particular, however: the immediate relatives of American citizens or of aliens legally residing in this country.

Present Immigration Policies Today, the Immigration Act of 1990, which became effective on October 1, 1991, is the basic law governing the admission of aliens to the United States. Like its predecessors, it was adopted only after years of intense debate, and many of

[20]The power to control the nation's borders is an inherent power of the United States, and that power includes the control of immigration. On the inherent powers, see Chapter 4, Section 1. In an early leading case on the point, the Supreme Court upheld the constitutionality of the Chinese Exclusion Act of 1882. That law generally barred Chinese from entering this country. The Court ruled that the power of the United States to "exclude aliens from its territory . . . is not open to controversy," *Chae Chan Ping* v. *United States*, 1889. The States have no power in the field, *The Passenger Cases*, 1849.

Interpreting Political Cartoons: Multicultural Awareness Ask students to name three biases against immigrants that are illustrated in this cartoon. (*Resentment at the competition for jobs, the perception that many immigrants cannot support themselves, and criticism of anyone "different."*)

Caption Answer Hindsight tells us that Native Americans had every right to view the passengers and crew of the Mayflower with suspicion.

Enrichment

Have students consider the problems and challenges facing recent immigrants to the United States. Ask students to imagine they are recent immigrants and to write letters that such immigrants might have written to those back home describing problems, challenges, setbacks, and opportunities. (Challenging)

Provide Guided Practice
Describe to students the various ways of acquiring citizenship and ask them to name each based on your description. Then do the same for the ways citizenship may be lost.

Provide Independent Practice
TRF **Teacher's Resource File**
You may wish to assign Section 4 Guided Reading and Review, Unit 5 File, p. 81, to help students master section objective content.

South of the Border An Immigration and Naturalization Service officer patrols the Mexican border, on the watch for people entering the country illegally.

its provisions are certain to be the subject of continuing controversy.

The new law provides for a substantial increase in the number of immigrants who may enter the United States each year. As many as 700,000 are to be admitted in 1992, in 1993, and in 1994. The annual limit is set at 675,000 for 1995 and beyond.

The current law continues the family-preference policy first put in place in 1965; at least a third of those persons admitted under its terms are to be the close relatives of American citizens or resident aliens. Those immigrants who have occupational talents in short supply in the United States—notably, highly skilled researchers, engineers, and scientists—also receive special preference.

Only those aliens who can qualify for citizenship can be admitted as immigrants. The law's list of "excludable aliens"—those barred because of some personal characteristic—is extensive. Among those excluded are, for example, criminals, persons with communicable diseases, drug abusers and addicts, illiterates, and mentally disturbed persons who might pose a threat to the safety of others.

Deportation Most of the civil rights set out in the Constitution are guaranteed to "persons." That term covers aliens as well as citizens. In one important respect, however, the status of aliens is altogether unlike that of citizens: Aliens may be subject to **deportation**—that is, a legal process in which aliens are legally required to leave the United States.[21]

Congress has provided that an alien may be deported on any one of several grounds. The most common today is illegal entry. Hundreds of thousands of aliens who enter with false papers, sneak in by ship or plane, or slip across the border at night are caught each year—most of them by the Border Patrol, the police arm of the Immigration and Naturalization Service. Conviction of any serious crime, federal or State, usually leads to a deportation order by the INS. In recent years several thousand aliens have been expelled on the basis of their criminal records, especially narcotics violators.

Undocumented Aliens

No one knows just how many undocumented aliens there are in the United States today. The Census Bureau has put their number at somewhere between three and a half and five million, and the INS at four to six million. Some authorities believe that the actual figure is at least twice those estimates.

However many there are, the number of undocumented aliens is increasing by at least half

[21]The Supreme Court has long held that the United States has the same almost-unlimited power to deport aliens as it has to exclude them. In an early major case, the Court ruled that (1) deportation is an inherent power, arising out of the sovereignty of the United States, and (2) deportation is not criminal punishment, and so does not require a criminal trial, *Fong Yue Ting* v. *United States*, 1893. Those major points remain basic to American law. Because deportation is a civil, not a criminal matter, several constitutional safeguards (for example, with regard to bail and ex post facto laws) do not apply. As but one illustration of this: In *Immigration and Naturalization Service* v. *Lopez-Mendoza*, 1984, the Court held that illegally seized evidence, which under the exclusionary rule cannot be used in a criminal trial, can be used at a deportation hearing.

a million a year, according to the INS. Most of these undocumented persons enter the country by slipping across the Mexican or Canadian border, usually at night. Some come with forged papers. Many are aliens who entered legally, as nonimmigrants, but have now overstayed their legal welcomes.[22]

Once here, most undocumented aliens find it fairly easy to become "invisible," especially in larger cities, and the understaffed INS finds it very difficult to locate them. Even so, immigration officials have apprehended more than a million undocumented aliens in each of the last several years. Nearly all are sent home. Most go voluntarily, but some leave only as the result of formal deportation proceedings.

The presence of so many undocumented persons has raised a number of difficult problems. Those problems have grown worse over the past several years and, until recently, not much had been done to meet them.

Take, as one illustration of those many problems, this: Until 1987, it was not illegal to hire undocumented aliens. As a result approximately 3.5 million persons who now hold jobs in this country came here illegally. Some employers were more than willing to hire undocumented aliens—because many of them are willing to work for substandard wages and under substandard conditions. Hundreds of thousands of undocumented aliens have taken jobs on farms, often as laborers; thousands more have become janitors and dishwashers, or seamstresses in sweatshops, or found other menial work. The increase in population has also added stress to the public schools and welfare services of several States—most notably California, Arizona, New Mexico, Texas, and Florida.

Many groups—labor, farm, business, religious, ethnic, civil rights, and others—have been troubled and divided by the problem of undocumented aliens. Finally, after wrestling with the issue for years, Congress passed the Immigration Reform and Control Act of 1986.

In its major provisions, that statute (1) offered a legalized status—amnesty—to many undocumented aliens and (2) made it unlawful for anyone to hire undocumented aliens.

The law's amnesty program was in effect for one year. From mid-1987 to mid-1988, those who could show that they entered this country before January 1, 1982, and had lived here "in an unlawful status" since then, could ask to have their stay legalized. Those who applied successfully became temporary legal residents. After 18 months (by late 1989/early 1990) they could become permanent residents and, eventually, naturalized American citizens.[23] More than 1.75 million aliens took advantage of the law's amnesty provisions.

By law, all prospective employees must now verify their citizenship. An employer who knowingly hires undocumented aliens can be fined from $250 to as much as $10,000 for each offense and, in the case of repeat offenders, can be jailed for as long as six months.

Section 4 Review

1. **Define:** citizen, jus soli, jus sanguinis, naturalization, alien, expatriation, denaturalization, deportation
2. By what two ways can a person become an American citizen?
3. How are individuals naturalized?
4. How may a person lose citizenship?
5. For what reasons can a person be deported?
6. What has Congress recently done about the undocumented aliens issue?

Critical Thinking

7. **Drawing Conclusions** (p. 19) Why do you think the current immigration law gives special preference to immigrants who have certain occupations?

[22]Well over half of all undocumented aliens have come from Mexico; most of the others come from other Latin American countries and from Asia. A majority of the Mexicans stay here only four to six months a year, working on farms or in other seasonal jobs. Most other illegal aliens hope to remain permanently.

[23]The law also provides temporary resident status for up to 350,000 aliens who can show that they have lived in the United States for at least three years and that they worked in American agriculture for at least 90 days in each of those years.

Monitor Comprehension

Answers to Section 4 Review
1. "Key Terms" are defined on the following pages:
- **a.** citizen, p. 561
- **b.** jus soli, p. 561
- **c.** jus sanguinis, p. 561
- **d.** naturalization, p. 562
- **e.** alien, p. 562
- **f.** expatriation, p. 564
- **g.** denaturalization, p. 564
- **h.** deportation, p. 566

2. Birth and naturalization.
3. Enter the U.S. legally, live here for five years (in one State for three months), and be 18; file a petition in district court; be literate in English; be of good moral character and attached to the principles of the Constitution; know fundamentals of U.S. history and government; take an oath or affirmation. **4.** Voluntarily renouncing it or through the process of denaturalization. **5.** Illegal entry; conviction of a serious crime; acts of disloyalty. **6.** Immigration Act of 1986 offered amnesty to many undocumented aliens and made it unlawful for anyone to hire an undocumented alien. **7.** Students should question whether or not the U.S. policies show evidence of bias or prejudice against certain groups.

Closure

Since the passage of the Chinese Exclusion Act in 1882, immigration to the United States has been restricted. In the next chapter, students will learn about other political and economic systems.

Assignment Assign Chapter 22, Section 1, pp. 575–581, for the next class period.

Teacher's Resource File
See the Unit 5 File, p. 82, for the Section 4 Quiz.

Reteach

Looking at the chart on page 563, ask students to write a paragraph that describes the various ways that citizenship can be acquired.

TEACHING

Critical Thinking

Demonstrating Reasoned Judgment

Objective

Determine whether significant progress has been made in the battle for civil rights for African Americans.

INSTRUCT

As students read the feature, have them list key evidence that they feel supports the statement and keep in mind why the other information does not support the statement.

Point out to students that it is important to be able to distinguish evidence from other information which does not necessarily support an argument. By doing so, one can make reasoned decisions. Once they have evaluated the evidence, you may wish to have students write a reaction paper regarding the statement in the feature.

Answers 1. (a) It was not very effective. (b) Progress has been made since the 1950s. **2.** (a) Statements 1, 3, 6, and 7. (b) Statements 1, 2, 3, 6, 7, and 8. (c) Statements 4, 5, and 9. **3.** (a) Answers will vary. (b) Answers will vary. (c) Students may suggest that they would like to know how the Civil Rights Act helped the plight of African Americans.

Critical Thinking

Demonstrating Reasoned Judgment

Demonstrating reasoned judgment means presenting evidence or reasoning that supports a given opinion or statement. It means being able to use your reasoning abilities to help formulate a final judgment or reach a conclusion about a piece of information.

The statement on this page about minority rights is followed by nine points of evidence that relate directly or indirectly to the statement. Use the steps below to practice using reasoned judgment about the statement and evidence.

1. Determine the main message of the statement. Before you can make an evaluation of a particular piece of information, you must make sure that you understand that information. Read the statement. (a) What is the statement's conclusion about the effectiveness of the 14th Amendment? (b) What is the statement's conclusion about civil rights today?

2. Summarize the meaning of each piece of evidence. Analyze the evidence to determine how each piece relates to the statement in question. (a) Which pieces of evidence relate directly to the subject of advances in civil rights for African Americans? (b) Which pieces relate indirectly to the topic of civil rights? (c) Which pieces provide no information about civil rights?

3. Identify the relationship of each piece of evidence to the statement. Consider how each piece of evidence relates to the statement. (a) In your opinion, does the evidence support the statement? (b) Based on this evidence, do you agree or disagree with the statement? (c) What additional information might you like to have to aid you in making your judgment?

Statement:

Despite the passage of the 14th Amendment in 1868, which guaranteed African Americans equal protection under the law, many parts of the nation instituted laws that effectively placed African Americans in an inferior status socially, politically, and educationally. Fortunately, this history of injustice toward minority groups is finally being addressed. Since the mid-1950s, this nation has made significant progress in the battle for civil rights for all citizens.

Evidence:

1. The United States armed forces were desegregated in 1948.

2. In 1896 the Supreme Court decided that communities could provide separate-but-equal facilities for white people and African Americans.

3. The United States Supreme Court declared public school segregation unconstitutional in 1954.

4. Between 1970 and 1990, the number of African-American elected officials in the South rose from over 500 to over 4,000.

5. Martin Luther King, Jr., was assassinated in Memphis, Tennessee, in 1968.

6. Integrated professional sports teams were first allowed to compete in Georgia in 1966.

7. The Civil Rights Act of 1964 was passed by the United States Congress.

8. In the 1960s, African Americans in many communities were unable to register to vote.

9. More than 28 million African Americans live in the United States.

TRF **Teacher's Resource File**

See the Unit 5 File, p. 83, for the Skill Application for this lesson.

Chapter-in-Brief

Scan all headings, photographs, charts, and other visuals in the chapter before reading the section summaries below.

Section 1 Diversity and Discrimination in American Society (pp. 545–549) The United States' population is largely white. Yet in recent decades, the populations of certain minority groups have grown significantly.

Historically, white America has been reluctant to yield an equal place in society to minority groups. For example, African Americans have been the subject of unjust treatment throughout much of the nation's history. Native Americans, Hispanic Americans, and Asian Americans also have suffered discrimination.

Women, though a majority of the population, have traditionally been denied the rights enjoyed by men. These inequities are still evident, especially in the workplace.

Section 2 Equality Before the Law (pp. 550–555) The Constitution's two Equal Protection clauses say that all people are to be treated equally. Governments, however, can create classifications of people. The Supreme Court has held that such classifications must pass the rational basis test. In the case of certain suspect classifications, the Court also can require the classification to meet the strict scrutiny test.

Historically, many States passed racial segregation laws. The Supreme Court allowed these laws with the separate-but-equal doctrine. The Court reversed itself in 1954, when it found in *Brown* v. *Topeka Board of Education* that separate was inherently unequal. Since that time, the Court has found segregation in many areas unconstitutional.

The Court also has held that classifications based on gender are unconstitutional unless they can pass the strict scrutiny and rational basis tests.

Section 3 Federal Civil Rights Laws (pp. 556–559) Congress enacted the first in a series of civil rights laws with its passage of the Civil Rights Act of 1957. The most far-reaching of the later acts, which include civil rights acts in 1960 and 1968, is the Civil Rights Act of 1964. All of the legislation comes down to this fact: Discriminatory practices based on race, color, sex, or national origin are illegal.

The Federal Government has used affirmative action to overcome the effects of discrimination. This has been widely criticized by those who feel that it is reverse discrimination. But the Supreme Court has found that affirmative action is constitutional as long as race or gender is not the only factor in the decision and as long as evidence of longstanding and flagrant discrimination exists.

Section 4 American Citizenship (pp. 561–567) According to the Constitution, there are two ways to become an American citizen. Those who are born in the United States, or to a parent who is a citizen and who has lived in the United States, become citizens at birth. Others can become citizens through naturalization.

Citizens can choose to renounce their citizenship. And naturalized citizens who acquired citizenship by deception or fraud can be denaturalized.

Since the late 1800s, United States policy consisted of setting quotas for immigration from different nations. Today, the nation has no quotas, but it does have a ceiling on the number of immigrants it allows.

In 1986, Congress passed legislation to address the issue of undocumented aliens. The law offered amnesty to certain undocumented aliens and made it illegal for employers to hire undocumented aliens.

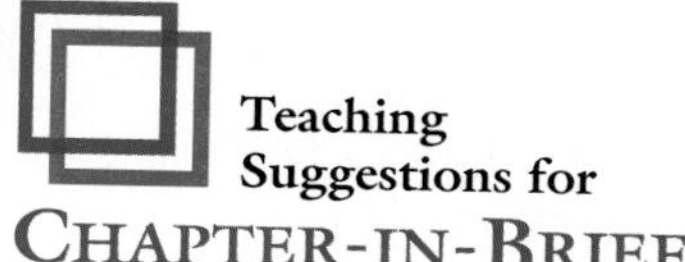

Teaching Suggestions for CHAPTER-IN-BRIEF

Below are some of the possible uses for the Chapter-in-Brief:

To Preview the Chapter You may want to assign the Chapter-in-Brief page and the Section Outlines from the Teacher's Resource File before beginning Chapter 21 to introduce students to the "Key Terms" and concepts in each section.

To Review the Chapter When students have completed Chapter 21, you might want to assign the Chapter-in-Brief as a tool for review, along with the Guided Reading and Reviews from the Teacher's Resource File.

To Omit the Chapter If you wish to skip Chapter 21, it may be helpful to assign the Chapter-in-Brief to students as a review before continuing to another chapter. You may also want to assign the Chapter 21 Test to assess student knowledge of the material. Then specific portions of Chapter 21 may be assigned to students needing reinforcement of "Key Terms" and concepts.

Teacher's Resource File See the Unit 5 File for the following materials:

- Section Outlines, pp. 71, 74, 77, 80.
- Guided Reading and Reviews, pp. 72, 75, 78, 81.
- Chapter 21 Test, pp. 73, 76, 79, 82.

ADDITIONAL RESOURCES

Bell, Derrick. *And We Are Not Saved: The Elusive Quest for Racial Equality.* Basic Books, 1987.

Blacks and the Constitution. Video. PBS Video, 1987. Color. 60 min.

Browning, Rufus P., *et al.* (eds.). *Racial Politics in American Cities.* Longman, 1990.

Cone, J. H. *Martin and Malcolm and America.* Orbis Books, 1991.

Craig, Barbara H. *Chada: The Story of an Epic Struggle.* Oxford, 1989.

"I Have a Dream": The Life of Martin Luther King. 16mm film. Bailey Film Associates, 1968. Color. 35 min.

Immigration: Growth of a Nation. Sound filmstrip. Random House Media, 1985. Color. 2 parts.

Levine, Herbert M. and Jean Edward Smith. *Civil Liberties and Civil Rights Debated.* Prentice Hall, 1988.

Sigelman, L. *Black Americans' Views of Racial Inequality.* Cambridge Univ. Press, 1991.

Takai, Ronald. *Strangers from a Different Shore: A History of Asian Americans.* Little, Brown, 1989.

Weisbrot, Robert. *Freedom Bound: A History of America's Civil Rights Movement.* Norton, 1989.

Weiss, Nancy J. *Whitney M. Young, Jr. and the Struggle for Civil Rights.* Princeton University Press, 1990.

Answers to
CHAPTER 21

Vocabulary and Key Terms

Matching
1. refugee
2. jus soli
3. Jim Crow law
4. expatriation
5. de jure segregation

True or False
1. True.
2. False—the correct term is *citizen.*
3. True.
4. True.
5. False—the correct term is *separate-but-equal doctrine.*

Word Relationships
1. Item *b* does not belong. The other three items refer to segregation resulting from laws or court decisions, whereas de facto segregation is segregation in fact but not by law.
2. Item *a* does not belong. The other three items refer to affirmative action. Alien is a person who is not a citizen.
3. Item *a* does not belong. The other three items refer to losing or renouncing citizenship; naturalization is the process of becoming a citizen.

Main Ideas

Section 1
1. That the United States population is made up of many different types of people. **2.** The United States began as a predominantly white country and became more so over time. The last 40 years has seen a sharp rise in the rate of minority, nonwhite population growth. **3.** White, male America has been consistently reluctant to share its dominant position with other groups. **4.** Women have been the targets of consistent discrimination.

Section 2
5. Equal treatment of people under the law. **6.** They must lead to the achievement of some legitimate governmental purpose. In some cases, they must also serve a compelling governmental interest. **7.** In the late 1800s, many States passed Jim Crow laws. The Supreme Court put forth the separate-but-equal doctrine in 1896—a decision that gave a constitutional basis to segregation. The separate-but-equal doctrine was finally overturned in 1954. In spite of the decline of de jure segregation, de facto segregation persists. **8.** The Court originally viewed gender-based distinctions as acceptable. Beginning in 1971, however, the Court has said that sex-based classifications must serve an important governmental objective.

Section 3
9. From the 1870 to the 1950s, no meaningful civil rights legislation was passed. Since 1957, Congress has passed a number of important civil rights acts.
10. (a) The most far-reaching law is the Civil Rights Act of 1964. (b) Prohibits discrimination at public accommodations; prohibits discrimination in any program receiving federal funds;

Chapter Review

Vocabulary and Key Terms

reservation (p. 574)
refugee (p. 549)
segregation (p. 551)
Jim Crow law (p. 551)
separate-but-equal doctrine (p. 552)
de jure segregation (p. 553)
de facto segregation (p. 553)
affirmative action (p. 557)
quota (p. 558)
reverse discrimination (p. 558)
citizen (p. 561)
jus sanguinis (p. 561)
jus soli (p. 561)
naturalization (p. 562)
alien (p. 562)
expatriation (p. 564)
denaturalization (p. 564)
deported (p. 566)

Matching: *Review the key terms in the list above. If you are not sure of a term's meaning, look up the term and review its definition. Choose a term from the list above that best matches each description.*

1. a person who leaves his or her home in order to escape the dangers of war, political persecution, or other causes
2. the law of the soil; a means by which one acquires citizenship
3. laws that required separate facilities for African Americans and whites
4. an act by which one forfeits citizenship
5. segregation as a result of laws

True or False: *Determine whether each statement is true or false. If it is true, write "true." If it is false, change the underlined word or words to make the statement true.*

1. The separation or isolation of one group from another is called <u>segregation</u>.
2. One who owes allegiance to a state and is entitled to protection by it is a <u>refugee</u>.
3. According to the concept of <u>*jus sanguinis*</u>, a person born to a parent who is an American citizen becomes a citizen him- or herself.
4. Many Native Americans today live on <u>reservations</u>.
5. The Supreme Court's decision in *Plessy* v. *Ferguson* established <u>affirmative action</u>.

Word Relationships: *Three of the terms in each of the following sets of terms are related. Choose the term that does not belong and explain why it does not belong.*

1. (a) Jim Crow law (b) de facto segregation (c) de jure segregation (d) separate-but-equal doctrine
2. (a) alien (b) reverse discrimination (c) affirmative action (d) quota
3. (a) naturalization (b) expatriation (c) deportation (d) denaturalization

Main Ideas

Section 1 (pp. 545–549)

1. What does it mean to say that the population of the United States is heterogeneous?
2. Briefly describe the trends in the composition of the population over the course of U.S. history.
3. Briefly describe the historical treatment of minority groups in the United States.
4. In what respect do women as a group resemble minority groups?

Section 2 (pp. 550–555)

5. What kind of equality does the Constitution guarantee?
6. According to the Supreme Court, what standards must laws that discriminate between groups meet?

7. Briefly describe the history of racial segregation from the late 1800s to today.
8. Briefly describe the history of the Supreme Court's view of classifications based on gender.

Section 3 (pp. 556–559)

9. Briefly describe the history of civil rights legislation between the 1870s and today.
10. (a) What was the major piece of civil rights legislation during the 1960s? (b) What are its major features?
11. Summarize the reasoning behind affirmative action programs. What is the main criticism of these programs?
12. Under what circumstances have affirmative action programs generally been allowed by the courts?

Section 4 (pp. 561–567)

13. Describe the means by which people can become citizens of the United States.
14. Describe the means by which people can lose citizenship.
15. Briefly describe immigration in the United States today.

Critical Thinking

1. **Making Comparisons** (p. 19) Recall what you read in Section 2 regarding the Supreme Court's attitude toward women. How has this attitude changed between the 1800s and today? How has society's attitude changed?
2. **Expressing Problems Clearly** (p. 19) Consider the doctrine of separate-but-equal. (a) Do you think it is possible for facilities that are segregated on the basis of race or gender to be truly equal? (b) Why or why not?
3. **Identifying Alternatives** (p. 19) Consider the process by which aliens can become naturalized United States citizens. (a) In your opinion, should this process be easier or more difficult? (b) What standards should be added or removed?

Getting Involved

1. **Writing Your Opinion** You are to give a speech before the United Nations on the value of diversity in the American population. Before you begin writing, brainstorm a list of the benefits this nation has received as a result of its diverse population. Open your speech with a statement that expresses your opinion on the topic. Then devote one paragraph to each of the benefits you identified in your list. Conclude with a statement in which you express your hopes for the future relations between the many peoples who make up American society. Review each paragraph to ensure that your ideas are stated positively and persuasively. Correct any errors and make a final draft.
2. **Cooperative Activity** Work as a class to create a package of proposed amendments and/or legislation to address the questions of civil rights raised in this chapter. Begin by holding a class discussion to generate a list of topics for the proposed amendments and legislation. Then divide into teams to create the wording for each proposed measure. When each team has completed its work, discuss as a class the strengths and weaknesses of each idea. Then have each team incorporate the comments of the class into a final draft. Finally, collect all the proposed measures in a single civil rights package.
3. **Class Debate** Hold a classroom debate on the following topic: *Resolved,* That United States immigration policy should set no limit to the numbers of immigrants. Select teams to debate each side of this issue. The rest of the class can evaluate each team's response.
4. **Creating a Political Cartoon** Create a cartoon to illustrate one of the concepts discussed in this chapter, such as affirmative action, separate but equal, or some other idea. Remember that you can use a combination of words and images in your cartoon.

and forbids discrimination by employers and unions in all job-related matters. **11.** Affirmative action attempts to overcome the harmful effects of past discrimination. Programs are criticized for causing reverse discrimination; they are not color blind. **12.** If race or sex is only one factor in the program and if the program seeks to overcome real imbalances resulting from past discrimination.

Section 4

13. By birth, if born to a United States citizen or if born in the United States. By naturalization, if both parents are naturalized or through the courts. Finally, large groups can be naturalized by a treaty or act of Congress. **14.** People can do so voluntarily, called expatriation. Naturalized citizens can be denaturalized if it is shown that they acquired citizenship fraudulently. **15.** The Immigration Law of 1990 allows 700,000 immigrants to enter from 1992 to 1994, and 675,000 after 1994. Only those who qualify for citizenship will be allowed to enter.

Critical Thinking

1. Students might suggest that women today are nominally and in many respects legally equal to men. However, students might also observe that there is evidence of continued discrimination against women. **2.** (a) Answers will vary, but students should realize that history has shown that separate facilities are inherently unequal. (b) Answers will vary. Students might say that the message that one group is better than another is inherent in the establishment of separate facilities. **3.** (a) Answers will vary. (b) Answers will vary. Make sure students can defend their answers based on a clear understanding of citizenship.

Getting Involved

1–4. Answers and results will vary, but students should demonstrate an understanding of the concepts in this chapter.

Managing the Unit

You may wish to review the following materials before beginning the unit to help plan your instruction.

Each chapter ends with a Chapter-in-Brief with suggestions for previewing, reviewing, or omitting the chapter.

Unit 6 Outline

Chapter 22 (pp. 574–603)
Comparative Political Systems
1 Great Britain
2 Japan
3 Mexico
4 The Former Soviet Union
■ **Chapter-in-Brief**, p. 601

Chapter 23 (pp. 604–627)
Comparative Economic Systems
1 Capitalism
2 Socialism
3 Communism
■ **Chapter-in-Brief**, p. 625

Pacing Charts,
pp. T28–T31

Unit 6

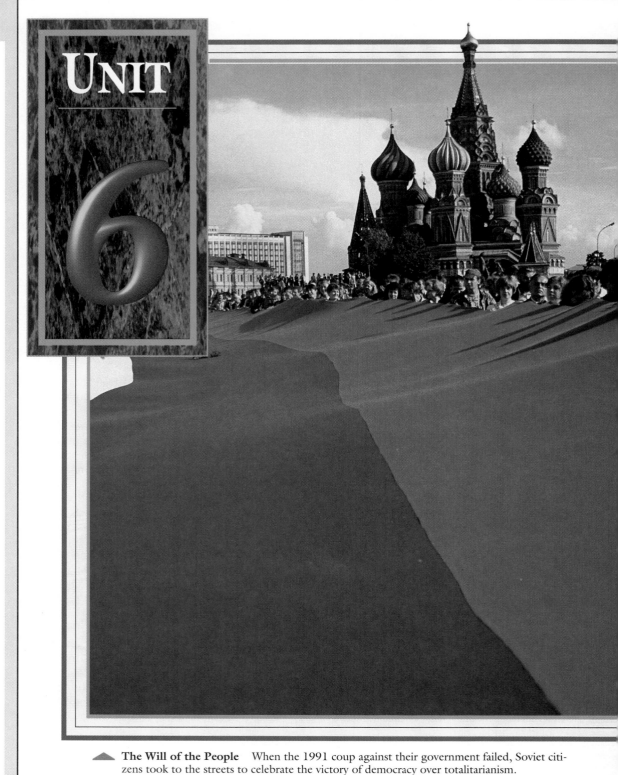

The Will of the People When the 1991 coup against their government failed, Soviet citizens took to the streets to celebrate the victory of democracy over totalitarianism.

Skills and Features

The following skill lessons and features are included in this unit.

Skill Lessons

Critical Thinking: Recognizing Ideologies (p. 600)
Citizenship: How to Start a Small Business (p. 624)

Debates/Case Studies

What *You* Can Do: Supporting Human Rights (p. 591)
What *You* Can Do: Working to End World Hunger (p. 612)

Comparative Political and Economic Systems

For three days beginning on August 19, 1991, the world held its breath while the Soviet Union sat like a seesaw balanced between past and future. People around the world waited to see if a sudden shift would drop the country back into what some described as the "old world of totalitarian darkness." For those three days, a group of hard-line Communist party stalwarts held Mikhail Gorbachev under house arrest. On their orders, tanks rolled into the streets, threatening to destroy the democratically elected Russian government. And then, in an astonishing triumph for democracy and freedom, it was over. The coup collapsed in the face of widespread public outrage. A shift did take place in the Soviet Union that summer. Ordinary citizens, believing in the principles of democracy, stood up to the tanks and with their actions thrust themselves hopefully into the future.

Did You Know That . . .

- Experts estimate that in the year 2100 the world's three most populous countries will be India, China, and Nigeria.
- Iraq spends six times more on its military than on health and education.
- Japan and Ireland have the lowest reported rate of murders in industrialized countries—fewer than 1 murder per 100,000 people.

Unit Focus

Activate Prior Knowledge Ask students to write down as many specific examples as they can think of about events in other countries during the past year. Tell students that such events are what make up the history of a nation. Ask: How do events in other countries affect the United States?

Interpreting the Visual Point out the photo of the celebration in the former Soviet Union in the unit opener. Ask students to consider the contrast between the ancient buildings in the photo's background and the modern-day event taking place in the foreground.

Did You Know That . . . Direct students to the items under "Did You Know That . . . ." Ask students to what extent they feel these statistics are related to the political and economic systems of these countries.

Journal Writing Suggested topics for the sixth unit include a comparison between the 1991 events in the former Soviet Union and the 1961 erection of the Berlin Wall, a creative piece on the changing world, or a critique of a recent action by a foreign country.

You may also want to utilize **CNN Video-link** to generate ideas for journal writing.

Bulletin Board Idea

Using the Poster Have students consider the political cartoon depicting shoppers on the wall poster titled "Freedom: A Global Perspective." Ask students to explain the cartoon. Where are these women shopping? What point is the cartoonist making about the conditions under which they live? Compare this view with the quote by George Bush. Ask students whether the people in the cartoon appear to be "energized." Discuss with the class the momentous changes that have occurred over the last few years in Eastern Europe and the former Soviet Union. Display a world map on the bulletin board with or near the wall poster. Use pins or flags to label those countries or regions that have, in recent years, chosen democracy and free market economies. How does the cartoon illustrate the difficulties these countries face?

Chapter 22 Resources

In the Teacher's Resource File The following materials are found in the Teacher's Resource File box.

Instructional Support: Unit 6 File

For the Section	For the Chapter
Outlines, pp. 2, 5, 8, 11	Skill Application, p. 14
Guided Reading and Reviews, pp. 3, 6, 9, 12	Case Study on Contemporary Issues, pp. 15–17
Quizzes, pp. 4, 7, 10, 13	Chapter Test, pp. 18–20
	Additional Test Questions, pp. 21–23

Enrichment Support Files

Participatory Government Activities, pp. 28–39
Simulations and Debates: U.S.-Japanese Relations
Historical and Legal Documents, p. 6
Comparative Government: A Multicultural View, pp. 4–5, 8–9, 12–13

Computer Test Bank and Assessment

Transparency Package, pp. 22, 47

Election Kit, p. 40

Chapter 22 Focus

Introduce the Chapter Tell students that in this chapter they will learn about the political systems of Great Britain, Japan, Mexico, and the former Soviet Union. They will read about how each system works and about their similarities and differences. Read with students the Chapter Preview and Objectives.

Writing Activity Direct students' attention to "Describe." Have them write a paragraph outlining their perceptions of the meaning of national identity.

Motivate for Learning Direct students' attention to "Predict." Discuss with students the former Soviet Union. Have students predict the future role of national identity in these new sovereign countries.

Chapter 22 Comparative Political Systems

Chapter Preview

In December, 1991, the Soviet Union was voted out of existence. Russia, Ukraine, Byelorussia, Kazakhstan, Kirghizia, and Armenia declared their independence from the union, and the Bush administration recognized the six former republics as independent, sovereign countries. But full diplomatic relations with six other former republics—Uzbekistan, Turkmenistan, Tajikistan, Moldavia, Georgia, and Azerbaijan—was withheld until the United States was satisfied that their governments met higher standards of democracy and stability.

The 12 "new" states are not new at all. Their traditions and histories are ancient; they have merely reclaimed the right to govern themselves in their own ways. Ironically, as the Soviet Union broke up, its western neighbors in the European Community worked toward greater union—each grappling to maintain national identities within that union. In this chapter, you will learn about other similarities and differences in four of the world's political systems.

Before you read this chapter:

- **Describe** the meaning of national identity.
- **Predict** the role of national identity in the former Soviet Union and the European Community by the year 2000.

As you read, focus on the main objective for each section. Understand:

1. The British Parliamentary system of government.
2. The characteristics of Japan's constitutional monarchy.
3. The characteristics of Mexico's system of government.
4. The history and break-up of the Soviet Union.

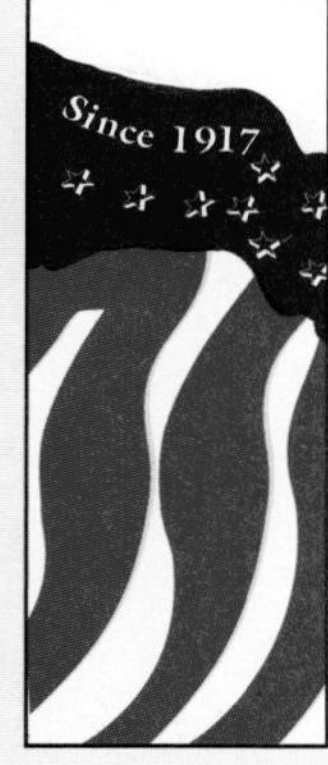

Magruder's American Government: *A Witness to Change* by William A. McClenaghan

At least since the end of World War II, students of United States history and government have also been students of the former Soviet Union. In a very real sense, the fate of our country has been inextricably linked with that of our cold-war foe. Nevertheless, this book has never questioned the superiority of the American way of life or the eventual outcome of the struggle between the two superpowers. In 1952, *Magruder's* made the following observation and prediction: *What guarantee is there that the dictatorship (as it exists in the U.S.S.R.) will ever end? With all power gathered in the hands of a few at the top, what is to prevent the few from perpetuating their rule?*

But man is independent by nature, and by suppressing this trait, communism is surely signing its own death warrant.

Today, Soviet communism is apparently gone. And though the dynamics that led to its downfall are clearly more complicated than the above quotation suggests, this country can rightfully celebrate—along with the people of the former Soviet Union—the spirit of freedom and independence that helped topple a dictatorship.

Momentous Changes in the Former Soviet Union The Ukrainian people in this photograph are taking part in a religious ceremony. By December of 1991, this former Soviet republic had announced its independence and its intention to join in a new commonwealth of nations.

1 Great Britain

Find Out:

- How are the British and American governments different and alike?
- What is the role of tradition and the unwritten constitution in British government?

Key Terms:

monarchy, by-election, coalition, minister, shadow cabinet

British government is democratic government. So, too, is American government; its roots are buried deep in English political and social history. Yet there are important differences between the two systems of government. Most of those differences grow out of this fundamentally important point: Unlike government in the United States, government in Great Britain[1] is unitary and parliamentary in form and rests upon an unwritten constitution.

[1]Great Britain is, officially, the United Kingdom of Great Britain and Northern Ireland. It contains four principal parts: England, with 80 percent of the population and more than half of the land area; Wales, conquered by England in the 13th century; Scotland, joined to England and Wales by the Act of Union that created Great Britain in 1707; and Northern Ireland, which became part of the United Kingdom in 1800.

SECTION 1
Great Britain

FOCUS

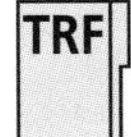

Teacher's Resource File See the Unit 6 File, p. 2, for the Section 1 Outline.

Objectives

22.1 Determine ways in which the British and American governments are different and alike.

22.2 Examine the role of tradition and the unwritten constitution in British government.

Bellringer Activity Hold up a picture of the British flag. See if students can identify it. Remind students that Great Britain is made up of the countries of England, Scotland, Wales, and Northern Ireland.

State the Purpose Like the United States, Great Britain is a democracy. The roots of American democracy stem from the British system of government, but the actual operation of the British government is quite different. In Section 1, students will compare the American and British governments.

ABCNEWS INTERACTIVE

The following video segment may be used to highlight aspects of foreign governments.

POWERS OF THE PRESIDENT GUIDEBOOK
Chapter 3: The Prime Minister and Parliament, p. 60

Vocabulary

Direct students' attention to "Key Terms" on page 575. Explain that each of these terms reflects a key feature of the British government. As students read through Section 1, have them identify the "Key Terms" and the ways in which each term is similar to or different from the American system of government.

Reading Strategy: Structured Overview

To help students gain an understanding of the British government, have them create a graphic organizer to outline the key points in Section 1. Write the words *executive, legislative,* and *judicial* on the board. As students read, they can fill in the chart using examples of each of these branches of government as they are manifested in Great Britain.

INSTRUCT

Discuss/Analyze The American and the British governments are both based on the same principles of democracy, yet each country executes its democracy in different ways. The United States government is relatively new compared to the parliamentary democracy of the British government.

Draw a chart on the board with two columns, labeled *Similarities* and *Differences.* Ask students to identify the ways in which the British and American governments are the same and yet different. You may want students to begin their discussion by explaining the difference between the U.S. Constitution and the written and unwritten constitution upon which the British system is based.

Draw a second chart on the board, also with two columns. Label the columns *Figureheads* and *Holders of Power.* Have students identify those elements of the British government that fall under each category. Remind students as they compare systems to discuss the role and function of the prime minister, the cabinet, the House of Lords, the House of Commons, the election process, and the monarch.

Outline Have students outline the section, using the main headings in the section as the main headings in their outline and filling in details with the section subheads.

The Unwritten Constitution

Actually, it is not strictly true to say that the British constitution is entirely unwritten. Parts of the constitution can be found in books and charters. However, no single document serves as the British constitution.

The written part of the British constitution includes historic charters, acts of Parliament, and innumerable court decisions. The unwritten part derives from customs and usages—practices that have gained acceptance over time. The written parts are called the law of the constitution, and the unwritten parts are called the conventions of the constitution.

The Law of the Constitution Many historic documents figure in Britain's written constitution. Perhaps the best known is the Magna Carta of 1215. Others include the Petition of Right of 1628 and the Bill of Rights of 1689. (See Chapter 2, Section 1.) Each of those documents was a landmark in the centuries-long struggle to limit the powers of the English monarch and advance the concept of due process of law.

Certain acts of Parliament also form a basic part of the British constitution. One example of these is the Representation of Peoples Act of 1969. That act lowered the voting age in all British elections from 21 to 18. In the United States, you will recall, such a change required a formal amendment to the Constitution.[2]

Finally, court decisions are another part of the law of the constitution. Centuries of court decisions have created a body of legal rules covering nearly every aspect of human conduct. Such decisions make up the common law. (See Chapter 25, Section 3 for a discussion of the common law in the American judicial system.)

The Conventions of the Constitution The truly unwritten part of the British constitution consists of the customs and practices of British politics. For example, no document says that Parliament must hold a new session each year. It just does. There are no written rules giving the lower house of Parliament the power to choose and dismiss a prime minister. That feature of British government developed over hundreds of years and is now a matter of custom.

[2]The 26th Amendment, effective in 1971.

Continuity and Change With its open-ended constitution, Britain has a flexible set of rules that is always evolving and open to change. A majority vote in Parliament can easily remove an old provision of the constitution or add a new one. The flexibility of this system can be very useful. But without the delays and safeguards that a system such as the American system would impose, there is always the danger of ill-considered and hasty action that might fundamentally alter the people's rights.

The Monarchy

In contrast to such republics as the United States and France, Britain has a hereditary ruler;
1.a so Great Britain is a **monarchy**. Its monarch bears the title of queen or king. While English monarchs once ruled with absolute power, their role has dwindled, and they are now little more than figureheads.[3] Because her powers and duties are controlled by Britain's unwritten constitution, Elizabeth II, Britain's queen since 1952, is known as a constitutional monarch.

In formal terms, all acts of the British government are performed in the name of the queen. As you will read shortly, however, the real power of government is exercised by the prime minister and other high officials.[4] The queen does appoint the prime minister, but her choice is subject to the approval of the House of Commons. So, traditionally, she chooses the leader of the majority party in that house to be prime

[3]Most present-day monarchs, especially in industrial democracies like Sweden, Norway, and Japan, are also figureheads. In the developing world, however, the monarchs of such nations as Saudi Arabia and Morocco still wield considerable power.

[4]The individual who symbolizes a nation's sovereignty is called the head of state, and the individual who directs the government, the head of government. In the United States, the President is both head of state and head of government. In Britain, the queen is head of state, and the prime minister is head of government.

TRF **Teacher's Resource File**
See the Historical and Legal Documents file, p. 6, for material to support the section.

minister. She has no power to dismiss the prime minister and no veto over acts of Parliament.

Today's British monarch reigns but does not rule. Nonetheless, the institution of monarchy serves an important function. The queen stands as a living symbol of the British state, as a focus of loyalty and pride. Periodic proposals to do away with the monarchy inevitably bring an outpouring of support for "our dear queen."

Parliament

Parliament is the central institution of British government. It holds both the legislative and the executive powers of the nation—powers that in the United States are divided between separate and independent branches of government. By its legislative power, Parliament passes Britain's laws. By its executive power, it chooses some of its members (the prime minister and the cabinet) to administer the departments of government and run the nation's affairs. In the British system, as in all parliamentary systems, government is built on the fusion of powers. The government's legislative and executive authority is fused—combined—in Parliament and the prime minister and cabinet.

Parliament is bicameral; its two houses are the House of Lords and the House of Commons. Of the two, the House of Commons is by far the more powerful body.

The House of Lords The upper chamber, the House of Lords, is an aristocratic body of more than 1,100 members. More than 750 of its members have inherited their positions. They hold noble titles—such as duke, marquess, earl, viscount, and baron—and are known as the hereditary peers. The other members are appointed for life by the queen. They include two archbishops and 24 bishops of the Church of England, law lords (eminent judges), and some 320 life peers. The life peers are persons who have been honored for their careers in science, literature, the arts, politics, or business. Attendance at sessions of the Lords rarely exceeds 200.

The House of Lords holds no real power over legislation. If it rejects a bill passed by the House of Commons, the Commons has only to approve the bill a second time, and it becomes law. The Lords can merely delay but not block a bill's passage.[5] The upper house can also amend a bill and return it to the lower house. The lower house can—and usually does—remove the amendment by a simple majority vote.

"Trooping the Color" This term describes the annual troop inspection led by Queen Elizabeth II of England. With no voice in government, the monarch is a symbol of British history and traditions.

Clearly, the House of Lords does not fit the pattern of a representative democracy. Various critics have urged that it be abolished—a deed that the House of Commons could readily accomplish by passing a law. Defenders of the upper house argue that it plays a useful role, however. By delaying passage of a controversial bill, they say, it may allow tempers to cool and

[5]The upper house has 30 days to act on a money bill and one year to act on other bills.

Illustrate Have students use their outlines of the section to create a diagram that shows the organization of the British Parliament. Their diagram should show the relationships among the following bodies: Monarch, House of Lords, House of Commons, Prime Minister, and Cabinet.

Analyze Explore with students the author's comment on page 576 regarding the flexible nature of the British system: "[W]ithout the delays and safeguards that a system such as the American system would impose, there is always the danger of ill-considered and hasty action that might fundamentally alter the people's rights." Do students agree or disagree with this statement? Based on the class discussion, you may wish to list the pros and cons of this aspect of the British system on the board.

INSTRUCT

Discuss Examine with students the differences between the British unitary form of government and the American federal form of government. Have students name some of the powers that State and local governments possess in the United States. (*Grant marriage licenses, establish public school systems, prohibit or allow gambling.*) Then explain to students that such powers do not belong to local government in Great Britain. Instead, power is vested only in Parliament.

give the lower house more time to weigh the full effects of a bill.

Besides its legislative role, the House of Lords does perform an important judicial function. Its nine law lords serve as the final court of appeals in both civil and criminal cases in the British court system. It is important to note that the British courts and judges, including the law lords, do not possess the power of judicial review. They cannot overrule a law or an act of government, even if they believe that it violates the constitution.

The House of Commons The lower house, known familiarly as the Commons, is a representative body. Its 650 members are called MPs, which stands for member of parliament. All are popularly elected from single-member districts, or constituencies, that are roughly equal in population. Currently, there are 523 constituencies in England, 38 in Wales, 72 in Scotland, and 17 in Northern Ireland.

A general election—one in which all seats in the Commons are at stake—takes place at least once every five years. Election dates are not firmly fixed. If an MP dies or resigns, a special
1.b election called a **by-election** is held in that MP's constituency to choose a replacement.

The Commons meets in a small, rectangular chamber within the majestic building of Parliament. The high-ceilinged House chamber was originally designed for just 350 members. It is, quite literally, a political arena. The members of rival parties sit on facing rows of benches, talking and sometimes hooting at one another.[6] An open space occupies much of the center of the chamber, with a raised chair at one end for the presiding officer (known as the speaker).[7] Leading members of the major parties sit on the front rows of benches. Those who occupy the remaining rows are known as backbenchers.

The majority party largely controls the work of the Commons. While any MP can introduce a bill, most measures are in fact offered by the prime minister and the cabinet. The prime minister and cabinet head the executive arm of British government. They form what, in the British and other parliamentary systems, is regularly called "the government"—what, in the United States, is referred to as the administration.

Eight standing committees consider bills and prepare them for final consideration by the full chamber. Committees in the Commons are generalists; any committee may consider any bill. Their main task is to put measures in proper form for final floor consideration. All bills sent to committee must be reported to the floor, where a party-line vote generally follows the will of the government.

The Prime Minister The prime minister, although formally appointed by the queen, is in fact responsible to the House of Commons. When a single party holds a majority in the Commons, as usually happens, that party's leader becomes prime minister. If no single party holds a majority, a coalition must be formed. In
1.c this sense, a **coalition** is a temporary alliance of parties for the purpose of forming a government. Two or more parties must agree on a common choice for prime minister and on a joint slate of cabinet members.[8]

The Cabinet The prime minister selects the members of the cabinet. Most cabinet members,
1.d or **ministers**, are members of the House of Commons. A few may sit in the House of Lords.

Collectively, the prime minister and the cabinet provide political leadership, both in the making and the carrying out of public policy. Individually, cabinet ministers head the various executive departments. One minister serves as foreign secretary—responsible for foreign affairs. Another serves as chancellor of the exchequer—responsible for finance. All told there are about 20 ministers, each with his or her own department and functions. The size of the cabinet

[6]MPs often heckle their rivals, loudly.

[7]The speaker is always a member of the House of Commons and is chosen by it. As an MP, the speaker must win reelection to the House of Commons at each general election—but the speaker always runs unopposed in those elections.

[8]Britain's last coalition government served during World War II, from 1940 to 1945. It was headed by Prime Minister Winston Churchill, a Conservative. Britain is the only parliamentary democracy in Europe that has not had a coalition government since World War II.

SPOTLIGHT ON: Behind the Scenes

In May 1979, Margaret Thatcher became the first woman prime minister in the history of the British government. A grocer's daughter educated at Oxford in chemistry and law, she was first elected to Parliament in 1959. In 1975, she was elected leader of the Conservative party—the first woman party leader in Britain. The Thatcher government cut taxes, privatized state-owned industry, waged war with Argentina over the Falkland Islands (1982), and brought Britain toward economic union with Western Europe.

John Major Margaret Thatcher's successor as British prime minister leads a country with an important position in world affairs.

varies from time to time, depending on the wishes of the prime minister.

The cabinet is accountable to the House of Commons. An almost daily feature of parliamentary sessions is question hour, when the cabinet ministers appear in the Commons to answer questions about their area of responsibility. Any MP may ask a question about any relevant subject.

Major opposition parties appoint their own teams of potential cabinet members. Each of these opposition MPs shadows, or watches, one particular member of the cabinet. If an opposition party should succeed in gaining a majority, its so-called **shadow cabinet** would then be ready to run the government.

Calling Elections

Britain has no fixed date for holding elections. A general election must be held at least once every five years, but one can take place at any time within that period.

The prime minister decides when a general election will occur. As a rule, elections are called at a time when conditions seem to favor the government and its candidates. If in fact they do, the prime minister's party will likely increase its majority or at the least preserve its control of the House of Commons. If they do not, the other major party may take over the government.

Occasionally, an election is triggered by quite different circumstances: when the government falls, as the result of losing the confidence, or support, of the House of Commons. Normally, a government with a clear majority of seats in the Commons has little trouble keeping that support. But the opposition can cut into the government's majority by winning a series of by-elections. Or, rarely, some majority party MPs may become upset with their party and vote against the government.

The government is acknowledged to have lost Parliament's support if it is defeated on some critical issue in the House of Commons. When the government loses such a vote of confidence, the government falls, and the prime minister asks the queen to dissolve Parliament—end its session—and call a new general election.

Provide Guided Practice Ask students to write down one clue to a term in Section 1. For example, a clue to the term *ministers* may be "Members of the cabinet." Tell students not to write the answer to the clue. After students have each written a clue, have them exchange papers to see if they can guess the answer to one another's clues. Then review all clues and answers as a class.

Provide Independent Practice

TRF **Teacher's Resource File** You may wish to assign Section 1 Guided Reading and Review, Unit 6 File, p. 3, to help students master section objective content.

Enrichment

Ask students to write a comparison of Parliament and the United States Congress. Ask students to consider the role that the British and United States constitutions have played in the formation and daily workings of each legislative branch. In conclusion, students should make their own analysis of which form of government is the most effective. (Challenging)

MONITOR COMPREHENSION

Answers to Section 1 Review
1. "Key Terms" are defined on the following pages:
a. monarchy, p. 576
b. by-election, p. 578
c. coalition, p. 578
d. minister, p. 578
e. shadow cabinet, p. 579
2. (a) No single document makes up the British constitution. (b) Law—historic documents, such as the Magna Carta; acts of Parliament; court decisions. Conventions—customs and practices of British government. **3.** She serves as a living symbol of the British state; performs ceremonial functions. **4.** (a) Only one house of the British legislature has any real power. It holds both legislative and executive powers. The House of Lords also has judicial powers. (b) The prime minister is a member of the legislature; does not act as chief executive or head of state; is not popularly elected. **5.** In Great Britain it is theoretically easier for third parties to influence government. Also, the fact that Parliament chooses the prime minister means that it is not possible for a voter to vote for members of different parties in elections to national office.

CLOSURE

Great Britain's government is, in theory, quite flexible compared to that of the U.S. But British traditions have served as a safeguard against instability. In Section 2, students will read about Japan, another parliamentary democracy.

Assignment Assign Section 2, pp. 581–585, for the next class period.

In rarer instances, changes within the majority party can lead to changes in the government. This is clearly illustrated by the Conservative party infighting that led to Prime Minister Margaret Thatcher's resignation in November 1990. In the face of harsh criticism from within her Conservative party, several Conservative MPs mounted a strong challenge to her leadership. Mrs. Thatcher resigned, thus ending a period of over 11 years as the government's leader. John Major, her minister of the exchequer, won the balloting at a Conservative party convention to become the party leader and the youngest prime minister in this century. In this way, the Conservatives retained control of the government without losing a vote of confidence or risking their seats in a general election. The policies that cost Mrs. Thatcher her position were gradually reversed by the new government.

The ability to change governments in these ways means that a prime minister who becomes ineffective or unpopular can be changed before his or her actions become too extreme or too damaging to the political system. The majority party, unless its majority is absolutely overwhelming, must be responsive to the opposition party and dissenters in its own ranks. These mechanisms are very different from the institutionalized checks and balances between the three branches of government found in the American political system.

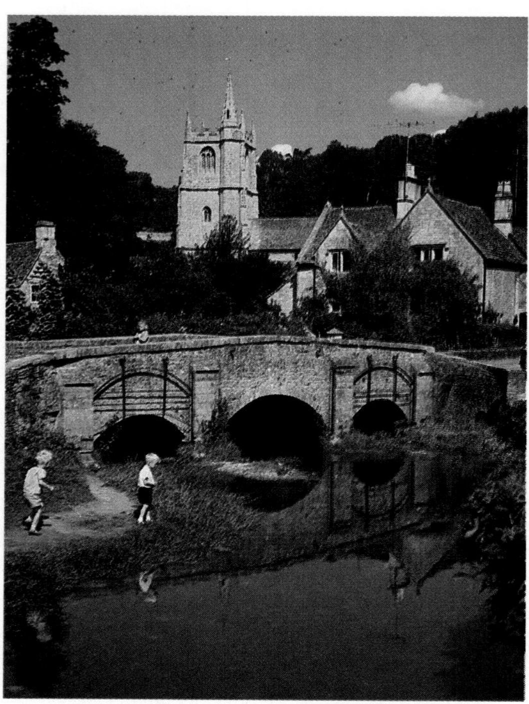

Local Government in England The less-populated villages dotting the English countryside are run by elected county councils.

The Party System

Because British voters do not elect candidates for nationwide office, the focus of elections in Great Britain is more localized than in the United States. While two major parties have dominated British politics in recent decades, the local focus makes it easier for smaller parties to exist. These may represent positions on specific issues or narrow ideological stands, or they may promote the interests of nationalist groups in Wales, Scotland, and Northern Ireland. Their existence can force the major parties to address these interests, or, if a party can get seats in the House of Commons, might even force a coalition to form by denying a larger party an outright majority.

The big two British political parties are the Conservative party and the Labour party. The Conservative party draws its main support from middle- and upper-class Britons. It tends to favor private economic initiatives and the traditions of the British class system. The Labour party appeals largely to working-class voters. It tends to favor government involvement in the economic system and a more socially equal society. In the past it has preached doctrinaire socialism. Under the current leadership of Neil Kinnock, however, the Labour party has moderated this approach and moved towards the mainstream of public opinion.

British parties are more highly organized and centrally directed than the major parties in American politics. High levels of party loyalty and party discipline characterize the British party system. Voter behavior clearly reflects that point. Voters in the constituencies regularly vote for candidates for the House of Commons on the basis of their party labels, not their individual qualifications.

TRF **Teacher's Resource File**
See the Unit 6 File, p. 4, for the Section 1 Quiz.

Reteach

Draw a diagram on the board that is similar to the one students created in "Instruct." The diagram should show the relationship among all elements of the British government discussed in the section. Build inaccuracies into the diagram. Have students identify the errors in your drawing.

Local Government

Recall that Britain has a unitary form of government (see Chapter 1, Section 2). Governmental power is centralized, or held at the national level. There is no division of powers by which some powers are vested in a national government while others belong to regional or local governments, as in the American federal system.

All local governments in Great Britain are creations of Parliament. To whatever extent those governments can deliver services or do anything else, it is only because the central government has created them, given them powers, and provided the financial means to carry them out.

The structure of local government in Britain depends on population density. In more heavily settled metropolitan areas, local government is centered in popularly elected district councils. In the shire counties, elected county councils are the principal institutions of local government.

The members of the local council are chosen by the voters in their district or county for four-year terms. Each council selects its chairperson from among its own members. In districts with enough population to be a borough or a town, the chairperson of the district council is known as the mayor; in larger cities, he or she is the lord or lady mayor.

Section 1 Review

1. Define: monarchy, by-election, coalition, minister, shadow cabinet

2. (a) In what sense does Britain have an unwritten constitution? (b) Describe the law of the constitution and the conventions of the constitution.

3. What is the essential role of the queen in British government today?

4. Cite three major differences between (a) the British Parliament and the U.S. Congress, and (b) the prime minister and the President.

Critical Thinking

5. Making Comparisons (p. 19) What is the major difference between the British and American two-party systems?

2 Japan

Find Out:

- What are the characteristics of Japan's parliamentary monarchy?
- In what ways is Japan's government centrally controlled?

Key Terms:

National Diet, prefecture, multi-seat district, consensus, dissolution

You are likely familiar with Japan as the efficient manufacturer and marketer of consumer electronics, automobiles, and video games. It is less likely that you are aware of the island nation's[9] consciously chosen path to political and technological modernization.

In this section, you will read about the government of Japan, which like Great Britain's, is a parliamentary democracy.

Japanese Government Before World War II

According to legend, the Japanese state was founded by the Emperor Jimmu in 660 B.C., but records indicate that it began to emerge about 1,000 years later, in the 4th century A.D. During the next 1,500 years, the country developed a political system in which territories were ruled by nobles (*daimyo*) backed by large families who owed only nominal loyalty to the imperial ruler living in the ancient city of Kyoto. Contacts with foreigners during that time were highly restricted.[10]

[9] Japan includes more than 2,000 islands. Its four main islands—Honshu, Hokkaido, Kyushu, and Shikoku—hold 98 percent of its land area and most of its 125 million people.

[10] Dutch and Portuguese traders had some contacts with the Japanese in the 16th and 17th centuries. The country was not opened to any meaningful Western contacts until 1853, however, when a U.S. naval squadron made a polite but firm visit. Japan and the United States concluded a commercial treaty the following year, and the Japanese then negotiated similar agreements with other Western powers.

SECTION 2
Japan

FOCUS

Teacher's Resource File See the Unit 6 File, p. 5, for the Section 2 Outline.

Objectives

22.3 Explain the characteristics of Japan's parliamentary monarchy.

22.4 Describe the ways in which Japan's government is centrally controlled.

Bellringer Activity Write the words *National Diet* on the board and ask students what image this phrase conjures up for them. Explain that the word *diet* has more than one meaning. In Section 2, students will read about the "national diet" of Japan—the body of legislators much like our own Congress.

State the Purpose Japan's government, like Great Britain's, is a parliamentary democracy. The relationship between the government and private enterprise in Japan has led to its strong place among the democratic industrialized nations of the world.

ABCNEWS INTERACTIVE

The following video segment may be used to highlight aspects of foreign governments.

POWERS OF THE CONGRESS GUIDEBOOK
Chapter 8: Comparing Governments (Presidential and Parliamentary), p. 83

Vocabulary

Direct students' attention to "Key Terms" on page 581. As they learn the meanings of *multi-seat district* and *prefecture*, ask students to compare these words with their equivalents in the American system of government.

Reading Strategy: Reinforcing Key Ideas

Have students skim Section 2 and write the main headings. As they read through the text, have students find facts that explain, or prove, each key idea.

INSTRUCT

Explain/Discuss Throughout its long history, Japan has undergone major changes in its governmental structure. Today, Japan's government is based on a parliamentary democracy, much like that of Great Britain.

Ask students to discuss the evolution of government in Japan. Have them give a brief overview of pre-World War II Japan and then discuss the changes that took place after the war. Invite students to speculate about reasons why the United States played such a large part in helping to form the present-day constitution and system of government in Japan. Ask them, too, to discuss ways in which the war changed the goals of Japan as a country.

To further the discussion, ask students to discuss the various aspects of Japanese government, including the National Diet and its two chambers; the bureaucratic structure of the government; the roles and structures of the executive, legislative, and judicial branches; and the policy of consensus politics.

Illustrate Draw a rough sketch on the board, similar to the one on page 585, showing the organization of the Japanese governmental system. Fill in only one label, and have students supply the remaining labels.

Yesterday and Today Japan's countryside remains much the same as it was in the days of the *daimyo*, Emperor Meiji, and the *samurai*, but 80 percent of Japan's population lives in crowded cities like Tokyo (right).

Japan freed itself in 1868 from the rule of a repressive military dictator, ending centuries of feudalism. An oligarchy of nobles backed by the legitimacy of Emperor Meiji then began a series of rapid changes. They openly studied and adopted Western forms, and rapidly pushed the country from isolation on the edge of Asia to an important position among the modern industrial nations.

As its industry grew and rights of suffrage spread to more of the population, the nation sought to secure the requirements for continued growth through the conquest of eastern Asia. The close partnership of the dominant political and economic elites gave rise to a form of fascism and militarism that pushed the Japanese into war with the United States, resulting in Japan's defeat at the end of World War II.

Japan was occupied by the United States for nearly seven years following the war, from 1945 to 1952. The occupation forces rewrote the country's old constitution and removed over 200,000 people from the top ranks of the military, the bureaucracy, and the major business conglomerates. The nation's remarkable postwar economic recovery was begun during the occupation and so, too, was the development of its present political system. Today, Japan is the leading democracy and the leading economic power in the largely undemocratic non-Western world.

The Constitution

The rewritten Constitution of 1947 made the government into a more effective parliamentary system. Suffrage was given to all citizens over the
1.a age of 20. The parliament, or **National Diet**, was formed with two, fully elected chambers. The larger, more powerful House of Representatives

TRF **Teacher's Resource File**
See the Comparative Government file, pp. 16–17, for material to support the section.

became the body from which the prime minister and cabinet were to be selected.

Unlike the British system, the judiciary has independent powers, and the Japanese Supreme Court can rule on the constitutionality of legislation. The powers of local government were increased and the top positions were made elective. The constitution contains quite an extensive listing of basic freedoms—in effect, a bill of rights.

Also part of the constitution is a unique antimilitary clause. The clause says that the Japanese people "forever renounce war as a sovereign right of the nation." It adds: "Land, sea, and air forces, as well as other war potential, will never be maintained."

United States officials insisted on the clause because they feared a revival of Japanese militarism. Later, they began to see Japan as an ally in the cold war. With encouragement from the United States, Japanese leaders since 1954 have given the clause a broad interpretation. They say that it rules out an army, a navy, and an air force, but not a so-called self-defense force. Thus, Japan has rebuilt its three military arms, calling them "ground, maritime, and air self-defense forces."

Also under the constitution, the Japanese emperor serves as the symbol of the state and the unity of the people. But, the emperor has no power to govern.

The National Diet

Under its constitution, Japan's National Diet is considered the highest organ of state power. The Diet contains an upper house, called the House of Councilors, and a lower house, called the House of Representatives. As in Britain, the lower house wields the greater power.

The prime minister and at least half of all Japan's cabinet ministers must be members of the Diet. Usually the prime minister comes from the lower house.

House of Councilors The House of Councilors has prestige but little power. Its 252 members sit for six years, in staggered terms. Three-fifths of the members are elected from districts that are based on Japan's **prefectures**—1.b the 47 political subdivisions into which Japan is divided. The remaining two-fifths of the seats are elected by the nation as a whole. Because it has fewer responsibilities than the lower house, the House of Councilors tends to serve an essentially deliberative, advisory role.

House of Representatives The House of Representatives has many important powers. It makes, and can also break, the prime minister. By a vote of no confidence, the House can force the prime minister either to resign or to dissolve the House of Representatives and call an early election. In addition, the lower house has full power to make treaties, raise funds, and make appropriations. On other matters, bills must be passed by both the lower and upper houses. But the lower house can override a negative vote in the upper house by passing a bill for a second time, by a two-thirds majority.

The 512 members of the House of Representatives are elected from 123 election districts. The Japanese system uses **multi-seat districts**, 1.c with voters in each electoral district choosing more than one representative. Representatives serve for four years—or less, if the house is dissolved and new elections take place sooner.

Consensus Politics The atmosphere in both houses of the National Diet is sedate compared to that in the legislative bodies in Britain and the United States. Japanese society places great stress on avoiding confrontation. Therefore, politicians seek to reach **consensus**—broad agree- 1.d ment—on issues. A political majority tries to avoid pushing through a bill against strong opposition from a minority. The two sides can usually work out some sort of compromise.

Most of the bills that are introduced in the National Diet are drawn up by the government or by the bureaucracy. As in other parliamentary democracies, government proposals usually become law.

Prime Minister and Cabinet

The prime minister and the cabinet perform the executive functions of government in the Japanese governmental system. The cabinet members serve as heads of major departments.

Provide Guided Practice Go through Section 2 and list the headings in the text on the board. Ask students to come forward and write key points and ideas under each heading.

Provide Independent Practice

TRF **Teacher's Resource File** You may wish to assign Section 2 Guided Reading and Review, Unit 6 File, p. 6, to help students master section objective content.

Enrichment

Ask students to create an oral report about some of the major technological advances forged by the Japanese since World War II. They may want to pick a particular product such as automobiles or cameras to use as an example. As part of their report, ask students to analyze the ways in which the Japanese government supports private industry. You might also want to ask students how technology influences the political policy of Japan. (Average)

Interpreting Tables Point out to students that this table shows the percentage increase in Japan's GNP since 1984. The Japanese GNP has been growing since at least 1984.

Caption Answer Based on the United States recession, Japan's GNP would either decrease or remain the same, but it would not likely increase.

Interpreting Charts Have students study the chart on page 585. Ask them what checks and balances the chart indicates in Japan's governmental system. (*Prime minister can dissolve the House of Representatives; House of Representatives can dismiss the prime minister.*)

Caption Answer By showing that the chain of command in Japan's government goes from the voters down to the cabinet; the emperor has no place in this line of command.

Japan's Annual GNP*

	Percentage Increase
1984	4.5%
1985	4.8%
1986	2.9%
1987	4.9%
1988	5.9%
1989	4.8%
1990 (projected)	5.1%
1991 (projected)	3.8%

*GNP, gross national product, is the total value of a nation's annual output of goods and services.
Source: The Washington Post National Weekly Edition, Dec. 31, 1990–Jan. 6, 1991.

Interpreting Tables Japan's bureaucracy, especially its Ministry of Trade and Industry, has played a large part in the country's economic success. Based on the recession in the United States in the early 1990s, would you expect Japan's GNP to increase, decrease, or stay the same in 1992?

Those members of the cabinet who are not members of Parliament are usually borrowed from the bureaucracy, an important part of the political system of which you will read shortly.

Voting to choose a prime minister takes place within the party and usually along party or factional lines. (Some parties are divided into factions.) The prime minister thus represents the majority party or a majority coalition within the House of Representatives.

The prime minister appoints the members of the cabinet. Membership in the cabinet is considered a great honor, and appointment may be a reward for faithful service to the prime minister. Under a system known as collective responsibility, cabinet members are considered to act as a group. A member who feels somehow unable to support a cabinet decision usually resigns rather than remain in conflict.

The prime minister has the power to dissolve the House of Representatives, but not the House
1.e of Councilors. This step, called **dissolution**, leads to immediate elections in which voters select a new House.

The Bureaucracy

The large Japanese bureaucracy, or civil service, enjoys unusual respect within Japanese society. It also wields great power. Top members of the bureaucracy are technocrats, or experts in technical and administrative affairs. They are drawn mainly from among the graduates of Tokyo University and several of Japan's other top national and private universities who compete to win civil service positions.

Japan's vast bureaucracy developed under the old imperial oligarchy. The bureaucracy undertook many tasks—in economic as well as administrative matters. The close cooperation between Japan's bureaucracy and the major corporations (*zaibatsu*) is a notable characteristic of Japanese society. The Ministry of Trade and Industry helps to coordinate the plans and strategies of both domestic and world trade. This close identification of public political and private economic policy is a key factor in Japan's ability to build one of the world's most dynamic capitalist economies.

The Party System

Japan's multi-party political system is dominated by one very powerful party, the Liberal Democratic party (LDP).[11] The supporters of the Liberal Democratic party include major business leaders, farmers, office workers, and people of the middle class. Since 1955, the LDP has provided all of Japan's prime ministers, although it has sometimes had to rule in coalition with another party.

The LDP itself is a coalition of several powerful interest groups that often disagree with one another. However, all of those factions support free enterprise, and they agree on the basically pro-Western foreign policy that Japan has

[11]The LDP's Kiichi Miyazawa became prime minister in 1991. The party has been torn by scandals in recent years. It lost its majority in the House of Councilors in 1989, but the LDP still holds 109 of the 252 seats in that body—more seats than those held by any other political party. With 60 percent of the seats in the more important lower house, the LDP still has solid control of the government.

SPOTLIGHT ON: Economics
One indicator of Japan's economic dynamism is the size of the country's trade surplus. Although Japanese imports totaled $236.7 billion in 1991, exports from the Pacific-island nation climbed to a record $314.6 billion, resulting in a trade surplus of $78.23 billion for the year—the largest trade surplus in the world. Nearly half of that surplus—$38.5 billion—resulted from trade with the United States. While U.S. exports of coal, wood products, oil, foodstuffs and other goods to Japan reached $53.1 billion in 1991, Americans bought $91.5 billion worth of Japanese exports.

followed since World War II. By custom, the leaders of the various factions within the party band together to support one of their number for prime minister.

Several other parties hold seats in the National Diet. The largest opposition group is the leftist Japan Socialist party, or JSP. The Socialists criticize Japan's current foreign policy and are against the return of militarism through the growth of the self-defense forces. Many of the Socialist supporters belong to the nation's large trade unions. Leftist and centrist factions jockey for power within the party. Other important political groups include the Japan Communist party (JCP) and the *Komeito*, or Clean Government party.

The Socialists have enjoyed growing political strength in recent years. After defeating the LDP in elections for the House of Councilors in 1989, they made major gains in the House of Representatives elections in 1990. The Socialists offered candidates in only 149 House races but won 136 of them. They now hold 53 more seats than they had in the previous House. Most observers of Japanese politics view these significant electoral victories as a protest vote against the recent shocking financial scandals within the LDP.

The Courts

Japan has an independent judicial system patterned on the American model—with trial courts at the local level, several intermediate appellate courts, and a Supreme Court. The courts hold the power of judicial review—the power to determine the constitutionality of laws passed by the Diet.

The Supreme Court has seldom struck down an act of the Diet. It has three times found the apportionment of seats in the Diet to be unconstitutional, however. By the high court's reckoning, votes cast in many lightly populated rural districts of Japan count four or five times as much as votes cast in many densely populated urban districts. That arrangement, the court has found, violates the constitution's guarantees of equal rights. But, to this point at least, the National Diet has done nothing in response to those decisions.

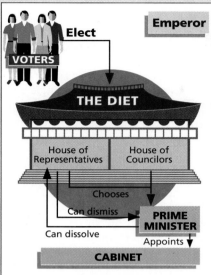

The Japanese Governmental System

VOTERS
Elect
Emperor
THE DIET
House of Representatives
House of Councilors
Chooses
Can dismiss
Can dissolve
PRIME MINISTER
Appoints
CABINET

Interpreting Charts Japan has a constitutional monarchy. In what way does this chart indicate that the emperor has no real power?

Section 2 Review

1. Define: National Diet, prefecture, multi-seat district, consensus, dissolution

2. What is one similarity and one difference between the Japanese constitution and the United States Constitution?

3. What exclusive powers does the Japanese House of Representatives hold?

4. What is collective responsibility?

5. What role does the bureaucracy play in the Japanese economy?

Critical Thinking

6. Recognizing Cause and Effect (p. 19) In what ways is World War II the most significant event in modern Japanese political history?

MONITOR COMPREHENSION

Answers to Section 2 Review
1. "Key Terms" are defined on the following pages:
a. National Diet, p. 582
b. prefecture, p. 583
c. multi-seat district, p. 583
d. consensus, p. 583
e. dissolution, p. 584
2. The Japanese constitution includes something similar to the Bill of Rights. But the Japanese constitution also prohibits the maintenance of a military. **3.** It can force the prime minister to resign or dissolve the House of Representatives, make treaties and appropriations, and raise funds. **4.** It is the system whereby cabinet members are considered to act as a group. **5.** The bureaucracy works in close cooperation with major industry to coordinate domestic and world trade. **6.** Students should observe that the war and its aftermath led to the democratization of the government. It also marked the point at which Japan began the economic development that has made it a leading economic world power.

CLOSURE

Since World War II, Japan has concentrated its efforts on technical and industrial development making it one of the leaders in technological advances today. In Section 3, students will read about the democratic system of government in Mexico.

Assignment Assign Section 3, pp. 586–590, for the next class period.

Teacher's Resource File
See the Unit 6 File, p. 7, for the Section 2 Quiz.

Reteach

Divide the class into three or four large groups. Have one student from each group write a sentence about the Japanese governmental system and then pass the paper along to the next student. The paper should circulate to each member of the group, with each student adding one sentence about the Japanese government. Finally, have a spokesperson from each group read the resulting document aloud.

SECTION 3
Mexico

FOCUS

Teacher's Resource File See the Unit 6 File, p. 8, for the Section 3 Quiz.

Objectives

22.5 Determine what historical events led to the development of the Mexican system of government.
22.6 Explain how Mexico's federal government is structured.
22.7 Examine ways in which the dominance of a single political party affects government in Mexico.

Bellringer Activity Have students look at the painting by Diego Rivera on page 587. Write on the board *Land, bread, and justice for all.* Tell students that the Mexican revolution of 1910 led to a new government that promised "land, bread, and justice for all," and a new constitution. Tell students they will learn about that government and that constitution in Section 3.

State the Purpose Mexico's current democratic government was influenced by the American system of government. The workings of that government, however, are steeped in the history and tradition of the Mexican people.

ABCNEWS INTERACTIVE

The following video segment may be used to highlight aspects of foreign governments.

POWERS OF THE CONGRESS GUIDEBOOK
Chapter 3: Elements of a Government, p. 78

3 Mexico

Find Out:

- What historical events led to the development of the Mexican system of government?
- What is the structure of Mexico's federal government?
- How does the dominance of a single political party affect government in Mexico?

Key Term:
nationalization

Mexico, the United States' neighbor to the south, has a political system that is, in form, influenced by its modeling on the American political system. But in operation, it is the product of a unique combination of Mexico's own history and the cultural makeup of its people. While Americans tend to think of Mexican history in terms of only a few specific historical events, its complex experience sets the basis for the system that exists today.

Mexico's Early Political History

The first evidence of important civilization in Mexico dates back to 1200 B.C. But Mexico is most commonly associated with the rich and complex Aztec civilization that gave way to Spanish colonialism in 1521 after Cortés defeated the Aztec emperor Cuauhtemoc in the battle of Tenochtitlán. During the next three centuries Spanish territorial claims expanded into North and South America. However, constant border disputes with England, France, and the newly independent United States seriously reduced Spain's area of domination by the early 19th century.

Independence from Spain Meanwhile, generations of Spaniards in Mexico intermixed with the native peoples, giving rise to a colonial elite with its own unique mestizo culture. Because of the decline of the Spanish empire and the conflicts over succession to the Spanish throne that followed, the Mexicans were able to declare their independence from Spain in 1821, establishing a monarchy with an elected emperor.

The Mexican monarchy lasted only two years before General Antonio López de Santa Anna deposed the emperor and set up a democratic republic with a constitution adopted in 1824. However, this republic was democratic only in the narrowest sense since most of the population, especially the Native Americans, could not participate.

Mexico's first constitution set the framework for dealing with several key issues and questions in the Mexican system: Should there be a centralized or federal government? How much power should a single political leader have? How could Mexico remain independent from its powerful neighbor to the north and other major world powers?

Over the next 100 years these issues appeared, disappeared, and reappeared with regularity in Mexican politics. Mexico experienced dictatorships and reform movements, one of which led to a revised constitution in 1857. There were periods of foreign invasion and interference as well as internal wars and revolution. Yet throughout this century of conflict, democratic reformers were able to gain political power at crucial times. The reformers reasserted the principles of Mexican independence and constitutional representative government.

In the early years of the 20th century, significant changes based on democratic principles occurred when a reform movement called the Regeneration Group and a leader named Venustiano Carranza sparked a revolution. They removed the dictatorship of Profirio Diaz and oversaw the writing of the Constitution of 1917.

The Constitution of 1917 The Mexican Constitution of 1917 was in many respects an updating of the document written in 1857. In fact, many of the features of the constitutions of 1824 and 1857 were included in the new document. The new constitution, however, created a system in which the government played a more active role in promoting the quality of Mexican social, economic, and cultural life. The rights of previously excluded portions of the population are also specified.

Reading Strategy: Problem Solving

Present to students the following problem: You are a member of the Mexican working class. For hundreds of years wealthy landowners have benefitted from Mexico's natural wealth, while the workers have barely managed to eke out a living. Mexico has gradually modernized, developing railroads and oil reserves, but still the workers do not benefit. What should you do?

Vocabulary

Direct students' attention to "Key Term" on page 586. Tell students that the term *nationalization* refers to something that happened to the Mexican oil industry in 1938. Ask students to think about what this might mean as they read the section.

▲ **Interpreting Political Art: Multicultural Awareness** This mural, painted by Mexican artist Diego Rivera in 1927, shows Mexican peasants planting the seeds that led to the country's 1910 revolution.

Mexico's Three Branches of Government

Like the United States, the Mexican Constitution sets up three independent branches of government—the executive led by the president, the legislature composed of two houses, and the judicial.

The President The president is the chief executive and is directly elected to a six-year term. The president has the power to appoint a cabinet and the attorney general, the top leadership of the military, and the judges of the federal courts. The president also has the power to propose constitutional amendments, which must be approved by two-thirds of the Congress and a majority of the state legislatures.

An important feature of the executive office is the constitutional rule preventing the president from being elected to successive terms. The intent of the rule is to prevent the possibility of a popular leader becoming a forceful dictator by continual reelection. While presidents cannot

Interpreting Political Art: Multicultural Awareness Tell students that it was peasants and middle-class Mexicans who finally stood up to the Mexican dictator; they were the people responsible for sowing the seeds of a new government.

INSTRUCT

Explain/Discuss Have students begin their discussion of Section 3 by talking about the specific elements of Mexico's federal government. Draw a chart on the board with two columns, titled *Mexico* and the *United States*, and two rows, titled *Government* and *Constitution*. Invite students to make comparisons between the Mexican government and the United States government as well as a comparison between the two countries' constitutions. Write students' observations on the board.

You might then want to ask students to discuss ways in which Mexico's history and culture influence the structure and function of its government. How are Mexico's history and culture different from United States history and culture? And how do these differences create a unique form of government for Mexico?

Illustrate Divide the class into small groups. Ask each group to locate one other painting by Diego Rivera or another Mexican artist that deals with the history of the country. Have each group write an explanation of the various elements in the painting and their significance to Mexican history and government.

Teacher's Resource File
See the Comparative Government file, pp. 4–5, for material to support the section.

INSTRUCT

Compare Explore with students the political party structure in Mexico. Point out that the Mexican government allows all registered parties to free and equal radio and television time during an election. Ask students to compare this situation with political party campaigning in the United States. Which system do they think would result in broader political representation in government? Ask students to compare the ability of minor parties to be heard in the United States and Mexico.

remain in office indefinitely, they do have considerably more power than a simple description of constitutional details suggests. This power comes from certain unique features of the Mexican political party system that you will read about in the pages ahead.

The Congress The Mexican Congress is a bicameral body with a Senate and a Chamber of Deputies.

There are 64 senators, two from each of the 31 Mexican states and two from the Federal District, which includes Mexico City. Senators are elected to six-year terms. The senators' terms are staggered so that half are elected at the time of the presidential election and half at a mid-term election three years later.

The Chamber of Deputies has 500 members. The deputies are elected to three-year terms and they cannot be reelected. Three hundred of the deputies are directly elected from districts of approximately 200,000 people. The rest of the seats are filled from the ranks of the various political parties based on the percentage of the total vote each receives in the national election. Thus, the Chamber of Deputies is elected on a mixed system of direct and proportional representation.[12]

The Congress meets from September 1 to December 31 each year. When it is not in session, a permanent committee of 15 deputies and 14 senators serves to approve presidential actions. Overall, because of their short sessions and the term limitations that produce a high rate of turnover, the Mexican Congress has far less power in governing the country than does the United States Congress.

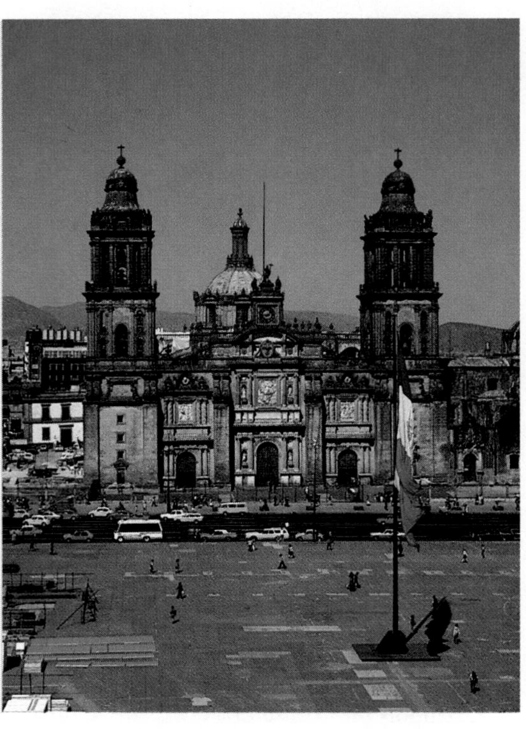

National Palace, Mexico City Mexico's three branches of government mirror those in the United States. This building contains the presidential and other executive offices of the Mexican government.

The Court System The Mexican judicial system is very similar to that in the United States. Although appointed by the political leadership, the judiciary is independent. Two systems of courts—the state and the federal—operate within Mexico's federal system. Each has its own separate jurisdiction.

The federal court system contains layers of circuit courts with federal district courts below. At the top is the Mexican Supreme Court. These courts have the power to judge cases that bear on federal law. In addition, they decide on constitutional issues. Each state court system has civil and criminal courts that are overseen by a Superior Court of Justice.

Political Parties

If what has been described so far were all there is to the Mexican political system, it would be of little interest, except as a governmental system based on a plan similar to the governmental struc-

[12]The proportional representation system was added to the constitution in 1963 in order to promote the existence of opposition parties. This maintains the democratic nature of the Mexican system. Each registered political party getting a minimum of 2.5 percent of the national vote is entitled to one seat in the Chamber of Deputies for every 1/2 percent it received, to a maximum of 20 seats.

ture of the United States. But like Japan, Mexican politics is marked by a high degree of consensus and a certain unchanging quality that is unlike anything in the American political system.

The Mexican national identity and independence from foreign domination are important ongoing themes in its national politics. These themes are represented by the country's main historical symbols—its precolonial past, the revolution against Spain, and the **nationalization**— 1.a
governmental acquisition of private industry for public use—of the oil industry in 1938. The carrier of this political tradition and the protector of these symbols is Mexico's dominant political party, the Institutional Revolutionary party (PRI).

The PRI was formed in 1928 as the National Revolutionary party by that period's most powerful politician, Plutarco Calles. It began to take its present form in 1938 under the control of then-President General Lazaro Cardenas del Rio. Fondly remembered by Mexicans for nationalizing the oil industry during his term in office, Cardenas put together a coalition of all the major interest groups and renamed it the party of the Mexican Revolution. Like his predecessor, Cardenas personally selected his party's next presidential candidate—in effect, the next president—and this has remained the practice in Mexican presidential politics ever since. This practice is called *tapadismo,* the veiled system.

The PRI's domination of Mexican politics has been so complete that it has selected every winning presidential candidate since the party's formation. Until the 1988 national election, the PRI had never lost an election to the Senate, and it traditionally has held an overwhelming majority in the Chamber of Deputies. This stronghold on the national branches of government has assured passage of laws written by the president, and also the likely approval of any constitutional amendments that might be proposed. PRI's dominance over Mexican politics extends to the state and municipal levels as well.[13]

Several parties oppose the dominance of the PRI. On the conservative side is the National Action party (PAN), which was formed in 1939. Its main appeal is among the conservative middle class and people who feel the Catholic Church should play a bigger role in the life of the country. Parties more radical than the PRI include the Mexican Communist party (PCM) and socialist parties of various types. These parties mainly attract urban workers and intellectuals. In 1982 a left coalition called the Unified Socialist party of Mexico (PSUM) was formed, which was led by the communists. But the radical parties have been highly fragmented in the last decade and show signs of remaining so.

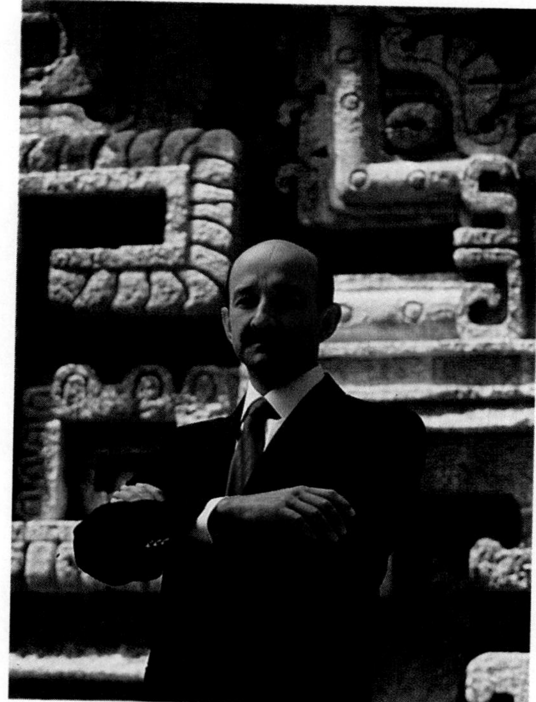

Pride in the Past The president of Mexico, Carlos Salinas, is proud to pose in front of symbols of Mexico's rich heritage.

[13]The PRI's worst showing in a national election came in 1988 when disenchantment with the government's economic policy was at a high level. Presidential candidate Carlos Salinas received only 50.36 percent of the vote compared to 70.99 percent of the vote received by Miguel de la Madrid in 1982. It also only won 260 of the 500 Chamber of Deputy seats, and lost 4 senate seats to a leftist coalition.

Provide Guided Practice
Write three headings on the board: *History, Government, Political Parties.* For *History* and *Political Parties,* draw a time line below the head and have students fill in important dates and events from the text. For *Government,* draw a flow chart of the Mexican governmental structure, with most of the boxes remaining blank. Have students fill in the blanks in the chart.

Provide Independent Practice
TRF **Teacher's Resource File**
You may wish to assign Section 3 Guided Reading and Review, Unit 6 File, p. 9, to help students master section objective content.

Spotlight on: Global Awareness
Mexican pride about its independence has been heightened by sometimes troubled relations with the United States. While U.S.-Mexican relations have been cordial since the 1930s, previous expansionist tendencies of the United States left Mexicans resenting "Yankee imperialism." When the United States went to war with Mexico in 1846, the result increased the size of the United States by one quarter (the present States of Texas, New Mexico, Arizona, California, Utah, and Nevada) and reduced Mexico's by almost one half.

Enrichment
Ask students to write about political parties in Mexico. Encourage students to use outside resources for a greater understanding of the role of the PRI and its opposition in Mexico. Students should present their findings in the voice of a member of an opposition party or a member of the PRI. (Average)

Interpreting Charts Ask students to name items which would be considered acceptable forms of identification.

Caption Answer Possible answers: no proof of citizenship, no identification, such as a driver's license.

Monitor Comprehension

Answers to Section 3 Review
1. The "Key Term" is defined on the following page:
a. nationalization, p. 589
2. Dictatorships and reform movements, foreign interference, and internal revolution. **3.** The three branches are independent. There is an executive branch led by a president, a judicial branch, and a bicameral legislature.
4. The PRI dominates Mexican politics to such a degree that passage of laws written by the president is assured as well as adoption of any proposed constitutional amendments. **5.** (a) Answers will vary. (b) When the people begin to lose faith in PRI in Mexico, other parties can gain power. The same may be said for Japan's LDP.

Closure

Mexico's democracy is the result of a long process. Today, the government resembles that of the United States, but differs as a result of Mexico's unique history and traditions. In Section 4, students will learn about the ongoing changes in the former Soviet Union.

Assignment Assign Section 4, pp. 592–599, for the next class period.

It is important to note that the Mexican system is different from the Japanese situation with the dominant LDP or the one-party communist state that existed in the Soviet Union. In Japan and the Soviet Union individuals founded their parties in order to gain political power. In Mexico, people already holding governmental power formed the PRI as an instrument of stability and continuity for their country.

Interestingly, the PRI has remained flexible to meet the changing needs of Mexican society. Ideologically liberal successors have been named by conservative presidents and conservatives by liberals, as was needed by the times. The government even provides financial support and facilities to the opposition parties. During elections all registered parties receive free, equal radio and television time. This provides outlets for the expression of diverse political viewpoints, even though political power has remained in the hands of a single political party for nearly 70 years.

How to Obtain a U.S. Passport

1. Complete a passport application form. You can pick up and submit this application at federal passport agencies, many local courthouses, and authorized post offices. (For the nearest federal passport agency, check the Federal Government listings in the telephone book under "State Department.")

2. Submit the application form. Include the following items:
- Proof of citizenship
  This can be in the form of:
  a) a previous US passport
  b) a certified birth certificate
  c) a naturalization certificate
- Two forms of current identification, one of which must bear your photograph or physical description, signature, and show an issue or expiration date.
- Two photographs, which must have been taken within the last six months, and must measure 2"x 2". The photo must be a full face shot with a plain white background.

3. Pay the passport fee. The following fees are applicable as of December, 1991:
- Under age 18: $40 (valid for five years)
- Over age 18: $65 (valid for ten years)

4. Wait for your application to be processed. The processing time for passport applications varies. You should apply for your passport well in advance of your proposed travel date.

Interpreting Charts Follow the steps given above on how to obtain an American passport. Identify two reasons why a person might not be eligible for a passport.

Local Government

Mexico is divided into 31 states and one Federal District of Mexico City. Each state is an autonomous unit with its own constitution. The state governments are headed by governors who are elected by direct popular election every six years. Each state also has a unicameral legislature with two classes of members who are directly elected. The deputies, like those at the national level, serve for three-year terms. The state senators serve for four-year terms.

Within the states, Mexico's political and economic organization is based on the principal of free municipalities. Thus, local government in Mexico is more like the United States than in highly centralized governmental systems such as Great Britain and France.

Section 3 Review

1. **Define:** nationalization
2. What type of events did Mexico experience in its first century after gaining independence from Spain?
3. In what ways are the three branches of Mexican government similar to those in the United States?
4. How does the political control of the PRI affect the balance of power between the executive branch and the legislative branch of government?

Critical Thinking

5. **Drawing Conclusions** (p. 19) (a) Can a country where one political party remains in continuing power truly be called democratic? (b) Use the examples of Japan and Mexico to support your answer.

★

Teacher's Resource File
See the Unit 6 File, p. 10, for the Section 3 Quiz.

Reteach

Write the three objectives for Section 3 on the board. Divide the class into three groups and ask each group to provide supporting details to answer each question. Each group should then share their answers with the rest of the class.

Supporting Human Rights

They can be so basic as to be necessary, such as the right to shelter and food. They can be denied by governments that are totalitarian dictatorships, that practice torture, that imprison people for their beliefs. "They" are human rights.

Although there are many ways of campaigning for human rights, each effort begins the same way—with an awareness of even one small aspect of this broad issue. It is awareness—and inspiration—that is the theme of the Reebok Human Rights Awards, presented annually by the Massachusetts-based sports shoe manufacturer, Reebok International, Ltd.

At the fourth annual awards ceremony in Boston in 1991, Reebok's chairman described the awards as "a way of combining a passion for young people and a commitment for human rights." The chairman introduced the keynote speaker, Jimmy Carter, as "the president who will be remembered for human rights."

Special awards were presented posthumously to the parents of three men who died within minutes of each other on the streets of Moscow in August 1991. What tragic chain of events links Dmitri Alexandrovich Komar, 22; Ilya Maratovich Krichevsky, 28; and Vladimir Alexandrovich Usov, 37, in the spirit of human rights?

For four tense days that August, the Soviet Union's hard road to democracy was gravely threatened when a hard-line group deposed leader Mikhail Gorbachev and refused to allow Russian President Boris Yeltsin and other officials to leave the parliament building in Moscow.

When tanks loyal to the junta converged outside the building, a human barrier formed in a spirit of solidarity with Yeltsin and the parliament under siege. Komar, a decorated veteran, entered one of the tanks in an attempt to persuade the crew to stop threatening civilians. He was shot and dragged behind the tank until Usov tried to free his body. Usov was shot for this act of courage. When a horrified spectator, Krichevsky, screamed at the tank crew to stop the violence, he was shot as well.

The unarmed victims were strangers in life, but are joined in death by their brave commitment to human rights. On receiving the Reebok award on Usov's behalf, his father said: "Each of our children made a statement and gave their lives for humanity."

The Reebok award recipients come from many parts of the world. Besides the young Soviets, the 1991 honorees included 11-year-old Ashley Black of Marlboro, New Jersey, who led a petition drive to stop video games "that teach hate and bigotry;" and 24-year-old Carlos Toledo of Guatemala for his work in Covenant House, an organization that works to protect and shelter street children.

Getting Involved

1. Identify a human rights abuse in your local community or the global arena. If you need to do research, your local library would be an ideal place. There, you could consult your local newspaper, various daily papers and news magazines, and books on the subject.

2. Formulate a plan for organizing volunteer efforts to help remedy this problem and identify resources that could be used in your plan.

3. Predict any problems or objections you might encounter in implementing your plan.

TEACHING

What You Can Do

Supporting Human Rights

Objective

Identify possible consequences of campaigning for human rights.

INSTRUCT

Before reading the feature, ask students to think of an example of someone working to protect human rights, or instances of violation of human rights. For example, students may mention Martin Luther King, Jr. as an example of the former and South Africa as an example of the latter.

Below are possible questions for postreading discussion:

- Why is it important for everyone to work together to protect human rights?
- What could you do to help in the struggle to achieve human rights for all people?

TRF **Teacher's Resource File**
See the Participatory Government Activities file, pp. 28–39, for material to support the lesson.

Section 4
The Former Soviet Union

Focus

Teacher's Resource File See the Unit 6 File, p. 11, for the Section 4 Outline.

Objectives

22.8 Determine how the reforms of Mikhail Gorbachev led to the end of Soviet communist government.
22.9 Examine how the role of the Communist party has changed in Soviet politics.
22.10 Explain how the former Soviet government was organized.

Bellringer Activity Read the following quote to the class: "I feel that my children will have a chance for a bright future because no one from this horrible gray building will tell them how to live, how to think, how to believe, or how to eat." Tell students that this statement, referring to the Communist party headquarters in Moscow, was made by a Soviet lawyer following the 1991 failed coup in the former Soviet Union.

State the Purpose The government of the Soviet Union has undergone extraordinary changes throughout the last century. In Section 4, students will read about the evolution of power in the Soviet Union.

4 The Former Soviet Union

Find Out:

- How did the reforms of Mikhail Gorbachev lead to the end of Soviet communist government?
- How did the role of the Communist party change in Soviet politics?
- How was the former Soviet government organized?

Key Terms:

perestroika, *glasnost*, purge, Supreme Soviet, interim government, Politburo

In August 1991 Soviet President Mikhail Gorbachev was vacationing in the Crimea when a group of Communist party leaders placed him under arrest. These party leaders objected to the democratic reforms that Gorbachev had begun in the communist government of the Soviet Union. They wanted a return to the policies of the old Soviet communist government. When the Soviet public heard of the attempted coup, protesters took to the streets, and popularly elected office holders denounced Gorbachev's arrest. The world anxiously awaited what would happen next. After several tense and uncertain days, the conspirators surrendered. Their coup had failed.

Extraordinary changes occurred in the Soviet Union since that failed coup. A four-month transition period followed. Then, on January 1, 1992, the Soviet Union was officially buried, and the Commonwealth of Independent States was born. The new commonwealth is a "union" in the loosest sense. It is a confederation of 12 of the 15 former Soviet republics, each of which retains the sovereignty usually associated with an independent country.[14]

Freedom Fighters: Moscow A hard-line military coup, intending to remove the existing Soviet government, lasted just four days in August 1991. These Soviet citizens, who defied the armed troops, were joined in spirit by the people of the world's democracies.

Reading Strategy: Who? What? When? Where? How? Why?

Ask students to skim Section 4 to glean an overview of the topics to be covered. Have them write the questions: who? what? when? where? how? and why? on a piece of notebook paper. As they come to each heading, have students write answers to their questions in order to help them understand the changing Soviet government.

Vocabulary

Direct students' attention to "Key Terms" on page 592. Ask them to keep a log of the words and as they read, to relate the words' meanings to reform in the Soviet Union.

The Changing Soviet Government

There were three distinct periods of Soviet government: (1) a totalitarian communist dictatorship, (2) a reform-minded communist government attempting to become more open and less repressive, and (3) a government in transition from centralized control to the loose confederation of the commonwealth.

The first period of Soviet government began with the communist revolution of 1917 and the emergence of the Communist party of the Soviet Union (the CPSU), which ruled the country with an iron fist.

The second period, which began in the mid-1980s, followed Mikhail Gorbachev's leadership. His program of ***perestroika***, the restructuring 1.a of political and economic life, attempted the fundamental alteration of the political system. The many and far-reaching changes that he put in place were illustrated by ***glasnost***, the policy of 1.b "openness" that included the government's expanded tolerance of dissent and freedom of expression. But the many and often far-reaching changes that Gorbachev initiated appeared to have embodied incompatible goals—establishing a democratic and open system of government while preserving the communist system. Gorbachev's program of trying to nurture political and economic reforms while preserving the Communist party and the Soviet bureaucracy and the elites they supported may have been impossible from the start.

The third period of Soviet government began with the failed coup of August 1991. It put into motion changes that were beyond the control of Gorbachev or the Communist party. Change in the Soviet Union became impossible to stop or even to control.

No one knows what the final form the new commonwealth will take; however, examining the Soviet system as it existed and as it evolved will help you understand a powerful lesson about government: No political system is immune from change or collapse.

[14]By late December 1991, the former Soviet republic of Georgia had not officially joined the new commonwealth, but approval from Georgia's legislature was expected before 1992.

MARX
LENNON
BY MARLETTE FOR NEW YORK NEWSDAY
" GORBACHEV'S GOING TOO FAST! "

By permission of Doug Marlette and Creators Syndicate.

Interpreting Political Cartoons Soviet President Gorbachev's mission was to undo the legacy of Marxist-Leninism, or communism. What does the cartoon say about this policy?

A Political History of the Soviet Union

The Soviet Union—once known officially as the Union of Soviet Socialist Republics—was the world's largest country in area. In the immediate aftermath of the 1991 coup, it still occupied one-sixth of all of the land surface of the earth.

The Soviet Union was the modern successor to the czarist Russian empire, which began to emerge in the 15th century and was formally established by Peter the Great in 1721. The Russian empire was ruled by a succession of tyrannical czars.

Heavy losses in the Russo-Japanese War of 1904–1905 and then in World War I began the collapse of czarist rule, and the empire was destroyed in the first of two revolutions in 1917. In March, scattered, spreading strikes and riots forced Czar Nicholas II to quit his office. Out of that first revolution came a short-lived attempt at democratic government. However, that government was overthrown on November 7, 1917—and out of that second coup, led by Vladimir Ilyich Lenin, the Communist party came to power.

Until 1991, the Soviet Union was composed of 15 regional units, the constituent republics, each of them inhabited by a major nationality group. The largest and most important of the

Interpreting Political Cartoons As students study the cartoon, ask them what the cartoon says about the historical legacies of the Soviet Union. (*The cartoon says that the historical legacies of such important figures as Karl Marx and Vladimir Lenin—figures that were responsible for shaping Soviet government in the twentieth century—are no longer applicable in the former Soviet Union.*)

Caption Answer It reinforced those who feared that Gorbachev's impatience for change would bring chaos—substituting American comedian Groucho Marx and musician John Lennon for Communist mentors Marx and Lenin.

ABCNEWS INTERACTIVE

The following video segment may be used to highlight aspects of foreign governments.

POWERS OF THE CONGRESS GUIDEBOOK
Chapter 5: Totalitarianism, p. 80

ACTIVITY: Cooperative Learning

Time: One class period **Activity:** Compare political systems by creating organizational charts. **Grouping:** Groups of four to six students **Purpose:** Assign one of the following to each group: Great Britain, Japan, Mexico, the Soviet Union before Gorbachev. Have students use information in the text to create an organizational chart of the government structure in that country. Then have students draw a chart of the government structure in the United States and compare its political system with that of the assigned country. **Roles:** Assign the following roles: manager, recorder, spokesperson.

Outcome: Have the spokesperson explain the group's charts to the class. Invite the class to suggest additions, deletions, and corrections to the information represented.

Teacher's Resource File
See the Comparative Government file, pp. 10–11, for material to support the section.

INSTRUCT

Explain/Discuss Ask students to discuss the ways in which the Soviet Union has undergone change throughout the last century. Begin the discussion by writing on the board the three distinct periods of Soviet political history: *totalitarian communist dictatorship, reform-minded communist government,* and a *government in transition.* As they discuss the three periods, invite students to talk about the leaders during each time period and their influence on Soviet government and society. Invite students to write notes on the board under the appropriate category during the discussion.

Ask students to discuss the events that led up to the coup in 1991 and to explain how the coup has influenced the transitional government of today.

constituent republics was the Russian Soviet Federal Socialist Republic—the RSFSR or, simply, Russia. It included more than 70 percent of the land area of the Soviet Union and contained more than half its population.[15]

Lenin Lenin was the architect of what became the Soviet Union. He began the task of transforming an ancient, tradition-bound, underdeveloped country into the world's first communist state. Lenin constructed a complex government with several layers of elected soviets, or councils. There were soviets at the factory level, farm level, city level, and regional and national levels. Despite that elaborate and representative structure, major policy decisions were made at the top by the Communist party leadership and passed down through the soviets.

Stalin Lenin's death in 1924 prompted a fierce struggle for power among his topmost lieutenants, and out of that conflict Josef Stalin emerged as the new Soviet leader.[16] Stalin consolidated his power over the next several years
1.c in a series of **purges**—the ruthless elimination of rivals and other dissidents.[17] By the mid-1930s Stalin had become, for all practical purposes, a dictator.

Under Stalin, the Soviet dictatorship began an intensive industrialization program and forced collectivization of the nation's agriculture. Farmers, workers, and others who resisted were imprisoned, shot, or sent to forced labor camps. At the appalling cost of millions of lives, Stalin was able to build the Soviet Union into a major industrial and military power.

[15]Ethnic Russians, who live mainly in the RSFSR, dominated the political and cultural life of the Soviet Union. But the nation contained millions of non-Russian peoples. The Soviet Union was made up of more than 100 distinct ethnic groups, speaking at least 100 different languages.

[16]Stalin was born Iosif Vissarionovich Dzhugashvili in 1879. He served as one of Lenin's closest aides and adopted the name Stalin (man of steel) some time before the revolution.

[17]Technically, a "purge" is a purification. Stalin "purified" the party and government by having his rivals—and millions of other dissidents—jailed, exiled, or executed in the 1930s and 1940s.

World War II brought a severe test of Stalin's leadership. Nazi Germany invaded the Soviet Union in mid-1941 and quickly seized control of most of European Russia. The Soviets suffered enormous casualties; at least 20 million Soviet citizens were killed during World War II. Finally, by early 1945, with the help of huge amounts of American aid, Soviet armies drove the Germans out of Eastern Europe.

At war's end, the Soviet Union was in control of all of Eastern Europe; and it had become one of the world's two superpowers, rivaling the United States in military power. Immediately, Stalin began the rebuilding of the nation's war-torn industry and agriculture. He also launched the aggressive foreign policy actions that soon brought on the cold war.

Soviet Leaders After Stalin Josef Stalin died in 1953, and Nikita Khrushchev became the leader of the Soviet Union. Under him the country began the process of "de-Stalinization." The levels of brutality and repression that had stained the Stalin era were diminished.

Khrushchev and later leaders did not hold the kind of absolute power that Stalin had. However, the person holding the positions of party chairman and Soviet premier exerted considerable control over Soviet society.

Gorbachev

Mikhail S. Gorbachev took control of the CPSU in 1985. From his first days in power, he pushed *perestroika*—his plan for the economic and political restructuring of the Soviet Union.

Like many others both within and outside his country, Gorbachev had long been aware of a number of major problems in the Soviet system. Among the most troublesome were:

— a rigid, inflexible government, burdened by slow-moving processes and an unresponsive bureaucracy.

— foreign and domestic policies too deeply rooted in the past and too tightly controlled by a small group of aging leaders.

— a stagnant economy plagued by widespread shortages of food, housing, and other consumer goods and by outmoded, inefficient, and unproductive workplaces.

SPOTLIGHT ON: Behind the Scenes

Stalin, more than any other leader in Russian history, used the secret police as an instrument of terror to consolidate his control over Soviet life. His great purge began in 1934, following the assassination of Muscovite party boss Serge Kirov. (Stalin himself is widely suspected to have ordered Kirov's murder, as a pretext for the crackdown that followed.) The terror intensified when Nicholas Ezhov took control of the N.K.V.D.—later, the K.G.B.—in 1936, and began massive arrests totalling a conservatively estimated 8 million people by 1941. Ezhov himself was arrested as an enemy of the state in 1938.

— tension among the various ethnic groups, each having a base within one of the republics, for greater national autonomy.

Originally, Gorbachev saw *perestroika* as a policy for changing the economy. His early efforts at economic reform made little headway, however—mostly because of (1) opposition from entrenched bureaucracies in the party and the government and (2) the apathetic reactions of an unconvinced Soviet people. So, the general secretary concluded, political reform had to come first.[18]

In 1988 Gorbachev put several proposals for major change in the Soviet political system before the party's central committee. He then submitted those same proposals to the **Supreme** 1.d
Soviet, the national legislature. His reforms were promptly adopted by the party and the Supreme Soviet.

The Consequences of Reform The Soviet Union's influence over its communist neighbors declined markedly as the reforms of *perestroika* and *glasnost* progressed. In the late 1980s it watched as Solidarity, a democratic workers' movement, unseated Poland's communist government and as other Eastern-bloc countries, that had once been directly under Moscow's control made overtures to the West.

In the closing months of 1989 a wave of independence swelled across Eastern Europe, sweeping aside even the most hardline communist governments such as East Germany and Romania. National independence movements in the Baltic Soviet republics of Lithuania, Latvia, and Estonia strengthened as the democratization of Eastern Europe took hold. By the middle of 1990, the large and powerful republics of Russia, Ukraine, and Byelorussia, joined by the Baltic republics and several smaller republics, had declared independence from the Soviet central authority. The newly elected president of the Russian Republic, Boris Yeltsin, further challenged the government and Gorbachev's leadership by resigning from the Communist party and having the laws of the Russian Republic declared sovereign over its population and territory.

Events had moved beyond Gorbachev's control. He wavered between siding with the hardline communists, who wanted reforms to stop, and supporting even more reforms. At the same time the political and economic foundation of the Soviet Union was falling apart.

The End of the Communist State The failed coup of August 1991 followed. Communist party leaders took the majority of the blame for this attack on the democratic movement, and party activities were even suspended for a brief time. Gorbachev returned to Moscow, but his power was severely undercut. With Yeltsin's collaboration Gorbachev called an unscheduled session of the legislature in September 1991 to

---

VOICES *on Government*

The Effect of the End of Communism on Soviet Youth

Natalie Koulik, a student in Richmond, Virginia, and a native of St. Petersburg in Russia.

"As a teen-ager, I was forced to join Komsomol, the Young Communist League. In the old days, I would not have passed my college entrance examinations if I had not been a member of the league. Only three years ago campus life at universities was controlled by Komsomol. But the Party has lost the support of Russian youth; its membership has plummeted from 100 percent to 10 percent. . . . *Glasnost* and *perestroika* inspired Russian youth to break from Communist party control."

---

[18]The economic aspects of *perestroika* are discussed in the next chapter.

Analyze Direct students' attention to the "Voices on Government" feature on page 595. Ask: How does this single quotation reflect all three periods of Soviet government? (*Ms. Koulik first discusses old strictures of the Communist government—being forced to join the Young Communist League in order to pass college entrance exams. This is the first period, totalitarian communist dictatorship. Then she refers to the fact that party membership has drastically declined. This is the last period, government in transition. Finally, she refers to* glasnost *and* perestroika, *which are indicative of the second period, reform-minded communist government.*)

INSTRUCT

Discuss Examine with students the changing role of the Communist party, or CPSU, in the former Soviet Union. What role do students envision the Communist party playing in the new Commonwealth of Independent States that has taken the place of the Soviet Union? Remind students of the quote that was read to them in the "Bellringer Activity." Given the history of the CPSU, do students think this person's feelings are indicative of much of Soviet society? Or, do they see a role for the Communist party in the independent nations?

1.e present proposals for an **interim government**—a new, transitional government. The legislature approved the proposals. An interim government was then set up awaiting the outcome of negotiations among the republics and between the republics and the central Soviet government.

The interim government agreed to the departure of the three Baltic republics (Latvia, Estonia, and Lithuania) from the union. And, when the remaining 12 republics insisted that they wanted an end to the old Soviet Union, the interim government dissolved itself and stepped down from power.

The features of the government of the former Soviet Union—its constitution, the role of the Communist party, and its formal structure—will now be examined.

The Soviet Constitution

The details of the old Soviet communist system were set out in the constitution of the Soviet Union. The most recent version of that document was adopted in 1977.

The 1977 Constitution In form, this document was similar to the constitutions of Western democracies—at least in the sense that it set out the structure and powers of Soviet government. It was not, however, a fundamental law nor was it a charter intended to limit government and the exercise of political power. The Western concept of constitutionalism was foreign to Soviet communist thought and practice.[19]

Like Western constitutions, the Soviet document contained several civil rights provisions. But Soviet citizens were not guaranteed such basic rights as those of free speech, press, and association in the way they are secured, for example, by the American Bill of Rights. The Soviet constitution declared the existence of those rights, but it also declared that "The exercise by citizens of rights and freedoms must not injure the interests of society and the state."

[19]To this point at least, the Soviet Union has been ruled by people, not by any written law. But there seems to be a new spirit of reliance on laws.

The constitution could be amended in fairly easy fashion, by a simple majority vote in the legislature. In recent years it had become top-heavy with many amendments prompted by the many Gorbachev reforms.

After the Coup In September 1991, in the aftermath of the failed coup against Gorbachev's government, the old constitution was abolished. In its place, a Declaration of Human Rights and Freedoms was approved.

Articles of this document stated: "The freedom of the individual, his or her honor and dignity are of supreme value in our society." No group, party, or state interests can be placed above the interests of the individual. The protection of "human freedoms as supreme social values" is the obligation of all agencies of the state. Other articles of the document guaranteed freedom of speech, freedom of conscience and religion, the right to peaceful assembly, and

President of the Russian Republic Boris Yeltsin's support of independence for the Soviet republics triumphed over Gorbachev's insistence on maintaining the Soviet Union.

the right to form political parties and unions independent of the government.

The Role of the Communist Party

Since the revolution of October 1917, the CPSU played a commanding role in the Soviet political system. Indeed, through more than 73 years, from the revolution on to 1990, the CPSU was the only political party in the Soviet Union. No other parties were allowed, and the communists' monopoly position was reinforced by the constitution. It declared the CPSU to be "the leading and directing force in Soviet society, the nucleus of its political system and of state and public organizations."

Before the Coup The CPSU was an elite party, composed of some 19 million specially chosen people. Those party members made up about nine percent of the Soviet Union's adult population.

The CPSU was organized like a giant pyramid. At the bottom were some 400,000 primary party organizations (once called cells), each headed by a party committee. The party hierarchy extended upward from the primary party organization, throughout the country. It followed a pattern known as parallel organization: The party's structure paralleled that of government in each of the 15 constituent republics; each layer of government—local, regional, republic, national—had its corresponding layer of party organization. Thus, at every level, party officials were able to oversee the work of the government.

At the top of the pyramid were the most important elements of the party's structure, the Central Committee of the CPSU, the Politburo, and the general secretary. The Central Committee of the CPSU was responsible for the party's affairs. It assembled once every six months—usually just before its governmental counterpart, the Supreme Soviet, met. Thus, Gorbachev's proposals for a new governmental structure in 1990 were first presented to the Central Committee.

The Central Committee elected the much
smaller **Politburo**—the body that in fact ran 1.f
the CPSU. The general secretary was the head of the Politburo. He presided over its meetings and his post allowed him to gain and exercise wide power. For most of the post-Stalin era, the general secretary also held the top post in the government.

The Politburo (political bureau) was a full-time decision-making body. Its members were the experienced, the powerful, and until very recently the elderly, heads of the party. Most of them also held key posts in the government—although the structure of the party was formally separate from that of the government. It was within this group that the coup against Gorbachev was plotted.

Before the attempted coup in August 1991, there were several indications that the party had lost at least some of its long-held power. First, the constitutional article guaranteeing the power of the CPSU was repealed in 1990, and a number of smaller political parties emerged within the Soviet Union. Second, Mikhail Gorbachev, clearly the most visible symbol of the Soviet political system, began to regularly present himself as the head of state, the president of the Soviet Union, rather than as the head of the party.

After the Coup Being a small, elite party with clearly identifiable offices, the CPSU was easily targeted and disbanded after the coup failed. Its assets were confiscated in several republics and localities. The once-privileged party officials suddenly faced unemployment. Statues of the party's founder, Lenin, were toppled; and the city of Leningrad became St. Petersburg (its old name under the czars).

The initial reaction against the CPSU moderated. Its existence, like that of other political parties, was guaranteed under the Declaration of Human Rights and Freedoms. The deep distrust of communism remains, however, and it appears that the CPSU will never have the power it once held.

The Government

The old totalitarian communist system in the Soviet Union allowed citizens to vote for members of the legislature. However, voters did not make choices. Generally, only one candidate ran

Provide Guided Practice Have students create a time line on the board, using a different color chalk for each of the three periods of Soviet government.

Provide Independent Practice

TRF **Teacher's Resource File** You may wish to assign Section 4 Guided Reading and Review, Unit 6 File, p. 12, to help students master section objective content.

Enrichment

Ask students to look through newspapers and news magazines from the past year to locate photographs relating to the final period in Soviet government, that of a government in transition. Title a bulletin board "Government in Transition" and post the photographs students locate along with descriptive captions explaining each. (Easy)

OR

TRF **Teacher's Resource File**
See the Unit 6 File, pp. 15–17, for the Case Study on Contemporary Issues for Chapter 22.

ACTIVITY: For Gifted Students

Theme: Leadership The Petition of Rights of 1628 in Great Britain, the defeat of Japan in World War II, the Mexican Constitution of 1917, and the failed Soviet coup of August 1991 each represent a revolutionary moment in time. Students may choose to develop a set of research questions to investigate the impact of that experience on national leadership. Through a review of primary source documents, news reports, interviews, and documentaries, students will be able to determine if there was a shift in government leaders or if popular support of the government required a change in leadership.

Global Awareness

The human freedom index measures 88 countries against 40 different indicators of human freedom. Some of the indicators include:

The right to . . .
- travel
- teach ideas and receive information
- ethnic language

The freedom from . . .
- forced or child labor
- torture or coercion
- capital punishment
- compulsory religion

The freedom for . . .
- political opposition
- social and economic equality for women and ethnic minorities

The legal right to . . .
- a nationality
- prompt trial

The personal right to . . .
- interracial, interreligious, or civil marriage
- determine the number of one's children

The Human Freedom Index*

The countries are ranked in order of the number of freedoms (out of 40) upheld in each country.

Rank	Country	Freedoms Upheld	Rank	Country	Freedoms Upheld
1	Sweden	38	49	Egypt	11
5	New Zealand	36	51	Poland	10
8	France	35	57	Haiti	9
11	Canada	34	58	Yugoslavia	8
12	Switzerland	34	60	Kuwait	8
15	Japan	32	63	Kenya	8
16	United Kingdom	32	68	Liberia	7
21	Italy	29	69	Bangladesh	7
22	Venezuela	29	71	Czechoslovakia	6
26	Botswana	26	72	Saudi Arabia	6
28	Argentina	25	74	Cuba	5
32	Panama	21	78	Vietnam	5
34	Israel	19	79	Pakistan	5
37	Peru	16	83	South Africa	3
38	Mexico	15	84	China	2
42	India	14	85	Ethiopia	2
44	Nigeria	13	86	Romania	1
47	Sri Lanka	11	88	Iraq	0

*The index is based on a 1985 study, *World Human Rights Guide*, by Charles Humana, a British academic. The 40 key indicators of freedom have been endorsed by international accords such as the Universal Declaration of Human Rights.

Source: United Nations Development Programme *Human Development Report*, 1991.

Interpreting Charts: Multicultural Awareness By showing how selected countries rate on measurements of freedoms, the chart illustrates the global scope of human rights violations. Since this index was based on a 1985 study, what changes might have occurred in the ranking of some countries?

for each office, and this candidate was either a CPSU member or a vocal supporter of the party.

The Legislature Under communist control, the Supreme Soviet was a kind of puppet theater, assembled for a few days each year to rubber-stamp the decrees of the CPSU.

Gorbachev's reforms altered the national legislature so that it was composed of two elements: the large Congress of People's Deputies and the smaller Supreme Soviet. Two-thirds of the 2,250 members of the Congress of People's Deputies were elected by the voters in districts throughout the country. The election of those deputies in 1989 marked the first time that competitive, multi-candidate elections had been held in the Soviet Union in more than 70 years.[20] The major job of the Congress of People's Deputies was that of choosing, from among its own members, the members of the Supreme Soviet, the other legislative chamber.

From 1989 to 1991, this Supreme Soviet met in spring and fall sessions, each lasting for three to four months. It operated under rules that allowed the introduction and debate of competing legislative proposals. It had several important powers—notably, to make laws, to approve the national budget, to confirm or reject the appointments of top government officials, and

[20]Even so, those elections were hardly democratic in the Western sense. The complex nominating process was very largely controlled by the CPSU; nine out of 10 of all of the candidates were party members. There was only one candidate on the ballot in 384 of the 1,500 districts.

Interpreting Charts: Multicultural Awareness Ask students what might be the purpose of such a ranking of nations. (*Possible answers: give nations a way to measure their performance objectively, inform the world of human rights violations in many countries.*)

Caption Answer Changes in Eastern Europe and the Soviet Union may have changed the status of some countries.

Interpreting Tables: Multicultural Awareness Have students look at the table footnote. Ask students to explain how this information might have affected the poll's outcome. (*Table reflects opinion of only half of the population the former Soviet Union. If the question had been asked after the coup, Soviet authorities, Soviet army, and Communist party would have received lower percentages.*)

Caption Answer The highest level of support (45%) was awarded to "Russian Republic authorities."

Monitor Comprehension

Answers to Section 4 Review

1. "Key Terms" are defined on the following pages:

- **a.** *perestroika*, p. 593
- **b.** *glasnost*, p. 593
- **c.** purge, p. 594
- **d.** Supreme Soviet, p. 595
- **e.** interim government, p. 596
- **f.** Politburo, p. 597

2. A totalitarian communist dictatorship, a reform-minded communist government, and a transitional government.

to declare war. And, importantly, it elected the president of the Soviet Union.

The Executive Gorbachev's restructuring of Soviet government in 1989 produced a new office, that of president of the Soviet Union elected by the Supreme Soviet. In early 1990, Gorbachev proposed the creation of a more Western-style presidency in which the presidency was to be filled by a direct vote of the Soviet people. Such an election had not taken place when the coup occurred.

As president, Gorbachev held the executive power of Soviet government. He appointed the other top officers of the government, set the lawmaking agenda for the Supreme Soviet, headed the defense establishment, and was responsible for the making and conduct of Soviet foreign policy.

The president had the power to veto any measure passed by the Supreme Soviet; but that body could override a presidential veto by a two-thirds majority in each of its chambers.

Interim Soviet Government The temporary interim government was administered by a State Council, Supreme Soviet, and Economic Council. Mikhail Gorbachev and the leaders of the republics were the members of the State Council. Each republic also sent representatives to the Economic Council.

A restructured Supreme Soviet became the highest legislative body, passing on legislation proposed by the State Council. The Supreme Soviet had two chambers: the Council of Union and the Council of Republics. In the latter chamber, the delegations of each republic had one vote.

The Soviet government operated under an emergency structure until the Commonwealth of Independent States was formed on January 1, 1992. The 12 republics of Russia, Ukraine, Moldavia, Uzbekistan, Turkmenistan, Armenia, Azerbaijan, Kazakhstan, Georgia, Tajikistan, Kirghizia, and Byelorussia are members of the commonwealth. However, three of the former Soviet republics—Latvia, Estonia, and Lithuania—will not be a part of the new country. They have officially declared their sovereignty and have been accepted as members of the United Nations.

Russian Confidence*

Who do you think would best handle the problems in the Soviet Union?	
Russian Republic authorities:	45%
Soviet authorities:	27%
Soviet army:	6%
Church:	3%
Communist party:	2%
KGB:	1%
None:	7%
No answer:	7%

*About half the people in the Soviet Union live in the Russian Republic. The question was asked before the August coup. Numbers do not add to 100 due to rounding.

Source: May 1991 Times Mirror Center For the People and the Press poll of 1,123 Russians.

Interpreting Tables: Multicultural Awareness Public opinion polls are still a novelty in Russian society, which stifled free speech under communism. How do these results reflect strong support for Boris Yeltsin, president of Russia?

Section 4 Review

1. **Define:** *perestroika*, *glasnost*, purge, Supreme Soviet, interim government, Politburo
2. Describe the three distinct periods of recent Soviet government.
3. What was the role of Lenin and Stalin in creating the Soviet communist state?
4. What major problems was Gorbachev attempting to correct with the introduction of *perestroika*?
5. How did the Declaration of Human Rights and Freedoms differ from the old Soviet constitution?
6. How has the role of the CPSU changed in the Soviet Union?

Critical Thinking

7. **Identifying Central Issues** (p. 19) How was the process of democratization in the Soviet Union incompatible with the one-party communist state?

3. Lenin constructed a complex system of government and Stalin built the Soviet Union into a major industrial and military power. **4.** Inflexible government, old-fashioned foreign and domestic policies, stagnant economy, and ethnic tension. **5.** The Declaration of Human Rights and Freedoms guarantees freedom of speech, freedom of conscience and religion, the right to peaceful assembly, and the right to form parties and unions independent of the government. **6.** The CPSU was originally disbanded, but the Declaration of Human Rights and Freedoms protects its existence. Though the CPSU is allowed to exist, it is unlikely that it will ever have the power it once had. **7.** Students may suggest that the one-party communist state has no opposition, i.e., it is a monopoly. Democracy is everyone being able to become involved in the way things are done, something which is completely incompatible with monopolistic rule.

Teacher's Resource File See the Unit 6 File, p. 13, for the Section 4 Quiz.

CLOSURE

The Soviet people and government have undergone dramatic change in just a few short years. In Chapter 23, students will read about the economic systems that mark differences in society throughout the world.

Assignment Assign Chapter 23, Section 1, pp. 605–611, for the next class period.

ACTIVITY: Teaching Heterogeneous Groups Divide the class into two groups. Have each group go through the text and write ten clues to an important term or concept in the chapter. Then have students take turns standing and asking the other group to identify the correct term or concept. The person asking the question should first identify the country to which the clue applies. For example, "Mexico. This happened to the oil industry in 1938." The other group would respond "Nationalization."

Reteach

Write several key steps in the history of the former Soviet Union on the board, but jumble their order. For example, you might place *Latvia, Estonia, and Lithuania are accepted as members of the United Nations* before *Gorbachev introduces the policy of perestroika*. Ask students to rearrange the events so that they are in the correct order.

TEACHING
Critical Thinking

Recognizing Ideologies

Objective

Identify the underlying ideologies in the Declaration of Independence.

INSTRUCT

As students read through the feature, have them list the factors that can help them recognize ideologies. As they read through the excerpt, have them pick out key words and phrases which help them to determine the ideologies involved.

In part 3 (c), you may wish to have students select an example of whether or not the United States has lived up to the ideology in the Declaration of Independence, and write a brief essay on that topic.

Answers 1. (a) Political. (b) Because it mentions government. **2.** (a) Students may say that every man is guaranteed the same rights as every other man. (b) The people give government leaders their power. (c) Government exists to protect human rights, and if it does not do so adequately, a new government may take its place. (d) The rights of the individual are what is important. **3.** (a) Answers will vary. (b) Equal rights should exist for all men and the government should work to protect those rights. (c) Students may suggest looking into the topic of slavery or women's rights as examples of how the U. S. has not lived up to this ideology.

Critical Thinking

Recognizing Ideologies

Recognizing ideologies means identifying underlying beliefs from actions or statements. This skill helps you to understand the basic reasons why people or governments act the way they do. By recognizing ideologies, you will be better able to establish a framework for understanding other people and for participating fully and effectively in society. Follow the steps below to practice this skill.

1. Know what an ideology is. An ideology is the body of ideas and beliefs on which a political, economic, or social system is based. Read the passage below, which comes from the United States Constitution. (a) What kind of system does the passage seem to be discussing—political, social, or economic? (b) On what do you base this conclusion?

2. Identify the basic ideas contained in an action or statement. Part of the skill of recognizing ideologies means being able to identify the broad themes that underlie any set of stated ideas. It is by piecing together and interpreting these broad themes that you are ultimately able to recognize the ideology present in a statement or action. Read the excerpt below again. (a) What is your understanding of the phrase "all men are created equal"? (b) What do you think the phrase "deriving their just powers from the consent of the governed" means? (c) What other broad concepts or ideas can you identify in the passage? (d) How would you summarize the ideology of the piece?

3. Consider the possible consequences of the ideology. Historically, some ideologies have been used as a basis for enslaving or oppressing a people. Other ideologies have formed the foundation of productive and successful political, economic, or social systems. It is therefore important to be able to evaluate the positive and negative potential behind any ideology you encounter. Read again the passage below, and answer the following questions. (a) What is your evaluation of the ideology presented in the statement below? (b) What are some of the positive aspects of the ideology stated there? (c) What evidence can you find from your knowledge of United States history to test whether or not the United States has lived up to this ideology through its actions and politics?

"We hold these truths to be self-evident, that all men are created equal, that they are endowed by their Creator with certain unalienable Rights, that among these are Life, Liberty and the pursuit of Happiness. That to secure these rights, Governments are instituted among Men, deriving their just powers from the consent of the governed; That whenever any Form of Government becomes destructive of these ends it is the Right of the People to alter or to abolish it, and to institute new Government, laying its foundation on such principles and organizing its powers in such form, as to them shall seem most likely to effect their Safety and Happiness."

—The Declaration of Independence

TRF **Teacher's Resource File**
See the Unit 6 File, p. 14, for the Skill Application to reinforce the skill lesson.

Chapter-in-Brief

Scan all headings, photographs, charts, and other visuals in the chapter before reading the section summaries below.

Section 1 Great Britain (pp. 575–581) Great Britain has a unitary government based on an unwritten constitution.

The monarch is the head of state who reigns but does not rule. Instead, the bicameral Parliament holds the legislative and executive powers. Most of this power is centered in the popularly elected House of Commons; the House of Lords has little authority, although its nine law lords do have judicial functions.

The prime minister and cabinet are members of Parliament who are chosen by Parliament from among the ranks of the majority party. If the prime minister loses the support of Parliament, his or her administration—the government—falls, and new elections are held.

Section 2 Japan (pp. 581–585) Throughout much of its centuries-long history, Japan's was a feudal society. However, more Western and democratic forms began to emerge in the late 1800s.

Japan's constitution of 1947 was written largely at the direction of American occupation authorities after World War II; it contains a unique antimilitary provision. The elected national legislature, the Diet, is bicameral. Most legislative power lies in the House of Representatives; the House of Councilors has little authority. The prime minister and cabinet are chosen by and are responsible to the House of Representatives. These officials are elected from the ranks of the majority party or coalition.

Japan's bureaucracy holds a unique position of prestige and power. It works closely with Japanese industry to coordinate policy.

Section 3 Mexico (pp. 586–590) An advanced civilization has existed in Mexico at least since the time of the Aztec empire. However, Spanish colonization destroyed that civilization.

Mexican independence came in 1821. Today, Mexican government is based on the Constitution of 1917. While its format is democratic, the government has been controlled by one party (PRI) for more than 60 years. Mexico's president can serve only one six-year term, but can hand-pick a successor.

The legislature is bicameral, but neither house is very powerful. The judiciary is independent and shares many of the same features of the United States court system.

Mexico's is a federal government, and state and local government have considerable autonomy.

Section 4 The Former Soviet Union (pp. 592–599) Soviet government was a dictatorship for more than 70 years. It has undergone broad and ongoing change since Mikhail Gorbachev gained power in 1985. A failed coup in the summer of 1991 introduced an element of crisis and uncertainty that makes the political situation in the nation very unstable.

Before the coup, the Soviet constitution was similar in form to Western-style constitutions. However, it did little to limit government or the ironclad control of the Communist party.

In the aftermath of the coup, a new constitution is anticipated. The role of the once dominant Communist party is uncertain but certainly diminished.

Under Gorbachev, Soviet government had been moving toward democracy. In January, 1992, a Commonwealth of Independant States broke up the Union. The form of any future permanent government—and of what was once the Soviet Union itself—remains in question.

Teaching Suggestions for CHAPTER-IN-BRIEF

Below are some of the possible uses for the Chapter-in-Brief:

To Preview the Chapter You may want to assign the Chapter-in-Brief page and the Section Outlines from the Teacher's Resource File before beginning Chapter 22 to introduce students to the "Key Terms" and concepts in each section.

To Review the Chapter When students have completed Chapter 22, you might want to assign the Chapter-in-Brief as a tool for review, along with the Guided Reading and Reviews from the Teacher's Resource File.

To Omit the Chapter If you wish to skip Chapter 22, it may be helpful to assign the Chapter-in-Brief to students as a review before continuing to another chapter. You may also want to assign the Chapter 22 Test to assess student knowledge of the material. Then specific portions of Chapter 22 may be assigned to students needing reinforcement of "Key Terms" and concepts.

Teacher's Resource File See the Unit 6 File for the following materials:

- Section Outlines, pp. 2, 5, 8, 11.
- Guided Reading and Reviews, pp. 3, 6, 9, 12.
- Chapter 22 Test, pp. 18–20.

ADDITIONAL RESOURCES

An Introduction to Capitalism, Socialism, and Communism. Sound filmstrip. National Geographic, 1985. Color. 7–12 min.

Barry, Donald. *Contemporary Soviet Politics.* Prentice Hall, 2nd ed., 1991.

Budge, Ian and David McKay. *The Changing British Political System: Into the 1990s.* Longman, 2nd ed., 1990.

Hammer, Darrell P. *The USSR: The Politics of Oligarchy.* Westview Press, 3rd ed., 1990.

Ishida, Takeshi and Ellis S. Krauss. *Democracy in Japan.* University of Pittsburgh Press, 1989.

James, Ian. *Inside Mexico.* Watts, 1989.

Kavanagh, Dennis and Anthony Selden. *The Thatcher Effect: A Decade of Change.* Oxford, 1989.

Macridis, Roy C. and Steven L. Burg. *Introduction to Comparative Politics: Political Regimes and Political Change.* HarperCollins, 1991.

Medish, Vadim. *The Soviet Union.* Prentice Hall, 4th ed., 1991.

Mexico (*Nations of the World Series*). National Geographic.

Treadgold, Donald W. *Twentieth Century Russia.* Westview Press, 7th ed., 1990.

Answers to CHAPTER 22 REVIEW

Vocabulary and Key Terms

Matching
1. purges
2. consensus
3. interim government
4. multi-seat district
5. National Diet

True or False
1. True.
2. True.
3. False—the correct term is *dissolution*.
4. False—the correct term is *coalition*.
5. False—the correct term is *perestroika*.

Word Relationships
1. *Perestroika:* plan for restructuring political and economic life. *Glasnost:* the policy of openness.
2. Prefecture: a political subdivision of Japan. Multi-seat district: the way that Japan elects its legislature.
3. Shadow cabinet: the members of a minority party who follow the activities of the British cabinet. National Diet: Japan's legislature.
4. Monarchy: rule by a king or queen. Minister: a cabinet member in a parliamentary system.

Main Ideas

Section 1
1. The British constitution consists of a written portion—the law of the constitution; and an unwritten portion—the conventions of the constitution. **2.** Little day-to-day function, but acts as head of state and serves ceremonial functions. **3.** Parliament has two houses: a largely powerless House of Lords and a powerful House of Commons. The legislature has both executive and legislative functions. **4.** The prime minister is chosen from the majority party or a coalition of parties in Parliament. The prime minister then selects the cabinet from Parliament.

Section 2
5. Japan's government was originally like that found in medieval Europe. A growing Westernization and a desire for continued growth led the nation to aggressive actions resulting in war with the United States.
6. (a) It renounces war and forbids the nation from establishing a military. The rule has been interpreted to allow a self-defense force. (b) The United States, which occupied Japan following World War II, insisted on the clause. **7.** (a) The Diet contains an upper house, the House of Councilors, and a lower house, the House of Representatives. The House of Representatives holds the greater power. (b) The prime minister is selected from the majority party or coalition in the House of Representatives. The prime minister then chooses the cabinet from the Diet or the bureaucracy. **8.** It is well respected and powerful in Japanese society. It cooperates closely with industry.

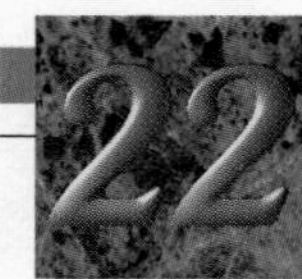

Chapter Review

Vocabulary and Key Terms

monarchy (p. 576)	prefecture (p. 583)	*glasnost* (p. 593)
by-election (p. 578)	multi-seat district (p. 583)	purges (p. 594)
coalition (p. 578)	consensus (p. 583)	Supreme Soviet (p. 595)
minister (p. 578)	dissolution (p. 584)	interim government (p. 596)
shadow cabinet (p. 579)	nationalization (p. 589)	Politburo (p. 597)
National Diet (p. 582)	*perestroika* (p. 593)	

Matching: *Review the key terms in the list above. If you are not sure of a term's meaning, look up the term and review its definition. Choose a term from the list above that best matches each description.*

1. Stalin's elimination of rivals and other dissidents
2. agreement among groups with varying interests
3. a transitional government intended to operate for a limited period of time
4. an electoral unit in which several people are elected to the same office
5. Japan's legislature

True or False: *Determine whether each statement is true or false. If it is true, write "true." If it is false, change the underlined word or words to make the statement true.*

1. <u>Nationalization</u> involves the takeover of private industries by the government.
2. A <u>by-election</u> is held to fill a vacant seat in Britain's House of Commons.
3. When the prime minister of Japan dissolves the House of Representatives, it is called <u>coalition</u>.
4. In parliamentary systems, a <u>minister</u> of several parties may take control in the absence of a majority party.
5. Gorbachev's program for restructuring the Soviet economy is known as <u>prefecture</u>.

Word Relationships: *Distinguish between words in each pair.*

1. *perestroika/glasnost*
2. prefecture/multi-seat district
3. shadow cabinet/National Diet
4. monarchy/minister

Main Ideas

Section 1 (pp. 575–581)

1. In what way is Great Britain's constitution different than the United States Constitution?
2. What is the role of the monarchy in the British government?
3. Briefly describe the organization of Britain's Parliament.
4. How are Britain's prime minister and cabinet members chosen?

Section 2 (pp. 581–585)

5. Briefly describe Japan's government before World War II.
6. (a) What is the antimilitary clause of Japan's constitution? (b) Why is it a part of their constitution?
7. (a) Briefly describe the organization of the National Diet. (b) How are the prime minister and cabinet chosen?
8. What are some unusual characteristics of the Japanese bureaucracy?

Section 3 (pp. 586–590)

9. Briefly describe Mexico's political history up to 1821.
10. Briefly describe Mexico's first 100 years of independence.
11. Briefly describe the three branches of government set up under the Constitution of 1917.
12. What is the special role of PRI in the Mexican political system?

Section 4 (pp. 592–599)

13. How did the Soviet government change over the course of its brief history?
14. Briefly describe Gorbachev's plans for *perestroika*.
15. What happened in the Soviet Union in the years following Gorbachev's ascent to political power?
16. (a) Briefly describe the anticipated future role of the Communist party. (b) Briefly describe the anticipated future form of government in the former Soviet Union.

Critical Thinking

1. **Recognizing Ideologies** (p. 19) What does the close cooperation between industry and the government suggest about the Japanese political and economic system? Would you support a similar system in the United States?
2. **Making Comparisons** (p. 19) Consider the practice of *tapadismo*, the handpicking of presidential successors practiced by the PRI in Mexico. (a) In what way is the selection of Republican and Democratic presidential candidates similar to the practice in Mexico? (b) In what ways is it different?
3. **Testing Conclusions** (p. 19) Recall the text's statement that Gorbachev's original goal of introducing democracy while at the same time preserving the communist system were possibly incompatible. What evidence can you find in the chapter to support that statement?
4. **Formulating Questions** (p. 19) What questions could you ask to discover why Great Britain retains its constitutional monarchy?

Getting Involved

1. **Writing Your Opinion** You are a citizen of the Soviet Union. It is the fall of 1991, just after the failed coup. Write a diary entry about your hopes for the future of your nation. Begin your entry by recounting the main events leading up to and including the coup. Then discuss your feelings about such issues as the fate of the Communist party, the possible breakaway of the republics that once made up the Soviet Union, your own personal future, and how the current disorder might affect you. As you write, keep in mind that you are writing from the point of view of a Soviet citizen living in a time of uncertainty. Revise your entry to correct any errors, and then make a final draft.
2. **Cooperative Activity** Hold a class constitutional convention in which you outline a new constitution. For this constitution, draw on the best characteristics of the governments discussed in the chapter. Begin by creating four teams to identify the strengths and weaknesses of each of the governments. Each group should consider such factors as the relationship between legislative and executive, the role and power of the parties, and the court system. Have each team present its findings to the class. Then, debate as a class which features you would like in your constitution, and hold brief votes to settle any disputes.
3. **Gathering Information** You are interested in finding out some basic information about a foreign country's governmental system. Use the Government Resources Handbook on page 690 to identify some sources you could use to find this information.

Section 3
9. Mexican civilization thrived for centuries. Spain invaded Mexico in 1521, beginning a period of Spanish colonization which lasted until 1821, when Mexico declared its independence. **10.** The period was turbulent and characterized by periods of dictatorship, foreign interference, and internal revolution. **11.** The branches are the executive, the legislative, and the judicial. They are independent. The legislative branch has two houses. **12.** The PRI dominates the politics of the nation. They have held a majority in the legislature and the presidency since the party was born in 1928.

Section 4
13. The government emerged as a totalitarian dictatorship. It entered a reform period upon the arrival of Gorbachev in 1985. It is now a government in transition. **14.** *Perestroika* was a plan for the political and economic restructuring of the Soviet Union. Its goals included a move toward more democratic and open government. **15.** The Soviet empire has crumbled. Twelve former Soviet republics have formed the Commonwealth of Independent States and three others—Latvia, Estonia, and Lithuania—have declared independence. **16.** (a) The Communist party exists in the former Soviet Union, but it will likely have none of its former power. (b) A Commonwealth of Independent States was formed. Lithuania, Latvia, and Estonia declared their independence.

Critical Thinking

1. Students might suggest that the cooperation indicates a widespread consensus on national goals that is shared by government, industry, and the people. **2.** (a) Students might observe that the selection of party candidates is performed in large part by the parties themselves. (b) Students should observe that presidential primaries give voters significant say over who is nominated. Also, because no one party dominates American politics, the selection of nominees is not as significant as it is in Mexico. **3.** The chapter suggests that hard-line communists were unwilling to cede their former power and that liberals were dissatisfied with the pace of change. Thus, Gorbachev had little support from either end of the ideological spectrum.
4. What would happen if there were no monarch in Great Britain? What do the people of Great Britain admire about their monarch? Does the monarchy serve any important political function in the British system?

Getting Involved

1–3. Answers and results will vary, but students should demonstrate an understanding of the concepts in this chapter.

Chapter 23 Resources

In the Teacher's Resource File
The following materials are found in the Teacher's Resource File box.

Instructional Support: Unit 6 File

For the Section	For the Chapter
Outlines, pp. 24, 27, 30	Skill Application, p. 33
Guided Reading and Reviews, pp. 25, 28, 31	Case Study on Contemporary Issues, pp. 34–36
Quizzes, pp. 26, 29, 32	Chapter Test, pp. 37–39
	Additional Test Questions, pp. 40–42

Enrichment Support Files

Participatory Government Activities, pp. 28–39
Simulations and Debates, pp. 35–70
Historical and Legal Documents, p. 12
Comparative Government: A Multicultural View, pp. 10–11, 12–13

Computer Test Bank and Assessment

Transparency Package, pp. 23, 48

Chapter 23 Focus

Introduce the Chapter Tell students that in this chapter they will learn about three different world economic systems—capitalism, socialism, and communism. Read with students the Chapter Preview and Objectives.

Writing Activity Direct students' attention to "Describe" under "Before you read this chapter." Have students explain briefly in writing the role they play in the United States economic system.

Motivate for Learning Direct students' attention to "Predict" under "Before you read this chapter." Lead students in a discussion of the present state of the American economy. Ask students to predict the effect politics has had on the United States economy.

Comparative Economic Systems

Chapter Preview

On December 7, 1991, ceremonies at Pearl Harbor, Hawaii, marked the Japanese attack that plunged the United States into World War II. Robert Reinhold, reporting for the *New York Times*, wrote: "The ceremonies . . . spoke volumes about the complex relationship that has since developed with Japan. The aged veterans who returned to the scene of their youthful terror . . . carried Japanese cameras, and the television monitors watched were made in Japan by Sony and Panasonic." In the postwar era, Reinhold's words reminded us, Japan's economy grew faster than any other in the world.

Today, the tiny island nation is a capitalistic model of efficiency and superior quality products. This chapter is about the ways in which economic life varies greatly from one country to another—the different ways that goods and services are produced, distributed, and consumed.

Before you read this chapter:

- **Describe** three ways that economics plays a part in your life.
- **Predict** how a country's political structure affects its economic success.

As you read, focus on the main objective for each section. Understand:

1. The fundamental principles of a free market system.
2. The nature of socialist political and economic thought.
3. The history of Soviet communism.

Magruder's American Government: *A Witness to Change* by William A. McClenaghan

Of all the changes to which *Magruder's American Government* has been witness in its 75 years, one of the greatest is the role of the Federal Government in the lives of the American people. The Great Depression and FDR's New Deal ushered in an era of governmental expansion that forever changed the nature of the United States government. In fact, that change continues today.

In 1948, Frank Magruder wrote: *The country is capitalistic, modified by certain socialistic trends. Among them may be mentioned the postal system, public power projects, progressive income taxes, old age pensions, and free public education. Some of these are so old and so well established that we seldom think of them as socialistic.*

Of course, those "socialistic trends" continued into the 1950s, 1960s, and beyond, as the American people sought and received a higher level of governmental services. For example, the U.S initiated such extensive federal programs as Medicare and Medicaid; and, more recently, proposals for some form of national health insurance have assumed a prominent position on the national political agenda.

Fueling the Economy Industry, whether large, like this airplane factory in France, or small, has a sizeable impact on a nation's economy. The structure of the economy, in turn, affects whether the nation's industry is owned privately or publicly.

1 Capitalism

Find Out:

- On what fundamental principle is capitalism based?
- What are the main characteristics of a free enterprise system?
- What are the basic types of business organizations?

Key Terms:

capital, capitalist, free enterprise system, entrepreneur, laws of supply and demand, monopoly

You have confronted these questions several times in this book: What are the functions a government ought to undertake? What should it have the power to do? What should it not be allowed to do? Certainly these questions can be asked of just about all areas of human activity, but they are raised most significantly in the realm of economic affairs.

Questions of politics and of economics are, in fact, inseparable. The most important economic questions faced by a nation are clearly political questions, as well. For example: What social services should a government provide? How should goods and services be distributed and exchanged within a nation? What types of income or property ought to be taxed?

SECTION 1
Capitalism

FOCUS

Teacher's Resource File
See the Unit 6 File, p. 24, for the Section 1 Outline.

Objectives

23.1 Explain on what fundamental principle capitalism is based.
23.2 Analyze the main characteristics of a free enterprise system.
23.3 Describe the basic types of business organizations.

Bellringer Activity Have students list the products they have bought within the last week. Be sure they include everything—from magazines to food products to clothing. Explain that their freedom to choose what and where they buy is one aspect of a capitalist society.

State the Purpose The United States economic system is based on the principles of capitalism and free enterprise. In Section 1, students will examine these fundamental principles of capitalism and determine ways in which this economic system is tied to the United States government.

ABCNEWS INTERACTIVE

The following video segment may be used to highlight aspects of economic systems.

POWERS OF THE CONGRESS GUIDEBOOK
Chapter 10: Capitalism, p. 86

Vocabulary

Direct students' attention to "Key Terms" on page 605. Ask students to explain the game *Monopoly*. Ask students to skim the text to determine why the concept on which this game is based is incompatible with free enterprise.

Reading Strategy: Predicting Content

Ask students to skim Section 1 and list the main and sub-headings that they find. Under each heading, ask them to write a sentence or phrase that predicts the content of each section. When they have finished reading Section 1, ask them to go back to their predictions and test them against the actual text.

Interpreting Graphics As students study the graphic, ask them what happens when there is a problem in one factor of production. (*This can result in problems in the other factors.*)

Caption Answer Create and expand industries, make investments in new technologies, and engage in activities that create jobs and contribute to a high standard of living.

INSTRUCT

Discuss/Analyze As students begin their discussion of Section 1, invite them to discuss the fundamental principles upon which a capitalist society such as the United States is based. Have them begin by describing the concept of private ownership and have them outline the four factors of production that contribute to the nation's economy—land, labor, management, and capital.

Lead students into a discussion of supply and demand, one of the characteristics of a free enterprise system. Ask students to identify the five characteristics of a free enterprise system: private ownership, guarantees for property rights, decentralized decision making, competition, and freedom of choice.

Because the global economy requires that the United States compete for markets with other countries, you may wish to discuss the labor and management of our national economy in contrast with that of Japan, Mexico, and South Korea, for example.

In this section, you will examine how the system called capitalism responds to those questions.

Private Ownership of Productive Property

Capitalism, the economic system found in the United States, Japan, and Germany to name a few prominent examples, is based on private ownership of productive property. Productive property is different from personal property, such as your toothbrush and your stereo. Personal property is typically privately owned under all the world's major economic systems. Productive property can be things such as a worker's tools, a farmer's fields, or a factory's machines. It can also take the form of original ideas, such as those in computer software, music, or inventions. These items are called productive since their use can produce other objects of economic value, income, or money.

What is distinctive about capitalism is that private individuals and companies own most of the productive property. They decide how their property is used, and the benefits of what it produces also become their property.

Four Factors of Production Four types of resources are especially important for any nation's economy. These basic resources are known as factors of production. One factor of production is land. Land can be put to a variety of economic uses for agriculture, mining, and forestry. A second factor of production is a human resource—labor. Men and women who work in mines, factories, offices, hospitals, and other places all provide labor that is an essential part of a nation's economy. Management, which is a special type of skilled labor, is a third factor of production. Management is the labor involved in organizing the other factors of production and making businesses run efficiently.

1.a The fourth factor of production is **capital**—the wealth, be it money, factories, or machinery—that is used to produce goods and services. Capital has to be made before it can be used. In other words, capital is a product of the economy that is then put back into the economy to make more products.

The Role of the Capitalist Someone who owns capital and puts it to productive
1.b use is called a **capitalist**. The term is most often applied to people who own large businesses or factories. Capitalists, using their privately owned productive property, create and expand industries, make investments in new technologies, and engage in activities that create jobs and contribute to the high standard of living for which modern capitalistic societies are admired. The United States economy is called capitalistic because it depends on the energy and drive of thousands of individual capitalists.

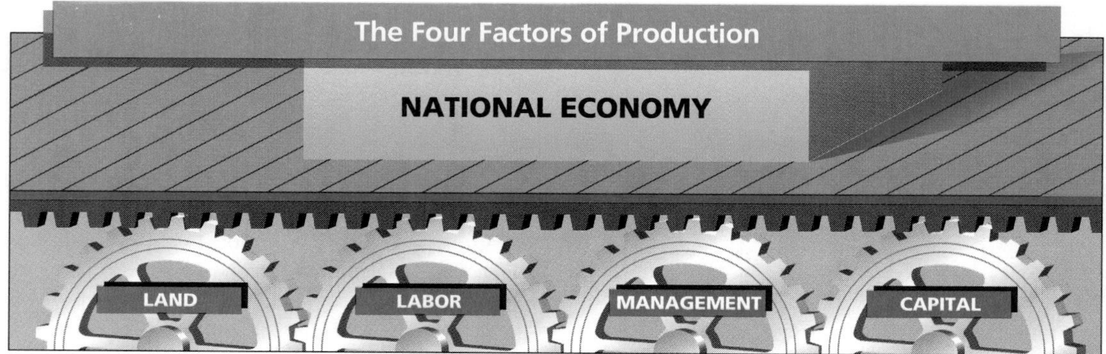

Interpreting Graphics The four factors of production work together to keep an economy moving forward. According to what you have read, what is the role of the capitalist in a capitalistic economic system?

Activity: For Gifted Students

Theme: Systems As part of their study of economic systems, students might consider the establishment of "regional economic communities" as a possible phenomenon in the next century. Explain to students that the creation of European and African Economic Communities has occurred with the expressed purpose of addressing overarching, regional economic issues. Students may choose to research these fledgling systems in order to map out the course of a North American Economic Community. Students may present their findings and recommendations in the form of a small group oral presentation.

SPOTLIGHT ON: Economics

One of the ways that businesses raise capital is through the sale of stock—that is, the selling of shares or certificates of ownership in a given company. More stocks are sold on the New York Stock Exchange, located on Manhattan's Wall Street, than anywhere else in the world. In 1990, almost 40 billion shares, valued at $1.33 trillion, were traded on Wall Street at an average rate of roughly 160 million shares a day. Stocks of lesser value are traded on New York's American Exchange (AMEX), where 3.3 billion shares were traded in 1990.

Drawing by Dan Fradon; ©1990 *The New Yorker Magazine, Inc.*

Interpreting Political Cartoons The move to a free market system does not bring instant wealth to a country. What does this cartoon suggest about the difficulties of such an adjustment?

The Free Enterprise System

A capitalistic economy is sometimes referred to as a **free enterprise system**. In such a system, 1.c
individuals are free to start and run their own businesses—their own enterprises. They are also free to dissolve those businesses. Free enterprise systems have five noteworthy characteristics.

Private Ownership In a free enterprise system, most of the means of production are privately rather than publicly owned. The owners are sometimes individuals. Often, however, they are groups of people who share ownership of a company.

Guarantees for Property Rights A free enterprise system can work only when property rights are guaranteed. In the United States, the 5th and 14th amendments to the Constitution declare that no person may "be deprived of life, liberty, or property without due process of law." The Constitution also requires that "just compensation" be paid to owners when private property is taken for public use.

Decentralized Decision Making Under capitalism, basic decisions about what to produce and how to produce it are left to private decision makers. Public officials do not order factories to produce products. Thus, if existing companies cannot meet the demand for a product, an enterprising capitalist might see a chance to make some money by starting up a new company. A person who takes the initiative and risk of starting or expanding a business is called an
1.d **entrepreneur**—an enterpriser.

Competition Because people are generally free to enter a new business at any time, a number of companies usually offer the same product or service. Companies must compete against one another for customers. Competition among multiple sellers helps to hold down prices and keep quality high, since customers are likely to buy from the

Discuss Ask students to consider the local hardware store. Then ask them to consider a large corporation in your community or in a nearby community. Tell students that these two types of businesses represent the ends of the spectrum in American business. Discuss with students the three types of business organizations—sole proprietorships, partnerships, and corporations—and the advantages and disadvantages of each.

Interpreting Political Cartoons Have students study the cartoon. Ask them what the cornucopia in the cartoon symbolizes. (*The cornucopia symbolizes the freedom of choice and high supply that are associated with the free enterprise system.*)

Caption Answer The cartoon suggests that there is a difficult period in which the "horn of plenty" is empty and the public is awaiting the prosperity associated with a free market economy.

Teacher's Resource File
See the Comparative Government file, pp. 16–17, for material to support the section.

Interpreting Political Cartoons As students study the cartoon, ask them to identify some of the economic problems that the Soviet Union was having in the 1980s. (*Huge consumer demand and extremely limited supply, which led to high prices.*)

Caption Answer The cartoon suggests that the Soviet Union did not yet fully understand the importance of the link between supply and demand.

company with the best product at the lowest price. Competition thus promotes efficiency since the producer has the incentive to keep costs low.

Under competitive conditions, the laws of supply and demand determine prices. Supply is the quantity of goods or services for sale. Demand is the desire of potential buyers for those goods and services. According to the **laws of supply and** 1.e
demand, when supplies become more plentiful, prices tend to drop. As supplies become limited, prices tend to rise. By the same token, if demand drops—that is, if there are few buyers—sellers will probably lower their prices in order to make a sale. If demand rises, sellers can raise prices.

Competition does not always work smoothly. Sometimes a single business becomes so successful that all of its rivals go out of business. A firm that is the only source of a product or service is called
a **monopoly**. Monopolies can be very powerful in 1.f
the marketplace. Practically speaking, they can charge as much as they want for a product. Since there is no other supplier of that good or service, the consumer must pay up or do without.

Political leaders in the United States decided late in the nineteenth century that monopolies were dangerous. American leaders were especially concerned about a type of monopoly called a trust.[1] The Federal Department of Justice has a division that analyzes business activities to determine if competition within an industry is threatened. It can, for example, stop the sale of a company if that sale might result in the elimination of competitive conditions in the marketplace.

[1]A device by which several corporations in the same line of business combine to eliminate competition and regulate prices. The Sherman Antitrust Act of 1890 remains the basic law against monopolies today. It prohibits "every contract, combination in the form of a trust or otherwise, or conspiracy in restraint of trade or commerce among the several States, or with foreign nations."

Interpreting Political Cartoons Healthy economies require a fine balance between supply and demand. What does this cartoon suggest about the Soviet Union's economy in the early 1990s?

Freedom of Choice A fifth characteristic of free enterprise is that consumers, entrepreneurs, and workers enjoy freedom of choice. Consumers can choose from a variety of products and services. Entrepreneurs can switch from one business to another. Workers can quit their jobs and take new ones. However, federal and State governments do place restrictions on freedom of choice. For example, the government prohibits the sale of products deemed hazardous to people's health or safety.

Laissez-Faire Theory

Early capitalist philosophers believed that, if only government did not interfere, the free enterprise system could work automatically. Adam Smith presented the classic expression of that view in *The Wealth of Nations*, in 1776. Smith claimed that when all individuals are free to pursue their own private interests, an "invisible hand" works to promote the general welfare. In short, Smith preached laissez-faire capitalism.[2]

Laissez-faire theory holds that government should play only a very limited, hands-off role in society. Governmental activity should be confined to: (1) foreign relations and national defense, (2) the maintenance of police and courts to protect private property and the health, safety, and morals of the people, and (3) those few other functions that cannot be performed by private enterprise at a profit. Properly, government's role in economic affairs should be restricted to functions intended to promote and protect the free play of competition and the operation of the laws of supply and demand.

Laissez-faire capitalism never in fact operated in this country. But it is clear that the concept had, and still has, a profound effect on the structure of the American economic system.

A Mixed Economy

Although the American economic system is essentially private in character, government has always played a large part in it. So, economists usually describe the American system as a mixed economy—one in which private enterprise and governmental participation coexist.[3]

[2]The term *laissez faire* comes from a French idiom meaning "to let alone."

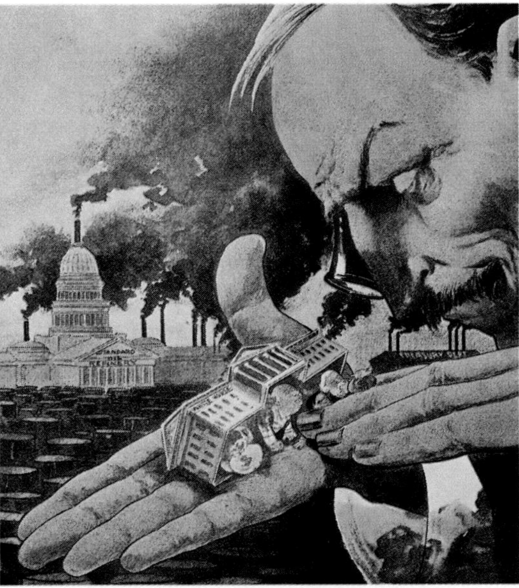

An "Invisible Hand" at Work Laissez-faire theory holds that government should not interfere with business. Yet business has often been charged with exerting undue influence on the United States government.

Many aspects of American economic life are regulated by government at every level. For example, the government prohibits trusts, protects the environment, and ensures the quality of food.

Many aspects of American economic life are promoted by government, as well. For example, the government constructs public roads and highways, provides such services as the postal system, the census, and weather reports, and offers many kinds of subsidies and loan programs.

The United States economy is also mixed in another sense: Government conducts some enterprises that might well be operated privately. Here, too, you can find examples at every level of government: public education, the postal system, various forms of transportation, and water and power systems.

[3]Recall, for example, the various powers of Congress discussed in Chapter 11. You will also read about the many powers of the State and local governments in Chapter 24.

Provide Guided Practice Ask students to identify various products that they might go into business to sell. Have the class identify the four resources for their business. (*The factors of production.*) Then have the class identify the characteristics of the free enterprise system that have an impact on their business and describe how their business might be affected by government policies.

Provide Independent Practice

TRF **Teacher's Resource File** You may wish to assign Section 1 Guided Reading and Review, Unit 6 File, p. 25, to help students master section objective content.

Enrichment

Divide the class into three or four groups. Have each group find at least four political cartoons concerning business practices in the United States. Then, have the members of each group show their cartoons to the class with an explanation of each. (Average)

OR

TRF **Teacher's Resource File**
See the Unit 6 File, pp. 34–36, for the Case Study on Contemporary Issues for Chapter 23.

Interpreting Graphs: Multicultural Awareness What effect do students think it would have on the United States economy if a country such as Japan or Canada stopped purchasing United States products? (*This would likely cause a sharp drop in the economy.*)

Caption Answer Canada conducts the most trade with the United States.

MONITOR COMPREHENSION

Answers to Section 1 Review
1. "Key Terms" are defined on the following pages:
- **a.** capital, p. 606
- **b.** capitalist, p. 606
- **c.** free enterprise system, p. 607
- **d.** entrepreneur, p. 607
- **e.** laws of supply and demand, p. 608
- **f.** monopoly, p. 608

2. Private owners. **3.** Private ownership, guarantees for property rights, decentralized decision making, competition, and freedom of choice. **4.** Sole proprietorships, partnerships, and corporations. **5.** Competition helps keep prices down and quality high. To keep costs low, producers need to run efficient operations.

Teacher's Resource File See the Unit 6 File, p. 26, for the Section 1 Quiz.

VOICES *on Government*

On the Importance of Savings to a Capitalist Economy

Kathleen Feldstein, economist and columnist

Martin Feldstein, former chief of the Council of Economic Advisors

"The funds that private individuals put into savings accounts or money market funds or bonds provide the source of business borrowing. For businesses to invest in new plants and equipment or in training programs or in research and development, they must be able to borrow. And if they can't borrow enough from Americans, they will turn to foreign investors. That is exactly the pattern that is evolving now. . . . Yet far from being understood, this phenomenon is stirring up latent fears of foreigners and renewed protectionist sympathy. The sad fact is that without foreign investment there would be very little capital available for our economy to grow."

Three Kinds of Business Organization

While the United States economy contains a number of gigantic companies with thousands of employees and with plants all over the world, most businesses in the United States are relatively small. Some 80 percent of businesses employ fewer than 20 people.

There are three basic types of business organizations—sole proprietorships, partnerships, and corporations. Each has its advantages and disadvantages.

Businesses owned by a single individual are sole proprietorships. Typical of businesses in this category might be a beauty shop, a garage, or a doctor's practice. A major advantage of sole proprietorships is that decisions can be made quickly, by the single owner. A major disadvantage is that the owner is personally liable for debts the business might build up.

Businesses owned by two or more individuals, called partners, are partnerships. An advantage is that a partnership can draw on the resources of more than one person for capital to start or expand the business. A disadvantage is that partnerships end if a partner leaves or dies.

Unlike partnerships, corporations have many owners, called shareholders.[4] A corporation might continue indefinitely because a shareholder's death does not affect the legal status of the corporation. In other words, the corporation exists as its own legal entity, independent from the existence of any stockholders.

Corporations can draw their capital from hundreds and even thousands of investors, thus enabling them to finance such costly projects as putting an earth satellite in orbit or building an oil pipeline. Shareholders are responsible only for the amount of money they have invested. If the business fails, they might lose that amount, but no more. The shareholders have limited liability, and are not held responsible for any debts the corporation might have.

One disadvantage of corporations is that their income is taxed twice. First, the corporation pays a tax on its profits. Then, individual shareholders pay a tax on their dividends.

Profit and Loss

What drives the capitalist economy? The best answer, most often, is profit.

To understand what profit is, you must first understand the idea of investment. An investment is a sum of money, or capital, that is put

[4] A share is a fraction of ownership in the corporation.

SPOTLIGHT ON: Behind the Scenes

Since 1978, the number of small businesses in the United States has increased by over 55 percent. Ninety-nine percent of the 19 million non-farm businesses in the United States are small businesses. Among these are some 13.2 million sole proprietorships, 1.8 million partnerships, and 4 million corporations. Fifty-five percent of the American work force is employed by small businesses. Small businesses also make 44 percent of all sales in America and produce 38 percent of the nation's gross national product—the total output of the nation's goods and services.

Top Purchasers and Suppliers of U.S. Exports and Imports

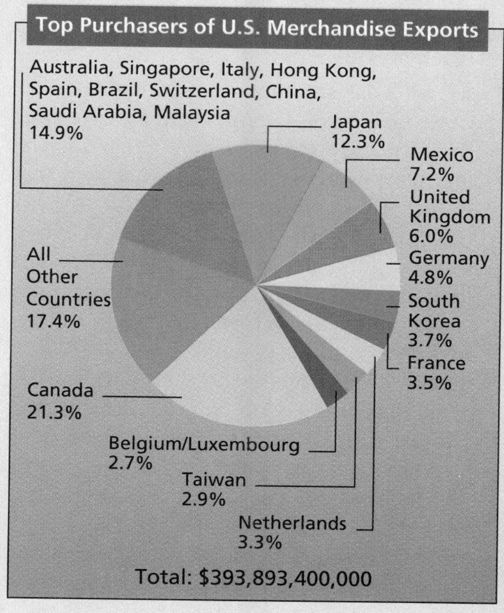

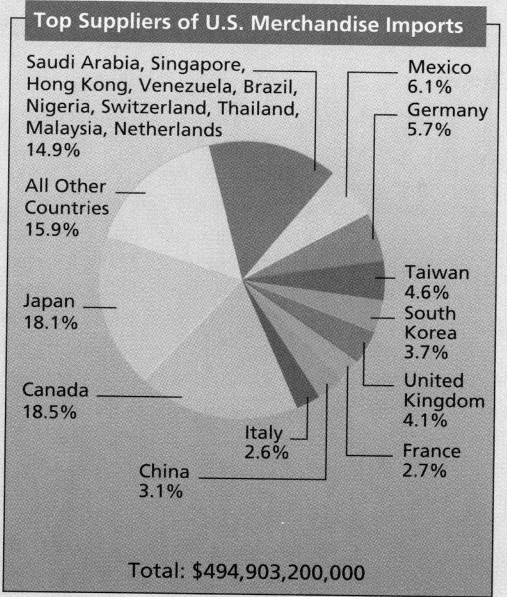

Source: *World Eagle*, October 1991; U.S. Dept. of Commerce, International Trade Administration, Office of Trade and Investment Analysis, *1990 U.S. Foreign Trade Highlights.*

Interpreting Graphs: Multicultural Awareness The United States economy does not exist in isolation but is linked with the economies of many other countries. Which country conducts the most trade with the United States?

into a business enterprise. For example, if you buy a car to start a business delivering groceries, what you pay for the car is an investment. The profit will be the amount of money earned from the business, after having subtracted the costs associated with earning that money—in this case, the purchase of the car and the costs of operating it, plus whatever you pay yourself. If earnings are less than the costs, the business has not made a profit; instead, it has taken a loss.

Taking risks and making investments, therefore, is an essential part of the capitalist system. Every year, many businesses fail for lack of profit. Businesses that survive tend to be those that have learned to make the most efficient use of the factors of production.

Section 1 Review

1. Define: capital, capitalist, free enterprise system, entrepreneur, laws of supply and demand, monopoly

2. Who controls most of the productive property in a capitalist economy?

3. What are the five characteristics of a free enterprise system?

4. What are the three basic business types in the United States?

Critical Thinking

5. Understanding Cause and Effect (p. 19) Explain how competition promotes efficiency.

★

Closure

The United States is based on the economic system known as capitalism. In a capitalist society, individually owned businesses control most of the productive property. In Section 2, students will read about another economic system—socialism—that seeks to distribute wealth more equitably among society.

Assignment Assign Section 2, pp. 613-617, for the next class period.

Activity: Cooperative Learning

Time: Two class periods **Activity:** Videotape a television ad for a business. **Grouping:** Three to four students **Purpose:** Have students choose a business and plan a 60-second television ad for it. Explain that the recorder should transcribe the script for the ad. After the spokesperson(s) has rehearsed, the camera operator can film the presentation. **Roles:** Have students assign the following roles: manager, recorder, spokesperson(s), camera operator. **Outcome:** Provide time for the class to view the ads.

Reteach

Write *free enterprise system* on the board and draw a circle around it. Then have students supply the five characteristics of a free enterprise system while you write them on the board with arrows pointing to the circle. Then give students specific factors of production that run the economy and have students name the broad category that they fit into. For example, you may say, "The workers on the assembly line at an auto plant." Students should respond "Labor."

TEACHING
What You Can Do

Working to End World Hunger

Objective

Examine how individuals can act to relieve the effects of social problems.

INSTRUCT

Before students begin reading the feature, ask them if they can think of a disturbing problem in the local or global community that they would like to do something about. Explain to students that they will read about a group of teenagers who recognized world hunger as a problem in the global community that they wanted to help solve.

Below are some possible questions for post-reading discussion:

- What community needs do you see that you would like to do something about?
- What could a group of students do to help satisfy this need?

TRF **Teacher's Resource File** See the Participatory Government Activities file, pp. 28–39, for material to support the lesson.

What You Can Do

Working to End World Hunger

When Mary Varilla, a high school student in Ridgefield, Connecticut, saw footage of an Ethiopian famine on television news reports in 1984, she became deeply concerned. She introduced the subject in a global issues discussion group at her school. After listening to Mary, others in the group shared her concern. Together, they decided that they wanted to do something to help victims of the famine. The group began by sponsoring school assemblies to educate students about world hunger. At these assemblies, students learned that the fight to end world hunger takes place on two fronts. Money raised through fund-raising and donations serves to provide emergency relief to those in immediate need. More importantly, money is also raised to help implement programs designed to prevent poverty and starvation in the future.

Mary and her group launched their fund-raising effort by soliciting support from local businesses, churches, synagogues, and other schools. The group's first joint project, a townwide walk-a-thon, attracted 2,000 participants and raised $60,000. After consulting with an experienced relief organization, they chose to send the money to Yifat Na Timuga, a poor, malaria-plagued town in Ethiopia in need of funds for three building projects already underway: a well to provide the town with clean water, homes for orphaned children, and a grain storage house.

Seeing the Results

By 1987, donations to Mary's group had slowed to a trickle. Many people questioned what their donations had accomplished, if anything. Mary and four of her classmates decided to find out for themselves. That summer, they embarked on a trip to Yifat Na Timuga to see the projects that they helped sponsor. The American teenagers were gratified by what they saw. A recently completed catch basin supplied the village with safe water for drinking, washing, and irrigation. They learned that people who had previously left the village were able to return because of the improved sanitary conditions. Children who before had to spend their days walking long distances to obtain clean water now had the time to attend school. The students also visited the orphanages that they helped to fund and enjoyed a challenging game of volleyball with a group of teens there.

Thousands of American teens have joined in the fight against hunger by educating those around them, raising funds, and working in relief projects. For some, the desire to stamp out hunger may become a lifetime commitment and a career goal. For others, the experience may simply be one chance to do some good. But by becoming active in fund-raising and service projects, students can make a difference—at home and around the world.

Getting Involved

1. Identify a need in your school, local, or global community similar to the one addressed in this case.

2. Formulate a plan for how you might organize volunteer efforts to help remedy this problem and identify resources that could be used in your plan.

3. Predict any problems you might encounter in implementing your idea. Also predict how you might solve those problems.

2 Socialism

Find Out:

- What are the historic roots of socialism?
- How are market economies different from command economies?
- What are the principal arguments for and against socialism?

Key Terms:

proletariat, bourgeoisie, welfare state, market economy, command economy

You know that in the United States, all people are entitled to equal protection under the law. Of course, this political equality is not the same as economic equality. As you have read, America's capitalistic system enables some to achieve greater financial rewards than others.

There is, however, an economic system that seeks to equitably distribute wealth through society. This section is about that system.

What Is Socialism?

Socialism is an economic and a political philosophy based on the idea that the benefits of economic activity—wealth—should be equitably distributed throughout a society. This fairness is achieved through the principle of collective—that is, public—ownership of the most important means by which goods and services are produced and distributed.

Socialism rejects the concepts of private ownership, individualism, and competition for profit that lie at the heart of capitalistic thought and practice. Instead, socialists emphasize cooperation and social responsibility in order to achieve this more equitable distribution of both income and opportunity. Political equality is not enough, they say. Real equality can come only when extreme differences in wealth across the population are reduced, and the public controls the centers of economic power in a society.

The roots of socialism lie deep in history. Almost from the beginning there have been those who have dreamed of a society built on socialist doctrine. Most earlier socialists foresaw a collective economy that would arise out of and then be managed by voluntary private action. With few exceptions, they believed that they could reach their goals without governmental action—and, so, early socialist doctrine is often called "private socialism."

The Industrial Revolution

Present-day socialism developed in large part as a reaction to the poverty and other miseries that accompanied the Industrial Revolution.

The Industrial Revolution occurred as the Western world moved from an agricultural to an industrial economy. It appeared most distinctly

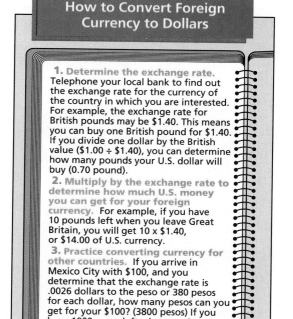

How to Convert Foreign Currency to Dollars

1. Determine the exchange rate. Telephone your local bank to find out the exchange rate for the currency of the country in which you are interested. For example, the exchange rate for British pounds may be $1.40. This means you can buy one British pound for $1.40. If you divide one dollar by the British value ($1.00 ÷ $1.40), you can determine how many pounds your U.S. dollar will buy (0.70 pound).

2. Multiply by the exchange rate to determine how much U.S. money you can get for your foreign currency. For example, if you have 10 pounds left when you leave Great Britain, you will get 10 x $1.40, or $14.00 of U.S. currency.

3. Practice converting currency for other countries. If you arrive in Mexico City with $100, and you determine that the exchange rate is .0026 dollars to the peso or 380 pesos for each dollar, how many pesos can you get for your $100? (3800 pesos) If you have 1000 pesos left when you leave Mexico, how many dollars should you expect to get? ($26)

Interpreting Charts The exchange rate between various currencies can change from day to day. In step 2, what would you get if the pound was worth $1.50 when you left Great Britain?

Section 2
Socialism

Focus

Teacher's Resource File See the Unit 6 File, p. 27, for the Section 2 Outline.

Objectives

23.4 Examine the historic roots of socialism.
23.5 Describe how market economies differ from command economies.
23.6 Explain the major arguments for and against socialism.

Bellringer Activity Ask students to agree or disagree with the following: Everyone should be guaranteed housing. Everyone should be assured of three meals a day. Athletes deserve to make over a million dollars a year. Tell students that these issues depend on the type of economic system in a country.

State the Purpose Socialism—the economic philosophy that wealth should be distributed equitably throughout a society—is a principle that takes various forms in different countries. In Section 2, students will read about the roots of socialism, the principles upon which it is based, and arguments for and against it.

Interpreting Charts Provide students with the following sample problem: You have £20 and the British pound is worth $1.65. How many dollars would you get? *($33)*

Caption Answer $15.

Vocabulary

Point out "Key Terms" on page 613. Ask students to explain what they think is meant by the words *market* and *command.* Place those words in the context of economics for students, and identify the differences between them.

Reading Strategy: Problem Solving

Ask students to devise a plan to eliminate homelessness in the United States. Who would be responsible for implementing their suggestions? Who would pay for their plan? As students read, ask them to decide whether their plan was based on capitalist or socialist ideology.

INSTRUCT

Discuss/Analyze Ask students to begin their discussion of Section 2 by defining *socialism* as an economic philosophy. Have them include an analysis of its present-day form and the roots from which it sprang.

Write *Characteristics of socialist economies* on the board. Have students provide the four characteristics given in the text (*nationalization, public services and the welfare state, taxation, and the command economy*) as well as supporting details for each.

Ask students to analyze the pros and cons of socialism. Discuss with students the criticisms of socialism (*overly bureaucratic, deadening of individual initiative, slow to progress, eliminates freedom of choice*) and the arguments given in support of this system (*evens out inequalities of wealth and power, gives people control over their daily lives*). Remind students of their responses in the "Bellringer Activity." Do they think that socialism would solve those issues with which they disagreed? Discuss why or why not as a class.

ABCNEWS INTERACTIVE

The following video segment may be used to highlight aspects of economic systems.

POWERS OF THE CONGRESS GUIDEBOOK
Chapter 26: Trade with Other Nations, p. 30

in Great Britain in the late 18th century and spread generally through Western Europe and to the United States in the 19th century. It was marked by rapid urbanization and the growth of large-scale manufacturing.

Many observers of 19th-century British factories and factory towns were appalled by the conditions they found. Men and women often worked 14- to 16-hour days—usually in filthy, noisy, and unsafe conditions. Small children regularly worked alongside their parents, for even less pay. Most factory workers and their families lived in dank, crowded, and unhealthful slums.

Those and other adverse effects of the Industrial Revolution led many to seek social and economic reforms. And those conditions led some to argue for much more radical change.

Karl Marx Clearly, Karl Marx (1818-1883), the father of modern-day socialism, was the most significant critic of capitalism to emerge in the 19th century. Much of his work and most of his extensive writings were done in collaboration with Friedrich Engels (1820-1895). Together, Marx and Engels wrote *The Communist Manifesto* in 1848—"to do for history," they said, "what Darwin's theory has done for biology."

Marx believed that capitalism was fatally flawed.
1.a The **proletariat**—the workers—were being so
1.b badly abused by the **bourgeoisie**—the capitalists—that they were certain to rise up and overthrow the capitalistic system. You will read more about Marx and his ideas in the next section.

Nationalization and Socialism In socialist economies such as Sweden's, key transportation and communications industries may be nationalized. Other businesses, such as this Swedish auto manufacturer, remain in private hands.

Socialists and Communists A powerful socialist movement took shape among European workers and thinkers during the middle and late 19th century. Almost all socialists accepted Marx's criticism of capitalism. But the movement was deeply split by the question of how best to achieve socialism. Some argued that a socialist society could come only out of a "violent and bloody revolution." Over time, those who took that view came to be called communists. Others argued that socialism could be attained by peaceful means, through the democratic process. Today, the terms *socialism* and *socialist* are usually used to identify those evolutionary socialists.

The British Labour party and the major "social democratic" parties of Western Europe are leading examples of that brand of socialism. At various times in recent history, these parties have controlled their governments and have instituted many socialist programs through democratic means.

Characteristics of Socialist Economies

Countries that have socialist governments typically enact one or more of the following measures to achieve the aims of socialist philosophy.

Nationalization Organizing enterprises under governmental control—often by taking over privately owned industries—is called nationalization. Recall that in the last chapter you read about nationalization in Mexico in the 1930s. In democratic countries such as Britain, the government might nationalize enterprises, paying the former owners what it calculates to be a fair price. In some countries, however, governments have nationalized industries without paying any compensation.

Nationalization sometimes, but rarely, includes all businesses in a country. Typically, nationalization is selective. Socialist governments usually want to control the country's most important industries, but they may allow many types of businesses to remain in private hands. Also, socialist countries might want certain important industries that are based upon newly emerging technologies to remain private since individual initiative and entrepreneurial risk-taking are very important during the early phases of a business.

A goal of many socialist governments is to give each company's workers a say in deciding how the company is run. Sweden's Social Democratic party, for example, has a plan for gradually transferring ownership of private companies to their workers. Elected worker representatives now sit on many companies' boards of directors.

Public Services and the Welfare State

Socialists stress the goal of assuring that everyone in a society is decently housed and fed. Stated another way, socialists aim to guarantee the public welfare by providing for the equal distribution of necessities and services. Public services are considered to be government's responsibility. Some of the earliest successes of the British Labour party included the adoption of pensions, health insurance, and unemployment insurance between 1908 and 1911. Other countries' programs may range from free university education to free housing for the poor.

Countries that provide extensive social services at little or no cost to the users are called **welfare** 1.c
states. In such countries, medical and dental services may be provided free or for a small charge. People who lose their jobs or who are physically unable to work receive government payments that are nearly as high as their former wages. All people above retirement age receive government pensions. Parents may receive government payments for each child until the child reaches the age of 18.

Taxation

All governments, capitalistic or socialist, get their funds from taxation. But because social welfare services are quite expensive, taxes in socialist countries tend to be high. It is not uncommon for taxes to take 50 or 60 percent of an individual's total income. Socialists tend to place most of the burden on the upper and middle classes, consistent with their philosophy of achieving a more equal distribution of wealth. Tax rates can amount to 90 percent of a wealthy person's income.

Health Care for All Many social services—including medical care—are provided to citizens of Canada by their government. Canadians also receive education and other services.

The Command Economy

Economies can be divided into two broad categories, depending on how basic decisions are made. Under capitalism, as you have seen, the government's role is a limited one. Key decisions are made by thousands of private individuals and companies through the give and take of the marketplace. For that
1.d reason, capitalistic economies are called **market economies**.

Under socialism, and also communism, decision making is much more centralized. Public bodies can plan how an economy will develop over a period of years. Governments set targets for production. They guide investment into specific industries. In theory, therefore, governments can direct the economy along desired paths. Thus, socialist and communist economies
1.e are called **command economies**.

A document called the five-year plan plays a key role in many command economies. The plan is a blueprint showing how leaders want the economy to develop over the next five years. (You will read about the use of five-year plans in the former Soviet Union in the next section.) Making a five-

Provide Guided Practice Ask students to indicate whether a list of statements refer to socialism or capitalism. That list might include the following: *Karl Marx criticized it. Adam Smith wrote of this system. Nationalization of industry. Free or inexpensive medical and dental care for everyone. High taxes. Large following in developing countries.*

Provide Independent Practice

TRF **Teacher's Resource File** You may wish to assign Section 2 Guided Reading and Review, Unit 6 File, p. 28, to help students master section objective content.

SPOTLIGHT ON: Political Talk

In the United States, the welfare state was established with a series of programs proposed by President Franklin D. Roosevelt known collectively as the New Deal. The phrase comes from FDR's acceptance speech to the 1932 Democratic convention pledging "a new deal to the American people," who were suffering the effects of the Great Depression. The New Deal laid the cornerstone of the welfare state with programs to provide old age pensions, unemployment relief, aid to the disabled, and aid to families with dependent children. The New Deal also gave the Federal Government a larger role in the management of the national economy.

Enrichment

Have students color code a world map based on whether each country has a capitalist or socialist economy. (Note: Following Section 3, students can fill in those countries with communist economies.) (Easy)

TRF **Teacher's Resource File**
See the Simulations and Debates file, pp. 35–70, for material to support this section.

Interpreting Tables: Multicultural Awareness Ask students which countries tend to have the highest and lowest prices. (*Tokyo tends to have the highest; Mexico City and Brasilia tend to have the lowest.*)

Caption Answer They are generally in the middle range for the countries shown.

Monitor Comprehension

Answers to Section 2 Review
1. "Key Terms" are defined on the following pages:
a. proletariat, p. 614
b. bourgeoisie, p. 614
c. welfare state, p. 615
d. market economy, p. 615
e. command economy, p. 615
2. Socialism rejects the capitalist ideas of private ownership, individualism, and competition for profit. **3.** Socialism was a reaction to the poverty and misery of the Industrial Revolution. **4.** Socialism breeds too many layers of bureaucracy; people are deprived of the freedom to decide how to use their income. Capitalism breeds inequality; workers have less control over their daily lives. **5.** Students may suggest that in a socialist society everyone works to put people back to work while in a capitalist society, it is primarily the individual's responsibility to find employment.

TRF **Teacher's Resource File** See the Unit 6 File, p. 29, for the Section 2 Quiz.

year plan is an intricate process drawing on experts from many areas of national life. The purpose is to set economic goals for the future and to plan how to achieve those goals most efficiently.

Socialism in Developing Countries

Socialism has won a large following in developing countries. There, public ownership and centralized planning are widespread.

One reason for socialism's appeal is that most developing countries are starting from scratch at building industry. Such countries have no tradition of locally controlled, large-scale industry. Large industries that do exist often are owned by foreign interests—firms that have a base in one country and holdings in many others. By nationalizing a foreign-owned company and placing local people in charge, a political leader can win broad public support.

Socialism also appeals to leaders who want to mobilize an entire nation behind a program of industrial growth. Through central planning, leaders can channel investment into the parts of the economy they think are most essential.

Birthplace of an Ideology The Industrial Revolution that so horrified Karl Marx began in Great Britain's textile mills. This is one of Britain's textile mills today.

Often, however, guided growth of this sort requires painful sacrifices by a nation's people. High taxes skim off a large part of people's income. The government may devote so much attention to one or two basic industries that the production of consumer goods or food may be neglected. Then public unrest may develop.

Political instability is a persistent problem in developing nations. It is one reason for the tendency of socialist and other governments in such nations to turn to authoritarian methods. Few developing nations have succeeded in establishing the democratic versions of socialism that are found in parts of the industrial world.

Major Criticisms of Socialism

Both capitalistic and socialist economies have their strengths and their weaknesses. For supporters of capitalism, it is easy to see weaknesses in the theory and practice of socialism. For supporters of socialism, on the other hand, it is capitalism that is riddled with faults.

Critics say socialist countries have a tendency to develop too many layers of bureaucracy. They say this complicates decision making and has a deadening effect on individual initiative. As a result, critics say, socialist economies are slower to take advantage of new technologies.

In the eyes of socialism's critics, the smooth running of an economy is too complex to be directed by central planners. Too many unpredictable events are involved, they claim. Too many clashing interests are at stake. For all its faults, the invisible hand of the market economy works more efficiently than the visible hand of the command economy, say socialism's critics.

Another criticism is that socialism deprives people of the freedom to decide for themselves how to use their income. Most of a person's income goes to taxes. Since earners get to keep only a part of their earnings, they have little incentive to work harder and earn more. Why work hard when your basic needs will be taken care of anyway? So ask socialism's critics.

In response, socialists point to the inequalities of wealth and power that exist under capitalism. Socialists argue that socialism evens out inequalities and thus is morally superior to capitalism. In their view, socialism makes political democra-

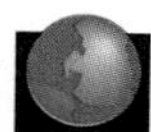

Global Awareness

Food Prices and Average Weekly Incomes for Selected Cities (Current Prices in U.S. Dollars)

	Brasilia	London	Madrid	Mexico City	Pretoria	Seoul	Tokyo	Washington D.C.
Sirloin Steak (1 kg*)	2.55	20.12	14.74	5.93	5.90	21.83	52.74	11.62
Whole Broilers (1 kg)	1.19	3.80	2.99	2.33	1.91	3.60	5.69	2.20
Large Eggs (1 doz)	0.80	3.13	1.91	0.71	0.94	2.39	1.95	0.99
Cheddar Cheese (1 kg)	3.36	7.48	12.24	6.27	4.16	11.70	13.72	11.85
Milk (1 liter**)	0.73	0.90	0.87	0.47	0.64	1.21	1.45	0.62
Butter (1 kg)	3.08	4.36	11.31	2.98	3.33	8.28	10.64	4.48
Apples (1 kg)	2.15	2.09	2.98	2.07	0.65	5.75	3.71	2.27
Flour (1 kg)	0.58	0.79	0.83	0.47	0.78	0.43	1.35	0.64
Rice (1 kg)	0.97	1.71	1.96	0.70	0.88	2.15	2.64	1.08
Sugar (1 kg)	0.58	1.16	1.18	0.59	0.59	0.82	1.67	0.97
Coffee (1 kg)	2.58	10.56	6.91	4.76	8.35	13.10	25.97	7.50
Potatoes (1 kg)	1.49	0.92	0.82	0.52	0.36	2.43	2.92	1.21
Average Weekly Income	$47	$281	$184	$44	$49	$95	$446	$404

*1 kg is equal to 2.205 pounds.
**1 liter is equal to 1.057 quarts.
Source: U.S. Department of Agriculture. Foreign Agriculture Service, *Agricultural Trade Highlights*, June 1991

Interpreting Tables: Multicultural Awareness The world's economies are closely related, yet they still differ greatly. How do the prices paid in the United States compare with those paid elsewhere?

cy work more smoothly by supplementing it with economic democracy.

Defenders of socialism also argue that it gives workers and ordinary citizens more control over their daily lives. Under capitalism, they say, a company's management can abruptly decide to close a factory that is no longer making money. The company has no obligation to ask its workers' opinions, even though such a decision can throw thousands out of work and disrupt an entire community. This could not happen under socialism, the argument goes. Workers and community leaders would sit on the company's board. They would help decide what was best for the entire work force and community—not just for the company's shareholders.

Section 2 Review

1. Define: proletariat, bourgeoisie, welfare state, market economy, command economy
2. How does socialism differ from capitalism?
3. What part did the Industrial Revolution play in the birth of modern socialism?
4. State two criticisms of socialism and two criticisms of capitalism.

Critical Thinking

5. Making Comparisons (p. 19) How might a socialist and capitalist government differ in its treatment of the problem of unemployment?

★

Closure

Socialism is the economic and political philosophy based on the idea that wealth should be equitably distributed among society. In Section 3, students will read about communism, an economic theory aimed at collective ownership of all productive property.

Assignment Assign Section 3, pp. 618-623, for the next class period.

Reteach

Have students individually or in small groups create comic books or leaflets that explain socialism and identify the arguments for and against this economic system.

SECTION 3
Communism

FOCUS

Teacher's Resource File See the Unit 6 File, p. 30, for the Section 3 Outline.

Objectives

23.7 Determine the basic concepts of Marx's communist theory.
23.8 Explain how communist theory was put into action in the Soviet Union.
23.9 Examine the ways in which Gorbachev's economic reforms lead to the "collapse" of communism in the former Soviet Union.

Bellringer Activity Ask students to write down a list of countries that come to mind when you say "communism." Explain that some formerly communist countries are abandoning that economic system.

State the Purpose Communism is the economic and political system that calls for collective ownership of all productive goods and services. In theory, everyone in society would work together for the good of all. In practice, communism has experienced a difficult history marked particularly by the politics of the former Soviet Union.

ABCNEWS INTERACTIVE

The following video segment may be used to highlight aspects of economic systems.

POWERS OF THE CONGRESS GUIDEBOOK
Chapter 9: Communism, p. 85

3 Communism

Find Out:

- What are the basic concepts of Marx's communist theory?
- How was communist theory put into action in the Soviet Union?
- How did Gorbachev's economic reforms lead to the "collapse" of communism in the former Soviet Union?

Key Terms:

five-year plan, collectivization

The word *communism* has a important place in the lexicon of recent American political history. Since the late 1940s, much of this nation's foreign policy has aimed at countering the influence of communism around the world. Yet for many Americans, the full meaning of the term is unclear.

Communism as it is known in today's world was born in Europe in the middle of the last century.[5] It is a political, economic, and social theory built by Karl Marx and then, especially in the Soviet Union, by Lenin and Stalin.[6]

Karl Marx's Communist Theory

Communism is often called a collective ideology. That is, it is a theory that calls for the collective, or state, ownership of all land and other productive property. As you have read, its basic concepts were first set out in *The Communist Manifesto*, written in 1848 by Karl Marx and Friedrich Engels. This political document condemned the misery and the exploitations of the Industrial Revolution in Europe, and it called upon oppressed workers across the continent to free themselves from "capitalist enslavement." The pamphlet ended with this rallying cry:

> "The proletarians have nothing to lose but their chains. They have a world to win. Workingmen of all countries, unite!"

In his major work, *Das Kapital* (first published in 1867), Marx analyzed the development and workings of capitalism from its historical roots. It presented Marx's view of capitalism based on four closely related concepts: (1) his theory of history, (2) the theory of value and capitalist accumulation, (3) his view of the nature of the state, and (4) the dictatorship of the proletariat.

Based on his ideology, Marx envisioned communism as a "free, classless society"—a society in which all social classes would vanish and all property would be owned by all people in common. There would be no exploitation of labor and no unemployment. Goods would be produced in abundance, and they would be available to all according to need. People would be happy to work hard, pleased to contribute their best for the benefit of all.

The Marxian View of History To Marx, all of human history has been a story of class struggle—of conflict among social classes competing for the control of labor and of productive property. In that view, there have always been two major and opposing classes in society—one an oppressor class and the other an oppressed class. Thus, in the Middle Ages the contending classes were the nobility and their serfs. In the modern world it is the bourgeoisie who keep the proletariat in submission.

Marx's doctrine held that the conflict between the classes would become so intense in the modern era that a revolt of the masses and the downfall of the bourgeoisie would be inevitable. The communist's political role was that of speeding up these revolutionary processes, by violence if need be.

The Labor Theory of Value In the communist view, the value of every commodity is set

[5]The word *communism* comes from the Latin *communis*, meaning "common, belonging to all." The idea of communal property dates back at least to the early Greeks. In the fourth century B.C., Plato proposed a system of communal property in *The Republic*.

[6]Stalin, and other communists in the Soviet Union and elsewhere, frequently referred to the ideology as Marxist-Leninism. Marx originally used the term *scientific socialism* to distinguish his thought from older and less extreme forms of socialism. In later years, Marx came to prefer the term *communism*.

Reading Strategy: Question Writing

Ask students to skim Section 3 and to write down the headings and subheadings. Then invite them to turn each heading into a question such as "What is Karl Marx's communist theory?" As they read, have them jot down answers to the questions they have created.

Vocabulary

Direct students' attention to "Key Terms" on page 618. Below are some additional words whose meanings may help students understand the section content.
—**lexicon:** the special vocabulary of a particular author, field of study, etc.
—**zealots:** people who are enthusiastically devoted to a purpose

by the amount of socially useful labor put into it. In short, labor creates all value. A pair of shoes or a rebuilt engine is each worth so much because it takes that much labor to produce it. Because the laborer made the shoes or rebuilt the engine, the communist argues that the laborer should receive that value in full.

Marxists reject the free enterprise notions of competition and profit. Competition, they say, forces the capitalist to drive workers' wages down to the lowest possible point. Profits are condemned as "surplus value," wrung from the grinding toil of the masses.

The Nature of the State Marx saw the state and its government as the instrument of the dominant class in society—a tool by which the capitalists maintained their power and privileged position. Other social institutions were also seen as playing a role in enforcing capitalist control over the masses. Thus, Marx described religion as "the opiate of the people." Religious beliefs, he wrote, are a drug fed to the masses, a hoax through which they are persuaded to tolerate their harsh lot in this life in the hope that someday they will gain what Marx called a "fictional afterlife."

The Dictatorship of the Proletariat Marx did not believe that the final form of communist society would appear immediately upon the overthrow of the bourgeoisie. He saw the need for a transitional phase during which the state would represent and enforce the interest of the masses. This was called, in Marx's terminology, the "dictatorship of the proletariat"—a period of authoritarian rule through which society must pass on the way to the goal of a classless society. He argued that once the goal of classlessness was realized, the need for the state and its government would disappear.

Marx also expected that the bonds of common interest between workers in different countries would be so strong that they would overshadow national identities and national loyalties. Thus, for example, he thought that French and German factory workers would come together on the basis of their shared economic situation—and so nationalism, a major cause of European wars, would be eliminated with the establishment of communism.

Communism in the Soviet Union

Marx was convinced that the world's most advanced industrialized countries, with their large working-class populations, were ripe for revolution. In particular, Marx expected that workers' revolutions would occur in France, Germany, and Great Britain, and then in the United States. But, that revolution actually occurred in the largely agricultural Russia in 1917; and with that upheaval came the creation of the world's first communist state.[7]

---

[7]In his later years, Marx did recognize the possibility that his theories might first be tested in practice in Russia. Lenin also took the Russia-first view, in the early 1900s. He thought that less advanced countries, with their comparatively small industrial populations, offered certain advantages to a revolutionary movement—notably, the effectiveness with which workers could be organized and controlled.

The First Marxist Karl Marx was an ardent critic of the capitalist system. He anticipated a violent rejection of capitalist ideals by the workers of the world.

INSTRUCT

Discuss/Analyze Communism has long been a foe to capitalism. The principles of communism as they played out in the Soviet Union were seen to lack any of the essential freedoms that guided the principles upon which the United States is based.

Trace the theoretical roots of communism created by Karl Marx in *The Communist Manifesto* of 1848. Have students analyze the various elements of communism laid out by Marx—the Marxian view of history, the labor theory of value, the nature of the state, and the dictatorship of the proletariat. Then ask students to discuss the ways in which communism was actually put into practice in the Soviet Union by Lenin and then later by Stalin. Ask them, too, to discuss Gorbachev's role in reforming some of the communist principles. Encourage students to compare the difference between the theory and the practice of communism.

Teacher's Resource File
See the Comparative Government file, pp. 10–11, for material to support the section.

INSTRUCT

Explain/Illustrate You may wish to discuss the effects of communism in Cuba, Vietnam, and China. Identify the reasons why those countries embraced Marxian theory, the effects on the standard of living for their citizens, and the current level of satisfaction or dissatisfaction of the people of those countries.

Bring to class news magazines from the past year and have students cut photographs and articles from the magazines that trace the collapse of communism in the Soviet Union. Display the clippings on a bulletin board.

In order to emphasize the enormous implications of the fall of Soviet communism, you may wish to discuss with students the comment made by President Bush in his 1992 State of the Union Address, in which he described the events as having "almost Biblical proportions." Also discuss with students the cuts in defense that the collapse allowed.

Farming Under Communism Contrary to Marx's original expectation, communism first took root in largely agricultural Russia, not in the industrialized centers of Europe.

Marx's analysis of capitalism did not provide a real blueprint—or anything close to one—for the formation of a communist society. This left the leaders of the Russian communist revolution with the task of interpreting his ideas for clues on what was to be done.

Communism Under Lenin In November 1917, Lenin and his followers seized power in Russia, established a communist government, and began at once their attempt to create their vision of a communist society. The new government ordered the nationalization of all banks and large businesses, and it moved to create workers' councils (soviets) in every enterprise to manage them. Outside the cities, Lenin encouraged the peasants to seize whatever land they could.

Lenin's government was immediately torn by civil war—three years of brutal conflict in which several groups challenged communist rule. Lenin, using both military force and terror on a broad scale, was able to defeat his foes, who were divided and poorly led. But by 1921 conditions had become extremely grave throughout the country. Peasant revolts had broken out in several places, and the threat of famine was widespread.

Lenin realized that the attempt to create an instant communist society had failed, and in 1921 he introduced the New Economic Policy, NEP. The NEP was a clear compromise between socialist principles and capitalism that was intended to revive agricultural production and promote manufacturing. The government continued to control what Lenin called the "commanding heights"—heavy industry, banking, foreign trade, wholesale commerce, and transportation. But private ownership of rural land and trade for profit were allowed to flourish. Said Lenin: "If we cannot go to communism directly, we shall zigzag to it through socialism."

By the time Lenin died in 1924, the Soviet Union had become a one-party state. All opposition to communism had been banned, and the communists had taken control of all of the country's social, political, and economic institutions.

Enrichment

Have students research the uprisings against communism in Bulgaria, China, and the former Soviet Union. Identify the role of young people in those events, analyzing the reasons for their dissatisfaction with communism and their effect on the outcomes of the uprisings. Have students present their findings in the form of a simulated television documentary. (Challenging)

Communism Under Stalin Lenin's death prompted a fierce struggle for power among his chief aides. Josef Stalin defeated his several rivals one by one, and he gained complete control of the Communist party and the government of the Soviet Union by 1928. For the next 25 years, Stalin ruled with an iron fist. As you have read, the Soviet economy and its influence abroad grew rapidly—but at a huge cost in human life and personal freedom.

Under Stalin, the 1930s were dominated by two major economic programs: the forced collectivization of Soviet agriculture and the rapid industrialization of the country's economy.

The NEP was ended in 1928. Stalin and others feared that its successes meant that free enterprise was gaining a foothold in the Soviet Union; and they also thought that steel and other heavy industries had received too little attention by the NEP. In its place came centralized economic planning for the entire country and the First Five-Year Plan.

The Five-Year Plans The **five-year plans** 1.a marked the first attempt by any society to combine large-scale centralized planning with the public ownership of the means of production as the basis for a nation's economic advancement. The First Five-Year Plan ran from 1928 to 1933.

The plan was dominated by two major goals: (1) **collectivization**—the combining of mil- 1.b lions of small peasant farms into giant collective, government-controlled farms, called *kolkhozy*, and (2) huge production increases in the nation's chemical, petroleum, machine tool, construction, steel, and other heavy industries.

Stalin ordered the creation of the *kolkhozy* in 1929. There was great resistance from the largest, most prosperous landholders whose numbers had grown under the NEP. They killed their livestock and destroyed farmland as an act of resistance. Party zealots from the cities invaded the rural areas, killing hundreds of thousands of peasant families and sending many more to labor camps in Siberia and Central Asia.

The First Five-Year Plan also aimed at bringing a greatly expanded industrial capacity to the Soviet Union. That goal was also emphasized in the Second and Third Five-Year plans.[8] By concentrating Soviet resources on the development of heavy industry, Stalin hoped to end the nation's economic backwardness and reduce its military vulnerability. The success of the collectivization of agriculture also depended on industrialization—because the farmers needed a source of farm machinery and gasoline.

The first three five-year plans were at least partial successes. The Soviet Union achieved rapid, if uneven, industrialization, but the need for consumer goods and urban services were ignored. Many products had to be rationed; housing shortages became common; and sewers, water systems, and other needs lagged behind a dramatic growth in urban population.

To spur greater production, Stalin also gave economic rewards and other incentives to party officials, bureaucrats, and factory managers. People with special talents—writers, artists, musicians, and athletes, for example—were also rewarded. Thus, Stalin created an elite class in the Soviet Union, a class that owed its privileged status to the Communist party and the state—and he also corrupted the Marxian ideal of the economic and social equality of all.

The Gorbachev Reforms

When Mikhail Gorbachev gained power in the Soviet Union in 1985, he inherited an economic system largely unchanged from the one built from 1928 to 1953 by Josef Stalin. It was an economic system directed by a totalitarian dictatorship. It was a very rigid command system driven by five-year plans created by central planners.

Gorbachev's first statements as leader of the Communist party pledged the continuation of the old policies. However, he acknowledged that rapid economic improvement was the government's most important goal. The ending of the Eleventh Five-Year Plan that year was marked by declining economic growth and worker output, which Gorbachev blamed on poor organization, complacency, and irresponsibility.

---

[8] The First Five-Year Plan, launched in 1928, was declared completed in 1932, nine months ahead of schedule. The second plan ran from 1932 to 1937 and the third from 1937 until it was interrupted by the German invasion of the Soviet Union in 1941.

Provide Guided Practice
Write down the subheadings found under "Karl Marx's Communist Theory" on pages 618–619. Ask students to call out various key points that illustrate each subheading.

Provide Independent Practice
TRF **Teacher's Resource File**
You may wish to assign Section 3 Guided Reading and Review, Unit 6 File, p. 31, to help students master section objective content.

SPOTLIGHT ON: Global Awareness

The economic stagnation Gorbachev pledged to combat was a long-term problem that had been plaguing the country for almost twenty years. Although five-year plans from the 1930s through the 1950s had produced steady—if erratic—economic growth and higher standards of living, that trend reversed during the rule of Premier Leonid Brezhnev (1964-1982). Growth in the Soviet GNP fell off sharply, from a peak of 5.2 percent in the late 1960s to 2 percent and falling by 1980, while growth in living standards dropped from 4.3 percent to 1.2 percent over the same period. Soviet citizens were critical of Brezhnev's regime after his death and refer to his tenure as the "stagnant years."

MONITOR COMPREHENSION

Answers to Section 3 Review
1. "Key Terms" are defined on the following pages:
a. five-year plan, p. 621
b. collectivization, p. 621
2. His theory of history, the labor theory of value, his view of the nature of the state, and the dictatorship of the proletariat. **3.** (a) France, Germany, Great Britain, and the United States. (b) These countries, with their large working-class populations, were ripe for revolution. **4.** It corrupted the ideal. Certain people were given economic incentives and this created a social elite. **5.** Liberals wanted to shift directly to capitalism while conservatives wanted a slower transition. **6.** Answers will vary. Students may suggest that when individuals own things themselves, they do not rely on others as much. Instability is created when the few own everything. On a whim, they can give to the people, or take from the people.

TRF **Teacher's Resource File**
See the Unit 6 File, p. 32, for the Section 3 Quiz.

New Economic Policies Several months later, Gorbachev abruptly broke with the past, criticizing a draft of the Twelfth Five-Year Plan for not putting enough emphasis on capital reinvestment in existing factories and not addressing consumer demand. He blamed previous leaders for not changing the shape of Soviet economic activity.

Gorbachev proposed instead a program that covered not only the period of the next plan, but also the two that followed until the year 2000. Thus he articulated the economic aspects of *perestroika*, his plan for the reorganization of the Soviet system. To show his seriousness he ousted the chairman of the central planning commission who had served for 20 years.

Gorbachev's plan for "radical reform" included more authority for local farm and factory managers, a more flexible pricing system, tying salaries to performance, and allowing enterprises to distribute production above planned levels "as they saw fit." In 1987, the "Law of Individual Labor Activity" was passed, permitting private profit-making activities in 40 categories. It even allowed state workers to quit their jobs to pursue these personal opportunities.

Further details of economic *perestroika* even included competition among state enterprises for contracts; self-financing of operations, which would allow the reduction of state subsidies; and the application of "full-scale profit and loss accounting." The proposals were approved by the party Central Committee in June 1987 and by the Supreme Soviet four days later.

In 1988 an official publication of the Communist party predicted the merging of socialism and capitalism in the Soviet Union.[9] It observed, "We cannot ignore the experience of mankind as a whole, including the nonsocialist world."

Political Changes Three years of bold proposals could not undo more than 60 years of entrenched bureaucracy. This, coupled with such

[9]The statement, from *Pravda*, was made by Vadim Medvedev, the official Communist party ideologist.

Quiet Revolution in the Soviet Union The decline of communism in the former Soviet Union was paralleled by the waning of Gorbachev's (left) power. After the failed coup of 1991, power shifted toward one-time rival Boris Yeltsin (center).

events as a terrible nuclear accident at Chernobyl, poor harvests, growing unrest in the republics, and the crumbling of its bloc of Eastern European allies, produced a failing economy by the beginning of 1990. Gorbachev was still in power, but his foundation was weak.

The Communist party was split into factions. One faction, the liberals, wanted the immediate shift to free market capitalism. The other group, the conservatives, wanted a slower transition. The conservatives feared that too swift a move would create severe unemployment and soaring prices, which would lead to social disorder. The liberals countered with the argument that "property in the hands of each individual is a guarantee of the stability of society."

Debate over the various reform plans raged for nearly seven months in 1990. A compromise "President's Plan" was finally adopted in October. It was less radical than the liberals wanted but much more radical than the conservative faction was willing to accept.

One month later, the first stock exchange in Soviet history was founded in Moscow, with the participation of 187 enterprises and banks. The foremost symbol of American capitalism, the New York Stock Exchange, provided technical assistance for the Soviets.

The End of Soviet Communism? The path of economic reforms in the former Soviet Union has been complicated by the failed overthrow of Gorbachev in August 1991 and the subsequent disintegration of the country. It seems certain, however, that whatever role the Communist party plays in the countries that replace the Soviet Union, Marxist-Leninist communism appears to be ended.

As an economic system and as a repressive totalitarian political system, communism still is a major force in today's world. You only have to look off the Florida coast to Cuba or to the world's most populous nation, China, to find examples of communist states.

Still, this much can be said: Communism is a system founded upon Marx's prediction of the inevitability of a workers' revolution against capitalism. The collapse of Soviet communism, however, has proven, instead, the power and inevitability of the forces of political and economic freedom.

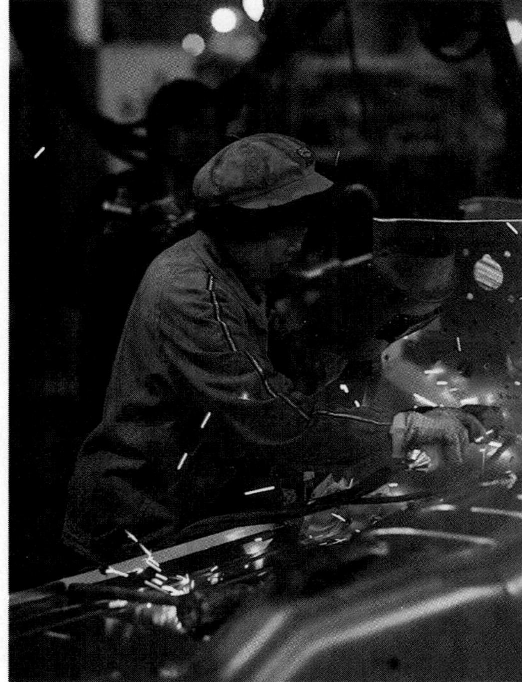

Bastion of Communism Though communism appears to be on the decline around the world, fully one-fifth of the planet's population lives and works under the communist government of China.

Section 3 Review

1. Define: five-year plan, collectivization
2. On what four closely related concepts did Marx build communist ideology?
3. (a) Where did Marx believe the first communist societies would appear? (b) Why?
4. How well did Soviet communism follow the socialist ideal of economic and social equality?
5. What were the differing views of liberals and conservatives about Gorbachev's reforms?

Critical Thinking

6. Drawing Conclusions (p. 19) Recall the statement on 623: "Property in the hands of each individual is a guarantee of the stability of society." What do you think this statement means?

★

Closure

Communism—the ownership of all goods and services by the state for the good of all—has been flawed when put into practice as a system for running a nation. The past year has seen the collapse of communism in its most powerful supporter—the Soviet Union.

Assignment Assign Chapter 24, Section 1, pp. 631–637, for the next class period.

Activity: Teaching Heterogeneous Groups

Review with students the elements discussed in the chapter concerning capitalism, socialism, and communism. For each of the three forms of government, have students create a comparison chart. Guide students in organizing their responses and in forming categories so that they can compare and contrast capitalist, socialist, and communist governments.

Reteach

In question and answer format, have students individually or in small groups pose questions to Karl Marx on the basic concepts of his theory such as: What is your view of history? How do you believe value should be determined for products? Students should compose answers to those questions. Using the same format, students then should pose questions to Gorbachev on how communist theory was put into practice in the former Soviet Union and how his economic reforms led to the collapse of communism in that country.

TEACHING
Citizenship

How to Start a Small Business

Objective
Identify the skills and knowledge required to start a small business and the benefits of doing so.

INSTRUCT

Before students read the feature, ask them how a small business can benefit the economic interests of the owner as well as the community. As they read the feature, have them draft a proposal for a small business that they would like to start. After reading the feature, allow students some time to get information from the SBA and the other sources mentioned. Then have each student submit a final proposal.

Answers 1. Students should have a product to sell in mind. **2.** Students should look up the address and phone number of the SBA, using the Government Resources Handbook to help them. **3.** Students should identify local sources of funds, such as the bank, a friend, or investors. **4.** Students may suggest that people will not frequent a business where the owner does not know his or her business or product. **5.** Have students use their product from Step 1 and create a plan for developing potential customers.

TRF **Teacher's Resource File** See the Unit 6 File, p. 33, for the Skill Application for this lesson.

Citizenship

How to Start a Small Business

On March 21, 1991, the Senate unanimously approved Patricia F. Saiki of Hawaii as the new head of the Federal Government's Small Business Administration (SBA). Saiki maintains that small businesses form the backbone of the country's economy. Successful small businesses help create new markets and jobs that spark economic growth for the entire nation. Follow the steps below to learn about starting a small business.

1. Know the risks. It is essential for anyone considering starting a business to be fully aware of the risks involved. Approximately three out of four new small businesses fail within a short period of time, often resulting in financial loss for the owner. To begin with, a small business must have a solid, marketable product—without it, no amount of money or planning can ensure success.

2. Contact the SBA. The SBA issues a wide variety of helpful publications and offers counseling, training programs, and financial assistance. A first step for anyone interested in opening a new business is to call the SBA or to write a letter stating his or her business plans. How could you use the Government Resources Handbook on page 690 to find the number and address of the SBA?

3. Ensure sufficient financing. Raising capital—the money needed to operate a business—is a basic task required in all successful business ventures. However, it can be a difficult and frustrating process. There are several sources available, and a business owner must consider the various options before making a decision. Some of these sources may be personal savings, friends and relatives, banks and credit unions. The SBA also offers a variety of loan programs. To be successful in obtaining loans, a person must be prepared to explain how much money is needed, why it is needed, and when it can be paid back.

4. Have a thorough knowledge of the business. For example, if a person is interested in opening a plumbing supply shop, it is essential that he or she know everything there is to know about the plumbing business. It is important also to know what kind of business information is available, where to get it, and how to use it. A few key sources of information include: the SBA District Office, the Small Business Development Center (SBDC), and the Small Business Institute (SBI). What might happen to a business person who does not know his or her business thoroughly?

5. Research the market. Having a good product and having the proper financing mean little if there is no demand for the product. The organizations mentioned in Step 4 can provide assistance in determining the best methods for recognizing customer needs and for creating a plan for developing potential customers.

Chapter-in-Brief

Scan all headings, photographs, charts, and other visuals in the chapter before reading the summaries below.

Section 1 Capitalism (pp. 605–611)
Capitalism is based on private ownership of productive property. Private individuals and companies decide how their property is used, and they own the benefits that their property creates. Those who own capital and put it to productive use are called capitalists.

A capitalistic economy is often called a free enterprise system. Such systems are characterized by: (1) private ownership of property, (2) the guarantee of property rights, (3) decentralized decision making, (4) competition, and (5) freedom of choice.

According to the laissez-faire theory, a capitalistic system works best with minimum interference from government. However, the United States government plays a significant role in the American economy.

There are three kinds of business organizations—sole proprietorships, partnerships, and corporations. No matter what the kind of business, the driving force is generally profit. In a capitalist economy, operating a business includes the potential of earning a profit—or of losing money.

Section 2 Socialism (pp. 613–617)
Socialism is an economic and political philosophy based on the idea that the benefits of economic activity should be equitably distributed.

Socialism developed in part as a reaction to the Industrial Revolution. Karl Marx was the key critic of capitalism. Those who believed that Marx's ideal could be achieved through democratic means came to be known as socialists.

Socialist economies often have nationalized industries. They also aim to guarantee social welfare through the equal distribution of necessities and services. In order to provide this level of service, taxes in socialist countries tend to be high.

Socialism is appealing to many developing nations. However, the costs and sacrifices required under such a system are difficult for such societies to bear.

In a socialist system, economic decision making is centralized. For this reason, such economies are called command economies. However, many critics feel that such central planning of a complex economy is impossible. Others criticize socialism because it denies individuals the right to decide how to use their incomes. Defenders of socialism say that capitalism leads to its own inefficiencies and inequities.

Section 3 Communism (pp. 618–623)
Communism calls for collective ownership of productive property. Its basic concepts came from Marx and the *Communist Manifesto*.

In spite of Marx's expectation that the worker's revolution would begin in industrialized Europe, it first took place in largely agricultural Russia. Led by Lenin, communists took control of what would become the Soviet Union. Later, under Stalin, the central government took complete control of the economy.

Stalin's system remained intact until the arrival of Gorbachev in 1985. Gorbachev introduced elements into the economy such as private property and even a stock exchange. Yet persistent problems in the economy and political structure helped produce dissatisfaction from both liberals and conservatives. One manifestation of this unrest was the failed 1991 coup. Although the future of the former Soviet Union is unclear, communism as it existed through the 1980s is apparently gone forever.

Though Soviet-style communism is apparently on the decline in most places, communism remains a force in places such as China and Cuba.

Teaching Suggestions for CHAPTER-IN-BRIEF

Below are some of the possible uses for the Chapter-in-Brief:

To Preview the Chapter You may want to assign the Chapter-in-Brief page and the Section Outlines from the Teacher's Resource File before beginning Chapter 23 to introduce students to the "Key Terms" and concepts in each section.

To Review the Chapter When students have completed Chapter 23, you might want to assign the Chapter-in-Brief as a tool for review, along with the Guided Reading and Reviews from the Teacher's Resource File.

To Omit the Chapter If you wish to skip Chapter 23, it may be helpful to assign the Chapter-in-Brief to students as a review before continuing to another chapter. You may also want to assign the Chapter 23 Test to assess student knowledge of the material. Then specific portions of Chapter 23 may be assigned to students needing reinforcement of "Key Terms" and concepts.

Teacher's Resource File See the Unit 6 File for the following materials:

- Section Outlines, pp. 24, 27, 30.
- Guided Reading and Reviews, pp. 25, 28, 31.
- Chapter 23 Test, pp. 37–39.

ADDITIONAL RESOURCES

Aganbegyan, Abel. *Inside Perestroika: The Future of the Soviet Economy.* Harper & Row, 1990.
Angel, R. C. *Explaining Economic Policy Failure.* Columbia University Press, 1991.
Communism: Its Rise and Fall in the 20th Century. Christian Science Monitor, 1990.
Hsu, Imanuel C. Y. *China Without Mao: The Search for a New Order.* Oxford, 2nd ed., 1990.
Milner, Henry. *Sweden: Social Democracy in Practice.* Oxford, 1989.
Ozinga, James R. *Communism: The Story of the Idea and Its Implementation.* Prentice Hall, 2nd ed., 1991.
Sakwa, Richard. *Gorbachev and His Reforms.* Prentice Hall, 1991.
Simpolicon: Simulation of Political and Economic Development. Computer software. Cross Cultural Software. Apple II series with 2 disk drives.
White, Stephen. *Gorbachev in Power.* Cambridge University Press, 1990.
Wilson, Frank L. *European Politics Today: The Democratic Experience.* Prentice Hall, 1990.

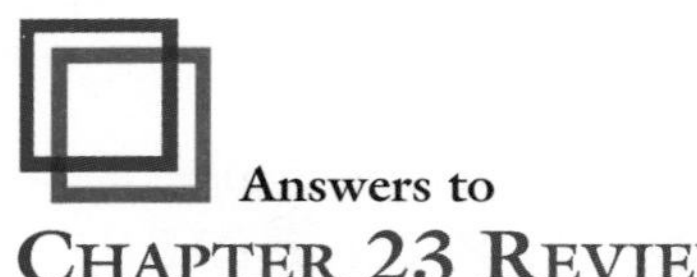

Answers to CHAPTER 23 REVIEW

Vocabulary and Key Terms

Matching
1. monopoly
2. bourgeoisie
3. free enterprise system
4. welfare state
5. command economy

True or False
1. False—the correct term is *proletariat.*
2. True.
3. True.
4. False—the correct term is *laws of supply and demand.*
5. True.

Word Relationships
1. welfare state
2. capitalist
3. entrepreneur
4. command economy
5. collectivization

Main Ideas

Section 1
1. Private individuals and companies control or own most of the productive property. **2.** Private ownership, guarantees of property rights, decentralized decision making, competition, and freedom of choice. **3.** (a) Laissez-faire theory says that an economic system will work best with the lowest degree of government intervention. (b) The United States is more accurately described as a mixed economy in which private enterprise and governmental participation coexist. **4.** Profit drives the capitalist economy. People take risks by investing their money in enterprises in the hopes of earning a profit. Thus, a business must make efforts to be efficient and make money in order to remain a good risk for investors.

Section 2
5. Marx believed that capitalism was fatally flawed, and that the proletariat would one day rise up and overthrow the bourgeoisie. **6.** Socialism describes a system that seeks to distribute the benefits of economic activity equitably throughout society. **7.** Socialist systems typically nationalize many industries. They are often welfare states, and they often have high taxes. **8.** Criticisms include: Socialism creates too many layers of bureaucracy; socialism destroys individual initiative by making economic security available to all; economies are too complicated to be controlled centrally; and socialism deprives people of their right to decide for themselves how to use their income.

Section 3
9. Marx saw history as a story of class struggle between social classes seeking control of labor and productive property. Marx predicted that that conflict would one day lead the proletariat to seize control. The labor theory of value held that the value of a product comes from the labor put into creating it. Therefore, the value should belong to the laborers who created it—not to a few wealthy property owners, as in the capi-

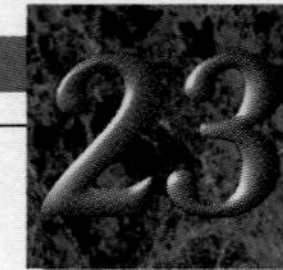

Chapter Review

Vocabulary and Key Terms

capital (p. 606)
capitalist (p. 606)
free enterprise system (p. 607)
entrepreneur (p. 607)
laws of supply and demand (p. 608)
monopoly (p. 608)
proletariat (p. 614)
bourgeoisie (p. 614)
welfare state (p. 615)
market economy (p. 615)
command economy (p. 615)
five-year plan (p. 621)
collectivization (p. 621)

Matching: *Review the key terms in the list above. If you are not sure of a term's meaning, look up the term and review its definition. Choose a term from the list above that best matches each description.*

1. a firm that is the only source of a product or service
2. in Marxist terms, the capitalists
3. an economic system in which individuals are free to start and run their own businesses
4. a government that assumes the role of promoter of citizen welfare through programs sponsored by the government
5. economic system in which the government directs the economy along a government-determined path

True or False: *Determine whether each statement is true or false. If it is true, write "true." If it is false, change the underlined word or words to make the statement true.*

1. Marx believed that the <u>bourgeoisie</u> would one day rise up and overthrow the capitalistic system.
2. An economy in which the economic decisions are made by thousands of private individuals and companies is called a <u>market economy</u>.
3. <u>Capital</u> consists of the wealth used to produce goods and services.
4. Under competitive conditions, the <u>free enterprise system</u> determines prices as a function of the quantity of goods available and customer need for those goods.
5. The <u>five-year plans</u> represented the first attempt by a society to combine large-scale centralized economic planning with public ownership of the means of production.

Word Relationships: *Replace the underlined definition with the correct term from the list above.*

1. Countries with socialist governments are sometimes referred to as <u>governments that provide citizens with extensive social services such as medical and dental care</u>.
2. <u>Someone who owns capital and puts it to productive use</u> creates and expands industries, invests in new technologies, and engages in activities that create jobs.
3. If existing companies do not see and meet demand, an <u>individual who takes the initiative of starting or expanding a business</u> may do so.
4. Socialist and communist economies are sometimes called <u>those in which governments can direct the economy along the desired path</u>.
5. Stalin's First Five-Year Plan included the goal of <u>the combining of millions of small peasant farms</u>.

Main Ideas

Section 1 **(pp. 605–611)**

1. What is the most distinctive characteristic of capitalism?
2. What are the hallmarks of a free enterprise system?
3. (a) Briefly describe the laissez-faire theory. (b) Why is it incorrect to call American capitalism laissez-faire capitalism?
4. Briefly describe the role of profit and loss in a capitalist system.

Section 2 **(pp. 613–617)**

5. Briefly describe Karl Marx's basic ideas about the capitalist system.
6. Briefly describe the meaning of the term *socialism.*
7. What are three characteristics commonly found in socialist countries?
8. What are the major criticisms of socialism?

Section 3 **(pp. 618–623)**

9. Briefly describe Marx's view of history and the labor theory of value.
10. Briefly describe communism under Lenin and Stalin.
11. Briefly describe the overall approach advocated by Gorbachev when he first assumed power in 1985.
12. What was the dispute between liberals and conservatives over Gorbachev's reforms?

Critical Thinking

1. **Formulating Questions** (p. 19) Create a list of questions you could use to evaluate the strengths and weaknesses of the capitalist system as it exists in the United States.
2. **Expressing Problems Clearly** (p. 19) Communist theory has always insisted on this guiding principle: "From each according to his ability, to each according to his need." Do you think that this principle represents a positive ideal? Explain your answer.
3. **Identifying Assumptions** (p. 19) Consider the common criticism of socialism on the grounds that it kills individual initiative. (a) What assumption about initiative underlies this criticism? (b) Is this assumption valid? Why or why not?

Getting Involved

1. **Writing Your Opinion** You are a newspaper editor in a country that operates under a command economy. Write a newspaper editorial in which you offer your opinion on the benefits and/or drawbacks of such a system. Review the characteristics of command economies as discussed in Sections 2 and 3. Consider the impact of such systems on individuals and on the country as a whole. Identify three arguments to support your general views on the benefits and drawbacks of a command economy. Begin the editorial by stating your overall opinion on the subject. Then, present your three arguments in a logical and orderly manner, devoting one paragraph to each. Remember, the purpose of an editorial is to communicate your opinion, so as you revise your first draft, make sure your arguments are as persuasive and clear as possible. Correct any errors, then draft a final copy.
2. **Class Debate** Hold a class debate on the following topic: *Resolved,* That the United States should more strictly observe the laissez-faire theory as put forward by Adam Smith. Select teams to debate each side of this topic. The rest of the class should evaluate each team's presentation.
3. **Gathering Information** Suppose you are interested in finding out some basic economic information about the United States, such as its gross national product, the per capita income, and other basic economic indicators. You would also like to compare these statistics with those of other leading countries. Use the Government Resources Handbook on page 690 to identify sources you might use to find this information.

Critical Thinking

1. Possible questions might include: What is the standard of living in the United States relative to countries under other economic systems? What percentage of the population experiences poverty in the American system? How evenly is the wealth distributed across the entire population? **2.** Answers will vary. Students might suggest that this principle is attractive because it recognizes that individuals have different needs and skills and that society has room for such differences. Others might criticize the principle because it unfairly rewards those who do not work as hard or effectively and punishes those who do. **3.** (a) Answers will vary. Students should observe that criticism assumes that people are motivated by the prospect of their own personal success and wealth; thus, taking away that prospect destroys a person's initiative. (b) Answers will vary.

Getting Involved

1–3. Answers and results will vary, but students should demonstrate an understanding of the concepts in this chapter.

talist system. **10.** Lenin brought communism to Russia, marked by nationalization of banks and large businesses, the establishment of workers councils, and the encouragement of peasants to seize land. However, Lenin had to introduce some free enterprise elements into the economy to avoid economic collapse. Stalin introduced the forced collectivization of Soviet agriculture and rapid industrialization. Stalin's five-year plans involved centralized planning of the entire economy. **11.** Gorbachev pledged a continuation of the old policies of communism. At the same time, he acknowledged the need for rapid economic growth. This led within a few months to significantly new economic policies—*perestroika*—that involved a move away from centralized control. **12.** Conservatives wanted a slow transition to a free market economy. Liberals wanted a more rapid shift to free market capitalism.

MANAGING THE UNIT

You may wish to review the following materials before beginning the unit to help plan your instruction.

Each chapter ends with a Chapter-in-Brief with suggestions for previewing, reviewing, or omitting the chapter.

UNIT 7 OUTLINE

PACING CHARTS,
pp. T28–T31

UNIT 7

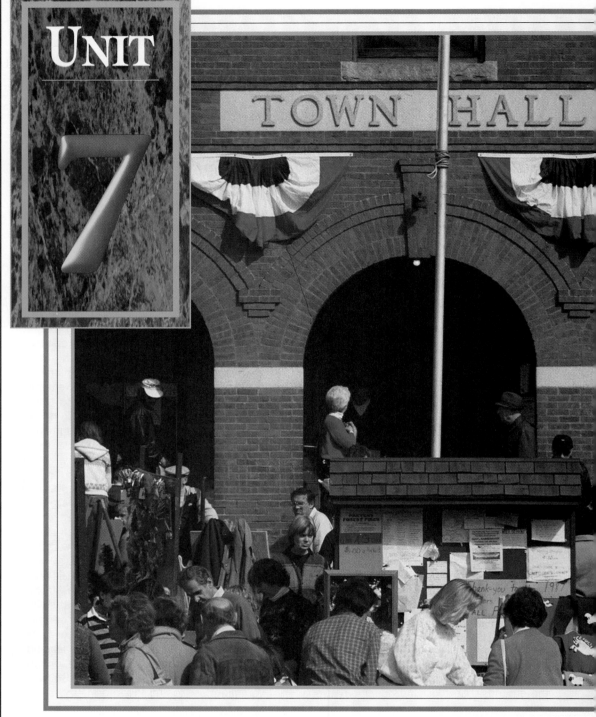

Participation in Government The town hall is the focal point of many community activities for these New Hampshire townspeople.

SKILLS AND FEATURES

The following skill lessons and features are included in this unit.

Skill Lessons

Citizenship: How to Write to Your Legislators (p. 658)
Citizenship: How to File a Claim in Small Claims Court (p. 682)

Debates/Case Studies

Debating Key Issues: Should the Government Require Students to Salute the Flag? (*West Virginia Board of Education* v. *Barnette*) (p. 649)
What *You* Can Do: Volunteering for Community Service (p. 672)

Participating in State and Local Government

In March 1991, at the venerable age of 97, Ernest W. Hibbard attended the annual town meeting in Hadley, Massachusetts. That fact taken by itself is in no way remarkable. New England town meetings may very well be the best exemplification of pure democracy in America. On town meeting day, any citizen may attend, speak on any question, and if old enough, vote. Mr. Hibbard was well acquainted with the process. He went to his first town meeting as a boy of 12. It was 1906, and the meeting was held in the afternoon when Ernest was scheduled to be in school. His father believed, however, that the boy would benefit more from attending town meeting than from his classes. Although he was too young to vote that day, the meeting must have made quite an impression on him: Ernest Hibbard didn't miss a single town meeting in the next 86 years— and his attendance serves as an enduring example of participation in government.

Did You Know That . . .

- Besides traditional law-enforcement activities such as crime investigation, patrol, and traffic enforcement, 50 percent of local police agencies have primary responsibility for animal control.
- A law still on the books in Oak Park, Illinois, prohibits roosters from crowing before 6 A.M.
- An old Virginia law makes it illegal to take a bath without a doctor's permission.

Unit Focus

Activate Prior Knowledge Ask students to identify the location of your town or city's seat of government. Ask how many students have ever been inside this building and for what purposes. Explain that all of these purposes relate to the functioning of local government.

Interpreting the Visual Point out the photo of the New Hampshire town hall in the unit opener. The event shown in the photo is a fall foliage festival. Ask: Even though this function had no governmental purpose, do you think it was useful to hold it at the town hall? Why or why not?

Did You Know That . . . Direct students to the items under "Did You Know That . . . ." Based on these facts, ask students to write one sentence classifying the overall purpose of State and local governments.

Journal Writing A journal may serve as a record of students' thoughts and ideas about their courses and related events in the world and their lives. It is an opportunity for students to create political cartoons, songs, poems, and stories as well as editorials and essays. Students should make entries at least once a week, and be sure to date each entry. Although journal writing generally is not graded, you should collect and review the journals at regular intervals. Suggested topics for the seventh unit include an opinion statement regarding a current State or local concern, or a song, poem, or political cartoon about local government in your community.

You may also want to utilize **CNN Video-link** to generate ideas for journal writing.

Bulletin Board Idea

Using the Poster Hang the wall chart of "The 3 Branches of American Government" on the bulletin board. Then have students find photographs of the representatives to the House and Senate from your State. Next, have students locate quotes from the representatives, newspaper articles about or by the representatives, and if possible, information from the representatives' offices. Hang all of this material on the bulletin board surrounding the wall chart. Ask students how many of them were aware before this time as to who their representatives to Congress were. Point out that these are the people whom the people of the State have entrusted to represent them in the making of national laws and policies. Discuss with students how comfortable they are about these people as their representatives and why they feel this way.

Chapter 24 Resources

In the Teacher's Resource File
The following materials are found in the Teacher's Resource File box.

Instructional Support: Unit 7 File

For the Section	For the Chapter
Outlines, pp. 2, 5, 8, 11	Skill Application, p. 14
Guided Reading and Reviews, pp. 3, 6, 9, 12	Case Study on Contemporary Issues, pp. 15–17
Quizzes, pp. 4, 7, 10, 13	Chapter Test, pp. 18–20
	Additional Test Questions, pp. 21–23

Enrichment Support Files

Supreme Court Cases, p. 17
Participatory Government Activities, pp. 20–27, 44–67
Simulations and Debates, pp. 26–31
Historical and Legal Documents, p. 50

Computer Test Bank and Assessment
Transparency Package, pp. 24, 49

Chapter 24 Focus

Introduce the Chapter Tell students that in this chapter they will learn about the structures and functions of State and local governments. Read with students the Chapter Preview and Objectives.

Writing Activity Direct students' attention to "Describe." Have students identify the governor of their State, and write a short description of the job he or she performs.

Motivate for Learning Direct students' attention to "Predict." Lead students in a discussion about the various functions of the State governments. Ask them to predict what would happen if the Federal Government took on these responsibilities.

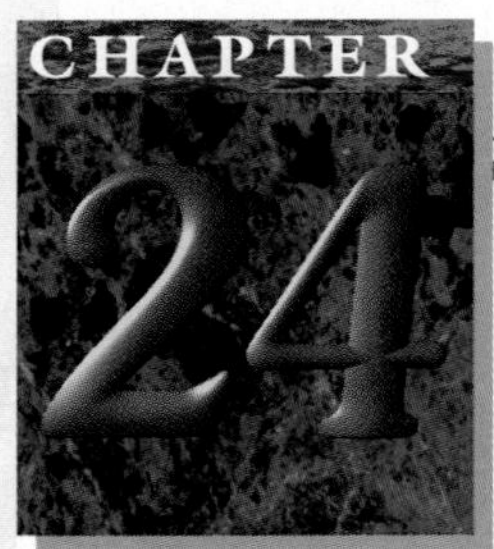

Chapter 24 Organization of State and Local Government

Chapter Preview

One day after Rose Mofford took office as acting governor of Arizona in 1988, the State's legislators faced an embarrassing problem. One hundred students from a Tucson junior high school appeared before an Arizona House committee to present a startling discovery: The Arizona State constitution stated that only a "male person" may occupy the offices of governor, secretary of state, treasurer, attorney general, or superintendent of public instruction.

The restriction, as it turned out, had no legal force because the United States Constitution took precedence. Even so, the embarrassed lawmakers quickly approved a constitutional amendment that dropped "male" from among the qualifications for those top State jobs. In this chapter, you will read about the overall shape of the office of governor and how State and local governments are organized.

Before you read this chapter:

- **Describe** what you know about the governor of your State.
- **Predict** what might occur if the Federal Government took over all the functions of State governments.

As you read, focus on the main objective for each section. Understand:

1. The structure, organization, and powers of State legislatures.
2. The overall shape of the office of governor.
3. The structure of local governments as creations of the State.
4. The governments of American cities.

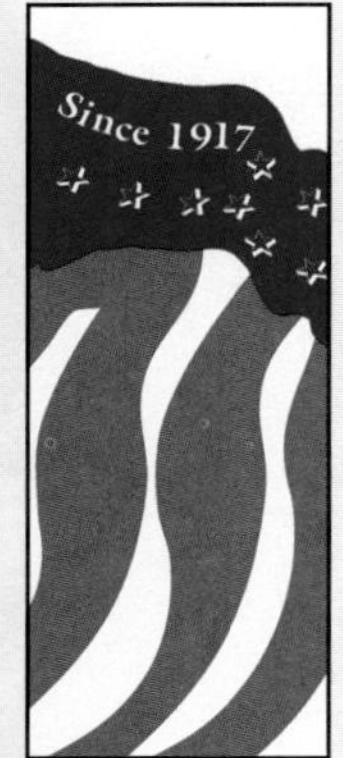

Magruder's American Government: *A Witness to Change* by William A. McClenaghan

Magruder's American Government has always expressed great faith in the American democratic system. Readers through the years have been left with little question that out system of democratic government is the best there is. Yet, at the same time, readers have also been reminded of the responsibilities the democratic system places upon the electorate. For example, read what *Magruder's* had to say about State legislatures—and about the voters who elected them—in the 1931 edition: *The public have gradually lost confidence in their State legisltures because the character of the legislators has deteriorated. This is due to the fact that the States extended suffrage more rapidly than they educated the voters in the proper use of the ballot.*

Notwithstanding this viewpoint, the United States has continued to seek wider suffrage, believing that a just government is best served by expanding the franchise tomore and more of its citizens. The Voting Rights Act, the 24th Amendment (outlawing poll taxes) and the 26th Amendment (lowering the voting age from 21 to 18) are just three examples of these efforts.

Presidential Hopeful from State Government Ranks Arkansas governor Bill Clinton takes his campaign to a high school in preparation for the highly visible New Hampshire presidential primary.

1 The State Legislatures

Find Out:

- What is a State constitution?
- What basic governmental functions does each State legislature perform?
- How are the State legislatures organized?

Key Terms:

initiative, referendum

The basic features of government at both the national and State levels in the United States are remarkably similar. At both levels the governmental structure is set out in a constitution that provides for legislative, executive, and judicial branches.

As you will see in this section, each State's constitution is that State's fundamental law. And, each State constitution establishes a legislative body that is, in effect, the powerhouse of that State's government.

The State Constitutions

Each State has a written constitution. That fact is, in itself, significant. From its very beginnings, American government has been based on written constitutions. In fact, the United States has sometimes been called "a land of constitutions."

The American experience with such documents dates from 1606 when King James I granted a charter to the Virginia Company. That act led to the settlement at Jamestown in the following year and, with it, the first government in British North America. Each of the other English colonies was established and governed on the basis of a written charter.

Since the first State constitutions were written in 1776, the States have drafted and approved nearly 150 of them. In a very real sense, each of the present-day State constitutions is a link in a chain of written documents that now stretches over nearly 400 years of American history.

A State constitution is that State's fundamental law. It sets out the way in which the government of that State is organized, and it distributes power among the various branches

SECTION 1
The State Legislatures

FOCUS

Teacher's Resource File
See the Unit 7 File, p. 2, for the Section 1 outline.

Objectives

24.1 Identify the significance of each State constitution.
24.2 Outline the basic governmental function of each State legislature.
24.3 Describe the organization of State legislatures.

Bellringer Activity Ask students to consider the following situation: You want to suggest that the school day be lengthened. Who would you go to with your proposal? How would you get your plan made into law?

State the Purpose State legislatures are responsible for the making of law at the State level. In each State, the legislature is established by a State constitution and possesses great powers to make public policy. In Section 1, students will learn about the structure of State legislatures, the requirements of their members, and the ways in which State legislatures operate and take action.

ABCNEWS INTERACTIVE

The following video segment may be used to highlight aspect of State legislatures and governments.

POWERS OF THE CONGRESS GUIDEBOOK
Chapter 62: The Federal System, p. 68

Vocabulary

Point out to students "Key Terms" on page 631. Have students review the text definition of the terms *initiative* and a *referendum*. Have students clarify the difference between the two terms.

Reading Strategy: Structured Overview

Write on the board: *State Legislature*. Then write as subheads: *Legislators, Legislature*. Have students scan the chapter and create subcategories under the subheads *Legislators* and *Legislature*. As students read, have them fill in details from the text.

INSTRUCT

Discuss/Analyze Have students recall the definition of the term *constitution.* (*Body of fundamental laws setting out the structure and purposes of government.*) Ask students to discuss why a constitution might be necessary at the State level. (*In the federal system, State governments play an important role and require the constraints of a constitution.*)

Have students compare what they have learned about the United States Congress with the text information about State legislatures and legislators. What are the similarities and differences in the size and structure of the legislatures, and the jobs of the legislators? (*Similarities: Most are bicameral, members are directly elected, State legislators serve the same lawmaking function of Congress. Differences: size of the legislatures, State legislators are generally paid far less than members of Congress.*)

What possible explanations can students find for the differences among State legislatures? (*Possible answers: Geographic differences, political tradition.*)

VOICES *on Government*

Brynhild Haugland, farmer and Republican State legislator for North Dakota, 1939 to 1990

On Serving as a Legislator

“No party [Democratic or Republican] has a monopoly on good people or good ideas. . . . There were 24 women in the legislature last year, but I have been the lone woman in some sessions. Still, no doors have ever been closed to me. The only limiting factor here is ability. . . . We are on the threshold of great change in this state, the nation and the world. Legislating is an ongoing process. . . . Most any good thing can be accomplished eventually if you aren't particular who gets the credit.”

of State government. It authorizes the exercise of power of government and puts limits on the exercise of governmental power. A State's constitution is superior to any and all other forms of State and local law within that State.

But remember this, too: Each State's constitution is subordinate to the United States Constitution; see Article VI, Section 2. No provision in any State constitution may conflict with any provision in any form of federal law.

The Legislature: Structure and Size

In every State, the legislature is the lawmaking branch of State government. Its basic function goes to the heart of democratic government: It is responsible for translating the public will into the State's public policy.

What is commonly called the legislature is officially known by that title in just over half the States. In several others, however, the constitution calls the legislature the General Assembly, and in a few the Legislative Assembly or the General Court.

Forty-nine of the 50 State legislatures are bicameral. The upper house is called the Senate in all States. The lower house is referred to as the House of Representatives in most, though some States call it the Assembly, General Assembly, or House of Delegates. Nebraska, the only State with a unicameral legislature, calls its single chamber the Legislature.

Size There is no exact figure for the ideal size of a legislative body. Two basic considerations are important, however. First, a legislature, and each of its houses, should not be so large as to hamper the orderly conduct of the people's business. Second, it should not be so small that the many views and interests within the State cannot be adequately represented. The upper house in most States has from 30 to 50 members. There are only 20 seats in Alaska's senate, however, and but 21 in the upper house in both Nevada and Delaware. Minnesota now has the largest upper house, with 67 members.

The lower house usually ranges between 100 and 150 members. However, only 40 members sit in the lower chamber in Alaska, 41 in Delaware, and 42 in Nevada. At the other extreme, Pennsylvania has 203 seats in its house, and New Hampshire has an almost incredible 400.

The State Legislators

You might find it surprising that the details of service in each of the 50 State legislatures are so much alike. However, all the States share traditions of government that help explain these similarities.

Qualifications Every State's constitution sets out certain requirements—of age, citizenship, and residence—for membership in the legislature. For example, most States require representatives to be at least 21 and senators to be 25. These qualifications do vary from State to State but, on the whole, they do not exclude a great many citizens.

SPOTLIGHT ON: Roots of Democracy

Systems of government in the States evolved from the governments of the colonies. These were modeled on the English system with the monarch at the top, the House of Lords under him or her, and the House of Commons at the bottom. For example, in the *charter* colonies, a charter was granted by the king, and citizens elected representatives to the upper and lower houses of the legislature. In the *proprietary* colonies, the proprietor, appointed by the king, chose the governor and the upper house, while the lower house was elected. In the *royal* colonies, the governor and councils were appointed by the king and the lower house was elected. Despite these differences, all the colonies were alike in having a governor and an upper and lower house, although Pennsylvania adopted a one-house legislature in 1701.

The realities of politics place still other qualifications on those who seek seats in their State legislatures. These qualifications, though informal, are even harder to meet than the formal ones. They have to do with a candidate's vote-getting abilities, and they are based on such characteristics as occupation, name familiarity, party identification, race, religion, national origin, and the like.

Election Voters voting in popular elections select the legislators in every State. Nearly everywhere, candidates for the legislature are usually nominated at party primaries, and opposing candidates face one another in a partisan general election. Legislative nominees are picked by conventions in only a few States—Delaware, for example. In only one State, Nebraska, are the candidates nominated in nonpartisan primaries. There the opposing candidates are not identified by party in the general election, either.

In most States the lawmakers are elected in November of even-numbered years. In four States—Mississippi, New Jersey, Virginia, and Louisiana—legislative elections are held in the odd-numbered years in the hope of separating State and local issues from national politics.

Terms Legislators serve either two-year or four-year terms. Senators are usually elected for longer terms than are their colleagues in the lower house. The rate of turnover in legislative seats is fairly high. In a given year, more than one-fourth of the 7,461 State legislators around the country are serving their first terms in office.

Compensation Far too often, capable men and women refuse to run for seats in State legislatures because of the financial sacrifices that such service entails. Salaries are generally too low, although most States provide some sort of additional allowances to help ease the financial burden of serving as a legislator.

Oregon provides a fairly typical example of the compensation offered to legislators by States. The basic salary is now $1,029 a month, or $24,686 for the biennium, a two-year period. In addition, each member receives an expense allowance: $73 for each day of the legislative session, which usually lasts for about 180 days, and for each day he or she attends interim committee meetings (meetings held between sessions). Each member also has an expense allowance of up to $550 for each month in which the legislature is not in session. The total compensation per member, including both salary and allowances, comes to about $27,000 a year.

Legislative Sessions Forty-two State legislatures now hold annual sessions, and the California legislature meets in a continuous two-year session. Only Arkansas, Kentucky, Montana,

How to Make Decisions

1. Decide What Your Options Are. Make a list of every option you can choose. For example, perhaps you are trying to decide between doing your homework or going to a movie with a friend.

2. Determine the Possible Outcomes of Each Option. Often, more than one outcome is possible as the result of a decision. List the various outcomes under each option. For example, if you do your homework you will be prepared for class, you will learn more, and so on. If you go to the movie, you will have a chance to visit with your friend and relax.

3. Assign a Value to Each Outcome. This is sometimes called assigning payoffs. All payoffs for each outcome should be in the same units. For example, dollars, time saved, lives saved, and so on. Doing your homework should help you get a better grade in the course. Going to a movie should have its own educational benefits and be enjoyable.

4. Make Your Decision. Compare the values of each outcome and the likelihood of achieving the value. For example, the likelihood that doing your homework will help you get a better grade may be 75% and the likelihood that going to a movie will be educational and enjoyable may be 95%. Based on this and the above information, decide which option to pursue.

Interpreting Charts Making decisions is one of the key responsibilities of a legislator. What outcomes of those decisions must legislators consider before they vote on an issue (Step 2)?

Next, have students examine the actual powers of Congress. Again, have students compare the State legislatures with what they have learned about Congress. (*Similarities: State legislatures and Congress have legislative powers, as well as executive and judicial powers; have presiding officers, use committee systems, and follow the same basic legislative process. Differences: Many States have direct legislation provisions, which do not exist at the national level. Some specific executive and judicial powers, such as the power of some State legislatures to appoint certain executive officials, are different from the executive powers of Congress.*)

Interpreting Charts Ask students to look at the chart and identify a decision they are facing in their lives. Have students use the steps in the chart to work towards a decision.

Caption Answer Legislators must weigh the specific outcomes of their voting behavior on individuals, businesses, and the entire State, as well as on voters who may carry their reactions to a legislator's behavior into the voting booth.

Interpreting Charts Direct students' attention to the chart on page 634. Ask them to consider what other information they might like to have if they were trying to compare local government among countries. (*Possible answers: Students might like to know the relative powers of the local governments compared to the provincial and national governments; for example, does the nation have a unitary system of government? A federal system?*)

Caption Answer Hungary has only two levels of local government, with only one unit at each level.

Nevada, North Dakota, Oregon, and Texas still meet on an every-other-year (biennial) basis.

Most States have turned to annual sessions only in the past decade or so, as it has become increasingly apparent that legislators cannot handle the legislative workload by meeting every other year for a few months. As a general rule, regular sessions, whether annual or biennial, are becoming longer and longer. All 50 governors, and just over half of the State legislatures too, can call special sessions to allow the lawmaking body to take up urgent matters for consideration between its regularly scheduled meetings.

Global Awareness

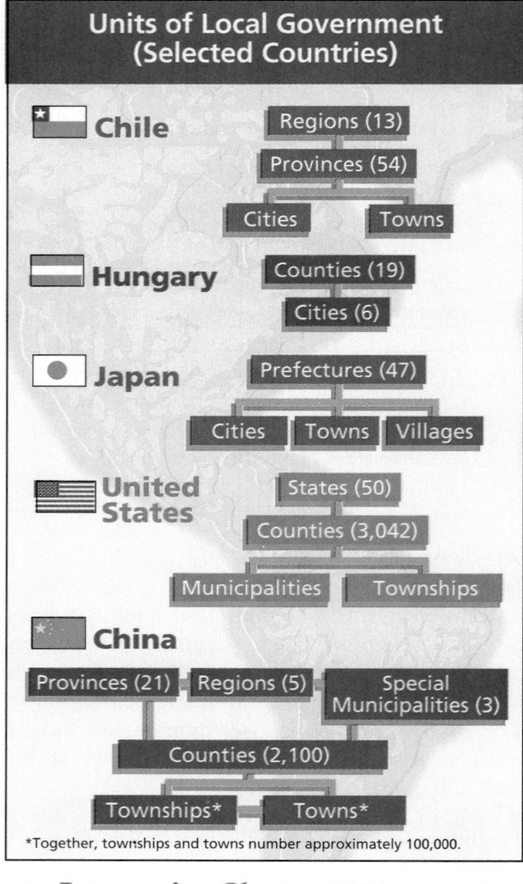

Interpreting Charts Which country has the least hierarchical government structure?

Powers of the Legislature

Identifying those powers that belong to a State legislature is a complicated matter. In each State the legislature has all of those powers (1) that the State constitution does not grant exclusively to the executive or judicial branches of the State's government or its local units, and (2) that neither the State constitution nor the United States Constitution denies to the legislature.

Legislative Powers State legislatures can pass any law that does not conflict with federal law or with any part of that State's constitution. Therefore, it is impossible to list all the powers of the State legislatures. However, most State constitutions do list several of the legislature's more important powers. Those most often mentioned include the powers to tax, spend, borrow, establish courts, define crimes and provide for their punishment, regulate commercial activities, and maintain public schools.

Every legislature's powers include the vital "police power"—the State's power to protect and promote the public health, safety, morals, and welfare. This broad power is the basis of thousands of State laws, including those that require vaccinations and prohibit the ownership of dangerous weapons, for example. You read about the police power in Chapter 20, Section 1.

Nonlegislative Powers All 50 State legislatures possess certain nonlegislative powers in addition to those they exercise in making law.

EXECUTIVE POWERS Some of a legislature's powers are executive in nature. For example, the governor's power to appoint certain officials is subject to approval by the legislature, or at least the upper house. In some States the legislature itself appoints certain executive officeholders. Thus, the secretary of state is chosen by the legislature in Maine, New Hampshire, and Tennessee.

JUDICIAL POWERS Each State legislature also has certain judicial powers. The chief illustration is the power of impeachment. In every State except Oregon, the legislature can remove any State executive officer or judge through that process.

Each legislature also has judicial powers with regard to its own members. Thus, disputes about the election or the qualifications of a member-elect are usually decided by the house involved in the matter. Then, too, because legislators themselves are not subject to impeachment (although in 15 States they can be recalled by voters), each chamber has the power to discipline any of its members, and in extreme cases even to expel them.

CONSTITUENT POWERS State legislatures play a role in constitution-making and the constitutional amendment process. Since this does not involve the making of statutes, this function—the constituent power—is a nonlegislative one.

Women in State Government Women are becoming increasingly prominent in State government. Massachusetts senator Patricia McGovern was the first woman to chair the Ways and Means Committee in her State.

Organization of the Legislature

In general terms, each State legislature is organized in much the same manner as Congress.

The Presiding Officers Those who preside over the sessions of the nation's 99 State legislative chambers are almost always powerful political figures—in the legislature itself and elsewhere in State politics.

The lower house in each of the 49 bicameral legislatures elects its own presiding officer, known everywhere as the speaker.

The senate chooses its own presiding officer in 22 States. In the other 28 States, the lieutenant governor serves as the president of the senate. Where the lieutenant governor does preside, the senate selects a president *pro tempore* to serve when the lieutenant governor is absent [1]

Except for the lieutenant governors, each of these presiding officers is chosen by a vote of the full membership in his or her legislative chamber. In fact those who fill leadership posts are usually picked by the majority party's caucus just before the legislature starts a new session.

The chief duties of those presiding officers center on the conduct of the legislature's floor business—and these duties are a major source of their power. The presiding officers refer bills to committee, recognize members who seek the floor, and interpret and apply the rules of their chamber to its proceedings.

Unlike the Speaker of the House in Congress, the speaker in nearly every State appoints the chairperson and other members of each house committee. The senate's president or president *pro tem* has the same power in just over half the States. The presiding officers regularly use the power to name committees as they use their other powers: to reward their friends, punish their enemies, and otherwise work their influence on the legislature.

The Committee System The committee system in State legislatures works much as it does in Congress. Much of the work of the legislature is done by committee members when

[1]The term *pro tempore* means "temporary." In practice this officer's title is generally shortened to president *pro tem*.

Provide Guided Practice
Work with the class to create a composite description of a typical State legislature using the information in the section. Make sure that the students' legislature is described in terms of size, structure, qualifications and characteristics of members, legislative and nonlegislative powers, the legislative process, and other characteristics discussed in the section.

Provide Independent Practice
TRF **Teacher's Resource File**
You may wish to assign Section 2 Guided Reading and Review, Unit 7 File, p. 3, to help students master section objective content.

Enrichment

Have students develop a campaign brochure for someone who is running for election to the State legislature. The brochure should clearly explain the candidate's understanding of the role of the legislature in State government. (Average)

Monitor Comprehension

Answers to Section 1 Review
1. "Key Terms" are defined on the following pages:
a. initiative, p. 636
b. referendum, p. 636
2. State constitutions serve as each State's fundamental law, but each is subservient to the Constitution. **3.** Legislators must meet varying official qualifications for age. They also must meet informal, political qualifications related to their ability to get votes. **4.** Possible answers: the power to impeach, to decide disputes about the elections, and to discipline its members. **5.** With direct initiative, the measure goes directly on the ballot. With indirect initiative, the proposal goes first to the legislature. **6.** Referendums may be mandatory, optional, or popular. **7.** (a) Possible answers: most legislatures are bicameral, the lower houses have a speaker, all legislatures use committees. (b) Possible answers: The role of the referendum and initiative, pay for legislators, size.

Closure

Point out that State legislatures are established by each State's constitution. The structure and operation of most State legislatures have both similarities to and significant differences from the United States Congress. In Section 2, students will learn about the executive branch of State governments and the office of the governor.

Assignment Assign Section 2, pp. 637–642, for the next class period.

they sort out those bills that will reach the floor and when they inform the full chamber on measures they have handled.

The standing committees in each house are generally set up by subject matter, such as committees on highways, education, and so on. A bill may be amended or even very largely rewritten in committee or, as often happens, ignored altogether[2] Joint committees—permanent groups made up of members of both houses—are being used increasingly in the State legislatures. These committees can produce substantial savings of legislative time and effort.

The Legislative Process

The major steps in the legislative process in a typical State legislature are much like those in Congress. You can review the legislative process in Congress by studying the diagram of the legislative process that appears on page 305, Chapter 12.

Legally, only a member may introduce a bill in either house in any of the State legislatures. So, in the strictest sense, legislators themselves are the source of all measures introduced. In broader terms, however, the lawmakers are the real source, the authors, of only a relative handful of bills.

A large number of bills come from public sources, from officers and agencies of State and local government. Every governor has a legislative program of some sort—and often an extensive and ambitious one.

Many bills are born in other public places too. Take, for example, a measure to increase the maximum penalty for some crime. That bill might be proposed by the attorney general. A bill to give cities a larger share of the money raised by the State's gasoline tax might be initiated in a city council or in some city manager's office.

[2]The "pigeonholing" of bills is as well known in the States as it is in Congress; see page 298. In fact, in most States one of the standing committees in each house is regularly the "graveyard committee," a body to which bills are sent to be buried. The judiciary committee, to which bills may be referred "on grounds of doubtful constitutionality," often fills this role. A vivid illustration of a graveyard committee existed for several years in the lower house in landlocked Oklahoma: the Committee on Deep Sea Navigation.

Bills also come from a wide range of private sources. In fact, the largest single source for proposed legislation in the States appears to be interest groups. As you may remember from Chapter 9, those groups and their lobbyists have one overriding purpose: to influence public policy to benefit their own special interests. Of course, some bills do originate with private individuals—business people, farmers, labor union members, and other citizens—who, for one reason or another, think that "there ought to be a law . . ."

Direct Legislation

Several States allow voters to take a direct part in the lawmaking process through the initiative and the referendum.

1.a **The Initiative** Through the **initiative** process, voters can propose by petition constitutional amendments in 17 States. In 21 States voters can use the initiative to initiate ordinary statutes, as well. Among these 21 States, the initiative takes two quite different forms: the more common direct initiative and the little-used indirect initiative.

In both the direct and indirect initiative, a certain number of qualified voters must sign initiative petitions to propose a law. The key difference between them lies in what happens to the proposed measure once enough valid signatures have been collected.

Where the direct initiative is used, the measure goes directly to the ballot, usually at the next general election. If the voters approve the measure, it becomes law. If not, it dies.

In the indirect initiative, the proposal goes first to the legislature. That body may pass it, making it a law. If it does not, the measure then goes to the voters. The number of voters who must sign petitions to initiate a statute varies from State to State.

1.b **The Referendum** A **referendum** is a process in which a legislative measure is referred to the State's voters for final approval or rejection. Three different forms of the referendum are now used among the States: mandatory, optional, and popular.

Teacher's Resource File
See the Unit 7 File, p. 4, for the Section 1 Quiz.

Teacher's Resource File
See the Historical and Legal Documents file, p. 50, for material to support the section.

Reteach

Have students work individually or in small groups to create a poster that illustrates the general characteristics and functions of State legislatures.

The mandatory referendum is involved whenever the legislature is required to refer a measure to the voters. Thus, in every State except Delaware, the legislature must submit proposed amendments to the constitution to the electorate. In several States some other measures also must go to the voters for final action—for example, measures to borrow funds.

An optional referendum measure is one that the legislature refers to the voters voluntarily. Such measures are rare. When one does appear on a State's ballot, it usually involves a "hot potato" question—that is, one lawmakers would rather not take direct responsibility for deciding themselves.

The popular referendum is the form most often connected with the idea of direct legislation. Under the popular referendum, the people may demand via a petition that a measure passed by the legislature be referred to them for final action. Most attempts to use the popular referendum in fact fail. Usually the opponents of a particular measure simply cannot gather the required number of signatures for their petitions to force a popular vote on the matter.

Section 1 Review

1. **Define:** initiative, referendum
2. How do each of the State constitutions fit within the scheme of federalism?
3. Name a few typical characteristics that are among the most important qualifications for the office of State legislator.
4. What are two judicial powers of State legislatures?
5. What is the difference between a direct and an indirect initiative?
6. What are the three types of referendum found among the states?

Critical Thinking

7. **Making Comparisons** (p. 19) Consider what you know about Congress and the State legislatures. (a) In what areas are they most alike? (b) In what areas are they the most different?

2 The Governor and State Administration

Find Out:

- What are the structural details of the typical governorship—its qualifications, selection, term, succession, and compensation?
- What are the governor's executive, legislative, and judicial powers?
- What are the titles and functions of the officers who share executive authority with the governor?

Key Terms:

item veto, pardon, commute, reprieve, parole

In colonial America, it was the actions of the royal governors that inspired much of the resentment that fueled the revolution. That attitude was carried over into the first State constitutions, in which the new State governors had little real authority.

In each of the 50 States, the office of governor has changed a great deal since those early days. In this section, you will explore the governorship today.

The Governorship

The governor is the principal executive officer in each of the 50 States. He or she is always a central figure in State politics and is often a well-known national personality, as well. Indeed, the governorships have produced several Presidents and many members of both houses of Congress.

Selecting the Governor As in the case of candidates for the State legislator, candidates for the governorship must meet both formal and informal requirements. Thousands of persons in every State could fulfill the formal requirements, which include American citizenship, a minimum age (usually 25 or 30), and residence in the State.

The informal qualifications, however, are more difficult to meet. Any person who wants

SECTION 2
The Governor and State Administration

FOCUS

Teacher's Resource File
See the Unit 7 File, p. 5, for the Section 2 Outline.

Objectives

24.4 Sketch the structural details of the average governorship: qualifications, selection, term, succession, and compensation.
24.5 Define the governor's executive, legislative, and judicial powers.
24.6 Identify the titles and functions of the officers sharing executive authority with the governor.

Bellringer Activity Write the name of your State's governor on the blackboard. Ask how many students recognize the name and the job he or she does. Once students have recognized that the person is the governor, ask students if they know when he or she was elected. When will the next gubernatorial election be? Has the governor been in the news lately? If so, why?

State the Purpose Section 2 examines the governorship and other parts of the executive branch of State government. The section begins by outlining the formal and informal qualifications for governor, selection, term, succession, and compensation. It explores the governor's various roles and powers. The section concludes with a discussion of other major State executive officers.

Vocabulary

Point out to students "Key Terms" on page 637. Have them clarify the differences among the terms *pardon, commute, reprieve,* and *parole.* Ask students which they consider the strongest form of "forgiving"?

Reading Strategy: Question Writing

Before students read the section, ask them to note the boldfaced headings in the text. Then have students convert each of the four headings into a question. As students read the section, have them look for and fill in answers to each of their questions.

INSTRUCT

Explain/Analyze Tell students that the office of governor bears many similarities to that of the U.S. President. Ask students to identify some of the similarities between the presidency and general characteristics of governorships. (*Details of eligibility, selection, term, and succession for governorship are similar. Governors have executive powers of appointing assistants and supervising executive employees; propose budgets to the legislature; and exert legislative influence through messages to the legislature and the power of the veto. Governors can exercise several judicial powers.*) Ask students to identify some of the key differences between the presidency and many governorships. (*Governors often share executive power with other officials, some of whom may be elected and some of whom may be appointed by the legislature. Many governors have the item veto, a powerful weapon not available to a President.*)

Ask students to discuss the governor's role as the political leader of the State government. In what ways does this position help the governor perform his or her job? (*Governors can use the power to put additional pressure on the legislature and other officials.*) How does the governor's political preeminence cause him or her difficulty in the State government? (*A governor often does not have official authority over executive branch officials, and is often held responsible politically for actions over which he or she has no control.*)

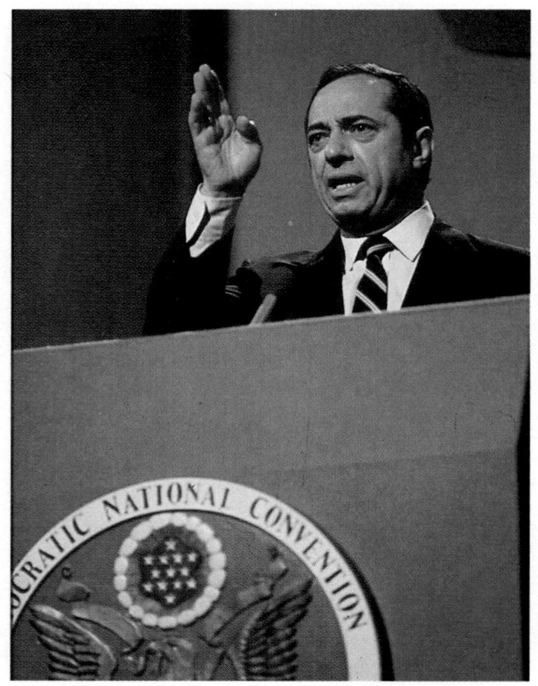

On the National Stage New York Governor Mario Cuomo increased his national visibility with his keynote address at the 1984 Democratic National Convention in San Francisco.

to be governor—or hold any other elected office, for that matter—must first satisfy certain political requirements. The candidate must be "available" and have those characteristics that will win the votes of the party's nominators and those of the voters in the general election. Exactly what, in particular, those characteristics are varies from State to State, and even from election to election. Race, sex, religion, personality, name familiarity, party membership, experience, stands on the issues, the ability to use television effectively—these and several other factors are all a part of the mix [3]

Selection In every State the governor is chosen by popular vote. In all but four States—Georgia, Louisiana, Mississippi, and Vermont—only a plurality is needed for election. The major parties' gubernatorial candidates are usually picked in primaries. Nearly half the States now provide for the joint election of the governor and lieutenant governor. In those States, each party's candidates for those offices run as a team, and the voter casts one vote to fill both posts.

Term The one-year gubernatorial term disappeared long ago. Governors are elected to four-year terms nearly everywhere today. Only three States—New Hampshire, Rhode Island, and Vermont—now provide for two-year terms.

Half the States place some limit on the number of terms governors may serve. Kentucky and Virginia have what amounts to a one-term limit; they forbid the governor to succeed himself/herself in office [4] In 27 other States, governors cannot serve more than two consecutive terms. Of these States, Arkansas, Delaware, Missouri, and North Carolina have an absolute two-term limit.

Succession Occasionally, a governor dies in office. Every so often, one resigns in midterm—to become a United States senator or to accept a presidential appointment, for example. No matter what the cause of the vacancy, the State constitution provides for a successor. In 43 States the lieutenant governor is first in the line of succession. In Maine, New Hampshire, New Jersey, and West Virginia, the president of the senate succeeds. In Arizona, Oregon, and Wyoming the office passes to the secretary of state.

---

[3]Only 11 women have ever won election to a governorship, and three of them are now in office: Joan Finney of Kansas, Barbara Roberts of Oregon, and Ann Richards of Texas. All three are Democrats and won election in 1990. Their eight predecessors: Nellie Ross (Wyoming, 1925–1927), Miriam Ferguson (Texas, 1925–1927, 1933–1935), Lurleen Wallace (Alabama, 1967–1968), Ella Grasso (Connecticut, 1975–1980), Dixy Lee Ray (Washington, 1977–1981), Martha Layne Collins (Kentucky, 1983–1987), Madeleine Kunin (Vermont, 1985–1991), Kay Orr (Nebraska, 1987–1991). Also, Rose Mofford (who had been secretary of state) succeeded to the governorship in Arizona in 1988, after that State's legislature impeached and removed Governor Evan Mecham; Governor Mofford served until 1991. The list of women governors includes but one Republican: Governor Orr of Nebraska.

[4]In both of these States a governor can serve one or more additional (but not successive) terms, however.

SPOTLIGHT ON: Behind the Scenes

One of the nation's most noteworthy governors is Ann W. Richards of Texas, elected in November 1990. After eight years as State treasurer, she defeated oilman-rancher Clayton Williams. Actions during her first year in office included persuading the Democrat-controlled legislature to approve a lottery; signing Texas's first income tax law into existence; and appointing far more minorities and women to office than her predecessors.

Removal The governor may be removed from office by the impeachment process in every State except Oregon. Only five governors have been ousted since Reconstruction, and only one—Arizona's Evan Mecham in 1988—has suffered that fate in the last 60 years.

The voters in 15 States have the power to recall the governor. This has happened only once, however—to Governor Lynn J. Frazier of North Dakota, in 1921. Removal did not keep him out of public office long: He was elected to the United States Senate the very next year.

Compensation A glance at the table on this page will show that gubernatorial salaries now average about $81,000 a year. The spread is fairly wide among the States, however, ranging from a low of $35,000 in Arkansas to a high of $135,000 in Maryland. Most States also provide the governor with an official residence, generally called the governor's mansion, and a more or less generous expense account.

The Governor's Executive Powers

The powers and duties of the governor of each State correspond to the three branches of government: executive, legislative, and judicial.

Unlike in the federal executive branch, the executive authority in most States is held by several separate, and independently chosen, officers. Only a part of that authority is held by the governor, who is in fact only a "first among equals." Yet, whatever the realities of the distribution of power may be, it is the governor to whom the people look for leadership in State affairs and hold responsible for the condition of the State. The governor is given a number of specific powers with which to accomplish that job.

Appointment and Removal A leading test of any administrator is his or her ability to select loyal and able assistants. Two major factors work against the governor's effectiveness here, however. First, of course, is the existence of other elected executives in State government. The people choose them and the governor cannot remove them.

Second, the State's constitution and statutes place restrictions on the governor's power to

Terms and Salaries of Governors

State	Term in Years	Annual Salary*
Alabama	4	$81,522
Alaska	4	$81,648
Arizona	4	$75,000
Arkansas	4	$35,000
California	4	$120,000
Colorado	4	$70,000
Connecticut	4	$78,000
Delaware	4	$80,000
Florida	4	$95,000
Georgia	4	$91,092
Hawaii	4	$94,780
Idaho	4	$75,000
Illinois	4	$97,370
Indiana	4	$77,200
Iowa	4	$76,700
Kansas	4	$74,235
Kentucky	4	$79,255
Louisiana	4	$73,440
Maine	4	$70,000
Maryland	4	$135,000
Massachusetts	4	$75,000
Michigan	4	$106,700
Minnesota	4	$109,053
Mississippi	4	$63,000
Missouri	4	$88,541
Montana	4	$54,672
Nebraska	4	$65,000
Nevada	4	$90,000
New Hampshire	2	$79,541
New Jersey	4	$130,000
New Mexico	4	$90,000
New York	4	$130,000
North Carolina	4	$123,300
North Dakota	4	$67,804
Ohio	4	$105,000
Oklahoma	4	$70,000
Oregon	4	$80,000
Pennsylvania	4	$105,000
Rhode Island	2	$69,900
South Carolina	4	$101,959
South Dakota	4	$63,232
Tennessee	4	$85,000
Texas	4	$93,432
Utah	4	$72,800
Vermont	2	$80,730
Virginia	4	$108,000
Washington	4	$112,000
West Virginia	4	$72,000
Wisconsin	4	$92,283
Wyoming	4	$70,000

*All states provide a residence as part of the salary with the exception of Arizona, Massachusetts, Rhode Island, and Vermont.
Sources: State constitutions and statutes and information furnished by appropriate State officials.

▲ **Interpreting Tables** Does there seem to be any correlation between the length of term of office and the salary offered?

Interpreting Tables Have students look at the table. Ask them if they can see any relationship between the physical size and population of a State and the salary it pays its governor? (*Possible answers: There is no absolute relationship between size and salary; e.g., the highest paying State is Maryland, which is quite small in area. There is a general relationship between a State's population and the governors salary. For example, many of the more populous States, such as California and New York, pay relatively high salaries, and many of the less populated States, such as Alaska, Vermont, and Wyoming, pay about the average or below. However, the relationship between population and salary is only general and does not apply in all cases.*)

Caption Answer No. Rhode Island, Vermont, and New Hampshire, each with a two-year gubernatorial term, offer between $69,900 and $80,730 per year—about average for governors' salaries.

ABCNEWS INTERACTIVE

The following video segment may be used to highlight aspects of State governments.

POWERS OF THE CONGRESS GUIDEBOOK
Chapter 62: The Federal System, p. 68

At the State's Helm Barbara Roberts, former secretary of state in Oregon, became governor in 1991. Roberts, Ann Richards (Texas), and Joan Finney (Kansas) are the only women holding the office of governor in the country.

hire and fire. In most States the constitution requires that most of the governor's major appointees be confirmed by the State senate. Moreover, the legislature often sets qualifications that must be met by those appointed to the offices it has created by statute. In a vigorous two-party State, for example, the law often requires that not more than a certain number of the members of each board or commission be from the same political party. Thus, a governor must appoint some members of the opposing party to posts in his or her administration.

Consider one more example: The law often requires that those persons the governor appoints to any of the State's professional licensing boards must themselves be licensed to practice in the particular field that that board regulates. Thus, only licensed realtors can be appointed to the real estate board; only licensed physicians can serve on the board of medical examiners; and so on.

In spite of these restrictions, the governor has the authority to fill many important posts. How a governor exercises this power is a key to his or her success.

Supervisory Powers The governor is empowered to supervise the work of thousands of men and women who staff the State's executive branch. But here again, the governor's authority in this field is often limited by the constitution and statutes of the State. Many State agencies are subject to the governor's direct control, but many are not. The governor's powers of persuasion and ability to operate through such informal channels as party leadership and appeals to the public can also make a significant difference in his or her ability to supervise the executive branch.

The Budget In most States the governor prepares the annual or biennial budget that goes to the legislature. The legislature may make changes in the governor's financial plan, of course. It may appropriate this or that amount, or nothing, for this agency and that program, as it chooses. But the governor's budget recommendations carry a great deal of weight.

The governor's budget-making power is an effective tool for controlling State administration. Although unable to appoint or remove the head of a certain agency, for example, the governor can use the budget-making power to affect that agency's programs. So the governor can have a real impact on the attitudes and behavior of many officials.

Military Powers Every State constitution makes the governor the commander in chief of the State militia—in effect, of the State's units of the National Guard. Governors may find it necessary to call out the National Guard to deal with such emergencies as prison riots or to aid in relief and prevent looting after a flood or some other natural disaster[5]

ACTIVITY: Teaching Heterogeneous Groups
Ask each student to formulate a list of five questions that he or she has about the content of the chapter. Then ask volunteers to present their questions to the students of their choice. If the selected students are unable to answer the questions, volunteers from the rest of the class can attempt answers.

The Governor's Legislative Powers

The State's principal executive officer has important formal legislative powers. These powers, together with the governor's own political clout, often make the governor in effect the State's chief legislator.

The Message Power The message power is really the power to recommend legislation. A strong governor can do much with it. A governor's program for legislative action is given to the lawmakers in a yearly State of the State address, in the budget, and in several special messages.

Special Sessions The governor in every State has the power to call the legislature into special sessions. On occasion, a governor has persuaded reluctant legislators to pass a bill by threatening to call them back in a special session if they adjourn the regular session without having done so.

The Veto Power Except for North Carolina, the governor in every State has the power to veto measures passed by the legislature. This power, as well as the threat to use it, is often the most potent power the governor has in influencing the work of the legislature.

In 43 States the governor's veto power includes the **item veto**. That is, the governor may veto 1.a
one or more items in a bill without rejecting the entire measure. The power is most often, but not always, restricted to items in appropriations bills. The item veto is regularly used to cancel inappropriate or unaffordable legislative appropriations.

The vote needed to override a governor's veto varies by State, but two-thirds of the full membership in each house is most common. In actual practice, less than 5 percent of all measures passed by the State legislatures are rejected by governors. However, when the veto power is used, it is quite effective. Less than 10 percent of all vetoes are overridden.

[5]In a national emergency, the National Guard may be called into federal service by the President. All of the States' National Guard units were federalized in 1940 and served as part of the nation's armed forces in World War II. Many units also saw combat duty in both Korea and Vietnam. A number were also called up in 1990, to serve during Operation Desert Shield. National Guard units are not often called into federal service in domestic crisis situations, however.

The Governor's Judicial Powers

In every State the governor has several judicial powers. Most of them are powers of executive clemency—powers of mercy that may be shown toward those convicted of crime.[6] For example, by the power to **pardon**, a governor may release a 1.b
person from the legal consequences of a crime. In most States, a pardon may be full or conditional, and it can be granted only after conviction.

With the power to **commute**, a governor 1.c
may reduce the sentence imposed by a court. Thus a death sentence may be commuted to life imprisonment. The power to **reprieve** post- 1.d
pones the execution of a sentence. The power to **parole** allows the release of a prisoner short 1.e
of the completion of the term to which he or she was originally sentenced.

The governor may have some or all of these powers. However, they are often shared with one or more boards. For example, a governor may share the pardoning or parole power with a board of pardons and/or a parole board.

Other Executive Officers

As you have already seen, in nearly every State the governor must share the control of his or her administration with a number of other elected officials. In most States, these offices are filled by popular election. The individuals who fill them must have a variety of different qualifications for these jobs.

The Lieutenant Governor The formal duties of the lieutenant governor are much like those of the Vice President at the national level—that is, there is little to do. He or she succeeds to the governorship if there is a vacancy in the office and presides over the senate in most States. Nevertheless, seven States

[6]An extradition request from another State also puts the governor in a judicial role.

Provide Guided Practice
Write the following headings on the board: *Executive powers, Legislative powers, Judicial powers.* Have students volunteer information from the section to be written in each column that describes characteristics of, or issues related to, the governorships of the States. (*Possible answers: Executive powers are often shared with other elected executive officials. They include military powers; a prominent role in the budget process; appointment, removal, and supervisory powers. Legislative powers include the message power and the power to call special sessions. Perhaps the most important legislative power is the item veto, which many governors hold. Judicial powers include the power to pardon, commute, offer reprieves and parole.*)

Provide Independent Practice
TRF **Teacher's Resource File**
You may wish to assign Section 2 Guided Reading and Review, Unit 7 File, p. 6, to help students master section objective content.

Enrichment

Have students look up one or two recent major messages delivered by their governor (for example, a State of the State address). What do these messages reveal about the governor's political agenda and the powers of the office? What does he or she want to see happen in your State? (Challenging)

Monitor Comprehension

Answers to Section 2 Review
1. "Key Terms" are defined on the following pages:
- **a.** item veto, p. 641
- **b.** pardon, p. 641
- **c.** commute, p. 641
- **d.** reprieve, p. 641
- **e.** parole, p. 641

2. A governor may die, resign, be removed by impeachment, or be recalled. **3.** It may pass laws restricting the governor's power to appoint members of boards or commissions. **4.** An item veto allows a governor to specifically veto a single provision of a measure. **5.** He or she succeeds to the governorship if there is a vacancy, and presides over the State senate in most States.
6. (a) The governor's formal and informal legislative powers give the governor's office great authority. (b) Because much of the governor's legislative power is political, the relationship between the governor and the legislature itself does not violate the separation of powers.

Closure

The governor is the principal executive officer in State government. State governors also have important legislative and judicial powers. Governors also typically share executive power with other executive officials.

In Section 3, students will read about some of the commonly found units of local government in the United States.

Assignment Assign Section 3, pp. 643–648, for the next class period.

seem to get along quite well without a lieutenant governor.

The Secretary of State The office of secretary of state exists everywhere but in Alaska, Hawaii, and Utah. The secretary of state is the State's chief clerk and record-keeper. He or she has charge of a great variety of public documents, records the official acts of the governor and the legislature, and usually administers the election laws. As with most of these other elected executives, the secretary of state has little real discretionary power or authority.

The Treasurer The treasurer is the custodian of State funds, often the State's chief tax collector, and regularly the State's paymaster.

Lawyer for the State of Alaska Alaska's attorney general, Charles E. Cole, was appointed by the governor and approved by a majority of the State legislature.

The treasurer's major job is to make payments out of the State treasury. Most of those payments go to meet the many agency payrolls of the State and to pay the bills for the various goods or services supplied to the State by its many suppliers.

The Attorney General The attorney general is the State's lawyer. He or she acts as the legal adviser to State officers and agencies as they perform their official functions, represents the State in court, and oversees the work of local prosecutors as they try cases on behalf of the State.

Much of the power of the office centers on the attorney general's formal written interpretations of constitutional and statutory law. These interpretations, called opinions, are issued to answer questions raised by the governor, other executive officers, legislators, and local officials regarding the lawfulness of their actions or proposed actions. In most States these opinions have the force of law unless successfully challenged in court.

Section 2 Review

1. Define: item veto, pardon, commute, reprieve, parole
2. Describe four circumstances under which a successor may take the place of a governor before that governor's usual term of office comes to an end.
3. List two ways in which a State legislature may place limits upon a governor's power to appoint officials.
4. What is the significance of the item veto to the legislative process at the State level?
5. What are the duties of the typical lieutenant governor?

Critical Thinking

6. Checking Consistency (p. 19) The governor is not only the State's principal executive officer, but is often the State's chief legislator also. (a) Explain how this is so. (b) Does this arrangement violate the principle of separation of powers?

★

TRF **Teacher's Resource File**
See the Unit 7 File, p. 7, for the Section 2 Quiz.

Reteach

Have students create a brochure entitled *The Governorship in the American Political System.* Students should use a question-and-answer format to identify the qualifications, selection, term, succession, compensation, powers, and functions of the office.

3 Counties, Towns, Townships, and Special Districts

Find Out:

- What are the major elements of county governments?
- How are towns and townships governed?
- What are the reasons behind the creation of special districts?

Key Terms:

county, parish, borough, township, special district

Washington has the White House, and your State has its own impressive capitol. These structures serve as functioning and symbolic centers for the Federal and State governments. In most communities, however, local government has no grand dome or stately mansion. Government in these places is visible mainly in the form of the day-to-day services that keep communities going.

In spite of its humble appearance, local government is vitally important in the lives of every American. As one measure of that fact, recall what you read earlier: Of the 83,237 units of government across the nation, 83,186 of these units are at the local level.

All local governments in the United States are creations of the States. Whether they are providing services, regulating activities, collecting taxes, or doing anything else, local governments can only act because the State has established them and permits them to. In this section, you will read about these units and about the complicated pattern of local government in the United States.

The Counties

The 3,042 counties cover nearly all of the United States. A **county** is a major unit of local government. Organized county governments are found in all States except Connecticut and Rhode Island. In Louisiana what are known elsewhere as counties are called **parishes**, and in Alaska they are known as **boroughs**. In addition to Connecticut and Rhode Island, there are

1.a
1.b
1.c

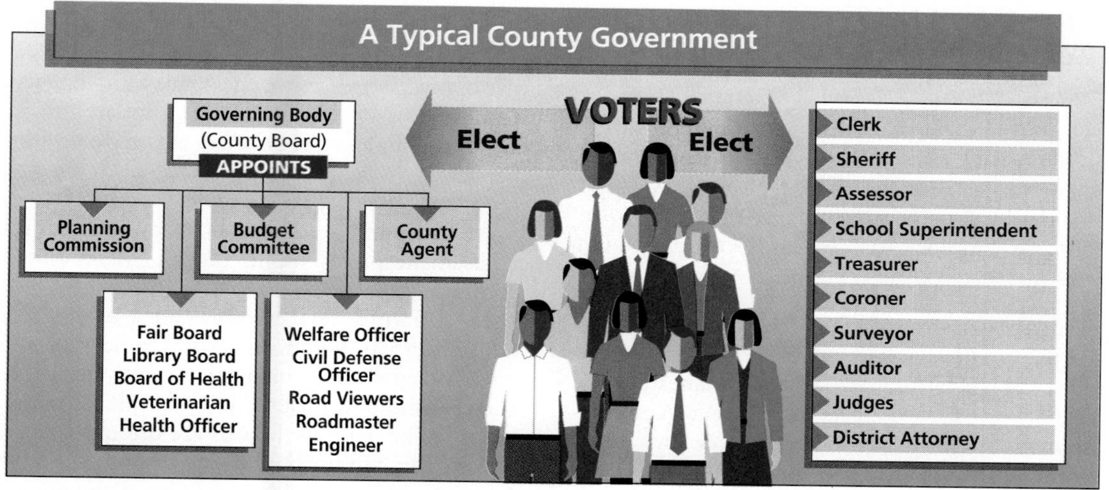

Interpreting Graphics In many States, the county board has both executive and legislative powers. Yet the board's executive power usually is shared with other elected officials. Why might such an arrangement cause confusion?

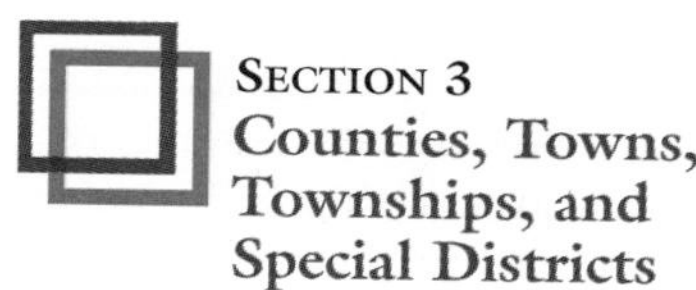

SECTION 3
Counties, Towns, Townships, and Special Districts

FOCUS

Teacher's Resource File See the Unit 7 File, p. 8, for the Section 3 Outline.

Objectives

24.7 Define the major elements of county government.
24.8 Describe how towns and townships are governed.
24.9 Explain why special districts are created.

Bellringer Activity Ask students to think about all the people who work in the school and in the police and fire departments in their community. Ask students if they know who employs these people. What is the unit of local government that provides these services for the people in their community?

State the Purpose There are more than 83,000 units of local government in the United States. Section 3 surveys some of the more common forms of local government.

Interpreting Graphics Ask students to speculate as to why some county officials are appointed and others are elected. (*Possible answer: Voters cannot be expected to knowledgeably elect so many officials.*)

Caption Answer With many people sharing executive power, no single person or body assumes the ultimate responsibility for making decisions.

Vocabulary

Point out "Key Terms" on page 643. Ask students to look up the words *parish* and *borough* in a dictionary. Have students compare various dictionary definitions of these words with the meanings given in the text. LEP

Reading Strategy: Relating to Topic

Ask students to think about how living within a particular school district affects their lives. How is their school district different from neighboring ones? What might their school experience be like in a much larger or smaller school system?

ABCNEWS INTERACTIVE

The following video segments may be used to highlight aspects of State governments.

Powers of the Congress Guidebook
Chapter 62: The Federal System, p. 68

INSTRUCT

Explain/Discuss Ask students to recall the definition of a unitary government from Chapter 1.(*A government in which all authority rests with a single, central government.*) Tell students that all State governments are unitary, and so all local governments are created by the States.

Discuss with students the different types of local governments commonly found in the United States. Using a map of the United States, such as the one on pages 712–713 of the text, point out the following areas and ask what kind of local government is predominantly found there: New England (*towns, with counties as judicial district*); New York and New Jersey west to the Dakotas, Kansas and Nebraska (*counties and townships*); the West and South (*counties*).

several places across the country where no organized county government exists. About 10 percent of the nation's population lives in those areas today.

The function of counties varies from region to region. Counties serve almost solely as judicial districts in the New England States. There, towns carry out most of the functions undertaken by counties elsewhere. Counties and townships share the functions of rural local government from New York and New Jersey west to the Dakotas, Nebraska, and Kansas. In the South and the West, counties are the major units of government in rural areas.

In terms of area, San Bernardino County in southern California is the largest in the United States. San Bernardino County covers 20,102 square miles. Arlington County in Virginia is the smallest, covering only 26 square miles. There is a marked variation in the area covered by each of the several counties within each State, too.

Counties also vary widely in terms of population. Nearly 9 million people now live in Los Angeles County in California. At the other end of the scale, only 107 residents were counted in Loving County, in western Texas, in the 1990 census. Most counties—in fact 75 percent of them—serve populations of fewer than 50,000.

Common Elements of County Governments

The structures of county government differ, often considerably. But, as you can see from the chart on page 643, they typically have four major elements: a governing body, elected officials, a number of boards, and appointed bureaucrats.

The Governing Body The governing body of the county is often called the county board. It is known by at least 20 other names among the States—for example: the board of commissioners, board of supervisors, police jury, fiscal court, county court, and board of chosen freeholders.

The members of the board, whatever its title, are almost always popularly elected. They are usually chosen from districts in the county rather than on an at-large basis. Terms of office run from one to eight years, but four-year terms are the most common.

Generally, county boards can be grouped into two types: boards of commissioners and boards of supervisors. The board of commissioners is the smaller and more common type. Found everywhere in the South and West, the board is also well known elsewhere. It most often has three or five members, but some have seven or more. The members, usually called commissioners, are elected only to these bodies. As a rule, they hold no other public office.

The board of supervisors is typically a much larger body, having an average of about 15 members but sometimes running to as many as 80 or more. The supervisors are elected from each of the several townships in the county, as in New York, Nebraska, and Wisconsin. Each supervisor is usually an officer of his or her township as well as a member of the countywide governing body.

The powers held by the county governing bodies are detailed in the State constitution and acts of the State legislature. However restricted they may be, the powers of these boards are generally both executive and legislative, despite the American tradition of separation of powers.

County governments' most important legislative powers are those dealing with finance. County boards levy taxes, appropriate funds, and incur limited debts. They also have a number of lesser legislative powers, many in the regulatory field. For example, county boards pass health and zoning ordinances and control amusement places found outside incorporated communities.

Most county boards carry out a number of administrative functions. They supervise the road program and manage county property such as the courthouse, jails, hospitals, parks, and the like. County boards are often responsible for the administration of welfare programs and the conduct of elections. They also appoint certain county officers, deputies, and assistants of many kinds, as well as most other county employees. In addition, they fix the salaries of most of those who work for the county.

As you will see, most of these governing bodies share their executive powers with other elected boards and officials. As a result, efficiency, economy, and accountability are often almost impossible to achieve.

Elected Officials A number of officials with countywide jurisdiction are separately elected. These other officers, and their principal duties, are most likely to include:

—The sheriff, who keeps the jail, furnishes police protection in rural areas, carries out the orders of the local courts, and is often the tax collector.

—The clerk, who registers and records such documents as deeds, mortgages, birth and marriage certificates, and divorce decrees. The county clerk often administers elections within the county, and acts as secretary to the county board and as clerk of the local courts.[7]

—The assessor, who appraises (sets the value of) all of the taxable property in the county.

—The treasurer, who keeps county funds and makes authorized payments from these funds.

—The auditor, who keeps financial records and authorizes payments to meet county obligations.

—The district attorney, who is the prosecuting attorney, carries out criminal investigations, and prosecutes those who break the law.

—The superintendent of schools, who is responsible for the administration of all or many of the public elementary and secondary schools in the county.

—The coroner, who investigates violent deaths and certifies the causes of deaths unattended by a physician.

Many other county officers are often elected. They include a surveyor, who surveys land and sets boundary lines; an engineer, who supervises the building of county roads, bridges, drains, and other improvements; and one or more judges of local courts.

[7]In several States a separate officer known as the recorder or the register of deeds has custody of those documents dealing with property transactions.

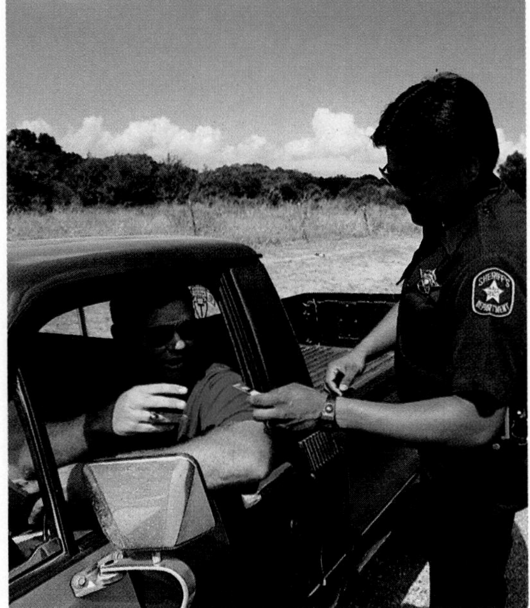

Covering All the Bases A county sheriff has a wide range of law enforcement responsibilities. Here, one of the sheriff's officers checks a motorist's driver's license.

Boards or Commissions These bodies, whose members are also sometimes elected, have authority over a number of county functions. They commonly include a fair board, a library board, a planning commission, a hospital board, a board of road viewers, a board of health, and, sometimes, a civil service commission. Members of the county board often serve *ex officio*—because of their office—on one or more of these other agencies.

County Bureaucracy Counties now employ approximately 2 million men and women. They, of course, do the day-to-day work of each of the nation's 3,042 counties.

Functions of Counties

Because counties are creations of the State, they are responsible for the administration of State laws and such county laws as the State's constitution and legislature allow them to make.

Have students identify some of the unique features of counties, towns, and townships. (*Possible answers: Counties are historically institutions of rural government. County boards have executive and legislative powers. They have a number of elected officials and specialized boards or commissions. Towns have town meetings. Townships also often have such meetings, or they have three- or five-member, popularly elected boards of trustees.*) Next, have students identify ways in which local governments are similar. (*Each provides services to the people who live there. With great variation from location to location, they build roads, care for the poor, provide sanitation services, maintain schools, and much more.*)

Finally, ask students to describe the role of special districts in the scheme of local government. (*They perform one or more related functions at the local level. They exist in great variety, most commonly for school purposes.*)

As students discuss the various forms of local government found in the United States, encourage them to offer whatever information they have about the local government where they live. Especially encourage discussion of local problems or issues and the way in which local government is trying to address those issues—for example, by building roads or hospitals.

Activity: Cooperative Learning

Time: Two class periods **Activity:** Make a chart of government in their State. **Grouping:** Groups of four to six students **Purpose:** Have students work together to make a chart of their State government that provides information such as the size and characteristics of the legislature, the names of key State officials, the number and names of counties and large cities, and other key information. Students can consult the Government Resources Handbook on page 690 for possible sources of information. **Roles:** Have students assign the following roles: manager, researcher(s), artist(s).

Outcome: Groups may refer to their charts as the class discusses the functions and services of each unit of government.

Inmates at Work in County Jail One function of county government is to manage county jails—an increasingly difficult task with the nation's jails becoming more and more crowded.

Historically, counties have been institutions of rural government. Most counties remain rurally oriented today. Though there is some difference from State to State, their major functions reflect their rural character. The most common ones are to keep the peace and maintain jails and other correctional facilities; assess property for tax purposes; collect taxes and spend county funds; build and repair roads, bridges, drains, and other such public works; and maintain schools. Counties record deeds, mortgages, marriage licenses, and other documents; issue licenses for such things as hunting, fishing, and marriage; administer elections; care for the poor; and protect the health of the people who live in the county.

Many counties have taken on other functions as they have become more urbanized. Two-thirds of the people in the United States today live within the boundaries of 375 of the nation's 3,042 counties. Several of these more heavily populated counties now offer many of the public services and facilities that are usually found in cities. They do such things as provide water and sewer service; have professionally trained police, fire, and medical units; and operate airports and mass transit systems. Some also enforce zoning and other land-use regulations, and many have built and operate auditoriums, sports stadiums, golf courses, and other recreational facilities.

Towns and Townships

The town or township is found as a separate unit of local government in nearly half the States. Although little known in the South or the West, it is found through the region stretching from New England to the Middle West.[8]

The New England Town In New England, the town is a major unit of local government. Except for just a few cities, each of the six States in the region is divided into towns. Each town generally includes all of the rural and the urban areas within its boundaries. The town is the unit that delivers most of those services that are the responsibility of cities and counties elsewhere in the country.

The roots of the New England town reach back to colonial beginnings. The Pilgrims landed at Plymouth Rock in 1620 as an organized congregation. They quickly set up a close-knit community in which their church and their government were almost one. Other Puritan congregations followed the Pilgrims' pattern. The desire to be near the church, the real or imagined threat from Native Americans, the severe climate, and the fact that the land was not suited to large farms or plantations led the settlers to form tight little communities. Their settlements were soon known as towns, as in England.[9]

At least in form, much of town government today is little changed from colonial times. The

[8]The term *town* is used in some States as the legal designation for smaller urban places; it is also sometimes used as another word for township. *Township* is also a federal public lands survey term, used to identify geographic units (often called congressional townships), each having exactly 36 square miles (36 sections).

[9]When a clan in England or in Northern Europe settled in a particular place, it usually built a wall around it. In Old English, the wall was a tun. In time the space within the wall became known as the tun, and then the town. As the New England towns grew in number and in population, it became necessary to survey their boundaries. The small and irregular shapes that resulted were called "townships" (town shapes). The suffix *ship* comes from the Old English word *scip*, meaning "shape."

Enrichment

Divide the class into groups. Have each group research one body of local government that has jurisdiction over their community. Have them learn the area of that body's jurisdiction and the functions it performs. (Average)

OR

Teacher's Resource File
See the Unit 7, pp. 15–17, for the Case Study on Contemporary Issues for Chapter 24.

main feature is the town meeting, long praised as the ideal vehicle of direct democracy. The town meeting is an assembly open to all the town's eligible voters. It meets yearly, and sometimes more often, to levy taxes, make spending and other policy decisions, and elect officers for the next year.

Between town meetings the board of selectmen/selectwomen, chosen at the annual meeting, manages the town's business. Typically, the board is a three-member body and has responsibilities for such things as roads, schools, care of the poor, sanitation, and so on. Other officers regularly selected at the annual meeting include the town clerk, a tax assessor, a tax collector, a constable, road commissioners, and school board members.

The ideal of direct democracy is still alive in many smaller New England towns. It has given way, however, to the pressures of time, population, and the complexities of public problems in many of the larger towns. There, representative government has largely replaced it. The officers of the town are often elected before the yearly gathering. Many of the decisions once made by the assembled voters are now made by the selectmen and -women. In recent years several towns have gone to a town manager system for the day-to-day administration of local affairs.

Townships Outside of New England, **townships** are found as units of local government in those States bounded by New York and New Jersey on the east and the Dakotas, Nebraska, and Kansas on the west. In none of those States do the townships blanket the State, however. Where they are found, townships are mostly county subdivisions. 1.d

In New York, New Jersey, and Pennsylvania, townships were formed as areas were settled and the people needed the services of local government. As a result, the township maps of those States often resemble crazy-quilts. But from Ohio westward, township lines are more regular. They mostly follow the lines drawn in federal public land surveys, and many are perfect squares.

About half of these States provide for annual township meetings, like those held in New England towns. Otherwise, most townships have much the same governmental mechanisms. The governing body is a three-member or five-member board, generally called the board of trustees or board of supervisors. Often, its members are popularly elected for two-year or four-year terms. In many places, however, the board's members serve because they hold other elected township offices, such as supervisor, clerk, and treasurer. There is often an assessor, a constable, a justice of the peace, and a body of road commissioners.

Unlike in New England, a municipality within a township, especially one of large size, usually exists as a separate governmental entity. Thus, township functions tend to be rural, involving such matters as roads, cemeteries, noxious weed control, drainage, and minor law enforcement. In some States, however, the township is also the basic unit of public school administration.

Many believe that townships have outlived their usefulness. More than half the States get along without them, suggesting that they are not indispensable. Many rural townships have been abolished in the past few decades, the victims of declining populations, improvements in transportation, and a host of other factors.

Some of the more densely populated townships appear to have brighter futures than their country cousins, however. This seems especially true in the suburban areas around some larger cities. Some States, like Pennsylvania, now allow townships to exercise many of the powers and furnish many of the services once reserved to cities.

Special Districts

There are now thousands of special districts across the country. A **special district** is an independent unit created to perform one or more related governmental functions at the local level. These districts are found in almost mind-boggling variety and in every State. 1.e

The school districts are by far the most widely found examples. Including them, there are more than 44,000 special districts today. The first of these districts was created by New York in 1812 for school purposes. By the 1950s, there were more than 50,000 school districts. Reorganizations have cut that number to less than 15,000 today.

Provide Guided Practice Ask for volunteers to call out the name of a State. For each State called, have students offer information about the type of local government commonly found there, and general characteristics of that type of government.

Provide Independent Practice

TRF **Teacher's Resource File** You may wish to assign Section 3 Guided Reading and Review, Unit 7 File, p. 9, to help students master section objective content.

SPOTLIGHT ON: Economics

Inequality among school districts is a perennial problem for local officials. A new approach to the problem of unequal or discriminatory establishment of school districts is to assign children to them on the basis of varying income levels rather than race. In the fall of 1992, the LaCrosse, Wisconsin school district became the first in the nation to bus approximately one-third of the district's 3,500 elementary students to various schools in order to integrate students from different economic levels. In this way, students from low-income areas have access to the educational options found in schools in higher-income areas.

Interpreting Maps Ask students why they think this water district is one of the most powerful governmental agencies in California. (*District represents interests of State's largest urban area.*)

Caption Answer San Diego County Water Authority.

Monitor Comprehension

Answers to Section 3 Review
1. "Key Terms" are defined on the following pages:

a. county, p. 643
b. parish, p. 643
c. borough, p. 643
d. township, p. 647
e. special district, p. 647

2. County commissioners and boards of supervisors. **3.** Governing boards share executive powers with other elected boards and officials. **4.** Examples: sheriff, clerk, assessor, auditor, district attorney. **5.** Form of direct democracy in which voters meet to make policy decisions. **6.** The first: New York, 1812. 1950s: More than 50,000 school districts. Today: 15,000. **7.** They are informed and interested about issues facing the town.

Closure

Local government varies in form and function. Counties, townships, towns, and special districts provide citizens with important services. In the next section, students will read about another unit of local government—cities and municipal areas.

Assignment Assign Section 4, pp. 650–657, for the next class period.

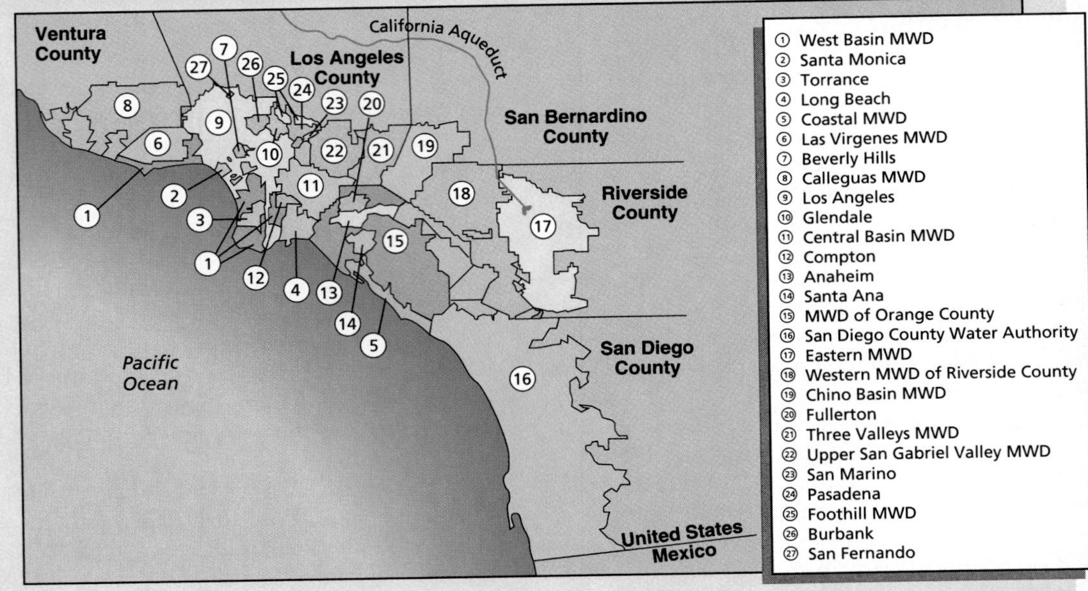

Interpreting Maps The metropolitan water district of southern California is made up of 27 member agencies from six counties. This special district has been called one of the most powerful government agencies in the State. What is the largest member agency in the MWD?

Most of the other special districts, which serve a wide range of purposes, have been created since the Depression of the 1930s, and their numbers are still growing. They are found most often, but by no means always, in rural and suburban areas. Many special districts have been created to provide water, sewage, or electrical service; to furnish fire, police, or sanitation protection; and to build and maintain bridges, airports, swimming pools, libraries, or parks. For example, fire protection might be provided in some out-of-the-way locale by setting up a special district. Others have been created for such purposes as soil conservation, housing, slum clearance, public transportation, irrigation, or reforestation. There are even, in many places, special districts for dog control or mosquito or other insect pest control purposes.

Section 3 Review

1. **Define:** county, parish, borough, township, special district
2. What are two major types of county boards?
3. What factors make county government generally inefficient?
4. List three elected officials commonly found in county government.
5. What is a town meeting?
6. Describe the history of school districts in the United States.

Critical Thinking

7. **Identifying Assumptions** (p. 19) Consider the idea of the New England town meeting. What does this method of town government assume about the citizens of the town?

TRF **Teacher's Resource File**
See the Unit 7 File, p. 10, for the Section 3 Quiz.

Reteach

Have students create a glossary that includes definitions of the following words: *county, town, township,* and *special district*. The glossaries should include information about where these forms of government are used and what their features are.

Debating Key Issues

Should the Government Require Students to Salute the Flag?

West Virginia Board of Education v. *Barnette*

Where should the division be made between the powers of the State and the personal freedoms of speech, thought, and religion? In the early 1940s, the West Virginia Board of Education made saluting the American flag compulsory in all West Virginia school rooms. The rule stipulated that any child who refused to salute the flag would be expelled from school, declared "unlawfully absent," and treated as a delinquent. The parents would be held legally responsible for their children's actions.

Several families in the West Virginia school system were members of the Jehovah's Witnesses. Their beliefs prohibited worship of any human-made image, including the flag. In federal district court, one Jehovah's Witness family—the Barnettes—filed a suit to prevent the school board from enforcing its flag-saluting law, claiming violation of the 1st and 14th amendments. The court decided in their favor. In 1943, the West Virginia board appealed to the Supreme Court.

Review the following arguments and evidence presented to the Supreme Court:

Arguments for the West Virginia Board of Education

1. The salute rule does not violate the 1st Amendment freedom of speech or religion. In this case, individual religious liberty must yield to political authority for the good of the nation. The mandatory salute promotes national unity.
2. The State's salute rule is not in violation of the 14th Amendment. Because it teaches children patriotism, it is a key part of the educational system. It does not abridge individual liberty, but rather promotes liberty for all.
3. The Federal Government does not have the authority to prohibit the State from instituting this law whose purpose is promoting citizenship and universal good.

Arguments for Barnette

1. The compulsory salute rule clearly violates the 1st Amendment. It suppresses free speech and denies freedom of religion. This rule sacrifices individual freedom by insisting on conformity to an exercise that has little, if anything, to do with national security.
2. The salute rule violates the 14th Amendment, which guarantees an individual's freedom regarding what he or she thinks, both secularly and religiously.
3. The Federal Government is sworn to uphold the Constitution and therefore has the power to nullify the flag rule. In a free country, patriotism will flourish without legislation. The freedom of religion is a far more powerful affirmation of patriotism than is a symbolic, coerced salute.

Getting Involved

1. Identify the constitutional grounds on which each side based its arguments.
2. Debate the opposing viewpoints presented in this case.
3. Predict how you think the Supreme Court ruled in this case and why. Then refer to the Supreme Court Glossary on page 764 to read about the decision.
4. Discuss the impact of the Court's decision on other personal freedoms. Under what circumstances, if any, should the government place limits on individual freedom?

TEACHING
Debating Key Issues

***West Virginia Board of Education* v. *Barnette*:**
Should the Government require students to salute the flag?

Objective
Determine whether or not people can be required to salute the flag under the 1st Amendment.

INSTRUCT

Before reading the feature, you may want to elicit student answers to the question in the title. Then when they have finished reading the feature, ask them if their answers have changed, and if so, why. Then work through the "Getting Involved" section, beginning with identifying the constitutional issues involved.

After the debate, ask students to explain which arguments they found to be most compelling. Have each student write an opinion paper—majority, concurring, or dissenting—based upon what they have read about the case. Then have students read the Supreme Court's decision to find out if the Court agreed with their views.

SUPREME COURT DECISION

The Court held that a compulsory flag salute was unconstitutional. "No official, high or petty, can prescribe what shall be orthodox in politics, nationalism, religion or other matters of opinion."

TRF **Teacher's Resource File**
See the Supreme Court Cases file, p. 17, for an activity that extends coverage of this case.

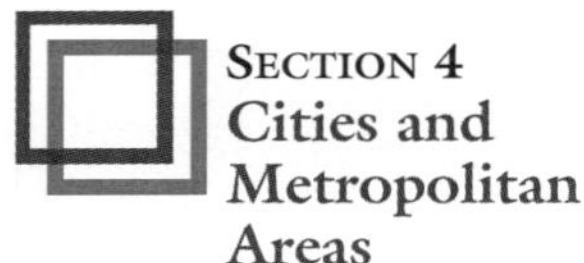

SECTION 4
Cities and Metropolitan Areas

FOCUS

Teacher's Resource File See the Unit 7 File, p. 11, for the Section 4 Outline.

Objectives

24.10 Analyze the various forms of city government.
24.11 Explain why city planning and zoning are vital.
24.12 Analyze why population has shifted from cities to suburbs.

Bellringer Activity Ask students to brainstorm a list of words and ideas they associate with the word *city*. Write these ideas down on the board. Ask students to discuss why they have these associations.

State the Purpose The cities and metropolitan areas of the United States have their own unique problems and needs. In this section, students will read how city and metropolitan governments address those needs and problems.

Interpreting Maps As students study the map, ask them to identify what the map implies about which level of government controls the various services listed in the legend. (*These are controlled on the local level.*)

Caption Answer National-State-County-City-District.

4 Cities and Metropolitan Areas

Find Out:

- What are the various forms of city government?
- Why are city planning and zoning vital?
- Why has population shifted so dramatically from cities to suburbs?

Key Terms:

mayor-council government, strong-mayor government, weak-mayor government, commission form, council-manager form, zoning, metropolitan area

How times have changed. In 1790, a mere five percent of the nation's population lived in the nation's few cities. Today, America's cities and their surrounding communities are home to nearly four of every five persons [10]

In this section, you will read about the government of American cities and their surrounding communities.

Forms of City Government

Although there are variations from city to city, each city has either (1) a mayor-council, (2) a commission, or (3) a council-manager form of government.

1.a **The Mayor-Council Form** The **mayor-council government** is the oldest and still the

[10]Depending on local custom and State law, municipalities may be known as cities, towns, boroughs, or villages. The use and meaning of these terms vary among the States. The larger municipalities are known everywhere as cities, and the usual practice is to use that title only for those communities with a significant population.

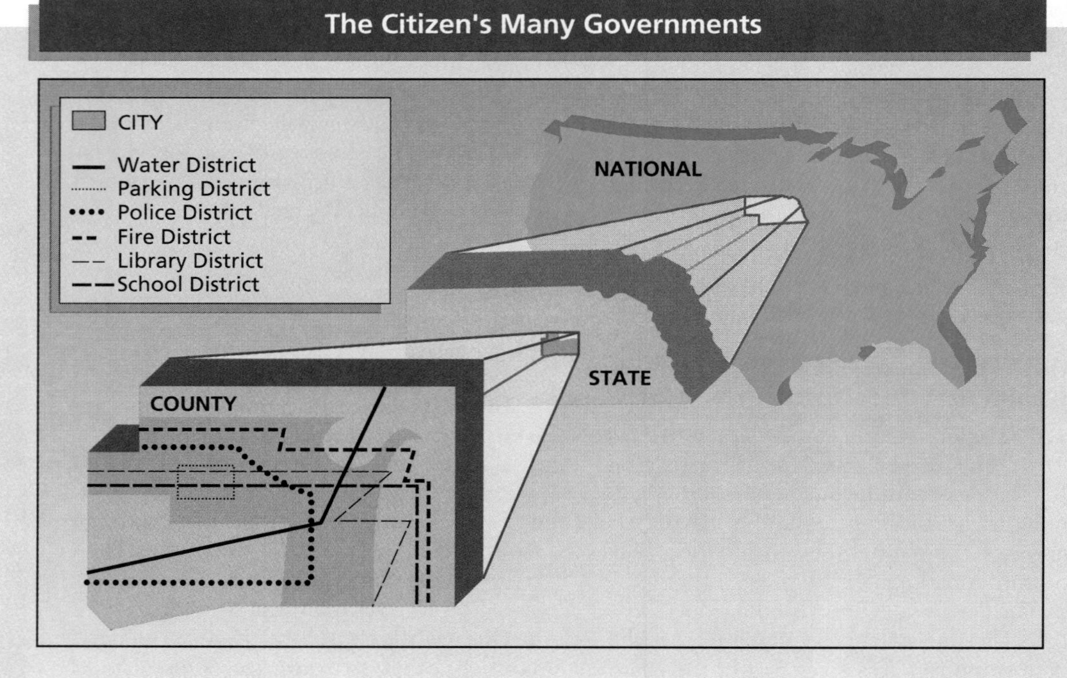

Interpreting Maps Many units of local government exist in this country. What is the chain of command from national government to the district level?

Reading Strategy: Predicting Content

Before students read the section, have them scan the boldfaced headings in the section. Tell students that these headings form an outline of the content of the section. Then have students write a prediction about the content of the section based on their preview of the section headings. Have students check the accuracy of their predictions as they read the section.

Vocabulary

Point out to students "Key Terms" on page 650. Have students prepare a chart displaying the characteristics of ***strong-mayor governments*** and ***weak-mayor governments,*** and listing possible advantages and disadvantages of each type.

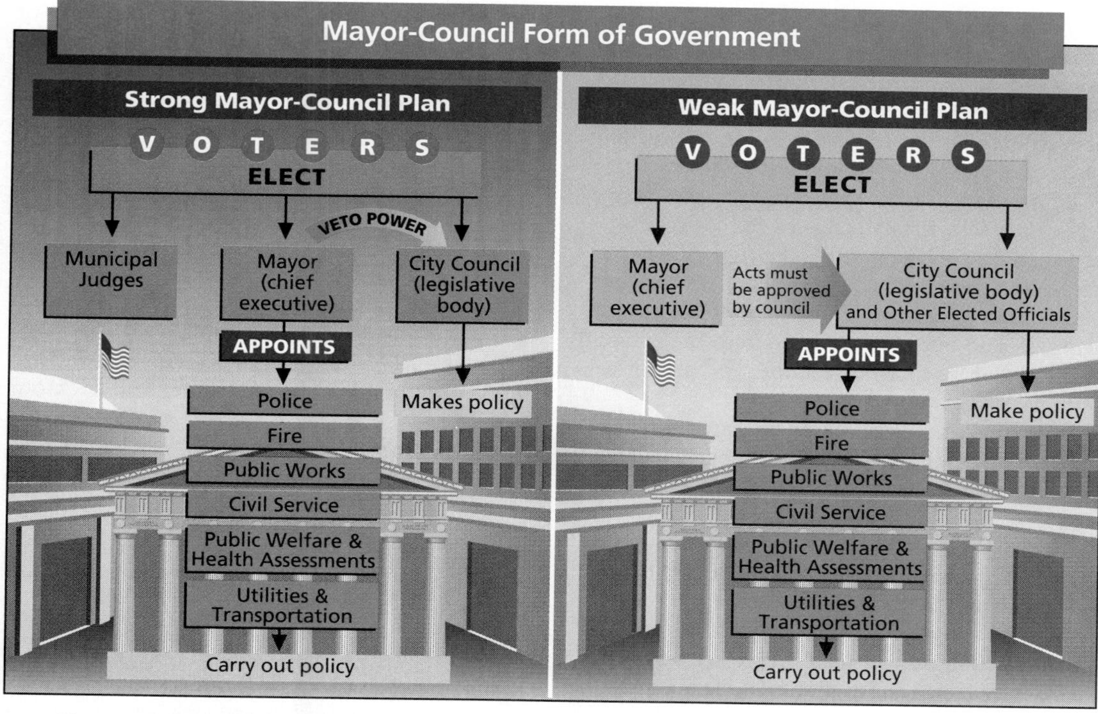

Interpreting Graphics Compare and contrast the mayor-council plans above. What prevents a mayor of a city governed under a weak mayor-council plan from having greater power?

most widely used type of city government. It features an elected mayor as the chief executive and an elected council as its legislative body.

The council is almost always unicameral. In fact, Everett, Massachusetts, is the only city in the United States that has a two-chambered council today. The typical council has five, seven, or nine members, but some larger cities have more. New York now has the largest council, with 51 members.

The members of the council are popularly elected everywhere. Terms of office run from one to as many as six years, but four-year terms are the most common. Council members are now most often elected from the city at-large, and that is the trend. Many cities, including several larger ones, however, choose their council members from wards (districts) within the city.

A move to nonpartisan city government began in the early 1900s. Its champions believed that (1) political parties were a major source for corruption in city government and (2) partisan contests at the Statewide and national levels have little to do with municipal problems and local issues. Today, less than a third of all cities still run their elections on a partisan basis.

Generally the mayor is also elected by the voters. In some places, however, the office is filled by appointment by the council from among its own members. The mayor presides at council meetings, usually may vote only to break a tie, and may recommend and usually veto ordinances. In most cities the veto can be overridden by the council.

Mayor-council governments are often described as either of the strong-mayor type, or the weak-mayor type, depending on the powers given to the mayor. This classification is useful for purposes of description. However, it blurs the importance of informal power in city politics.

INSTRUCT

Explain/Discuss Help students to understand that cities are home to millions of Americans. City governments are the local governments of a significant percentage of the population.

Ask students to discuss the various forms of city government, including the benefits and drawbacks of each. Suggest that students use the various graphics on pages 651–653 to help them understand the differences among these various forms. Ask students if any of these methods make more sense to them, and if so, why. Have them compare each form to the structure of the executive and legislative branches at the national and State levels. For example, ask how the role of the mayor is different from that of the President and governor? (*Strong-mayor plan, with a powerful chief executive and a separate legislature, is most like federal and State governments. In the others, executive power is largely held by a commission or council. The mayor has little real power.*)

Interpreting Graphics As students study the graphic, ask them what purpose the veto power in the strong mayor-council plan serves. (*It gives the mayor power to check and balance the power of the legislative branch.*)

Caption Answer The mayor's acts must be approved by the council. Yet the mayor has no veto power to check and balance the council.

SPOTLIGHT ON: Behind the Scenes

How are the two largest cities in the country run? In New York, David Dinkins, the country's highest-paid mayor, is assisted by a city manager and a council of 51 members. Both mayor and council members serve four-year terms. In Los Angeles, Mayor Tom Bradley works with the country's highest-paid city manager, and a council of 15 members. Terms of office are also four years. One interesting difference between the cities: New York has 35,605 law enforcement employees; Los Angeles has 10,478. One reason for this difference is that New York's population is approximately twice that of Los Angeles.

Interpreting Graphics Direct students' attention to the graphic on page 652. Ask students to suggest possible problems that might arise from the fact that each commissioner heads a department in addition to being part of the city council. (*The council members have legislative and executive powers. There is no separation of powers.*)

Caption Answer The commission form of local government does not actually have a system of checks and balances since the legislative and executive functions are contained within the same governmental body—the commissioners.

ABCNEWS INTERACTIVE

The following video segment may be used to highlight aspects of the State government.

POWERS OF THE CONGRESS GUIDEBOOK
Chapter 62: The Federal System, p. 68

1.b In a **strong-mayor government**, the mayor heads the city's administration, usually has the power to hire and fire employees, and prepares the budget. Typically, the mayor is otherwise able to exercise strong leadership in the making of city policy and the running of its affairs.

1.c In a **weak-mayor government**, the mayor has much less formal power. Executive duties are shared with such other elected officials as the clerk, treasurer, city engineer, police chief, and council members. Powers of appointment, removal, and budget are shared with the council or exercised by that body alone; the mayor seldom has a veto power.

Most mayor-council cities operate under the weak-mayor rather than the strong-mayor plan. But the latter form is generally found in larger cities.

The success of the mayor-council form depends in very large measure on the power, ability, and influence of the mayor. In weak-mayor cities, responsibility for action or inaction is hard to fix.

The strong-mayor plan helps to solve the problems of leadership and responsibility. Still, it has three large weaknesses. First, it depends very heavily on the capacities of the mayor. As you have seen in the case of other elected officials, political and administrative talents are not often combined in the same person.

Second, a major dispute between the mayor and the council can stall the workings of city government. This is another way of saying that the mayor-council form incorporates the principles of separation of powers and checks and balances—with all their benefits and drawbacks.

Third, the mayor-council form is quite complicated and so is often little understood by the average citizen.

The Commission Form Only a few American cities now have a commission form of government.[11] The largest of these are Portland, Oregon; Mobile, Alabama; and Jackson, Mississippi.

1.d The **commission form** is simple. Three to nine, but usually five, commissioners are

[11] The commission form was born in Galveston, Texas, in 1901. A tidal wave had swept the island city the year before, killing 7,000 persons and laying much of it to waste. The old mayor-council regime was too incompetent and corrupt to cope with the emergency. The Texas legislature gave Galveston a new charter, providing for five commissioners to make and enforce the law in the stricken city. Intended to be temporary, the arrangement proved so effective that it soon spread to other Texas cities and then elsewhere in the country. Its popularity has waned, however. In 1960 Galveston's voters approved a new city charter providing for council-manager government.

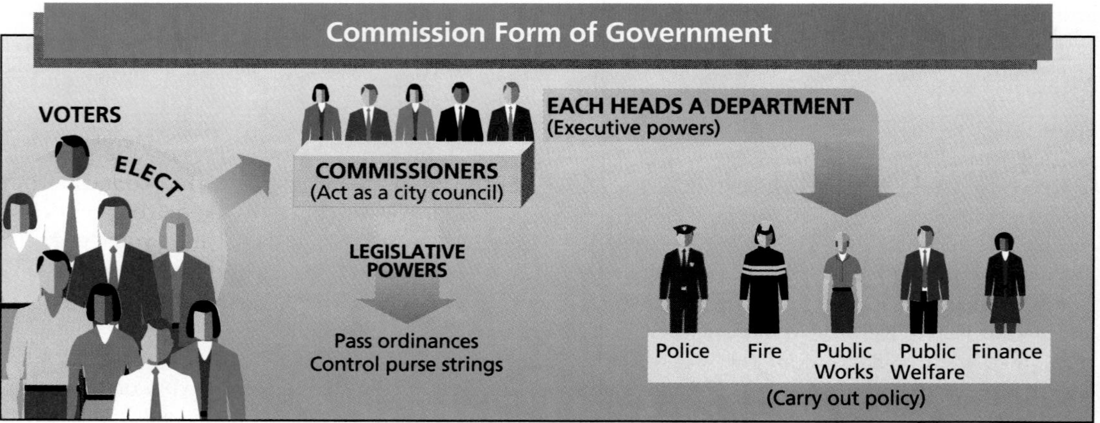

Interpreting Graphics This form of government is one of the most uncomplicated systems for a city or town. Does a system of checks and balances exist in the commission form of government? Why or why not?

popularly elected. Together, they form the city council, pass ordinances, and control the purse strings. Individually, they head the different departments of city government—police, fire, public works, finance, parks, and so on. Thus, both legislative and executive powers are centered in one body.

Depending on the city, either the voters or the commissioners themselves choose one of the commissioners to serve as the mayor. Like the other commissioners, the mayor heads one of the city's departments. He or she also presides at council meetings and represents the city on ceremonial occasions. The mayor generally has no more authority than the other commissioners and rarely has the veto power.

The commissioners are usually elected for two-year or four-year terms, and almost always from the city at-large and on nonpartisan ballots. Unlike their counterparts in mayor-council and council-manager cities, they regularly serve as full-time officers.

The commission form has three chief defects. First, the lack of a single chief executive (or, the presence of several chiefs among equals) makes it difficult to fix responsibility. This also means that the city generally has no effective political leadership.

Second, there is a built-in tendency toward "empire-building," in which each commissioner tries to draw as much of the city's money and influence as possible to his or her own department.

Finally, there is a lack of coordination at the topmost levels of policymaking and administration. Each commissioner is likely to equate the citywide public good with the peculiar interests and functions of his or her department.

The Council-Manager Form The **council-manager form** is a modification of the mayor-council form. It features (1) a strong council, of usually five or seven members, elected at-large on a nonpartisan ballot, (2) a weak mayor, chosen by the voters, and (3) a manager, the city's chief administrative officer, named by the council. 1.e

The council is the city's policy-making body. The manager carries out the policies the council makes and is directly responsible to that body for the efficient administration of the city. The manager serves at the council's pleasure and may be dismissed by the council at any time and for any reason.

Today, most city managers are professionally trained career administrators. As chief administrator, the manager directs the work of all city

Interpreting Graphics Have students examine the graphic on page 653. Ask them to consider the possible functions of the mayor in this form of government. (*Possible answers: The mayor stands as the political figurehead of the government, the face of the government for the people.*) Does this system offer a more clear separation of powers than the commission form? (*Possible answers: Yes, since the council is not directly responsible for executive control of departments. No, since the manager, who performs much of the executive function, works directly for the council and can be dismissed by it at any time.*)

Caption Answer The manager is appointed, not elected.

Interpreting Graphics In the council-manager form of government, a professional manager sees that necessary services are performed for the residents of the city. What keeps the actions of a manager from becoming strictly politically motivated?

Activity: For Gifted Students

Theme: Power American cities have been the breeding ground for the most powerful political machines in this nation's history. Students can report on the history and influence of such political machines as the Daly machine in Chicago or the Tammany Hall machine in New York City. Students should investigate the means by which these machines obtained and kept power over city government over an extended period of time. Students should also look into the events that brought about the decline and fall of the machine. Students can present their findings in the form of a written or oral report.

INSTRUCT

Discuss Have students recall their responses to the "Bellringer Activity" at the beginning of the section. Have students compare the list they generated with the municipal functions discussed on page 654. In their opinions, do students think that cities have been able to provide adequately the level of services necessary for a good quality of life?

As students discuss this issue, have them consider the challenges that cities face. For example, you might ask students to consider the difficulties of growth. Ask students how cities have tried to meet this challenge. *(Zoning)* Have students consider the potential problems related to zoning. How would they feel if they owned property that had its value cut in half by a zoning ordinance?

Next have students discuss the relationship between cities and suburbs. Ask students to summarize the causes and impact of the phenomenon of suburbanitis. (*Higher income city residents leave the city for the suburbs, taking with them resources the city needs to provide services.*) Ask students to consider how the move toward providing services across a metropolitan area helps overcome some of the difficulties of suburbanitis. (*It helps prevent the irreversible flow of resources out of the city. Because services are provided and paid for across an area that includes inner cities and suburbs, the resources that left the city when higher income people moved to the city are still available to it.*)

departments and has the power to hire and fire all city employees. The manager also prepares the budget for council consideration, and then controls the spending of the funds the council appropriates.

The council-manager plan has the backing of nearly every student of municipal affairs, and its use has spread widely. It is now found in more than 8,000 communities, including a majority of all of those cities with populations between 25,000 and 250,000.

The council-manager plan has three major advantages over either the mayor-council or the commission forms of city government. First, it is simple in form. Second, it is clear who has the responsibility for policy, on the one hand, and for its application, on the other. Third, it relies on highly trained experts who are skilled in modern techniques of budgeting, planning, computerization, and other administrative tools.

Some critics of the plan hold that it is undemocratic because the chief executive is not elected. Others say that it does not offer strong political leadership. This is a particular shortcoming, they argue, in larger cities, where the population is often quite diverse and its interests are competitive.

Municipal Functions

A city exists primarily to provide services to those who live within its boundaries.

Consider just a few of the many things that most or all cities do: provide police and fire protection; build and maintain streets, sidewalks, bridges, street lighting systems, parks and playgrounds, swimming pools, golf courses, libraries, hospitals, schools, correctional institutions, daycare centers, airports, public markets, parking facilities, auditoriums, and sports arenas. They furnish such public health and sanitation services as sewers and waste-water treatment, garbage collection and disposal, and disease prevention and eradication programs. Cities operate water, gas, light, and transportation systems. They regulate traffic; building practices; air, water, and noise pollution; and public utilities.

Many cities build and manage public housing projects, clear slums, provide summer youth camps, build and operate docks and other harbor facilities, and maintain tourist attractions.

City Planning

With few exceptions, most American cities developed haphazardly, without a plan, and with no eye to the future. The results of this shortsightedness can be seen almost everywhere. The most obvious, and damaging, examples can be seen in what is often called the core area or the inner city, the older and usually overcrowded central sections of larger cities.

Industrial plants were placed anywhere their owners chose to build them. Rail lines were run through the heart of the community. Towering buildings shut out the sunlight from the too-narrow streets below. Main roads were laid out too close together and sometimes too far apart. Schools, police and fire stations, and other public buildings were squeezed onto cheap land or

City Hall in Dallas, Texas Dallas is one of the largest cities in the United States with a council-manager government.

SPOTLIGHT ON: Political Talk

One response to the problem of inner-city decay common in the 1950s and 60s was called—euphemistically at times—"urban renewal." Urban renewal programs were instituted when planners deemed an area of a city blighted. Although well-intentioned, federally sponsored urban renewal programs often replaced functional, if somewhat unsightly, working-class neighborhoods with housing projects for the poor or luxury accommodations for the rich. Between 1949 and 1961, some 150,000 buildings, most residential, were demolished, displacing some 500,000 persons. By 1967, the number of buildings destroyed topped 400,000 and the number of displaced persons topped 1.4 million.

TRF **Teacher's Resource File**
See the Simulations and Debates file, pp. 26–31, for material to support the section.

put where the political organization could make a profit. Examples are endless.

Planning Growth Fortunately, many cities have seen the need to create order out of their random growth. Most have established some sort of planning agency, usually a planning commission, supported by a trained professional staff. A number of factors have prompted this step. The need to correct past mistakes has often been an absolutely compelling one, of course. Then, too, many cities have recognized the advantages that can result, and the pitfalls that can be avoided, through well-planned and orderly development. Importantly, cities have been spurred on by the Federal Government. Most federal grant and loan programs require that cities that seek aid must first have a master plan as a guide to future growth.

Washington, D.C., is one of the few cities in the nation that has been a planned city from its beginning. Its basic plan was approved by Congress before a single building was erected in 1790. The original plan has been followed fairly closely through the years. The National Capitol Planning Commission guides the city's development today.

City Zoning The practice of dividing a city into a number of districts, or zones, and regulating the uses to which property in each of them may be put, is called **zoning**. Generally, a 1.f
zoning ordinance places each parcel of land in the city into one of three zones: residential, commercial, or industrial. Each of these is then divided into subzones. For example, each or several residential zones may be broken down into several areas. One may be just for single-family residences. Another may allow both one-family and two-family dwellings. In still another, apartment houses and other multifamily units may be allowed.[12]

[12]Most zoning ordinances also prescribe limits on the height and area of buildings, determine how much of a lot may be occupied by a structure, and set out several other such restrictions on land use. They often have "set-back" requirements, which state that structures must be placed at least a certain distance from the street and from other property lines.

"The zoning commission would like to point out an irregularity!"

Interpreting Political Cartoons Zoning commissions have many responsibilities that relate to the overall plan for a city's development. What is one of the roles of the zoning commission, according to this cartoon?

Zoning is really a phase of city planning—and an important means for assuring orderly growth. It began to come into general use only as recently as the 1920s. Zoning still meets opposition from many who object to this interference with their right to use their property as they choose. Even so, nearly every city of any size in the United States is zoned today. The only major exception is Houston, where zoning was turned down by popular vote.

Zoning ordinances must be reasonable. Remember that the 14th Amendment prohibits any State, and thus its cities, from depriving any person of life, liberty, or property without due process of law. Each of the 50 State constitutions contains a similar provision.

Clearly, zoning does deprive a person of the right to use his or her property for certain purposes. Thus, if an area is zoned only for single-

Interpreting Political Cartoons After students have had a chance to look at the cartoon, ask them why it might be of concern for a community to have buildings of similar size. (*Possible answer: Such regulations help ensure that neighborhoods remain residential as opposed to commercial.*)

Caption Answer To make sure the designs of residences are in compliance with the zoning board's specifications.

Provide Guided Practice Write the following on the board: *Mayor-council form, commission form,* and *council-manager form.* Ask students to volunteer explanations of how these forms of city government work. Then have students discuss which form is best equipped to deal with the problems facing today's cities, including growth planning and suburbanitis. Encourage students to suggest alternatives to traditional city governments for the provision of certain services. For example, students might suggest establishing a metropolitan-area–wide organization to perform some functions.

Provide Independent Practice

TRF **Teacher's Resource File** You may wish to assign Section 4 Guided Reading and Review, Unit 7 File, p. 12, to help students master section objective content.

Enrichment

Have students hold a debate in which they argue the merits of different forms of city government. If you wish, hold several debates to compare mayor-council form to commission form, commission form to council-manager form, and so on. (Easy)

Interpreting Political Cartoons Ask students to examine the cartoon on page 656. What does the cartoon suggest about the cause and effect of urban problems such as pollution and suburban sprawl. (*The initial cause of the decision to commute to work sets in motion the series of effects shown in the cartoon.*)

Caption Answer The cartoon suggests that many urban problems result from the large number of commuters.

MONITOR COMPREHENSION

Answers to Section 4 Review
1. "Key Terms" are defined on the following pages:
a. mayor-council government, p. 650
b. strong-mayor government, p. 652
c. weak-mayor government, p. 652
d. commission form, p. 652
e. council-manager form, p. 652
f. zoning, p. 655
g. metropolitan area, p. 656
2. Mayor-council, commission, or council-manager. **3.** Providing police and fire protection, building and maintaining streets, and furnishing public health and sanitation services. **4.** Most cities grew up haphazardly, creating problems of crowding and poor management of space and other resources. **5.** As more and more people fled the cities for the suburbs, they left behind a population that was unable to supply the financial resources to provide for city services.

family dwellings, one cannot build an apartment house or a service station on his or her property in that zone. Zoning can also reduce the value of a particular piece of property—for example, a choice corner lot may be much more valuable with a drive-in restaurant on the property than a house.[13]

While zoning may at times deprive a person of liberty or property, the key question always is this: Does it do so without due process? That is, does it do so unreasonably?

The question of reasonableness is one for the courts to decide. The Supreme Court first upheld zoning as a proper use of the police power in *Euclid* v. *Amber Realty Co.*, 1926, a case involving an ordinance enacted by the city council of Euclid, Ohio.

Suburbanitis and Metropolitan Areas

The growth and sprawl of urban areas have raised many problems for cities, as well as for residents of the suburbs that surround those cities.

Suburbanitis Most larger cities, and many smaller ones, suffer from what has been called "suburbanitis." Today, nearly 115 million Americans—more than 45 percent of the population—live in suburbs.

The nation's suburbs began to grow at a rapid rate in the years immediately after World War II—in the late 1940s, and then on through the 1950s and 1960s. The suburban growth rate slowed somewhat in the 1970s, but it rebounded in the 1980s and on into the 1990s—especially around the Sun Belt cities of the South and West.

This dramatic shift in population can be explained on several grounds. Many quite understandable desires have helped to bring it about, including needs for more room; cheaper land; less smoke, dirt, noise, and congestion; and greater privacy. Suburban growth has sharpened a great many problems for core cities. As many of the better-educated, high-income families have moved out, they have taken their civic, financial, and social resources with them. They have left behind a central city, which in contrast to its suburbs has much higher percentages of older persons, low-income families, and minorities. The cities also have more older buildings and substandard housing, more unemployment, and higher crime rates. Inevitably, both the need for and the stress on city services have multiplied.

Metropolitan Areas Suburbanites face their share of problems too. Water supply, sewage disposal, police and fire protection, transportation, and traffic control are only some of them. Duplication of such functions by city and suburb or by city and county can be wasteful and dangerous. More than one fire has burned on while neighboring fire departments quibbled over which of them was responsible for fighting it.

Attempts to meet the needs of **metropolitan**
1.g **areas**—that is, of the cities and the areas around them—have taken several forms. Over the years, annexation has been the standard means. Outlying

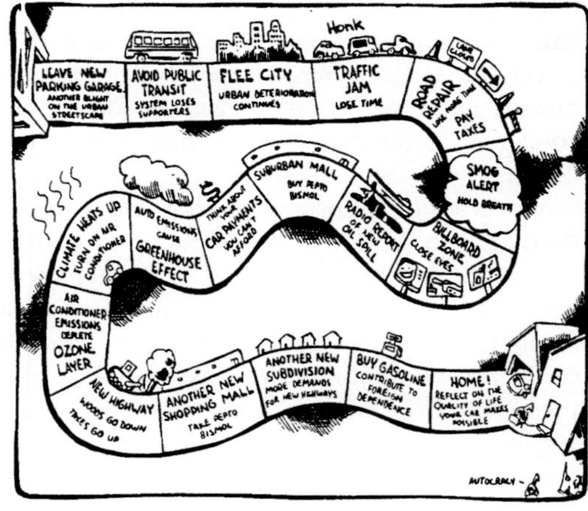

Interpreting Political Cartoons The current "suburbanitis" plague has created many problems, caused by thousands of people living in the suburbs and working in the city. What does this cartoon say about commuting to work?

[13]However, nonconforming uses in existence before a zoning ordinance is passed are almost always allowed to continue. Most ordinances give the city council the right to grant exceptions, called variances, in cases where property owners might suffer undue hardships.

areas have simply been brought within a city's boundaries. But many suburbanites resist annexation. Cities, too, have often been slow to take on the burdens involved.

Another approach involves the creation of special districts, which you have already studied. The best known and most common are school districts, but there are now more than 29,000 sanitary, water, fire protection, and other special districts across the country. Many of them have been created especially to meet the problems of heavily populated urban areas. Their boundaries frequently cut across county and city lines to include the entire metropolitan area, and they are often called metropolitan districts.

These metropolitan districts are generally set up for a single purpose; for example, for park development, as in the Cleveland Metropolitan Park Development District. There is no reason why a district's authority cannot be expanded to cover other functions, however. The Metropolitan District Commission (MDC), created by Massachusetts, until 1992 had its own police department and controlled park development for the city of Boston and neighboring communities. The MDC also had a number of planning functions in the district as a whole. Boston has only about a third of the district's population; the balance lives within 40 other municipalities.

Yet another approach to the challenges facing metropolitan areas is increasing the authority of counties. Among local governments around the country, counties are generally the largest in area and are most likely to include those places demanding new and increased services.

The functions of many urban counties have grown in recent years, as you have already seen. Dade County (Miami), Florida, has undertaken the nation's most ambitious approach to metropolitan problems. In 1957 its voters approved the first home rule charter designed "to create a metropolitan government." Under it, a countywide metropolitan government (Metro) is responsible for areawide functions. These include fire and police protection; an integrated water, sewer, and drainage system; zoning; expressway construction; and the like. Miami and the other 26 cities within the county continue to perform the strictly local functions and services.

Metropolitan Government in Florida An officer of the Dade County metropolitan government is one of the participants in this ambitious countywide system, which includes Miami and 26 other cities.

Section 4 Review

1. **Define:** mayor-council government, strong-mayor government, weak-mayor government, commission form, council-manager form, zoning, metropolitan area
2. What are the three major forms of city government?
3. Cite three examples of municipal functions.
4. Why did city planning become so necessary?
5. How has the growth of the suburbs affected central or core cities?
6. What is the purpose of a metropolitan district?

Critical Thinking

7. **Testing Conclusions** (p. 19) Based on what you have read in this section, do you agree or disagree with this statement: Citizens prefer to have a single leader whom they can look to for leadership and hold responsible for errors.

★

6. These bodies have developed to provide services for entire metropolitan areas, thus avoiding the need to duplicate such services in nearby areas. 7. Answers will vary. Students might point out that most large cities have systems in which a single person, such as a mayor, is the identifiable leader, even though that person often has little real power.

Teacher's Resource File See the Unit 7 File, p. 13, for the Section 4 Quiz.

Closure

Point out that each of the three forms of city government has its advantages and disadvantages. Yet no matter what the form, each city government aims to provide services to city residents and to deal with such issues as growth and the phenomenon of "suburbanitis."

Assignment Assign Chapter 25, Section 1, pp. 663–667, for the next class period.

Reteach

Have students work individually or in small groups to create a poster showing the three major types of city government. The poster should also communicate some of the challenges facing the governments of cities and some of the solutions used to meet those challenges.

TEACHING
Citizenship

How to Write to Your Legislators

Objective

Identify guidelines for writing an effective letter.

INSTRUCT

Before students read the Citizenship feature, ask them to list various public issues that are of importance to them. Once students have read the feature, have them select one of the issues from their lists, and, using the guidelines in the lesson, write to their senator or representative regarding this issue. Remind students that they can use this information when writing to State and local officials as well.

Answers 1. (a) Students should consult the *Government Resources Handbook* on page 690 for possible sources. (b) Possible answers: So the people can have access to their elected representatives, so those officials can keep in touch with what is going on in their district.
2. There is more time to influence the shape and content of the bill. **3.** Students may suggest calling or writing their legislator's offices. **4.** Few people respond positively to threats. An appeal to reason is more likely to influence a lawmaker. **5.** (a) They receive a lot of correspondence and cannot waste time. (b) Little work would get done that could help the people in general.

Citizenship

How to Write to Your Legislators

Most elected officials pay close attention to mail from their constituents. Senator Phil Gramm (R., Texas) says that, after years in Congress, "I am more convinced than ever of the wisdom of the 'average' citizen and the value of his advice." Every day, your representatives receive dozens to hundreds of letters from "the folks back home," and all of them must be answered. The volume of constituent mail has become so great that handling it now takes a large amount of staff time. The use of computer-driven personalized form letters enable legislators to respond quickly and has eased the burden considerably.

Congressman Morris Udall (D., Arizona) suggests several guidelines for writing an effective letter. Use the following steps when writing to your lawmakers.

1. Address your letter properly. You can send your letter to Washington or to your State representative's or senators' local offices. The proper addresses in Washington, D.C. are:

Representative ______________

House Office Building
Washington, D.C. 20515

or:

Senator ______________

Senate Office Building
Washington, D.C. 20510

Answer these questions: (a) How would you locate your State representative's and senators' local offices? (b) Why do those offices exist?

2. Make sure the letter is timely. Most members of Congress say that letters that deal with public policy matters, and especially views on pending legislation, are the most welcome. Do not wait until a bill is out of committee or has passed the House (or Senate). Also, do not try to instruct your lawmaker on every issue. Answer the question: Why might it be best to write a lawmaker before the matter in question has gotten out of committee or passed one of the two houses?

3. Identify the bill or issue that prompts your letter. It is preferable to mention the bill or issue in the first paragraph and to be as specific as you can. Give the bill number, or mention its popular title—for example, the Minimum Wage Bill or the S&L Bailout Bill. Answer the question: What is the best way to learn your legislator's stand on a bill or issue?

4. Give the reasons for the stand you take. Be specific and constructive. Do not make threats or promises or berate your lawmaker, and do not pretend to wield vast political influence. Such an approach is unnecessary and ineffective. Senator Stephen M. Young (D., Ohio) sometimes replied to abrasive letters with notes like this one, "I'm sending you a letter received this morning, evidently from some crackpot who signed your name." Answer the question: Why might it be more effective to try to use reason than threats when communicating with lawmakers?

5. State other purposes clearly and briefly. Many constituents write seeking information on everything from how to obtain a passport to the best ways to prune and fertilize roses. Many others ask for help—with everything from untangling a problem with the Social Security Administration to a mother's plea that her soldier son be stationed somewhere closer to home. (a) Why is it important to be brief and to the point when writing legislators? (b) What might happen if all legislators were regularly expected to respond to such types of questions and requests?

TRF **Teacher's Resource File**
See the Unit 7 File, p. 14, for the Skill Application for this lesson.

TRF **Teacher's Resource File**
See the Participatory Government Activities file, pp. 44–67, for material to support the chapter.

Chapter-in-Brief

Scan all headings, photographs, charts, and other visuals in the chapter before reading the section summaries below.

Section 1 The State Legislatures (pp. 631–637) Each State's constitution is that State's fundamental law. State legislators are popularly elected, serve similar terms, and meet similar qualifications.

Each legislature has certain nonlegislative powers. These powers are similar to the nonlegislative powers of Congress. One difference is that some State legislatures have the power to appoint certain executive officers.

Legislative activity in the States also resembles that of Congress. Presiding officers exert a strong influence, and much of the work takes place in committees. One key difference is that many States allow voters to take a direct part in lawmaking through the initiative and referendum.

Section 2 The Governor and State Administration (pp. 637–642) The governor is the principal executive officer in all 50 States. He or she is popularly elected everywhere, usually to four-year terms.

Governors share their executive authority with such other offices as lieutenant governor, attorney general, and secretary of state, and treasurer. Nevertheless, governors tend to be the persons to whom voters look for leadership.

A governor's powers regularly include the power to appoint and remove certain officials, and the power to supervise employees. Governors also prepare the budget.

Governors also possess legislative powers, such as the message power and the power to call legislative sessions. Another key legislative power is the veto power.

Section 3 Counties, Towns, Townships, and Special Districts (pp. 643–648) All local governments are creations of the States. Nearly every government in the United States is a local government.

Counties or their equivalent exist in all but two States. Their functions vary depending on the region. Counties also vary in their structures, which generally include county boards, plus elected officials such as sheriffs, clerks, and others.

As a unit of government, towns and townships are found in about half the States. Towns are the major unit of government in New England. Townships are subdivisions of counties, and they tend to have primarily rural functions.

There are many special districts in every State. These units are used to provide a wide variety of services, including education, water and sewage, police and fire, and airport and park services.

Section 4 Cities and Metropolitan Areas (pp. 650–657) Cities exist to provide services to their citizens. As a means of fulfilling that task, city governments take one of three forms: (1) mayor-council, (2) commission, or (3) council-manager. The mayor-council form is the most popular, and it has two major variations—the strong mayor type and the weak mayor type.

Historically, cities often grew up haphazardly. Today, however, many cities have established some sort of planning agency. Zoning is another method cities use to manage growth and change.

Recent population shifts from many cities to the suburbs has left cities with fewer resources to deal with growing problems. One response has been the organization of metropolitan districts to provide services to entire metropolitan areas.

Teaching Suggestions for

CHAPTER-IN-BRIEF

Below are some of the possible uses for the Chapter-in-Brief:

To Preview the Chapter You may want to assign the Chapter-in-Brief page and the Section Outlines from the Teacher's Resource File before beginning Chapter 24 to introduce students to "Key Terms" and concepts in each section.

To Review the Chapter When students have completed Chapter 24, you might want to assign the Chapter-in-Brief as a tool for review, along with the Guided Reading and Reviews from the Teacher's Resource File.

To Omit the Chapter If you wish to skip Chapter 24, it may be helpful to assign the Chapter-in-Brief to students as a review before continuing to another chapter. You may also want to assign the Chapter 24 Test to assess student knowledge of the material. Then specific portions of Chapter 24 may be assigned to students needing reinforcement of "Key Terms" and concepts.

Teacher's Resource File See the Unit 7 File for the following materials:

- Section Outlines, pp. 2, 5, 8, 11.
- Guided Reading and Reviews, pp. 3, 6, 9, 12.
- Chapter 24 Test, pp. 18–20.

ADDITIONAL RESOURCES

The Book of the States, 1990–1991. The Council of State Governments, 1990.

Cronin, Thomas E. *Direct Democracy: The Politics of Initiative, Referendum, and Recall.* Harvard University Press, 1989.

Government in the United States. Sound filmstrip. National Geographic, 1976. Color. 5 parts, 14–17 min.

Grant, Donald R. and Lloyd B. Omdahl. *State and Local Government in America.* Allyn and Bacon, 5th ed., 1987.

Harrigan, John J. *Politics and Policy in the States and Communities.* HarperCollins, 4th ed., 1991.

Levy, John M. *Contemporary Urban Planning.* Prentice Hall, 2nd ed., 1991.

Morlan, Robert L. and David Martin (eds.). *Capitol, Courthouse, and City Hall.* Longman, 7th ed., 1987.

The Municipal Yearbook. International City Management Association, Annual.

Rosenthal, Alan. *Governors and Legislatures: Contending Powers.* CQ Press, 1990.

Answers to CHAPTER 24

Vocabulary and Key Terms

Matching
1. item veto
2. council-manager form
3. commute
4. county
5. commission form

True or False
1. True.
2. False—the correct term is *metropolitan area.*
3. False—the correct term is *strong-mayor government.*
4. False—the correct term is *initiative.*
5. False—the correct term is *parole.*

Word Relationships
1. Item *b* does not belong. Other items represent units of local government, whereas zoning refers to a means of managing development and growth in cities.
2. Item *a* does not belong. Other items refer to a governor's judicial powers, whereas referendum refers to a means by which citizens participate in the lawmaking process.
3. Item *d* does not belong. Other items refer to types of city government. Special district refers to a unit of local government established to manage a specific issue.
4. Item *b* does not belong. Other items refer to legislative processes. Parole is the release of a prisoner before the completion of his or her sentence.

Main Ideas

Section 1
1. Answers could include the following: Most legislatures are bicameral; the upper house is generally smaller than the lower house. Legislatures make laws, and they also possess certain executive, judicial, and constituent powers. State legislatures perform work in committees, and they have presiding officers who help guide the legislatures' efforts. **2.** Answers could include the following: State legislators are elected, and must meet slightly varying qualifications of age, citizenship, and residence. Legislators generally serve two- or four-year terms. Salaries vary greatly, but are generally relatively low. **3.** Direct legislation refers to methods by which voters can take direct part in the lawmaking process—the initiative and referendum.

Section 2
4. Both are the chief executive officers. Both are elected by the people, and most governors serve four-year terms. Both must meet certain qualifications of age, residence, and citizenship, as well as much more difficult political standards. Both have executive, legislative, and judicial powers. **5.** Governors generally do not have the degree of authority within the executive branch that the President enjoys. They must often share that authority with elected executive department officials. **6.** Because they are elected, they are not as responsi-

Chapter Review

Vocabulary and Key Terms

initiative (p. 636)
referendum (p. 636)
item veto (p. 641)
pardon (p. 641)
commute (p. 641)
reprieve (p. 641)
parole (p. 641)
county (p. 643)
parish (p. 643)
borough (p. 643)
township (p. 647)
special district (p. 647)
mayor-council government (p. 651)
strong-mayor government (p. 652)
weak-mayor government (p. 652)
commission form (p. 652)
council-manager form (p. 653)
zoning (p. 655)
metropolitan area (p. 656)

Matching: *Review the key terms in the list above. If you are not sure of a term's meaning, look up the term and review its definition. Choose a term from the list above that best matches each description.*

1. a governor's power to reject certain provisions of measures passed by the legislature
2. a modification of the mayor-council form of government featuring a strong council, a weak mayor, and a manager who is the city's chief administrative officer
3. the power of a governor to reduce the sentence imposed by a court
4. the major unit of local government in most States outside of New England
5. a form of city government consisting of three to nine popularly elected commissioners who form the city council

True or False: *Determine whether each statement is true or false. If it is true, write "true." If it is false, change the underlined word or words to make the statement true.*

1. What are known as counties in most other States are called <u>boroughs</u> in Alaska.
2. Cities and the areas around them are known as <u>special districts</u>.
3. In a <u>mayor-council government</u>, the mayor heads the city administration, can hire and fire many employees, prepares the budget, and generally exercises strong leadership.
4. In a number of States, citizens can propose constitutional amendments or statutes via the <u>referendum</u>.
5. <u>Reprieve</u> means the release of a prisoner before the completion of his or her sentence.

Word Relationships: *Three of the terms in each of the following sets of terms are related. Choose the term that does not belong and explain why it does not belong.*

1. (a) township (b) zoning (c) county (d) parish
2. (a) referendum (b) pardon (c) reprieve (d) commute
3. (a) mayor-council government (b) weak-mayor government (c) commission form (d) special district
4. (a) initiative (b) parole (c) item veto (d) referendum

Main Ideas

Section 1 (pp. 631–637)

1. Briefly describe the notable features of the State legislatures, their organization, and structure.

2. Briefly describe the general characteristics of the job of State legislator.
3. What is direct legislation?

Section 2 (pp. 637–642)

4. In what general ways are State governors similar to the President?
5. In what general ways are most governorships different from the presidency?
6. Why is it significant that many executive department officials are elected?

Section 3 (pp. 643–648)

7. How are local governments created?
8. What are the major forms of local government in the United States?
9. In what ways does the function of counties vary from region to region?
10. What are the most common types of special districts?

Section 4 (pp. 650–657)

11. (a) What are the basic forms of city government? (b) What variations exist of the mayor-council form?
12. (a) Briefly describe how most cities in the United States developed. (b) How have cities responded to growth?
13. Briefly describe the phenomenon and impact of "suburbanitis."
14. What are some of the issues that led to the creation of metropolitan districts?

Critical Thinking

1. **Recognizing Ideologies** (p. 19) Recall that many States have provisions for the initiative or referendum. What does the existence of these methods of direct legislation suggest about the role of the people in government?
2. **Making Comparisons** (p. 19) You read that many governors share executive power with several other elected officials. In your opinion, is effective government served by distributing power among several officials?
3. **Drawing Conclusions** (p. 19) Different regions of the country rely on different means of local government. (a) Explain how differences from region to region might affect the selection of a form of government. (b) How might the form of local government affect the democratic process?

Getting Involved

1. **Writing Your Opinion** You are a legislator in a State that is considering adding initiative and referendum to your State constitution. Write a speech in which you argue in favor of or against the initiative and referendum. Begin by stating your feelings on the topic. Then, write one paragraph for each of the reasons you do or do not support the proposed change. Remember that your speech should aim to persuade other lawmakers to support your position. It should also appeal to the voters. Revise your first draft to ensure that your arguments are clearly presented and politically sound. Correct any errors, then draft a final copy.
2. **Cooperative Activity** Work as a class to create a development plan for a new city. Begin by brainstorming a list of the features an ideal city should seek to develop. Select five items on which everyone agrees. These five items will then be translated into a written city plan. To create this plan, divide the class into five groups, and assign each group one of the items. The groups should then create a written guideline for implementing their items. Ask the class to offer suggestions and improvements for each guideline.
3. **Creating a Poster** Consider what you have read in this chapter about local government. Create a poster that illustrates your understanding of the place of local government in the American political system. Your poster should use a combination of words and pictures to communicate its message.

ble to the governor as they would be if they were appointed. The governor may not remove them at his or her will.

Section 3

7. State governments create every local government. **8.** Counties (and boroughs and parishes), towns and townships, and special districts. **9.** In New England, they are largely judicial districts. From New York and New Jersey west to the Dakotas, Nebraska, and Kansas, they share government functions with townships in rural areas. In the South and West, they are the main unit of rural government. **10.** School districts are the most common type of special district. They exist for many other purposes as well, including water and sewage treatment, electrical service, and more.

Section 4

11. (a) Mayor-council form, commission form, or council-manager form. (b) Mayor-council governments may be of the weak- or strong-mayor type, depending on the extent of the powers granted to the mayor. **12.** (a) Haphazardly, with little or no consideration of how that growth would lead to problems in the future. (b) Many cities actively plan their growth. **13.** This term refers to the growth of suburbs, which depleted many cities of affluent residents and the businesses they supported, leaving behind core cities that are disproportionately poor and in need of costly services. **14.** People living in metropolitan areas realized that it was needlessly expensive to duplicate costly services in many neighboring communities. Thus, they joined together to a create districts that cover the entire metropolitan area.

Critical Thinking

1. Students should note that the initiative and referendum suggest that the people are/ought to be directly involved in the making of public policy. **2.** Students might say that government works more efficiently when a single person has the authority to make decisions by him- or herself; others, that the democratic ideal is best served when authority is distributed among several elected representatives. **3.** (a) Students might suggest that local custom, tradition, and needs; and differences in the distribution of the population and in physical geography might affect the form a government might take. (b) Students may suggest that form of government selected determines whether people will be directly involved, as in a town meeting, or be represented by others.

Getting Involved

1–3. Answers and results will vary, but students should demonstrate an understanding of the concepts in this chapter.

Chapter 25 Resources

In the Teacher's Resource File

The following materials are found in the Teacher's Resource File box.

Instructional Support: Unit 7 File

For the Section
Outlines, pp. 24, 27, 30, 33
Guided Reading and Reviews, pp. 25, 28, 31, 34
Quizzes, pp. 26, 29, 32, 35

For the Chapter
Skill Application, p. 36
Case Study on Contemporary Issues, pp. 37–39
Chapter Test, pp. 40–42
Additional Test Questions, pp. 43–45

Enrichment Support Files

Participatory Government Activities, pp. 28–39
Simulations and Debates: Mock Trial; Jury Deliberation; Educational Reform

Computer Test Bank and Assessment

Transparency Package, pp. 25, 50

Chapter 25 Focus

Introduce the Chapter Tell students that in this chapter they will learn about the functions of State government, including how the State courts operate and the services the State provides. Read with students the Chapter Preview and Objectives.

Writing Activity Direct students' attention to "Describe." Have students identify three services that the State provides. Once they have done so, ask them to write a short paragraph describing how each of these services benefits the citizens of the State. Have students recall what they read in Chapter 16 about the financing of the Federal Government.

Motivate for Learning Direct students' attention to "Predict." Lead students in a discussion of the ways in which a State might go about raising the money it needs to provide services for its citizens.

State and Local Government in Action

Chapter Preview

In 1845 Henry David Thoreau built a sparse, one-room cabin in the lush, green woods surrounding Walden Pond in Concord, Massachusetts. He lived there alone for more than two years, writing his book *Walden, or Life in the Woods.* Over the years, the historic site has been threatened by a growing suburbia—by people using the site for swimming, hiking, and picnicking, for example, and most recently, by the desire of developers to build an office and condominium complex within a stone's throw of the pond. Almost immediately, strong opinions emerged on both sides of the controversy. Naturalists, who wished to conserve the history and beauty of the site, locked horns with those who saw the economic rewards development would bring.

The debate has raged for five years over how this land should be used: development, recreation, or reservation? In this chapter you will see how the many functions of State government play a role in the outcome of these types of questions.

Before you read this chapter:

- **Describe** three services that States provide for their citizens.
- **Predict** how States obtain the revenue to provide these services.

As you read, focus on the main objective for each section. Understand:

1. The many services provided by States for their citizens.
2. The major sources of State and local government revenues.
3. The different kinds of law applied by State courts.
4. The overall organization of the State court systems.

Magruder's American Government: *A Witness to Change* by William A. McClenaghan

When the first edition of *Magruder's American Government* appeared in 1917, the concept of juvenile justice was a relatively new one in American society. As that book reported, "Juvenile Courts to try children have recently been established in many cities. In times past, children were tried by the same court as adults." In fact, *Magruder's* could have added that the trying of children as adults was still the practice in several parts of the country.

Of course, the establishment of juvenile courts only partially solved the problem of providing justice for young people. Below is Frank Magruder's 1917 account of the disposition of a case involving two children who had been involved in a fight: "The mother of the larger boy, being present, was directed to go into an adjoining room and whip her boy in the presence of an officer."

Today, juvenile court systems stress the child's welfare rather than his or her punishment. However, as the *Magruder's* you are reading points out, courts have, in recent years and in extraordinary cases, sought the death penalty for crimes committed by individuals as young as 15 years old.

Participating in Local Government As many teenagers have learned, working on a political campaign requires hard work and energy. Participation has its rewards, however, such as the chance to meet new people and feel a part of the community.

1 Providing Important Services

Find Out:
- What are some of the many services provided by the States?
- What factors help to influence a State's economy and budget?

Key Term:
urbanization

You may have noticed while reading the last chapter and other points in this book how similar the State governments are in form to the Federal Government. For example, each has three branches of government, all but one have bicameral legislatures, each has its own constitution, and so on. Given these similarities, it is easy to overlook the many unique features and functions of your own State government, and the many services it provides to its citizens.

In this section, you will read about State governments and their important role in the day-to-day lives of their citizens.

What State Governments Do

Over the course of this book, you have read many times about the key role of the States in the American federal system. Recall that there was a widespread distrust among the Framers of a strong, central government, and so they created a system in which the States held many important powers. As you read in Chapter 4, Section 1, the Constitution reserves to the States all those powers not expressly delegated to Congress and not specifically denied to the States. These reserved powers are broad—in fact, they are too numerous to list here. In addition, the exercise of these powers varies greatly from one State to the next. Again, that fact

SECTION 1
Providing Important Services

FOCUS

Teacher's Resource File See the Unit 7 File, p. 24, for the Section 1 Outline.

Objectives
- **25.1** Identify some of the many services provided by the States.
- **25.2** Analyze factors that help to influence a State's economy and budget.

Bellringer Activity Invite students to identify geographical features of your State, characteristics of its population, its population patterns, and problems it faces, all of which distinguish it from other States. Ask students to consider how these differences might affect the services that your State government provides to people of the State.

State the Purpose State governments provide many services to their citizens. These services fall into several broad categories that are the same in all States, though each State varies in the specific services it provides. In this section, students will learn some of the categories of services provided by the States.

ABCNEWS INTERACTIVE

The following video segment may be used to highlight aspects of State governments.

POWERS OF THE CONGRESS GUIDEBOOK
Chapter 11: The Federal System, p. 87

Vocabulary

Point out "Key Term" on page 663. Ask students to identify a word they know that is a part of the word *urbanization.* After students have identified the word *urban,* have them look up the word in the dictionary and check its meaning there. LEP

Reading Strategy: Problem Solving

Before students read the section, ask them to imagine that they have just been elected governor of a new State. Have them create a list of the types of services that they think their new government should provide to the people of the State. As students read, have them compare their lists to the content of the section.

Interpreting Charts As students read the chart, ask them to consider why volunteers are so important in the United States. (*Many services are available only if people are willing to give their time to provide them.*)

Caption Answer Because if one is going to give his or her time to an organization, it is important to know about that organization.

INSTRUCT

Explain/Discuss Make sure that students correctly identify five categories of services that States provide—education, public welfare, public safety, highways, and other services.

Have students discuss ways in which States cooperate, or co-administer programs, with the Federal Government. Ask students if they can identify any benefit in having the Federal Government and the States cooperate in providing services. (*The Federal Government has more financial resources and the ability to distribute resources fairly across the nation.*)

Analyze with students the ways in which budgets may vary from State to State. Have students provide examples of differences that they know of between States. Ask students to consider why these differences may affect the kinds of services offered in a State or the way they are provided. For example, how might the State's role in providing and maintaining roadways be different in a largely rural State as opposed to an urban one?

How to Volunteer

1. Choose a volunteer organization that reflects your interests. Start by listing two or three of your interests. Next, do research to match one of your interests with a volunteer organization. You can do this by contacting your local government. Many cities keep directories of local volunteer organizations. Or you might talk with your parents, teachers, guidance counselors, friends, and neighbors. For example, suppose your interests include reading, pursuing a career in health care, and being outdoors. Your research might put you in touch with a tutoring organization, a hospital volunteer program, or a conservation group.

2. Determine how much time you can spend on volunteer work each week or month. Because American society depends heavily on volunteer help, your commitment is essential. Decide before you volunteer how often you can realistically expect to be able to work outside your regular activities. Be sure to let the person who is organizing the volunteer work know from the start what your time commitment is, and remember—even a minimal time commitment will probably mean a great deal to the individual or organization that you are helping.

3. Decide whether you will need a means of transportation. Is the organization or home at which you will volunteer within walking distance? If not, can someone at the organization or your parents give you a ride? Can you make use of public transportation?

Interpreting Charts Read these suggestions on how to be a good volunteer. Why do you think thoughtful research is emphasized in Step 1?

reflects the conscious aim of the Framers and the federal system they created.

Along with the powers reserved to the States come some important responsibilities. Like the Federal Government, State governments generally aim to fulfill the lofty purposes set forward in the preamble to the Constitution; that is, they seek to "establish justice, ensure domestic tranquility, provide for the common defense, promote the general welfare, and secure the blessings of liberty . . . "

You have already read about one of the ways that State governments perform their function. They establish local governments of all types. As you read in Chapter 24, these various local units provide a great many services to those who live within their borders.

States also take a direct role in providing services to the people of the State. The services they provide fall into a number of broad categories.

Education The education of the State's residents is one of the most important responsibilities that the States have taken upon themselves. It is also the most expensive entry in every State budget, representing about one-third of overall State expenditures. The cost of providing education has risen sharply in recent decades and continues to increase year to year.

As you have read, the education of schoolchildren at the primary and secondary levels is, to a significant degree, a responsibility of local governments. As you will read shortly, local taxes, especially property taxes, provide a significant proportion of the funding for primary and secondary schools.

Of course, the States do provide some financial assistance to their local governments for the purposes of education. The level of this aid varies from State to State—and widely. Some States contribute well over half of the cost of educating primary and secondary students. Other States contribute a fraction of that amount. In addition, the States set guidelines in order to maintain high quality in the schools. For example, State laws set minimum qualifications for teachers, establish curricula and screen the quality of educational materials, establish the minimum length for the school year, and much more.

At the college and university levels, the States play a major role. States understand that the ability to provide highly trained college graduates is a key to the success of businesses in the State—and to the decisions of other businesses to locate there. Every State has its own public higher education system, and in some States that system is extensive, including several universities, technical universities, and community colleges. California's system is the largest such system in the nation. The University of California alone has nine campuses, and California State University has 19. In addition, the State has an extensive system of community

SPOTLIGHT ON: Constitutional Issues
The Constitution is silent about the Federal Government's responsibility to promote education, so this field is the responsibility of the States. However, the Federal Government has gone a long way toward encouraging States to support education. In 1862, the Morrill Act granted each State 30,000 acres of public land for each of the State's representatives and senators in Congress. States were to sell the land in order to raise money to create and maintain colleges for agriculture and the mechanical arts. Today, every State and Puerto Rico receives federal funds to help support land-grant universities.

TRF **Teacher's Resource File**
See the Simulations and Debates file, "Educational Reform," for material to support the section.

Interpreting Political Art: **Multicultural Awareness** This mural is painted on the side of a high school in San Francisco. The lamp of learning in the mural represents the high value placed on education by the community.

colleges—colleges that offer two–, rather than four–year, programs of study.

Education at State universities and colleges is generally much less expensive than that obtained at private institutions. On average, tuition at four-year public colleges and universities is about one-fifth that of private four-year institutions. Nevertheless, many State universities, such as the University of California (Berkeley) and the University of Michigan (Ann Arbor), are included among the ranks of the world's finest institutions.

Public Welfare The States take an active role in promoting the health and welfare of their citizens. States pursue this goal by a variety of means.

Most States fund ambitious public health programs. States operate public hospitals and offer direct care to millions of citizens. They immunize children against dangerous childhood diseases—measles and mumps, for example. With the Federal Government, the States administer such programs as Medicaid, Medicare, and Aid to Families with Dependent Children. In addition, States have many similar programs of their own to care for their needy.

Recent soaring costs in the health-care industry have placed a great strain on many States' ability to care for their people. Many governors, State legislators, mayors, and other public officials are among the leading advocates of some sort of national health-insurance plan.

Beyond the direct provision of health care, States do much to ensure the public health and welfare. State efforts to protect the environment are one such example; many enforce stringent antipollution laws. States also inspect factories and other workplaces to protect worker health and safety. And, they license health-care practitioners to ensure quality care. (Licensing also serves another purpose—that of providing revenue to the States.) Again, the list of services in this area goes on and on.

Public Safety The first State police outfit was the legendary Texas Rangers, established in 1835. Today, every State maintains a police force to preserve law and order. A State's police are perhaps most visible as they patrol the State's roads and highways. However, State law-enforcement forces perform many other vital

Interpreting Political Art
Have students study the mural. Ask them to identify some of the symbols used in the painting and what their meanings are. (*Possible answers: The eagle might represent freedom; the people represent youth.*)

Provide Guided Practice
Divide the class into two teams. Choose a volunteer from the first team. If that person can name correctly one of the five categories of State services, have that student call on a student on the other team to give an example. Then have a person from the second team give a category and call on someone on the first team to give an example. Repeat the activity, using reasons why State budgets vary. You may wish to develop a motivational scoring system.

Provide Independent Practice
TRF **Teacher's Resource File**
You may wish to assign Section 1 Guided Reading and Review, Unit 7 File, p. 25, to help students master section objective content.

ACTIVITY: For Gifted Students

Theme: Interdependence Have students study the relationship between their State and their community in providing educational services. Students may explore the following questions: How is educational funding determined by their State? Who serves on their State Board of Education and how are they elected? How does the State influence the practices of their local school district? Students may use news articles, periodicals, interviews, etc., to collect data on these questions. Students may develop recommendations regarding the direction of educational planning for their State and present them in a written report.

Enrichment

Have students look in the telephone book to find State departments that have offices in and near your community. Have students make a written list of several of those departments, with a brief explanation of the primary responsibility of each. (Easy)

OR

TRF **Teacher's Resource File**
See the Unit 7 File, pp. 37–39, for the Case Study on Contemporary Issues for Chapter 25.

Interpreting Graphs Ask students which area's expenses remained about the same from 1985–1988. What possible reasons can they give for that fact? (*Highways; slowdown in construction.*)

Caption Answer The "All Other" category, followed by education.

MONITOR COMPREHENSION

Answers to Section 1 Review
1. The "Key Term" is defined on the following page:
a. urbanization, p. 666
2. Education. **3.** Public health programs, environmental protection, factory inspections, licensing of health-care practitioners, maintenance of a police force, and a corrections system. **4.** The degree to which a State is urbanized; physical geography; and the State government's needs, strengths, and future. **5.** Examples might include an agricultural State requiring services to aid that industry, or an urbanized State requiring complex transportation systems.

CLOSURE

States all provide similar kinds of services to their residents, with variations due largely to differences in geography, population patterns, and economy. As students read the next section they will learn how State governments are financed through their powers of taxation and how State budgets are made.

Assignment Assign Section 2, pp. 667–671, for the next class period.

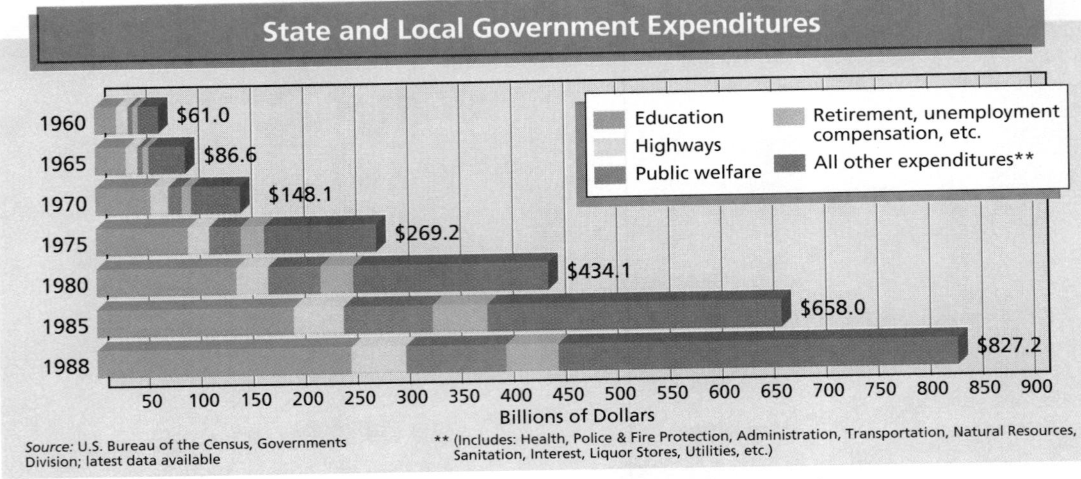

Interpreting Graphs This graph breaks down the various expenditures for which State and local governments are responsible. Over time, which expense has increased the most?

services. Depending on the State, they may function as the primary police force in many rural communities. The State police departments also offer a centralized file for fingerprints and other information, and they provide training and many other services in support of local law-enforcement agencies.

Each State has its own corrections system for those who are convicted of committing State crimes. Thus States operate prisons, penitentiaries, and a variety of other facilities, including reformatories specifically designed for juvenile offenders.

Highways Building and maintaining the roads and highways of the State is an enormous job, and it regularly ranks second or third in each State's budget in terms of spending.

Again, the Federal Government is a partner with the States in the funding of many highways. However, a great many roadways are built solely with State funds, not with money from the Federal Government.

Once the roads are built, States must maintain them. The States also look after the physical safety of the roads and make repairs as needed. You have already read about the role of the State police in ensuring the safety of drivers on the road. In addition, States license drivers to ensure their competence. They set speed limits. And, in many States, the State requires the periodic inspection of vehicles to ensure their safety.

Other Services As noted earlier, the many services that the States provide to their citizens are too numerous to be listed here. You have just read about some of the more obvious ones. But no less important are such functions as the setting aside of public lands for conservation and recreation; the regulation of businesses and the commerce they conduct within the State; the protection of consumers from a variety of dangers and inconveniences; and many, many more.

Differences Among the States

If you have ever traveled around the United States, you know that the variety in the geography and in the people is truly amazing. That variety has made this nation rich in every sense of that word. The variety found among the States also helps to explain some of the differences in what, and how much, the different States provide to their citizens.

One key characteristic that influences State budgets is the degree to which the State is urban-
1.a ized. **Urbanization** is defined as the percentage of the population of a State living in cities of more than 250,000 people or in suburbs of cities

Teacher's Resource File
See the Unit 7 File, p. 26, for the Section 1 Quiz.

Reteach

Have students create a diagram that shows the relationship between the following components: the State government, the State's geography, the State's citizens, and the Federal Government. The diagram should arrange these features to show how they influence one another.

with more than 50,000. The budgets of those States that have a high percentage of their population living in urbanized areas—States such as California and New Jersey—tend to reflect the special challenges of governing urbanized communities. For example, the management of roads and traffic is more complicated in urban areas, and thus requires more money to achieve.

Similarly, less urbanized States, such as Vermont and West Virginia, have budgets that reflect their own special needs.

Another factor influencing State budgets is the physical geography of a State. Again, a look at the map on page 712 will confirm what you already know: Each State is different in its size, shape, and physical features. Such issues as location relative to major national and world markets, energy supplies, natural resources, and agricultural resources help shape the State's economy and its budget. Thus, each State government considers its own needs, its own strengths, and its own future as it produces its operating plans. These budgets can differ widely in their size and shape, depending in large part on where that State is located.

Section 1 Review

1. **Define:** urbanization
2. In general, what is the most expensive item in the budgets of the States?
3. What are some of the ways in which States try to protect their citizens' health, welfare, and safety?
4. What are three factors that can influence the shape of an individual State's budget and the services it provides?

Critical Thinking

5. **Recognizing Cause and Effect** (p. 19) Briefly explain how the unique physical features of a State might influence the shaping of a State's budget and the services it provides.

★

[1]Remember, the power to tax is also limited by any number of practical considerations—important economic and political factors in each State.

2 Financing State Government

Find Out:

- What are the powers of the State and local governments to tax?
- What are the different types of State and local revenue?
- What is the State budget and how is it made?

Key Terms:

sales tax, regressive tax, income tax, progressive tax, property tax, assessment, inheritance tax, estate tax

You know by now that government is an expensive proposition, and it is becoming more so from year to year. Altogether, the 50 States and their thousands of local governments now take in and spend more than one trillion dollars a year.

In this section, you will read about how the State and local governments get their money, and how they decide how to spend it.

Raising Revenue at the State and Local Level

This year the States will take in some $400 billion in taxes, and all their local units will collect more than $200 billion. In addition, the 50 States and their local governments will also receive $400 billion or so from a number of nontax sources. Recall that taxes are charges made to raise money for public purposes.

The power to tax is one of the major powers reserved to each of the States. In the strictly legal sense, then, it is limited only by those restrictions imposed by the Federal Constitution and by its own fundamental law.[1]

Federal Limitations The Federal Constitution places only a few restrictions on State and local taxing powers.

INTERSTATE AND FOREIGN COMMERCE As you have already seen, the Constitution forbids the States the power to "lay any imposts or

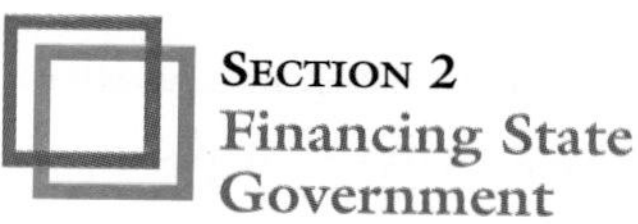

SECTION 2
Financing State Government

FOCUS

Teacher's Resource File See the Unit 7 File, p. 27, for the Section 2 Outline.

Objectives

25.3 Describe the powers of the State and local governments to tax.
25.4 Identify the different types of State revenue and local revenue.
25.5 Explain what the State budget is and how it is made.

Bellringer Activity Before you begin the section, ask students to make guesses about how much it costs per student to operate a school, including classes, sports, music, and other activities. After students have made their guesses, tell them that as a national average, it costs about $5,300 per student per year.

State the Purpose States require a great deal of money to provide all the services they provide. The States have broad powers to tax, yet those powers are limited by the Constitution, by the States' own laws and constitutions, and by practical considerations. In Section 2, students will learn how the States raise revenue and how they make and execute budgets.

ABCNEWS INTERACTIVE

The following video segment may be used to highlight aspects of State revenues and budgeting.

POWERS OF THE CONGRESS GUIDEBOOK
Chapter 21: Collecting Revenues, p. 25

Vocabulary

Point out "Key Terms" on page 667 to the students. Before students read the section, have students predict the meaning of the terms *sales tax, income tax, property tax,* and *inheritance tax.* Have students check their definitions against those given in the text.

Reading Strategy: Predicting Content

As a preparation for reading, have students read the boldfaced headings in this section. Tell students that these headings form an outline of the content in the section. Then have students predict the content of the section based on their preview of the section headings. As they read, students should compare their predictions with the section content.

INSTRUCT

Discuss/Analyze Help students understand the restrictions on States' power to tax. Ask students to discuss the role of politics in limiting the power of a State government to raise taxes. How does the fact that the Federal Government taxes individuals affect the power of the States to do so? (*Citizens may feel that they pay enough to the Federal Government and may politically punish State officials who seek to raise taxes.*)

Discuss with students the major sources of State and local revenue. Do students think that States should engage in more business activities or permit gambling and other revenue-raising activities to lower their reliance on taxes? (*No: Such activities are not beneficial to good government or a healthy society. Yes: Whatever a government can do to obtain revenue and lower taxes is positive.*) What about borrowing more? Ask students to consider why there are so many types of taxes. (*So no one activity or item is taxed at too high a rate; so that the burden of taxation is spread as thinly as possible across society.*) Have students explain their understanding of progressive and regressive taxes. Which, in their opinion, is the most fair?

Have students explain the importance of a State budget and what an executive budget is. (*A budget represents the political decisions of a government as to how it will spend its money. The executive budget is one prepared by the governor, who has the power to administer the money appropriated by the legislature.*)

duties on imports or exports" and "any duty of tonnage."[2] In effect, the States are here prohibited from taxing interstate and foreign commerce. The Supreme Court has often held that because the Constitution gives to Congress the power to regulate that trade, the States are generally forbidden to do so.

THE NATIONAL GOVERNMENT AND ITS AGENCIES Ever since the Supreme Court's decision in *McCulloch* v. *Maryland*, 1819, the States have been forbidden to tax the Federal Government or any of its agencies or functions. They are forbidden to do so because, as Chief Justice Marshall put it in *McCulloch*: "The power to tax involves the power to destroy."

THE 14TH AMENDMENT The Due Process and Equal Protection clauses place limits on the power to tax at the State and local levels. Essentially, the Due Process Clause requires that taxes be (1) imposed and administered fairly, (2) not so heavy as to actually confiscate property, and (3) imposed only for public purposes.

The Equal Protection Clause forbids the making of unreasonable classifications for taxing purposes such as those based on race, religion, nationality, political party membership, or similarly unreasonable factors.

State Constitutional Limitations Each State's constitution limits the taxing powers of that State and also those of its local governments. For example, most State constitutions exempt the properties of churches, private schools, museums, cemeteries, and the like from taxation. Many set maximum tax rates, and some prohibit certain kinds of taxes.

Types of State and Local Revenue

Beyond the limits just noted, a State can levy taxes as it chooses. The legislature decides what taxes the State will levy, and at what rates. It also decides what taxes the local units can levy.[3]

The Sales Tax The sales tax is the most productive source of income among the 50 States today. It accounts for just about a third of all tax monies the States collect each year.

1.a A **sales tax** is a tax placed on the sale of various commodities; it is paid by the purchaser. It may be either general or selective in form. A general sales tax is one applied to the sale of most commodities. A selective sales tax is one placed only on the sale of certain commodities, such as cigarettes, liquor, or gasoline.

Today, 45 States levy a general sales tax.[4] The rates range among the States from a low of 3 percent in Colorado, North Carolina, and Wyoming to a high of 8 percent in Connecticut.

Every State now levies a selective sales tax on gasoline and other motor fuels, alcoholic beverages, insurance policies, and cigarettes. Most States also have additional selective sales taxes.

There are two major reasons why the sales tax is so widely used. First, it is relatively easy to collect. Second, it is a fairly dependable revenue producer. But notice that it is a **regressive**
1.b **tax**—one that is the same for all people and not geared to the ability to pay. Therefore, it falls most heavily on those with lower incomes.

1.c **The Income Tax** The **income tax**, levied on the income of individuals and/or corporations, yields almost a third of State tax revenues today. Forty-three States levy an individual income tax; 45 have some form of corporate income tax.[5]

The individual income tax is usually a **pro-**
1.d **gressive tax**—that is, the higher the income, the higher the tax rate. The rates vary among the States, from 1 or 2 percent on lower incomes in most States to 10 percent or more on the highest incomes in some States.

The corporate income tax rates are most often uniform, a certain fixed percentage of income. Only a few States set the rates on a graduated—progressive—basis. The progressive

[2] Article I, Section 10, Clauses 2 and 3.

[3] A State constitution sometimes grants certain taxing powers directly to local governments, but this is not at all common.

[4] All except Alaska, Delaware, Montana, New Hampshire, and Oregon. Each of these States does impose various selective sales taxes, however.

[5] Nevada, South Dakota, Texas, Washington, and Wyoming levy neither type of income tax. Alaska and Florida impose only the corporate tax.

income tax is held by many to be the fairest form of taxation, especially because it may be closely geared to the ability to pay.

The Property Tax The **property tax** is the 1.e chief source of income for local governments today. It accounts for approximately 80 percent of all of their tax receipts.

A government levies the property tax on (1) real property—land, buildings, and improvements that go with the property if sold, or (2) personal property—either tangible or intangible. Tangible personal property includes all movable wealth that is visible and the value of which can be easily assessed, such as television sets, automobiles, and air conditioners. Examples of intangible personal property include such things as stocks, bonds, mortgages and bank accounts. Because one can hide intangibles from the tax assessor, many States do not tax them. In others, they are taxed at a lower rate than tangible personal property.

The process of determining the value of the property to be taxed is known as **assessment**. 1.f The task is usually carried out by an elected county, township, or city assessor.

Several arguments support the property tax. Because government protects property—and often enhances its value—property can properly be required to contribute to the support of government. It is also a dependable source of revenue.

Similarly, there are some major criticisms of the property tax. For one, the tax is not geared to the ability to pay. Although the amount of real property one owns may have been a fair measure of one's wealth in earlier history, it is not today. Second, it is all but impossible to assess all taxable property on a fair and equal basis.

Inheritance or Estate Taxes Every State except Nevada levies inheritance or estate taxes, so-called "death taxes." An **inheritance tax** is 1.g one levied on the beneficiary's share of an estate, and an **estate tax** is one levied directly 1.h on the full estate itself.

Business Taxes A wide variety of business taxes, in addition to the corporate income tax, are important sources of revenue in most States.

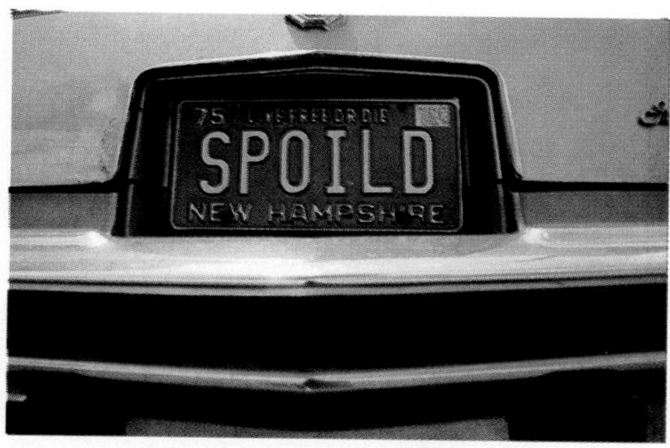

▲ **Live Free or Die** New Hampshire's State motto is reflected in the absence of a sales tax in that State.

Over half the States impose severance taxes. These are taxes placed on the removal of such natural resources as timber, oil, gas, minerals, and fish from the land or water.

Every State has several different license taxes. These are fees that permit persons to engage in a business, occupation, or activity that is otherwise unlawful. All States require that corporations be licensed to do business in the State. Certain kinds of businesses—chain stores, amusement parks, bars and taverns, and transportation lines—must also have an additional license to operate. Then, too, most or all States require the licensing of doctors, lawyers, dentists, morticians, barbers, hairdressers, plumbers, engineers, electricians, and many others.

Nearly half the States have levies known as documentary and stock transfer taxes. These are charges made on the recording, registering, and transfer of such documents as mortgages, deeds, and securities. Some States also impose capital stock taxes, which are levied on the total assessed value of the shares of stock issued by a business concern.

Other Taxes State and/or local governments impose a number of other taxes. More than half the States levy amusement taxes—usually on the tickets of admission to theaters, sports events, circuses, and the like. Payroll taxes produce huge sums—in all, well over $100 billion among the States today. But money produced by these taxes is held in trust

Provide Guided Practice Ask students to work in small teams to create a flowchart showing the process by which State governments raise money and then prepare a budget for the spending of those revenues. The chart should indicate the many sources of revenue, including various types of taxes, borrowing, and other sources.

Provide Independent Practice

TRF **Teacher's Resource File** You may wish to assign Section 2 Guided Reading and Review, Unit 7 File, p. 28, to help students master section objective content.

Enrichment

Have students create a graph that shows their State's major sources of revenue and how much income the State raises from each source. (Average)

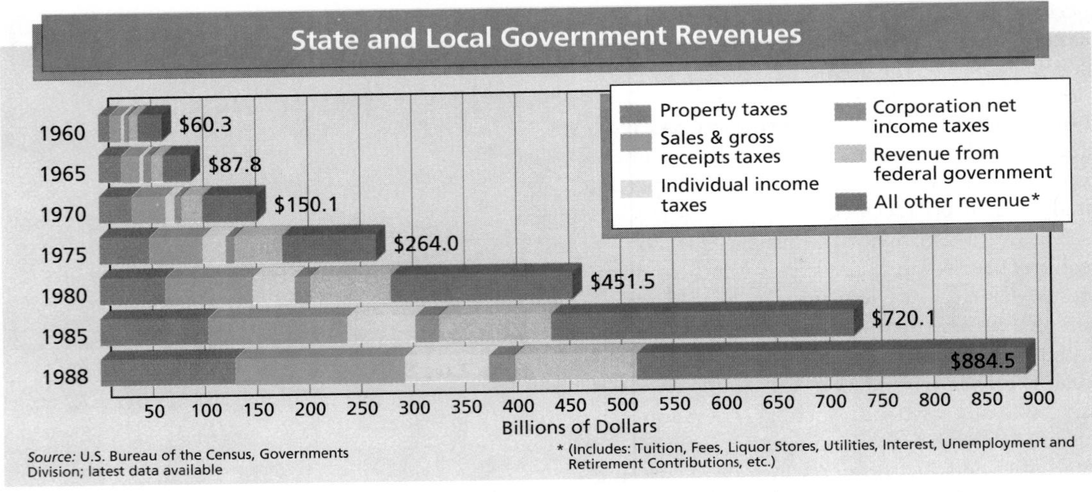

Interpreting Graphs After examining the growth of State and local government finances, compare this graph to the graph on page 666. In which years have expenditures of State and local governments exceeded revenues?

funds for such social welfare programs as unemployment compensation, accident insurance, and retirement programs.

All States levy license taxes for other than business purposes too, such as those for motor vehicles and motor vehicle operators, and hunting, fishing, and marriage licenses.

Nontax Receipts

State and local governments now take in some $400 billion a year from a wide range of nontax sources. A large portion of that huge amount comes from the Federal Government each year.

Each of the States and many of their local governments make money from a number of different publicly operated business enterprises. Toll bridges and toll roads are found in many parts of the country; several States are in the ferry business. North Dakota markets a flour sold under the brand-name "Dakota-Maid" and is also in the commercial banking business. California operates a short railway line in San Francisco.

Eighteen States are in the liquor-dispensing business, selling it through State-operated stores.[6] Many cities own and operate their water, electric power, and bus transportation systems.

Other nontax sources include court fines, the sale or leasing of public lands, interest from such sources as loans, investments, and late tax payments, and much else.

Several States have relaxed their once-strict antigambling laws, hoping to attract dollars, jobs, and tourists. State-run lotteries now make close to $8 billion a year for 32 States.[7]

Borrowing

States and their local governments often must borrow money for unusually large undertakings, such as public buildings or toll bridges and

[6]Alabama, Idaho, Iowa, Maine, Michigan, Mississippi, Montana, New Hampshire, North Carolina, Ohio, Oregon, Pennsylvania, Utah, Vermont, Virginia, Washington, West Virginia, Wyoming. North Carolina's stores are operated by the counties; Wyoming's liquor monopoly operates only at the wholesale level.

[7]Arizona, California, Colorado, Connecticut, Delaware, Florida, Idaho, Illinois, Indiana, Iowa, Kansas, Kentucky, Maine, Maryland, Massachusetts, Michigan, Minnesota, Missouri, Montana, New Hampshire, New Jersey, New York, Ohio, Oregon, Pennsylvania, Rhode Island, South Dakota, Vermont, Virginia, Washington, West Virginia, Wisconsin.

Interpreting Graphs As students look at the graph, ask them which source of revenue brings in the most money. (*Sales taxes.*) Ask students whether or not they think this places too big a burden on consumers. (*Some may say yes, sales taxes make it more expensive to purchase goods, and, therefore, put a financial burden on less wealthy consumers. Others may say that sales taxes are a way to spread the tax burden among more people.*)

Caption Answer 1960 and 1975.

Monitor Comprehension

Answers to Section 2 Review 1. "Key Terms" are defined on the following pages:

- **a.** sales tax, p. 668
- **b.** regressive tax, p. 668
- **c.** income tax, p. 668
- **d.** progressive tax, p. 668
- **e.** property tax, p. 669
- **f.** assessment, p. 669
- **g.** inheritance tax, p. 669
- **h.** estate tax, p. 669

2. States cannot levy taxes on imports, exports, and any duty of tonnage. States cannot tax the Federal Government or any of its agencies or functions. Taxes must be fair and may be imposed only for public purposes. **3.** Sales, income, property, inheritance, and estate taxes. **4.** Income, severance, license, documentary, and stock transfer taxes. **5.** Nontax receipts, such as business activities and lotteries, and borrowing. **6.** Answers will vary. Students should defend their arguments logically.

Spotlight on: Economics

Today, many States are operating flourishing and lucrative lottery businesses. In New York, for example, revenue from the lottery was just short of one billion dollars in both 1990 and 1991. This was a marked increase over recent years, and it represented a much-needed supply of revenues for a State struggling with severe budgetary problems. In spite of the success of lotteries at raising revenue for State programs, a number of States are troubled by the concept of legalized, government-sponsored gambling, and so refuse to introduce lotteries.

highways, that cannot be paid for out of current income. That borrowing is most often done by issuing bonds, much as the Federal Government does. Generally, State and local bonds are fairly easy to market because the interest from them is not taxed by any level of government.

Many State and local governments have, in times past, had to default on their debts. Thus, most State constitutions now place detailed limits on the power to borrow.

The State Budget

In Chapter 16, Section 3, you read that a budget is a financial plan, a plan for the control and use of public money, personnel, and property. It is also a political document, a statement  of public policy.

Forty-seven States have now adopted the executive budget. That is, they have given the governor two vital powers: (1) the power to prepare the State budget, and (2) the authority to administer the funds the legislature has appropriated. In most States the governor has the help of a budget agency, appointed by and answering to the governor.[8]

The basic steps in the budget process are much the same at the State and local levels as they are at the federal level:

1. Each agency prepares estimates of its needs and expenditures in the upcoming fiscal period.
2. Those estimates are reviewed by an executive budget agency.
3. The revised estimates and supporting information are brought together in a budget for the governor to present to the legislature.
4. The budget is considered, the necessary funds are appropriated, and any necessary revenue measures are passed by the legislature.
5. The execution of the budget approved by the legislature is supervised by the governor.
6. The execution of the budget is given an independent check, the postaudit.

[8]Responsibility for the preparation of the budget is shared by the governor and the legislature in the other three States: Mississippi, South Carolina, and Texas.

VOICES on Government

On Budget Reductions

Sharon Pratt Dixon,
mayor of Washington, D.C.

“Reducing the budget will not be easy, but the ‘Let's Have It All’ decade of the 1980s is over. A lot of jurisdictions in this country are going through a ‘downsizing’ process. . . . It is time for a strong dose of financial discipline and an honest deal for our citizens. Enough is enough. Necessity may have to be the mother of invention. One way or another, this government is going to provide a dollar's worth of services for a dollar's worth of taxes. We can accept nothing less.”

Section 2 Review

1. Define: sales tax, regressive tax, income tax, progressive tax, property tax, assessment, inheritance tax, estate tax

2. What restrictions does the Federal Constitution place on the taxing powers of the States?

3. What are the main forms of State taxes to which individuals are subject?

4. What are the main State taxes to which businesses are subject?

5. What are the other sources of State revenue?

Critical Thinking

6. Expressing Problems Clearly (p. 19) In your opinion, should a tax be applied at the same rate to all people, or should those who have more be expected to pay at a higher rate?

★

Teacher's Resource File See the Unit 7 File, p. 29, for the Section 2 Quiz.

Closure

Remind students that States and local units raise money through taxation and nontax sources of revenue. States and local units are limited in their ability to tax by several factors. The States decide how to spend their revenue in their budgets, which are generally prepared by the governor.

As students read the next section they will learn the kinds of law applied in the State court systems, and how State courts operate.

Assignment Assign Section 3, pp. 672–674, for the next class period.

Activity: Teaching Heterogeneous Groups

Have students work in groups to create circle, or pie, graphs that illustrate (1) the sources of your State's revenues and (2) the expenditures for your particular locality. Students should refer to Section 1 to review some of the services generally provided by State governments and to Section 2 to review different types of State and local revenues. They should then consult the *Government Resources Handbook* on page 690 or their State, city, town, or county treasurer's office to find out the specific sources of revenue for their State and how those revenues are spent.

Reteach

Have students suppose they are the governors of States with executive budgets. Tell the students to write letters to their biggest supporters in the legislature, explaining the budget process and where the money is to come from.

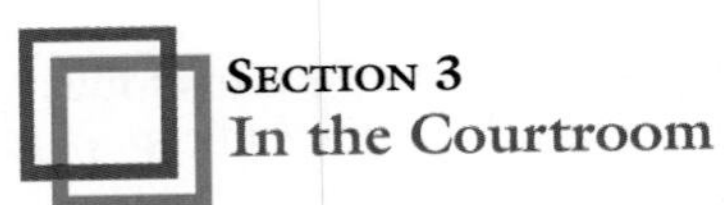

SECTION 3
In the Courtroom

FOCUS

Teacher's Resource File
See the Unit 7 File, p. 30, for the Section 3 Outline.

Objectives
25.6 Identify the different kinds of law applied in State courts.
25.7 Explain what a grand jury is and how it functions.
25.8 Explain what a petit jury is and how it functions.

Bellringer Activity Ask students if they know the meaning of the word *peers.* (*A person of the same rank, value, ability, etc.*) Ask students why they think that the court cases in their State are often decided by "juries of one's peers."

State the Purpose State courts are responsible for protecting individual rights, for determining the innocence or guilt of persons accused of crimes, deciding civil disputes, and more. Much of the work of State courts is performed by juries. In Section 3, students will learn about the activities of their State courts.

ABCNEWS INTERACTIVE
The following video segment may be used to highlight aspects of the State court systems.

POWERS OF THE SUPREME COURT GUIDEBOOK
Chapter 20: Judicial Review, p. 83

See also Enrichment Questions and Activities beginning on page 161.

3 In the Courtroom

Find Out:

- What kinds of law are applied in State courts?
- What are the functions of a grand jury?
- What is a petit jury and how does it function?

Key Terms:
common law, precedent, criminal law, civil law, petit jury

The principal function of the State courts is to decide disputes between private persons and between private persons and government. And, because nearly all of them can exercise the power of judicial review, they act as potent checks on the conduct of all of the other agencies of both State and local government.

In this section, you will read about the laws that are applied in State courts and about one of the ways those courts decide matters of the law.

Kinds of Law Applied in State Courts

The law—the code of conduct by which society is governed—is made up of several different forms,[9] including:

CONSTITUTIONAL LAW As you have read, the highest form of law in this country is based on the provisions of the United States Constitution and the State constitution, and judicial interpretations of them.

STATUTORY LAW This form of law consists of the law—statutes—enacted by legislative bodies, including the United States Congress, the State legislature, the people (through the initiative or referendum), and city councils and other local legislative bodies.

ADMINISTRATIVE LAW This form of law is composed of the rules, orders, and regulations that are issued by federal, State, or local executive officers, acting under proper constitutional and/or statutory authority.

COMMON LAW The common law makes up a large part of the law of each State except
1.a Louisiana.[10] **Common law** is unwritten, judge-made law that has developed over centuries from those generally accepted ideas of right and wrong that have gained judicial recognition. State courts apply common law except when it is in conflict with written law.

The common law originated in England. It
1.b developed as judges followed **precedent** and abided by earlier court decisions—that is, as they applied the rule of *stare decisis,* "let the decision stand."[11] Most legal disputes in American courts are fought out very largely over the application of precedents.

EQUITY This is a branch of the law that supplements common law. Whereas the common law applies to or provides a remedy for matters *after* they have happened, equity seeks to stop wrongs before they occur.

To illustrate this point, suppose your neighbors plan to add a room to their house. You think that a part of the planned addition will be on your land, and you know that it will destroy your rose garden. You can prevent the construction by getting an injunction.

Criminal and Civil Law

You have probably heard reference to criminal law and civil law. These are two other bases by which the law is commonly classified.

Criminal Law That portion of the law that defines public wrongs—offenses against the

[9]In its overall sense, the term *law* may be defined as the whole body of "rules and principles of conduct which the governing power in a community recognizes as those which it will enforce or sanction, and according to which it will regulate, limit, or protect the conduct of its members"; *Bouvier's Law Dictionary,* 3rd revision, vol. II, pp. 1875–76.

[10]Because of the early French influence, Louisiana's legal system is largely based on French legal concepts, derived from Roman law. The common law has worked its way into Louisiana law, however.

[11]American courts generally follow the rule. A decision, once made, becomes a precedent—a guide to be followed in all later, similar cases, unless compelling reasons call for its abandonment and the setting of a new precedent.

Reading Strategy: Question Writing
As a preparation for reading, have students read each of the main boldfaced headings in the section. Then have students convert each of these headings into a question. As students read the section, have them write down answers to the questions they have written.

Vocabulary
Direct students' attention to "Key Terms" on page 672. Have students carefully note the difference between the meaning of the terms *common law, civil law,* and *criminal law.*

public order—and provides for their punishment is the **criminal law**. A criminal case is one 1.c brought by the State against a person accused of committing a crime. The State as the prosecution is always a party in a criminal case.

Crimes are of two kinds: felonies and misdemeanors. A felony is the greater crime and may be punished by a heavy fine and/or imprisonment or even death. A misdemeanor is the lesser offense, punishable by a small fine and/or a short jail term.

Civil Law The **civil law** is that portion of the 1.d law relating to human conduct, to disputes between private parties, and to disputes between private parties and government not covered by criminal law. Civil cases in the legal system are usually referred to as suits and often lead to the award of money or a fine. Civil law can involve a wide range of issues, including divorce and custody disputes, torts—private wrongs against a person or property—and contracts.

The Jury System

A jury is a body of persons selected according to law who hear evidence and decide questions of fact in a court case. There are two basic types of juries in the American legal system: (1) the grand jury and (2) the petit jury.

The grand jury is used only in criminal proceedings. The petit jury is the trial jury, and it is used in both civil and criminal cases.

The Grand Jury The grand jury has from six to 23 persons, depending on the State. Where larger juries are used, generally at least 12 jurors must agree that an accused person is probably guilty before a formal accusation is made. Similarly, with smaller juries, an extraordinary majority is needed to indict, or bring the formal charge.

When a grand jury is impaneled, or selected, the judge instructs the jurors to find a true bill of indictment against any and all persons whom the prosecuting attorney brings to their attention and who they think are probably guilty. The judge also instructs them to bring a presentment, or accusation, against any persons whom they, of their own knowledge, believe have violated the State's criminal laws.

"Your honor, the jury finds the defendant weakly developed as a central character, overshadowed by the principal witness, unconvincingly portrayed as a victim of society, and guilty as charged."

Interpreting Political Cartoons The drama of the courtroom has sometimes been portrayed in movies and books. What does this cartoon say about the potential drama in the justice system?

The grand jury meets in secret. To preside over its sessions, either the judge appoints or the jurors select one of their number to serve as the foreman or -woman. The prosecuting attorney presents witnesses and evidence against persons suspected of crime. The jurors may question those witnesses and summon others to testify against a suspect.

After receiving the evidence and hearing witnesses, the grand jury deliberates, with only the jurors themselves present. With the completion of their review, they move to the courtroom where their report, including any indictments they may have returned, is read in their presence.

The grand jury is expensive, cumbersome, and time-consuming. Hence, most of the States today depend more heavily on a much simpler process of accusation: the information.

An information is a formal charge filed by the prosecutor, without the action of a grand jury. The information is now used for most minor offenses. More than half the States now use it in most of the more serious cases, as well. The use

Interpreting Political Cartoons Ask students to suggest how movies and television present courtroom scenes as drama and entertainment.

Caption Answer The cartoon portrays the jury as criticizing the trial as if it were a novel or movie.

INSTRUCT

Explain/Analyze Help students to understand the different kinds of law applied in the State courts. Ask students to think of reasons why common law plays such a large part of the law of each State. (*Represents centuries of legal tradition.*)

Ask students to think of examples of criminal and civil law. (*A civil dispute might include a custody battle; a criminal case would include murder, robbery, or other crimes.*)

Have students analyze the strengths and weaknesses of the grand and petit jury. Discuss an alternative to the jury system and what the dangers might be in such a system.

Provide Guided Practice Write the following words on the blackboard: *The law* and *the jury system*. Ask students to volunteer information about the section to place in each column. Elicit responses about the many kinds of law heard in State courts and about grand juries and petit juries.

Provide Independent Practice

TRF **Teacher's Resource File** You may wish to assign Section 3 Guided Reading and Review, Unit 7 File, p. 31, to help students master section objective content.

SPOTLIGHT ON: Roots of Democracy

Prior to the year 1100, law in England consisted of customary law and canon law. After the conquest of England in 1066, the Normans introduced new legal procedures. William the Conqueror (1027-1087) began the development of common law by attempting to separate church and secular authority and by strengthening the feudal courts. Under Henry I (1068–1135) there was established a system of writs. The writs were issued by a sheriff as a summons to appear before the curia, the king's justices, to answer questions concerning the alleged wrong-doing. These appearances before the curia were not organized under customary law as was usual for the time, but were driven by a belief in a need for legal equity.

Eventually, the frequent use of the royal court led to the creation of a separate Court of Common Pleas (c. 1190). By 1297 the law of the royal courts had become known as "common law."

Enrichment

Have students work in small groups to create fictional court cases based on different kinds of law. Have each group describe its case, outline the arguments, and explain the process and bases on which the case was decided. (Challenging)

Monitor Comprehension

Answers to Section 3 Review
1. "Key Terms" are defined on the following pages:
a. common law, p. 672
b. precedent, p. 672
c. criminal law, p. 673
d. civil law, p. 673
e. petit jury, p. 674
2. Possible answers: constitutional, statutory, administrative, common, equity, civil, and criminal law. **3.** (a) It developed from generally accepted ideas of right and wrong. (b) Judges followed precedent and abided by earlier court decisions. **4.** To determine whether there is enough evidence against a person to justify a formal accusation. **5.** (a) A formal charge against a person brought to the grand jury's attention by a prosecutor. (b) An accusation based on a grand jury's own knowledge. (c) A formal charge filed by the prosecutor. **6.** Answers will vary. Students may suggest that an accused person is better off with the decision of a whole jury than the decision of one judge.

Closure

Remind students that State courts decide cases based on many kinds of laws. States use the jury system, including grand juries and petit juries, to hear and decide many cases.

In Section 4, students will learn how the State court systems are organized and how judges are selected.

Assignment Assign Section 4, pp. 676–681, for the next class period.

of the information has much to recommend it. It is far less costly and time-consuming. Then, too, since grand juries most often follow the prosecutor's recommendations, many argue that a grand jury is really unnecessary.

The Petit Jury As you have seen, the **petit**
1.e **jury** is the trial jury. It hears the evidence in a case and decides the disputed facts. The number of trial jurors may vary. As it developed in England, the jury consisted of "12 men good and true." Although 12 is still the usual number, a lesser number, often six, now fills jury boxes in several States. Today, women everywhere are qualified to serve on juries.

In over a third of the States, jury verdicts need not be unanimous in civil and minor criminal cases. Rather, some extraordinary majority is needed. If a jury cannot agree on a verdict (a so-called hung jury), either another trial with a new jury takes place or the matter is dropped.

Misdemeanor cases and civil proceedings in which only minor sums are involved are often heard without a jury. In several States even the most serious of crimes may be heard without a jury—if the accused, fully informed of his or her rights, waives the right to trial by jury.

Selection of Jurors Jurors are picked in more or less the same way in most States. Periodically, some county official[12] or special jury commissioners prepare a list of persons eligible for jury service. Depending on the State, the lists are drawn from the poll books, the county tax rolls, motor vehicle and drivers license lists, and even public utility and telephone company billings.

The sheriff serves each person with a court order, a writ of *venire facias,* meaning "you must come." Persons under 18 and those over 70 years of age, illiterates, the ill, and criminals are commonly excluded. In many States those in occupations vital to the public interest—physicians, druggists, teachers, firefighters, and the like—are also excused.

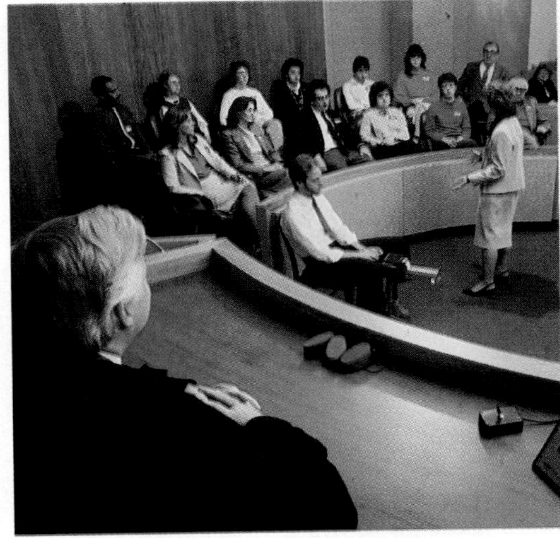

Trial by Jury Jurors have decided the guilt or innocence of their peers since ancient times. In the United States, jury duty is an obligation of citizenship.

As with the grand jury, the States are moving away from the use of the trial jury. The greater time and cost of jury trials are leading reasons. The competence of the average jury and the impulses that may lead it to a verdict are often questioned, as well.

Section 3 Review

1. Define: common law, precedent, criminal law, civil law, petit jury
2. What are four kinds of law that State courts apply?
3. (a) How did common law originate? (b) What makes precedents a key part of common law?
4. What is the primary duty of a grand jury?
5. (a) What is an indictment? (b) A presentment? (c) An information?

Critical Thinking

6. Drawing Conclusions (p. 19) In your opinion, would justice be better served by relying more or less on juries? Explain your answer.

★

[12] Most often it is the clerk of the court, the sheriff, or the county governing body, and sometimes the presiding judge, and in New England, officers of the town.

Activity: Cooperative Learning

Time: Two periods **Activity:** Design a game illustrating how petit juries work. **Grouping:** Groups of six or more **Purpose:** Have students create and play a game of "jury." Each group should create a list of evidence related to an imaginary crime committed by an imaginary suspect. After each team has completed its list, have teams exchange lists. Each team will then act as a jury to reach a verdict in another team's case. **Roles:** Assign the following roles: recorder; jury foreperson, jury members. **Outcome:** Have each jury deliberate over the evidence and reach a unanimous verdict. Have each jury discuss its verdict with the team that created the evidence.

Teacher's Resource File
See the Unit 7 File, p. 32, for the Section 3 Quiz.

Reteach

Ask students to write a short guide for jurors in State courts. The guide should discuss the kinds of law that the jurors might expect to be involved in court cases and what their possible roles will be as members of a grand or petit jury.

What You Can Do

Volunteering for Community Service

When you think of citizenship participation, what comes to mind? The first thing you might think of is voting. While there is no doubt that casting a ballot ranks as an important means of citizenship participation, there is another way to participate as a citizen—and you don't need to be of voting age. Volunteering for community service is a means of citizenship participation available to everyone, whether or not they are eligible to vote.

There are countless ways to work as a community volunteer. Volunteers work in hospitals, schools, nursing homes, and shelters, just to name a few places. They visit shut-ins, build playground equipment, read books to children at libraries—the list goes on and on. The citizenship chart on page 664 outlines steps that help you decide where and how to volunteer. For now, read on to learn about a high school student whose volunteer work made a difference in Oak Park, Illinois.

Whitney Heidenrich, a student at Oak Park and River Forest High School, decided to help children who are victims of abuse, neglect, or abandonment. Through her school service club, she became a volunteer "big sister" at the Hephzibah Children's Association Shelter in Oak Park. The shelter offers temporary care to area children suffering from abuse, neglect, or abandonment; tries to reunite children with their parents; or, in severe cases, helps them find foster or adopted families. After completing specialized training, Whitney and 40 other students made a commitment to spend at least one hour a week with a child at the shelter.

Whitney was paired up with a ten-year-old girl who described herself this way: "Some kids don't have families to care for them and give them clothes and things to eat. One of them is me." After her mother died, the girl's father remarried. Her father and stepmother, she said, "just didn't want me." While the shelter worked to find her a new family, she counted on regular visits from 17-year-old Whitney.

Whether it's helping with homework, reading books, baking cookies, playing video games, or just talking quietly together, Hephzibah's volunteer siblings are an important part of the lives of their little "brothers" and "sisters." Whitney said this about the arrangement: "I feel I'm someone she can talk to. I think she needs that. It's just that much more attention she gets."

The volunteer siblings think they get as much from the program as they give. Every month, they meet with staff members of the shelter to discuss treatment methods for child abuse. And, like Whitney, they get the satisfaction that comes from knowing their efforts make a difference.

Getting Involved

1. Identify a need in your community similar to the one addressed in this case. You might start by doing research at your local library or by calling your local government to inquire about children's shelters. Or, identify any need in your community that might benefit from volunteer service.

2. Formulate a plan for how you might organize volunteer efforts to help remedy this problem and identify resources which could be used in your plan.

3. Predict any problems you might encounter in implementing your plan. How might you solve them in order to carry out your plan?

TEACHING

What You Can Do

Volunteering for Community Service

Objective

Identify ways to help out as a community volunteer.

INSTRUCT

Before students read the feature, ask them if they or anyone in their household have ever volunteered for any organization in the community. They may mention political campaign volunteers, candy stripers, or participants in a Big Brother/Big Sister program. Tell students that they are going to read about how one student got involved as a volunteer.

Below are some possible questions for postreading discussion:

- For what organizations could students volunteer?
- How much time is required to "make a difference" as a volunteer?
- How could volunteers be organized at school to help a cause?

TRF **Teacher's Resource File**
See the Participatory Government Activities file, pp. 28–39, for material to support the lesson.

SECTION 4
The Courts and Their Judges

FOCUS

Teacher's Resource File
See the Unit 7 File, p. 33, for the Section 4 Outline.

Objectives

25.9 Describe how State court systems are organized.
25.10 Describe the methods by which judges are selected in the various States.

Bellringer Activity Before you begin the section, ask students to describe their images of judges. Who are they and what are they like? Where do students think they acquired their images of judges?

State the Purpose Though each State's court system is different, there are similarities in their organization and in the processes by which their judges are selected. In Section 4, students will read about this organization and judge selection process.

ABCNEWS INTERACTIVE

The following video segment may be used to highlight aspects of the State court systems.

POWERS OF THE SUPREME COURT GUIDEBOOK
Chapter 29: Justices of the Supreme Court, p. 97

4 The Courts and Their Judges

Find Out:

- How are State court systems organized?
- What are the methods by which judges are selected in the various States?

Key Term:
appellate jurisdiction

They deal with everything from traffic tickets to murder, from disputes over nickels and dimes to settlements involving millions. They are the State courts and the judges who sit in them. In this section, you will read about the way these courts are organized.

Organization of State Court Systems

Each of the State constitutions creates a court system for that State, and most of them leave the many details of its organization to the legislature. The following are some of the common features of those State and local court systems.

Justices of the Peace Justices of the peace—JPs—stand on the lowest rung of the State judicial ladder. They preside over what are commonly called justice courts.

JPs are almost always popularly elected. Mostly, JPs try misdemeanors—cases involving such petty offenses as traffic violations, disturbing the peace, public drunkenness, and the like. They can almost never settle civil disputes involving more than a few hundred dollars. They do issue certain kinds of warrants, hold preliminary hearings, and often perform marriages.[13]

[13]Recall, a warrant is a court order authorizing, or making legal, some official action, for example, a search warrant or an arrest warrant. A preliminary hearing is generally the first step in a major criminal prosecution. There the judge decides if the evidence is in fact enough to hold that person—bind that person over—for action by the grand jury or the prosecutor.

Magistrates' Courts Magistrates are the city cousins of JPs. For the most part, magistrates handle those minor civil complaints and misdemeanor cases that arise in an urban setting. They preside over what are generally called magistrates' courts or, in some places, police courts. Those courts are much like the justice courts, with just about the same jurisdiction. Magistrates, like JPs, are usually popularly elected and for short terms.

Municipal Courts Municipal courts are found in most of the nation's larger cities and many of its middle-sized and small ones. The jurisdiction of municipal courts is citywide. They can often hear civil cases involving several thousands of dollars as well as the usual run of misdemeanors. Many municipal courts are organized into divisions, which hear cases of a given kind, for example, civil, criminal, small claims, traffic, and probate divisions.

Consider the small claims division, often called the small claims court. Many people cannot afford the costs of suing for the collection of a small debt.

Small claims courts are designed for just such situations. In them, a person can bring a claim for little or no cost. The proceedings are usually informal, and the judge often handles the matter without attorneys for either side.

Juvenile Courts Individuals under 18 years of age are generally not subject to the justice of the courts in which adults are tried. Minors who are arrested for some offense or otherwise come to the attention of the police or other authorities may appear in juvenile courts.

The juvenile justice system is designed to address the special needs and problems of young people. This system generally emphasizes rehabilitation more than punishment. However, under certain circumstances juvenile courts do refer certain offenders to an adult criminal court for trial.

General Trial Courts Most of the more important civil and criminal cases heard in the United States are heard in the States' general trial courts.

Each State is divided into a number of judicial districts, or circuits, each generally covering one or

Reading Strategy: Structured Overview

As a preparation for reading, write the section's main boldfaced headings across the top of the chalkboard as students read them to you. List the subheadings under each main heading. Have students skim the text under each subheading, and ask volunteers to provide details as you list them on the board.

Vocabulary

Point out "Key Term" on page 679 to the students. Have students recall this term from Chapter 18 and explain in their own words what each of the two components of the term means.

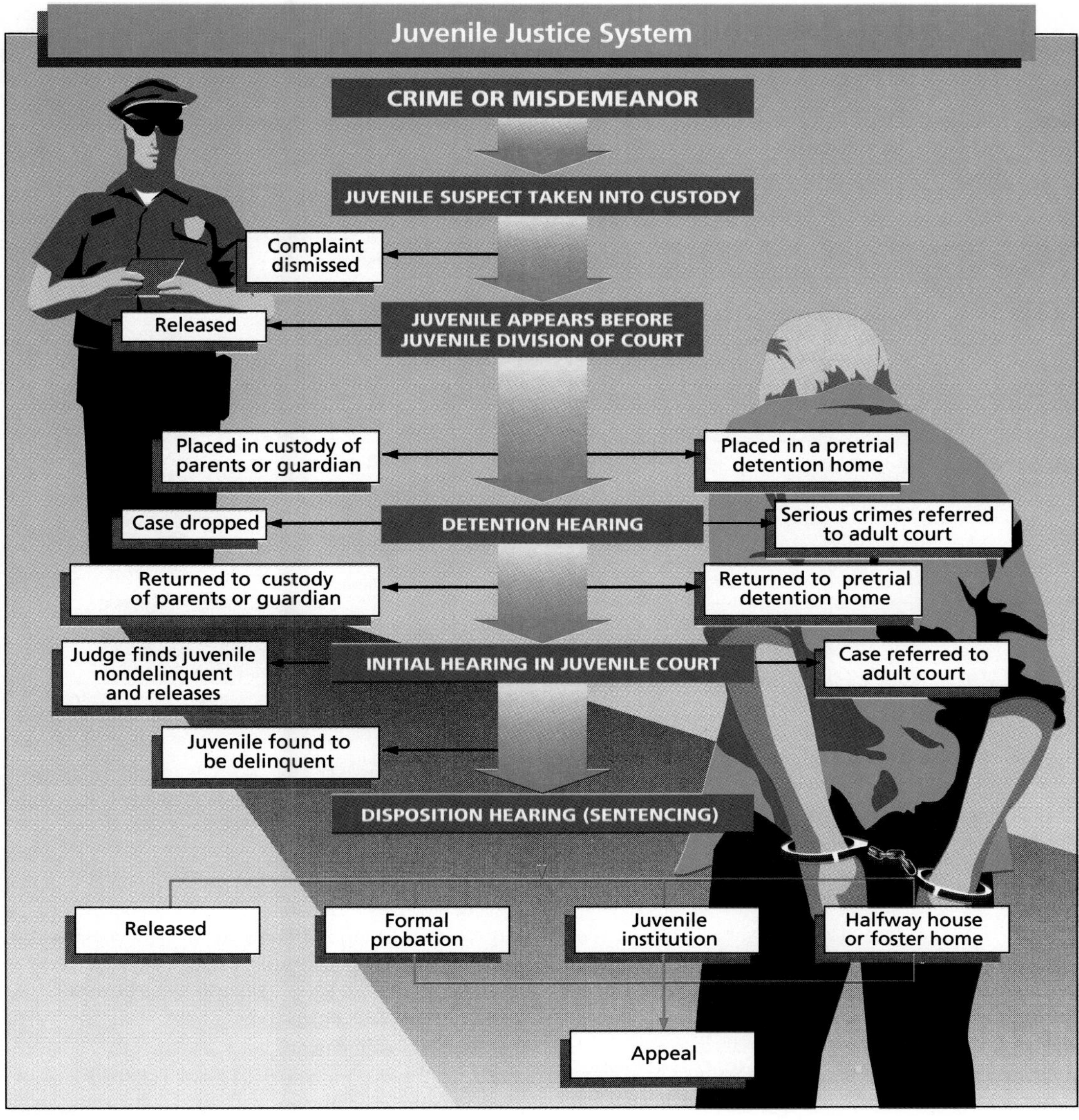

Interpreting Charts Delinquency is conduct that is out of step with accepted social behavior or is against the law. How does the chart show that the justice system makes every effort to rehabilitate, rather than to punish, juvenile offenders?

more counties. For each district there is a general trial court, known variously as district, circuit, chancery, county, or superior courts, or courts of common pleas. Most legal actions brought under State law are begun in these courts.

These general trial courts are courts of "first instance." That is, they exercise original jurisdiction over most of the cases they hear. When cases do come to them on appeal from some lower court, a trial *de novo* (a new trial, as

Interpreting Charts Have students look at the chart. Ask them to notice and comment on the number of steps that a person must pass through in the juvenile justice system before sentencing.

Caption Answer Possible answers: The chart shows that even those who are judged delinquent may receive a sentence that does not include detention in a juvenile institution, but rather release, probation, or placement in a halfway house or foster home.

INSTRUCT

Discuss/Analyze Have students recall what they learned about the dual court system in Chapter 18. Remind them that they learned about the federal system then. Now, they will learn about the State systems, which also have several layers.

Ask students to consider the various types of courts found in the typical State court system. Ask students to discuss the advantages of having several layers of courts. (*It enables courts to address specific kinds of cases, which increases the efficiency of the system.*)

Discuss with students the idea of a unified court system. Ask students to describe what advantages they think such a system would offer. Ask students to explain the difference between geographical and functional organization. (*Geographic organization divides the State into regions in which a court hears cases. Functional organization establishes courts to hear certain types of cases.*)

SPOTLIGHT ON: Behind the Scenes

Special treatment for juvenile offenders is a relatively recent phenomenon in the United States. It has been only within the last 100 years or so that young people have been treated differently under the law than adults. For example, as recently as 1899, 322 boys ages nine to sixteen were imprisoned in the city of Chicago for crimes ranging from assault with a deadly weapon to picking up coal on the railroad tracks. In prison, they shared cells with adult criminals. This raised an outcry for a new system, and the Illinois Juvenile Court Act of 1899 established the first separate, noncriminal court for the children of Chicago. The juvenile court movement spread rapidly, and by the 1920s every State had some legal provision for delinquent youth.

Interpreting Charts: Multicultural Awareness As students study the chart, ask them if they can see any relationship between crime rates and the number of police in the countries shown in the chart. (*Possible answer: No, the chart shows that countries with low police ratios may have high crime rates, as in Canada. However, countries with low police ratios may have high crime rates, as in the United States, or low crime rates, as in Panama or Kuwait.*)

Caption Answer The number of people per police officer is the highest in Canada, the lowest in Kuwait.

INSTRUCT

Analyze Ask students to identify the qualities they feel a judge ought to have. Analyze with students the benefits and drawbacks of selecting judges by vote and by appointment. Based on what they have learned about the American voter and the State governors and legislatures, do students feel more comfortable with the idea of judges being elected or appointed?

Invite a student volunteer to explain the Missouri Plan in his or her own words. Have other students agree or disagree as to whether the description was accurate and correct it as they understand it. In this way, reach a class consensus as to what the Missouri Plan is, then have the class evaluate the plan.

Global Awareness

Crime Rates and Police Protection, Selected Countries

	Offenses Reported to the Police Per 100,000 People					
		Personal		Property		
Country	Total*	Murder	Assault	Burglary	Automobile theft	Population per Police Officer**
Australia	7,264	4.2	81.3	1,787.3	838.8	450
Finland	7,324	1.1	36.9	902.9	199.7	640
Hungary	1,719	4.2	58.1	250.7	47.8	710
Kenya	448	5.4	20.7	60.0	14.5	1,500
Jordan	700	2.3	18.1	49.4	14.7	630
Kuwait	667	5.3	21.8	57.0	11.1	80
Panama	711	4.7	2.6	—	92.8	180
Peru	244	1.2	10.5	130.6	8.0	730
Canada	11,169	5.7	124.0	1,426.8	334.4	8,640
Thailand	314	12.4	18.5	9.5	2.4	530
United States	5,480	8.6	346.1	1,344.6	507.8	345

0 500 1000 1500

*Figure for total offenses reported includes crimes other than those listed in the table.
**Includes full-time, paid professionals performing domestic security functions. Includes administrative staff but excludes clerical employees.

Source: Encyclopaedia Britannica, *1990 Book of the Year*

Interpreting Charts: Multicultural Awareness Compare these crime rates and police protection statistics. Which country has the most people per police officer? The least?

though the case had not been heard before) is usually held.

The trial court is seldom limited as to the kinds of cases it may hear. Although its decision on the facts in a case is usually final, disputes over questions of law may be carried to a higher court.

In the more heavily populated districts of some States, cases involving such matters as the settlement of estates or the affairs of minors are heard in separate trial courts. Where they are found, these tribunals are often called surrogate, probate, or orphans' courts.

Intermediate Appellate Courts All but a few States now have one or more intermediate appellate courts. They are courts of appeal that stand between the trial courts and the State's supreme court. These appellate courts serve to ease the burden of the high court.

Like the trial courts, the appellate courts have different names among the States, but they are most often called the court of appeals[14] Most work of these courts involves the review of cases decided in the trial courts. That is, these appeals
1.a courts exercise mostly **appellate jurisdiction**. Their original jurisdiction, where it exists, is limited to a few specific kinds of cases—election disputes, for example. In exercising their appellate

[14]In New York the general trial court is called the supreme court; the intermediate appellate court is the appellate division of the supreme court; the State's highest court is known as the Court of Appeals.

jurisdiction, these courts do not hold trials. Rather, they hear oral arguments from attorneys, study the briefs—written arguments—that attorneys submit, and review the record of the case in the lower court.

Ordinarily, an appellate court does not concern itself with the facts in a case. Rather, its decision turns on whether the law was correctly interpreted and applied in the court below. Its decision may be reviewed by the State's high court, but its disposition of a case is usually final.

The State Supreme Court The State's supreme court is the highest court in its judicial system.[15] Its major function is to review the decisions of lower courts in those cases that are appealed to it.

The size of each State supreme court is fixed by each State constitution. In most States five or seven justices sit on the high bench.

The justices, including a chief justice, are appointed by the governor in 23 States. They are selected by the legislature in four States, and by the voters in the other 23.

The State supreme court is the court of last resort in the State's judicial system. It has the final say in all matters of State law. But, remember, many cases also raise questions of federal law. So, some State supreme court decisions may be reviewed by the United States Supreme Court. In fact, however, not very many of them are.[16] Recall, an appeal from a State's high court will be heard in the federal Supreme Court only if (1) a "federal question"—some matter of federal law—is involved in the case and (2) the Supreme Court agrees to hear that appeal.

[15]The State's highest court is known by that title in 45 States. But in Maine and Massachusetts it is called the Supreme Judicial Court; in Maryland and New York, the Court of Appeals; and in West Virginia, the Supreme Court of Appeals. Two States actually have two high courts. In Oklahoma and in Texas, the Supreme Court is the highest court in civil cases, and a separate Court of Criminal Appeals is the court of last resort in criminal cases.

[16]However, you did look at several such cases in Chapters 19, 20, and 21, most especially cases involving the 14th Amendment's Due Process and Equal Protection clauses.

In short, most State supreme court decisions are final. The oft-heard claim "I'll fight this case all the way to the United States Supreme Court" is almost always just so much hot air.[17]

Unified Court Systems

The typical State court system is organized geographically rather than by types of cases. Thus, the general trial courts are most often organized so that each hears those cases arising within its own district, circuit, or county, no matter what the subject matter may be.

In these map-based systems, a judge must hear cases in nearly all areas of the law. A backlog of cases can and often does build up in some courts while judges sit with little to do in others. Moreover, uneven interpretations and applications of the law may and sometimes do occur from one part of the State to another.

To overcome these difficulties, a number of States have begun to abandon geographical organization in recent years. They have turned, instead, to a unified court system, one that is organized on a functional, or case-type, basis.

In a completely unified court system, there is technically only one court for the entire State. It is presided over (administered by) a chief judge or judicial council. There are a number of levels within the single court, such as supreme, intermediate appellate, and general trial sections. At each level within each section, divisions are established to hear cases in certain specialized or heavy caseload areas of the law—criminal, juvenile, family relations, and other areas that need special attention.

In such an arrangement, a judge can be assigned to that section or division to which his or her talents and interests seem best suited. To relieve overcrowded dockets, judges may be moved from one section or division to another.

[17]State law regularly gives its lower courts final jurisdiction over many types of minor cases. That is, review cannot be sought in a higher State court. In those cases, the lower court is the State's court of last resort. If any review is to be had, it can be only in the United States Supreme Court. Such reviews are extremely rare.

Provide Guided Practice As a class, create an outline on the chalkboard of a guide for new United States citizens. The guide should be designed to explain the State court systems and their judges. Ask students to volunteer information about the contents of the guide, such as the types of courts in the State, variations in organization, and variations in methods of judge selection. Also have students suggest ways to organize this information in the guidebook.

Provide Independent Practice

TRF **Teacher's Resource File** You may wish to assign Section 4 Guided Reading and Review, Unit 7 File, p. 34, to help students master section objective content.

Enrichment

Have students perform research into the organization of State and local courts in your community, including the process by which judges are selected. (Average)

Interpreting Tables: Multicultural Awareness Have students look at the table. Ask students to explain whether or not they are surprised by the numbers in the table, and if so, why.

Caption Answer To a large extent it does, because many of the western States such as California, Hawaii, Alaska, Montana, Washington, and New Mexico have among the highest percentages of women judges.

Interpreting Political Cartoons Have students look at the cartoon on page 681. Ask them whether or not they think judges' past conduct affects their ability to be fair judges of other people's behavior.

Caption Answer Probably election, as the cartoonist seems to be pointing out that judges should be answerable to the public.

MONITOR COMPREHENSION

Answers to Section 4 Review
1. The "Key Term" is defined on the following page:
   a. appellate jurisdiction, p. 678

2. Justices of the peace. **3.** They help ease the burden placed on the State's highest court. **4.** The State supreme court reviews the decisions of lower courts in those cases that are appealed to it. **5.** Popular election, appointment by the governor, and appointment by the legislature.

Minority and Women Judges*, Selected States

State	Minorities	Women
Hawaii	70.5%	11.5%
New Mexico	25.0%	12.5%
California	13.5%	10.5%
Maryland	9.8%	7.9%
Michigan	8.9%	8.3%
Texas	8.5%	6.2%
New York	7.4%	9.7%
North Carolina	7.2%	5.0%
Illinois	6.2%	4.3%
Colorado	5.6%	11.3%
Delaware	5.3%	19.1%
Connecticut	5.1%	8.0%
Virginia	4.8%	2.3%
Florida	4.6%	7.8%
New Jersey	4.6%	6.5%
Washington	4.5%	13.0%
Nevada	4.5%	7.7%
Pennsylvania	4.4%	4.0%
Alabama	4.3%	6.0%
Alaska	3.9%	21.0%
Georgia	3.2%	4.1%
West Virginia	3.1%	3.1%
Minnesota	2.7%	7.8%
Utah	2.4%	6.0%
Ohio	2.4%	4.2%
Idaho	2.4%	2.4%
Louisiana	2.2%	4.7%
Rhode Island	2.1%	10.6%
Missouri	1.8%	5.3%
Mississippi	1.8%	2.7%
Indiana	1.4%	6.0%
Kansas	1.3%	11.6%
Oklahoma	0.8%	9.3%
Nebraska	0.8%	3.4%
Montana	0.0%	14.3%
Maine	0.0%	10.6%
Wyoming	0.0%	7.3%
North Dakota	0.0%	5.3%
Arkansas	0.0%	3.6%
New Hampshire	0.0%	2.7%
South Dakota	0.0%	2.5%
Federal Judiciary	**10.5%**	**7.4%**

*Minorities and females have been found to be better represented in those states that appoint, rather than elect, judges.
Source: Reprinted from *U.S. News & World Report*, January 20, 1986. Copyright 1986 U.S. News & World Report.

Interpreting Tables: Multicultural Awareness Women first began to win equal rights in the western States, some say because women played such a large role in settling the frontier. Does this table reflect a progressive attitude toward women in the western States?

Selection of Judges

More than 15,000 judges sit in the State and local courts today. They are most often chosen in one of three ways: by (1) popular election, (2) appointment by the governor, or (3) appointment by the legislature.

Popular election is by far the most widely used method by which judges are picked around the country. The voters choose about three-fourths of all judges sitting in American courts today.

In fact, in 11 States popular election is the only method by which judges are chosen. In most of the other States, most or at least some judges are also chosen at the polls. About half of all judicial elections are nonpartisan contests today.[18]

Selection by the legislature is the least commonly used of the three major methods. The legislature now chooses all or at least most judges in only four States: Connecticut, Rhode Island, South Carolina, and Virginia.

The governor appoints nearly a fourth of all State judges today. In three States—Delaware, Massachusetts, and New Hampshire—all judges are named by the governor. In several other States, the governor has the power to appoint all or many of them, but under a Missouri Plan arrangement, as you will see in just a moment.

How Should Judges Be Selected? Most people believe that judges should be independent, that they should "stay out of politics." Whatever method of selection is used, then, should be designed with that goal in mind.

Nearly all authorities agree that selection by the legislature is the most political of all the methods of choice—and few favor it. So, the question is really: Which is better, popular election of judges or appointment by the governor?

Those who agree on popular election generally make the democratic argument. Because judges "say the law," interpret and apply it, they should be chosen by and answer directly to the people. Some also argue that the concept of

[18]Except that vacancies caused by deaths or by midterm resignations are usually filled by appointments made by the governor. The 12 States are Arkansas, Kentucky, Louisiana, Minnesota, Montana, Nevada, North Carolina, North Dakota, Pennsylvania, West Virginia, and Wisconsin

"We all make mistakes, as Your Honor knows, having been twice reprimanded by the New York State Commission on Judicial Conduct."

▲ **Interpreting Political Cartoons** The manner of selecting judges varies from State to State. Do you think this cartoonist would favor popular election or appointment of judges?

separation of powers is undercut if the executive (the governor) has the power to name the members of the judicial branch.

Those who favor appointment by the governor argue that the judicial function should be carried out only by those who are well qualified. Proponents of executive appointment insist it is the best way to ensure that those who preside in courts will have the qualities most needed in that role: absolute honesty and integrity, fairness, and the necessary training and ability in the law.

Popular election is both widely used and widely supported. Moves to abandon it have been strongly opposed by party organizations. So, most moves to revise the method of judicial selection have kept at least some element of voter choice.

The Missouri Plan For nearly 70 years now, the American Bar Association (ABA) has sponsored an approach that combines the election and appointment processes. Because its adoption in Missouri in 1940 involved much political drama, and so attracted wide attention, the method is often called the Missouri Plan.

Missouri's version of the plan is more or less typical of its shape in those other States where it is now used. The governor appoints the seven justices of the State's supreme court, the 32 judges of the court of appeals, and all judges who sit in certain of the State's trial courts The governor must make each appointment from a panel, or list, of three names recommended by a judicial nominating commission. The commission is made up of a sitting judge, several members of the bar, and private citizens.

Each judge named by the governor then serves until the first general election after he or she has been in office for at least a year. The judge's name then appears on the ballot, without opposition. The voters decide whether or not that judge should be kept in office.

If the vote is favorable, the judge then serves a regular term—six years for a trial court judge and 12 years for one who sits on a higher court in Missouri. Thereafter, the judge may seek further terms in future retain-reject elections. Should the voters reject a sitting judge, the process begins again. In nearly half the States, some form of the Missouri Plan is now used for selecting at least some judges.

Section 4 Review

1. **Define:** appellate jurisdiction
2. What courts are frequently found at the lowest, most local level in a State's court system?
3. Why do nearly all States now have intermediate appellate courts?
4. What is the primary function of each State's supreme court?
5. What three methods are used to select State judges?
6. Why is the Missouri Plan so favored by nearly all students of judicial administration?

Critical Thinking

7. **Identifying Alternatives** (p. 19) Consider the role and function of judges in the State courts. In your opinion, what would be the best way to select quality judges?

★

6. It combines the election and the appointment processes, enabling private citizens and State officials to have a say in which judges are in office.
7. Answers will vary. Students may suggest election, appointment by elected officials, or a combination of both such as the Missouri Plan. Students should be prepared to explain the reasons for their choices.

Teacher's Resource File
See the Unit 7 File, p. 35, for the Section 4 Quiz.

CLOSURE

Remind students that State court systems contain a variety of different courts. They also differ in their organization, and there is a growing move toward unified court systems. Finally, the selection of judges in different States also varies, with some States opting for popular election, others empowering the legislature or governor to appoint judges, and still others using a combination of appointment and election.

Reteach

Have students write a brief letter to the editor promoting a unified court system and the Missouri Plan for selecting judges. In their advertisements, have students explain these two plans and how they promise to offer improvements over conventional plans for organizing courts and selecting judges.

TEACHING
Citizenship

How to File a Claim in Small Claims Court

Objective

Organize pertinent information in order to file a claim in small claims court.

INSTRUCT

Before students read the Citizenship feature, ask them to recall any situations from their lives in which they have had a disagreement with a merchant. As they read through the feature, have them consider how they handled their complaint and how they might respond differently if the same situation were to occur again.

Answers 1. Suggest that students obtain an application form. **2.** Students may suggest that it will save money for themselves and the court. **3.** Students may suggest that the clearer and more accurate the form and the information on it, the quicker and more accurately the application can be processed. **4.** Students may suggest that their presentation will be more credible if presented in a calm and reasoned manner.

TRF **Teacher's Resource File** See the Unit 7 File, p. 36, for the Skill Application for this lesson.

How to File a Claim in Small Claims Court

Small claims courts are usually city or county courts designed to resolve claims involving small amounts of money. The maximum value of a small claim varies depending on where you live, but can range up to $5,000. No lawyers are necessary to bring a claim in small claims court, which makes the court easier and less expensive for the public to use. Follow the steps below to learn how to file a claim in small claims court.

1. Obtain an application form. To find out where the small claims court in your area is located, consult a local telephone directory. The information section at the front of the directory may include information about the small claims court in your area. Or, look under the name of your city or county for a listing of the courthouse. Once you have found the number of the court, ask for a small claims court application form.

2. Consider mediation. In some locations, mediation services are available as an alternative to small claims court. Mediation is a process in which a mediator assists two parties in finding their own resolution to their dispute without going to court. Your small claims application form may include information about mediation. If you are interested in this service, follow the directions on the form. Why might mediation be a good alternative to going to court?

3. Complete and return the application form. If you decide to follow through with your claim, complete the application form. Be sure to include all the requested information, and be as thorough and clear as possible in your responses. Though you do not need to hire a lawyer, filing a small claim will involve a small fee, usually around $10. The completed form and payment may be mailed or delivered in person to the clerk-magistrate's office where you are filing your claim. Why do you think it is important to fill out the forms completely and accurately?

4. Prepare for the trial. Your success at small claims court will depend on your presentation before the judge who will hear your case. In order to make a good presentation, it is important to prepare for your day in court. Bring to court any and all witnesses, checks, bills, photographs, or copies of letters that will help you prove your case. Both sides will have an opportunity to present their version of the dispute. When—and only when—the judge asks you to speak, make your presentation calmly and politely. Notice of the judge's decision will either be given or sent to each side. Why do you think it is important to make your case calmly and politely?

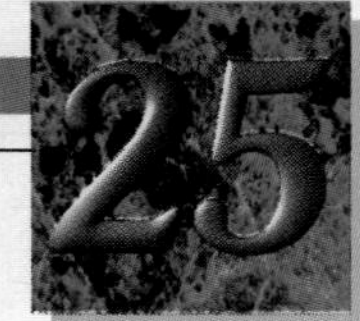

Chapter-in-Brief

Scan all headings, photographs, charts, and other visuals in the chapter before reading the section summaries below.

Section 1 Providing Important Services (pp. 663–667) The federal system is one in which the States have many important powers and provide many important services.

States provide services directly to citizens. For example, States spend the largest portion of their budgets on education. Their most direct involvement is in higher education.

States are directly involved in the promotion of public health and welfare. In cooperation with the Federal Government and on their own, States administer a variety of programs. They also protect public safety, build and maintain roadways, protect the environment, and more.

Differences in the geography of the States lead to differences in each State's budget. Factors such as availability of resources and location have a powerful impact on the local economy.

Section 2 Financing State Government (pp. 667–671) State and local governments rely on a variety of methods to raise revenues. Most States—and a number of local governments—have general and/or selective sales taxes. These taxes are solid revenue producers, but they are regressive.

Other widely used taxes include the income tax, the property tax, and a variety of business taxes. In addition, State and local governments raise funds by running businesses and State lotteries. They also rely on borrowing.

The State budget is the means by which States plan the control and use of State money. Most States use the executive budget.

Section 3 In the Courtroom (pp. 672–674) State courts apply several forms of law, including constitutional law, statutory law, administrative law, common law, and equity law. Law is also classified as either criminal or civil.

A jury is a body of persons selected to hear evidence and decide questions of fact in a court case. Grand juries decide whether or not there is enough evidence to justify a formal accusation against a person. Petit juries hear evidence and decide the disputed facts.

Jurors are picked from among the State's citizens. Many States are deemphasizing the use of both grand juries and trial juries. Among the criticisms of juries is their cost and their competence. However, the system has a long and honorable place in the development of American law.

Section 4 The Courts and Their Judges (pp. 676–681) Each State constitution creates its own court system. There are, however, many common features among the States. For example, many State systems include justices of the peace and magistrates' courts. Municipal and juvenile courts are also common.

Most important civil and criminal cases heard in United States courts are heard in the States' general trial courts. All but a few States now have one or more intermediate appellate courts. The highest court in a State's judicial system is the State's supreme court.

Many States are moving to a unified court system. These systems abandon the geographic organization of the courts in favor of organization on a functional, or case-type, basis.

Judges in State and local courts are chosen by either (1) popular election, (2) appointment by the governor, or (3) appointment by the legislature. Popular election is the most widely used form.

One method used for selecting judges in a growing number of States is the so-called Missouri Plan, which combines appointment by the governor and popular election.

Teaching Suggestions for CHAPTER-IN-BRIEF

Below are some of the possible uses for the Chapter-in-Brief:

To Preview the Chapter You may want to assign the Chapter-in-Brief page and the Section Outlines from the Teacher's Resource File before beginning Chapter 25 to introduce students to "Key Terms" and concepts in each section.

To Review the Chapter When students have completed Chapter 25, you might want to assign the Chapter-in-Brief as a tool for review, along with the Guided Reading and Reviews from the Teacher's Resource File.

To Omit the Chapter If you wish to skip Chapter 25, it may be helpful to assign the Chapter-in-Brief to students as a review before continuing to another chapter. You may also want to assign the Chapter 25 Test to assess student knowledge of the material. Then specific portions of Chapter 25 may be assigned to students needing reinforcement of "Key Terms" and concepts.

Teacher's Resource File See the Unit 7 File for the following materials:

- Section Outlines, pp. 24, 27, 30, 33.
- Guided Reading and Reviews, pp. 25, 28, 31, 34.
- Chapter 25 Test, pp. 40–42.

ADDITIONAL RESOURCES

Baum, Lawrence. *American Courts: Process and Policy.* Houghton Mifflin, 2nd ed., 1990.

Carp, Robert A. and Ronald Stidham. *Judicial Process in America.* CQ Press, 1989.

The County Yearbook: The Authoritative Source Book on County Governments. National Association of Counties and the International City Management Association, Annual.

Davis, Samuel M. *Rights of Juveniles: The Juvenile Justice System.* Clark Boardman, 1989.

Dead End. 16mm film. MTI Teleprograms, 1979. Color. 12 min.

Facts and Figures on Government Finance, 1989. Tax Foundation, 1990.

Poletown Lives! 16mm film. Information Factory, 1983. Color. 52 min.

U.S. Bureau of the Census: State Government Finances in 1989. Government Printing Office, 1990.

Van Horn, Carl E. (ed.). *The State of the States.* CQ Press, 1989.

Answers to CHAPTER 25 REVIEW

Vocabulary and Key Terms

Matching
1. income tax
2. inheritance tax
3. criminal law
4. precedent
5. property tax

True or False
1. False—the correct term is *civil law.*
2. False—the correct term is *estate tax.*
3. True.
4. True.
5. True.

Word Relationships
1. common law
2. appellate jurisdiction
3. assessment
4. regressive tax
5. urbanization

Main Ideas

Section 1
1. States provide services in the fields of education, health and welfare, public safety, highways; and they provide many other services, such as maintenance of recreation areas, regulation of business and industry, and more. **2.** Education is generally the most costly. **3.** Differences in the physical geography of a State, its location, and the degree to which it is urbanized.

Section 2
4. States are limited by certain federal limitations; e.g., States cannot tax interstate commerce, any agency of the Federal Government, or in such a way as to violate due process and equal protection. States often also have their own constitutional limits, and there are political limits as well. **5.** Answers could include sales, income, property, inheritance and estate, and various business taxes. **6.** Many States operate businesses, many run lotteries or permit other forms of gambling, and all States gather revenue through a variety of fines, leases, and other means. States also have the power to borrow money. **7.** State budgets are plans for the control of public money. Thus they are political documents that set priorities and decide who gets what.

Section 3
8. Answers include constitutional law, statutory law, administrative law, common law, equity, and criminal and civil law. **9.** Criminal law defines public wrongs and provides for their punishment. Cases in criminal law are always brought by the State. Civil law deals with disputes between private parties, and with disputes between private parties and government not covered by criminal law.
10. (a) Grand juries decide whether or not an accused person is probably guilty of a crime and should stand trial. (b) A petit jury is the trial jury; it hears evidence in a case and decides disputed facts.
11. Jurors are selected from among the eligible citizens by some county official or special jury commissioners. The list of eligible citizens may be drawn

Chapter Review

Vocabulary and Key Terms

urbanization (p. 666)	assessment (p. 669)	civil law (p. 673)
sales tax (p. 668)	inheritance tax (p. 669)	petit jury (p. 674)
regressive tax (p. 668)	estate tax (p. 669)	appellate jurisdiction (p. 678)
income tax (p. 668)	common law (p. 672)	
progressive tax (p. 668)	precedent (p. 672)	
property tax (p. 669)	criminal law (p. 673)	

Matching: *Review the key terms in the list above. If you are not sure of a term's meaning, look up the term and review its definition. Choose a term from the list above that best matches each description.*

1. a tax on individual and corporate income
2. what is levied on a beneficiary's share of an estate
3. the body of law that defines public wrongs and provides for their punishment
4. previous court decisions that serve as the basis for later cases
5. what is levied on tangible and intangible personal wealth and on land and buildings

True or False: *Determine whether each statement is true or false. If it is true, write "true." If it is false, change the underlined word or words to make the statement true.*

1. Common law is that which relates to disputes between private persons.
2. An inheritance tax is levied directly on the estate of a person.
3. A tax that is based upon a person's ability to pay is called a progressive tax.
4. The tax paid by the purchaser upon the sale of a commodity is a sales tax.
5. The petit jury often consists of 12 people, and it hears the evidence and decides questions of fact in a case.

Word Relationships: *Replace the underlined definition with the correct term from the list above.*

1. Much of the law applied in the State courts is based on that body of law made up of generally accepted standards of rights and wrongs.
2. State appellate courts have the authority to review the decisions of inferior courts.
3. Local governments must conduct the process of determining the value of property for purposes of taxation in order to determine property taxes.
4. The sales tax is criticized for being a tax levied at a flat rate so that it falls most heavily on those least able to pay.
5. One factor that impacts the budget of a government is the percentage of people living in cities of a certain size.

Main Ideas

Section 1 (pp. 663–667)

1. Briefly describe the major categories of services that States provide to their citizens.
2. What is the most costly of these services?
3. What kinds of differences exist among the States that influence the shapes of their budgets?

Section 2 (pp. 667–671)

4. What are the general limits of a State's power to tax?
5. List the major categories of taxes that exist at the State and local level.
6. What are the main sources of nontax revenue available to the States?
7. In what sense is the State budget "more than bookkeeping entries and dollar signs"?

Section 3 (pp. 672–674)

8. What kinds of law applied in State courts are discussed in Section 3?
9. What is the difference between civil and criminal law?
10. (a) What is the role of the grand jury in the State court system? (b) What is the role of the petit jury?
11. How are jurors selected?

Section 4 (pp. 676–681)

12. Briefly describe the types of courts found in the typical State judicial system.
13. What are unified court systems?
14. How are judges selected at the State level today?
15. What are the main features of the Missouri Plan for selecting judges?

Critical Thinking

1. **Formulating Questions** (p. 19) State and local governments spend the largest share of their budgets on education, highways, public welfare, and retirement and unemployment compensation for workers. Write a list of questions you could use to explore whether or not you agree with these spending priorities.
2. **Making Comparisons** (p. 19) Review the concepts of regressive and progressive taxes discussed in Section 2. (a) Which of these kinds of taxes do you think is most fair? (b) Explain your reasoning.
3. **Expressing Problems Clearly** (p. 19) In your opinion, what should be the characteristics required of all judges in the State judicial system?

Getting Involved

1. **Writing Your Opinion** Recall what you have read in Section 4 about criticisms of the grand jury and petit jury in the State judicial systems. Write a letter to the governor in which you argue for or against the continued use of such juries. To help organize your thoughts, create a chart in which you list the pros and cons of grand juries and petit juries. Once you have decided on a position, begin by explaining your purpose in writing and stating your overall position on the matter. Then, explain in separate paragraphs the different reasons for your position. If you advocate an alternative or improvement to the jury system, be sure to include it. Revise to correct errors and to ensure the clarity of your letter, then draft a final copy.
2. **Cooperative Activity** Hold a class committee hearing to decide how to distribute $6 billion in State funds among several competing interests. First, assign teams of two or three individuals to represent four interests: (1) education, (2) highways, (3) public welfare, and (4) public safety. Each team will attempt to persuade the committee to approve its request for $2 billion. Allow each team time to prepare and deliver a brief presentation to the class explaining why they require the funding. (For purposes of the activity, assume that $2 billion represents an appropriate request from each department.) After each team has finished, discuss as a class how to divide the $6 billion among the groups. Submit various proposals to a class vote. The plan that receives the most votes wins.
3. **Gathering Information** Using the Government Resources Handbook on page 690, identify possible sources you could use to find out about the amount of tax revenue and the kinds of taxes collected in your State.

from poll books, tax rolls, motor vehicle and drivers license lists, or other sources. Those under 18 and over 70, those who can't read, the ill, and convicted criminals are often excluded, as are people in certain occupations.

Section 4

12. Justices of the peace and magistrate courts hear minor civil and misdemeanor cases. Municipal courts exist in many cities to hear civil and misdemeanor cases; they may have divisions, such as small claims and traffic. Juvenile courts hear cases involving those under 18. General trial courts hear most important civil and criminal cases. Intermediate appellate courts and, above them, State Supreme Courts review cases from the lower courts. **13.** These are court systems organized on a functional—case-type—basis. **14.** Judges are either popularly elected, appointed by the governor, or appointed by the legislature. **15.** It involves the initial appointment of judges from a panel selected by a special committee. The appointed judges serve for a period of time before being subject to a vote by the people. If voters approve, the judge continues to serve for a regular term.

Critical Thinking

1. Possible questions: What additional programs seek money from the State? What do other States spend on similar programs? What unusual characteristics of the State affect spending in these fields? **2.** (a) Answers will vary. Student answers should reflect an understanding of progressive and regressive taxes. (b) Students who favor progressive taxes might suggest that those who have more should contribute a higher share. Those who favor regressive taxes might argue that taxes should not vary according to who is paying them. **3.** Answers will vary, but might include knowledge of the State legal system, knowledge of the law, responsiveness to public sensitivities, or other characteristics.

Getting Involved

1–2. Answers and results will vary, but students should demonstrate an understanding of the concepts in the chapter. **3.** Possible answers include each State's *State Manual* or *Blue Book*, or *The Book of the States*, or *The United States Statistical Abstract*. Some such information is also available in almanacs, such as *The Information Please Almanac, Atlas, and Yearbook.*

Stop The Presses

Bury me on my face; for in a little while everything will be turned upside down

–Diogenes

On this and the following pages you will find a number of last-minute additions, changes, and corrections which, for reasons of timing, could not be included in the main body of the text itself.

Soviet Union Dissolved

■ The Soviet Union, born out of the October Revolution in 1917, is no more. The one-time superpower, America's arch cold war foe, collapsed and, as noted on page 592, was formally dissolved in the closing days of 1991. The Union of Soviet Socialist Republics has been succeeded by a Commonwealth of Independent States—a loose confederation of 11 of the 15 constituent republics of the old Soviet Union. The 11 member-states of the new commonwealth, each now also sovereign states in the world community, are identified on page 599.

As this book went to press, the United States Department of State had approved the following list of updated names for the former republics:

- Byelorussia is now Byelarus.
- Moldavia is now Moldova.
- Kirghizia is now Kyrghyzstan.

The former republics are joined together mostly for economic and military purposes. (As of early 1992, Georgia, torn by civil war, remained outside the confederation. The three Baltic republics, Lithuania, Latvia, and Estonia, broke away from the Soviet Union in September of 1991, three months before the Soviet collapse; they have no intention of joining the Commonwealth of Independent States.)

The Commonwealth of Independent States established a capital at Minsk, in Byelarus. A Commonwealth Council, composed of the heads of the member-states, is to coordinate the affairs of the confederation until it can agree on a more defined structure.

The 11 member-states have declared themselves equal members of their confederation. But, clearly, Russia is more prominent than the others. As it was in the old union, Russia is the heart of the new bloc of states. Russia has replaced the Soviet Union as the largest country in the world. It covers nearly 6.6 million square miles, more than 75 percent of the area covered by the old Soviet Union. Its resource-rich landmass stretches from the edge of Eastern Europe across Northern Asia to the Pacific Ocean, a distance of some 4,000 miles. The Russian population, now about 150 million, includes more than half of the people of the former Soviet Union. *Pages 4, 11, 443–447, 592–599.*

—Russia has taken the Soviet Union's membership in the United Nations, including the permanent seat in the Security Council, with its veto power. Russia and the two other former Soviet republics already members of the world body, Byelarus and Ukraine, are now pushing UN membership for the other members of the Commonwealth of Independent States. *Pages 450–453.*

—The future of the Commonwealth of Independent States is at best uncertain, and this is a matter of grave concern to the United States and the rest of the world. All of its members are beset by the consequences of the disintegration of the Soviet Union. Their economies are in shambles, and most of them are plagued by deep-seated ethnic conflicts.

The Commonwealth of Independent States has declared that its members will abide by all international agreements to which the Soviet Union was a party—including its disarmament treaties. The Soviets based their long-range nuclear weapons in four of the republics—in Russia, Byelarus, Ukraine, and Kazakhstan. Those four states have promised that that weaponry will be controlled by a unified military command. Decisions regarding the use of those weapons, including their disposal, are to be made by Russia's president, Boris Yeltsin, subject to the approval of the presidents of Byelarus, Ukraine, and Kazakhstan. Those three states have also agreed to the transfer of all tactical (short-range) nuclear weapons to Russia, where they are to be dismantled under joint supervision. (By treaty, the United States is also a party to that dismantling process; and Congress has appropriated $400 million to help with and speed up that effort.)

The Commonwealth of Independent States has also created a temporary central command structure for the conventional armed forces of the former Soviet Union. Several of the member-states have declared that they intend to maintain their own separate military forces also. *Pages 436–437, 443–447.*

Supreme Court Update

■ THE SUPREME COURT HAS HEARD ARGUMENTS in a major church-state case, *Weisman* v. *Lee,* and it will likely decide that case by June 1992. The case, from Providence, Rhode Island, poses this question: Can religious prayers be offered as part of a public school's graduation ceremonies? Many authorities believe that the High Court will use this case as a vehicle to abandon the *Lemon* test. They predict that the Court will adopt, instead, a rule that will allow government to take actions that favor organized religions so long as those actions do not involve the coercion of any person. Such a rule would very likely permit such things as organized prayer in public schools and greatly expanded public aid to parochial schools. *Pages 490–495.*

—Another important case on the High Court's docket, *United States* v. *Montana,* involves the method by which seats in the House of Representatives are redistributed among States after each decennial census. Under the 1991 reapportionment, which was based on the 1990 census, the average congressional district will include some 575,000 persons. If that plan becomes effective, Montana will lose one of its two seats in the House—and Montana's one representative will represent that State's entire population—some 803,000 persons. That, the State argues, would violate "the goal of equal representation for equal numbers of people"—a constitutional standard the Supreme Court has applied to legislative redistricting cases since the 1960s. *Pages 238–240.*

Beginning in 1992, members of both houses of Congress will receive $129,500 in salary. The Speaker of the House will earn $166,200. These new figures represent a 3.5 percent cost-of-living increase in pay over the figures given in Chapter 10. *Page 252.*

Election Preview

■ THE FEDERAL ELECTION COMMISSION HAS given $10.6 million to each of the two major parties for their 1992 national conventions. The FEC will add a cost-of-living adjustment to those subsidies sometime before the conventions are held. *Pages 175–179.*

New Cabinet Member

■ PRESIDENT BUSH HAS APPOINTED ANOTHER woman to the cabinet. Barbara Franklin became secretary of commerce in early 1992. She succeeded Robert Mossbacher, who resigned that post to become the general chairman of the President's 1992 reelection committee. *Page 374.*

Population Shifts

■ THREE OUT OF EVERY FOUR AMERICANS NOW live in urban areas. The Census Bureau reports that the nation's urban population totaled 187.1 million (75.2 percent) and the rural population 61.7 million (24.8 percent) in 1990. (For census purposes, any community of at least 2,500 residents is classed as urban. About 15 percent of all urban dwellers now live in small towns of approximately that size.)

There are, on average, more than 2,000 people per square mile in urban America. The average comes to only 18 persons per square mile in rural areas. California ranked as the least rural State in 1990, with only 7 percent of its population living in rural areas. Vermont was the most rural State, with 68 percent of its population living outside of any urban place. *Pages 643–657.*

Stop The Presses Photographic essay: The Break-up of the Soviet Union

These images, made as 1991 drew to a close, capture the days and weeks surrounding the break-up of the Soviet Union. *Top:* The Russian legislature approved the formation of the Commonwealth of Independent States on December 12, 1991. *Middle:* This historic vote heralded the formal dissolution of the Soviet Union, whose flag, shown flying over the Kremlin, was lowered for the last time on December 31, 1991. *Bottom:* As the new year began, the new Russian state took steps toward a market economy by removing price controls on many goods. Prices once controlled by the Soviet government soared out of reach of the average Russian consumer. Despite the increase in prices, many Russians scooped up goods as quickly as they were unloaded, as shown in the photograph.

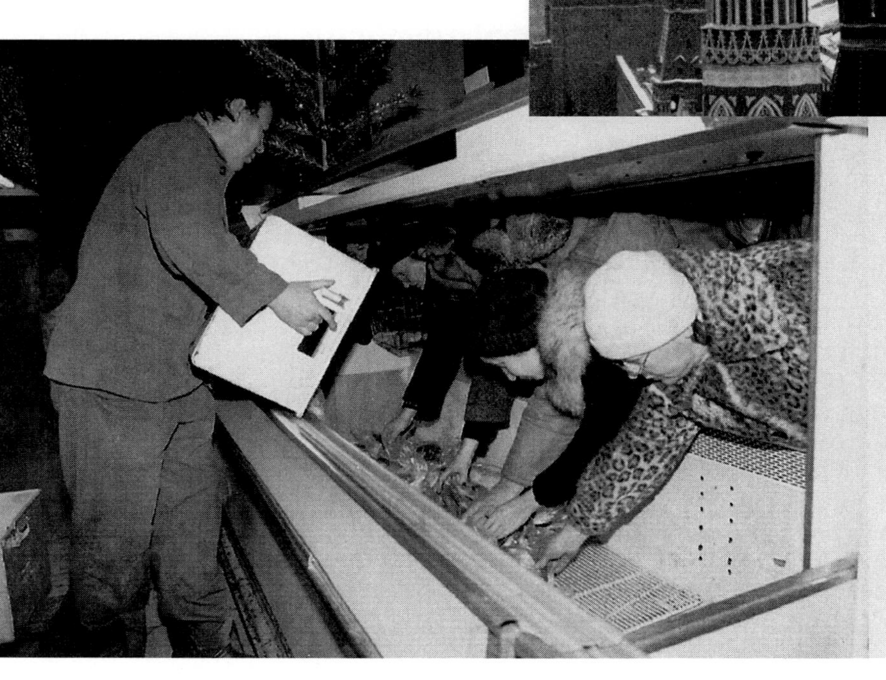

Reference Section

Government Resources Handbook

Public and Private Resources

The Founders believed that, if democratic government were to work effectively, citizens of the democratic state must be informed of the actions of their government. In order for the people to be informed, the Founders believed that most actions of the government must be open and available for scrutiny. The Constitution states in Article I, Section 5:

"Each House shall keep a journal of its proceedings, and, from time to time, publish the same, excepting such parts as may, in their judgment, require secrecy; and the yeas and nays of the members of either House, on any question, shall, at the desire of one-fifth of those present, be entered on the journal."

In the course of carrying out its duties, Congress, of course, has seen fit to publish much more than the journals of its daily activities. Likewise, the executive agencies annually release thousands of publications about their activities, as well as making public the incredible amount of statistical information they collect. And law libraries are stacked to the roof with volume after volume of the proceedings of national and State courts.

In addition to the information published by the government, many private sources publish information that is very useful to an understanding of American government and politics. These sources are sometimes superior to public sources because they summarize information from many sources, they offer commentary and insight, and they reduce the time it might take to collect information.

As a student of American government and as a citizen of a democracy, you should make yourself aware of some of the most important publications about our government. The following pages offer you such information.

Government Publications

When you begin to search for information about government, the best place to start is your public library. Become familiar with your library and the many indexes that can lead you to a source. Also ask your librarian what other sources the library can offer you in locating the information you want.

Another place to begin looking for public sources of information is your local telephone directory. The "blue pages," or Government Listing Section, is usually located at the back of the white pages of the directory. Look particularly under United States Government, Government Printing Office.

Nearly all federal agencies publish pamphlets and reports to describe their work and to provide general or specialized information to the public. Most of them will supply a list of available publications. (The addresses of the public information offices of the principal federal agencies are cited in the *United States Government Manual*; see below.) Some of these publications can be obtained from the particular agencies on request. Many of them are available at a nominal price from the Superintendent of Documents, Government Printing Office, Washington, D.C. 20402.

Most of the many publications produced by federal agencies—including congressional committee hearings and reports—can be found in any of the more than 1,000 depository libraries across the country. A depository library is one to which the Government Printing Office regularly sends copies of the materials it publishes. A call to the local branch of the Government Printing Office can help you locate the closest depository library. There are also more than 8,500 public libraries in the United States, and many hundreds of other more specialized and private libraries that contain the most useful of the government's publications.

The Government Printing Office's information sheet, *Document Sales*, outlines the procedure for ordering government publications. It also describes two very useful Government Printing Office indexes: (1) the free monthly list of *Selected United States Government Publications*—highlighting newly issued or still popular publications for sale, and (2) the *Monthly Catalog of United States Government Publications*—a much more extensive, comprehensive listing of all federal agency publications.

Among the most useful of the government publications are the following:

United States Government Manual. Published annually by the National Archives and Records Administration. The *Manual* describes the creation, organization, and work of every unit in the executive, legislative, and judicial branches of the Federal Government. It also contains up-to-date organization charts and lists persons holding upper-level governmental posts.

Congressional Directory. Published once every two years with an annual supplement by the congressional Joint Committee on Printing, the *Directory* contains some of the material found in the *Government Manual,* but focuses on the legislative branch. It includes autobiographical sketches of all members of Congress, lists congressional committees and committee assignments, identifies office and committee staff personnel, tabulates statistics for recent congressional elections, and reprints the map of each congressional district.

Statistical Abstract of the United States. Published annually by the Census Bureau in the Department of Commerce. The *Abstract* is an extensive and comprehensive compilation of recent and current statistical data on virtually every aspect of American economic, social, and political life. Its hundreds of charts, graphs, and tables cover such topics as population, immigration, public finance, and law enforcement. (Your librarian can also point you to many other useful items published by the Census Bureau.)

Congressional Record. Published for every day that Congress is in session, and bound and indexed annually by the congressional Joint Committee on Printing. The *Record* contains everything that is said (and much that is not) and reports all the actions taken on the floor in either house. A twice-monthly *Congressional Record Index* contains the same information. (Each member of Congress has an allotment of subscriptions of the *Record,* to be mailed to whomever he or she chooses. Your local or school librarian might wish to contact your member of Congress to see about obtaining a copy.)

Weekly Compilation of Presidential Documents. Published every Monday by the White House. It reprints the President's public messages, speeches, and other statements; the text of press conferences; and a checklist of bill signings, appointments, and White House press releases.

Historical Statistics of the United States, Colonial Times to 1970. This volume, first published in 1976 by the Bureau of the Census, is a supplement to the annual *Statistical Abstract.* It takes much of the data reported in the annual publications and reports the information on an historical basis.

Budget of the United States Government. Published annually by the Office of Management and Budget. The budget document provides a summary of the budget for the year, special analyses of the budget, historical tables, organization charts of the United States Government, and details of new policy initiatives.

State Manual, or Blue Book. Published once every year or two, usually by each State's office of the secretary of state, it often contains the text of the State's constitution, brief descriptions of State and local governmental structure and agencies, recent election results, lists of State and local officials, and much historical, descriptive, and other data about the State.

The Book of the States. Published every two years by the Council of State Governments. It contains a wealth of factual and comparative data on the organization, procedures, and major functions of State governments and several essays on current developments in State government and politics.

Guides and Indexes

Several privately published guides to printed materials will help you find information in a variety of publications. Guides are published monthly, quarterly, or annually, and most are available in a public library.

In addition to these printed publications, many libraries now have computers that access guides which are updated on a weekly or daily basis. On-line computer services, which allow someone to locate (and possibly retrieve) a publication or item of information while sitting at a computer terminal, are also available to individuals and schools. These on-line computer services are worth investigating as new storage and retrieval systems make these services more available and useful to the public.

Books in Print. This book is a continuing list of all hardbound books, new and old, that are published in the United States and currently available. The books are indexed by author, title, publisher, and ISBN.

Paperbound Books in Print. This is a continuing catalog of all paperback books published and currently available in the United States.

Readers' Guide to Periodical Literature. The *Periodical Guide* contains an index of all articles appearing in most magazines and other periodicals of any significant circulation in the country.

The Public Affairs Information Service. This index provides a continuing listing by subject of current books, pamphlets, periodical articles, government documents, and other library materials on a broad range of topics in public affairs.

The Social Science Index. This index is a more specialized, academically oriented catalog of periodical articles in the social sciences. You will find listings of articles on political science, public administration, economics, and criminology in addition to the other social sciences.

Most major (and many smaller) newspapers publish indexes to their daily editions, typically on a bi-weekly or monthly and annual basis. The *New York Times Index* and the *Wall Street Journal Index* are outstanding examples of this kind of very valuable research tool and can be found in larger libraries.

General Reference Works

Many general reference works will prove very useful to an understanding of American government and politics. A few of the important works published by governmental agencies are listed on the previous page. The list of works published by private sources is extremely long and grows yearly. Here are several books that you will likely be able to find in your school or local library. Most of these books are revised and updated on a regular basis.

The American Political Dictionary by Jack Plano and Milton Greenberg. (Published by Holt, Rinehart and Winston)

Safire's Political Dictionary by William Safire. (Published by Random House)

Encyclopedia of American History, edited by Richard B. Morris and Henry Steele Commager. (Published by Harper & Row)

The *Encyclopedia of the American Constitution,* edited by Leonard W. Leby, Kenneth L. Karst, and Dennis J. Mahoney. (Published by Macmillan, 4 volumes)

History of U.S. Political Parties by Arthur M. Schlesinger, Jr. (Published by Bowker, 4 volumes)

Documents of American History, edited by Henry Steele Commager. (Published by Prentice Hall, 2 volumes)

Summaries of Leading Cases on the Constitution by Paul Bartholomew and Joseph Menez. (Published by Littlefield, Adams)

Politics in America: Members of Congress in Washington and at Home, edited by Alan Ehrenhart. (Published by Congressional Quarterly Press)

Several publications by *Congressional Quarterly* are cited at various points in this textbook. Among the several excellent reference works published by *Congressional Quarterly* are these volumes:

Congressional Quarterly's Guide to U.S. Elections. This books is a massive collection of returns for all House and Senate elections since 1924, all gubernatorial elections since 1788, and all presidential elections and national nominating conventions.

Congressional Quarterly's Guide to Congress. This is a comprehensive study of the origins, history, power, and procedures of the nation's lawmaking body.

Congressional Quarterly's Guide to the United States Supreme Court. This guide is one of the most extensive compilations of information ever published about the Court, its members, history, and the cases it has decided.

Congressional Quarterly's Guide to the Presidency. This guide provides in-depth information about the presidency and the executive agencies.

Washington Information Directory. This book provides information about all the Political Action Committees and political organizations that have offices in Washington.

Almanacs

Almanacs are handy reference tools that contain a wealth of up-to-date information on a variety of topics. Most almanacs give you ready access to data about politics, the economy, population, history, and other areas of vital information. Because almanacs are inexpensive, one-volume books that are published annually, you should easily be able to find a current edition in a library or bookstore, or even in your classroom. Some of the best-known almanacs are listed below.

The World Almanac and Book of Facts. This general almanac contains close to 1,000 pages and 10,000 listings, most of which are useful to students of American government. The book contains separate sections with the previous year in review, time lines on world and American history, and listings for each State in the Union and each country in the world.

Information Please Almanac. Much like *The World Almanac* in size and scope, this almanac also contains special consumer features on such issues as drug abuse, taxes, first aid, science, law enforcement, etc.

The Universal Almanac. This new almanac features larger, easier-to-read type than most other almanacs. It also incorporates more graphics than other almanacs. The larger-than-average international section is very useful for comparative government statistics.

The Statesman's Yearbook. Published for over 125 years, this specialized British almanac features close to 1700 pages of information about the countries of the world. Entries are listed by country and include information about the history, population, geography, climate, government, defense, international relations, economy, energy, natural resources, industry, trade, communications, religion, education, and social welfare of a nation.

The Almanac of American Politics. More expensive and more specialized than the other almanacs, this reference work is devoted exclusively to information about the 535 members of the United States Congress. This almanac describes each congressional district and gives detailed information about its representative, including his or her voting record on key issues.

Encyclopaedia Britannica, Book of the Year. This volume is not strictly an almanac; it is the yearly supplement to the encyclopedia. However, the last few hundred pages contain up-to-date statistical information about all the countries of the world, similar to the information you would find in an almanac.

Periodicals

A vast amount of basic information can be found in the news stories, feature articles, and commentaries in magazines and other periodicals. To locate articles, use one of the references or guides listed.

Many periodicals—such as *Time, Newsweek,* or *U.S. News & World Report*—provide general news coverage. However, keep in mind that many periodicals reflect a strong liberal or conservative perspective on their coverage of current events. For example, the *National Review* has a conservative bent and *The New Republic* offers a contrasting liberal perspective.

Most libraries will carry at least several of these well-respected magazines:

American Heritage
The Atlantic
Business Week
Commentary
Common Cause Magazine
Congressional Digest
Congressional Quarterly Weekly Report
Forbes
Fortune
Harper's
Insight
National Civic Review
National Journal
National Review
Nation's Business
The New Republic
Newsweek
Public Opinion
Senior Scholastic
Time
U.S. News & World Report
World Press Review

A number of more specialized scholarly journals are also available in many libraries. The following are among the most useful for students of American government:

American Journal of Political Science
The American Political Science Review
The Annals of the American Academy of Political and Social Sciences
Foreign Affairs
Foreign Policy
Journal of International Affairs
The Journal of Politics
Public Administration Review
Public Opinion Quarterly
Publius: The Journal of Federalism
State Government

Private Organizations

A large number of private organizations publish informative pamphlets and other materials on American government and politics, focusing especially on various public policy questions. To find the names and addresses of an organization, see *The Encyclopedia of Associations,* a reference work published yearly that is a guide to national and international organizations.

A sampling of some of the most prominent organizations are listed below:

The American Federation of Labor and Congress of Industrial Organizations (AFL-CIO), 815 16th Street, NW, Washington, D.C. 20006

The American Enterprise Institute for Public Policy Research, 4720-A Boston Way, Lanham, MD 20706

Chamber of Commerce of the United States, 12615 H Street, NW, Washington, D.C. 20062

The Committee for Economic Development, 477 Madison Avenue, New York, NY 10022

Common Cause, 2030 M Street, NW, Washington, D.C. 20036

The Democratic National Committee, 430 Capitol Street, SE, Washington, D.C. 20003

The Foreign Policy Association, 205 Lexington Avenue, New York, NY 10016

The League of Women Voters of the United States, 1730 M Street, NW, Washington, D.C. 20036

The National Association for the Advancement of Colored People (NAACP), 4815 Mt. Hope Drive, Baltimore, MD 21215

The National Municipal League, 55 W. 44th Street, New York, NY 10036

The Republican National Committee, 310 1st Street, SE, Washington, DC 20003

Books

This unit-by-unit listing is not intended as an exhaustive bibliography. It is, instead, a sampling of many recently published volumes useful to the study of American government.

Unit 1

Allen, W.B. *et al.* (eds.) *The Essential AntiFederalist.* University Press of America, 1987.

Barone, Michael. *Our Country: The Shaping of America from Roosevelt to Reagan.* Free Press, 1990.

Bowen, Catherine Drinker. *Miracle at Philadelphia: The Story of the Constitution.* Little, Brown, 1986.

Bowman, Ann O'M. and Richard C. Kearney. *State & Local Government.* Houghton Mifflin, 1990.

Cox, Archibald. *The Court and the Constitution.* Houghton Mifflin, 1987.

Dahl, Robert A. *Democracy and Its Critics.* Yale University Press, 1989.

Miles, Rosaline. *The Women's History of the World.* Harper & Row, 1990.

Moyers, Bill. *A World of Ideas.* Doubleday, 1989.

Press, Charles and Kenneth VerBerg. *State and Community Governments in a Dynamic Federal System.* Harper Collins, 3rd ed., 1991.

Roskin, Michael G., *et al. Political Science: An Introduction.* Prentice Hall, 4th ed., 1991.

Rossiter, Clinton. *1787: The Grand Convention.* Norton, 1987.

Unit 2

Abramson, Jeffrey and Gary R. Orren. *The Electronic Commonwealth: The Impact of News Media Technologies on Democratic Politics.* Basic Books, 1990.

Asher, Herbert B. *Polling and the Public: What Every Citizen Should Know.* CQ Press, 1987.

Conway, Jill K., *et al. Learning About Women: Gender, Politics, and Power.* University of Michigan Press, 1989.

Conway, M. Margaret. *Political Participation in the United States.* CQ Press, 2nd ed., 1990.

Dunham, Pat. *Electoral Behavior in the United States.* Prentice Hall, 1991.

Jackson, Brooks. *Broken Promises: Why the Federal Election Commission Failed.* Brookings, 1990.

Magleby, David B. and Candice J. Nelson. *The Money Chase: Congressional Campaign Finance Reform.* Brookings, 1990.

Mahood, H.R. *Interest Group Politics in America: A New Intensity.* Prentice Hall, 1990.

Mickelson, Sig. *From Whistle Stop to Sound Bite: Four Decades of Politics and Television.* Praeger, 1989.

Nogel, Jack H. *Participation.* Prentice Hall, 1987.

Pohlmann, Marcus D. *Black Politics in Conservative America.* Longman, 1990.

Sherill, Robert. *Why They Call It Politics.* Harcourt Brace Jovanovich, 5th ed., 1990.

Vogel, David. *Fluctuating Fortunes: The Political Power of Business in America.* Basic Books, 1989.

Unit 3

Aberbach, Joel D. *Keeping a Watchful Eye: The Politics of Congressional Oversight.* Brookings, 1990.

Abourezk, James G. *Advise and Dissent: Memoirs of South Dakota and the U.S. Senate.* Laurence Hill, 1990.

Bailey, Christopher J. *The U.S. Congress.* Blackwell, 1989.

Barry, John M. *The Ambition and the Power: The Fall of Jim Wright.* Viking, 1990.

Cochran, Charles E. *et al. American Public Policy.* St. Martin's Press, 3rd ed., 1990.

Fenno, Richard F., Jr. *The Making of a Senator: Dan Quayle.* CQ Press, 1989.

Fowler, Linda L. and Robert D. McClure. *Political Ambition: Who Decides to Run for Congress.* Yale University Press, 1989.

Power in Congress: Who Has It, How They Got It, How They Use It. CQ Press, 1987.

Warmuth, Francis D. and Edwin B. Fumage. *To Chain the Dog of War: The War Powers of Congress.* University of Illinois Press, 2nd ed., 1989.

Wolpe, Bruce C. *Lobbying Congress: How the System Works.* CQ Press, 1990.

Unit 4

Barnet, Richard J. *The Rockets' Red Glare: When America Goes to War—The Presidents and the People.* Simon & Schuster, 1990.

Burnham, David. *A Law Unto Itself: Power, Politics and the IRS.* Random House, 1990.

Crabb, Cecil V. and Kevin V. Mulcahy. *American National Security: A Presidential Perspective.* Brooks/Cole, 1991.

Cronin, Thomas E. (ed.) *Inventing the American Presidency.* University Press of Kansas, 1989.

DiClerico, Robert E. *The American President.* Prentice Hall, 3rd ed., 1990.

Hastedt, Glenn P. *American Foreign Policy: Past, Present, Future.* Prentice Hall, 2nd ed., 1991.

Heard, Alexander. *Made in America: The Nomination and Election of Presidents.* Harper Collins, 1991.

Heilbroner, Robert and Peter Bernstein. *The Debt and the Deficit: False Alarms/Real Possibilities.* Norton, 1989.

Hughes, Barry B. *Continuity and Change in World Politics.* Prentice Hall, 1991.

McNamara, Robert S. *Out of the Cold: New Thinking for American Foreign and Defense Policy in the 21st Century.* Simon & Schuster, 1989.

Noonan, Peggy. *What I Saw at the Revolution: A Political Life in the Reagan Era.* Random House, 1990.

Pfiffner, James. *The Managerial Presidency.* Brooks/Cole, 1991.

Whitney, David C. and Robin V. Whitney. *The American Presidents: Biographies of the Chief Executives from Washington Through Bush.* Prentice Hall, 7th ed., 1990.

UNIT 5

Bell, Derrick. *And We Are Not Saved: The Elusive Quest for Racial Equality.* Basic Books. 1987.

Browning, Rufus P. *et al.* (eds.). *Racial Politics in American Cities.* Longman, 1990.

Canedy, Susan. *America's Nazis: A Democratic Dilemma.* Markgraf, 1990.

Fenwick, Lyndon B. *Should the Children Pray? A Historical, Judicial and Political Examination of Public School Prayer.* Baylor University Press, 1990.

Irons, Peter. *The Court of Their Convictions: Sixteen Americans Who Fought Their Way to the Supreme Court.* Free Press, 1989.

Keenan, Joseph. *The Constitution of the United States: Origins, Documents, and Interpretations.* Dorsey, 2nd ed., 1988.

Levine, Herbert M. and Jean Edward Smith. *Civil Liberties and Civil Rights Debated.* Prentice Hall, 1988.

Louthan, William C. *The United States Supreme Court: Lawmaking in the Third Branch of Government.* Prentice Hall, 1991.

Takai, Ronald. *Strangers from a Different Shore: A History of Asian Americans.* Little, Brown, 1989.

UNIT 6

Barry, Donald D. *Contemporary Soviet Politics.* Prentice Hall, 2nd ed., 1991.

Budge, Ian and David McKay. *The Changing British Political System: Into the 1990s.* Longman, 2nd ed., 1990.

Campbell, Colin *et al. Politics and Government in Europe Today.* Harcourt Brace Jovanovich, 1990.

Communism: Its Rise and Fall in the 20th Century. Christian Science Monitor, 1990.

Ishida, Takeshi and Ellis S. Krauss. *Democracy in Japan.* University of Pittsburgh Press, 1989.

Macridis, Roy C. *Modern Political Systems: Europe.* Prentice Hall, 7th ed., 1990.

Macridis, Roy C. and Steven L. Burg. *Introduction to Comparative Politics: Political Regimes and Political Change.* Harper Collins, 1991.

Ozinga, James R. *Communism: The Story of the Idea and Its Implementation.* Prentice Hall, 2nd ed., 1991.

Salisbury, Harrison. *Tiananmen Square: Thirteen Days in June.* Little, Brown, 1989.

Wilson, Frank L. *European Politics Today: The Democratic Experience.* Prentice Hall, 1990.

UNIT 7

Baum, Lawrence. *American Courts: Process and Policy.* Houghton Mifflin, 2nd ed., 1990.

The Book of the States, 1991-1992. The Council of State Governments, 1990.

Cronin, Thomas E. *Direct Democracy: The Politics of Initiative, Referendum and Recall.* Harvard University Press, 1989.

Grant, Donald R. and Lloyd B. Omdahl. *State and Local Government in America.* Allyn and Bacon, 5th ed., 1987.

Jacob, Herbert, *et al. Politics in the American States.* Scott, Foresman, 5th ed., 1990.

Harrigan, John J. *Politics and Policy in the States and Communities.* Harper Collins, 4th ed., 1991.

Henry, Nicholas. *Governing at the Grassroots: State & Local Politics.* Prentice Hall, 3rd ed., 1987.

U.S. Bureau of the Census: State Government Finances in 1989. Government Printing Office, 1990

Van Horn, Carl E. (ed.). *The State of the States.* CQ Press, 1989.

The Executive Departments: Public Agencies and Functions*

Department of State

Established: 1789

Head: Secretary of State

Telephone: (203) 647-4000

The State Department's primary objective is to promote the long-range security and well-being of the United States. Its major functions include advising the President in forming and executing foreign policy, negotiating treaties and agreements with foreign nations, speaking for the United States in the United Nations and other international organizations, and representing the United States at more than 800 international conferences each year.

Bureau of Economic and Business Affairs. Designs and carries out policy regarding foreign economic matters, including resources and food, energy issues, trade controls, finance and development, aviation, and maritime affairs.

Regional Bureaus. Responsible for U.S. foreign affair activities in five geographic regions: the Bureaus of African Affairs, European and Canadian Affairs, East Asian and Pacific Affairs, Inter-American Affairs, and Near Eastern and South Asian Affairs.

Bureau of Public Affairs. Provides information on foreign policy to the American people through conferences, briefings, and speaking and media engagements. This bureau also produces and distributes publications, videotapes, and films on U.S. foreign policy.

* The agencies listed on these pages are the major units in the 14 cabinet departments. For information on other agencies in each of them, see *The Government Manual*.

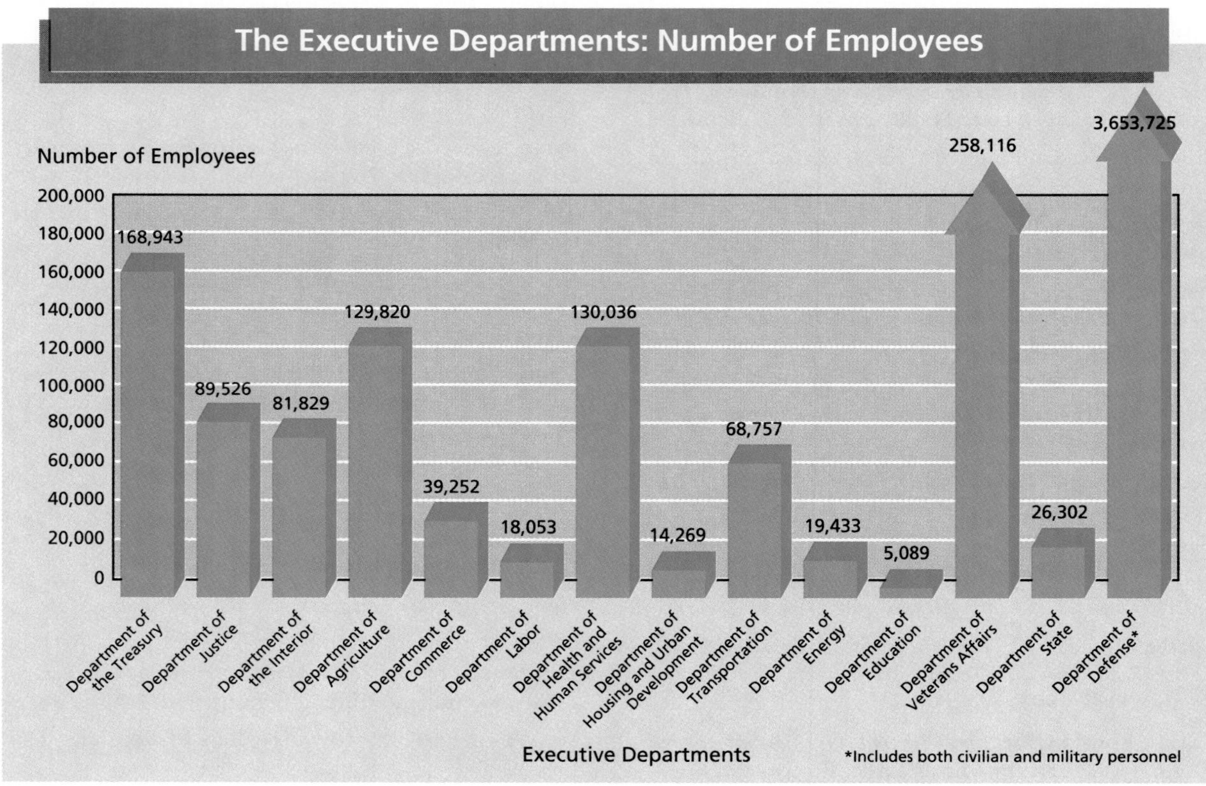

This graph summarizes the size of each of the nation's executive departments, ranging from a low of 5,089 employees for the Department of Education to a high of 3,653,725 employees for the Department of Defense.

Bureau of Intelligence and Research. Coordinates programs of intelligence, research, and analysis for the department and other federal agencies. Gathers and analyzes information essential to foreign policy determination and execution.

Bureau of Consular Affairs. Administers and enforces laws concerning immigration and nationality, issues passports and visas, and is responsible for the protection and welfare of American citizens and interests abroad.

Bureau of Politico-Military Affairs. Develops policy and provides direction on issues that affect U.S. security policies, military assistance, nuclear policy, and arms control matters.

Office of the Chief of Protocol. Advises the National Government, the President, the Vice President, and the secretary of state on matters of diplomatic procedure according to international laws and customs; responsible for coordinating visits of foreign officials and conducting ceremonial functions and public events.

United States Foreign Service. Maintains embassies, consulates, missions, and other offices throughout the world. Ambassadors representing the President have full responsibility for conducting foreign policy within their country of assignment and informing the President about any developments that affect the welfare and security of the American people. The ambassadors' responsibilities include negotiating agreements, explaining U.S. foreign policy, and maintaining cordial relations with the host country's government and people.

Other Bureaus

- Bureau of International Organization Affairs
- Bureau of Human Rights and Humanitarian Affairs
- Bureau for Refugee Programs
- Bureau of Oceans and International and Scientific Affairs

Department of the Treasury

Established: 1789

Head: Secretary of the Treasury

Telephone: (202) 566-2000

The Treasury Department is the Federal Government's leading financial agency. Its major functions include the collection of tax revenue and customs duties, borrowing and the management of the public debt, criminal law enforcement (notably tax evasion, smuggling, and counterfeiting), accounting for public monies, the manufacture of coins and currency, and the supervision of national banks.

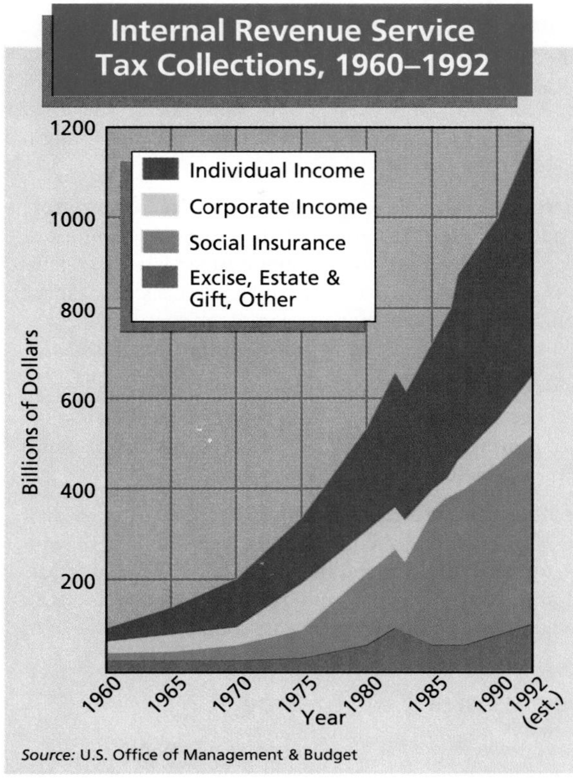

Computer technology has greatly speeded the processing of tax returns. According to the graph, which shows various types of tax collections, the individual income tax has generated the most income since 1965.

Internal Revenue Service. Administers, enforces most federal tax laws; collects nearly all federal taxes (including, especially, personal and corporate income, social security, excise, estate, and gift taxes).

United States Customs Service. Administers, enforces customs laws; collects duties on imports; combats smuggling and other illegal practices in international trade.

Bureau of the Public Debt. Supervises most federal borrowing; manages the public debt.

Bureau of Alcohol, Tobacco, and Firearms. Administers and enforces federal laws governing firearms and explosives, and those covering the production, use, and distribution of alcohol and tobacco products.

Financial Management Service. Government's central bookkeeper and principal financial reporting agency.

Bureau of Engraving and Printing. Designs, engraves, prints all currency (paper money), treasury bonds and notes, postage stamps, food coupons, and similar financial items issued by the Federal Government.

United States Mint. Manufactures all U.S. coins; holds stocks of gold and silver; operates mints in San Francisco, California; Philadelphia, Pennsylvania; Denver, Colorado; and West Point, New York; the assay office in San Francisco, California; and the bullion depository in Fort Knox, Kentucky.

Office of the Comptroller of the Currency. Headed by the comptroller of the currency; administers federal banking laws and generally supervises the operations of some 4,600 national banks; directs staff of more than 2,000 bank examiners to assure the soundness of the operations and financial condition of all national banks.

Office of Thrift Supervision. Monitors and regulates the approximately 2,600 savings and loan institutions covered by Savings Association Insurance Fund (SAIF), which insures deposits in S & L's.

United States Secret Service. Protects the President and Vice President, the members of their immediate families, former Presidents and their wives or widows, presidential and vice-presidential candidates, and visiting heads of foreign states; enforces laws against counterfeiting.

Department of Justice

Established: 1870

Head: Attorney General

Telephone: (202) 514-2000

The Department of Justice is the nation's largest law firm. Among its major responsibilities, it furnishes legal advice to the President and heads of the other executive departments; represents the United States in court; enforces most federal criminal laws; enforces federal civil rights, antitrust, public lands, immigration and naturalization laws, and supervises the federal penal system.

Solicitor General. Represents the United States in the Supreme Court; decides which lower court decisions the Federal Government should appeal to the High Court and the position the United States should take in these cases.

Antitrust Division. Handles court cases involving violations of antitrust laws, other federal statutes covering illegal business practices.

Environment and Natural Resources Division. Handles most civil (noncriminal) cases involving public lands and natural resources, wildlife resources, Native American lands and claims; prosecutes civil and criminal cases arising out of federal environmental protection laws.

Tax Division. Handles civil and criminal cases arising out of the tax laws; often acts as in-court attorney for the Internal Revenue Service.

Civil Rights Division. Handles both civil and criminal cases involving acts of discrimination prohibited by the various federal civil rights laws.

Civil Division. Handles most civil cases to which the United States is a party (all civil cases not handled by one of the other divisions).

Criminal Division. Handles most court cases involving federal crimes (all criminal cases not handled by one of the other divisions).

Immigration and Naturalization Service. Administers and enforces the immigration laws (involving aliens who seek to enter or remain in the United States) and the naturalization laws (relating to aliens who seek citizenship).

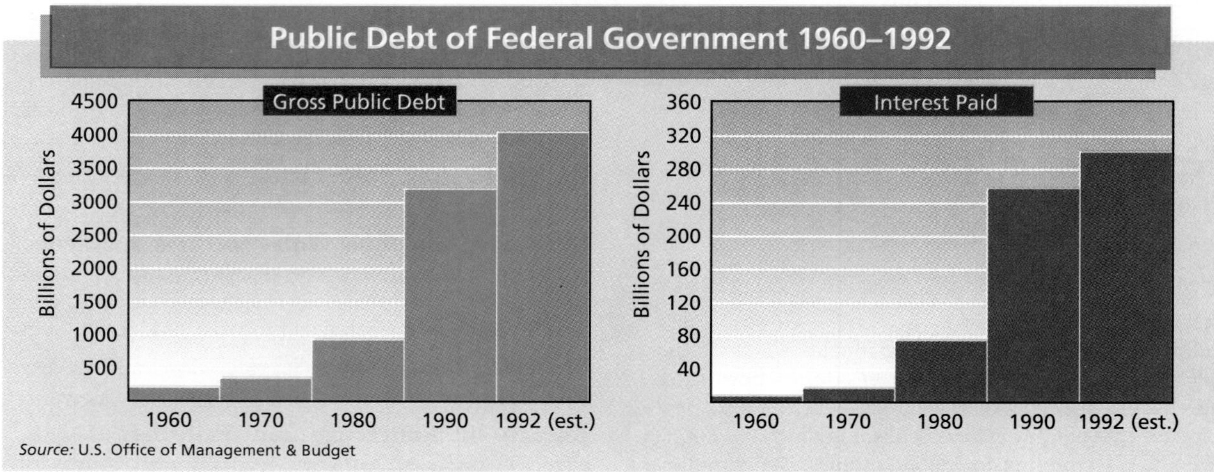

Federal borrowing is supervised by the Bureau of the Public Debt. The interest payment on the United States public debt has increased by approximately $230 billion since 1980.

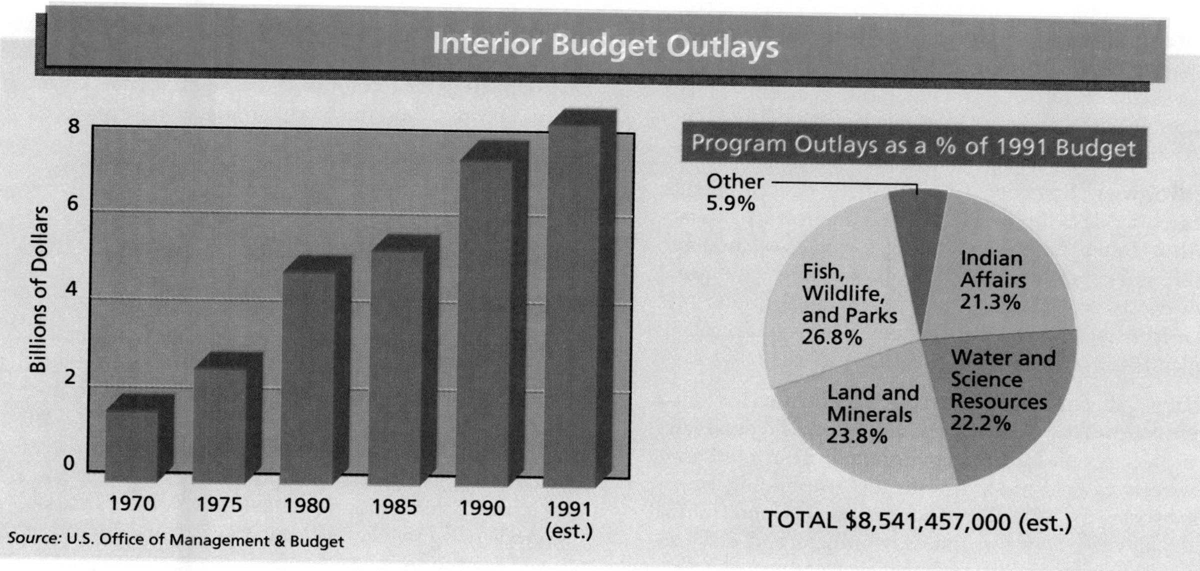

The Department of the Interior is the government's major conservation agency. These graphs show the amount of money spent by this department since 1970 (left) and the breakdown of the department's budget for 1991 by agency.

United States Marshals Service. The oldest federal law enforcement agency; its nearly 3,000 officers protect federal courts, execute federal court orders, arrest most federal fugitives, operate the Witness Security Program, and respond to such emergency situations as terrorist incidents.

Federal Bureau of Investigation. Principal investigative arm of the Justice Department; handles all violations of federal law except those specifically assigned to another federal law enforcement agency; gathers and reports facts, locates witnesses, compiles evidence in those cases.

Drug Enforcement Administration. Administers and enforces laws relating to controlled substances (principally narcotics and dangerous drugs).

Bureau of Prisons. Operates the federal penal system (including six penitentiaries and more than 60 correctional institutions, prison camps, detention centers, medical centers, and other jail facilities).

Department of the Interior

Established: 1849

Head: Secretary of the Interior

Telephone: (202) 208-3100

The Interior Department is the Federal Government's major conservation agency. Its principal work involves the management of more than 500 million acres of public lands; conservation, development, and use of mineral, water, fish, and wildlife resources; reclamation of arid lands; operation of federal hydroelectric power facilities; administration of the national parks system; and responsibility for Native American reservations.

Bureau of Land Management. Controls, manages some 270 million acres of public lands (located chiefly in the West and Alaska); manages timber, oil, gas, minerals, rangeland, recreation, and other resources of those lands; leases public lands for such purposes as grazing and the commercial development of oil, gas, minerals, and other resources.

Minerals Management Service. Leases the offshore (outer continental shelf) lands for oil, gas, and other resource development.

Bureau of Reclamation. Builds, operates water projects to reclaim arid and semiarid lands in the western States; most projects are multipurpose. That is, in addition to water conservation, storage, and irrigation, they serve such other purposes as hydroelectric power generation, flood control, municipal and industrial water supply, navigation, and outdoor recreation.

National Park Service. Administers the more than 350 units of the National Park System (including national parks, national monuments, scenic rivers, lakeshores and seashores, recreation areas, and historic sites); plays host to more than 300 million tourist visits each year.

United States Fish and Wildlife Service. Responsible for protecting and increasing the nation's fish and wildlife resources; maintains more than 450 wildlife refuges, 70 fish hatcheries, a number of laboratories, and a nationwide network of wildlife law enforcement agents.

Geological Survey. Conducts surveys and other research to describe (map) the geography and geology of the United States and to locate oil, gas, mineral, water, and other natural resources; studies such natural hazards as earthquakes, volcanoes, and floods. Its detailed maps and reports now cover more than half of the land area of the United States.

Office of Surface Mining Reclamation and Enforcement. Administers and enforces federal laws to protect people and the environment from the harmful effects of coal mining; regulates stripmining activities; works to reclaim abandoned mines and mined lands; aids the States in the development and enforcement of their own similar regulatory programs.

Bureau of Mines. Conducts research and issues factual reports on mining techniques, mine health and safety, environmental pollution, the recycling of solid wastes, and nearly all other phases of mining activity in this country.

Bureau of Indian Affairs. Administers educational, public health, and other social assistance and economic development programs for the nation's Native American and Alaskan Native population, especially the approximately 600,000 Native Americans who now live on or near some 260 reservations.

Office for Territorial and International Affairs. Works to promote the economic, social, and political development of the territories of the Virgin Islands, Guam, American Samoa, and the Northern Marianas.

Department of Agriculture

Established: 1889

Head: Secretary of Agriculture

Telephone: (202) 447-2791

The Department of Agriculture reflects this fundamentally important point: the nation's farms produce the food upon which all of us must depend, and they also produce a goodly share of the raw materials essential to the nation's manufacturing industries. The USDA's several agencies have wide-ranging responsibilities in the areas of agricultural conservation and rural development, marketing, credit, crop stabilization, and research and education.

Farmers Home Administration. Makes low-interest, long-term loans to farmers, ranchers, and farm groups unable to get credit at reasonable terms from other (private) lenders; also guarantees loans from private lenders. Most FHA loans are made for the purchase, enlargement, improvement, or operation of family-sized farms.

Rural Electrification Administration. Makes low-interest, long-term loans to farm cooperatives and other rural-based nonprofit groups to provide electric power and/or telephone service to people in rural areas; also guarantees loans from private lenders.

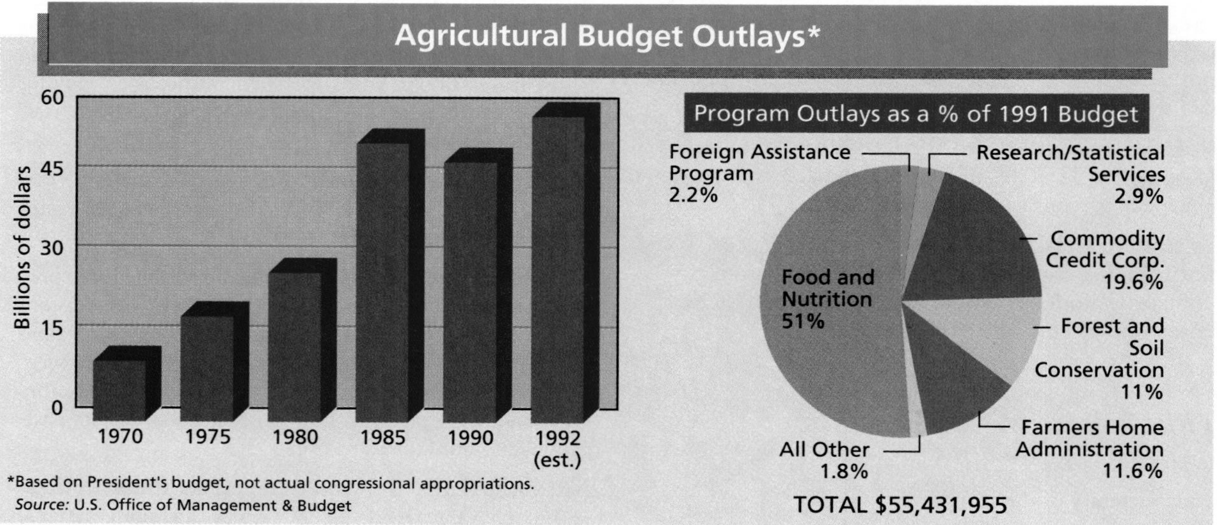

According to the pie graph at right, outlays by the Food and Nutrition Service, whose programs are described on the next page, represented 51 percent of the expenditures of the Department of Agriculture in 1991.

Agricultural Cooperative Service. Helps farmers to form and run cooperatives, especially to market their crops and to purchase farm supplies.

Agricultural Marketing Service. Aids farmers to market their products; issues daily reports on crop conditions, demands, prices, and other local and national market data, through press, radio, television; enforces several laws that prohibit fraud and other deceptive market practices.

Animal and Plant Health Inspection Service. Conducts inspections and may impose quarantines to prevent, control, or eradicate animal and plant pests and diseases; regulates the manufacture and sale of chemical and other products used to control such pests and diseases; administers laws for humane treatment of livestock and circus, zoo, and laboratory animals.

Food and Nutrition Service. Administers the food stamp program (coupons for low-income persons and families to increase their food purchasing power); provides grants and/or foodstuffs for other food assistance programs (most notably, the National School Lunch Program).

Food Safety and Inspection Service. Inspects poultry and meat processing plants and grades their products under federal laws that set safety, quality, and label standards.

Federal Grain Inspection Service. Weighs and inspects all grain exports from the United States; oversees State and private inspection of grain marketed within the country.

Agricultural Stabilization and Conservation Service. Administers several price support, commodity loan, and subsidy payment programs to "stabilize" (maintain, bolster) farm incomes and market prices for certain crops.

Commodity Credit Corporation. Holds (stores) crops purchased or accepted as payments of loans under the various programs administered by the ASCS; reduces surplus crop holdings (mostly by donations to federal, State, and private welfare agencies and programs).

Federal Crop Insurance Corporation. Offers (sells directly) and contracts with private companies to provide insurance to producers of most widely grown crops, to protect them against unavoidable losses from such causes as weather, insects, and diseases.

Agricultural Research Service. Conducts basic and applied research programs; makes grants to support research at State agricultural experiment stations and land-grant universities; provides financial support for the Cooperative Extension Service (which operates through land-grant universities and county extension agents, to promote "beyond-the-classroom" education and other farm-related activities, especially in rural areas); administers grants and other financial aid for higher education in food and agricultural sciences, veterinary medicine.

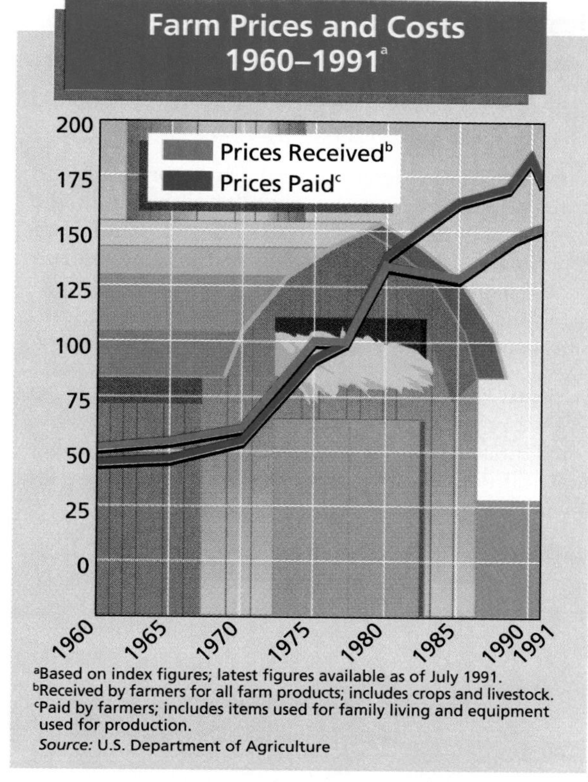

The graph above shows the increasing disparity between prices received by farmers for their goods and prices paid by farmers for their operating expenses.

Forest Service. Manages the national forest system (156 national forests, 19 national grasslands, and land use projects on 191 million acres in 44 States, the Virgin Islands and Puerto Rico); sells timber and issues oil, gas, mineral, grazing leases; provides outdoor recreation facilities and protects scenic areas and wildlife habitat; makes grants for forestry research.

Soil Conservation Service. Directs and/or provides financial and other assistance for a broad range of soil conservation, watershed protection, and related programs; promotes the creation of and gives technical help to local soil conservation districts (which now number about 3,000 and cover more than 90 percent of the nation's farms and farmlands).

Department of Commerce

Established: 1903

Head: Secretary of Commerce

Telephone: (202) 377-2000

Many of the Federal Government's programs to promote business and the overall well-being of the nation's economy are centered in the Commerce Department. Its several agencies are charged with this broad mission: to promote international trade, spur the nation's economic growth, and encourage technological advancement.

Bureau of the Census. Takes a census of the nation's population every 10 years (as required by the Constitution); collects, analyzes, and publishes other statistical data about the people and the economy of the nation.

National Institute of Standards and Technology. Formerly, the National Bureau of Standards; maintains the uniform standards of all weights and measures that, by law, can be used in the United States; conducts advanced scientific and other experimental research and testing; provides scientific/technological services to government, private industry.

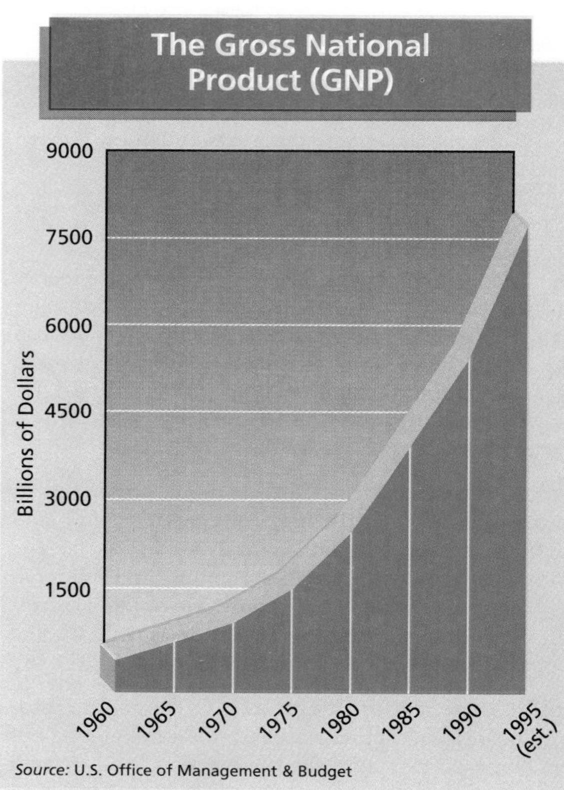

The GNP measures, in dollar terms, the total annual national output of goods and services. This graph shows the rise in the GNP since 1960.

Patent and Trademark Office. Issues more than 90,000 patents a year (patents of invention, good for 17 years; patents of design, good for 14 years; and plant patents, good for 17 years); registers some 60,000 trademarks each year (good for 10 years and renewable).

National Oceanic and Atmospheric Administration. Operates the National Weather Service, which forecasts and reports weather conditions; makes satellite observations of weather and other features of the earth's environment; conducts oceanic, atmospheric, seismological and other environmental research; publishes nautical and aeronautical maps, charts, and other reports; administers the Sea Grant program (grants for marine research, education).

United States Travel and Tourism Administration. Works with the travel industry, here and abroad, to attract tourists and other foreign visitors to this country.

National Technical Information Service. Central federal service for machine processable data files and computer software in engineering, medical, and other scientific and technical fields.

Minority Business Development Agency. Promotes and coordinates federal and other public and private efforts to help organize and strengthen businesses owned and operated by members of minority groups; furnishes management and technical assistance to minority firms.

Bureau of Economic Analysis. Collects and analyzes data to provide a detailed picture of the structure, condition, and prospects of the nation's economy; reports on the gross national product (the GNP, the total annual national output of goods and services, measured in dollar terms).

International Trade Administration. Promotes American interests in foreign trade, enforces federal laws to protect American industry against unfair foreign competition, maintains a network of Foreign Commercial Service offices to report on business conditions and investment opportunities abroad, and conducts trade fairs and operates trade centers in other countries.

Bureau of Export Administration. Enforces laws that control the export of products, materials, and technology for reasons of national security.

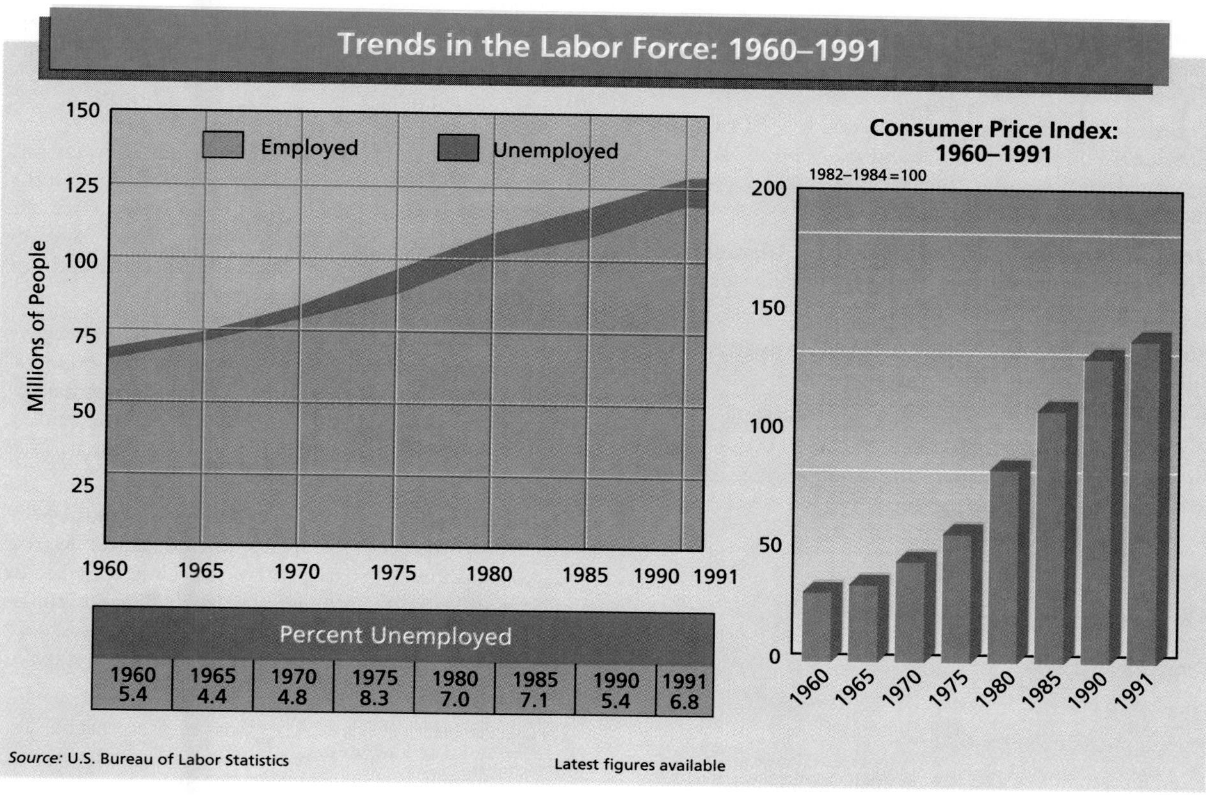

These graphs show the number of employed and unemployed in the labor force since 1960 (left) as well as the consumer price index, which is based on average prices paid for day-to-day items such as food, clothing, shelter, transportation, fuels, drugs, and other goods and services.

Department of Labor

Established: 1913

Head: Secretary of Labor

Telephone: (202) 523-6666

For more than 75 years now, the Labor Department's job has been the one Congress first assigned to it in 1913: "to foster, promote, and develop the welfare of the wage earners of the United States, to improve their working conditions, and to advance their opportunities for profitable employment."

Employment and Training Administration. An umbrella agency that performs numerous functions through numerous units: through the United States Employment Service, aids the States to operate a system of local employment offices; through the Federal Unemployment Insurance Service, supervises the States' administration of their unemployment compensation programs (largely financed by a federal tax on employers); through the Office of Job Training Programs, makes grants for and administers job training, work experience, and public service employment programs; through the Bureau of Apprenticeship and Training, works to improve the standards of apprenticeship and training for skilled jobs.

Employment Standards Administration. An umbrella agency: through the Wage and Hour Division, enforces federal minimum wage and maximum hours laws; through the Office of Federal Contract Compliance Programs, enforces laws prohibiting discrimination in employment on all federally supported construction projects; through the Office of Workers' Compensation Programs, administers laws providing injury and accident benefits for federal employees.

Office of Labor-Management Standards. Administers the Labor-Management Reporting and Disclosure (Landrum-Griffin) Act of 1959 and other statutes, regulating the internal procedures and finances of labor unions, protecting rights of members.

Bureau of Labor-Management Relations. Offers a wide range of services to improve and facilitate relations between labor and management in collective bargaining and other areas.

Pension and Welfare Benefits Administration. Enforces federal laws regulating conduct of private pension, welfare plans.

Veterans' Employment and Training Service. Works with the VA and other public and private agencies to ensure the reemployment and other work benefit rights of veterans.

Occupational Safety and Health Administration. Enforces federal laws that set minimum safety and health standards in most work situations.

Mine Safety and Health Administration. Enforces federal laws setting minimum safety and health standards for mining operations.

Bureau of Labor Statistics. Collects, analyzes, and publishes data on employment, unemployment, hours of work, wages, prices, productivity, and several other topics in the field of labor economics.

Department of Defense

Established: 1949

Head: Secretary of Defense

Telephone: (703) 545-6700

The Department of Defense is responsible for providing the military forces needed to prevent war and protect the security of our country. The major elements of these forces are the army, navy, Marine Corps, and air force, consisting of about 2.0 million men and women on active duty. In addition, the Department of Defense employs about 1.6 million civilians. Central headquarters of the department is at the Pentagon, the "world's largest office building."

Joint Chiefs of Staff. The principal military advisers to the President, the National Security Council, and the secretary of defense. The Joint Chiefs of Staff are the highest-ranking military officers of the army, navy, air force, and Marine Corps and are subject to the authority of the President and the secretary of defense.

Department of the Army. Organizes, trains, and equips active duty and reserve forces for the preservation of peace, security, and the defense of our nation. The army's mission focuses on land operations, training soldiers with modern weapons and equipment that enable them to respond quickly.

Department of the Navy. The primary mission of the Department of the Navy, including its Marine Corps component, is to protect the United States by effectively carrying out war at sea. Responsibilities include seizing or defending advanced naval bases; supporting, as required, all other military forces; and maintaining freedom of the seas.

Department of the Air Force. Responsible for providing an air force that is capable of preserving the peace and security of the United States internationally and in space.

Service Academies. The United States Military Academy (West Point, New York), the United States Air

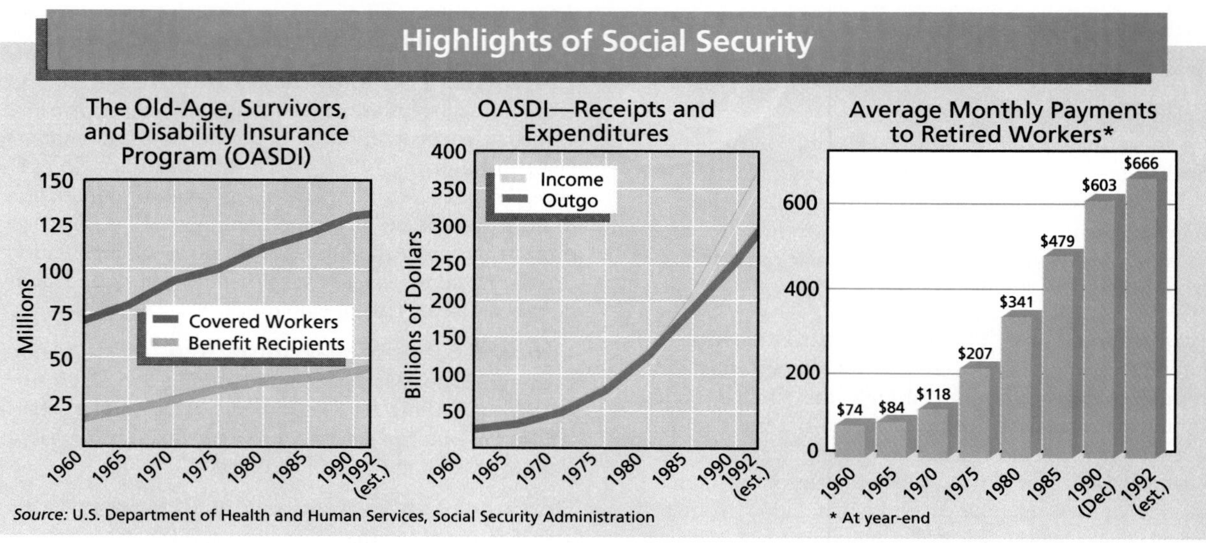

According to the bar graph, the average monthly payment to a single retiree increased almost three times from 1975 to 1992.

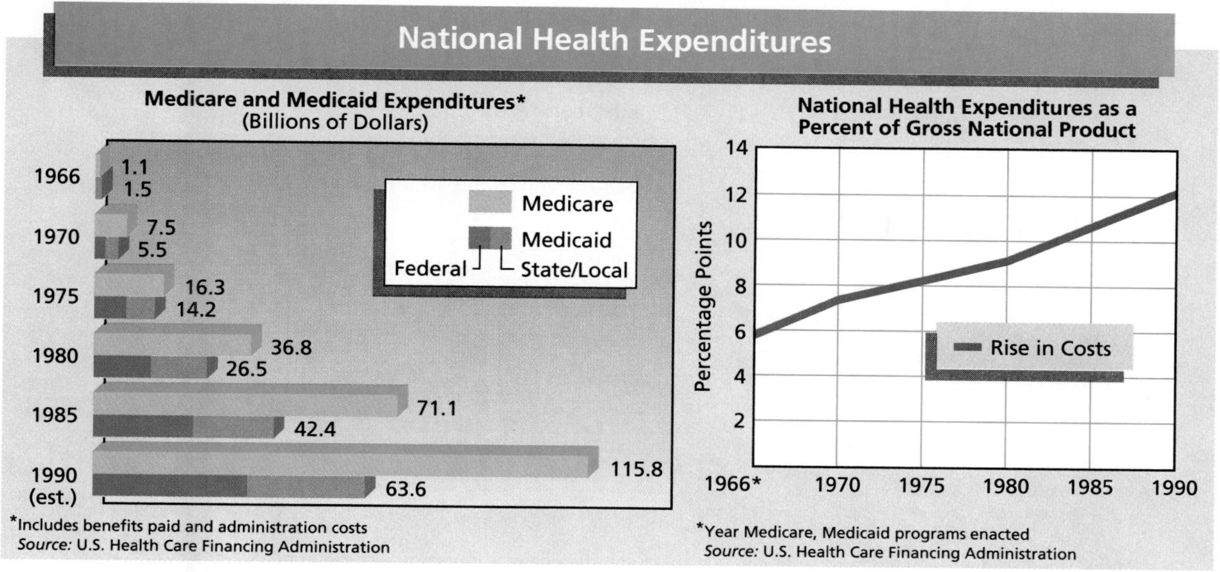

These graphs show the breakdown of funds spent on Medicare and Medicaid (left) and the percentage of the GNP taken by health expenditures. According to the line graph, national health expenditures as a percent of GNP doubled between 1966 and 1990.

Force Academy (Colorado Springs, Colorado), and the United States Naval Academy (Annapolis, Maryland) all offer theoretical and practical officer training as well as a four-year comprehensive college education.

Department of Defense Agencies. Various defense agencies established for specific purposes include:

- National Security Agency
- Defense Communications Agency
- Defense Investigative Service
- Defense Mapping Agency

Department of Health and Human Services

Established: 1953

Head: Secretary of Health and Human Services

Telephone: (202) 619-0251

The Department of Health and Human Services administers several welfare, public assistance, and public health programs and also has a number of research, educational, and regulatory functions in those areas. HHS has described itself as "a department of people serving people, from newborn infants to our most elderly citizens."

Office of Human Development Services. An umbrella agency: through the Administration on Aging, makes grants, gives other support to State and local programs to provide social services to older persons; through the Administration for Native Americans, makes grants, gives other support to social and economic development programs for Native Americans, Alaskan Natives, and Native Hawaiians; through the Administration on Developmental Disabilities, makes grants, gives other support to rehabilitation and similar programs for persons with disabilities.

Public Health Service. An umbrella agency: through the Centers for Disease Control, conducts research and treatment programs for the prevention and control of communicable and other diseases; through the Food and Drug Administration, conducts research and administers federal laws that prohibit the manufacture, shipment, or sale of impure and unsafe foods, drugs, cosmetics, medical devices, and other items; through the Health Resources and Services Administration, makes grants to strengthen State, local, and private nonprofit hospital and other health care facilities and programs; funds centers to train health professionals serving AIDS patients; provides medical and other health care services to certain groups (e.g., Coast Guard personnel and their dependents, federal prisoners, Native Americans); through the National Institutes of Health, makes grants to support medical research and operates several research institutes (e.g., the National Cancer Institute, the National Institute of Allergy and Infectious Diseases, and the National Institute of Environmental Health Sciences).

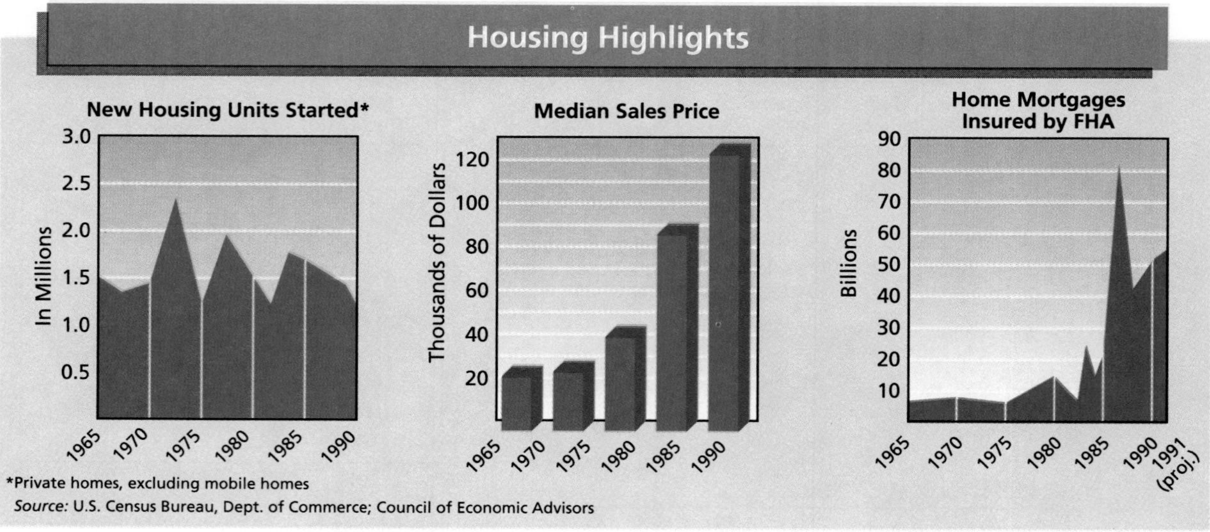

Major trends in housing statistics can be seen on these graphs. The major portion of most families' incomes goes to housing, which now costs more than six times what it did in 1965.

Social Security Administration. Administers several major elements of the social security program, especially: (1) the Old-Age, Survivors, and Disability Insurance (OASDI) program—under which compulsory payroll taxes paid by employers, employees, and the self-employed finance payments (pensions and other benefits) to persons covered under the program when they retire or become permanently disabled and to their dependents or survivors; (2) the Supplemental Security Income (SSI) program—which gives direct federal assistance (payments) to needy aged, blind, and disabled persons.

Health Care Financing Administration. Administers two other major elements of the social security program: (1) Medicare—a health insurance program for most elderly persons (those over 65 who receive OASDI benefits), to help pay at least most of their hospital, medical, and other health care bills (financed by a combination of compulsory payroll taxes and optional monthly fees); and (2) Medicaid—a federal grant program, to help the States pay the hospital, medical, and other health care bills of some 27 million low-income Americans—mostly children, pregnant women, and elderly nursing home patients.

Family Support Administration. Administers the other principal element of the social security program: Aid to Families with Dependent Children (AFDC)—under which federal grants help the States give financial assistance to children who lack adequate parental support; administers federal laws that require States to enforce child support obligations of absent parents.

Department of Housing and Urban Development**

Established: 1965

Head: Secretary of Housing and Urban Development

Telephone: (202) 708-1422

The Department of Housing and Urban Development is the principal federal agency concerned with the nation's housing needs and with the development and rehabilitation of its urban communities. HUD conducts a number of insurance, rent subsidy, and grant programs.

Assistant Secretary for Community Planning and Development. Administers several grant programs to aid State and local government efforts to improve housing conditions in urban areas (e.g., water, sewer, and slum clearance projects; rehabilitation of residential housing units; rental assistance for low-income families).

Assistant Secretary for Housing (Federal Housing Commissioner). Administers several programs, including: (1) mortgage insurance programs—the Federal Government guarantees loans made by private lenders (mortgages) for the purchase of private housing (mostly

**HUD and two other departments (Energy and Education) are not organized in quite the same way as the other Cabinet departments. Most of their functions and programs are administered directly by a number of assistant secretaries (rather than by several bureaus, services, or similar line agencies).

single-family residences and such multifamily units as apartment houses and condominiums); (2) loan programs—to help public and private borrowers finance housing projects for the elderly (e.g., nursing homes) and people with disabilities; (3) the Rent Supplement Program—in which HUD pays a portion of the rents of low-income families.

Assistant Secretary for Public and Indian Housing. Administers several programs, including: (1) public housing programs in which loans, subsidies, and other aid are given to local agencies to build and operate public housing projects (mostly for low-income families); and (2) housing programs for Native Americans—to provide low-income public housing, and promote private home ownership on and near reservations.

Department of Transportation

Established: 1967

Head: Secretary of Transportation

Telephone: (202) 366-4000

Most of the Federal Government's activities relating to the movement of persons and goods by ground, water, or air are located in the Department of Transportation. DOT's several agencies conduct a number of promotional and regulatory programs covering matters ranging from highway construction to offshore maritime safety to commercial air traffic.

United States Coast Guard. Enforces federal maritime laws (laws relating to the high seas and the navigable waters of the United States—e.g., smuggling, ship safety, port security, and spillage, pollution, and other marine environmental protection statutes); maintains ships and other vessels, aircraft, and communications facilities, especially for search and rescue operations; operates an extensive network of aids to navigation (e.g., lighthouses, buoys, icebreakers, radio and other electronic devices); operates the U.S. Coast Guard Academy (at New London, Connecticut).

Federal Aviation Administration. Enforces federal laws regulating air commerce (including, for example, aircraft safety, pilot licensing, and air traffic), operates an extensive network of aids to air navigation (e.g., air traffic control towers and centers, radio and other electronic communications facilities), makes grants for the construction and improvement of public airports, and conducts a wide range of aviation-related research projects.

Federal Highway Administration. Administers several grant programs to aid State and local construction and maintenance of highways and other roads (including the 42,500-mile interstate freeway system); makes grants for such other purposes as highway safety (e.g., traffic signs and signals, projects to eliminate traffic hazards) and beautification; enforces federal highway safety laws (e.g., laws regulating the movement of such dangerous cargoes as

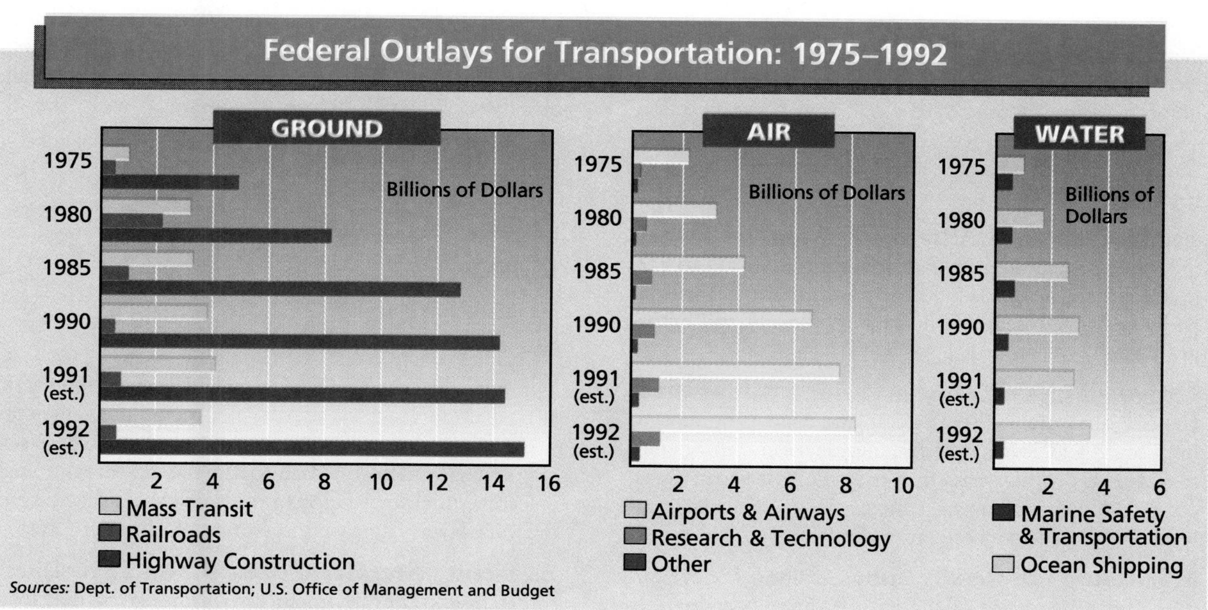

As the first graph shows, federal outlays for railroads peaked in the early 1980s and have decreased steadily since that time. The graphs also show outlays for air and water transportation.

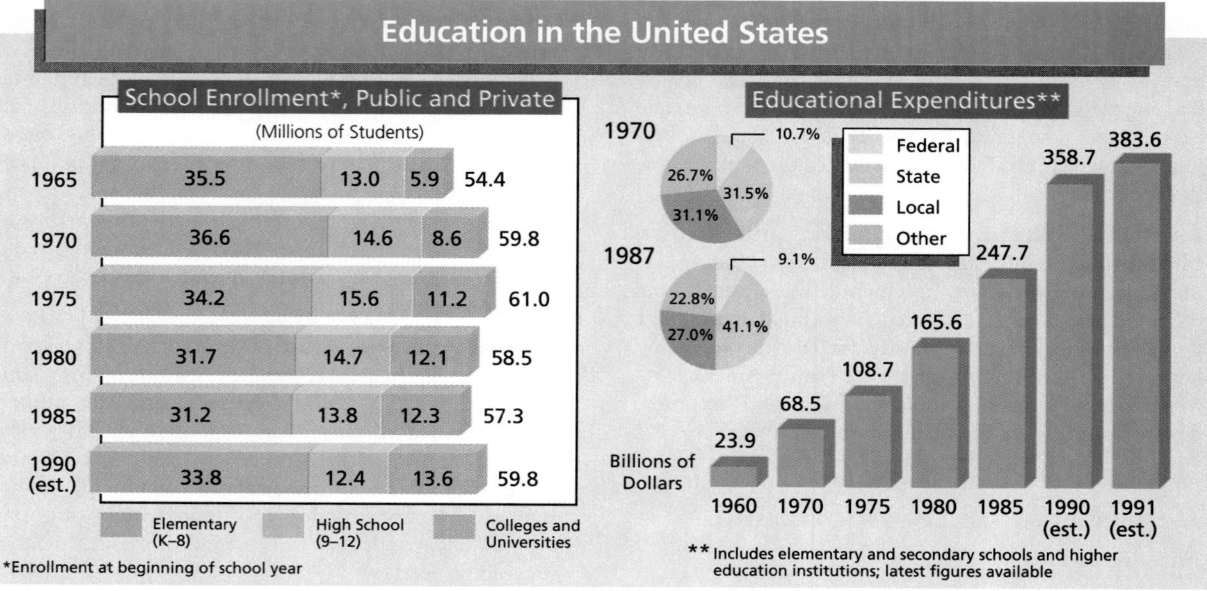

Source: U.S. Dept. of Education, National Center for Educational Statistics

As shown on the graph at left, enrollment in colleges and universities has increased steadily since 1965. In 1987, State government was responsible for the bulk of educational expenditures, as the pie graph at right shows.

explosives and hazardous wastes); builds and maintains roads in such federal areas as national parks, national forests, and Native American reservations; conducts research on a wide range of highway-related matters.

National Highway Traffic Safety Administration. Enforces federal motor vehicle safety laws, makes grants to support State and local motor vehicle safety and accident-prevention programs (including driver training), and conducts research on matters relating to motor vehicle safety.

Federal Railroad Administration. Enforces federal rail safety laws, gives financial and other aid to certain railroads (especially those in financial difficulty), and conducts research on most phases of rail transportation.

Urban Mass Transportation Administration. Administers several grant and loan programs to help State and local governments develop and operate bus, rail, and other mass transit systems in urban areas; conducts research covering most phases of urban mass transportation and its operational efficiency.

Maritime Administration. Promotes development and operations of the nation's merchant marine, subsidizes shipbuilding and certain ship operating costs (to counter foreign competition), conducts research programs to improve the merchant marine, and trains officers for the merchant marine (at the U.S. Merchant Marine Academy, at Kings Point, New York).

Saint Lawrence Seaway Development Corporation. Operates that part of the Seaway within the United States (the American side of the stretch between Montreal and Lake Erie), sets and collects tolls and otherwise works in close cooperation with the St. Lawrence Seaway Authority of Canada.

Department of Energy

Established: 1977

Head: Secretary of Energy

Telephone: (202) 486-5000

The functions of the Department of Energy reflect the critical importance of the development, use, and conservation of the nation's energy resources. DOE's several agencies focus on such matters as high-technology research, nuclear weapons programs, the marketing of federal power, energy conservation, and much more.

Assistant Secretary, Fossil Energy. Directs research and development programs involving fossil fuels—coal, petroleum, and gas (e.g., study and demonstration projects relating to mining, drilling, and other methods of fuel extraction); manages the Strategic Petroleum Reserve and other petroleum storage projects.

Assistant Secretary, Nuclear Energy. Directs research and development programs involving fission energy (e.g., projects relating to nuclear reactor development and the disposal of reactor wastes).

Assistant Secretary, Defense Programs. Directs nuclear weapons research, development, testing, and production programs.

Assistant Secretary, Conservation and Renewable Energy. Directs research and development programs designed to promote more efficient uses (conservation) of energy and to increase the production and use of solar, wind, tidal, and other energy from renewable sources; makes grants to support State and local efforts in those areas (e.g., local projects to weatherize housing).

Energy Information Administration. Collects, analyzes, and publishes a broad range of data relating to energy (e.g., information on energy resources, production, and consumption).

Economic Regulatory Administration. Enforces laws regulating aspects of energy production, sale, and use (e.g., laws regulating drilling on leased federal lands, placing controls on fossil fuel exports, requiring increased industrial use of coal in place of oil and natural gas).

Bonneville Power Administration. Markets electric power generated by the vast network of federal multipurpose dams (constructed and operated by the Army Corps of Engineers and Interior's Bureau of Reclamation) in the Pacific Northwest. (Smaller-scale operations are also conducted in four other regions.)

Department of Education

Established: 1979

Head: Secretary of Education

Telephone: (202) 401-1571

Nearly 60 million Americans attend school. The Department of Education administers a number of programs designed to aid the States and their local units in the field of public education.

Assistant Secretary for Special Education and Rehabilitative Services. Makes grants for research and to support teacher training and other State and local programs for the education of children with disabilities and for rehabilitation programs for those children.

Assistant Secretary for Postsecondary Education. Administers several grant programs to support and expand instructional and other educational services and facilities in colleges, universities, and similar institutions; administers several different types of student grant and loan programs.

Assistant Secretary for Vocational and Adult Education. Administers grants and other programs to support and expand State and local efforts in vocational training and adult education.

Assistant Secretary for Elementary and Secondary Education. Administers grant programs to support a variety of State and local efforts in preschool, elementary, and secondary education, including grants to local school districts for Native American and migrant education.

Assistant Secretary for Educational Research and Improvement. Directs research and administers grant programs to support State and local school efforts in a wide range of instructional service and resource areas (e.g., basic skills, library and laboratory resources, and education on health, abuse of alcohol and other drugs).

Department of Veterans Affairs

Established: 1989

Head: Secretary of Veterans Affairs

Telephone: (202) 233-4000

The Department of Veterans Affairs reflects a historic concern for the welfare of those men and women who have served in the nation's armed forces. Today, the Department operates a number of programs that make a broad range of benefits available to more than 27 million veterans and their dependents.

Veterans Health Services and Research Administration. Provides hospital, nursing home, domiciliary care, outpatient medical and dental care to eligible veterans; operates 172 hospitals, more than 300 clinics and other facilities in this country and in the Philippines.

Veterans Benefits Administration. Provides pensions and other compensations for service-connected (and many nonservice-connected) disabilities; administers vocational rehabilitation, job training, and other educational assistance programs; administers veterans' home-loan guarantee and life insurance programs.

National Cemetery System. Maintains more than 100 cemeteries for veterans around the country; provides headstones and markers for graves of veterans.

U.S. DATA BANK The United States: A Statistical Profile*

State	Capital	Population (in thousands)			Area in Square Miles	% Land Federally Owned	Population per sq. mi.
		1990	1980	% Change			
United States	**Washington, D.C.**	**248,709**	**226,544**	**+9.8**	**3,618,770**	**30.3**	**70.2**
Alabama	Montgomery	4,040	3,894	+3.8	51,705	1.7	79.6
Alaska	Juneau	550	402	+36.9	591,004	81.1	0.96
Arizona	Phoenix	3,665	2,717	+34.8	114,000	44.5	32.3
Arkansas	Little Rock	2,350	2,286	+2.8	53,187	7.1	45.1
California	Sacramento	29,760	23,668	+25.7	158,706	44.5	190.8
Colorado	Denver	3,294	3,272	+14.0	104,091	29.8	31.8
Connecticut	Hartford	3,287	3,108	+5.8	5,018	0.4	678.5
Delaware	Dover	666	594	+12.1	2,045	2.4	340.8
Florida	Tallahassee	12,937	9,747	+32.7	58,664	9.4	239.6
Georgia	Atlanta	6,478	5,463	+18.6	58,910	4.0	111.8
Hawaii	Honolulu	1,108	965	+14.9	6,471	6.9	172.6
Idaho	Boise	1,006	944	+6.7	83,564	60.6	12.2
Illinois	Springfield	11,430	11,427	0.0	56,345	1.4	205.6
Indiana	Indianapolis	5,544	5,490	+1.0	36,185	2.0	154.6
Iowa	Des Moines	2,776	2,914	-4.7	56,275	0.4	49.7
Kansas	Topeka	2,477	2,364	+4.8	82,277	1.3	30.3
Kentucky	Frankfort	3,685	3,660	+0.7	40,410	5.5	92.0
Louisiana	Baton Rouge	4,219	4,206	+0.3	47,752	22.6	96.9
Maine	Augusta	1,227	1,125	+9.2	33,265	0.8	39.8
Maryland	Annapolis	4,781	4,217	+13.4	10,460	3.1	489.2
Massachusetts	Boston	6,016	5,737	+4.9	8,284	1.6	767.6
Michigan	Lansing	9,295	9,262	+0.4	58,527	9.8	165.4
Minnesota	St. Paul	4,375	4,076	+7.3	84,402	4.7	55.0
Mississippi	Jackson	2,573	2,521	+2.1	47,689	5.5	54.8
Missouri	Jefferson City	5,117	4,917	+4.1	69,697	4.6	74.3
Montana	Helena	799	787	+1.6	147,046	29.4	5.5
Nebraska	Lincoln	1,578	1,570	+0.5	77,355	1.1	20.5
Nevada	Carson City	1,201	801	+50.1	110,561	78.9	10.9
New Hampshire	Concord	1,109	921	+20.5	9,279	13.0	123.7
New Jersey	Trenton	7,730	7,365	+5.0	7,787	3.4	1,041.9
New Mexico	Santa Fe	1,515	1,303	+16.3	121,593	33.1	12.5
New York	Albany	17,990	17,558	+2.5	49,108	0.8	381.0
North Carolina	Raleigh	6,628	5,880	+12.7	52,669	7.1	136.1
North Dakota	Bismark	638	653	-2.1	70,702	4.4	9.2
Ohio	Columbus	10,847	10,798	+0.5	41,330	1.3	264.9
Oklahoma	Oklahoma City	3,145	3,025	+4.0	69,956	2.0	45.8
Oregon	Salem	2,842	2,633	+7.9	97,073	52.3	29.6
Pennsylvania	Harrisburg	11,881	11,865	+0.1	45,308	2.3	265.1
Rhode Island	Providence	1,003	947	+5.9	1,212	0.7	960.3
South Carolina	Columbia	3,486	3,121	+11.7	31,113	6.1	115.8
South Dakota	Pierre	696	691	+.8	77,116	5.5	9.17
Tennessee	Nashville	4,877	4,591	+6.2	42,144	5.1	118.3
Texas	Austin	16,986	14,226	+19.4	266,807	1.6	64.9
Utah	Salt Lake City	1,722	1,461	+17.9	84,899	60.0	21.0
Vermont	Montpelier	562	511	+10.0	9,614	6.0	60.8
Virginia	Richmond	6,187	5,347	+15.7	40,767	7.5	156.3
Washington	Olympia	4,866	4,132	+17.8	68,139	29.6	73.1
West Virginia	Charleston	1,793	1,950	-8.0	24,232	9.1	74.5
Wisconsin	Madison	4,891	4,706	+4.0	56,153	5.4	90.1
Wyoming	Cheyenne	453	470	-3.4	97,809	46.5	4.7
Washington, D.C		606	638	-4.9	69	28.4	8,783.0

*All data for 1989, except 1990 population figures and 1988 election results.
Sources: Bureau of the Census; General Services Administration; 1991 *Statistical Abstract*

710

The United States: A Statistical Profile

State	% Urban	Population: African American (in thousands)	Population: Spanish Origin† (in thousands)	% Foreign Born**	% High School Graduates	Two-Party Vote, 1988 Presidential Election††: George Bush (Republican) Votes	%	Michael Dukakis (Democrat) Votes	%
United States	**77.5**	**29,986**	**22,354**	**6.2**	**71.1**	**48,881,278**	**53.4**	**41,805,374**	**45.6**
Alabama	67.4	1,020	24	1.0	63.2	815,576	59.2	549,506	39.9
Alaska	41.1	22	17	3.9	86.9	118,817	59.7	72,105	36.2
Arizona	79.0	110	688	6.0	80.6	702,541	60.0	454,029	38.8
Arkansas	40.1	373	19	0.9	67.6	466,578	56.4	349,237	42.2
California	95.7	2,208	7,687	14.8	78.6	5,054,917	51.1	4,702,233	47.6
Colorado	81.5	133	424	3.8	83.2	728,177	53.1	621,453	45.3
Connecticut	92.4	274	213	8.5	80.6	750,241	52.0	676,584	46.9
Delaware	66.3	112	15	3.4	80.7	139,639	55.9	108,647	43.5
Florida	90.8	1,759	1,574	10.9	77.9	2,616,597	60.9	1,655,851	38.5
Georgia	65.0	1,746	108	1.7	71.1	1,081,331	59.7	714,792	39.5
Hawaii	75.5	27	81	14.0	82.3	158,625	44.7	192,364	54.3
Idaho	20.4	3	52	2.3	77.3	253,881	62.1	147,272	36.0
Illinois	82.7	1,694	904	7.3	77.2	2,310,939	50.7	2,215,940	48.6
Indiana	68.5	432	98	1.9	78.0	1,297,763	59.8	860,643	39.7
Iowa	44.0	48	32	1.7	83.4	545,355	44.5	670,557	54.7
Kansas	53.8	143	93	2.0	82.2	554,049	55.8	422,636	42.5
Kentucky	46.5	262	21	0.9	64.7	734,281	55.5	580,368	43.9
Louisiana	69.5	1,299	93	2.1	70.9	883,702	54.3	717,460	44.1
Maine	35.9	5	6	3.8	76.9	307,131	55.3	243,569	43.9
Maryland	92.8	1,189	125	4.6	80.7	876,167	51.1	826,304	48.2
Massachusetts	90.4	300	287	8.4	80.7	1,194,635	45.4	1,401,415	53.2
Michigan	80.1	1,291	201	4.4	77.0	1,965,486	53.5	1,675,783	45.7
Minnesota	67.7	94	53	2.7	85.5	962,337	45.9	1,109,471	52.9
Mississippi	30.1	915	15	0.9	67.7	557,890	59.9	363,921	39.1
Missouri	66.2	548	61	1.8	75.9	1,084,953	51.8	1,001,619	47.9
Montana	23.9	2	12	2.3	83.6	190,412	52.1	168,956	46.2
Nebraska	48.5	57	36	1.9	82.2	398,447	60.1	259,646	39.2
Nevada	82.9	78	124	6.7	84.0	206,040	58.9	132,738	37.9
New Hampshire	56.1	7	11	4.2	82.2	281,537	62.5	163,696	36.3
New Jersey	100.0	1,036	739	10.3	79.4	1,740,604	56.2	1,317,541	42.6
New Mexico	48.4	30	579	4.2	74.6	270,341	51.9	244,497	46.9
New York	91.1	2,859	2,214	13.4	76.7	3,081,871	47.5	3,347,882	51.6
North Carolina	56.7	1,456	76	1.5	71.3	1,237,258	58.0	890,167	41.7
North Dakota	40.3	3	4	2.3	81.1	166,559	56.0	127,739	43.0
Ohio	79.0	1,154	139	2.7	77.6	2,416,549	55.0	1,939,629	44.1
Oklahoma	59.4	233	86	1.8	75.4	678,367	57.9	483,423	41.3
Oregon	68.5	46	112	4.2	83.9	560,126	46.6	616,206	51.3
Pennsylvania	84.8	1,089	232	3.6	76.8	2,300,087	50.7	2,194,944	48.4
Rhode Island	92.5	38	45	8.8	72.7	177,761	43.9	225,123	55.7
South Carolina	60.6	1,039	30	1.4	69.8	606,443	61.5	370,554	37.6
South Dakota	29.5	3	5	1.4	78.3	165,415	52.9	145,560	46.5
Tennessee	67.7	778	32	1.0	65.4	947,233	57.9	679,794	41.5
Texas	81.6	2,021	4,339	6.0	74.3	3,036,829	56.0	2,352,748	43.3
Utah	77.5	11	84	3.5	88.2	428,442	66.2	207,352	32.0
Vermont	23.4	1	3	4.2	81.8	124,331	51.1	115,775	47.6
Virginia	72.5	1,162	160	3.2	74.3	1,309,162	59.7	859,799	39.2
Washington	81.7	149	214	5.8	88.2	903,835	48.5	933,516	50.0
West Virginia	36.4	56	8	1.1	68.0	310,065	47.5	341,016	52.2
Wisconsin	67.4	39	93	2.7	81.1	1,047,499	47.8	1,126,794	51.4
Wyoming	29.6	3	25	1.9	85.6	106,867	60.5	67,113	38.0
Washington, D.C.	100.0	399	32	***	72.9	27,590	14.3	159,407	82.6

† Persons of Spanish origin may be of any race.
†† *Source: Congressional Quarterly.* The percentages are of all votes cast (the total vote, including votes cast for minor party candidates).
** 1980 population figures. (Latest data available from Bureau of the Census) *** Data not available.

711

PACIFIC OCEAN
WASHINGTON
Seattle
Olympia
Tacoma
Spokane
Columbia
Portland
Salem
OREGON
IDAHO
Boise
Snake R.
Pocatello
MONTANA
Great Falls
Missouri R.
Helena
Butte
Yellowstone
Calgary
Regina
CANADA
NORTH DAKOTA
Bismarck
SOUTH DAKOTA
Pierre
WYOMING
Casper
Cheyenne
NEBRASKA
Platte R.
CALIFORNIA
Sacramento
San Francisco
Oakland
Los Angeles
San Diego
NEVADA
Humboldt R.
Reno
Carson City
Las Vegas
Great Salt Lake
Ogden
Salt Lake City
UTAH
COLORADO
Denver
Pueblo
Colorado
Arkansas R.
KANSAS
ARIZONA
Phoenix
Tucson
NEW MEXICO
Albuquerque
Santa Fe
Rio Grande
Pecos
El Paso
Amarillo
Oklahoma City
TEXAS
Fort Worth
Austin
San Antonio
Corpus Christi
ALASKA
Barrow
Cape Prince of Wales
Bering Strait
SEWARD PEN.
Nome
BERING SEA
Yukon R.
Fairbanks
Klondike
NUNIVAK ISLAND
Anchorage
PRIBILOF ISLANDS
KENAI PEN.
Seward
ALEUTIAN ISLANDS
Dutch Harbor
ALASKA PEN.
Kodiak
GULF OF ALASKA
Juneau
Sitka
Ketchikan
Prince Rupert
QUEEN CHARLOTTE ISLANDS
PACIFIC OCEAN
750 Miles
750 Kilometers
HAWAII
KAUAI
NIIHAU
OAHU
Honolulu
Pearl Harbor
MOLOKAI
LANAI
MAUI
KAHOOLAWE
HAWAII
Hilo
PACIFIC OCEAN
100 Miles
100 Kilometers

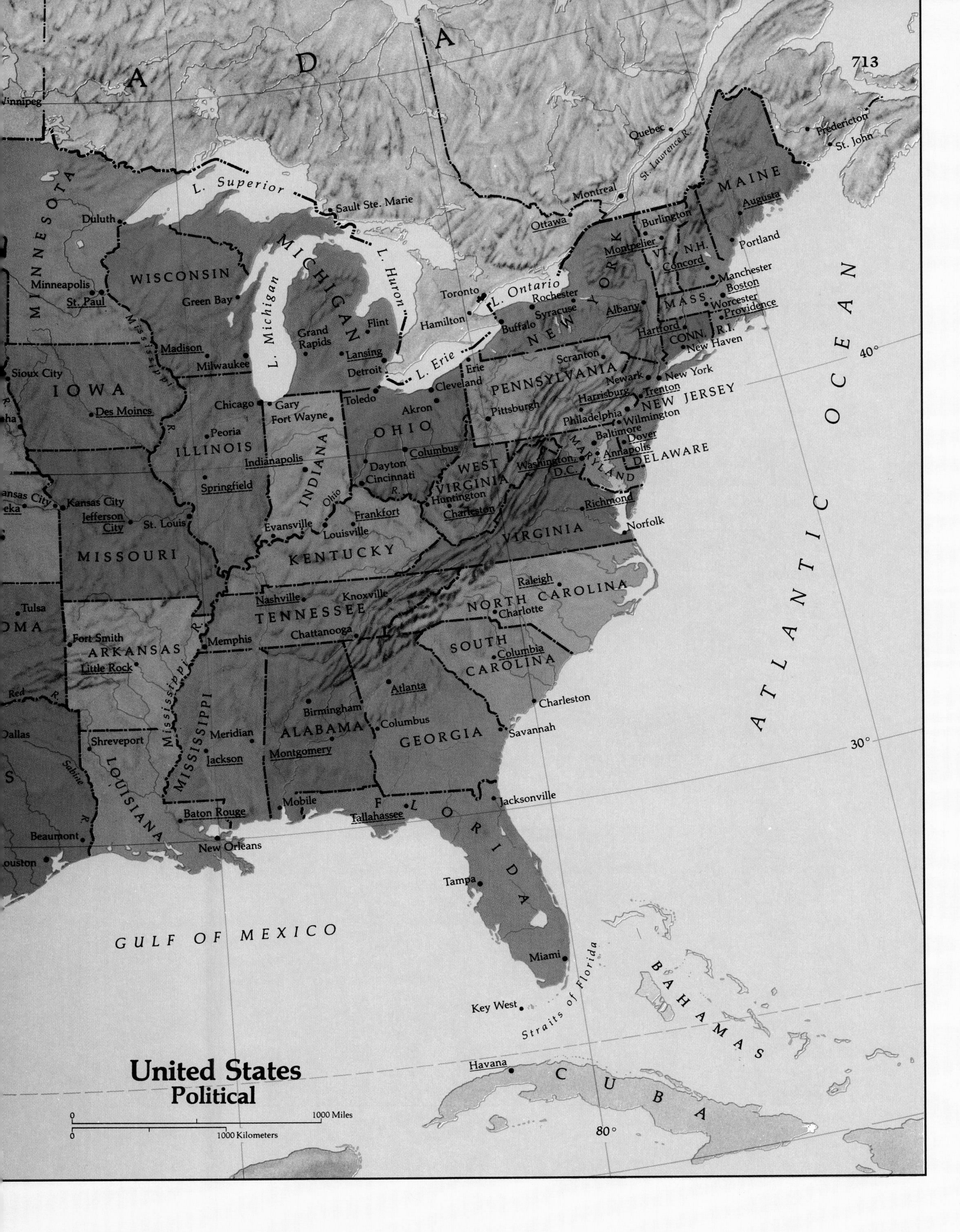
C A N A D A
Winnipeg
Quebec
St. Lawrence R.
Fredericton
St. John
Montreal
Ottawa
L. Superior
Sault Ste. Marie
Duluth
MINNESOTA
Minneapolis
St. Paul
WISCONSIN
Green Bay
Madison
Milwaukee
Mississippi R.
L. Michigan
MICHIGAN
L. Huron
Flint
Grand Rapids
Lansing
Detroit
Toronto
Hamilton
L. Ontario
Rochester
Syracuse
Buffalo
L. Erie
Erie
NEW YORK
Albany
Burlington
Montpelier
VT.
N.H.
Concord
MAINE
Augusta
Portland
Manchester
Boston
MASS.
Worcester
Providence
R.I.
Hartford
CONN.
New Haven
New York
Newark
Trenton
NEW JERSEY
Scranton
PENNSYLVANIA
Harrisburg
Philadelphia
Pittsburgh
Wilmington
Dover
Baltimore
Annapolis
DELAWARE
MARYLAND
Washington, D.C.
Sioux City
IOWA
Des Moines
Chicago
Gary
Fort Wayne
Toledo
Cleveland
Akron
Peoria
ILLINOIS
Indianapolis
INDIANA
OHIO
Columbus
Dayton
Cincinnati
Ohio R.
Springfield
WEST VIRGINIA
Huntington
Charleston
Richmond
Norfolk
VIRGINIA
Kansas City
Jefferson City
St. Louis
MISSOURI
Evansville
Louisville
Frankfort
KENTUCKY
Raleigh
NORTH CAROLINA
Charlotte
Nashville
Knoxville
TENNESSEE
Chattanooga
Memphis
Tulsa
Fort Smith
ARKANSAS
Little Rock
Red R.
SOUTH CAROLINA
Columbia
Atlanta
Charleston
Birmingham
Columbus
ALABAMA
GEORGIA
Savannah
Dallas
Shreveport
Meridian
MISSISSIPPI
Jackson
Montgomery
Sabine R.
LOUISIANA
Baton Rouge
Mobile
Tallahassee
Jacksonville
FLORIDA
Beaumont
New Orleans
Houston
Tampa
GULF OF MEXICO
Miami
Key West
Straits of Florida
BAHAMAS
ATLANTIC OCEAN
40°
30°
80°
Havana
CUBA
United States
Political
0
1000 Miles
0
1000 Kilometers

World Data Bank

The tables and graphs in this World Data Bank provide you with an opportunity to compare the governments, economies, and certain qualities of life for selected countries. Similar comparisons are found in the Global Awareness charts on the following pages in your textbook:

World Population Growth and Distribution

Population Growth 1650-2000

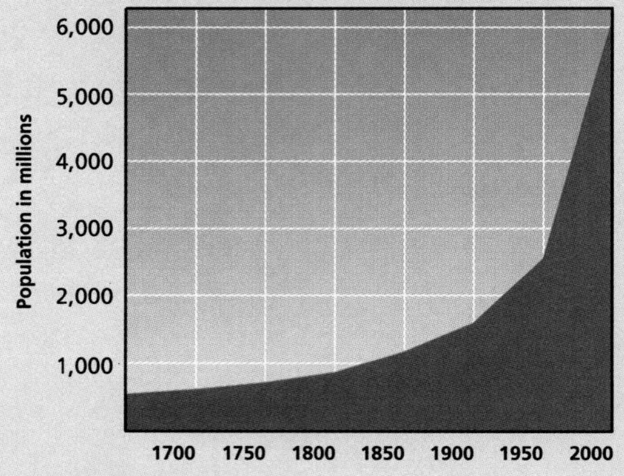

Sources: U.S. Bureau of the Census
Population Division of the United Nations

Population Distribution by Region: 1990

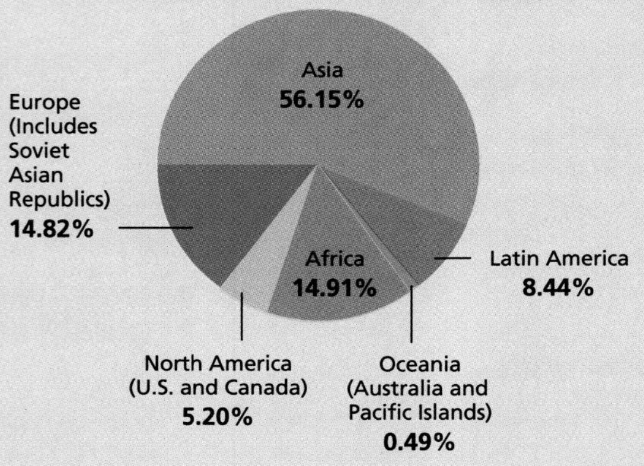

Source: U.S. Bureau of the Census

Education in Selected Countries

COUNTRY	% of Children in Age Group in Primary Schools	% of Children in Age Group in Secondary Schools	% of Population over Age 25 with Some College	% of Government Budget Spent on Education	% of Population over Age 25 that Is Literate
United States	97	90	32.2	7.5	95.5
Algeria	88	45	0.3	6.1	44.7
Brazil	82	15	5.0	3.3	79.3
Cameroon	75	15	0.3	2.6	55.2
Cuba	95	69	5.9	6.3	96.0
Japan	100	96	14.3	5.1	100.0
Nepal	56	18	6.8	3.0	20.7
Poland	99	73	5.7	3.8	99.2
Sweden	96	81	15.4	7.6	100.0

World Population Density

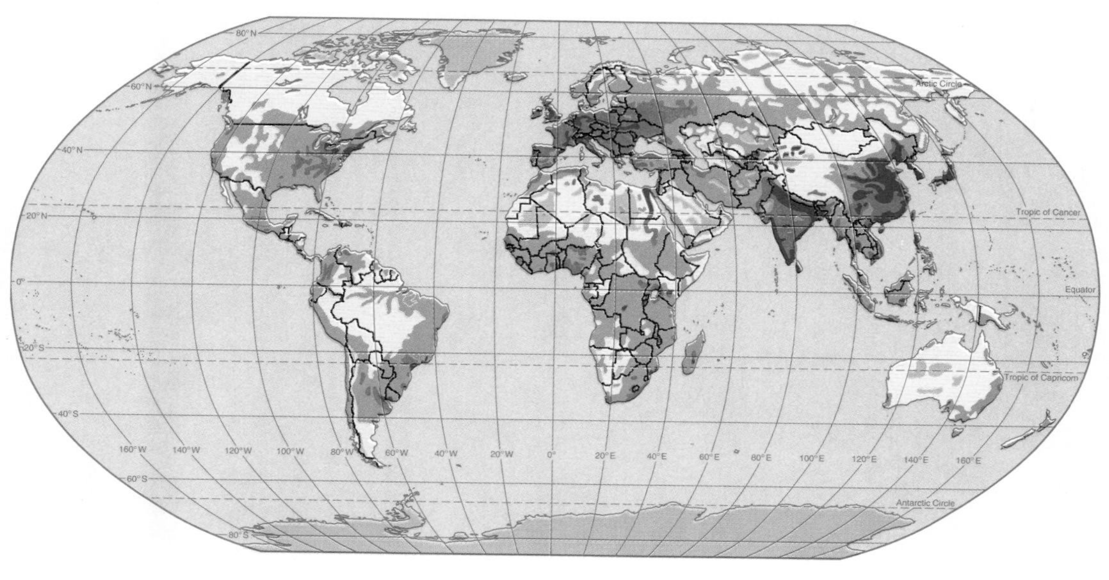

Per sq. mi.	Over 250	125–250	60–125	2–60	Under 2	Uninhabited
Per sq km	Over 100	50–100	25–50	1–25	Under 1	Uninhabited

Economic and Health Statistics for Selected Countries: 1989[1]

COUNTRY	Per Capita GNP	Life Expectancy at Birth (Female)	Infant Mortality Rate[2]	Average Daily Calorie Consumption
United States	**$ 17,592**	**79**	**9.1**	**3,642**
Argentina	**$ 2,134**	**74**	**32.0**	**3,191**
Canada	**$ 19,020**	**80**	**7.3**	**3,425**
China	**$ 360**	**70**	**33.0**	**2,628**
India	**$ 350**	**58**	**91.0**	**2,204**
Japan	**$ 15,030**	**82**	**5.0**	**2,858**
Mexico	**$ 2,373**	**73**	**42.0**	**3,148**
United Kingdom	**$ 14,535**	**78**	**13.3**	**3,218**
Zaire	**$ 260**	**54**	**107.0**	**2,160**

[1] The year 1989 is used because this is the most recent year for which data is available for all countries.
[2] Number of deaths before age one per 1,000 live births.

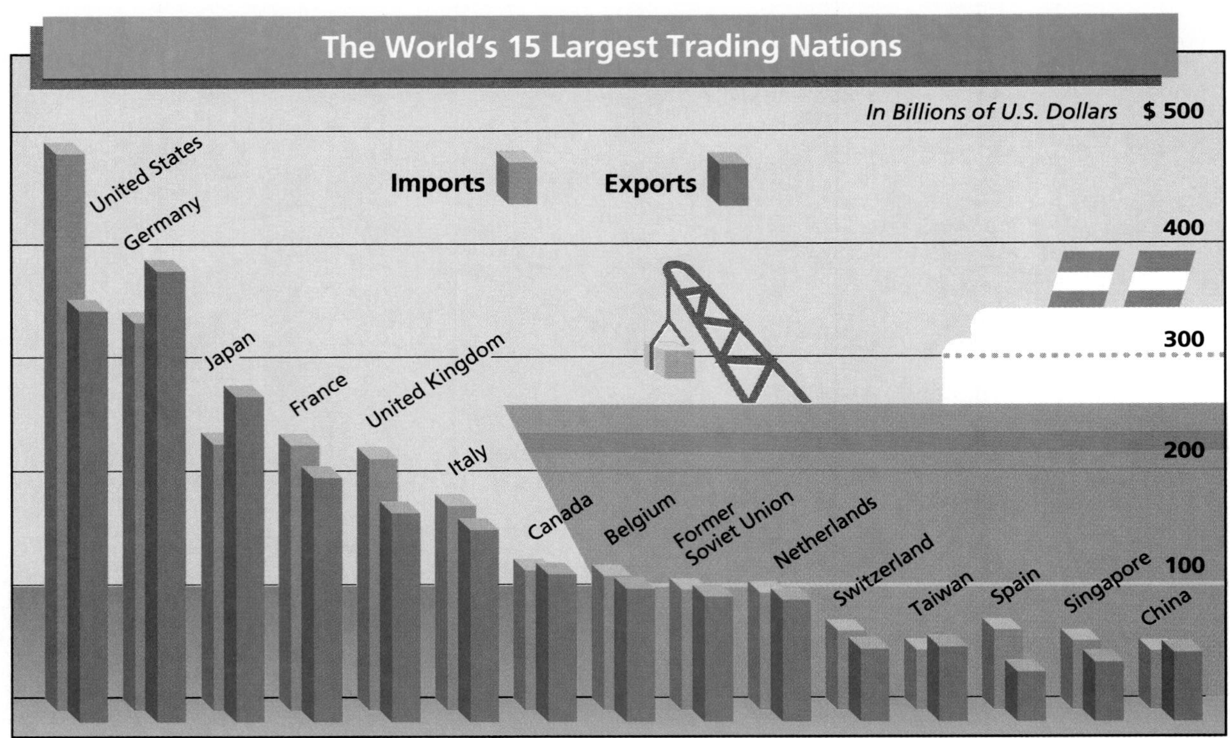

The World's 15 Largest Trading Nations
In Billions of U.S. Dollars
$ 500
400
300
200
100
Imports
Exports
United States
Germany
Japan
France
United Kingdom
Italy
Canada
Belgium
Former Soviet Union
Netherlands
Switzerland
Taiwan
Spain
Singapore
China

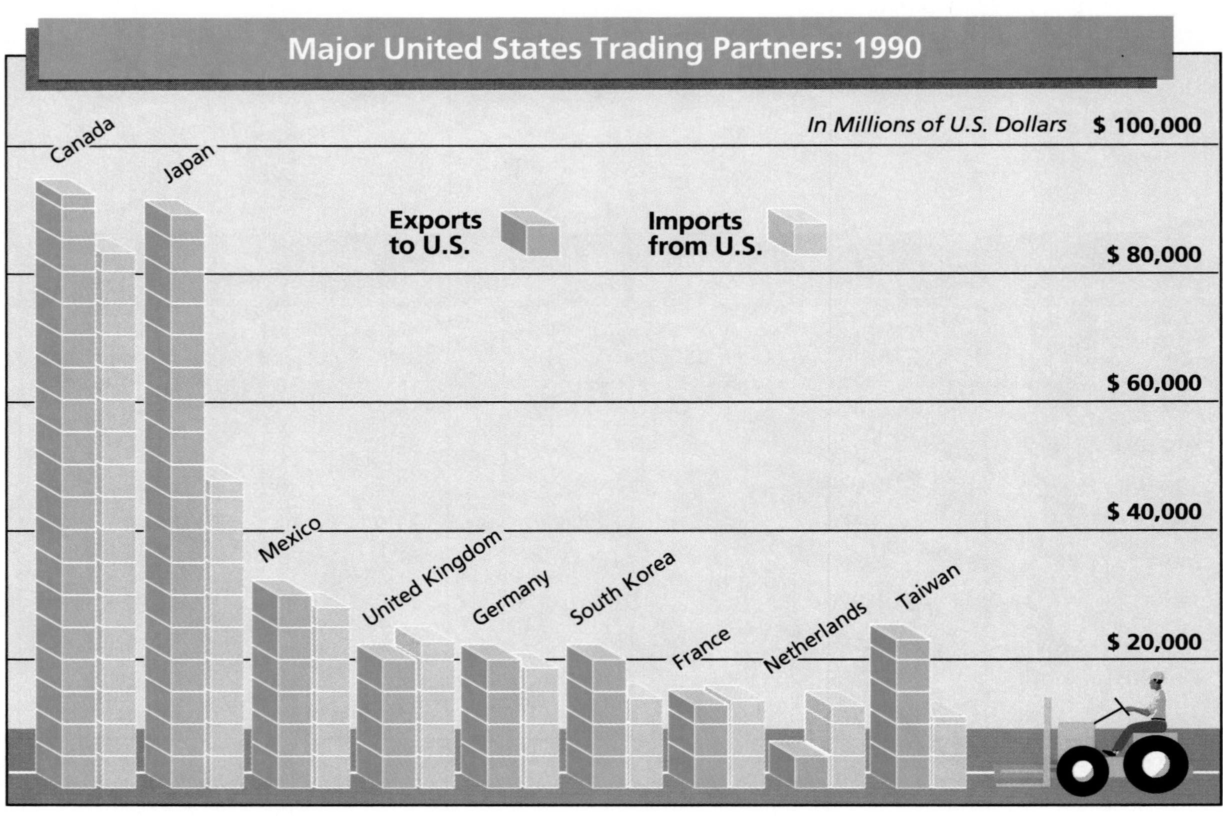

Major United States Trading Partners: 1990
In Millions of U.S. Dollars
$ 100,000
$ 80,000
$ 60,000
$ 40,000
$ 20,000
Exports to U.S.
Imports from U.S.
Canada
Japan
Mexico
United Kingdom
Germany
South Korea
France
Netherlands
Taiwan

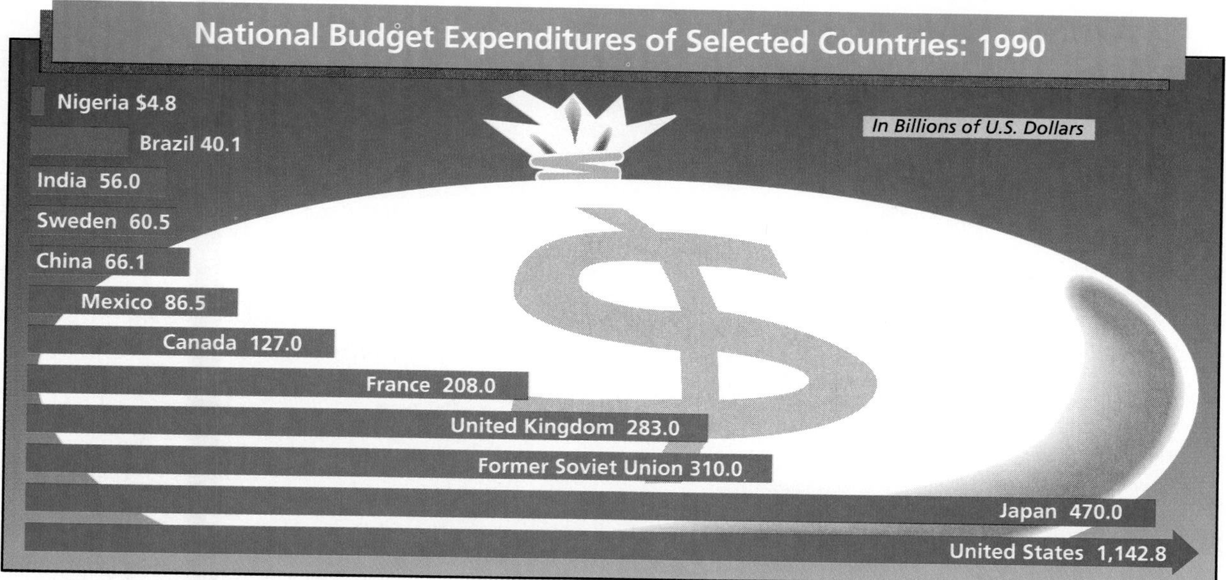
National Budget Expenditures of Selected Countries: 1990
In Billions of U.S. Dollars
Nigeria $4.8
Brazil 40.1
India 56.0
Sweden 60.5
China 66.1
Mexico 86.5
Canada 127.0
France 208.0
United Kingdom 283.0
Former Soviet Union 310.0
Japan 470.0
United States 1,142.8

Source: The World Almanac and Book of Facts, 1992

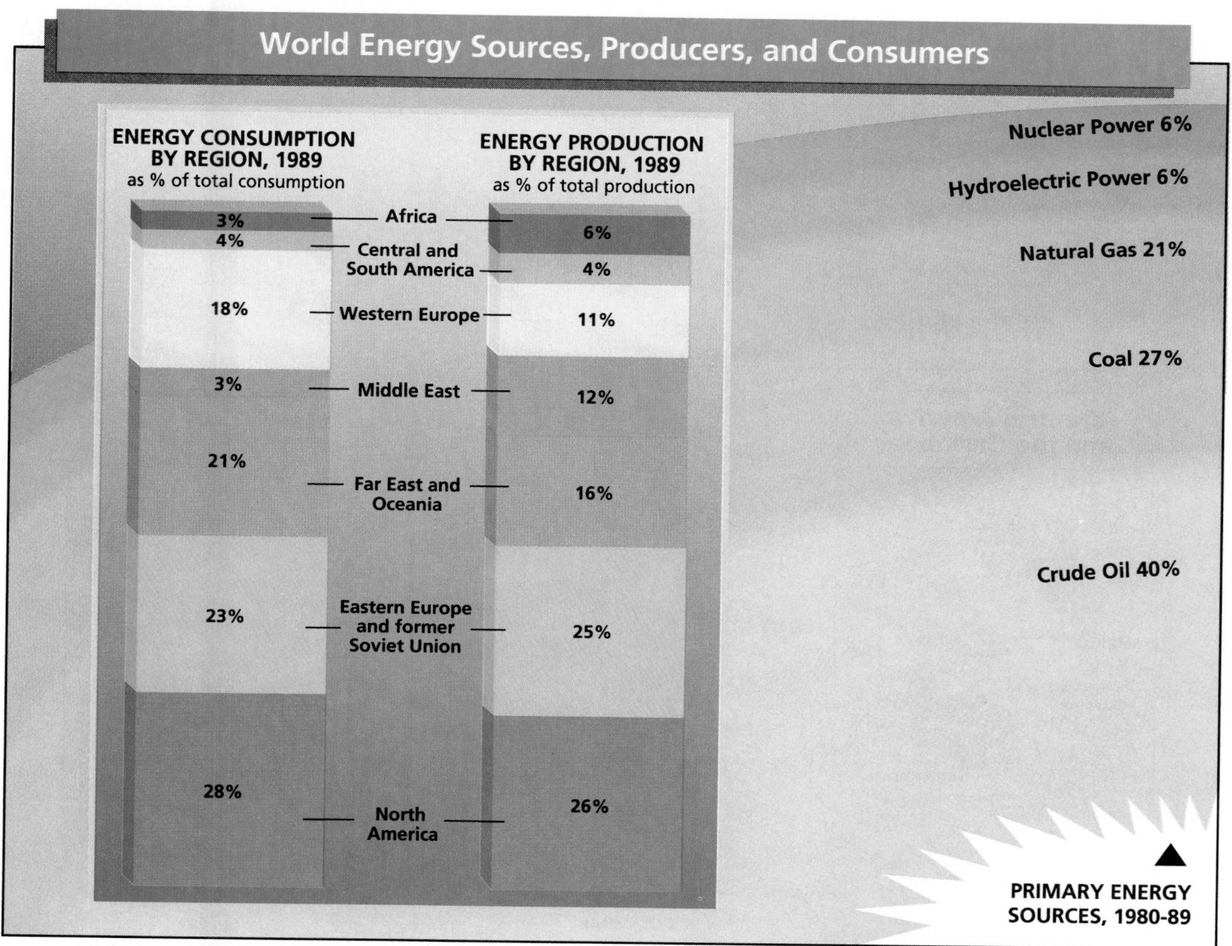
World Energy Sources, Producers, and Consumers
ENERGY CONSUMPTION BY REGION, 1989
as % of total consumption
ENERGY PRODUCTION BY REGION, 1989
as % of total production
Africa 3% 6%
Central and South America 4% 4%
Western Europe 18% 11%
Middle East 3% 12%
Far East and Oceania 21% 16%
Eastern Europe and former Soviet Union 23% 25%
North America 28% 26%
Nuclear Power 6%
Hydroelectric Power 6%
Natural Gas 21%
Coal 27%
Crude Oil 40%
PRIMARY ENERGY SOURCES, 1980-89

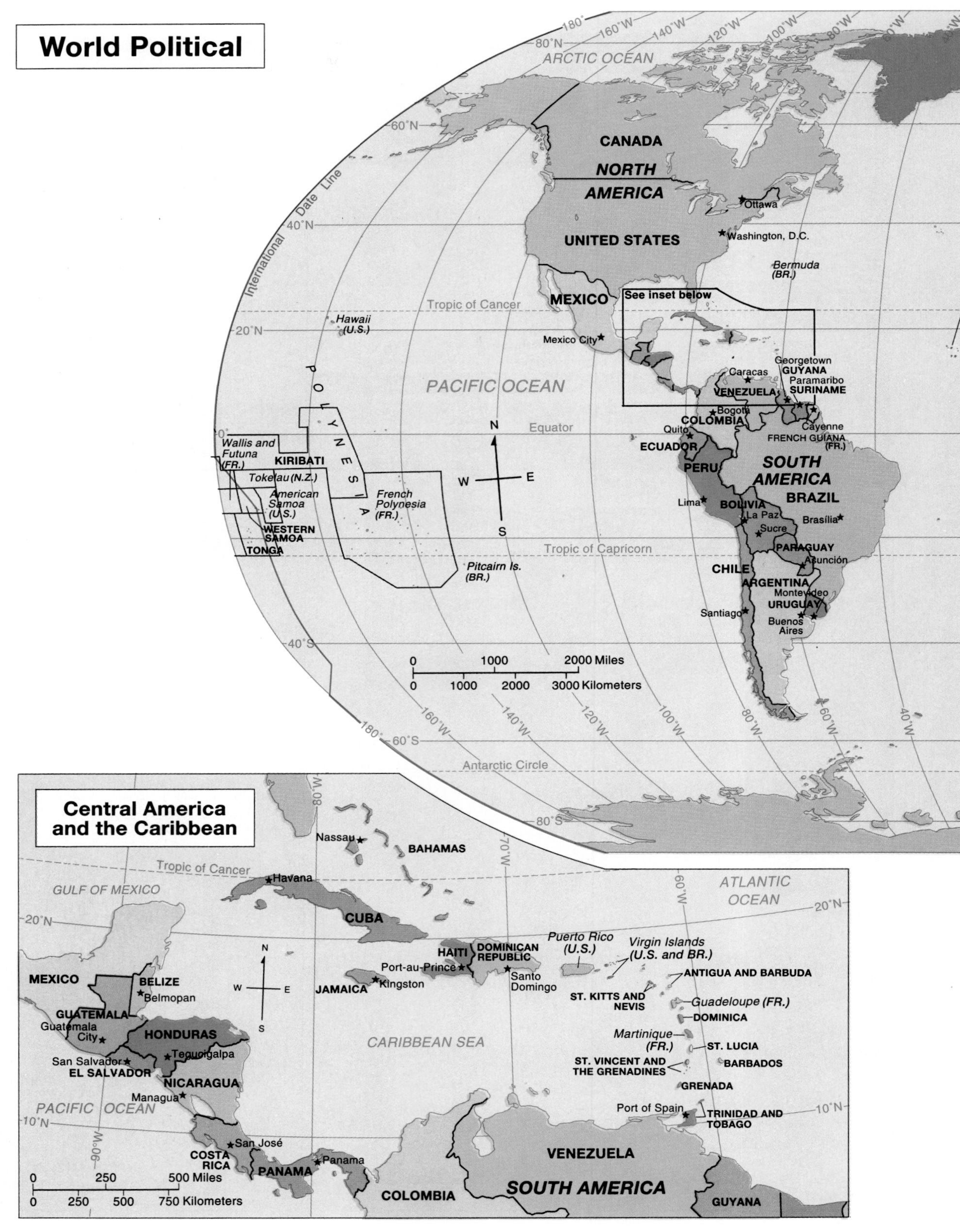
World Political
ARCTIC OCEAN
CANADA
NORTH AMERICA
Ottawa
Washington, D.C.
UNITED STATES
Bermuda (BR.)
MEXICO
See inset below
Mexico City
Tropic of Cancer
Hawaii (U.S.)
International Date Line
PACIFIC OCEAN
POLYNESIA
Equator
Wallis and Futuna (FR.)
KIRIBATI
Tokelau (N.Z.)
American Samoa (U.S.)
WESTERN SAMOA
TONGA
French Polynesia (FR.)
Pitcairn Is. (BR.)
Caracas
VENEZUELA
Georgetown
GUYANA
Paramaribo
SURINAME
Cayenne
FRENCH GUIANA (FR.)
Bogotá
COLOMBIA
Quito
ECUADOR
PERU
Lima
SOUTH AMERICA
BRAZIL
Brasília
BOLIVIA
La Paz
Sucre
PARAGUAY
Asunción
Tropic of Capricorn
CHILE
ARGENTINA
Santiago
Montevideo
URUGUAY
Buenos Aires
0 1000 2000 Miles
0 1000 2000 3000 Kilometers
Antarctic Circle
Central America and the Caribbean
GULF OF MEXICO
Tropic of Cancer
Nassau
BAHAMAS
Havana
CUBA
ATLANTIC OCEAN
HAITI
DOMINICAN REPUBLIC
Port-au-Prince
Santo Domingo
Puerto Rico (U.S.)
Virgin Islands (U.S. and BR.)
ANTIGUA AND BARBUDA
ST. KITTS AND NEVIS
Guadeloupe (FR.)
DOMINICA
Martinique (FR.)
ST. LUCIA
ST. VINCENT AND THE GRENADINES
BARBADOS
GRENADA
Port of Spain
TRINIDAD AND TOBAGO
MEXICO
BELIZE
Belmopan
JAMAICA
Kingston
GUATEMALA
Guatemala City
HONDURAS
Tegucigalpa
San Salvador
EL SALVADOR
NICARAGUA
Managua
CARIBBEAN SEA
PACIFIC OCEAN
San José
COSTA RICA
PANAMA
Panama
COLOMBIA
VENEZUELA
SOUTH AMERICA
GUYANA
0 250 500 Miles
0 250 500 750 Kilometers

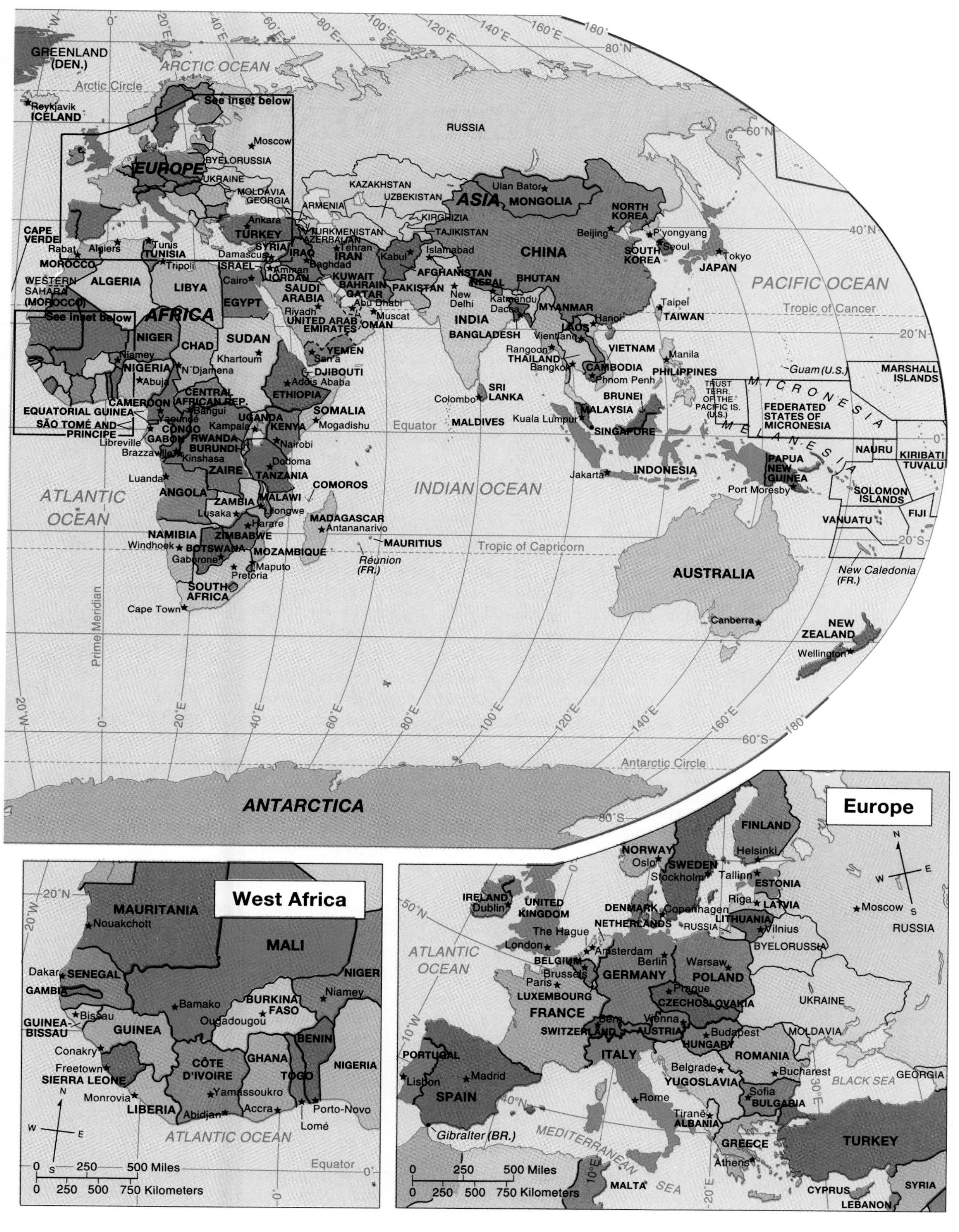
GREENLAND (DEN.)
ARCTIC OCEAN
Arctic Circle
Reykjavik
ICELAND
See inset below
Moscow
RUSSIA
EUROPE
BYELORUSSIA
UKRAINE
MOLDAVIA
GEORGIA
ARMENIA
KAZAKHSTAN
UZBEKISTAN
Ulan Bator
ASIA
MONGOLIA
NORTH KOREA
KIRGHIZIA
TURKMENISTAN
AZERBAIJAN
TAJIKISTAN
Beijing
P'yongyang
Seoul
SOUTH KOREA
Tokyo
JAPAN
CHINA
Ankara
TURKEY
SYRIA
IRAQ
Tehran
IRAN
Kabul
Islamabad
Baghdad
Damascus
ISRAEL
Amman
JORDAN
Cairo
EGYPT
KUWAIT
BAHRAIN
QATAR
SAUDI ARABIA
Riyadh
Abu Dhabi
UNITED ARAB EMIRATES
Muscat
OMAN
AFGHANISTAN
PAKISTAN
NEPAL
BHUTAN
New Delhi
Katmandu
Dacca
INDIA
BANGLADESH
MYANMAR
Hanoi
Taipei
TAIWAN
PACIFIC OCEAN
Tropic of Cancer
CAPE VERDE
Rabat
Algiers
Tunis
TUNISIA
Tripoli
MOROCCO
WESTERN SAHARA (MOROCCO)
ALGERIA
LIBYA
AFRICA
NIGER
CHAD
SUDAN
Khartoum
YEMEN
San'a
DJIBOUTI
Addis Ababa
ETHIOPIA
Niamey
NIGERIA
N'Djamena
Abuja
CENTRAL AFRICAN REP.
Bangui
CAMEROON
Yaoundé
EQUATORIAL GUINEA
SÃO TOMÉ AND PRINCIPE
CONGO
GABON
Libreville
Brazzaville
Kinshasa
UGANDA
Kampala
KENYA
Nairobi
RWANDA
BURUNDI
ZAIRE
Dodoma
TANZANIA
SOMALIA
Mogadishu
Luanda
ANGOLA
ZAMBIA
Lusaka
MALAWI
Lilongwe
Harare
ZIMBABWE
COMOROS
MADAGASCAR
Antananarivo
MAURITIUS
Réunion (FR.)
NAMIBIA
Windhoek
BOTSWANA
Gaborone
MOZAMBIQUE
Maputo
Pretoria
SOUTH AFRICA
Cape Town
ATLANTIC OCEAN
INDIAN OCEAN
Equator
Tropic of Capricorn
Prime Meridian
Colombo
SRI LANKA
MALDIVES
Vientiane
LAOS
Rangoon
THAILAND
Bangkok
VIETNAM
CAMBODIA
Phnom Penh
Manila
PHILIPPINES
BRUNEI
MALAYSIA
Kuala Lumpur
SINGAPORE
INDONESIA
Jakarta
Guam (U.S.)
TRUST TERR. OF THE PACIFIC IS. (U.S.)
MARSHALL ISLANDS
MICRONESIA
FEDERATED STATES OF MICRONESIA
MELANESIA
NAURU
KIRIBATI
TUVALU
PAPUA NEW GUINEA
Port Moresby
SOLOMON ISLANDS
VANUATU
FIJI
AUSTRALIA
New Caledonia (FR.)
Canberra
NEW ZEALAND
Wellington
Antarctic Circle
ANTARCTICA
West Africa
MAURITANIA
Nouakchott
MALI
Dakar
SENEGAL
GAMBIA
Bamako
BURKINA FASO
Ougadougou
Niamey
NIGER
Bissau
GUINEA-BISSAU
GUINEA
Conakry
Freetown
SIERRA LEONE
Monrovia
LIBERIA
CÔTE D'IVOIRE
Yamassoukro
Abidjan
GHANA
Accra
TOGO
Lomé
BENIN
Porto-Novo
NIGERIA
ATLANTIC OCEAN
Equator
0 250 500 Miles
0 250 500 750 Kilometers
Europe
FINLAND
Helsinki
NORWAY
Oslo
SWEDEN
Stockholm
Tallinn
ESTONIA
Riga
LATVIA
Moscow
RUSSIA
IRELAND
Dublin
UNITED KINGDOM
DENMARK
Copenhagen
LITHUANIA
Vilnius
NETHERLANDS
The Hague
London
Amsterdam
Berlin
Warsaw
POLAND
BYELORUSSIA
ATLANTIC OCEAN
BELGIUM
Brussels
Paris
LUXEMBOURG
GERMANY
Prague
CZECHOSLOVAKIA
UKRAINE
FRANCE
SWITZERLAND
Bern
Vienna
AUSTRIA
Budapest
HUNGARY
MOLDAVIA
PORTUGAL
Lisbon
Madrid
SPAIN
ITALY
Rome
Belgrade
YUGOSLAVIA
ROMANIA
Bucharest
BLACK SEA
GEORGIA
Sofia
BULGARIA
Tirane
ALBANIA
Gibralter (BR.)
MEDITERRANEAN SEA
GREECE
Athens
TURKEY
MALTA
CYPRUS
LEBANON
SYRIA
0 250 500 Miles
0 250 500 750 Kilometers

THE DECLARATION OF INDEPENDENCE

In Congress, July 4, 1776

THE UNANIMOUS DECLARATION OF THE THIRTEEN UNITED STATES OF AMERICA

When in the Course of human events, it becomes necessary for one people to dissolve the political bands which have connected them with another, and to assume among the powers of the earth, the separate and equal station to which the Laws of nature and of Nature's God entitle them, a decent respect to the opinions of mankind requires that they should declare the causes which impel them to the separation.

The opening paragraph of the Declaration describes the basic purpose of the document: to set out the reasons why the former colonists declared their independence.

THE POLITICAL THEORY OF THE DECLARATION

We hold these truths to be self-evident, that all men are created equal, that they are endowed by their Creator with certain unalienable Rights, that among these are Life, Liberty and the pursuit of Happiness. That to secure these rights, Governments are instituted among Men, deriving their just powers from the consent of the governed; That whenever any Form of Government becomes destructive of these ends it is the Right of the People to alter or to abolish it, and to institute new Government, laying its foundation on such principles and organizing its powers in such form, as to them shall seem most likely to effect their Safety and Happiness. Prudence, indeed, will dictate that Governments long established should not be changed for light and transient causes; and accordingly all experience hath shown, that mankind are more disposed to suffer, while evils are sufferable, than to right themselves by abolishing the forms to which they are accustomed. But when a long train of abuses and usurpations, pursuing invariably the same Objects evinces a design to reduce them under absolute Despotism, it is their right, it is their duty, to throw off such Government, and to provide new Guards for their future security.

The Declaration was written by a five-member committee appointed by the Second Continental Congress on June 11, 1776. The document was very largely the work of Thomas Jefferson, who chaired the committee. Its other members (John Adams, Benjamin Franklin, Roger Sherman, and Robert Livingston) made minor changes in Jefferson's original draft before the final version was reported to Congress. Jefferson drew heavily from the ideas of English philosopher John Locke to declare these "self-evident" truths: the equality of all men; the natural rights of men, granted to them by God; the principle of limited government; government only by the consent of the governed; and the right to rebel against tyrannical government.

THE "INJURIES AND USURPATIONS"

Such has been the patient sufferance of these Colonies; and such is now the necessity which constrains them to alter their former Systems of Government. The history of the present King of Great Britain is a history of repeated injuries and usurpations, all having in direct object the establishment of an absolute Tyranny over these States. To prove this, let Facts be submitted to a candid world.

He has refused his Assent to Laws, the most wholesome and necessary for the public good.

He has forbidden his Governors to pass Laws of immediate and pressing importance, unless suspended in their operation till his Assent should be obtained; and when so suspended, he has utterly neglected to attend to them.

He has refused to pass other Laws for the accommodation of large districts of people, unless those people would relinquish the right of Representation in the Legislature, a right inestimable to them and formidable to tyrants only.

He has called together legislative bodies at places unusual, uncomfortable, and distant from the depository of their public records, for the sole purpose of fatiguing them into compliance with his measures.

He has dissolved Representative Houses repeatedly, for opposing with manly firmness his invasions on the rights of the people.

He has refused for a long time, after such dissolutions, to cause others to be elected; whereby the Legislative powers, incapable of Annihilation, have returned to the People at large for their exercise; the State remaining in the mean time exposed to all the dangers of invasions from without, and convulsions within.

He has endeavored to prevent the population of these States; for that purpose obstructing the Laws for Naturalization of Foreigners; refusing to pass others to encourage their migration hither, and raising the conditions of new Appropriations of Lands.

He has obstructed the Administration of Justice, by refusing his Assent to Laws for establishing Judiciary powers.

He has made Judges dependent on his Will alone for the tenure of their offices, and the amount and payment of their salaries.

He has erected a multitude of New Offices, and sent hither swarms of Officers to harass our people and eat out their substance.

He has kept among us in time of peace, Standing Armies, without the Consent of our legislatures.

He has affected to render the Military independent of, and superior to, the Civil Power.

He has combined with others to subject us to a jurisdiction foreign to our constitutions, and unacknowledged by our laws; giving his Assent to their Acts of pretended Legislation:

For quartering large bodies of armed troops among us;

For protecting them, by a mock Trial, from punishment for any Murders which they should commit on the Inhabitants of these States;

For cutting off our Trade with all parts of the world;

For imposing taxes on us without our Consent;

For depriving us, in many cases, of the benefits of Trial by Jury;

For transporting us beyond Seas, to be tried for pretended offenses;

For abolishing the free System of English Laws in a neighboring Province, establishing therein an Arbitrary government, and enlarging its Boundaries, so as to render it at once an example and fit instrument for introducing the same absolute rule into these Colonies;

For taking away our Charters, abolishing our most valuable Laws, and altering, fundamentally, the Forms of our Governments;

For suspending our own Legislatures, and declaring themselves invested with Power to legislate for us in all cases whatsoever.

He has abdicated Government here, by declaring us out of his Protection, and waging War against us.

He has plundered our seas, ravaged our Coasts, burned our towns, and destroyed the lives of our people.

He is at this time transporting large Armies of foreign Mercenaries to complete the works of death, desolation and tyranny, already begun with circumstances of Cruelty and perfidy scarcely paralleled in the most barbarous ages, and totally unworthy the Head of a civilized nation.

He has constrained our fellow Citizens taken Captive on the high Seas to bear Arms against their Country, to become the executioners of their friends and Brethren, or to fall themselves by their Hands.

He has excited domestic insurrections amongst us, and has endeavored to bring on the inhabitants of our frontiers the merciless Indian Savages whose known rule of warfare is an undistinguished destruction of all ages, sexes, and conditions.

In every stage of these Oppressions We have Petitioned for Redress in the most humble terms. Our repeated Petitions have been answered only by repeated injury. A Prince whose character is thus marked by every act which may define a Tyrant, is unfit to be the ruler of a free people.

Nor have We been wanting in attentions to our British brethren. We have warned them from time to time of attempts by their legislature to extend an unwarrantable jurisdiction over us. We have reminded them of the circumstances of our emigration and settlement here. We have appealed to their native justice and magnanimity, and we have conjured them by the ties of our common kindred to disavow these usurpations, which, would inevitably interrupt our connections and correspondence. They too have been deaf to the voice of justice and of consanguinity. We must, therefore, acquiesce in the necessity, which denounces our Separation, and hold them, as we hold the rest of mankind, Enemies in War, in Peace Friends.—

The body of the Declaration sets out the long list of grievances felt by the colonists and cites their repeated but unsuccessful attempts to redress them by peaceful means.

The Formal Proclamation of Independence

We, therefore, the Representatives of the United States of America, in General Congress, Assembled, appealing to the Supreme Judge of the world for the rectitude of our intentions, do, in the Name, and by the Authority of the good People of these Colonies, solemnly publish and declare, That these United Colonies are, and of right ought to be Free and Independent States; that they are Absolved from all Allegiance to the British Crown, and that all political connection between them and the State of Great Britain, is and ought to be totally dissolved, and that as Free and Independent States, they have full Power to levy War, conclude Peace, contract Alliances, establish Commerce, and to do all other Acts and Things which Independent States may of right do. And for the support of this Declaration, with a firm reliance on the protection of Divine Providence, we mutually pledge to each other our Lives, our Fortunes and our sacred Honor.

The final paragraph of the Declaration makes the formal pronouncement of independence from Great Britain, and claims for the United States all of the rights to which an independent nation is entitled.

JOHN HANCOCK
President of the
Continental Congress
1775–1777

NEW HAMPSHIRE
Josiah Bartlett
William Whipple
Matthew Thornton

MASSACHUSETTS BAY
Samuel Adams
John Adams
Robert Treat Paine
Elbridge Gerry

RHODE ISLAND
Stephan Hopkins
William Ellery

CONNECTICUT
Roger Sherman
Samuel Huntington
William Williams
Oliver Wolcott

NEW YORK
William Floyd
Philip Livingston
Francis Lewis
Lewis Morris

NEW JERSEY
Richard Stockton
John Witherspoon
Francis Hopkinson
John Hart
Abraham Clark

DELAWARE
Caesar Rodney
George Read
Thomas M'Kean

MARYLAND
Samuel Chase
William Paca
Thomas Stone
Charles Carroll
of Carrollton

VIRGINIA
George Wythe
Richard Henry Lee
Thomas Jefferson
Benjamin Harrison
Thomas Nelson, Jr.
Francis Lightfoot Lee
Carter Braxton

PENNSYLVANIA
Robert Morris
Benjamin Rush
Benjamin Franklin
John Morton
George Clymer
James Smith
George Taylor
James Wilson
George Ross

NORTH CAROLINA
William Hooper
Joseph Hewes
John Penn

SOUTH CAROLINA
Edward Rutledge
Thomas Heyward, Jr.
Thomas Lynch, Jr.
Arthur Middleton

GEORGIA
Button Gwinnett
Lyman Hall
George Walton

An Outline of the Constitution of the United States

"The American Constitution is the most wonderful work ever struck off at a given time by the brain and purpose of man."

—William E. Gladstone

Preamble

Article I Legislative Department

- Section 1. Legislative Power; the Congress
- Section 2. House of Representatives
- Section 3. Senate
- Section 4. Elections and Meetings
- Section 5. Legislative Proceedings
- Section 6. Compensation, Immunities, and Disabilities of Members
- Section 7. Revenue Bills; President's Veto
- Section 8. Powers of Congress
- Section 9. Powers Denied to Congress
- Section 10. Powers Denied to the States

Article II Executive Department

- Section 1. Executive Power; the President; Term; Election; Qualifications; Compensation; Oath of Office
- Section 2. President's Powers and Duties
- Section 3. President's Powers and Duties
- Section 4. Impeachment

Article III Judicial Department

- Section 1. Judicial Power; Courts; Terms of Office
- Section 2. Jurisdiction
- Section 3. Treason

Article IV Relations of States

- Section 1. Full Faith and Credit
- Section 2. Privileges and Immunities of Citizens
- Section 3. Protection Afforded to States by the Nation

Article V Provisions for Amendment

Article VI Public Debts; Supremacy of National Law; Oath

- Section 1. Validity of Debts
- Section 2. Supremacy of National Law
- Section 3. Oaths of Office

Article VII Ratification of Constitution

1st Amendment. Freedom of Religion, Speech, Press, Assembly, and Petition

2nd Amendment. Bearing Arms

3rd Amendment. Quartering of Troops

4th Amendment. Searches and Seizures

5th Amendment. Criminal Proceedings; Due Process; Eminent Domain

6th Amendment. Criminal Proceedings

7th Amendment. Civil Trials

8th Amendment. Punishment for Crimes

9th Amendment. Unenumerated Rights

10th Amendment. Powers Reserved to the States

11TH AMENDMENT. Suits Against States

12TH AMENDMENT. Election of President and Vice President

13TH AMENDMENT. Slavery and Involuntary Servitude
- Section 1. Slavery and Involuntary Servitude Prohibited
- Section 2. Power of Congress

14TH AMENDMENT. Rights of Citizens
- Section 1. Citizenship; Privileges and Immunities; Due Process; Equal Protection
- Section 2. Apportionment of Representation
- Section 3. Disqualification of Officers
- Section 4. Public Debt
- Section 5. Power of Congress

15TH AMENDMENT. Right to Vote—Race, Color, Servitude
- Section 1. Suffrage Not to Be Abridged
- Section 2. Power of Congress

16TH AMENDMENT. Income Tax

17TH AMENDMENT. Popular Election of Senators
- Section 1. Popular Election of Senators
- Section 2. Senate Vacancies
- Section 3. Inapplicable to Senators Previously Chosen

18TH AMENDMENT. Prohibition of Intoxicating Liquors
- Section 1. Intoxicating Liquors Prohibited
- Section 2. Concurrent Power to Enforce
- Section 3. Time Limit on Ratification

19TH AMENDMENT. Equal Suffrage—Sex
- Section 1. Suffrage Not to Be Abridged
- Section 2. Power of Congress

20TH AMENDMENT. Commencement of Terms; Sessions of Congress; Death or Disqualification of President-Elect
- Section 1. Terms of President, Vice President, Members of Congress
- Section 2. Sessions of Congress
- Section 3. Death or Disqualification of President-Elect
- Section 4. Congress to Provide for Certain Successors
- Section 5. Effective Date
- Section 6. Time Limit on Ratification

21TH AMENDMENT. Repeal of 18th AMENDMENT
- Section 1. Repeal of Prohibition
- Section 2. Transportation, Importation of Intoxicating Liquors
- Section 3. Time Limit on Ratification

22ND AMENDMENT. Presidential Tenure
- Section 1. Restriction on Number of Terms
- Section 2. Time Limit on Ratification

23RD AMENDMENT. Inclusion of District of Columbia in Presidential Election System
- Section 1. Presidential Electors for District of Columbia
- Section 2. Power of Congress

24TH AMENDMENT. Right to Vote in Federal Elections—Tax Payment
- Section 1. Suffrage Not to Be Abridged
- Section 2. Power of Congress

25TH AMENDMENT. Presidential Succession; Vice Presidential Vacancy; Presidential Inability
- Section 1. Presidential Succession
- Section 2. Vice Presidential Vacancy
- Section 3. Presidential Determination of Inability

26TH AMENDMENT. Right to Vote—Age
- Section 1. Suffrage Not to Be Abridged
- Section 2. Power of Congress

The Constitution of the United States

PREAMBLE

We the People of the United States, in Order to form a more perfect Union, establish Justice, insure domestic Tranquility, provide for the common defence, promote the general Welfare, and secure the Blessings of Liberty to ourselves and our Posterity, do ordain and establish this Constitution for the United States of America.

The Preamble states the broad purposes the Constitution is intended to serve—to establish a government that provides for greater cooperation among the States, ensures justice and peace, provides for defense against foreign enemies, promotes the general well-being of the people, and secures liberty now and in the future. The phrase *We the People* emphasizes the twin concepts of popular sovereignty and of representative government.

Article I

LEGISLATIVE DEPARTMENT

Section 1. *Legislative Power; The Congress*

All legislative powers herein granted shall be vested in a Congress of the United States, which shall consist of a Senate and House of Representatives.

Section 1. Legislative power, Congress Congress, the nation's lawmaking body, is bicameral in form; that is, it is composed of two houses: the Senate and the House of Representatives. The Framers of the Constitution purposely separated the lawmaking power from the power to enforce the laws (Article II, the Executive Branch) and the power to interpret them (Article III, the Judicial Branch). This system of separation of powers is supplemented by a system of checks and balances; that is, in several provisions the Constitution gives to each of the three branches various powers with which it may check, restrain, the actions of the other two branches.

Section 2. *House of Representatives*

1. The House of Representatives shall be composed of members chosen every second year by the people of the several States, and the electors in each State shall have the qualifications requisite for electors of the most numerous branch of the State legislature.

Clause 1. Election Electors means voters. Members of the House of Representatives are elected every two years. Each State must permit the same persons to vote for United States representatives as it permits to vote for the members of the larger house of its own legislature. The 17th Amendment (1913) extends this requirement to the qualification of voters for United States senators.

2. No person shall be a Representative who shall not have attained to the age of twenty-five years, and been seven years a citizen of the United States, and who shall not, when elected, be an inhabitant of that State in which he shall be chosen.

Clause 2. Qualifications A member of the House of Representatives must be at least 25 years old, an American citizen for seven years, and a resident of the State he or she represents. In addition, political custom requires that a representative also reside in the district from which he or she is elected.

3. Representatives ~~and direct taxes~~* shall be apportioned among the several States which may be included within this Union, according to their respective numbers, ~~which shall be determined by adding to the whole number of free persons, including those bound to service for a term of years and excluding Indians not taxed, three fifths of all other persons~~. The actual enumeration shall be made within three years after the first meeting of the Congress of the United States, and within every subsequent term of ten years, in such manner as they shall by law direct. The number of Representatives shall not exceed one for every thirty thousand, but each State shall have at least one Representative; and, until such enumeration shall be made, the State of New Hampshire shall be entitled to choose three, Massachusetts eight, Rhode Island and Providence Plantations one, Connecticut five, New York six, New Jersey four, Pennsylvania eight, Delaware one, Maryland six, Virginia ten, North Carolina five, South Carolina five, and Georgia three.

Clause 3. Apportionment The number of representatives each State is entitled to is based on its population, which is counted every 10 years in the census. Congress reapportions the seats among the States after each census. In the Reapportionment Act of 1929, Congress fixed the permanent size of the House at 435 members with each State having at least one representative. Today there is one House seat for approximately every 575,000 persons in the population.

---

*The black lines indicate portions of the Constitution altered by subsequent amendments to the document.

The words "three-fifths of all other persons" referred to slaves and reflected the Three-Fifths Compromise reached by the Framers at Philadelphia in 1787; the phrase was made obsolete, was in effect repealed, by the 13th Amendment in 1865.

4. When vacancies happen in the representation from any State, the executive authority thereof shall issue writs of election to fill such vacancies.

CLAUSE 4. VACANCIES The executive authority refers to the governor of a State. If a member leaves office or dies before the expiration of his or her term, the governor is to call a special election to fill the vacancy.

5. The House of Representatives shall choose their Speaker and other officers; and shall have the sole power of impeachment.

CLAUSE 5. OFFICERS; IMPEACHMENT The House elects a Speaker, customarily chosen from the majority party in the House. Impeachment means accusation. The House has the exclusive power to impeach, or accuse, civil officers; the Senate (Article I, Section 3, Clause 6) has the exclusive power to try those impeached by the House.

Section 3. *Senate*

1. The Senate of the United States shall be composed of two Senators from each State ~~chosen by the legislature thereof~~ for six years; and each Senator shall have one vote.

CLAUSE 1. COMPOSITION, ELECTION, TERM Each State has two senators. Each serves for six years and has one vote. Orginally, senators were not elected directly by the people, but by each State's legislature. The 17th Amendment, added in 1913, provides for the popular election of senators.

2. Immediately after they shall be assembled in consequences of the first election, they shall be divided, as equally as may be, into three classes. The seats of the Senators of the first class shall be vacated at the expiration of the second year; of the second class, at the expiration of the fourth year; and of the third class, at the expiration of the sixth year; so that one-third may be chosen every second year~~; and if vacancies happen by resignation, or otherwise, during the recess of the legislature of any State, the execution thereof may make temporary appointments until the next meeting of the legislature, which shall then fill such vacancies~~.

CLAUSE 2. CLASSIFICATION The senators elected in 1788 were divided into three groups so that the Senate could become a "continuing body." Only one-third of the Senate's seats are up for election every two years.

The 17th Amendment provides that a Senate vacancy is to be filled at a special election called by the governor; State law may also permit the governor to appoint a successor to serve until that election is held.

3. No person shall be a Senator who shall not have attained to the age of thirty years, and been nine years a citizen of the United States, who shall not, when elected, be an inhabitant of that State for which he shall be chosen.

CLAUSE 3. QUALIFICATIONS A senator must be at least 30 years old, a citizen for at least nine years, and a resident of the State from which elected.

4. The Vice President of the United States shall be President of the Senate, but shall have no vote, unless they be equally divided.

CLAUSE 4. PRESIDING OFFICER The Vice President presides over the Senate, but may vote only to break a tie.

5. The Senate shall choose their other officers, and also a President pro tempore, in the absence of the Vice President, or when he shall exercise the office of President of the United States.

CLAUSE 5. OTHER OFFICERS The Senate chooses its own officers, including someone to preside when the Vice President is not there. That senator is called the Senate's president pro tempore.

6. The Senate shall have the sole power to try all impeachments. When sitting for that purpose, they shall be on oath or affirmation. When the President of the United States is tried, the Chief Justice shall preside; and no person shall be convicted without the concurrence of two-thirds of the members present.

CLAUSE 6. IMPEACHMENT TRIALS The Senate conducts the trials of those officials impeached by the House. The Vice President presides unless the President is on trial, in which case the chief justice of the United States takes charge of the proceedings. To convict an official two-thirds of the members present must vote a guilty verdict.

No President has ever been convicted. In 1868 the House impeached President Andrew Johnson but the Senate acquitted him of the charges by one vote. In 1974 the Judiciary Committee of the House of Representatives recommended to the House that President Richard M. Nixon be impeached, but he resigned from office before further action could be taken.

7. Judgment in cases of impeachment shall not extend further than to removal from office, and disqualification to hold and enjoy any office of honor, trust, or profit under the United States; but the party convicted shall, nevertheless, be liable and subject to indictment, trial, judgment, and punishment, according to law.

CLAUSE 7. PENALTY ON CONVICTION The only punishment allowed for an official who is convicted in an impeachment case is removal from office and disqualification from holding any other federal office. However, the convicted official may still be tried in a regular court of law for the same offense.

Section 4. *Elections and Meetings*

1. The times, places, and manner of holding elections for Senators and Representatives, shall be prescribed in each State by the legislature thereof: but the Congress may at any time, by law, make or alter such regulations, except as to the places of choosing Senators.

CLAUSE 1. ELECTION In 1842 Congress required that representatives be elected from districts within each State with more than one seat in the House. The districts in each State are drawn by that State's legislature. Six States now (1991) have only one seat in the House: Alaska, Delaware, North Dakota, South Dakota, Vermont, and Wyoming. The 1842 law also directed that representatives be elected in each State on the same day: the Tuesday after the first Monday in November of every even-numbered year. In 1914 Congress also set that same date for the election of senators.

2. The Congress shall assemble at least once in every year, and such meeting shall be on the first Monday in December, unless they shall by law appoint a different day.

CLAUSE 2. SESSIONS Congress must meet at least once a year. The 20th Amendment (1933) changed the opening date to January 3.

Section 5. ***Legislative Proceedings***

1. Each House shall be the judge of the elections, returns, and qualifications of its own members, and a majority of each shall constitute a quorum to do business; but a smaller number may adjourn from day to day, and may be authorized to compel the attendance of absent members, in such manner, and under such penalties, as each House may provide.

CLAUSE 1. ADMISSION OF MEMBERS; QUORUM In 1969 the Supreme Court held that the House cannot exclude any member-elect who satisfies the qualifications set out in Article I, Section 2, Clause 2.

A majority in the House (218 members) or Senate (51) constitutes a quorum. In practice, both houses often proceed with less than a quorum present. However, any member may raise a point of order (demand a "quorum call"). If a roll call then reveals less than a majority of the members present, that chamber must either adjourn or the sergeant at arms must be ordered to round up absent members.

2. Each House may determine the rules of its proceedings, punish its members for disorderly behavior, and, with the concurrence of two-thirds, expel a member.

CLAUSE 2. RULES Each house has adopted detailed rules to guide its proceedings. Each house may discipline members for unacceptable conduct; expulsion requires a two-thirds vote.

3. Each House shall keep a journal of its proceedings, and, from time to time, publish the same, excepting such parts as may, in their judgment, require secrecy; and the yeas and nays of the members of either House, on any question, shall, at the desire of one-fifth of those present, be entered on the journal.

CLAUSE 3. RECORD Each house must keep and publish a record of its meetings. The *Congressional Record* is published for every day that either house of Congress is in session, and provides a written record of all that is said and done on the floor of each house each session.

4. Neither House, during the session of Congress, shall, without the consent of the other, adjourn for more than three days, nor to any other place than that in which the two Houses shall be sitting.

CLAUSE 4. ADJOURNMENT Once in session, neither house may suspend (recess) its work for more than three days without the approval of the other house. Both houses must always meet in the same location.

Section 6. ***Compensation, Immunities, and Disabilities of Members***

1. The Senators and Representatives shall receive a compensation for their services, to be ascertained by law, and paid out of the treasury of the United States. They shall, in all cases, except treason, felony, and breach of the peace, be privileged from arrest during their attendance at the session of their respective Houses, and in going to, and returning from, the same; and for any speech or debate in either House, they shall not be questioned in any other place.

CLAUSE 1. SALARIES; IMMUNITIES Senate and House members set their own salaries and are paid by the United States government. This provision establishes "legislative immunity." The purpose of this immunity is to allow members to speak and debate freely in Congress itself. Treason is strictly defined in Article III, Section 3. A felony is any serious crime. A breach of the peace is any indictable offense less than treason or a felony; this exemption from arrest is of little real importance today.

2. No Senator or Representative shall, during the time for which he was elected, be appointed to any civil office under the authority of the United States, which shall have been created, or the emoluments whereof shall have been increased during such time; and no person, holding any office under the United States, shall be a member of either House during his continuance in office.

CLAUSE 2. RESTRICTIONS ON OFFICE HOLDING No sitting member of either house may be appointed to an office in the executive or in the judicial branch if that position was created or its salary was increased during that member's current elected term. The second part of this clause—forbidding any person serving in either the executive or the judicial branch from also serving in Congress—reinforces the principle of separation of powers.

Section 7. ***Revenue Bills, President's Veto***

1. All bills for raising revenue shall originate in the House of Representatives, but the Senate may propose or concur with amendments as on other bills.

CLAUSE 1. REVENUE BILLS All bills that raise money must originate in the House. However, the Senate has the power to amend any revenue bill sent to it from the lower house.

2. Every bill which shall have passed the House of Representatives and the Senate, shall, before it become a law, be presented to the President of the United

States; if he approve, he shall sign it, but if not, he shall return it, with his objections, to that House in which it shall have originated, who shall enter the objections at large on their journal, and proceed to reconsider it. If, after such reconsideration, two-thirds of the House shall agree to pass the bill, it shall be sent, together with the objections, to the other House, by which it shall likewise be reconsidered, and, if approved by two-thirds of that House, it shall become a law: But in all such cases the votes of both Houses shall be determined by yeas and nays, and the names of the persons voting for and against the bill shall be entered on the journal of each House respectively. If any bill shall not be returned by the President within ten days (Sunday excepted) after it shall have been presented to him, the same shall be a law, in like manner as if he had signed it, unless the Congress, by their adjournment, prevent its return, in which case it shall not be a law.

CLAUSE 2. ENACTMENT OF LAWS; VETO Once both houses have passed a bill, it must be sent to the President. The President may (1) sign the bill, thus making it law; (2) veto (reject) the bill, whereupon it must be returned to the house in which it originated; or (3) allow the bill to become law without signature, by not acting upon it within 10 days of its receipt from Congress, not counting Sundays. The President has a fourth option at the end of a congressional session: If he does not act on a measure within 10 days, and Congress adjourns during that period, the bill dies; the "pocket veto" has been applied to it. A presidential veto may be overridden by a two-thirds vote in each house.

3. Every order, resolution, or vote, to which the concurrence of the Senate and House of Representatives may be necessary (except on a question of adjournment), shall be presented to the President of the United States; and before the same shall take effect, shall be approved by him, or, being disapproved by him, shall be repassed by two-thirds of the Senate and House of Representatives, according to the rules and limitations prescribed in the case of a bill.

CLAUSE 3. OTHER MEASURES This clause refers to joint resolutions, measures Congress often passes to deal with unusual, temporary, or ceremonial matters. A joint resolution passed by Congress and signed by the President has the force of law, just as a bill does. As a matter of custom, a joint resolution proposing an amendment to the Constitution is not submitted to the President for signature or veto. Concurrent and simple resolutions do not have the force of law and, therefore, are not submitted to the President.

Section 8. *Powers of Congress*

The Congress shall have power

1. To lay and collect taxes, duties, imposts, and excises, to pay the debts, and provide for the common defence and general welfare of the United States; but all duties, imposts, and excises, shall be uniform throughout the United States;

CLAUSE 1. The 18 separate clauses in this section set out 27 of the many expressed powers the Constitution grants to Congress. In this clause Congress is given the power to levy and provide for the collection of various kinds of taxes, in order to finance the operations of the government. All federal taxes must be levied at the same rates throughout the country.

2. To borrow money on the credit of the United States;

CLAUSE 2. Congress has power to borrow money to help finance the government. Federal borrowing is most often done through the sale of bonds on which interest is paid. The Constitution does not limit the amount the government may borrow.

3. To regulate commerce with foreign nations, and among the several States, and with the Indian tribes;

CLAUSE 3. This clause, the Commerce Clause, gives Congress the power to regulate both foreign and interstate trade. Much of what Congress does, it does on the basis of its commerce power.

4. To establish an uniform rule of naturalization, and uniform laws on the subject of bankruptcies, throughout the United States;

CLAUSE 4. Congress has the exclusive power to determine how aliens may become citizens of the United States. Congress may also pass laws relating to bankruptcy.

5. To coin money, regulate the value thereof, and of foreign coin, and fix the standard of weights and measures;

CLAUSE 5. Congress has the power to establish and require the use of uniform gauges of time, distance, weight, volume, area, and the like.

6. To provide for the punishment of counterfeiting the securities and current coin of the United States;

CLAUSE 6. Congress has the power to make it a federal crime to falsify the coins, paper money, bonds, stamps, and the like of the United States.

7. To establish post offices and post roads;

CLAUSE 7. Congress has the postal power, the power to provide for and regulate the transportation and delivery of mail; "post offices" are those buildings and other places where mail is deposited for dispatch; "post roads" include all routes over or upon which mail is carried.

8. To promote the progress of science and useful arts, by securing, for limited times, to authors and inventors, the exclusive right to their respective writings and discoveries;

CLAUSE 8. Congress has the power to provide for copyrights and patents. A copyright gives an author or composer the exclusive right to control the reproduction, publication, and sale of literary, musical, or other creative work. A patent gives a person the exclusive right to control the manufacture or sale of his or her invention.

9. To constitute tribunals inferior to the Supreme Court;

CLAUSE 9. Congress has the power to create the lower federal courts, all of the several federal courts that function beneath the Supreme Court.

10. To define and punish piracies and felonies, committed on the high seas, and offences against the law of nations;

CLAUSE 10. Congress has the power to prohibit, as a federal crime: (1) certain acts committed outside the territorial jurisdiction of the United States, and (2) the commission within the United States of any wrong against any nation with which we are at peace.

11. To declare war, grant letters of marque and reprisal, and make rules concerning captures on land and water;

CLAUSE 11. Only Congress can declare war. However, the President, as commander in chief of the armed forces (Article II, Section 2, Clause 1), can make war without such a formal declaration. Letters of marque and reprisal are (were) commissions authorizing private persons to outfit vessels (privateers) to capture and destroy enemy ships in time of war; they are forbidden in international law by the Declaration of Paris of 1856, and the United States has honored the ban since the Civil War.

12. To raise and support armies; but no appropriation of money to that use shall be for a longer term than two years;

13. To provide and maintain a navy;

CLAUSES 12 and 13. Congress has the power to provide for and maintain the nation's armed forces. It established the air force as an independent element of the armed forces in 1947, an exercise of its inherent powers in foreign relations and national defense. The two-year limit on spending for the army insures civilian control of the military.

14. To make rules for the government and regulation of the land and naval forces;

CLAUSE 14. Today these rules are set out in a lengthy, oft-amended law, the Uniform Code of Military Justice, passed by Congress in 1950.

15. To provide for calling forth the militia to execute the laws of the Union, suppress insurrections, and repel invasions;

16. To provide for organizing, arming, and disciplining the militia, and for governing such part of them as may be employed in the service of the United States, reserving to the States respectively the appointment of the officers, and the authority of training the militia, according to the discipline prescribed by Congress;

CLAUSES 15 and 16. In the National Defense Act of 1916, Congress made each State's militia (volunteer army) a part of the National Guard. Today, Congress and the States cooperate in its maintenance. Ordinarily, each State's National Guard is under the command of that State's governor; but Congress has given the President the power to call any or all of those units into federal service when necessary.

17. To exercise exclusive legislation in all cases whatsoever, over such district (not exceeding ten miles square) as may, by cession of particular States, and the acceptance of Congress, become the seat of the Government of the United States, and to exercise like authority over all places, purchased by the consent of the legislature of the State in which the same shall be, for the erection of forts, magazines, arsenals, dockyards, and other needful buildings; and

CLAUSE 17. In 1791 Congress accepted land grants from Maryland and Virginia and established the District of Columbia for the nation's capital. Assuming Virginia's grant would never be needed, Congress returned it in 1846. Today, the elected government of the District's 69 square miles operates under the authority of Congress. Congress also has the power to acquire other lands from the States for various federal purposes.

18. To make all laws which shall be necessary and proper for carrying into execution the foregoing powers, and all other powers vested by this Constitution in the Government of the United States, or in any department or officer thereof.

CLAUSE 18. This is the Necessary and Proper Clause, also often called the Elastic Clause. It is the constitutional basis for the many and far-reaching implied powers of the Federal Government.

Section 9. ***Powers Denied to Congress***

1. The migration or importation of such persons as any of the States now existing shall think proper to admit, shall not be prohibited by the Congress prior to the year one thousand eight hundred and eight; but a tax or duty may be imposed on such importation, not exceeding ten dollars for each person.

CLAUSE 1. "Such persons" referred to slaves. This provision was part of the Commerce Compromise, one of the bargains struck in the writing of the Constitution. Congress outlawed the slave trade in 1808.

2. The privilege of the writ of habeas corpus shall not be suspended, unless when, in cases of rebellion or invasion, the public safety may require it.

CLAUSE 2. A writ of habeas corpus, the "great writ of liberty," is a court order directing a sheriff, warden, or other public officer, or a private person, who is detaining another to "produce the body" of the one being held in order that the legality of the detention may be determined by the court.

3. No bill of attainder or *ex post facto* law shall be passed.

CLAUSE 3. A bill of attainder is a legislative act that inflicts punishment without a judicial trial. See Article I, Section 10, and Article III, Section 3, Clause 2. An *ex post facto* law is any criminal law that operates retroactively to the disadvantage of the accused. See Article I, Section 10.

4. No capitation, ~~or other direct tax~~, shall be laid, unless in proportion to the census or enumeration hereinbefore directed to be taken.

CLAUSE 4. A capitation tax is literally a "head tax," a tax levied on each person in the population. A direct tax is one paid directly to the government by the taxpayer—for example, an income or a property tax; an indirect tax is one paid to another private party who then pays it to the government—for example, a sales tax. This provision was modified by the 16th Amendment (1913), giving Congress the power to levy "taxes on incomes, from whatever source derived."

5. No tax or duty shall be laid on articles exported from any State.

CLAUSE 5. This provision was a part of the Commerce Compromise made by the Framers in 1787. Congress has the power to tax imported goods, however.

6. No preference shall be given by any regulation of commerce or revenue to the ports of one State over those of another, nor shall vessels bound to, or from, one State, be obliged to enter, clear, or pay duties, in another.

CLAUSE 6. All ports within the United States must be treated alike by Congress as it exercises its taxing and commerce powers. Congress cannot tax goods sent by water from one State to another, nor may it give the ports of one State any legal advantage over those of another.

7. No money shall be drawn from the treasury, but in consequence of appropriations made by law; and a regular statement and account of the receipts and expenditures of all public money shall be published from time to time.

CLAUSE 7. This clause gives Congress its vastly important "power of the purse," a major check on presidential power. Federal money can be spent only in those amounts and for those purposes expressly authorized by an act of Congress. All federal income and spending must be accounted for, regularly and publicly.

8. No title of nobility shall be granted by the United States; and no person holding any office of profit or trust under them shall, without the consent of the Congress, accept of any present, emolument, office, or title, of any kind whatever, from any king, prince, or foreign state.

CLAUSE 8. This provision, preventing the establishment of a nobility, reflects the principle that "all men are created equal." It was also intended to discourage foreign attempts to bribe or otherwise corrupt officers of the government.

Section 10. *Powers Denied to the States*

1. No State shall enter into any treaty, alliance, or confederation; grant letters of marque and reprisal; coin money; emit bills of credit; make anything but gold and silver coin a tender in payment of debts; pass any bill of attainder, *ex post facto* law, or law impairing the obligations of contracts, or grant any title of nobility.

CLAUSE 1. The States are not sovereign governments and so cannot make agreements or otherwise negotiate with foreign states; the power to conduct foreign relations is an exclusive power of the National Government. The power to coin money is also an exclusive power of the National Government. Several powers forbidden to the National Government are here also forbidden to the States.

2. No State shall, without the consent of the Congress, lay any imposts or duties on imports or exports, except what may be absolutely necessary for executing its inspection laws; and the net produce of all duties and imposts, laid by any State on imports or exports, shall be for the use of the treasury of the United States; and all such laws shall be subject to the revision and control of the Congress.

CLAUSE 2. This provision relates to foreign, not interstate, commerce. Only Congress, not the States, can tax imports; and the States are, like Congress, forbidden the power to tax exports.

3. No State shall, without the consent of Congress, lay any duty of tonnage, keep troops, or ships of war, in time of peace, enter into any agreement or compact with another State, or with a foreign power, or engage in war, unless actually invaded, or in such imminent danger as will not admit of delay.

CLAUSE 3. A duty of tonnage is a tax laid on ships according to their cargo capacity. Each State has a constitutional right to provide for and maintain a militia; but no State may keep a standing army or navy. The several restrictions here prevent the States from assuming powers that the Constitution elsewhere grants to the National Government.

Article II

EXECUTIVE DEPARTMENT

Section 1. *President and Vice President*

1. The executive power shall be vested in a President of the United States of America. He shall hold his office during the term of four years, and together with the Vice President, chosen for the same term, be elected as follows:

CLAUSE 1. EXECUTIVE POWER, TERM This clause gives to the President the very broad "executive power," the power to enforce the laws and otherwise administer the public policies of the United States. It also sets the length of the presidential (and vice-presidential) term of office; see the 22nd Amendment (1951), which places a limit on presidential (but not vice-presidential) tenure.

2. Each State shall appoint, in such manner as the legislature thereof may direct, a number of Electors, equal to the whole number of Senators and Representatives, to which the State may be entitled in the Congress; but no Senator or Representative, or person holding an office of trust or profit, under the United States, shall be appointed an Elector.

CLAUSE 2. ELECTORAL COLLEGE This clause establishes the "electoral college," although the Constitution does not use that term. It is a body of presidential electors chosen in each State, and it selects the President and

Vice President every four years. The number of electors chosen in each State equals the number of senators and representatives that State has in Congress.

~~3. The Electors shall meet in their respective States, and vote by ballot for two persons, of whom one, at least, shall not be an inhabitant of the same State with themselves. And they shall make a list of all the persons voted for, and of the number of votes for each; which list they shall sign and certify, and transmit, sealed, to the seat of the Government of the United States, directed to the President of the Senate. The President of the Senate shall, in the presence of the Senate and House of Representatives, open all the certificates, and the votes shall then be counted. The person having the greatest number of votes shall be the President, if such number be a majority of the whole number of Electors appointed; and if there be more than one, who have such majority, and have an equal number of votes, then, the House of Representatives shall immediately choose, by ballot, one of them for President; and if no person have a majority, then, from the five highest on the list, the said House shall, in like manner, choose the President. But in choosing the President, the votes shall be taken by States, the representation from each State having one vote; a quorum for this purpose shall consist of a member or members from two-thirds of the States, and a majority of all the States shall be necessary to a choice. In every case, after the choice of the President, the person having the greatest number of votes of the Electors shall be the Vice President. But if there should remain two or more who have equal votes, the Senate shall choose from them, by ballot, the Vice President.~~

CLAUSE 3. ELECTION OF PRESIDENT AND VICE PRESIDENT This clause was replaced by the 12th Amendment in 1804.

4. The Congress may determine the time of choosing the Electors, and the day on which they shall give their votes; which day shall be the same throughout the United States.

CLAUSE 4. DATE Congress has set the date for the choosing of electors as the Tuesday after the first Monday in November every fourth year, and for the casting of electoral votes as the Monday after the second Wednesday in December of that year.

5. No person, except a natural-born citizen, or a citizen of the United States at the time of the adoption of this Constitution, shall be eligible to the office of President; neither shall any person be eligible to that office, who shall not have attained to the age of thirty-five years, and been fourteen years a resident within the United States.

CLAUSE 5. QUALIFICATIONS The President must have been born a citizen of the United States, be at least 35 years old, and have been a resident of the United States for at least 14 years.

6. ~~In case of the removal of the president from office, or of his death, resignation, or inability to discharge the powers and duties of the said office, the same shall devolve on the Vice President~~, and the Congress may by law provide for the case of removal, death, resignation or inability, both of the President and Vice President, declaring what officer shall then act as President, and such officer shall act accordingly, until the disability be removed, or a President shall be elected.

CLAUSE 6. VACANCY This clause was modified by the 25th Amendment (1967), which provides expressly for the succession of the Vice President, for the filling of a vacancy in the Vice Presidency, and for the determination of presidential inability.

7. The President shall, at stated times, receive for his services a compensation, which shall neither be increased nor diminished during the period for which he shall have been elected, and he shall not receive, within that period, any other emolument from the United States, or any of them.

CLAUSE 7. COMPENSATION The President now receives a salary of $200,000 and a taxable expense account of $50,000 a year. Those amounts cannot be changed during a presidential term; thus, Congress cannot use the President's compensation as a bargaining tool to influence executive decisions. The phrase "any other emolument" means, in effect, any valuable gift; it does not mean that the President cannot be provided with such benefits of office as the White House, extensive staff assistance, and much else.

8. Before he enter on the execution of his office, he shall take the following oath or affirmation:

"I do solemnly swear (or affirm), that I will faithfully execute the office of President of the United States, and will, to the best of my ability, preserve, protect, and defend the Constitution of the United States."

CLAUSE 8. OATH OF OFFICE The chief justice of the United States regularly administers this oath or affirmation, but any judicial officer may do so. Thus, Calvin Coolidge was sworn into office in 1923 by his father, a justice of the peace in Vermont.

Section 2. ***President's Powers and Duties***

1. The President shall be Commander in Chief of the army and navy of the United States, and of the militia of the several States, when called into the actual service of the United States; he may require the opinion, in writing, of the principal officer in each of the executive departments upon any subject relating to the duties of their respective offices, and he shall have power to grant reprieves and pardons for offences against the United States, except in cases of impeachment.

CLAUSE 1. MILITARY, CIVIL POWERS The President, a civilian, heads the nation's armed forces, a key element in the Constitution's insistence on civilian control of the military. The President's power to "require the opinion, in writing" provides the constitutional basis for the cabinet. The President's power to grant reprieves and pardons, the power of clemency, extends only to federal cases.

2. He shall have power, by and with the advice and consent of the Senate, to make treaties, provided two-thirds of the Senators present concur; and he shall nominate, and, by and with the advice and consent of the Senate, shall appoint ambassadors, other public ministers, and consuls, judges of the Supreme Court, and all other officers of the United States whose appointments are not herein otherwise provided for, and which shall be established by law; but the Congress may by law vest the appointment of such inferior officers, as they think proper, in the President alone, in the courts of law, or in the heads of departments.

CLAUSE 2. TREATIES, APPOINTMENTS The President has the sole power to make treaties; to become effective, a treaty must be approved by a two-thirds vote in the Senate. In practice, the President can also make executive agreements with foreign governments; these pacts, which are frequently made and usually deal with routine matters, do not require Senate consent. The President appoints the principal officers of the executive branch and all federal judges; the "inferior officers" are those who hold lesser posts.

3. The President shall have power to fill up all vacancies that may happen during the recess of the Senate, by granting commissions which shall expire at the end of their next session.

CLAUSE 3. RECESS APPOINTMENTS When the Senate is not in session, appointments that require Senate consent can be made by the President on a temporary basis, as "recess appointments."

Section 3. *President's Powers and Duties*

He shall, from time to time, give to the Congress information of the state of the Union, and recommend to their consideration such measures as he shall judge necessary and expedient; he may, on extraordinary occasions, convene both Houses, or either of them, and in case of disagreement between them, with respect to the time of adjournment, he may adjourn them to such time as he shall think proper; he shall receive ambassadors and other public ministers; he shall take care that the laws be faithfully executed, and shall commission all the officers of the United States.

The President delivers a State of the Union Message to Congress soon after that body convenes each year. That message is delivered to the nation's lawmakers and, importantly, to the American people, as well. It is shortly followed by the proposed federal budget and an economic report; and the President may send special messages to Congress at any time. In all of these communications, Congress is urged to take those actions the Chief Executive finds to be in the national interest. The President also has the power: to call special sessions of Congress; to adjourn Congress if its two houses cannot agree for that purpose; to receive the diplomatic representatives of other governments; to insure the proper execution of all federal laws; and to empower federal officers to hold their posts and perform their duties.

Section 4. *Impeachment*

The President, Vice President, and all civil officers of the United States, shall be removed from office on impeachment for, and conviction of, treason, bribery, or other high crimes and misdemeanors.

The Constitution outlines the impeachment process in Article I, Section 2, Clause 5 and in Section 3, Clauses 6 and 7.

Article III

JUDICIAL DEPARTMENT

Section 1. *Courts, Terms of Office*

The judicial power of the United States shall be vested in one Supreme Court, and in such inferior courts as the Congress may from time to time ordain and establish. The judges, both of the Supreme and inferior courts, shall hold their offices during good behavior, and shall, at stated times, receive for their services a compensation which shall not be diminished during their continuance in office.

The judicial power conferred here is the power of federal courts to hear and decide cases, disputes between the government and individuals and between private persons (parties). The Constitution creates only the Supreme Court of the United States; it gives to Congress the power to establish other, lower federal courts (Article I, Section 8, Clause 9) and to fix the size of the Supreme Court. The words "during good behavior" mean, in effect, for life.

Section 2. *Jurisdiction*

1. The judicial power shall extend to all cases, in law and equity, arising under this Constitution, the laws of the United States, and treaties made, or which shall be made, under their authority; to all cases affecting ambassadors, other public ministers, and consuls; to all cases of admiralty and maritime jurisdiction; to controversies to which the United States shall be a party; to controversies between two or more States, ~~between a State and a citizen of another State~~, between citizens of different States, between citizens of the same State claiming lands under grants of different States, ~~and between a State, or the citizens thereof, and foreign states, citizens, or subjects~~.

CLAUSE 1. CASES TO BE HEARD This clause sets out the jurisdiction of the federal courts; that is, it identifies those cases that may be tried in those courts. The federal courts can hear and decide—have jurisdiction over—a case depending on either the subject matter or the parties involved in that case. The jurisdiction of the federal courts in cases involving States was substantially restricted by the 11th Amendment in 1795.

2. In all cases affecting ambassadors, other public ministers and consuls, and those in which a State shall be a party, the Supreme Court shall have original jurisdiction. In all the other cases before mentioned, the

Supreme Court shall have appellate jurisdiction, both as to law and fact, with such exceptions and under such regulations as the Congress shall make.

CLAUSE 2. SUPREME COURT JURISDICTION Original jurisdiction refers to the power of a court to hear a case in the first instance, not on appeal from a lower court. Appellate jurisdiction refers to a court's power to hear a case on appeal from a lower court, from the court in which the case was originally tried. This clause gives the Supreme Court both original and appellate jurisdiction. However, nearly all of the cases the High Court hears are brought to it on appeal from the lower federal courts and the highest State courts.

3. The trial of all crimes, except in cases of impeachment, shall be by jury; and such trial shall be held in the State where the said crimes shall have been committed; but when not committed within any State the trial shall be at such place or places as the Congress may by law have directed.

CLAUSE 3. JURY TRIAL IN CRIMINAL CASES A person accused of a federal crime is guaranteed the right to trial by jury in a federal court in the State where the crime was committed; see the 5th and 6th amendments. The right to trial by jury in serious criminal cases in the State courts is guaranteed by the 6th and 14th amendments.

Section 3. ***Treason***

1. Treason against the United States shall consist only in levying war against them, or in adhering to their enemies, giving them aid and comfort. No person shall be convicted of treason unless on the testimony of two witnesses to the same overt act, or on confession in open court.

CLAUSE 1. DEFINITION Treason is the only crime defined in the Constitution. The Framers intended the very specific definition here to prevent the loose use of the charge of treason—for example, against persons who criticize the government. Treason can be committed only in time of war and only by a citizen or a resident alien.

2. The Congress shall have power to declare the punishment of treason, but no attainder of treason shall work corruption of blood, or forfeiture except during the life of the person attainted.

CLAUSE 2. PUNISHMENT Congress has provided that the punishment that a federal court may impose on a convicted traitor may range from a minimum of five years in prison and/or a $10,000 fine to a maximum of death; no person convicted of treason has ever been executed by the United States. No legal punishment can be imposed on the family or descendants of a convicted traitor. Congress has also made it a crime for any person (in either peace or wartime) to commit espionage or sabotage, to attempt to overthrow the government by force, or to conspire to do any of these things.

Article IV

RELATIONS AMONG STATES

Section 1. ***Full Faith and Credit***

Full faith and credit shall be given in each State to the public acts, records, and judicial proceedings of every other State. And the Congress may, by general laws, prescribe the manner in which such acts, records, and proceedings shall be proved, and the effect thereof.

Each State must respect—recognize the validity of—the laws, public records, and court decisions of every other State.

Section 2. ***Privileges and Immunities of Citizens***

1. The citizens of each State shall be entitled to all privileges and immunities of citizens in the several States.

CLAUSE 1. RESIDENTS OF OTHER STATES In effect, this clause means that no State may discriminate against the residents of other States; that is, a State's laws cannot draw unreasonable distinctions between its own residents and those of any of the other States. See Section 1 of the 14th Amendment.

2. A person charged in any State with treason, felony, or other crime, who shall flee from justice, and be found in another State, shall, on demand of the executive authority of the State from which he fled, be delivered up, to be removed to the State having jurisdiction of the crime.

CLAUSE 2. EXTRADITION The process of retaining a fugitive to another State is known as "interstate rendition" or, more commonly, "extradition." Usually, that process works routinely; some extradition requests are contested however—especially in cases with racial or political overtones. A governor may refuse to extradite a fugitive; but the federal courts can compel an unwilling governor to obey this constitutional command.

~~3. No person held to service or labor in one State, under the laws therof, escaping into another, shall, in consequence of any law or regulation therein, be discharged from service or labor, but shall be delivered up on claim of the party to whom such service or labor may be due.~~

CLAUSE 3. FUGITIVE SLAVES This clause was nullified by the 13th Amendment, which abolished slavery in 1865.

Section 3. ***New States; Territories***

1. New States may be admitted by the Congress into this Union; but no new State shall be formed or erected within the jurisdiction of any other State, nor any State be formed by the junction of two or more States, or parts of States, without the consent of the legislatures of the States concerned as well as of the Congress.

CLAUSE 1. NEW STATES ONLY Congress can admit new States to the Union. A new State may not be created by taking territory from an existing State without the consent of that State's legislature.

Congress has admitted 37 States since the original 13 formed the Union. Five States—Vermont, Kentucky, Tennessee, Maine, and West Virginia—were created from parts of existing States. Texas was an independent republic before admission. California was admitted after being ceded to the United States by Mexico. Each of the other 30 States entered the Union only after a period of time as an organized territory of the United States.

2. The Congress shall have power to dispose of and make all needful rules and regulations respecting the territory or other property belonging to the United States; and nothing in this Constitution shall be so construed as to prejudice any claims of the United States, or of any particular State.

CLAUSE 2. TERRITORY, PROPERTY Congress has the power to make laws concerning the territories, other public lands, and all other property of the United States.

Section 4. ***Protection Afforded to States by the Nation***

The United States shall guarantee to every State in this Union a republican form of government, and shall protect each of them against invasion; and on application of the legislature, or of the executive (when the legislature cannot be convened), against domestic violence.

The Constitution does not define "a republican form of government," but the phrase is generally understood to mean a representative government. The Federal Government must also defend each State against attacks from outside its border and, at the request of a State's legislature or its governor, aid its efforts to put down internal disorders.

Article V

PROVISIONS FOR AMENDMENT

The Congress, whenever two-thirds of both Houses shall deem it necessary, shall propose amendments to this Constitution, or, on the application of the legislatures of two-thirds of the several States, shall call a convention for proposing amendments, which, in either case, shall be valid, to all intents and purposes, as part of this Constitution, when ratified by the legislatures of three-fourths of the several States, or by conventions in three-fourths thereof, as the one or the other mode of ratification may be proposed by the Congress; provided ~~that no amendment which may be made prior to the year one thousand eight hundred and eight shall in any manner affect the first and fourth clauses in the ninth section of the first Article; and~~ that no State, without its consent, shall be deprived of its equal suffrage in the Senate.

This section provides for the methods by which formal changes can be made in the Constitution. An amendment may be proposed in one of two ways: by a two-thirds vote in each house of Congress, or by a national convention called by Congress at the request of two-thirds of the State legislatures. A proposed amendment may be ratified in one of two ways: by three-fourths of the State legislatures, or by three-fourths of the States in conventions called for that purpose. Congress has the power to determine the method by which a proposed amendment may be ratified. The amendment process cannot be used to deny any State its equal representation in the United States Senate. To this point, 26 amendments have been adopted. To date, all of the amendments except the 21st Amendment were proposed by Congress and ratified by the State legislatures. Only the 21st Amendment was ratified by the convention method.

Article VI

NATIONAL DEBTS, SUPREMACY OF NATIONAL LAW, OATH

Section 1. ***Validity of Debts***

All debts contracted and engagements entered into, before the adoption of this Constitution, shall be as valid against the United States under this Constitution, as under the Confederation.

Congress had borrowed large sums of money during the Revolution and later during the Critical Period of the 1780s. This provision, a pledge that the new government would honor those debts, did much to create confidence in that government.

Section 2. ***Supremacy of National Law***

This Constitution, and the laws of the United States which shall be made in pursuance thereof, and all treaties made, or which shall be made, under the authority of the United States, shall be the supreme law of the land; and the judges in every State shall be bound thereby, anything in the constitution or laws of any State to the contrary notwithstanding.

This section sets out the Supremacy Clause, a specific declaration of the supremacy of federal law over any and all forms of State law. No State, including its local governments, may make or enforce any law that conflicts with any provision in the Constitution, an act of Congress, a treaty, or an order, rule, or regulation properly issued by the President or his subordinates in the executive branch.

Section 3. ***Oaths of Office***

The Senators and Representatives before mentioned, and the members of the several State legislatures, and all executive and judicial officers, both of the United States and of the several States, shall be bound, by oath or affirmation, to support this Constitution; but no religious test shall ever be required as a qualification to any office or public trust under the United States.

This provision reinforces the Supremacy Clause; all public officers, at every level in the United States, owe their first allegiance to the Constitution of the United States. No religious qualification can be imposed as a condition for holding any public office.

Article VII

RATIFICATION OF CONSTITUTION

The ratification of the conventions of nine States shall be sufficient for the establishment of this Constitution between the States so ratifying the same.

The proposed Constitution was signed by George Washington and 37 of his fellow Framers on September 17, 1787. (George Read of Delaware signed for himself and also for his absent colleague, John Dickinson.)

Done in Convention, by the unanimous consent of the States present, the seventeenth day of September, in the year of our Lord one thousand seven hundred and eighty-seven, and of the Independence of the United States of America the twelfth. *In Witness* whereof, we have hereunto subscribed our names.

Attest: William Jackson,
SECRETARY

George Washington, PRESIDENT AND DEPUTY FROM VIRGINIA

NEW HAMPSHIRE
John Langdon
Nicholas Gilman

MASSACHUSETTS
Nathaniel Gorham
Rufus King

CONNECTICUT
William Samuel Johnson
Roger Sherman

NEW YORK
Alexander Hamilton

NEW JERSEY
William Livingston
David Brearley
William Paterson
Jonathan Dayton

PENNSYLVANIA
Benjamin Franklin
Thomas Mifflin
Robert Morris
George Clymer
Thomas Fitzsimons
Jared Ingersoll
James Wilson
Gouverneur Morris

DELAWARE
George Read
Gunning Bedford, Jr.
John Dickinson
Richard Bassett
Jacob Broom

MARYLAND
James McHenry
Dan of St. Thomas Jennifer
Daniel Carroll

VIRGINIA
John Blair
James Madison, Jr.

NORTH CAROLINA
William Blount
Richard Dobbs Spaight
Hugh Williamson

SOUTH CAROLINA
John Rutledge
Charles Cotesworth Pinckney
Charles Pinckney
Pierce Butler

GEORGIA
William Few
Abraham Baldwin

AMENDMENTS

The first 10 amendments, the Bill of Rights, were each proposed by Congress on September 25, 1789, and ratified by the necessary three-fourths of the States on December 15, 1791. These amendments were originally intended to restrict the National Government—not the States. However, the Supreme Court has several times held that most of their provisions also apply to the States, through the 14th Amendment's Due Process Clause.

1st Amendment. ***Freedom of Religion, Speech, Press, Assembly, and Petition***

Congress shall make no law respecting an establishment of religion, or prohibiting the free exercise thereof, or abridging the freedom of speech, or of the press; or the right of the people peaceably to assemble, and to petition the government for a redress of grievances.

The 1st Amendment sets out five basic liberties: The guarantee of freedom of religion is both a protection of religious thought and practice and a command of separation of church and state. The guarantees of freedom of speech and press assure to all persons a right to speak, publish, and otherwise express their views. The guarantees of the rights of assembly and petition protect the right to join with others in public meetings, political parties, pressure groups, and other associations to discuss public affairs and influence public policy. None of these rights is guaranteed in absolute terms, however; like all other civil rights guarantees, each of them may be exercised only with regard to the rights of all other persons.

2nd Amendment. ***Bearing Arms***

A well-regulated militia being necessary to the security of a free state, the right of the people to keep and bear arms shall not be infringed.

Each State has the right to maintain a militia, a volunteer armed force for its own protection; however, both the

National Government and the States can and do regulate the possession and use of firearms by private persons.

3RD AMENDMENT. ***Quartering of Troops***

No soldier shall, in time of peace, be quartered in any house, without the consent of the owner; nor, in time of war, but in a manner to be prescribed by law.

This amendment was intended to prevent what had been common British practice in the colonial period; see the Declaration of Independence. This provision is of virtually no importance today.

4TH AMENDMENT. ***Searches and Seizures***

The right of the people to be secure in their persons, houses, papers, and effects, against unreasonable searches and seizures, shall not be violated; and no warrants shall issue, but upon probable cause, supported by oath or affirmation, and particularly describing the place to be searched and the persons or things to be seized.

The basic rule laid down by the 4th Amendment is this: Police officers have no general right to search for or seize evidence or seize (arrest) persons. Except in particular circumstances, they must have a proper warrant (a court order) obtained with probable cause (on reasonable grounds). This guarantee is reinforced by the exclusionary rule, developed by the Supreme Court: Evidence gained as the result of an unlawful search or seizure cannot be used at the court trial of the person from whom it was seized.

5TH AMENDMENT. ***Criminal Proceedings; Due Process; Eminent Domain***

No person shall be held to answer for a capital, or otherwise infamous, crime, unless on a presentment or indictment of a grand jury, except in cases arising in the land or naval forces, or in the militia, when in actual service, in time of war, or public danger; nor shall any person be subject, for the same offence, to be twice put in jeopardy of life or limb; nor shall be compelled, in any criminal case, to be a witness against himself; nor be deprived of life, liberty, or property, without due process of law; nor shall private property be taken for public use, without just compensation.

A person can be tried for a serious federal crime only if he or she has been indicted (charged, accused of that crime) by a grand jury. No one may be subjected to double jeopardy—that is, tried twice for the same crime. All persons are protected against self-incrimination; no person can be legally compelled to answer any question in any governmental proceeding if that answer could lead to that person's prosecution. The 5th Amendment's Due Process Clause prohibits unfair, arbitrary actions by the Federal Government; a like prohibition is set out against the States in the 14th Amendment. Government may take private property for a legitimate public purpose; but when it exercises that power of eminent domain, it must pay a fair price for the property seized.

6TH AMENDMENT. ***Criminal Proceedings***

In all criminal prosecutions, the accused shall enjoy the right to a speedy and public trial, by an impartial jury of the State and district wherein the crime shall have been committed, which district shall have been previously ascertained by law; and to be informed of the nature and cause of the accusation; to be confronted with the witnesses against him; to have compulsory process for obtaining witnesses in his favor; and to have the assistance of counsel for his defence.

A person accused of crime has the right to be tried in court without undue delay and by an impartial jury; see Article III, Section 2, Clause 3. The defendant must be informed of the charge upon which he or she is to be tried, has the right to cross-examine hostile witnesses, and has the right to require the testimony of favorable witnesses. The defendant also has the right to be represented by an attorney at every stage in the criminal process.

7TH AMENDMENT. ***Civil Trials***

In suits at common law, where the value in controversy shall exceed twenty dollars, the right of trial by jury shall be preserved; and no fact, tried by a jury, shall be otherwise re-examined in any court of the United States than according to the rules of the common law.

This amendment applies only to civil cases heard in federal courts. A civil case does not involve criminal matters; it is a dispute between private parties or between the government and a private party. The right to trial by jury is guaranteed in any civil case in a federal court if the amount of money involved in that case exceeds $20 (most cases today involve a much larger sum); that right may be waived (relinquished, put aside) if both parties agree to a bench trial (a trial by a judge, without a jury).

8TH AMENDMENT. ***Punishment for Crimes***

Excessive bail shall not be required, nor excessive fines imposed, nor cruel and unusual punishment inflicted.

Bail is the sum of money that a person accused of crime may be required to post (deposit with the court) as a guarantee that he or she will appear in court at the proper time. The amount of bail required and/or a fine imposed as punishment must bear a reasonable relationship to the seriousness of the crime involved in the case. The prohibition of cruel and unusual punishment forbids any punishment judged to be too harsh, too severe for the crime for which it is imposed.

9TH AMENDMENT. ***Unenumerated Rights***

The enumeration in the Constitution of certain rights shall not be construed to deny or disparage others retained by the people.

The fact that the Constitution sets out many civil rights guarantees, expressly provides for many protections against government, does not mean that there are not other rights also held by the people.

10TH AMENDMENT. ***Powers Reserved to the States***

The powers not delegated to the United States by the Constitution, nor prohibited by it to the States, are reserved to the States respectively, or to the people.

This amendment identifies the area of power that may be exercised by the States. All of those powers the Constitution does not grant to the National Government, and at the same time does not forbid to the States, belong to each of the States, or to the people of each State.

11TH AMENDMENT. ***Suits against States***

The judicial power of the United States shall not be construed to extend to any suit in law or equity, commenced or prosecuted against one of the United States by citizens of another State or by citizens or subjects of any foreign state.

Proposed by Congress March 4, 1794; ratified February 7, 1795, but official announcement of the ratification was delayed until January 8, 1798. This amendment repealed part of Article III, Section 2, Clause 1. No State may be sued in a federal court by a resident of another State or of a foreign country; the Supreme Court has long held that this provision also means that a State cannot be sued in a federal court by a foreign country or, more importantly, even by one of its own residents.

12TH AMENDMENT. ***Election of President and Vice President***

The Electors shall meet in their respective States, and vote by ballot for President and Vice President, one of whom, at least, shall not be an inhabitant of the same State with themselves; they shall name in their ballots the person voted for as President, and in distinct ballots the person voted for as Vice President; and they shall make distinct lists of all persons voted for as President, and of all persons voted for as Vice President, and of the number of votes for each, which lists they shall sign, and certify, and transmit, sealed, to the seat of the Government of the United States, directed to the President of the Senate; the President of the Senate shall, in the presence of the Senate and the House of Representatives, open all the certificates, and the votes shall then be counted; the person having the greatest number of votes for President shall be the President, if such number be a majority of the whole number of Electors appointed; and if no person have such a majority, then, from the persons having the highest numbers, not exceeding three, on the list of those voted for as President, the House of Representatives shall choose immediately, by ballot, the President. But in choosing the President, the votes shall be taken by States, the representation from each State having one vote; a quorum for this purpose shall consist of a member or members from two-thirds of the States, and a majority of all the States shall be necessary to a choice. And if the House of Representatives shall not choose a President, whenever the right of choice shall devolve upon them, before the fourth day of March next following, then the Vice President shall act as President, as in case of death, or other constitutional disability, of the President. The person having the greatest number of votes as Vice President, shall be the Vice President, if such number be a majority of the whole number of Electors appointed; and if no person have a majority, then, from the two highest numbers on the list, the Senate shall choose the Vice President; a quorum for the purpose shall consist of two-thirds of the whole number of Senators; a majority of the whole number shall be necessary to a choice. But no person constitutionally ineligible to the office of President shall be eligible to that of Vice-President of the United States.

Proposed by Congress December 9, 1803; ratified June 15, 1804. This amendment replaced Article II, Section 1, Clause 3. Originally, each elector cast two ballots, each for a different person for President. The person with the largest number of electoral votes, provided that number was a majority of the electors, was to become President; the person with the second highest number was to become Vice President. This arrangement produced an electoral vote tie between Thomas Jefferson and Aaron Burr in 1800; the House finally chose Jefferson as President in 1801. The 12th Amendment separated the balloting for President and Vice President; each elector now casts one ballot for someone as President and a second ballot for another person as Vice President. Note that the 20th Amendment changed the date set here (March 4) to January 20, and that the 23rd Amendment (1961) provides for electors from the District of Columbia. This amendment also provides that the Vice President must meet the same qualifications as those set out for the President in Article II, Section 1, Clause 5.

13TH AMENDMENT. ***Slavery and Involuntary Servitude***

SECTION 1. Neither slavery nor involuntary servitude, except as a punishment for crime, whereof the party shall have been duly convicted, shall exist within the United States, or any place subject to their jurisdiction.

SECTION 2. Congress shall have power to enforce this article by appropriate legislation.

Proposed by Congress January 31, 1865; ratified December 6, 1865. This amendment forbids slavery in the United States and in any area under its control. It also forbids other forms of forced labor, except punishments for crime; but some forms of compulsory service are not prohibited—for example, service on juries or in the armed forces. Section 2 gives to Congress the power to carry out the provisions of Section 1 of this amendment.

14TH AMENDMENT. ***Rights of Citizens***

SECTION 1. All persons born or naturalized in the United States, and subject to the jurisdiction thereof, are citizens of the United States and of the State wherein they reside. No State shall make or enforce any law which shall abridge the privileges or immunities of citizens of the United States; nor shall any State deprive any person of life, liberty, or property, without due process of law, nor deny to any person within its jurisdiction the equal protection of the laws.

Proposed by Congress June 13, 1866; ratified July 9, 1868. Section 1 defines citizenship. It provides for the acquisition of United States citizenship by birth or by naturalization. Citizenship at birth is determined according to the principle of *jus soli*—"the law of the soil," where born; naturalization is the legal process by which one acquires a new citizenship at some time after birth. Under certain circumstances, citizenship can also be gained at birth abroad, according to the principle of *jus sanguinis*—"the law of the blood," to whom born. This section also contains two major civil rights provisions: the Due Process Clause forbids a State (and its local governments) to act in any unfair or arbitrary way; the Equal Protection Clause forbids a State (and its local governments) to discriminate against, draw unreasonable distinctions between, persons.

Most of the rights set out against the National Government in the first eight amendments have been extended against the States (and their local governments) through Supreme Court decisions involving the 14th Amendment's Due Process Clause.

SECTION 2. Representatives shall be apportioned among the several States according to their respective numbers, counting the whole number of persons in each State, excluding Indians not taxed. But when the right to vote at any election for the choice of electors for President and Vice President of the United States, Representatives in Congress, the executive and judicial officers of a State, or the members of the legislature thereof, is denied to any of the male inhabitants of such State, being twenty-one years of age and citizens of the United States, or in any way abridged, except for participation in rebellion or other crime, the basis of representation therein shall be reduced in the proportion which the number of such male citizens shall bear to the whole number of male citizens twenty-one years of age in such State.

The first sentence here replaced Article I, Section 2, Clause 3, the Three-Fifths Compromise provision. Essentially, all persons in the United States are counted in each decennial census, the basis for the distribution of House seats. The balance of this section has never been enforced and is generally thought to be obsolete.

SECTION 3. No person shall be a Senator or Representative in Congress, or elector of President and Vice President, or hold any office, civil or military, under the United States, or under any State, who, having previously taken an oath, as a member of Congress, or as an officer of the United States, or as a member of any State legislature, or as an executive or judicial officer of any State, to support the Constitution of the United States, shall have engaged in insurrection or rebellion against the same, or given aid or comfort to the enemies thereof. But Congress may, by a vote of two-thirds of each House, remove such disability.

This section limited the President's power to pardon those persons who had led the Confederacy during the Civil War. Congress finally removed this disability in 1898.

SECTION 4. The validity of the public debt of the United States, authorized by law, including debts incurred for payment of pensions and bounties for services in suppressing insurrection or rebellion, shall not be questioned. But neither the United States nor any State shall assume or pay any debt or obligation incurred in aid of insurrection or rebellion against the United States, or any claim for the loss or emancipation of any slave, but all such debts, obligations, and claims shall be held illegal and void.

Section 4 also dealt with matters directly related to the Civil War. It reaffirmed the public debt of the United States; but it invalidated, prohibited payment of, any debt contracted by the Confederate States and also prohibited any compensation of former slave owners.

SECTION 5. The Congress shall have power to enforce, by appropriate legislation, the provisions of this article.

15TH AMENDMENT. ***Right to Vote—Race, Color, Servitude***

SECTION 1. The right of citizens of the United States to vote shall not be denied or abridged by the United States or by any State on account of race, color, or previous condition of servitude.

SECTION 2. The Congress shall have power to enforce this article by appropriate legislation.

Proposed by Congress February 26, 1869; ratified February 3, 1870. The immediate purpose of this amendment was to guarantee to newly freed slaves their right to vote. It has a much broader application today.

16TH AMENDMENT. ***Income Tax***

The Congress shall have power to lay and collect taxes on incomes, from whatever source derived, without apportionment among the several States, and without regard to any census or enumeration.

Proposed by Congress July 12, 1909; ratified February 3, 1913. This amendment modified two provisions in Article I: Section 2, Clause 3, and Section 9, Clause 4. It gives to Congress the power to levy an income tax, a direct tax, without regard to the populations of any of the States.

17TH AMENDMENT. ***Popular Election of Senators***

The Senate of the United States shall be composed of two Senators from each State, elected by the people thereof, for six years; and each Senator shall have one vote. The electors in each State shall have the qualifications requisite for electors of the most numerous branch of the State legislatures.

When vacancies happen in the representation of any State in the Senate, the executive authority of such State shall issue writs of election to fill such vacancies: Provided, That the legislature of any State may empower the executive thereof to make temporary appointment until the people fill the vacancies by election as the legislature may direct.

This Amendment shall not be so construed as to affect the election or term of any Senator chosen before it becomes valid as part of the Constitution.

Proposed by Congress May 13, 1912; ratified April 8, 1913. This amendment repealed those portions of Article I, Section 3, Clauses 1 and 2 relating to the election of senators. Senators are now elected by the voters in each State. If a vacancy occurs, the governor of the State involved must call an election to fill the seat; the governor may appoint a senator to serve until the next election, if the State's legislature has authorized that step.

18TH AMENDMENT. ***Prohibition of Intoxicating Liquors***

~~SECTION 1. After one year from the ratification of this article the manufacture, sale or transportation of intoxicating liquors within, the importation thereof into, or the exportation thereof from the United States and all territory subject to the jurisdiction thereof for beverage purposes is hereby prohibited.~~

~~SECTION 2. The Congress and the several States shall have concurrent power to enforce this article by appropriate legislation.~~

~~SECTION 3. This article shall be inoperative unless it shall have been ratified as an Amendment to the Constitution by the legislatures of the several States, as provided in the Constitution, within seven years of the date of the submission hereof to the States by Congress.~~

Proposed by Congress December 18, 1917; ratified January 16, 1919. This amendment outlawed the making, selling, transporting, importing, or exporting of alcoholic beverages in the United States. It was repealed in its entirety by the 21st Amendment in 1933.

19TH AMENDMENT. ***Equal Suffrage—Sex***

The right of citizens of the United States to vote shall not be denied or abridged by the United States or by any State on account of sex.

Congress shall have power to enforce this article by appropriate legislation.

Proposed by Congress June 4, 1919; ratified August 18, 1920. No person can be denied the right to vote in any election in the United States on account of his or her sex.

20TH AMENDMENT. ***Commencement of Terms; Sessions of Congress; Death or Disqualification of President-Elect***

SECTION 1. The terms of the President and Vice President shall end at noon on the 20th day of January, and the terms of Senators and Representatives at noon on the 3d day of January, of the years in which such terms would have ended if this article had not been ratified; and the terms of their successors shall then begin.

SECTION 2. The Congress shall assemble at least once in every year, and such meeting shall begin at noon on the 3d day of January, unless they shall by law appoint a different day.

Proposed by Congress March 2, 1932; ratified January 23, 1933. The provisions of Sections 1 and 2 relating to Congress modified Article I, Section 4, Clause 2, and those provisions relating to the President, the 12th Amendment. The date on which the President and Vice President now take office was moved from March 4 to January 20. Similarly, the members of Congress now begin their terms on January 3. The 20th Amendment is sometimes called the "Lame Duck Amendment" because it shortened the period of time a member of Congress who was defeated for reelection (a "lame duck") remains in office.

SECTION 3. If, at the time fixed for the beginning of the term of the President, the President-elect shall have died, the Vice President-elect shall become President. If a President shall not have been chosen before the time fixed for the beginning of his term, or if the President-elect shall have failed to qualify, then the Vice President-elect shall act as President until a President shall have qualified; and the Congress may by law provide for the case wherein neither a President-elect nor a Vice President-elect shall have qualified, declaring who shall then act as President, or the manner in which one who is to act shall be selected, and such person shall act accordingly until a President or Vice President shall have qualified.

This section deals with certain possibilities that were not covered by the presidential selection provisions of either Article II or the 12th Amendment. To this point, none of these situations has occurred. Note that there is neither a President-elect nor a Vice President-elect until the electoral votes have been counted by Congress, or, if the electoral college cannot decide the matter, the House has chosen a President or the Senate has chosen a Vice President.

SECTION 4. The Congress may by law provide for the case of the death of any of the persons from whom the House of Representatives may choose a President whenever the right of choice shall have devolved upon them, and for the case of the death of any of the persons from whom the Senate may choose a Vice President whenever the right of choice shall have devolved upon them.

Congress has not in fact ever passed such a law. See Section 2 of the 25th Amendment, regarding a vacancy in the vice presidency; that provision could some day have an impact here.

SECTION 5. Sections 1 and 2 shall take effect on the 15th day of October following the ratification of this article.

SECTION 6. This article shall be inoperative unless it shall have been ratified as an Amendment to the Constitution by the legislatures of three fourths of the several States within seven years from the date of its submission.

Section 5 set the date on which this amendment came into force. Section 6 placed a time limit on the ratification process; note that a similar provision was written into the 18th, 21st, and 22nd amendments.

21ST AMENDMENT. *Repeal of 18th Amendment*

SECTION 1. The eighteenth article of Amendment to the Constitution of the United States is hereby repealed.

SECTION 2. The transportation or importation into any State, Territory, or possession of the United States for delivery or use therein of intoxicating liquors, in violation of the laws thereof, is hereby prohibited.

SECTION 3. This article shall be inoperative unless it shall have been ratified as an Amendment to the Constitution by conventions in the several States, as provided in the Constitution, within seven years from the date of the submission hereof to the States by the Congress.

Proposed by Congress February 20, 1933; ratified December 5, 1933. This amendment repealed all of the 18th Amendment. Section 2 modifies the scope of the Federal Government's commerce power set out in Article I, Section 8, Clause 3; it gives to each State the power to regulate the transportation or importation and the distribution or use of intoxicating liquors in ways that would be unconstitutional in the case of any other commodity. The 21st Amendment is the only amendment Congress has thus far submitted to the States for ratification by conventions.

22ND AMENDMENT. *Presidential Tenure*

SECTION 1. No person shall be elected to the office of the President more than twice, and no person who has held the office of President, or acted as President, for more than two years of a term to which some other person was elected President shall be elected to the office of the President more than once. But this Article shall not apply to any person holding the office of President when this Article was proposed by the Congress, and shall not prevent any person who may be holding the office of President, or acting as President, during the term within which this Article becomes operative from holding the office of President or acting as President during the remainder of such term.

SECTION 2. This article shall be inoperative unless it shall have been ratified as an Amendment to the Constitution by the legislatures of three fourths of the several states within seven years from the date of its submission to the States by the Congress.

Proposed by Congress March 24, 1947; ratified February 27, 1951. This amendment modified Article II, Section I, Clause 1. It stipulates that no President may serve more than two elected terms. But a President who has succeeded to the office beyond the midpoint in a term to which another President was originally elected may serve for more than eight years. In any case, however, a President may not serve more than 10 years. Prior to Franklin Roosevelt, who was elected to four terms, no President had served more than two full terms in office.

23RD AMENDMENT. *Presidential Electors for the District of Columbia*

SECTION 1. The District constituting the seat of Government of the United States shall appoint in such manner as the Congress may direct:

A number of electors of President and Vice President equal to the whole number of Senators and Representatives in Congress to which the District would be entitled if it were a State, but in no event more than the least populous State; they shall be considered, for the purposes of the election of President and Vice President, to be electors appointed by a State; and they shall meet in the District and perform such duties as provided by the twelfth article of Amendment.

SECTION 2. The Congress shall have power to enforce this article by appropriate legislation.

Proposed by Congress June 16, 1960; ratified March 29, 1961. This amendment modified Article II, Section I, Clause 2 and the 12th Amendment. It included the voters of the District of Columbia in the presidential electorate; and provides that the District is to have the same number of electors as the least populous State—three electors—but no more than that number.

24TH AMENDMENT. *Right to Vote in Federal Elections—Tax Payment*

SECTION 1. The right of citizens of the United States to vote in any primary or other election for President or Vice President, for electors for President or Vice President, or for Senator or Representative in Congress, shall not be denied or abridged by the United States or any State by reason of failure to pay any poll tax or other tax.

SECTION 2. The Congress shall have power to enforce this article by appropriate legislation.

Proposed by Congress September 14, 1962; ratified January 23, 1964. This amendment outlawed the poll tax, or any other tax, as a condition for taking part in the nomination or election of any federal officeholder—that is, in any process connected with selecting the President, Vice President, or members of Congress. From 1966 on, the Supreme Court has several times held that the 14th Amendment's Equal Protection Clause forbids any tax-paying qualification for voting in any State or local election.

25TH AMENDMENT. ***Presidential Succession, Vice Presidential Vacancy, Presidential Inability***

SECTION 1. In case of the removal of the President from office or of his death or resignation, the Vice President shall become President.

Proposed by Congress July 6, 1965; ratified February 10, 1967. Section 1 revised the inexact wording of the provision relating to presidential succession in Article II, Section 1, Clause 6. In effect, it wrote into the Constitution the precedent set by Vice President John Tyler, who succeeded to the presidency on the death of William Henry Harrison in 1841.

SECTION 2. Whenever there is a vacancy in the office of the Vice President, the President shall nominate a Vice President who shall take office upon confirmation by a majority vote of both Houses of Congress.

This section provides for the filling of a vacancy in the office of Vice President. Prior to its adoption, the office had been vacant on 16 occasions and had remained unfilled for the remainder of each term involved. When Spiro Agnew resigned the office in 1973, President Richard Nixon selected Gerald Ford in accord with this provision; and, when President Nixon resigned in 1974, Gerald Ford became President and then chose Nelson Rockefeller as Vice President.

SECTION 3. Whenever the President transmits to the President *pro tempore* of the Senate and the Speaker of the House of Representatives his written declaration that he is unable to discharge the powers and duties of his office, and until he transmits to them a written declaration to the contrary, such powers and duties shall be discharged by the Vice President as Acting President.

Until the adoption of the 25th Amendment, no procedure had been adopted to determine when or whether the President is so incapacitated as to be unable to perform the powers and duties of the presidency.

SECTION 4. Whenever the Vice President and a majority of either the principal officers of the executive departments or of such other body as Congress may by law provide, transmit to the President *pro tempore* of the Senate and the Speaker of the House of Representatives their written declaration that the President is unable to discharge the powers and duties of his office, the Vice President shall immediately assume the powers and duties of the office as Acting President.

Thereafter, when the President transmits to the President *pro tempore* of the Senate and the Speaker of the House of Representatives his written declaration that no inability exists, he shall resume the powers and duties of his office unless the Vice President and a majority of either the principal officers of the executive department or of such other body as Congress may by law provide, transmit within four days to the President *pro tempore* of the Senate and the Speaker of the House of Representatives their written declaration that the President is unable to discharge the powers and duties of his office. Thereupon Congress shall decide the issue, assembling within forty-eight hours for that purpose if not in session. If the Congress, within twenty-one days after receipt of the latter written declaration, or, if Congress is not in session, within twenty-one days after Congress is required to assemble, determines by two-thirds vote of both Houses that the President is unable to discharge the powers and duties of his office, the Vice President shall continue to discharge the same as Acting President; otherwise, the President shall resume the powers and duties of his office.

This section deals with the possibility of a circumstance in which a President will not be able to detemine the fact of incapacity. To this point, Congress has not established the "such other body" referred to here. This section contains the only typographical error to be found in the Constitution; in its second paragraph, the word "department" should in fact read "departments."

26TH AMENDMENT. ***Right to Vote—Age***

SECTION 1. The right of citizens of the United States, who are eighteen years of age or older, to vote shall not be denied or abridged by the United States or by any State on account of age.

SECTION 2. The Congress shall have the power to enforce this article by appropriate legislation.

Proposed by Congress March 23, 1971; ratified July 1, 1971. This amendment provides that the minimum age for voting in any election in the United States cannot be more than 18 years. (Note that this amendment does not prevent any State from setting the minimum voting age in that State at less than 18.)

HISTORICAL DOCUMENTS

The Code of Hammurabi

The code of Hammurabi, believed to date before 1750 B.C., is a series of laws decreed by Hammurabi, the ruler of the city of Babylon when that ancient city was at the peak of its power. Inscribed on stone columns over seven feet high, these laws were intended to inform the people of what they could and could not do. They were written down and codified so that judges and administrators would have a uniform set of rules to follow in deciding disputes and imposing penalties for crimes. The Code consists of 280 sections that deal with such matters as land tenure, property rights, trade and commerce, family relations, and the administration of justice. Selected sections of the Code are excerpted below:

■ If a man practice (robbery) and be captured, that man shall be put to death. . . .

■ If a man has come forward in a lawsuit for the witnessing of false things, and has not proved the thing that he said, if that lawsuit is a capital case, that man shall be put to death. If he came forward for witnessing about corn or silver, he shall bear the penalty (which applies to) that case.

■ If a man has concealed in his house a lost slave or slave-girl belonging to the Palace or to a subject, and has not brought him (or her) out at the proclamation of the Crier, the owner of the house shall be put to death.

■ If a fire has broken out in a man's house, and a man who has gone to extinguish it has cast his eye on the property of the owner of the house and has taken the property of the owner of the house, that man shall be thrown into the fire.

■ If a man is subject to a debt bearing interest, and Adad (the Weather-god) has saturated his field or a high flood has carried (its crop) away, or because of lack of water he has not produced corn in that field, in that year he shall not return any corn to (his) creditor. He shall . . . not pay interest for that year.

■ If a man has donated field, orchard or house to his favourite heir and has written a sealed document for him (confirming this), after the father has gone to his doom, when the brothers share he (the favorite heir) shall take the gift that his father gave him, and apart from that they shall share equally in the property of the paternal estate.

■ If an artisan has taken a child for bringing up, and has taught him his manual skill, (the child) shall not be (re)claimed. If he has not taught him his manual skill, that pupil may return to his father's house.

■ If a man aid a male or female slave . . . to escape from the city gates, he shall be put to death . . . .

■ If a man be in debt and sell his wife, son, or daughter, or bind them over to service, for three years they shall work in the house of the purchaser or master; in the fourth year they shall be given their freedom. . . .

■ If a builder has made a house for a man but has not made his work strong, so that the house he made falls down and causes the death of the owner of the house, that builder shall be put to death. If it causes the death of the son of the owner of the house, they shall kill the son of the builder.

■ If a man would put away [divorce] his wife who has not borne him children, he shall give her money to the amount of her marriage settlement and he shall make good to her the dowry which she brought from her father's house and then he may put her away.

■ If a son has struck his father, they shall cut off his hand.

■ If a man has destroyed the eye of a man of the "gentleman" class, they shall destroy his eye. If he has broken a gentleman's bone, they shall break his bone. If he has destroyed the eye of a commoner or broken a bone of a commoner, he shall pay one mina (about $300) of silver. If he has destroyed the eye of a gentleman's slave, he shall pay half the slave's price.

■ If a gentleman's slave strikes the cheek of a man of the "gentleman" class, they shall cut off (the slave's) ear.

■ If a gentleman strikes a gentleman in a free fight and inflicts an injury on him, that man shall swear "I did not strike him deliberately," and he shall pay the surgeon.

The Magna Carta

The Magna Carta (Great Charter) was wrested from King John by several barons of the realm, at Runnymede in 1215. One of the great documents of liberty, the Magna Carta rested on the feudal principle that the king and nobles had mutual contractual obligations. Its provisions limited the power of the crown and firmly planted the principle that the king, like other Englishmen, is subject to law. It became a symbol of political liberty and the foundation of constitutional government. Here are excerpts from 13 of its 63 articles:

1. That the English church shall be free, and shall have her rights entire, and her liberties inviolate; and we will that it be thus observed; and our will is that it be observed in good faith by our heirs forever.

2. We also have granted to all the freemen of our kingdom, for us and for our heirs forever, all the underwritten liberties, to be had and holden by them and their heirs, of us and our heirs forever. . . .

12. No scutage or aid shall be imposed in our kingdom, unless by the general council of our kingdom; except for ransoming our person, making our eldest son a knight and once for marrying our eldest daughter; and for these there shall be paid no more than a reasonable aid.

14. And for holding the general council of the kingdom concerning the assessment of aids, except in the three cases aforesaid, and for the assessing of scutage, we shall cause to be summoned the archbishops, bishops, abbots, earls, and greater barons of the realm, singly by our letters. And furthermore, we shall cause to be summoned generally, by our sheriffs and bailiffs all others who hold of us in chief, for a certain day, that is to say, forty days before their meeting at least, and to a certain place. And in all letters of such summons we will declare the cause of such summons. And summons being thus made, the business shall proceed on the day appointed, according to the advice of such as shall be present, although all that were summoned come not.

15. We will not in the future grant to any one that he may take aid of his own free tenants, except to ransom his body, and to make his eldest son a knight, and once to marry his eldest daughter; and for this there shall be paid only a reasonable aid. . . .

36. Nothing from henceforth shall be given or taken for a writ of inquisition of life or limb, but it shall be granted freely, and not denied. . . .

39. No freeman shall be taken or imprisoned, or disseised [deprived], or outlawed, or banished, or in any way destroyed, nor will we pass upon him, nor will we send upon him, unless by the lawful judgment of his peers, or by the law of the land.

40. We will sell to no man, we will not deny to any man, either justice or right.

41. All merchants shall have safe and secure conduct to go out of, and to come into, England, and to stay there and to pass as well by land as by water, for buying and selling by the ancient and allowed customs, without any unjust tolls, except in time of war, or when they are of any nation at war with us. . . .

42. It shall be lawful, for the time to come, for any one to go out of our kingdom and return safely and securely by land or by water, saving his allegiance to us (unless in time of war, by some short space, for the common benefit of the realm).

60. All the aforesaid customs and liberties, which we have granted to be holden in our kingdom, as much as it belongs to us, all people of our kingdom, as well clergy as laity, shall observe, as far as they are concerned, towards their dependents.

61. And whereas, for the honor of God and the amendment of our kingdom, and for the better quieting the discord that has arisen between us and our barons, we have granted all these things aforesaid. Willing to render them firm and lasting, we do give and grant our subjects the underwritten security, namely, that the barons may choose five and twenty barons of the kingdom, whom they think convenient, who shall take care, with all their might, to hold and observe, and cause to be observed, the peace and liberties we have granted them, and by this our present Charter confirmed. . . .

63. . . . It is also sworn, as well on our part as on the part of the barons, that all the things aforesaid shall be observed in good faith, and without evil duplicity. Given under our hand, in the presence of the witnesses above named, and many others, in the meadow called Runnymede, between Windsor and Staines, the 15th day of June, in the 17th year of our reign.

Madison's *Notes*: Debate of June 6 on the Virginia Plan

James Madison's *Notes* enable readers today to gain a glimpse of the debates that took place behind closed doors at the Constitutional Convention held in Philadelphia in the summer of 1787. Excerpted here are portions of Madison's *Notes* on the debate of June 6 on the Virginia Plan's call for a bicameral (two house) legislature.

MR. PINCKNEY [S.C.], according to previous notice and rule obtained, moved "that the first branch of the national legislature be elected by the state legislatures, and not by the people," contending that the people were less fit judges in such a case, and that the legislatures would be less likely to promote the adoption of the new government if they were to be excluded from all share in it.

MR. RUTLEDGE [S.C.] seconded the motion.

MR. GERRY [MASS.]: Much depends on the mode of election. In England the people will probably lose their liberty from the smallness of the proportion having a right of suffrage. Our danger arises from the opposite extreme; hence in Massachusetts the worst men get into the legislature. Several members of that body had lately been convicted of infamous crimes. Men of indigence, ignorance, and baseness spare no pains, however dirty, to carry their point against men who are superior to the artifices practised. He was not disposed to run into extremes. He was as much principled as ever against aristocracy and monarchy. It was necessary, on the one hand, that the people should appoint one branch of the government in order to inspire them with the necessary confidence. . . . His idea was that the people should nominate certain persons in certain districts, out of whom the state legislatures should make the appointment.

MR. WILSON [PA.]: He wished for vigor in the government, but he wished that vigorous authority to flow immediately from the legitimate source of all authority. The government ought to possess not only, first, the *force* but, second, the *mind or sense* of the people at large. The legislature ought to be the most exact transcript of the whole society. Representation is made necessary only because it is impossible for the people to act collectively. . . .

MR. SHERMAN [CONN.]: If it were in view to abolish the state governments, the elections ought to be by the people. If the state governments are to be continued, it is necessary, in order to preserve harmony between the national and state governments, that the elections to the former should be made by the latter. The right of participating in the national government would be sufficiently secured to the people by their election of the state legislatures. The objects of the Union, he thought, were few: (1) defense against foreign danger; (2) against internal disputes and a resort to force; (3) treaties with foreign nations; (4) regulating foreign commerce and drawing revenue from it. These, and perhaps a few lesser objects, alone rendered a confederation of the states necessary. All other matters, civil and criminal, would be much better in the hands of the states. . . .

COLONEL MASON [VA.]: Under the existing Confederacy, Congress represent the *states,* not the *people* of the states; their acts operate on the *states,* not on the individuals. The case will be changed in the new plan of government. The people will be represented; they ought therefore to choose the representatives. The requisites in actual representation are that the representatives should sympathize with their constituents, should think as they think and feel as they feel, and that, for these purposes, [they] should even be residents among them. Much, he said, had been alleged against democratic elections. He admitted that much might be said; but it was to be considered that no government was free from imperfections and evils and that improper elections, in many instances, were inseparable from republican governments. . . .

MR. MADISON [VA.] considered an election of one branch, at least, of the legislature by the people immediately as a clear principle of free government, and that this mode, under proper regulations, had the additional advantage of securing better representatives as well as of avoiding too great an agency of the state governments in the general one. He differed from the member from Connecticut (Mr. Sherman) in thinking the objects mentioned to be all the principal ones that required a national government. Those were certainly important and necessary objects; but he combined with them the necessity of providing more effectually for the security of private rights and the steady dispensation of justice.

Interferences with these were evils which had more, perhaps, than anything else produced this Convention. Was it to be supposed that republican liberty could long exist under the abuses of it practised in some of the states? . . .

All civilized societies would be divided into different sects, factions, and interests, as they happened to consist of rich and poor, debtors and creditors, the landed, the manufacturing, the commercial interests, the inhabitants of this district or that district, the followers of this political leader or that political leader, the disciples of this religious sect or that religious sect. In all cases where a majority are united by a common interest or passion, the rights of the minority are in danger. What motives are to restrain them? . . .

Conscience, the only remaining tie, is known to be inadequate in individuals; in large numbers, little is to be expected from it. . . .

What has been the source of those unjust laws complained of among ourselves? Has it not been the real or supposed interest of the major number? Debtors have defrauded their creditors. The landed interest has borne hard on the mercantile interest. The holders of one species of property have thrown a disproportion of taxes on the holders of another species.

The lesson we are to draw from the whole is that where a majority are united by a common sentiment, and have an opportunity, the rights of the minor party become insecure. In a republican government the majority, if united, have always an opportunity. . . .

MR. DICKINSON [DEL.] considered it as essential that one branch of the legislature should be drawn immediately from the people and as expedient that the other should be chosen by the legislatures of the states. This combination of the state governments with the national government was as politic as it was unavoidable. In the formation of the Senate, we ought to carry it through such a refining process as will assimilate it as near as may be to the House of Lords in England. He repeated his warm eulogiums on the British constitution. He was for a strong national government but for leaving the states a considerable agency in the system. The objection against making the former dependent on the latter might be obviated by giving to the Senate an authority permanent and irrevocable for three, five, or seven years. Being thus independent, they will speak and decide with becoming freedom.

MR. READ [DEL.]: Too much attachment is betrayed to the state governments. We must look beyond their continuance. A national government must soon of necessity swallow all of them up. They will soon be reduced to the mere office of electing the national Senate. He was against patching up the old federal system; he hoped the idea would be dismissed. It would be like putting new cloth on an old garment. The Confederation was founded on temporary principles. It cannot last; it cannot be amended. If we do not establish a good government on new principles, we must either go to ruin or have the work to do over again. . . .

MR. PIERCE [GA.] was for an election by the people as to the first branch and by the states as to the second branch, by which means the citizens of the states would be represented both *individually* and *collectively.*

GENERAL PINCKNEY wished to have a good national government and at the same time to leave a considerable share of power in the states. An election of either branch by the people, scattered as they are in many states, particularly in South Carolina, was totally impracticable. He differed from gentlemen who thought that a choice by the people would be a better guard against bad measures than by the legislatures. . . .

The state legislatures also, he said, would be more jealous and more ready to thwart the national government if excluded from a participation in it. The idea of abolishing these legislatures would never go down.

MR. WILSON would not have spoken again but for what had fallen from Mr. Read; namely, that the idea of preserving the state governments ought to be abandoned. He saw no incompatibility between the national and state governments, provided the latter were restrained to certain local purposes; nor any probability of their being devoured by the former. . . .

On the question for electing the first branch by the state legislatures as moved by Mr. Pinckney, it was negatived.

The Federalist No. 10
(James Madison)

One of the 26 essays believed to have been written by James Madison, the tenth of *The Federalist* papers presents Madison's observations on dealing with the "mischiefs of factions" and the advantages of a republican (representative) form of government over that of a pure democracy. This essay was first published on November 23, 1787.

Among the numberous advantages promised by a well-constructed Union, none deserves to be more accurately developed than its tendency to break and control the violence of faction. The friend of popular governments never finds himself so much alarmed for their character and fate as when he contemplates their propensity to this dangerous vice. He will not fail, therefore, to set a due value on any plan which, without violating the principles to which he is attached, provides a proper cure for it. The instability, injustice, and confusion introduced into the public councils have, in truth, been the mortal diseases under which popular governments have everywhere perished; as they continue to be the favorite and fruitful topics from which the adversaries to liberty derive their most specious declamations.

The valuable improvements made by the American constitutions on the popular models, both ancient and modern, cannot certainly be too much admired; but it would be an unwarrantable partiality to contend that they have as effectually obviated the danger on this side, as was wished and expected. Complaints are everywhere heard from our most considerate and virtuous citizens, equally the friends of public and private faith, and of public and personal liberty, that our governments are too unstable, that the public good is disregarded in the conflicts of rival parties, and that measures are too often decided, not according to the rules of justice and the rights of the minor party, but by the superior force of an interested and overbearing majority. However anxiously we may wish that these complaints had no foundation, the evidence of known facts will not permit us to deny that they are in some degree true.

It will be found, indeed, on a candid review of our situation, that some of the distresses under which we labor have been erroneously charged on the operation of our governments; but it will be found, at the same time, that other causes will not alone account for many of our heaviest misfortunes; and, particularly, for that prevailing and increasing distrust of public engagements, and alarm for private rights, which are echoed from one end of the continent to the other. These must be chiefly, if not wholly, effects of the unsteadiness and injustice with which a factious spirit has tainted our public administrations.

By a faction, I understand a number of citizens, whether amounting to a majority or minority of the whole, who are united and actuated by some common impulse of passion, or of interest, adverse to the rights of other citizens, or to the permanent and aggregate interests of the community.

There are two methods of curing the mischiefs of faction: the one, by removing its causes; the other, by controlling its effects.

There are again two methods of removing the causes of faction: the one, by destroying the liberty which is essential to its existence; the other, by giving to every citizen the same opinions, the same passions, and the same interests.

It could never be more truly said than of the first remedy that it was worse than the disease. Liberty is to faction what air is to fire, an ailment without which it instantly expires. But it could not be less folly to abolish liberty, which is essential to political life, because it nourishes faction, than it would be to wish the annihilation of air, which is essential to animal life, because it imparts to fire its destructive agency.

The second expedient is as impracticable as the first would be unwise. As long as the reason of man continues fallible, and he is at liberty to exercise it, different opinions will be formed. As long as the connection subsists between his reason and his self-love, his opinions and his passions will have a reciprocal influence on each other; and the former will be objects to which the latter will attach themselves. The diversity in the faculties of men, from which the rights of property originate, is not less an insuperable obstacle to a uniformity of interests. The protection of these faculties is the first object of government. From the protection of different and unequal faculties of acquiring property, the possession of different degrees and kinds of property immediately results; and from the influence of these on the sentiments and views of the respective proprietors ensues a division of the society into different interests and parties.

The latent causes of faction are thus sown in the nature of man; and we see them everywhere brought into different degrees of activity, according to the different circumstances of civil society. A zeal for different opinions concerning religion, concerning government, and many other points, as well of speculation as of practice; an attachment of different leaders ambitiously contending for preeminence and power; or to persons of other descriptions whose fortunes have been interesting to the human passions, have, in turn, divided mankind into parties, inflamed them with mutual animosity, and rendered them much more disposed to vex and oppress each other than to cooperate for their common good. So strong is this propensity of mankind to fall into mutual animosities that, where no substantial occasion presents itself, the most frivolous and fanciful distinctions have been sufficient to kindle their unfriendly passions and excite their most violent conflicts. But the most common and durable source of factions has been the various and unequal distribution of property.

Those who hold and those who are without property have ever formed distinct interests in society. Those who are creditors and those who are debtors fall under a like discrimination. A landed interest, a manufacturing interest, a mercantile interest, a moneyed interest, with many lesser interests, grow up of necessity in civilized nations and divide them into different classes, actuated by different sentiments and views. The regulation of these various and interfering interests forms the principal task of modern legislation and involves the spirit of party and faction in the necessary and ordinary operations of the government.

No man is allowed to be a judge in his own cause, because his interest would certainly bias his judgment and, not improbably, corrupt his integrity. With equal, nay, with greater reason, a body of men are unfit to be both judges and parties at the same time; yet what are many of the most important acts of legislation but so many judicial determinations, not indeed concerning the rights of single persons, but concerning the rights of large bodies of citizens? And what are the different classes of legislators but advocates and parties to the causes which they determine? Is a law proposed concerning private debts? It is a question to which the creditors are parties on one side and the debtors on the other. Justice ought to hold the balance between them. Yet the parties are, and must be, themselves the judges; and the most numerous party or, in other words, the most powerful faction must be expected to prevail.

Shall domestic manufactures be encouraged, and in what degree, by restrictions on foreign manufactures? [These] are questions which would be differently decided by the landed and the manufacturing classes, and probably by neither with a sole regard to justice and the public good. The apportionment of taxes on the various descriptions of property is an act which seems to require the most exact impartiality; yet there is, perhaps, no legislative act in which greater opportunity and temptation are given to a predominant party to trample on the rules of justice. Every shilling with which they overburden the inferior number is a shilling saved to their own pockets.

It is in vain to say that enlightened statesmen will be able to adjust these clashing interests and render them all subservient to the public good. Enlightened statesmen will not always be at the helm. Nor, in many cases, can such an adjustment be made at all without taking into view indirect and remote considerations, which will rarely prevail over the immediate interest which one party may find in disregarding the rights of another or the good of the whole. The inference to which we are brought is that the *causes* of faction cannot be removed and that relief is only to be sought in the means of controlling its *effects*.

If a faction consists of less than a majority, relief is supplied by the republican principle, which enables the majority to defeat its sinister views by regular vote. It may clog the administration, it may convulse the society; but it will be unable to execute and mask its violence under the forms of the Constitution. When a majority is included in a faction, the form of popular government, on the other hand, enables it to sacrifice to its ruling passion or interest both the public good and the rights of other citizens. To secure the public good and private rights against the danger of such a faction, and at the same time to preserve the spirit and the form of popular government, is then the great object to which our inquiries are directed. Let me add that it is the great desideratum by which this form of government can be rescued from the opprobrium under which it has so long labored and be recommended to the esteem and adoption of mankind.

By what means is this object attainable? Evidently by one of two only. Either the existence of the same passion or interest in a majority at the same time must be prevented, or the majority, having such coexistent passion or interest, must be rendered, by their number and local situation, unable to concert and carry into effect schemes of oppression. If the impulse and the opportunity be suffered to coincide, we well know that neither moral nor religious motives can be relied on as an adequate control. They are not found to be such on the injustice and violence of individuals and lose their efficacy in proportion to the number combined together, that is, in proportion as their efficacy becomes needful.

From this view of the subject it may be concluded that a pure democracy, by which I mean a society consisting of a small number of citizens who assemble and administer the government in person, can admit of no cure for the mischiefs of faction. A common passion or interest will, in almost every case, be felt by a majority of the whole; a communication and concert result from the form of government itself; and there is nothing to check the inducements to sacrifice the weaker party or an obnoxious individual. Hence it is that such democracies have ever been spectacles of turbulence and contention; have ever been found incompatible with personal security or the rights of property; and have in general been as short in their lives as they have been violent in their deaths. Theoretic politicians, who have patronized this species of government, have erroneously supposed that by reducing mankind to a perfect equality in their political rights, they would, at the same time, be perfectly equalized and assimilated in their possessions, their opinions, and their passions.

A republic, by which I mean a government in which the scheme of representation takes place, opens a different prospect and promises the cure for which we are seeking. Let us examine the points in which it varies from pure democracy, and we shall comprehend both the nature of the cure and the efficacy which it must derive from the Union.

The two great points of difference between a democracy and a republic are: first, the delegation of the government, in the latter, to a small number of citizens elected by the rest; secondly, the greater number of citizens, and greater sphere of country, over which the latter may be extended.

The effect of the first difference is, on the one hand, to refine and enlarge the public views by passing them through the medium of a chosen body of citizens, whose wisdom may best discern the true interest of their country, and whose patriotism and love of justice will be least likely to sacrifice it to temporary or partial considerations. Under such a regulation, it may well happen that the public voice, pronounced by the representatives of the people, will be more consonant to the public good than if pronounced by the people themselves, convened for the purpose. On the other hand, the effect may be inverted. Men of factious tempers, of local prejudices, or of sinister designs may, by intrigue, by corruption, or by other means, first obtain the suffrages, and then betray the interests of the people. The question resulting is, whether small or extensive republics are more favorable to the election of proper guardians of the public weal; and it is clearly decided in favor of the latter by two obvious considerations:

In the first place, it is to be remarked that, however small the republic may be, the representatives must be raised to a certain number, in order to guard against the cabals of a few; and that, however large it may be, they must be limited to a certain number, in order to guard against the confusion of a multitude. Hence, the number of representatives in the two cases not being in proportion to that of the two constituents, and being proportionally greater in the small republic, it follows that, if the proportion of fit characters be not less in the large than in the small republic, the former will present a greater option, and consequently a greater probability of a fit choice.

In the next place, as each representative will be chosen by a greater number of citizens in the large than in the small republic, it will be more difficult for unworthy candidates to practice with success the vicious arts by which elections are too often carried; and the suffrages of the people being more free, will be more likely to center in men who possess the most attractive merit and the most diffusive and established character.

It must be confessed that in this, as in most other cases, there is a mean, on both sides of which inconveniences will be found to lie. By enlarging too much the number of electors, you render the representative too little acquainted with all their local circumstances and lesser interests; as by reducing it too much, you render him unduly attached to these and too little fit to comprehend and pursue great and national objects. The federal Constitution forms a happy combination in this respect: the great and aggregate interests being referred to the national, the local and particular to the state legislatures.

The other point of difference is the greater number of citizens and extent of territory which may be brought within the compass of republican than of democratic government; and it is this circumstance principally which renders factious combinations less to be dreaded in the former than in the latter. The smaller the society, the fewer probably will be the distinct parties and interests composing it; the fewer the distinct parties and interests, the more frequently will a majority be found of the same party; and the smaller the number of individuals composing a majority, and the smaller the compass within which they are placed, the more easily will they concert and execute their plans of oppression. Extend the sphere and you take in a greater variety of parties and interests; you make it less probable that a majority of the whole will have a common motive to invade the rights of other citizens; or if such a common motive exists, it will be more difficult for all who feel it to discover their own strength and to act in unison with each other. Besides other impediments, it may be remarked that, where there is a consciousness of unjust or dishonorable purposes, communication is always checked by distrust in proportion to the number whose concurrence is necessary.

Hence, it clearly appears that the same advantage which a republic has over a democracy, in controlling the effects of factions, is enjoyed by a large over a small republic—is enjoyed by the Union over the states composing it. Does the advantage consist in the substitution of representatives whose enlightened views and virtuous sentiments render them superior to local prejudices and to schemes of injustice? It will not be denied that the representation of the Union will be most likely to possess these requisite endowments. Does it consist in the greater security afforded by a greater variety of parties, against the event of any one party being able to outnumber and oppress the rest? In an equal degree does the increased variety of parties comprised within the Union increase this security? Does it, in fine, consist in the greater obstacles opposed to the concert and accomplishment of the secret wishes of an unjust and interested majority? Here, again, the extent of the Union gives it the most palpable advantage.

The influence of factious leaders may kindle a flame within their particular states but will be unable to spread a general conflagration through the other states. A religious sect may degenerate into a political faction in a part of the Confederacy; but the variety of sects dispersed over the entire face of it must secure the national councils against any danger from that source. A rage for paper money, for an abolition of debts, for an equal division of property, or for any other improper or wicked project will be less apt to pervade the whole body of the Union than a particular member of it; in the same proportion as such a malady is more likely to taint a particular county or district than an entire state.

In the extent, and proper structure of the Union, therefore, we behold a republican remedy for the diseases most incident to republican government. And according to the degree of pleasure and pride we feel in being republicans, ought to be our zeal in cherishing the spirit and supporting the character of Federalists.

The Federalist No. 51
(James Madison)

To what expedient, then, shall we finally resort, for maintaining in practice the necessary partition of power among the several departments as laid down in the Constitution? The only answer that can be given is that as all these exterior provisions are found to be inadequate the defect must be supplied, by so contriving the interior structure of the government as that its several constituent parts may, by their mutual relations, be the means of keeping each other in their proper places. Without presuming to undertake a full development of this important idea, I will hazard a few general observations which may perhaps place it in a clearer light, and enable us to form a more correct judgment of the principles and structure of the government planned by the convention.

In order to lay a due foundation for that separate and distinct exercise of the different powers of government, which to a certain extent is admitted on all hands to be essential to the preservation of liberty, it is evident that each department should have a will of its own; and consequently should be so constituted that the members of each should have as little agency as possible in the appointment of the members of the others. Were this principle rigorously adhered to, it would require that all the appointments for the supreme executive, legislative, and judiciary magistracies should be drawn from the same fountain of authority, the people, through channels having no communication whatever with one another. Perhaps such a plan of constructing the several departments would be less difficult in practice than it may in contemplation appear. Some difficulties, however, and some additional expense would attend the execution of it. Some deviations, therefore, from the principle must be admitted. In the constitution of the judiciary department in particular, it might be inexpedient to insist rigorously on the principle; first, because peculiar qualifications being essential in the members, the primary consideration ought to be to select that mode of choice which best secures these qualifications; second, because the permanent tenure by which the appointments are held in that department must soon destroy all sense of dependence on the authority conferring them.

It is equally evident that the members of each department should be as little dependent as possible on those of the others for the emoluments annexed to their offices. Were the executive magistrate, or the judges, not independent of the legislature in this particular, their independence in every other would be merely nominal.

But the great security against a gradual concentration of the several powers in the same department consists in giving to those who administer each department the necessary constitutional means and personal motives to resist encroachments of the others. The provision for defense must in this, as in all other cases, be made commensurate to the danger of attack. Ambition must be made to counteract ambition. The interest of the man must be connected with the constitutional rights of the place. It may be a reflection on human nature that such devices should be necessary to control the abuses of government. But what is government itself but the greatest of all reflections on human nature? If men were angels, no government would be necessary. If angels were to govern men, neither external nor internal controls on government would be necessary. In framing a government which is to be administered by men over men, the great difficulty lies in this: You must first enable the government to control the governed; and in the next place, oblige it to control itself. A dependence on the people is, no doubt, the primary control on the government; but experience has taught mankind the necessity of auxiliary precautions.

This policy of supplying, by opposite and rival interests, the defect of better motives might be traced through the whole system of human affairs, private as well as public. We see it particularly displayed in all the subordinate distributions of power; where the constant aim is to divide and arrange the several offices in such a manner as that each may be a check on the other—that the private interest of every individual may be a sentinel over the public rights. These inventions of prudence cannot be less requisite in the distribution of the supreme powers of the State.

But it is not possible to give to each department an equal power of self-defense. In republican government, the legislative authority necessarily predominates. The remedy for this inconveniency is to divide the legislature into different branches; and to render them, by different modes of election, and different principles of action, as little connected with each other as the nature of their common functions and their common dependence on the society will admit. It may even be necessary to guard against dangerous encroachments by still further precautions. As the weight of the legislative authority requires that it should be thus divided, the weakness of the executive may require, on the other hand, that it should be fortified. An absolute negative on the legislature appears, at first view, to be the natural defense with which the executive magistrate should be armed. But perhaps it would be neither altogether safe nor alone sufficient. On ordinary occasions it might not be exerted with the requisite firmness, and on extraordinary occasions it might be perfidiously abused. May not this defect of an absolute negative be supplied by some qualified connection between this weaker department and the weaker branch of the stronger department, by which the latter may be led to support the constitutional rights of the former, without being too much detached from the rights of its own department?

If the principles on which these observations are founded be just, as I persuade myself they are, and they be applied as a criterion to the several State constitutions, and to the federal Constitution, it will be found that if the latter does not perfectly correspond with them, the former are infinitely less able to bear such a test.

There are, moreover, two considerations particularly applicable to the federal system of America, which place that system in a very interesting point of view.

First. In a single republic, all the power surrendered by the people is submitted to the administration of a single government; and the usurpations are guarded against by a division of the government into distinct and separate departments. In the compound republic of America, the power surrendered by the people is first divided between two distinct governments, and then the portion allotted to each subdivided among distinct and separate departments. Hence a double security arises to the rights of the people. The different governments will control each other, at the same time that each will be controlled by itself.

Second. It is of great importance in a republic not only to guard the society against the oppression of its rulers, but to guard one part of the society against the injustice of the other part. Different interests necessarily exist in different classes of citizens. If a majority be united by a common interest, the rights of the minority will be insecure. There are but two methods of providing against this evil: The one by creating a will in the community independent of the majority—that is, of the society itself; the other, by comprehending in the society so many separate descriptions of citizens as will render an unjust combination of a majority of the whole very improbable, if not impracticable. The first method prevails in all governments possessing an hereditary or self appointed authority. This, at best, is but a precarious security; because a power independent of the society may as well espouse the unjust views of the major as the rightful interests of the minor party, and may possibly be turned against both parties. The second method will be exemplified in the federal republic of the United States. While all authority in it will be derived from and dependent on the society, the society itself will be broken into so many parts, interests, and classes of citizens, that the rights of individuals, or of the minority, will be in little danger from interested combinations of the majority. In a free government the security for civil rights must be the same as that for religious rights. It consists in the one case in the multiplicity of interests, and in the other in the multiplicity of sects. The degree of security in both cases will depend on the number of interests and sects; and this may be presumed to depend on the extent of country and number of people comprehended under the same government. This view of the subject must particularly recommend a proper federal system to all the sincere and considerate friends of republican government, since it shows that in exact proportion as the territory of the Union may be formed into more circumscribed Confederacies, or States, oppressive combinations of a majority will be facilitated: the best security, under the republican forms, for the rights of every class of citizens, will be diminished; and consequently, the stability and independence of some member of the government, the only other security, must be proportionally increased. Justice is the end of government. It is the end of civil society. It ever has been and ever will be pursued until it be obtained, or until liberty be lost in the pursuit. In a society under the forms of which the stronger faction can readily unite and oppress the weaker, anarchy may as truly be said to reign as in a state of nature, where the weaker individual is not secured against the violence of the stronger: And as, in the latter state, even the stronger individuals are prompted by the uncertainty of their condition to submit to a government which may protect the weak as well as themselves. So, in the former state, will the more powerful factions or parties be gradually induced, by a like motive, to wish for a government which will protect all parties, the weaker as well as the more powerful. It can be little doubted that if the State of Rhode Island was separated from the Confederacy and left to itself, the insecurity of rights under the popular form of government within such narrow limits would be displayed by such reiterated oppressions of factious majorities that some power altogether independent of the people would soon be called for by the voice of the very factions whose misrule had proved the necessity of it. In the extended republic of the United States, and among the great variety of interests, parties, and sects which it embraces, a coalition of a majority of the whole society could seldom take place on any other principles than those of justice and the general good; and there being thus less danger to a minor from the will of the major party, there must be less pretext, also, to provide for the security of the former, by introducing into the government a will not dependent on the latter; or, in other words, a will independent of the society itself. It is no less certain that it is important, notwithstanding the contrary opinions which have been entertained, that the larger the society, provided it lie within a practicable sphere, the more duly capable it will be of self-government. And happily for the *republican cause*, the practicable sphere may be carried to a very great extent by a judicious modification and mixture of the *federal principle.*

The Federalist No. 78
(Alexander Hamilton)

We proceed now to an examination of the judiciary department of the proposed government. In unfolding the defects of the existing Confederation, the utility and necessity of a federal judicature have been clearly pointed out. It is the less necessary to recapitulate the considerations there urged as the propriety of the institution in the abstract is not disputed; the only questions which have been raised being relative to the manner of constituting it, and to its extent. To these points, therefore, our observations shall be confined.

The manner of constituting it seems to embrace these several objects: 1st. The mode of appointing the judges. 2nd. The tenure by which they are to hold their places. 3rd. The partition of the judiciary authority between different courts and their relations to each other.

First. As to the mode of appointing the judges: this is the same with that of appointing the officers of the Union in general and has been so fully discussed in the two last numbers that nothing can be said here which would not be useless repetition.

Second. As to the tenure by which the judges are to hold their places: this chiefly concerns their duration in office, the provisions for their support, the precautions for their responsibility.

According to the plan of the convention, all judges who may be appointed by the United States are to hold their offices *during good behavior*; which is conformable to the most approved of the State constitutions, and among the rest, to that of this State. Its propriety having been drawn into question by the adversaries of that plan is no light symptom of the rage for objection which disorders their imaginations and judgments. The standard of good behavior for the continuance in office of the judicial magistracy is certainly one of the most valuable of the modern improvements in the practice of government. In a monarchy it is an excellent barrier to the despotism of the prince; in a republic it is a no less excellent barrier to the encroachments and oppressions of the representative body. And it is the best expedient which can be devised in any government to secure a steady, upright, and impartial administration of the laws.

Whoever attentively considers the different departments of power must perceive that, in a government in which they are separated from each other, the judiciary, from the nature of its functions, will always be the least dangerous to the political rights of the Constitution; because it will be least in a capacity to annoy or injure them. The executive not only dispenses the honors but holds the sword of the community. The legislature not only commands the purse but prescribes the rules by which the duties and rights of every citizen are to be regulated. The judiciary, on the contrary, has no influence over either the sword or the purse; no direction either of the strength or of the wealth of the society, and can take no active resolution whatever. It may truly be said to have neither FORCE nor WILL but merely judgment; and must ultimately depend upon the aid of the executive arm even for the efficacy of its judgments.

This simple view of the matter suggests several important consequences. It proves incontestably that the judiciary is beyond comparison the weakest of the three departments of power; that it can never attack with success either of the other two; and that all possible care is requisite to enable it to defend itself against their attacks. It equally proves that though individual oppression may now and then proceed from the courts of justice, the general liberty of the people can never be endangered from that quarter; I mean so long as the judiciary remains truly distinct from both the legislature and the executive. For I agree that "there is no liberty if the power of judging be not separated from the legislative and executive powers." And it proves, in the last place, that as liberty can have nothing to fear from the judiciary alone, but would have everything to fear from its union with either of the other departments; that as all the effects of such a union must ensue from a dependence of the former on the latter, notwithstanding a nominal and apparent separation; that as, from the natural feebleness of the judiciary, it is in continual jeopardy of being overpowered, awed, or influenced by its coordinate branches; and that as nothing can contribute so much to its firmness and independence as permanency in office, this quality may therefore be justly regarded as an indispensable ingredient in its constitution, and, in a great measure, as the citadel of the public justice and the public security.

The complete independence of the courts of justice is peculiarly essential in a limited Constitution. By a limited Constitution, I understand one which contains certain specified exceptions to the legislative authority; such, for instance, as that it shall pass no bills of attainder, no *ex post facto* laws, and the like. Limitations of this kind can be preserved in practice no other way than through the medium of courts of justice, whose duty it must be to declare all acts contrary to the manifest tenor of the Constitution void. Without this, all the reservations of particular rights or privileges would amount to nothing.

Some perplexity respecting the rights of the courts to pronounce legislative acts void, because contrary to the Constitution, has arisen from an imagination that the doctrine would imply a superiority of the judiciary to the legislative power. It is urged that the authority which can declare the acts of another void must necessarily be superior to the one whose acts may be declared void. As this doctrine is of great importance in all the American constitutions, a brief discussion of the grounds on which it rests cannot be unacceptable.

There is no position which depends on clearer principles than that every act of a delegated authority, contrary to the tenor of the commission under which it is exercised, is void. No legislative act, therefore, contrary to the Constitution, can be valid. To deny this would be to affirm that the deputy is greater than his principal; that the servant is above his master; that the representatives of the people are superior to the people themselves; that men acting by virtue of powers may do not only what their powers do not authorize, but what they forbid.

If it be said that the legislative body are themselves the constitutional judges of their own powers and that the construction they put upon them is conclusive upon the other departments, it may be answered that this cannot be the natural presumption where it is not to be collected from any particular provisions in the Constitution. It is not otherwise to be supposed that the Constitution could intend to enable the representatives of the people to substitute their *will* to that of their constituents. It is far more rational to suppose that the courts were designed to be an intermediate body between the people and the legislature in order, among other things, to keep the latter within the limits assigned to their authority. The interpretation of the laws is the proper and peculiar province of the courts. A constitution is, in fact, and must be regarded by the judges as, a fundamental law. It therefore belongs to them to ascertain its meaning as well as the meaning of any particular act proceeding from the legislative body. If there should happen to be an irreconcilable variance between the two, that which has the superior obligation and validity ought, of course, to be preferred; or, in other words, the Constitution ought to be preferred to the statute, the intention of the people to the intention of their agents.

Nor does this conclusion by any means suppose a superiority of the judicial to the legislative power. It only supposes that the power of the people is superior to both, and that where the will of the legislature, declared in its statutes, stands in opposition to that of the people, declared in the Constitution, the judges ought to be governed by the latter rather than the former. They ought to regulate their decisions by the fundamental laws rather than by those which are not fundamental.

This exercise of judicial discretion in determining between two contradictory laws is exemplified in a familiar instance. It not uncommonly happens that there are two statutes existing at one time, clashing in whole or in part with each other and neither of them containing any repealing clause or expression. In such a case, it is the province of the courts to liquidate and fix their meaning and operation. So far as they can, by any fair construction, be reconciled to each other, reason and law conspire to dictate that this should be done; where this is impracticable, it becomes a matter of necessity to give effect to one in exclusion of the other. The rule which has obtained in the courts for determining their relative validity is that the last in order of time shall be preferred to the first. But this is a mere rule of construction, not derived from any positive law but from the nature and reason of the thing. It is a rule not enjoined upon the courts by legislative provision but adopted by themselves, as consonant to truth and propriety, for the direction of their conduct as interpreters of the law. They thought it reasonable that between the interfering acts of an *equal* authority that which was the last indication of its will should have the preference.

But in regard to the interfering acts of a superior and subordinate authority of an original and derivative power, the nature and reason of the thing indicate the converse of that rule as proper to be followed. They teach us that the prior act of a superior ought to be preferred to the subsequent act of an inferior and subordinate authority; and that accordingly, whenever a particular statute contravenes the Constitution, it will be the duty of the judicial tribunals to adhere to the latter and disregard the former.

It can be of no weight to say that the courts, on the pretense of a repugnancy, may substitute their own pleasure to the constitutional intentions of the legislature. This might as well happen in the case of two contradictory statutes; or it might as well happen in every adjudication upon any single statute. The courts must declare the sense of the law; and if they should be disposed to exercise WILL instead of JUDGMENT, the consequence would equally be the substitution of their pleasure to that of the legislative body. The observation, if it prove anything, would prove that there ought to be no judges distinct from that body.

If, then, the courts of justice are to be considered as the bulwarks of a limited Constitution against legislative encroachments, this consideration will afford a strong argument for the permanent tenure of judicial offices, since nothing will contribute so much as this to that independent spirit in the judges which must be essential to the faithful performance of so arduous a duty.

This independence of the judges is equally requisite to guard the Constitution and the rights of individuals from the effects of those ill humors which the arts of designing men, or the influence of particular conjunctures, sometimes disseminate among the people themselves, and which, though they speedily give place to better information, and more deliberate reflection, have a tendency, in the meantime, to occasion dangerous innovations in the government, and serious oppressions of the minor party in the community. Though I trust the friends of the proposed Constitution will never concur with its enemies in questioning that fundamental principle of Republican government which admits the right of the people to alter or abolish the established Constitution whenever they find it inconsistent with their happiness; yet it is not to be inferred from this principle that the representatives of the people, whenever a momentary inclination happens to lay hold of a majority of their constituents incompatible with the provisions in the existing Constitution would, on that account, be justifiable in a violation of those provisions; or that the courts would be under a greater obligation to connive at infractions in this shape than when they had proceeded wholly from the cabals of the representative body. Until the people have, by some solemn and authoritative act, annulled or changed the established form, it is binding upon themselves collectively, as well as individually; and no presumption, or even knowledge of their sentiments, can warrant their representatives in a departure from it prior to such an act. But it is easy to see that it would require an uncommon portion of fortitude in the judges to do their duty as faithful guardians of the Constitution, where legislative invasions of it had been instigated by the major voice of the community.

But it is not with a view to infractions of the Constitution only that the independence of the judges may be an essential safeguard against the effects of occasional ill humors in the society. These sometimes extend no farther than to the injury of the private rights of particular classes of citizens, by unjust and partial laws. Here also the firmness of the judicial magistracy is of vast importance in mitigating the severity and confining the operation of such laws. It not only serves to moderate the immediate mischiefs of those which may have been passed but it operates as a check upon the legislative body in passing them; who, perceiving that obstacles to the success of iniquitous intention are to be expected from the scruples of the courts, are in a manner compelled, by the very motives of the injustice they mediate, to qualify their attempts. This is a circumstance calculated to have more influence upon the character of our governments than but few may be aware of. The benefits of the integrity and moderation of the judiciary have already been felt in more States than one; and though they may have displeased those whose sinister expectations they may have disappointed, they must have commanded the esteem and applause of all the virtuous and disinterested. Considerate men of every description ought to prize whatever will tend to beget or fortify that temper in the courts; as no man can be sure that he may not be tomorrow the victim of a spirit of injustice, by which he may be a gainer today. And every man must now feel that the inevitable tendency of such a spirit is to sap the foundations of public and private confidence and to introduce in its stead universal distrust and distress.

That inflexible and uniform adherence to the rights of the Constitution, and of individuals, which we perceive to be indispensable in the courts of justice, can certainly not be expected from judges who hold their offices by a temporary commission. Periodical appointments, however regulated, or by whomsoever made, would, in some way or other, be fatal to their necessary independence. If the power of making them was committed either to the executive or legislature there would be danger of an improper complaisance to the branch which possessed it; if to both, there would be an unwillingness to hazard the displeasure of either; if to the people, or to persons chosen by them for the special purpose, there would be too great a disposition to consult popularity to justify a reliance that nothing would be consulted but the Constitution and the laws.

There is yet a further and a weighty reason for the permanency of the judicial offices which is deducible from the nature of the qualifications they require. It has been frequently remarked with great propriety that a voluminous code of laws is one of the inconveniences necessarily connected with the advantages of a free government. To avoid an arbitrary discretion in the courts, it is indispensable that they should be bound down by strict rules and precedents which serve to define and point out their duty in every particular case that comes before them; and it will readily be conceived from the variety of controversies which grow out of the folly and wickedness of mankind that the records of those precedents must unavoidably swell to a very considerable bulk and must demand long and laborious study to acquire a competent knowledge of them. Hence it is that there can be but few men in the society who will have sufficient skill in the laws to qualify them for the stations of judges. And making the proper deductions for the ordinary depravity of human nature, the number must be still smaller of those who unite the requisite integrity with the requisite knowledge. These considerations apprise us that the government can have no great option between fit characters; and that a temporary duration in office which would naturally discourage such characters from quitting a lucrative line of practice to accept a seat on the bench would have a tendency to throw the administration of justice into hands less able and less well qualified to conduct it with utility and dignity. In the present circumstances of this country and in those in which it is likely to be for a long time to come, the disadvantages on this score would be greater than they may at first sight appear; but it must be confessed that they are far inferior to those which present themselves under the other aspects of the subject.

Upon the whole, there can be no room to doubt that the convention acted wisely in copying from the models of those constitutions which have established *good behavior* as the tenure of their judicial offices, in point of duration; and that so far from being blamable on this account, their plan would have been inexcusably defective if it had wanted this important feature of good government. The experience of Great Britain affords an illustrious comment on the excellence of the institution.

Anti-Federalist Responses: Arguments Against the Adoption of the Constitution

When the Constitutional Convention of 1787 produced the new Constitution, many thoughtful, patriotic people from all over the country opposed its adoption. These Anti-Federalists, as they were known, had a number of objections to the Constitution. Five of their most significant objections were these: (1) The new Constitution was a document written by and for the primary benefit of a wealthy and powerful aristocracy. (2) The Constitution lacked a bill of rights. (3) The Constitutional Convention was not authorized to do anything but amend the Articles of Confederation; therefore, the Constitution was an illegal document. (4) States would be wholly subordinate to the new National Government and lose their sovereignty. (5) The powers given to the new United States Government were so extensive as to lead inevitably to tyranny and despotism. The following documents provide a sampling of Anti-Federalist arguments.

Richard Henry Lee

Lee from Virginia wrote the best-known Anti-Federalist essays of the time, "Letters from the Federal Farmer to the Republican." These excerpts are from these letters written in October 1887.

The present moment discovers a new face in our affairs. Our object has been all along to reform our federal system and to strengthen our governments—to establish peace, order, and justice in the community—but a new object now presents. The plan of government now proposed is evidently calculated totally to change, in time, our condition as a people. Instead of being thirteen republics under a federal head, it is clearly designed to make us one consolidated government. . . . This consolidation of the states has been the object of several men in this country for some time past. Whether such a change can ever be effected, in any manner; whether it can be effected without convulsions and civil wars; whether such a change will not totally destroy the liberties of this country, time only can determine. . . .

The Confederation was formed when great confidence was placed in the voluntary exertions of individuals and of the respective states; and the framers of it, to guard against usurpation, so limited and checked the powers that, in many respects, they are inadequate to the exigencies of the Union. We find, therefore, members of Congress urging alterations in the federal system almost as soon as it was adopted. . . .

We expected too much from the return of peace, and, of course, we have been disappointed. Our governments have been new and unsettled; and several legislature, [by their actions] . . . have given just cause of uneasiness. . . .

The conduct of several legislatures touching paper-money and tender laws has prepared many honest men for changes in government, which otherwise they would not have thought of—when by the evils, on the one hand, and by the secret instigations of artful men, on the other, the minds of men were become sufficiently uneasy, a bold step was taken, which is usually followed by a revolution or a civil war. A general convention for mere commercial purposes was moved for—the authors of this measure saw that the people's attention was turned solely to the amendment of the federal system; and that, had the idea of a total change been started, probably no state would have appointed members to the Convention. The idea of destroying, ultimately, the state government and forming one consolidated system could not have been admitted. A convention, therefore, merely for vesting in Congress power to regulate trade was proposed. . . .

The plan proposed appears to be partly federal, but principally, however, calculated ultimately to make the states one consolidated government.

The first interesting question therefore suggested is how far the states can be consolidated into one entire government on free principles. In considering this question, extensive objects are to be taken into view, and important changes in the forms of government to be carefully attended to in all their consequences. The happiness of the people at large must be the great object with every honest statesman, and he will direct every movement to this point. If we are so situated as a people as not to be able to enjoy equal happiness and advantages under one government, the consolidation of the states cannot be admitted.

* * *

There are certain unalienable and fundamental rights, which in forming the social compact ought to be explicitly ascertained and fixed. A free and enlightened people, in forming this compact, will not resign all their rights to those who govern, and they will fix limits [a bill of rights] to their legislators and rulers, which will soon be plainly seen by those who are governed, as well as by those who govern; and the latter will know they cannot be passed unperceived by the former and without giving a general alarm. These rights should be made the basis of every constitution; and if a people be so situated, or have such different opinions, that they cannot agree in ascertaining and fixing them, it is a very strong argument against their attempting to form one entire society, to live under one system of laws only.

* * *

It may also be worthy our examination how far the provision for amending this plan, when it shall be adopted, is of any importance. No measures can be taken toward amendments unless two-thirds of the Congress, or two-thirds of the legislature of the several states, shall agree. While power is in the hands of the people, or democratic part of the community, more especially as at present, it is easy, according to the general course of human affairs, for the few influential men in the community to obtain conventions, alterations in government, and to persuade the common people that they may change for the better, and to get from them a part of the power. But when power is once transferred from the many to the few, all changes become extremely difficult; the government in this case being beneficial to the few, they will be exceedingly artful and adroit in preventing any measures which may lead to a change; and nothing will produce it but great exertions and severe struggles on the part of the common people. Every man of reflection must see that the change now proposed is a transfer of power from the many to the few, and the probability is the artful and ever active aristocracy will prevent all peaceful measures for changes, unless when they shall discover some favorable moment to increase their own influence.

* * *

It is true there may be danger in delay; but there is danger in adopting the system in its present form. And I see the danger in either case will arise principally from the conduct and views of two very unprincipled parties in the United States—two fires, between which the honest and substantial people have long found themselves situated. One party is composed of little insurgents, men in debt, who want no law and who want a share of the property of others—these are called levelers, Shayites, etc. The other party is composed of a few but more dangerous men, with their servile dependents; these avariciously grasp at all power and property. You may discover in all the actions of these men an evident dislike to free and equal government, and they will go systematically to work to change, essentially, the forms of government in this country—these are called aristocrats. . . .

. . . The fact is, these aristocrats support and hasten the adoption of the proposed Constitution merely because they think it is a stepping-stone to their favorite object. I think I am well-founded in this idea; I think the general politics of these men support it, as well as the common observation among them that the proffered plan is the best that can be got at present; it will do for a few years, and lead to something better. . . .

Luther Martin

Martin, the leading Anti-Federalist from Maryland, attended the Constitutional Convention as a delegate. In this excerpt from a speech before the Maryland State legislature on November 29, 1787, he defends his decision to leave the Convention before its work was finished.

It was the states as states, by their representatives in Congress, that formed the Articles of Confederation; it was the states as states, by their legislatures, who ratified those Articles; and it was there established and provided that the states as states (that is, by their legislatures) should agree to any alterations that should hereafter be proposed in the federal government, before they should be binding; and any alterations agreed to in any other manner cannot release the states from the obligation they are under to each other by virtue of the original Articles of Confederation. The people of the different states never made any objection to the manner in which the Articles of Confederation were formed or ratified, or to the mode by which alterations were to be made in that government—with the rights of their respective states they wished not to interfere. Nor do I believe the people, in their individual capacity, would ever have expected or desired to have been appealed to on the present occasion, in violation of the rights of their respective states, if the favorers of the proposed Constitution, imagining they had a better chance of forcing it to be adopted by a hasty appeal to the people at large (who could not be so good judges of the dangerous consequence), had not insisted upon this mode . . . .

It was also my opinion that, upon principles of sound policy, the agreement or disagreement to the proposed system ought to have been by the state legislatures; in which case, let the event have been what it would, there would have been but little prospect of the public peace being disturbed thereby; whereas the attempt to force down this system, although Congress and the respective state legislatures should disapprove, by appealing to the people and to procure its establishment in a manner totally unconstitutional, has a tendency to set the state governments and their subjects at variance with each other, to lessen the obligations of government, to weaken the bands of society, to introduce anarchy and confusion, and to light the torch of discord and civil war throughout this continent. All these considerations weighed with me most forcibly against giving my assent to the mode by which it is resolved that this system is to be ratified, and were urged by me in opposition to the measure.

. . . [A] great portion of that time which ought to have been devoted calmly and impartially to consider what alterations in our federal government would be most likely to procure and preserve the happiness of the Union was employed in a violent struggle on the one side to obtain all power and dominion in their own hands, and on the other to prevent it; and that the aggrandizement of particular states, and particular individuals, appears to have been much more the subject sought after than the welfare of our country . . . .

When I took my seat in the Convention, I found them attempting to bring forward a system which, I was sure, never had entered into the contemplation of those I had the honor to represent, and which, upon the fullest consideration, I considered not only injurious to the interest and rights of this state but also incompatible with the political happiness and freedom of the states in general. From that time until my business compelled me to leave the Convention, I gave it every possible opposition, in every stage of its progression. I opposed the system there with the same explicit frankness with which I have here given you a history of our proceedings, an account of my own conduct, which in a particular manner I consider you as having a right to know. While there, I endeavored to act as became a freeman and the delegate of a free state. Should my conduct obtain the approbation of those who appointed me, I will not deny it would afford me satisfaction; but to me that approbation was at most no more than a secondary consideration—my first was to deserve it. Left to myself to act according to the best of my discretion, my conduct should have been the same had I been even sure your censure would have been my only reward, since I hold it sacredly my duty to dash the cup of poison, if possible, from the hand of a state or an individual, however anxious the one or the other might be to swallow it . . . .

William Findley, Robert Whitehill, and John Smilie

Findley, Whitehill, and Smilie—who were delegates to the Pennsylvania State convention—believed that they and other opponents of the Constitution were prevented from expressing their views because of the political maneuverings of the Federalists. This excerpt is from "The Address and Reasons of Dissent of the Minority of the Convention of the State of Pennsylvania to their Constituents," which the three men published in the *Pennsylvania Packet and Daily Advertiser* on December 18, 1787.

The Continental Convention met in the city of Philadelphia at the time appointed. It was composed of some men of excellent character; of others who were more remarkable for their ambition and cunning than their patriotism; and of some who had been opponents to the independence of the United States. The delegates from Pennsylvania were, six of them, uniform and decided opponents to the constitution of the commonwealth [the Articles of Confederation]. The convention sat upward of four months. The doors were kept shut, and the members brought under the most solemn engagements of secrecy. Some of those who opposed their going so far beyond their powers, retired, hopeless, from the convention; others had the firmness to refuse signing the plan altogether; and many who did sign it, did it not as a system they wholly approved but as the best that could be then obtained; and notwithstanding the time spent on this subject, it is agreed on all hands to be a work of haste and accommodation. . . .

Our objections are comprised under three general heads of dissent, viz.:

We dissent, first, because it is the opinion of the most celebrated writers on government, and confirmed by uniform experience, that a very extensive territory cannot be governed on the principles of freedom otherwise than by a confederation of republics, possessing all the powers of internal government but united in the management of their general and foreign concerns. . . .

We dissent, secondly, because the powers vested in Congress by this Constitution must necessarily annihilate and absorb the legislative, executive, and judicial powers of the several states, and produce from their ruins one consolidated government, which from the nature of things will be *an iron-handed despotism*, as nothing short of the supremacy of despotic sway could connect and govern these United States under one government.

As the truth of this position is of such decisive importance, it ought to be fully investigated, and if it is founded, to be clearly ascertained; for, should it be demonstrated that the powers vested by this Constitution in Congress will have such an effect as necessarily to produce one consolidated government, the question then will be reduced to this short issue, viz.: whether satiated with the blessings of liberty, whether repenting of the folly of so recently asserting their unalienable rights against foreign despots at the expense of so much blood and treasure, and such painful and arduous struggles, the people of America are now willing to resign every privilege of freemen, and submit to the dominion of an absolute government that will embrace all America in one chain of despotism; or whether they will, with virtuous indignation, spurn at the shackles prepared for them, and confirm their liberties by a conduct becoming freemen. . . .

We dissent, thirdly, because if it were practicable to govern so extensive a territory as these United States include, on the plan of a consolidated government, consistent with the principles of liberty and the happiness of the people, yet the construction of this Constitution is not calculated to attain the object; for independent of the nature of the case, it would of itself necessarily produce a despotism, and that not by the usual gradations but with the celerity that has hitherto only attended revolutions effected by the sword.

To establish the truth of this position, a cursory investigation of the principles and form of this Constitution will suffice.

The first consideration that this review suggests is the omission of a Bill of Rights ascertaining and fundamentally establishing those unalienable and personal rights of men, without the full, free, and secure enjoyment of which there can be no liberty, and over which it is not necessary for a good government to have the control—the principal of which are the rights of conscience, personal liberty by the clear and unequivocal establishment of the writ of habeas corpus, jury trial in criminal and civil cases, by an impartial jury of the vicinage or county, with the common law proceedings for the safety of the accused in criminal prosecutions; and the liberty of the press, that scourge of tyrants, and the grand bulwark of every other liberty and privilege. The stipulations heretofore made in favor of them in the state constitutions are entirely superseded by this Constitution. . . .

Anonymous

This excerpt is from an essay that appeared in the *Boston Gazette and the Country Journal* on November 26, 1787. Its anonymous author used the misleading pen name, "A Federalist."

I am pleased to see a spirit of inquiry burst the band of constraint upon the subject of the new plan for consolidating the governments of the United States as recommended by the late Convention. If it is suitable to the genius and habits of the citizens of these states, it will bear the strictest scrutiny. The people are the grand inquest who have a right to judge of its merits. The hideous demon of aristocracy has hitherto had so much influence as to bar the channels of investigation, preclude the people from inquiry, and extinguish every spark of liberal information of its qualities.

. . . Those furious zealots who are for cramming it [the Constitution] down the throats of the people without allowing them either time or opportunity to scan or weigh it in the balance of their understandings bear the same marks in their features as those who have been long wishing to erect an aristocracy in this commonwealth. Their menacing cry is for a rigid government; it matters little to them of what kind, provided it answers that description.

As the plan now offered comes something near their wishes, and is the most consonant to their views of any they can hope for, they come boldly forward and demand its adoption. They brand with infamy every man who is not as determined and zealous in its favor as themselves. They cry aloud the whole must be swallowed or none at all, thinking thereby to preclude any amendment; they are afraid of having it abated of its present rigid aspect. They have striven to overawe or seduce printers to stifle and obstruct a free discussion, and have endeavored to hasten it to a decision before the people can duly reflect upon its properties.

In order to deceive them, they incessantly declare that none can discover any defect in the system but bankrupts who wish no government, and officers of the present government who fear to lose a part of their power. These zealous partisans may injure their own cause, and endanger the public tranquility by impeding a proper inquiry; the people may suspect the whole to be a dangerous plan, from such covered and designing schemes to enforce it upon them. Compulsive or treacherous measures to establish any government whatever will always excite jealousy among a free people. Better remain single and alone than blindly adopt whatever a few individuals shall demand, be they ever so wise. I had rather be a free citizen of the small republic of Massachusetts than an oppressed subject of the great American empire. Let all act understandingly or not at all. . . .

It will first be allowed that many undesigning citizens may wish its adoption from the best motives, but these are modest and silent when compared to the greater number who endeavor to suppress all attempts for investigation. These violent partisans are for having the people gulp down the gilded pill blindfolded, whole and without any qualification whatever. These consist generally of the noble order of Cincinnatus, holders of public securities, men of great wealth and expectations of public office, bankers and lawyers. These, with their train of dependents, form the aristocratic combination. The lawyers in particular keep up an incessant declamation for its adoption; like greedy gudgeons they long to satiate their voracious stomachs with the golden bait. The numerous tribunals to be erected by the new plan of consolidated empire will find employment for ten times their present numbers; these are the loaves and fishes for which they hunger. They will probably find it suited to their habits, if not to the habits of the people. . . .

Articles of Confederation

In force from March 1, 1781 to March 4, 1789

To all to whom these Presents shall come, we the undersigned Delegates of the States affixed to our Names send greeting. Whereas the Delegates of the United States of America in Congress assembled did on the fifteenth day of November in the Year of our Lord One Thousand Seven Hundred and Seventy seven, and in the Second Year of the Independence of America agree to certain articles of Confederation an perpetual Union between the States of Newhampshire, Massachusetts-bay, Rhode-island and Providence Plantations, Connecticut, New York, New Jersey, Pennsylvania, Delaware, Maryland, Virginia, North-Carolina, South-Carolina and Georgia in the Words following, viz. "Articles of Confederation and perpetual Union between the states of Newhampshire, Massachusetts-bay, Rhode-island and Providence Plantations, Connecticut, New-York, New-Jersey, Pennsylvania, Delaware, Maryland, Virginia, North-Carolina, South-Carolina and Georgia.

[ART. I.] The Stile of this confederacy shall be "The United States of America."

[ART. II.] Each state retains its sovereignty, freedom and independence, and every Power, Jurisdiction and right, which is not by this confederation expressly delegated to the United States, in Congress assembled.

[ART. III.] The said states hereby severally enter into a firm league of friendship with each other, for their common defence, the security of their Liberties, and their mutual and general welfare, binding themselves to assist each other, against all force offered to, or attacks made upon them, or any of them, on account of religion, sovereignty, trade, or any other pretence whatever.

[ART. IV.] The better to secure and perpetuate mutual friendship and intercourse among the people of the different states in this union, the free inhabitants of each of these states, paupers, vagabonds and fugitives from Justice excepted, shall be entitled to all privileges and immunities of free citizens in the several states; and the people of each state shall have free ingress and regress to and from any other state, and shall enjoy therein all the privileges of trade and commerce, subject to the same duties, impositions and restrictions as the inhabitants thereof respectively, provided that such restriction shall not extend so far as to prevent the removal of property imported into any state, to any other state of which the Owner is an inhabitant; provided also that no imposition, duties or restriction shall be laid by any state, on the property of the united states, or either of them.

If any Person guilty of, or charged with treason, felony, or other high misdemeanor in any state, shall flee from Justice, and be found in any of the united states, he shall upon demand of the Governor or executive power, of the state from which he fled, be delivered up and removed to the state having jurisdiction of his offence.

Full faith and credit shall be given in each of these states to the records, acts and judicial proceedings of the courts and magistrates of every other state.

[ART. V.] For the more convenient management of the general interests of the united states, delegates shall be annually appointed in such manner as the legislature of each state shall direct, to meet in Congress on the first Monday in November, in every year, with a power reserved to each state, to recall its delegates, or any of them, at any time within the year, and to send others in their stead, for the remainder of the Year.

No state shall be represented in Congress by less than two, nor by more than seven Members; and no person shall be capable of being a delegate for more than three years in any term of six years; nor shall any person, being a delegate, be capable of holding any office under the united states, for which he, or another for his benefit receives any salary, fees or emolument of any kind.

Each state shall maintain its own delegates in a meeting of the states, and while they act as members of the committee of the states.

In determining questions in the united states, in Congress assembled, each state shall have one vote.

Freedom of speech and debate in Congress shall not be impeached or questioned in any Court, or place out of Congress, and the members of congress shall be protected in their persons from arrests and imprisonments, during the time of their going to and from, and attendance on congress, except for treason, felony, or breach of the peace.

[ART. VI.] No state without the Consent of the united states in congress assembled, shall send any embassy to, or receive any embassy from, or enter into any conference, agreement, or alliance or treaty with any King, prince or state; nor shall any person holding any office of profit or trust under the united states, or any of them, accept of any present, emolument, office or title of any kind whatever from any king, prince or foreign state; nor shall the united states in congress assembled, or any of them, grant any title of nobility.

No two or more states shall enter into any treaty, confederation or alliance whatever between them, without the consent of the united states in congress assembled, specifying accurately the purposes for which the same is to be entered into, and how long it shall continue.

No state shall lay any imposts or duties, which may interfere with any stipulations in treaties, entered into by the united states in congress assembled, with any king, prince or state, in pursuance of any treaties already proposed by congress, to the courts of France and Spain.

No vessels of war shall be kept up in time of peace by any state, except such number only, as shall be deemed necessary by the united states in congress assembled, for the defence of such state, or its trade; nor shall any body of forces be kept up by any state, in time of peace, except such number only, as in the judgment of the united states, in congress assembled, shall be deemed requisite to garrison the forts necessary for the defence of such state; but every state shall always keep up a well regulated and disciplined militia, sufficiently armed and accounted, and shall provide and constantly have ready for use, in public stores, a due number of field pieces and tents, and a proper quantity of arms, ammunition and camp equipage.

No state shall engage in any war without the consent of the united states in congress assembled, unless such state be actually invaded by enemies, or shall have received certain advice of a resolution being formed by some nation of Indians to invade such state and the danger is so imminent as not to admit of a delay, till the united states in congress assembled can be consulted: nor shall any state grant commissions to any ships or vessels of war, nor letters of marque or reprisal, except it be after a declaration of war by the united states in congress assembled, and then only against the kingdom or state and the subjects thereof, against which war has been so declared, and under such regulations as shall be established by the united states in congress assembled, unless such state be infested by pirates, in which case vessels of war may be fitted out for that occasion, and kept so long as the danger shall continue, or until the united states in congress assembled shall determine otherwise.

[ART. VII.] When land-forces are raised by any state for the common defence, all officers of or under the rank of colonel, shall be appointed by the legislature of each state respectively by whom such forces shall be raised, or in such manner as such state shall direct, and all vacancies shall be filled up by the state which first made the appointment.

[ART. VIII.] All charges of war, and all other expences that shall be incurred for the common defence or general welfare, and allowed by the united states in congress assembled, shall be defrayed out of a common treasury, which shall be supplied by the several states, in proportion to the value of all land within each state, granted to or surveyed for any Person, as such land and the buildings and improvements thereon shall be estimated according to such mode as the united states in congress assembled, shall from time to time direct and appoint. The taxes for paying that proportion shall be laid and levied by the authority and direction of the legislatures of the several states within the time agreed upon by the united states in congress assembled.

[ART. IX.] The united states in congress assembled, shall have the sole and exclusive right and power of determining on peace and war, except in the cases mentioned in the sixth article—of sending and receiving ambassadors—entering into treaties and alliances, provided that no treaty of commerce shall be made whereby the legislative power of the respective states shall be restrained from imposing such imposts and duties on foreigners, as their own people are subjected to, or from prohibiting the exportation or importation of any species of goods or commodities whatsoever—of establishing rules for deciding in all cases, what captures on land or water shall be legal, and in what manner prizes taken by land or naval forces in the service of the united states shall be divided or appropriated.—of granting letters of marque and reprisal in times of peace—appointing courts for the trial of piracies and felonies committed on the high seas and establishing courts for receiving and determining finally appeals in all cases of captures, provided that no member of congress shall be appointed a judge of any of the said courts.

The united states in congress assembled shall also be the last resort on appeal in all disputes and differences now subsisting or that hereafter may arise between two or more states concerning boundary, jurisdiction or any other cause whatever; which authority shall always be exercised in the manner following. Whenever the legislative or executive authority or lawful agent of any state in controversy with another shall present a petition to congress stating the matter in question and praying for a hearing, notice thereof shall be given by order of congress to the legislative or executive authority of the other state in controversy, and a day assigned for the appearance of the parties by their lawful agents, who shall then be directed to appoint by joint consent, commissioners or judges to constitute a court for hearing and determining the matter in question: but if they cannot agree, congress shall name three persons out of each of the united states, and from the list of such persons each party shall alternately strike out one, the petitioners beginning, until the number shall be reduced to thirteen; and from that number not less than seven, nor more than nine names as congress shall direct, shall in the presence of congress be drawn out by lot, and the persons whose names shall be so drawn or any five of them, shall be commissioners or judges, to hear and finally determine the controversy, so always as a major part of the judges who shall hear the cause shall agree in the determination: and if either party shall neglect to attend at the day appointed, without shewing reasons, which congress shall judge sufficient, or being present shall refuse to strike, the congress shall proceed to nominate three persons out of each state, and the secretary of congress shall strike in behalf of such party absent or refusing; and the judgment and sentence of the court to be appointed, in the manner before prescribed, shall be final and conclusive; and if any of the parties shall refuse to submit to the authority of such court, or to appear to defend their claim or cause, the court shall nevertheless proceed to pronounce sentence, or judgment, which shall in like manner be final and decisive, the judgment or sentence and other proceedings being in either case transmitted to congress, and lodged among the acts of congress for the security of the parties concerned: provided that every commissioner, before he sits in judgment, shall take an oath to be administered by one of the judges of the supreme or superior court of the state, where the cause shall be tried, "well and truly to hear and determine the matter in question, according to the best of his judgment, without favour, affection or hope of reward:" provided also that no state shall be deprived of territory for the benefit of the united states.

All controversies concerning the private right of soil claimed under different grants of two or more states, whose jurisdictions as they may respect such lands, and the states which passed such grants are adjusted, the said grants or either of them being at the same time claimed to have originated antecedent to such settlement of jurisdiction, shall on the petition of either party to the congress of the united states, be finally determined as near as may be in the same manner as is before prescribed for deciding disputes respecting territorial jurisdiction between different states.

The united states in congress assembled shall also have the sole and exclusive right and power of regulating the alloy and value of coin struck by their own authority, or by that of the respective states—fixing the standard of weights and measures throughout the united states.—regulating the trade and managing all affairs with the Indians, not members of any of the states, provided that the legislative right of any state within its own limits be not infringed or violated—establishing and regulating post-offices from one state to another, throughout all the united states, and exacting such postage on the papers passing thro' the same as may be requisite to defray the expences of the said office-appointing all officers of the land forces, in the service of the united states, excepting regimental officers.—appointing all the officers of the naval forces, and commissioning all officers whatever in the service of the united states—making rules for the government and regulation of the said land and naval forces, and directing their operations.

The united states in congress assembled shall have authority to appoint a committee, to sit in the recess of congress, to be denominated "A Committee of the States," and to consist of one delegate from each state; and to appoint such other committees and civil officers as may be necessary for managing the general affairs of the united states under their direction—to appoint one of their number to preside, provided that no person be allowed to serve in the office of president more than one year in any term of three years; to ascertain the necessary sums of Money to be raised for the service of the united states, and to appropriate and apply the same for defraying the public expences—to borrow money, or emit bills on the credit of the united states, transmitting every half year to the respective states an account of the sums of money so borrowed or emitted,—to build and equip a navy—to agree upon the number of land forces, and to make requisitions from each state for its quota, in proportion to the number of white inhabitants in such state; which requisition shall be binding, and thereupon the legislature of each state shall appoint the regimental officers, raise the men and cloath, arm and equip them in a soldier like manner, at the expence of the united states, and the officers and men so cloathed, armed and equipped shall march to the place appointed, and within the time agreed on by the united states in congress assembled: But if the united states in congress assembled shall, on consideration of circumstances judge proper that any state should not raise men, or should raise a smaller number than its quota, and that any other state should raise a greater number of men than the quota thereof, such extra number shall be raised, officered, cloathed, armed and equipped in the same manner as the quota of such state, unless the legislature of such state shall judge that such extra number cannot be safely spared out of the same, in which case they shall raise officer, cloath, arm and equip as many of such extra number as they judge can be safely spared. And the officers and men so cloathed, armed and equipped, shall march to the place appointed, and within the time agreed on by the united states in congress assembled.

The united states in congress assembled shall never engage in a war, nor grant letters of marque and reprisal in time of peace, nor enter into any treaties or alliances, nor coin money, nor regulate the value thereof, nor ascertain the sums and expences necessary for the defence and welfare of the united states, or any of them, nor emit bills, nor borrow money on the credit of the united states, nor appropriate money, nor agree upon the number of vessels of war, to be built or purchased, or the number of land or sea forces to be raised, nor appoint a commander in chief of the army or navy, unless nine states assent to the same: nor shall a question on any other point, except for adjourning from day to day be determined, unless by the votes of a majority of the united states in congress assembled.

The congress of the united states shall have power to adjourn to any time within the year, and to any place within the united states, so that no period of adjournment be for a longer duration than the space of six Months, and shall publish the Journal of their proceedings monthly, except such parts thereof relating to treaties, alliances or military operations as in their judgment require secresy; and the yeas and nays of the delegates of each state on any question shall be entered on the Journal, when it is desired by any delegate; and the delegates of a state, or any of them, at his or their request shall be furnished with a transcript of the said Journal, except such parts as are above excepted, to lay before the legislatures of the several states.

[Art. X.] The committee of the states, or any nine of them, shall be authorised to execute, in the recess of congress, such of the powers of congress as the united states in congress assembled, by the consent of nine states, shall from time to time think expedient to vest them with; provided that no power be delegated to the said committee, for the exercise of which, by the articles of confederation, the voice of nine states in the congress of the united states assembled is requisite.

[ART. XI.] Canada acceding to this confederation, and joining in the measures of the united states, shall be admitted into, and entitled to all the advantages of this union: but no other colony shall be admitted into the same, unless such admission be agreed to by nine states.

[ART. XII.] All bills of credit emitted, monies borrowed and debts contracted by, or under the authority of congress, before the assembling of the united states, in pursuance of the present confederation, shall be deemed and considered as a charge against the united states, for payment and satisfaction whereof the said united states, and the public faith are hereby solemnly pledged.

[ART. XIII.] Every state shall abide by the determinations of the united states in congress assembled, on all questions which by this confederation are submitted to them. And the Articles of this confederation shall be inviolably observed by every state, and the union shall be perpetual; nor shall any alteration at any time hereafter be made in any of them; unless such alteration be agreed to in a congress of the united states, and be afterwards confirmed by the legislatures of every state.

And whereas it hath pleased the Great Governor of the World to incline the hearts of the legislatures we respectively represent in congress, to approve of, and to authorize us to ratify the said articles of confederation and perpetual union. Know ye that we the undersigned delegates, by virtue of the power and authority to us given for that purpose, do by these presents, in the name and in behalf of our respective constituents, fully and entirely ratify and confirm each and every of the said articles of confederation and perpetual union, and all and singular the matters and things therein contained: And we do further solemnly plight and engage the faith of our respective constituents, that they shall abide by the determinations of the united states in congress assembled, on all questions, which by the said confederation are submitted to them. And that the articles thereof shall be inviolably observed by the states we respectively represent, and that the union shall be perpetual. In Witness whereof we have hereunto set our hands in Congress. Done at Philadelphia in the state of Pennsylvania the ninth Day of July in the Year of our Lord one Thousand seven Hundred and Seventy-eight, and in the third year of the independence of America.

JOSIAH BARTLETT
JOHN WENTWORTH Junr
August 8th 1778
On the part & behalf of
the State of New Hampshire

JOHN HANCOCK
SAMUEL ADAMS
ELBRIDGE GERRY
FRANCIS DANA
JAMES LOVELL
SAMUEL HOLTEN
On the part and behalf of
the State of Massachusetts Bay

WILLIAM ELLERY
HENRY MARCHANT
JOHN COLLINS
On the part and behalf
of the State of Rhode-Island
and Providence Plantations

ROGER SHERMAN
SAMUEL HUNTINGTON
OLIVER WOLCOTT
TITUS HOSMER
ANDREW ADAMS
On the part and behalf of
the State of Connecticut

JA[S] DUANE
FRA[S] LEWIS
W[M] DUER.
GOUV MORRIS
On the Part and Behalf of
the State of New York

JNO WITHERSPOON
NATH[L] SCUDDER
On the Part and in Behalf of
the State of New Jersey.
Nov[r] 26, 1778.—

ROB[T] MORRIS
DANIEL ROBERDEAU
JON[A] BAYARD SMITH.
WILLIAM CLINGAN
JOSEPH REED
22[d] July 1778
On the part and behalf of
the State of Pennsylvania

THO M:KEAN
Feby 12 1779
JOHN DICKINSON
May 5th 1779
NICHOLAS VAN DYKE,
On the part & behalf of
the State of Delaware

JOHN HANSON
March 1 1781
DANIEL CARROLL d[o]
On the part and behalf
of the State of Maryland

RICHARD HENRY LEE
JOHN BANISTER
THOMAS ADAMS
JN[O] HARVIE
FRANCIS LIGHTFOOT LEE
On the Part and Behalf of
the State of Virginia

JOHN PENN
July 21st 1778
CORN[S] HARNETT
JN[O] WILLIAMS
On the part and Behalf
of the State of N[o] Carolina

HENRY LAURENS
WILLIAM HENRY DRAYTON
JN[O] MATHEWS
RICH[D] HUTSON.
THO[S] HEYWARD Jun[r]
On the part & behalf of
the State of South-Carolina

JN[O] WALTON
24th July 1778
EDW[D] TELFAIR.
EDW[D] LANGWORTHY
On the part and behalf of
the State of Georgia

The Emancipation Proclamation

Issued by President Abraham Lincoln on January 1, 1863.

Whereas on the 22d day of September, A.D. 1862, a proclamation was issued by the President of the United States, containing, among other things, the following, to wit:

"That on the 1st day of January, A.D. 1863, all persons held as slaves within any State or designated part of a State the people whereof shall then be in rebellion against the United States shall be then, thenceforward, and forever free; and the Executive Government of the United States, including the military and naval authority thereof, will recognize and maintain the freedom of such persons and will do no act or acts to repress such persons, or any of them, in any efforts they may make for their actual freedom.

"That the executive will on the 1st day of January aforesaid, by proclamation, designate the States and parts of States, if any, in which the people thereof, respectively, shall then be in rebellion against the United States; and the fact that any State or the people thereof shall on that day be in good faith represented in the Congress of the United States by members chosen thereto at elections wherein a majority of the qualified voters of such States shall have participated shall, in the absence of strong countervailing testimony, be deemed conclusive evidence that such State and the people thereof are not then in rebellion against the United States."

Now, therefore, I, Abraham Lincoln, President of the United States, by virtue of the power in me vested as Commander-in-Chief of the Army and Navy of the United States in time of actual armed rebellion against the authority and government of the United States, and as a fit and necessary war measure for suppressing said rebellion, do, on this 1st day of January, A.D. 1863, and in accordance with my purpose so to do, publicly proclaimed for the full period of one hundred days from the first day above mentioned, order and designate as the States and parts of States wherein the people thereof, respectively, are this day in rebellion against the United States the following, to wit:

Arkansas, Texas, Louisiana (except the parishes of St. Bernard, Plaquemines, Jefferson, St. John, St. Charles, St. James, Ascension, Assumption, Terrebonne, Lafourche, St. Mary, St. Martin, and Orleans, including the city of New Orleans), Mississippi, Alabama, Florida, Georgia, South Carolina, North Carolina, and Virginia (except the forty-eight counties designated as West Virginia, and also the counties of Berkeley, Accomac, Northhampton, Elizabeth City, York, Princess Anne, and Norfolk, including the cities of Norfolk and Portsmouth), and which excepted parts are for the present left precisely as if this proclamation were not issued.

And by virtue of the power and for the purpose aforesaid, I do order and declare that all persons held as slaves within said designated States and parts of States are, and henceforward shall be, free; and that the Executive Government of the United States, including the military and naval authorities thereof, will recognize and maintain the freedom of said persons.

And I hereby enjoin upon the people so declared to be free to abstain from all violence, unless in necessary self-defense; and I recommend to them that, in all cases when allowed, they labor faithfully for reasonable wages.

And I further declare and make known that such persons of suitable condition will be received into the armed service of the United States to garrison forts, positions, stations, and other places, and to man vessels of all sorts in said service.

And upon this act, sincerely believed to be an act of justice, warranted by the Constitution upon military necessity, I invoke the considerate judgment of mankind and the gracious favor of Almighty God.

Supreme Court Glossary

Cases discussed in "Debating Key Issues" appear without constitutional references.

Baker v. *Carr,* 1962

(14th Amendment, Equal Protection Clause) Rapid population growth in Nashville and reluctance of the rural-dominated Tennessee legislature to redraw State legislature districts led Mayor Baker of Nashville to ask for federal court help. The federal district court refused to enter the "political thicket" of State legislature redistricting and the case was appealed. The Court directed a trial to be held in a Tennessee federal court. The case led to the 1964 *Westberry* decision, which created the "one man, one vote" equal representation concept.

Bethel School District #403 v. *Fraser,* 1986

(1st Amendment, freedom of speech) A high school student gave a sexually suggestive political speech at a high school assembly to elect student officers. The school administration strongly disciplined the student, Fraser, who argued that school rules unfairly limited his freedom of political speech. Fraser's view was upheld in State court. Oregon appealed to the Supreme Court, which found that although ". . . the use of an offensive form of expression may not be prohibited when an adult speaker uses it to make a political point . . . the same latitude of expression is not permitted to children in a public school."

Betts v. *Brady,* 1942

(6th Amendment, right to counsel) A Maryland man named Betts was unable to pay for an attorney but was denied court-appointed counsel under Maryland law. Defending himself, he was found guilty. When he appealed, the Court further developed the "special circumstances" rule it had begun in 1932, saying that although "right to counsel" was not absolutely guaranteed by the 6th Amendment in State court trials, there were some "special circumstances" where counsel was required. The Court preferred, over the next 20 years, to review the "right to counsel" cases on a case-by-case basis. Overturned by *Gideon*, 1963.

Bob Jones University v. *United States,* 1983

(14th Amendment in conflict with 1st Amendment) Bob Jones University, a private school, denied admission to applicants in an interracial marriage or who "espouse" interracial marriage or dating. The Internal Revenue Service then denied tax exempt status to the school because of racial discrimination. The university appealed, claiming that their policy was based on the Bible. The Court upheld the IRS ruling, stating that ". . . (T)he Government has a fundamental overriding interest in eradicating racial discrimination in education."

Brown v. *Board of Education of Topeka,* 1954

(14th Amendment, Equal Protection Clause) Probably no 20th century Supreme Court decision so deeply stirred and changed life in the United States as *Brown*. A 10-year-old Topeka girl was not permitted to attend her neighborhood school because she was an African American. The Court heard arguments about whether segregation itself was a violation of the Equal Protection Clause and found that it was, commenting that "in the field of public education the doctrine of 'separate but equal' has no place. . . . Segregation is a denial of the equal protection of the laws." The decision overturned *Plessy*, 1896.

California v. *Greenwood,* 1988

(4th Amendment, illegal evidence) Acting on a tip that Billy Greenwood was selling narcotics, police examined trash bags that had been picked up from Greenwood's house. Items associated with drug use were found in the garbage and were listed in the application for a search warrant. The subsequent search revealed further evidence that was used in a trial to obtain a conviction. When Greenwood appealed the "warrantless search," the Court said that garbage bags left in the street are accessible to "criminals, children, scavengers, snoops, and other members of the public." Greenwood could not reasonably have expected that the contents of the garbage would remain private. The evidence was admissible.

The Civil Rights Cases, 1883

(14th Amendment, Equal Protection Clause) The Civil Rights Acts of 1875 included punishments for businesses that practiced discrimination. The Court ruled on a number of cases involving the Acts in 1883, finding that the Constitution, "while prohibiting discrimination by governments, made no provisions . . . for acts of racial discrimination by private individuals." The decision limited the impact of the Equal Protection Clause, giving tacit approval for segregation in the private sector.

Dennis v. *United States,* 1951

(1st Amendment, freedom of speech) The Smith Act of 1940 made it a crime for any person to work for the violent overthrow of the United States in peacetime or war. Eleven Communist party leaders, including Dennis, had been convicted of violating the Smith Act, and they appealed. The Court upheld the Act. Much modified by later decisions, the Dennis case focused on anti-government speech as an area of controversy.

Dred Scott v. *Sanford*, 1857

(6th Amendment, individual rights) This decision upheld property rights over human rights by saying that Dred Scott, a slave, could not become a free man just because he had traveled in "free soil" States with his master. A badly divided nation was further fragmented by the decision. "Free soil" federal laws and the Missouri Compromise line of 1820 were held unconstitutional because they deprived a slave owner of the right to his "property" without just compensation. This narrow reading of the Constitution, a landmark case of the Court, was most clearly stated by Chief Justice Roger B. Taney, a States' rights advocate.

Edwards v. *South Carolina*, 1963

(1st Amendment, freedom of speech and assembly) A group of mostly African-American civil rights activists held a rally at the South Carolina State Capitol, protesting segregation. A hostile crowd gathered and the rally leaders were arrested and convicted for "breach of the peace." The Court overturned the convictions, saying that "The 14th Amendment does not permit a State to make criminal the peaceful expression of unpopular views."

Engel v. *Vitale*, 1962

(1st Amendment, Establishment Clause) The public school Regents of New York required the recitation of a 22-word nonsectarian prayer at the beginning of each school. A group of parents filed suit against the required prayer, claiming it violated their 1st Amendment rights. The Court found New York's action to be unconstitutional, observing, "There can be no doubt that . . . the Regents' prayer is a religious activity. . . ."

Escobedo v. *Illinois*, 1964

(6th Amendment, right to counsel) In a case involving a murder confession by a person known to Chicago-area police and who was not afforded counsel while under interrogation, the Court extended the "exclusionary rule" to illegal confessions in State court proceedings. Carefully defining an "Escobedo Rule," the Court said, "where . . . the investigation is no longer a general inquiry . . . but has begun to focus on a particular subject . . . (and where) the suspect has been taken into custody . . . the suspect has requested . . . his lawyer, and the police have not . . . warned him of his right to remain silent, the accused has been denied . . . counsel in violation of the 6th Amendment."

Everson v. *Board of Education*, 1947

(1st Amendment, Establishment Clause) In a case known as "the New Jersey School Bus Case," the Court considered the use of public funds for the operation of school buses in New Jersey, including buses carrying students to parochial schools. The Court permitted New Jersey to continue the payments, saying that the aid to children was not governmental support for religion. The decision, however, strongly stated that the "wall of separation of church and state" must be kept "high and impregnable." This was the first clear incorporation of 1st Amendment limits on States.

Ex Parte Milligan, 1866

(Article II, executive powers) An Indiana man was arrested, treated as a prisoner of war, and imprisoned by a military court during the Civil War under presidential order. He claimed that his rights to a fair trial were interfered with and that military courts had no authority outside of "conquered territory." He was released because "the Constitution . . . is a law for rulers and people, equally in war and peace, and covers . . . all men, at all times, and under all circumstances." The Court held that presidential powers to suspend the writ of *habeas corpus* in time of war did not extend to creating another court system run by the military.

Feiner v. *New York*, 1951

Decision: The Court upheld the disorderly conduct conviction of Feiner, observing that "it is one thing to say that the police cannot be used as an instrument of suppression of unpopular views, and another to say that . . . they are powerless to prevent a breach of the peace." Free speech, therefore, may be limited when a clear and present danger exists. (See "Debating Key Issues" feature on page 137.)

Furman v. *Georgia*, 1972

(8th Amendment, capital punishment) Three different death penalty cases, including *Furman*, raised the question of racial imbalances in the use of death sentences by State courts. Furman had been convicted and sentenced to death in Georgia. In deciding to overturn existing State death-penalty laws, the Court noted that there was an "apparent arbitrariness of the use of the sentence. . . ." Many States rewrote their death-penalty statutes and these were generally upheld in *Gregg* v. *Georgia*, 1976.

Gibbons v. *Ogden*, 1824

(Article I, Section 8, Commerce Clause) This decision involved a careful examination of the power of Congress to "regulate interstate commerce." Aaron Ogden's exclusive New York ferry license gave him the right to operate steamboats to and from New York. He said that Thomas Gibbon's federal "coasting license" did not include "landing rights" in New York City. Federal and State regulation of commerce conflicted. The Court strengthened the power of the United States to regulate any interstate business relationship. Federal regulation of television, pipelines, and banking are all based on *Gibbons.*

Gideon v. *Wainwright*, 1963

Decision: Gideon won a new trial and was found not guilty with the help of a court-appointed attorney. The "Gideon Rule" upheld the 6th Amendment's guarantee of counsel for all poor persons facing a felony charge, a further incorporation of Bill of Rights guarantees into State constitutions. (See "Debating Key Issues" feature on page 527.)

Gitlow v. *New York*, 1925

(1st Amendment, freedom of speech) For the first time, the Court considered whether the 1st and 14th amendments had influence on State laws. The case, involving "criminal anarchy" under New York law, was the first consideration of what came to be known as the "incorporation" doctrine, under which, it was argued, the provisions of the 1st Amendment were "incorporated" by the 14th Amendment. Although New York law was not overruled in the case, the decision clearly indicated that the Supreme Court could make such a ruling. Another important incorporation case is *Powell* v. *Alabama*, 1932.

Gregg v. *Georgia*, 1976

Decision: The Court upheld the Georgia death sentence, finding that it did not violate the cruel and unusual punishment clause of the 8th Amendment. The Court stated for the first time that "punishment of death does not invariably violate the Constitution." (See "Debating Key Issues" feature on page 64.)

Griswold v. *Connecticut*, 1965

(14th Amendment, Due Process Clause) A Connecticut law forbade the use of "any drug, medicinal article, or instrument for the purpose of preventing conception." Griswold, director of Planned Parenthood in New Haven, was arrested for counseling married persons and after conviction, appealed. The Court overturned the Connecticut law, saying that "various guarantees (of the Constitution) create zones of privacy . . ." and questioning, ". . . would we allow the police to search the sacred precincts of marital bedrooms . . . ?" The decision is significant for raising for more careful inspection the concept of "unenumerated rights" in the 9th Amendment, later central to *Roe*, 1973.

Hazelwood v. *Kuhlmeier*, 1988

Decision: The Court upheld the principal's action because the school official acted as the publisher of the newspaper. "1st Amendment rights of students . . . are not automatically coextensive with the rights of adults in other settings. . . ." School officials had full control over school-sponsored activities "so long as their actions are reasonably related to legitimate pedagogical concerns. . . ." (See "Debating Key Issues" feature on page 39.)

Heart of Atlanta Motel v. *United States*, 1964

Decision: The Court upheld the law, saying, "If it is interstate commerce that feels the pinch, it does not matter how 'local' the operation which applies the squeeze. . . . The power of Congress to promote interstate commerce also includes the power to relate the local incidents thereof, including local activities . . . which have a substantial and harmful effect upon that commerce." Segregation by race of private facilities engaged in interstate commerce was found unconstitutional. (See "Debating Key Issues" feature on page 274.)

In Re Gault, 1967

(14th Amendment, Due Process Clause) Prior to the Gault case, proceedings against juvenile offenders were generally handled as "family law," not "criminal law" and provided few due process guarantees. Gerald Gault was assigned to six years in a State juvenile detention facility for an alleged obscene phone call. He was not provided counsel and not permitted to confront or cross-examine the principal witness. The Court overturned the juvenile proceedings and required that States provide juveniles "some of the due process guarantees of adults," including a right to a phone call, to counsel, to cross-examine, to confront their accuser, and to be advised of their right to silence.

Island Trees School District v. *Pico*, 1982

(1st Amendment, freedom of speech) A number of books were removed by the school board from the library at Island Trees High School, New York. When a group of students sued to have the books returned, the case reached the Supreme Court. The Court reversed the decision of the school board, saying that though school boards have "comprehensive power to manage local schools, their discretion must be exercised in a manner which [protects] . . . the 1st Amendment rights of students."

Katz v. *United States*, 1967

(4th Amendment, electronic surveillance) The Court reversed *Olmstead*, 1928, in this decision about wiretapping. Arrested for illegal gambling after using a public phone to transmit information about betting, Katz claimed that the electronic bug, used without a warrant, was a violation of his 4th Amendment rights. The Court expanded the protections of the 4th Amendment, observing that persons, not just property, are protected against illegal searches. Whatever a citizen "seeks to preserve as private, even in an area accessible to the public, may be constitutionally protected."

Korematsu v. *United States*, 1944

Decision: The Court upheld the military order, noting that "pressing public necessity [World War II] may sometimes justify the existence of restrictions which curtail the civil rights of a single racial group . . ." but added that "racial antagonism never can . . . [justify such restrictions]." Only Japanese Americans were interned during World War II. (See "Debating Key Issues" feature on page 369.)

Lemon v. *Kurzman*, 1971

(1st Amendment, Establishment Clause) In overturning State laws regarding aid to church-supported schools in this and a similar Rhode Island case, the Court created the *Lemon* test limiting "excessive entanglement of government with religion." The Court noted that any State law about aid to religion must meet three tests: (1) purpose of the aid must be clearly secular, not religious, (2) its primary effect must neither advance nor inhibit religion, and (3) it must avoid "excessive entanglement of government with religion."

Mapp v. *Ohio,* 1962

(4th and 14th amendments, illegal evidence and Due Process Clause) Admitting evidence gained by illegal searches was permitted by some State constitutions before *Mapp*. Cleveland police raided Ms. Mapp's home without a warrant and found obscene materials. She appealed her conviction, saying that the 4th and 14th amendments protected her against improper police behavior. The Court agreed, extending "exclusionary rule" protections to citizens in State courts, saying that the prohibition against unreasonable searches would be "meaningless" unless evidence gained in such searches was "excluded." This case further developed the concept of "incorporation" begun in *Gitlow*, 1925.

Marbury v. *Madison,* 1803

(Article III, judicial powers) Chief Justice Marshall established "judicial review" as a power of the Supreme Court. After defeat in the 1800 election, President Adams appointed many Federalists to the federal courts, but the commissions were not delivered. New Secretary of State James Madison refused to deliver them. Marbury sued in the Supreme Court. The Court declared a portion of the Judiciary Act of 1789 unconstitutional, thereby declaring the Court's power to find acts of Congress unconstitutional.

Massachusetts v. *Shepperd,* 1984

(4th Amendment, illegal evidence) A search in Massachusetts was based on a warrant issued on an improper form. Shepperd argued that the search was illegal and the evidence was inadmissible under *Mapp*, 1962. Massachusetts argued that the police acted in "good faith," believing that the warrant was correct. The Court agreed with Massachusetts, noting that the "exclusionary rule should not be applied when the officer conducting the search had acted with the reasonable belief that he was following proper procedures." This was the first of several exceptions to the Exclusionary Rule handed down by the Court in the 1980s, including *Nix*, 1984, and *United States* v. *Leon*, 1984.

McCulloch v. *Maryland,* 1819

(Article I, Section 8, Elastic Clause) Called the "Bank of the United States" case. A Maryland law required federally chartered banks to use only a special paper to print money, which amounted to a tax. William McCulloch, the cashier of the Baltimore branch of the bank, refused to use the paper, claiming that States could not tax the Federal Government. The Court declared the Maryland law unconstitutional, commenting ". . . the power to tax implies the power to destroy."

Miller v. *California,* 1973

(1st Amendment, freedom of the press) In *Miller*, the Court upheld a stringent application of California obscenity law by Newport Beach, California, and attempted to define what is obscene. The "Miller Rule" included three tests: (1) That the average person would, applying contemporary community standards, find that the work appealed to the prurient interest; (2) that the work depicts or describes, in an offensive way, sexual conduct defined by State law; and (3) that "the work, taken as a whole, lacks serious literary, artistic, political or scientific value. . . ."

Miranda v. *Arizona,* 1966

(5th, 6th, and 14th amendments, rights of the accused) Arrested for kidnapping and sexual assault, Ernesto Miranda signed a confession including a statement that he had "full knowledge of his legal rights. . . ." After conviction, he appealed, claiming that without counsel and without warnings, the confession was illegally gained. The Court agreed with Miranda that "he must be warned prior to any questioning that he has the right to remain silent, that anything he says can be used against him in a court of law, that he has a right to an attorney and that if he cannot afford an attorney one will be appointed for him. . . ." Although later modified by *Nix*, 1984, and other cases, *Miranda* firmly upheld citizen rights to fair trial in State courts.

Missouri v. *Cruzan,* 1990

(9th Amendment, right to die) A Missouri woman was in a coma from an automobile accident in 1983. Her family, facing astronomical medical bills and deciding that "her life had ended in 1987," directed the health care providers to end intravenous feeding. The State of Missouri opposed the family's decision. The family went to court and the Supreme Court ruled that "States could require clear and convincing" evidence that Cruzan would have wanted to die, although the Court did not require other States to meet the Missouri standard. Following the ruling, another hearing was held in Missouri at which "clear and convincing evidence" was presented to a judge. The intravenous feeding was ended and Cruzan died on December 26, 1990.

Mueller v. *Allen,* 1983

Decision: The Court upheld the law, stating that it met the *Lemon* test (*Lemon*, 1972), and that the deduction was available to all parents with children in school. Although it was of greater benefit to parents of children in private schools, each parent had the choice of which school their children attended. (See "Debating Key Issues" feature on page 415.)

New Jersey v. *T. L. O.,* 1985

Decision: The court set a new standard for searches in schools in this case, stating that the school had a "legitimate need to maintain an environment in which learning can take place," and that to do this "requires some easing of the restrictions to which searches by public authorities are ordinarily subject. . . ." The Court thus created a "reasonable suspicion" rule for school searches, a change from the "probable cause" requirement in the wider society. (See "Debating Key Issues" feature on page 467.)

New York Times v. *United States,* 1971

Decision: The Court cited the 1st Amendment guarantee of a free press and refused to uphold the injunction against publication, observing that "it is the obligation of the government to prove that actual harm to the nation's security would be caused by the publication. . . ." The decision limited "prior restraint" of the press. (See "Debating Key Issues" feature on page 197.)

Nix v. *Williams,* 1984

(4th Amendment, illegal evidence) A man was convicted of murdering a 10-year-old girl after he led officers to the body. He had been arrested, but not advised of his rights, in a distant city, and in transit, he had conversed with a police officer. Williams agreed that the child should have a proper burial and directed the officer to the body. Later, on appeal, Williams's attorneys argued that the body should not be admitted as evidence because the questioning was illegal. The Court disagreed, observing that search parties were within two and one-half miles of the body. "Evidence otherwise excluded may be admissible when it would have been discovered anyway." The decision was one of several "exceptions to the exclusionary rule" handed down by the Court in the 1980s.

Olmstead v. *United States,* 1928

(4th Amendment, electronic surveillance) Olmstead was engaged in the illegal sale of alcohol. Much of the evidence against him was gained through a wiretap made without a warrant. Olmstead argued that he had "a reasonable expectation of privacy," and that the *Weeks* decision of 1914 should be applied to exclude the evidence gained by the wiretap. The Court disagreed, saying that Olmstead "intended to project his voice to those quite outside . . . and that . . . nothing tangible was taken." Reversed by subsequent decisions, this case contains the first usage of the concept of "reasonable expectation of privacy" that would mark later 4th Amendment decisions.

Plessy v. *Ferguson,* 1896

(14th Amendment, Equal Protection Clause) A Louisiana law required separate seating for white and African-American citizens on public railroads, a form of segregation. Herman Plessy argued that his right to "equal protection of the laws" was violated. The Court held that segregation was permitted if facilities were equal. The Court interpreted the 14th Amendment as "not intended to give Negroes social equality but only political and civil equality. . . ." The Louisiana law was seen as a "reasonable exercise of (State) police power . . ." Segregated public facilities were permitted until *Plessy* was overturned by the *Brown* v. *Board of Education* case of 1954.

Powell v. *Alabama,* 1932

(6th Amendment, right to counsel) The case involved the "Scottsboro Boys," seven "young negro men" accused of sexual assault. This case was a landmark in the development of a "fundamentals of fairness" doctrine of the Court over the next 40 years. The Scottsboro boys were quickly prosecuted without the benefit of counsel and sentenced to death. The Court overturned the decision, stating that poor people facing the death penalty in State courts must be provided counsel, and commenting, ". . . there are certain principles of Justice which adhere to the very idea of free government, which no [State] may disregard." The case was another step toward incorporation of the Bill of Rights into State constitutions.

Regents of the University of California v. *Bakke,* 1970

Decision: The Court ruled narrowly, providing an admission for Bakke, but not overturning "affirmative action," preferring to take discrimination questions on a case-by-case basis. (See "Debating Key Issues" feature on page 560.)

Reynolds v. *United States,* 1879

(1st Amendment, Free Exercise Clause) Called the "Mormon Case," this decision involved George Reynolds, an "old order" Mormon with multiple wives. An anti-Mormon law forbidding bigamy was passed by Congress, and Reynolds was prosecuted. He claimed that his religious belief overrode federal laws and that the law was unconstitutional. The Court ruled that "freedom of religion means freedom to hold an opinion or belief, but not to take action . . . subversive to good order."

Roe v. *Wade,* 1973

(9th Amendment, right to privacy) A Texas woman challenged a State law forbidding the artificial termination of a pregnancy, saying that she "had a fundamental right to privacy." The Court upheld a woman's right to choose in this case, noting that the State's "important and legitimate interest in potential life" became "compelling" at the end of the first trimester, and that before then ". . . the attending physician, in consultation with his patient, is free to determine, without regulation by the State, that . . . the patient's pregnancy should be terminated." The decision struck down State regulation of abortion in the first three months of pregnancy and was modified by *Webster*, 1989.

Rostker v. *Goldberg,* 1981

Decision: The Court did not support the challenge, observing that "the purpose of the registration is to develop a pool of potential combat troops . . ." and that "Congress and the Executive have decided that women should not serve in combat." Since the matter of using women in combat had received considerable attention in Congress, with debates, hearings, and committee actions, the Court agreed that Congress did not act unthinkingly or reflexively. (See "Debating Key Issues" feature on page 295.)

Roth v. *United States,* 1957

(1st Amendment, freedom of the press) A New York man named Roth operated a business that used the mail to invite people to buy materials considered obscene by postal inspectors. The Court, in its first consideration of censorship of obscenity, created the "prevailing community standards" rule, which required a "consideration of the work as a whole." In its decision, the Court defined as obscene that which offended "the common conscience of the community by present-day standards. . . ." In a case decided the same day, the Court applied the same "test" to State obscenity laws.

Schenck v. *United States,* 1919

(1st Amendment, freedom of speech) Charles Schenck was an officer of an antiwar political group who was arrested for alleged violations of the Espionage Act of 1917, which made active opposition to the war a crime. He had urged thousands of young men called to service by the draft act to resist and to avoid induction. The Court limited free speech in time of war, stating that Schenck's words, under the circumstances, presented a "clear and present danger. . . ." Although later decisions modified the decision, the Schenck case created a precedent that 1st Amendment guarantees were not absolute.

School District of Abington Township, Pennsylvania v. *Schempp,* 1963

(1st Amendment, Establishment Clause) A Pennsylvania State law required reading from the Bible each day at school as an all-school activity. Some parents objected and sought legal remedy. When the case reached the Court, it agreed with the parents, saying that the Establishment Clause and Free Exercise Clause both forbade States from engaging in religious activity. The Court created a rule holding that if the purpose and effect of a law "is the advancement or inhibition of religion," it "exceeds the scope of legislative power."

Sheppard v. *Maxwell,* 1966

(6th Amendment, right to a fair trial) Dr. Samuel Sheppard was convicted of murdering his wife in a trial widely covered by national news media. Sheppard appealed his conviction, claiming that the pretrial publicity had made it impossible to get a fair trial. The Court rejected arguments about "press freedom," overturned his conviction, and ordered a new trial. As a result of the Sheppard decision, some judges have issued "gag" orders limiting pretrial publicity.

South Dakota v. *Dole,* 1986

Decision: The Court upheld the right of the national government to limit highway funds to States that did not qualify under the rules of "entitlement." All States that wished to continue to receive full federal highway aid were required to raise the legal age to purchase and consume alcohol to 21 years. In recent years the Federal Government has attached similar strings to federal aid in a number of instances, including mandating maximum speed limits on interstate highways. (See "Debating Key Issues" feature on page 87.)

Tennessee Valley Authority v. *Hiram G. Hill, Jr., et al.,* 1978

Decision: The Court found the injunction against TVA's completion of the nearly finished dam, which the interior secretary found would harm an endangered fish species, to be proper to prevent violation of the Endangered Species Act. (See "Debating Key Issues" feature on page 221.)

Texas v. *Johnson,* 1989

(1st Amendment, freedom of speech) Dousing with kerosene and burning a U.S. flag taken from the flagpole at the 1984 Republican National Convention in Dallas, Gregory Johnson led a protest against national policies outside the convention center. He was arrested and convicted under a Texas law prohibiting the desecration of the Texas and United States flags. Johnson's conviction was overturned in the highest criminal court in Texas, and the State appealed. The Court ruled the Texas law an unconstitutional limit on "freedom of expression," noting that "although the State had a legitimate interest in encouraging proper treatment of the flag, it may not foster its own view of the flag by punishing a person for burning the flag as a means of political protest."

Thompson v. *Oklahoma,* 1988

(8th Amendment, capital punishment) An Oklahoma youth was 15 years old when he committed a capital murder. At age 16 he was sentenced to death for the slaying. In hearing an appeal of the case, the Court overturned the death sentence, holding that "the 8th and 14th amendments prohibit the execution of a man who was sentenced to death for a crime he committed at 15 years of age." A death penalty was cruel and unusual punishment for a 15 year old.

Tinker v. *Des Moines Public Schools,* 1969

Decision: The Court agreed with the Tinkers, upholding students' 1st Amendment rights, noting that "students do not abandon their civil rights at the schoolhouse gate . . ." and that the wearing of black armbands was "peaceful expression of political opinion. . . ." Schools would need to show evidence of the possibility of "substantial disturbance" before free speech could be limited at school. (See "Debating Key Issues" feature on page 498.)

United States v. *Nixon,* 1974

Decision: The Court overruled the President and ordered him to surrender the tapes, thereby limiting executive privilege. The President's "generalized interest in confidentiality . . ." was subordinate to "the fundamental demands of due process of law in the fair administration of criminal justice." (See "Debating Key Issues" feature on page 322.)

Walz v. *Commission of New York,* 1970

(1st Amendment, Establishment Clause) State and local governments routinely exempt church property from taxes. Walz claimed that such exemptions were a "support of religion," a subsidy by government. The Court disagreed, noting that such exemptions were just an example of a "benevolent neutrality" between government and churches, not a support of religion. Governments must avoid taxing churches, because taxation would give government a "control" over religion, prohibited by the "wall of separation of church and state" noted in *Everson*, 1947.

Webster v. *Reproductive Health Services*, 1989

(9th Amendment, right to privacy) A 1986 Missouri law stated that (1) life began at conception, (2) unborn children have rights, (3) public funds could not be used for abortions not necessary to save the life of the mother, and (4) public funds could not be used for abortion counseling. Health care providers in Missouri filed suit, challenging the law, claiming it was in conflict with *Roe*, 1973, and intruded into "privacy questions." A 5-4 Court upheld the Missouri law, stating that the people of Missouri, through their legislature, could put limits on the use of public funds. The *Webster* decision narrowed the protection of *Roe*.

Weeks v. *United States*, 1914

(4th Amendment, illegal evidence) A search without proper warrant was made in San Francisco and evidence was used by a postal inspector to prosecute Mr. Weeks. Weeks claimed that the evidence was gained by an illegal search, and thus was inadmissible. The Court agreed, applying for the first time an "exclusionary rule" for illegally gained evidence in federal courts. The decision stated ". . . if letters and private documents can thus be seized and used as evidence . . . his right to be secure against such searches . . . is of no value, and . . . might as well be stricken from the Constitution." See also *Mapp* v. *Ohio*, 1962; *Massachusetts* v. *Sheppard*, 1904; and *Nix* v. *Williams*, 1904.

West Virginia Board of Education v. *Barnette*, 1942

Decision: The Court held that a compulsory flag salute violated the 1st Amendment's exercise of religion clause and was, therefore, unconstitutional. ". . . no official, high or petty, can prescribe what shall be orthodox in politics, nationalism, religion, or other matters of opinion. . . ." (See "Debating Key Issues" feature on page 649.)

Westside Community Schools v. *Mergens*, 1990

(1st Amendment, Establishment Clause) A request by Bridget Mergens to form a student Christian religious group at school was denied by an Omaha high school principal. Mergens took legal action, claiming that a 1984 federal law required "equal access" for student religious groups. The Court ordered the school to permit the club, stating, "a high school does not have to permit any extracurricular activities, but when it does, the school is bound by the . . . Act of 1984. Allowing students to meet on campus and discuss religion is constitutional because it does not amount to a 'State sponsorship of a religion.'"

Wilkins v. *Missouri*, 1989

(8th Amendment, capital punishment) A 16-year-old abused juvenile runaway in Missouri robbed a convenience store and stabbed the attendant several times, stating that "a dead person can't talk." He was sentenced to death. The Court decided that the death penalty for a 16 year old did not constitute "cruel and unusual punishment," commenting that "we discern neither a historical nor a modern societal consensus forbidding the imposition of capital punishment on any person who murders at 16 or 17 years of age." With *Thompson*, 1988, this case clearly sets the age of 16 as the minimum age for the imposition of capital punishment.

Wisconsin v. *Yoder*, 1972

(1st Amendment, Free Exercise Clause) Members of the Amish religious sect in Wisconsin objected to sending their children to public schools after the eighth grade, claiming that such exposure of the children to another culture would endanger the group's "self-sufficient agrarian lifestyle essential to their religious faith." The Court agreed with the Amish, while noting that the Court must move carefully to weigh the State's "legitimate social concern when faced with religious claim for exemption from generally applicable educational requirements."

GLOSSARY

Number(s) after each definition refer to page(s) where the term is defined.

Act of admission A congressional act admitting a United States territory into the Union as a State. p. 83
Administration The officials and agencies of the executive branch that carry out public policies. p. 382
Affirmative action Policy that requires that both public and private organizations take positive steps to overcome the effects of past discrimination. p. 557
Albany Plan of Union Plan put forward by Benjamin Franklin in 1754 that aimed at uniting the 13 colonies for trade, military, and other purposes; never enacted. p. 32
Alien One who is not a citizen (or national) of the state in which he/she lives. pp. 487, 562
Ambassador A personal representative appointed by the head of a nation to represent that nation in matters of diplomacy. p. 429
Amendment A change in, or addition to, a constitution or a law. p. 60
Amnesty A general pardon offered to a group of law violators. p. 368
Anarchy The total absence of government. p. 17
Anti-Federalists Those persons who opposed the adoption of the Constitution in 1787–1788. p. 47
Appellate jurisdiction Authority of a court to review decisions of inferior (lower) courts; see original jurisdiction. pp. 464, 678
Apportionment Distribution of seats in a legislative body among electoral districts. p. 238
Articles of Confederation Document by which the first U.S. government was established after the American Revolution; allowed few important powers to the central government. p. 36
Assessment The process of determining the value of property for purposes of taxation. p. 669
At-large Election of an officeholder by the voters of an entire governmental unit (e.g., a State or county) rather than by the voters of a district, a subdivision of that area. p. 241

Bail Money the accused may be required to post (deposit with the court) as a guarantee that he/she will appear in court at the proper time. p. 536
Ballot Device by which a voter registers a choice in an election. p. 168
Bankruptcy Court action to release a person or corporation from unpaid debts. p. 267
Bench trial A trial held without a jury; civil or criminal proceeding at which the judge decides questions of fact as well as questions of law. p. 532
Bicameral An adjective, describing a legislative body composed of two houses. p. 28
Bill A proposal presented to a legislative body for possible enactment as a law. p. 297
Bill of attainder Legislative act that inflicts punishment upon a person or group without a trial. p. 529
Bill of Rights First 10 amendments to the Constitution. pp. 62, 486
Blanket primary A nominating election in which voters may switch from one party's primary to another on an office-to-office basis; see direct primary. p. 162
Block grant One type of federal grants-in-aid; block-grant monies are to be used in some particular but broadly defined area of public policy (e.g., education or highways); see grants-in-aid. p. 85
Borough A major unit of local government in Alaska, similar to counties in other States; also in some States a small town, village. p. 643
Bourgeoisie In Marxist terms, the social class of the capitalists. p. 614
Boycott Refusal to buy or sell an opponent's goods in order to influence his/her behavior. p. 32
Bureaucracy Any large, complex administrative structure; a hierarchical organization with job specialization and complex rules. p. 381
Bureaucrat Person with defined responsibilities in a bureaucracy. p. 381
By-election A special election held to fill a vacant seat in Britain's House of Commons. p. 578

Cabinet Presidential advisory body, traditionally composed of the heads of the executive departments and other officers the President may choose. p. 373
Capital Wealth used to produce goods and services. p. 606
Capitalist One who controls and uses the capital by which goods and services are produced under a free enterprise system; see free enterprise. p. 606
Caucus A meeting of a group of like-minded persons to select the candidates they will support in an election; see party caucus. p. 158
Certificate A method of putting a case before the Supreme Court; used when a lower court is not clear about the procedure or the rule of law that should apply in a case and asks the Supreme Court to certify the answer to a specific question. p. 475
Certiorari, writ of Order issued by a higher court directing a lower court to send up the record of a case for its review. p. 474
Checks and balances System of overlapping the powers of the legislative, executive, and judicial branches, to permit each branch to check the actions of the others; see separation of powers. p. 57
Chief administrator Term for the President as head of the administration of the Federal Government. p. 316

Chief citizen Term for the President as the representative of the people, working for the public interest. p. 316
Chief diplomat Term for the President as the main architect of foreign policy and spokesperson to other countries. p. 316
Chief executive Term for the President as vested with the executive power of the United States. p. 316
Chief legislator Term for the President as architect of public policy and the one who sets the agenda for Congress. p. 316
Chief of party Term for the President as the leader of his or her political party. p. 316
Chief of state Term for the President as the head of the government of the United States, symbol of all the people of the nation. p. 316
Citizen One who owes allegiance to a state and is entitled to its protection. p. 561
Civil law That body of law relating to human conduct, including disputes between private persons and between private persons and government, not covered by criminal law. p. 673
Civil liberties Guarantees of the safety of persons, opinions, and property from the arbitrary acts of government. p. 486
Civil rights Refers to positive acts of government that seek to make constitutional guarantees a reality for all; e.g., prohibition of discrimination. p. 486
Closed primary Form of the direct primary in which only declared party members may vote; see open primary, direct primary. p. 162
Cloture Procedure that may be used to limit or end floor debate in a legislative body. p. 306
Coalition A union of persons or groups of diverse interests; an alliance of parties for the purpose of forming a government. pp. 100, 578
Coattail effect Influence that a popular candidate for a top office (e.g., President or governor) can have on the voters' support of other candidates of his/her party on the same ballot. p. 167
Collective security Basic purpose of the U.N. and a major goal of American foreign policy, to create a system in which participating nations agree to take joint action to meet any threat to or attack on another member. p. 443
Collectivization Stalin's plan of combining small peasant farms. p. 621
Command economy Economic system in which the government directs the economy. p. 615
Commander in chief Term for the President as commander of the nation's armed forces. p. 316
Commerce and Slave Trade Compromise An agreement during the Constitutional Convention of 1787 protecting the interests of slaveholders by forbidding Congress the power to tax the export of goods from any State, and, for 20 years, the power to act on the slave trade. p. 44
Commerce power Exclusive power of Congress to regulate interstate and foreign trade. p. 264
Commission form Form of city government in which elected commissioners serve collectively as the city council and separately as heads of the city's administrative department. p. 652
Committee chairman Member who heads a standing committee in a legislative body. p. 289
Committee of the Whole A committee that consists of an entire legislative body; used for a procedure in which a legislative body expedites its business by resolving itself into a committee of itself. p. 301
Common law That body of law made up of generally accepted standards of rights and wrongs developed over centuries by judicial decisions rather than in written statutes. p. 672
Commutation The power to reduce (commute) the length of a sentence or fine for a crime. pp. 384, 641
Compromise The process of reconciling competing views and interests in order to find the position most acceptable to the largest number. p. 17
Concurrent jurisdiction Power shared by federal and state courts to hear certain cases. p. 464
Concurrent powers Powers held by the National Government and the States in the federal system. p. 78
Concurrent resolution Measure passed by both houses of a legislature that does not have the force of law nor require the chief executive's approval; often used to express the legislature's opinion or for internal rules or housekeeping. p. 297
Concurring opinion Written explanation of the views of one or more judges who support a decision reached by a majority of the court but disagree with the grounds for that decision. p. 476
Confederation Form of government in which an alliance of independent states creates a central government of very limited power; the member states have supreme authority over all matters except in those few areas in which they have expressly delegated power to the central government. p. 11
Conference committee Temporary joint committee created to reconcile any differences between the two houses' versions of a bill. p. 294
Connecticut Compromise Agreement during the Constitutional Convention that Congress should be composed of a Senate, in which the States would be represented equally, and a House, in which representation would be based upon a State's population. p. 43
Consensus General agreement among various groups on fundamental matters. p. 583
Constituents All persons represented by a legislator or other elected officeholder. p. 250
Constitution Body of fundamental law, setting out the basic principles, structures, processes, and functions of a government and placing limits upon its actions; may be written or unwritten. p. 35
Constitutionalism Basic principle that government and those who govern are bound by the fundamental law; the rule of law; see limited government. p. 56
Containment Basic feature of American foreign policy since World War II, to contain Soviet communism within its own boundaries as a way to reduce its influence and force its eventual collapse. p. 443

Continuing resolution Measure that, when signed by the President, allows an agency to function on the basis of appropriations made the prior year. p. 419
Continuous body Governing unit such as the Senate whose seats are never all up for election at the same time. p. 246
Copyright The exclusive, legal right of a person to reproduce, publish, or sell his or her own literary, musical, or artistic creations. p. 268
Council-manager form Form of city government with an elected council as the policy-making body and an appointed administrator responsible to the council for the running of the city's government. p. 653
County A major unit of local government in most States; created by the State; principal powers lie in the fields of law enforcement, roads, schools, welfare. p. 643
Criminal law That body of law that defines crimes and provides for their punishment. p. 673
Custom duty Tax (tariff) on goods brought into the United States. p. 410

De facto segregation Segregation that exists "in fact," not as a result of laws or governmental actions; see de jure segregation, segregation. p. 553
Defendant In a civil suit, the person against whom a court action is brought by the plaintiff; in a criminal case, the person charged with the crime. p. 464
Deficit Yearly shortfall between revenue and spending. p. 413
De jure segregation Segregation that exists as a result of some law or governmental action; see de facto segregation, segregation. p. 553
Delegated powers Those powers (expressed, implied, inherent) granted to the National Government by the Constitution. p. 75
Democracy System of government in which supreme authority rests with the people; see direct democracy, representative democracy. p. 13
Denaturalization Court revocation of naturalized citizenship through due process of law. p. 564
Deportation Legal process in which aliens are legally required to leave the United States. p. 566
Deterrence Basic feature of American foreign policy; to maintain massive military strength in order to prevent any attack upon this country or its allies. p. 443
Dictatorship Form of government in which those who rule cannot be held responsible to the will of the people. p. 12
Diplomatic immunity Practice in international law under which ambassadors and other diplomatic officials have special privileges and are not subject to the laws of the state to which they are accredited. p. 430
Direct democracy A democratic system of government in which the people participate directly in decision making. p. 13
Direct primary The most widely used method of making nominations in American politics; an intraparty nominating election at which those who vote choose a party's candidates to run in the general election; see closed primary, open primary. p. 161
Direct tax A tax that must be paid by the person on whom it is levied; see indirect tax. p. 262
Discharge petition A procedure to bring a bill to the floor of the legislative body when a committee has refused to report it. p. 298
Dissenting opinion Written explanation of the views of one or more judges who disagree with (dissent from) a decision reached by a majority of the court; see majority opinion. p. 476
Dissolution Act of dissolving a governing body such as a house of representatives. p. 584
Division of powers Basic principle of federalism; the constitutional provisions by which governmental powers are divided on a geographic basis (in the United States, between the National Government and the States). p. 74
Double jeopardy Trial a second time for a crime of which the accused was acquitted in a first trial; prohibited by the 5th and 14th amendments. p. 530
Draft Process by which people enter compulsory service in the military. p. 437
Due process/Due Process Clause Constitutional guarantee, set out in the 5th and 14th amendments to the National Constitution and in every State's constitution, that government will not deprive any person of life, liberty, or property by any unfair, arbitrary, or unreasonable action, and that government must act in accord with established rules. pp. 488, 517

Economic protest parties Political parties rooted in periods of economic discontent. p. 115
Electoral college Group of persons (presidential electors) chosen in each State and the District of Columbia every four years who make a formal selection of the President and Vice President. p. 328
Electorate All of the persons entitled to vote in a given election. pp. 112, 130, 346
Eminent domain Power of a government to take private property for a public use. p. 270
Enabling act A congressional act that allows the people of a United States territory to prepare a constitution as a step toward admission as a State in the Union. p. 83
English Bill of Rights Drawn up by Parliament in 1689 to prevent abuse of power by English monarchs; forms the basis for much in American government and politics today. p. 27
Entitlement Benefits that federal law says must be paid to those persons who meet the eligibility requirements set for those payments. p. 416
Entrepreneur A person who organizes, operates, and assumes the risks of a business enterprise. p. 607
Espionage Spying for a foreign power. p. 506
Establishment Clause Part of the 1st Amendment prohibiting either the establishment of a religion or the sanctioning of an existing religion by the government. p. 490.
Estate tax A tax levied directly on the estate of a deceased person; see inheritance tax. pp. 410, 669
Excise tax Tax levied on the production, transportation, sale, or consumption of goods or services. p. 410

Exclusionary rule Evidence gained by illegal or unreasonable means cannot be used at the court trial of the person from whom it was seized; based upon Supreme Court interpretation of the 4th and 14th amendments. p. 524

Exclusive jurisdiction Power of the federal courts alone to hear certain cases. p. 464

Exclusive powers Most of the delegated powers; those held by the National Government alone (exclusively) in the federal system. p. 78

Executive agreement Pact made by the President with the head of a foreign state; a binding international agreement with the force of law but which (unlike a treaty) does not require Senate consent. pp. 66, 361

Executive order Rules, regulations issued by a chief executive or his/her subordinates, based upon either constitutional or statutory authority and having the force of law. p. 356

Expatriation Act by which one renounces (forfeits, gives up) citizenship. p. 564

Ex post facto law Criminal law applied retroactively to the disadvantage of the accused; prohibited by the Constitution. p. 529

Expressed powers Those delegated powers of the National Government that are given to it in so many words by the Constitution; also sometimes called the "enumerated powers." p. 75

Extradition Legal process by which a fugitive from justice in one State is returned (extradited) to it from another State. p. 90

Federal budget Detailed estimate of federal income and outgo during the coming fiscal year, and a work plan for the execution of public policy. p. 371

Federal government, Federalism Form of government with governmental powers divided between a central government and several regional governments; this geographically based division of powers is made by an authority superior to both the central and the regional governments. In the United States, the division of powers between the National Government and the 50 States is made by the Constitution. pp. 10, 59

Federalists Those persons who supported the adoption of the Constitution in 1787–1788. p. 47

Filibuster Various tactics (usually prolonged floor debate) aimed at defeating a bill in a legislative body by preventing a final vote on it; often associated with the U.S. Senate; see cloture. p. 304

Five-year plan Attempt to combine large-scale centralized planning with the public ownership of the means of production as the basis for a nation's economic advancement; used in Soviet Union. p. 621

Floor leader Members of the House and Senate picked to carry out party decisions and steer legislative action to meet party goals. p. 286

Foreign aid Economic and military aid to other countries as a means of fulfilling foreign policy goals. p. 447

Foreign policy The actions and stands that a nation takes in every aspect of its relationships with other countries; everything a nation's government says and does in world affairs. p. 426

Formal amendment A modification in the Constitution brought about through one of four methods set forth in the Constitution. p. 60

Franchise Suffrage, the right to vote. p. 129

Framers The group who came together in 1787 to draft the Constitution of the United States. p. 40

Free enterprise system An economic system based on private ownership, individual initiative, profit, and competition; see capitalist, private enterprise. p. 607

Free Exercise Clause Part of the 1st Amendment guaranteeing to each person the right to believe whatever that person chooses in matters of religion. p. 496

Full Faith and Credit Constitution's requirement (Article IV, Section 1) that each State accept (honor the validity of, give full faith and credit to) the public acts, records, and judicial proceedings of every other State. p. 89

General election Regularly scheduled election at which the voters choose public officeholders. p. 158

Gerrymandering The drawing of electoral district lines to the advantage of a party or group. pp. 138, 242

Gift tax Tax imposed on the making of a gift by a living person. p. 410

Glasnost Policy of openness in the former Soviet Union, including government's expanded tolerance of dissent and freedom of expression. p. 593

Government That complex of offices, personnel, and processes by which a state is ruled, by which its public policies are made and enforced. p. 3

Grand jury Body of 12 to 23 persons convened by a court to decide whether or not there is enough evidence to justify bringing a person to trial; see indictment, information, presentment, petit jury. p. 529

Grants-in-aid program Financial aid granted by one government to another (e.g., by the National Government to the States), with the funds available subject to certain conditions and to be used for certain purposes; see block grants. p. 84

Grass roots Of or from the common people, the average voter; used to describe opinion and pressure on public policy. p. 226

Habeas corpus, writ of Court order that a prisoner be brought before the court and that the detaining officer show cause why the prisoner should not be released; designed to prevent illegal arrests and unlawful imprisonments. p. 528

Ideological party Political party based on a particular set of beliefs, a comprehensive view of social, economic, and political matters. p. 114

Impeachment Formal charge (accusation of misconduct) brought against a public official by the lower house in a legislative body; trial, and removal upon conviction, occurs in the upper house. p. 275

Implied powers Those delegated powers of the National Government implied by (inferred from) the

expressed powers; those "necessary and proper" to carry out the expressed powers; see delegated powers, expressed powers. p. 75
Income tax A tax levied on individual and corporate income. p. 668
Independent agency Agency created by Congress outside of the cabinet departments. p. 388
Independent Voter who does not identify with or regularly support a particular party. p. 150
Indictment Accusation by a grand jury; a formal finding by that body that there is sufficient evidence against a named person to warrant his/her criminal trial. p. 529
Indirect tax A tax levied on one party but passed on to another for payment. pp. 263, 650
Informal amendment A change made in the Constitution not by actual written amendment, but by the experience of government under the Constitution; the methods include: (1) legislation passed by Congress; (2) actions taken by the President; (3) decisions of the Supreme Court; (4) the activities of political parties; and (5) custom. p. 65
Information Formal charge of crime brought against a named person by the prosecutor directly, rather than by a grand jury; see indictment. p. 530
Inherent powers Those delegated powers of the National Government that belong to it because it is the national government of a sovereign state. p. 75
Inheritance tax A "death tax" levied on the beneficiary's share of an estate; see estate tax. p. 669
Initiative Petition process by which a certain percentage of voters can put a proposed constitutional amendment or statute on the ballot for popular approval or rejection. p. 636
Injunction Court order that requires or forbids some specific action. p. 139
Interest group Private organization that tries to influence public policy. pp. 190, 211
Interim government Government set up to serve during the transition from a previous government. p. 596
Interstate compact Formal agreement between or among States, authorized by the Constitution (Article I, Section 10). p. 88
Isolationism Basic part of American foreign policy until World War II; a policy of refusing to become generally involved in world affairs. p. 425
Item veto Power held by 43 State governors (but not the President) to eliminate (veto) one or more provisions (items) in a bill without rejecting the entire measure; see veto. p. 641

Jim Crow law Law to isolate and separate one group of people from another on the basis of race. p. 551
Joint committee Legislative committee composed of members of both houses. p. 294
Joint resolution Legislative measure that must be passed by both houses and approved by the chief executive to become effective; similar to a bill, with the force of law, and often used for unusual or temporary purposes. p. 297
Judicial review Power of the courts to determine the constitutionality of the actions of the legislative and executive branches of government. p. 58
Jurisdiction Power of a court to try and decide a case. p. 462
Jus sanguinis Acquisition of American citizenship at birth, because of the citizenship of one or both parents; the "law of the blood," to whom born. p. 561
Jus soli Acquisition of American citizenship at birth, because of birth in the United States; the "law of the soil," where born. p. 561

Keynote address Speech given at a party convention to set the tone for the convention and the campaign to come. p. 336

Labor union Organization of workers who share the same type of job or who work in the same industry; see interest group. p. 216
Legal tender Any kind of money that a creditor must by law accept in payment for debts. p. 266
Libel Publication of statements that wrongfully damage another's reputation; see slander. p. 499
Liberal constructionist One who believes that the provisions of the Constitution, and in particular those granting power to government, are to be construed in broad terms. p. 260
Limited government Basic principle of the American system of government; that government is limited in what it may do, and each individual has certain rights that government cannot take away; see constitutionalism, popular sovereignty. pp. 26, 56
Literacy Ability to read and write; tests of literacy once used in several States to prevent voting by certain groups. p. 135
Lobbying Activities of an agent (lobbyist) for a pressure group, usually to influence public policy. p. 224

Magna Carta The Great Charter establishing the principle that the power of the monarchy was not absolute in England; forced upon the king by his barons in 1215, and protecting such fundamental rights as trial by jury. p. 27
Majority opinion Written statement by a majority of the judges of a court in support of a decision made by that court. p. 476
Major party A dominant party in a governmental system (e.g., the Republicans and Democrats in American politics); see minor party. p. 99
Mandate The instructions or commands a constituency gives to its elected officials concerning policies. p. 190
Market economy Economic system in which the government's role is a limited one and key decisions are made by private individuals and companies through the give and take of the marketplace. p. 615
Mass media Those means of communication that reach large audiences, especially television, newspapers, radio, and magazines. p. 198

Mayor-council government The most common form of city government in this country, featuring an elected mayor as chief executive and an elected council as the legislative body. p. 650
Media Means of communicating with people, such as the press, radio, and television. p. 355
Medium A means of transmitting information; the singular form of *media*. p. 198
Metropolitan area Term for the large cities and the surrounding separate (but economically and socially integrated) communities. p. 656
Minister Cabinet member in a parliamentary government. p. 578
Minor party One of the less widely supported political parties in a governmental system; see major party. p. 102
Miranda rule A listing of the Constitutional rights that suspects must be advised of before police questioning: (1) they have a right to remain silent; (2) anything they say may be used against them in court; (3) they have a right to an attorney before questioning begins; (4) an attorney will be appointed for them by the court if they cannot afford one; (5) they may bring the questioning to an end at any time. p. 535
Monarchy Government with an hereditary ruler. p. 576
Monopoly A firm that is the only source of a product or service. p. 608
Multi-seat district Electoral districts in which voters choose more than one representative. p. 583
Multiparty system Political system in which three or more major parties compete for public offices; see one-party, two-party system. p. 105

National Diet Japanese parliament. p. 582
Nationalization Governmental acquisition of private industry for public use. p. 589
Naturalization Legal process by which a person born a citizen of one country becomes a citizen of another. p. 562
Necessary and Proper Clause Part of the Constitution that gives Congress the power to make all laws "necessary and proper" for executing its powers; has been used to expand greatly congressional power. p. 271
New Jersey Plan An alternative to the Virginia Plan offered at the Constitutional Convention of 1787, differing chiefly in the matter of how states should be represented in Congress. p. 43
Nomination Process of selecting (naming) candidates for office. pp. 158, 230

One-party system Political system in which only one party exists, or in which only one party has a reasonable chance of winning elections. p. 105
Open primary Form of the direct primary in which any qualified voter may participate without regard to his/her party allegiance. p. 162
Opinion leader Any person who has a more than usual influence on the views of others. p. 188
Original jurisdiction Power to hear a case first, before any other court. p. 464
Oversight function Review by legislative committees of the policies and programs of the executive branch. p. 250

Pardon Release from the punishment or legal consequences of a crime, by the President (in a federal case) or a governor (in a State case). pp. 368, 641
Parish The Louisiana term for counties. p. 643
Parliamentary government Form of government in which the executive leadership (usually, a prime minister and cabinet) is chosen by and responsible to the legislature (parliament), as well as being members of the legislature, as in Great Britain. p. 11
Parole Release of a prisoner short of the completion of the term of a sentence. p. 641
Party caucus A meeting of party leaders and/or members to conduct party business. p. 287
Party identification Person's sense of attachment, loyalty to a political party. p. 149
Passport Certificate issued by a government, identifying a person as a citizen of a country and authorizing that person to travel, live abroad. p. 430
Patent A license issued to an inventor granting the exclusive right to manufacture and sell his or her invention for a limited period of time. p. 269
Patronage Practice of giving government jobs to supporters and friends; see spoils system. p. 396
Payroll tax Tax levied on employers and their employees, and on self-employed persons. p. 409
Perestroika In the former Soviet Union, policy to restructure political and economic life. p. 593
Petit jury Body of (usually) 12 persons who hear the evidence and decide questions of fact in a court case; see trial jury, grand jury. p. 674
Petition of Right Challenged the idea of the divine right of kings, declaring in 1628 in England that even a monarch must obey the law of the land. p. 27
Picketing Patrolling of a business site by workers on strike; an attempt to inform the public and to persuade others not to deal with the employer involved. p. 504
Plaintiff In civil law, the party who brings a suit or some other legal action against another (the defendant) in court. p. 464
Platform Written declaration of the principles and policy positions of a political party, usually adopted at that party's convention. p. 337
Pluralistic society One consisting of several distinct cultures and groups. p. 104
Plurality In an election, at least one more vote than that received by any other candidate; a plurality may or may not be a majority of the total vote. p. 103
Pocket veto Type of veto a chief executive may use after a legislature has adjourned; it is applied when the chief executive does not formally sign or reject a bill within the time period allowed to do so; see veto. p. 307
Police power Power of a State to act to protect and promote the public health, safety, morals, and welfare. p. 519

Politburo The highest policy-making committee of the Communist party in the former Soviet Union. p. 597
Political action committee (PAC) Political arm of a special interest group that seeks to influence elections and public policy decisions. p. 174
Political efficacy Influence or effectiveness in politics and the workings of government. p. 142
Political party Organized group that seeks to control government through the winning of elections and the holding of public office. p. 99
Political socialization Complex process by which individuals acquire their political attitudes and opinions. p. 145
Polling place Particular location where those voters who live in a particular area (see precinct) vote in an election. p. 167
Poll tax Tax (now unconstitutional) paid in some States before a person was allowed to vote. p. 136
Popular sovereignty Basic principle of the American system of government; that the people are the only source of any and all governmental power, that government must be conducted with the consent of the governed. pp. 35, 55
Precedent Previous court decisions that influence the ruling of later and similar cases. p. 672
Precinct The smallest unit of election administration; a local voting district. p. 122
Prefecture Political subdivision into which Japan is divided. p. 583
Presentment Formal accusation of crime brought by a grand jury of its own motion. p. 530
Presidential electors The persons elected by the voters to represent them in making a formal selection of the President and Vice President. p. 327
Presidential government Form of government characterized by a separation of powers between independent and coequal executive and legislative branches, as in the United States. p. 11
Presidential primary Election at which a party's voters (1) choose some or all of a State party organization's delegates to that party's national convention, and/or (2) express a preference among various contenders for the party's presidential nomination. p. 331
Presidential succession Manner in which a vacancy in the presidency is to be filled. p. 324
President of the Senate The presiding officer of a senate: in Congress, the Vice President of the United States; in a State's legislature, either the lieutenant governor or a senator. p. 286
President *pro tempore* The member of the United States Senate, or of the upper house of a State's legislature, chosen to preside in the absence of the president of the Senate. p. 286
Probable cause Reasonable ground, a good basis for the belief that something is true—e.g., that a crime has been committed. p. 523
Progressive tax Any tax in which each step in the rate schedule is geared to the taxpayer's ability to pay (e.g., an income tax); see regressive tax. pp. 407, 668
Proletariat In Marxist terms, the workers in a capitalist system. p. 614
Propaganda A technique of persuasion, aimed at influencing public opinion to create a particular popular belief. p. 223
Property tax A tax levied on (1) real property (land and buildings), or (2) personal property (tangible and intangible personal wealth); see assessment. p. 669
Public affairs Events and issues that concern the people at large. p. 213
Public debt All of the money borrowed by the government over the years and not yet repaid, plus the accrued interest on that money. p. 413
Public-interest group An organization that seeks to influence public policies on behalf of the "public good," as distinguished from those groups that serve a private interest; see interest group. p. 220
Public opinion Those attitudes shared by a significant number of persons on matters of government and politics; expressed group attitudes. p. 186
Public opinion poll A formal survey of public attitudes. p. 191
Public policy All of those things a government decides to do. pp. 3, 211
Purge Ruthless elimination of rivals and dissidents as practiced by Stalin. p. 594

Quasi-legislative, quasi-judicial Ability of government bodies with certain executive (administrative) functions to exercise certain rule-making and decision-making powers (e.g., the several federal independent regulatory commissions). p. 391
Quorum Least number of members who must be present for a legislative body to conduct business. p. 301
Quota Rules requiring certain numbers of jobs or promotions for certain groups. p. 558
Quota sample In scientific polling, a group chosen to be interviewed in which the members of each of several groups are included in proportion to their percentage in the total population; see random sample, sample. p. 193

Random sample In scientific polling, a sample to be interviewed drawn such that each member of the population has an equal chance to be included in it; see quota sample, sample. p. 192
Ratification Formal approval, final consent to the effectiveness of a constitution, constitutional amendment, or treaty. p. 36
Reapportionment Redistribution of political representation on the basis of population changes, usually after a census; see apportionment. p. 239
Recognition The exclusive power of a President to recognize, establish formal diplomatic relations with, foreign states. p. 362
Redress Satisfaction of a claim brought in court. p. 478
Referendum Process in which a measure passed by a legislature is submitted (referred) to the voters for final approval or rejection. p. 636

Refugee One who leaves his or her home to seek refuge from war, persecution, or other danger. p. 549

Regional security alliance Defensive alliance formed by negotiating a mutual defense treaty with countries that agree to take collective action to meet aggression in various parts of the world. p. 448

Register List of viable job candidates maintained by the Office of Personnel Management in the federal recruiting and hiring process. p. 398

Registration Procedure of voter identification, intended to prevent fraudulent voting; also known as enrollment. p. 134

Regressive tax Any tax levied at a flat rate, i.e., falls most heavily on those least able to pay it (e.g., a sales tax); see progressive tax. pp. 409, 668

Representative democracy A system of government in which a small group of persons chosen by the people to act as their representatives expresses the popular will. p. 13

Representative government System of government in which public policies are made by officials who are selected by the voters and held accountable to them in periodic elections; see democracy. p. 27

Reprieve An official postponement of execution of a sentence; see pardon. pp. 368, 641

Reservation Areas of public land set aside by a government for use by a Native-American group. p. 547

Reserved powers Those powers held by the States in the American federal system. p. 77

Resolution Measure relating to the internal business of one house in a legislature, or expressing that chamber's opinion on some matter, without the force of law; see concurrent resolution, joint resolution. p. 297

Reverse discrimination A description of affirmative action by critics of that policy; holds that giving preference to females and/or nonwhites discriminates against members of the majority group; see affirmative action. p. 558

Rider Provision, unlikely to pass on its own merit, added to an important bill certain to pass so that it will "ride" through the legislative process. p. 297

Right of legation The right of a nation to send and receive diplomatic representatives. p. 429

Rule of law See constitutionalism. p. 56

Runoff primary A second primary, involving the two front-runners in the first contest; held where election law requires a majority vote for nomination. p. 163

Sabotage Destructive act intended to hinder a nation's war or defense effort. p. 506

Sales tax A tax paid by the purchaser on the sale of commodities; the single most important source of income among the States. p. 668

Sample In scientific polling, a small number of people chosen as a representative cross-section of the total population to be surveyed; see quota sample, random sample. p. 192

Search warrant Court order authorizing a search of a suspect's property or person. p. 519

Sedition Spoken, written, or other action promoting resistance to lawful authority; especially advocating the violent overthrow of a government. p. 506

Segregation Separation or isolation of a racial or other group from the rest of the population in education or other areas of public or private activity. p. 551

Select committee Legislative committee created for a limited time and for some specific purpose; also known as special committee. p. 293

Seniority rule Unwritten rule in both houses of Congress, that the top posts in each chamber will (with rare exception) be held by "ranking members," i.e., those with the longest records of service; applied most strictly to committee chairmanships. p. 289

Separate-but-equal doctrine Long held by the Supreme Court, that the 14th Amendment's Equal Protection Clause did not forbid racial segregation so long as the separate facilities for African Americans were equal to those provided for whites; overturned in *Brown* v. *Topeka Board of Education,* 1954. p. 552

Separation of powers Basic principle of the American system of government, that the executive, legislative, and judicial powers are divided among three independent and coequal branches of government; see checks and balances. pp. 56, 541

Session The regular period of time during which a legislative body conducts business. p. 237

Shadow cabinet In a parliamentary system, leading members of the opposition who are likely to be cabinet ministers should their party win a majority at the next election. p. 579

Shield law Law found in some States designed to protect reporters against being forced to disclose confidential news sources. p. 502

Single-interest group Political action committee that concentrates effort on one issue. p. 224

Single-issue party Political party that concentrates on a single public policy issue. p. 115

Single-member district Electoral district from which one person is chosen by the voters for each office on the ballot; see at-large. pp. 103, 241

Slander Speech that wrongfully damages a person's reputation; see libel. p. 499

Sound bite Short, sharply focused television news report. p. 204

Sovereign Supreme, absolute power of a state within its own territory. p. 4

Speaker of the House The presiding officer of the House of Representatives, chosen by and from the majority party in the House. p. 285

Special district Local unit of government, created to perform (usually) a single public function in a locale (e.g., a school or library district). p. 647

Special session An extraordinary session of a legislative body. p. 238

Splinter party Political party that has split away from one of the major parties. p. 115

Split-ticket voting Voting for candidates of more than one party in the same election; see straight-ticket voting. pp. 122, 150

Spoils system Practice of awarding government jobs, contracts, and other favors to friends and supporters; see patronage. p. 395
Standing committee Permanent committee in a legislative body to which bills in a specified subject-matter area are referred; see select committee. p. 290
State A body of people, living in a defined territory, organized under a government and having the power to make and enforce law without the consent of any higher authority. p. 4
Straight-ticket voting Voting for the candidates of one party in an election; see split-ticket voting. p. 149
Straw vote Unscientific measurement of public opinion; usually asking the same question of a large number of people. p. 191
Strict constructionist One who advocates a narrow interpretation of the Constitution's provisions, in particular those granting power to government. p. 260
Strong-mayor government Variety of mayor-council form of city government, featuring a mayor with broad executive powers (e.g., to hire and fire, to prepare budget, to veto ordinances). p. 652
Subcommittee Division of existing committee that is formed to address specific issues. p. 298
Suffrage Right to vote. p. 129
Supply and demand, laws of A basic feature of a capitalistic economy; when supplies of goods, services become plentiful, prices tend to drop; when supplies become scarcer, prices tend to rise. p. 608
Supreme Soviet National legislature of the former Soviet Union. p. 595
Symbolic speech Expression of beliefs, ideas by conduct rather than in speech or print. p. 503

Tax return Declaration of taxable income and the exemptions and deductions claimed; filed with the Internal Revenue Service. p. 408.
Term The specified length of time served by elected officials in their elected offices. p. 237
Three-fifths Compromise An agreement at the Constitutional Convention of 1787 that slaves should be counted as three-fifths of a person for purposes of determining the population of a state. p. 44
Township A term used for a subdivision of a county in many States; see county. p. 647
Trade association Interest group representing a segment of the business community. p. 216
Treason Crime of disloyalty which, says the Constitution, "shall consist only in levying war against (the United States), or in adhering to their enemies, giving them aid and comfort"; can be committed only in wartime. p. 506
Treaty Formal agreement made between or among sovereign states. p. 361

Two-party system Political system in which the candidates of only two (major) parties have a reasonable chance of winning elections; see multiparty, one-party system. p. 102

UN Security Council United Nations council bearing the UN's major responsibility for maintaining international peace. p. 451
Unconstitutional Contrary to constitutional provisions and so invalid. p. 59
Unicameral An adjective describing a legislative body with one chamber; see bicameral. p. 29
Unitary government Form of government in which all of the powers of the government are held by a single agency, as in Great Britain; local governments are completely subordinate to and have only those powers given to them by the central government. p. 10
Urbanization Percentage of population of a State living in cities of more than 2,500 people or in suburbs of cities with more than 50,000. p. 666

Veto Chief executive's power to reject a bill passed by a legislature; literally (Latin) "I forbid"; see item veto, pocket veto. p. 307
Veto power A constitutional power that enables the President (or a governor) to return legislation to the Congress (or the State legislature) unsigned with reasons for his objection; see pocket veto. pp. 307, 587
Virginia Plan Offered at the Constitutional Convention; called for a bicameral legislature in which representation in both houses would be based on population or financial support for the central government. p. 42
Visa A permit to enter another state, obtained from the country one wishes to enter. p. 430

Ward Local unit of party organization; also, a district within a city for city council elections. p. 122
Weak-mayor government Variety of mayor-council form of city government, featuring a mayor with little real power. p. 652
Welfare state A government that assumes the role of promoter of citizen welfare through programs sponsored by the government. p. 615
Whip Assistants to the floor leaders, responsible for monitoring and marshalling votes. p. 287
Winner-take-all An almost obsolete system whereby the presidential aspirant who won the preference vote in a primary automatically won the support of all the delegates chosen in the primary. p. 332

Zoning Practice of dividing a city or other unit of government into districts (zones) and regulating by law (a zoning ordinance) the uses of land in each of them. p. 655

INDEX

Note: Entries with a page number followed by an (n) denote reference to a footnote on that page; those followed by a (p) denote a photo.

ACKNOWLEDGMENTS

PICTURE RESEARCH: Toni Michaels
EDITORIAL SERVICES: Mary Ashford, Amy Helfer, Peter T. Lacey
DESIGN SERVICES: Marie E. McAdam, Mark McKertich
PRODUCTION: Jean C. Thomas

COVER PHOTO (front/back cover and title pages): Paul Conklin
FRONT MATTER: Page viii, ©Tannenbaum/Sygma; **ix**, ©Mark Antman/The Image Works; **x**, ©Owen Franken/Stock Boston; **xii**, ©Bob Daemmrich/Stock Boston; **xiii**, Sovfoto/Eastfoto.
BACKGROUND PHOTO OF AMERICAN FLAG appearing once in each chapter: Scott Slobodian/TSW

UNIT 1

Page 1, ©Cliff Feulner/The Image Bank; **3**, ©Tannenbaum/Sygma; **6**, By permission of Johnny Hart and Creators Syndicate, Inc.; **8**,"Unveiling of the Statue of Liberty." Quilt by Katherine Westphal, 1964. National Museum of American Art—Smithsonian Institution. Gift of the Artist. Photo. Art Resource; **11**, ©John Running/Stock Boston; **13**, ©Yivo Institute for Jewish Research; **16**, ©Alan Carey/The Image Works; **18**, Courtesy, Mexican American Legal Defense Educational Fund; **25**, ©Bob Daemmrich/The Image Works; **27**, **29**, ©The Granger Collection; **31**, ©Library of Congress; **33**, "Washington Studying the Plans of Battle" (Night Scene) by Dunsmore. Courtesy, The Fraunces Tavern Museum; **34L**, ©Independence National Historic Park Collection; **34R**, ©Bettmann Archive; **38**, ©The Granger Collection; **40**, ©Robert Llewellyn; **41**, ©The Granger Collection; **43**, ©Burr Shafer; **46**, ©Independence National Historic Park; **49L**, ©The Bettman Archive; **49C**, ©The Library Company of Philadelphia; **49R**, ©The Granger Collection; **55**, ©Robert Llewellyn; **57**, ©Crandall/The Image Works; **62**, ©The Granger Collection; **66L**, R, ©Bettmann Archive; **67**, ©Taylor/Albuquerque Tribune, NM/Rothco; **73**, ©The Dallas Morning News; **74**, ©Liederman/Rothco; **81**, ©Cary Wolinsky/Stock Boston; **84**, ©Rob Crandall/Picture Group; **85**, ©Bob Daemmrich/The Image Works; **88**, ©Manfred Gottschalk/Tom Stack & Associates; **91**, ©Bob Daemmrich/The Image Works.

UNIT 2

Pages 96–97, ©Robert Llewellyn; **99**, ©Trippett/Sipa Press; **101**, ©DeWitt Collection, The University of Hartford; **103**, ©Arthur Grace/Sygma; **104**, Reprinted with special permission of King Features Syndicate, Inc.; **106L**, Cynthia Johnson/Gamma Liaison; **106R**, Dunagin's People by Ralph Dunagin. Reprinted with special permission of NAS, Inc.; **112**, Edmund Sullivan/DeWitt Collection, The University of Hartford; **120L**, ©Trippett/Sipa Press; **120R**, ©Paul Conklin/Monkmeyer Press; **121L**, Courtesy, Republican National Committee; **121R**, ©AP/Wide World Photos; **124**, ©1984 by HERBLOCK in the Washington Post; **129**, ©Lisa Quinones/Black Star; **130L**, ©The Granger Collection; **130R**, ©Library of Congress; **134**, By Dana Summers. ©1991, Washington Post Writers Group. Reprinted with permission; **135**, ©Ernst Haas/Magnum; **139**, ©UPI/Bettmann Newsphotos; **140**, ©Paul Conklin; **142**, ROB ROGERS reprinted by permission of UFS, Inc.; **150L**, ©Bob Daemmrich/The Image Works; **150R**, ©Bob Daemmrich/Stock Boston; **151**, OLIPHANT COPYRIGHT 1991 UNIVERSAL PRESS SYNDICATE. Reprinted with permission. All rights reserved; **157**, ©Wally McNamee/Woodfin Camp & Associates; **159**, ©The Granger Collection; **160**, **161**, Edmund Sullivan/Dewitt Collection, University of Hartford; **163**, Dunagin's People by Ralph Dunagin. Reprinted with special permission of NAS, Inc.; **164**, ©Frank Siteman/The Picture Cube; **165**, ©Chris Gulker/The Picture Group; **167**, ©AP/Wide World Photos; **168**, file photo; **169L**, Indiana State Election Committee; **169R**, Massachusetts State Election Committee; **170T**, ©Mary Heaton; **170C**, ©Reprinted with special permission of King Features Syndicate, Inc.; **170B**, ©Charles Gupton/Stock Boston; **173**, ©by HERBLOCK in the Washington Post; **176**, ©J.L. Atlan/Sygma; **179**, ©Paul Conklin; **185**, ©L. Downing/Woodfin Camp & Associates; **186**, Reprinted with special permission of King Features Syndicate, Inc.; **187**, ©Gabe Kirchheimer/Black Star; **190**, ©Bob Daemmrich/Stock Boston; **191**, file photo; **192**, By permission of Mike Luckovich and Creators Syndicate; **193**, ©Bettmann Newsphotos; **195**, ©Ellis Herwig/The Picture Cube; **196**, ©Bettmann Newsphotos; **200**, ©Spencer Grant/The Picture Cube; **201**, Courtesy, National Public Radio; **203**, ©Huston Westover/F-Stop Pictures; **204**, Reprinted with special permission of King Features Syndicate, Inc.; **211**, ©Bob Daemmrich/Tony Stone Worldwide; **212**, ©Dennis Brack/Black Star; **214**, ©Wally McNamee/Woodfin Camp & Associates; **217L**, ©Paul Conklin; **217R**, ©Gary Sigman/Black Star; **219L**, ©Luana George/Black Star; **219R**, ©Joe Cempa/Black Star; **220**, Reprinted with special permission of King Features Syndicate, Inc.; **222**, ©Mark Antman/The Image Works; **225**, ©Dennis Brack/Black Star.

UNIT 3

Pages 232–233, Courtesy, the Supreme Court Historical Society, photograph Ralph D. Jones; **235**, ©U.S. House of Representatives; **237**, OLIPHANT copyright 1990 UNIVERSAL PRESS SYNDICATE. Reprinted with permission. All rights reserved; **242**, ©The Granger Collection; **243**, ©Steve Magnuson; **245**, Courtesy, Barbara Mikulski; **246**, ©Library of Congress; **249**, ©Library of Congress; **259**, ©AP/Wide World Photos; **260T**, Courtesy, Norman Y. Mineta; **260B**, Reprinted by permission, Tribune Media Services; **263**, C.P. Houston, Houston Chronicle; **265**, ©Holt Confer/The Image Works; **266T**, ©The Granger Collection; **267**, ©Steve Starr/Picture Group; **269**, "The Senate" (1935) William Gropper. Oil on canvas, 25 1/8"x33 1/8" (63.8x84.2 cm). Collection, The Museum of Modern Art, New York. Gift of A. Conger Goodyear; **275**, **277**, ©Dennis Brack/Black Star; **283**, ©Rick Friedman/Black Star; **285T**, ©Dennis Brack/Black Star; **285B**, ©The Bettmann Archive; **286**, **287**, ©Wide World Photos; **289**, ©1991 Tom Darcy/N.Y. Newsday. Dist. by L.A. Time Syndicate; **296L**, **R**, **298**, Courtesy, U.S. House of Representatives; **299**, Marty LaVor © 1989; **300**, ©Cornell Capa/Magnum;

301T, ©Paul Conklin; **301B**, ©Shepard Sherbell/SABA Press Photos; **303**, ©Mark Reinstein/Uniphoto; **304**, ©AP/Wide World Photos; **308**, ©Bob Daemmrich/The Image Works.

UNIT 4

Pages 312–313, ©Arthur Grace/Stock Boston; **315**, ©Wally McNamee/Woodfin Camp and Associates; **316**, ©Cynthia Johnson/Gamma Liaison; **317**, ©UPI/Bettmann Newsphotos; **319T**, **ML**, ©The Granger Collection; **319MR**, ©Wide World Photos; **319B**, ©Dennis Brack/Black Star; **324**, ©Library of Congress; **326**, ©J.L. Atlan/Sygma; **328**, Reprinted by permission: Tribune Media Services; **329**, ©The Granger Collection; **333**, ©Paul Conklin; **334L**, ©Wide World Photos; **334R**, ©Ohman/Tribune Media Services; **336**, **337**, **339R**, ©Paul Conklin; **339L**, ©Dennis Brack/Black Star; **347**, Sipa/Special Features; **353**, ©Dennis Brack/Black Star; **354**, Chicago Historical Society; **357**, ©AP/Wide World Photos; **358**, ©Bob Henriques/Magnum; **359a**, ©The White House Historical Association; Photograph by the National Geographic Society; **359b–h**, ©The Granger Collection; **359i**, ©Wide World Photos; **359j**, ©Dennis Brack/Black Star; **360**, ©George Tames; **362**, ©The Bettmann Archive; **363**, ©Hernandez/Sipa Press; **365L**, file photo; **365R**, ©Abbas/Magnum; **368**, ©AP/Wide World Photos; **372**, ©Owen Franken/Stock Boston; **373**, ©Library of Congress; **375**, ©Courtesy, U.S. Department of the Interior; **381**, ©Bodhan/Stock Boston; **384**, BERRY'S WORLD reprinted by permission of NEA, Inc.; **386TL**, ©The Granger Collection; **386TR**, ©Susan Van Etten; **386BL**, Library of Congress; **386BR**, OLIPHANT© 1991 UNIVERSAL PRESS SYNDICATE. Reprinted with permission.; **388**, Courtesy, The Small Business Administration; **389**, ©Bob Daemmich/The Image Works; **392**, Government Bureau, 1956, by George Tooker. The Metropolitan Museum of Art, George A. Hearn Fund, 1956. (56.78); **395**, Reprinted by permission, Tribune Media Services; **396L**, ©The Bettmann Archive; **396R**, ©Library of Congress; **405**, ©Perry Alan Werner/The Image Works; **407**, **408**, **409**, ©Reprinted with special permission of King Features Inc.; **410**, ©Granitsas/The Image Works; **410** inset, ©Nancy Ploeger/Monkmeyer Press; **412**, ©Dennis Brack/Black Star; **413**, ©Mike Roemer/Gamma Liaison; **416**, ©David Burnett/Woodfin Camp & Associates; **418**, ©Dennis Brack/Black Star; **419**, By permission of Johnny Hart and NAS, Inc.; **420**, Internal Revenue Service; **425**, Atlanta Journal/Stocksouth/Sygma; **426**, ©National Archives; **428**, ©Xinhua/Sygma; **429**, ©Wide World Photos; **430**, ©Barry Iverson/Woodfin Camp & Associates; **431**, Drawing by Stevenson; ©1986 The New Yorker Magazine; **432**, ©C. Arbron/Sygma; **434**, ©Paula Bronstein/Black Star; **436**, NASA; **437**, ©John Ficara/Woodfin Camp & Associates; **437 top**, ©Wally McNamee/Woodfin Camp & Associates; **441**, Official Panama Canal Photo; **442**, Library of Congress; **444**, ©The Bettmann Archive; **445**, ©Owen Franken/Stock Boston; 447, ©L. Downing/Woodfin Camp & Associates; **451**, ©Hazel Hankin/Stock Boston.

UNIT 5

Pages 458–459, ©Peter Gridley/FPG; **461**, ©Catherine Karnow/Woodfin Camp & Associates; **464**, ©Paul Conklin; **469**, ©The Bettmann Archive; **471**, **473**, ©Ken Heinen; **477**, Terry Thompson/Sygma; **485**, ©B. & J. McGrath/The Picture Cube; **487**, ©Bob Daemmrich/Stock Boston; **488**, ©AP/Wide World Photos; **491**, ©John O'Connor/Monkmeyer Press; **492**, ©Miro Vintoniv/Stock Boston; **494**, ©Paul Conklin; **496**, ©Frank Siteman/The Picture Cube; **500**, ©Bob Rashid/Monkmeyer Press; **502**, ©Ura Wexler/Folio; **503**, ©Randy Taylor/Sygma; **507**, ©The Bettmann Archive; **509**, ©Mike Mazzaschi/Stock Boston; **511**, ©Reprinted with special permission of King Features Syndicate, Inc.; **517**, ©Robert Llewellyn; **518**, ©Ken Heinen; **519**, ©Bob Daemmrich/The Image Works; **521**, ©Mary Heaton; **523**, ©Bob Daemmrich/Stock, Boston; **525**, Painting by Hank Virgona. Photograph Courtesy, of American Heritage Picture Collection; **530**, ©Bob Daemmrich/Stock, Boston; **533**, Reprinted with special permission of King Features Syndicate, Inc.; **534**, ©James Wilson/Woodfin Camp & Associates; **545**, ©Paul Conklin; **548**, ©Bob Daemmrich/Stock Boston; **550**, Courtesy, Larry Echohawk; **551**, Library of Congress; **552**, Krichlow, Ernest "White Fence #1," 1975, 48"x40". O.C/Museum, NCAAA; **553**, Robert Kelly/Life Picture Service; **553 inset**, Gordon Parks/Life Picture Service; **556**, ©Kolvoord/Texastock; **565**, ©1980 Don Wright; **566**, ©Alon Reininger/Woodfin Camp & Associates.

UNIT 6

Pages 572–573, ©Peter Turnley/Black Star; **575**, ©Vladimir Sichov/Sipa Press; **577**, ©Tim Graham/Sygma; **579**, ©P.F. Gero/Sygma; **580**, ©Herbert Lanks/Monkmeyer Press; **582L**, Inge Morath/Magnum; **582R**, ©Peter Menzel/Stock Boston; **587**, Laura Platt Winfrey; **588**, Peter Menzel/Stock Boston; **589**, ©Christopher Morris/Black Star; **592**, ©Vladimir Sumovsky/Sygma; **593**, By permission of Doug Mariette and Creator's Syndicate; **595**, Courtesy, Richmond Newspapers; **596**, ©Klaus Reisinger/Black Star; **605**, ©Richemond/The Image Works; **607**, Drawing by Dan Fradon; ©1990 The New Yorker Magazine, Inc.; **608**, ©Wiley Miller, San Francisco Examiner; **609**, New York Public Library. Photograph Courtesy, of American Heritage Picture Collection; **610**, Courtesy, Martin and Kathleen Feldstein; **614**, Courtesy, Volvo Cars of North America; **615**, ©A. Farquhar/Valan Photos; **616**, ©Patrick Ward/Stock Boston; **619**, ©The Granger Collection; **620**, ©Herbert Lanks/Monkmeyer Press; **622**, ©Sovfoto/Eastfoto; **623**, ©Peter Turnley/Black Star; **624**, ©Herb Snitzer/Stock Boston.

UNIT 7

Pages 628–629, ©Craig Blouin/F-Stop Pictures; **631**, ©Doug Bruce/Picture Group; **632**, Courtesy, Brynhild Haugland; **635**, ©Susan Van Etten; **638**, ©Randy Taylor/Sygma; **640**, Courtesy, Governor Barbara Robert's Office; **642**, Courtesy, Charles E. Cole; **645**, **646**, ©Bob Daemmrich/The Image Works; **654**, ©Michael Sullivan/Texasstock; **655**, Reprinted by permission: Tribune Media Services; **656**, Toles ©1989, The Buffalo News, reprinted with permission of Universal Press Syndicate. All rights reserved; **657**, ©Michal Heron/Woodfin Camp & Associates; **663**, ©Bob Daemmrich/Stock Boston; **665**, Courtesy, Judy Jamerson; **669**, ©Phillip Jon Bailey/Stock Boston; **671**, ©J. L. Atlan/Sygma; **673**, Drawing by Cheney; ©1988 The New Yorker Magazine, Inc.; **674**, ©Stacey Pick/Stock Boston; **681**, Drawing by Stevenson; ©1981 The New Yorker Magazine, Inc.; **682**, ©Rhoda Sidney/Monkmeyer Press; **688 all**, ©AP/Wide World Photos.